THE FAMILY, SEX AND MARRIAGE

THE FAMILY, SEX AND MARRIAGE

In England 1500–1800

LAWRENCE STONE

HARPER & ROW, PUBLISHERS
New York, Hagerstown, San Francisco, London

International Standard Book Number:
0–06–014142–5

Library of Congress Catalog Card
Number: 77–50

TO MY FAMILY, WITHOUT WHOM . . .

The problems, being existential, are universal; their solutions, being human, are diverse ... The road to the grand abstractions of science winds through a thicket of singular facts.

(C. Geertz, *The Interpretation of Cultures*, New York, 1973, p. 363.)

Contents

**PART THREE: THE RESTRICTED PATRIARCHAL
NUCLEAR FAMILY 1550–1700**

PART FOUR: THE CLOSED DOMESTICATED NUCLEAR FAMILY 1640–1800

PART FIVE: SEX

Graphs

Illustrations

Acknowledgements

Some of the basic ideas in this book were presented to the Columbia University Seminar on the Nature of Man, the Social Science Seminar at the Institute for Advanced Study at Princeton, a *Past and Present* Conference in London, and the History Department Colloquium at Princeton, to the members of all of which I am grateful for some very trenchant criticisms and helpful suggestions. Without them I would never have eliminated some of the more extravagant claims and implausible hypotheses, and would never have got clear in my own mind the essentials of my very complicated argument. I am particularly grateful for constructive suggestions from Robert Darnton, W.J.Goode, Margaret Mead, Robert K.Merton, Theodore K.Rabb and Edward P.Thompson. I also owe a great debt, of a somewhat ambiguous kind, to Clifford Geertz. He has provided me with invaluable intellectual stimulus and new insights, and has also driven me to think out where my craft as an historian differs from his as an anthropologist. The main themes of the book and some of the evidence were presented to students and faculty at Cambridge University as the Trevelyan Lectures in November 1975. From the reactions of the audience, especially those of J.H.Plumb and E.A.Wrigley, I also learned much. None of these persons and groups, however, should be assumed to be in agreement with the argument, for which I must, alas, take full responsibility.

I am also grateful to Michael MacDonald, who generously allowed me to make use of some of his unpublished findings from the case-books of the Reverend Richard Napier; to the archivist at Brasenose College, Oxford, who permitted me to examine transcripts of the Legh MSS; to Miriam Slater, who has allowed me to quote from her unpublished dissertation; and to Natalie Davis, whose mimeographed bibliography on 'Society and the Sexes in Early Modern Europe' drew my attention to many sources I should otherwise have missed. Ansley Coale very kindly answered a number of technical questions about demography. For financial support for this project, I am indebted to the National Science Foundation (Grants GS28832X and GS39877X) and to the Princeton University Research Board. A preliminary version of Chapter 4 of this book was published by the University of Pennsylvania Press,[1] to which I am grateful for permission to reproduce a revised and expanded text. I am indebted to Mrs Mary Hyde for her generosity in allowing me to quote some items from Mrs Thrale's Children's Book which will be published in her forthcoming *The Thrales of Streatham Park*. P.Laslett kindly provided me with the figures for pre-nuptial conceptions and illegitimacy for Graphs 15 and 16 from his forthcoming *Family Life and Illicit Love in Earlier Generations*. R.B.Latham kindly allowed me to read the proofs of the last volume of his definitive edition of Pepys' *Diary*, which include the previously expurgated passages. I am also grateful to Mrs V.B.Elliott for supplying me with some information from her work on Kent marriage records of the early seventeenth century. I owe the figures upon which Graph 12 is based to the kindness of Professor J.C.Sommerville. He has also allowed me to quote from an unpublished paper. For individual references and suggestions I am indebted to P.Clark, M.H.Crawford, N.Z.Davis, D.H.Fischer, E.Gilliam, P.Goubert, A.T.Grafton, L.H.Rosenband, M.Shanley, Morton Smith, S.R.Smith, M.Smuts, S.E.Spock, L.A.Tilly, S.Watkins, C.S.Weiner, and others whose names I have doubtless overlooked.

I am very grateful to my devoted secretary, Mrs Betty Ann Berry, who typed and retyped version after version of an increasingly illegible and bulky manuscript with remarkable speed, accuracy and palaeographical skill. Finally, I owe a very large debt to my wife. It is, naturally, from interaction with her that I have learned whatever I know at first hand about the ups and downs of family life. She has read the manuscript several times and provided me with a not always welcome stream of suggestions and criticisms, most of which I have accepted, and some rejected. She helped me with the horribly tedious chore of checking footnotes, and in doing so managed to eliminate a number of serious misinterpretations caused by overhasty reading of documents. She has done her best to prune what has become, unfortunately, a somewhat luxuriantly overgrown tree, although I could not always bring myself to perform the radical surgery she recommended. The only possible excuse for allowing a book to reach such an inordinate length is the value and intrinsic interest of the case histories which bulk so large. The quirky oddity of human beings revealed in these not always very edifying stories may help to mitigate the tedium of reading so many pages, while the examples provided may stimulate other scholars to develop alternative models and explanations.

Throughout the book, spelling, capitalization and punctuation have been modernized, on the grounds that the gain in readability far outweighs the loss in accuracy of transcription. In the period of Old Style dating, the year is taken to begin on 1 January.

Lawrence Stone
Princeton

PART ONE

Introduction

CHAPTER 1

Problems, Methods and Definitions

'The public life of a people is a very small thing compared to its private life.'
(G.d'Avenel, *Les Français de mon Temps*, Paris, 1904, p. 1)

'To judge fairly of those who lived long before us ... we should put quite apart both the usages and the notions of our own age ... and strive to adopt for the moment such as prevailed in theirs.'
(Lady Louisa Stuart, c. 1827, in *Letters and Journals of Lady Mary Coke*, ed. J.A.Horne, Edinburgh 1889, I, p. xxxv)

'We have very little of correctly detailed domestic history, the most valuable of all as it would enable us to make comparisons ...'
(*The Autobiography of Francis Place*, c. 1823–26, ed. M.Thale, Cambridge, 1972, p. 91)

I THE PATTERN OF CHANGE

i. The Problem

Despite its dauntingly massive appearance, the subject of this book can be stated fairly simply. It is an attempt to chart and document, to analyse and explain, some massive shifts in world views and value systems that occurred in England over a period of some three hundred years, from 1500 to 1800. These vast and elusive cultural changes expressed themselves in changes in the ways members of the family related to each other, in terms of legal arrangements, structure, custom, power, affect and sex. The main stress is on how individuals thought about, treated and used each other, and how they regarded themselves in relation to God and to various levels of social organization, from the nuclear family to the state. The microcosm of the family is used to open a window on to this wider landscape of cultural change. The subject is thus one which was recommended to historians by Dr Johnson in *The Idler*: 'The mischievous consequences of vice and folly, of irregular desires and predominant passions, are best discovered by those relations which are levelled with the general surface of life, which tell not how any man became great, but how he was made happy, not how he lost the favour of his Prince, but how he became discontented with himself.'[1]

The critical change under consideration is that from distance, deference and patriarchy to what I have chosen to call Affective Individualism. I believe this to have been perhaps the most important change in *mentalité* to have occurred in the Early Modern period, indeed possibly in the last thousand years of Western history. This is not the first time that questions of this sort have been asked, for they are similar to some of those with which both Max Weber and Joseph Burckhardt wrestled more than three-quarters of a century ago. They too were obsessed with the complex inter-relationships thanks to which changes in culture emerged from changes in religion, social structure, political organization, economics, literacy and so on. Neither Weber nor Burckhardt solved these problems either to their own or to posterity's full satisfaction, and I cannot hope to succeed where scholars of such pre-eminent distinction have partly failed. But it is worth making a new effort, using a much narrower focus, in a different national context and in the light of another seventy-five years or so of historical scholarship, if only because these issues are so central to the evolution of Western civilization.

ii. The Stages in Family Evolution

The pattern of change, which for the sake of brevity is here inevitably grossly over-simplified and over-schematized, is as follows. In the sixteenth century, and almost certainly for at least a millennium before it, the characteristic type, especially among the social elite, was what I have chosen, for lack of a better term, to call the Open Lineage Family, since its two most striking features were its permeability by outside influences, and its members' sense of loyalty to ancestors and to living kin. The principal boundary circumscribed the kin, not its sub-unit, the nuclear family. This was a society where neither individual autonomy nor privacy were respected as desirable ideals. It was generally agreed that the interests of the group, whether that of the kin, the village, or later the state, took priority over the wishes of the individual and the achievement of his particular ends. 'Life, liberty and the pursuit of happiness' were personal ideals which the average, educated sixteenth-century man would certainly have rejected as the prime goals of a good society. Conventional wisdom was that happiness could only be anticipated in the next world, not in this, and sex was not a pleasure but a sinful necessity justified only by the need to propagate the race. Individual freedom of choice ought at all times and in all respects to be subordinated to the interests of others, whether lineage, parents, neighbours, kin, Church or state. As for life itself, it was cheap, and death came easily and often. The expectation of life was so low that it was highly imprudent to become too emotionally dependent upon any other human being. Outside court circles, where it flourished, romantic love was in any case regarded by moralists and theologians as a kind of mental illness, fortunately of short duration; the latter advised that even affection should be prudently limited by the prospect of the early death of its subject. Of course by no means everyone heeded this advice, but for this and other reasons affective relations seem generally to have been cool, and those that existed were widely diffused rather than concentrated on members of the nuclear family.

As a result, relations within the nuclear family, between husband and wife and parents and children, were not much closer than those with neighbours, with relatives, or with 'friends' – that group of influential advisors who usually included most of the senior members of the kin. Marriage was not an intimate association based on personal choice. Among the upper and middling ranks it was primarily a means of tying together two kinship groups, of obtaining collective economic advantages and securing useful political alliances. Among peasants, artisans and labourers, it was an economic necessity for partnership and division of labour in the shop or in the fields. For both men and women it was the price of economic survival, while for the latter it was the only career available. So far as society was concerned, it was a convenient way of channelling the powerful but potentially disruptive instinct of sexual desire – which it was assumed could be satisfied by any reasonably presentable member of the other sex – and it made possible the production and rearing of legitimate children. In a highly authoritarian and patriarchal society, it was only natural and reasonable that mate selection should primarily be made by parents, kin and 'friends', rather than by the bride and groom. Nor did most young people resent such a system, since for them the association in marriage was only one of many social relationships, and personal accommodation to circumstances, necessity and authority was an ingrained pattern of behaviour. In outward appearances of symbol and ritual, deference was king in early modern society, although underlying resentments certainly existed, bubbling to the surface occasionally during peasant revolts. But for most people most of the time, obedience came easily, even in so critical a matter as the choice of a life partner for bed and board. Only those entirely without property and who had long ago left home were free to marry solely on the basis of personal choice, and even then the motives might well be more practical than affective.

The household into which the married couple moved was characterized by its lack of well-defined boundaries. Although they did not normally live in their parents' house, as in most other societies, the relationship of a married man or woman to parents, kin, friends and neighbours remained almost as close as those with each other or their children. All these groups, as well as school and Church, shared in the common tasks of upbringing and socializing children and in controlling and arbitrating marital conflicts and disputes. Privacy, like individualism, was neither possible nor desired. The poor lived in one- or two-room houses where one person could never be alone. Among the middle ranks, servants – children of other families – were everywhere, rooms were few and non-specialized in function, and bedrooms and even beds were often shared. Even the rich, with ample house-space, were constantly spied upon and interrupted by their domestic servants.

In the village community, the neighbours kept a watchful eye on each other. The gigantic flood of denunciations of domestic moral transgressions that poured annually into the archdeacons' courts between about 1475 (when good record-keeping began) and 1640 show that little went on in the home that was not noticed and reported by the neighbours. Privacy was clearly a rarity, which the rich lacked because of the architectural layout of their houses and the prying ubiquity of their servants, and the poor lacked because of confinement in a one- or two-room hovel.

In such a society relations with one's own children were not particularly close. Richer families put their infants out to wet-nurse, and when they returned, the advice of moralists, theologians and writers of domestic advice books, at least after the Reformation, was that the first duty of parents was ruthlessly to crush the wills of young children by physical force, as the only hope of containing Original Sin. Most children of all classes left home very early, between the ages of seven and fourteen, to work in other people's houses as servants or apprentices, to serve in a magnate's household, or to go to school.

To conclude, therefore, the early sixteenth-century home was neither a castle nor a womb. Lacking firm boundaries, it was open to support, advice, investigation and interference from outside, from neighbours and from kin;

and internal privacy was non-existent. Inside the home the members of the nuclear family were subordinated to the will of its head, and were not closely bonded to each other by warm affective ties. They might well feel closer to other members of the kin, to fellow members of a guild, or to friends and neighbours of the same sex whom they met daily in an ale-house. It is important also to realize that the total amount of affective feelings was limited. Not only was attachment widely diffused, but there was not much of it. The family, therefore, was an open-ended, low-keyed, unemotional, authoritarian institution which served certain essential political, economic, sexual, procreative and nurturant purposes. It was also very short-lived, being frequently dissolved by the death of husband or wife, or the death or early departure from the home of the children. So far as the individual members were concerned, it was neither very durable, nor emotionally or sexually very demanding. The closest analogy to a sixteenth-century home is a bird's nest.

The second type of family which first overlapped and then very slowly replaced the Open Lineage Family over a period of about a century and a half, and then only in certain social strata, was what I call – to stress the differences – the Restricted Patriarchal Nuclear Family. This type, which began in about 1530, predominated from about 1580 to 1640, and ran on to at least 1700, saw the decline of loyalties to lineage, kin, patron and local community as they were increasingly replaced by more universalistic loyalties to the nation state and its head, and to a particular sect or Church. As a result, 'boundary awareness' became more exclusively confined to the nuclear family, which consequently became more closed off from external influences, either of the kin or of the community. But at the same time, both state and Church, for their own reasons, actively reinforced the pre-existent patriarchy within the family, and there are signs that the power of the husband and father over the wife and the children was positively strengthened, making him a legalized petty tyrant within the home.

After 1640 a series of changes in the state, the society and the Church undermined this patriarchal emphasis, while continuing the decline of external pressures on the increasingly nuclear family. The result was the evolution among the upper bourgeoisie and squirarchy of a third type, the Closed Domesticated Nuclear Family, which evolved in the late seventeenth century and predominated in the eighteenth. This was the decisive shift, for this new type of family was the product of the rise of Affective Individualism. It was a family organized around the principle of personal autonomy, and bound together by strong affective ties. Husbands and wives personally selected each other rather than obeying parental wishes, and their prime motives were now long-term personal affection rather than economic or status advantage for the lineage as a whole. More and more time, energy, money, and love of both parents were devoted to the upbringing of the children, whose wills it was no longer thought necessary to crush by force at an early age. Education loomed larger and larger in parents' minds, and among the wealthier members of society the new orientation towards children led to an active desire to limit their numbers in order to improve their life-chances. Patriarchal attitudes within the home markedly declined, and greater autonomy was granted not only to children but also to wives.

The home itself became increasingly private. Externally, it was more and more closed off from prying neighbours, and complaints in the archdeacons' courts about domestic deviations fell off dramatically. It was also more closed off from the kin, whose role in the choice of marriage partners withered away. After marriage, social ties with relatives were now increasingly confined to parents, uncles and aunts. Contacts with cousins diminished. Internally, the home became more private. The houses of the rich were planned on the corridor and hallway system instead of that of suites of rooms leading out of each other; rooms became more specialized in function, as well as more numerous; as far down the social scale as the farmer or tradesman, more bedrooms, studies, closets, and withdrawing-chambers were built, where members of the family could get away from each other and from the servants, even if in fact many continued to live in the kitchen. In some social groups, there occurred a rejection of the traditional Christian suspicion and hostility to sexuality, and even a glorification of sensuality for its own sake.

Further stages in the diffusion of this new family type did not take place until the late nineteenth century, after a period of nearly a century during which many of the developments that have been described had gone into reverse. When forward movement picked up again at the end of the nineteenth century, it involved a spread of the domesticated family ideal up into the higher court aristocracy and down into the masses of artisans and respectable wage-earners who composed the bulk of the population.

But the four key features of the modern family – intensified affective bonding of the nuclear core at the expense of neighbours and kin; a strong sense of individual autonomy and the right to personal freedom in the pursuit of happiness; a weakening of the association of sexual pleasure with sin and guilt; and a growing desire for physical privacy – were all well established by 1750 in the key middle and upper sectors of English society. The nine-teenth and twentieth centuries merely saw their much wider social diffusion.

iii. The Cultural Stratification of Family Types

Early Modern English society was composed of a number of very distinct status groups and classes: the court aristocracy, the county gentry, the parish gentry, the mercantile and professional elite, the small property owners in town and country, the respectable and struggling wage-earners, and the totally destitute who lived on charity and their wits. These constituted more or less self-contained cultural units, with their own communication networks, their own systems of value and their own patterns of acceptable behaviour. Internal cultural divisions between social groups ran much deeper than they do today, when the differences are as much between generations as between classes. As time went on and as writing and printing spread to become the main vehicle for the diffusion of ideas, the degree to which different social strata used or were affected by this new means of expression brought with it still more marked divisions. The result was less the supersession of one family pattern and set of familial values by another than the provision of a widening number of quite different patterns.

Attitudes and customs which were normal for one class or social stratum were often quite different from those which were normal in another. Such changes as took place sometimes affected one class but not others; for example, the rising rates of pre-marital pregnancy and illegitimacy affected the peasantry, the artisans, and the poor in the late eighteenth century, but not the upper middle class, the gentry and the aristocracy. Other changes, for example the drift towards a more child-oriented attitude, affected different groups at widely different times, taking a century or more to flow from one to another. Other powerful influences were confined to a single class. Thus possession of property to be handed down vitally affected family structures and marriage arrangements among the propertied classes, but left the propertyless masses untouched. Conversely, the pressures of urbani-zation and industrialization profoundly affected the poor, but hardly impinged on the lives of the nobility in any significant way. Even religion, which was so powerful a force in the early seventeenth century and again in the nineteenth century, affected the more literate middling social strata far more deeply than the pleasure-seeking court aristocracy or the illiterate poor. Magical beliefs remained deeply embedded in the minds of the lower ranks who constituted the majority of the population, so that the religious enthusiasm of the age created a dissociation of sensibility rather than a restructuring of the values and beliefs of the society as a whole. Once again, there was a fragmentation of cultural norms. Stratified diffusion of new ideas and practices is the key to any realistic understanding of how family change took place. Generalizations about family change have therefore always to be qualified by a careful definition of the class or status group, the literate or the illiterate sector, the zealously godly or the casually conformist, which is under discussion. Patterns of behaviour found in the leading sectors of value-change, the professional and gentry classes, do not necessarily apply to the court aristocracy, the urban lower-middle class, the rural smallholder, or the landless labourer.

A further difficulty is that patterns of behaviour which were the norm in the metropolis of London were certainly not common in the provincial towns, much less in the rural countryside where the bulk of the population lived. Our evidence is heavily weighted towards persons who visited London regularly, even if they did not live there, and whose values may well have been very different from those of their country cousins who never set eyes on the metropolis. Lower down the social scale we have glimpses which suggest the existence of regional differences, especially between the inhabitants of the Lowland and the Highland zones, between provincial towns and isolated villages, and between forest areas and areas of settled arable farming. These are all problems that will only be resolved by intensive research at the local level.

Simple models of family evolution may work perfectly well for primitive and culturally homogeneous societies unaffected by the technology of printing, the social consequences of demographic growth or the rise of capitalism, the economic consequences of gigantic wealth alongside abject poverty and unemployment, and the intellectual consequences of Puritanism, Newtonian Science and the Enlightenment. But they will not work for so sophisticated, so diversified and so changing a society as seventeenth- and eighteenth-century England, where there is a plurality of cultural worlds, and a consequent plurality of family styles and values. Thus of the three ideal types of family which have been identified, each overlapped the other by anything up to a century, and none of them ever fully died out.

2   EVIDENCE AND INTERPRETATION

i. Sources

Every possible type of evidence has been examined to pick up hints about changes in values and behaviour at the personal level. The greatest reliance has been placed on personal documents, diaries, autobiographies, memoirs, domestic correspondence, and the correspondence columns of newspapers. Other sources which have been used are the more popular and most frequently reprinted handbooks of advice about domestic behaviour, before 1660 written mainly by moral theologians and after 1660 mainly by laymen, with doctors becoming increasingly prominent after about 1750; reports of foreign visitors; imaginative literature, concentrating on the most popular novels, plays and poems of the day; art, especially conversation-pieces and caricatures; architectural house plans showing circulation patterns and space use; modes of address within families, between husband and wife and parents and children; folk customs such as bundling and wife-sale; legal documents such as wills, inventories, marriage contracts, and litigation over divorce or sexual deviation; and finally, demographic statistics about birth, marriage, death, pre-nuptial conceptions and bastardy.

To identify and describe changes in values, this rag-bag of evidence has been picked over and the finds assembled to try to create a coherent composite picture. The principal weakness of the data base does not lie in sampling, since all the most readily accessible surviving personal documents and all the most popular didactic, literary and artistic works have been examined. The preservation rate of the first is poor, and undoubtedly there has survived only a fragment of what once existed. But there is no reason to suppose that there is any inherent bias between what was kept and what was thrown away, except that much correspondence of an explicitly sexual or embarrassingly intimate character has undoubtedly been destroyed. It can therefore be assumed that what we have today is fairly representative of what has been lost, and that what is in print is representative of what still remains in manuscript.

Interpretation is more of a problem, since the most revealing materials, namely diaries, memoirs, autobiographies and letters, can rarely be checked from an independent source. We have, for example, no records kept by Mrs Pepys or Mrs Boswell to act as controls on the accuracy of the reporting of their husbands, who were the two greatest diarists in the English language. This material needs to be treated with the same critical scrutiny which the historian gives to documents in political history: an exchange of love letters needs to be handled with exactly the same sceptical caution as an exchange of diplomatic notes – no more, no less. But these personal records are peculiarly difficult to interpret. As E. H. Carr has warned, 'no document can tell us more than what the author of the document thought – what he thought happened, what he thought ought to happen or would happen, or perhaps only what he wanted others to think he thought, or even only what he himself thought he thought.'[2] A good deal of this kind of material, unfortunately, probably falls into the last two categories. A second difficulty is that these are highly personal documents and, therefore, often very idiosyncratic, reflecting the quirks and quiddities of the individual psyche of the author, as well as the shared norms of social and moral behaviour of persons of his social class, education and time. They must, therefore, be examined in bulk, to make sure that one is not taking the exception for the rule, given the known wide variations of family patterns even within a single class at a certain time in a limited area.

Autobiographies are particularly suspect forms of evidence. This is partly because some tended to copy stereotyped models from the past such as St Augustine, Plutarch, Seneca or Marcus Aurelius, while others developed new stereotypes, like the Quaker model; partly because they were often very selective in what they recorded, being written with a view to placing the authors in a good light for posterity and leaving the world with some useful moral lessons; partly because even when they appeared most frank and intimate, like Rousseau's *Confessions* or Casanova's *Memoirs*, they were often involved in deliberate fantasy or role-playing.[3] They can be enormously revealing in what they tell, but only in areas which are not contaminated by the influence of these ulterior motives. Moreover, every autobiographer is something of a psychological oddity. As Francis Place admitted, 'to the charge which will be made against me of egotism, I at once and beforehand plead guilty. No man ever wrote about himself without being an egoist.'[4] Egoists although autobiographers may all be, their value to the historian depends on their sensitivity, perception and obsession to provide accurate detail about themselves. They provide a unique revelation of their inner experiences which they believe, rightly or wrongly, to have been influential in moulding their lives.

ii. Problems of Interpretation

It has to be admitted that the nature of the surviving evidence inexorably biases the book towards a study of a small minority group, namely the literate and articulate classes, and has relatively little to say about the great majority of Englishmen, the rural and urban smallholders, artisans, labourers and poor. The bias undoubtedly exists, but its consequences are mitigated by the fact that everything suggests that the former were the pacemakers of cultural change. Distortion of the record can be avoided if it is always remembered that the principle of stratified cultural diffusion and the persistence of distinctive, class-determined sub-cultures are the two keys to a proper understanding of the complicated history of family evolution in any society as socially differentiated as Early Modern England.

This problem is compounded during the sixteenth and early seventeenth centuries by the extreme loquacity of the Puritans and their compelling anxiety to commit their thoughts and beliefs to paper. It is known that Puritans were at all times only a small minority, even of the middling sort and the gentry, and yet it is their didactic literature – sermons, moral theology and advice books – and their personal documents – letters, diaries and autobiographies – which predominate in the surviving records. They therefore appear to be typical of the culture, although in fact they may have been no more than a supremely articulate and eloquent minority whose passionate and well-advertised views only partly influenced the behaviour of the silent majority.

An even more serious difficulty is caused by the fact that between the sixteenth and the eighteenth centuries there was a dramatic increase in the amount and type of printed material. There was rapidly growing emphasis on the novel, which itself evolved from a picaresque narrative of external adventures, like *Robinson Crusoe*, to an in-depth discussion of love, property and marriage, which were the dominant themes of the genre from Samuel Richardson to Jane Austen. There was also a substantial increase in literacy and in the capacity to handle the language, especially by women. The question therefore arises whether what appears to be a growth of affect may in fact be no more than a growth in the capacity to express emotions on paper, stimulated by growing familiarity with writing and influenced by the reading of novels. The possibility that nature may have been imitating art does not seriously affect the hypothesis, but it would be seriously undermined if it could be shown that the stiff, wooden, remote and rather unfriendly tone of sixteenth- and early seventeenth-century correspondence was no more than the product of literary clumsiness. Fortunately, however, there is sufficient independent evidence from advice books and con-temporary comment to make it fairly certain that the change is in the message, not merely in familiarity with the medium.

There remain, however, some formidable methodological problems in handling this kind of data. For one thing, many of the most important questions deal with values, states of mind, and intimate habits of thought which do not usually find their way on to paper. One is therefore often obliged to infer hidden attitudes from overt actions, or even from gross statistical trends. This can be a risky procedure, since similar actions may at different times and under different social conditions spring from a variety of motives. Contraception, for example, may be caused by strict economic necessity, the need to avoid starvation; or by a preference shift towards conspicuous consumption; or by a more compassionate attitude of husbands towards their wives; or by a change in moral theology; or by improved contraceptive technology. Moreover, much of the evidence appears at first sight to be contradictory. This may be the result of incomplete or inaccurately matched data, or of genuine ambiguities arising from a changing situation to which some groups and individuals responded more rapidly than others, creating a whole series of overlapping sub-cultures. Even within the individual, differing modes of behaviour may also be strictly compartmentalized. Thus the Renaissance elite in the Italian cities were filling their houses with sculptured and painted *putti*, while continuing to empty them of flesh-and-blood babies by sending them out to wet-nurses.[5] The late sixteenth-century nobility were developing a passion for genealogy and family history, at almost the same time as they were busy dismembering the inherited estates upon which this family continuity had depended. Puritan desire to preserve male parental authority was in practice undermined by Puritan zeal for holy matrimony. Ideas about the innocence of the child led for a time not to his liberation but to his repression, since innocence was interpreted as liability to sin. A subject so riddled with paradoxes is clearly not easy to handle.

Even if all these qualifications and difficulties are constantly borne in mind, any generalization on these complex and obscure subjects inevitably runs into the objection that any behavioural model of change over time imposes an artificial schematization on a chaotic and ambiguous reality. This is, of course, true in the sense that a survey of family types at any one moment in time will reveal the same complexities as a geological survey. Strata are piled upon strata in layers that earth movements have pushed and pulled out of place, so that older formations lie on the surface in places, while very recent formations are beginning to develop here and there. Similarly, older family types survive unaltered in some social groups at the same time as other groups are evolving quite new patterns. There will, therefore, be a plurality of co-existing types, without there being any single pattern predominant among all social classes, or even necessarily within a single class. Model building, therefore, involves an attempt to identify Weberian ideal types out of the welter of historical evidence, and to highlight features which seem to have been dominant in certain social groups, but were far from universal at any given time.

iii. Historiography

Until very recently, indeed until the last ten years or so, serious historical study of the family in a given society has been hamstrung by the domination of four theories, all borrowed from the social sciences and all of which have turned out to be partly wrong or misapplied. The first was the Parsonian functionalist assumption that the family is part of an unchanging social order, and that its purpose is system-maintenance, an hypothesis that effectively barred the possibility of independent change over time, and of the development of actively dysfunctional traits. The second was the Freudian assumption that the oral, anal and sexual experiences of infancy and very early childhood are decisive in moulding character, which once set can only with the greatest difficulty be modified later on. This blocked the study of personality growth and evolution throughout life in response to the ongoing influences of culture, family and society.

As David Riesman has put it, 'there has been a tendency in current social research, influenced as it is by psychoanalysis, to overemphasize and overgeneralize the importance of very early childhood in character formation. Even within this early period an almost technological attention has sometimes been focused on what might be called the tricks of the child-rearing trade: 'feeding and toilet training schedules. . . .' This emphasis 'assumes that once the child has reached, say, the weaning stage, its character structure is so formed that, barring intensive psychiatric intervention, not much that happens afterwards will do more than bring out tendencies already set.'[6] No-one doubts that child-rearing practices strongly affect the adult personality, but acceptance of the theories of more recent developmental ego-psychologists like Erikson and Hartmann opens up a new range of possibilities for the historian.[7] These theories involve hypotheses about the continued plasticity of the ego far into adulthood as it responds, through a series of crises, to the twin challenges of maturation and the influences of the family, the culture and the environment.

A third false theory was the Freudian assumption that sex – the id – is the most powerful of all drives, and has not changed over the ages; hence the oedipal conflict, and the tragic frustrations of civilized man. The eternally repeated Freudian drama of the conflict of the id, the ego and the super-ego stands outside history and is unaffected by it. But in fact the sexual drive is itself not uniform, but is heavily dependent on an adequate protein diet and the amount of physical exhaustion and psychic stress. It also varies enormously from individual to individual. Secondly, and more importantly, we know that the super-ego has at times repressed and at times released this drive, according to the dictates of cultural conventions, especially religious conventions. Nothing could be more false than that the sexual experiences and responses of middle-class Europeans in the late nineteenth century were typical of those of all mankind in the past, or even of Europeans in the previous three centuries, or even of all classes in late Victorian society. The fourth mistake was an extrapolation from the biological assumption that generativity and nurturance are innate traits of all animals. This has led to the false beliefs that marital fertility must have been uncontrolled and therefore cannot have varied significantly in pre-modern times, and that mothers must always have striven to keep their children alive and well. Neither of these is true, either in the animal world or in man.

We now know that very significant changes over time took place in the Early Modern period in family functions, in emotional relationships, in character formation, in attitudes towards and the practice of sexuality, and towards the number of children born and the care taken, within marriage, over their subsequent preservation. The precise historical context, the economic, political, religious and social systems, the specific social group and its culture and values, turn out to be at least as important as any of these allegedly unchanging characteristics.[8]

These misleadingly static theories of the social scientists did not do too much harm, however, since the problems of the family, kinship, marriage, love and sex were until very recently not ones thought worthy of serious concern by the historical profession. Indeed it is only in the last decade that the historians have come to recognize the urgent need for a careful investigation of these matters in the past. Two specialized periodicals have recently started, dealing respectively with the history of the family and the history of the child, while two international journals have recently devoted whole issues to the history of the family and sex. Some pathbreaking pioneer studies of certain broad aspects of the question in western European history have very recently been published, and are acting as stimuli to an enormous amount of new research now in progress on both sides of the Atlantic.[9]

3 METHODOLOGY

i. The Approach

The historian of the family is faced with the usual problem, but in its most intractable form, of how best to interweave fact and theory, anecdote and analysis. As Levi-Strauss has well said, 'biographical and anecdotal history

... is low-powered history, which is not intelligible in itself, and only becomes so when it is transferred *en bloc* to a form of history of a higher power than itself.... The historian's relative choice ... is always confined to the choice between history which teaches more and explains less and history which explains more and teaches less.'[10] This book oscillates between analysis, which tries to explain, and anecdote, which tries to teach, in the perhaps vain hope that it may thus be possible to have the best of both worlds.

In dealing with the anecdotal material, the alternatives are to offer brief extracts from a large range of sources, or to use selected case studies to illustrate a point in depth. In this book the second method has been adopted, since in so sensitive an area as family relations only fairly detailed accounts can bring out the nuances of the situation. This choice has been deliberately made in full awareness that the method is open to the charge that the case studies selected are unrepresentative of the whole sample. All that can be said in defence is that a deliberate effort has been made to find representative examples and to eliminate exceptional sports.

The illustrative value of these anecdotes is beyond question. As Roger North remarked in the late seventeenth century, 'these may seem trivial passages, not worth remembering, but being exactly true, are part of the natural history of mankind which is everyone's interest to know.'[11] It cannot be denied, however, that the task of the historian of the family is greatly complicated by the inexplicable quirks of individual behaviour in this area of human relations. Some adults will react to a repressive childhood by granting great freedom to their own children, while the majority will routinely follow the repressive tradition. Some husbands will react to an unhappy arranged marriage by granting their own children freedom of choice of spouses, while the majority will routinely follow the arranged marriage tradition. One can, therefore, never be sure whether or not the individual example is typical or a sport, even of his or her own class and time and place. As Dr Zeldin has rightly warned, 'The history of domestic relations cannot be written in the same way as the history of international relations, and any description of them must be tentative and incomplete.'[12]

This book has been constructed along the following lines. Firstly, every effort has been made to maximize the size and variety of the data base by drawing upon the largest amount of evidence from the widest number of different types of sources. Secondly, it has been recognized that there is no such thing as a characteristic family type applicable to all ranks of society at a given time. The enormous differences of income, inheritance patterns, status and culture dictated similar differences in family relationships. Thirdly, one of the prime objectives has been to identify uniformities, and to set up a plausible typology, while recognizing that one is dealing only in ideal types, and that in any case no single typology will apply to all ranks in society. Fourthly, trans-national comparisons have been made with France and New England, in order to try to separate those features which were common to most of western Europe at a given time from those which were peculiar to England. Fifthly, in the interests of parsimony, those factors have been stressed which appear to have had the strongest effect upon the widest range of cultural and institutional arrangements. Central to the whole enterprise is the endeavour to chart changes in *mentalité* which found expression in changing family types, and to demonstrate how those particular changes came about.

ii. Six Points of View

Changes in the family are tackled from six points of view. The first is biological: the harsh facts of birth, nuptiality, marriage and death which not only governed the structure but also influenced the emotional content of family life.

The second is sociological: the relationship between the nuclear unit and other forms of social organization, notably the kin, the community, the school, the Church and the state.

The third is political: the distribution of power within the family, the patterns of authority and deference that existed between the head of the lineage and its members, between husbands and wives and parents and children, and the way these patterns related to cultural arrangements in the society as a whole.

The fourth is economic: the role of marriage as a method of transferring real and personal property; the role of the family as a unit of economic production in agriculture or cottage industry, as well as a unit of bourgeois and upper-class consumption; and the allocation of work responsibilities between husband, wife and children.

The fifth is psychological: the affective place of the family in the lives of the individuals who composed it, the degree of intensity and the hierarchy of priorities which they brought to their relationships with each other – husband and wife, parents and young children, parents and adult married children, sibling and sibling.

The sixth is sexual: the attitude adopted, in theory and in practice, towards an instinct which forms the basic biological bonding of the family.

Of course, any division of the material along these lines would be merely for analytical convenience. Some aspects are rather more limited and self-contained than others, but in practice all to some degree act and react upon the others. Consequently, except for demography and sex, the others have all been interwoven into the chronological analyses.

iii. Inadequate Methods

Because all these aspects are inextricably involved in any study of family change, stress on any one element tends to lead to sterility or myopia, or both. Procrustean tactics cannot cope with a Protean problem. Historical demography using family reconstitution has provided an enormously powerful tool in revealing the biological components of human life in the past; but it has inevitably failed to deal with the realities of human relationships, of how people treated one another and felt about one another. On the other hand, old-fashioned studies of domestic relations based on handbooks of behaviour and anecdotes culled from upper-class records are hardly more revealing of life as it was actually led by the majority even of that restricted class. Even less helpful are isolated studies of particular groups within the family. Histories of childhood suffer from the major defect that the study is unintelligible unless it is related to the history of the adults who controlled the children's lives and moulded their minds. Nor is it possible to write a history of women without linking it to the history of two other human groups: men, who have exploited, dominated, supported, or even cherished them; and also children, whose gestation, production, nurturance and upbringing has hitherto taken up much of their time and energies. The treatment of women by men, and the treatment of children by adults, can only be understood in the light of the cultural norms of the society as a whole.

The family is thus the only viable unit of study, firstly, since it provides the forum within which all these individuals interact, and where all the problems of this interaction are raised, if not resolved. Secondly, it is the only viable unit since it forces the historian to take into consideration the wider political, social, economic, intellectual, educational and religious forces which are all constantly at work in modifying the nature of the family, and changing the attitudes of those who compose it both towards one another and towards the outside world. The main difficulty about studying family history is how to handle an institution the essential functions of which – as a union for legitimate sexual reproduction and as a biological link between parents and children – does not, and by its nature cannot, alter; and yet how to discover, prove, date and explain important shifts in attitudes and relationships which, provided that one takes a long view covering several centuries, have clearly taken place.

In trying to grapple with this baffling phenomenon, it is tempting to fall back on the diffusion of ideas. But here still further difficulties arise. It is one thing to establish that in 1693 John Locke published a widely read book which advocated that boys at school should not be regularly beaten for minor academic lapses and that by the mid-eighteenth century some of the most elite schools had, indeed, given up this practice. But between the idea and the action there yawns a vast gap. We do not know who read Locke, nor do we know how the readers responded to him. What seems to be involved is a far broader and prior shift in attitudes towards the child, which made the readership more responsive to Locke's message. Or, to take another example, medical and didactic writers since the time of Galen had been urging mothers to breast-feed their children, but it was only in the late eighteenth century that a majority of English upper-class mothers began to follow the advice. Here again, the key factor seems to be less the enunciation of the idea than a deep-seated change in the response of the readers, which at last made them more receptive to the advice. Only after the book becomes popular does it become an independent variable in its own right, which leaves the ultimate causal problem still unexplained.

iv. Linear or Cyclical Models

Any simple linear or cyclical model for such profound changes is bound to fail, for four reasons. The first is the social stratification of cultural values, as a result of which one status group, say the elite at court, will have a totally different set of familial values and behaviour patterns from those of the peasantry in the villages. The second is the temporal stratification of cultural values, and the slowness and irregularity of cultural change. As a result one set of values and its corresponding behaviour pattern is already obsolete and is generating its opposite a little before it reaches its apogee. To give but one example, in the late eighteenth century romantic love, sexual hedonism and child-rearing permissiveness were about to reach their peak among the elite just at the moment when the repressive doctrines of proto-Victorian morality were beginning to emerge to replace them. The third is the multiplication of possible mixes in cultural values, as a result of which it is extremely unlikely that the particular combination adopted by a social group in one period will be exactly repeated in another. A given group may, for example, opt for openness or privacy, collectivism or individualism, domestic fusion of roles or specialization, hierarchy or egalitarianism, calculation or emotion, asceticism or hedonism, discipline or licence, sin and guilt or pleasure, ancestor-worship or the rejection of lineage, sexual and age-group segregation or joint participation. Given this wide range of options – and of points between – it is highly unlikely that any one set of choices governing family structure, functions and relationships will be exactly replicated in another place or at another time or in another social group. Fourthly, the society in which the family evolved from the sixteenth to the eighteenth centuries changed in such extraordinary and erratic ways as to make a linear or a cyclical pattern most improbable. Two changes of incalculable significance were the growth of literacy and of printing, which created great divergences between high and low cultures, and the growth of geographical and social mobility, which ripped large numbers of individuals out of their familiar domestic environment and cast them adrift to find new attachments and new values.

4 DEFINITION OF TERMS

In order to understand what follows, it is first necessary to define with some care what is meant by 'family', 'household', 'lineage', 'kin', 'marriage' and 'divorce'. On close inspection these apparently simple words turn out to have complicated and ambiguous meanings.

i. Family

a. Definition and Functions. The word 'family' can be used to mean many things, from the conjugal pair to the 'family of man', and it is therefore imperative to begin with a clear definition of what the word will mean in this book. Here it is taken as synonymous neither with 'household' – persons living together under one roof – nor with 'kin' – persons related by blood or marriage. It is taken to mean those members of the same kin who live together under one roof. The functions which this institution can fill and has filled are many and varied, although in very few societies has it embraced all of them at any one time. They include sexual, emotional, social and economic elements, although the degree to which any one of them is present will vary from period to period, from culture to culture, and from class to class. At the biological level, family and marriage provide for the reproduction and nurture of legitimate children. The second function is to canalize and control the drive for sexual play and pleasure, which is so extraordinarily constant in the human species, persisting all the year round and to a more advanced age than is needed for reproductive purposes. The emotional function – which is by no means always present – is to form an attachment arising out of close and regular physical proximity to another human being, whether the relationship be husband to wife or parent to child. More often, the family serves a minimum negative psychic function of the avoidance of loneliness.

As a social system, the nuclear family has two castes – male and female – and two classes – adult and child. The male caste always dominates the female, and the adult class the child, but the latter, if he lives, is guaranteed upward social mobility since in time he becomes an adult.[13] In the Early Modern period, a female adult took precedence over a male child, but only up to the age of about seven.

The family was the main instrument for the social control of children, although it also acted, or was supposed to act, as a control mechanism for adults and as a stabilizing factor in society. As Thomas Fuller put it in the mid-seventeenth century: 'Though bachelors be the strongest stakes [i.e., the best soldiers], married men are the best binders in the hedge of the Commonwealth.'[14] Thus most Early Modern societies regarded single young men or women in particular as a potential menace to the social order, and in some English towns and in New England in the seventeenth century they were obliged to live in a patriarchal household rather than at liberty by themselves. The declared object was the prevention of 'much sin and iniquity which ordinarily are the companions and consequences of a solitary life.'[15] Then, as today, the establishment of a family meant the assumption of serious responsibilities for others and thus was regarded as an important factor in social stability and cohesion. The family was expected to act as the principal agent for the socialization of children, their orientation and adaptation to the religion, the culture and the morality appropriate to their country and their class. It also had considerable police functions, for parents were held responsible for the delinquency of their children. The family was expected to nurture the helpless, particularly the very young and that minority of adults who survived to old age. Finally, the family served as an agent of social placement, conferring status and providing job opportunities through contacts and influence supplied by its connections, and those of the kin.

The family also had a number of important economic functions. Marriage was for centuries one of the most common mechanisms for the transfer and redistribution of property and capital, inevitably second to direct inheritance in the male line, but leaving purchase and sale a very poor third.[16] In many cases, moreover, especially among the peasants and artisans, the family was a unit of economic production, all members working together in a common economic enterprise in the fields or at a cottage industry.

b. Types. Until very recently, it was generally believed that at some indeterminate date western European society moved from one family type to another. It was alleged that at first the typical unit was the extended stem family, consisting of two or more generations of married couples linked in father and son chains, who lived permanently under one roof. At some point this was replaced by the nuclear family of parents and unmarried children with which we are familiar today. This orthodoxy has now been replaced by a new one, according to which the European family has always been nuclear, at any rate since reliable records begin in the early sixteenth century. This hypothesis is based on census data, which prove that in many areas of western Europe in the Early Modern period, including England, less than ten per cent of all households contained kin relatives in addition to the conjugal family of parents and unmarried young children.[17]

There are four reasons why this new orthodoxy is as unsatisfactory as the old. The first is that there were some areas of Europe, particularly to the south and east, at different periods of time, where the extended family (vertically through generations) or the enlarged family (horizontally through kin) continued to predominate, the architecture of the average farmhouse reflecting this situation. Consequently, a generalization that may be true for England and other parts of north-west Europe cannot safely be used for the whole continent. It is not true, for example, of very many areas of France south of the Loire in the seventeenth and eighteenth centuries.[18] Secondly, at the highest social level, among the aristocracy, it was not at all uncommon in the sixteenth and seventeenth centuries for an enlarged or stem family to cohabit in a rambling country house, whether in England or elsewhere. For example, when in 1632 Dudley, son and heir of Dudley third Lord North, married, his father obliged him and his wife to reside with him at the family seat in the country at Kirtling, while for the first three years the house also held young Dudley's widowed sister. Lord North charged the couple heavily for the privilege, demanding first £200 a year and later £400 a year as the family increased. It was not until 1650, eighteen years after the marriage, that Dudley, his wife, and his ten surviving children were at last allowed to set up their own household in another family seat.[19]

Among the impoverished members of the lesser gentry, married children also sometimes lived in the same house as their parents for longer than the first year or so. When the son of William Blundell of Crosby Hall married in 1667, his father could not afford to set the couple up on an estate of their own, and they therefore took up permanent residence in Crosby Hall. In 1687, when the Reverend Matthew Henry married into a well-to-do family, the young couple boarded for some years with the wife's parents at Chester.[20]

Apart from these exceptions to a hypothetical rule, there are three more fundamental flaws in the theory that the Western family has always been nuclear. In the first place, it ignores the developmental sequence of all families, since it is based solely on census data, which merely represent a cross-section of the family situation at a fixed moment in time. Owing to the demographic attrition of old people in pre-modern societies, the proportion of conjugal families with grandparents still alive at any one time could never have been more than about twenty-seven per cent, of whom only a proportion would be widowed.[21] The census evidence shows that the proportion of three-generation families was about eight to fifteen per cent, which therefore proves that it was quite normal for widowed grandparents to live with their children. The European family expanded and contracted like a concertina, moving from the extended stem family to the nuclear and back again, as it passed through various stages. To take a hypothetical but average case, a young couple might begin their married life for a year or two in the house of one of their parents, thus becoming part of an extended stem family. But they would very soon move out on their own and set up a nuclear family, usually first without and then with children. Eventually the children would grow up and leave home for apprenticeship, school, or service in someone else's house. Very soon after, in some cases the father of one of the couple would die and the widowed mother would move in with them, or in other cases both might move in since the old father was no longer able to work. The family thus became extended stem again. Soon afterwards the eldest son would marry, and he and his bride might also move in for a short period, so that it might become a fully extended stem family of three generations. Then the old couple or the widow would die, the married children would move away, and the family would become nuclear once again. It is clear that census data is quite unable to illustrate this complicated family life-cycle as it passed through various stages of fission and fusion.[22]

Another objection is that the new orthodoxy ignores the importance of economic resources. Generally, the richer the family, the larger the size and the more complex the type of house, and consequently of family. Most commonly, the very rich provided for widowed mothers in separate but usually nearby dower houses, but in some cases they took in an aged parent to live with them in the house.[23] With a small army of servants, plenty of house-space, and much entertaining, the three-generation expanded family was not an unusual type among wealthy landed families.

The lesser gentry and yeomen, who owned only one, fairly large house, normally allocated the widow a separate part of it for her residence. For example, in 1596 Charles Scott of Godmersham, Kent, died leaving his home and the bulk of his estate to his eldest son, but stipulating that part of the house should be set aside for his widow 'so that none shall meddle with that end'. Lower still down the social scale, among the peasantry of Cambridgeshire, for example, it was normal for a man to stipulate in his will that a room be set aside in the house for his widow for her lifetime, so long as she did not remarry, as many did. Robert Salmon of Willingham left his cottage to his only daughter, but ordered that his widow should have a bedroom in the kitchen with access to the kitchen fire. If the two women could not agree to share, the daughter was to build the widow a shack on the back of the house, with its own fireplace. Similarly, in 1589 William Brasier gave his widow house-room, access to the kitchen fire, and meat and drink in the house bequeathed to his son. If these arrangements did not work out, the widow was to have an annuity of £3 a year to live by herself. There can be little doubt that most widows in peasant families lived in the same house with one of their children, even if their numbers were small due to high mortality and a high rate of remarriage.[24]

There are also examples among artisans of fathers dividing up the house-rooms among his children, presumably intending them either to partition off the space for habitation or to agree to one buying the others out. For example, in 1728 a Worcestershire cooper died leaving a personal estate worth a mere £1 5s. He had one son and two daughters, and he left each of the latter, presumably in lieu of a dowry, ten square yards of his workshop.[25]

At the bottom of the social scale, the very poor possessed too little land to feed, and too few rooms to house, more than the members of the nuclear family: they just could not afford the extended or stem family, since they lacked the necessary resources to maintain it. For this reason an increase in the number of nuclear families may mean no more than an increase in the number of paupers and landless labourers in the society, who are unable to house and feed more than their own wives and young children.[26]

Lastly, cohabitation is only one – and not the most important – clue to family type and structure. Other critical variables are whether or not production is shared in a common economic enterprise; whether the members of the family go out to work independently of each other; whether or not consumption is shared, with one kitchen cooking a single meal, or whether there are separate marketing and separate kitchens. More important than any of these mechanical criteria is the strength of the emotional ties, the amount of shared functions, activities and social contacts, for kin – or neighbour – bonding can be very close and intimate without co-residence under a single roof. The key definition of the nuclear family is that the ties that bind its members together are stronger than those which bind any one member to outsiders, whether relatives, friends, associates or patrons. But recent studies of contemporary society have shown some kin linkages flourishing despite geographical separation, and despite the pressures of modern urban industrial society.[27] Parts of 'the world we have lost' turn out to be still here after all.

One may conclude, therefore, that there has been little significant change in formal family organization in north-west Europe over the past five hundred years. In terms of residence, neither has there been a shift from an enlarged family full of kin relatives or an extended stem family of several generations to a simple nuclear or conjugal one, nor has the nuclear family always been predominant. It is true that at any given moment in time most families since the sixteenth century in England have been nuclear in type, but most of the individuals who composed them at some stage of their lives either belonged to, or were to belong in future to, families of a different type. The family in north-west Europe has for centuries been like an amoeba, reproducing itself, expanding and contracting through an infinitely repetitive cyclical movement governed by age, custom, mortality, and economic resources.

As we shall see, however, this stability of residential form conceals enormous changes in the reality of human relationships. These latter changes reduce to relative triviality arguments over changes in household size, composition and structure, or over whether we are dealing with different residential types of family.

ii. Household

A household consists of persons living under one roof. The core of any household is clearly the family, namely members related by blood or marriage, usually the conjugal pair and their unmarried children, but sometimes including grandparents, one married child, or occasionally kin relatives. But most households also included non-kin inmates, sojourners, boarders or lodgers, occupying rooms vacated by children or kin, as well as indentured apprentices and resident servants, employed either for domestic work about the house or as an additional resident labour force for the fields or the shop. This composite group was confusingly known as a 'family' in the sixteenth and seventeenth centuries, so that Ralph Josselin could note in his diary that one of his maidservants was 'the first that married out of my family'. Throughout this book the group of inmates in a single house will be described as a household, but it should be noted that in many households, the relations with children were not all that much closer than the relations with domestic servants, so that the use of the word 'family' to mean the 'household' made good psychological sense at that time. In most cases, however, these domestic servants were not members of the kin, however distant (although there is one case in the Josselin family where a boy was an apprentice in the house of his father's sister's husband's sister's husband!).[28] In contemporary theory, servants were equated with children as subordinate members of the household. Cleaver and Dod's popular manual of the early seventeenth century (which merely repeated much of the work of Robert Cawdrey published in 1562) stated the standard doctrine very clearly: 'The householder is called *Pater Familias*, that is father of a family, because he should have a fatherly care over his servants as if they were his children.' Thus the late seventeenth-century Boston Puritan minister, Cotton Mather, regarded it as his duty to teach his servants – even negroes – both the word of God to lead them to baptism, and also the art of reading and writing.[29] It was because of their legal and moral subordination to the head of the household that no-one, not even the Levellers, suggested that the electoral franchise should be extended to children or servants or women. They were not free persons.

It was precisely because its junior members were under close supervision that the state had a very strong interest in encouraging and strengthening the household. In a society almost entirely without a police force, it was a most valuable institution for social control at the village level. It helped to keep in check potentially the most unruly element in any society, the floating mass of young unmarried males; and it provided the basic unit for taxation. No wonder both Church and state looked on marriage with approval, and the sixteenth-century moral theologians spoke eulogistically about it as 'appointed by God Himself to be the fountain and seminary of all other sorts and kinds of life in the Commonwealth and the Church.'[30]

In the Early Modern period, living-in servants were not the rarity that they are today, but a normal component of all but the poorest households.

From the time of the first censuses in the early sixteenth century to the mid-nineteenth century, about one third or more of all households contained living-in servants. In the country, many of the men were agricultural labourers, hired at annual fairs and living in dormitories on the farm, while in the towns many were apprentices serving a seven-year term. But most women servants worked in the home on domestic chores, and what is so striking about the pre-modern household, especially in the towns, is the ubiquity of maidservants. In Coventry in 1523 they formed a quarter of the adult population, while in Prescot in Lancashire as late as 1851 over one-third of all women employed outside their homes were in domestic service.[31] These figures prove that the practice of employing female domestic servants extended far down the social and economic scale.

In addition to these ubiquitous servants, the pre-modern household, at any rate of the artisan, shopkeeper or small husbandman, also commonly included lodgers, who filled the house-space vacated by departed children, and whose rent went to swell the family income. These lodgers, who were especially common in urban households, were usually unmarried young persons in their late teens or early twenties, who worked for employers elsewhere. With the breakdown of the paternalistic practice of apprentices living in their masters' homes in the late eighteenth century, the number of lodgers living in a household but not under the control of its head must have increased considerably.

This diverse assemblage of persons, the married couple, perhaps aged parents or unmarried relatives, children and step-children of various ages, domestic servants, living-in labourers or apprentices and paying lodgers, composed the household. Because of the shifting diversity of composition, and because the number of servants kept, and of children surviving and still at home, varied directly with the wealth of the houseowner, all censuses reveal a very wide range in the number of persons in different households. Consequently, the discovery that from the mid-sixteenth to the mid-nineteenth centuries the average English household consisted of about 4·75 persons does not of itself have any historical significance.[32] At the very highest level, among the greater aristocracy, the early sixteenth-century household consisted of up to a hundred persons who lived together in castles and rambling manor houses, and ate together in the great communal halls. All members were bound together by the ideal of 'good lordship' dispensed by the head of the household and 'faithfulness' or 'faithful affection' displayed by his followers, and in particular by those who lived with him in his household. The late sixteenth and seventeenth centuries saw the decline, both as an ideal and as a practice, of the great noble household and its replacement by a new ideal of loyalty to the state.[33]

Apart from this change at the highest aristocratic level, the only fundamental changes in the household in the last five hundred years have been the removal of unmarried agricultural workers and apprentices to lodgings on their own; the disappearance of living-in domestic servants in all households except a handful of the very richest; the postponement from about age twelve to about age eighteen of the departure from the household of the children; and the increase in the proportion of households containing widowed parents. All but the first have occurred during the last hundred years, long after the period under discussion in this book.

iii. Lineage and Kin

The lineage are relatives by blood or marriage, dead, living, and yet to be born, who collectively form a 'house'. The kin are those members of the lineage who are currently alive and who by virtue of the relationship are recognized to have special claims to loyalty, obedience or support. Among the nobility and squirarchy, the kin formed the core around which was constructed that wider system of 'good lordship' centered in the great household. What bound such a group together was a strong sense of loyalty to the ancestral ties of blood, that is of hereditary lineage, a system of thought which affected a whole range of values and attitudes. Allegiance to lineage and kinship creates a system which gives priority to the permanent interests of the 'house', its maintenance, continuity, function and economic well-being for century after century. The living members, the kin, are regarded as no more than the trustees of the lineage's name, property and blood. The interests of, and loyalty to, the lineage are paramount, and all other interests and loyalties are secondary. It was precisely this relation of the individual to his lineage which provided a man of the upper classes in a traditional society with his identity, without which he was a mere atom floating in a void of social space.

As this traditional society eroded, however, under the pressures of Church, state, and a market economy, different values came to the fore. These included the interest of the state in obtaining efficient and honest servants who were best fitted for their tasks; the interest of the individual in obtaining freedom to maximize his economic gains and freedom to pursue his personal goals; and the claims and interests of intermediate organizations, such as churches and professional groups. These new values undermined allegiance by the kin, and the result was a crisis of confidence among the aristocracy. They desperately tried to relight the dying embers of lineage loyalty, first by an artificial revival of the cult of chivalry, and then by symbolic reaffirmations of the significance of ancestry. Heraldic emblazonment became more and more gaudy and elaborate, with coats of arms proliferating; huge genealogies were constructed, tracing lineal descent back to some mythical figure in the distant past, possibly even one from the Old Testament; and local churches were converted into lineage shrines by stuffing them full of large and elaborate family tombs bright with painted coats of arms.

As one proceeds further away from the Highland zone and closer to London, and further down the social scale through gentry, bourgeoisie, peasants and artisans, the concept of kinship carried less and less of the baggage of ideological commitment to 'honour' and 'faithfulness', etc., to which most great magnates and their followers paid more than mere lip-service. In these less exalted circles, lineage meant little, and kinship was more an association for the exchange of mutual economic benefits than a prime focus of emotional commitment. Further down still, among the propertyless, the community of friends and neighbours was probably more important in both respects, especially in the urban environment.

iv. Marriage

In the Early Modern period, marriage was an engagement which could be undertaken in a bewildering variety of ways, and the mere definition of it is fraught with difficulties. Up to the eleventh century, casual polygamy seems to have been general, with easy divorce and much concubinage. The result was many bastards and many half-siblings, who acted as a reserve for inheritance if the official male heir failed. As late as 1020, the Northumbrian Priests' Law still found it necessary to insist that 'we forbid that any man should have more wives than one; and she is to be lawfully betrothed and wedded'. Pagan Anglo-Saxon society was clearly very casual about the solemn contract of marriage. In this respect at least they were individualists *avant la lettre*. This view of the laity that marriage was a personal affair of no concern to external authorities was one which slowly weakened, but which persisted right through the middle ages and beyond, became partly embedded in canon law, and was the cause of a great deal of trouble and confusion in the Early Modern period. In the early middle ages all that marriage implied in the eyes of the laity seems to have been a private contract between two families concerning property exchange, which also provided some financial protection to the bride in case of the death of her husband or desertion or divorce by him. For those without property, it was a private contract between two individuals, enforced by the community sense of what was right. A church ceremony was an expensive and unnecessary luxury, especially since divorce by mutual consent followed by remarriage was still widely practised. It was not until the thirteenth century that the Church at last managed to take over control of marriage law, to assert at least the principle of monogamous indissoluble marriage, to define and prohibit incest, to punish fornication and adultery, and to get bastards legally excluded from property inheritance.[34]

Although by the sixteenth century marriage was fairly well defined, before 1754 there were still numerous ways of entering into it. For persons of property it involved a series of distinct steps. The first was a written legal contract between the parents concerning the financial arrangements. The second was the spousals (also called a contract), the formal exchange, usually before witnesses, of oral promises. The third step was the public proclamation of banns in church, three times, the purpose of which was to allow claims of pre-contract to be heard (by the seventeenth century nearly all the well-to-do evaded this step by obtaining a licence). The fourth step was the wedding in church, in which mutual consent was publicly verified, and the union received the formal blessing of the church. The fifth and final step was the sexual consummation.[35]

But it cannot be emphasized too strongly that according to ecclesiastical law the spousals was as legally binding a contract as the church wedding, although to many laity it was no more than a conditional contract. Any sort of exchange of promises before witnesses which was followed by cohabitation was regarded in law as a valid marriage. It was for this reason that Quaker marriages were upheld by Chief Justice Hale in the late seventeenth century, and that in 1585 a man who changed his mind sold for ten shillings his rights over a girl by spousals. When the money was not paid, he forbade the banns.

In remoter areas, especially the Scottish border country, Wales and the extreme south-west, the betrothal ceremony itself, the 'handfast', continued to be treated by many of the poor as sufficient for a binding union without the blessing of the Church. There is some evidence that even in the Lowland zone quite large numbers of the poor were not getting married in church in the late seventeenth century.[36] Indeed the church wedding had not been elevated to the position of a sacrament until 1439, and it was only in 1563, after the Reformation, that the Catholic Church first required the presence of a priest for a valid and binding marriage.[37]

The Anglican Church naturally did not recognize this Catholic innovation, and since it took no measures of its own, the situation was left in considerable confusion. Alone among the Christian Churches of Europe, the Anglican Church retained unaltered the medieval law of marriage, and continued to leave matrimonial litigation in the hands of ecclesiastical courts. As the Anglican Church tightened its grip on society in the sixteenth and seventeenth centuries, both the laity and the clergy came increasingly to regard the wedding in church as the key ceremony, but the civil lawyers who ran the courts continued to recognize the spousals before witnesses. Spousals could take two forms, one of which was the contract *per verba de futuro*, an oral promise to marry in the future. If not followed by consummation (which was assumed to imply consent in the present), this was an engagement which could be legally broken by mutual consent at a later date. If followed by consummation, however, it was legally binding for life. The contract *per verba de praesenti*, however, by which the pair exchanged before witnesses such phrases as 'I do take thee to my wife' and 'I do take thee to my husband', was regarded in ecclesiastical law as an irrevocable commitment which could never be broken, and which nullified a later church wedding to someone else. It was this ceremony, not the one in church, which created the binding legal obligation, although a church wedding was necessary if a widow wanted later to claim right of dower, or children to claim an inheritance. This was because the civil courts, which controlled property, only recognized a church wedding, whereas the Church courts had been obliged in the twelfth century to recognize a contract without a wedding.[38]

The Church courts therefore declared a marriage in church to be adulterous and of no validity if there could be proved a prior oral contract *per verba de praesenti* by one of the pair with another person, or a contract *per verba de futuro* followed by consummation. To make matters worse, the canons of 1604 stipulated that a church wedding must take place between the hours of 8 a.m. and noon in the church at the place of residence of one of the pair, after the banns had been read for three weeks running. Marriages performed at night, in secular places like inns or private houses, or in towns or villages remote from the place of residence, would subject the officiating clergyman to serious penalties. The canons also forbade the marriage of persons under twenty-one without the consent of parents or guardians. The catch, however, was that although such marriages were now declared illegal, they were nonetheless valid and binding for life: this was a paradox the laity found hard to understand.[39]

This post-1604 situation resulted in a brisk trade carried on by unscrupulous clergymen, operating in districts which were immune from superior ecclesiastical supervision, who would marry anyone for a fee, no questions asked. This was a commerce which became more and more widespread and scandalous in the late seventeenth and early eighteenth centuries, when parent-child relations on the issue of control of marriage were becoming more and more strained, and more and more children were defying their parents and running away (plate 2). Shadwell described a clergyman who 'will marry a couple at any time; he defies licence and canonical bann, and all those foolish ceremonies'. If the playwrights are to be believed, some clergymen were even more obliging. Captain Basil in Farquhar's *The Stage Coach* reported: 'We saw a light in the parson's chamber that travelled with me, went up and found him smoking his pipe. He first gave us his blessing, then lent us his bed.' Many London churches, which were by various legal quirks unlicensed or exempt from superior jurisdiction, specialized in quick marriages. Between 1664 and 1691 some forty thousand marriages took place in St James's, Duke Place, while 'there's such a coupling at Pancras that they stand behind one another, as 'twere in a country dance'. The most flourishing trade of all was done by decayed clergymen in the vicinity of the Fleet in London, particularly in the first half of the eighteenth century when official weddings were heavily taxed, and those around the Fleet were both legally valid and very cheap. Notice-boards advertised 'Marriages performed within', and touts encouraged passers-by with the invitation 'Sir, will you be pleased to walk in and be married?' (plate 1). For the poor within walking distance of London, Fleet marriages were a financial godsend, but many drunken, hasty and exploitative unions were also sealed in these sordid surroundings, and once performed they could never be dissolved. These venal clergymen were also prepared, for a fee, to back-date a registration to legitimize children already born, or even to supply a man for a woman seeking a husband in a hurry.[40]

There are two pieces of evidence which strongly indicate that the position of the Church courts, that the old pre-Christian oral spousals formed an indissoluble union without the blessing of a clergyman, was still not properly understood by the public in the late seventeenth century, although it had been part of ecclesiastical law since the twelfth century. One is that already cited: the flood of persons who were willing to pay money to any clergyman, however disreputable, who was prepared to perform the marriage service over them in any place, however sordid. These persons clearly thought that a clerical blessing was needed to legitimize the union, otherwise they would not have wasted their money in these squalid marriage-parlours. The second piece of evidence comes from the questions sent in to the popular newspaper the *Athenian Mercury*, which during the 1690s flourished on answering readers' queries. A significant proportion of these questions concerned the degree to which verbal spousals were binding and prevented a subsequent marriage to another person, a fact many readers clearly found hard to believe. The readers were apparently mainly of the urban middle class, with only a tiny sprinkling of nobility and gentry, while the editor, John Dunton, and his assistants were Presbyterian noncon-formists. The latter clung to a fairly austere ethical code of conduct, according to which violations of contractual obligations were wrong. The replies they gave were mostly legally correct (though they failed to stress the critical difference between spousals *de futuro* and *de praesenti*), but they had to be repeated over and over again, since the readership found it so hard to believe that a verbal engagement without clerical blessing had full legal validity.[41]

To sum up the situation in the late seventeenth and early eighteenth centuries, the ecclesiastical courts were recognizing as a valid and indissoluble contract a ceremony which they were also declaring illegal and a punishable offence for the officiating clergyman. Meanwhile, the common law courts were applying a different set of rules for the purpose of establishing claims to the inheritance of property. The upper and middle ranks of society believed and practised the law as defined by the common law courts, while popular pundits in the press, like John Dunton, were publicizing a not entirely accurate version of the ecclesiastical law. Meanwhile, many of the poor were practising their own forms of concubinage following an exchange of words, some but not all of which were legal in the eyes of the ecclesiastical courts. The Church canons said one thing about the conditions under which a clerical wedding ceremony was legal, the Church courts quite another about what made it valid.

Before the Act of 1753, therefore, there is no simple answer to the problem of defining what was, and what was not, a marriage. There were many ways of entering into the married state. Some of the poor lived in a form of concubinage, while between 1694 and 1754 hundreds of thousands of others went through the cheaper form of ceremony of a clandestine wedding in a London ale-house, coffee-house or even brothel, carried out by a professional clerical marriage-maker. The upper classes and prosperous bourgeoisie normally evaded all canonical restrictions on time and place by obtaining a special licence. Perhaps not much more than half the population were being married strictly according to the rules of canon law and of those that were at least half had already entered into full sexual relations.[42]

Because of their concern to defend and pass on their property, the nobility were inevitably disturbed by this hopeless legal tangle, and particularly by the ease with which penniless adventurers could entice or seduce their daughters and heiresses and irrevocably marry them without parental knowledge or consent, at any place and at any time of day. Moreover, a claim, true or false, to a secret pre-contract, supported by bribed witnesses, was an irritatingly easy way for a child to block a marriage arranged by the parents, to which he or she was averse (though the *Athenian Mercury* wrongly claimed that contracts without parental consent had no validity). Feelings were particularly strong between 1677 and 1714, a period when parent-child tensions over control of marriage were rising and when commercialized clandestine marriages were becoming a public scandal (and were the theme of over one third of all comedies played on the London stage). During this time, the House of Lords repeatedly tried to change and simplify the law, only to be defeated again and again in the House of Commons.[43]

It was not until 1753 that Lord Hardwicke's Marriage Act was passed, which at last brought coherence and logic to the laws governing marriage. From 1754 only the church wedding, not the verbal spousals, was legally binding, so that a prior oral contract was no longer a cause for the annulment of a later marriage in church; secondly, all church marriages had to be entered in the parish register and signed by both parties; thirdly, all marriages which occurred at times or in places defined as illegal by the 1604 canons were now also declared invalid; fourthly, no marriage of persons under twenty-one was valid without the consent of parents or guardians; and fifthly, enforcement of the law was transferred from the feeble control of the Church courts to the secular courts, which were empowered to impose up to fourteen years' transportation on clergymen who disobeyed the law.[44] From now on, the only recourse for runaway couples defying their parents was the long and expensive flight to Scotland, especially to Gretna Green, where the new Marriage Act did not apply, and where there sprang up a new trade in commercialized marriage on the spot with no questions asked (plates 3 and 4).[45]

The debate over the passage of the Bill provides revealing evidence about current attitudes to marriage among the propertied classes. The prime reason for the Bill was frankly stated as being the fact that 'both men and women of the most infamous character had opportunities of ruining the sons and daughters of the greatest families in England, by the convenience of marrying in the Fleet and other unlicensed places; and marrying had become as much a trade as any mechanical profession.'[46] The solution was to deny the validity of the religious ceremony unless it conformed to certain conditions, including parental consent if under twenty-one. This necessarily involved the rejection of the ceremony as a sacrament, an indissoluble union before God. Advocates of the reform complacently declared that 'we have in this age got the better of this as well as a great many other superstitious opinions . . .' so as 'to render Christianity consistent with common sense.' Marriage was now regarded as a contract like any other, subject to statutory controls for the public good, for 'this adding of a sanctity to the marriage is inconsistent with the good of every society and with the happiness of mankind in general.' The Bill was thus clearly only made possible by the growing secularization of elite society and by the acceptance of the idea that personal happiness could be achieved by public legislation. Its proponents would have preferred to restrict the clause demanding parental consent to persons of 'fortune and rank', but recognized that 'this is impossible in this country.'

The second object of the Bill was to do away with secret pre-contracts and secret marriages, which made bigamy all too easy (plate 5). Public registration of the marriage was now an essential part of the ceremony. It was argued, with some plausibility, that under existing conditions in which marriage could be made by mere verbal contract, by the blessing of a wandering clergyman in an ale-house, by a private chaplain in a private house, or by a commercial clerical marriage-maker in one of the unlicensed London churches, a man could have as many wives as he wished. 'Every man may privately have a wife in every corner of this city, or in every town he has been in, without it being possible for them to know of one another.' Another speaker agreed that 'the crime of polygamy [is] now so frequent.'[47]

The main reason for opposition to the Bill was the fear that since parents would in future have the whip hand over their children until twenty-one, the aristocracy would be able to create a closed, and increasingly wealthy, caste by keeping their heiresses exclusively for marriage within their own ranks and by snapping up all the heiresses of socially ambitious and wealthy commoners. Opponents of the Bill argued that 'riches is the blood of the body politic: it must be made to circulate,' and how better than by the marriage by free choice of commoners' children to those of noblemen? One also raised the fear of aristocratic racial degeneration: 'what sort of breed their offspring will be we may easily judge, if the gout, the gravel, the pox and madness are always to wed together.' Thirdly, they protested that the Bill would infringe the natural right of minors to marry whom they pleased, and would lead to a revival of arranged and loveless marriages, like those on the continent of Europe, with the consequent institutionalization of adultery by both sexes as a normal convention of polite society.

The final argument of the opponents of the Bill was that it would make marriage for the poor both slow and expensive, resulting in a rise in concubinage, bastardy and infanticide. By making verbal spousals invalid, some feared that the Bill would also allow men to seduce girls on promise of marriage and then abandon them with impunity.[48]

Except for the last, regarding the high cost of marriage and easy evasion of promises, these arguments had few merits, and were not justified by subsequent events. The scandals and general disadvantages to society of clandestine marriages and secret pre-contracts were such that the Bill carried. After 1754, it was at long last clear what was a valid marriage and what was not, and open registration of the union was called for, if not in fact always carried out. The unknown number of the poor who were unwilling or unable to go through the ceremony in the church were henceforth obliged to live in concubinage, since their private exchanges of verbal promises were no longer legally binding. Before the Act came into force in 1754 the public had been left in a state of considerable and reasonable confusion about the state of the law concerning marriage. After 1754 the law was absolutely clear, although it is by no means certain how many of the poor or the Dissenters were able or willing to comply with it.

v. Separation and Divorce

At this period there was no divorce permitting remarriage in the Anglican Church. For marriages which broke down, usually because of adultery, there was only separation of bed and board, accompanied by a financial settlement. This was currently called 'divorce', but it did not allow either party to remarry. Moreover the many medieval impediments which could create a nullity were now blocked up. These had been so numerous that a rich man with a good lawyer could probably obtain one, although the records of ecclesiastical courts show that the average man did not use this device. He almost certainly simply divorced himself or ran away without going to law. After the Reformation, an annulment could only be obtained on the three grounds of a pre-contract to someone else, consanguinity within the Levitical degrees, or male impotence over a period of three years – the last not an easy matter to prove.[49] A man or woman whose spouse had left home and had not been heard of for a period of seven years was also free to remarry, on the assumption that the missing spouse was dead. If he or she returned, however, either the first marriage took priority over the second or the woman was permitted to choose which husband she preferred.[50]

For most people in England, therefore, marriage was an indissoluble union, breakable only by death; this point was emphasized by Defoe in 1727, and by that acidulous spinster Miss Weeton in a sarcastic poem in 1808 about a discontented husband:

> 'Come soon, O Death, and Alice take.'
> He loudly groan'd and cry'd;
> Death came – but made a sad mistake,
> For Richard 'twas that died.[51]

Unlike the other Protestant churches, the Anglican Church, largely because of historical accident at its inception, failed to provide for remarriage by the innocent party in cases of separation for extreme cruelty or adultery. This question remained in some doubt throughout Elizabeth's reign, but was finally clarified by number 107 of the canons of 1604, which forbade the remarriage of 'divorced' persons. To the aristocracy this created an intolerable situation, since it meant that a nobleman whose wife committed adultery before producing a son was precluded from marrying again and begetting a legal male heir to carry on the line and inherit the property. It was to circumvent this difficulty that in the late seventeenth century, as the concept of marriage as a sacrament ebbed with the waning of religious enthusiasm, divorce by private Act of Parliament became a possible avenue of escape for wealthy noblemen and others who found themselves in this predicament. But this was a very expensive procedure, and it was almost entirely confined, especially before 1760, to those who had very large properties at stake to be handed on to a male heir by a second marriage. Between 1670 and 1799, there were only one hundred and thirty-one such Acts, virtually all instituted by husbands, and only seventeen passed before 1750 (Graph 1).[52]

At the other end of the social scale, among the propertyless, there were also alternatives to death as a means of finally dissolving an unsatisfactory marriage. In a society without a national police force, it was all too easy simply to run away and never be heard of again. This must have been a not infrequent occurrence among the poor, to judge by the fact that deserted wives comprised over eight per cent of all the women aged between thirty-one and forty listed in the 1570 census of the indigent poor of the city of

DIVORCES BY ACT OF PARLIAMENT

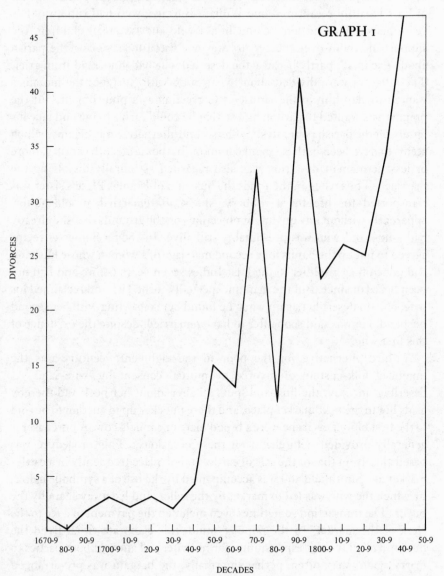

GRAPH I

DIVORCES

1670-9   90-9   10-9   30-9   50-9   70-9   90-9   10-9   30-9   50-9
      80-9   1700-9   20-9   40-9   60-9   80-9   1800-9   20-9   40-9

DECADES

Norwich. The tragic victims of this solution to marital discord or economic stress were the wives and children, who were left destitute and inevitably became charges on the community. In 1762, for example, the parish officials of East Hoathly recaptured one William Burrage, who had run away five years before. He had left behind him a wife and six small children, the support of whom over these years was estimated to have cost the parish about £50 in all, partly because the deserted wife had gone mad from grief. The villagers were divided about what to do with Burrage: the moralists wanted to clap him in the House of Correction as a punishment, but the pragmatists wanted to pardon him so that he could earn a living and take his family off the parish poor rates.[53] The second alternative was bigamy, which seems to have been both easy and common. In the eighteenth century, more or less permanent desertion was also regarded as morally dissolving the marriage. Thus when in the 1790s the husband of Francis Place's sister was transported for life for a robbery, she soon remarried an old suitor, apparently without any qualms or objections on the grounds that she already had a husband who was presumably still alive. In 1807 a Somerset rector agreed to put up the banns for a second marriage of a woman whose husband had gone off as a soldier to the East Indies seven years before and had not been heard of since. But the man unexpectedly turned up and reclaimed his wife, only to desert her again when he found her consorting with her second husband. He was said soon after to have remarried, despite the existence of this first wife.[54]

A third alternative for the poor in the eighteenth century was the unofficial folk-custom of divorce by mutual consent by 'wife-sale'. As described in 1727, the husband 'puts a halter about her neck and thereby leads her to the next market place, and there puts her up to auction to be sold to the best bidder, as if she were a brood mare or a milch-cow. A purchaser is generally provided beforehand on these occasions.' This procedure was based closely on that of the sale of cattle. It took place frequently in a cattle-market like Smithfield and was accompanied by the use of a symbolic halter, by which the wife was led to market by the seller, and led away again by the buyer. The transaction sometimes even included the payment of a fee to the clerk of the market. In the popular mind, this elaborate ritual freed the husband of all future responsibility for his wife, and allowed both parties to marry again. Very often, perhaps normally, the bargain was pre-arranged with the full consent of the wife, both purchaser and price being agreed upon beforehand. The latter varied widely, from a few pence to a few guineas. Sometimes the husband actually paid to have his wife taken off his hands. In 1796 a Sheffield steel-burner sold his wife for sixpence to a fellmonger and then gave the purchaser half a guinea to take her out of town to Manchester on the next coach. At other times, the price was higher, for example in 1797 when a London butcher sold his wife for three guineas and a crown to a hog-driver. A little higher up the social scale there is even some evidence of the use of written contracts: one has survived from 1768 which was made between a clothworker and a gentleman (for six guineas), being duly signed and witnessed like an ordinary deed of sale. In this case, the transaction took place without the wife's knowledge or consent, but neither here nor in any other case is the object of sale recorded as having raised any objection. She presumably calculated that any purchaser was likely to treat her better than a husband who was prepared to sell her publicly for a modest sum in order to get rid of her.

It appears that this procedure was almost exclusively confined to the lower classes, and was centered mostly in the big towns and the west of England. It had a medieval origin, but evidence for it becomes far more frequent in the late eighteenth century, then dies away in the nineteenth, the last recorded case being in 1887. Whether this means that the practice was on the increase in the late eighteenth century is doubtful. It seems more likely that the newspapers were picking up more of these cases and reporting them, since they were increasingly regarded as scandalous to bourgeois morality. By the 1790s, reports usually ended with some hostile comment about 'such depraved conduct in the lower order of people'. To the labouring classes, however, this ritualized procedure was clearly regarded as a perfectly legitimate form of full divorce, to be followed by remarriage, despite its illegality in both secular and ecclesiastical courts, and despite increasing condemnation in the public press. Indeed the courts made intermittent and half-hearted attempts to stop it, Lord Mansfield treating it as a criminal offence, a conspiracy to commit adultery.[55]

One may conclude, therefore, that in the late seventeenth and eighteenth centuries, full divorce and remarriage was possible by law for the very rich and by folk custom for the very poor, but impossible for the great majority in the middle who could not afford the cost of the one or the social stigma and remote risks of prosecution of the other.

CHAPTER 2

The Demographic Facts

Birth, copulation and death,
That's all the facts when you come to brass tacks,
Birth, copulation and death.
(T.S.Eliot, Sweeney Agonistes)

'*Man that is born of Woman is of few days and full of trouble. He cometh forth like a flower and is cut down. He fleeth also as a shadow and continueth not.*' (*Emblems of Mortality*, London, 1789, p. 39, (quoting Job XIV. 1), illustrated in *Early Childrens Books and their Illustration*, ed. G.Gottlieb, Pierpont Morgan Library, New York, 1975, no. 86)

The best way to start an analysis of family structure is to establish the demographic facts, which inexorably dictated so many of its basic features, including even such apparently independent variables as emotional commitment. These facts did not alter very dramatically over time, but they varied widely from class to class, and it is necessary to distinguish between the landed, professional and mercantile rich, the top three to five per cent who dominated the society, and the plebeians of moderate, modest or marginal wealth who formed the vast majority.

I MARRIAGE

i. Nuptiality

Among the landed classes in pre-Reformation England, nuptiality – the proportion of surviving children who married – was determined by family strategy. The three objectives of family planning were the continuity of the male line, the preservation intact of the inherited property, and the acquisition through marriage of further property or useful political alliances. Given the very uncertain prospects of survival, the first could only be ensured by the procreation of the largest possible number of children in the hope that at least one male child would live to marriageable age. The second could only be assured by restricting the claims of the children on the patrimony through primogeniture. This meant excluding younger sons and daughters from the bulk of the inheritance, which delayed their marriage, and in many cases meant depriving them of the opportunity to marry at all. The third could best be achieved by marrying them, and marrying them into wealthy and influential families, which in the case of daughters demanded the provision of large cash portions, and in the case of younger sons required substantial annuities or two-life leases of property. The second objective thus directly clashed with the third, and if the former were given priority, as it often was, it meant the sacrifice of daughters by putting them into nunneries, and the extrusion of younger sons to fend for themselves as military adventurers or clergy or otherwise. The ideal of virginity so valued by the Catholic Church provided the theological and moral justification for the existence of nunneries, which contained considerable numbers of upper-class girls placed there by their fathers in order to get rid of them. Many, but by no means all, of these girls probably found the religious life a satisfying alternative career to an arranged marriage. For those women who sought power, the life of an abbess was clearly preferable even to that of an aristocratic wife.[1]

With the abolition of nunneries in the mid-sixteenth century, this delicate mechanism that made possible vigorous procreation and the avoidance of costly marriages was upset. This abrupt change coincided with a period during which the desire to preserve intact the family patrimony was at its weakest and when it became morally obligatory upon the landed classes to marry off their daughters. The marriage market was flooded with girls who had hitherto been consigned to nunneries, but who now had to be married off, at considerable cost, to their social equals. Despite a heavy and growing drain on the family resources, more than ninety-five per cent of all surviving daughters born in the late sixteenth century to the English nobility eventually married. Among boys from this landed elite, the eldest son and heir at this period almost always married, since his prime duty was to produce a male heir to carry on the line, but about one fifth of the younger sons were obliged to remain bachelors for life.

In the late seventeenth and eighteenth centuries, there was a distinct trend towards bachelordom among owners of medium to large country houses in three sample countries (Graph 2). The cause of this is a mystery, although some may have been homosexual and now more willing to admit their deviation in the more tolerant atmosphere of the eighteenth century. At the same time, property arrangements indicate an intensification among landed families of the desire to preserve intact the family patrimony for transmission to the male heir. This meant that there was less of either money or property to spare for younger sons and daughters, many more of whom were consequently obliged to forgo marriage. As a result, despite the improvement of record-keeping, the proportion of recorded daughters who reached the age of fifty and never married rose from ten per cent in the sixteenth century to fifteen per cent in the early seventeenth century and to nearly twenty-five per cent between 1675 and 1799 (Graph 3). As this crisis developed, some neglected daughters became desperate and grabbed at the first man who came along.[2] For younger sons, there was a similar sharp rise in the proportion who never married from the sixteenth to the seventeenth century, although after 1600 the recorded proportion of bachelors hovered between twenty and twenty-six per cent (Graph 3). In the eighteenth century contemporaries certainly thought that the proportion was actually increasing, and it was this growth of bachelordom which led Daniel Defoe to complain about the consequent rise in both spinsters and prostitutes.[3] Whether the same decline in nuptiality was also true of the children of the urban patriciate is at present unknown, but it is not unlikely.

For those below the rural and urban elite, there is extensive French evidence to suggest that in the eighteenth century about ten per cent of all men aged fifty were still unmarried and between eight and fifteen per cent of all women, which is not far off the level in France in 1968. There was no role for old maids in villages, and they were nearly all concentrated in the towns.[4] The evidence for England is still very patchy, but one census, for the town of Lichfield in 1695, shows that nine per cent of all women aged over thirty were still spinsters, which suggests the basically similar but rather higher nuptiality that one would expect in a Protestant country.[5]

To sum up, the available evidence suggests that a distinctive feature of pre-modern England was the exceptionally low nuptiality of the daughters and the younger sons of the rural (and perhaps also the urban) elite, the cause of which was the custom of primogeniture. For the rest of the population, marriage was the normal condition, applying to about ninety per cent of the children of the lower middle class, the peasantry and the poor and almost all the male heirs of the rich. It was not universal, however, and by comparison with non-western societies, a nuptiality rate of ninety per cent is low. This means that some ten per cent of women were withdrawn

NUPTIALITY OF SQUIRES AND ABOVE (AGED 21 +)

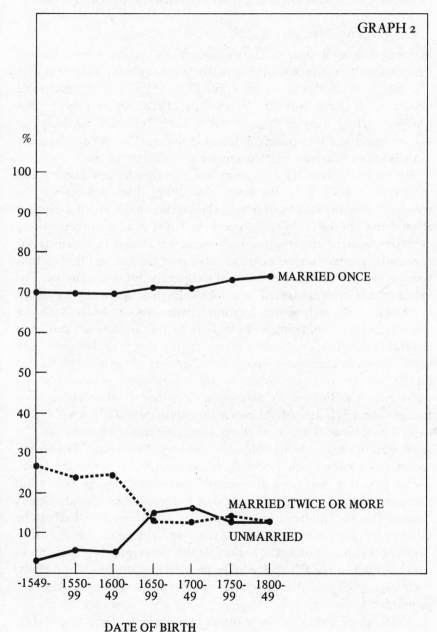

GRAPH 2

MARRIED ONCE

MARRIED TWICE OR MORE

UNMARRIED

DATE OF BIRTH

from the reproductive pool in each generation, assuming that the illegitimacy rate was as low as it appears to be from the parish registers.

ii. Age at First Marriage

Marriage is the legal *rite de passage* which marks the transition from youthful independence to joint responsibility in the creation of a new nuclear family. The age at which this transition occurred is, therefore, of considerable importance. It is also a subject which is closely linked with nuptiality, since whether a child married late, or never, both depended on economic circumstances and the strategy of family planning. The two are therefore causally linked, and are separated only for analytical purposes.

The evidence about age of marriage for the upper landed classes is less satisfactory than it is for the lower classes, but there is enough to be reasonably certain of facts and trends. Daughters married on the average at about twenty in the late sixteenth century, rising to about twenty-two to twenty-three in the late seventeenth and eighteenth. When it comes to boys it is essential to make a clear distinction between the son and heir and his younger brothers, since they followed completely different patterns. The median age at first marriage of heirs for the English squirarchy was about twenty-one in the early sixteenth century, twenty-two in the late sixteenth century, twenty-four rising to twenty-six in the seventeenth and early eighteenth centuries, and twenty-seven to twenty-nine in the late eighteenth to early nineteenth centuries (Graph 4).[6] There were three probable reasons for this slow rise in the median age of marriage of heirs of squires. The first was a greater willingness by parents to allow their children rather more freedom of mate choice, a development the explanation of which will appear later. This greater freedom of choice inevitably meant allowing them to reach maturity before being obliged to make up their minds. The second reason was based on medical grounds. It was widely believed that sperm was a vital fluid that controlled growth, and excessive discharge before full maturity would, therefore, stunt physical and intellectual growth. Others believed that the children of early marriages were themselves likely to be weaklings: 'young marriages beget starvelings,' argued the ninth Earl of Northumberland. Thomas Cogan thought that the average height of upper-class Englishmen was falling due to the physical immaturity of the parents, while others believed that childbirth was excessively dangerous for very young girls.[7]

A final cause for the slow rise of marriage age of heirs of squires and their wives was the growing duration of higher education, which now took the

PROPORTION OF PEERS' CHILDREN (AGED 50+)
WHO NEVER MARRIED

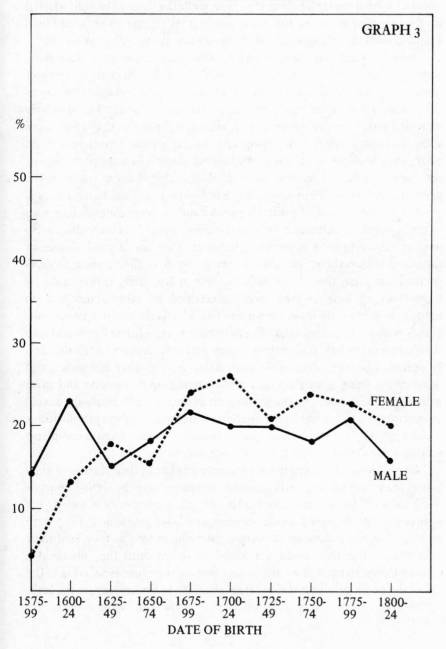

GRAPH 3

FEMALE

MALE

DATE OF BIRTH

form of a few years at the university, often followed by a few years at the
Inns of Court, and then two or three years on the Grand Tour. Even in the
eighteenth century, when the university and the Inns of Court were less frequented, boys stayed at school to a later age, while the Grand Tour often lasted
for four years or more. All this could postpone the return to a settled life in
England until the young man was twenty-two or twenty-three years old.[8]

Those younger sons who married, who were probably a decreasing
proportion of the whole, did so considerably later than their sisters or elder
brother. By the eighteenth century, they were on the average marrying in
their early to middle thirties, which makes them one of the two most elderly
marrying groups in the whole society, although the brides they chose were
some ten years younger. The reason for the delay is clear. Before they could
marry they needed to accumulate, by individual effort in some profession or
occupation, sufficient income and capital to enable them to maintain the
gentlemanly style of life in which they had been brought up. Early marriage
would have meant a socially inferior partner and a severe economic handicap
in the struggle for reintegration into the elite world of their childhood. So
long as they remained unmarried, however, they had a good chance of
maintaining something very close to the life style of their upbringing. As
professional men, they could earn enough to live fairly comfortably by
themselves, so long as they were entertained by others, and had no
obligation to entertain others in return, like Thackeray's Major Pendennis.
If they were lawyers, they could live in chambers at an Inn of Court and take
their meals in the hall, saving their money for those elegances of clothes and
equipment which kept them in the rank of the men of quality. For society and
conviviality, there were the clubs which sprang up in London and in so
many provincial towns in the eighteenth century, while as always sexual
satisfaction of a sort could be obtained from the large numbers of prostitutes
– although not without serious risk of disease – or else from a compliant
serving-maid or housekeeper, or semi-permanent mistress.

The only other social group which married as late as their thirties or even
forties in the seventeenth and eighteenth centuries were the eight-hundred-
odd Fellows of Oxford and Cambridge colleges, a number of whom by the
eighteenth century were themselves younger sons of gentlemen. They were
precluded by the college statutes from marrying as long as they held their
Fellowships, but they could not afford to resign until they obtained a
Church living. In most cases, this meant waiting their turn for a living in the
gift of their college, a wait which often lasted ten to fifteen years in the early
eighteenth century, rising to nearly twenty at the end of the century. By

MEDIAN AGE AT FIRST MARRIAGE OF PEERS' CHILDREN
AND HEIRS OF SQUIRES AND ABOVE

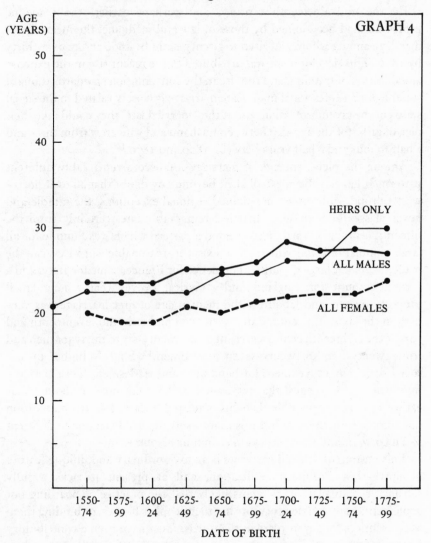

DATE OF BIRTH

then, they were the latest marrying group in the whole society, and a sympathetic speaker in the House of Commons in the debate on the University Reform Bill in 1854 drew an affecting picture of the elderly don feasting his eyes on the distant Paradise of a college living, 'with perhaps a venerable Eve waiting for him in the Garden.'[9]

By the mid-nineteenth century, and perhaps earlier, the academic profession had been joined by those of law and medicine, the mean age of marriage among whom had risen to twenty-eight by 1800 and to over thirty by 1870. This development was attributed to the recent rise in the expense and duration of training, and the rise in the consumption standards thought suitable for a professional man. Late marriage is closely related to the social status of the given profession. But if they married late, they could take their pick of girls, for the age-gap between husband and wife grew from three and a half to four and a half years between 1800 and 1870.[10]

Among the plebs, the age of marriage followed a remarkably different pattern. It has now been established beyond any doubt that all over north-west Europe, with some unexplained regional exceptions, the middle and lower classes of both sexes married remarkably late, certainly from the fifteenth century onward. This created a pattern which was 'unique for all large populations for which data exist or reasonable surmises can be made.'[11] A very large quantity of evidence for France, some for Italy, and a certain amount for England and America, proves that among small property-owners and labourers the median age of first marriage was very high in the sixteenth century and went even higher in the seventeenth and part of the eighteenth centuries, rising from twenty-six to thirty for men and from twenty-four to twenty-seven for women.[12] Slightly higher up the social scale, among yeomen, husbandmen, and tradesmen, there is a very little evidence to suggest that marriage may have taken place about a year earlier.[13] It is just possible that this is related to earlier sexual maturation due to better nutrition,[14] but it is more likely to have been due to different social customs and easier access to economic resources.

This custom of delayed marriage is an extraordinary and unique feature of north-west European civilization, and at present it lacks a fully satisfactory explanation. It seems likely that the practice of boarding out adolescents as unmarried servants in other people's houses, or binding them as apprentices for seven years in the towns, must have been a contributory factor in causing the delay. In 1556 the Common Council of London, disturbed by the growth of poverty caused by 'over-hasty marriages and over-soon setting up of households by the youth', decreed that nobody was to be admitted as a Freeman of London until the age of twenty-four. This effective marriage bar was extended across the country by the Statute of Artificers of 1563, which set a limit of twenty-one in the countryside and twenty-four in corporate towns. For children who were a charge on the parish poor rate, the Act of 1601 empowered the overseers to apprentice them at the age of ten until the age of twenty-four, thus virtually enslaving them for fourteen years and delaying any possibility of marriage.[15]

By far the most important cause, however, since it affected a large proportion of the population, was the need to wait, either to save up enough money to buy the necessary household goods, or to inherit the cottage, shop or farm, and so be in an economic position to support a family. In societies where girls marry soon after puberty, this problem is solved by the newly married couple's living in the same house as one of their parents for some years – the stem-family. In north-western Europe, it was the custom for the newly married couple to set up house on their own immediately or very soon after marriage. When and why this became the custom is unknown, but under these conditions, either a lengthy period of saving, or the death or retirement of a parent, was a necessary prerequisite for marriage.

This economic explanation, dependent on the custom of new residence outside the home, is supported by the data about adult mortality. If a man married at twenty-seven or twenty-eight, his first son was probably born about two years later, when he was thirty. The expectation of life for a thirty-year old male in the seventeenth and early eighteenth centuries seems to have been about twenty-two to twenty-six years, which coincides with the average age at marriage of the son. Even among the squirarchy, the median age at first marriage coincided with the median age at inheritance (Graphs 4 and 5). In Brittany and Anjou in the late eighteenth century just about half of those marrying for the first time had already lost their fathers.[16] All this suggests that there was an inverse causal relationship between the rate of adult mortality and the age of marriage, mediated through property inheritance.[17] Given the high mortality rates among adults of pre-modern society, and the need for some capital to set up a family, the delayed marriage system makes good economic sense, especially in areas such as England where the father did not normally retire and hand over the farm in return for food and shelter.[18]

In the early eighteenth century *The Spectator* published an imaginary offer of marriage from a peasant suitor, which ran as follows: 'I am now my own man and may match where I please, for my father is taken away, and now I am come into my living, which is ten yardland and a house; . . . and all my brothers and sisters are provided for; besides I have good household stuff.'[19] This imaginary case is supported by statistical evidence that farmers did indeed marry particularly late. Other influences which forced couples to postpone marriage were the ability of the local authorities in 'closed' villages to prevent either the possibility for 'squatting' on waste land, or the construction of new houses, for fear that the inhabitants would become a burden on the poor rate; and efforts, for similar reasons, by town authorities to keep out lodgers. On the other hand the possibility of female or child employment facilitated early marriage. Thus it is noticeable that textile workers tended to marry early, partly because unmarried girls could quickly accumulate a dowry through their earnings, and partly because wives and young children could be gainfully employed in spinning.[20]

Most of the factors listed are economic at bottom, and it seems clear that the critical determinant was the possibility of obtaining the resources to maintain an independent household at the desired level of living standards. Among the very poor, this would be a bare subsistence, which is why the age of marriage in Ireland after the famine of 1848 rose to thirty-eight for men and thirty for women, with a nuptiality rate as low as seventy-five per cent. The artisan needed to buy his tools, the shopkeeper to buy his stock, while among the lower middle and middle classes the decisive factor would have been the desire to acquire sufficient capital and income to set up house and live in the style to which they were accustomed or to which they aspired. Thus James Lackington, a Methodist bookseller, who married in 1770, did so after a courtship which had lasted no less than seven years.[21]

It has also been argued that post-Reformation Christianity has favoured late marriage, by encouraging asceticism and thrift, and the nuclear family over the kin. It is impossible to prove this suggestion, although there are striking correlations in eastern Europe and the Balkans between Christianity and late marriage, and Islam and early marriage.[22]

There are several consequences which must have followed from the late marriage pattern, which since the sixteenth century has been normal among the poor and the lower middle classes, and since the eighteenth century among the professional classes and the younger sons of the landed classes (two categories which to some extent overlap). In view of the low recorded level of illegitimacy it is reasonable to assume that for many young men this delay involved considerable sexual denial at a time of optimum male sexual drive, despite the usual non-procreative outlets.[23] If one follows Freudian theory, this could lead to neuroses of the kind that so regularly shattered the calm of Oxford and Cambridge colleges at this period; it could help to

MEDIAN AGE AT FATHER'S DEATH OF HEIRS
OF SQUIRES AND ABOVE

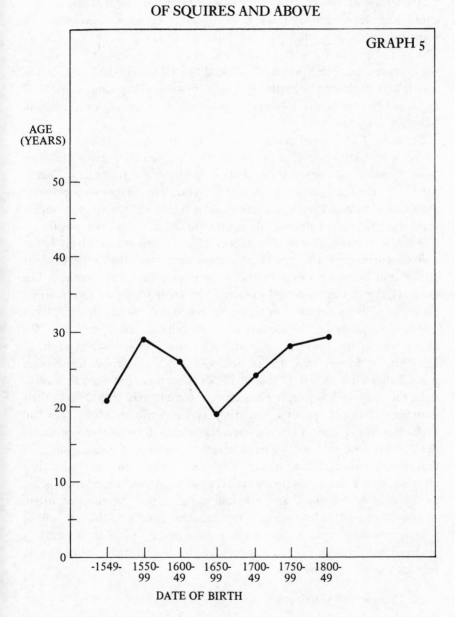

GRAPH 5

AGE
(YEARS)

DATE OF BIRTH

explain the high level of group aggression, which lay behind the extraordinary expansionist violence of western nation states at this time. It could also have been a stimulus to capitalist economic enterprise, by providing a cheap youthful labour force, stimulating saving in order to marry, and generating activist social and economic dynamism.[24] Certainly the delay caused severe problems of social control among the lower classes, which were dealt with by ensuring so far as possible that young people lived in households as family workers, apprentices or servants, rather than in lodgings by themselves.[25]

Secondly, like the relatively low nuptiality rate, late marriage put a severe brake on demographic growth, by withholding sexually mature women from reproduction for some ten of their twenty-five fertile years. This is partly why the demographic growth of England, even in its spurts between 1520 and 1620 and after 1740, was so slow relative to the rates currently experienced by under-developed countries in the late twentieth century.

Thirdly, it means that families tended to be formed consecutively rather than concurrently, marriage taking place as often as not after the death of the father, and in most cases after the death of one parent or another. The generation gap was stretched out, and the stem family of two married generations living together in the same house was inevitably rare. Even among the squirarchy, the median age of inheritance after the death of the father was in the twenties, only rising to thirty after 1750 (Graph 5). Fourthly, it means that, unlike societies where marriage takes place immediately after puberty, the individuals concerned, provided they came from the more or less propertyless classes, were largely free to make their individual choice of a partner, since they were now mature adults; they had been away from home for ten years or more; and their fathers were probably dead. What little evidence we have, mainly from French sources, suggests that selection was made on a basis of hard-headed common sense rather than emotion, with a view to obtaining a cook, a nurse, a housekeeper, an assistant in the field or the shop, and a sexual partner. For the rural or urban smallholder, artisan, tradesman, shopkeeper or common labourer, a wife was an economic necessity, not an emotional luxury, while for a woman a husband was also an economic necessity, to do the heavy work and to provide a subsistence income.[26]

iii. Duration of Marriage

If the age of first marriage was very late for all save the male heirs and the daughters of the landed classes, the duration of marriage was generally very short. It is a curious fact that, if one adopts the reasonable criterion of durability, marriages in the mid-twentieth century were more stable than at almost any other time in history, despite the high divorce rate. In the United States in 1955, the average marriage lasted thirty-one years before it was broken either by the death of one or other of the partners or by divorce, the latter accounting for one-third of total dissolutions.[27] In the seventeenth and eighteenth centuries, however, marriages were broken very much earlier by the premature death of one spouse or another, since all pre-modern societies had a fairly high death rate among young adults. In the sixteenth century, the chance of dying in one's twenties or thirties was as great as it is today in one's sixties. Even in early nineteenth-century England, the mortality rate among adults between twenty-five and forty was about one per cent a year. Consequently there was a two per cent chance of one spouse or the other dying each year, which means that not far off thirty per cent of all marriages were broken up by death in the first fifteen years.[28]

Among the peasantry in eighteenth- and even nineteenth-century France, death rates were far higher, and marriages consequently on the average only lasted from twelve to seventeen years, frequently followed by remarriage and the creation of a second family.[29] In England the only evidence as yet available covers a single village. It suggests that the median duration of first marriages among the poor was about seventeen to nineteen years, rising to twenty-two in the late eighteenth century. For the children of the squirarchy, the median duration of first marriages was twenty-two years in the early seventeenth century, falling to nineteen in the period of high mortality in the late seventeenth century, but rising to thirty as mortality fell in the late eighteenth century (Graph 6).[30] If one assumes that mortality among young adults was higher among the peasantry than the aristocracy, and that the English poor were less impoverished, and therefore healthier than the French, this scanty English evidence matches the French very well.[31] It seems safe to assume that among the bulk of the population the median duration of marriage in Early Modern England was probably somewhere about seventeen to twenty years.

From these facts can be drawn one very firm conclusion about the pre-modern family, namely that it was, statistically speaking, a transient and temporary association, both of husband and wife and of parents and children. Whether it was actually perceived this way at the time is more difficult to determine, but the incessant preaching on the imminence of death must have been a constant reminder of the essential transience of all human relationships. In practice the probability of a durable marriage was low, since it was likely to be broken before very long by the death of the husband or the wife. Indeed, it looks very much as if modern divorce is little more than a functional substitute for death. The decline of the adult mortality rate after the late eighteenth century, by prolonging the expected duration of marriage to unprecedented lengths, eventually forced Western society to adopt the institutional escape-hatch of divorce. Marriage must, therefore, have lasted longest during the Victorian period, when declining mortality rates had not yet been offset by rising divorce rates.

Secondly, throughout the Early Modern period, a couple marrying had less than fifty per cent statistical probability of life together for more than a year or two after their children had left home. It is only in the twentieth century that the sharp reduction in the age at which the last child is born, coupled with the sharp decline in adult mortality rates, has created the expectation of up to twenty years of life together after the departure of the children. Thus among American Quakers in the mid-twentieth century, the average expectation of joint life after marriage for a woman is as long as forty-four years.[32]

Thirdly, remarriage was very common, about a quarter of all marriages being a remarriage for the bride or the groom. Among the squirarchy and above, about twenty-five per cent married again in the late sixteenth and seventeenth centuries and about fifteen per cent in the eighteenth, of whom about five per cent married a third time or more (Graph 2). Why the remarriage rate declined so sharply in the eighteenth century remains a mystery, unless it was due to declining adult mortality. Among the plebs the same pattern applies. In Manchester in the 1650s in one-third of all marriages one of the partners had been married before. This means that in the seventeenth century the remarriage rate, made possible by death, was not far off that in our own day, made possible by divorce. In both periods, consecutive legal polygamy has been extremely common. Many of the remarriages were by the fathers of young children whose wives had died in childbirth, and who, therefore, urgently needed a nurse, housekeeper, cook, washerwoman and sexual partner. On the other hand many women who lost their husbands, especially poor women, could not find a new partner, so that in Lichfield in 1695 no fewer than thirty-one per cent of all women over thirty were widows.[33]

One consequence of high child and adult mortality rates, coupled with the practice of fostering out of the home at an early age, was that parent-child relations were even more tenuous than those of husband and wife. It was a society in which there were very large numbers of orphans, and only a

MEDIAN DURATION OF FIRST MARRIAGE

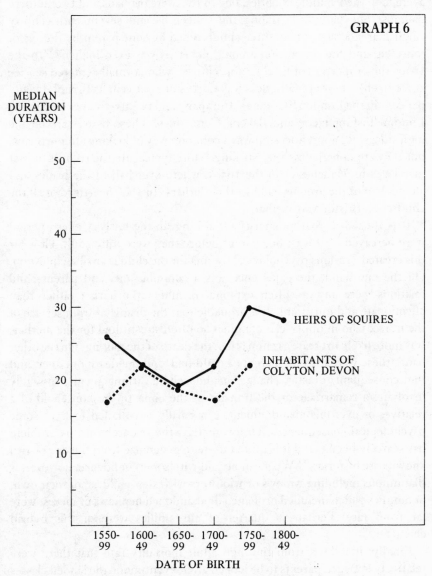

GRAPH 6

MEDIAN
DURATION
(YEARS)

HEIRS OF SQUIRES

INHABITANTS OF
COLYTON, DEVON

DATE OF BIRTH

minority of adolescent children had two living parents. Of those marrying for the first time in Brittany and Anjou in the late eighteenth century, on the average in their middle twenties, one in five were orphans and two in three had lost one parent.[34] Among the sixteenth- and seventeenth-century English aristocracy, one in three children had lost one parent by the age of fourteen, and the proportion among plebeians was even higher.[35] In the 1630s the proportion of English apprentices (who normally entered service at fourteen) who were fatherless was thirty-four per cent at Bristol, twenty per cent in the London Stationers' Company and twenty-five per cent in the London Fishmongers' and Bakers' Companies. These figures are on the high side, since apprenticeship was a common way of looking after orphans, but they are nonetheless very striking. More typical are the records of first marriages in Manchester in the 1650s, where over half of the brides and almost half of the grooms had lost their fathers. In 1696 one-third of all the children in Bristol were orphans.[36]

It is thus clear that a majority of children in the Early Modern period were bereaved of at least one parent before they were fully adult. How far this created a serious psychological trauma for the child is an open question. On the one hand, the experience was a common one, and parent-child relations were anyway often exploitative and authoritarian rather than affectionate and nurturant. It is arguable that the dismissal from service of the nurse, who in upper-class families so often substituted for the mother, was more likely to create a trauma than the death of the mother. On the other hand, these were the only parents a child had, and the death of either, and the consequent drastic change in household arrangements, possibly involving a remarriage or the transfer of the child to the household of a relative, or even his abandonment, can hardly have failed to have some psychological consequences. Unfortunately, the research on this problem has scarcely begun, and it is quite unsafe to generalize from the one or two known case histories.[37] What can be said with some confidence, however, is that unions including widows or widowers with step-children of their own, or families which included orphaned or abandoned nephews or nieces, were far from rare. Perhaps a quarter of all families were of this hybrid character.[38]

Finally, it follows from the high adult mortality rate that there were relatively few aged parents to be looked after, even among the landed classes (Graph 7). Gregory King's figures for Lichfield in 1695 suggest that only about five per cent of the population was over the age of sixty, as compared with fourteen per cent in America today. Among the will-making part of

EXPECTATIONS OF LIFE AT 21 OF
HEIRS OF SQUIRES AND ABOVE

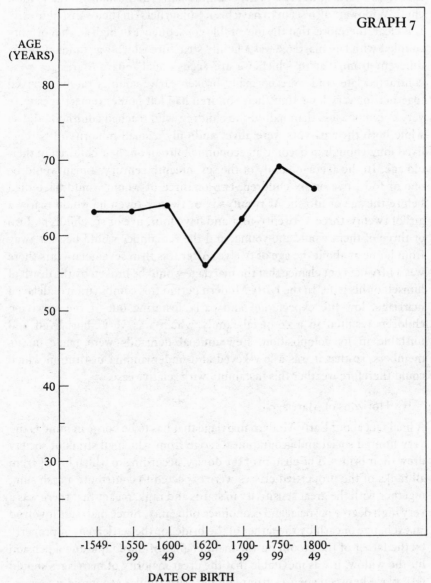

GRAPH 7

the population, bereaved parents were obligatorily looked after by the children. So long as they did not remarry, most widows had a legal right to a room and board, and access to the communal fire, in the house of their eldest child. Widowers also seem to have been 'sojourners' in their sons' houses.[39] It is clear, therefore, that the inexorable consequence of high adult mortality coupled with late marriage was a family structure which was fundamentally different from that to which we are accustomed today. Marriages were contracted late, and were normally broken early; couples rarely survived together for very long after their children had left home; remarriages were very common; less than half of the children who reached adulthood did so while both their parents were alive; and only a small minority of parents lived long enough to become an economic burden on their children in their old age. In the average family of the seventeenth century, a man would be one of four, five or six children, two or three of whom would have died before the age of fifteen. At twenty-six or twenty-seven he would marry a girl of twenty-three or twenty-four and have four, five or six children. Two or three of them would die young, and the remainder would be sent away from home at about the age of twelve. After less than seventeen years there was a fifty per cent chance that the marriage would be broken by the death of himself or his wife. In the Early Modern period this combination of delayed marriage, low life expectation and early fostering out of the surviving children resulted in a conjugal family which was very short-lived and unstable in its composition. Few mutual demands were made on its members, so that it was a low-keyed and undemanding institution which could therefore weather this instability with relative ease.

iv. Horizons of Marriage

A final fact about Early Modern marriage that has to be borne in mind is the very limited social and geographical range from which all strata of society drew their brides. The custom of the dowry, according to which brides from all ranks of the propertied classes were expected to contribute a cash sum, together with the great sensitivity to status and rank, meant that there was a very high degree of social and economic endogamy. Since marriage involved an exchange of cash by the father of the bride for the settlement of property by the father of the groom for the maintenance of the couple and a pension for the widow, it was inevitable that the great majority of marriages should take place between spouses from families with similar economic resources. Since men were acutely conscious of the value of status, this was a quality which might be traded in for money, for example by the marriage of the son and heir of an impoverished nobleman to the heiress of a rich merchant. By and large, however, the fact that most families aspired to maintain status and enlarge connections through marriage meant that in most cases like would marry like. To give but one example, ninety per cent of the known marriages of Lancashire gentry in the early seventeenth century were with other gentry families. Of the handful who married down, almost all were younger sons of minor families.[40] In Kent in the first half of the seventeenth century, about half of all knights, gentry, yeomen and husbandmen married girls from the same status group, while a third of the clergy married daughters of clergy. Occupational endogamy among artisans and craftsmen was inevitably less close; but among the commoner trades, about one in five of clothiers, tailors, butchers, shoemakers and sailors married daughters of members of their own occupation. The causes of these high levels of endogamy probably varied from group to group. The knights were so few in number that their rate of intermarriage is remarkable: they must have been snapping up most of each other's daughters. That a third of clergymen married other clergymen's daughters is also remarkable, but since the profession included such a wide range of status and income levels, it is impossible to tell just what it means. In the artisan trades, many young men must have married their master's daughter and joined the family enterprise; while seamen probably formed a self-contained and isolated cultural group. All the same, the generally high level of status, profession and trade endogamy suggests, but does not prove, a correspondingly high level of parental control over both occupation and marriage in early seventeenth-century Kent.[41]

The geographical horizons of marriage were also very limited, although the higher one moves up the social scale, the wider they become. Only with the aristocracy, and only by the early seventeenth century, however, was there a genuinely national marriage market even at this elevated level.[42] The squirarchy, men who carried the title of esquire, knight or baronet, were far more limited in their range, at any rate up to the 1630s, and probably beyond. In the early seventeenth century, sixty per cent of the squirarchy of Lancashire and fifty per cent of that of Dorset married within the county. By about 1700 regional marriage markets were developing for the squirarchy, such as the service performed by the annual fair at Bury St Edmunds. It was attended by 'an infinite number of knights' daughters from Norfolk, Cambridgeshire and Suffolk,' and in practice was 'more a market for ladies than merchandises.' In the eighteenth century a national marriage market for the squirarchy also developed at the balls, assemblies and parties that constituted the season at London in the spring and at Bath in the early summer. By the 1740s these were now well-established institutions where the elite young of both sexes from all over the country could freely meet and mingle.[43]

In Hertfordshire, a county heavily affected by its proximity to London, the proportion of squires and above who married within the county was about thirty per cent in the sixteenth century, falling to about twenty per cent in the seventeenth and eighteenth centuries. If one includes the contiguous counties and London, slightly less than half chose brides from within this restricted area throughout the period. In the more isolated Northamptonshire, however, the changes were more marked. There was a sharp drop from about thirty to forty per cent marrying within the county in the sixteenth century to about twenty per cent thereafter, sinking still further to fifteen per cent in the late eighteenth century. If one takes Northamptonshire and the contiguous counties as a regional unit, the proportion marrying within it fell from seventy per cent in the sixteenth century to fifty per cent in the seventeenth and early eighteenth century to forty per cent in the late eighteenth century. The effect of the development of national marriage markets in London and Bath is very clear. The same is true even of remote Northumberland, where the proportion marrying girls from other northern families fell steadily from ninety per cent in the late sixteenth century to sixty per cent in the late seventeenth to fifty-five per cent in the late eighteenth.[44]

Lower down the social scale, among the small parish gentry and those who merely called themselves 'gentlemen' or 'Mr', the degree of local endogamy was naturally considerably higher. Of men of this class in Lancashire, almost eighty per cent married girls from within the county in the first half of the seventeenth century, thus forming an almost wholly self-contained group bound, or divided, by a complex network of kinship ties and rivalries.[45] At the level of agricultural labourers, husbandmen and artisans, studies of several villages, six in Lancashire, and one near York, indicate that as late as 1800 about two-thirds of all grooms who married where they were born chose brides from the village itself, about ninety per cent from within ten miles and all but a negligible proportion from within twenty miles.[46] Those who emigrated to towns or elsewhere naturally married further afield, but for those who stayed behind, the limits were set by the distance a suitor was prepared to walk or ride to visit a girl, and by the restricted range which most boys and girls travelled to take up employment as living-in servants.

2 BIRTH

It is commonly supposed that pre-modern homes were swarming with children. This is an illusion derived from a number of striking but in fact exceptional examples. No-one who has once read about it will easily forget the family size of the early eighteenth-century Scottish architect James Smith. Before dying at the age of thirty-seven in 1699 giving birth to twins, his first wife provided him with eighteen children. He then married again and fathered fourteen more, making thirty-two in all, most of whom survived and one of whom he named 'Climacteric Smith', since the child was born in his father's seventieth year.[47]

The normal reality was very different. Since the female age of marriage was commonly between twenty-three and twenty-seven, and the menopause began at about forty,[48] the period during which the average wife could give birth was fairly limited. Moreover, many marriages did not last through the full female reproductive span, owing to the premature death of one spouse or the other. There were, of course, some social groups – French Canadians and Hutterites in America for example – with very high fertility rates indeed. In France, in those rare families in which marriage took place when the bride was twenty or under, and in which both partners lived to the completion of the reproductive span, the number of children born was naturally very large, varying from place to place from an average low of 6·6 to a high of 10·8.[49] But most families were neither formed at the age of twenty nor completed without interruption by death. The average number of children born to one wife was therefore very much lower, only four or less in upper-class England (Graph 8) and six or eight among the yeomen and freeholders in the much healthier conditions of New England.

A third reason for this relatively low fertility is that (except in areas like Brittany and Flanders) the interval between births was on the average between twenty-four and thirty months. One explanation for birth intervals of this length is foetal wastage through miscarriages, still-births and possibly induced abortions. The one parish register so far discovered to record still births shows a very high and rising rate of between four and ten per cent of live births between 1581 and 1710. The rate, which is a bare minimum since it omits unnamed children and possibly others, rose sharply in the late seventeenth century, for reasons which are not at present clear, unless induced abortions were on the increase or maternal nutrition was on the decline.[50]

More important, however, was the contraceptive effects of lactation on most women, and especially those whose diet was insufficient to maintain body-weight. Lactation, which commonly lasted for eighteen months or more, induces amenorrhoea in most cases for about six months for well-fed women and eighteen months for women suffering from malnutrition. It therefore serves as an effective contraceptive, while some women in the more literate classes may have followed medical advice against a lactating woman having sexual intercourse. There is no evidence, however, that there was any superstitious taboo among the poor against intercourse at this time.[51]

Finally, birth intervals lengthened very significantly with age, either because of declining female fecundity or male virility, or because of greater incentive to and expertise in contraceptive practices, or some combination of these.[52]

The other significant fact to notice about family size is that, unlike today, the rich had more children than the poor.[53] One reason for this is that the former married younger wives, and remarried more rapidly and more frequently if their first wives died before the completion of the period of fertility. Another reason is that their wives were more fertile before the eighteenth century, since they lacked the contraceptive protection of lactation, the children being normally put out to wet-nurses instead of being nursed by their mother. Thirdly, they were better fed and better housed. There is reason to think that unhealthy living conditions, bad hygiene, rotten food and a chronic state of malnutrition may have been powerful causes of the low fertility, as well as the high infant mortality, of the poor. One or other of the two partners must often have been too sick for intercourse, while serious malnutrition, which must have been common among the bottom third of the population living on the bare margin of subsistence, is now known to reduce the male sexual appetite and very seriously to affect female fecundity. It not only weakens resistance to disease and so raises the death rate of children and young adults, but it also impairs the sexual functioning of the living. The menarche is delayed; normal adolescent sterility of girls lasts unusually long; the menstrual cycle of adult women is either irregular or stopped altogether, thus preventing ovulation; there is higher pregnancy wastage through miscarriages; and the amenorrhoea normal during the lactation period lasts longer. The caloric intake per capita thus affects births as well as deaths.[54]

Under these circumstances, it is hardly surprising that the rich always had more children than the poor, until the time when they began to practise birth control, as a result of which the relationship was reversed. This

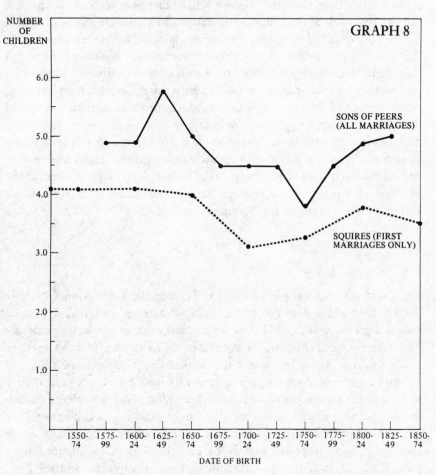

MEAN NUMBER OF CHILDREN BORN

GRAPH 8

NUMBER
OF
CHILDREN

SONS OF PEERS
(ALL MARRIAGES)

SQUIRES (FIRST
MARRIAGES ONLY)

6.0

5.0

4.0

3.0

2.0

1.0

1550-
74
1575-
99
1600-
24
1625-
49
1650-
74
1675-
99
1700-
24
1725-
49
1750-
74
1775-
99
1800-
24
1825-
49
1850-
74

DATE OF BIRTH

happened among the generation born after 1640 among the bourgeoisie of Geneva; between 1650 and 1750 among the children of the English squirarchy (Graph 8) and after 1700 among French dukes and peers. The practice did not begin among the poor in France before the late eighteenth century, spreading out from Paris and the south-west region. In England it seems to have been practised in one English village between 1650 and 1720, but this is very weak evidence on which to build a national generalization.[55]

Nor only were the rich more fertile than the poor, but it seems very likely that a higher proportion of their children survived to adulthood. Although they handed their children over to the sometimes dubious care of wet-nurses, they had no strong economic incentive to infanticide by negligence, while their children were much better fed, clothed and housed, and should therefore have been healthier – although they were also subjected to the harmful, indeed often lethal, attentions of doctors. Even so, it is astonishing to discover that the proportion of the squirarchy and above who died leaving no son to inherit was twenty-five per cent, rising to over forty per cent as the practice of contraception reduced family size after 1650 (Graph 9). Heiresses were common, and became commoner.

3   DEATH

i. Mortality Rates

The most striking feature which distinguished the Early Modern family from that of today does not concern either marriage or birth; it was the constant presence of death. Death was at the centre of life, as the cemetery was at the centre of the village. Death rates in France were four or five times as high as they are today, which means that in a village of one thousand persons in the seventeenth century, some fifty would die every year, mostly infants, children and young adults, so that at least once a week the church bell would toll, and a funeral procession would wind its way along the village street. Death was a normal occurrence in persons of all ages, and was not something that happened mainly to the old. Urban populations were particularly at risk, due to contaminated water supplies, and no early modern city reproduced itself; even to maintain their size, all were dependent on a constant influx from the healthier countryside.

It appears to be a fact that for the last two-thirds of the sixteenth century mortality rates declined for a time, during a temporary easing of the ancient threat of bubonic plague and before the ravages of smallpox began. But the relief was only relative, and it did not last into the seventeenth century,

PROPORTION OF SQUIRES AND ABOVE WHO LEFT NO SON

GRAPH 9

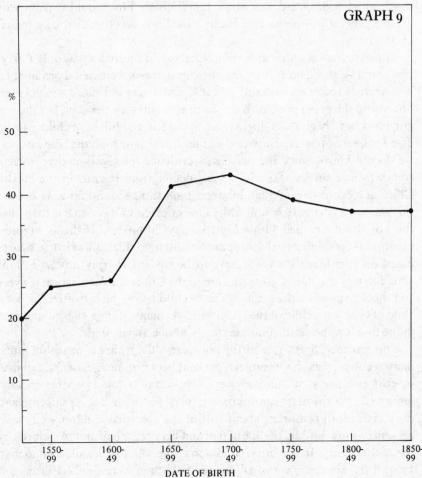

DATE OF BIRTH

when death rates rose again to very high levels. The cause of this rise is unknown, but it was perhaps because the expansion of world commerce carried with it from continent to continent hitherto unknown diseases and new strains of viruses and bacteria, to which local immunity had not been built up by long exposure. In addition, smallpox seems to have become both much more widespread and much more lethal. This would explain why greater general prosperity and cheaper food was accompanied by a higher death rate.

The expectation of life at birth in England in the 1640s was only thirty-two years. Of those born alive, the ones most at risk were new-born infants. The average recorded mortality rate in the first year in France was between fifteen and thirty per cent, with the mean at twenty-one per cent, but the real rate must have been much higher due to unrecorded births of children who died in the first few days or weeks of life.[56] Just how high the true rate was we do not know, since the only hard evidence for a pre-modern society comes from a survey taken by a local doctor from records in the Health Office of a canton near Milan between 1798 and 1800. So far as is known, this was not a particularly unhealthy time or place, and yet no less than one-third of all infants died within fourteen days of birth.[57] If this is a typical example of pre-industrial European infant mortality, all existing figures based on parish registers will have to be revised sharply upwards. This situation was also one of great concern to the Church. Ecclesiastical lawyers and theologians took the position that 'a child before he is baptized is not a child of God but a child of the Devil,' and yet many of these babies who died in the first few days had almost certainly not been baptized.[58]

The recorded death rate of the one-year-olds, which is probably much more accurate, was about eighteen per cent between the ages of one and five, so that prospects of survival were significantly, but not dramatically, improved once the first year was passed (plate 6). In the late seventeenth and early eighteenth centuries, about half of the recorded children of French peasantry were dead by the age of ten, and between a half and two-thirds by the age of twenty. In the cities, conditions were worse still, and in London in 1764, forty-nine per cent of all recorded children were dead by the age of two, and sixty per cent by the age of five.[59] The situation was distinctly better in rural England than in France, so far as we can tell at present, but even so, between a quarter and a third of all children of English peers and peasants were dead before they reached the age of fifteen (Graph 10).

There is growing reason to suspect that a proportion of the infant deaths of the poor were due to culpable neglect. Infants in the Early Modern period

PROPORTION OF CHILDREN BORN WHO DIED
BEFORE AGE 15

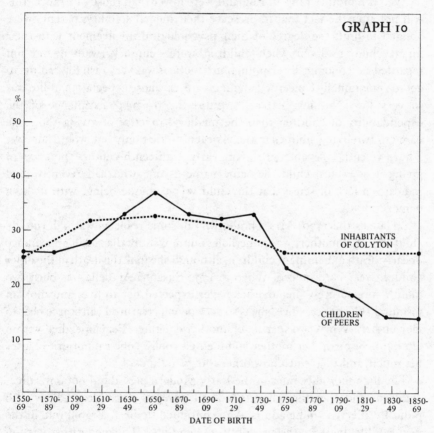

GRAPH 10

%

INHABITANTS
OF COLYTON

CHILDREN
OF PEERS

1550-
69 1570-
89 1590-
09 1610-
29 1630-
49 1650-
69 1670-
89 1690-
09 1710-
29 1730-
49 1750-
69 1770-
89 1790-
09 1810-
29 1830-
49 1850-
69

DATE OF BIRTH

were exposed to lack of attention by the mother in the first critical weeks; premature weaning; accidental smothering in bed with their parents; the transfer of the infant to the care of a wet-nurse (with the high probability of death by neglect); abandonment in doorways; or deposit in parish workhouses or foundling hospitals, which were often almost equally lethal if less offensive to the public than the spectacle of dead babies littering the streets.[60]

Even if mortality rates in England were lower than those of France, this will not alter the fact that to preserve their mental stability, parents were obliged to limit the degree of their psychological involvement with their infant children. Even when children were genuinely wanted and not regarded as economically crippling nuisances, it was very rash for parents to get too emotionally concerned about creatures whose expectation of life was so very low. Nothing better illustrates the resigned acceptance of the expendability of children than the medieval practice of giving the same name to two living siblings in the expectation that only one would survive. The sixteenth-, seventeenth- and early eighteenth-century practice of giving a new-born child the same name as one who had recently died indicates a lack of sense that the child was a unique being, with its own name.[61]

As late as the 1770s Mrs Thrale, who in some respects was a devotedly child-oriented mother, was nonetheless unmoved by the sickly appearance or early death of her infant children, although she took the death of the older children very hard indeed. When in 1770 Susanna Arabella was born two months prematurely, her mother never expected her to live, and took an instant dislike to her, since 'she is so very poor a creature I can scarce bear to look on her.' When two years later another daughter, Penelope, died within ten hours of birth, her mother commented coolly, 'one cannot grieve after her much, and I have just now other things to think of.'[62]

The high mortality rates of the Early Modern period did not only affect children, and therefore the attitude of parents to children. They also radically affected young adults, who continued to die at a rapid rate in the prime of life, between the ages of twenty and fifty. The modern association of death with the aged bears no relation to reality at any earlier period, when relatively few died at a ripe old age. English death rates may have been lower, but among Anjou peasants in the seventeenth and eighteenth centuries, and among Lyons townspeople in the eighteenth century, the proportion of the survivors who died increased each decade of life after twenty, but the actual numbers who died in their twenties was about the

EXPECTATION OF LIFE AT BIRTH OF
SONS OF PEERS

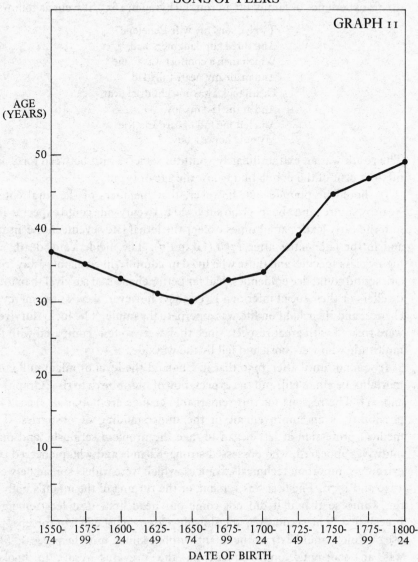

GRAPH 11

same as the numbers who died in their sixties. Even in the 1840s the expectation of death next year for young adults in England was eight times greater than it is in America today.[63] All affective relationships were thus at the mercy of sudden and unexpected death. When Sir John Gibson summed up his experience of family life in rough rhyme in 1655, it went as follows:

> Twelve sons my wife Penelope
> And three fair daughters had,
> Which then a comfort was to me
> And made my heart full glad.
> Death took away my children dear
> And at the last my joy,
> And left me full of care and fear,
> My only hopes a boy.[64]

The result was an extraordinarily youthful society, with between forty and fifty per cent of the population below the age of twenty.

It should be pointed out, however, that members of the rural elite – wealthy squires and above – who survived to twenty-one could expect to live into the early sixties at all times except the lethal late seventeenth century, and to the late sixties after 1750 (Graph 7). The incidence of death was highly class specific, and those who lived in comfort, lived mainly away from cities, and could flee epidemics, had far better chances of survival than town dwellers or their social inferiors. Even they, however, were at the mercy of chance, and their hold on life was a perpetual gamble. The lucky survivors were treated with great respect, since they were so few, compared with the multitude who were born and fell by the wayside.

It was not until after 1750 that in England the level of infant and child mortality began to fall, and the expectation of life at birth to rise (Graphs 10 and 11). The reasons for this remarkable change are not at all clear. One possibility is an improvement in the understanding of obstetrics. The medical profession at last began to take the problem seriously, and male midwives appeared, who possessed stronger hands and who pioneered two extremely important technical advances, which were widely spread between 1730 and 1770. The first was version, or the turning of the infant's body in the womb so that if it did not come out head first, it at least emerged breech first. The second was the slow development of efficient forceps, the use of which would extract the infant without killing it in the process. This was an enormous improvement on the previous resort to hooked instruments, which certainly killed the infant and were quite likely to tear into the mother's uterus as well.[65]

Both developments were the product of the growing profession of male midwives, whose rise in numbers and popularity was looked upon with deep suspicion both by the ignorant female midwives, whose livelihoods were threatened by their advent, and also by their professional medical colleagues, who associated the trade with that of abortionists. The first male midwife to achieve knighthood was Sir David Hamilton in 1780 – an event that so outraged a conservative colleague that he spread the couplet:

> 'Rise up, Sir David,' said the Queen
> The first cunt-knight that e'er was seen.

It seems likely that the transmission by the male midwives of their new-found expertise and their raising of the technical qualifications of the female midwives may have done something to reduce the death rate of infants during delivery.[66] Another suggestion for the post-1770 decline in infant mortality is that it was caused by the increase in the supply of cow's milk to urban areas, which saved many infant lives.[67] Better personal hygiene, facilitated by the spread of easily washable cotton clothing, may have helped. The greater opportunities for child employment during the early phases of industrialization may also have provided poor parents with a greater incentive to preserve their children, and a greater ability to feed them and keep them alive. The decline in child mortality was probably due, to a significant extent, to the effectiveness of inoculation against smallpox, which became normal among the elite in the latter half of the eighteenth century. How widespread the practice was lower down the social scale is still a matter for dispute.[68]

ii. Examples

The psychological and practical effects upon family life of the high mortality rates of Early Modern England can easily be judged by looking at almost any tomb of the period. For example, at Yarnton, in Oxfordshire, there is a memorial to Sir Thomas Spencer and his family. Sir Thomas died aged forty-six in 1685, while his widow survived him for twenty-seven years. But he lived to bury not only two infant sons (called successively Thomas) and two infant daughters, but also his only surviving son and heir, William, who died aged twenty-six. The tomb shows Sir Thomas flanked by his dead heir, his widow and his four surviving daughters and co-heiresses (plate 8).

Similar evidence of high mortality can be culled from the genealogy of any well-documented family of the period. The story of the upper squirarchy family of the Verneys of Middle Claydon in Buckinghamshire

during the middle and late seventeenth century will serve as well as any.[69]
In 1625 the mayor of Abingdon and his wife both died of the plague, leaving
a seven-year-old orphan girl, Mary. Relatives bought her wardship from the
Crown and sold her at the age of thirteen to Sir Edmund Verney, to be
married to his sixteen-year-old son and heir, Ralph. Ralph lived on to the
age of eighty-three, but Mary died at thirty-four, having given birth to six
children. Of the six, two died in infancy and two when aged four and eight.
Seven of Ralph's eleven brothers and sisters lived to the age of fifty and over
(one died at eighty-eight and another at ninety-two) and six were married,
and yet between them they only produced two sons who survived to
maturity. Ralph's eldest son, Edmund, married at twenty-six a girl who
turned out to be a life-long and incurable melancholic, but who managed to
produce three children. Their eldest son died unmarried of a fever at the age
of twenty in the lifetime of his father (who died aged fifty-two); the second
son died unmarried of a fever at the age of twenty-two four years later; and
the surviving daughter died in childbirth at the age of twenty-one, the infant
also dying a month later. With the death of all three children, the direct line
thus came to an end.

Ralph's second son, John, had been a Turkey merchant and married very
late, after he had first made a fortune in Aleppo. Six years after his return to
London, at the age of forty, he married a sixteen-year-old girl. She bore him
four children (who all lived) and then died six years later, at the age of
twenty-two. Six years later still, now aged fifty-two, John married the
thirty-one-year-old daughter of a baronet to serve as a stepmother to his
four young motherless children. She produced a child who died almost
immediately, and a year later, once again pregnant, she succumbed to
smallpox and died after only two years of marriage. So he tried again and
married a twenty-five-year-old girl, who lived, but failed to produce a child.

The Wandesfords were also a moderately successful upper gentry family,
making their way in the world by successful marriages and legal careers.
Sir Christopher Wandesford was Master of the Rolls, Lord Justice, and
finally Lord Deputy in Ireland after the recall of his patron, Sir Thomas
Wentworth, in 1640. No sooner had he reached this pinnacle of his career in
the prime of life at forty-eight than he fell ill of a fever which killed him
within a couple of weeks. Of his seven children, one died at the age of two,
one at ten, one at twenty-eight and two at thirty, leaving only two, one son
and one daughter, Alice, to live their lives to the full span of sixty or more.
Alice married William Thornton in 1651 and gave birth to eight children, of
whom five died within two years of birth. Of the three surviving children,

the one son, on whom the hopes of the family depended, died prematurely at the age of thirty, leaving only two daughters out of the eight births to complete a full life span.[70]

The life of Alice's only surviving sister Catherine was even more tragic, largely due to the exceptional fertility of the Wandesford girls. Married very early to Sir Thomas Danby of Thorp Perrow, by the time she died at the age of thirty, she had had six miscarriages and ten children, of whom only seven survived their mother. She only managed to produce her last child by a breech delivery of 'such extremity that she was exceedingly tormented with pains.' After the delivery she could not sleep and could scarcely eat until she died of fever a fortnight later. As her sister Alice commented, 'Although she was married to a good estate, yet did she enjoy not much comfort.' Death was a welcome release to her.[71]

The two previous examples have concerned gentry families, but a final case of a plebeian family can show the same processes at work lower down the social scale. It concerns the family of Jacob Bee, a skinner, glover, and ale-house keeper at Durham. His father, Nicholas, married first in 1621, but his wife died childless within two years, so in 1624 he married a widow of unknown age. She produced five living children in the next nine years, of whom only one or possibly two survived to adulthood, the others dying at the ages of one, four and nine. Nicholas' only son, Jacob, married in 1658 at the early age of twenty-two, and he and his wife lived together for no less than fifty-one years. But they produced only five children, one of whom survived to adulthood, and all of whom died in their parents' lifetime. Two children died at the age of four, one at six and one at nine. The only surviving son Nicholas married his first wife in 1681 at the age of twenty-three. She produced one daughter a year later, but in 1684 her second child died at birth, and she died of the results of the childbirth nine days later. Nicholas soon remarried and had three more children, only one of whom is known to have married. The other two may, therefore, have died young.[72] This is a family with relatively low natural fertility, but just as subject to high mortality as the Verneys and Wandesfords.

iii. The Causes of Death

In many respects these stories are largely typical of the life experiences of any family in the seventeenth century. On the other hand, it has to be emphasized that the wives in the first two cases were exceptionally fertile, and also that this seems to have been a particularly unhealthy period. It was not until 1665 that the great scourge of England, bubonic plague, which had a death rate among its victims of about seventy per cent, finally and mysteriously died away after half a century of particularly severe recrudescence, with major outbreaks in London in 1603, 1625, 1636 and 1665, and many even more lethal outbreaks in country towns.[73] One of the things that made the plague so psychologically shattering was that fear of contagion destroyed the bonds of family solidarity: 'then all friends leave us, then man or woman sits and lies alone and is a stranger to the breath of his own relations . . . ; if a man be sick of the plague, then he sits and lies all alone,' since not even his nearest and dearest dared approach him.[74]

Second only to the plague was the newer and now extremely common disease of smallpox, which if it did not so frequently kill, yet left many of the survivors either blinded altogether or pockmarked and disfigured for life. It seems likely that in the early eighteenth century smallpox was an all but universal disease, with a death rate among its victims of about sixteen per cent. There is mounting evidence of a peculiarly high mortality rate in the late seventeenth and early eighteenth centuries, and it seems likely that one cause was this new scourge of smallpox, not yet brought under control by inoculation.[75]

Physical isolation was no insurance against smallpox. Alice Thornton first had a mild infection at the age of six in 1631, and contracted it a second time at the age of sixteen, when she nearly died. The disease also ravaged her surviving children. Both her daughters, Alice and Katherine, contracted it in 1666–67, losing all their hair and ruining their complexions as a result. The third surviving child, Robert, also went down with it, although with rather less devastating results; 'he never recovered his sweet beautiful favour and pure colour in his cheeks; but his face grew longish; his hair did not fall off.' In view of this constant threat, against which medical science was almost helpless when it was not positively harmful, it is not surprising that Alice Thornton concluded in 1664: 'we are so frail of nature that none can assure themselves health or life one day.'[76] Many beautiful young girls were suddenly rendered hideous to look at by this horrible disease. In 1745 the pretty seventeen-year-old Joanna Cumberland caught the disease: 'when it had kept her in torments for eleven days, having effectually destroyed her beauty, [it] finally put an end to her life.'[77] One example of those who lived but were disfigured for life was the fourteen-year-old daughter of Thomas Wright, who got smallpox in 1782: 'I regretted very much the ravage this nauseous disorder had made in her fine countenance, which was so great that if I had been absent for the time, I should have been unable at first to have recognized my own child.' As a girl of three in 1747,

Mrs Catherine Cappe caught smallpox and was disfigured for life by it, an event which more or less determined, for the worse, the whole of her future life. As Oliver Goldsmith put it in 1760:

> Lo, the smallpox with horrid glare
> Levelled its terrors at the fair;
> And, rifling every youthful grace,
> Left but the remnant of a face.[78]

So terrifying was this disease that it was sometimes difficult to find a clergyman willing to bury anyone who had died of it, and after the 1760s no prudent family would hire a servant who had not already had it or been inoculated against it. In 1766 Tom Watts of Bletchley had himself inoculated 'as he has a design to go to London for a place,' and he knew that this was an essential requirement for employment in a genteel household. By the end of the century, it was recognized as a parental duty to have all one's children inoculated 'to alleviate the frightful disease.'[79]

Apart from endemic diseases like smallpox, small children were exposed to a host of other dangers. According to Dr William Cadogan in 1748, the most common causes of infantile mortality were fever at teething time, and intestinal worms. Other causes were inadequate milk supply from mother or wet-nurse; poisoning from pewter dishes and lead nipple-shields; lack of fresh air; and excessive swaddling.[80] Inadequate diet in infancy deformed many children by rickets, while the unbalanced diet of the rich made more than one in twelve of the late sixteenth- and early seventeenth-century peers the victims of years of agony from stones in the kidney or the bladder.[81]

The almost total ignorance of both personal and public hygiene meant that contaminated food and water was a constant hazard. Personal standards of hygiene were no better at the very top of the social pyramid than at the bottom. In 1665 the court of Charles II fled from the great plague in London, and took refuge in the Oxford colleges. They did not go back to London until early the next year, 'leaving at their departure their excrements in every corner, in chimneys, studies, coal-houses, cellars.' In the same year Samuel Pepys, when one night he was sleeping in a strange house and found that the maid had forgotten to provide a chamber-pot, did not light a candle and fumble his way to the privy, but simply deposited his excrement – twice – in the fireplace.[82]

In towns in the eighteenth century, the city ditches, now often filled with stagnant water, were commonly used as latrines; butchers killed animals in their shops and threw the offal of the carcasses into the streets; dead animals were left to decay and fester where they lay; latrine pits were dug close to wells, thus contaminating the water supply. Decomposing bodies of the rich in burial vaults beneath the church often stank out parson and congregation; urban cemeteries became overcrowded as the population grew, and the decaying bodies, constantly disturbed to make way for others, began to pollute the air of the neighbourhood. A special problem in London in the early eighteenth century was the 'poor's holes', large, deep, open pits in which were laid the bodies of the poor, side by side, row upon row. Only when the pit was filled with bodies was it finally covered over with earth. 'How noisesome the stench is that arises from these holes so stowed with dead bodies, especially in sultry seasons and after rain.'[83]

In 1742 Dr Johnson described London as a city 'which abounds with such heaps of filth as a savage would look on with amazement.' There is corroborative evidence that indeed great quantities of human excrement were 'cast into the streets at night time when the inhabitants shut up their houses.' It was also dumped on the surrounding highways and ditches so that visitors to or from the city 'are forced to stop their noses to avoid the ill smell occasioned by it.' It was not until the 1750s that local regulations for sewage disposal and paving and lighting Acts at last improved the sanitary conditions of London. In the old town of Edinburgh, however, as late as the 1760s most houses had no latrines at all. At the beat of a drum at 10 p.m. everyone emptied the day's excrements out of close-stools and chamber pots into the street, where they lay all night until cleaned up early the next morning. English visitors found the stench so nauseating that they could not take a walk before breakfast. In the bustling industrial town of Sheffield in the 1770s, channels filled with garbage and excrement ran down the centre of every street, while wandering pigs roamed up and down and acted as scavengers. Once a quarter the sluices of the dam of Barker Pool above the town were opened, and the streets were flooded with water for a proper cleansing. In London in the 1780s in the big slum tenement houses, there was a single inside privy shared by many families, so that 'there was always a reservoir of putrid matter in the lower part of the house. . . . But few houses were drained from the basement.' It was not until the very end of the eighteenth century that the English began to feel boastful about the state of their national sanitation, even though in fact it only applied to the rich. A caricature of 1796 illustrated 'National Conveniences' – the English water-closet, the Scotch bucket, the French latrine, and the Dutch lake.[84]

The result of these primitive sanitary conditions was constant outbursts of bacterial stomach infections, the most fearful of all being dysentery, which swept away many victims of both sexes and of all ages within a few hours or days. Stomach disorders of one kind or another were chronic due to poorly balanced diet among the rich, and the consumption of rotten and insufficient food among the poor.[85] The prevalence of intestinal worms was the one scientific justification for the current medical practice of regular violent purges and emetics to empty the bowels and colon. R.L.Edgeworth recollected that in the 1750s he had to take two nine-day courses of physic a year 'to fortify my stomach and to kill imaginary worms.' Edgeworth was lucky, since for many in the eighteenth century worms were far from imaginary. Indeed, worms were a common complaint among the rich as well as the poor; for example, in 1779 the Countess of Pembroke's daughter Charlotte 'was forced to take some pretty strong worm medicines, which got rid of a great number.' A Mr Evans, 'the famous man for curing worms at Knightsbridge,' had a very active practice indeed among the rich in the late eighteenth century. Sometimes recourse to him was too late, as in the case of Mr Carter's son, as 'the creatures had eaten into the intestines and the boy died.' On other occasions, his cures were ineffective, as in the case of Mrs Thrale's eldest daughter, who was 'grievously tormented with worms' in 1771 when she was taken to Mr Evans, and still 'mightily tormented' with them ten years later. Worms were a slow, disgusting and debilitating disease that caused a vast amount of human misery and ill health in the eighteenth century. Some of the remedies also were extremely dangerous, often consisting of swallowing pills of mercury or tin.[86]

In the many poorly drained marshy areas, recurrent malarial fevers were common and debilitating diseases, while everyone was at the mercy of a miscellany of swift and incurable bacterial and viral infections which carried off young and old at a few days' notice. Perhaps even more heartbreaking was the slow, inexorable, destructive power of tuberculosis, or 'consumption' as it was then called, which seems to have been one of the commonest causes of death at this time, especially among children and adolescents. James Boswell's wife endured eleven years of spitting blood and slow physical deterioration before the disease finally killed her.

For women, childbirth was a very dangerous experience, for midwives were ignorant and ill-trained, and often horribly botched the job, while the lack of hygienic precautions meant that puerperal fever was a frequent sequel. All too common were such stories as one recorded succinctly by Oliver Heywood in 1684: 'Mistress Earnshaw of York was in sore labour, had her child pulled from her by piecemeal, died at last, left a sad husband.' Because of this high mortality from childbirth, at all periods from the sixteenth to the nineteenth century, in three out of four cases of all first marriages among the squirarchy that were broken by death within ten years, the cause was the death of the wife (plate 7).[87]

Finally, there was the constant threat of accidental death from neglect or carelessness or association with animals like horses – which seem to have been at least as dangerous as automobiles – or elements like water.[88] From the series of accidents and diseases experienced by Simonds D'Ewes, the son of a wealthy lawyer in the early seventeenth century, for example, it is hardly surprising that, after surviving so many hazards, he became convinced that he was one of the Elect of God.[89]

The medical profession was almost entirely helpless to deal with human disease, since the scientific theory upon which treatment was based was disastrously wrong, and since virtually nothing was known about the importance of personal and public hygiene. The standard treatment was to aid nature by the forcible evacuation of evil 'humours' through bloodletting, induced vomiting, and the constant application of purges and enemas to clean out the stomach and bowels. No single disease had been properly diagnosed, except bubonic plague and smallpox, and there was no proper system of classification. Many of the remedies prescribed by reputable doctors hardly differed from the magical formulas of the witch doctors: for example, for apoplexy, swallow a glass of urine of a healthy person, mixed with salt, to induce vomiting; for gout, apply live earthworms to the affected part until they begin to swell. London virtuosi and members of the Royal Society were as helpless and credulous as any rural practitioner. Robert Boyle advised blowing dried and powdered human excrement into the eye as a remedy for cataract, while Robert Hooke took medicines made up of powdered human skull, among other ingredients.

There were only three effective remedies for specific diseases, and even they only became available in the course of the eighteenth century: quinine for fever, ipecacuanha for dysentery, and smallpox inoculation for smallpox.[90] With these exceptions, it is generally true that in most cases medical treatment did more harm than good and that on balance doctors certainly killed more people than they cured. In these circumstances it is hardly surprising that those who were not too convinced of the efficacy of either prayer or medicine tended to flock to the numerous astrologers, magicians, 'white witches' and 'wise women' who were such formidable rivals to the established professions of medicine and the Church in the sixteenth and seventeenth centuries.[91] Both faith healing and herbal remedies probably did more good than professional medical attention, so that the preference for the former was based on rational calculation, not mere superstition.

The last cause of infant and child death was the indifference and neglect of many parents. The rich sent their children away to paid wet-nurses for the first year, despite the known negligence of nurses, which resulted in a death rate double that of maternally fed babies. The poor were sometimes obliged to leave their children tied up in swaddling-clothes for hours to wallow in their own excrement while they went out to work; poverty also obliged them to put the infants with them in their own beds, where they occasionally rolled over and smothered them in their sleep; like the parents, the infants were fed badly and irregularly; and if things got desperate, the parents might simply abandon the infants in the street rather than watch them starve. Part of the very high infant mortality must have been due to this neglect, itself the product of poverty and ignorance. But at the same time the neglect was caused in part by the high mortality rate, since there was small reward from lavishing time and care on such ephemeral objects as small babies. It was a vicious circle.[92]

4   CONCLUSION

Under existing social and technological conditions, the availability of land and food set limits to the numerical size at which a population could be supported, which was effectively controlled by natural, social and cultural practices, affecting both birth and death.

The result was a population of which about half was under twenty and only a handful over sixty; in which marriage was delayed longer than in any other known society; in which so many infants died that they could only be regarded as expendable; and in which the family itself was a loose association of transients, constantly broken up by death of parents or children or the early departure of children from the home. It is impossible to stress too heavily the impermanence of the Early Modern family, whether from the point of view of husbands and wives, or parents and children. None could reasonably expect to remain together for very long, a fact which fundamentally affected all human relationships.[93] Death was a part of life, and was realistically treated as such.

It would be foolish, however, to adopt a reductionist position that there is a simple and direct correlation between the level of mortality and the amount and degree of affect at any given moment in history. Mortality in England was abnormally high in the fifteenth century, abnormally low in the sixteenth, high again in the late seventeenth and early eighteenth, and began a prolonged secular fall in about the middle of the eighteenth century. This see-saw oscillation does not coincide with what little we know about affective relationships, which seem to have begun to improve when mortality was at a peculiarly high level, between 1650 and 1750. There is clearly an important intervening variable: the cultural norms and expectations of society. On the other hand, it is fairly clear that the relative lack of concern for small infants was closely tied to their poor expectation of survival and that there is on the average a rough secular correlation between high mortality and low gradient affect. The high gradient affect characteristic of modern Western societies is unlikely to develop on a mass scale before child and young adult mortality have declined and before child numbers have been reduced by contraception.

PART TWO

The Open Lineage Family 1450–1630

CHAPTER 3

Family Characteristics

'The intent of matrimony is not for man and wife to be always taken up with each other, but jointly to discharge the duties of civil society, to govern their families with prudence, and educate their children with discretion.'
(Restatement of the traditional position in *The Lady's Magazine*, V, 1774, p. 240.)

I   STRUCTURE AND VALUES

The most striking characteristic of the late medieval and early sixteenth-century family, at all social levels, was the degree to which it was open to external influences, a porosity that is in contrast to the more sealed off and private nuclear family type that was to develop in the seventeenth and eighteenth centuries. Not only its individual members, but the nuclear family itself was strongly other-directed. The principal external agencies varied from class to class: among the landed elite being mainly the kin and the 'good lord'; and among the peasantry, artisans and labourers being mainly the neighbours. In both cases the nuclear family had only weak boundaries to separate it from wider definitions of social space.

i. Nobility and Gentry

In the late middle ages the nuclear family of the landed elite was no more than a loose core at the centre of a dense network of lineage and kin relationships. The degree to which the kin interacted with the nuclear core depended on social rank. It was dominant among the great aristocracy, very influential among the squirarchy, and still important among the parish gentry. The reason for this is the preoccupation with the preservation, increase and transmission through inheritance and marriage of the property and status of the lineage, of the generations of ancestors stretching back into the remote past. The larger the property and status, and the more ancient the family on its ancestral acres, the more intense was the preoccupation with the lineage, and thus the greater the participation of the kin in the formation and daily life of the conjugal family. The degree of loyalty to lineage thus depended on the size of the property and on the lack of social or geographical mobility. As a result the conjugal family among all ranks of the propertied classes was inextricably enmeshed with, and strongly supported by, the kin. A great many of the functions now performed by the nuclear family, and a great many of the emotions now focused upon it, were then shared with the kin. The family at this period cannot, therefore, be looked at in isolation, since at every turn it was being affected by and interacting with kin relatives. Since the kin formed a community, marriage meant not so much intimate association with an individual as entry into a new world of the spouse's relatives, uncles, nephews and distant cousins: 'I was married into my husband's family,' recalled Mary, Countess of Warwick, as late as the early seventeenth century, in a revealing phrase.[1] Kinship was an institution whose purpose was the mutual economic, social and psychological advancement of the group, and in which the principle of patriarchy – the leadership of the head of the clan – was very strong, although tempered by the influence of the grand family council. Any such society, hierarchical, patriarchal, authoritarian and kin-oriented, inevitably gives very low priority to the short-term quest for psychological or emotional gratification by the individual, and very high priority to the long-term economic and patronage interests of the lineage as a whole. These lineage and kin relationships provided society with its political framework, and formed the principal bonding of patronage and 'good lordship' on the one hand, and loyalty and deference on the other. These were the key articulating principles of the society, which began to decline in England in the late sixteenth century, but which lasted in Scotland until the late seventeenth.[2]

To understand the moral premises upon which such a society is based, it is necessary to rid ourselves of three modern Western culture-bound preconceptions. The first is that there is a clear dichotomy between marriage for interest, meaning money, status or power, and marriage for affect, meaning love, friendship or sexual attraction; and that the first is morally reprehensible. In practice in the sixteenth century, no such distinction existed; and if it did, affect was of secondary importance to interest, while romantic love and lust were strongly condemned as ephemeral and irrational grounds for marriage. The second modern preconception is that sexual intercourse unaccompanied by an emotional relationship is immoral, and that marriage for interest is therefore a form of prostitution. The third is that personal autonomy, the pursuit by the individual of his or her own happiness, is paramount, a claim justified by the theory that it in fact contributes to the well-being of the group. To an Elizabethan audience the tragedy of Romeo and Juliet, like that of Othello, lay not so much in their ill-starred romance as in the way they brought destruction upon themselves by violating the norms of the society in which they lived, which in the former case meant strict filial obedience and loyalty to the traditional friendships and enmities of the lineage. An Elizabethan courtier would be familiar enough with the bewitching passion of love to feel some sympathy with the young couple, but he would see clearly enough where duty lay.

Marriage among the property-owning classes in sixteenth-century England was, therefore, a collective decision of family and kin, not an individual one. Past lineage associations, political patronage, extension of lineage connections, and property preservation and accumulation were the principal considerations. Property and power were the predominant issues which governed negotiations for marriage, while the greatest fear in a society so acutely conscious of status and hierarchy was of social derogation in marriage, of alliance with a family of lower estate or degree than one's own. In the late middle ages, the current head of one of the larger landed families was regarded as no more than a temporary custodian of the family estates, which were the permanent assets of the lineage and were tied up in unbreakable entails, under which the bulk of them passed to the eldest son by the convention of primogeniture. The other children, both daughters and younger sons, were at the economic mercy of their father or elder brother, who could allocate to them as much or as little as he chose of the personal estate in cash or two-life leases.[3] He could also grant them parts of the unentailed estates, and often did so, but was unable to give them any share of the entailed landed property. The current head thus wielded great power over daughters and younger children. But he was quite unable either to disinherit his eldest son or, very often, to provide adequately for the other children to secure for them marriages that might be advantageous to the family interests. Landowners found that this was a straitjacket which cramped their freedom of action and did not necessarily always contribute to the long-term welfare of the lineage.

The prime factor affecting all families which owned property was therefore the principle of primogeniture, for the preservation and protection of which the entail was designed. No study of the English landed family makes any sense unless the principle and practice of primogeniture is constantly borne in mind. It was something which went far to determine the behaviour and character of both parents and children, and to govern the relationship between siblings. Owing to the demographic insecurity which threatened all families, a father tried to see to it that the heir to the estate was married fairly early. This was the most important strategic decision of a generation, and it was made by the father and the family council of elders, negotiating directly with equivalent representatives of the family of the bride.

Under such a system, both the elder and the younger children suffered. The latter normally inherited neither title nor estate, unless one of them happened to be heir to his mother's property, and they were therefore inevitably downwardly mobile, until they had made their own fortunes in some profession or occupation. Some were kept hanging around on or near the estate, as a kind of walking sperm-bank in case the elder son died childless and had to be replaced. As for the elder sons, their entrepreneurial drive was sapped by the certainty of the inheritance to come, until which time they were condemned to live a kind of shadow existence waiting for their father to die, when they would at last come into their own. James Boswell, who for years was in just this situation, once talked bitterly about his 'narrow and dependent state'.[4] Both heirs and younger sons were thus willy-nilly forced into the Micawberish situation of waiting for something to turn up, namely an early death of father or brother.

The third inter-related factor, along with entails and primogeniture, which governed the structure of the English family at all levels of the propertied classes from the sixteenth century on through the nineteenth century, was the dowry system. In England, brides who were not landed heiresses were unable, because of primogeniture, to provide landed property, but were expected instead to bring with them as a dowry a substantial cash sum, called a 'portion'. In the sixteenth and early seventeenth centuries, this money went directly to the father of the groom, who often used it himself as a dowry in marrying off one of his own daughters. In return, the father of the groom guaranteed the bride an annuity, called a 'jointure', if she survived her husband as a widow. Marriage, therefore, always involved a transfer of a significant amount of real or personal property from the family of the bride to that of the groom, with a reverse commitment in the future of a significant proportion of annual income.

Several important consequences followed from this. The first was that there was a high probability of strong class endogamy, that women would tend to marry spouses from a similar economic bracket, since only they were suitable recipients of the cash portion and were able to guarantee the appropriate jointure in return. Secondly, the system gave great power to the head of the family in controlling the marriages of his children, since he alone could provide the necessary portions for his daughters and guarantee the necessary jointures for his sons' widows. Not only the male heir and the daughters, but also the younger sons, were at his mercy. Thirdly, under such conditions marriages tended to be arranged by parents rather than by the children themselves. As we shall see, this patriarchal authority was only undermined after 1660, when the 'strict settlement' deprived the father of his power to give or to withhold, by stipulating the provision allocated to each unborn child at the time of the parents' marriage. Fourthly, rich wives were valuable – and widows more valuable still (especially widows past the childbearing age) – as prizes to be fought for. To obtain likely brides, a sixteenth-century family often relied on a marriage broker to make the first suggestions and contacts, and the financial preliminaries were often settled between the parents before the pair had even set eyes on each other. In Catholic families, for example, the broker would often be a Catholic priest, whose itinerant life, moving from country house to country house, put him in an excellent position to know the market.[5] Conversely, the dowry system, and the cultural obligation to marry off the girls, meant that daughters were a serious economic drain on the family finances, though they were useful in cementing political connections. Under these conditions, personal factors entered into the strategy of marriage only in so far as it was important to ensure a healthy genetic strain for breeding.

It should be emphasized that lineage and kinship was only one of three foci of loyalty for the greater and lesser landowners of the fifteenth and early sixteenth centuries. The second highly prized value was that of 'good lordship' – a reciprocal exchange of patronage, support and hospitality in return for attendance, deference, respect, advice and loyalty. This 'lordship' embraced not only the wider ramifications of the kin, but also the household retainers and servants, the client gentry and the tenants on the estates, all comprising a collective 'affinity'. The kin was, therefore, merely one component of this larger whole, under which all the others were subsumed. Its physical manifestation was the great house with its open hospitality, its lack of privacy, and its constant crowds of attendants, retainers, servants, clients and suitors. Its psychological manifestation was a particularist system of values, by which personalized loyalty and lordship was the highest and most prized of qualities, taking precedence over those of obedience to the Ten Commandments, of submission to the impersonal dictates of the law, and of deference to the personal authority of the king. It was a bounded, localized, highly personal world, which had yet to be affected by wider notions of loyalty to more universalistic codes and ideals.[6]

Not only was this network of patronage the cement that held sixteenth-century society together; it also determined the life-chances of every individual in it. For this was a society run by what Weber defined as a 'patrimonial bureaucracy', in which offices, favours and rewards were all distributed not according to merit or need, but according to partiality. Primogeniture and patriarchy meant that power tended to drift into the hands of the oldest males, and that in every family, village and county, and even at court, there was a constant struggle to win the approval of, or establish some reciprocal claim upon, some individual – often an old man – who controlled the levers of power. In such a society marriage, with its attendant family settlement, was a critical ingredient for the extension of the network of patronage connections, and was therefore strictly controlled by the elders of both families.

The third highly prized value was not collective, like lineage or lordship, but personal: that of honour. Honour was itself in part, of course, derived from lineage and from lordship, but there was more to it than that. A relic of late medieval ideas about chivalry, it demanded public recognition of individual worth, a high reputation in the peer-group world of gentlemen as a person deserving respect and 'worship'. This honour was best achieved and maintained by vigorous, even combative, self-assertion, military glory in the field, a scrupulous maintenance of good faith, backed by good lineage origins and good marriage connections.[7] One's honour was something worth fighting for, and even dying for to protect, which explains the code of the duel. It was a value that was to persist into the eighteenth century, when it merged with the new sense of individualism. As a result, many gentlemen would continue to fight duels over 'giving the lie'.

What is significant about these three interlocking sets of values is that they all took priority both over loyalty to the nuclear family unit against the outside world, and over obedience to the sovereign state. The new world of the late sixteenth century was to substitute ideas of obedience to the state, adherence to a particular brand of Christian faith and devotion to the nuclear family for these medieval values, which were still cherished and fostered in the early sixteenth century.

Because they served such important social, economic and political functions, it follows that lineage loyalties, kin networks, and the ties of 'good lordship' will persist longest where the alternative support system, namely the state and the law, are weakest, and that they will tend to revive and expand in times of national political or economic crisis. It is not surprising, therefore, that it was in the turbulent and weakly governed upland areas of the north of England that a lineage and lordship culture flourished most strongly in the early sixteenth century, centered around the great and ancient 'houses' of the Nevilles, the Percys, the Cliffords, and the Dacres. In 1569 a Dacre follower told Leonard Dacre that 'the poor people . . . favour you and your house, and cry and call for you and your blood to rule them.' He added that Dacre's brother was willing 'to suffer death patiently . . . so that . . . you and your blood in name might continue with your ancestor's living.' But in that year the final showdown occurred between this old particularist lineage and lordship culture and the new universalistic culture of the nation state. The Rebellion of the Northern Earls proved conclusively that the old culture was already hollow, and no longer able to sustain the challenge of outright rebellion against the sovereign.[8]

ii. Plebs

Those classes below the nobility and gentry, who for convenience may be subsumed under the status category of 'plebs', comprised the vast bulk of the population, most of whom were resident in villages or small towns. One would suppose that those who owned land, however small, planned their marriages and inheritance strategies to preserve the property and extend the influence of the lineage. They were presumably also open to similar pressures from the kin as the rich, but to a lesser extent since personal contact involving travel and hospitality was restricted by poverty, and communication in writing was restricted by lack of literacy.

But until there has been carried out in England a comprehensive study of inheritance customs among the peasantry, we do not know the extent to which primogeniture was practised among the English peasantry of the sixteenth century and before. To the extent that it was, the principle had very important effects. It tended to produce low nuptiality, since many younger sons could not afford to marry; late marriage for those who did marry since the eldest sons were often dependent on their fathers' death or retirement to be able to afford it, while the younger sons had first to make their own way in the world; much migration to the towns or new lands, since only one son could remain on the home farm; low population density, since farms remained large; and relatively high fertility within marriage, since there was no very strong incentive to keep down the number of children .[9] At the peasant level, the key issue was whether the father was willing to retire from work and hand the farm over to a son or son-in-law in return for stipulated pension rights for the lifetime of himself and his wife. This was a common practice in central Europe, but apparently less normal in Early Modern England.

The one detailed study available, based on wills in the late sixteenth and early seventeenth centuries in Cambridgeshire, suggests that these fathers were exercising great latitude in their dispositions. Primogeniture prevailed, but there was a general tendency to carve off small tenements to provide a livelihood for younger sons. In most cases, the bulk of the property was passed on to the eldest son, but for generation after generation the inheritance became smaller through provisions made for widows and younger sons. This fragmentation process weakened the economic strength of the smallholder and helped to force him into liquidation in crisis periods of harvest failures, which came in the early seventeenth century. In one rich fenland village, partible inheritance was the norm, and fragmentation therefore even greater, since it was so much easier to earn a subsistence living on a tiny holding with access to the fens.[10] If these findings are confirmed elsewhere, the decline of the small landowner in England was due as much to cultural patterns of inheritance as to economic pressure from the nobility and gentry.

Below the peasantry, the propertyless poor lacked any sense of lineage or of status, and possessed neither the house room nor the surplus food to be able to shelter and feed a relative in a crisis. Control over the marriage of children was weak since they mostly left home somewhere between the ages of seven and fourteen to go into domestic or agricultural service as living-in servants, or to serve out a term of apprenticeship, also living in the master's house. They were therefore removed at an early age from the direct control of their natural parents, and when they came to marry, some ten or fifteen years after they first left home, they were inevitably fairly free to choose a spouse for themselves. In any case, the family and kin interest in the marriage of the propertyless was low since no money or land changed hands, and the incentive to interfere was consequently limited. Marriage among the poor, we must assume, was far more a personal than a family and kin affair. Kin were very useful, on the other hand, for economic advancement and job placement, and the role of uncles in the life of the poor should not be underestimated. Among the propertied peasants and artisans, moreover, marriage control remained strong owing to the need to share out the property in order to give the young married pair a start in life.

Interference in the affairs of the nuclear family among the plebs, however, came mainly not from the kin but from the neighbours in the village community. The economic life of every open-field village was strictly controlled by community decisions in the manorial court, while the laws of copyhold tenure often interfered with the freedom of a widow to remarry while retaining her plot of land. All aspects of the economic planning of the family – who could plough when, who could sow or reap what and where, how many cattle of what type could be permitted to graze where – came under collective control in the open-field system.

Secondly, domestic life in the village was unable to develop so long as it was overshadowed by the luxuriant growth of neighbourly activity and scrutiny.[11] During the late sixteenth and early seventeenth centuries, this intrusive scrutiny actually intensified due to the rise of ethical Puritanism and the increased activity of the Church courts in controlling personal morality. Everyone gossiped freely about the most intimate details of domestic relations, and did not hesitate to denounce violations of community norms to an archdeacon's visitation enquiry, so that people were constantly testifying in court about the alleged moral peccadilloes of their neighbours.

2   AFFECTIVE RELATIONSHIPS

i. The Society

Any discussion of emotional relationships in general is inevitably a most hazardous undertaking, since the evidence is so scanty, ambiguous and divergent that the stock historical methodology of demonstration by example is even less convincing than usual. What follows is, therefore, no more than a highly impressionistic account of what could and should be the subject of a much more intensive investigation.

Such personal correspondence and diaries as survive suggest that social relations from the fifteenth to the seventeenth centuries tended to be cool, even unfriendly. The extraordinary amount of casual inter-personal physical and verbal violence, as recorded in legal and other records, shows clearly that at all levels men and women were extremely short-tempered. The most trivial disagreements tended to lead rapidly to blows, and most people carried a potential weapon, if only a knife to cut their meat. As a result, the law courts were clogged with cases of assault and battery.[12] The correspondence of the day is filled with accounts of brutal assaults at the dinner-table or in taverns, often leading to death. Among the upper classes, duelling, which spread to England in the late sixteenth century, was kept more or less in check by the joint pressure of the Puritans and the King before 1640, but became a serious social menace after the Restoration. Friends and acquaintances felt honour bound to challenge and kill each other for the slightest affront, however unintentional or spoken in the careless heat of passion or drink. Casual violence from strangers was also a daily threat. Brutal and unprovoked assaults by gangs of idle youths from respectable families, such as the Mohawks, were a frequent occurrence in eighteenth-century London streets; and the first thing young John Knyveton was advised to do when he came to the fashionable western suburbs of London in 1750 was to buy himself a cudgel or a small sword, and to carry it for self-defence, especially after dark.[13] Dr Johnson noted that when in the late seventeenth century his mother had lived in London, 'there were two sets of people, those who gave the wall and those who took it: the peaceable and the quarrelsome.' By 1737, however, pedestrians normally kept to the right, and there were no more quarrels of punctilio about keeping to the wall side of the pavement.[14] This indicates a change of manners to a more orderly, more disciplined, and less personally aggressive society.

The amount of mugging in the streets seems to have risen in the early eighteenth century, and London was then a very dangerous place. Shopkeepers and tavern-keepers complained that they were losing money since 'their customers are afraid when it is dark to come to their houses and shops for fear that . . . they may be blinded, knocked down, cut or stabbed.' It was only with the introduction of a more efficient police system, better paving and lighting, and perhaps an improvement in the morals and sobriety of the drifting poor in the late eighteenth century, that crime in the streets seems to have abated. A guidebook of 1802 at last found it possible to assert that 'no city . . . is more free from danger to those who pass the streets at all hours.'[15]

This habitual violence was not confined to the cities. In some villages throughout the sixteenth and much of the seventeenth centuries, both feuding among kin factions and personal hostility of one individual towards another were so intense that in the more backward areas it proved impossible to impose the normal discipline of parish worship. The villagers would not assemble under the same roof, much less join together in the same ritual of communion or church service. When in the mid-sixteenth century John Gilpin tried to bring Christianity to the border areas in Northumberland, he was thwarted by the refusal of many parishioners to enter the same building as those from a family with whom they were feuding. They were willing enough to listen to him, but not to go into the church together.[16]

In the 'face-to-face society' of the traditional village, whose virtues are so often praised in this more impersonal and mobile world of the twentieth century, it was possible for expressions of hatred to reach levels of frequency, intensity and duration which are rarely seen today, except in similar close-knit groups like the Fellows of Oxford and Cambridge colleges. It is an unfortunate fact of life that close propinquity does not necessarily lead to brotherly love, or even to easy-going toleration. It is equally likely to generate hostility which in a pre-modern society frequently spilled over into open violence.

It is significant that the one large-scale study of crime in medieval England, in the early fourteenth century, shows that violence was far more frequently directed outside the family than within it. Only eight per cent of homicides, for example, were within the family, compared with over fifty per cent in England today. When it occurred, intra-family violence seems to have been mainly caused by disputes over property, or to have been a product of frustration with general conditions of life, which led to violence ending in unintended tragedy. Of course, a great deal of casual wife-beating or child-battering, which today would end up in the courts, simply went unrecorded in medieval and Early Modern times. What is so striking, however, is that the family was more a unit for the perpetration of crime – a third of all group crimes were by family members – than a focus for crime. It is tempting to argue that the family that slayed together, stayed together.[17] One conclusion one can draw from this evidence is that familial emotive ties were so weak that they did not generate the passions which lead to intra-familial murder and mayhem. Neither Othello nor Oedipus nor Cain were familiar figures in fourteenth-century England, any more than they were, so far as is known, in the sixteenth century.

Habits of casual violence are not incompatible with habits of casual friendliness and hospitality, and it is the relative absence of evidence of the latter which is perhaps more revealing about the inner dynamics of the society. The violence of everyday life seems to have been accompanied by much mutual suspicion and a low general level of emotional interaction and commitment. Alienation and distrust of one's fellow man are the predominant features of the Elizabethan and early Stuart view of human character and conduct. In the 1590s the astrologer Simon Forman was constantly drawing lessons from Shakespeare to remind himself not to be too trustful. 'Never admit any party without a bar between', in case he attacks you physically. 'Beware . . . of noblemen and of their fair words, and say little to them, lest they [hang] thee for thy good will.' 'Beware of trusting feigned beggars or fawning fellows.'[18] Wary suspicion was the only reliable guide for survival in the jungle of human society.

A 'Letter of Advice to a Son' was a very common form of literary and moral exercise among the landed classes at this period. These documents normally express a thoroughly pessimistic view of human nature, full of canny and worldly-wise hints about how to conduct personal relations which leave little room for generosity, faith, hope or charity. A not untypical, if a little extreme, example of this genre is provided by Sir William Wentworth's 'Advice' to his son Thomas, the future Earl of Strafford, written in 1607.[19] The basic assumption is that no one is to be trusted, since anyone and everyone – wife, servants, children, friends, neighbours, or patrons – are only kept loyal by self-interest, and may, therefore, at any moment turn out to be enemies. The only safe way to manoeuvre through the world is by the exercise of extreme self-control, outward reserve, secrecy, and even duplicity. 'Be very careful to govern your tongue, and never speak in open places all you think . . . But to your wife, if she can keep council (as few women can) or to a private faithful friend, or some old servant that hath all his living and credit under you, you may be more open.' Judges, juries, under-sheriffs, and men of influence are to be courted both with flattery and with judicious gifts; but 'give little or nothing beforehand' in case the recipient pockets it for himself. As for noblemen, 'be careful not to make them hate you'. 'He that will be honoured and feared in his country must bear countenance and authority, for people are servile, not generous, and do reverence men for fear, not for love of their virtues.' 'Nothing but fear of revenge or suits can hold men back from doing wrong.' Even kinsmen, 'if any of all these have lands or goods joining with you, in no case trust them too much.' 'Ever fear the worst.' 'Whosoever comes to speak with you comes premeditate for his advantage.' 'In any case, be suspicious of the conscience of any that seems more saintlike than others and smooth like oil.' 'Never persuade yourself that any man is honest', without long experience of dealing with him. As for servants, 'trust them not more than you need must in matters that may greatly concern your danger.' To keep a hold on servants, never reward them with fixed life annuities, but always with things that can be revoked, like tenancies at will. Be suspicious of the advice of lawyers 'who live by the suits and contentions of others.' Tenants 'notwithstanding all their fawning and flattery . . . seldom love their landlord in their hearts.' Therefore, give no long leases but keep them as tenants at will. Even a wife is to be subjected to the same treatment, being assured a small fixed jointure for her widowhood and kept in line with promises of more on condition of continual good behaviour. All this reflects a thoroughly cynical view of the human condition and social relationships, including those with wives, kinsfolk and friends.

This general approach to life can be duplicated in many other examples of this genre of 'Advices', even if the somewhat paranoid overtones are peculiar to William Wentworth. Shakespeare's interpretation of King Lear merely underscores the moral that a father who gives up real power, in the expectation of obtaining the love and attention of his children instead, is merely exhibiting a form of insanity. His inevitable disappointment would have come as no surprise to an Elizabethan audience.[20] The use of the word 'friend' in the sixteenth and early seventeenth centuries does much to illuminate this climate of opinion. Used in the singular, the word did indeed often mean a loved one, as when in 1628 Sir Fulke Greville arranged that the inscription on his tombstone should record that he had been 'friend to Sir Philip Sidney.' It certainly had this meaning if qualified for clarity as 'a choice special friend', 'my dear friend', etc. But it was also frequently used to mean not a person to whom one had some emotional attachment, but someone who could help one on in life, with whom one could safely do business, or upon whom one was in some way dependent. Significantly enough, it was not until the mid-eighteenth century that the word unambiguously took on its original and its modern meaning, being defined by Dr Johnson as 'one who supports you and comforts you while others do not', someone 'with whom to compare minds and cherish private virtues.' It was in this sense that in the late 1740s Miss Talbot exclaimed with satisfaction 'How rich have I been in friends, dear Miss Carter, and such friends as fall to the lot of few.'[21]

Used in the plural, as 'my friends', the word before the eighteenth century always meant no more than 'my advisors, associates and backers.' This category often indicated a relative, particularly a parent or an uncle by blood or marriage. But it could also include a member of the household, such as a steward, chaplain or tutor; or a neighbour; or a political associate sharing a common party affiliation; or a person of high status and influence with whom there was acquaintance and from whom there was hope of patronage.[22] Sir William Wentworth certainly recognized the existence of 'a private faithful friend', 'your familiar fast friend'. But he warned that 'your friend afterward may become your enemy', and when it came to the serious decisions of life, such as marriage or money transactions, he told his son to turn to 'the council of their faithful aged friends', 'your wise faithful friends', 'your wise ancient friends', 'some aged faithful friend', etc. These are elderly family associates and kinsmen, not necessarily men who might have ties of personal affection for his son, since the choice of these 'friends' is specified as '3 or 4 or 5 knights or esquires that were faithful to your father, for those are likest to be faithful to you'.

It was 'friends' who were the key advisors in the critical decision of marriage, not only among the nobility and gentry, but down to the lower middle classes. Thus, in the early seventeenth century, Frances Lane found herself trapped into an engagement with a shoemaker. 'Her friends, father and mother, liking of a stranger, would persuade her to marry him, but she fancied him not. Yet her friends were very willing thereunto, and it was concluded in a week.' As late as the 1820s, in the full romantic period, Lady Louisa Stuart commented that 'a young man's *friends*, in this sense meaning parents, guardians, old uncles and the like, are rarely propitious to love.' Indeed they were not, but the survival of the phrase in the nineteenth century to mean no more than conservative and hard-boiled matrimonial councillors is evidence of how long the old usage persisted, long after 'friend' in the singular had taken on its modern meaning.[23]

Overwhelming evidence of the lack of warmth and tolerance in interpersonal relations at the village level is provided by the extraordinary amount of back-biting, malicious slander, marital discord and unfaithfulness, and petty spying and delation which characterized life in the villages of Essex in the late sixteenth century. The Church courts were deluged with accusations and complaints by neighbour against neighbour, and one gets the impression of a society in which privacy was non-existent, spying and prying and questioning was a universal pastime, especially of the women, and tongues were continually wagging about the shortcomings and moral lapses of others in the village. Delation for sexual transgressions in particular seems to have been a standard and regular occupation, the reward for which was to see the guilty parties condemned to stand in a white sheet in the market place or the church to confess their misdemeanour. As for pregnant unmarried women, they were treated with a ruthless cruelty which only the fear that the child would become a burden on the local poor-rate can explain. The Elizabethan village was a place filled with malice and hatred, its only unifying bond being the occasional episode of mass hysteria, which temporarily bound together the majority in order to harry and persecute the local witch.[24]

This was not an easy-going society suddenly disorientated by the advent of Puritanism, for a village curé in Anjou, writing in 1700 – admittedly a wretched period – found exactly the same set of human relations among his peasant flock. They married for economic interest, not inclination; grown-up children did not look after sick or impoverished parents; parents did not look after sick or helpless children. There was no concept of 'home' in the village. Outside the family, brutality was the norm, and savage physical assaults were common. Quarrels, beatings and lawsuits were the predominant pastimes of the village. A late-eighteenth-century doctor, writing about the Auvergne, which is admittedly notorious for its backwardness, was shocked to find that 'people do not feel that true happiness consists of kindness to those about you, who will always respond in like manner.'[25] The evidence from both England and France suggests that it is rash to assume that the economic and ritual cooperation needed to live in an Early Modern village also necessarily meant strong communal solidarity in emotional terms. It might, and again it might not.

To argue that in the sixteenth and seventeenth centuries interpersonal relations were at best cold and at worst hostile does not at all mean that this was a society in which emotion played a minor role. Rather, emotion was deflected into other channels, primarily into passionate religious enthusiasm, where hatred of believers in different Christian churches or sects seems to have been at least as important a psychological bonding as identity with one's own fellow-believers. Tempers were short, and both casual violence and venomous and mutually exhausting litigation against neighbours were extremely common, and soaked up much psychic energy. Finally, from time to time emotional tensions obtained release in collective acts of persecution of some scapegoat, denounced as a witch or a heretic. In all these cases, it is noticeable that hate seems to have been more prominent an emotion than love.

What is being postulated for the sixteenth and early seventeenth centuries is a society in which a majority of the individuals that composed it found it very difficult to establish close emotional ties to any other person. Children were neglected, brutally treated, and even killed; adults treated each other with suspicion and hostility; affect was low, and hard to find. To an anthropologist, there would be nothing very surprising about such a society, which closely resembles the Mundugumor in New Guinea in the twentieth century, as described by Margaret Mead.

There seem to have been four causes for the development of such a culture. The first was the frequency with which infants at that period were deprived of a single mothering and nurturing figure to whom they could relate during the first eighteen months or two years of life. Upper-class babies were mostly taken from their real mothers and put out to wet-nurses.

These nurses were often cruel or neglectful, and they often ran out of milk, as a result of which the baby had to be passed from nipple to nipple, from one unloving mother-substitute to another. If the infant stayed with one wet-nurse, then it became deeply attached to her, as a result of which the weaning process at about eighteen months inflicted the trauma of final separation from the loved substitute mother-figure and a return to the alien and frightening world of the natural mother. In 1829 William Cobbett asked rhetorically: 'Who has not seen these banished children, when brought and put into the arms of their mother, screaming to get from them and stretching out their little hands to get back to the arms of the nurse?' In 1776 a French propagandist for Rousseauesque ideas about maternal breast-feeding, Etienne Aubry, painted a picture of precisely this scene. The upper-class father is standing aloof, the elegant natural mother is eagerly grasping for the baby as the peasant nurse reluctantly surrenders it, while the baby squirms and wriggles, looking away from her mother and longingly back at the nurse.[26] In Cobbett's opinion, which is supported by modern psychology, the infant never succeeds in transferring its affections from the wet-nurse back to the natural mother after weaning. Only the children of the very rich, like Shakespeare's Juliet, enjoyed a wet-nurse who lived in the home and stayed on with them later as a nurse throughout their childhood. The more normal experience was that of James Boswell's son, who was put out to one wet-nurse on his birth in October 1775, and transferred to another in November. When his daughter's nurse left after feeding the child for eighteen months, 'the separation was a distress to both.'[27]

Another psychological consequence of wet-nursing was the anxiety experienced by many adults about who they really were. The fairy stories of the time are full of accounts of changelings whose real identity had been concealed by an exchange carried out by the wet-nurse. It was not unreasonable to suppose that if an infant child of wealthy parents were to die in the care of the wet-nurse, the latter might well be tempted to conceal the event by substituting her own infant or that of a neighbour. Thus Susan Sibbald, who was born in 1783 and put out to a smuggler's wife to be nursed, lived with a nagging fear that she had been changed in the cradle and was a smuggler's child, which would explain why her mother seemed to dislike her.[28]

A study of modern psychiatric patients from wealthy homes where they have been neglected by their parents and left in the hands of nannies, servants and boarding-schools – exactly the experience of the majority of sixteenth and seventeenth-century children from the upper classes – reveals a clearly defined 'deprivation syndrome'. Its seven features are chronic low-grade depression; a sense of abandonment; a feeling of emptiness; deep dependency needs; an inability to maintain human relations; psychotic-like attacks of rage; and a tendency to erect projective defences against the world, giving a paranoid colouration to their character.[29] The first three feelings can usually only be surmised, but are always found in the autobiographies of religious enthusiasts when describing their pre-conversion state of mind. The last three, which show up in outward behaviour, are overwhelmingly obvious in all the documentation of the period. Most men and women of the sixteenth and seventeenth centuries, from all walks of life, to differing degrees, show very clear evidence of all the overt symptoms of parental deprivation. Whether rich or poor, they nearly all suffered from neglect or ill-treatment in one form or another.

Quite apart from the psychological wounds inflicted by the practice of wet-nursing, which was confined largely to the rich, many children of all classes suffered the loss by death of one parent or another at an early age. There is evidence to suggest that throughout the Early Modern period nearly one in ten of all children under three, and one in five of all children living at home, had experienced this loss. [30] But since this was common to the sixteenth, seventeenth and eighteenth centuries, it cannot be identified as a cause of the pre-1660 coolness. Thirdly, the practice of tight swaddling in the first months or even year of life, resulting in what is virtually a prolongation of the inter-uterine condition of total immobility, is thought to isolate the infant from its surroundings.[31] Thus there could be, and often was, a combination of sensory deprivation, motor deprivation and affect deprivation in the first critical months of life, the consequences of which upon the adult personality are now thought to be very serious and long lasting in reducing the capacity for warm social relationships. It has been connected, for example, with the violent and orgiastic nature of adult gratifications in Russia.[32]

Finally, there was the deliberate breaking of the young child's will, first by the harshest physical beating and later by overwhelming psychological pressures, which was thought to be the key to successful child-rearing in the sixteenth and seventeenth centuries. These four factors, the lack of a unique mother figure in the first two years of life, the constant loss of close relatives, siblings, parents, nurses and friends through premature death, the physical imprisonment of the infant in tight swaddling-clothes in early months, and the deliberate breaking of the child's will all contributed to a 'psychic numbing' which created many adults whose primary responses to others were at best a calculating indifference and at worst a mixture of suspicion and hostility, tyranny and submission, alienation and rage.

It is not being claimed that everyone in the sixteenth and early seventeenth centuries suffered from this psychic numbing, for this would be both ridiculous and untrue. There were certainly plenty of cheerful and affectionate Wives of Bath in real life as well as in the works of Shakespeare. But it is remarkable how difficult it is to find in the correspondence and memoirs of that period that ease and warmth which is so apparent in the eighteenth century. So far as the surviving evidence goes, England between 1500 and 1660 was relatively cold, suspicious, and violence-prone. It should be emphasized that this is a comparative judgement, not an absolute one, and it may be skewed by the relative paucity of evidence before 1640, the relative dominance of that evidence by the Puritans, and the relative clumsiness and unfamiliarity with the use of the written word to express emotions. But enough legal and other evidence survives to indicate that the difference between periods is a reality, not merely a product of distorted evidence.

ii. Husbands and Wives

In the sixteenth century, relations between spouses in rich families were often fairly remote. Living in big houses, each with his or her own bedroom and servants, husband and wife were primarily members of a functioning social universe of a large household and were rarely in private together. It has been seen that their marriage was usually arranged rather than consensual, in essence the outcome of an economic deal or a political alliance between two families. The transaction was sealed by the wedding and by the physical union of two individuals, while the emotional ties were left to develop at a later date. If they did not take place, and if the husband could find sexual alternatives through casual liaisons, the emotional outlet through marriage was largely non-existent for either husband or wife.

In any case, the expectations of felicity from marriage were pragmatically low, and there were many reasons why disappointment was minimal. The first is that the pair did not need to see very much of one another, either in elite circles, where they could go their own way, or among the plebs, where leisure activities were segregated, with the men resorting to the ale-house, and the women to each other's houses. In 1687, when the arranged marriage was coming under severe criticism from all quarters, Aphra Behn described how domestic life was managed among noble families in London society: 'My lord keeps his coach, my lady hers; my lord his bed, my lady hers; and very rarely see one another unless they chance to meet in a visit, in the Park, the Mall, the Tour, or at the basset table, where they civilly salute and part, he to his mistress, she to play.'[33]

The second reason why such a system was so readily accepted was the high adult mortality rates, which severely reduced the companionship element in marriage and increased its purely reproductive and nurturance functions. There was a less than fifty-fifty chance that the husband and wife would both remain alive more than a year or two after the departure from the home of the last child, so that friendship was hardly necessary.[34] William Stout's comment on a marriage in 1699 could stand as an epitaph for many sixteenth- and seventeenth-century couples: 'they lived very disagreeably but had many children.'[35]

Eighteenth-century middle-class observers of social relations among the labouring classes, peasants and urban *petite bourgeoisie* in France could find no trace of affection in the marital relationship. Their observations may be biased by class and background, but if they are at all accurate, they must reflect a permanent feature of the traditional European society. All over France, 'If the horse and the wife fall sick at the same time, the ... peasant rushes to the blacksmith to care for the animal, and leaves the task of healing his wife to nature.' If necessary, the wife could be replaced very cheaply, while the family economy depended on the health of the animal. This peasant pragmatism was confirmed by traditional proverbs, such as 'rich is the man whose wife is dead and horse alive.' The same lack of marital sentiment was evident in the towns. '*L'amitié*, that delicious sentiment, is scarcely known. There are in these little towns only marriages of convenience; nobody appreciates that true happiness consists in making others happy, who always reward us in kind.'[36]

This rather pessimistic view of a society with little love and generally low and widely diffused affect needs to be modified in two ways if it is accurately to reflect the truth. Romantic love and sexual intrigue was certainly the subject of much poetry of the sixteenth and early seventeenth centuries, and of many of Shakespeare's plays. It was also a reality which existed in one very restricted social group: the one in which it had always existed since the twelfth century, that is the households of the prince and the great nobles. Here, and here alone, well-born young persons of both sexes were thrown together away from parental supervision and in a situation of considerable freedom as they performed their duties as courtiers, ladies and gentlemen in waiting, tutors and governesses to the children. They also had a great deal of leisure, and in the enclosed hot-house atmosphere of these great houses, love intrigues flourished as nowhere else. That this was so in sixteenth-century England we know from the first intimate secular autobiography in the language, that of the gentleman musician Thomas Wythorne.[37] In the middle years of the sixteenth century, he served as music teacher and tutor in a number of noble households, and his autobiography is primarily an account of complex love intrigues among his fellow attendants, and of temptations to adultery from his female married employers. By his own account, he spent his time fending off the amorous advances of ladies. No doubt this is a one-sided view of the situation, but the atmosphere of constant erotic and romantic intrigue carries with it the ring of truth. These were the circles in which the content of the love poetry and theatre of the Elizabethan period was fully understandable, since it formed the background to their lives.

The second modification of the pessimistic general description of affective relations concerns a far wider group, including many who were subjected to the loveless arranged marriage, which was normal among the propertied classes. It is clear from correspondence and wills that in a considerable number of cases, some degree of affection, or at least a good working partnership, developed after the marriage. In practice, as anthropologists have everywhere discovered, the arranged marriage works far less badly than those educated in a romantic culture would suppose, partly because the expectations of happiness from it are not set unrealistically high, and partly because it is a fact that sentiment can fairly easily adapt to social command. In any case, love is rarely blind, in the sense that it tends to be channelled along socially acceptable lines, towards persons of the other sex of similar background. This greatly increases the probability that an arranged marriage, provided it is not undertaken purely for mercenary considerations and that there is not too great a discrepancy in age, physical attractiveness or temperament, may well work out not too badly. This is especially the case where leisure is segregated, so that the pair are not thrown together too much, and where both have a multitude of outside interests and companions to divert them. In a 'low affect' society, a 'low affect' marriage is often perfectly satisfactory.

The final modification to be made to the bleak affective picture is that, owing to the high adult death rate and the late age of marriage, by no means all marriages among persons of property in the sixteenth century were arranged by the parents, since many of them were dead: marriages by choice certainly occurred, although freedom of choice was far more difficult to achieve for women other than widows. For example, in 1598 the rising young shipwright Phineas Pett married Anne Niccols. Both his parents were dead, but he had two powerful and influential brothers to contend with, upon whom he depended for patronage in his career. He records that 'I did not neglect my wooing, having taken such a liking of the maiden that I determined resolutely (by God's help) either to match with her or never to marry any; the which I with much difficulty ... at length achieved, all my own kindred being much against my matching with her.'[38] Other examples of young men successfully defying the wishes of their kin would not be hard to find, even if they were the exception to the rule.

Many young men who were freed by parental death to make their own choice were still motivated primarily by financial considerations. For example, in Thomas Wythorne's unsuccessful suit to a young widow, her fortune of £20 a year was the prime attraction for him. But the widow seems to have been more concerned with personal factors, which is apparently why the arrangements broke down. She expected to be visited every day, while Wythorne thought that every other day was quite enough to show serious intent.[39]

iii. Parents and Children

Between upper-class parents and children, relations in the sixteenth century were also usually fairly remote. One reason for this was the very high infant and child mortality rates, which made it folly to invest too much emotional capital in such ephemeral beings. As a result, in the sixteenth and early seventeenth century very many fathers seem to have looked on their infant children with much the same degree of affection which men today bestow on domestic pets, like cats and dogs. Montaigne commented: 'I have lost two or three children in infancy, not without regret, but without great sorrow.' The phrase 'two or three' indicates a degree of indifference and casual unconcern which would be inconceivable today. The most one normally could expect from a father at that time was the laconic entry in the account book of Daniel Fleming of Rydal in 1665: 'Paid for my loving and lovely son John's coffin: 2s. 6d.' John was two years and nine months old when he died.[40] In the seventeenth century there is no doubt whatever that 'restraint of emotional outpouring characterized infant departures as well as entries into the uncertain temporal scene', an observed psychological fact which stands in striking contrast with the evidence for the very late eighteenth and the nineteenth centuries.[41] There is no evidence, for example, of the purchase of mourning – not even an armband – on the death of very small children in the sixteenth, seventeenth and early eighteenth centuries, nor of parental attendance at the funeral. If the former had been common practice, it would certainly have appeared in the many surviving household account books.

The longer a child lived, the more likely it was that an affective bond would develop between it and its parents. Thus when in 1636 the wealthy antiquary Simonds D'Ewes and his wife lost their only son at the age of twenty-one months, after having already lost three sons who only lived a matter of days or weeks, he commented on the difference in the quality of their response. Part of the reaction was admittedly generated by D'Ewes' passionate desire to have a male heir to carry on the name and line, his fear that this child was his last chance, and his very articulate expression of his feelings, but part of it went deeper: 'We both found the sorrow for the loss of this child, on whom we had bestowed so much care and affection, and whose delicate favour and bright grey eye was so deeply imprinted on our hearts, far to surpass our grief for the decease of his three elder brothers, who dying almost as soon as they were born, were not so endeared to us as this was.'[42] Quite apart from the powerful disincentive to psychological involvement caused by the high infant mortality rate, most upper-class parents, and many middle- and lower-class ones, saw relatively little of their children because of the common practice of 'fostering out'. In the upper classes, babies were put out to wet-nurse at birth, usually away from home, for between twelve and eighteen months. Before the age of two infants were regarded with some distaste as smelly and unformed little animals lacking the capacity to reason. 'I could never well endure to have them brought up or nursed near about me,' remarked Montaigne, and even Locke regarded small children as animals controllable only by fear of pain.[43] Sometimes the relation to the wet-nurse was the closest affinity in the child's life, especially when she was taken into the household and continued to live there after weaning. Shakespeare's Juliet was deeply attached to her nurse, but had only stiff and formal relations with her mother, who could not even remember her exact age. In his *Civile Conversation* of 1581, Stephen Guazzo tells a story of a child saying bitterly to its mother: 'You bore me but nine months in your belly, but my nurse kept me with her teats the space of two years. ... So soon as I was born, you deprived me of your company, and banished me your presence.'[44] In 1790 the Russian Alexander Radishchev gave a very similar description of 'the young master's wet-nurse', now a serf's widow who was about to be sold. 'To this day she feels a certain tenderness for him. Her blood flows in his veins. She is his second mother, and he owes his life more to her than to his natural mother. The latter conceived him in lust and did not take care of him in childhood. The nurse really brought him up.' The same was true of the French dauphin, the future Louis XIII, who was born on 26 September 1601, and whose mother did not take him in her arms and fondle him until seven months later, on 19 March 1602.[45]

One of the reasons for this system of sending new-born infants out to mercenary wet-nurses for the first year or more was that it made the appalling level of infant mortality much easier to bear. Admittedly the death rate of infants fed by hired wet-nurses seems to have been about twice that of infants fed by their mothers, but at least the parents did not see them or know about them.[46] The child thus only entered the home and his parents only began to get acquainted with him after he had survived the first extremely dangerous months of life elsewhere.

Not only were the infants of the landed, upper bourgeois and professional classes in the sixteenth and seventeenth centuries sent out to hired wet-nurses for the first twelve to eighteen months, but thereafter they were brought up mainly by nurses, governesses and tutors. Moreover they seem normally to have left home very young, sometime between the ages of seven and thirteen, with about ten as the commonest age, in order to go to boarding-school. Lower down the social scale they also left home at between seven and fourteen to begin work as domestic servants, labourers or apprentices, but in all cases living in their masters' houses rather than at home or in lodgings. What one sees at these middle- and lower middle-class levels is a vast system of exchange by which parents sent their own children away from home – usually not very far – and the richer families took in the children of others as servants and labourers. As a result of this custom, some very fragmentary census data suggest that from just before puberty until they married some ten years later, about two out of every three boys and three out of every four girls were living away from home. Nearly one-half of all husbandman households and nearly one-quarter of craftsman and tradesman households contained living-in servants or apprentices.[47] The reason for this mass exchange of adolescent children, which seems to have been peculiar to England, is far from clear. All we do know is that this was a medieval practice, for an Italian visitor in about 1500 reported as follows: 'The want of affection in the English is strongly manifested towards their children: for after having kept them at home till they arrive at the age of 7 or 9 years at the utmost, they put them out, both males and females, to hard service in the houses of other people. ... Few are born who are exempted from this fate, for everyone, however rich he may be, sends away his children into the houses of others, whilst he, in return, receives those of strangers into his own. . . . I, for my part, believe that they do it because they like to enjoy all their comforts themselves, and that they are better served by strangers than they would be by their own children.'[48] This is a highly implausible explanation of a social practice which was clearly of great antiquity. Its true causes are lost in the obscurity of time, and all the historian can do is to establish that the export of children was a peculiarly English cultural phenomenon and to speculate about the consequences of it.

One result was that members of the importing families lived, ate, and, at the lower social levels where rooms were few, even slept in the company of members of another family. Domestic relations must consequently have been more formal and more restrained than they need to be today because of the constant presence in the house of strangers, who were likely to gossip with the neighbours about what they observed or overheard inside the home. But it was only when the bourgeois demand for privacy developed in the early eighteenth century, that this became a common source of complaint.[49]

There are also far more important consequences to the 'exporting' families of this widespread process of adolescent 'fostering out'. Firstly, it greatly reduced the oedipal and other tensions which inevitably arise between parents and adolescent children struggling to assert their independence and master the problems of their budding sexuality. As a result, the choice of a marriage partner was the one major issue of conflict between parents and children at this time. Secondly, it reduced the danger of incest in those classes of society where housing was poor and there were insufficient bedrooms. Thirdly, it meant that neither upper-class nor labouring and artisan class parents saw very much of their children, since the latter spent so short a time within the confines of the home, possibly no more than between the ages of two, when they returned from the wet-nurse, and somewhere betwen seven and fourteen. When a child married, even if his or her spouse had been chosen by the parents, the pair normally set up house independently, often at some distance.[50] A fourth result of this practice of fostering out was the strong contemporary consciousness of adolescence (then called 'youth'), as a distinct stage of life between sexual maturity at about fifteen and marriage at about twenty-six. So far as the middle and labouring classes were concerned, of the four obvious transit points between childhood and adulthood, two – entering the work-force and leaving home – took place together at a very early age, at about ten to twelve; the other two – marriage and the setting up of an independent household – also took place together, but at a very late age, at about twenty-five to twenty-eight. In between came a long period of sexual moratorium and social dependency, at work and away from home but without the responsibilities of marriage and housekeeping. The principle vices of that stage of ego development were defined as lust and pride, which clergy and masters struggled to control. Some groups of youth, especially boys at boarding-school and apprentices in big cities, particularly London, developed fierce peer-group loyalties and the well-defined characteristics of a sub-culture. The most striking evidences of this were the organized political activities of the London apprentices during the English Revolution, and the many mass riots and rebellions in eighteenth-century public schools.[51]

The autobiography of Sir Simonds D'Ewes provides a revealing account of childhood in an upper-class kin-oriented patriarchal family in the early seventeenth century.[52] His father was Paul D'Ewes, a successful Middle Temple lawyer and later holder of the lucrative office of one of the Six Clerks in Chancery, and his mother was Cecilia, daughter of Richard Simonds, a wealthy Dorset landowner. Cecilia was an heiress worth £10,000, and her marriage with Paul D'Ewes in 1594, when she was only fourteen, had been arranged between her father and her future husband, with financial considerations uppermost on both sides. Owing to the extinction of collateral lines, a male heir to the marriage would be the only surviving representative of both the D'Ewes and the Simonds families and was, therefore, desperately wanted by both the parents and the maternal grandparents. Teenage women in the seventeenth century seem to have been relatively infertile, and it is not surprising that it was not until six years later that a child was conceived of the marriage, during a visit in March 1602 to Cecilia's parents' house of Coxden in Chardstock, Dorset. Paul then returned to London to his law practice and did not return until midsummer, while Cecilia remained with her parents. When he arrived, she told him that 'her father intended to take that child ... because it had been begotten and was now likely to be born in his house, and so he claimed it for his own.' The child, named Simonds after the surname of his maternal grandfather, was born in December after a difficult and bungled delivery which so damaged his right eye that he could never use it for reading. His first months were spent at Coxden, where his mother nursed him herself and his father visited them during the legal vacations. His father was worried about the management of his own house and estate in Suffolk and was determined to move his wife back there to look after the property. So when Simonds was five months old they set out over rough country roads in a poorly sprung coach; the jolting so affected the child that he nearly died after the first twenty miles to Dorchester. Since the child could clearly not be moved again, a wet-nurse was found in the town, and after seeing him settled in for a couple of weeks, his mother left him and proceeded on to Suffolk. After some months with the wet-nurse, Simonds moved back to his grandfather's house at Coxden, where he remained for the next seven years, during which time his parents only visited him twice. His grandfather spent a lot of time in London on law business, his grandmother was old and sick, and he was mostly thrown into the company of ill-disciplined servants who taught him drinking, swearing and 'corrupt discourses'. Part of the time he spent as a boarder with the local clergyman, who ran a small school and taught him to read and write English and study the Bible.

When he was eight years old his grandfather, much to his dismay, returned him to his parents, whom he hardly knew. Although his mother screeched for joy when she saw her child again, she in fact saw very little of him since he was immediately sent off to boarding-school at Lavenham. Within eight months, both his maternal grandparents had died, leaving Simonds as the heir to a great estate, with his father as trustee on his behalf. The boy was suddenly removed from school to attend the funeral of his grandfather at Coxden. Since this was the country he knew and loved and since he still hardly knew his parents, he persuaded them to let him stay there and go to school with another local clergyman, where he remained for three years learning Latin. His mother left his father in London, and spent six months at Coxden to be near him, during which time he saw enough of her to become deeply attached to her and to be converted to her own brand of intense Puritan faith. Three years later, he left the west country and returned to London, where he entered yet another school as a boarder for two years. But being dissatisfied with the master's erudition, he got his parents to move him to the grammar school at Bury, near the new family country seat of Stow Hall, where he spent his vacations. In 1618, at the age of sixteen, he left school and went up to St John's College, Cambridge. Soon after he arrived there, however, he was suddenly summoned home to attend the death-bed of his mother, who was the only one of his parents to whom he had any deep attachment, and whose premature death at thirty-eight he took very hard indeed.

It cannot be pretended that Simonds D'Ewes was typical of his age. For one thing, he was rare in being the sole male heir to both his father's and his maternal grandfather's estates, so that two families were competing for him. All the same, it is a story that could only have occurred in the early seventeenth century, and there are several interesting conclusions to be drawn from it. As a child, his principal attachments had been to his maternal grandparents rather than to his own parents, and he neither saw much of his father nor cared much for him. Almost all his childhood and adolescence was spent away from home, at the house of his wet-nurse, with his grandparents, at five different boarding-schools, and finally at university. It was a fragmented and peripatetic existence, lacking any stable geographical or affective base, and as such is probably not too unlike the childhood experiences of many upper-class children in the sixteenth and early seventeenth centuries. When he came to write his autobiography, he displayed both the all-pervasive influence of his Puritan beliefs and a great sensitivity to the nuances of domestic relations. He was a transitional figure, half-way between the kin-oriented anonymity of the past and the affective individualism of the future.

D'Ewes' peripatetic life was far from unusual. It was natural and reasonable that in times of economic stress children were transferred to whichever more affluent member of the kin was prepared to have them. For years in the late seventeenth century William Blundell of Crosby Hall looked after his grandson since his son was too poor to educate him.[53] Among the lower middle class, which was more prone to economic crisis than the gentry, these arrangements were commoner still. The ironmonger William Stout of Lancaster never married, because of an unfortunate love affair, and settled down as a bachelor, with a spinster sister as his housekeeper. But he was fond of children, so that for twenty years in the early eighteenth century 'we had always two of my brother Leonard's children with us: took them at two years old and kept them till they were six years old and capable to go to Bolton school.' One of the children was more or less adopted by William, who kept him from the age of two to fifteen and taught him Latin, writing and mathematics. Later on in the eighteenth century, when the father of Samuel Bamford lost his job as Governor of the Manchester Workhouse, the two sons were sent to live with an uncle, and the daughter to live with a friend. This was a necessary form of mutual self-help that was an invaluable support in times of economic stress. Sometimes children were simply handed over for good without much question to whoever seemed willing to look after them. John Sydenham was the son of a land-factor, born in 1721. His mother had died when he was young, and so he went to live with his grandfather. In 1734 the family was visited by an unknown wealthy relative, who had an only son who was sickly and mentally defective. The relative said to John's father: 'Roger, will you give me your elder son? You have three sons. I fear mine will be dead before I get home. Give him to me fresh and part with him willingly, and I will take good care of him.' John's father readily agreed, and off he went from home at the age of thirteen.[54] In these lower middle-class circles, even in the early eighteenth century, economic circumstances made it inevitable that children were shifted about from one house to another in the hopes of providing them with a better preparation for life. The willingness of parents to discard their children in this way, however, provides an illuminating insight into parent-child relations, which lacked the exclusive, monopolistic quality of more recent times.

Not only did children not live with their parents for very long in the sixteenth and seventeenth centuries, but such relations as existed were, as will be seen, normally extremely formal, while obedience was often enforced with brutality. Under these circumstances, the one close tie – though not necessarily one of love – which could and often did develop between parents and children among the elite was between the father and his surviving eldest son, who was designed to inherit the title, position and property.[55] He was highly prized since he was the guarantee of that family continuity for which so much else was ruthlessly sacrificed. The key to all understanding of interpersonal relationships among the propertied classes at this time is a recognition of the fact that what mattered was not the individual but the family. But in many cases, fathers remained remote even from their only son and heir upon whom all hope of lineal descent rested. The relations of Simonds D'Ewes and his father are a case in point.

Younger sons, and particularly daughters, were often unwanted and might be regarded as no more than a tiresome drain on the economic resources of the family. The attitude towards his daughters of William Blundell, an impoverished Lancashire Catholic gentleman of the mid-seventeenth century, provides an illuminating example of parental attitudes. In 1653 he reported with sardonic malice the birth and almost immediate death of his sixth daughter and ninth child: 'My wife has much disappointed my hopes in bringing forth a daughter, which, finding herself not so welcome in this world as a son, hath made already a discreet choice of a better.' When his surviving daughters grew up in the 1670s, he shipped two of them off to nunneries abroad, without informing their mother of his plans, at the cut-rate cost of £10 and £15 each a year for life. When they complained from their foreign nunneries that they almost never got letters from home, he retorted coldly that 'When business requires no more, your mother or I do commonly write to our children once (and seldom oftener) in little less tha a year. We hope they will be pleased with this, for we have too much business and too much charge in the world to comply with all our dear relations according to the measure of our love.'[56] Lower down the social scale, where servants were fewer and the family was thrown together on a more intimate footing, the loss of infants was also accepted with resignation. Ralph Josselin was not particularly upset either by the death of his ten-day-old child, or that of the thirteen-month-old one. Even the deaths in rapid succession of a twenty-year-old daughter and the twenty-nine-year-old son and heir did not produce the passionate outburst of despair which might have been expected. Ralph certainly grieved, but he consoled himself with the thought that the dead 'were being received into heaven'. Belief in the immortality of the soul, and confidence that the children had gone to Heaven and nowhere else, were a great help in assuaging the sorrow generated by the commonplace of death in the seventeenth century. In any case the ties with children were loosened very early, since they were mostly sent out of the home in their early teens. All seven of Josselin's surviving children left home between the ages of ten-and-a-half and fifteen-and-a-half to go to boarding-school, to serve an apprenticeship, or to take a job as a servant.[57]

Even when they survived to adulthood, fathers in the seventeenth century tended to take much the same cold-blooded attitude towards their children. In 1676 the son of Adam Martindale, a humble nonconformist minister and schoolmaster, married a poor girl instead of a rich one, against his father's will. Three years later, at the age of thirty, he died. His father's only recorded reaction was a long complaint about the financial loss this death caused him. There was first the premature death of 'an only son in the best of time . . ., whose education had cost me so dear', so that all the investment was wasted. Secondly, the son was the youngest life in a three-life lease of some property, the value of which was consequently much reduced. Furthermore his son owed him money; and he also had to pay both for the funeral and for looking after the grandchild. Altogether, he reckoned bitterly that his son had cost him about £80 to £90 by being so perverse as to die.[58]

At the bottom of the social scale, among the really poor, the absence of birth control, and the constant struggle to find enough food to feed the hungry mouths, must have made children less than welcome. In circles where the labour of the wife in the field or in the shop was essential to the economic security of the family, any interruption to bear and then to feed another child could be a serious inconvenience. Research that has been done upon the peasantry in France suggests that the prevalent responses were indifference to the deaths of infants or young children, resignation before the deaths of adolescents and young adults, and sheer egocentric panic in the face of epidemics. Their attitudes thus hardly differed from those of their social superiors whose wealth made them only marginally more immune than their inferiors to the ever-present possibility of imminent death.[59]

For upper-class mothers the situation was rather more complicated. Under conditions where wet-nurses, nurses and servants had the care of the infant child, the maternal bond was given little opportunity to develop, and mothers were, therefore, often almost as remote and detached from their infant children as fathers. On the other hand, even a mother who had barely set eyes on her infant between its birth and its early death was inevitably affected by the wastage of so much effort and pain in pregnancy and labour. At the very minimum, there would be a strong sense of disappointment and even despair, even if there were no personal attachment to the particular infant for its own sake.

In gentry families where Christian piety was very highly developed (whether of Anglican, Puritan or Catholic variety is immaterial), where it was thought proper whenever possible for the mother to nurse her own children, and at a time when pregnancies and childbirth were painful and difficult for the mother, close ties might develop between mother and child at an early stage. For example, in the 1650s and 1660s, Mrs Alice Thornton was obviously strongly attached at any rate to those of her nine children who lived for more than a matter of hours or days.[60] Mrs Thornton's piety made her an exception among gentry parents, but her maternal responses to her children must have been familiar among the middle and lower classes, where breast-feeding was normal and physical contact a day-to-day occurrence. In these cases, the natural maternal instincts were allowed to develop, and in the early seventeenth century the popular psychological practitioner the Reverend Richard Napier treated a number of women who were mentally disturbed by the death of infant children.[61] On the other hand the unmistakable evidence for the abandonment of children in hard times from the fifteenth century onwards – a practice which spread in the eighteenth century as demographic pressures increased – and the way in which young children were driven by their parents into factories and mines for very long hours at very early ages in the late eighteenth century, both suggest that a most important feature of parent/children relationships among the lower classes was the necessity of the former to obtain some economic benefits from the latter. At this very marginal economic level, little else could be expected.

iv. Siblings

As for the relations between siblings among the upper classes, primogeniture inevitably created a gulf between the eldest son and heir and his younger brothers who, by accident of birth order, were destined to be thrown out into the world and would probably become downwardly mobile. In the mid-seventeenth century Sir Christopher Guise commented on 'the malice of cadets, who are often the most unnatural enemies of their own house, upon no stronger provocation than what nature and their own melancholy thoughts present them.'[62] Between brother and sister, however, this embittered sense of envy did not exist, and there is evidence of the frequent development of very close ties indeed. Since upper-class boys were often kept at home with a private tutor until they went off to university at sixteen or seventeen, there was time for these relationships to mature and deepen. When John Wandesford got smallpox in 1642, his sixteen-year-old sister Alice was so attached to him that she broke the strict quarantine enforced by her parents by exchanging messages tied round the neck of the family dog, as a result of which she also contracted the disease. And when eleven years later her eldest brother George was accidentally drowned in crossing the river Swale, she nearly died of grief. When Ralph Josselin's two grown-up children Thomas (aged twenty-nine) and Anne (aged twenty) died within a few days of each other in 1673, their father observed that they were 'loving in their lives, and in their death they were not divided, lying in the same grave.' When Sylvester Douglas was first sent off to school at the age of eight, he missed his sister so much that he ran away from school and made the long and lonely walk home in order to be with her.[63]

There is reason to suspect that in the sixteenth and seventeenth centuries the brother-sister relationship was often the closest in the family. In the eighteenth century, when family bonding generally became much closer, there are still signs that brother-sister ties were particularly intimate. When Lady Mary Wortley Montagu lost her brother in 1713, 'In him she appeared to think she had lost her best, if not her only, natural friend.' When Robert Robinson died in 1756, both his sisters were deeply moved. Elizabeth said, 'I know not how to reconcile myself to the loss of one of the companions of my youth.' As for Sarah, it was reported that 'she bears her loss patiently, but it touches her heart very sorely.' When in 1800 Dorothea Herbert's brother Otway died from a fall from a horse at the age of twenty-nine, she gave way to despair: 'Thus bereft of my darling brother, all the pangs of Hell seemed to lay hold on me.'[64] It may be an obvious and perhaps permanent feature of family life, but there can be little doubt that there was something very special about brother–sister relationships among the landed classes at this period. They were far closer than brother–brother ties, which were always threatened by the gulf of primogeniture, and closer than child–parent relations even at the most affectionate stage in the late eighteenth century, since parents and children were inevitably physically separated from each other for a good part of every day, even in the most devoted of families, as well as being psychologically separated by the generation gap.

3 CONCLUSION

To sum up this welter of fragmentary evidence is not an easy task. It appears that before the age of about two, infants were not regarded by upper-class parents as fully human. They were smelly, noisy little creatures, driven by instinct, not reason, incapable of communicating except at the animal level, and with only the most precarious hold on life. It seemed eminently reasonable not to care about them very much – and hardly anyone did, except the Church, which was increasingly anxious to see them properly baptized before they died. After two, however, there was a distinct change. In the first place, their life expectations significantly improved, while among the propertied classes they re-entered the family home for the first time after being out at wet-nurse. They were weaned and ate food like grown-ups; they could talk and reason and were liable to discipline and punishment in order to fit them for adult society. At this period children are at their most amusing and endearing, while their occasional temper tantrums were handled by nurses and governesses. From two to seven was, therefore, a period in which affection often developed between elite parents and children. Children may have been regarded more as playthings, toys to divert the mind, but some genuine human relationship was established, which sometimes became very close. For example, in the first decade of the century, the dauphin Louis and his father Henri IV became extremely attached to one another at just this period of the child's life. At some time between seven and fourteen, however, most children would leave home, usually for good, so that the period of close parent–child bonding was a relatively short one at all levels of society.

As has been pointed out, it would be a mistake to think that there was never any affective bonding between parent and child and husband and wife at this period. Confined by the rules of the social system, which dictated marriage in the interests of the lineage and a strong preference for male over female children, bonding and even choice undoubtedly existed, especially at the lowest levels of society. In the one instance in which we can examine the thoughts and behaviour of the medieval peasant in some detail – unfortunately in a somewhat untypical, isolated and heretical mountain village in the Pyrenees in the early thirteenth century – we find some latitude in the choice of partner, even some love, and more signs that mothers, who all breast-fed their babies, were not entirely indifferent to their fate. On the other hand, married life was brutal and often hostile, with little communication, much wife-beating and frequent mutual threats of denunciation to the Inquisition for heresy. Moreover, it is a sinister fact that twice as many male children appear in the stories told to the Inquisitor as female ones, although there is no obvious reason for this being so. There were also a lot of bachelor shepherds in the village. It looks as if many female infants may have been quietly allowed to die, while male children were cherished since they would eventually become useful contributors to the family labour force, and future providers of support for parents in old age. On the whole, this unique record tends to support the theory that affect was both low and diffused in traditional Western society, though it also makes clear that free choice, and even love, were sometimes possible within the rigid but stress-resistant structure around which the society functioned.[65]

About all that can be said with confidence on the matter of emotional relations within the sixteenth- and early seventeenth-century family at all social levels is that there was a general psychological atmosphere of distance, manipulation and deference; that high mortality rates made deep relationships very imprudent; that marriages were arranged by parents and kin for economic and social reasons with minimal consultation of the children; that evidence of close bonding between parents and children is hard, but not impossible, to document; and that evidence of close affection between husband and wife is both ambiguous and rare. Moreover, belief in the immortality of the soul and the prospect of salvation was a powerful factor in damping down such grief as might be aroused by the loss of a child, spouse or parent.

By the eighteenth century intimacy and involvement (which may result in love or hate or a combination of both) were regarded as key ingredients of family life. In the sixteenth century however, family relationships were characterized by interchangeability, a lack of individual commitment so that substitution of another wife or another child was easy, and by conformity to external rules of conduct. The family group was held together by shared economic status and political interests, and by the norms and values of authority and deference. This was a family type which was entirely appropriate to the social and economic world of the sixteenth century, in which property was the only security against total destitution, in which connections and patronage were the keys to success, in which power flowed to the oldest males under the system of primogeniture, and in which the only career opening for women was in marriage. In these circumstances the family structure was characterized by its hierarchical distribution of power, the arranged marriage and the fostering out of children. It was a structure held together not by affective bonds but by mutual economic interests.

It was, moreover, an institution that lacked firm boundaries. It was part of a wider network of relationships, linked to the kin by ties of dependence, loyalty, reciprocity and mutual aid, and to the patron by the network of allegiance to the principles of 'good lordship'. The significance of these factors was at its maximum at the highest levels of society, among the aristocracy and greater gentry, and diminished the lower one descends in the social scale. But they applied to all owners of property down to the lower middle class of small freeholders, artisans and shopkeepers, and were irrelevant only to the very poor lacking either property or influence.

The sixteenth-century family of origin did not have very much to do with the socialization of children, since the latter were so soon sent away from home. Thanks to the principle of interchangeability, the substitute parents, the masters of the servants or apprentices, in many cases played a more important role in socializing the child than his natural parents, while for a tiny minority the school and university served the same function. But all these agencies inculcated the same set of values, stressing in particular the need for deference and obedience to superiors, and the need for patronage to succeed in the world. It was a lesson reinforced by the Church, with its Sunday homilies on obedience, and by the state with its panoply of public shame and torture instruments, running from the stocks to the gallows, to be employed on those who disobeyed its edicts and lacked influential friends.

Finally, it should be stressed that no modern value judgements are involved in this description of a now vanished familial world. To contemporaries it certainly appeared perfectly normal, and was, as has been repeatedly argued, entirely congruent with the values of the society as a whole. The vantage point from which this family system has been examined is not that of our own day, but that of the eighteenth century. The central theme of this book is the extraordinary changes in attitudes towards the individual and towards emotion that occurred between 1660 and 1800, and if the sixteenth century seems somewhat bleak and impersonal, it is by contrast with the warmth and autonomy of the eighteenth century. This change is partly, of course, a change of verbal style and of cultural expression, but there are sufficient concrete changes, which cannot be disposed of by these arguments, to prove that it is also an historical reality.

PART THREE

The Restricted Patriarchal Nuclear Family 1550–1700

CHAPTER 4

The Decline of Kinship, Clientage and Community

'The attachment of relatives to one another was warmer, and the duties founded on consanguinity were extended to a wider circle. Even distant relationship was considered as constituting an obligation to reciprocity of love and good offices. To keep alive the bond of union, relatives in all circumstances addressed one another by their kindred names, as "uncle", "aunt", "niece", "cousin".'

(T.Somerville, reflecting on eighteenth-century Scotland – which changed well over a century later than England – in *My Own Life and Times 1741–1814*, Edinburgh, 1861, p. 368.)

I INTRODUCTION

Between about 1500 and 1700 the English family structure at the upper levels began a slow process of evolution in two related ways. Firstly, the importance of the nuclear core increased, not as a unit of habitation but as a state of mind: as its boundaries became more clearly defined, so the influence of the kin and clientage correspondingly declined. Secondly the importance of affective bonds to tie the conjugal unit together began to increase. These two changes were the product of three concurrent and interrelated changes: the decline of kinship and clientage as the main organizing principles of landed society; the rise of the powers and claims of the state, encouraged by the Protestant reformers, both taking over some of the economic and social functions previously carried out by the family, the kin and the clientage, and subordinating kin and client loyalties to the higher obligations of patriotism and obedience to the sovereign; and the missionary success of Protestantism, especially its Puritan wing, in bringing Christian morality to a majority of homes, especially among the gentry and urban bourgeoisie, both in sanctifying holy matrimony and in making the family serve as a partial substitute for the parish.

At the same time, these and other forces were at work to bring about a third important development: the reinforcement for a time among these same social groups of the pre-existing patriarchal aspects of internal power relationships within the family. This occurred partly because the nuclear family became more free from interference by the kin, especially the wife's kin, and partly because of wider religious, legal and political changes which enhanced the powers of the head of the household.

The period is, therefore, one in which two overlapping family types can be seen to co-exist among the upper and middle ranks, each slowly but imperfectly replacing the other. The first was the late medieval Open Lineage Family, exposed to influence from kinship and clientage in which the conjugal unit of husband, wife and unmarried children was of relatively lesser importance than the wider kinship affiliation of the cousinhood, and even than the wider attachments of 'good lordship'. The second was the Restricted Patriarchal Nuclear Family of the late sixteenth century, in which loyalty became increasingly focused inward on the conjugal core and outward on the state rather than on kin relatives by blood or marriage, or on clients and patrons.

2 THE LANDED CLASSES: THE DECLINE OF KINSHIP AND CLIENTAGE

Between 1500 and 1750 it is clear that there was a decline in the role played in landed society by both kinship and clientage. One indication is that claims to cousinhood ties in the subscription of letters occur far less frequently in the late seventeenth and eighteenth centuries than in the sixteenth or early seventeenth, presumably because it was no longer so useful in creating a favourable predisposition in the recipient. It would, for example, be hard to find a parallel in the eighteenth century for the claim to cousinhood advanced in the early seventeenth century by Thomas Wentworth in a letter to Sir Henry Slingsby. The connection was indeed there, but there were no fewer than seven links in the genealogical chain which joined the two, three of them by marriage through the female line.[1] Kinship connections certainly continued to be important for many purposes, especially economic aid and job placement, but they were increasingly limited to the closer relatives. Uncles and aunts, fathers-in-law, brothers-in-law and sons-in-law were still called upon to serve surrogate or interchangeable roles with members of the nuclear family.

Another significant pointer to a change in both kinship and clientage relations is the decay of 'hospitality' among the aristocracy and greater gentry, which was a common burden of complaint in the seventeenth century. When in the late sixteenth century Lord Burghley advised his son, 'Let thy kindred and allies be welcome to thy table, grace them with thy countenance and ever further them in all honest actions', he was giving advice that was already becoming out of date.[2] The practice of open-handed hospitality, shown not only to members of the extended family but to any friend or even to casual passers-by of gentlemanly status, was one which dated back at least to the days of Beowulf. It was certainly an ideal to which everyone paid respect at least up to 1640, and was something about which one boasted on one's tombstone. There was, of course, more to this ideal than personal honour defined by generosity demonstrated by open-handed support of kin relatives, clients and allies, for it extended to a whole way of life, including the retaining of hordes of largely idle servants and the keeping of an open table for all comers. Its symbolic function was to make manifest the exercise of patronage over clients and to ensure the maintenance of status. The decline of these habits of the late sixteenth and early seventeenth centuries was evidence of a lessening preoccupation with the preservation of connections with the inner circle of kin as well as with the outer layer of retainers and supporters. It involved a major reorientation of consumption patterns, caused by the growth of a more inward-looking, more private and more urbanized life-style for the aristocratic family. It was characterized by the withdrawal of the family from the great hall to the private dining-room and by the increasing habit of residing for long periods in London to enjoy the 'season'.[3]

The decay of the gigantic and fantastically expensive funeral ritual attended by literally hundreds of kindred, cousins, retainers, domestic servants and poor was another symbol of the same shedding by the social elite of outer layers of familial and extra-familial client ties, and a slow withdrawal to a more private domestic existence.[4] The decline of these late feudal practices represented primarily a decline of traditional 'good lordship', of the function of a great household as a centre of patronage for kin, clients, retainers, servants and tenants. This decline was caused by the rise of other, more modern forms of political connections based on current issues such as religion, foreign and domestic policy, party and personality. But this decline of good lordship carried with it a weakening of ties to the kin, and a narrowing of the focus of concern down to the interests and pleasures of the nuclear core.

More concrete evidence than these indicators of a decline of expenditure on, and attention paid to, the ramifications of the kin and clientage network is provided by the very clear decline in the concept of kin responsibility for individual crimes and actions. In the early and mid-sixteenth century, at any rate in the Highland zone of the north and west, the royal writ and the royal law courts were less important as law enforcement agencies than the blood feud and the vendetta. Under the vendetta there is collective kin responsibility for individual action, as opposed to the legal theory of individual responsibility: the law will punish the individual criminal but no one else; the vendetta is perfectly satisfied by the punishment of the criminal's brother, father, uncle or nephew, which is a classic example of the principle of interchangeability. By the end of the sixteenth century, this custom had virtually died out in England.[5] Henry VIII was the last English king to punish whole families, such as the De La Poles, for the treason of one member.

The traditional penal solidarity of the clan, by which the kin or immediate family of a fallen politician suffered punishment with him, first went out among the patriciate of Florence in the fifteenth century.[6] A century later it happened in England, but in France the custom lived on into the eighteenth century. In the late seventeenth century, Louis XIV exiled the family of Fouquet, and imprisoned that of Cartouche. Moreover, the penal solidarity of the family in the payment of taxes remained a part of French law until it was abolished in 1775, being finally denounced as 'this odious law which, from the fault of a single man, incriminates a whole family.'[7] In Russia the practice only died out in the mid-twentieth century. Thus from Florence in the fifteenth century to Russia in the twentieth one can observe the slow diffusion in the West of the principle of individual legal responsibility, affecting first the kin and later members of the nuclear family itself.

In national politics, there took place a slow decline first in kinship then in clientage as the central organizing principle of political groupings. In the fifteenth century, the Wars of the Roses were almost entirely a struggle of aristocratic kinship factions and alliances for control of royal authority and patronage. In the sixteenth century, kin groupings remained powerful in politics, but slowly gave way to religious conviction and personal ambition as the state strengthened its grip on society and began to attract loyalties to itself. Even so, much of the political in-fighting of the century revolved around certain kinship rivalries, in particular that between the Howards and the Dudleys, until the last, illegitimate, Dudley finally went into exile at the end of the century, and the Howards hitched themselves on to James I's coat-tails to share in the spoils of the court. It has been shown conclusively that clientage was a primary cement of political faction in the Elizabethan period,[8] but its influence was much weakened in the early seventeenth century because of the emergence of fundamental issues of religious and constitutional principle and the distribution of the burden of taxation.

The degree to which kinship, clientage and even family loyalties had become subordinated to the principle of autonomy of choice of political and religious ideology became clear during the English Revolution of the 1640s, when one aristocratic family in seven was divided father against child or brother against brother.[9] If the divisions within the nuclear core were so frequent, it is obvious that the cousinhood was even more hopelessly fragmented, and that clientage was equally weak. Other loyalties now took precedence among the elite of the English political nation, although how far this change penetrated down the society is at present unknown. No one knows, for example, whether yeoman or merchant families divided father against son, brother against brother in the Civil War.

Another striking example of how kinship was eroding in the seventeenth century is provided by the contrast in marriage patterns between the traditional Highlands of Scotland and the more modernized Lowlands. In the former, the clans Macdonald and Mackenzie remained all-powerful, and marriages of the clan head, and of the heads of cadet branches, were almost entirely confined within the clan, as an important means of cementing its solidarity. In the latter, however, less than eight per cent of marriages took place within the clan. This proves that there had developed a completely different society in Lowland Scotland with completely different values, and consequently using a completely different matrimonial strategy.[10]

At the end of the seventeenth century, the English political nation was bitterly divided into two parties, going under the labels of Whigs and Tories. In binding together these political groupings, there were four main elements: clientage, meaning dependence on a political patron; kinship; professional ties; and personal friendship. Kinship was certainly a help, and was used by politicians to increase their influence. Thus Harley carefully cultivated the remotest of cousins, and found it advantageous to find ways of signing his letters 'your most faithful and humble servant and kinsman.' But for every family connection which carried clear political associations, there were three or four about which nothing is known. There may have been no connection, or the kin may in fact have been split down the middle. Thus of the ten MPs and candidates of the Bertie kin in the reign of Queen Anne, seven were Tories, two Whigs, and one a Whiggish waverer.[11] Kinship often remained useful in the formation of the Whig factions in the eighteenth century, such as the Walpole group, the Pelham Whigs or

Rockingham Whigs, but it was no more than one element among several, and not necessarily the most important or the most durable one. The impermanence and unreliability of these connections in English eighteenth-century politics, as compared with those of the early sixteenth century, suggest that in the Early Modern period kinship was replaced by 'bastard kinship', just as in the late middle ages the ties of feudalism had been replaced by those of 'bastard feudalism'.

In local affairs, kin ties undoubtedly continued to be important well into the eighteenth century. As the English elite was fissured down religious lines in the late sixteenth and seventeenth centuries, fairly strict religious endogamy developed among Catholics and Puritans, but in this case the lines of kinship followed and reinforced the ties of religion, not vice-versa.[12] After the middle of the seventeenth century, the amount of social mobility shrank significantly, so that relatively little new blood was coming in to the squirarchy to keep the system fluid. Meanwhile in each county for century after century the squires had been intermarrying with one another, until the web of cross-cousinhood became so dense and so universal that it lost its meaning. If everybody is everyone else's cousin, the connection does not matter any more, which is why the recent discovery that Charles I was a remote cousin of John Hampden does nothing to advance our understanding of the English Revolution of the seventeenth century.[13]

Another test of the declining role of kinship is the moral legitimacy accorded to nepotism as a factor in recruitment to state and private offices. It is, of course, a truism that ties of blood and clientage remained very important and respectable elements in appointments in Church and state well into the middle of the nineteenth century. It would be very interesting to know how far it remained entirely respectable to use nepotism to favour a close relative within the nuclear family, such as a son or a brother, but not to favour a cousin from the remoter layers of the kin. There are suggestions that this was the case by the early seventeenth century in England.[14] There is also some evidence that nepotism generally was meeting increasing competition from two alternative sets of values. In the first place, many offices, especially in the law and the army, were obtained by purchase from the incumbent or his superior, and here money was usually more important than kinship. To the extent that saleable offices increased in the seventeenth century, as they did, this undermined the importance of kinship. Secondly, here and there, in the two sectors of administration in which efficiency was absolutely essential for the life of the nation, the Treasury to supply and handle public funds and the navy to protect England's shores and to blast open the sea lanes of the world for English goods and English merchants, there are signs, beginning with Samuel Pepys in the late seventeenth century, of the development of a more impersonal, meritocratic, professional spirit.[15]

It is also noticeable that although hereditary office-holding, as legally established in France by the *Paulette* in the early seventeenth century, was never officially accepted in England, the practice of sons succeeding fathers seems to have become increasingly common in the middle ranks of offices in the seventeenth century.[16] Hereditary office was seen, rightly, as a threat to the independent authority of the state, and was always opposed by the crown. It is true that well into the nineteenth century public office in England continued to serve as a system of outdoor relief largely monopolized by the hereditary elite. Generation after generation of younger or illegitimate sons were found comfortable berths in the public service, either at home or in the colonies. But each time there had to be a struggle, and each time there was competition to the ties of blood or marriage from the alternative principles of money and merit. Moreover, the influence was primarily exercised by fathers for sons, or sometimes uncles for nephews, and only rarely for more distant members of the kin. It was thus a product of the bonding of the nuclear family rather than of the lineage.

To conclude, everything points to a very slow erosion of the significance of kinship ties among the landed classes, but there is also good reason to suppose that they persisted and continued to play a part in family strategy and local and national politics well into the nineteenth century. A slow trend should not be mistaken for radical change. Moreover, with the decline of ideological passion in national politics after 1720, there was a positive revival of the power of patronage networks and clientage, until ideological conflict rose again towards the end of the century.

3   THE MIDDLE RANKS: THE MODIFICATION OF KINSHIP

Lower down the social scale, changes in the ties of kinship are more difficult to determine. On the one hand, the same factors as were affecting the elite – especially religious loyalties – were also influencing the middle ranks of society. Just as with the elite, there is plenty of evidence that the closer kin relatives, particularly paternal and maternal uncles, continued to play a large part in family decisions, especially when the parents died and the children had to be found jobs or husbands. In 1637–40 a young Cambridge graduate, the Reverend Ralph Josselin, used one uncle's credit to borrow money to tide him over, stayed with another when he was unemployed, and found his first church living by the good offices of the first uncle, who in fact paid £10 of his £44-a-year income. Nearly a century later, the Reverend John Thomlinson was lodged, launched on a clerical career, and found a variety of possible financially attractive brides through the patronage and connections of his two uncles, despite the fact that his father was still alive. On the other hand, Josselin's links to more distant kin relatives, such as cousins, were very remote and casual. Of his thirty-odd first cousins, his elaborate diary over a period of forty-two years mentions only three of them more than five times, and only fourteen even once. 'Cousins, it seems, were not of great emotional or economic importance to Josselin.'[17]

Among the peasantry, the same pattern seems to have prevailed. In one Leicestershire village in the sixteenth and seventeenth centuries, peasant wills show that it was only those who had no nuclear family obligations, or who had already fulfilled them by other means, who left real or personal property to members of the kin. 'The wider kin circle was therefore relatively unimportant.' This evidence is supported by an examination of wills in a Worcestershire village between 1676 and 1775, which shows over half of the testators making bequests to the nuclear family, and only a quarter to kin relatives.[18] By this test, the economic role of the kin among small property-owners in the village was now very limited.

It is clear, however, that among certain groups circumstances dictated that kinship ties should remain strong, because of the need for surrogates, and that in others the ties waxed and waned according to the degree of economic stress or geographical mobility. Thus kin ties were important at Salem, Massachusetts, in the eighteenth century due to the very high mortality at sea of young husbands, and the consequent need of support for the bereaved. Similarly, among the artisans and small men of Lancashire in the late nineteenth century, when individuals were subjected to the intense stresses of migration from the countryside to the city and the search for employment in an alien environment, members of the kin outside the nuclear core were active as temporary hosts for the migrants and as agents for job placement.[19] It seems likely that this was a revival of an older custom in response to an unprecedented social upheaval, not the healthy survival of a traditional practice.

Certain groups, however, continued to lay considerable stress on kin ties for social, political or economic purposes. Intermarriage was very commonly used as social bonding among parish gentry families within the county in the early seventeenth century.[20] It was also used for economic bonding among the recently mobile mercantile elites in London and the major cities. In these latter circles, economic circumstances – the need for capital and for reliable business associates – stimulated the search for marriage and kinship connections, which were more carefully cherished than among other social groups. They were particularly common among successful wealthy bourgeoisie without ambitions to transform their children into gentlemen. These upwardly mobile groups might cut the ties of blood which bound them to their humbler relatives back home, but would cement business connections with their economic peers or superiors by a new set of kinship relations. Much joint investment with, and much borrowing from, kin relatives continued to take place throughout the eighteenth century, although the growth of country banks and joint stock companies provided increasingly important alternatives.[21]

A few examples will serve to illustrate this point. An extraordinarily tight web of family ties linked the twenty-eight men who in 1580 formed the Court of Aldermen, the ruling elite of the City of London. Of these twenty-eight, three were sons of aldermen, nine sons-in-law, two brothers, six brothers-in-law, and one had married an alderman's widow. Many of them were also linked to other aldermanic families by marriages of their children. There were some fifteen cluster families whose connections by blood or marriage in one way or another embraced two thirds of the sixty-four men who held office as Lord Mayor and served as aldermen throughout the whole Elizabethan period. What is most significant, however, is that these clusters did not form coherent groups in terms of trading interests, wealth or political connections, so that this evidence for family linkage in the higher echelons of the London business elite should not be pushed too far. Nor was it a closed world by any means, for the cluster families did not dominate the scene, and outsiders could fight their way in. But family ties, mostly fairly close ones, certainly helped to cement pre-existing bonds of friendship and mutual economic and political interests, and also helped to ease the access of outsiders into this elite world. Newcomers were easily co-opted and absorbed through marriage.[22]

In the early seventeenth century, the same picture holds true. Between one third and one half of all London merchants who were active in trade to the Levant had fathers, fathers-in-law or brothers already in the Levant Company when they first joined it. In the 1630s twenty-three men linked by birth or marriage to the Elizabethan members of the Company probably controlled half its trade. Another merchant group in this period were the new men in the American trades, who were also linked by numerous family ties. But this was a two-way process in which common economic interests stimulated marriage alliances, and marriage alliances stimulated economic partnership. 'Their interconnected ties of business, sometimes formed on the basis of previous kinship ties, had themselves been strengthened by the establishment of new family links.'[23]

This use of marriage ties to develop or to cement commercial alliances among urban patriciates was a practice which flourished in the sixteenth and seventeenth centuries and only began to weaken in the eighteenth. As late as 1788 the biographer of a Leeds parson reasserted the now decaying principle that men 'must respect the attachments of friendship and blood; and their attempts to draw close these natural or artificial ties must be deemed, not only innocent, but even laudable. The claims of merit can, therefore, have no place where they would interfere with duties of prior obligation.' Up to a point, these principles indeed still applied among the eighteenth-century merchants of Leeds and Hull, where the family firm predominated, and Robert Pease could explain 'we keep entirely together to help one another'. Even in Hull, however, there is clear evidence that by the late eighteenth century more and more partnerships, loans, etc., were being contracted outside the family.[24] Even among the urban patriciates, the bonds of kinship were on the decline.

In the socialization of the child, his training for life responsibilities, the seventeenth century saw a partial transfer of function among the middle and upper ranks from both the kin and nuclear family to impersonal educational institutions such as dame schools, private schools, grammar schools and colleges, which provided literacy and piety for the many, and classics and piety for the few. The removal during the day of the male child from the house between the ages of six and ten for education in basic literacy was a revolutionary innovation in the life of most families from the lower middle class upwards. For those with greater means and higher aspirations, attendance at a boarding grammar school, private school or academy meant that the functional role of both family and kin was still further reduced, since the child left the home altogether and entered an institution.[25]

4   THE CAUSES OF CHANGE

i. Political

It has already been noted that the strength of kinship and clientage ties is correlated with the existence of hard times, which for the upper classes takes the form of a breakdown of law and order or shattering economic changes. The see-saw relationship between the kin and the state during the middle ages has been well put by Professor Georges Duby: 'The family [he means the kin] is the first refuge in which the threatened individual takes shelter when the authority of the state weakens. But as soon as the political institutions afford him adequate guarantees, he shakes off the constraints of the family, and the ties of blood are loosened. The history of lineage is thus a succession of contractions and expansions whose rhythm follows the modifications of the political order.'[26] Since the power of the state to enforce law and order has virtually never slackened since the sixteenth century, it follows that the functional decline of the kin and clientage in the sixteenth and seventeenth centuries was an irreversible change in social organization. The consequent relative isolation of the nuclear family enhanced the prominence of the last two areas over which it retained some control: the nurturance and socialization of the infant and young child, and the psycho-sexual satisfaction of the husband and wife. This process can hardly be called the rise of the nuclear family, but rather its reorientation to serve two narrower, more specialized functions.

The modern state is a natural enemy to the values of the clan, of kinship, and of good lordship and clientage links among the upper classes, for at this social and political level they are a direct threat to the state's own claim to prior loyalty.[27] Aristocratic kinship and clientage lead to faction and rebellion, such as the Wars of the Roses or the Fronde, to the use of kin loyalty and client empires by entrenched local potentates to create independent centres of power, and to make the working of the jury system of justice impossible by the subordination of objective judgement to ties of blood or local loyalty. In the sixteenth century, the state in England increasingly assumed monopoly powers of justice and punishment, military protection, welfare, and the regulation of property. This takeover was accompanied by a massive propaganda campaign for loyalty, inculcating the view that the first duty of every citizen is obedience to the sovereign, that man's highest obligation is to his country, involving the subordination of all other considerations and loyalties, even life itself. Medieval society had been held together by vague claims of obedience to the most powerful kinship network of all, headed by the king. This royal network soon began to seek to exploit and to extend the powers of the central government for its own benefit. Later, however, it developed a new desire for impersonal and efficient service, and a new demand for prior obedience to the sovereign it had created. It also developed a new sense of responsibility for the welfare of those it ruled over. Early Modern society was thus transformed from an association of cousins in the kin into an association of subjects to the sovereign monarch, and of citizens of the commonwealth. Rebellion against the divinely ordained sovereign became not merely dangerous, but impious and immoral, as is shown by the fact that failed conspirators in Tudor England now invariably confessed the sinfulness of their actions just before their execution.[28]

This fundamental shift in human values and in the social arrangements that went with them in the period from 1560 to 1640 has been well described by one historian as a shift from a 'lineage society', characterized by bounded horizons and particularized modes of thought, to the more universalistic standard of values of a 'civil society'. In 1603 George Bowes, who lived in the north, where the transformation was most marked, told his children that their first duty was to 'fight the battles of God and the King', thus placing loyalty to the national religion and the head of the nation state above all other considerations of kin loyalty, patronal clientage or personal attachments. The causes of this vast change are clear enough: the Reformation, with its powerful drive for the christianization of society and its claim to overriding moral allegiance through the preaching of the Word; grammar school and university education in the rhetoric of Humanism with its stress on loyalty to the prince; Inns of Court education in respect for an abstraction, the common law, as superior to any private or local loyalties to individuals; the growth of more commercialized relationships between man and man; the rise of 'possessive market individualism' that was slowly beginning to erode old communal affiliations.[29] Finally there was the institutional expansion of the nation state: the growth of its bureaucratic size, organization and powers, as literacy and record-keeping expanded and were taken over by the laity; the extension of its claims to universal obedience to the sovereign; and the persistent and progressive intrusion by the central authorities into local government, local jurisdiction and local patronage networks. These were not autonomous processes, but were driven forward by the massive transformation of popular and elite ideas about where prior loyalty lay. Fuelled initially by a general desire for security, the expansion of the bureaucratic nation state soon took on an independent life of its own.

The consequent decline of kinship and clientage was a major cause of the rise of the nuclear family. Their movements were linked like a pair of scales. But as loyalty to kinship declined, it shifted not only inward towards the nuclear core, but also outward towards the state, whose policies and actions were to no small extent responsible for the decline of the kin. The chief instrument for forging loyalty to the new nation state of the sixteenth century was the flood of official propaganda placing greater emphasis on the need for authority and obedience. Two very important methods used to strengthen the power of the state were first the destruction of the political power of aristocratic kinship and clientage; and secondly, a deliberately fostered increase in the power of the husband and father within the conjugal unit, that is to say, a strengthening of patriarchy.

The strengthening of family responsibilities finds ideal expression in Thomas More's *Utopia*, where family firms, family trades, family political units, and family military units are the rule, and corporate bodies between the family and the state are virtually non-existent. Whereas Plato's ideal society had involved the destruction of the family, that of More involved the destruction of all other social units but the family.[30] Among the upper landed classes, the country gentry and nobility, this growing concentration on the nuclear family is reflected in the formulation of lengthy genealogies which pay only cursory attention to collateral branches, and are mainly concerned with tracing the male line backward in time. Similarly, the growing complexity of coats of arms recorded alliances in the male line of the heirs by primogeniture of the nuclear family, not kin connections, while the same emphasis is reflected in the increasing stress laid upon ever larger and more elaborate family tombs in the sixteenth century. It is noticeable that the family mausoleums of the period contain the remains of the male heirs of the nuclear family and their wives from generation to generation, but only rarely adult younger children or kin relatives. The rule of primogeniture is clearly reflected in the disposal of the bodies after death.

ii. Religious

This shift of emphasis towards the nuclear family was given powerful support by Reformation theology and practice. The medieval Catholic ideal of chastity, as a legal obligation for priests, monks and nuns and as an ideal for all members of the community to aspire to, was replaced by the ideal of conjugal affection. The married state now became the ethical norm for the virtuous Christian, its purpose being more than what Milton described contemptuously, referring to the Pauline view, as 'the prescribed satisfaction of an irrational heat ..., the promiscuous draining of a carnal rage.' The great Puritan preacher William Perkins now described marriage as 'a state in itself far more excellent than the condition of a single life' – a clear contrast to the contemporary Catholic view of Cardinal Bellarmine that 'marriage is a thing humane, virginity is angelical' – in other words that it is no more than an unfortunate necessity to cope with human frailty. This sanctification of marriage – 'holy matrimony' – was a constant theme of Protestant sermons of the sixteenth century, which were directed to all classes in the society, and is to be found in both Puritan and Anglican moral theology of the early seventeenth century from William Gouge to Jeremy Taylor.[31]

It was Archbishop Cranmer who in England first officially added a third to those two ancient reasons for marriage, the avoidance of fornication and the procreation of legitimate children. In his Prayer Book of 1549 he added the motive of 'mutual society, help and comfort, that the one ought to have of the other, both in prosperity and in adversity.'[32] Later on in the sixteenth century Robert Cawdrey, as revised by Cleaver and Dod, and then Thomas Gataker, William Perkins and William Gouge, authors of the most popular family handbooks of their day, also emphasized that the purposes of marriage included spiritual intimacy. This doctrine was taken directly from the writings of the early continental reformers. Calvinist Geneva was certainly a male-dominated society, but Calvin stressed the ideal of the companionate marriage, women participated with their husbands in the singing of psalms, and wife-beating was actively discouraged by the consistories.[33] A second important influence on English thought was Bullinger, repeated by Robert Cleaver, who described marriage as a union 'with the good consent of them both, to the end that they may dwell together in friendship and honesty, one helping and comforting the other, eschewing ... uncleanness, and bringing up their children in the fear of God.'

This theme was developed still further by mid-and late-seventeenth-century Puritans, particularly by the Presbyterian Richard Baxter, who reversed the order of marriage motives in the prayer book, and put mutual comfort and support before procreation – an order of priorities first adopted by William Tyndale as far back as 1528, and followed by a number of later Puritan divines. Marriage for Puritans was an extension of Covenant theology, and was regarded as a sanctified contract, with binding mutual obligations. They all agreed in regarding the wife as subordinate to the husband: 'second helper' for Robert Cleaver, 'servant' for Augustine Niccholes in 1615, and 'assistant' for Thomas Gataker in 1620. But they were equally agreed in stressing the mutuality of the obligations, and they increasingly tended to emphasize companionship and friendship as the prime considerations. They regarded marriage both as a free personal contract and as a religious contract, which caused Benjamin Wadsworth in America to argue that couples who failed to love each other not only wronged each other but also disobeyed God. 'The indisputable authority, the plain command of the great God, required husbands and wives to have and manifest very great affection, love and kindness to one another.' On the other hand, this love had to be kept within the strict bounds of moderation, and subordinate to 'the light of the spirit'.[34]

Having beaten back efforts to legalize divorce with remarriage by the innocent party for the adultery or desertion of the wife, which was recognized by most Reformed churches abroad, the Tudor Protestants had no alternative but to urge the importance of affective ties as a necessity for marriage, in addition to the old Pauline arguments. Although they were as respectful as ever of the need for social equality and economic security as prime factors in mate selection, they were nonetheless obliged to oppose the strongly commercial attitude to marriage which had been prevalent in the late middle ages and the early sixteenth century, by which bride and groom had been bartered by their parents without their consent.[35] Since the Puritan moral theologians were equally insistent upon the need for filial obedience to parents, the result was often to place the dutiful child in an impossible conflict of role models. They had to try to reconcile the often incompatible demands for obedience to parental wishes on the one hand and expectations of affection in marriage on the other. Puritans solved this dilemma by arguing that affection could and would develop after marriage, provided that no violent antipathy manifested itself at a first brief interview.[36]

In England in the 1630s this new attitude to marriage gave rise to some extravagant hyperbole, used by both laity and Anglican theologians. In 1638 Robert Crosse spoke of marriage as 'an earthly paradise of happiness', though he added the conventional warnings against 'an oversottish and doting affection' and 'unlawful and raging lusts'. In 1642 Daniel Rogers thought that 'husbands and wives should be as two sweet friends' and Jeremy Taylor declared that 'the marital love is a thing pure as light, sacred as a temple, lasting as the world.'[37] It is no accident that Charles 1 and Henrietta Maria were 'the first English royal couple to be glorified as husband and wife in the domestic sense', even if this development owed as much to the rarefied cult of neo–Platonic love in court circles as it did to the attitude of the contemporary Anglican moral theologians.[38]

It should be noted that hardly any of these Protestant or Puritan writers were willing to carry their ideas about the spiritual nature of the marital union to the point of giving it priority over all other considerations. It was left to Milton, tormented by his own unhappy marriage and influenced partly by Renaissance thought and partly by previous Puritan theologians, to demote all other ends to marriage – the procreation of children, sexual control, the public interest in law and order, and the clerical interest in an ecclesiastically blessed *rite de passage*. For him the prime object of marriage was 'the apt and cheerful conversation of man with woman, to comfort and refresh him against the solitary life.' The logical conclusion to this step was to advocate – as Milton did, three hundred years ahead of his time and with almost no contemporary support – divorce and remarriage in cases of hopeless temperamental incompatibility. The argument was very simple, based on the proposition that 'Where love cannot be, there can be nothing left of wedlock but the empty husk of outside matrimony.' By minimizing the sexual and procreative functions of marriage, he easily came to the conclusion that 'natural hatred is a greater evil in marriage than the accident of adultery'. On the other hand, Milton had very strong views about the subordinate function of women – 'Who can be ignorant that woman was created for man, and not man for woman?' – and he therefore demanded divorce only when the 'unfitness' lay with the wife, not the husband. It could be demanded by both parties or by the husband alone, but not by the wife alone.[39] Milton thus carried the Protestant concept of holy matrimony about as far as it could go without abandoning the sexual superiority of the male. The roots of affective individualism in seventeenth-century Puritan sectarianism are clearly demonstrated in these writings.

The intensification of married love brought about by the stress on holy matrimony played a part in the shift from a kin-oriented to a nuclear family. In the Open Lineage Family, where affect was low and widely diffused, the lack of privacy and the self-interest of the kin put a damper on intensive marital emotional bonding. But with the churches now ringing with sermons encouraging such bonding, the influence of the kin tended to decline, as the married couple presented a more unified front towards the external world. The rise of married love and the decline of kin influence were therefore mutually reinforcing trends. The former also was important in helping to detach the couple psychologically from their parents. This major shift in moral allegiances was well understood by the preachers who advocated married love, one of whom frankly stated that 'it is a less offence for a man to forsake father and mother and to leave them succourless ... than it is for him to do the like towards his lawful married wife.' The opposition of parents and kin to the principle and practice of married love was based on a perceived threat to their power and interests.[40]

A final effect of the Reformation was to reduce the incest taboos from cousins in the sixteenth degree, as well as those spiritually linked by common godparents, to close blood relatives limited to the Levitical degrees. Even first cousins could now marry. The purpose of this change was to block the scandalous divorce proceedings of the pre-Reformation church, as well as to return to sound biblical precedent, but it incidentally struck a blow against the whole concept of kinship and affinity.[41]

There were also more profound, although less easily demonstrable, effects on the family of the change from pre-Reformation Catholicism to Anglican Protestantism. In post-Tridentine Catholic Europe, the parish, the youth group and the confraternity were serious competitors for loyalty with the state, the kin, and the conjugal household.[42] In Protestant countries, however, the Reformation swept away a whole set of rites, practices, symbols, beliefs, and institutional organizations which had hitherto provided both a framework of social support for community loyalties and a method of handling personal psychological crises. Civic pride had been reaffirmed by the frequent processions in which the statue sacred to the city had been paraded through the streets. Local loyalties had focused around wayside shrines and holy places. The tensions and frustrations of social life had been relieved by occasional periods of festive licence – May Day ceremonies, harvest festivals, saints' day celebrations, or the rituals of social inversion.[43] The pre-Reformation Church had also provided means for handling personal problems of guilt, pain and death. Guilt could be assuaged by means of confession and the remission of sins. Fear of the hereafter was diminished by the way-station of Purgatory, which could be passed through quickly by arranging for masses for the dead. Pain and sickness might be relieved by pilgrimages to famous relics and ritual prayers to miracle-working images of the Virgin or the saints. There was always hope.

Sometimes slowly, more often quickly and violently, the Reformation destroyed the social and psychological supports upon which both the community and the individual had depended for comfort and to give symbolic meaning to their existence. Miracle-working images and relics were defaced and destroyed, chantries endowed for masses for the dead were suppressed, the priests dispersed and the property nationalized. Purgatory was declared inoperative. Confession to priests was forbidden, and their power to remit sins declared a pious fraud. May Day festivities, churchales, religious processions, the celebration of saints' days were all denounced as mere relics of pagan superstition, to be suppressed along with the physical cult objects – the maypole or the sacred images – around which they had been organized. Man now stood alone before his Maker, with nothing but his conscience, the Bible and the preachers to guide him, deprived of all the old psychological props, collective rituals, and opportunities for blowing off steam.

There were only two beneficiaries of this drastic elimination of sacred ritual by the Protestant zealots. The first was the nation state which now laid claim to those loyalties which had hitherto gone to the community, the city, the parish or the confraternity. By destroying intermediary social organizations, myths and relics, Protestantism – and later the counter-Reformation in Europe – enormously strengthened a process which was already under way for other reasons: the rise of the authoritarian, all-embracing, inquisitorial, all-demanding nation state, and its embodiment in the divinely ordained person of the King.

The second beneficiary of the Reformation was the household and its head, which filled the vacuum left by the decline of the Church and its priests as the central institution for moral and religious instruction. The only competitor with the head of the household was now some of the more charismatic Puritan preachers who by correspondence at a distance exercised great influence over a number of pious upper-class wives and mothers.[44]

The parish church ceased to be used for a wide range of village functions. In the past it had acted as the library, the central news agency, the place for whipping unruly servants or disobedient schoolchildren, the site of political elections, the arena for cock-fighting or drinking-parties for the benefit of the clergyman. Many of these activities were now either transferred to the home, the inn or specialized buildings, or suppressed altogether.[45]

The transfer of religious and moral functions was even clearer. Attendance at service in church remained a formal Sunday obligation, but devotional piety shifted to the daily attendance at family prayers; moral control by the priest was partially replaced by moral direction by the head of the household; and Church catechisms were partially replaced by catechisms for the household, about a hundred of which were published between 1550 and 1600 alone. Edward Dering's popular *Catechism* was described by its author as 'very needful to be known to all householders whereby they may better teach and instruct their families in such points of Christian religion as is most meet.' Marriage sermons stressed the need for the bridal couple 'never to neglect family prayer.'[46] In the more pious households, husbands and wives would confess their sins to each other at home, instead of to the priest in church.[47] In many other cases the private diary was the substitute for the confessional, although the forgiveness of the latter is much easier on human frailty than the self-torture of the former. The Protestant ideal, as described by Robert Cawdrey in 1562, was that each family head should have 'a church in his house'. In towns in southern England by the early seventeenth century, the Bible was available in most upper and middle and even lower-middle class homes, and daily public readings from it by the head of the household, fortified by a rousing sermon in the church on Sunday, replaced the ritual of the sacrament as the main vehicle of religious expression.[48] At the risk of oversimplification, it could be said that Reformation Protestantism was a religion of literacy, domestic prayer, and the family bible in the family home, all buttressed by the public sermon, whereas counter-Reformation Catholicism was a religion of visual display, the worship of the sacred image or relic in the holy place, and the administration by the priest in the church of a magical sacrament during a public ceremony conducted in an unknown language.

This general tendency to substitute the household for the church was carried a stage further by the Puritans, who tended to elevate a select few chosen for their godliness. This selectivity thrust the burden of maintaining piety more exclusively back on to the household, and the end product might well be a sect – a separated church constructed from the voluntary association of a group of godly families. Although this outcome was not visible at first, the essence of Puritanism was a family church, and this implication of its drive for purity is clear to us today.[49] Since all could not aspire to these heights of godliness, the religious unit would inevitably tend to cease to be the parish, embracing all who lived in a geographical area, whether saints or sinners, and would become a collection of private, self-selected families, drawn from any level of social class, but in practice mostly from the yeoman, husbandman, artisan and tradesman level, with some gentry leadership at the top. This aspect of Puritanism became particularly noticeable after the Restoration in 1660, when the nonconformists, driven back on themselves by prohibition of public worship, were inevitably the most vigorous supporters of the now decaying practice of regular family prayers, morning and night.[50]

Whether in Anglican or Puritan households, there was, in varying degrees, a new emphasis on the home and on domestic virtues, and this was perhaps the most far-reaching consequence of the Reformation in England. The household was the inheritor of many of the responsibilities of the parish and the Church; the family head was the inheritor of much of the authority and many of the powers of the priest. The transubstantiated Host, carefully preserved at the east end of the church, was replaced by the informal sharing of the symbolic bread and wine, taken in the sixteenth century seated with one's hat on, around a rough table set in the middle of the church, in imitation of pictures of the Last Supper. More important was the weekly sermon, notes on which were often taken in the newly invented shorthand. But the purpose of the note-taking was to provide a basis for later discussion of the contents in the privacy of the home, while these public ceremonies were at least partly replaced or reinforced by family prayers. These took place daily in the home, a prominent feature of which was now the Holy Bible on a lectern in the hall, or taken from a bible-box. It was a book which also, significantly enough, often served at all levels of society to record the family genealogy. Thus the Word of God was to some degree removed from the parish church and transferred to the private home: the Holy Spirit was partly domesticated.

It is significant corroboration of this argument that when in 1845 Jules Michelet launched his attack on the powers of the Catholic priesthood in France, exercised in particular over women through the confessional, he did it in the name of the family. His argument was that through the confession box, it was the priest who controlled the wife rather than her husband, and who knew all her secret thoughts and desires better than he did. As a result, families were divided in their opinions between the father on the one hand and the wife and daughters on the other. 'His own house becomes uninhabitable.' Michelet's ideal was a family in which the husband was the undisputed master of his home, and the wife was his loyal companion and associate. 'Let the family hearth become firm and strong, then the tottering edifice of religion, political religion, will quietly settle down.'[51] The battle that Michelet was fighting in mid-nineteenth-century France was one that in England had been won by the end of the sixteenth century.

5 PEASANTS, ARTISANS AND THE POOR: THE DECLINE OF COMMUNITY

Although the evidence is fragmentary in the extreme, it is fairly clear that neither kinship nor clientage had played anything like the same role among peasants, artisans and poor as they did among their betters. At this social level, it was the community of neighbours whose influence on and control over family life had been of the greatest importance. This influence and control increased or became more institutionalized in some areas, weakened and all but disappeared in others.

i. Intensified Regulation

The most important factor in changing family relationships among the plebs were economic changes in the village and the town. These seem to have happened through two overlapping processes, the first of which may have increased community interference in the economic life of the family, and the second of which may have decreased and in the long run more or less ended it. The first was the enormous demographic growth of the rural population between about 1520 and 1620, which placed the old open-field system under tremendous strain. The manorial courts were obliged to step in to limit squatting on waste land, to regulate the number of cattle allowed on the common pasture, and generally to arbitrate an equitable division of fixed assets between increasing numbers of claimants.

The degree to which individual action was regulated by the manorial court is hardly comprehensible to generations brought up in conditions of entrepreneurial freedom. To take but one example, the manorial court at Whitfield in Northumberland between 1558 and 1744 closely regulated every aspect of economic and, indeed, personal life. Steeping flax or hemp in water where horses drink or in running water, letting scabbed or infected cattle on to the common lands, not adhering to the prescribed weights and measures, stopping up the public ways and footpaths, taking in lodgers, erecting cottages, shooting with guns or cross-bows, and not ringing pigs, were all offences punishable by fine. So also were failing to repair hedges, scolding, chiding, brawling, or singing scandalous songs, and a host of offences against the many economic monopolies and powers exercised by the lord of the manor.[52] The open-field peasant lived in a communally-regulated world, and both the economic and the personal freedom of the head of the household were strictly limited.

Similarly in the towns, the shrinkage of urban industry induced first the local guilds and then Parliament to step in with a battery of defensively autarkic regulations, while the persistence of ancient traditions about the just price in an inflationary age stimulated more and more intensive efforts to regulate the markets. Wherever one looks in the period between 1540 and 1640 there appears a clash between traditional community interests and growing aspirations for family entrepreneurial freedom, a clash whose first consequence was an intensification of public regulation.

Another area in which there was a positive intensification of public interference in family life was in the field of morals. The steady advance of Christianity throughout the century, and the growing censoriousness about sin which accompanied it, led to growing interference by Church authorities, supported by neighbours and parish officials, to make all inhabitants conform to the new community norms. Domestic life in the village was conducted in a blaze of publicity.

The clergy struggled to persuade the lower classes to abandon altogether the traditional habit of censensual unions unblessed by the church. There was an earnest effort to ensure that all sexual unions, whether of clergy and their pre-Reformation 'housekeepers' or of the poor, should now be recognized and sanctified by a formal Christian sacrament. Some tentative evidence of the success of this pressure upon the lower classes is the apparent decline in illegitimacy rates in the backward north and north-west from about four per cent in the 1590s, before educated Protestant ministers first became available in large numbers in these areas, to about one and a half per cent in the mid-seventeenth century when the Puritan supremacy was at its height. The registered rural illegitimacy rate in the whole country was on the average only about three per cent even in the Elizabethan period, which suggests that the practice of either consensual unions or of casual fornication followed by abandonment was relatively rare, or else – more likely – that most illegitimate children were either not registered at all or were registered as legitimate.[53] But since Puritans were likely to be more strict in registering bastardy than conventional Anglicans, the recorded decline over the next fifty years is convincing evidence of the success of the Protestant, and especially Puritan, ministers in christianizing the marriage practices of the poor, as well as in introducing an element of sexual constraint into those of the rich. For all members of society, clergy, men of property and the poor, the ideal state was now that of marriage. But this marriage had to be arranged either by or with the knowledge and approval of parents, accompanied by the consent of the bride and groom, and sanctified and legitimated by the Church.

A powerful means of enforcing public standards of morality on family life was through denunciations to the archdeacons' courts, however ineffectual the latter may have been in punishing transgressors. Neither fornication nor adultery was easy in so public an arena as a village, although of course there was plenty of both. Neighbours gossiped about the most intimate details of family relationships, and were quick to complain to the ecclesiastical courts of anything that violated local mores. Reputed seducers of maidens were duly reported on the basis of hearsay only. They thought it wrong that a boy over seventeen should continue to sleep in the same bed as his mother. They were very suspicious about the household of husband and wife, one manservant and one maid, which only contained two beds, so that the husband slept in a bed with both his wife and the maid. They even knew about, and complained of, unusually enthusiastic or deviant sexual behaviour between man and wife. They complained when a husband turned a blind eye to the adultery of his wife, and were quick to denounce cases of bigamy or trigamy. They lurked about to catch the curate in bed with a girl. While approving of a husband's power to discipline an unruly wife, they objected to noisy and excessive brutality or use of foul language which disturbed the peace of the village, as much as they objected to the female propensity to scolding and slander.[54]

An alternative to the archdeacons' courts, whose powers were limited to the more or less voluntary compliance with shame punishments such as standing in church in a white sheet during a service, was enforcement of the moral code by the local secular authorities. In the late Elizabethan period, any constable was empowered to break into any house in which he suspected fornication or adultery to be in progress and, if his suspicions were confirmed, to carry the offenders to jail or before a Justice of the Peace. This was a power that was used up to about 1660, but died out after the Restoration, although it remained in the standard handbook on local justice.[55] Convicted offenders were often ordered to be whipped in the sixteenth and early seventeenth centuries.

If the ecclesiastical and secular authorities failed to take action, the villagers might be provoked into resorting to their traditional forms of public shame punishment. The commonest form was 'rough music,' or a serenade with the beating of pots and pans by the village youth marching around the house of one of those who offended parish norms, perhaps by marrying someone decades younger than him- or herself. A cuckolding spouse or a notoriously hen-pecked husband might find themselves publicly humiliated by a 'skimmington', being paraded round the village seated backwards on a donkey. A slanderous or shrewish wife classified as a 'common scold' might be strapped in a 'cucking-stool' in her own doorway, or ducked in the village pond by the mob. These were ancient practices which went on at least into the eighteenth century.[56] There was a 'moral economy' of village culture which was both supportive and coercive at the same time. Neighbours not only helped each other in crises, but also reported each other's transgressions to the authorities or took direct action themselves. This is true of villages at all times and in all places, but particularly so of England in the sixteenth and early seventeenth centuries, thanks to the combination of a cool psychological atmosphere and a censorious religious creed and Church.

Finally there was the pressure of the godly community of Puritans, led by their minister, who kept a vigilant eye on the domestic lives of their members and did not hesitate to interfere when they detected evidence of sin. In some ways, therefore, the family life of the poor was more heavily regulated by public pressures between 1580 and 1660 than at any time before or since. It became even more open to public inspection than it had ever been, or was ever to be again.

But against this intensification of exposure to community controls must be set a series of developments which were tending in the opposite direction, and conferring greater freedom on the nuclear family.

ii. Weakened Regulation

Among these classes, the very high geographical mobility of English society in the late sixteenth and seventeenth centuries, which has now been established beyond reasonable doubt, made it very difficult for kinship associations to retain their old strength. Both muster rolls of male adults liable to military service and detailed census returns of two villages suggest a rural population turnover as high as fifty per cent or more in ten years. While removal by death accounted for some twenty per cent of those who disappeared, there are still some thirty per cent or more who moved on elsewhere in a given ten-year span, which indicates that the seventeenth-century English village was far from being a static or isolated unit. In one Worcestershire village, eighty per cent of the seventy-five surnames disappeared from the parish records between 1666 and 1750. Village continuity was preserved by a mere five large and enduring families, which inevitably intermarried a great deal. Similarly, a study of witnesses in rural court cases between 1580 and 1640, who were all men well above the poverty line, show that two-thirds had moved to a different parish during their lives, even if about half of them had only moved five miles. A 1782 census of a Bedfordshire village showed that only a third of the heads of households, of either sex, had been born in the village, although most of them came from less than ten miles away. Thus among the lower, lower-middle and middle class groups, geographical mobility was remarkably high, and at least half the population died in a different parish from that in which they were born.[57]

Much of this geographical mobility can be accounted for merely by youths and young girls going out into service or apprenticeship and moving on from master to master. But what is also involved is both the emigration of youth away from the parental home, and the migration of whole nuclear families from place to place, thus breaking the bonds of kinship. Most of this flow was certainly short-range migration of less than sixteen miles, for marriage or work as a servant. But a significant amount of it was longer range, from the more densely populated rural areas into the forests and the under-populated Highland zone, and even more from the countryside into the towns. Nearly three-quarters of Canterbury residents who served as witnesses in court cases between 1580 and 1640 were immigrants into the city from elsewhere. But the truly massive influx was into London. The population of London and its surburbs increased from about sixty thousand in 1500 to about five hundred and fifty thousand in 1700, despite the fact that the urban death rate was so high that the city was far from reproducing itself. This staggering growth was, therefore, caused by a constant and massive flow of immigrants from the countryside, estimated to be at least eight thousand a year net in the late seventeenth and early eighteenth centuries. Once entered into the anonymity of the city, these immigrants often tended to remain transients without deep roots. A London parson in the days of Elizabeth remarked that every twelve years or so 'the most part of the parish changeth, ... some going and some coming.' A sample of deponents in lawsuits in Stepney between 1580 and 1639 shows that only nine per cent had been born in that parish or neighbouring Whitechapel, and only fourteen per cent in London and Middlesex. Moreover, the evidence of apprenticeship records suggest that a good deal of the artisan immigration to London in the sixteenth century was of a very long-range variety, with nearly half the immigrants coming from the north of England. Only at the end of the seventeenth century did London immigrants begin to come predominantly from the surrounding areas.[58]

This very high rate of mobility from place to place, most of it short range but some of it over long distances, and sustained for over a century, must have done more than anything else to weaken the ties of kinship among the lower levels of society. Travel was both slow and expensive, and removal for only sixteen miles meant a four-and-a-half-hour walk to reach home. Moreover, correspondence among illiterates was difficult if not impossible. Many of these movements must therefore have detached the adolescent children, and later the nuclear pair, from their parents and kin in the village. For these large numbers who were mobile, the web of kin relations that enveloped them in the home village was now more or less cut, which necessarily threw them back on the isolated conjugal family. Some migrants no doubt found temporary shelter with a kin relative, but before long the nuclear pair, or the lonely adolescent, were on their own in alien corn, and only a minority could hope to marry into a wider kin which could offer support in the new surroundings. In such circumstances the key reference group, whose goodwill was necessary for support and control, were not the now distant kin, but the odd relative settled in the town, and the neighbours: community was replacing kin as the main external force in family life.

Finally it should be noted that those who were socially upwardly mobile as well as geographically laterally mobile would have a special incentive to shed their embarrassing kin connections as they struggled to get themselves accepted in their new status niche.

As society became more dense, more complex and more organized, there developed a series of semi-public bodies – town authorities, parish overseers of the poor, schools, and later even banks – which took over many of the functions previously performed not only by the nuclear family, but also by the kin, and the patron. This was a very slow and very relative process, however, and far more important at this stage was a shift in functions and values away from the kin towards the state, or towards local institutions pushed into existence by state action.

The principal area in which the function of peasant kinship can be shown to have been on the decline in the seventeenth century is that of aid and welfare for the helpless, the sick and the indigent. In traditional societies these problems are handled by the conjugal family, the kin and the neighbours, with some minor help from the church. In sixteenth-century England, rapid demographic growth in the villages, urban immigration, the impoverishment of the towns, and the ravages of price inflation meant that support from the extended network of the kin and from neighbours in the community became inadequate for large numbers of orphans, widows, cripples, sick, and aged, while structural unemployment of the able-bodied first became a problem. During the century, welfare for those unable to support themselves had perforce to be progressively taken over by public bodies. In the early sixteenth century, some towns were obliged to organize their own poor relief system, paid out of taxes, and in the second half of the century the practice spread to the countryside on a voluntary and emergency basis only. In about 1600 a nationwide system based on local compulsory taxation and expenditure was instituted, and during the seventeenth century it became a fully functioning organization run by the parish, which effectively relieved the kin, the conjugal family and the neighbours of their previous sense of obligation to provide relief to the sick and the indigent to save them from starvation. In addition to these public arrangements, private legacies from the wealthy built and endowed a significant number of orphanages, hospitals and almshouses for the old, and set up supplementary funds for poor relief in a fair number of villages.[59]

A rather similar transfer of responsibility occurred, over a long period of time, in the socialization of the child, part of which was slowly transferred from the family to the school. In the sixteenth and seventeenth centuries this must have affected most yeoman and husbandman families, but could have had relatively little impact on the rural labourers. In the towns, however, not only artisans but many of the poor were literate by 1640. At the end of the eighteenth century the Sunday schools, with their provision of free education on a day which did not interfere with the income-producing labour of the child, at last began to affect the lives of the bottom third of the society, the unskilled labouring poor. These were parents who were 'unable to give them instruction and it is feared some of them have no heart for it.' For this large group of children at the bottom of the social system, after about 1790 the Sunday schools increasingly took over the function of surrogate parents, performing all the tasks of socialization in morals, hygiene, piety and literacy that the actual parents were unable or unwilling to perform.[60] Family responsibility for the socialization of children thus declined in stages from the sixteenth to the early nineteenth centuries, slowly spreading downward from class to class.

There were several slow economic changes which tended to free the peasant family. The enclosure of open fields at last gave the family head full control over the exploitation of his property, while the development of trading in inns and ale-houses outside market restrictions, and the flight of industry into the countryside to escape guild regulations, had the same result. The putting-out system in cloth manufacture and the development of home industry, particularly spinning, strengthened the family as an economic unit of production by making the home the place of work and by providing employment there for wives and children.

Finally the slow rise of a force of landless labourers and cottagers, which developed throughout the sixteenth, seventeenth and eighteenth centuries, meant the growth of a group of persons whose only ties to their employer were the strictly economic ones of the wage-earner to the man who pays him. These new poor lacked the paternal ties of the landlord to his tenants or the farmer to his living-in servants. Once again, the bonds tying the individual to intermediate institutions or patrons were weakened, although in this case the effect on family life is very uncertain.

iii. Conclusion

To sum up, the degree of community control over the family of the plebs in some respects decreased and in others increased between 1540 and 1640. On the one hand, religious factors were intensifying the moral interference of the community in intimate domestic affairs, while demographic pressures were in some ways intensifying the economic regulation of free enterprise upon those still bound by the rulings of the manorial court over the use of the open fields. On the other hand, there were increasing numbers who were evolving into independent family producers, and geographical mobility was loosening community controls.

At the higher level of the social elite, however, the trend is less ambiguous; there was a clear decline in allegiance to kinship and clientage, with a corollary growth of loyalty outward to the state and the religion and inward to the family. The effects on family life of this withdrawal of the kin may not have been altogether for the good. Wives maltreated by their husbands were now less able to turn to their kin for support and defence. Intervention by the elders of the kin to settle marital quarrels was now less easy and less welcome. The kin could no longer so readily serve as mediators between the parents and the children in the case of a direct clash between the two on the issue of the choice of a spouse. The partial withdrawal of external support and intervention thus made family life more liable to explosive conflict between husband and wife, and parents and children. On the other hand, the partial withdrawal of the kin was an essential preliminary step to clear the way for the subsequent development of the domesticated family and the selection of spouses by the choice of the individuals on the basis of prior affection. But this would not occur for a long time, until the late seventeenth and the eighteenth centuries. Kinship ties did not disappear overnight, but merely slowly, if irregularly, receded over several centuries as they became less desirable and less necessary. Thus, when the gentleman merchant John Verney was considering marriage in 1671, one of his options was a Miss Edwards. Her father took care to tell John that the girl 'brought in no kindred with her, neither of great persons to be a charge by way of entertainment, nor of mean to be a charge by way of charity and their neediness.'[61] Kinship was clearly now regarded more as a potential burden than a potential opportunity.

CHAPTER 5

The Reinforcement of Patriarchy

'If ever thou purpose to be a good wife, and to live comfortably, set down this with thyself: mine husband is my superior, my better; he hath authority and rule over me; nature hath given it to him . . . God hath given it to him.'
(W. Whately, *The Bride Bush*, London, 1617, p. 36)

I GENERAL CAUSES

The enhancement of the importance of the conjugal family and the household relative to the kinship and clientage at the upper levels of society was accompanied by a positive reinforcement of the despotic authority of husband and father – that is to say, of patriarchy. Both Church and state provided powerful new theoretical and practical support, while two external checks on patriarchal power declined as kinship ties and clientage weakened. At the same time, a new interest in children, coupled with the Calvinist premise of Original Sin, gave fathers an added incentive to ensure the internalized submissiveness of their children. It cannot be proved conclusively that in reality the powers of fathers over children and of husbands over wives in the upper and middle ranks most exposed to this propaganda became greater than they had been in the middle ages. But this seems a plausible hypothesis, given the fact that patriarchy for its effective exercise depends not so much on raw power or legal authority, as on a recognition by all concerned of its legitimacy, hallowed by ancient tradition, moral theology and political theory. It survives and flourishes only so long as it is not questioned and challenged, so long as both the patriarchs and their subordinates fully accept the natural justice of the relationship and of the norms within which it is exercised. Willing acceptance of the legitimacy of the authority, together with a weakness of competing foci of power, are the keys to the whole system.

i. The State

It has plausibly been argued that patriarchy within the family is a characteristic of societies with strong authoritarian state systems, a phase of development characteristic of sixteenth- and early seventeenth-century England, between the more simple semi-tribal, feudal or community organizations of medieval society, and the participatory limited monarchy and later mass democracy of the late seventeenth century onwards.[1] The question of deciding which is the cause and which the effect is irrelevant, since authoritarian monarchy and domestic patriarchy form a congruent and mutually supportive complex of ideas and social systems. The growth of patriarchy was deliberately encouraged by the new Renaissance state on the traditional grounds that the subordination of the family to its head is analogous to, and also a direct contributory cause of, subordination of subjects to the sovereign. In 1609 James I informed his somewhat dubious subjects that 'The state of monarchy is the supremest thing upon earth', one of his arguments being that 'Kings are compared to fathers in families: for a King is truly *parens patriae*, the politic father of his people.' When some twenty-five years later Robert Filmer argued the case for absolute monarchy, he used exactly the same logic: 'We find in the Decalogue that the law which enjoins obedience to Kings is delivered in the terms of: "Honour thy Father".' (As a strong anti-feminist, he discreetly omits 'and Mother.')

In 1618 Richard Mocket published a book, *God and the King*, in which he made the connection even clearer. All subjects were the children of the king, and bound by the Fifth Commandment to honour and obey him. James I was so delighted with this book that he ordered it to be studied in schools and universities and bought by all householders, thus ensuring it a very wide sale.[2] Both the products of the printing press and homilies and catechisms in church were harnessed to the task of spreading the message.

In New England the standard catechism, by John Cotton, ran as follows:

Question: What is the Fifth Commandment?
Answer: Honour thy father and mother that thy days may be long. ...
Question: Who are here meant by father and mother?
Answer: All our superiors, whether in family, school, church and commonwealth.
Question: What is the honour due to them?
Answer: Reverence, obedience, and (when I am able) recompense.[3]

In France the old lines of argument were if possible made even more explicit. In 1639 a royal declaration stated that 'the natural respect of children towards their parents is the bond of the legitimate obedience of subjects towards their sovereigns.' In this year the final touches were given to eighty years of legislation in France which had progressively strengthened paternal power, especially over the marriage of children. Conservatives like Bossuet argued that 'one makes Kings on the model of fathers', and liberals like Montesquieu, who believed strongly in paternal authority as a symbol of the authority of the law, nonetheless saw a clear relationship between 'the servitude of women' and 'despotic government.'[4]

There are good reasons to think that this support given by the state to the principle of patriarchy paid off in generating an internalized sense of obligation of obedience to the absolute king as the father of his people. Despite Charles I's long record of duplicity and illegal actions, very many individuals were in the last resort unable to shake off the ideological chains with which they had so long been bound. Men like Hyde were exasperated enough to destroy the machinery of royal government in 1640–41, but not enough to take up arms against the king in 1642. Even more striking is the response of the vast crowd in Whitehall in 1649, when Charles I's head was severed from his body. Seventy years later, an old woman could still recall with horror the 'dismal groan' that she heard from the crowd as a child, while a boy remembered as long as he lived 'such a groan as I never heard before, and desire I may never hear again.'[5] This mass response to a public execution must surely have been a reflection of a feeling by the crowd that it had witnessed an act of national patricide: the father of his people had been publicly murdered.

When in the same year Arthur, Lord Capel, was tried and executed for leading an unsuccessful royal rebellion, he defended himself on the grounds of obedience to the Fifth Commandment: he was rallying, he argued, in defence of the nation's father. This same patriarchal theory, reinforcing the traditional habits of deference and authority which were basic to the social structure and value system of seventeenth-century England, must surely have helped to smooth the path to the Restoration of Charles II in 1660.[6]

What seems to have happened is that a diffuse concept of patriarchy inherited from the middle ages that took the form of 'good lordship' – meaning dominance over kin and clientage – was vigorously attacked by the state as a threat to its own authority. Patriarchy was now reinforced by the state, however, in the much modified form of authoritarian dominance by the husband and father over the woman and children within the nuclear family. What had previously been a real threat to the political order was thus neatly transformed into a formidable buttress to it.

ii. The Protestant Church

At first sight it might appear that the stress laid in this chapter upon the role of Protestantism in fostering patriarchalism in the English middle- and upper-class family is contradicted by the admitted fact that the most extreme forms of patriarchalism are to be found now, and were probably also in the Early Modern period, among the deeply Catholic peasantry of Portugal, Spain, southern France and southern Italy, and the Orthodox Christians of the Balkans and Greece. This is perfectly correct, but since the patriarchal family is even more deeply entrenched in the Moslem world on the southern shore of the Mediterranean it is clear that the phenomenon is not a religious one dependent on the particular type of Christianity, but a regional cultural feature common to Catholic Christians, Orthodox Christians and Moslems around the Mediterranean basin, and peculiarly well developed among the most impoverished peasantry.[7] Middle- and upper-class patriarchy in sixteenth- and early seventeenth-century England is something different, which needs a quite different explanation.

The success of the Reformation church in encouraging holy matrimony and in stressing the moral and religious responsibilities of the household has already been explained. What has not been sufficiently emphasized, however, is the way in which the role of the head of the household was also strengthened. From this point of view, if not that of either theology or the sociology of religion, the principal result of the Reformation was the heavy responsibility placed by Protestantism upon the head of the household to supervise the religious and moral conduct of its members. In 1528 Luther himself boasted of bringing order, discipline and obedience to the family, as well as to society as a whole. 'Among us,' he wrote, there was now knowledge of the Scriptures and also of 'marriage, civil obedience, the duties of father and mother, father and son, master and servant.' The triumphant emphasis on patriarchy as one of the benefits of the Lutheran Reformation is here unmistakable. All the magisterial Reformed Churches stressed the subordination of wives to husbands, summed up in John Milton's terse description of sex-typed obligations: 'He for God only, she for God in him.' Nor was this all. The shift to Protestantism meant the loss by the wife of control over the domestic rituals of religious fasting and feasting on the appropriate days. Thirdly, the concept that the Bible was the key to all knowledge placed a premium on literacy as the main means to salvation, but the wide educational gap between men and women in the sixteenth century placed the latter at a new and serious disadvantage. Lastly, the doctrine of the priesthood of all believers meant in practice that the husband and father became the spiritual as well as the secular head of the household. The aggrieved or oppressed wife could no longer rely on the priest to provide a counter-poise to potential domestic tyranny arising from this new authority thrust upon her husband.[8]

Not all heads of households were capable of fulfilling these heavy responsibilities, nor were all wives willing so abjectly to subordinate their wills. Moreover, the identity of the husband and father with the family religious confessor placed severe strains on many wives and children, who found themselves trapped in a situation where they had no-one to turn to for escape or alternative counsel. In many pious upper-class households in the seventeenth century, the power of the head of the household was oppressive in its completeness. Sir George Sondes certainly made his family and servants attend church services twice on Sundays. But 'all the week after, it was my constant course to pray with my family, once if not twice every day; and if I had not a [chaplain] in my house, I performed the office myself.' As for Sir Nathaniel Barnardiston, 'towards his children he executed the office of an heavenly father to their souls ... and many times he would take them into his closet and there pray over them and for them.' In the 1630s the Kentish Puritan gentleman Thomas Scott spent 'the evening with my wife, children and family in hearing prayers.' Supper was prefaced by a reading from the Bible, and after it 'my wife reads Dr Preston's sixth sermon. My daughter-in-law reads line by line, and she and all the rest of my family ... sing Psalm 5.'[9] These family exercises were by no means confined to Puritans, and in the high Anglican household of Sir Christopher Wandesford, apparently in the 1630s when he was Master of the Rolls in Ireland, there were family prayers three times a day, at 6 a.m., 10 a.m. and 9 p.m. After his death, his widow would assemble her children every day before breakfast to pray together and read or repeat psalms and chapters of the Bible, after which the children knelt to receive their mother's blessing. In this all-enveloping atmosphere of domestic piety, in many gentry and bourgeois homes not only had the household replaced the parish, but the father had replaced the priest. The link between Protestant religion and family patriarchy was made by the Presbyterian Thomas Edwards in 1646, when he vigorously opposed the granting of religious toleration on the grounds that 'they should never have peace in their families more, or ever after have command of wives, children, servants.'[10]

In 1715, just as the political and religious values that lay behind patriarchy were visibly crumbling, Daniel Defoe tried to prop some of them up in his didactic handbook *The Family Instructor*. He stressed the role of the head of the household as the moral and religious ruler over all the residents, including servants and apprentices: 'Masters of families are parents, that is guardians and governors, to their whole house, though they are fathers only to their children.'[11]

iii. The Law

A change in legal arrangements for the inheritance of property, which in origin probably had nothing to do with the motives of either Church or state, nonetheless powerfully reinforced the trend to patriarchy within the nuclear family. During the middle ages control over landed property through entail meant that the head of the family was no more than a life tenant of most of the estates, with little freedom to dispose of them at his pleasure. In the late fifteenth century, the lawyers found a way to break entails without too much difficulty, and some confusing legislation of the 1530s had the result of still further widening the breach. This greatly strengthened the ability of the current head of the family to dispose of the property as he chose, although it also greatly weakened his capacity to prevent his heir from doing the same thing.[12] He could now quite easily either sell land to meet current needs or split it up amongst his children as he thought fit. The increase in this freedom of action of the current owner meant an increase in his capacity to punish or reward his children or siblings. Thus it meant the further subordination of the children, including the heir, to the father, and of younger sons and daughters to their elder brother if he inherited the estate before they married.

It would be wrong to assume that this major transformation in the disposal of property within the family flowed from specific feats of ingenuity performed by certain lawyers. After all, lawyers strive to please their clients, and the root cause of the changes must therefore lie in changing attitudes towards family responsibility held by different generations of landed proprietors. To account for these changes, one is compelled to enter into the realm of speculation. There can be little doubt that the landed classes of the late fifteenth and early sixteenth centuries underwent a severe crisis of confidence; their medieval military functions were eroded, but nothing else was available to take its place as a justification for their enormous wealth and power. They first threw themselves into a romantic revival of the ancient chivalric ideal, but that was too brittle to sustain the weight placed upon it, and it soon collapsed.[13]

The reckless alienation of property by the great old families at this period can be explained in part as a reaction to the takeover of many of their functions by state-appointed lesser men, and to the frustration and sense of despair this loss of power engendered. Many other late sixteenth-century landowners were new men, recently risen upon the ruins of Church property, who had not had time to develop a mystique about the sanctity of the family estates, and who therefore felt free to alienate them, either to provide for their younger children or to support current consumption. There can be no doubt that these generations faced severe problems about the disposition of younger sons, since so few job openings were available. The military career was very insecure, since there was no standing army and there were long intervals of peace. The law was mostly occupied by elder sons of small gentry, positions in the Reformation Church were now despised, doctors were not gentlemen, and the state bureaucracy was very small, with hardly any local offices at all. Since openings in socially respectable professions were so scarce, the best – indeed, in many cases, the only – way to provide for surplus sons seemed to be to settle upon them a portion of the family estates, so that they could continue to support the life style of minor gentry.

All these explanations are plausible, but all that we know for certain is that between about 1480 and 1660 more flexible legal arrangements considerably increased the power of the head of the household over his children, and to a lesser extent over his wife. The authority of the family council of kin elders to interfere in these dispositions was now significantly reduced, although a grossly inequitable distribution of goods and property would lead to adverse public criticism. The current owner of the estates could now not only bribe his children with promises of more; he could threaten them with total exclusion from the inheritance. He possessed the power to manipulate the distribution of his property, either to serve his own selfish interests or to preserve and increase in perpetuity the family status and property through primogeniture, or to control and direct his children in making the two most crucial decisions of their lives: choice of a spouse and choice of a career. Only later did this power come to be seen as a temptation to dissipate the estates which was a danger to the patrimony, as well as harmful to the interests of daughters and younger sons, who were entirely at the mercy of their father or elder brother.

iv. Education

The invention of the printing press, the distribution of books, the emphasis laid on the Book – that is the Bible – as the repository of all wisdom, inevitably had the effect of widening the social and cultural gap between those who could read, especially those who could read Latin, and those who could not. Although the mid-sixteenth century saw the emergence of a number of highly educated noblewomen, in general access both to sacred truth and to new learning was monopolized by men, thus increasing their prestige and influence and reducing that of women. In Elizabethan England this discrepancy between the sexes in terms of education was true at all levels of society; from the male artisans who could sign their names to the male elite who could write letters and read the Bible, and often also Cicero. Most of their wives were unable to emulate their husbands in these respects, which significantly reinforced their sense of inferiority.

v. Conclusion

To sum up, the power of the husband and father was greatly enhanced by his inheritance from the pre-Reformation priest of the duty to indoctrinate his family in piety and morality through daily family prayers and Bible reading. He was relieved of some of his social responsibilities by the state, but strongly encouraged by it to exercise his delegated authority as the priest-ruler of his microcosmic empire. He was given greater power over the family property, including that of his wife or his children, and enjoyed considerable freedom to exercise physical coercion backed by the full force of law and custom. He was more free than ever before from control and guidance from his own or his wife's kin, and to a considerable extent from interference by the parish priest. As a result, the husband and father for a time became the family despot, benevolent or malign according to temperament and inclination, lording it over his wife and his children. Almost the only check left upon his will was now the moral consensus of friends and neighbours, themselves also deeply affected by these patriarchal values. But this mostly affected the plebs, and community feeling, as expressed in violent public acts against domineering wives, was on the whole supportive of patriarchy.

It should be emphasized, however, that the common practice of fostering out, and the high level of geographical mobility caused by this social custom and by economic dislocations, meant that among the poor the control of the father over his children was limited to the relatively short period before they left home. After that point, patriarchal authority over them was exercised not by their natural father, but by the master whose living-in servants or apprentices they became. Thus, among the lower classes the patriarchal principle and practice remained powerful, but was exercised mainly upon the children of other people after they had reached the age of about ten to fourteen.

2   PARENTS AND CHILDREN

i. Areas of Permissiveness

All the evidence we have suggests that infants were fed on demand, and were not weaned until a year or eighteen months, often fairly slowly. Among the more prosperous classes it was normal before the mid-eighteenth century to send the children out to mercenary wet-nurses, who may or may not have given the infants the milk and the attention that they needed. It is very uncertain, therefore, to what extent children at this period suffered the oral trauma of weaning to anything like the degree that Freudian theory would suggest.

It also seems fairly certain that children throughout the Early Modern period were not subjected to early and severe toilet training, which has become so marked a feature of nineteenth- and twentieth-century child rearing. This was a time when personal and public hygiene was largely disregarded. Men and women rarely, if ever, washed their bodies, and they lived in the constant sight and smell of human faeces and human urine. Many houses, even palaces, lacked latrines, while public conveniences in the streets or public places were largely nonexistent. When in 1667 Mrs Pepys was seized with diarrhoea in the theatre, she had no option but to go off to a corner of Lincoln's Inn walks, where 'she did her business'. Close-stools and chamber pots were scattered around the wealthier houses and used when convenient, then emptied directly into the street. Samuel Pepys was a wealthy man, whose house in Seething Lane in London in the 1660s had a privy which drained into a vat in the cellar. From time to time the vat had to be emptied by night-soil men with buckets which they carried through the kitchen to a cart outside the door, a process which Pepys found nauseating. But Pepys himself and his rich friends were far from fastidious. One day he suddenly opened the door of his dining-room to find the wife of his patron, the Countess of Sandwich, 'doing something upon the pot'.[14]

The standards of the French court were similar to those of the English, and 'in the neighbourhood of the Louvre, in several parts of the court, on the great stairway and in the passages, behind the doors, and just about everywhere, one sees a thousand ordures, one smells a thousand intolerable stenches, caused by the natural necessities which everyone performs there every day.'[15]

In such a society, the toilet training of infants could obviously not be a matter of serious concern. In any case, the practice of swaddling meant that unless the nurse was prepared frequently to unwind and wind up the bands, which was a very tedious business, the infant child would be left for hours to lie in its own excrement. The only specific example of toilet training we have from the sixteenth or seventeenth centuries concerns the French dauphin Louis in the first years of the latter century. His training began at about sixteen months, and was supposed to be completed by two years, when he began to sleep in a proper bed, sometimes with the adults. By three he was regularly excreting into a chamber pot. The total lack of references to this problem in child-rearing manuals of the time strongly reinforces the hypothesis that children were left to learn to control their sphincters more or less at their own pace. Bed-wetting at a late age, however, was severely punished by flogging or worse, since it seriously inconvenienced the adults. When Eugene, one of William Byrd's servants, wetted his bed twice in a week, his master made him drink a pint of urine each time. Eugene never did it again. The first references to toilet training in domestic manuals occur at the end of the seventeenth century, and they are more concerned with instilling regular habits to evacuate the colon daily than with training in cleanliness.[16]

The principal interference with the infantile bowels, in those classes which could afford the harmful ministrations of doctors, was the constant application of purges and suppositories and enemas to ensure their forcible evacuation. Dr Héroard began to interfere with the excretory processes of the infant Louis from the age of two weeks and continued this close anal supervision for the rest of his life: it was, indeed, his prime preoccupation, as it was for other doctors of the period.[17] In this respect, the child was no worse off than the adult, except that his system was less able to stand the punishment it received, which no doubt raised the infantile mortality rate among the children of the rich, and that it may have stimulated a fixation at the anal stage of ego development.

Passage through the oral and anal stages of infantile development was thus probably relatively easy, with milk on demand, late weaning and late toilet training. It may well be that the genital stage of childhood was equally free from repression, and that the main problem in this area was premature over-stimulation. There is some little evidence to suggest that adults found the genital stage of childhood sexuality amusing rather than horrifying. This encouragement of sexual play may have been no more than one aspect of a general tendency to treat children from about two to seven as amusing pets to entertain the grown-ups. It was the one period in a child's life when his parents and other adults treated him other than harshly or with indifference.[18]

It should be emphasized that none of this historical evidence from the Early Modern period disproves Freud's theory about how at different stages of infantile development different erogenous zones become the foci of sexual stimulation, thus providing a logical explanation for the later relationship between oral, anal and genital pleasure. Nor does the historical record do anything to belittle the importance of sublimation, or of the unconscious operating with a secret dynamism of its own. What it does, however, is to cast very great doubt upon the assumption that the particular kinds of infantile traumas upon which Freud laid so much stress have been suffered by the whole of the human race at all times and in all places. It is now fairly clear that four of the main traumas (oral, anal, genital and oedipal) which Freud looked for and found among his patients and therefore assumed to be universal, are dependent on experiences which were peculiar to the late Victorian European middle-class society from which his patients came. As we shall see, children in the Early Modern period suffered a different, and perhaps even more psychologically disturbing, series of traumatic experiences.

ii. Areas of Repression

If children were weaned very late and were not severely toilet trained in the seventeenth century, and if there was no great emphasis on the repression of infant sexuality, in other ways they were treated with the utmost severity. For one thing, their physical mobility was severely reduced. For the first four months or so after birth, they were tightly bound in bandages so that they were unable to move either head or limbs. They were completely immobilized (plate 12). Only after about four months did they gain the use of their arms, but not their legs.[19] Although this was an immemorial custom over all of Europe, there is one indication that it may have been rather different in seventeenth-century England. In 1628 the French-born noblewoman Charlotte de la Trémouille, Countess of Derby, wrote home indignantly, 'I wish you could see the manner in which children are swaddled in this country. It is deplorable.'[20] Whether she meant that English children were more constrained than French, or less, is not at all clear.

The medical reasons behind this practice of swaddling were that 'for tenderness the limbs of a child may easily and soon bow and bend and take diverse shapes.' There was also a widespread popular fear that unless restrained the infant might tear off its ears, scratch out its eyes or break its legs. Finally, it was extremely convenient for the adults, since modern investigation shows that swaddling in fact slows down the infant's heartbeat and induces far longer sleep and less crying.[21] Swaddling also allowed the infant to be moved about like a parcel and left unattended in odd corners or hung on a peg on a wall without danger to life or limb and without overt protest. Psychological theories about how such treatment in infancy leads to adult passivity and docile obedience to the state, for example in Russia, hardly seems to be confirmed by the turbulent history of sixteenth- and seventeenth-century England and France where the same swaddling techniques were universally practised.[22] The long-term psychological effects of such restraints – if any – are therefore still unknown, while the convenience for parents or nurses is beyond dispute.

Once removed from the swaddling bandages, the boys were left free, but the girls were encased in bodices and corsets reinforced with iron and whalebone to ensure that their bodies were moulded to the prevailing adult fashion. Dressed in miniature adult clothes, they were expected to conform to the ideal of adult feminine shape and carriage, and in particular to maintain an upright posture and to walk slowly and gracefully. The contraptions used to achieve these ends often frustrated them, leading instead to the distortion or displacement of the organs, and sometimes even death. When in 1665 George Evelyn's two-year-old daughter Elizabeth died, the doctor told him that 'her iron bodice was her pain, and had hindered the lungs to grow'; the surgeon who examined the body 'found her breast bone pressed very deeply inwardly, and he said two of her ribs were broken, and the straightness of the bodice upon the vitals occasioned this difficulty of breathing and her death.'[23]

During the period from 1540 to 1660 there is a great deal of evidence, especially from Puritans, of a fierce determination to break the will of the child, and to enforce his utter subjection to the authority of his elders and superiors, and most especially of his parents. John Robinson, the first pastor of the Pilgrim Fathers in Holland, was only reflecting current ideas when he observed that 'surely there is in all children ... a stubbornness, and stoutness of mind arising from natural pride, which must in the first place be broken and beaten down.' 'Children should not know, if it could be kept from them, that they have a will in their own, but in their parents' keeping.'[24] In the seventeenth century the early training of children was directly equated with the bating of hawks or the breaking-in of young horses or hunting dogs. These were all animals which were highly valued and cherished in the society of that period, and it was only natural that exactly the same principle should be applied to the education of children, especially now that parents began to care more about them.

In the middle ages, schools had used physical punishment to enforce discipline, and the characteristic equipment of a schoolmaster was not so much a book as a rod or a bundle of birch twigs. The emblem of *Grammar* on Chartres Cathedral porch is a master threatening two children with a scourge; at Oxford University the conferring of the degree of Master of Grammar was accompanied by presentation of a birch as symbol of office and by the ceremonial flogging of a whipping-boy by the new Master.[25] But only an infinitesimal minority, mostly from the lower classes, was subjected to such discipline in the middle ages, since so few undertook the study of Latin grammar. Those who did so were presumably highly motivated to learn and therefore did not need brutal methods to make them work. Moreover, even in the schools, at any rate in France, there is a good deal of evidence to show that many punishments took the form of fines. Flogging began to be substituted for fines in the fifteenth century, but only in the case of the poor who could not pay the fines and were thought socially suitable for physical punishment, and even then only the very young.[26]

In the early sixteenth century, there were a number of significant changes; firstly flogging became the standard routine method of punishment for academic lapses for all schoolchildren, regardless of rank or age; secondly a far larger proportion of the population began to go to school, and therefore became liable to this discipline; thirdly, as education changed from a minority privilege to a widespread social obligation, many more schoolboys were poorly motivated to learn, and therefore created disciplinary problems most easily solved by the use of force. As a result corporal punishment at school became a standard practice applied to rich and poor, old and young, regardless of rank. In the late sixteenth and seventeenth centuries it was normal for the social elite to send boys to school rather than to have them taught at home by a private tutor. The argument in favour of elite boys going to public schools was that by mingling with other boys of all kinds, rich and poor, virtuous and vicious, friends and enemies, 'they learn the pratique of the world', as Roger North put it.[27]

There can be no doubt, therefore, that more children were being beaten in the sixteenth and early seventeenth century, over a longer age span, than ever before. It looks as if the greater evidence of brutality in the sixteenth-century home and school is a reflection of a harsher reality, not merely of a larger and more revealing body of written records. Whipping was now so normal a part of a child's experience that when a seventeenth-century moral theologian wished to convey to children some idea of Hell, the best way he could think of describing it was as 'a terrible place, that is worse a thousand times than whipping'. As for Heaven, it was a place where children 'would never be beat any more'.[28]

Scholastic punishments normally took two forms. The first and most common was to lay the child over a bench, or alternatively to horse him on the back of a companion, and to flog his naked buttocks with a bundle of birches until the blood flowed. The second was to strike his hand or mouth with a ferula, a flat piece of wood which expanded at the end into a pear-shape with a hole in the middle. One blow with this instrument was enough to raise a most painful blister.

There can be no doubt whatever that severe flogging was a normal and daily occurrence in the sixteenth- and seventeenth-century grammar school, and some of the most famous headmasters of the most elitist schools of their day, like Dr Busby of Westminster School or Dr Gill of St Paul's, were notorious for their savagery. Indeed, some of them seem to have been pathological sadists, and John Aubrey's account of Dr Gill's 'whipping-fits' suggests a man who had become the slave of a perverted sexual obsession. But what is significant is that elite parents were willing to give him a free hand over their sons without censure or restraint, since flogging was then regarded as the only reliable method of controlling both children and adults. In 1622 Henry Peacham reported that scholars were 'pulled by the ears, lashed over the face, beaten about the head with the great end of the rod, smitten upon the lips for every slight offence with the ferula.' Peacham deplored these sadistic excesses but explained them by the fact that schoolmasters believed that 'there is no other method of making a scholar but by beating him.' The routine normality of the practice allowed Ben Jonson to describe a schoolmaster as a man accustomed to 'sweeping his living from the posteriors of little children'.[29]

Nor was there any escape for the children. In the early sixteenth century Peter Carew ran away from Exeter Grammar School and took refuge on one of the turrets of the city wall, threatening to throw himself down if a master tried to recapture him. His father was summoned, seized the boy, had him coupled to a hound, led him home, and chained him in a dog-kennel until he managed to escape.[30]

It seems likely that institutionalized brutality was standard in public schools and grammar schools, but varied from master to master in the countless small private schools run by clergymen for a handful of local children and boarders in the seventeenth century. Some were miniature concentration camps run by sadists, while others were humane and understanding. But these latter cases, when they are mentioned in the records, are always described as exceptions to the rule. Thus Simonds D'Ewes records that he was never flogged by his London schoolmaster Henry Reynolds, explaining that 'he had a pleasing way of teaching, contrary to all others of that kind. For the rod and the ferula stood in his school rather as ensigns of his power than as instruments of his anger, and were rarely made use of for the punishment of delinquents. For he usually rewarded those who deserved well ... and he accounted the primative punishment of not rewarding the remiss and negligent equipolent to the severest correction.'[31] But D'Ewes was an exceptionally diligent and able student, always one of the best in the class, and as such was presumably normally free of the punishments meted out to his more dim-witted or idle companions.

The extension of flogging even reached into university education. During the late sixteenth century the colleges of Oxford and Cambridge had received for the first time a huge influx of sons of the wealthy laity, to house whom they had greatly enlarged their accommodation. The key feature of the sixteenth-century college was the application to lay children of the strict, prison-like conditions previously applied to regular clergy in monasteries and colleges. This was the time when the college assumed its now familiar function of acting *in loco parentis*, with all the aids of high walls, gates closed at 9 p.m., and strict internal surveillance by the tutors. This was also the time, between 1450 and 1660, when colleges freely used physical punishments on their younger students, normally, but not always, under the age of eighteen, either by public whippings in the hall or over a barrel in the buttery, or else by putting them in stocks in the hall. By the medieval statutes of Balliol and Lincoln Colleges, the college head had powers of physical punishment, but in the sixteenth century this authority was greatly extended, and delegated to deans and even tutors.[32] Aubrey, who entered Oxford in 1642, noted that there 'the rod was frequently used by the tutors and deans on his pupils, till Bachelors of Arts'.[33]

It should be emphasized that this widespread and constant use of flogging as the prime method of spreading a knowledge of the classics was the last thing that the Humanist educational reformers had in mind when they pressed for a classical training of the European elite. From Guarino to Vives to Erasmus, and from Elyot to Ascham to Mulcaster, they were to a man opposed to the indiscriminate use of severe physical punishments. They all advised that to spare the rod was to spoil the child, but they also believed that children could and should be enticed into the classics, not driven like cattle, and should be punished only for moral failures such as obstinacy or idleness, not for stupidity.[34] What happened in practice was that a man like Mulcaster, successively headmaster of Merchant Taylors' and St Paul's in the reign of Elizabeth, practised what he preached and ran his schools on model humanist lines. But the majority of lazier and less dedicated schoolmasters extended the medieval tradition of flogging on an ever increasing scale as classical education spread, since it was the easiest and least troublesome means of drilling Latin grammar into large numbers of thick or resistant skulls. Renaissance school practice thus eventually came to bear little relation to Renaissance educational theory: the subject matter was more grammatical, the method of learning more by rote memorizing, the discipline more brutal. In practice, post-Renaissance education, because of its insufferably tedious content and method of instruction, demanded effective repression of the will, the imagination, the emotions, and even intellectual curiosity. In part, at least, the increased use of physical punishment was therefore a natural accompaniment of the spread of this degenerate kind of classical learning as a subject of study in school and home. This connection was suggested by Locke, who asked, 'Why ... does the learning of Latin and Greek need the rod, when French and Italian needs it not? Children learn to dance and fence without whipping; nay arithmetic, drawing, etc., they apply themselves well enough to without beating'.[35]

In the very early sixteenth century, when Humanism was still riding high, some families in their domestic discipline in the home followed a different drummer. The Italian Stephen Guazzo had denounced as 'butchers' the many fathers of children who 'beat them continually, like slaves, for the least fault in the world', advice echoed by Thomas Becon in his catechism of 1550. The Humanist Sir Thomas More reminded his children that 'I never could endure to hear you cry. You know, for example, how often I kissed you, how seldom I whipped you. My whip was invariably a peacock's tail. Even this I wielded hesitantly and gently, so that sorry welts might not disfigure your tender seats. Brutal and unworthy to be called father is he who does not himself weep at the tears of his child.' But More was an exceptional man, as he himself hinted. His fellow Humanist, the Spaniard

Vives, recalled that 'there was nobody I did more flee, or was more loath to come nigh, than my mother when I was a child', and he himself advised parents that 'cherishing marreth sons, but it utterly destroyeth daughters'. This severity was powerfully reinforced by the first wave of Protestantism, and by her own account her pious parents led Lady Jane Grey a miserable life in the 1530s and 1540s. 'When I am in presence either of father or mother, whether I speak, keep silence, sit, stand or go, eat, drink, be merry or sad, be sewing, playing, dancing, or doing anything else, I must do it, as it were, in such weight, measure, and number, even so perfectly as God made the world, else I am so sharply taunted, so cruelly threatened, yea presently sometimes with pinches, nips and bobs, and some ways I will not name for the honour I bear them, so without measure misordered that I think myself in Hell.'[36] One recognizes in this bitter description the paradigm of the perfectionist parents, who were to dominate middle- and upper-class English upbringing for the next hundred years.

The fostering-out system by which children were sent away from home at an early age to act as servants or living-in apprentices in someone else's house meant that perhaps two out of every three households contained a resident adolescent who was not of the family. These servants and apprentices were even more exposed than the children to brutal punishments. In 1599 Simon Forman 'did bethong my boy [servant] with a rope's end.' In 1665 Pepys, who was by no means a cruel man, 'made my wife, to the disturbance of our house and neighbours, to beat our little girl [a maidservant], and then we shut her down into the cellar, and there she lay all night.'[37] Apprentices were usually indentured at the age of fourteen for seven years, and in London were sufficiently numerous to form a distinct adolescent subculture of their own. They were exposed to almost limitless sadism from their masters, mitigated only by the fact that the bolder spirits among them could, and sometimes did, sue their torturers for assault. These law suits reveal a female apprentice who was stripped naked, strung up by her thumbs and given twenty-one lashes; a boy who was beaten so severely that he could not stand upright and who spat blood for a fortnight; another who was flogged, salted and then held naked to a fire; another who was beaten so severely with a boat-hook that his hip was broken; and so on.[38].

Only psychotic parents treated their own children with such calculated ferocity, but whipping was the normal method of discipline in a sixteenth- or seventeenth-century home, mitigated and compensated for, no doubt, by a good deal of fondling when the child was docile and obedient. Both rewards and punishments took physical rather than psychological forms.

Up to the age of seven, the children were mostly left in the care of women, primarily their mother, nurse, and governess. Many of these women were demonstratively affectionate, but they all believed in the current doctrine of the need to crush the will. Roger North, a son of Dudley, fourth Lord North, recalled in old age that his upbringing in the mid-seventeenth century 'was in general severe but tender'. If the children were disobedient, their mother 'would reduce us to terms by the smart of correction; and which was more grievous, would force us to leave crying and condescend to the abject pitch of thanking the good rail [i.e. the rod], which she said was to break our spirits, which it did effectively.' As a successful product of the system, Roger North believed in it, and thought that the relaxation of discipline he perceived in his old age at the end of the century was leading to profligacy and debauchery.[39]

But not all children reacted so positively, and it is hardly surprising that this treatment meant that many children grew up with a fear and even hatred of their parents, particularly in the seventeenth century, when the ideological underpinnings of repression were breaking down. Gilbert Burnet, who was born in 1630, recalled in his old age that he was subjected to 'much severe correction; . . . the fear of that brought me under too great an uneasiness, and sometimes even to a hatred of my father. The sense of this may have perhaps carried me in the education of my children to the other extreme of too much indulgence.' Richard Norwood had a regular nightmare of parental rejection: 'Usually in my dreams I methought I saw my father always grievously angry with me.' Joseph Lister was regularly beaten by his mother, while Thomas Raymond recalled bitterly about his father: 'upon all occasions felt the effects of his choler, which was of great mischief unto me, being of a soft and timorous complexion'. Robert Boyle recalled that his father had 'a perfect aversion for fondness' to or from his children, while John Aubrey, who was always inclined to wild and hysterical exaggeration, claimed implausibly that in his youth, parents 'were as severe to their children as their schoolmasters; and their schoolmasters as masters of the House of Correction'. 'Fathers and mothers slashed their daughters . . . when they were perfect women.' As a result, 'the child perfectly loathed the sight of his parents as the slave his torture'. Aubrey is clearly not to be taken literally, and his remarks are significant primarily since he, like North and Burnet, was contrasting conditions before 1640 with the more amiable parent-child relations that he thought prevailed when he was writing in the late seventeenth century.[40] All three claimed to have lived through a period of marked change in the treatment of children.

In 1622 Robert Burton summed up the early seventeenth-century situation in critical, but accurate terms: 'Parents, and such as have the tuition and oversight of children, offend many times in that they are too stern, always threatening, chiding, brawling, whipping or striking; by means of which their poor children are so disheartened and cowed that they never after have any courage, a merry hour in their lives, or take pleasure in anything.'[41]

This severity towards children seems to have been as common in seventeenth-century France as in England, which suggests that the importance of Puritanism should not be exaggerated. In France, Pierre Charron also spoke of the 'almost universal' custom of 'beating, whipping, abusing and scolding children, and holding them in great fear and subjection'.[42] About the only case in which this disciplinary process in the home can be followed in great detail is that of the young son and heir of Henri IV of France, the future Louis XIII. The child was first whipped at the age of two, and the punishments continued after he became king at the age of nine. He was whipped on the buttocks with a birch or a switch, administered first by his nurse, the time being immediately he woke up on the morning after the transgression, which was usually obstinacy. The whippings increased in frequency when he was three, and on one occasion his father whipped him himself when in a rage with his son. As he grew older, his nurse could not control him, and the child was held down by soldiers while she beat him. At the age of ten, he still had nightmares of being whipped, and the threats to whip him only stopped at the age of thirteen, not long before his marriage.[43] If this was the treatment meted out to a future and even a reigning king in the early seventeenth century, on the instructions of his father, it is clear that the contemporaries quoted were describing no more than the reality about late sixteenth- and early seventeenth-century domestic relations between parents, governesses and children in the home. Admittedly mitigated by much physical caressing and fondling, including genital play, whipping was a regular part of the experience of a child.

As one might expect, there were even examples in the early seventeenth century of what is known today as the 'battered child syndrome' in which maternal or paternal hatred of the child reaches pathological proportions. Lady Abergavenny 'in a passion killed her own child about seven years old. She having been a great while whipping it, my Lord being grieved to hear it cry so terribly, went into the room to plead for it, and she threw it with such force on the ground she broke the skull; the girl lived but four hours after it.'

Indeed, it is clear that children often had as much or more to fear from their mothers than from their fathers, presumably because the psychological frustrations and anxieties of the former were vented on their helpless children. When flogging was the normal punishment it was hard for a mother to know how to satisfy her husband that discipline was being properly enforced. But many seem to have erred on the side of cruelty, so that Endymion Porter was careful to write to his wife, 'I would have you cut George's hair somewhat short, and not to beat him overmuch'.[44]

The breaking of the will was thus generally accepted as the prime aim of early education, and, as with animals, physical punishment was the standard method employed for the purpose. There were clear gradations of punishment, according to the recalcitrance of the child. Beatings could be mild or severe; on the hands, the face, or the buttocks; clothed or naked; administered by the nurse, the governess or tutor, or the mother or the father; using the hand or a birch rod. In addition, there was a whole armoury of moral terrors, from the fear of death and condemnation to the eternal torments of Hell, to the fear of ogres, witches and ghosts, who were frequently used by nurses to terrorize children into silence and obedience: the fairy tales of the period were shot through with cannibalism, murder and other horrors. On the other hand, typical Victorian punishments like locking up in dark cupboards and deprivation of food do not seem to have been used before the eighteenth century, since they depended on psychological pressure rather than physical force.

What makes this training different from what was to follow was not only its reliance on physical punishment, but also the absence of any graduated system of rewards. The advice to maintain coolness and distance between parents and children must have prevented the use of the giving or withdrawal of love as a method of control. The main rewards were physical fondling of the very young, which must mainly have been limited to nurses and servants by the doctrine of parental distance, and the cold comfort of moral approbation.

This extension of the use of physical punishment throughout the whole educational system at home and in school merely reflected a growing use of this method of social control throughout the society, including naturally the home. A late sixteenth-century Dutchman, appropriately enough called Batty, who was rapidly translated into English, developed the theory that the providence and wisdom of God had especially formed the human buttocks so that they could be severely beaten without incurring serious bodily injury.[45] The late sixteenth and early seventeenth centuries were for

England the great flogging age: every town and every village had its whipping-post, which was in constant use as a means of preserving social order.

This stress on domestic discipline and the utter subordination of the child found expression in extraordinary outward marks of deference which English children were expected to pay to their parents in the sixteenth and early seventeenth centuries. It was customary for them when at home to kneel before their parents to ask their blessing every morning, and even as adults on arrival at and departure from the home. This was a symbolic gesture of submission which John Donne believed to be unique in Europe. The children of the widowed Lady Alice Wandesford in the 1640s knelt daily to ask her blessing, and in 1651 her twenty-eight-year-old eldest son knelt for her blessing before leaving on a journey. Even when grown up, sons were expected to keep their hats off in their parents' presence, while daughters were expected to remain kneeling or standing in their mother's presence. 'Gentlemen of thirty and forty years old', recalled Aubrey, 'were to stand like mutes and fools bareheaded before their parents; and the daughters (grown women) were to stand at the cupboard-side during the whole time of their proud mother's visit, unless (as the fashion was) leave was desired, forsooth, that a cushion should be given to them to kneel upon, ... after they had done sufficient penance in standing.' Well into his middle age Sir Dudley North 'would never put on his hat or sit down before his father, unless enjoined to it'. Elizabeth, Countess of Falkland, always knelt in her mother's presence, sometimes for an hour at a time, despite the fact that she had married above her parents into the peerage, and that she was 'but an ill kneeler and worse riser'. In 1654 Thomas Cobbett, a Puritan émigré minister, recommended that children 'should rise up and stand bare before their parents when they come to them or speak to them'.[46] In the first half of the seventeenth century a son, even when grown up, would commonly address his father in a letter as 'sir', and sign himself 'your humble obedient son', 'your son in continuance of all obedience', or 'your most obedient and loving son'. In the 1680s Edmund Verney as an undergraduate at Oxford cautiously began his letters home 'Most honoured father', while those he received began with the peremptory word 'Child'. As late as 1715 the Earl of Coventry's daughter Anne regularly addressed her father in her letters as 'Dear Sir,' and concluded with 'Your very obedient humble servant and dutiful daughter.'[47]

A New England book of etiquette of 1715, which copied English works of the previous century, had the following advice to offer to children in the home:

1. Make a bow always when you come home, and be immediately uncovered.
2. Be never covered at home, especially before thy parents or strangers.
3. Never sit in the presence of thy parents without bidding, tho' no stranger be present.
    . . . .
6. Never speak to thy parents without some title of respect, viz.: Sir, Madam, etc.
7. Approach near thy parents at no time without a bow.
8. Dispute not nor delay to obey thy parents' commands.[48]

In some of the more devout households of early eighteenth-century America, these deferential customs were apparently still maintained. It was reported that the children of the great theologian, preacher, scholar and administrator Jonathan Edwards 'were uncommonly respectful to their parents. When their parents came into the room, they all rose instinctively from their seats, and never resumed them until their parents were seated; and when either parent was speaking, no matter with whom they had been conversing, they were immediately silent and attentive.'[49]

This pattern of extreme deference to parents in the home was in full conformity with behaviour norms of the society at large. Thus the doffing of the hat, the bowing, and the respectful forms of address to superiors were all part of the disciplinary rules of late sixteenth- and early seventeenth-century colleges. The 1612 Statutes of Wadham College, Oxford, ordered that when a Bachelor met a Master, he should take his hat off once, either on greeting or on leaving; undergraduates, however, were to keep their hats off all the time they were in the presence of Bachelors or Masters, while all members of the college were to treat the Warden with the greatest respect. The Oxford University Statutes of 1636 prescribed that 'the juniors shall show due and suitable reverence to their seniors both in public and private, that is, undergraduates to Bachelors, Bachelors of Arts to Masters, and in like manner Masters to Doctors; that is, by yielding to them the best places at meetings, by giving way when they meet, and by uncovering the head at a suitable distance and by a reverent greeting and address.'[50]

It would be quite wrong to suppose that in the sixteenth and early seventeenth centuries conformity to these behaviour patterns aroused widespread resentment. Human beings – and especially children – can adapt fairly easily to a very wide range of expectations, from the repressive to the permissive, so long as the rules are clearly understood and generally accepted. Under conditions in which everyone knows and accepts his place, the deferential system provides a comfortable framework for all social relationships, at least as comfortable as the egalitarian norms of American society today. They only cease to work harmoniously when the premises on which they are based come under challenge. The prescriptions, therefore, represented ideals congruent to a particular phase of English development, both in the family and in society generally, which was confined to the sixteenth and early seventeenth centuries. The full significance of these symbolic gestures and use of words to indicate filial deference becomes apparent only when they are contrasted with the very different modes of the late seventeenth and eighteenth centuries.

One of the most effective methods used to socialize children in the seventeenth century was to teach them, at a very early age, to be afraid of death and of the possibility of eternal damnation. It was standard advice in the sixteenth and seventeenth centuries to tell them to think much about death; and since it was then so likely a prospect for a child, it was reasonable that they should be well prepared. The advice offered to children of John Norris in 1694 merely repeated the by now rather outdated wisdom of the past century:

be ... much ... in the contemplation of the four last things, Heaven, Hell, Death and Judgment. Place yourselves frequently upon your deathbeds, in your coffins, and in your graves. Act over frequently in your minds the solemnity of your own funerals; and entertain your imaginations with all the lively scenes of mortality. Meditate much upon the places, and upon the days of darkness, and upon the fewness of those that shall be saved; and be always with your hourglass in your hands, measuring out your own little span and comparing it with the endless circle of eternity.[51]

The Boston Puritan Cotton Mather, at the same period, himself an anachronism in his own time, was always impressing on his children the imminence of death, of themselves or their friends or their father, and turning the subject to moral profit. Once he decided that 'I would oblige each of the children to retire and ponder on that question: what should I wish to have done if I were now adying. And report unto me their answer to the question, of which I may take unspeakable advantage, to inculcate piety upon them.'[52]

One example from the diary of Samuel Sewall of Boston, who was an enlightened and loving parent, will serve to illustrate the use of this very common psychological control device, employed especially by Puritans on both sides of the Atlantic. When in 1690 a little boy aged nine died of smallpox, Sewall took the opportunity to tell his eight-year-old son Samuel about it, and to warn him 'what need he had to prepare for death'. Sam seemed not to be impressed at the time, but later that day 'he burst out into a bitter cry and said he was afraid he should die'. Nervous children could be temporarily driven hysterical by this treatment. One afternoon in 1696, Sewall's fifteen-year-old daughter Betty 'a little after dinner burst out in an amazing cry, which caused all the family to cry too'. She explained that 'she was afraid she should go to Hell, her sins were not pardoned', a conclusion she reached from a sermon her father read to her and from her own reading of Cotton Mather. Five weeks later she was still distraught and came to her father as soon as he was awake, to tell him that she 'was afraid [she] should go to Hell, like Spira, not Elected'. Ten weeks later she was still in the same profound melancholia, and could hardly read her prescribed chapter of the Bible for weeping. Six months later, she was still not cured, and was a prey to fits of passionate weeping, saying that she 'was a reprobate, loves not God's people as she should'. [53]

iii. The Causes of Repression

This evidence all suggests strict subordination of children to parents and a high degree of severity adopted in their upbringing in the sixteenth century. Paradoxically enough, this was the first result of a greater interest in children. So long as no-one cared about them very much, they could be left to run wild, or in the hands of nurses, servants and tutors. But the Reformation – and in Catholic Europe the Counter-Reformation – drive for moral regeneration brought with it an increasing concern to suppress the sinfulness of children. A pedagogic movement, which had begun a century earlier with the Italian Renaissance as a glorification of the purity and innocence of the child, was twisted in its late sixteenth- and early seventeenth-century northern religious transplantation into a deadly fear of the liability of children to corruption and sin, particularly those cardinal sins of pride and disobedience. The threat of religious, intellectual and political chaos triggered off by the Reformation induced moral theologians – who were the most articulate leaders of educated opinion – to agree that the only hope of preserving social order was to concentrate on the right disciplining and education of children. This accounts in large measure for the sudden access of interest in pedagogy in the second and third decades of the sixteenth century, and the swamping of the more gentle and affectionate ideas of the Humanists. [54]

The doctrine of Original Sin strongly encouraged the stress on repression rather than encouragement as the core of educational theory (plate 13). 'If thou smite him with the rod, thou shalt deliver his soul from Hell', was a quotation from the Bible that Protestants took very seriously indeed.[55] In their standard handbook on the family of the early seventeenth century, the Puritan preachers Robert Cleaver and John Dod warned parents that 'the young child which lieth in the cradle is ... altogether inclined to evil' – a piece of conventional wisdom which Richard Allestree merely repeated half a century later in 1663. Oliver Heywood recollected that his mother 'though she was very indulgent to us, yet she was severe and sharp against sin'.[56] Many late sixteenth- and seventeenth-century mothers were both caring and repressive at the same time, for the simple reason that the two went together.

Because of this conviction of the innate sinfulness of the child, the only solution seemed to be to crush his will. For the child was both the hope of the future – the embodiment of parental ambitions to create a generation of virtue and godliness that would presage the Second Coming – and, at the same time, the negation of all such aspirations, the incarnation of Original Sin, the victim from birth of the manifold and endless temptations of the Devil. Puritans in particular, therefore, were profoundly concerned about their children, loved them, cherished them, prayed over them and subjected them to endless moral pressure. At the same time they feared and even hated them as agents of sin within the household, and therefore beat them mercilessly. Even the gentle John Bunyan was severe with children (plate 13).

In the 1520s William Tyndale gave forewarning of what was in store for Protestant children: 'if thou wilt not obey, as at His commandment, then are we charged to correct thee, yea and if thou repent not and amend thyself, God shall slay thee by his officers and punish thee everlastingly'. Calvin had decreed the death penalty as the punishment for disobedience to parents, and in the 1640s both Connecticut and Massachusetts turned the precept into legislation, although so far as is known only a handful of children were ever executed for this crime. In Connecticut, the magistrates were authorized in 1642 to commit a child to the House of Correction on complaint from his parents about 'any stubborn or rebellious carriage', while Massachusetts in 1646 imposed the death penalty for any child over sixteen who 'shall curse or smite their natural father or mother', or even refuse to obey their orders.[57]

Not only were most of the most popular child-rearing handbooks written by Puritans, but Puritans seem to have been exceptionally prominent among authors of books for children published before 1700. Of those authors whose religious opinions can be identified, twice as many were Puritans or

Dissenters as were conformist Anglicans, despite the enormous pre-ponderance of the latter in the population both before 1640 and after 1660.[58] This may be partly because nonconformists are better recorded and more easily identified than Anglicans, but even so the discrepancy is both striking and persuasive: Puritans were abnormally concerned about children and their upbringing.

One reason for this particular emphasis in Puritan circles on the education of children, and their salvation from the hands of the Devil, is that it was only by the mass conversion of the younger generation that they could hope to create or perpetuate the godly society to which they aspired. Before 1642 they lacked political authority in England; in their brief hour of triumph in the 1640s and 1650s they tried desperately to convert the masses by Draconian moral legislation; and after 1660 they once more became a persecuted minority. In New England they predominated politically, but saw the next generations steadily backsliding before their eyes. No wonder they beat their children and prayed over them, for they were the only hope for the future.

The second reason for the severity of the treatment accorded to children at this time is the rapid spread of knowledge of the Bible, and Protestant treatment of the book as an authoritative source on all subjects. The *Apocrypha* and *Proverbs* contain some extremely harsh instructions about how to bring up children. Sirach in the *Apocrypha*, who was quoted with approval by the Elizabethan musican and tutor Thomas Wythorne, was particularly severe, and yet his advice struck a congenial chord among sixteenth-century parents. 'If thou play with him, he shall bring thee to heaviness. Laugh not with him lest thou weep with him also, and lest thy teeth be set on edge at last.. . .' The advice is to keep psychological distance. No hint of tenderness is to be permitted, since this would undermine authority and destroy deference.[59]

These recommendations were taken up by Protestant moral theologians and repeated to a wide audience. 'Bow down his neck while he is young', quoted Thomas Becon from the *Apocrypha* in his catechism of 1550, 'and beat him on his sides while he is a child, lest he wax stubborn and be disobedient unto thee, and so bring sorrow to thy heart'. In the newly sanctified conjugal marriage, the duty of the wife and mother was to assist her husband in the task of the repression of their children. She 'holds not his hand from due strokes, but bares their skins with delight to his fatherly stripes'.[60] The last factor to be born in mind is that immature children were regarded as mere animals lacking the capacity to reason, and therefore to be broken in just as one would break in a puppy, a foal or a hawk.

The psychological coolness and physical severity that characterized the upbringing of children in late sixteenth- and early seventeenth-century England can thus be explained in terms of specific factors peculiar to the culture of the time. They were part of the traditional cultural baggage of the age, a set of values which were deeply internalized and were congruent with the social organization. They were probably accepted by children as part of the natural order of things, just as the harshly hierarchical and authoritarian character of the society as a whole was accepted by the adults. By putting the treatment of children in the sixteenth century into this broader context, it becomes intelligible and even reasonable.

It is possible, however, that there were deeper psychological causes, although they hardly seem necessary to explain the phenomenon. One theory has it that this obsession with childish 'stubbornness' or 'obstinacy' was caused by the personal insecurity of the parents in a hierarchical society; that there existed in all pre-modern societies a constant tension between the natural desire for freedom of the individual will and the pressing need for social order. According to this theory, parents were determined to break the wills of their children since their own wills were constantly being subordinated to those of others.[61] It is perfectly true that in the hierarchical, deferential society of Early Modern Europe, men and women were constantly obliged to emphasize their subordination to superiors by overt marks of respect, particularly by removing their hats in their presence or giving them the wall in the street. Conversely, they constantly asserted their superiority over inferiors by insisting on identical marks of respect and obedience from those below them. It was indeed a society in which the free expression of the will could not be tolerated. Since all authoritarian societies depend on authoritarian child-rearing practices, Early Modern England was no exception to the rule.

The cause of this passion for crushing the will of the child went deeper than this, however, since it was applied with particular emphasis to the social elite, including kings. It was at the most elite public schools like Eton and Westminster that flogging was then at its most ferocious – and where it has lasted longest, indeed into our own day. The instructions given by Henri IV to the governess of the future Louis XIII, when the child was six years old, were clear and explicit: 'I wish and command you to whip him every time that he is obstinate or does something bad . . . I know from experience that I myself benefited, for at his age I was much whipped. That is why I want you to whip him and to make him understand why.'[62] The motivation in whipping a future king was clearly not to teach deference in a deferential society, since he was destined to become the apex of the pyramid: it was to teach him to control his will.

Another theory has it that the process was an infinitely repetitive one related to individual psychology. 'Fathers whipped their sons for their own good because they themselves were whipped as children. These fathers had been thwarted in their own infantile efforts to be autonomous', leaving them with 'a pervasive sense of shame and doubt'.[63] But there is absolutely no evidence that Henri IV himself suffered from any such feelings: he seems to have been the very epitome of the well-adjusted, dynamic and commanding extrovert personality. In any case, his father had died early and he had been brought up by a strong-minded mother. The theoretical objection to such an explanation is that it is incapable of explaining change, since each successive generation is automatically obliged, by the very fact of its own childhood experience, to impose the same experience on its children. And yet there were to be very significant changes during the eighteenth century in this very area of the enforcement on the young child of obedience to superiors.

A more convincing theory has it that the deferential society is itself a reflection of the defence mechanism of the ego when it discovers a basic conflict between its own impulses to autonomy and the strict canons of obedience ruthlessly enforced by its parents. Thus the deferential behaviour of the children is a defensive response to ego repression, as the only way to survive, while the authoritarian and remote behaviour of the parents is an expression of the original desire for autonomy, which now at last finds an outlet in the bullying of their own children.[64] This thesis makes good sense, and could also be applied to explain the persistence for so long of the traditional experience of an English public school, where in the first year the boy is a virtual slave at the mercy of the older boys and in the last he turns the tables and in his turn acts as a cruel and arbitrary tyrant towards his juniors.

iv. Control of Occupation and Marriage

Paternal absolutism in the family was not only the basis for order in the society at large. It also had specific ends in view within the family system of the age, for obedience which began in little things was expected to lead to obedience in big ones. The practical benefit to be gained by parents from the extraordinary measures taken to break the child's will at an early stage was that later on he would accept with passive resignation their decisions in the two most important choices of his life, that of an occupation, and that of a marriage partner.

a. Choice of Occupation. The choice of a career did not affect girls, for whom the only option was marriage. But it was the parents who decided, with the interests of the family primarily in mind, whether a boy was to be prepared to fulfil the duties of a country gentleman or to be given specialized training for the Church, the law, trade, or some other occupation. When Sir Peter Legh forced his younger son Thomas to adopt a clerical career in 1619–22, against his repeated objections and declarations of a total lack of vocational interest, all the young man could do was to write acidly to his father that 'I ... trust you have begged of God, together with my consent unto your will, his acceptance of my weak endeavours and performances'.[65]

This was not an exceptional case, for in upper-class circles it was the father who decided while they were still children which of the younger sons should be educated at the university to go into the Church, which should learn Latin and go on to the Inns of Court to become a lawyer, and which should be apprenticed in London to become a merchant. Each case involved long planning ahead and a heavy financial investment; the choice had to be made by the age of fourteen, and once begun there was no turning back. The only children of this class who were free were those who were trained for nothing in particular, and were allowed to hang about the family home or were sent off to make their own way in the world as best they could. By the seventeenth century education was already dictating career-choice, which is why parents were so angry when their children balked. In 1685 Edmund Verney wrote furiously to his nineteen-year-old eldest son, Ralph: 'I hear you hate learning and your mind hankers after travelling. I will not be taught by my cradle how to breed it up; it is insolence and impudence in any child to presume so much as to offer it.' The memory of this mild act of insubordination still rankled some months later, when young Ralph died suddenly of a fever. His father saw the hand of God in the tragedy and hastened to press the moral home to his second, and now only, son: 'I ... exhort you to be wholly ruled and guided by me, and to be perfectly obedient to me in all things according to your bounden duty. ... For should you do otherwise and contrary in the least, ... I am afraid that you will be in that evil circumstance snatched away by death in your youth, as your poor brother was last week.' One wonders whether Edmund remembered this warning when the boy died four years later. It was not until the eighteenth century that fathers began to give their children more freedom of choice in the selection of a career or occupation, as attitudes towards patriarchal power slowly shifted. In 1708 *The British Apollo* told its readers that 'it is a custom not more common than imprudent to dispose of children in ways of living not at all agreeable to their genius and inclinations'.[66] The habit persisted, but criticism was mounting.

b. Marriage Arrangements in the Propertied Classes. The choice of marriage partner concerned both boys and girls and was especially important in a society where there were large financial and political stakes in marriage and where divorce was virtually impossible. Almost all children until the end of the sixteenth century were so conditioned by their upbringing and so financially helpless that they acquiesced without much objection in the matches contrived for them by their parents. The moral justification for parental control was derived, as has been seen, from the social values of the society and from the Fifth Commandment. 'Honour thy father and mother' was a sacred precept reiterated by both Protestant preachers and state propagandists, and interpreted to mean strict obedience. When this argument began to fail after the middle of the seventeenth century, one defender of traditional behaviour tried in 1663 to base filial obedience on the sanctity of private property: 'Children are so much the goods, the possessions of their parent, that they cannot, without a kind of theft, give away themselves without the allowance of those that have the right in them'. This was an ingenious attempt to shore up ancient but decaying patterns of authority by using new economic theories, but it was not very convincing.[67]

A pragmatic calculation of family interest was the accepted viewpoint of the sixteenth century, and the one upon which the approach to marriage in real life was normally based. The elite, however, were also subjected by the poets and playwrights to propaganda for an entirely antithetical ideal of romantic love, as expressed for example in Shakespeare's *Sonnets* and plays. There was a long tradition of love poetry in the late sixteenth and seventeenth centuries that ran directly across the norms and practices of its readers, although, as has been seen, love intrigues played a central role in the life of the young attendants at court and in noble households. Rochester in about 1675 summed up the values expressed in this type of literature:

> Love, the most generous passion of the mind,
> The softest refuge innocence can find,
> The safe director of unguarded youth,
> Fraught with kind wishes and secured with truth.
> That cordial drop Heaven in our cup has thrown
> To make the nauseous draught of life go down.[68]

Until romanticism temporarily triumphed in the late eighteenth century, there was thus a clear conflict of values between the idealization of love by some poets, playwrights and the authors of romances on the one hand, and its rejection as a form of imprudent folly and even madness by all theologians, moralists, authors of manuals of conduct, and parents and adults in general. Everyone knew about it, some experienced it, but only a minority of young courtiers made it a way of life, and even they did not necessarily regard it as a suitable basis for life-long marriage.

The accepted wisdom of the age was that marriage based on personal selection, and thus inevitably influenced by such ephemeral factors as sexual attraction or romantic love, was if anything less likely to produce lasting happiness than one arranged by more prudent and more mature heads. This view finds confirmation in anthropological studies of the many societies where love has not been regarded as a sound basis for marriage, and where one girl is as good as another, provided that she is a good housekeeper, a breeder, and a willing sexual playmate. Dr Johnson was not merely being a cranky eccentric when he persisted in taking this now outmoded view in the late eighteenth century. He argued that 'marriages would in general be as happy, and often more so, if they were all made by the Lord Chancellor, upon a due consideration of the characters and circumstances, without the parties having any choice in the matter'.[69] In the early sixteenth century, these were views which would not have excited any comment or controversy.

In any case, most children inevitably took the same calculating attitude towards marriage as their parents, so that intergenerational conflict was reduced because they shared the same objectives. In 1639 Christopher Guise was the twenty-two-year-old son and heir of a moderately wealthy Gloucestershire gentry family, living on an allowance of £80 a year. He was unwilling to get married, 'having observed some young married couples to live in a very narrow compass'. Three years later, however, at the urging of his parents, he married the daughter of Sir Lawrence Washington, who was clearly a good financial catch. He did it merely in order to get the family estate firmly settled on him, and to extract from his father £400 a year as present maintenance (and future jointure for his widow). 'I was at last content to make all sure, at the loss of my loved liberty.' He was not held in marriage bonds very long, however, since his wife died within seven weeks 'and left me again at liberty', although a little melancholy. Back from the Civil War in 1645, and overwhelmed with debt, 'I found myself in a manner enforced to look after another match', and finally managed to capture the daughter of a wealthy Londoner. When she too died in 1659 he took back to live with him an ex-mistress from earlier days, who looked after him until he died eleven years later, and in return was rewarded with a substantial cash sum, a life annuity of £100 a year for herself, and another of £50 a year for her son, who was presumably an illegitimate child of Sir Christopher.[70] It is a revealing story of the benefits and defects of the mercenary marriage system, and the role of mistresses as an emotional escape-hatch.

In the middle ages and the early sixteenth century, it was customary for noblemen and gentlemen to sign contracts by which their children's marriages were sold long in advance of maturity, or to leave instructions in their wills about whom the children were to marry. They were still doing so in the more backward north right up to the end of the sixteenth century. In 1558 Michael Wentworth specified in his will that 'if any of my daughters will not be advised by my executors, but of their own fantastical brain bestow themselves lightly upon a light person, then I will that daughter to have' only £66 instead of the £100 which was promised to the obedient. This was powerful posthumous economic blackmail.

When high politics were at stake, extreme measures were sometimes resorted to. It is alleged that in the early seventeenth century, Sir Edward Coke, the ex-Chief Justice, not only abducted his daughter by force from her mother – which is certainly true – but also had her 'tied to a bed-post and severely whipped', in order to force her consent to marriage with the mentally unstable brother of the Duke of Buckingham, a manoeuvre that was designed to restore her father's lost favour at Court.[71] The marriage duly took place, soon followed by the wife's desertion of her husband for a more congenial lover.

It is significant that up to 1640 the landed classes continued to endure, although with increasing discontent, the practice of wardship, by which the marriages of young fatherless heirs and heiresses of landed property were put up for sale by the Crown. The Court of Wards was tolerated as long as the society upon which it levied its tribute had itself little respect for individual freedom of choice, and treated its own children with as little consideration for personal feelings as did the Court itself. Thus in 1567 the first Lord Rich made provision in his will for his illegitimate son Richard. He directed his executors to purchase from the Crown 'one woman ward or some other woman' with an estate of £200 a year clear 'for a marriage ... to the said Richard'. If Richard were to refuse the girl, he lost all his inheritance, for the executors were then 'to sell the said ward ... to the uttermost advantage'. The possibility that the girl ward might refuse

Richard clearly did not cross Lord Rich's mind. It was not until a century later, at the Restoration, that the Court of Wards was finally abolished, in part at least due to a growth of novel ideas about personal autonomy, and in part in order to restore control of marriage to the family, and to remove this form of inheritance tax upon the elite.[72]

Only a handful of children resisted parental dictation before the end of the sixteenth century, and their rebellion was soon crushed. In 1436 an unwilling girl was forced into a betrothal by her parents in Armagh, Ireland. During the ceremony, at which she wept and resisted, her mother hit her with a stick until it broke, while her father knocked her down. In the mid-fifteenth century, Elizabeth, daughter of Agnes Paston, obstinately insisted on choosing her own husband. To bring her to heel, her mother put her in virtual solitary confinement, forbidden to speak either to visitors or to male servants. In addition, 'she hath since Easter the most part been beaten once in the week or twice, and sometimes twice on a day, and her head broken in two or three places'.[73] It is hardly surprising that few children had the strength of will to resist such treatment.

In the sixteenth century, violence was less necessary since the duty of filial obedience had been more successfully internalized. On the rare occasions when children threatened to marry to suit themselves, parents were quick to emphasize the traditional need to consider the interests of the lineage and the obligation to obey one's parents. In 1658 the fourth Lord Mountgarret's eldest son, Richard Butler, fell in love with Emilia Blundell, the daughter of an impoverished gentleman. When he learned what was in the wind, his lordship wrote a stern fatherly letter to his son. 'I am informed that you are so miserably blinded as to incline to marry, and so with one wretched act to undo both the gentlewoman and yourself, and (as much as in you lies) to dash all my designs which concern my self and house. Son, I charge you by the bond of nature and duty which you owe me, that you presume not to proceed in so desperate a purpose, as a thing which I detest and abhor. And therefore lay these words close in to your heart, and read in them as high indignation of mine, as if they were far more sharper. . . . Be not you wanting in the obedience of a son in a matter of so great importance as this to me and my family: but let this . . . suffice to keep you from plunging yourself into ruin. . . . If it do not, I shall take order that the blow smart there where in justice it should.'[74]

This firm reminder of where morality and family duty lay, coupled with the final ominous threat, was sufficient to break off the match.

In the seventeenth century, the control of marriage extended beyond that of parents over children to that of patrons over clients. Thus when in 1678 the Reverend William Butterfield asked Sir Ralph Verney for his dead father's living of Middle Claydon, Sir Ralph temporized, 'desiring first to see him married'. Having no one particularly in mind, the young man consulted Sir Ralph, who recommended a Miss Sarah Lovett. William obediently 'goes a-wooing might and main to Miss Lovett'. He was lent Sir Ralph's son Edmund's hat to improve his appearance, but it did not fit. Even so, in the end he won both the wife and the living.[75] It is very doubtful whether Butterfield found anything strange or unpleasant about this manoeuvre. He wanted the living, and without it he could not afford to marry. He had no personal preference of his own, and naturally turned to an older man for advice. And whom else should he ask but his prospective patron? Once given the hint he went to work and won the lady's consent, and was no doubt fully satisfied with his bargain.

Authoritarian control by parents over the marriages of their children inevitably lasted longest in the richest and most aristocratic circles, where the property, power and status stakes were highest. The enormous complexities of arranging for the marriage of a young girl of high aristocratic family in the mid-seventeenth century is well brought out by the case of Betty Livingstone, a daughter of the first Earl of Newburgh.[76]Born in 1649, she was dumped in the remote country house of her paternal aunt Dorothy Lady Stanhope, when her father fled the country to avoid arrest by Parliament for his royalist intrigues. She stayed there after her father's return to England in 1660, since meanwhile her mother had died, and he had married again. In 1663, when she was fourteen, through the influence of her half-brother the Duke of Richmond, she was given a place at the court of Charles II as maid of the Privy Chamber of the Queen. But in two years she ran up such heavy debts that she withdrew again to her aunt in the country.

At this point, at the age of fifteen-and-a-half, her various relatives began to plan her marital future for her. First, her aunt arranged a marriage with Lord Brudenell, son and heir to the Earl of Cardigan, but she rejected him out of hand because he was a Catholic. Three years later, at eighteen-and-a-half, Betty fell in love with Lord Annesley, eldest son of the Earl of Anglesey, but her aunt refused to agree to the match since she had grander plans for her. Lord Roos, future first Duke of Rutland, was in the process of divorcing his wife by Act of Parliament (at that time a very unusual and difficult procedure), and it was proposed that as soon as he was free, Betty should marry him. Meanwhile, a stop was put to the affair with Lord Annesley by the latter's father's arranging behind his back to marry him to

Elizabeth Manners, Lord Roos' sister. But Lord Annesley was secretly defying his father and urging Betty to run away from home and marry him privately. Encouraged secretly by her father, she wrote a letter of agreement, but the messenger handed it to Annesley's father instead of to Annesley himself. His father opened it, and told his son that he would disinherit him if he did not immediately marry Elizabeth Manners, the agreement for which had finally been concluded between the two fathers totally without the knowledge of those most concerned. Lord Annesley was convinced that his father meant what he said, and in fear of losing his inheritance he backed out of his promise to Betty and duly married Elizabeth Manners.

Lord Roos' divorce was hanging fire in Parliament, so that he could not press his suit. Betty's father, therefore, now stepped in and ordered her to marry Robert Delaval, son and heir of Sir Ralph Delaval. The young man came to visit, and Betty found him not at all to her taste. But she agreed to marry him on condition that her debts incurred at court were first paid off with £1,000 which she had inherited, rather than that it should go to her marriage portion. A fearful family row followed, during which her father threatened to remove her from her aunt's and carry her away as a virtual prisoner to his own country house. But she stuck to her guns, finally won her – purely financial – point, and then obediently married Robert Delaval. The marriage was a most unhappy one, since when he was not struck down by asthma, the husband was off on heavy drinking-bouts with a set of debauched companions. But no doubt the marriage was doomed from the start, since Betty never pretended to like her husband and bitterly regretted the loss of her independence: 'That pleasing word of liberty being now no more to be pronounced by me as what I have a right to, I cannot but, at the first putting on of shackles, find their weight heavy.' In a remorseful moment, she once admitted that it was her own sharp tongue which often goaded her husband into his excesses, so there were clearly faults on both sides.

These were not the only parents of the high aristocracy in the north who still continued in the late seventeenth century to exercise full control over marriage, although directed now against increasingly obstinate and defiant children. When the daughter of Lord Wharton married in 1687, perfectly respectably but against his will, he made the local parson refuse her the sacrament, and bullied her into surrendering her legal rights to a £3,000 portion.[77]

Occasional examples of this sort of behaviour occurred even in the early years of the eighteenth century. When in 1719 the son and heir of the Duke of Richmond was married to the immature daughter of Lord Cadogan, 'the marriage was made to cancel a gambling debt; the young people's consent having been the last thing thought of: the Earl of March was sent for from school, and the young lady from the nursery; a clergyman was in attendance and they were told that they were immediately to become man and wife. The young lady is not reported to have uttered a word; the gentleman exclaimed "They are surely not going to marry me to that dowdy".' But the marriage took place, and the pair immediately parted, the groom to set off with his tutor for some years on the Grand Tour, the bride to go home to her mother. By now, however, the circumstances seem to have been sufficiently unusual to arouse comment. It is also true, that, entirely by serendipity, the marriage eventually turned out to be a fairy-tale success. The young man returned from the Grand Tour some years later, noticed a beautiful young woman sitting near him at the theatre, and found that it was his own wife. According to the story, they lived happily ever after.[78] But this was a subsequent bonus of the gods, bestowed upon what had been a ruthlessly arranged, purely mercenary marriage of the most old-fashioned kind.

These are stories about the very topmost levels of aristocratic society, who by virtue of their rank also had strong ties to the court. It shows that in some families in these circles, the principle of dictatorial control of parents over the marriage of their children, and the general acceptance of financial considerations as the sole basis of marriage, remained almost unimpaired as late as 1720, at a time when both were disappearing among the squirarchy, and had vanished among the bourgeoisie.

Indeed, among the Scottish high aristocracy, these high-handed, but now archaic, ways of handling marriage continued unimpaired well into the mid-eighteenth century. In the 1740s, Caroline, daughter of the second Duke of Argyll, fell in love with the brilliant and attractive Lord Quarendon, but was obliged by her father to marry the dull, worthy, but wealthy and high-ranking Lord Dalkeith instead. 'She was led to the altar more dead than alive and there plighted her unwilling vows.' Another daughter, Mary, was bargained over by the parents like a prize animal at a fair, and was finally sold to the son of the Earl of Leicester, despite the fact that both father and son were notorious rakes. She wept daily and treated her fiancé scornfully before the marriage, in revenge for which he coolly refused to go to bed with her on their wedding night. She retaliated by refusing to go to bed with him at all, thus frustrating the whole purpose of the match, which was to produce a son and heir. To punish her, she was carried off to the family seat at Holkham and virtually imprisoned there, being referred to jocularly by the household servants as 'our Virgin Mary'. Finally, a separation had to be arranged.[79]

Only if a girl of aristocratic family possessed enormous persistence, obstinacy and strength of will could she hope to marry the individual of her choice. But it could be done. In 1625 there was born Mary, daughter of that most successful of all early seventeenth-century self-made men, the wilful and imperious first Earl of Cork. In 1639, when she was only fourteen, Mary's father agreed to marry her to Mr Hamilton, son of Lord Clandeboys, who was worth some £7,000 or £8,000 a year. When the parents were agreed, the boy came to visit Mary, her father 'designing suddenly that we should be married'. But she flatly refused, for 'my aversion to him was extraordinary', and after some terrible scenes with her father, she finally forced the latter to break off the match. But this was no more than the exercise of a veto by the child, a concession which by then had been generally made by most parents. For two years she continued to refuse matches to young men of money and title offered her by her father. But what was far more serious was that she set her heart on Charles Rich, younger son of the second Earl of Warwick, and told her father that she would marry him or no-one. This time her father was beside himself with fury at her impertinence, banished her to the country, and refused her permission to come into his presence. Her fanatical religious piety enabled her to withstand all these pressures, and in the end it was her father, not she, who gave way. The mercenary old royalist was forced to allow his daughter to marry a younger son, without prospects, of the leading Puritan and parliamentarian family in the country.[80] Owing to the death without heirs of his elder brother, Charles eventually inherited the family title and fortune, and Mary became Countess of Warwick. But this was sheer luck, and not something that her embittered father could have counted on.

Lower down in the social scale, among the squires and wealthy lawyers of the early seventeenth century, patriarchal authority had to struggle to maintain itself. A typical example of the new complexities is provided by the account Simonds D'Ewes gives of his own marriage. [81]. In 1626 he was twenty-four years old, a Middle Temple lawyer, and already more or less financially independent in his own right as the co-heir to his late maternal grandfather's estate. He was, therefore, economically free to marry, so long as he was not seeking an heiress, in which case he was dependent on a firm property settlement from his father. But Simonds was a genealogical snob, who wished to marry into ancient stock, and also aspired to ally himself to a landed heiress. He therefore needed his father's consent to a settlement which would provide a suitable jointure for the bride after his own death, and would settle the D'Ewes estate upon him in reversion. His father, on the other hand, was a greedy man who wanted not a landed heiress but a bride with a large cash portion, which under current arrangements would go to himself and not to his son.

Simonds first proposed to his father two co-heiresses of ancient family, but in each case the negotiations never got off the ground. His father then made some proposals for daughters of great City merchants with large cash portions, whom Simonds rejected. Then her uncle made an opening proposal for a match with Anne, the daughter and heiress of the late Sir William Clopton, of an ancient and wealthy Suffolk family. This led to tedious and complex negotiations between Simonds' father on the one hand and Anne's grandmother and guardian on the other. Everything seemed settled, when his father suddenly broke off negotiations, having heard of an alternative offer bringing a cash portion of £5,000. Simonds learned who the girl was and told his father that he had seen her, but 'finding her face rough and unpleasant, I could upon no terms affect her'. His father then gave way, and the draft financial arrangements with the Cloptons were finally concluded.

At this point, Simonds had not yet met the prospective bride, who was anyway only thirteen-and-a-half years old. He had seen her two or three times seven years before when she was only a child, but not since. He therefore had a preliminary interview with Anne to inspect her physical appearance, 'whose person gave me absolute and full content as soon as I had seriously viewed it'. She was a reasonably pretty girl and he was satisfied; she presumably raised no objection to him (after all she was only a child still), and the marriage contract was, therefore, finally signed.

Thereafter, he saw more and more of Anne, who rapidly became devoted to him, while his own affection to his child bride also deepened. But her grandmother was unwilling to agree to an immediate marriage, allegedly for two reasons. The first was that the girl was too young for sexual intercourse, which might stunt her growth and endanger her health. Secondly, she was afraid that the child's 'good will and affections was no solid or real love grounded on judgement, and might thereafter alter and lessen again after marriage'. Here was the traditional fear of love as a temporary fever. However, Simonds, who was afraid that either his father or her grandmother might at any moment change their minds if a better offer presented itself, finally overcame their objections by promising to remain chaste for a period after the marriage, which he in fact did for eight months.

He was soon as devoted to his young wife as she was to him, and he persuaded her to participate in his private fasting and prayers, seeking assurances that she as well as he could be counted among the Elect.

This is a complicated story, with many different strands of cultural behaviour involved in it. It shows the continuing control of parents over the marriage, even of grown-up sons, well into the early seventeenth century, as well as the way they bartered heiresses while they were still mere children and not even sexually mature. On the other hand it also shows a son exercising the right of refusal on grounds of dislike of the physical appearance of a bride proposed by his father, an argument the latter accepted. It also shows that after all the financial negotiations had been concluded, the contract was not actually signed until the groom had inspected the bride and found her physically satisfactory. The mutual love and affection, cemented by common Calvinist zeal, which subsequently developed between the bride and groom was an accident, which merely aroused the suspicion of the bride's grandmother, who had no faith in the enduring quality of such emotions. The story thus perfectly illustrates the transitional pattern of marriage among the early seventeenth-century English landed classes as they moved uneasily between one set of values based on kin interest and marriage arranged by others with a view to financial advantage, and another set based on allowing children a right of veto in order to provide a better chance of marital harmony. The result was an awkward interplay of forces, which in this particular case turned out to everyone's satisfaction.

Even among the squirarchy, however, pressure was still being exercised on daughters in the late seventeenth century, although the sense of guilt about such behaviour was clearly increasing. In 1684 the twenty-one-year-old Lettice, daughter of Richard Legh of Lyme, was being pursued by an elderly peer, whose cause was actively supported by her mother.[82] She was saved by the fact that 'my lord will not permit of her being pressed beyond her inclination', but she remained in constant dread of having some husband or other more or less forced upon her. The third daughter, Fanny, was her own mistress, since she had inherited a legacy, and was therefore free of financial constraints from her parents. Her mother was very annoyed at her lack of influence, and wrote irritably – and ungrammatically – to her son: 'knowing she has her portion in her own power, if she marry a tinker, I would rather she were buried alive than she should be so cast away'. In fact, of course, such fears were groundless, and Fanny chose an eminently suitable neighbouring squire.

By 1690 the last daughter, Betty, was still unmarried, probably because she was not much of a catch, except in financial terms. But in that year she was persuaded to engage herself to a fifty-year-old widower, Streynsham Master, carrying with her a huge portion of £15,000 provided by her father. The contract was signed, the wedding preparations were in full swing, and the marriage ceremony was set for two days later, when Betty made a last desperate attempt to escape. She wrote to Master asking him to release her and 'not to insist more of this business', reminding him that 'you cannot say that ever I have given you encouragement'. Master wrote back a tactful note, agreeing that the marriage would not proceed 'without your free and voluntary consent', but pointing out in a sentence that reveals the true nature of the marriage, 'how much it consists with your interest and circumstances, to which a small indisposition of mind or body ought to submit'. One can only guess the pressures that were brought to bear, but three days later the marriage finally took place, only one day behind schedule. Master was a dull, worthy old man, and there is no evidence that Betty ever became particularly attached to him. But she was content, and bore him three children, in whom she became wholly absorbed. In 1692, she was 'so infinitely fond of her nursery that she cannot look off it one hour. She is a very good nurse and has abundance of milk.'

These illustrations of marriage arrangements show very clearly how things were slowly changing. At first, in the early sixteenth century, children were bought and sold like cattle for breeding, and no-one thought that the parties concerned had any right to complain. But Protestant moral theology, with its stress on 'holy matrimony' slowly forced a modification of this extreme position, which was only maintained in its pure state through the seventeenth century in the highest ranks of the aristocracy where the stakes of property and power were largest. To retain 'holy matrimony', which the theologians thought desirable in itself, as well being as a way to reduce adultery, it was necessary that the couple should be able to develop some affection for each other. It was therefore thought necessary to concede to the children the right of veto, the right to reject a spouse chosen by the parents on the grounds that the antipathy aroused by a single interview was too great to permit the possibility of the future development of affection. This right of veto could only be used with caution and probably only once, or at most twice, while for women there was always the risk that its exercise might condemn them to spinsterhood, if their parents failed to provide another suitor.

A second philosophical trend that was beginning to make itself felt in the early seventeenth century, most markedly expressed in the growing hostility to the system of royal wardship, was the concept of personal autonomy or 'liberty', a notion which only came to fruition in the late seventeenth and eighteenth centuries, and discussion of whose origins and importance must be postponed for the time being. Patriarchal disposition of children in marriage was therefore already under attack long before 1660.

Finally, it is apparent that high adult mortality provided many children with some freedom of choice by removing their parents from the scene at an early age. If a boy was the heir to the estate, he was then more or less free to suit himself. Thus in 1624, long after his father's death, Sir Thomas Wentworth decided to court Arabella, the sixteen-year-old daughter of the Earl of Clare. 'He grew passionately in love with her after his first acquaintance, insomuch that for 3 or 4 months before they were married, he missed not 3 days from being most part of the afternoons in her company.'[83] Even girls were freed by the death of both their parents. When the nineteen-year-old orphan Mary Abell was being wooed by the neighbouring Verneys for their son Edmund, mainly with a view to uniting the two estates, it was reported that she 'is resolved to marry where she thinks she may live happy, and if there be a liking between the young folk, there may be a match'.[84]

On the other hand, popular attitudes on such fundamental issues changed with glacial slowness, varying from family to family, as well as from class to class, while the law was naturally even slower to change. In 1706 a gentleman died leaving a will which entirely disinherited his son, on the grounds that the latter had married against his wishes. Although the son contested the will, the jury voted to uphold it.[85] There was clearly a very long period of conflict between parents and children, lasting right through the seventeenth century before the old patriarchal attitudes to marriage were finally discredited.

c. Marriage Arrangements in the Lower Classes. Because the key to the system of controlled marriage was the exchange of property, it theoretically follows that children lower down the economic scale would enjoy greater freedom of choice. Whether this is so is not at present known for certain. Harrington thought that the arranged marriage system did not press 'so heavy on the lower sort, being better able to shift for themselves, as upon the nobility and gentry'. On the other hand, a large proportion of the population owned some property, and there is plenty of evidence for arranged marriages among the yeomanry in the sixteenth century. For example, in 1514 a Lancashire girl was forced by her uncle and her 'friends', under threat of losing her inheritance in land, to marry a man she actively disliked. She fled from him a month later after a severe beating, and sued for a separation, explaining that 'but only for the fear of loss of my land I would never be with him an hour'. In his will of 1599 William Shaftoe curtly decreed: 'To my daughter Margery, 60 sheep, and I bestow her in marriage upon Edward, son of Reynold Shaftoe of Thockerington.' When in 1632 the eldest son of Adam Martindale's artisan father came to marry, his father expected him to marry a girl with a portion of at least £120, and was furious when he chose one with only £40. The casebooks of Richard Napier suggest that the choice of marriage partner was the principal issue which divided parents and children at all social levels above that of the absolute poor in the early seventeenth century.[86]

Among the propertyless at the bottom of society, however, children even in the sixteenth century were probably very much freer to choose a spouse than their superiors, as they certainly were in the eighteenth century. In the first place, their parents had little economic leverage over them since they had little or nothing to give or bequeath them. In the second place, most of the children left home at the age of ten to fourteen in order to become apprentices, domestic servants, or living-in labourers in other people's houses. This very large floating population of adolescents living away from home were thus free from parental supervision and could, therefore, make their own choice of marriage partners as soon as they were out of apprenticeship. The only thing that held them back was the need to accumulate sufficient capital to set up house and to start a shop or trade, which was the principal cause for the long delay in marriage into the middle twenties.

The fact that the children of the poor were freer to make their own choices than the children of the rich did not mean, however, that affective considerations weighed more than the same prudential ones that would govern choice if made for them by their parents. Among the peasantry of northern France in the eighteenth century (and presumably for centuries before), it was reported that 'passion plays little role in alliances. People want wives simply to have children, to have a housekeeper who can make a good stew and bring something to eat out to the fields, and who can spin for the shirts and mend the clothes.' The division of labour between the sexes at this period meant that marriage was a much more comfortable and convenient arrangement than living singly, and the personal attractiveness of the spouse mattered less than her dowry, health and practical competence. One piece of statistical evidence to support this contention is

1. A Fleet wedding: two clergymen are crowding round the coach to offer their services, 1747.

2. Elopement from boarding school, 1798.

3. Flight to Gretna Green, pursued by the father. By T. Rowlandson, 1785.

4. A wedding at Gretna Green.
By T. Rowlandson, 1811.

5. The bigamist, 1787.

The CHILD.

*Man that is born of a Woman, is of few Days, and
full of Trouble. He cometh forth like a Flower,
and is cut down: He fleeth also as a Shadow, and
continueth not.*

JOB xiv. 1.

Man, who conceiv'd in the dark Womb,
   Into the World is brought,
Is born to Times with Misery,
   And various Evil fraught.

And as the Flow'r soon fades and dies,
   However fair it be,
So sinks he also to the Grave,
   And like a Shade does flee.

E 2

6. Death takes a child, *Emblems of Mortality*, 1789.

7. Death takes a wife and child: tomb of Lady Margaret Leigh and her infant, both dead in childbirth. Fulham, Middlesex, *c.* 1605.

8. Death cripples a family: tomb of Sir Thomas Spencer and family. Yarnton, Oxfordshire, *c.* 1712.

'Dedicated to the immortal memory of Sir Thomas Spencer alias Spenser Bart., Lord of this Manor of Yarnton, who died the 6th of March 1684/5 aged 46 years, and of Dame Jane his wife (daughter of Sir John Gerrard of Lamer in the County of Herts., Bart.), who died the 30th of April 1712 aged 74 years, and of their nine children: of which five died in his life-time (viz) Thomas, Thomas, Jane, Margaret, all infants, and William who lived to the age of 26 years and was a gent. of great hopes and died unmarried the 13th of September 1683; and four survived him, all daughters and co-heirs.'

9. *Opposite* The romantic
approach to death: the husband
supports his dying wife and tries
to repel the figure of Death.
Tomb of Lady Elizabeth
Nightingale. By T. F. Roubiliac,
Westminster Abbey, 1761.

10. *Right* The stock heraldic
figure: Sir Richard Knightley.
Fawsley, Northamptonshire,
c. 1535.

11. Realistic portraiture:
Elizabeth, wife of Sir Moyle
Finch. Eastwell, Kent (now in
the Victoria and Albert
Museum), 1623–28.

12. The swaddled child. Infant of Sir John St John. Lydiard Tregoze, Wiltshire, *c.* 1634.

13. Original sin: *Divine Emblems*, by J. Bunyan, 1686 (1790 ed.).

Of Man by Nature.

FROM God he's a back-slider,

Of ways he loves the wider;

With wickednefs a sider,

More venom than a spider.

   In sin he's a confider,

A make-bate and divider;

Blind reafon is his guider,

The devil is his rider.

Upon the Difobedient Child.

CHILDREN, when little, how do they delight u
When they grow bigger, they begin to fright u
Their finful nature prompts them to rebel,
And to delight in paths that lead to hell.
Their parents love and care they overlook,
As if relation had them quite forfook.
They take the counfels of the wanton, rather
Than the moft grave inftructions of a father
They reckon parents ought to do for them,
Though they the fifth commandment do conten
They fnap, and fnarl, if parents them controu
Although in things moft hurtful to the foul,
They reckon they are mafters, and that we
Who parents are, fhould to them fubject be
If parents fain would have a hand in chufin
The children have a heart ftill in refufing.

G

that in Europe about twenty per cent of all first marriages in the seventeenth and eighteenth centuries were with wives five or more years older than their husbands, as against the six to eight per cent which is normal under today's conditions, when sentiment and sexual attraction are the decisive considerations. One detailed study of marriage in an Early Modern European peasant society, based on a careful study of all the evidence, has concluded that 'in a peasant society, an engagement of marriage may have nothing of the character of an intimate, private understanding between two lovers. In a peasant marriage contract, the economic unit, with its human and material requirements, is the dominant consideration. Personal preferences have a lower priority.'[87] Very little information is at present available for England, but there is no reason to suppose that attitudes there were at all different before the nineteenth century.

d. Conclusion. In the sixteenth and seventeenth centuries in England, the children of the rich could and did marry early, but only rarely to the person of their own choice. The children of the lower-middle classes were a little freer, but economic considerations and parental pressures were still predominant. The absolute poor were more or less free to select their own mates without concern for portions and jointures, since neither had much to contribute. But they looked for an efficient economic assistant rather than an affectionate companion, and lack of capital meant that they were unable to marry until they were twenty-six or more. Paradoxically enough, the lower one descends in the social scale, the greater the freedom of choice of a spouse. It was the only area of civil liberties in which this inverse social correlation existed, but even so, the choice was usually made for economic and not affective reasons, and for lack of money had usually to be postponed until the late twenties.

This picture of a severe repression of the will of the child, extending to his or her choice of a spouse, is supported by a sufficient range of evidence to be beyond possibility of challenge. This should not be taken to mean, however, that parents were not attached to their children. Indeed, it is the argument of this chapter that the repression was itself a by-product of a greater concern for the moral and academic training of children and, therefore, a function of greater attention being paid to them. There are plenty of examples from the seventeenth century of families being shattered by the deaths of children, especially those who lived sufficiently long for deep affective ties to develop, and who were the potential male heirs to the family name and property.

For example, the gentleman antiquary John Evelyn and his wife were devastated by the death of their only son, Richard, in 1658. One reason for the sorrow was that already by five-and-a-half he was developing into one of those child prodigies so admired by the age, and who therefore delighted his pedantic father. At three-and-a-half he knew a hundred words of French; at under five he knew the active and passive verbs of grammar and was moving on to nouns; at five he could read easily, including his father's crabbed handwriting. At five-and-a-half he was dead. 'After six fits of a quartern ague ... we lost the prettiest and dearest child that ever parents had, a prodigy for wit and understanding, for beauty of body a very angel, and for endowments of mind of incredible and rare hopes.' A month later Evelyn was still deeply depressed by the loss, and his wife 'is still in tears, and in every corner of this house she hears the voice and sees the face of her dear companion, that strangely cheerful and beautiful child'.[88] Even in the iron age of the late sixteenth and early seventeenth centuries, when the treatment of children was at its harshest, the death of one who conformed to the highest expectations of his parents was inevitably a shattering blow. Although self-centred pride in the late child's accomplishments was clearly an important factor in John Evelyn's thinking, the love for his child of himself and his wife does something to mitigate the otherwise bleak impression of domestic relationships at that period and in that class. Coming at the very end of that period, it was a harbinger of things to come, and is perhaps an indication that attitudes were already changing.

v. Results of Repression

Despite the probable absence of much trauma, in the Freudian sense, at the oral, anal or genital stages, the severity of the childhood upbringing deeply affected the personality of large numbers of adults in the sixteenth and early seventeenth centuries. The objects of the training at home and at school were to maintain a psychological distance between parents and children, to instil awe and deference, to suppress the imagination, to discipline the intellect and to control the emotions. The methods included infantile abandonment to a wet-nurse, imprisonment in swaddling bands in the first months of life, the constant use of physical punishment, an educational discipline which depended on memorizing and repetition of grammatical forms rather than a study of content and meaning, the instillation of fear of Hell and Damnation, and early ejection from the home. It is hardly surprising that such an upbringing should tend to produce adults who were cold, suspicious, distrustful and cruel, unable to form close emotional relationships with others, and liable to sudden outbursts of aggressive hostility towards each other.

3 HUSBAND AND WIFE

i. Subordination of Wives

There is evidence to suggest that a similar trend towards greater patriarchy in husband-wife relations was also developing in the sixteenth century. But, just as with patriarchal power over children, strong countervailing forces began to operate towards the end of that century and in the seventeenth century, so that the picture is by no means clear. For a considerable period, two conflicting trends were at work at the same time, and the growing authority of the husband can only be seen in a relatively pure form during the first half of the sixteenth century.

At this time a woman's legal right to hold and dispose of her own property was limited to what she could specifically lay claim to in a marriage contract. By marriage, the husband and wife became one person in law – and that person was the husband. He acquired absolute control of all his wife's personal property, which he could sell at will. By a judicial interpretation, a husband's debts became by law a prior charge on his wife's jewels and other personal property, although it is fair to add that the husband also became responsible for his wife's debts. A husband always had full rights during his lifetime over his wife's real estate, and by an act of 1540 he was empowered to make long leases for three lives or twenty-one years and to pocket the fines.

As Widow Blackacre put it in Wycherley's *Plain Dealer*, 'matrimony to a woman [is] worse than excommunication in depriving her of the benefit of the law'. Defoe's *Roxana* was even more critical of the legal impotence of a wife: 'the very nature of the marriage contract was . . . nothing but giving up liberty, estate, authority and everything to a man, and the woman was indeed a mere woman ever after – that is to say a slave'.[89] This legal subjection of women to husbands or fathers was the reason why the franchise was always restricted to male householders, a position which even the radical Levellers in the late 1640s never questioned. Women were self-evidently not free persons, and therefore were no more eligible for the vote than children.

In the sixteenth century a widow's rights over real estate were in practice weakened by the rise of the legal device of the use to feoffees, which could bar her from her dower; moreover, until the end of the seventeenth century, her medieval common-law right to a share of the personal estate was effective only in Wales, the province of York and the city of London.[90] If women entered the agricultural and servicing labour market, as they did in considerable numbers in the sixteenth and seventeenth centuries, they were everywhere paid at a rate which was at most only one half of that of men: the differential may even have widened.[91]

On the other hand the custom of leasing lands for three lives or ninety-nine years, whichever might be the longer, meant that in the many cases in which the husband predeceased the wife, the latter became a life tenant of the property. Thus when in 1626 Henry Hellier of Sonning, Berkshire, named his wife and young son in a three-life copyhold, he in fact made it possible for his widow to inherit the property for her lifetime, even after a second marriage.[92] At this modest social level in the rural community, therefore, a widow's property rights were well protected by the three-life lease. This custom persisted in the north and west as late as the nineteenth century, but there was a movement to leases for years in the south and east in the seventeenth and eighteenth centuries, which must, quite unintentionally, have reduced the rights of widows in these areas.

In some ways the status of wives, as well as their legal rights, seems to have been on the decline in the sixteenth century, despite the 'monstrous regiment of women' who by genealogical accident became queens at that period. Thomas More's *Utopia* is remarkable in that the subjection of wives to husbands is the one authoritarian feature in an otherwise egalitarian society. Some Elizabethans revived the Platonic doubts whether a woman could be considered as a reasoning creature; others questioned whether she had a soul.[93]

Despite a century-long trickle of books in praise of women, many lay commentators in the late sixteenth and seventeenth centuries remained thoroughly ambivalent in their attitude towards them. In a sermon before Queen Elizabeth, Bishop Aylmer trod cautiously between the two poles of opinion:

Women are of two sorts: some of them are wiser, better learned, discreeter, and more constant than a number of men; but another and worse sort of them are fond, foolish, wanton, flibbergibs, tattlers, triflers, wavering, witless, without council, feeble, careless, rash, proud, dainty, tale-bearers, eavesdroppers, rumour-raisers, evil-tongued, worse-minded, and in everyway doltified with the dregs of the devil's dunghill.

From the baroque richness of the vocabulary in the latter section, there can be little doubt about what the bishop really thought of women, despite his care to mollify his highly sensitive queen. Others were less tactful in expressing their feelings. Thomas Fuller thought that they were 'of a servile nature such as may be bettered by beating', but nevertheless advised against it. John Smith of Nibley recorded a local Gloucestershire saying, 'a woman, spaniel and a walnut tree, the more they are beaten, better they be', but added doubtfully '*sed quaere de hoc*'. Others relapsed into total cynicism. In a play by George Wilkins, Ilford advised that 'women are the purgatory of men's purses, the paradise of their bodies, and the hell of their minds: marry none of them'. The ninth Earl of Northumberland was equally severe: 'toys and vanities in their youths are the subjects they are bent to; miserableness and psalms in their latter days'.[94] It is highly significant of popular attitudes towards women in the early seventeenth century that Joseph Swetnam's *The Arraignment of Lewd, Idle, Froward and Unconstant Women*, a savage anti-feminist piece of polemic, went through no less than ten editions between its first publication in 1616 and 1634, although it also generated some fierce rebuttals.[95]

The Protestant preachers and moral theologians were as zealous as the laity in advocating the total subordination of wives. In Matthew's Bible of 1537 there was an ominous gloss to 1 Peter 3, noting that a husband, if his wife is 'not obedient and helpful to him, endeavoureth to beat the fear of God into her head, and that thereby she may be compelled to learn her duty and do it'. In Calvin's Geneva, which formed so important a model for much of Protestant Europe, women's legal rights declined, while their inferior position was emphasized by their exclusion from the priesthood and from the consistory.[96] William Gouge, in his popular manual *Of Domesticall Duties* of 1622 and 1634, flatly declared that 'the extent of wives' subjection doth stretch itself very far, even to all things'. He even argued that 'though an husband in regard of evil qualities may carry the image of the devil, yet in regard to his place and office, he beareth the image of God'. The old arguments from the Bible were dredged up and repeated to support this position. 'We cannot but think that the woman was made before the Fall that the man might rule over her.' There was, Gouge thought, good reason 'that she who first drew man into sin should now be subject to him, lest by the like womanish weakness she fall again'. The only concession that he was prepared to make was that a husband may not beat his wife, and even this was a moral, not a legal, position. By law, a husband could chastise a wife, and even if the number of wife-beaters was not so very much greater in the sixteenth century than in the nineteenth, the different attitudes of the law could make a significant difference to husband–wife relations. Even when advocating married love, Robert Cawdrey never forgot the need for male mastery: 'we would that the man when he loveth should remember his superiority'.[97]

Of greatest impact, in the sense that it must have reached the widest audience, over the longest period of time, was the Homily on Marriage, which was the eighteenth of the many from which all parsons were ordered by the Crown to read in church every Sunday from 1562 onwards. It left the audience in no doubt about the inferior status, rights and character of a wife: 'the woman is a weak creature not endued with like strength and constancy of mind; therefore, they be the sooner disquieted, and they be the more prone to all weak affections and dispositions of mind, more than men be; and lighter they be, and more vain in their fantasies and opinions'. For the sake of domestic peace, however, the husband is advised not to beat his wife, as is his right, but to take account of the psychological fact that a woman is 'the weaker vessell, of a frail heart, inconstant, and with a word soon stirred to wrath'. Women were bluntly reminded that 'ye wives be in subjection to obey your husbands ... for the husband is the head of the woman, as Christ is the head of the Church'. As the Reverend John Sprint reminded women in a sermon in 1699, absolute obedience and extraordinary care to 'please their husbands' were, therefore, the first necessities for a happy and Christian marriage.[98] The ideal woman in the sixteenth and seventeenth centuries was weak, submissive, charitable, virtuous and modest, like the wife of the Massachusetts minister in the 1630s whom he publicly praised for her 'incomparable meekness of spirit, towards myself especially'. Her function was housekeeping, and the breeding and rearing of children. In her behaviour she was silent in church and in the home, and at all times submissive to men. As contemporaries were well aware, modes of address are significant indicators of social realities. Women habitually signed letters to their husbands 'your faithful and obedient wife'. In 1622 the Puritan moral theologian William Gouge was insistent that wives should address their spouses respectfully as 'Husband', and to avoid such demeaning endearments as 'sweet, sweeting, heart, sweetheart, love, joy, dear, duck, chick or pigsnie', as well as such egalitarian modes as the first name. Some women were clearly using familiar modes of address, and some of this male chauvinist propaganda may have been designed to hold back the trend. On the other hand, eighteenth- and early nineteenth-century evidence from all over Europe shows peasant wives addressing their husbands in deferential terms, never sitting down at the table at which the men and boys were eating, and always walking a step or two behind their husbands. These are concrete symbols of patriarchy in the family which were presumably also normal in sixteenth- and seventeenth-century England, even if contemporary evidence is at present lacking. It looks as if the sense of inferiority was fully internalized by most women, so that even a courageous and independent gentlewoman like Mrs Anne Hutchinson in the middle of the seventeenth century admitted her sex's 'ignorance and weakness of judgement, which in the most knowing women is inferior to the masculine understanding of men'.[99] Clear evidence of feminist claims to equality do not emerge into the open until the ferment of ideas in the aftermath of Revolution in the late 1640s.

But it would, of course, be absurd to claim that the private reality fully matched the public rhetoric, and there are plenty of examples of Elizabethan women who dominated their husbands. Their monopoly of certain work responsibilities, their capacity to give or withhold sexual favours, their control over the children, their ability to scold, all gave them useful potential levers of power within the home. All that is here claimed is that the theoretical and legal doctrines of the time were especially insistent upon the subordination of women to men in general, and to their husbands in particular, and that many women accepted these ideas. Defoe's Roxana grimly reflected that 'a wife is looked upon as but an upper servant'. The treatment of wives by their husbands naturally differed widely from individual to individual, but one gets the impression that the casual insouciance expressed in the diary of the small Lancashire gentleman Nicholas Blundell on 24 September 1706 was far from uncommon in the seventeenth century: 'My wife felt the pains of labour coming upon her. Captain Robert Fazakerley and I went a-coursing'.[100]

The subordination of wives to husbands certainly applied to the upper and upper-middle classes, but the situation is less clear among artisans, shopkeepers, smallholders and unskilled labourers. In these classes at any period of pre-industrial society, husband, wife and children tended to form a single economic unit, like the crew of a ship, in which the role of the wife was critical. When the husband was away, she looked after his affairs for him. On a smallholding, she had limited but very clearly defined duties over which she had full control: she managed the dairy and poultry side of the business, and marketed the produce. If there was cottage industry, she was in charge of spinning the yarn, knitting, glove-stitching and lace-making.[101] If her husband was a day labourer, on the other hand, she and her children were likely to do no more than assist him in the back-breaking work in the fields. She might also set up an ale-house in the home, or sell perishable goods from door to door. In the cloth-manufacturing areas, the family was even more a wholly interdependent economic unit, since the putting-out system prevailed and spinning was exclusively done by women and children. In the early eighteenth century, Defoe observed that in the wool-manufacturing areas of the West Riding of Yorkshire, cloth was made in every house, 'women and children carding and spinning; all employed from the youngest to the oldest, scarce anything above four years old but its hands were sufficient for its own support'. Later on in the eighteenth century similar conditions prevailed in the first stages of the development of the cotton industry round Manchester. In the towns, the wife helped to manage the shop, or helped the craftsman at his trade. She also added a critical element to the family budget by sewing, dressmaking or lace-making. At the lowest levels, she would take in laundry or act as a charwoman, carter, street-cleaner, prostitute, beggar or thief. At any rate in the eighteenth and early nineteenth centuries, when our evidence is ample, the lower-class wife managed the domestic economy, being responsible for the spending of the pooled family income. In such circumstances, regardless of the current legal or moral theories, and regardless of how her husband treated her in terms of status or deference, she was at least an important economic asset.[102]

This does not mean, however, that the economic contribution of the wife to the family budget necessarily gave her higher status and greater power, and that her progressive removal from the labour force as capitalism spread prosperity slowly downward was the cause of her social degradation. This was a theory of Engels, but the historical evidence suggests that it is untrue.[103] All members of the household were allotted tasks by the head of the household, and in this respect working women, especially if they were employed in the family holding, in the home or shop, were more like servants than partners. So far as we know, the money they earned was controlled by the husband, who anyway was in legal theory entitled to it. All that productive work entailed for most married women in the sixteenth, seventeenth and eighteenth centuries was, therefore, a crushing burden of labour added on to their normal household chores of marketing, cleaning, cooking and child care. The work did not bring any compensation in an independent income to spend on personal luxuries, nor greater status, nor greater participation in male leisure activities. The lot of a working wife was probably like that of many women today in underdeveloped countries, and as described by an early nineteenth-century visitor to the Scottish Highlands. 'Here, as in all semi-barbarous countries, the woman seems to be regarded rather as the drudge than the companion of the man ... I wish you but saw with what patience these poor females continue thus dumbly employed, for the greater part of a long summer's day.' As a result of their work load, 'I scarcely saw a Gairlock woman of the humbler class turned of thirty, who was not thin, sallow and prematurely old'.[104] Poverty is an acid that erodes both physical beauty and affective relations.

Finally, it has to be remembered that relatively few married women worked outside the home in the Early Modern period. Even as late as 1851, only twenty-five per cent of all women were employed, and they were almost all unmarried girls in domestic service or the textile industry. As late as 1911, only ten per cent of married women in England were employed. The history of the twentieth century offers no support for the theory that there is any correlation between the growth of women's legal and political rights and the growth of their contribution to the labour force, and the same lack of correlation is probably also true of the past.[105] Authority and respect do not necessarily follow from economic participation, which may well be no more than a disguised form of domestic slavery. Joint participation in leisure activities and family decision-making is a far better indication of a wife's status and autonomy than her role in the family economy.

Another test of the sense of independence displayed by women in the late sixteenth century, when many were gainfully employed, is whether or not the crimes they committed were similar in scale and type to those of men. The evidence suggests, on the contrary, that married and unmarried women were as submissive and as dependent as the conduct books suggested that they ought to be. They had a minimal share in crimes of theft, commercial fraud and violence, and when violence took place they were usually aiding their menfolk. They were prominent only in defamation, especially accusations against other women of sexual incontinence. The only two areas where they showed a spirit of independence was in leading food riots, and in adhering to dissident religious opinions, whether Puritan or Catholic, but in both cases they were relying on the higher moralities of the just price and the true faith to spur them to defy the law.

Finally, women were treated in the courts as financially dependent on men, so that those without men, such as spinsters, widows and deserted wives, bulked large on the poor relief rolls. Everything suggests, therefore, that women in the late sixteenth century did indeed regard their sex role as one of dependence and inferiority, just as the theoretical literature indicated. Men in want stole; women turned to men – husbands or sexual clients – or to public charity; men brawled, women slandered; men took direct action against the law when they felt aggrieved, women only in accordance with a higher moral code. The fact that many women worked does not seem to have affected their sense of identity as a member of an inferior and subordinate sex.[106]

The reasons for the apparent positive decline in the status and rights of wives in the sixteenth and early seventeenth centuries are not entirely clear. One obvious cause was the decline of kinship, which left wives exposed to exploitation by their husbands, since they lost the continuing protection of their own kin. Secondly, the end of Catholicism involved the elimination of the female religious cult of the Virgin Mary, the disappearance of celibate priests, who through the confession box had hitherto been so very supportive of women in their domestic difficulties, and the closing off of the career option of life in a nunnery. Puritanism was unable to fill the same role for more than a tiny minority of educated female zealots who attached themselves to charismatic preachers, while post-Reformation English society had nothing but contempt for spinsters. A third important factor was the emphasis placed by the state and the law on the subordination of the wife to the head of the household as the main guarantee of law and order in the body politic.

Finally it could be argued that the Protestant sanctification of marriage and the demand for married love itself facilitated the subordination of wives. Women were now expected to love and cherish their husbands after marriage and were taught that it was their sacred duty to do so. This love, in those cases where it in fact became internalized and real, made it easier for wives to accept that position of submission to the will of their husbands upon which the preachers were also insisting. By a paradoxical twist, one of the first results of the doctrine of holy matrimony was a strengthening of the authority of the husband over the wife, and an increased readiness of the latter to submit herself to the dictates of the former. Sir Kenelm Digby complacently remarked in the late 1630s that one should be careful to choose an obedient wife, 'which none can promise to himself . . . whose will is not wholly in his power by love'. [107] This is similar to the paradox by which the first result of an increased concern for children was a greater determination to crush their sinful wills by whipping them.

ii. The Education of Women

There is one socially very restricted, short-lived and paradoxical exception to the rule that literacy and classical education widened the gap between the sexes. For a brief period, during the middle third of the sixteenth century, there was a vigorous drive for female classical education by Renaissance Humanists like Vives and Erasmus. Perhaps encouraged by Queen

Catherine of Aragon, no fewer than seven ambitious treatises on this theme appeared in England between 1523 and 1538. Sir Thomas More was merely repeating the standard arguments of this school when he wrote 'if the female soil be in its nature stubborn, and more productive of weeds than fruit, it ought, in my opinion, to be more diligently cultivated with learning and good instruction'. 'I do not see why learning . . . may not equally agree with both sexes.'[108]

As a result of this active propaganda by influential English Humanist educators, there appeared for a short time a handful of aristocratic women who were as expert as men in classical grammar and language: women like Lady Jane Grey, Queen Elizabeth, and the daughters of Sir Anthony Cooke. It would have broken Catherine of Aragon's heart if she had lived to discover that the women who followed her advice were almost all ardent Protestants. In 1548 John Udall proudly drew Queen Catherine Parr's attention to

the great number of noble women at that time in England not only given to the study of humane sciences and strange tongues but also so thoroughly expert in Holy Scriptures that they were able to compare with the best writers.

Queen Elizabeth herself was a product of this efflorescence of the theological and classically learned noblewoman, and was thoroughly familiar with, and read and spoke easily, Latin, Greek, French and Italian. In 1580 the schoolmaster Richard Mulcaster could still boast:

Do we not see in our country some of that sex so excellently well trained and so rarely qualified in regard both to the tongues themselves and to the subject-matter contained in them, that they may be placed along with, or even above, the most vaunted paragons of Greece or Rome?[109]

Though he did not know it, Mulcaster was writing the swan-song of the movement. This period when a learned education was given to aristocratic women did not last much longer than forty years, from about 1520 to 1560. In 1561 there appeared in translation Castiglione's *The Courtier*, which put forward a different ideal of womanhood, one who had a sprinkling of letters, but whose prime qualities were now the social graces – skill in music, painting, drawing, dancing and needlework. This new courtly ideal, and the Protestant, especially Puritan, ideal of the woman as the docile housewife, the diligent upholder of holy matrimony in a subservient role to the husband, spelt the end of the learned lady. It had been Luther's view, repeated by countless Protestant moral theologians, that 'Women should remain at home, sit still, keep house, and bear and bring up children'.[110] As a result, the rise of Protestantism in the late sixteenth and early seventeenth centuries coincided with the decline of the learned lady in England. The model fell into disrepute, and in 1694 William Wotton summed up the change. In the sixteenth century, learning 'was so very modish that the fair sex seemed to believe that Greek and Latin added to their charms; and Plato and Aristotle, untranslated, were frequent ornaments of their closets'. But in the seventeenth century 'this humour in both sexes abated by degrees'.[111] To the late seventeenth-century playwrights, would-be learned ladies like the Duchess of Newcastle became figures of fun, to be satirized and ridiculed for their pedantic and unattractive folly. 'Plato in petticoats' was not a popular figure in Restoration drama or Restoration society.

During the seventeenth century, this masculine literary education for noble and gentle women was replaced by the traditional feminine accomplishments and graces needed to catch a husband, such as music, singing, dancing, needlework and embroidery, and no more than the basic elements of reading and writing in English and also French. Perhaps the most striking feature of English women's education for several centuries was to be their fluency in French. This change can be seen in a number of examples of the early seventeenth century. In the 1630s Lady Anne Halkett's parents 'paid masters for teaching my sister and me to write, speak French, play on the lute and virginals, and dance, and kept a gentlewoman to teach us all kinds of needlework'. Even these modest accomplishments were often neglected, and it is astonishing how many women from knightly or even noble homes in the early and even middle seventeenth century were unable to write a literate letter. Very many were like the mid-seventeenth-century Elizabeth Legh, wife of Sir Thomas Chicheley, Master of the Ordinance, or Lady Lettice Goring, daughter of the Earl of Cork; they could hardly form their letters, their grammar was atrocious, and their spelling largely phonetic. In 1652 Sir Ralph Verney gently admonished his twelve-year-old goddaughter, the daughter of the royal doctor, to abandon her plans to study Hebrew, Greek, Latin and shorthand, and to stick to subjects more suitable for girls: 'believe me, a Bible (with the common prayer) and a good plain catechism in your mother tongue, being well read and practised, is well worth all the rest, and much more suitable to your sex. I know your father thinks this false doctrine, but be confident your husband will be of my opinion. In French you cannot be too cunning, for that language affords many admirable books fit for you, as romances, plays, poetry, stories of illustrious not learned women ... and in brief all manner of good housewifery.' To her father he wrote: 'Let not your girl learn Latin nor shorthand; the difficulty of the first may keep her from that vice, for so I must esteem it in a woman'. His objection to shorthand was that 'the pride of taking sermon notes had made multitudes of women most unfortunate', a reference, presumably, to the current enthusiasm of many women for extremist religious preachers.

Even women agreed with these lowered educational aspirations, and in 1662 Mrs Elizabeth Josceline, before the birth of her first child, told her husband how she wanted the child educated if it were a daughter and if she herself should die in childbirth (both mother and child in fact died within nine days): 'I desire her bringing up may be learning the Bible as my sisters do, good housewifery, writing and good work; other learning a woman need not'.[112] John Winthrop even believed that female learning led to madness and was convinced that the wife of the Governor of Connecticut had lost her reason by too much reading and writing. 'If she had attended to her household affairs, and such things as belong to women, and had not gone out of her way and calling to meddle in such things as are proper to men, whose minds are stronger, etc., she had kept her wits.'[113]

In the 1630s Sir Christopher Wandesford's daughters were brought up with those of Sir Thomas Wentworth, the Lord Deputy of Ireland, and may be regarded as enjoying what was then the current ideal education for upper-class women. They were taught English, reading and writing, together with a spoken and written knowledge of French, but this was the limit of the academic side of their education. Great stress was laid upon 'pious, holy and religious instructions' in addition to which they were taught singing, dancing, music (the lute and the theorbo) and such 'suitable housewifery' as working silk and making sweetmeats.[114]

Margaret, the daughter of Sir Thomas Lucas, and future Duchess of Newcastle (who tried without much success to make a name for herself as an intellectual author in later life), was given much the same rather casual training in the graces and virtues needed to catch a husband: 'singing, dancing, playing on music, reading, writing, working and the like, yet we were not kept strictly thereto, they were rather for formality than benefit; for my mother cared not so much for our dancing and fiddling, singing and prating of several languages, as that we should be bred virtuously, modestly, civilly, honourably, and on honest principles'. All that was lacking here was the severe religious indoctrination given to the Wandesfords.[115] Similarly when in 1682 the eight-year-old Molly Verney was sent away to school in Chelsea to learn dancing and other social graces and asked for permission to learn the expensive art of japanning boxes, her father readily agreed, with the comment that 'I admire all accomplishments that will render you considerable and lovely in the sight of God and man'. His programme for her further education was to train her in behaviour in the household of a lady of quality, in preparation for marriage to a country squire of substantial but moderate means. A kindly and affectionate father, as Edmund Verney undoubtedly was towards Molly, could think of no more appropriate goal for a girl to aspire to, nor a better way to achieve it than the acquisition of such elegant but unintellectual accomplishments.[116]

If this was the case among upper-class women in the seventeenth century, it is not difficult to imagine conditions lower down the social scale. The education of the daughters of yeomen was confined to a very little reading and writing, barely enough for religious and functional use, together with sewing and the management of domestic affairs. In this class reading and writing was barely necessary; many were in the condition of the wife of Edward Duffield, a Suffolk yeoman, who 'could not write or read a written hand'. Among the population in general, only one woman in three could even sign her name in a marriage register in 1754, which was not much more than half the proportion of men, and there is every reason to suppose that the proportion was if anything worse in the seventeenth century.[117] Women at all levels of society were an educationally deprived group compared with men.

4 RESPONSES TO FAMILY DEATH

Responses to sickness and death in the family are governed by four factors: cultural, the traditional treatment of death in the particular class, society and time; theological, the prevailing eschatology about God's role in determining every event in this world and about the prospects of life after death; sociological, the degree of affective bonding between the dying individual and the other members of his family; and pseudo-scientific, the degree of interference in the process permitted to the medical profession, regardless of whether this intervention has any real prospect of success. All societies have developed rituals for handling the alarming episode of death: there are rituals to comfort the dying, by establishing models of a 'good death' carried out to the bitter end in public; rituals for the disposal of the physical remains, usually involving the neighbourhood in a funeral procession and a post-funeral feast that re-focuses attention again on the living; and rituals of mourning that ease the adjustment of the bereaved by the imposition of rigid patterns of graded behaviour.

i. Publicity

In the sixteenth and seventeenth centuries, death in the family was treated significantly differently from the way it was treated in the eighteenth century, and in almost the exact reverse of the way it is treated in Anglo-Saxon countries today. Elaborate public rituals were performed both over the process of death and over the funeral; the first served to mitigate the fear of death for the dying and the second the separation anxieties and grief among the bereaved.

All, including children, were accustomed to death-bed scenes, which were public spectacles attended by both relatives and neighbours. 'Death should be public, or else why / Are neighbours called when people die?' asked Bernard de Mandeville in 1707. To the moral sensibilities of Early Modern man, it was perfectly respectable to want to watch a death – even a death by execution – which is why Dr Johnson was so irritated when in 1783 the humanitarian trend of the day confined hangings to the privacy of the prison yard. 'The age is running mad after innovation,' he grumbled, 'Tyburn itself is not safe from the fury of innovation. ... The public was gratified by a procession; the criminal was supported by it.' He rightly saw that for the dying, publicity had the enormous psychic benefit of diverting attention from fear of death itself to the struggle to put on an impressive show for the spectators. 'Scarce any man dies in public but with apparent resolution, from that desire of praise that never quits us.'[118]

After death, the grief of the bereaved was assuaged by a series of formal ceremonies about the corpse, which was laid out in state for public inspection. As a result, from childhood upwards, everyone had seen many corpses, not only of criminals rotting on gibbets in chains, but also of neighbours, kin and close relatives, such as brothers, sisters, mothers and fathers formally on display for the last rites of respect and mourning for the dead.

The rituals which surrounded the funeral and the mourning of a member of the high aristocracy were on so opulent and public a scale that no place was left for private grief. The body was disembowelled and carefully embalmed to preserve it more or less intact and free from smell for subsequent display to the dependants and neighbours who streamed in to pay their respects. The funeral procession, which took place some weeks later, might run into hundreds of persons, while the whole church was draped in black from floor to roof-beams. In the sixteenth and seventeenth centuries, it was not unusual to spend a year's gross income upon one of these posthumous displays, in which pomp and pageantry and display were used to demonstrate the wealth and power and influence of the lineage. The burial of the individual was turned into a public demonstration of the prestige of the family, and an ostentatious symbol of the transfer of authority and status from the dead man to his successor.[119]

Nor were the funeral procession and the subsequent, often very drunken, funeral feast the end of the affair, for there followed the formal reception of mourners by the widow. One of the last occasions when this already obsolete practice was carried out was at the death of the first Duke of Kingston in 1726. The widow had to

see company, that is, to receive in person the compliments of condolence which every lady on her grace's visiting list was bound to tender, in person likewise. And this was the established form: the apartments, the staircase, and all that could be seen of the house, were hung with black cloth; the duchess, closely veiled with crape, sat upright in her state-bed under a high black canopy; and at the foot of the bed stood ranged, like a row of mutes in a tragedy, the grandchildren of the deceased duke – Lady Frances Pierrepont, Miss Wortley herself, and Lady Gower's daughters. Profound silence reigned; the room had no light but from a single wax taper; and the condoling visitors, who curtseyed in and out of it, approached the bed on tiptoe; if relations, all, down to the hundredth cousin, in black-glove-mourning for the occasion.[120]

So highly ritualized a ceremonial did much to make death endurable for the survivors, by providing them with a public and socially accepted mode of catharsis. Death was incorporated into the pattern of daily life, by being given the special treatment accorded to other *rites de passages*.

ii. Christian Eschatology

Long before the Reformation took hold, the Italian Humanists had developed an attitude to death that saw it as a personal and deeply disturbing, since meaningless, tragedy. They rejected both the passive resignation of the stoic philosophers and the active comfort offered by the Christian apologists that the dead were, if not in Heaven, at least in the way-station of Purgatory, from which they could be sprung by the prayers of the living. Between the Reformation and the late seventeenth century, however, the beliefs that officially controlled and guided responses to death in England were firstly that Purgatory does not exist, for the dead were long ago predestined for Heaven or Hell, and there is nothing the living can do about it; and secondly, that every event in this world, including every death, is the planned result of God's inscrutable purpose. The puzzle, therefore, was to determine what sinful act, perpetrated by whom, had been the cause of the misfortune. This belief was widely spread through all sections of society, although it had some competition at the higher levels from the equally deterministic theories of contemporary astrology, and among the lower levels from popular belief in white and black magic. Among those who believed in witchcraft, sickness and death might not be God's work but Satan's, operating directly through one of his human agents.

For most of the middle and upper classes, however, the Christian eschatology was the most commonly accepted explanation of sickness or death. It was most confidently believed in by the Puritans, and it is in the Puritan response to death that some of the most characteristic features of this mode of thought can be seen in their purest and most extreme form. For many Puritans, sickness or death, either of themselves or of a member of their immediate family, raised acute anxieties, because of the paradoxical ambiguities of their theological position. On the one hand, death was a blessing, a merciful deliverance from the miseries of this world into the comforts of the next; on the other, it was 'a most terrible calamity'; it was the curse of Adam, as a result of whose action 'sin entered the world, and death by sin'. It might have been supposed that both Puritans and Calvinist Anglicans, confident about their presence among the Elect, would have faced death with tranquil equanimity. But most of them, both in England and in New England, remained in a constant state of uncertainty about their salvation, worrying whether their confidence might not after all be a device of the Devil to lull them into a false sense of security. They were extremely conscious of the subtlety and wiles of the Devil, and persisted in stressing the potential torments of Hell well into the eighteenth century, long after their Anglican colleagues had abandoned this method of stimulating religious devotion. Many of the more devoted Puritans, therefore, took their approaching death very hard – harder, indeed, than their more sinful and unregenerate neighbours.[121]

To Puritans, it was not only such general calamities as plague, smallpox or bad weather leading to famine which were the work of God for his own inscrutable purposes. To them every piece of good or bad fortune in the daily life of the individual was also directly and knowingly caused by God, the former being a reward for virtue, the latter a punishment for sin. Consequently when it came to the sickness or death of a member of their own immediate family, these disasters often raised anxiety rather than leading to comfortable resignation, since they had to be the result of somebody's sin, either that of the victim or of one of his family, perhaps their own. Some had no hesitation in blaming the victim. In the early seventeenth century Adam Martindale's sister went up to London without her parents' permission, and on her return caught smallpox and died. Adam took it as God's punishment on her for her disobedience to her father.Even minor sins like vanity were also punished by God in horribly appropriate ways, according to Martindale. 'My sister, that was too proud of her [appearance], became extreme ugly before she died, her face being sadly discoloured, and so swelled that scarce any form of visage was discernable.'[122]

Others tended to blame themselves for the misfortunes of members of their family. When Ralph Josselin's daughter had an ague, he thought it might be a punishment for his own sins; and when his ten-day-old son died in 1648, he regarded it as a punishment imposed on him by God for his excessive fondness for playing chess. He also decided that in future 'I should be more careful of my family to instruct them in the fear of God'.[123] Similarly, when the infant son of Mary, fourth Countess of Warwick fell ill, 'my conscience told me it was for my backsliding. Upon which conviction I presently retired to God; and by earnest prayer begged of him to restore my child, and did then solemnly promise to God, if he would hear my prayer, I would become a new creature.' To the astonishment of the doctor, the child promptly recovered.[124]

The same attitude prevailed among the Puritans in Massachusetts. When Cotton Mather's daughter fell into the fire and burned herself badly, her father wrote: 'Alas, for my sins the just God throws my child into the fire.' Other accidental burns to other children led him not to install fire guards or hire babysitters, but to preach a sermon on the subject of 'What use ought parents to make of disasters befallen their children'. He told himself that 'on every observable miscarriage of any person in my family, I must make my flight unto the blood of my Saviour, as a family sacrifice, that so the wrath of God may be turned away from my family'.After the death of his rascally son Increase – of whom despite everything he was more fond than that all-too-perfect specimen of a Puritan child, Samuel – he wrote: 'I exceedingly loathed and judged myself before the Lord for the sins of that child, being on some account my own'. When another colonial Bostonian left his children without supervision and returned to find one drowned in the well, he did not attribute the accident to his own negligence, but ascribed it to a punishment of God upon him for his breaking of the Sabbath by working on a Sunday.[125]

Nor was it merely a case of parents blaming themselves for the death of their children, for children also blamed themselves for the death of their parents. In 1612 the nineteen-year-old Alice Critchlow, the daughter of a Puritan minister, lost her mother 'whom she tenderly affected and for whose death she made excessive sorrow'. For two years she remained in a state of total psychic collapse, overwhelmed by the sense of guilt. Stimulated by an over-zealous young Puritan minister, she was convinced that her sinfulness had caused her mother's death, and that she was beyond redemption 'still suffering God's terrors and refusing to be comforted'.[126] Many Puritans, on both sides of the Atlantic, clearly believed that God held all members of the nuclear family as hostages for the good behaviour of any one of them.

On the other hand death was more easily accepted by those Puritans who were totally convinced that they were among the Elect, and therefore blameless. Such a one was the early seventeenth-century antiquary Simonds D'Ewes, who after sixty separate days of fasting and prayer was fully convinced by many signs that he was among the saved. When his fourth and last son died at the age of two, he therefore took it not as a sign of God's displeasure with him, but rather, like Job, as a test of his faith: 'I began to consider that this great affliction was sent upon me still to humble me more and more, and to wean me from the love of the profits and preferments of this life'.[127] In 1664 Mary Countess of Warwick's only son, now an exquisitely handsome and vigorous young man of twenty, recently married to a Cavendish, and the sole hope of the family, suddenly went down with smallpox and died. When he heard the news, the boy's father 'cried out so terribly that his cry was heard a great way'. But Mary professed to take it more calmly, moulding her recorded reactions on the conventional stereotype of the pious and submissive Christian. She confessed 'I loved him at a rate that . . . I could with all the willingness in the world have died either for him or with him, if God had only seen it fit. Yet I was dumb and held my peace, because God did it, and [I] was constantly fixed in the belief that this affliction came from a merciful Father, and therefore would do me good.' She described it as 'that sad but just chastisement of me'.[128]

Similar assurance of salvation buoyed up the late seventeenth-century nonconformist minister Oliver Heywood in his hour of trial. When his deeply beloved wife of thirty years fell very ill of fever in 1701, he followed exactly the precept 'Trust in God and keep your powder dry'.

I did make full account she would die, and put her into God's hands, seemed content to part with her, having good hopes of her safe arrival in Heaven. But 1. God set me a praying for recovery, with submission of his will. 2. God helped several others, ministers and Christians, to plead affectionately for her. 3. God directed her thoughts to a careful prudent nurse to attend her, Sarah Brooke, who had experience of the like distemper, and was exceeding diligent and active about her. 4. Mr. John Bearcliff, apothecary in Halifax, came to see her, did what he could for her. So that by the blessing of God in 3 weeks time she was better.[129]

It was not merely sickness or death, but the most trivial misfortunes in life which were attributed by the pious Puritan to the direct will of God. When in 1706 Samuel Sewall of Boston got up in bed in the night and pissed in a pot whose bottom fell out, thus wetting himself and the bed, his only comment was that 'there's no security but in God, who is to be sought by prayer'. He explained the accident on the grounds that he had been too tired that night to say his prayers.[130]

The most illuminating example of these beliefs at work in late seventeenth-century Puritan circles comes from Sewall's friend, the leading Boston minister, preacher and theologian, Cotton Mather. When he got a cold, he noted, 'I must enquire after sin as the cause of sickness'. When he had a toothache, he asked himself, 'Have I not sinned with my teeth? How? By sinful, graceless, excessive eating, and by sinful speeches, for there are *literae dentales* used in them.' Whenever a child of his fell sick, he resorted to prayer and fasting, and sometimes came away convinced that God had assured him 'the child should yet live', that 'the child should recover'. Sometimes he would write boldly, 'I lay in the dust before the Lord and obtained mercy for my child'. He seemed to regard the sickness and deaths of his children as instruments to test his will and his virtue. It was on his own spirit of devotion, and of proper resignation to God's inscrutable will, that their future life or death depended. There are hints that he regarded these trials as beneficial means towards his own spiritual advancement, his pain at their suffering or death being a yardstick to assess his own approach towards salvation, and the efficacy of his intercessions with God.

It was not until the slow and painful death of his wife in 1702 that his belief in the power of prayer was shaken. As she grew worse day by day and week by week, despite his prayers and fasting, he was deeply disturbed on not one but two counts: 'Lord, how aggravated a calamity must be her death if such a sting as the disappointment of my particular faith must be added unto it'.[131]

When he finally had to admit defeat, that his prayers were of no avail, he knelt by the bedside, took his wife's hand in his, and 'solemnly and sincerely gave her up unto the Lord'. He then symbolically put her hand away and did not touch her again until she died two hours later. 'This was the hardest, and perhaps the bravest, action that I ever did', he remarked. After her death he

comforted himself on both counts: 'Had she lived, it would probably have
been in continual weakness and languor and sorrow that would have been at
last uneasy to us all. . . . My health would infallibly have been destroyed [by
fasting and prayer on her behalf] if she had recovered a little more, and so far
that should I have run the venture of sleeping with her, my feeble
constitution would infallibly have run into a consumption.' Satisfied on this
point, he then asked himself why his prayers were ineffective; the
explanation being that 'she, herself, in the Court of Heaven, put in a bar to
it'.[132] Sometimes his practice of giving one of his family up to God when he
thought they were dying turned out to be premature. When his daughter
Nanny was in an agony of fever and was speechless in 1703, he knelt by her
bedside and declared that he surrendered her to God, upon which she
recovered her voice, saying, 'I heard my father give me away today. But I
shall not die this time, for all that'. And indeed she recovered two days later.
Thereafter, Cotton seems to have surrendered his dying children to God out
of their hearing. When Sammy was ill in 1709, he 'resigned the child unto
the Lord', adding that 'I did not ask that the child might live and be a rebel
and a traitor to God. No, I had rather have him die in his infancy than live in
cursed and loathsome wickedness.' When in 1713 little Jerusha was dying,
Cotton 'would endeavour exceedingly to glorify God by making a sacrifice
of the lovely child'. When his beloved Kathy was dying in 1716, he wrote 'I
would say, "My Father, kill my child if it be thy pleasure to do so"'.[133]

This deep faith was clearly critical to Cotton in enabling him to explain to
himself the deaths of his children, upon whom he had devoted so much
attention, although so little love. On the one hand, he believed that God
helps those who help themselves, and he was the leader, in the face of
fanatical and ferocious popular hostility, in introducing the practice of
inoculation against smallpox into Boston in 1721, going to the length of
having his son Sammy inoculated to set an example. On the other hand, he
remained strong in his faith in the value of prayer, which on occasion he put
to less laudable purposes than comfort in moments of domestic grief. In
1711, having decided that his own life was of great importance to the welfare
of his family, 'I must, therefore, not only make my own fervent prayer for it
unto the God of my life, but also oblige the children to pray for it
continually'. Five years later, he convinced himself that his wife's only
daughter by her former husband was being maltreated by her husband, 'a
sorry, sordid, froward, and exceedingly wicked fellow'. Cotton, therefore,
kept three whole days of prayer, the principle purpose of which was to ask
God for the death of the man, so that 'the poor child might be delivered from

his insupportable tyrannies'. Soon after the third day of prayer, the previously healthy young man was suddenly stricken with a languishing disease from which he died six months later, despite the ministrations of five skilled doctors. Cotton, who some years before had played a very equivocal role in the persecution of the Salem witches, concluded from this satisfactory chain of events 'how much must a praying life be more than ever encouraged and animated with me'.[134]

It is clear from this account that for Cotton Mather in Boston, as for Oliver Heywood in England, the doctrine of particular providences helped him to cope with the problems of sickness and death which were all around him and which again and again blighted his hopes of domestic happiness. For him, and for those like him, the consolations of religion were based on three beliefs: that sickness and death were the wages of sin, either of the individual concerned or of other members of the nuclear family; that God directly decides on each individual case, on its merits; and that God's wrath can be averted, or even diverted on to others, by the power of prayer. Together they formed a coherent explanation for suffering and death in the world. It was also one which was curiously close to the beliefs of the rural masses in the power of charms, wise men and witches. There is little evidence in Mather's diaries that he was emotionally deeply committed to any of his children. His concern with them was that they should bring him credit and not shame in the community, and that they should by their lives and their deaths serve as witnesses and instruments in his complicated life-long tussle with God.

In England the only group who preserved a similar implicit faith in the direct intervention of divine Providence well into the eighteenth century were the nonconformists. The Reverend Matthew Henry, a nonconformist clergyman in Chester, was reacting just like the Mathers in Boston to the deaths of his children.[135] Puritan doctrine provided spiritual comfort about the future of the dead, although it often left the living with a nagging sense of personal guilt. The rise of doubts about this Puritan eschatology in the early eighteenth century can be traced in the diary of the Lancashire nonconformist Richard Kay in the 1730s and 1740s. As a practising doctor Kay was brought daily face to face with sickness and death, which, given the current standards of medical knowledge, he was almost helpless to alleviate. Slowly he began to wonder whether all this suffering could possibly be deliberately inflicted by an all-wise and beneficent deity. When a child fell into a stone pit and broke a thigh, he asked, somewhat doubtfully, 'Lord, teach us some instructive lesson by every providence that befalls us, or any we are concerned with'. He died at the early age of thirty-five, after much personal physical suffering, and before his growing doubts had undermined his belief in the particular providences of God.[136]

iii. Conclusion

Given the constant liability to sickness, pain or sudden death, the bonds that tied the family together could hardly be more durable than the lines of life itself. The institution was subjected to the endless strain of frequent sickness, often leading to prolonged pain and incapacity or to early bereavement. In 1702 the Reverend Matthew Henry noted with surprise that no-one close to him had died in the last three years. 'Since I set out in the world, I never was so long without the death of children or others near and dear to me.'[137] Family correspondence is filled with such dismal news, the exchange of which formed a bond of a kind between distant relatives, who otherwise had nothing to say to each other.

These frequent deaths were taken as a warning against excessive affective involvement with others. It was for this reason that moral theologians of the seventeenth century, who were such enthusiastic advocates of married love, nonetheless advised moderation in the affections: 'Let this caution be minded, that they don't love inordinately, because death will soon part them'. Thus despite his insistence on the virtues of holy matrimony, Richard Baxter was careful to warn his readers to limit their commitments, and to 'prepare for the loss of children and friends. It is your unpreparedness that maketh it seem unsupportable.' The advice was followed, and when Thomas Shepherd's beloved wife died, he concluded: 'this made me resolve to delight no more in creatures, but in the Lord'.[138] His resolution may not have lasted, but at the time it was clearly a comforting thought. For those, like the Verneys, who were not particularly pious, the consolations of religion were only partly successful in mitigating the horror of their precarious lives, and they were therefore inevitably a grim and rather callous lot. Others, like Mrs Alice Thornton and Ralph Josselin, were sustained by an all-consuming faith in the promise of an afterlife offered by Christianity, which alone enabled them to endure a series of losses without losing heart or withdrawing entirely into themselves. These were typical responses for the sixteenth and seventeenth centuries, but were very different from those of the eighteenth century, when the rise of affective bonding in the companionate family and the decline in religious faith caused the emergence of a different set of attitudes to the problem of death.[139]

5 CONCLUSION

During the sixteenth and seventeenth centuries there took place a series of important changes in the structure of the English middle- and upper-class family, in its social and economic functions, and in affective relationships within it and towards the groups outside it. Under pressure from the state and from Protestant moral theology, it shifted from a predominantly open structure to a more restrictedly nuclear one. The functions of this nuclear family were now more and more confined to the nurture and socialization of the infant and young child, and the economic, emotional and sexual satisfaction of the husband and wife. Within this nuclear core with its more limited and more specialized functions, power flowed increasingly to the husband over the wife and to the father over the children. Although it cannot be proved that the power of the husband and father was more authoritarian and patriarchal than had been in the late middle ages, there are certainly theoretical reasons why this should have been so. He was now less hampered by interference from the kin, either his own or that of his wife, both Church and state were unanimous in reinforcing his authority and pressing new duties on him, and he was now more concerned about the right education of his children, and therefore more likely to interfere with their freedom from a very early age.

There were a variety of causes for the reinforcement of the authority of the father and husband within the family. There was the pressure of state propaganda for an authoritarian state and therefore an authoritarian family; Protestant Reformation emphasis on the role of the household rather than the Church as the agency for moral and religious control; Calvinist views about Original Sin and the need for severe measures towards children to defeat the Devil and punish wickedness; the spread of classical education which exposed more and more children to flogging in school; legal changes in women's rights over property, and the capacity of the family head to dispose of his estates as he wished; the critical need to be able to control a child's choice of marriage partner, education and career; the urge to break the will of one's child because one's own will had also been broken in childhood.

All these are true and necessary causes but they are not, perhaps, entirely sufficient. There is some deeper underlying force at work in the society, both in Protestant and in Catholic areas. Sixteenth- and early seventeenth-century Europe saw a breakdown of old values and sense of order. The unity of Christendom had been irreparably shattered by the Reformation, and the pieces were never put together again. The result was that from henceforth there were various options in terms of religious ideology, faith and practice, and no-one could be completely certain which was right and which was wrong. The first result of this uncertainty was extreme fanaticism. Internal doubts could only be appeased by the most ferocious treatment of those who disagreed. The authoritarian family and the authoritarian nation state were the solutions to an intolerable sense of anxiety, and a deep yearning for order.[140]

The extraordinary obsession with flogging in the sixteenth and seventeenth centuries is evidence of this nagging fear that only the most drastic of measures taken to suppress any form of dissent, deviation or disobedience would suffice to hold together the shaky framework of ordered society. As a result, this was the period when Catholics were flogged to teach them not to believe in the saints and the Virgin Mary; radical Protestant sectaries were flogged for separating themselves from the state Church in order to worship together; vagrants were flogged for being homeless; unmarried mothers were flogged for violating the sexual rules and threatening to raise poor rates; adulterers were flogged for breaking the family monopoly of all sexual activity; children were flogged by parents and schoolmasters to break their wills and to drill Latin grammar into them; wives were flogged by husbands for any act of disobedience by the former, or merely to relieve the frustrations or satisfy the pleasure of the latter. It was the great age of the whip, the sovereign panacea for all social disorders. Family patriarchy was no more than one aspect of a much wider and deeper phenomenon.

Having made this general statement about the growth of patriarchy in the home, one caveat must be entered. In any familial relationship, the degree of affective bonding and the distribution of power over decision-making will, in the last resort, depend on the personal characters of the husband and the wife. All that is here being claimed is that at this particular period in history, law, custom, state propaganda, moral theology and family tradition all conspired to create a set of internalized values and expectations. These values stressed the nuclear family against the kin, maintained coolness and distance in interpersonal relations within the nuclear core, and created expectations of authority and respect by the husband and father, and of submission, obedience and deference by the wife and the children. This being the case, it is reasonable to suppose that in a majority of cases reality conformed, to some degree, to the ideal. It would have taken a woman gifted with great strength of character, independence of mind and tactical skill to be able to wear the trousers in the sixteenth century. Many women undoubtedly possessed these attributes and dominated their families like matriarchs, but to do so they had to struggle against all the standard conventions of their time. This made their task much more difficult, and their success much rarer than at other times when the values of the society were less severely patriarchal. Similarly, many children contrived, at great personal cost, to defend their identity and their willpower against the combined onslaughts of parents, governesses and schoolmasters. But the odds were at this period heavily stacked against them. The period from 1530 to 1660 may consequently be regarded as the patriarchal stage in the evolution of the nuclear family.

It may also be that the generation of children that was hardest hit was that of the late sixteenth century. They were the first to be exposed to the full pressure of Calvinist moral theology. They were also more numerous and better educated than ever before, while their career opportunities were wider and their marriages financially more critical since the society was wealthier. And yet they were also exposed to the love poetry and the plays of Shakespeare and others, which offered an alternative model to that of blind obedience to paternal dictates. It is hardly surprising that there were already signs in the early seventeenth century that some of these conflicts were rising to the surface.

But it was only with the decline of religious, social, economic and political tensions after 1660 that there came a relaxation of the need for familial authoritarianism. As a result, this patriarchal family phase was only a temporary one which had hardly become established before it was undermined by a new set of values. One key aspect of this stage of development, the reinforcement of patriarchal authoritarianism, was already under challenge by the middle of the seventeenth century; another, the weakness of affective bonds between husband and wife and parents and children within the family, was about to undergo a very rapid change. A third, the eschatology that reduced the pain of death within the family, was about to be fundamentally transformed. The situation which has been described was, therefore, characteristic of a transitional stage, squeezed in between the more kin-, client- and community-oriented and more financially bonded family of the late middle ages and the more private, more domestic and affectively bonded family of the eighteenth century.

PART FOUR

The Closed Domesticated Nuclear Family 1640–1800

CHAPTER 6

The Growth of Affective Individualism

'To every individual in nature is given an individual property by nature, not to be invaded or usurped by any: for everyone as he is himself, so he hath a self propriety, else he could not be himself. ... For by natural birth all men are equally and alike born to like propriety, liberty and freedom.'
> (R.Overton, *An Arrow against all Tyrants*, London, 1646, in G.E.Aylmer [ed.], *The Levellers in the English Revolution*, London, 1975, pp. 68–69.)

'All men are naturally in ... a state of perfect freedom to order their actions and dispose of their possessions and persons as they think fit, within the bounds of the law of nature, without asking leave or depending upon the will of any other man.'
> (J.Locke, *Two Treatises on Government*, London, 1689, Second Treatise, sect. 4.)

I INTRODUCTION

The sixteenth-century trend towards increasingly authoritarian relationships within the middle- and upper-class family was progressively overtaken in the late seventeenth and eighteenth centuries by an opposite trend toward greater freedom for children and a rather more equal partnership between spouses. It was a development that was accompanied by a further walling-off of the nuclear family from either interference or support from the kin, and a further withdrawal from the community. Thirdly, there developed much warmer affective relations between husband and wife and between parents and children, which was itself a powerful reason for the declining influence of kin and community. A fourth feature was the identification of children as a special status group, distinct from adults, with its own special institutions, such as schools, and its own information circuits, from which adults now increasingly tried to exclude knowledge about sex and death.

A fifth and last development, which emerged only among the landed elite and hardly affected the bourgeois and professional classes, was the increasingly open recognition and acceptance of sensuality. One result was the open inclusion of eroticism in marital relations as well as in the extra-marital liaisons to which it had previously been, in theory and perhaps also in practice, largely confined. Further discussion of this fourth feature, however, will be postponed until the problem of sexuality is taken up in Part Five of this volume.

Apart from eroticism, these trends first became prominent in wealthy merchant and professional households in the city in the last third of the seventeenth century. From there they spread to the upper landed classes, gathering strength rapidly in the early eighteenth century, and reaching a climax towards 1800.

These changes in human relations within the microcosm of the family cannot be explained except in terms of changes in the macrocosm of the total cultural system, a major reorientation of meaning among those sectors of society which experienced these changes. This being so, the search for explanation must carry us to areas far removed from the family itself, since what is involved is a change in how the individual regarded himself in relation to society (the growth of individualism) and how he behaved and felt towards other human beings, particularly his wife and children on the one hand, and parents and kin on the other (the growth of affect). Before beginning a discussion of this very difficult subject, it should be clearly understood that what is being put under the microscope is a secondary, but highly significant, tendency at work within what still remained at all levels a deferential society based, although to a diminishing extent, on the time-honoured principles of hierarchy and obedience. These principles found open expression in the elaborate rituals of doffing of hats in the presence of superiors; the giving of the wall when passing in the street; the meticulous ordering of official processions such as funerals, by which every rank was allotted his appropriate place; the socially graded arrangements for seating in churches, with the squirarchy hidden behind their high box pews in the chancel, the middle ranks placed at the upper end of the nave, each within his family pew, and the poor clustered on benches at the back; and the regulations in Oxford colleges, whereby each status rank doffed his hat to the one above him, undergraduates to BAs, BAs to MAs, MAs to Fellows, Fellows to the Head. Similarly, the array of huge family tombs which filled the chancels of so many English parish churches in the sixteenth and seventeenth centuries were, like the elaborate genealogies so lovingly drawn up by the heralds, evidence of a widespread and cultivated ancestor-worship, which supported the authority of the elders in the family over the younger members of it.

These elaborate rituals and symbols had profound psychological significance, their purpose being to buttress the social order and protect it from the chaos threatened by the Reformation and redistribution of church property and the growing inequalities of wealth and poverty. In the long run, these efforts were successful in containing the threat of social disintegration, and by the early eighteenth century a period of calm began. By 1720 the old Dissenters were conformist Unitarians and the Catholics were a negligible minority group; the Church was a mere docile appendage of the state and a tool of the establishment; and the social elite had at last settled their century-long political quarrels. Between aristocracy, national squirarchy, local gentry, professional men and wealthy merchant oligarchs, between court and country, there was friction and tension, but no longer bitter and irreconcilable differences. The 'quality' were once more reunited on basic issues.

It was precisely because of this underlying unity of the elites, and of the largely unquestioning habits of deference by those below, re-emphasized daily in action and in prayer, reinforced by the solemn ritual of the death sentence and execution of lower-class criminals against property, that the state apparatus could remain so relatively weak in eighteenth-century England without a total collapse of social order. It was a close thing, anarchy lay only just below the surface, and the authority of the elite was tempered by the fear and reality of a mob riot. But authority held, for, as Burke pointed out, political liberty was – and is – bought at the price of internalized respect for social discipline. Individual autonomy – contemporaries called it 'freedom' or 'liberty' – therefore, was a new luxury which could now safely be indulged in by the well-to-do, and which modified and mitigated the rigidities of a society whose fundamental cohesion was preserved by habits of obedience to legitimate authority, two of the most important aspects of which were the subordination of children to parents, and of women to men.

Individualism is a very slippery concept to handle. Here what is meant is two rather distinct things: firstly, a growing introspection and interest in the individual personality; and secondly, a demand for personal autonomy and a corresponding respect for the individual's right to privacy, to self-expression, and to the free exercise of his will within limits set by the need for social cohesion: a recognition that it is morally wrong to make exaggerated demands for obedience, or to manipulate or coerce the individual beyond a certain point in order to achieve social or political ends. Because these are now such familiar tenets of Western society, they should not be taken for granted. They are culturally determined values, which most societies in world history have despised or deplored, and which most still do. Normally, individualism is equated with narcissism and egocentricity, a selfish desire to put one's personal convenience above the needs of the society as a whole, or those of sub-units such as the kin or the family. The emergence in late seventeenth- and eighteenth-century England of a different set of values, which placed the individual above the kin, the family, the society and even, in some eighteenth-century judicial pronouncements, the state, is therefore a very unusual phenomenon, which requires very careful demonstration and explanation.

It should be noted that the development of personal introspection and the growth of toleration for other individuals stem from what are in some ways antithetical psychological impulses. The most powerful influence behind the first was the overpowering sense of sin and the preoccupation with individual salvation that was the hallmark of the Puritan personality in the seventeenth century, and was greatly stimulated by literacy and the habit of private reading and meditation. The interest in the self sprang from the urgent need to discipline the self – the 'sphincter morality' as the Freudians describe it. Puritanism, introspection, literacy and privacy form a single affinity group of characteristics. They do not, however, necessarily lead to a willingness to respect the liberty or privacy of others. On the contrary, both in England and in New England, they led directly to the creation of a suspicious and inquisitorial society, constantly on the watch to spy out the sins of others and to suppress all deviations from the true way.

The spirit of toleration for the autonomy of others derives as much from indifference as from principle. With its stress on the liberation of other individuals and their freedom in the pursuit of personal goals, it is a feature of the opposite personality type, extrovert, easy-going, and willing to tolerate diversity, if only for the sake of peace. What seems to have happened was this. In the late sixteenth and early seventeenth centuries, two different world views, the Puritanically ascetic and the secularly sensual, were competing for the allegiance of the ruling classes. Between 1640 and 1660 the former won, abused its victory by attempting to impose its values by force, and then collapsed. The result was a strong reaction to hedonism, while Puritanism persisted as a viewpoint adhered to by a minority.

There was thus a major oscillation between two predominant personality types in England in the seventeenth century. Both types, in their different ways, made their contribution, the first to the growth of introspection and the second to the growth of respect for the autonomy of others. Puritanism in its death throes left behind it certain critically important legacies. Despite its authoritarian inclinations, it also emphasized the importance of the individual conscience and of private prayer to God, and in defeat after 1660 it had no option but to plead for religious toleration from the majority. Secondly, its stress on the importance of holy matrimony – meaning marriage bound by mutual affection – helped to undermine its contrary emphasis on the need for strict filial obedience to parents. But it was the post-1660 cultural supremacy of the anti-Puritan character type which built on this foundation decisively to change attitudes towards authority, affection and sex within the middle and upper ranks of society.

2   AFFECTIVE INDIVIDUALISM IN SOCIETY

i. Self-awareness

In the seventeenth century there is clear iconographic and literary evidence for a new interest in the self, and for recognition of the uniqueness of the individual. This is a development common to Europe, and which apparently has its origins in two different strands of thought: the secular Renaissance ideal of the individual hero as expressed in the autobiography of Cellini or the essays of Montaigne; and religious introspection arising from the Calvinist sense of guilt and anxiety about salvation. In England, both influences were at work, although the second seems to have been the most important, at any rate before 1660.

Changes in the predominant type of funerary memorials of the wealthy provide a significant clue to changes in attitudes. In the sixteenth and early seventeenth centuries tombs were nearly all depersonalized family monuments. The contracts specified a featureless stock effigy representing the deceased, to be set within an elaborate architectural framework chiefly noticeable for the display of brightly painted coats of arms that emphasized the antiquity and status connections of the family (plate 10). It was a display of family pomp and position, not a memorial to the individuality of the dead.[1] In the 1620s portraiture was introduced from abroad by Nicholas Stone, and in the late seventeenth century the most common type thereafter became a personalized bust, based on personal sittings or a death mask, although still surrounded by a formal architectural setting with family coats of arms (plate 11). Thus the contract for a late seventeenth-century tomb of the Earl of Dorset specifies that the images should be likenesses passed as satisfactory by the court painter, Lely.[2] In the eighteenth century, there developed the free-standing allegorical figure holding a realistic relief portrait of the deceased, with a poem recounting his virtues and lamenting his death. It was now a highly personal and wholly secular object. Although these were usually installed in the traditional place, the parish church, some of the richer families began to build mausoleums on their own grounds, modelled on prototypes from pagan antiquity, thus detaching the memorials of the family dead from Christian ritual and the Christian public place of worship.[3]

A similar development was the personal portrait in oils or watercolours, first around the court by Hilliard, Van Dyck, Dobson and Lely, and later spreading into the country through visits by itinerant painters from London.

It is true, of course, that this change is in part due to a long-delayed spread of Renaissance artistic styles and fashions, but the fact that these styles laid such emphasis on the individual is nonetheless significant. Those who commissioned these monuments and portraits now wished to commemorate for posterity a personalized image, not a faceless item on a genealogical tree.

At the same time, there developed a series of almost wholly new genres of writing, the intimately self-revelatory diary, the autobiography and the love letter. Partly, of course, these products were the result of a shift from an oral to a written culture among the laity. Literacy is probably a necessary pre-condition for the growth of introspection. But there is more to it than this. In the first place, writing and reading, unlike the telling of tales by the fireside, are inherently lonely occupations. Unless he is reading aloud, which often happened in the seventeenth and eighteenth centuries, the individual is carrying on an interview between himself and the writing on the page, and this inanimate object, this page of paper covered with lines in ink, provided the essential means of communication for the new sensibility. The growth of literacy, moreover, created a literature of self-exploration, from the novel to the love letter. Secondly, there is overwhelming evidence that a desire to investigate the self was greatly stimulated by Calvinist theology and morality. Most of the English diaries and autobiographies written before 1700 were religious in inspiration, their numbers were far larger than those found in Catholic countries, and a disproportionately large proportion of them were the work of Puritans. The Puritan was constantly searching his soul, performing a moral and spiritual stock-taking to discover whether or not he was among the Elect of God. If literacy and Calvinist predestinarian theology were the driving forces, the emergence of these new, intensely personal, literary modes signifies the consequent development of a new, more inner-directed personality.

The first of the new genres of writing was the diary. As David Riesman has put it, 'the diary-keeping that is so significant a symptom of the new type of character may be viewed as a kind of inner time-and-motion study by which the individual records and judges his output day by day. It is evidence of the separation between the behaving and the recording self.'[4] Although the best of these diaries are carefully crafted with an eye to literary form and dramatic plot development, and are sometimes written up from notes or memory days or even weeks later than the events they describe, they nonetheless provide a gold-mine for the social historian. It is thanks to their diaries that Samuel Pepys is someone we know better than any man who ever lived before him, and James Boswell perhaps better than any man who has ever lived.

The second new type of document was the introspective autobiography. 'I write not my gests, but myself and my essence,' explained Montaigne. This particular form first appeared in England in 1576 with the autobiography of Thomas Wythorne, just a year before the first adult self-portrait, by Nicholas Hilliard. The motives behind these productions were mixed. The vast majority of the late sixteenth- and seventeenth-century autobiographies were inspired by a desire to record a profound religious experience, and therefore were mainly written by Puritan nonconformists, many of them Quakers: over two hundred and twenty of this type (many written by women) have survived for the period before 1725. Others were no more than picaresque adventure stories, like that of Lord Herbert of Cherbury, others were inspired by a desire to record for posterity the revolutionary changes they had lived through, like the autobiography of Lord Clarendon. Others were designed to put the authors in a good light, and to convey an uplifting moral message to their children. It was not until the late seventeenth century that the autobiography commonly became both secular and introspective, a record of personal emotions rather than of external events or religious experiences.[5] Lady Halkett is the first English woman whose autobiography is primarily the story of her chequered love-life, and it is at just this time that there is a quantum jump in the number of love letters, like those of Dorothy Osborne to William Temple.

These are all signs of the spirit of secular individualism emerging out of the ashes of religious enthusiasm after 1660, and it would be difficult to exaggerate the significance and novelty of this widespread evidence of a desire for personal self-expression in the late seventeenth and the eighteenth centuries. It demonstrates a wholly new scale and intensity of interest in the self. It is no longer a matter of isolated works written centuries apart by exceptional men of religious genius like St Augustine or Luther; from the seventeenth century onwards there bursts on to paper a torrent of words about intimate thoughts and feelings set down by large numbers of quite ordinary English men and women, most of them now increasingly secular in orientation. There are known to have survived over three hundred and sixty English diaries and over two hundred autobiographies, all written before 1700. Since only twelve autobiographies were written before 1600, only one of which was of the personal type, it is evident that the genre was a seventeenth-century phenomenon, gathering popularity and becoming less religious in motivation and content in the eighteenth.[6]

Undoubtedly a great stimulus to these developments was provided by the disruptions of the Civil Wars, and their aftermath of exile for the defeated. These events tore many families apart, and the only lifeline that bound them was the letter. Many women found themselves not only suddenly saddled with unusual responsibilities, but also dependent on the art of writing to hold their families together.

These same trends inevitably were reflected in the imaginative literature of the day, and were indeed partly responsible for the evolution of the novel from a surface tale of picaresque adventure, like *Robinson Crusoe*, to a deep probe into personal psychology, like *Wuthering Heights*. This was a process which took a long time to develop, and it was only with Richardson in the middle of the eighteenth century that the novel became primarily preoccupied with feelings. Richardson was a pioneer, and had to cast his novels in the form of a series of letters, for lack of a better technical way of conveying his message. But the interest in self-expression was evident long before, for example in Defoe's *Roxana*, and the late eighteenth century sees the full development of the romantic novel, whose central theme was the struggle of love and personal autonomy against family interest and parental control.

This change in the content of novels coincided with a change in quantity. There was an explosion of novels published in the late eighteenth century, stimulated by a reduction in book costs made possible by cheaper paper and larger sales. The latter were made possible because of the new demand provided by the growing army of educated and leisured women, whose needs were met by the invention and spread of the circulating subscription library. The first such library was set up in Bath in 1725, the next was in London in 1739, and by the 1780s they were to be found in all the major market towns of England. These libraries were by then buying some four hundred copies of an average printing of about one thousand. As one heroine of a novel said in 1786: 'I subscribed to a circulating library and read, or rather devoured . . . from ten to fourteen novels a week.'[7]

To sum up the modalities in the growth of self-awareness in the sixteenth and seventeenth centuries, they seem principally to have been the effect of Calvinism in stimulating guilty introspection, the consequences of literacy in generating private reading and correspondence, and the substitution of the novel of feeling for that of adventure, itself the product of demand from a growing mass of educated and leisured women.

ii. Autonomy

The second aspect of individualism was the rising demand for autonomy, which found practical expression in growing resistance to attempts to put extreme pressure on the individual's body and soul. The rise of the sovereign nation state and the religious divisions of the Reformation in the early sixteenth century had increased both the scale and the intensity of those pressures, so that there eventually developed a head-on clash between two systems of values: the one demanded total conformity in deeds and words and even in secret thoughts to the collective will as expressed by the state and the official Church; the other insisted on the right of the individual to a certain freedom of action and inner belief. In the sixteenth century, the first trend was visible all over Europe, as dissidents and deviants were interrogated, tortured and often killed. Treason laws were extended to the spoken word without action, and heresy laws demanded inner agreement with official dogmas which not only changed from year to year, but were concerned with issues, like the real presence in the sacrament, which could not be decided by reason alone. England and Holland were the two countries where opposition to such excessive demands for conformity of belief first officially developed, although they were certainly opposed to the 'Radical Reformation' of Anabaptists and other sects, which were ferociously crushed out of existence by the authorities everywhere, both Catholic and Protestant.

The first clear sign of the new attitude in official circles occurred in the late sixteenth century when Lord Burghley protested against Archbishop Whitgift's inquisitory procedures to investigate private religious opinions, on the grounds that they were making 'windows into men's souls', which he regarded as an illegitimate intrusion into personal privacy. In the middle of the seventeenth century, the English state was headed for a time by Oliver Cromwell, a man who genuinely believed in the virtue of granting 'liberty to tender consciences'. During the heady revolutionary atmosphere of the late 1640s, radicals were busy denouncing all infringements on the freedom of the individual to think as he pleased about religion. 'Why should we hate and destroy one another?' asked the Leveller Richard Overton, 'Are we not all the creatures of one God, redeemed by one Lord Jesus Christ?' Persecution 'is the utter enemy of all spiritual knowledge, a hinderer of its increase and growth. For no man knoweth but in part, and what we know we receive it by degrees, now a little and then a little. . . . Nay, is it not frequent among us that the thing that we judged heresy we now believe is orthodox?'

These and other libertarian ideas of the Levellers of the late 1640s derived partly from religious sectarianism and its stress on the individual conscience, now extended to a contract theory according to which submission to authority is based exclusively on prior voluntary agreement; partly to secular ideas about natural law and the proprietory right every individual had in himself which could not justly be violated by anyone else; partly from ideas about the common law, based on a misunderstanding of the meaning of Magna Carta; and partly from an interpretation of English history based on the false theory of 'the Norman yoke', according to which there had been a golden age of primitive popular democracy in the Anglo-Saxon period, before kings, lords and all the apparatus of tyranny were fastened on England by the Norman Conquest of 1066.[8]

The Levellers were crushed, but some trace of their belief in religious toleration lived on as a minority opinion, as did Milton's bold plea for the abolition of political and religious censorship: 'Let truth and falsehood grapple. Whoever knew truth put to the worse in a free and open encounter?'[9] Moreover, their ideas about an individual's natural property right in himself, and the consequent contractual basis for the state, were eventually incorporated into conventional political thinking, and became a part of standard Whig orthodoxy in the eighteenth century.

More important in this respect, however, was almost certainly the deep-rooted 'country' ideology of fidelity to an ancient 'balanced constitution' that protected the personal and property rights of men of substance from intrusion by the state. First coherently formulated in the parliamentary battle over the Petition of Right in 1628, in the crucible of Civil War and in the political struggles from 1660 to 1720, this ideology took powerful hold of the country squires, and was the inspiration for their political behaviour throughout the eighteenth century. In its fully developed form, it ran something like this: 'The Country consists of men of property: all others are servants. The business of Parliament is to preserve the independence of property, on which is founded all human liberty and human excellence. The business of government is to govern, and that is a legitimate authority; but to govern is to wield power, and power has a natural tendency to encroach. It is more important to supervise government than to support it, because the preservation of independence is the ultimate political good.'[10]

By the late seventeenth century such very different political theorists as Hobbes and Locke both agreed that the individual preceded society. Hobbes' conclusion was that life in the pre-societal world was 'nasty, brutish and short' and that authoritarian controls were the only preservative of public order. But Hobbes was largely without influence, and it was Locke, who built his society on a compact of individuals for the preservation of their private properties, who was the popular theorist for the post-1688 Whig state. Nor is it mere coincidence that the first work in England to idealize the life of the noble savage, Aphra Behn's *Oroonoko*, was published in 1688, the year of the overthrow of Divine Right monarchy.

Although passed through Parliament and accepted by the social elite largely for pragmatic reasons of political necessity rather than idealistic conviction, the fact remains that by 1689 a limited religious toleration was the law of the land, the sovereign powers of the executive were strictly limited, and a few years later political censorship of newspapers and pamphlets was allowed to lapse.

Finally, between 1688 and 1714 large numbers of Tory preachers and politicians were obliged to eat their words and to renounce very quickly two generations of fervent subscription to the doctrines of the Divine Right of Kings and of Non-Resistance to the will of an anointed King. The fact that the change took place so swiftly, and with such relatively little moral soul-searching, suggests that the rhetoric was already something of a hollow façade concealing a void. By 1741, a Tory, David Hume, could say that 'to talk of a King as God's Viceregent on earth, would but excite laughter in everyone.'[11] What had been an accepted political truism in 1540 and 1640 had become a mere joke in 1740.

The Reverend William Butterfield, who was rector of Middle Claydon, not vicar of Bray, described how his own beliefs had evolved. Before 1688, 'Passive Obedience and Non-Resistance and no salvation out of the episcopal communion were the common topics of the court, and popular sermons the test of loyalty and good affection to the Church of England, and the high road to preferment.' After 1688 he 'discharged my mind from those slavish principles of government in the state', and with respect to religion came to the conclusion that 'the more fundamental and essential doctrines of faith and good life being first secured, matters of opinion and external modes and forms of worship and discipline are not to be imposed or urged farther than is consistent with peace and charity.' The new scale of values placed personal morality above religious dogma, as expressed in Pope's famous couplet of 1733:

> For modes of faith let graceless zealots fight
> He can't be wrong whose life is in the right.

The very title of Joseph Trapp's anti-Methodist treatise of 1739 is itself sufficient indication of the change of mood away from the fanaticism of the early and mid-seventeenth century: *The Nature, Folly, Sin and Danger of being Righteous Overmuch* – a message visually reinforced by Hogarth in about 1760 with a popular print entitled *Enthusiasm Delineated*.[12]

This shift of opinion against doctrinal or moralistic enthusiasm inevitably had important repercussions in all spheres of life, including relations within the family. This is because it led to a vigorous debate about divine providence and agnosticism. By 1754 *The Gentleman's Magazine* was complaining that 'the libertine of fashion' was constantly attending 'the disputing societies, where he hears a deal about free will, free agency and predestination, till at length he is convinced that a man is at liberty to do as he pleases. . . .' When coupled with the belief that man's overriding passion is 'the innate desire that is in every man of happiness in general', this conviction led directly not only to a rational defence of suicide when only misery was in prospect, but also to a far more selfish pursuit of personal gratification in domestic life than had previously been thought consistent with a well-ordered society.[13]

iii. Philosophical Ideas

At the root of all the most significant changes of the late seventeenth and eighteenth centuries lies a progressive reorientation of culture towards the pursuit of pleasure in this world, rather than postponement of gratification until the next. One aspect was a growing confidence in man's capacity to master the environment and to turn it to his use and benefit. This reorientation of human goals was made possible by the shift away from an attitude of passive resignation before disease, exploitation, poverty and misery, as being the will of God, relieved only by the promise of reward after death. Man was now freed to seek his own personal pleasure here and now, no longer hedged in by the narrow boundaries laid down by moral theology or traditional custom. This new attitude could lead to anything, from the experimental breeding of specialized dogs and horses and cattle, to the use of sex for pleasure rather than procreation by taking contraceptive measures, and to challenging the wishes of one's parents over the choice of a spouse.

The evidence of rational, this-worldly secularization is too well known to need recapitulation here.[14] What is significant in religion is not so much the growth of Deism and atheism as the growth of an attitude of indifference towards the authority of the clergy, the scriptures and moral theology. One suggestive piece of evidence of this change is the slump between 1650 and 1740 of the number of editions of the Bible published in England, despite the continued spread of literacy (Graph 12). This is not to say that the Bible – and The Pilgrim's Progress – were not still the staple diet of all literate Englishmen, but they had now to compete with novels and with a flood of textbooks on all aspects of nature and the physical world.

It was in the late seventeenth century that English physical scientists and astronomers destroyed traditional ideas about the hierarchically organized universe. Although many scientists, like Leibnitz, strongly denied that their finds were subversive of the hierarchical principle, in fact their work tended to cast doubt upon the theory of the Great Chain of Being, which bound every man, woman and child in a web of dependency and subordination to the will of others and ultimately of the universe. Newton may have been 'the last of the Magi', a superstitious crank, but he was also undoubtedly (if unintentionally), a great liberator of the human mind. In his clockwork universe, Man was now an isolated atomized individual, set free to act as he chose. More important, however, in its influence on society at large, was probably the diffusion through the Royal Society of the Baconian hope that science would supply the technology which would enable man to master nature. Once there was hope of escape from unpredictable catastrophe, it became possible and reasonable to assert one's right to determine and plan one's own future. The first medical breakthrough that gave families some confidence that this might be true was the great success of smallpox inoculation in saving many children's lives, sight and beauty. This suggested that passive acceptance of one's fate was no longer the only, or even the best, response to the problems of life on earth. But there is no direct one-to-one relationship between needs and cognitive systems, so that this argument should not be pressed too hard. It should also be remembered that

Protestantism was a very practically oriented religion, so that, for example, the leading Puritan minister in early eighteenth-century Boston, Cotton Mather, was also the first to introduce the smallpox inoculation. The roots of eighteenth-century self-help lie in religion as well as science.

This sense of control over the environment, and particularly over animal breeding, inevitably led men to choose their wives as one would choose a brood mare, with a great care for their personal genetic inheritance, and to train their children with the same patience and attention as they had long devoted to their horses, dogs or hawks. Often men of infinite leisure, they had plenty of time on their hands which in the eighteenth century could be spent in educating their children in the home. The Lockean model of the child as a plain sheet of paper exactly conformed to current scientific views of the effects of careful nurture in the improvement of domesticated animals.

Other influences were at work to encourage the growth of possessive individualism in economic affairs. Commercial, industrial and agricultural expansion, with individual entrepreneurs using new technologies to increase production, were all powerful motors for cultural change. Evidence of a growing acceptance of the idea of possessive individualism is to be found in the emphasis placed both by the eighteenth-century common law[15] and by political theorists like John Locke on the sanctity of private property; in the new, more favourable attitude adopted towards enclosures of common lands and open fields; and in the abandonment of many of those safeguards against untrammelled and amoral free enterprise which had been erected, by both Anglicans and Puritans, to enforce traditional ideas about the just price, the wickedness of usury, etc.[16]

Another manifestation of the rise of individualism was the revival of the code of honour of the duel which had been more or less held in check before the Restoration by the combined efforts of the Puritans, who regarded it as mere legitimized murder, and the King, who disliked having his friends and courtiers killing one another. In the early years of the eighteenth century duelling rose to a new peak as every gentleman, or bully, stood on the smallest punctilio of offended personal honour. 'Every gaming-table, despicable brothel, tavern, coffee-house, masquerade, the theatres, and even festive meetings, produced its duellist, and the universal fashion of wearing swords allowed no time for passion to subside, or reason to reflect; a walk into the street or into an adjoining room, enabled the parties to wound each other in an instant; revenge and pain maddened them; and death frequently ensued to both.'[17]

EDITIONS OF THE BIBLE AND TESTAMENT

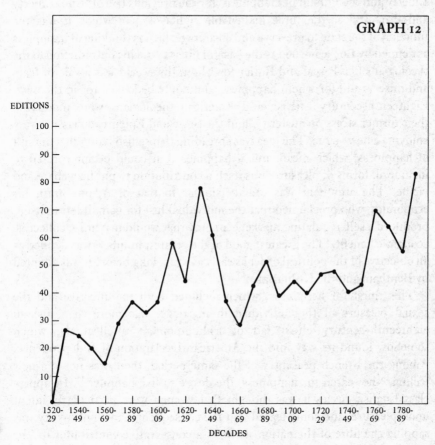

GRAPH 12

EDITIONS

DECADES

One of the most important intellectual innovations of the late seventeenth and eighteenth centuries was to place the selfish pursuit of pleasure in this world at the centre of human psychological motivation. When in the Declaration of Independence of 1776 Thomas Jefferson substituted 'Life, Liberty and the Pursuit of Happiness' for the previous trio of 'Life, Liberty and Property' as the three inalienable rights of man which it was the function of the state to preserve and encourage, he was thinking of happiness as defined by Locke in 1690 as the basis of liberty, and in contradiction to the theologians like Pascal and Butler for whom this world was a vale of tears and misery, and for whom happiness could only be looked for in the next. Eighteenth-century English and American theologians were modifying their former stress on austerity, and the Stoic and Epicurean classics were enjoying a new vogue. The idea was spreading that selfish individual pursuit of happiness, which meant moral happiness but could be interpreted to include all forms of pleasure, was itself a contribution to public welfare and virtue. The argument was exactly similar to that of Adam Smith for economics, who proclaimed that the individual lust for gain, if left to itself, produced a self-regulating market economy that would maximize collective economic benefit. 'The greatest good of the greatest number' was defined as an objective of the political order as early as 1725, long before it was adopted by Bentham and the Utilitarians.[18]

This thirst for happiness, which included both the affective and the sexual pleasure of the individual in marriage, was more than just an eighteenth-century elitist fad of Enlightenment intellectuals, which somehow found its way into the American Declaration of Independence. Among the French peasantry of the same period, there was noted a new feeling, 'the search for happiness, the desire to live happily.'[19] In upper-class English circles it was thought that women were particularly intent upon pleasure, and some feared that the consequent growth of luxury was sapping the fibre of the nation. In 1773 a conservative contributor to *The Lady's Magazine* complained that women 'are incessantly talking about pleasures, and speak of them with a degree of enthusiasm which deceives themselves. . . . The sex endeavour in vain to perpetuate pleasure by varying and refining it. Their invention has multiplied the objects of amusement and created new ones every day.' There was undeniably a remarkable growth of a fashionable leisure industry in the eighteenth century, based in large measure on the increase in the number of women lacking full employment and educated for ornament and amusement.[20] This by-product of the growing wealth, education and luxurious tastes of the middling and higher ranks of society was itself a powerful stimulus to the rise of personal autonomy. That it found expression in opulent frivolity and ever-changing fashions was one of the costs of the liberation of increasing numbers of women from the burden of productive work.

Another broad philosophical movement, which gathered strength throughout the mid and late eighteenth century, was a growing antipathy to cruelty. The origins of this sentiment may be traced back to some obscure zone of English Puritan thought, since its first clear expression is to be found in *The Liberties of the Massachusetts Colony*, adopted by the General Court in 1641. This document placed strict limits on the use of judicial torture to extract information, and forbade husbands to beat their wives or maltreat their servants or apprentices. It even, for the first time in history, legislated to protect domestic animals: 'No man shall exercise any tyranny or cruelty towards any brute creatures which are usually to be kept for man's use.' Since 1641 was the last year in which the English state formally ordered the use of torture on a political prisoner, the same motives must have been working in England to place restraints on the treatment of prisoners by the Parliamentary leaders and Oliver Cromwell, despite the hatreds generated by a bitter civil war.[21]

Late seventeenth-century evidence for this trend of Puritan thought is hard to find, and the spread of revulsion against cruelty in the eighteenth century seems to have been concurrent with, and related to, the spread of Enlightenment ideas throughout Europe. Even then, it was at all times a state of mind confined to a relatively small part of the population. But it was a highly articulate and ultimately very influential part, which slowly learned to employ all the devices of mass persuasion available in what was increasingly an educationally literate and politically open society. Organized in societies formed for the purpose of promoting this or that change, the reformers used the spreading bulk of newspapers, as well as pamphlets, sermons, novels, cartoons and prints, to influence a wider public and then mobilized that public through the machinery of the mass petition to bring pressure on Parliament. They were responsible in the end for such things as the abolition of the slave trade, the suppression of most cruel sports, prison reform, and reform in the treatment of the mentally sick. It is too facile to point out that the most successful of these endeavours affected others than the reformers themselves, and that it was therefore only too easy for the English elite to incorporate the concept of benevolence into their set of cultural imperatives. They had little to lose economically and much to gain in terms of naval power, by the abolition of the slave trade, policed by themselves. The cruel sports which were suppressed were those mainly patronized by the poor – cock-throwing, bull-baiting, bear-baiting, dog-fighting, etc. – while blood sports patronized by the upper classes, like shooting and fox-hunting, went unaffected. Nevertheless, the movement was a genuinely moral one involving the upsurge of new attitudes and emotions, which acquired an enormous stimulus thanks to the development in the mid-eighteenth century of a new ideal type, namely the Man of Sentiment, or the Man of Feeling, the prototype of the late eighteenth-century Romantic. Conformity to this new ideal positively reinforced the legitimacy of the ruling class.

Be that as it may, this new attitude was directly reflected in children's books of the late eighteenth century, which inculcated the need to avoid cruelty to animals and violence and brutality towards human beings. The connection between maltreatment of animals and maltreatment (and murder) of human beings was the theme of Hogarth's popular set of openly propagandist prints, *The Four Stages of Cruelty*, published in 1751. Years later, Hogarth remarked that he thought 'the publication of them has checked the diabolical spirit of barbarity to the brute creation, which, I am sorry to say, was once so prevalent in this country.' Ten years later there was published a most successful book for young teenagers, *The Newtonian System of Philosophy adapted to the Capacities of young Gentlemen and Ladies ... by Tom Telescope*. This work inculcated into the young the same distaste for cruelty to animals, and extended the moral to include slaves and others. 'Kindness to animals, yes, but greater kindness to human beings is the burden of Tom's final lecture.'[22]

This moralizing was often wrapped up in a package which to modern tastes seems nauseously sentimental, but the message was new and clear. One has to steel oneself to read such boring, moralistic and sentimental contemporary best-sellers as Richardson's *Pamela*, or the archetype of the new trend, Henry Mackenzie's *The Man of Feeling* of 1770, in which there is an outburst of weeping (by either sex) on average every ten-and-a-half pages. But behind the flow of tears there lies a new attitude towards man's inhumanity to man. For about half a century, from 1770 to 1820, it was fashionable to express emotional anguish concerning cruelty, a distress which finally opened the way to remedial legislation and institutional reform. The sickly romanticism that surrounded this movement was ephemeral, and Lady Louisa Stuart recalled that when in 1826 she tried to read aloud *The Man of Feeling* to a group of friends, they now laughed instead of cried.[23]

Prominent among the leaders of the movement for humanitarian reform were nonconformists, especially Quakers over the slave trade and Evangelicals over cruel sports. These same men were also, inevitably, responsible for the movement of moral repression that began in earnest to affect all classes after 1770: the Society for the Suppression of Vice was founded in 1801, two years after the founding of the Royal Institution for Bettering the Condition and Increasing the Comforts of the Poor. Material aid and moral reformation went hand in hand. In its effect on family life, the connection between hostility to cruelty to animals and to cruelty to children is clear enough, while both slaves and women were ultimately beneficiaries, along with felons and madmen, of the drive for legal protection for the helpless. At the same time, the Romantic movement encouraged a more openly emotional involvement in family relationships. Thus some of the improvements in the treatment of wives and children of the middle and upper classes, particularly in the latter half of the eighteenth century, were spin-offs from this growing desire to ameliorate the human lot and to reduce the amount of sheer physical cruelty in the world. Why this movement should have emerged with such power at this particular moment in history remains a mystery, but its success undoubtedly owes much to the evangelistic enthusiasm of its leading protagonists and their skilful use of the new media of mass communications that had only recently become available.

3   AFFECTIVE INDIVIDUALISM IN THE FAMILY

i. Attacks on Patriarchy

The most direct and explicit link between political theory and family life occurs in John Locke's *Two Treatises on Government*, published in 1689, but written a decade earlier. The first Treatise attacked Robert Filmer's *Patriarcha*, which had based the authority of the king in the state on the analogy of the authority of the father in the family, and in the process it redefined the latter as well as the former. Marriage was stated to be a mere contractual relationship giving 'common interest and property', but not, for example, the power of life and death over a wife. It was argued that the power of the father over his children is merely a utilitarian by-product of his duty to nourish them until they can look after themselves. It is thus only a limited and temporary authority, which automatically ends when the child grows up. In any case, paternal authority is irrelevant to the authority of a king, to which adults voluntarily submit on condition that he acts for their own good.[24] The practical need to remodel the political theory of state power in the late seventeenth century thus brought with it a severe modification of theories about patriarchal power within the family and the rights of the individual.

In 1691 Guy Miège tried to save the situation by the bizarre argument that 'The law of Nature has put no difference (or subordination) amongst men, except it be that of children to their parents or of wives to their husbands. So that with relation to the law of Nature, all men are born free.'[25]

This neat trick by which the law of nature as the basis for a contractual system of government was reconciled with the continued subordination of women and children naturally did not go unchallenged. The issue had already been debated on the stage in 1697, when in Vanbrugh's play *The Provoked Wife* Lady Brute applies Locke's breakable contract theory of the state to her own situation: 'The argument's good between the King and the people, why not between the husband and the wife?' In 1701 Mary Chudleigh also criticized men because

> Passive Obedience you've transferred to us
> . . . .
> That antiquated doctrine you disown,
> 'Tis now your scorn, and fit for us alone.

In 1706 Mary Astell asked 'If absolute sovereignty be not necessary in a state, how comes it to be so in a family? Or if in a family, why not in a state? . . . Is it not then partial in men to the last degree to contend for and practise that arbitrary dominion in their families which they abhor and exclaim against in the state? . . . If all men are born free, how is it that all women are born slaves?'[26]

The incompatibility of domestic patriarchy with the political theory of contractual obligation became so glaring that the moral theologians were forced to modify their position. In 1705 Bishop Fleetwood set out the new doctrine, which in effect undermined the traditional absolute authority of the father and husband. 'There is no relation in the world, either natural or civil and agreed upon, but there is a reciprocal duty obliging each party . . . I only mention this to make it very evident that the obligation of children to love, honour, respect and obey their parents is founded originally upon the parents' love and care of them.' Marriage was now similarly a contract, with mutual rights and obligations, whose nature could be debated endlessly. It was still the duty of wives to be 'submissive, subject and obedient to their husbands', but it was also the duty of husbands to 'love their wives', a duty which carried obligations of affection, fidelity and care.[27]

In 1724 Bernard de Mandeville added his satirical pen to the continuing debate. By making fun of a father who was still 'preaching nothing but Passive Obedience and Non-Resistance to his daughter', he helped to undermine parental authority over the marriage of their children. He put into the mouth of the opponent of this view the Lockean idea that 'when we come to be of age, we are no more tied to so strict an obedience to their commands'. He also took the side of wives against husbands, describing an offer of marriage as 'that the person to whom he pays his devotion would be so kind as to oblige herself solemnly, before witnesses, on the penalty of being damned, to be his slave as long as she lives, unless he should happen to die before her.'[28]

Domestic patriarchy was also coming under attack from religious dissenters. After the Restoration, the radical dissenting sects were well aware of the importance of patriarchal power in the household as an obstacle to their proselytizing mission. In 1666 John Bunyan denounced 'mad-brained blasphemous husbands that are against the godly and chaste conversation of their wives; also you that hold your servants so hard to it that you will not spare them time to hear the Word.' He was driven by his frustrations to demand a relaxation of household patriarchy as a means of exposing women, children and servants to his preaching. Others felt the same way, and the publisher and bookseller John Dunton in about 1705 flatly declared that rigidly patriarchal heads of households 'are no better than domestic tyrants, and the perfect enemies to peace within doors'.[29]

Another philosophical trend, towards the pursuit of individual happiness as an ideal, also had profound repercussions on ideas about power relationships within the family. Under this new scale of values, marriage ceased to be mainly an artificial but necessary constraint placed upon man's otherwise unbridled lust, and became instead a prime source of personal pleasure, both emotional and sexual. Those who wished to reduce the amount of adultery were concerned to make marriage a companionate bond freely entered into, so that sexual passion could be more comfortably confined to the marriage bed. This new pragmatism planned to make the individual's selfish desire for happiness contribute to the common good. As such, it was a potent force eroding the legitimacy of patriarchal control of marriage arrangements among the propertied classes.

It is symptomatic of how far this new attitude had penetrated the thinking of the landed classes that when the clause in Lord Hardwicke's Marriage

Bill, making parental consent obligatory for all under twenty-one, was being debated in Parliament in 1753, there was opposition to it on ethical as well as self-interested grounds. It was said that the clause involved 'controlling all the emotions of love and genuine affection in youth by the frigid maxims of avarice and ambition imbibed by age.' The result would be to enforce 'a splendid and wretched state of legal prostitution in which the happiness of the party was sacrificed to the pride of family.' Twenty years later a female writer to *The Lady's Magazine* was alleging that 'no law was ever made since the Revolution that has occasioned so many broken hearts, unhappy lives, and accumulated distresses as this has.' Behind the windy rhetoric there clearly lies a passion for individual welfare as opposed to family interest, which would never have found wide acceptance at an earlier period. The contrast with Lord Halifax's cynical and pessimistic *Advice to a Daughter* of 1688 could hardly be greater.[30] The opinions of Romeo and Juliet were now emerging from the mouths of their parents.

The practical consequences of this slow shift of opinion soon showed up in many areas. The mounting criticism of the sale by auction of the wardship and marriage of fatherless heirs and heiresses by the Crown in the seventeenth century, culminating in the abolition of the court at the Restoration, is one piece of evidence of the spread of a sense that each individual has certain innate rights which should not be bartered away by anyone else. This sentiment was directly applied to marriage by the political philosopher James Harrington in the 1650s: 'Whereas it is a mischief beyond any that we can do to our enemies, we persist to make nothing of breaking the affection of our children.'[31] This observation was the product of a new attitude towards the proper responsibility of parents and children in matrimonial decision-making. Practices which had been acceptable to most children in 1560 or 1600 were now being challenged by theologians and philosophers as well as by the children themselves.

Another way this criticism of patriarchy made itself felt was in the establishment of new property arrangements among wealthy landowners. It will be remembered that between about 1500 to 1660, the current owner was relatively free to dispose of his estates as he wished, which gave him a formidable weapon to help impose his will upon his children. The threat of partial or even complete disinheritance as a penalty for disobedience was a very real one. During the early seventeenth century, progressive attempts were made by current owners to tighten up the legal arrangements again so as to preserve the family patrimony, and to reduce the freedom of their successors to alienate it. These efforts culminated in the development in the middle of the century of a legal device called the 'strict settlement'. Under its provisions, the powers of the current owner were once again reduced to those of a life trustee, since he had willed away his rights to his unborn children in a settlement drawn up before his marriage.[32]

This resulted in a third set of family property arrangements, by which the owner was again no more than a life tenant, but careful provisions were now made for the settlement of annuities or marriage portions on all children before they were born. The owner could thus neither alienate the property nor deprive any of his children of their arranged inheritances. He could reward favourites by giving them more, but he could not punish those who displeased him by giving them less. The rights of each member of the family were thus clearly defined and carefully preserved against encroachment by any other member. The difference that the strict settlement made was not in changing the distribution of property among the children so much as in reducing the arbitrary control of the father over that distribution and therefore his power to enforce his own will upon them over such critical issues as marriage. That this was the issue at stake was clearly seen at the time, and in 1715 Defoe described 'the mischievous consequence of leaving estates to children entirely independent of their parents' as 'a fatal obstruction to parental authority.'[33] This was an exaggeration, but not an unreasonable distortion of the new reality of a decline in patriarchy within the family. More enlightened parents, however, came to regard it as morally wrong to manipulate their children by the exercise of economic blackmail. Thus in 1775 Mrs Hester Thrale, who was by temperament a dictatorial and authoritarian parent, was given power by her husband to settle her own inherited estate on her children in any manner she wished. Her lawyer pointed out to her that 'I had a right to leave it to whichever of my children I pleased, or to keep such a right in reserve for the greater encouragement of them to duty and attention. But I scorned to create such paltry dependencies and resolved to entail it according to birth alone, that there might be no temptation in me to practise, or in them to suspect, so mean partiality.'[34]

The concept of individualism, the respect for the rights of others, that lay behind Mrs Thrale's self-satisfied comment, is clearly of decisive importance in guiding this change. A second possibility is that the change was in part a product of a revival of confidence among large landowners in the long-term economic and political prospects of their families. Having weathered the economic crisis of the late sixteenth century and the political crisis of the early seventeenth century, the survivors dug in, seized power over patronage and consolidated their gains. The experience of the Civil War confiscations convinced many of the need for legally water-tight vesting of title in trustees rather than in the name of the current owner. In any case there was a rising interest in the long-term continuity of the family heritage. By now the newly enriched gentry of the sixteenth century were well established, several generations of younger sons had built up a reserve bank of male heirs if direct succession failed, and their estates were beginning to acquire the lustre of ancient possession. The current owners were therefore increasingly anxious to ensure family perpetuity, particularly since the first sufferers from any new limitations on property transfers would be not themselves but their heirs. They could, therefore, be virtuous at the next generation's expense.

Another feature of late seventeenth- and eighteenth-century marriage settlements was that far greater care was taken to protect the property rights of the wife. Not only was an allowance of pocket-money – 'pin money' – specified in the marriage contract, but increasingly she was managing to keep more of her own property under her personal control. Partly, this was due to a series of judicial decisions in the law courts, which went a long way towards protecting married women's property. Partly, also, it was because an increasing number of women, especially widows, were taking the precaution of vesting their property in separate trustees before marriage, so that their husbands could not touch it. Men who found their powers hampered in this way often took it very badly. When Sir John Guise made his second marriage in 1710, it was under the novel system of the separation of estate and goods. He found it most unsatisfactory, causing him eight years of hell, and he advised his posterity 'Let all men and women, I say, avoid these things.'[35]

At first sight this reaffirmation of the principle of primogeniture to preserve in perpetuity the family estates appears to run contrary to the spirit of individualism, which might seem to argue for partible inheritance. In fact, however, the careful provisions for younger sons, daughters and widows secured the rights of all parties, and thus undermined the principle of patriarchal power. By this means, primogeniture was successfully harmonized with individualism, although admittedly it preserved a highly inegalitarian distribution of family resources.

Less tangible indication of the same underlying trend of thought can be seen in attitudes towards family prayers, towards death, and towards personal and bodily privacy.

ii. Decline of Family Prayers

The general decline in religious enthusiasm in the late seventeenth and eighteenth centuries carried away with it the role of the husband and father as the religious head of the household, symbolized by the regular assembly of all members, often twice a day, to hear him lead the family in prayer and obtain his blessing. The corrosive influence of the individual religious conscience bred of sectarian radical ideas in destroying this traditional hierarchical custom is well brought out in the autobiography of the later Ranter, Laurence Clarkson. His religious career began in his teens in the 1630s by defiance of the views of his cautiously conformist Arminian father. He found himself unable to accept the Book of Common Prayer and, therefore, was driven to reject his father. 'The next thing I scrupled was asking my parents' blessing; that oftentimes in the winter mornings, after I have been out of my bed, I have stood freezing above, and durst not come down till my father was gone abroad. And the reason, I was satisfied the blessing or prayers of a wicked man God would not hear, and so should offend God to ask him blessing. For either of these two ways I must down on my knees and say "Father, pray to God to bless me", or "Give me your blessing, for God's sake", either of which I durst not use with my lips.'[36]

This appeal to the individual conscience generated by religious radicalism was one factor in the undermining of family prayers, but far more important was the general decline of religious enthusiasm and religious practice in the reaction against the rule of the Puritans after the Restoration. In the 1660s, Samuel Pepys, who seems to have been fairly average in his respect for religious observance, only held a family service once a week, on Sunday evenings, when the maid read a passage from the Bible and Pepys led the family prayers. In 1692 John Dunton in the *Athenian Mercury* urged his numerous bourgeois readers to keep up the old practice of family prayers in the home, one reason being that it 'conciliates respect and reverence to the head of it' – a frank confession of its function in reinforcing patriarchy. It was the current decline in family prayers, Dunton thought, which was responsible for the rise of 'atheism, profaneness and all kinds of villainy'. An anonymous pamphleteer of about 1700 and Defoe in 1715 reiterated the complaint that family worship and religious instruction were dying.[37] Three-quarters of a century later it was dead: in 1778 James Boswell lamented 'that there was no appearance of family religion today, not even reading of chapters. How different from what was the usage in my grandfather's day, or my mother's time.'[38]

It is no coincidence that this formal ritual of regular, daily, collective family prayers developed in the sixteenth century, along with patriarchalism; declined in the eighteenth century as a more egalitarian, individualistic and companionate family type developed; revived again in the nineteenth century along with the Victorian patriarchal family;[39] and died out once again in the twentieth century with the revival of the more egalitarian and permissive family type. The rise and fall of family prayers coincided not only with the rise and fall of religious enthusiasm, but also with the rise and fall of patriarchy in the family.

iii. Changing Attitude to Death

An important result of the decline in religious enthusiasm in the late seventeenth and eighteenth centuries was the decline in the belief that every event, and in particular every death, is the result of the deliberate, if inscrutable, will of God. This faith in the direct intervention of God in all aspects of human affairs was directly challenged by a new theological view of Providence, expressed by a single sentence of Lord Halifax, written in 1688: 'take heed of running into that common error of applying God's judgements upon particular occasions.'[40] This was the logical conclusion of the new theology of Free Will, and view of God as a remote watchmaker presiding over the maintenance of a mechanical universe. Now the sickness or death of a wife or a husband or a child could no longer be resignedly accepted as the purposeful will of God. In conventional Anglican circles, the old attitude towards death was collapsing in the early eighteenth century, as ideas about the randomness of personal misfortune and a more pragmatic view of the possibilities of human intervention were spreading. In 1740, the *Gentleman's Magazine* ruminated dubiously that 'it is a wonderful part of the providence of God that so many little creatures seem to be born only to die' ... God, who does nothing in vain, has wise ends, no doubt, and purposes worthy of Himself to serve.' Scepticism was clearly creeping in, despite the formal reassertion of the beneficence of God's Providence. Only the Wesleyan Methodists still clung throughout the eighteenth century to 'the doctrine of a particular providence'. John Wesley learned it from William Law's *Serious Call to a Devout and Holy Life* and interpreted it 'practically, so as to apply it to every circumstance of life'.[41]

The public ritual of the death-bed scene, the formal paying of respect to the corpse, the elaborate funeral ceremony, and the formal period of mourning all persisted into the eighteenth and nineteenth centuries. But the decay of belief that every death is directly willed by God, together with the growth of a more affectionate relationship between husbands and wives and parents and children, changed the meaning of the death of a spouse or a child. Previously, death had been a highly formalized ritual, a *rite de passage* on the way to Heaven, the chief actor being the dying man, ideally repentant, resigned to God's will, and fortified by the consolations of religion. The centre of attention now shifted from the behaviour of the dying to the response of the living, for whom death was now no more than a meaningless personal bereavement, the extinction of a loved one. Individualism destroyed the concept of the substitution of one person for another, and opened the way for what Professor Ariés has described as the grief-laden obsession with 'Thy Death'.[42] This marks a change in cultural attitudes towards death which definitely pre-dated any change in the rates of mortality and seems to be wholly unconnected with any social or economic transformation. It is a product of the growth of individualism and the change in religious eschatology.

One result of the change is the appearance on tombs of the widow, seated or kneeling in an attitude of mourning beside the effigy of her dead husband. Later, in the full romantic phase of the late eighteenth century, the skeletal figure of Death was prominently displayed, coming to claim his victim (plate 9).

Evidence of the new sensibility is provided by changes in public attitudes towards churchyards. From being multi-purpose places where the dead lay, the children played, the grown-ups talked, bargained, made love and quarrelled, and the cattle grazed, they became places set apart for the dead alone, ringed by walls, and invested in romantic melancholia. It is no accident that Thomas Gray's *Elegy written in a Country Churchyard*, first published in 1751, achieved an immediate and enormous success, not so much for its intrinsic poetic merits, as Gray shrewdly realized, as for 'the affecting and pensive cast of its subject'. It was part of a whole genre of literary products of the 1740s and 1750s, ranging from Dr Young's *Night Thoughts* to James Harvey's *Meditations on the Tombs*, which exploited this popular interest in the theme that all flesh is grass and our time on earth is short.[43]

The death of an infant or young child was no longer shrugged off as a common event on which it would be foolish to waste much emotion. A good example of the new response by a conventional eighteenth-century Christian is that of James Boswell to the death of his five-month-old son David in 1777. 'I was calm as I could wish, and resigned to the dispensations of God. My wife was in real grief, but composed her mind better than I could have expected.' Boswell carried the corpse upstairs and laid it on a table in the drawing-room. The next day, 'I was tenderer today than I imagined, for I cried over my little son, and shed many tears. At the same time I had really a pious delight in praying with the room locked, and leaning my hands on his alabaster frame as I knelt.' The next day the corpse was put in its coffin, and Boswell read the funeral service over it, before it was removed to the cemetery. There is no suggestion in this account of anything but a purely domestic and private mourning, carried out in full romantic style, with all the emphasis on the response of the bereaved. As usual, no member of the family attended the funeral.[44]

The death of an adolescent child had inevitably always been far more traumatic for the parents, but even here there are changes. There was an intensification of grief in the eighteenth century, and it was expressed not only more openly, and more bitterly, but also less ritually, in a more personal, more introspective manner. Members of the nuclear family now dramatized their sense of loss in violently expressive, and no doubt highly therapeutic ways. One may suspect that the changing response owed something to the growth of literacy, which encouraged a more private form of grief, as well as the growth of a more child-centered family and the decline in belief in God's far-sighted but inscrutable providence. In the 1740s, when Richard Cumberland was a schoolboy at Westminster, his seventeen-year-old sister Joanna came up to London to visit him, caught smallpox and died after eleven days of agony. The family was shattered by the blow. 'My father, who tenderly loved her, submitted to the afflicting dispensation in silent sadness, never venting a complaint. My mother's sorrows were not under such control, and, as to me, devoted to her as I had been from the cradle, the shock appeared to threaten me with such consequences' that he was removed from school and taken home to recover from what appears to have been a total psychological collapse.[45]

Similarly in 1759 when Arthur Young's elder married sister died in childbirth, their mother was completely broken by the event. She 'grieved so much for her loss that she could never be persuaded to go out of mourning, but mourned till her own death, nor did she ever recover her cheerfulness.' As for Arthur Young himself, his marriage turned out unhappily, and all his hopes were centered on his beloved daughter 'Bobbin'. When in 1797 the fourteen-year-old girl caught tuberculosis and died, Young suffered a blow from which he never recovered. 'There fled the first hope of my life', he later noted. He adopted the romantic plan of burying the girl's corpse under the family pew in the church, 'fixing the coffin so that when I kneel, it will be between her head and her dear heart.' There is an obsession here with the physical remains that does not match the formal statements of confidence in the afterlife of the soul, but which occurs again and again in the eighteenth century.[46] The fashionable preoccupation with melancholy presupposed a certain scepticism about the prospects of another and a happier world after death.

At the height of the romantic period, the sufferings of parents at the death of a child reached an extreme intensity. In 1821 the little son of William and Barbara Ponsonby died slowly of fever over a period of twelve days, to the horror and despair of his parents. 'William's heart seems breaking, as he stands pale and motionless all day and almost all night at the foot of that little bed', wrote the child's grandmother; 'to see them hanging over him and trying to warm his little cold hands in theirs made my heart ache almost to breaking.' This was a time when even the death of an infant only a few weeks old was the cause for an outpouring of grief. When in 1814 the two-month old baby of Lady Caroline Capel died (her thirteenth child), the mother was overwhelmed. Her daughter reported that 'our baby, since she was born has never been touched but by those who loved her. During her illness, she was always in her mother's arms; died upon her mother's breast; was laid out by her sisters; watched day and night by her mother and sisters; by them laid in her coffin; and by them conveyed to her grave.'[47] Some years earlier, in 1790, the wife of a Kidderminster doctor had lost her baby with even more gruesome psychological results: 'This unhappy mother refused for several days to part with the remains of her child. She dressed the corpse as the living baby had been dressed, and kept it with her day and night till the mob threatened to tear down the house.'[48]

These numerous stories of extreme grief at the death of a child in the late eighteenth and the beginning of the nineteenth centuries mark a new phase in middle and upper-class responses to infant and child mortality. Among the classes sufficiently affluent to afford such luxuries, emotional anguish for the death of a baby was now both a social convention and a psychological reality, one which was later used to reinforce the profound religiosity of the mid-Victorian propertied classes. It is not merely that many more women were literate and were, therefore, putting their emotions on record. The nature and quality of those emotions were themselves changing.

Not only was the attitude of adults to death changing in significant ways, but there is some reason to think that for children death itself was becoming less familiar. Partly, this was due to the decline of both child and adult mortality rates in the late eighteenth century, to the removal of hangings to the privacy of the prison yard, and to the decline of the elaborate rituals which used to surround a death in the family. In any society the first physical contact with death is bound to be a shock to a child, but unfamiliarity makes the shock greater. In 1791 the two-and-a-half-year-old son of Thomas Butt of Worcester was taken by the maid for a walk through the churchyard, where he accidentally ran into 'the corpses of two little children on their progress to the grave'. The child, who could barely talk, came home deeply disturbed. 'Two little children, big me', he said, 'put in coffins – close. Naughty servants put these – to go underground – deep – deep – buried – death.'[49]

Up to about the 1770s parents of all classes generally thought that it was a valuable experience to expose young children to corpses, and even to executions. In 1757 the twelve-year-old Thomas Holcroft was taken by his shoemaker father to see a hanging, which in those days was a process of slow strangulation. 'His convulsive struggles to my young and apprehensive imagination were intolerable. I soon turned my eyes away, unable to look any longer.' In 1772 Lord Spencer took his eleven-year-old daughter down into a dark crypt at Toulouse, where there were stacked hundreds of macabre black mummified corpses. When the girl showed fear, 'Papa ... said I must conquer it and go and touch one of them, which was very shocking.' By now, however, other parents were trying to shelter their children from death, instead of deliberately exposing them to it. When in 1774 her aunt died in her father's house, where her three children were staying, Mrs Philip Francis hastily removed them to their school, 'for I thought it would be terrifying to children to be in the house with a corpse.'[50] It is difficult today to realize how relatively new it was to have such a thought, and how short-lived it was. It was part of the trend to treat children as different in kind from adults: persons from whom certain basic facts of life, first rather tentatively about death, and later in the Victorian period very positively about sex, should be withheld as unsuitable.

This new attitude to death, when coupled with the increasing number of companionate marriages, meant that the early and unexpected death of a spouse now more frequently had traumatic effects on the survivor. For example in 1778 Boswell met in a London street David Ross, who had married the famous courtesan Fanny Murray (to whom Wilkes had addressed his *Essay on Woman*). Ross broke down in the street and 'cried for the death of his wife', a response for which one can find no parallel in the sixteenth or early seventeenth centuries, when death was accepted as God's will. Again when in 1793 Lord Herbert lost in childbirth his wife after only seven years of marriage, he was deeply affected. 'I suffer martyrdom from the horrid and continued struggle to keep down the appearance of being overcome with grief, and though I do keep it down, I believe most surprisingly, I suffer the more for it when alone.'[51]

The dying, as well as the survivors, were affected by the decline of confidence in the consolations of religion. George Crabbe testified that to the rural poor around 1800, death was now a psychologically frightening and physically painful event:

> I've seldom known, though I have often read,
> Of happy peasants in their dying bed,
> Whose looks proclaim'd that sunshine of the breast,
> That more than hope, that Heaven itself express'd.
> What I behold are feverish fits of strife,
> 'Twixt fears of dying and desire for life.
> Those earthly hopes, that to the last endure,
> Those fears, that hopes superior fail to cure.[52]

Death was now an ugly business, without religious meaning or consolation. The great cultural change between attitudes to death in the sixteenth and early seventeenth centuries on the one hand and in the eighteenth century on the other was succinctly, if cynically, summed up by Lady Mary Wortley Montagu in 1749: 'The money formerly given to monks for the health of the soul now is thrown to doctors for the health of the body, and generally with as little real prospect of success.'[53]

The Evangelicals, and especially the Methodists, were the only group in the late eighteenth century which exploited to the full for purposes of the discipline of children the ancient threat of death and damnation. John Wesley and his followers were very ambivalent about Original Sin. They laid great stress on its inevitability, but they conceded its mitigation by the Prevenient Grace of baptism. They sometimes spoke of infants as symbols of unspotted purity and innocence, and at other times urged one another to 'teach them that they are sinful, polluted creatures', 'little more than an animal'. They believed that 'the great end of life is to prepare for death', and were convinced that education was an uphill struggle against depravity. Since they genuinely cared for children, and expressed tenderness and love for them, they rejected brutal physical punishment, and instead resorted to the old Puritan practice of instilling in children the fear of death, an event individually determined by God. 'Read often treatises of Death and Hell and of Judgment', advised Thomas White. Since they believed so strongly that little children should realize that 'time is short ... eternity is endless', they made a special point of exposing them to the physical realities of death. 'Present my respects to your son, and tell him that last week I buried three young persons', wrote one Evangelical to another. In Mrs Sherwood's most popular early nineteenth-century novel *The Fairchild Family*, the children were deliberately exposed to the dead. 'Have you ever seen a corpse, my dears?' asked Mrs Fairchild, before taking the children to see the putrefying body of a neighbour, or a condemned criminal's rotting remains hanging in chains from a gibbet.[54]

Isaac Watts' *Divine Songs in Easy Language for the Use of Children*, which was first published in 1715, was one of the best-sellers of the late eighteenth and early nineteenth centuries, selling some eight million copies between 1775 and 1850. Some of the poems spoke of the infant child as pure and innocent, unsullied by the world, while others harped on less genial themes.

> There is an hour when I must die
> Nor do I know how soon 'twill come.
> A thousand children young as I
> Are called by death to hear their doom
> . . . .
> There is a dreadful Hell
> And everlasting pains.
> There sinners must with devils dwell
> In darkness, fire and chains.

Disobedience to parental wishes was singled out as a crime especially repugnant to God.

> Have ye not heard what dreadful plagues
> Are theatened by the Lord
> To him that breaks his father's law
> Or mocks his mother's word?
> . . . .
> The ravens shall pick out his eyes
> And eagles eat the same.

Out of the nine illustrations in a book of *Poetry for Young Persons* of 1827, five were concerned with death, three being graveyard scenes, one a death bed and one a dying child, while the *Evangelical Magazine*, published from 1793 onward, was full of luridly graphic accounts of pious death-bed episodes.

The attitude to death of the Evangelicals of the 1790s was thus precisely similar to that of Puritans like Cotton Mather in the 1690s, and the poems of

Isaac Watts provide a direct chain of continuity. Hell and Damnation was the constant theme of prayer, threat and meditation, and death was seen as the result of the personal decision of God, which the pious Christian should accept without complaint. *A Mother's Thanksgiving for the Death of her Child* was the revealing title of one of Wesley's poems, and children themselves were constantly reminded that they were 'a sinner born/A child and heir of Hell.'[55] This seventeenth-century eschatology, which was to become more widespread again in the nineteenth century, was in direct contrast to the more conventional eighteenth-century position adopted among the educated classes, that death was no more than a personal physiological accident unplanned by God, the main significance of which was its psychological effect upon the survivors.

iii. Personal Privacy

The most striking change in the life-style of the upper classes in the seventeenth and eighteenth centuries was the increasing stress laid upon personal privacy.[56] From the middle ages through to the sixteenth century, the great household had functioned more like a modern commune than a modern family. Everyone, all the time, was on public display. In the seventeenth century, however, the master and mistress of the household staged a withdrawal. The superfluously large horde of domestic servants was trimmed to a functional size. The family ceased to dine in public on high table in the great hall with the servants, and withdrew to the private dining-room. In the eighteenth century the adult family often served themselves from a 'dumb waiter' in order to ensure total privacy. They ceased to ride conspicuously through town and countryside at the head of a great cavalcade or retinue and withdrew to the shuttered coach and the curtained sedan chair. Private rooms, like 'the study', 'my lord's chamber', 'my lady's chamber', were built for individual seclusion. Billiard-rooms, and later smoking-rooms, were built to divide the sexes. And the house was split into four basic subdivisions: the public rooms for mass entertaining; the family rooms; the servants' quarters with their own access staircases; and the nursery area for the children.

The great houses of the fifteenth and sixteenth centuries had been constructed of interlocking suites of rooms without corridors, so that the only way of moving about was by passing through other people's chambers. In the late seventeenth and the eighteenth centuries, however, house plans allocated space to corridors, which now allowed access without intruding upon privacy. In some of the older courtyard houses, as at Beechwood

(Hertfordshire) in 1702, Althorp (Northamptonshire) in the 1790s and Wilton (Wiltshire) in 1801, a thin addition was added to the inner walls, containing corridors which at last permitted circulation without an invasion of other people's bedrooms. Inventories of goods show a decline in the practice of putting truckle beds here, there and everywhere. Most bedrooms were transferred upstairs, leaving the ground floor for living-quarters. Although public rooms remained large, there was a proliferation of smaller rooms where daily life was increasingly led.[57]

The motive was partly to obtain privacy for individual members of the family, but more especially to provide the family itself with some escape from the prying eyes and ears of the ubiquitous domestic servants, who were a necessary evil in every middle- and upper-class household. It is significant that the first protests against the invasion of privacy caused by servants came from the middle classes, who were the worst sufferers since their houses had less space for escape and who were the first to become sensitive to the problem. In 1725 Daniel Defoe complained that 'you are ... always at the mercy of every newcomer to divulge your family affairs, to inspect your private life, and treasure up the sayings of yourself and friends. A very great confinement, and much complained of in most families.' Many years later Dr Johnson warned acidly:

> They first invade your table then your breast,
> Explore your secrets with insidious art,
> Watch the weak hour and ransack all the hearts,
> Then soon your ill-paid confidence repay,
> Commence your lords, and govern or betray.[58]

That Dr Johnson was speaking no more than the truth was amply proven at the trials for noble adultery of the eighteenth century. The key witnesses in these trials were always servants, whose prying curiosity clearly made sexual privacy almost impossible for anyone of standing who wished to conduct a discreet affair in his or her own home. Always, at all times of day or night, servants were spying through cracks in the wainscoting, peering through keyholes, listening at doors to hear the rhythmic creaking of beds, and carefully inspecting the bedlinen for tell-tale stains. The architectural innovations of the eighteenth century were a help, but they offered inadequate protection from such watchful and prurient curiosity.[59]

These trends to architectural privacy mainly affected the wealthy, but in the seventeenth and eighteenth centuries the housing of all classes down to that of yeomen and tradesmen became more varied, more subdivided and more specialized in function, and thus afforded greater privacy.[60] The provision of such facilities does not necessarily mean, however, that they were always used. George Crabbe the younger describes the house of his great-uncle, a very wealthy yeoman farmer of the late eighteenth century, with an income of £800 a year. He lived in a large house with all the gentlemanly appurtenances, including a marble-paved hall, drawing-room, and dining-parlour. But these rooms were only used 'on great and solemn occasions', such as rent day or the occasional visit of a neighbouring nobleman. At all other times, the family and their visitors lived entirely in the old-fashioned kitchen, along with the servants.[61]

One piece of evidence that farmers, shopkeepers and artisans now wanted more privacy in the home was that apprentices and unmarried wage labourers were increasingly removed from the households of their masters. According to Francis Place, this was already taking place among labourers and apprentices in London in the third quarter of the eighteenth century. In 1753 an MP remarked that urban day labourers now lived in lodgings rather than in their masters' houses, and in the 1770s Joseph Brasbridge recorded that his apprentice slept at his father's house, so that 'I had ... no control over him after the business of the day was ended.' The removal of agricultural servants from the farmhouse took place in the very remote and backward area of South Lindsey in Lincolnshire in the second quarter of the nineteenth century. It was thus between 1750 and 1850 that there occurred this major change in living arrangements.[62] As a result, paternal control of employers over their adolescent labour force declined, and the non-monetary component of rewards – free food and free lodging – were replaced by wages in money. This in turn signified the cultural erosion of paternalism in the relations of employers and employees, and the increasing isolation of the domestic nuclear household. So far as can be seen, this was not a development fought for by servants seeking personal freedom in the teeth of paternalist opposition from masters, but was one that for different reasons suited the new ideas about domestic life of both parties. The change brought greater liberty for the servants and greater privacy for the masters.[63]

As for the poor, who constituted the majority of the population, they continued well into the nineteenth century to live in one- or two-roomed houses. Under these conditions, privacy was neither a practical possibility nor, one imagines, even a theoretical aspiration. As George Crabbe delicately, but firmly, put it in 1807:

> See! Crowded beds in those contiguous rooms,
> Beds but ill parted by a paltry screen
> Of paper'd lath or curtain dropp'd between.
> Daughters and sons to yon compartments creep
> And parents here beside their children sleep.
> Ye who have power, these thoughtless people part,
> Nor let the ear be first to taint the heart.

The common practice among the poor of the sharing of beds by two, three, or even four persons made even visual sexual privacy impossible. In Elizabethan Essex, court records quite incidentally turn up evidence of a man having intercourse with a girl while her sister was in the same bed and of a case in which the girl's mother was in the same bed. There was simply nowhere else to go, and there is every reason to suppose that this indifference to sexual privacy persisted well into the nineteenth century; in fact, until working-class housing began to be slightly less grossly overcrowded. At the age of four Francis Place, who was born in 1771, was still sleeping with his two-year-old brother in a bed alongside that of their parents. When he grew up, for the first nine years of their married life he and wife lived, ate, slept and worked in a single room, during which time they conceived three children. As late as the early nineteenth century, Henry Mayhew regarded as one of the main causes of the loose sexual morality of the poor 'the single bed-chamber in the two-room cottage'. And yet in some areas the two-room cottage was itself a luxury: in one slum parish of Bristol in 1838, forty-five per cent of all families lived in one multipurpose room, while another thirty-eight per cent lived in no more than two.[64]

v. Bodily Privacy

One aspect of this trend to individualism and privacy was an outgrowth of the Renaissance Humanist stress on 'civility', defined as a set of external behaviour traits which distinguished the civilized from the uncivilized.[65] Spreading outwards and downwards from the princely courts of Europe, this aspect of Renaissance thought was particularly stressed by Erasmus. One of the features of this new 'civility' was the physical withdrawal of the individual body and its waste products from contact with others. It is no coincidence that the fork, the handkerchief and the nightdress arrived more or less together and spread slowly together in the late seventeenth and early eighteenth centuries. A plentiful supply of plates, knives, forks, and spoons were now provided by the host, to be changed at each course. They were meant for personal use only, and were no longer to be dipped in the communal dish after being put in the mouth. There was no longer any chance of a mingling of the salivas of different persons around a dinner-table. Another aspect of the same trend was the rise of personal cleanliness. Spitting was frowned upon. Shaving the head and using wigs, which became common among the elite in the late seventeenth century, though no doubt mainly adopted to stay in fashion, was one way to keep down lice. Finally, the habit of washing the body, and the introduction of wash-basins and portable bathtubs into the bedroom began to spread among wealthy households in the late eighteenth century.

The motive behind all these refinements of manners is clear enough. It was a desire to separate one's body and its juices and odours from contact with other people, to achieve privacy in many aspects of one's personal activities, and generally to avoid giving offence to the 'delicacy' of others. The odour of stale sweat, which had been taken for granted for millennia, was now beginning to be thought offensive; spitting and nose-blowing were now to be carried out discreetly, and indeed the former was actively discouraged. Both sexual activity and excretion became more private, preparing the way for nineteenth-century prudery. The development of these new behaviour patterns clearly had nothing to do with problems of hygiene and bacterial infection, which were never even mentioned in the conduct books. It had exclusively to do with conforming to increasingly artificial standards of gentlemanly behaviour, which were internalized in the young at an early age (the apogee of this development being the intensive toilet training of the infant in the nineteenth and twentieth centuries).

The essence of this movement was to create a culture in which the elite, the gentleman and the lady, were clearly distinguished by a whole set of immediately recognizable external behaviour traits. Even their language now began to divide on status lines. In the sixteenth century the prime characteristics of language were local dialect rather than national status patterns, but by the eighteenth century there was a fashionable language taught at school and used in the upper-class home, which overrode the provincial dialects of the uneducated. A new word was invented for this elite: 'the quality', a word whose significance is clear enough.

4   CONCLUSION: THE CAUSES OF CHANGE

In the sixteenth century and earlier, the standard world view was that all individuals in society are bound together in the Great Chain of Being, and all are interchangeable with each other. One wife or one child could substitute for another, like soldiers in an army. The purpose in life was to assure the continuity of the family, the clan, the village or the state, not to maximize the well-being of the individual. Personal preference, ambition and greed should always be subordinated to the common good.

The second view, which developed in the sixteenth and seventeenth centuries, was that each individual thinks of himself as unique, and strives to impose his own will on others for his selfish ends. The result is a Hobbesian state of nature, the war of all against all, which can only be brought under control by the imposition of stern patriarchal power in both the family and the state.

The third view, which developed in the late seventeenth and early eighteenth centuries, was that all human beings are unique. It is right and proper for each to pursue his own happiness, provided that he also respects the right of others to pursue theirs. With this important proviso, egotism becomes synonymous with the public good.

i. Causes of the Rise of Individualism

The causes of the evolution of this third view have been spelt out at length. They involve a complex of semi-independent developments spread out over more than a century, each evolving at its own tempo. The result was not, however, a mere intersection of curving lines, but the shift of a whole system of values, which dominated the thinking of substantial numbers of the English elite.

Contemporaries were vaguely aware that apparently wholly disparate developments might somehow have linkages to each other. Thus in 1761 the *Annual Register* remarked that 'Time, which has enclosed commons and ploughed up heaths, has likewise cultivated the minds and improved the behaviour of ladies and gentlemen of the country.'[66] How time performed these miracles, and how they were connected, the writer prudently left obscure. To him they were apparently tied together only by the commonality of the word 'cultivation' in treating of agriculture and manners. One can, perhaps, try to be a little clearer than that in sorting out the causes of the change.

a. Economic. It is not difficult to list economic changes that were helping to create greater personal and familial autonomy, and a relaxation of community discipline. Progressive enclosure of the common fields was destroying co-operative village farming; guild and corporation controls of production and distribution in the towns were weakening; the growth of a market economy was encouraging new economic strata and new economic organizations, particularly the family trading or artisanal shop, and the free wage labourer; population pressures and the gigantic growth of London were generating geographical mobility and giving an increasing proportion of the society some experience of the quality of life in a big city, where earned income mattered more than ascribed status, production more than consumption, and where the principal ties were with one's workmates in the shop; new attitudes to property were developing, by which men now had economic rights divorced from social obligations; human relationships were increasingly seen in economic terms, governed by the rules of the free market. All these trends helped to stimulate the growth of 'possessive individualism' as applied to economic behaviour. Novel ideas about the elasticity of demand, due to man's infinite desire for more and new goods, were based on the identical psychological principle. Man was egotistical, vain, envious, greedy, luxurious and ambitious. His main desire was to differentiate himself from his neighbours in some way or another. As Nicholas Barbon put it in 1690, 'The wants of the mind are infinite. Man naturally aspires, and as his mind is elevated, his senses grow more refined and more capable of delight. His desires are enlarged, and his wants increase with his wishes, which is for everything which is rare, can gratify his senses, adorn his body, and promote ease, pleasure, and pomp of life.'[67]

How far this theory of pleasure-seeking economic individualism in turn stimulated individualism in other spheres of life cannot, of course, be proved one way or the other. But it seems plausible to suppose that there was some carry-over. Dr Johnson was undoubtedly correct when he pointed out to Boswell the corrosive influence of a monetary market economy on feudal dependencies and kinship networks. The cultural lag between Scotland and England is sufficient proof of the critical importance of this basic economic factor. Boswell

talked of the little attachment which subsisted between near relations in London. Sir, said Johnson, in a country so commercial as ours, where every man can do for himself, there is not so much occasion for that attachment. No man is thought the worse of here whose brother was hanged. In uncommercial countries many of the branches of a family must depend on the stock; so, in order to make the head of the family take care of them, they are represented as connected with his reputation, that, self-love being interested, he may exert himself to promote their interest. You have first large circles, or clans; as commerce increases, the connection is confined to families. By degrees, that too goes off, as having become unnecessary and there being few opportunities of intercourse.[68]

b. Social. One critical social development was the emergence to a position of economic, and to a limited extent political and social, eminence of a wealthy entrepreneurial bourgeoisie. There are two reasons why persons from this background are likely to be more receptive than others to the principle of affective individualism. Firstly, their whole way of life is based on a strict code of personal behaviour, emphasizing thrift, hard work and moral self-righteousness. The association of so many of this class with nonconformity in the late seventeenth century and with Evangelicalism in the late eighteenth and early nineteenth centuries is no coincidence, since there is a psychological congruity between these religious beliefs and the day-to-day achievement-oriented behaviour of an economically upwardly mobile social group. In their striving to achieve respectability, they are particularly likely to be affected by popular didactic works of religious or secular morality, especially in the area of home life. Cast adrift by their economic and professional success from the cultural moorings of the class from which they have emerged, they adopt whatever doctrine seems most appropriate to their new condition of life. Because of their high level of literacy and their sense of moral purpose, they are avid readers of current didactic literature. Upwardly mobile themselves, they care for their children and are anxious to give them the benefits of the elite education which they themselves may have lacked. Often deeply religious, in the seventeenth century they were strongly affected by the current stress on holy matrimony and marital affection. Their business experience make them value autonomy and self-reliance as the way to succeed in this world. They are therefore the first to shed the ties to their own kin (although they use marriage ties to cement business connections), to stress merit and the sanctity of contracts, to develop close affective relations within the home, and to lavish care and attention upon their children.

This new social class, with its new familial values, first appeared, so far as we know, in fifteenth-century Florence, and to judge from seventeenth-century Dutch economy, politics and art, it also flourished among the wealthy mercantile patriciate of Amsterdam in the seventeenth century. Indeed, it is probably partly from this Dutch model that the English bourgeoisie of the late seventeenth century derived its domestic values and its self-confidence, for this was a period in which Dutch influence on English culture and economy was at its maximum. On the other hand, the development of a prosperous bourgeoisie alone is not sufficient to generate affective individualism. Only under certain cultural circumstances will they serve as carriers of the new ideology, as is shown by the fact that Renaissance

Genoa had a wealthy bourgeoisie like Florence, and Renaissance Venice a wealthy ennobled bourgeoisie, but both failed to develop either the nuclear affective family or the autobiography.[69]

The second social fact of central importance is the predominance – politically, socially and culturally – of the squirarchy in England, resulting from its consolidation of control over local government, and its near monopoly of high prestige and status. It was in the interests of this landed elite, in loose alliance with the commercial and professional upper bourgeoisie, that there were invented the new ideas about a limited contract state, religious toleration, and a Bill of Rights. Stimulated and sustained by the 'country' ideology, it was the concept and reality of individual liberties and individual property rights among this group which was so carefully nurtured and protected in the eighteenth century by the common law and by cultural convention. The political events of the seventeenth century were crucial in this respect.

Thanks to the extraordinary homogeneity of English elite society, and the ease of cultural and social connections between the landed classes and the wealthy bourgeoisie from the late seventeenth century, the latter's ideas about domestic behaviour soon spread to the squirarchy, with Locke's *Some Thoughts upon Education* and Addison's *Spectator* as the key instruments of their propagation. Together, the upper bourgeoisie and the squirarchy thus formed the elite which not only dominated political, social and economic life in the eighteenth century, but which served as the carrier of these new cultural values in personal and family life. There had been bourgeois cultures before and elsewhere, but nowhere else had they spread their values through the landed elite as well. The reasons the squires were so open to these familial ideas lie partly in the high degree of intermarriage between them and the bourgeoisie; partly in the congruence of the ideas with the political 'country' ideology of the contract state which had been evolved to justify squirarchy control of the political machine; and partly in their congruence with ideas about 'holy matrimony' that had been passed on from the moral theologians, first Puritan and then Arminian, in the first half of the seventeenth century.

c. Ideological and Political. These purely economic and social changes provide a necessary, but certainly not a sufficient, cause for the rise of individualism, and on another occasion in 1778 Dr Johnson admitted that something else was involved. He recognized the obvious fact of the general decline of social deference.

Subordination is sadly broken down in this age. No man now has the same authority which his father had – except a gaoler. No man has it over his servants; it is diminished in our colleges, nay in our grammar schools. . . . There are many causes, the chief of which is, I think, the great increase of money . . . Gold and silver destroy feudal subordination. But besides there is a general relaxation of reverence. No son now depends upon his father as in former times. Paternity used to be considered as of itself a great thing which had a right to many claims. That is, in general, reduced to very small bounds.[70]

Dr Johnson was thus forced to recognize the rise of autonomy as an ideal, independent of the corrosive effect of the market economy. What he was noting had been observed by Defoe over half a century before, when he reported a conversation in which a fictional cloth-worker refused to address a clothier as 'master'. 'Not my master, an it please your worship, I hope I am my own master.'[71] There is more to this remark than a mere change in economic organization. It symbolizes a cultural change, a decay of patriarchy and deference as an ideal and a practice, involving the decline of the authority of both employers and household heads.

Dr Johnson made no attempt to explain this change, nor to relate it to the complex but convergent set of ideas, some of them inherited from the egalitarian and individualistic movements thrown up by the English Revolution, which were current from the late seventeenth century.

The most important underlying trend which allowed vent to this desire for autonomy in the late seventeenth century was the recovery of psychological balance, the dying away of the siege mentality of the late sixteenth and early seventeenth centuries, which saw everywhere a conspiracy of evil, planning the satanic capture of the world. In this more relaxed atmosphere, the pressure for unquestioning obedience and conformity within the family, as within the society, naturally declined.

In the late seventeenth century, this psychological relaxation and the failure of the great Puritan experiment at moral regeneration from 1640 to 1660 led to the (temporary) collapse of Puritanism as a major religious and moral force in English life. As it withdrew into isolated nonconformity, however, Puritanism bequeathed a number of essential – if unintended – legacies to the more secularized society that succeeded it. The 'Puritan ethic' of thrift, sobriety and hard work survived the decline of Puritanism to find its finest exponents in Benjamin Franklin and Samuel Smiles, and was internalized in the eighteenth-century bourgeois family. Secondly, respect for the individual conscience directed by God was one element of Puritanism (which, in many other ways, was repressive and authoritarian) that survived to help create not only the desire to provide religious toleration for 'tender consciences', but also to induce a respect for personal autonomy in other aspects of life. Thirdly the stress by the Puritans on the need for holy matrimony was ultimately incompatible with the patriarchal authority which they also extolled. How could paternal control over the choice of a marriage partner be maintained, if the pair were now to be bound by ties of love and affection? The concession of some element of choice was an inevitable by-product of such thinking, and it is no accident that it was the late seventeenth-century nonconformists who led the way in demanding freedom for children in the choice of spouse.

Other religious views also led to wholly unforeseen consequences. Slowly, the Protestant churches began to place mutual comfort as one of the main – sometimes even *the* main – purpose of marital sex, no longer viewed as an instinct mainly limited to the purpose of procreation. This immediately cast doubt on the previous hostility to sex during pregnancy since it could not lead to procreation. This forced the French Catholic Church, which interfered minutely in such matters through the confession box, to reconsider its condemnation of any other sexual position than the 'missionary' one, since penetration from the rear, or the woman on top would obviously be less potentially damaging to a child in the womb. By such twists and turns, the moral theologians opened the door to the eighteenth-century treatment by many laity of sexual pleasure as an end in itself, free from the centuries-old sense of sin and guilt imposed by the Christian Church.

A fifth area where the moral theologians led the laity into unforeseen problems was the dilemma over paid wet-nursing. There was general medical agreement, supported by modern statistics about contemporary conditions, that wet-nursing was far more dangerous for the child than nursing by the mother. It was also held that sexual excitement in a nursing mother spoiled her milk, while if by chance she should become pregnant, the milk would dry up altogether and the suckling child would therefore die. Since nursing normally lasted a year to eighteen months, the moral theologians, with their concern for holy matrimony and the avoidance of 'unnatural practices' and of adultery, were forced to choose between advising the resumption of sexual relations with a nursing mother – thus endangering the life of the child – or forbidding it – thus risking adultery by the sex-starved husband. When in doubt they tended to prefer the former.

A final important development, which seems to have been an accidental by-product of Puritan theology and its accompanying haunting sense of guilt, was the growth of self-awareness. This is shown by the fact that the bulk of diaries and autobiographies of the seventeenth century come from the pens of Puritans. Deprived of the comforts of the confession box and driven by anxiety over their salvation into a strict moral account-keeping, they took to writing diaries as a means both of confession of sin and of checking up of their moral balance-sheet. They also wrote autobiographies to stress the significance in their lives of their conversion experience. It is no coincidence that the two most intimate English diarists of the seventeenth and eighteenth centuries, Samuel Pepys and James Boswell, were both brought up under Puritan direction, and were haunted thereafter by a lingering sense of guilt about their exuberant enjoyment of all the pleasures of life, especially those of the flesh.

Thus the effective christianization in the late sixteenth and early seventeenth centuries, for the first time, of large sectors of the population had profound effects on family life which lasted long after religious enthusiasm had ebbed, and hardly any of which were either intended or anticipated. It was the reaction to the excesses of Puritanism, however, which provided other important contributions to the trend towards individual autonomy. One was the eighteenth-century hostility to 'enthusiasm' of all kinds and the consequent growth of a willingness to tolerate most forms of Christian sectarianism provided they did not disturb the public peace. When toleration at last became a positive virtue, a great step had been taken in the direction of autonomy. Without in any way meaning to do so, the march of natural science in the late seventeenth century greatly aided the rise of latitudinarianism and eventually even of Deism, and thus contributed to this mood of sceptical toleration. 'This is, I believe, the first age that has scorned a pretence to religion,' remarked a woman in Henry Fielding's *The Modern Husband* in 1732.

Another result of the decline of Puritanism was the rejection of the concept of Original Sin, of the infant child as being born an agent of the Devil. For this pessimistic theory was substituted the idea, given immense publicity by Locke's *Some Thoughts on Education* of 1693, that an infant is a *tabula rasa*, a blank sheet upon which the adults can imprint either good or evil. This did not do much to mitigate the desire to mould the child, but it did a lot to stimulate a show of love and affection in the home, and to reduce physical brutality in the schools.

If 1660 saw the end of the rule of the Puritans, 1688 saw the end of the absolutist monarchical state. There is no need to rehearse the century-long struggle of the English landed classes represented in Parliament and aided by powerful elements in the urban bourgeoisie, by which the power of the Crown and the executive was effectively checked between 1620 and 1714. The successful reduction of authoritarianism in the political constitution gave extraordinary freedom to the propertied classes. England was ruled by aristocrats in the interests of the squirarchy and the bourgeoisie. This comfortable arrangement was eventually reflected in upper-class family arrangements where there took place a relaxation of the tyranny of fathers over children and husbands over wives, and also in school education where brutal flogging by masters was increasingly condemned in theory, and reduced – but not abolished – in practice.

The connection between the decline of absolute monarchy in the state and the decline of patriarchal authoritarianism in the family was made very explicit in the debate between Robert Filmer and John Locke in the 1680s. After forty years of inconclusive wrestling with this inconvenient theoretical problem by the defenders of limited monarchy and by Republicans, Locke at last cleared the way in the first of his *Two Treatises on Government*. He realized that he had to destroy the ancient argument, so forcibly restated by Filmer in his *Patriarcha*, at last published in 1680, that the authority of a King and that of a father were directly linked by scriptural authority and the natural laws of hierarchy. He therefore abandoned scripture, and relied solely on natural law, which was now becoming the normal basis for philosophical discussion. He argued that conjugal society was formed by voluntary contract for the purpose of begetting and rearing children. There was no need for absolute sovereignty in marriage to achieve these limited ends, but merely leadership by the stronger and wiser of the two, namely the man. The marriage contract could therefore include a wide variety of dispositions about a wife's property, and in logic could be dissolved at will once its purpose was fulfilled, that is when the children left home. For fear lest this argument might not prove convincing, Locke advanced a second, that the relationship of absolute monarchy to domestic patriarchy was in any case not direct and logical, but merely a rhetorical analogy, so that even if patriarchy did exist in the family, it would not prove that absolute sovereignty must exist in the society. Locke therefore covered himself on the political front, even if the public rejected his very advanced arguments about the voluntary, limited, variable and terminable nature of the marriage contract. But the fact that he put forward these radical arguments about marriage in the first Treatise did not escape the notice of contemporaries, as we shall see. They posed a real problem for political Whigs anxious to maintain paternal authority in the home, and they helped to undermine the psychological, although not the legal, foundations of domestic patriarchy in England.[72]

It was in the atmosphere created by this relaxation of psychological tension, this decline in religious enthusiasm, and this new political theory that in the mid-eighteenth century some of the ideas of the Enlightenment were enabled to take root. Thus family relationships were powerfully affected by the concept that the pursuit of individual happiness is one of the basic laws of nature, and also by the growing movement to put some check on man's inhumanity to man or animals which is so prominent a feature of eighteenth-century intellectual and political life. It is difficult not to believe that the prolonged campaign to reduce the regular flogging of children for minor academic lapses at school, and the abandonment in some circles of the use of all physical punishment in the home, was not connected with this general trend against casual brutality in day-to-day life. The vanguard of the movement was composed partly of Enlightenment thinkers – Voltaire was prominent in these areas – partly, especially in England, of the Dissenters and Evangelicals, and partly of the average, educated MP and JP, clergyman and schoolmaster. It was almost entirely a middle- and upper-class movement, of persons who prided themselves on being 'Men of Sentiment' or 'Men of Feeling'. Some of the first effects of this movement were to create a far more permissive mode of child-rearing in certain classes, and probably also in some measure to improve the conditions of wives. Public opinion, for example, no longer approved of wife-beating as a pastime for frustrated and drunken husbands, any more than it approved of ferocious punishment of apprentices or servants. The arbitrary power of the head of the household physically to discipline those living under his roof, whether members of the family or not, was very significantly reduced. Moreover, it was proto-Enlightenment, and then later Enlightenment ideas which made possible the striking improvements in female education which took place in the eighteenth century, the purpose and result of which was to make them better mothers and more companionate wives.

By the early eighteenth century, complete identification had been made between the pursuit of gratification by the individual and the welfare of the public. In 1733 Alexander Pope concluded one section of his *Essay on Man* with the words: 'Thus God and Nature link'd the general frame/And bade self-love and social be the same.' He then went even further, concluding the next section with the claim 'That Reason, Passion answer one great aim/That true Self-Love and Social are the same.'[73] In these two couplets Pope drags in God, Nature, Reason and Passion to support a proposition which can only be described as a transformation of human consciousness. For the first time, some men were beginning to believe – with very little justification – that the egocentric pursuit of self-interest contributed to the public good rather than to its destruction. Secondly, Pope's identification of passion and reason as working to the same end rather than as polar opposites harmonized emotion and logic. It thus prepared the way for the rise of romantic love as a respectable component of marital strategy and married life.

Pope's blithe assumption of the identity of self-love and the public good had many taproots, most of which we have already mentioned. In religion, there was the old Puritan and nonconformist belief that in the last resort the dictates of the private conscience are the ultimate guide to behaviour, and will in the long run lead to the salvation of mankind. In political thought, John Locke had already popularized the theory that each individual has an inalienable right to life, liberty and property, to protect and secure which is the sole basis and justification for the social contract on which the political power of the state depends. In economics Adam Smith was later to popularize the idea that, thanks to the 'hidden hand', the sum of each individual's greedy acquisitive instincts will maximize the economic benefits of the community. In psychology, Locke and others had already laid down that each man has a natural property in himself, not to be violated by any, and that the pursuit of happiness is man's instinctive and legitimate aspiration, the satisfying of which is the true aim of the good society.

ii. Causes of English Leadership Over Europe

In order to answer the subsidiary question, not why individualism grew in this period, but why England took the lead over continental Europe, it is necessary to separate developments which were peculiar to England from those which were common throughout the whole of western Europe.

This-worldly secularism, literacy, the pursuit of happiness, humanitarianism, physical and bodily privacy, and personalized death were common to the whole of Western culture. But it was the high development of the market economy in England that made possible and necessary the theory of economic individualism; the legacies from Puritanism of respect for the individual conscience, the ideal of holy matrimony, and the admission by Protestant theology that sex could be for purposes other than procreation were also ideas very limited in their geographical scope; the development of a large, wealthy, powerful and cultivated upper bourgeoisie was confined to Holland, England and France; the seizure of power by the gentry after a bloody civil war and the creation of a state based on the theory of a mutual contract between sovereign and people were purely English; the strong sense of cautious pragmatism engendered by such an historical experience and so delicately balanced a polity was very English; the cultural homogeneity of upper bourgeoisie and gentry, which allowed ideas to flow freely from the one to the other, was also peculiarly English, as was the absence of censorship and the creation of a large unified market of 'the quality' for literary production of all kinds; the role of London as the only political, economic and cultural centre of the country was unique; the development of the novel of sensibility, and the enormous growth of novel-reading thanks to the generalized institution of circulating libraries, were especially English phenomena. One can thus identify some specifically English features over and above those shared by all of Europe, which adequately explain the wide and early diffusion of new familial ideals and practices throughout the middle and upper ranks of English society. As a result, nowhere else, so far as we know, did the landed classes accept so readily the wide ramifications of the ideology of individualism, the notion that self-interest coincided with the public welfare.

iii. Causes of the Growth of Affect

The abandonment of the principle of human interchangeability and the rise of the concept that each person is unique, and cannot be exactly replicated or replaced is adequately explained by these convergent forces. The rise of affect, however, is only partly a product of individualism, and seems to have its roots also in a basic personality change. In the sixteenth and early seventeenth centuries there predominated a personality type with 'low gradient' affect, whose capacity for warm relationships was generally limited, and who diffused what there was of it widely among family, kin, and neighbours. In the eighteenth century there predominated among the upper bourgeoisie and squirarchy a personality type with 'steep gradient' affect, whose general capacity for intimate personal relationships was· much greater, and whose emotional ties were now far more closely concentrated on spouse and children. The cause of this personality change is not known, but it seems plausible to associate it with a series of changes in child rearing, which created among adults a sense of trust instead of one of distrust.[74] There were also two ideas which helped to stimulate affect in the eighteenth century. The first was the new confidence that the pursuit of happiness, best achieved by domestic affection, was the prime legitimate goal in life. The second was the new ideal of the 'Man of Sentiment' who was easily moved to outbursts of indignation by cruelty and to tears of sympathy by benevolence. Finally there was the slow structural shift that first weakened the power of the kin, and then that of the parents. With this shift in power went a change in concepts of duty and obligation.

These two trends towards individualism and towards affect came together to form Affective Individualism, the development of which in bourgeois and squirarchy family life in the late seventeenth and eighteenth centuries is the theme of the next three chapters.

CHAPTER 7

Mating Arrangements

'Who marrieth for love without money hath good nights and sorry days.'
(J.Ray, *A Collection of English Proverbs*, Cambridge, 1670, p. 17.)

'There is a certain trifle not much thought of in modern marriages called love.'
(D.Defoe, *Review*, 1704 (Facsimile ed., ed. A.W.Secord) vol. III,
Supplementary Journal, no. 1, p. 9.)

*'Parents require in the man fortune and honour, which are requisite to make the
married state comfortable and honourable. The young lady may require personal
accomplishments and complaisance, which are requisite to render a union
agreeable.'*
(*The Lady's Magazine*, V, 1774, p. 82.)

I THEORY

i. Power and Motives

Changes in mating arrangements among classes owning substantial
amounts of property depend on changes in two theoretically distinct, but
practically interrelated, issues. The first is the distribution of power over
decision-making between the parents and the children; and the second is the
distribution of weight attached to various factors in making the choice.

In terms of power to make a match, four basic options are available in a
society. The first is that the choice is made entirely by parents, kin, and
family 'friends', without the advice or consent of the bride or groom. The
second option is that the choice is made as before, but the children are
granted a right of veto, to be exercised on the basis of one or two formal
interviews which take place after the two sets of parents and kin have agreed
on the match. It is a right which can only be exercised once or twice, and
tends to be more readily conceded to the groom than to the bride. The

principle that underlies this concession is that mutual compatibility is desirable to hold a marriage together, and that this will slowly develop between any couple which do not exhibit an immediate antipathy towards each other on first sight. In a deferential society, this is a reasonable assumption. The third option, made necessary by the rise of individualism, is that choice is made by the children themselves, on the understanding that it will be made from a family of more or less equal financial and status position, with the parents retaining the right of veto. The fourth option, which has only emerged in this century, is that the children make their own choice, and merely inform their parents of what they have decided.

Within this range of options, the richer and more well-born the family, the greater is the power likely to be exercised by parents. Furthermore, at that time eldest sons were particularly exposed to parental pressure, since under primogeniture they inherited the bulk of the estate and their marriage was therefore critical to the future of the family. Daughters were also in a weak position since their only viable future lay in marriage. It was not much use for a critic to complain in 1703 that 'a woman ... has been taught to think marriage her only preferment, the sum total of her endeavours, the completion of all her hopes.'[1] The teaching merely conformed to reality. This being the case, the most free were younger sons.

Just as there are only four basic options concerning the distribution of decision-making, so there are only four basic options in the motives of choice. The first and most traditional motive for marriage is the economic or social or political consolidation or aggrandizement of the family. If these are the objectives, marriage is primarily a contract between two families for the exchange of concrete benefits, not so much for the married couple as for their parents and kin – considerations subsumed by contemporaries under the single rubric of 'interest'. This tended to be the predominant motive at the top and also towards the bottom of the social scale. In 1786 Mary Wollstonecraft correctly pointed out that 'in many respects the great and little vulgar resemble, and in none more than the motives which induce them to marry.'[2]

The second motive is personal affection, companionship and friendship, a well-balanced and calculated assessment of the chances of long-term compatibility, based on the fullest possible knowledge of the moral, intellectual and psychological qualities of the prospective spouse, tested by a lengthy period of courtship. The third is physical attraction, stimulated by some degree of mutual sexual experimentation before marriage, a possibility on the whole only open to young people of high rank away from home, in attendance in noble households or the royal court, or people of low rank among whom physically intimate courting was customary. The result would be a narrowly focused lust, a physical obsession with the body of a particular person. The eighteenth century described men affected by this powerful emotion as 'cunt-struck'.[3] Mostly, however, this was assumed to be a force operating outside the bounds of marriage, something for which the man in its grip was prepared to abandon all other obligations, responsibilities and interests – work, home, wife, children, friends, reputation, everything. The third possible personal motive was romantic love as portrayed in fiction and on the stage, a disturbance in the mental equilibrium resulting in an obsessive concentration upon the virtues of another person, a blindness to all his or her possible defects, and a rejection of all other options or considerations, especially such mundane matters as money.

By 1660 the shift from the first to the second option in the distribution of power over decision-making had already taken place in all but the highest ranks of the aristocracy: it had been conceded, in the interests of 'holy matrimony', that children of both sexes should be given the right of veto over a future spouse proposed to them by their parents. Between 1660 and 1800, however, there took place the far more radical shift from the second to the third option, with the children now normally making their own choices, and the parents being left with no more than the right of veto over socially or economically unsuitable candidates. At the same time there was inevitably a marked shift of emphasis on motives away from family interest and towards well-tried personal affection. Almost everyone agreed, however, that both physical desire and romantic love were unsafe bases for an enduring marriage, since both were violent mental disturbances which would inevitably be of only short duration. Francis Bacon was repeating the wisdom of the ages when he wrote of love that 'in life it doth much mischief, sometimes like a siren, sometimes like a fury.' Despite the flood of poems, novels and plays on the themes of romantic and sexual love, they played little or no part in the daily lives of men and women of the late seventeenth and eighteenth centuries. Bacon was right when he said that 'the stage is more beholding to love than the life of man'. It was part of a fantasy world, rather than a reality, for all but a handful of idle young courtiers and attendants in noble households. Thus by the eighteenth century both interest and love were equally rejected, and in 1703 it was observed that 'there is no great odds between his marrying for the love of money or for the love of beauty; the man does not act in accordance with reason in either case'.[4]

Although some, especially women, were seeking the emotion of romantic love as a basis for marriage at the end of the eighteenth century, the important shift came earlier, from giving priority to economic and social considerations to giving equal or more weight to solidly based and well-tried mutual affection. This is where the major transformation occurred in the eighteenth century, with the result, as we shall see, of a marked rise in more companionate relationships between husband and wife after marriage. By the middle of the eighteenth century, few would have taken the cynical view of Thomas, second Lord Lyttelton, that 'after all that sentimental talkers and sentimental writers may produce upon the subject, marriage must be considered as a species of traffic, and as much a matter of commerce as any commodity that fills the warehouse of a merchant. ... One marries for connections, another for wealth, a third from lust, a fourth to have an heir, to oblige his parents, and so on.' They would have agreed with him in his contempt for romantic love, but objected that he omitted the prime consideration: companionship and friendship. A better insight into current attitudes at the height of the romantic movement at the end of the eighteenth century was offered by a writer in *The Lady's Monthly Museum* in 1799.

Some few grovelling spirits among the ladies may, indeed, form a systematic plan of advancing their interests, or gratifying their ambition, by a matrimonial connection. Some, even, who pass current in the muster-roll of virtuous women, may yet be base enough to dispose of their persons, by a species of legal prostitution, to the highest bidder. But are there not many amiable females, who surrender themselves into the arms of the enraptured object of their fondest regards, from the tenderest, from the most exalted principles of esteem and affection? Others, again, mistake the transient glow of passion, or the fond delirium of imagination, for the fervours of a rational attachment, and rush presumptuously into the marriage state without reflection: while some placid souls, ... bestow themselves on the first man with whom it may be convenient to unite, merely as the casualties of the moment may favour them, or as their friends may advise, without being directed by any motives of love or interest.[5]

It is obvious that at the root of both these changes in the power to make decisions about marriage, and in the motives that guided these decisions, there lie a deep shift of consciousness, a new recognition of the need for personal autonomy, and a new respect for the individual pursuit of happiness.

Besides this shift in basic attitude from deference to autonomy, there are also three sociological conditions required for the development of relatively free individual mate selection based on psychological compatibility, or perhaps love. The first is that the nuclear family has become relatively independent of the kin, so that decisions about marriage are no longer made by a grand family council of elders, whose main concern is necessarily to defend and advance the interests of the clan rather than to gratify the personal wishes of the individuals, although usually they will genuinely seek to find a compatible mate. The second is that close parent–child bonding has developed, so that parents are reasonably satisfied that their own values have been internalized in their children and the latter will therefore make their selection from within the socially appropriate group. Thirdly, parents must be willing to grant adolescents considerable freedom to meet on neutral ground with members of the other sex and to develop their own courting rituals of conversation, dancing, etc.

ii. Propagandists

The principal early evidence for this shift of consciousness and these sociological changes comes from the wealthy bourgeois and professional classes towards the end of the seventeenth century. There was, however, an earlier trend of thought in the same direction among the Arminian clergy and the Cavalier poets around the court in the 1630s, especially in the entourage of Queen Henrietta Maria where a cult of neo-platonic love flourished. The extravagant praise of married love by divines like Jeremy Taylor has already been noted. Secular writers also took up the same theme. Sir Kenelm Digby, for example, combined the sensuality of the current poetic idiom with the new cult of domesticity. 'Oh, the flat contents that are in marriages for temporal conveniences!' he exclaimed. 'Certainly one must affectionately desire what one would take much pleasure to enjoy.' The ideal wife he defined as one with whom 'together with all the other commodities of marriage, one may enjoy the sweetness of a full friendship, have the means to disburden oneself of all cares, in most important affairs receive faithful counsel, and whose very countenance will comfort one. . . .' As one who had made Lady Venetia Stanley first his mistress then his wife, in defiance of the wishes of his mother and the prospects of financially much more advantageous matches, he naturally thought that parental claims for obedience in this area should not be carried too far. Shortly afterwards, in 1645, Lord North was the first in English history to take the extreme radical position, publicly urging 'parents to leave their children full freedom with their consent in so important a case'. By 1700 Sir Richard Newdigate abandoned all but his financial interest in his son's marriage: 'let him marry whom he will, so I have the portion.'[6] It is clear, therefore, that there is a rather thin stream of aristocratic and gentry opinion in favour of giving children freedom of choice in marriage and of placing companionship above interest that ran strongly in the 1630s and 1640s and thereafter fell away to a trickle. But its existence probably does much to explain why, when similar bourgeois ideas were propounded to the landed classes in the early eighteenth century by Addison and others, they took to them so readily. They had already been softened up to receive them.

The best evidence for change in this area in the late seventeenth century is provided by the correspondence columns of the *Athenian Mercury* in the 1690s, a very successful paper published by Presbyterian dissenters and read mainly by the bourgeoisie. When a correspondent asked, 'Whether it is lawful to marry a person one cannot love, only in compliance with relations and to get an estate', he got an unequivocal answer. 'Such a practice would be the most cruel and imprudent thing in the world – society is the main end of marriage. Love is the bond of society, without which there can neither be found in that state pleasure, or profit or honour.' Similarly when a woman asked 'whether 'tis convenient for a lady to marry one she has an aversion for, in obedience to her parents', she was told that 'Parents are not to dispose of their children like cattle, nor to make them miserable because they happened to give them being. They are indeed generally granted a negative voice, nor, I am sure, will that always hold if they are signally unreasonable. But that they have an irresistible, despotical positive vote, none but a Spaniard will pretend, and I am sure our English ladies will very unwillingly grant.'[7]

When in 1706 Mary Astell complained that 'a woman, indeed, can't properly be said to choose, all that is allowed her is to refuse or accept what is offered', she did not seem to realize what an advance this was on the situation two or three generations before. She felt passionately that 'they only who have felt it know the misery of being forced to marry where they do not love', but was bothered by the ease with which, under the new situation of free choice, a woman could be hoodwinked by an artful suitor: 'he may call himself her slave a few days but it is only in order to make her his all the rest of his life.' The only motive for marriage that Mary Astell would admit was settled and well-reasoned affection. She rejected the influence of both money and beauty since 'the man does not act in accordance to reason in either case, but is governed by irregular appetites.'[8]

In the first decade of the eighteenth century, that archetypal bourgeois propagandist Daniel Defoe expressed the most advanced male position: 'the limit of a parent's authority in this case of matrimony either with son or daughter, I think, stands thus: the negative, I think, is theirs, especially with a daughter; but I think, the positive is in the children's.' This is a very tentative statement peppered with deprecatory 'I thinks', but it was nonetheless a revolutionary position to adopt. When dealing with marriage for money, both Defoe and *The Spectator* dropped all hesitation, denouncing 'family marriage for the preserving of estates in the lines and blood of houses, keeping up names and relations and the like precedent ends', as the equivalent of violent rape, since the women are always forced to comply. 'Forcing to marry is, in the plain consequences, not only forcing to crime, but furnishing an excuse to crime.' Defoe's reasons for adopting this position were also very clear. 'As marriage is a state of life in which so much of humane felicity is really placed ... it seems to me the most rational thing in the world that the parties concerned, and them alone, should give the last strokes to its conclusion; that they only should be left to determine it, and that with all possible freedom.' For 'to say love is not essential to a form of marriage is true; but to say it is not essential to the felicity of the married state ... is not true.' This being the case, Defoe proceeded to challenge the earlier notions 'that love, while necessary to marriage, could safely be left to develop of its own after the wedding'; that 'they will lie together till they love afterwards'; that 'property begets affection'. On the contrary, he argued that 'where there is no pre-engagement of the affection before marriage, what can be expected after it? ... There is not one in ten of those kinds of marriages that succeed.'[9]

Addison in *The Spectator* hammered home the same point to the squirarchy: 'Those marriages generally abound most with love and constancy that are preceded by a long courtship. The passion should strike root and gather strength before marriage be grafted on to it.' He was clearly in full agreement with one of his correspondents who angrily rejected the advice of the conservatives, which he described as: 'Marry first and love will come after, or pigs love by lying together.' Steele took the same line in *The Tatler*, asserting cautiously but clearly that 'a generous and constant passion in an agreeable lover, where there is not too great a disparity in other circumstances, is the greatest happiness that can befall the person beloved.' All now agreed that all a parent might lawfully do was to 'command her not to marry this or that person'. In other words, the power of veto, which had already been conceded to the child, was now all that was left of parental authority, the positive choice passing to the children themselves.[10]

These two interlocked themes of the conflict between parental choice and choice by the spouses themselves, and between economic and affective reasons for choice, are also reflected in the theatre of the day. As early as 1668 Althea in Sedley's *Mulberry Garden* commented:

> Under what tyranny are women born!
> Here we are bid to love, and there to scorn:
> As if unfit to be allowed a part
> In choosing him that must have all our heart.

In 1673, however, the heroine in Ravenscroft's *The Careless Lover* rejected this pessimism and frankly declared her independence: 'But Uncle, it is not now as it was in your young days. Women then were poor, sneaking, sheepish creatures. But in our age we know our own strength and have wit enough to make use of our talents.' In Colley Cibber's *Non-Juror* of 1717, the heroine asked bluntly: 'Do you think a man has any more charms for me for my father's liking him? No, sir. . . .'[11]

For over half a century, from the 1680s to the 1740s, the arranged marriage exclusively for interest, as practised by the aristocracy, also came under growing assault from the fashionable playwrights and artists of the day. Aphra Behn launched the attack in the 1680s with extreme statements of the new system of values: 'As love is the most noble and divine passion of the soul, so it is that to which we may justly attribute all the real satisfactions of life; and without it man is unfinished and unhappy.' 'Oh how fatal are forced marriages!' lamented Lady Fulbank in *The Lucky Chance* of 1686, 'How many ruins one such match pulls on.' Half a century later, in Garrick's *Lethe* of 1740, Lord Chalkstone remarks: 'I married for a fortune; she for a title. When we had both got what we wanted, the sooner we parted the better.'[12] The possible tragic consequences and the mutual frustration of the schemes of both parents who planned such mercenary matches were brought vividly before a mass public of all walks of life by the publication in 1745 of the six prints of Hogarth's *Marriage à la Mode*. The first shows the old merchant and the earl haggling over the financial details of the marriage of the former's daughter to the latter's son; the second shows the extravagance and lack of harmony in their married life – the husband has returned from a night out, spent with a girl; the wife has been at home at an all-night card party; the third, the way the husband sought and found his sexual pleasures elsewhere, with the result that he is in a quack doctor's office complaining about the venereal disease of his mistress and himself; the fourth, the wife attended by her own lover and by a host of hairdressers, eunuch singers, fashionable ladies, etc.; the fifth, the death of the husband as the result of a duel when he finds his wife in a bagnio with her lover; and the sixth, the death by suicide of the wife on hearing of the execution of her lover for the murder of her husband; she is being kissed by her daughter, a child of syphilitic constitution with rickety legs and an open sore on her face. Since there is no male heir, everyone has lost; to symbolize the collapse of the project, the wife's old merchant father is grimly pulling her wedding ring off the finger of his dying daughter, before the breath is out of her body.[13]

The continued, though declining, obsession with property among the landed classes explains why in 1701 even so ardent a champion of women's rights as Mary Astell was claiming no more for a girl than the right of veto of a clearly incompatible partner, a position already conceded, even to girls, by more advanced parents for at least half a century: 'Modesty requiring that a woman should not love before marriage, but only make choice of one whom she can love hereafter; she who has none but innocent affections being easily able to fix them where duty requires.'[14]

It is also significant that Lord Halifax's *Advice to a Daughter*, which was first published in 1688 and represented the traditional view of marriage arrangements, was continually republished throughout the eighteenth century, running to seventeen editions in English before 1791, besides several in French translation.[15] He explained to his daughter the bitter truth of her situation.

It is one of the disadvantages belonging to your sex, that young women are seldom permitted to make their own choice; their friends' care and experience are thought safer guides to them than their own fancies, and their modesty often forbiddeth them to refuse when their parents recommend, though their inward consent may not entirely go along with it. In this case there remaineth nothing for them to do but to endeavour to make that easy which falleth to their lot, and by a wise use of everything they may dislike in a husband, turn that by degrees to be very supportable, which, if neglected, might in time beget an aversion.

You must first lay it down for a foundation in general, that there is inequality in the sexes, and that for the better economy of the world, the men, who were to be the law-givers, had the larger share of reason bestowed upon them, by which means your sex is the better prepared for the compliance that is necessary for the better performance of those duties which seem to be most properly assigned to it.

He told her that a separation from a hated husband involved a sordid washing of dirty linen and should be avoided if possible. He explained the reason for the double sexual standard, to prevent doubts about the legitimacy of offspring and their right of inheritance, and advised her to look the other way if her husband should embark on extra-marital liaisons. 'To expostulate in these cases looketh like declaring war and preparing reprisals.' Anyway, 'an indecent complaint makes a wife much more ridiculous than the injury that provoketh her to it'. If he turns out to be an alcoholic, 'it will be no new thing if you should have a drunkard for a husband', and the drink may make him more affectionate and tolerant. If he is short-tempered, he needs to be handled with extreme tact and discretion. If he is mean, he needs to be cajoled to spend more generously ... and so on. These are counsels of resignation and despair, and yet they were widely read and approved of in aristocratic circles until nearly the end of the eighteenth century, presumably because they fitted in so well with the egocentric desires of husbands and with the stark realities of married life for women in these elevated circles. In any case, few husbands can have had *all* these vices, which was presumably some comfort to the girls who read the book. There are several late seventeenth-century examples of marriage among the baronetage and aristocracy, which show that Halifax's precepts were accepted by many elite parents, although they were beginning to encounter signs of resistance among the children.

In *Tom Jones*, published in 1749, Henry Fielding set out the two views of marriage, the old and the new. Her aunt, Mrs Western, advised Sophia that 'the alliance between the families is the principal matter. You ought to have a greater regard for the honour of your family than for your own person.' She also told her that marriage was 'a fund in which prudent women deposit their fortunes to the best advantage'. Her father, Squire Western, who had treated her mother like 'a faithful upper-servant all the time of their marriage', locked Sophia in her room until she would agree to marry the man of his choice, who would be 'one of the richest men in the county'. By way of contrast, there was Squire Allworthy, who 'thought love the only foundation of happiness in a married state, as it can only produce that high and tender friendship which should always be the cement of this union.' He therefore would tolerate neither any use of parental compulsion, nor marriage motivated by lust for a beautiful person or by avarice for a great fortune or by snobbery for a noble title. Sophia herself took the same position, promising that she would not marry without her father's consent, but obstinately refusing to marry a man chosen by him and not by herself. In this novel Fielding presents somewhat ideal stereotypes of the two extremes in attitudes to marriage, and the plot revolves around the clash between the two.[16]

It is the current intense interest in this conflict of ideals that explains the

enormous popularity of Richardson's novel *Clarissa Harlowe* in the middle
of the eighteenth century, especially, it is said, among the bourgeoisie.[17]
The heroine of the novel, who comes from an aspiring gentry family, after
much moral heart-searching finally refuses a purely mercenary match with
the disagreeable Mr Solmes, which had been arranged for her by her
parents. She elopes instead with a dissolute squire, who rapes her when
under the influence of drugs. She then dies, consumed with guilt, but as
morally pure as when the story began.

On the surface this is a tale written in protest against parental dictation
and mercenary marriage; but as a contemporary young woman pointed out
to Richardson at the time, the author shows his partial acceptance of the
authority of parents to dispose of their children by attributing to Clarissa so
heavy a load of guilt for disobeying the highly unreasonable and immoral
order of her father to marry Mr Solmes. Mrs Chapone asked Richardson 'if
then what she did was just and reasonable, why is she continually afflicting
her soul with remorse and fear . . . as if he [her father] had really the power of
disposing of her happiness in the next world as well as in this?' She adopted
the argument of John Locke, that parental authority derives from the
responsibility for nurture, and therefore diminishes as a child reaches the
age of discretion, so that 'when he comes to the state that made his father a
freeman, the son is a freeman too . . . (and if his son, I presume his daughter
too).' Mrs Chapone thought that after they were twenty-one, children were
bound to do no more than 'reverence and honour' their parents. Even so, she
made only limited claims to freedom of choice. 'Take notice, dear Sir, that I,
as well as Clarissa, only insist on a *negative* and that it never entered into my
mind to suppose a child at liberty to dispose of herself in marriage without
the consent of her parents.' But she firmly rejected the older idea that love
could and should follow marriage, using the very practical arguments that
this would be even more difficult after marriage than before; firstly because
the tyrannical powers legally given to husbands encourage them to be
disagreeably authoritarian, and secondly because men get meaner and more
exclusively concerned with money as they grow older, and therefore become
less lovable. She concluded: 'Who is to be the judge in nice or dubious
cases? . . . I readily answer: the child, because it is the *child*'s happiness and
the *child*'s conscience only which are concerned', supporting her case with
reference to the sermons of Bishop William Fleetwood of Ely, published in
1737.[18]

This literary evidence shows that there was a prolonged public argument
during the late seventeenth and eighteenth centuries about a child's freedom

of choice of a marriage partner, with more liberal views slowly but steadily becoming more common among authors catering both to the middling ranks of commercial and professional people, and also to the wealthy landed classes.

A concurrent prolonged argument was also proceeding about the respective weight of 'interest' and love as motives for marriage. In 1704 a wealthy man in love with a poor lady, who reciprocated the love, put his dilemma to Defoe in *The Review*: 'If I marry her, I am ruined; if I lie with her, she is.' Defoe's reply was without equivocation. By his own admission the man could afford to marry, and 'mutual love [is] the essence of matrimony and makes it a heavenly life.' This early eighteenth-century propaganda does not mean, of course, that cynical marriages with a strict eye to material interests did not continue to take place. As late as 1792 a caricaturist produced a whole series devoted to this theme, entitled *Matrimonial Speculation*, although the fact that he did so suggests that all the motives were now regarded by the audience as reprehensible.[19]

Even those who were most ardent advocates of basing the choice on mutual affection were equally firm in condemning the two other possible personal motives for marriage: sexual desire and romantic love. Although sympathetic towards prudent attachment, the eighteenth century thus firmly rejected the popular image of the twin bases of modern marriage.

iii. Attitude to Sexual Desire

Evidence of hostility to sexual desire as a basis for choice of a marriage partner can be found in every commentator of the seventeenth and eighteenth centuries, and it would be merely wearisome to stack up a pile of quotations to prove so uncontested and unchanging a point. Even Defoe, who has already been shown to be a pioneering 'liberal' on the marriage issue, thought that marriage for lust 'brings madness, desperation, ruin of families, disgrace, self-murders, killing of bastards, etc.'[20]

On the other hand, it was generally assumed that young widows, suddenly deprived of regular sexual satisfaction by the loss of a husband, were likely to be driven by lust in their search for a replacement. A proverb that goes back at least to the Elizabethan period, and probably much further, has it that 'He that wooeth a widow must go stiff before'. Suitors of widows were expected to make aggressive sexual advances, unlike suitors of virgins, who in upper-class circles were virtually untouchable before marriage. The Elizabethan Thomas Wythorne, who took a strict view of pre-nuptial sexual relations, thought it possible that he lost the young widow he was wooing because of his failure to attempt seduction.[21]

The only other group whose marriages were to some extent based on sexual passion was presumably the propertyless poor, who indulged in the common practice of intimate courting known as 'bundling' and premarital sexual relations. Among the upper classes, the aristocracy, who were still largely subjected to the arranged marriage system, continued to follow their normal adulterous pursuits as the flesh moved them. It was only in the late eighteenth century that there appeared signs of a new upper-class ideal, to channel sexual desire into the marriage bond and keep it there. This was a natural by-product of allowing greater freedom of mate selection within the prescribed social class, and was epitomized in a late eighteenth-century French painting by Prud'hon, which shows Venus and Cupid, the two traditional deities of sexual desire, now for the first time joined by Hymen, the Goddess of Marriage. In 1772 Helvetius suggested that marriage actually heightened sexual passion: 'I was scorched by Cupid, who was consuming my soul; Hymen, far from quenching the flames, fanned them up.'[22] But this was not the normal eighteenth-century view, which remained as traditionally suspicious of lust as a secure basis for marriage as it had now become of economic or social advancement.

iv. Attitude to Romantic Love

The key elements of the romantic love complex are the following: the notion that there is only one person in the world with whom one can fully unite at all levels; the personality of that person is so idealized that the normal faults and follies of human nature disappear from view; love is often like a thunderbolt and strikes at first sight; love is the most important thing in the world, to which all other considerations, particularly material ones, should be sacrificed; and lastly, the giving of full rein to personal emotions is admirable, no matter how exaggerated and absurd the resulting conduct may appear to others.

There can be no doubt that at all times a few young people at all levels of society have defied the conventional wisdom of the day which condemned such mental disturbances, and have fallen head over heels in love. But given the hostility towards socially or financially unbalanced matches, and given the great influence over choice of partners still exercised by parents, 'friends', and masters, it is hardly surprising that these love affairs often failed to end in a happy marriage. The waiting-room of a popular psychological practitioner like the Reverend Richard Napier in the early seventeenth century saw not a few victims of unrequited or unfulfilled love.

How commonly passionate pre-marital love developed in defiance of the wisdom of the day it is impossible to say, but it is fairly certain that it happened to no more than a minority of either men or women.[23] Ever since the twelfth century it had been familiar to court and aristocratic households, and Shakespeare's comedies were built around the theme of love, often, but not always, ending in marriage. In the early seventeenth century, the melancholia induced by unrequited love was an increasingly familiar theme both to dramatists and to scholars like Robert Burton. It seems likely, therefore, that love before marriage, however rare it may have been in the sixteenth century, may have been on the increase in the early seventeenth century and after. Ralph Josselin, a clergyman and the son of a small farmer, himself described the classic case of love at first sight, which struck him suddenly when as a poor curate he preached his first sermon in 1639: 'the first Lord's day, being October 6, my eye fixed with love upon a maid, and her's upon me, who afterwards proved my wife.'[24]

According to contemporaries, the growth of marriage for love in the eighteenth century was caused by the growing consumption of novels. Always a stock-in-trade of the theatre, romantic love was the principal theme of the novel, whose astonishing rise to popularity was so marked a feature of the age. In 1723 Swift was still taking the traditional view that love was 'a ridiculous passion which hath no being but in plays and romances'. Even in the middle of the eighteenth century, most influential men and women were still firmly opposed to the idea, but by then they were fighting a losing battle against the mounting flood of romantic novels and poems. In 1773 a writer in *The Lady's Magazine* complained that 'there is scarce a young lady in the kingdom who has not read with avidity a great number of romances and novels, which tend to vitiate the taste'. By the end of the century, the rise of the circulating library had greatly stimulated both output and consumption, and in 1799 a (fictitious) mother complained to *The Lady's Monthly Museum* that her daughter

reads nothing in the world but novels – nothing but novels, Madam, from morning to night. . . . The maid is generally dispatched to the library two or three times in the day, to change books. One week she will read in the following order: *Excessive Sensibility, Refined Delicacy, Disinterested Love, Sentimental Beauty*, etc. In the next come *Horrid Mysteries, Haunted Caverns, Black Towers, Direful Incantations*, and an endless list of similar titles.

The mother believed, not unreasonably, that 'a continued repetition of such reading seems, by infusing false and romantic notions, to injure, rather than to improve, the natural feelings of sensibility.' This had been the standard attitude towards romance, and the blue-stocking Elizabeth Montagu remarked tartly of Abraham Cowley's poems on the subject, 'his love verses are insufferable'. Dr Gregory in 1762 repeated the ancient wisdom to his daughters: 'Do not give way to a sudden sally of passion, and dignify it with the name of love. Genuine love is not founded in caprice.'[25]

Despite these valid objections, romantic love and the romantic novel grew together after 1780, and the problem of cause and effect is one that is impossible to resolve. All that can be said is that for the first time in history, romantic love became a respectable motive for marriage among the propertied classes, and that at the same time there was a rising flood of novels filling the shelves of the circulating libraries, devoted to the same theme. An extraordinarily large number of these novels were now written not merely for women, but also by women (Graph 13). As *The Times* remarked satirically in 1796, 'four thousand and seventy-three novels are now in the press from the pens of young ladies of fashion'. The results of massive exposure to this pulp literature was clear enough to contemporaries. Thanks to notions imbibed from this reading, young people fell headlong into the arms of whoever took their fancy, and, if their parents raised objections, they ran away to Scotland to get married in a hurry. 'Of all the arrows which Cupid has shot at youthful hearts,' remarked *The Universal Magazine* as early as 1772, '[the modern novel] is the keenest. There is no resisting it. It is the literary opium that lulls every sense into delicious rapture. . . . In contempt of the Marriage Act [demanding parental consent if under twenty-one] post-chaises and young couples run smoothly on the North Road.'[26] (Plate 3.) In 1792 *The Bon Ton Magazine* warned its female readers that under the influence of romanticism, 'women of little experience are apt to mistake the urgency of bodily wants with the violence of a delicate passion'. In short, they were likely to mistake male lust for the emotion they read about in novels (plate 14).[27] Both Dr Johnson and Mary Wollstonecraft regarded them as the same thing, romantic love being no more than a purely artificial emotion invented by novelists and adopted by men as a cover for sexual desire. The latter argued that 'in the choice of a husband, [women] should not be led astray by the qualities of a lover, for a lover the husband . . . cannot long remain.' She went so far as to claim that 'love and friendship cannot subsist in the same bosom', then backed off to concede that women should 'be contented to love but once in their lives; and after marriage, calmly let passion subside into friendship'.[28]

Anthropological studies of the many societies in which sentiment is

WOMEN NOVELISTS AND NOVELS
PUBLISHED BY WOMEN

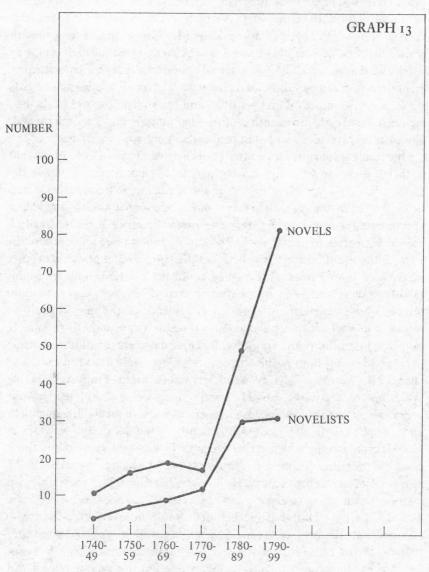

GRAPH 13

NUMBER

NOVELS

NOVELISTS

DATE OF FIRST PUBLICATION

unknown tend to support La Rochefoucauld's observation that 'people would never fall in love if they had not heard of love talked about'. It is a product, that is, of learned cultural expectations, which became fashionable in the late eighteenth century thanks largely to the spread of novel-reading. It took even so clear-sighted a woman as Mrs Cappe quite a long time to realize that 'the heroine of the novel is not exactly fitted for the exemplary wife', and that passion based on external appearance 'may consist with very great defects of temper and moral character.'[29] Not all young men or girls were, or are, so practical and sensible, and the romantic novel of the late eighteenth and early nineteenth centuries has much to answer for in the way of disastrous love affairs and of imprudent and unhappy marriages.

One result of romanticism was that girls between 1780 and 1810 gave vent to their feelings in ways which were particularly unrestrained. It was the sudden death of Mary Hays' first lover and her failure to find another which drove her from the ideal of reserve and submission hitherto considered appropriate for women to a career as a minor literary figure and finally a radical supporter of the French Revolution and women's liberation. In 1779, at the age of nineteen, she began exchanging love letters with a young neighbour, John Eccles. Before they could get married, however, John rapidly sickened and died. This shattering event threw Mary into a catatonic trance, whose violence and duration is evidence of the new attitude to romantic love which young women now thought it appropriate to adopt: 'I sank into insensibility and stupidity, for three days refused all refreshment. . . . I talked calmly but very incoherently – my eyes were fixed and I scarcely changed my position.'[30] Mary was clearly rather proud of these remarkable symptoms of frustrated passion, rather than seeing them, as previous generations would have done, as signs of unfortunate mental derangement and a deplorable failure to submit patiently to the inscrutable wisdom of God. It is not so much the fact that romantic love existed, for that is nothing new: it is the radically different attitude towards it which is so striking in the mid and late eighteenth century. By becoming fashionable, it inevitably also became much more common, and the response to its frustration more extreme. In 1794 Dorothea Herbert fell deeply in love with a man who eventually abandoned her. Years later, she was still in profound and bitter despair. 'What could induce the specious rogue to seduce my affections, betray me to lingering torments, and then desert me for ever, is a problem I never could solve. Ah, my poor heart, what cruelties did it suffer. What more than Hell-born woe when the monster struck his last blow and left me forever benighted in intolerable despair.'[31]

Another woman who was destroyed by her notions of romantic love was Lucy, daughter of George, first Lord Lyttelton. After a series of abortive infatuations, she finally received, and accepted on the spot, an offer from Arthur Annesley, son and heir of Lord Anglesey, a handsome, wealthy but very unstable young playboy with a reputation for mercurial shifts of sexual interest. At first the marriage went well, and a year later Lucy was still wildly in love with her husband. 'I pronounce a wedded life the nearest state of solid bliss allowed us on earth.' Even after four years she was writing to 'my dearest love', telling him that 'I shall sleep tonight in *our* bed and hug my lonely pillow.' By 1775, however, Arthur had resumed his promiscuous philandering, and the marriage was coming apart because of Lucy's jealousy. Her brother, himself a professional rake, tried to tell her to see life as it really was and not as it appeared in novels. Her misery, he told her, 'proceeds in part from your ignorance of the human heart, and your romantic ideas of conjugal happiness, perhaps arising from splendid descriptions of it in the fashionable novels of the age.' He told her to stop nagging, and to 'wink at these little sallies of youthful fire, and that disposition to gallantry and even to predilection in gallantry.' The fact of the matter was that Arthur was now tired of her and her demonstrative and jealous affection. She lived a short and unhappy life. Six of her seven children died very young; she herself died only sixteen years after her marriage; and very shortly afterwards Arthur remarried with an eighteen-year-old girl. In this case, romantic love had turned very sour indeed.[32]

It was stories like this that made William Cobbett remark in 1829 that 'few people are entitled to more compassion than young men thus affected [by love]; it is a species of insanity that assails them, and it produces self-destruction in England more frequently than in all other countries put together.' Whether or not his statistics on suicide for thwarted love are correct, he was certainly expressing the standard view when he advised young men to choose their brides for such enduring companionate qualities as chastity, sobriety, industry, frugality, cleanliness, knowledge of domestic affairs, good temper and beauty – in that order.[33]

v. Conclusion

The extent to which the new values were put into practice by the readers of these plays, novels and didactic treatises is very hard indeed to determine. In a period of flux, some families opted for one pattern of marriage and some for another. Moreover there were very considerable differences in the responses at different social and economic levels in the society, so that very careful distinctions have to be made. One social group, the lower middle class, seems to have accepted one aspect of the new ideas, namely that the choice should lie with the children, but rejected the other, that prior affection rather than financial gain and prudential calculation should be the basis of the choice. A letter to *The Spectator* vigorously condemned those 'ladies who are too nicely bent on the sordid principles of gain, interest and ambition, without one serious thought or reflection on their future state and tranquillity.'[34] Another social group, namely the gentry and squirarchy, accepted the need for affection, but the parents still continued to exert a good deal of influence. The picture is therefore a very confused one, which can best be described by giving a series of real-life examples, beginning with the middling ranks of society, moving down to the lower middle class, then up to the squirarchy, and finishing with the high aristocracy.

2 PRACTICE

i. The Middling Ranks

a. Decision-makers. An example of a child's still displaying traditional attitudes of deference and filial obedience, and of a father's rejecting the decision-making role, is provided by the story of how the Reverend Nicholas Carter responded to the marriage offers made to his brilliant daughter Elizabeth, who was born in 1717. In this case the father specifically refused to take on himself the responsibility which his daughter was, at any rate ostensibly, anxious to press upon him.[35]

A far more ambiguous story about parental attitudes concerns Catherine, the daughter of Admiral Yeo. She was secretly wooed by a naval surgeon, Mr B, but he not only had nothing but his lieutenant's salary to live on, but also was the son of a personal enemy of her father. To put a stop to the courtship, her father 'locked me up for two months, during which space I never saw a creature but the person who brought me victuals. I was suffered neither pen, ink or paper.' Her release only came when Mr B's ship sailed, not to return for four years. On her release she was courted by the son of a rich tradesman, but she did not like either his person or his Presbyterian religion. The next suitor was an old lecher, to escape from whose attentions she went into the country to stay with a farmer. There she was courted by an apparently rich mercer, Mr Jemmat, who professed to have a fortune of £3,000. Catherine agreed to marry him 'not for love indeed, but to avoid the persecutions of a too rigid father, whose behaviour was insupportable'. But she jumped out of the frying-pan into the fire. Mr Jemmat turned out to be insanely jealous, a habitual drunkard, and on the verge of financial ruin. Within three years he was bankrupt.[36] What is interesting about this story is that Admiral Yeo was only trying to exercise a right of veto, admittedly enforced by incarceration, and that Miss Yeo herself chose Mr Jemmat, so that she had only herself to blame for her misfortunes.

Of course, at any period in history a father who believes that his cherished son and heir is throwing himself away on a worthless girl, and by doing so is endangering a promising career, is bound to be resentful and hostile. What was new about the eighteenth century was that this hostility was no longer effective in stopping children marrying to suit themselves. In 1761 at the age of twenty-one, Philip Francis, the brilliant but impecunious son of the Reverend Philip Francis, DD, the translator of Horace, fell in love with the daughter of a retired small businessman without any financial resources whatsoever, who added to the family income by singing at private parties. His father was naturally furious at the social discrepancy, declaring that even if the girl had £10,000, he would be opposed to the match. But his three-month ban on all communications between the two was defied, and in 1762 the marriage took place, resulting in a four-year breach between father and son, who had hitherto been on fairly intimate terms. Eventually, it was the father who had to adapt himself to the new situation in which children felt morally justified in putting personal choice before parental desires and family ambitions.[37]

There can be no doubt that public opinion in landed and bourgeois circles in the late eighteenth century was turning decisively against parental dictation of a marriage partner. The silversmith Joseph Brasbridge tells the story of an attorney at Banbury, a Mr Aplin, who took on as his articled clerk a poor but bright young boy of humble origins, Richard Bignell. Bignell and Aplin's daughter, who also worked in her father's office, fell in love and when the period of his clerkship was expired, Bignell asked Aplin for his daughter's hand, only to be rejected 'with the utmost scorn'. When he later discovered that the young couple had secretly married, Mr Aplin turned his daughter out of doors and refused to have anything more to do with her. What is so interesting is the reaction of the attorney's middle-class and gentry clientele in Banbury to this traditional treatment of disobedient children. 'The people in the town and neighbourhood, condemning the father's harshness and, willing to encourage the young man's industry, gradually withdrew their business from Mr Aplin and transferred it to Mr Bignell.'[38] It would be hard to find a more convincing demonstration of the new attitude to parental control over marriage among provincial townspeople and county gentry at the end of the eighteenth century.

b. Motives. In the eighteenth century the importance of money was far less generally accepted as a crucial factor in marriage than it had been in the seventeenth. In the late seventeenth century the two motives were jostling for priority within the mind of a single suitor, like the successful Turkey merchant John Verney, who in the 1670s was looking around for a wife. He came from upper gentry stock, but was by profession a member of the commercial bourgeoisie, so that the origin of his system of values is a little obscure. When he first came back from Aleppo in 1674, he embarked on a cold-blooded search for a mercenary marriage. He was soon approached by a sixty-year old wealthy London citizen anxious to marry off his nineteen-year-old daughter. Although Mr Edwards promised a good estate to go with her and that she was 'a good housewife', he was very reluctant to allow John Verney even to take a look at the girl before the financial details were ironed out. But at last he agreed to stage an 'accidental' meeting in the street, so that the prospective groom could assure himself that there was 'nothing disgustful' about the girl. During the meeting, the girl (who was totally ignorant of what was afoot) did not exchange a single word with John Verney, but the sight of her allowed him to report coolly to his father that 'though her beauty is not like to prefer her to the title of a duchess, yet she is a very passable woman and well-shaped'. He was content to pursue the negotiations on the grounds that 'the gentlewoman is a passable handsome woman and her father able, if he be but willing, to give her money enough.' In the end the financial negotiations broke down, but it is clear that on both sides of this match there was no suggestion of consulting the feelings of the prospective bride, who was not even told that she was under consideration, much less of the need for prior affection by either the bride or the groom.[39]

When John Verney tried again six years later in 1680, however, he fell in love with a fifteen-year-old girl long before the marriage negotiations were concluded. At a point when her father was raising impossible obstacles and he thought the match had fallen through, he wrote asking for a 'lock of your delicate hair' as a keepsake. After everything had been straightened out and the marriage had taken place, he and his young bride remained devoted to each other. When she left for a visit soon after the birth of their first child, he wrote letters to her headed 'Dearest dear' or 'Dearest Heart', thanking her for 'tender expressions' and giving details of the growth of 'pretty precious'. Some years later, after the birth of two children and when a third was *in utero*, he concluded a letter with a phrase revealing the depth of his domestic felicity. He sent her 'everything that the lovingest of husbands can express to the best of wives, and love to the little ones, not forgetting the kicker in the dark.'[40]

These matrimonial ventures by a man who was both the younger son of a baronet and a Turkey merchant in the 1670s and 1680s show very clearly the way in which two very different attitudes towards marriage were in sharp competition in these circles at that time, affecting all three elements in the situation: the degree to which property and money should be the prime considerations in marriage; the degree to which the marriage should be arranged by the parents without much consideration for the wishes of the prospective groom or bride; and the degree to which prior love should serve as an essential basis for a stable and successful marriage. Between 1674 and 1680 the mind of John Verney seems to have moved from one position to another on all three issues. In the end, he and his wife provided an early model of the new domesticated affective nuclear family, but he could equally easily have married Miss Edwards for her money, and experienced the most conventional of arranged marriages.

Another example a century later shows much the same ambivalence still at work. George Butt was the son of a not very prosperous doctor at Lichfield, whose family had come down in the world but who through influential connections obtained a church living, which he supplemented by private teaching. In 1773 he was ready to marry, and fell desperately in love with the sister of a pupil, the beautiful Mary Woodhouse. But Mary suddenly died, leaving George a shattered and heartbroken man. At this point, while he was still in deep mourning for his love, his father stepped in and urged him to marry Martha, the heiress of a rich Coventry merchant, Henry Sherfield. Martha was a little woman with a long sad face and sharp features badly disfigured by smallpox – the very opposite of the beautiful Mary. She was also temperamentally the antithesis of George, but her 'fortune rendered her a desirable match under the pecuniary circumstances of the family.' So George 'consented to his father's earnest wish', while Martha Sherfield obediently did what her father told her. According to their daughter, there was no enthusiasm on either side, and they had little in common. A piquant detail is that he named his first daughter Mary Martha, combining the names of his dead love Mary Woodhouse and his living wife Martha.[41]

The story of how the barrister Mr Elers found his bride in the 1740s shows that more old-fashioned seventeenth-century styles still persisted into the eighteenth century. His friend and client Mr Grosvenor fell heavily into debt due to gambling losses and sought to recoup by a wealthy marriage. And so when his friend Mr Hungerford offered him the hand of his only daughter and heiress, Mr Grosvenor accepted her unseen. As a precaution, he took Mr Elers down with him to the Hungerford house in the country in order to examine the title deeds and draw up the necessary conveyances. When they arrived, they found that Miss Hungerford 'had not much beauty, grace or dignity; she was a plump, good-natured, unfashioned girl with little knowledge of any sort and with no accomplishments'. Mr Grosvenor confided in Mr Elers that 'the girl is a sad encumbrance on the estate'. When Mr Elers mildly disagreed, Grosvenor said, 'Suppose you were to take the whole bargain off my hands?' 'Most willingly', replied Elers. Mr Hungerford readily agreed to the change of the prospective bridegroom; 'the young lady ... submitted with blushes and becoming filial duty to the wishes of her parents', and Elers gained a landed fortune of £800 a year. As a result, he gave up his London practice and retired to live the life of a country gentleman. But he had no talent for estate management, disliked field sports, and found the conversation of the neighbouring squires a bore. He became idle and apathetic. His wife was tiresomely fertile and kept producing healthy children who were very expensive to look after; and so he eventually got into financial difficulties. It is a story with several morals.[42]

ii. The Lower Middle Class

a. Decision-Makers. At this lower social level, where the economic leverage of parents was weak since they did not have much to give as a bribe or to withhold as a threat, and in which their social control was weak since the children had already left home, patriarchal authority seems to have been in full decay by the late seventeenth century, if not earlier. A further reason for this is that the very late age of marriage, which was customary in these circles, meant that in many cases the parents were already dead and so unable to control the marriage, and that in all cases the spouses were fully adult men and women, who could not easily be controlled, least of all from a distance. It seems inevitable that parental control of marriage among the lower classes must have been severely limited by all these factors. Only those with expectations of inheritance of a little property, such as a peasant son who was waiting to inherit a yardland or so from his father, or an artisan or shopkeeper's son with hopes of inheriting the tools, the shop and the goodwill, could be expected to pay very much attention to parental directions or advice, if they did not coincide with his own inclinations.

This advice, however, was increasingly falling on deaf ears. As early as the middle of the seventeenth century, the Reverend Ralph Josselin was struggling vainly to control the marriage of his children. Various prospective suitors were brought to stay in the house and were carefully inspected, but it was the children who had chosen them, and not the parents. Away in service in London, the daughters found their own potential husbands. Josselin was distressed when his son John married without his knowledge, but merely commented resignedly: 'God pardon his errors'. The patriarchal authority that Josselin perhaps wished to exercise over the choice of marriage partner for his children was clearly neither very resolutely attempted nor very successfully enforced. He was normally consulted, the family opinion carried great weight, but the initiative lay with the absent children, both girls and boys, who themselves first selected their potential mates for submission to inspection by their parents.[43]

A typical example of marriage arrangements among the lower middle classes of the late seventeenth century is that of John Dunton, the nonconformist bookseller and publisher. Once he was established in business in about 1682 and could afford a wife, he began to look around him. In Dr Annesley's Meeting House, he caught sight of one of the doctor's daughters 'that almost charmed me dead'. Finding that she was already engaged, he switched his attentions to the second daughter, Iris. He asked the doctor's permission to court her, and obtained it, after enquiries about his character and finances, with the promise that Iris was entirely free to accept or reject him as she chose (she had already rejected one persistent suitor). She in fact accepted him, and the marriage turned out to be very successful. Despite his own impetuosity, the advice he gave to others about marriage was to prepare the ground with a long courtship, in order to discover 'how far our humours would agree. I consider how much the happiness of a married life depends on this particular.' After marriage he recommended that 'both of us should make mutual abatements in our opposite humours'. Despite this stress on a marriage based on affection, Dunton in the 1680s was adamant in insisting on the moral obligation of parental consent, thus displaying his ambiguous position half-way between one system of values and another. 'Neither did I ever know a child in my life, that married against his parent's consent ... but the curse of God has followed either them or their off-spring.' He was also strongly opposed to both 'mere concupiscence' and 'secular advantage' as legitimate motives for marriage.[44]

In the eighteenth century, the opinion of the parents was often ignored. The diary of James Frelwell, a Yorkshire yeoman in the 1720s and 1730s, records many cases of children marrying by free choice without the advice or consent of parents. His cousin's only daughter married at the age of seventeen 'without her parents' knowledge, much less with their consent', but they were forced to accept the situation and teach the young man the family trade of tanning. Both James's sisters married against the wishes of their parents or brothers, and indeed without their knowledge.[45] It was a situation which Frelwell seems to have accepted with philosophical resignation. William Cole, on the other hand, was still shocked in 1766 when he learned that his godson had married a Miss Plumtree 'without the knowledge and consent of her parents'. The girl had been left a fortune by her aunt, which made her financially independent of her father, but perhaps what upset Cole most was 'that she made the offer herself'. This was a reversal not only of parent–child power relations, but also of traditional sex roles in the mating process.[46]

b. Motives. In lower middle-class circles, where capital was a critical factor in getting a start in life by buying a shop or starting a business, it was inevitable that financial considerations should continue to play a very large part in marriage plans, even though the decisions were left to the children themselves. Defoe's Moll Flanders, who moved in these circles, soon came to the sad conclusion that 'marriages are here the consequence of politic schemes, for forming interests, carrying on business', and that love had no share or very little in the matter. After a bitter experience she decided that 'money only made a woman agreeable ... the money was the thing'.[47] In other words, in terms of marriage, a woman in the late seventeenth and eighteenth centuries was still regarded in these circles less as a companion or a sex object than as property, and to some extent also as a status object.

The ambiguities of the motives for lower middle-class marriage in the late eighteenth century are well revealed by the correspondence of the Cumberland brothers in the late 1770s, when both were in their middle twenties. Richard was a parson in Gloucestershire, and George a clerk in the Exchange Assurance Office in London. George thought that Richard ought to get married and they engaged in a debate about the qualities desirable in a wife. Richard declared himself 'proof against beauty', thinking 'neatness and good nature everything in a wife'. He would accept someone whom he found attractive with no more money than 'just enough to pay fees and preliminaries'; failing that he would settle for 'one of the common run' with money enough 'to make amends for trifling deficiencies, and of an amiable temper – supposing a probability of our making each other as happy as the generality of married people'. Richard's expectations were clearly not high. Indeed he was soon congratulating himself 'on having escaped a most dangerous temptation, that of connecting myself with a partner for life, for the sake perhaps of a few hundreds to begin with, a very common case with young men in my situation'. George, on the other hand, was seriously courting a Miss Townshend and Richard wrote advising discretion. He conceded that 'she is a woman of honour, taste and spirit', but questioned whether she also possessed such virtues as 'economy, prudence, a love of home and domestic amusements'. But the key issue was financial: 'The question is, will your united incomes, added to any reasonable expectancies you may have, enable you to enter the state of matrimony without experiencing any of those self-denials which I suspect you are neither disposed to submit to?'[48] Not surprisingly, the brothers remained bachelors.

When in 1748 John Wesley was considering marriage with Mrs Murray, he listed the arguments *pro* and *con*. In favour were, in this order, her qualities as a housekeeper, a nurse, a companion, a friend, and as 'a fellow labourer in the gospel of Christ'. Finally, 'she is and would be a continual defence (under God) against unholy desires and inordinate affections'. Against her were her low birth, her position as Wesley's servant, her travelling with him for six months already, which would lead to suspicion that she had been his mistress before marriage, and the fact that she was pre-contracted to another man. Despite the vigorous opposition of his brother and other advisers, Wesley decided in favour, but – after much indecision – the lady finally opted for her other suitor. Wesley was thwarted, and three years later made what turned out to be a most unhappy marriage with another widow, as a matter of convenience rather than love or affection, and as a protection against sexual temptation from his many female admirers. In both cases the alleged motives were prudential, but in the case of Mrs Murray affect was in fact a prime consideration, whereas convenience predominated in his later unfortunate choice of Mrs Vazeille.[49]

Very similar prudential considerations governed the second marriage in 1765 of Thomas Turner, an educated Sussex schoolmaster turned shop-keeper. After four years of an irregular and somewhat drunken life as a widower, he had determined to remarry so as to have someone to keep him company in the evenings and stop him from drinking too much. To his diary he frankly confided his motives in marrying a rather dull, badly educated, and unattractive farmer's daughter:

The girl, I believe, as far as I can discover, is a very industrious sober woman and seemingly endowed with prudence and good nature, with a serious and sedate turn of mind. She comes of reputable parents, and may perhaps, one time or other, have some fortune. As to her person, I know it's plain (so is my own), but she is cleanly in her person and dress, which I will say is something more than at first sight it may appear to be towards happiness. She is, I think, a well-made woman. As to her education, I own it is not liberal; but she has good sense and a desire to improve her mind, and has always behaved to me with the strictest honour and good manners – her behaviour being far from the affected formality of the prude, on the one hand; and on the other, of that foolish fondness too often found in the more light part of the sex.

Two weeks after the marriage he was still not much more enthusiastic about his choice. 'I have, it's true, not married a learned lady, nor is she a gay one; but I trust she is good natured and one that will use her utmost endeavours to make me happy. As to her fortune, I shall one day have something considerable, and there seems to be a flowing stream.' In Turner's case, the main attractions of marriage were clearly the escape from loneliness and the expectation of money, rather than any real affection.[50]

Among the lower middle ranks and the more respectable elements of the poor there is statistical evidence to indicate a trend towards a later marriage age, due to a prudent desire to accumulate the necessary economic resources before embarking on such an expensive undertaking. In 1778 George Crabbe, then an unsuccessful and unqualified surgeon, fell in love. But the girl 'was too prudent to marry where there seemed to be no chance of a competent livelihood; and he, instead of being in a position to maintain a family, could hardly by labour which he abhorred earn daily bread for himself'. The match was therefore postponed for the time being. It is not surprising, therefore, to find Crabbe in 1807 giving warm approval to those of the rural poor who had the prudence to delay marriage until they had the economic means to support a family.

> Reuben and Rachel, though as fond as doves,
> Were yet discreet and cautious in their loves;
> Nor would attend to Cupid's wild commands,
> Till cool reflection bade them join their hands.
> When both were poor, they thought it argued ill
> Of hasty love to make them poorer still;
> Year after year, with savings long laid by,
> They bought the future dwelling's full supply;
> Her frugal fancy cull'd the smaller ware,

The weightier purchase ask'd her Reuben's care;
Together then their last year's gain they threw,
And lo! an auction'd bed, with curtains neat and new.
Thus both, as prudence counsell'd, wisely stay'd
And cheerful then the calls of Love obey'd[51]

Others, however, no doubt influenced by novel-reading, were cheerfully putting love before prudence, as Crabbe was well aware. In 1751, that hard-boiled and highly sophisticated young surgeon John Knyveton, who was then working in a London hospital, tells of a young woman patient who had to have a leg amputated after an injury to her knee. She was a country girl from Norfolk who had fallen in love with a farmer's son, but had been packed off to London by her guardian who disapproved of the connection. One day the farmer's son appeared in the hospital ward, having finally discovered where she was. Despite her maimed condition, their love was renewed and they were married the next day at the bedside. In his professional capacity Knyveton learned from this episode that, as the head surgeon told him, 'there be no medicine like love'. He also meditated that 'this strange, intoxicating distemper of love, which I have heard described as a disease . . . [is] surely one affection above all others that one would pray to be inoculated with'. These sentiments were apparently shared by all the other patients in the ward, who observed the scene 'half of them in tears, and the other half unwonted quiet, according to their several temperaments'. This is a true story of nature imitating art.[52]

iii. The Labouring Poor

Among social groups so poor that no money or property was involved, but only the economic and sexual union of two impecunious young people, even the most imperious of parents were unable to exercise control. Francis Place's father was an authoritarian brute, if his son is to be believed. But when in 1790 at the age of nineteen he declared his intention of marrying a seventeen-year-old girl as soon as he could raise the money for a few sticks of furniture, neither his mother nor even his father raised any objection. The bride's mother, however, strongly disapproved of the match, thinking Place to be too young, too poor and too bad-tempered. But the pair simply put up the banns without her permission and got married anyway. When Place's sister decided to marry a scoundrel of a butcher, she also had her way, despite the concerted pressure of all her family against it.[53] Parents in these circles were naturally consulted, but their opinions were easily and apparently frequently rejected.

iv. The Squirarchy and Nobility

Among the wealthier landed classes, the two issues of power and motive are too inextricably mixed to be usefully disentangled. The most fruitful way of examining conflict and change in these classes is therefore to examine the conduct of marriage negotiations from the point of view first of men and then of women.

a. Men. A typical but particularly well-documented example of late seventeenth-century marriage arrangements, as conducted in conservative aristocratic and courtly circles, concerns those in 1665 for the union of Jemima, a daughter of the first Earl of Sandwich, and Philip, the eldest son of Sir George Carteret.[54] The idea of a match was first broached by her mother to the family client Samuel Pepys in February, and in June the Sandwich parents decided to go ahead with the plans and authorized Pepys to make the first moves. The object was partly financial but more to cement a politico-administrative alliance, since both fathers were now very high officials in the Admiralty. Pepys, therefore, approached a Carteret client, Dr Clerk, who approved the match on the egotistical grounds that 'being both men relating to the sea, under a kind aspect of His Majesty, already good friends, and both virtuous and good families, their alliance might be of good use to us'. In other words, the two clients hoped to benefit from a cementing of the alliance of their influential patrons. The financial details were rapidly worked out – a marriage portion of £5,000 from Sandwich and a jointure for Jemima, if she were widowed, of £800 a year from Carteret; the approval of the King and of the Duke of York was secured; and the contract was signed and sealed on 5 July. It was not until this moment that Jemima was sent for from the country to be informed what fate her parents had decided for her. The only person at all bothered by this procedure was her mother, Lady Sandwich, who confided in Pepys her doubts 'whether her daughter will like of it or no, and how troubled she is for fear of it, which I do not fear at all'. Her anxiety seems to have arisen not from doubts about her daughter's happiness, but from the fear of the political damage that would be done if she unexpectedly turned recalcitrant.

By 15 July Jemima had arrived, the trousseau had been bought, and the time had come to introduce the couple to one another. Pepys was put in charge of taking the young Philip Carteret down to meet his bride. As a man of the world himself, with a winning way with women, whom he was constantly pawing and kissing, he was irritated to discover that he had on his hands a most bashful and tongue-tied young man. So shy was Philip that he did not even speak to Jemima or touch her at the introduction or all through dinner. Lord Sandwich suggested leaving the pair alone after dinner for a while, but Pepys advised against it; 'lest the lady might be too much surprised'. He was afraid of the effect of Philip's clumsy bashfulness. When he took Philip off to bed, he asked him how he liked his bride. The young man expressed approval 'but in the dullest, inspid manner that ever lover did'. Next day was Sunday, and Pepys instructed Philip to take Jemima by the hand and lead her as they came and went to and from church, but he was still too shy even to approach her. Later on that day, the pair were deliberately left alone for two periods of about an hour each in order to get acquainted as best they could. Pepys then took Jemima aside and asked her 'how she liked the gentleman and whether she was under any difficulty concerning him. She blushed and hid her face awhile, but at last I forced her to tell me. She answered that she could readily obey what her father and mother had done, which was all she could say, or I expect.' It was indeed all she *could* say, seeing that both sets of parents were determined on the match; it already had the approval of the King and his brother; the contract was already signed and sealed; and the trousseau had already been purchased. Jemima was trapped, as indeed was Philip also, and the effort to ascertain her feelings was clearly merely perfunctory. Over the next few days, Jemima remained solemn and discreet, Philip as shy and tongue-tied as ever. Meanwhile Jemima had to have minor surgical attention, to prepare her for the marriage. On 31 July the pair were married with due pomp and ceremony, although Pepys found 'the young lady mighty sad', and the wedding dinner a stiff and joyless affair. Later he attended Philip into the bridal chamber, kissed Jemima, drew the curtains around the four-poster, and withdrew. The next day he found the pair 'pleased this morning with their night's lodging', although whether they were really pleased or not, indeed whether the match was in fact consummated that night, is far from clear. At all events, Jemima did not become pregnant until fifteen months later. History does not relate how they got on with each other for the rest of their short married life, which lasted until Philip was killed at the battle of Solebay seven years later, leaving his widow with three children.

An instructive example of the ambiguities which were already creeping into marriage arrangements among the squirarchy is provided by the occasion in 1687 when George and Nancy Nicholas planned to marry their twenty-one-year-old daughter Jenny to an elderly baronet of merchant stock, Sir John Abdy. Her mother greedily counted up the assets: an estate worth £1,500 a year, no father or mother to support, a well-furnished house, and an offer of a jointure of £600 a year on the old man's death. 'Here are many qualifications for making a wife happy.' Jenny, however, was very reluctant to accept her aged suitor, and even the family patriarch, old Sir Ralph Verney, was for once on the side of the children. 'Cousin Jenny Nicholas cannot marry an old man, and I cannot blame her, for old age is very disagreeable unto youth; and I presume her father and mother have too much kindness for her than to force her.' Her mother (who herself had been forced by her father to reject a suitor twenty-five years before) admitted that the suitor was not young nor 'so fine a bred man as Sir Ralph Verney', and declared that her daughter 'is perfectly left to herself – 'tis she must live with him'. Whether or not Mrs Nicholas lived up to her principles, the next that is heard is that the marriage had been concluded. It may be that Jenny was attracted by the money and position, and found Sir John agreeable enough to marry; or it may be that the traditional pattern of marriage arranged by the parents for money and status triumphed over the new principle of a child's right of veto, and that a good deal of pressure was in fact successfully exerted.[55]

At exactly the same period, however, Anne Duchess of Hamilton was convinced that her daughters should only marry men they were attracted to, and therefore put no pressure on them. Moreover, the son and heir, James, who was away in London at court, was busy pursuing wealthy English brides of his own choice without consulting his father, upon whom he was nonetheless dependent for a legal settlement, without which he could not marry.[56] This was an exceptional case since the young man was far away and had the backing of the King, but his father's resignation to the situation suggests that even in exalted ducal circles, attitudes were having to be modified in the light of changing circumstances in the late seventeenth century.

A little later the eighteen-year-old William Lord North received a financially very attractive offer to marry a girl, unseen, and he seemed inclined to accept. But his elderly guardian Roger North counselled extreme prudence. He pointed out that the offer contained a lot about money, but 'not a word about her person or wit'. He therefore strongly advised personal inspection before any commitment, for 'they may produce a monster, or one that neither you can love nor she your lordship. Whatever the fortune is, the person must not be disagreeable, if your lordship intend to live comfortably'.[57] In this case it was the youth who was thinking about money, and the old bachelor who was thinking about affection, which shows that the clash of values was not a simple generational conflict.

An interesting early eighteenth-century example from the gentry of how attitudes were changing is the story of Nicholas Blundell of Crosby Hall. An impoverished Catholic squire, Nicholas had done the right thing by his family and in 1703 had married for money. They had made an unhappy pair, and twenty-two years later, when his own daughters came on the marriage market, he was determined not to make the same mistake again. He reflected that 'it is my chief aim to settle my daughters to their own liking, that they may make choice of a man they can love, and I will do my endeavour to propose such to them whose circumstances may make them happy'. This was a little ambiguous, but when it came to the point he flatly declared that 'it was always my promise to her [Mary] that I would not oblige her to marry against her will'. Among the lesser gentry of Lancashire in 1725 this was apparently still a rather novel attitude, but Nicholas told himself that 'if I be reflected on for not compelling her, I would rather be taxed with that than give any occasion of being esteemed a harsh or unkind parent'.[58]

The story which best epitomizes the transitional position from one mode of behaviour to another in the early eighteenth century is that of the negotiations in 1710–11 to marry Mary, the daughter of a very wealthy self-made Sheffield attorney, Joseph Banks of Scofton, to the son and heir of Colonel Talbot of Thornton-le-Street in Yorkshire.[59] Himself now a substantial landowner and accustomed in his business to act as agent for dukes and landed gentry, Banks had adopted the traditional marriage habits of the class to which he aspired. On the other hand, as a professional man of bourgeois origins, he also brought with him the idea that the personal choice of the two individuals was paramount. A few months before the story opens, Banks had burned his fingers in abortive negotiations for Mary's marriage to another landed son and heir, in which he thought he had been financially double-crossed. This time, negotiations were carried on via two intermediaries, that for Banks being a cousin, the Reverend William Steer of Sheffield, who first proposed the match. Throughout June, July, August and September 1710, the fathers exchanged financial information and offers in an atmosphere of total secrecy, neither the two young people nor even Banks' wife being informed of what was going on. There were considerable financial problems, for the Talbots turned out to be far less wealthy than Banks had expected and Colonel Talbot demanded an excessively large marriage portion, half of which was to go to himself. However, by the end of September these matters had been straightened out, and 'Mally' at last knew what was going on. The two fathers met on neutral ground and agreed on the financial terms. Banks then stipulated and the Colonel agreed 'that the young people should have an interview, and if they liked one another the matter was done, but if otherwise there was to be an end'. Enquiries about young Roger Talbot turned up nothing derogatory, except 'his loving a pot', or an inclination to drink to excess. After the visit, Steer reported optimistically on 11 October that Mary 'looks on him (as far as she can learn by their short acquaintance) to be so good humoured that she can reasonably propose to live happily with him'. This seemed good enough for Steer, who was of the old school and thought that 'they seldom fail to be happy that marry into an honest family', and therefore that family standing was more important than personal inclination.

But Mary was, in fact, very uncertain; other visits may have followed, and Mary was now writing to her mother in a much more discouraging tone. In January Joseph Banks wrote to Mary, placing the final decision fairly and squarely on her. 'I leave it to thyself. But after I have gone so far, without more reasons than I knew, to go off would not look well.' On the other hand, Mary was still young (only twenty), and she could probably do better for herself financially. 'Pray God direct thee. I leave it to thyself.' Encouraged by this letter, Mary wrote Steer a firm refusal of the offer. 'I cannot for my life think him agreeable . . . and I think that man and woman must run a great hazard of living miserably all their lives where there is not a mutual inclination beforehand. . . . My Papa has left me entirely to choose which way I please in this affair.' The fact of the matter was that Mary had heard that Roger had got dead drunk at Pontefract on the way home from his visit, and decided not to tie herself to a lifelong alcoholic. Her father himself agreed: 'I . . . cannot blame her, for the apprehension of want of government that way must be very dreadful'.

So far as it goes, this story is one of a perfect compromise between old-fashioned economic horse-trading between the fathers and the new rules of granting total freedom of choice to the young people, in this case exercised entirely on the principle of the need for prior affection. On the other hand, this veto power exercised by Mary was a card which could hardly be played more than once, at most twice, and the records do not tell us whether there was any more enthusiasm on her part some time later, when she made the far more socially and financially advantageous marriage to a local notable, Sir Francis Whichcote, third Baronet. It is, however, reasonable to suppose that her father's choice was then more prudent, and that, in view of the good will she had shown the first time, she may have been consulted at an earlier stage of the negotiations.

Even if the children of the nobility were allowed full freedom of choice to accept or reject the partners proposed to them, it by no means follows that they were necessarily swayed exclusively by 'fancy' – as Joseph Banks called it – rather than by the older and more practical considerations of money and status. The higher one goes up the social scale, the more likely this is to be true. When in 1716 Thomas Pelham-Holles, Duke of Newcastle, married Henrietta Godolphin, the granddaughter of the Duke of Marlborough, it was on Newcastle's side an arranged marriage for money, since he had to have between £20,000 and £30,000 to clear off his debts. 'Harriot' seems to have been a pawn in a game played by her grandmother, and she does not appear to have been consulted at all. On the other hand Newcastle was very careful to cross-question the Marlborough agent, Sir John Vanbrugh, about his prospective bride's character, since he was afraid to 'find himself tied for life to a woman not capable of being a useful and faithful friend, as well as an agreeable companion'.[60]

Later on in the eighteenth century, the motives for marriage among the aristocracy were still confused, but all sides were beginning to recognize the need for prior affection. In the 1780s the Earl of Pembroke was heavily in debt and therefore urged his heir Lord Herbert to find a bride 'as beautiful as you please, and as rich as Croesus ... *ou nous sommes tous ... foutus*'. The latter first made an offer to Caroline, daughter of the Duke of Marlborough, but was rejected. Her brother explained that 'she has not that kind of liking for you, without which she is determined not to marry any man. ... She likes you very well, but not as a lover.' This was now thought, on all sides, to be a sufficient reason for refusal. Lord Herbert also made some very half-hearted overtures to the only daughter and heiress of Sir Richard Child of Osterley, the fabulously wealthy banker. In this he seems to have been following up an earlier suggestion of his governor and friend Major Floyd, who asked him: 'have you ever seen her, and do you think you could bring yourself to lay your chaste leg over her for the dirty consideration of two or three hundred thousand pounds?' But nothing came of this, and a year later, Lord Herbert got himself engaged to a penniless cousin, Elizabeth Beauclerk, and had to ask his father not only for his blessing but for an extra £1,000 a year with which to set up house. His father's philosophical acceptance of the *fait accompli* was highly illuminating about the new scale of values. He pointed out 'how very much the situation of our affairs stand in need of at least thirty thousand pounds. ... It would have been lucky for us had you found a thirty thousand pounder as agreeable to you as Elizabeth.' Having made the point, however, Pembroke dropped it, and gave his approval of the match without further argument, on the grounds that 'the greatest pleasure I can feel is to know that you are happy. If you are happy my dearest George, I must be so. ... *N'en parlons plus*.'[61] As we have seen, seventeenth-century fathers did not treat similar acts of independence by the male heir, and similar family financial disasters, with anything like such easy-going good humour. When in 1805 Lord Duncannon, son and heir of the Earl of Bessborough, became engaged to Maria Fane, daughter of the Earl of Westmorland, he merely wrote to his mother to request his parent's approval. There is no suggestion of prior choice by or consultation with his father, who wrote to his son about the matter very calmly – although admittedly from both the social and the financial points of view the bride was perfectly acceptable. 'Your mother has showed me your letter ... and I can assure you I approve, as far as I am acquainted with the circumstances of the match you wished to make, neither did I want you to marry a very great fortune. I only represented to you it was necessary that the lady should have some fortune, otherwise you would have great difficulties in your living. ...'[62] The limits imposed by parents even in these circles were now mild indeed compared with those current a century or more earlier.

b. Women. So far, marriage in elite landed circles has been looked at exclusively from the point of view of the men, the fathers and the sons, but there is available a little evidence from the women themselves, which serves to put match-making at this period in a rather different perspective.

A detailed and absorbing example from a woman's point of view of the confusion of values existing among the upper classes in the mid-seventeenth century is provided by the autobiography of Lady Anne Halkett, which is one of the first in England to be mainly the history of a chequered love life.[63] She was a woman strongly influenced by her sense of religious duty, which had been instilled into her at an early age. As the daughter of Thomas Murray, a court official and Provost of Eton, she had been brought up in a strict Anglican tradition, in many ways as austere as that practised by the Puritans. This piety was the main driving force in her life, and as a result she had difficulty in accommodating to her complicated emotional entanglements. She also believed in the traditional view about obedience to at least a parental veto in marriage: 'I ever looked upon marrying without consent of parents as the highest act of ingratitude and disobedience that children could commit, and I resolved never to be guilty of it'. On the other hand, she was modern enough to refuse to allow a parent or anyone else to dictate her feelings or tell her whom to marry, an attitude which infuriated her mother.

Her situation was further complicated by the chaos and disorder of civil war and revolution, particularly since she and her friends and relatives were all on the losing side and were constantly in hiding or on the move.

Her story opens in 1644, when Lord Howard of Escrick, an impoverished royalist nobleman in exile, sent his eldest son and heir, Thomas, to stay in her sister's household. Lord Howard's intention was 'to marry him to some rich match that might improve his fortune', and in particular 'to marry a rich citizen's daughter that his father had designed for him'. But instead the young man fell head over heels in love with the twenty-one-year-old Anne, although she did her best to discourage him, knowing well the opposition of both his father and her mother (her father had died twenty years before). She was nevertheless very fond of him, and even in the face of violent parental opposition arranged a secret meeting with him (with her sister present as chaperone). When the young man nearly fainted with emotion, Anne sat on his knee to comfort him, but she remained resolute in her determination to obey her mother. The next day Thomas Howard departed 'and left me to the severities of my offended mother, whom nothing could pacify'. Her mother threatened that if Anne ever saw Thomas Howard again, she would 'turn me out of her doors and never own me again', an order that Anne ingeniously frustrated by agreeing to another secret meeting with the young man, but with her eyes blindfolded. She reiterated her refusal to marry without parental consent, but vowed to be faithful to him, while he exchanged many similar vows of his undying devotion to her. When she got to hear of this further meeting, her mother was naturally even more enraged and demanded again that Anne cease to think about Thomas Howard, a demand for thought-control that Anne obstinately refused to give. About two years later, however, in 1646, Thomas married – willingly or not is unknown – a daughter of the Earl of Peterborough, and this episode, therefore, came to an end.

Soon after the death of her mother in 1647 or 1648, Anne went to live in her brother's house in London, where she met an Irish royalist colonel, Joseph Bampfield, who was then engaged on a series of secret missions for the imprisoned king. Excited by the conspiratorial activities of the colonel and her devotion to the royalist cause, she took a prominent and dangerous part in helping Bampfield to smuggle the king's younger son James, Duke of York (the future James II) out of the country. The colonel had not seen his wife for over a year, a fact which he explained away to Anne's satisfaction by the fact that she and her friends were all Parliamentarians. The intimacy throve on royalist plotting, and soon afterwards in 1649 he announced one day that his wife was dead and asked Anne to marry him. Anne by then had convinced herself that she was in love with this romantic secret agent, and she engaged herself to marry him as soon as the political situation made it possible. But he was in hiding, and she had to leave London in a hurry to avoid arrest for her complicity in the plot to smuggle out the Duke of York. She therefore took refuge at Naworth Castle with her friend Lady Howard and her husband Sir Charles. There she heard, almost simultaneously, two shattering pieces of news. The first was the arrest of the colonel and his grave danger of execution, and the second (from her brother and sister) that the colonel was a rogue and a liar and that his wife was in fact still alive. On hearing this news 'I fell so extremely sick that none expected life for me'. But the colonel made a daring and successful escape from prison; and she persuaded herself that the story about the wife was false. She indignantly repudiated rumours that she 'designed to marry a man that had a wife'. Meanwhile her brother-in-law had accidentally met Colonel Bampfield in a boat going to Flanders and had promptly challenged him to a duel for trifling with the affections of his sister-in-law while he was a married man. The colonel denied the accusation but fought the duel, very badly wounding Anne's brother-in-law in the hand.

By now she had moved on to Edinburgh, where the ubiquitous colonel turned up and asked for an interview, which threw her into another hysterical collapse. 'The conflict betwixt love and honour was so great and prevalent that neither would yield to other, and betwixt both I was brought into so great a distemper that I expected now an end to all my misfortunes.'

The colonel was busy plotting for a rising in Scotland on behalf of Charles II, and among his fellow conspirators was Sir James Halkett, an elderly widower with four children, some of whom were nearly grown-up. Sir James saw more and more of Anne, and eventually asked her to marry him. She refused on the grounds of her prior engagement to Colonel Bampfield, whose protestations about his wife's death she continued more or less to believe. She told Sir James that 'nothing but the death of Colonel Bampfield could make me ever think of another'. Meanwhile, there took place the invasion of Scotland by Charles II and the crushing defeat of the Scottish royal army by Cromwell at Dunbar. Anne fled with the royalist nobility into the Highlands.

A year later in 1653 confirmation that Mrs Bampfield was alive and well caused a further psychological collapse. When she recovered, Sir James revived his suit, which she eventually accepted, and she agreed to marry him as soon as she had fully cleared up her financial affairs. Anne returned to

London for this purpose in 1654, when the colonel, who was now (entirely unknown to her) acting as a double agent for both Charles II and Cromwell, turned up for the last time. He asked her flatly whether or not she was married to Sir James Halkett, because if she was he would not bother her again. 'I hated lying, and I saw there might be some inconvenience to tell the truth, and (Lord pardon the equivocation) I said "I am" out loud, and secretly said "not".' Thus she was finally freed from a nine-year involvement with the colonel, which was clearly the most passionate emotional experience of her life, and in 1656, at the age of thirty-three, she married her patient elderly suitor, Sir James Halkett.

This is a story which could only have happened in the seventeenth century. The extreme piety which dominated her life was typical of her age, as was that reverence for parental wishes which prevented her from giving herself to either of her first two lovers, and the code of the duel which drove her brother-in-law to risk his life in a challenge on her behalf but against her wishes. Both fornication and bigamy were unthinkable for her, and on delicate occasions she took a chaperone with her to interviews with her suitors. At the same time the Civil Wars and their aftermath caused constant interruptions of relations and the impossibility of establishing even such a simple fact as whether or not the wife of a prominent gentleman were still alive. These separations not only stimulated literacy, since writing was now a prime means of keeping in touch, they also stimulated a strong, if ephemeral, sense of independence among many women who suddenly found responsibility thrust upon them. One instance of Anne's new-found spirit of independence was her adoption of the practice of going to plays and amusement gardens with female friends, each paying her own way, after she overheard some gentlemen complaining about the cost of taking a lady to the theatre. Her emotional attachment to the colonel was also a product of war, being stimulated by his glamorous role as a secret royalist agent. But once he was shown up as a liar and a fraud, and once the upheavals of war were over, she made a practical prosaic match of the most traditional kind, and settled down once more in the subordinate role of dutiful wife and mother. She was a woman who moved uncertainly between two worlds: the one, in which she had been brought up and in which she was to live out her last decades, was based on female subordination to men, and marriage for interest not attraction; the other, which boiled up for a while in the crucible of war, was one of excitement, glamour, intrigue, love and feminine independence, literacy and responsibility. Her conflict between love and honour is characteristic of the plots of contemporary classical drama.

Another ambiguously revealing seventeenth-century case history written by a woman is the story of the marriage of Alice Wandesford with William Thornton in 1651.[64] Alice's late father had been an ally of the Earl of Strafford, and the children were staunch Anglicans. Although the son and heir George was a minor and had taken no part whatever in the Civil Wars, his property was sequestered as a royalist delinquent in 1651. Under these circumstances, his uncle William approached a relative, Richard Darley, who was all-powerful in the local Parliamentary County Committee, and struck a bargain with him. Darley promised to get the sequestration lifted in return for a marriage between his nephew William Thornton and Alice Wandesford, who was likely to inherit a fairly ample estate. As Alice commented bitterly: 'Thus the bargain was struck betwixt them before my dear mother or myself ever heard a syllable of this matter ... in a case on which all the comfort of my life, or misery, depended.' Alice had not even met Mr Thornton and, in any case, had a strong preference for remaining single. But she was willing to sacrifice herself in the family interests if the gentleman was acceptable to her. When she met Mr Thornton, she found that he seemed to be 'a very godly, sober and discreet person' and so consented reluctantly to the marriage: 'I thought it rather duty in me to accept my friends' desires for a joint benefit than my own single retired content.' The wedding took place on 15 December 1651, and it is hardly surprising that immediately after the service Alice was struck by an illness which in retrospect we can perhaps identify as psychosomatic, a bodily reaction of protest against her predicament, rather than as mere indigestion. At 2 p.m. on the wedding day she was suddenly struck by 'a violent pain in my head and stomach, causing a great vomiting and sickness at my heart, which lasted eight hours before I had any intermission'. However suspicious we may be of Alice's account of her life, what comes through very clearly is the complex pressures that could be brought to bear on an upper-class girl in the mid-seventeenth century and the way in which her freedom of choice was circumscribed, even if she were left theoretically free to make her own decisions. It also illustrates some of the tensions that these pressures could create at a time when the concept of greater freedom of choice was becoming more widespread, and some of the ways women took to resolve them.

By the early eighteenth century, some of the more high-spirited and independent girls in the higher aristocratic circles would no longer tolerate these authoritarian dispositions of their hearts and bodies by their parents or 'friends'. Mary, daughter of a younger son of the Marquess of Dorchester, had long been courted by an elderly suitor, Mr Wortley, to whom she was attached. But Mr Wortley and her father quarrelled over the financial arrangements, and the latter broke off the match. In 1710 Mary commented bitterly that 'people in my way are sold like slaves, and I cannot tell what price my master will put upon me.' But when her father ordered her to marry someone she positively hated, she dug in her toes and refused to agree. Her father 'told me he was very much surprised that I did not depend on his judgment for my future happiness', and threatened she would live out her life as an old maid since 'he would never so much as enter into a treaty with any other.' Her relatives were no help since they sided with her father. 'They found no necessity of loving; if I lived well with him, that was all was required of me; and that if I considered this town [London], I should find very few women in love with their husbands, and yet many happy.' Finally, after first giving in to the blackmail, Mary finally solved her problems by eloping with Mr Wortley, with the secret support of her brother.[65] She was clearly in advance of her time in these high aristocratic circles.

The autobiography of Mary Granville (later Mrs Delany) reveals similar conflicts at a similar period and at a similar social level.[66] Mary was born in 1700, the daughter of a younger son of a Groom of the Bedchamber and with close aristocratic and court connections. Her parents and relatives were staunch Tories and were driven from court and office by the Hanoverian succession in 1714. She therefore grew up a well-connected, lively and intelligent girl, but without a fortune. Judging by her story, however, she must have been extremely attractive to men. Her first suitor was a Mr Twyford, who paid court to her at the early age of fifteen and asked her to marry him. Mary's father 'told him I had no fortune, and it was very probable, for this reason, his friends would not approve of his choice'. When Mr Twyford found that his parents, especially his mother, flatly refused their consent, he asked Mary to marry him privately, a step she refused to take. Some three years later, after she was married, she learned that this rebuff and her marriage had driven Mr Twyford into an hysterical collapse:

His mother's cruel treatment of him and absolute refusal of her consent for his marrying me affected him so deeply as to throw him into a dead palsy. He lost the use of his speech, though not of his senses, and when he strove to speak, he could not utter above a word or two, but he used to write perpetually and I was the only subject of his pen. He lived in this wretched state about a year after I was married. When he was dead, they found under his pillow a piece of cut paper, which he had stolen out of my closet.

At the age of seventeen, Mary was invited to stay with her uncle Lord

Lansdowne at Longleat, where she was thrown in the company of a Mr Alexander Pendarves, a very wealthy Cornish Tory landowner. He found Mary very attractive, and Lord Lansdowne, who probably planned the whole thing in advance, saw an opportunity of providing his impoverished niece with a rich husband, while at the same time consolidating his own Tory political influence in Cornwall. Neither Lord and Lady Lansdowne nor her other aunt Lady Stanley regarded the personal feelings of this seventeen-year-old girl towards her sixty-year-old suitor as of the slightest importance. Indeed, they easily convinced themselves that she would see things their way, and called her 'childish, ignorant and silly' to raise objections to a marriage which was so clearly in her own best interests.

The trouble was that Mary could not abide her suitor's 'large, unwieldly person and his crimson face'. 'I thought him ugly and disagreeable; he was fat, much afflicted with gout, and often sat in a sullen mood, which I concluded was from the gloominess of his temper.' For two months Mr Pendarves followed Mary about the enormous house, and Mary fled from him in apprehension and disgust. He was anxious to declare his intentions, but was deterred by Mary's attitude, and was only provoked into action by jealousy of a young man who was staying in the houses, a younger son of Edward Villiers, Earl of Jersey, whose attentions Mary clearly found far more acceptable than his own. He therefore approached Lord Lansdowne, who 'readily embraced the offer and engaged for my compliance; he might have said obedience, for I was not entreated but commanded.' Seizing a suitable opportunity, Lord Lansdowne summoned her to a talk. He 'took me by the hand, and after a very pathetic speech of his love and care of me, and of my father's unhappy circumstances, my own want of fortune, and the little prospect I had of being happy if I disobliged those friends that were desirous of serving me, he told me of [Pendarves'] passion for me, and his offer of settling his whole estate on me; he then, with great art and eloquence, told me all his good qualities and vast merit, and how despicable I should be if I could refuse him because he was not young and handsome.' In a state of shock, Mary stammered out her willingness to obey his commands, excused herself, and fled to her room, where she wept for two hours until ordered to come down to supper. But she was trapped. 'I had nobody to advise with; every one of the family had persuaded themselves that this would be an advantageous match for me – no-one considered the sentiments of my heart; to be settled in the world, and ease my friends of an expense and care, they urged that it was my duty to submit, and that I ought to sacrifice everything to that one point.' Her one hope was that her parents would support her, but instead they were delighted at so rich a catch as Mr Pendarves. To Mary, however, he was repellent. In the first place, he was sixty years old, forty-three years older than herself. 'As to his person he was excessively fat, of a brown complexion, negligent in his dress, and took a vast quantity of snuff, which gave him a dirty look: his eyes were black, small, lively and sensible; he had an honest countenance, but altogether a person rather disgusting than engaging. He was good-natured and friendly, but so strong a "party man" [i.e., a Tory], that he made himself many enemies. ... He was very sober for two years after we married, but then he fell in with a set of old acquaintance, a society famed for excess in wine, and to his ruin and my misery was hardly ever sober. This course of life soured his temper, which was naturally good, and the days he did not drink were spent in a gloomy sullen way, which was infinitely worse to me than his drinking; for I did not know how to please or entertain him, and yet no one ever heard him say a snappish or cross thing to me.' In this character sketch, Mary does her best to be fair to poor Mr Pendarves, but, as we shall see, she does not ask herself to what extent her dislike of him might have been responsible for his moroseness and his drinking.

So married they were 'with great pomp' early in 1717, after which they progressed slowly back to the family seat at Roscrow in Cornwall, accompanied by the blessings of Mary's aunt Lady Stanley, 'wishing you and Mr Pendarves all happiness together, riches, honour and length of days' – as if this was all that was needed for happiness. On arrival at Roscrow, Mary found to her horror that it was a gloomy and dilapidated old structure, which had not been lived in for thirty years. At this point, for the first time, she collapsed in a fit of weeping. However, Mr Pendarves, whom even Mary admitted was a kindly and affectionate old gentleman, gave her a free hand in restoring the house, which cheered her up for a time.

Whether Mr Pendarves attempted sexual relations with her and whether she submitted with frigidity and loathing or openly rebuffed him is naturally not stated in her autobiography. But inevitably he was jealous of his pretty young wife, who was pursued by a succession of hopeful men. There was Mr Pendarves' nephew Mr Basset of Tehidy, a man of gallantry, married to a very dull wife, whose attentions to Mary caused poor Mr Pendarves to sulk. There was a dear young friend of Mr Pendarves who left his wife and stayed in the house for months on end. He finally avowed his love for Mary, was rebuffed, and threatened suicide. He was got rid of by the simple expedient of telling him that the Pendarves were moving back to London.

Soon afterwards Mr Pendarves, worried by debts and also, one may suspect, by his failure to win the affection of his wife, took to alcohol in order to drown his pain. His drinking bouts were only interrupted by violent attacks of gout, when he was confined to bed. 'As soon as he was able to go abroad, he returned to his society, never came home sober, and has frequently been led between two servants to bed at six and seven o'clock in the morning. Unhappy cruel state! How many tears have I shed. ...' One may suspect that for Mr Pendarves, this may have been one solution to the torment of sleeping in the same bed as an attractive young woman for whom he had great affection, but who found him physically revolting.

Meanwhile, Mary was beseiged by suitors. There was the Earl of Clare (married to Mary's aunt) who once wrote her a letter when Pendarves was laid up with gout, in which he deplored 'my unhappy situation in being nurse to an old man and declared most passionately his admiration for me'. Another admirer was the young Herminius, Lord Baltimore, a handsome and well-bred young man, whom Mary clearly found most attractive. But Mary remained faithful to her husband for seven years until finally in 1726 she woke up one morning to find herself lying beside a dead man with a blackened face. The initial shock was great, but the new state of widowhood was, as she frankly admitted, 'not unwelcome', although Mr Pendarves had not signed his will, so that she was not the great heiress she had anticipated. Moreover, honesty forced her to admit that Mr Pendarves had been 'very obliging in his behaviour to me, and I have often reproached myself bitterly for my ingratitude (if it can be so called) in not loving a man who had so true an affection for me'.

Three years after the death of Mr Pendarves, Lord Baltimore met her one Saturday at the opera and blurted out that he 'had been in love with me for five years'. She put him off for the moment, and they parted in order to think things over. Since she was a widow, and he had already succeeded to his estate, they had no one to please but themselves. Two days later he came to visit her and declared that he was 'determined never to marry unless he was well assured of the affection of the person he married. My reply was "can you have stronger proof (if the person is at her own disposal) than her consenting to marry you?" He replied that was not sufficient. I said he was unreasonable, upon which he started up and said, "I find, Madam, this is a point in which we shall never agree"', and promptly left, never to return. Not so long afterwards, he married the daughter of the enormously wealthy Sir Theodore Janssen, upon the news of which Mary fell very ill indeed. She turned violently against the whole male sex, declaring her distaste for men as a species: 'everyday my dislike strengthens; some few I will except, but very few, they have so despicable an opinion of women and treat them by their words and actions so ungenerously and inhumanly.'

On the other hand, there are two interpretations which can be put on this last episode. The first is that Lord Baltimore meant what he said, that he fully believed in the ideal of positive prior affection before marriage, and demanded a reciprocal statement from Mary of affection (and perhaps consent to sleep together), which she refused to give because she preferred flirtation to commitment, being basically frigid. The other is that in the forty-eight hours since his first declaration, he had had second thoughts, had decided after all to look for a richer wife, and had used the demand for a declaration of love, and maybe consent to fornication, as an excuse to get out of a difficult situation.

The whole story of Mary Granville illustrates the see-saw battle between family wishes and personal choice, between interest, money and affection, that was waged in the hearts and minds of the English elite in the early eighteenth century. Mary's marriage to Mr Pendarves was a classic case of an arranged marriage purely for money and influence. Mr Twyford's love for Mary and his paralysis and death, apparently caused by his parents' refusal to allow him to marry, illustrate the opposite pole of pure romantic love. The constant attempts on her virtue made by married relatives and acquaintances show the way the arranged marriage positively encouraged adulterous attempts on the chastity of married women, while Mary's refusal of her suitors, and her subsequent attitude to men may well have been caused by frigidity induced by cohabitation with the odious Mr Pendarves. The case of Lord Baltimore shows a young man torn between love and money, unable to make up his mind as to which came first, but apparently opting in the end for money, possibly because he could not obtain reciprocal affection.

Among the high aristocracy as late as the 1780s, some girls still allowed themselves to be guided by their parents into more or less blind marriages. There were, however, two critical differences from the old-style arranged marriage. In the first place the parental motive, at least ostensibly, was the future happiness of the daughter, not the best financial or political interests of the family at large. Secondly, the means employed to obtain compliance was love and not authority. The new affectionate parent-child relations were now used with great effect, especially by mothers, to get their daughters to do what they wanted. Thus, when in the 1780s Harriet Spencer, daughter of Lord Spencer, became engaged to Lord Duncannon, the son and heir of the Earl of Bessborough, she told a friend that 'I had not the least guess about it till the day papa told me. ... I wish I could have known him a little better first, but my dear papa and mama say that it will make them the happiest of creatures, and what would I not do to see them happy?' everything she could learn about the young man was in his favour, so that she concluded that 'I have a better chance of being reasonably happy with him than with most people I know'. On these terms she accepted him, and indeed the marriage turned out reasonably well.[67]

Respect for parental wishes, reinforced by these tight bonds of affection, were now especially deeply internalized for young women brought up in an atmosphere of fairly intense but conventional piety. Hester Lynch Salusbury was the only daughter of an impoverished branch of a rich and very well-connected family.[68] Her expectations rose dramatically when her uncle married an elderly and rich heiress, Miss Penrice of Offley Place, and planned to make his niece his heiress. In 1761 both her uncle and her mother were extremely anxious that she should marry a rich, handsome, well-educated brewer, Henry Thrale. Although Mr Thrale paid more attention to her mother than to her, Miss Salusbury seemed willing enough to go along with these arrangements, in order to please her mother and for the sake of the anticipated inheritance from her uncle. But her father objected to Mr Thrale and, according to her, she decided that she 'durst not commit a positive offence against God by disobliging my father, who had the sole right to dispose of me, and whom therefore I would obey at the hazard of all my temporal hopes'. But in 1762 that obstacle was cleared from the path by her father's death from apoplexy, and the pressure on her from her mother and uncle increased. In 1763 Mr Thrale finally got himself to the point of making her an offer, which she accepted. As she later put it, 'Mr Thrale was originally [my mother's] choice for me, not mine for myself, however we never differed either on that or any other occasion – her pleasure was my delight, her will my law'.

These later, clearly self-serving, remarks made at a time she had long been thoroughly disillusioned about her marriage, should not be taken as entirely true. But she was certainly devoted to her mother, and there seems little doubt that she had no affection for her prospective husband, nor he for her. As she wrote in 1787, 'ours was a match of mere prudence and common good liking, without the smallest pretensions to passion on either side. I knew no more of him than of any other gentleman who came to the house.' They had not spent more than five minutes alone together before the evening of their wedding day, as they prepared to go to bed together for the first time. Mr Thrale had his own lower-class mistress to provide him with love and sexual satisfaction, and was looking for a docile, well-born, well-educated girl to be the mother of his children, who would be content to live quietly at his suburban villa at Streatham Park and at his London house by the brewery in the very unfashionable end of town at Southwark. He was also, no doubt, attracted by her present and future financial assets – about £30,000 in all – and by her prospects from her uncle of a great deal more. As for Miss Salusbury, she was anxious to please her mother; she found Mr Thrale a rich, even-tempered and handsome sort of man to whom she could have no obvious objection; and she hoped by the marriage to consolidate her claims on her uncle's large estate. On both sides, it was a marriage of convenience. Mrs Thrale almost certainly also hoped to win her husband's affection after marriage, but she failed completely in the effort. He came eventually to admire her intelligence and good business sense, but never showed any affection for her personally. Part of the trouble may have been Mrs Thrale's continued psychological dependence on her mother, whom she continued to visit every day, and who eventually moved in with them. When her mother died in 1773, Mrs Thrale wrote that she 'left me destitute of every *real*, every *natural* friend, for ... Mr Thrale and Dr Johnson [who also lived mostly in the house] are the mere acquisitions of chance'. In many ways, this was a very old-fashioned sort of marriage, in the role played by parental wishes, the predominant economic considerations, and the total lack of prior mutual affection or even pretence at it. The causes were the financial aspirations of Mrs Thrale's mother, who was anxious to escape from her predicament of well-born but impoverished gentility, and the social aspirations of Mr Thrale, who was anxious to dignify his brewing business by marrying into the pedigreed gentry.

This was an exceptional situation, and among the squirarchy many mothers by the late eighteenth century thought it wrong to exercise the new weapon of affection, that was now at their disposal, to influence in any way the marriage choices of their daughters. In 1792 a Mrs Drake told a friend that her daughter Mariana had decided to marry a Mr Evance. She was worried since he was twenty years older than her daughter, but 'the choice is entirely hers. . . . In a matter of so much import to the future happiness of a child, a mother *must feel*, as marriage is certainly a lottery'.[69] In this case, the mother, whatever her real feelings, now thought it appropriate to claim that she had freely conceded the right of choice to her child, and that her sole concern was her daughter's personal happiness, not money or social benefits.

c. Conclusion. It is clear that the eighteenth-century aristocracy and squirarchy were hopelessly torn in their sense of priorities and values in matrimonial projects and that no single or simple pattern will serve to explain the complex reality. Choices varied from person to person; the pressures varied from parent to parent. The only certain facts which emerge are that the least free were the heirs and heiresses to great fortunes, unless their parents were dead and they had obtained full financial control; secondly, that even if they were free, young people might well opt for money rather than love or lust; thirdly, that the loveless marriage was now generally regarded as a direct encouragement to adultery by both parties; fourthly, that marriage at the free choice of bride and groom and based on solid emotional attachment was increasingly common by the end of the century; and fifthly, that some noble and gentry parents were using the ties of affection that now bound their children to them in order to direct their choice. One can make the theoretical assumption that it is only in circles where the cult of individualism and privacy has taken hold that well tested affection is either generally sought after by young people, or is necessarily a better way of handling a decision of critical importance, which is always largely a gamble, however and by whom it is decided. A second theoretical assumption is that freedom of choice can most easily be conceded by parents in closely integrated groups with internalized norms, where there is little chance that the children will come into close contact with members of a lower social class; where the property at stake in the marriage is not too great; where the risk of seduction by penniless adventurers is small; and where the age of marriage is postponed at least to the mid-twenties, when a sensible choice is more likely to be made than in the late teens.

Finally the society must have devised means by which young people can mix freely and test out each other's character and temperament, so as to be in a position to make a rational choice based on settled affection. This was not permitted before the end of the seventeenth century, when at last there developed a series of institutions by which the courting process could go on among the elite. The balls, card parties and assemblies in the county town, particularly at the four assizes or at the major annual fairs or horse-racing events, were important mechanisms for the new style of local match-making. The building of assembly rooms in town after town during the eighteenth century is evidence of its importance. On the national level, the development of the London season, lasting from early in the New Year to June, and the subsequent season at a major watering place like Bath, provided the necessary facilities for the development of acquaintances across county boundaries. By the middle of the eighteenth century, there were both a series of county marriage markets, centered on the facilities of the county towns, and a national marriage market, centered on London and Bath. After Lord Hardwicke's Marriage Act came into force in 1754, parents could allow a child to associate with others rather more freely, since they were at least certain that he or she could no longer contract a secret but binding engagement with an unsuitable person, and could only make a clandestine marriage by travelling all the way to Scotland.

This development of a national marriage market in London and Bath greatly widened the pool of potentially satisfactory spouses, from the parental point of view. So long as the gentry were confined to marrying within their own class and within their own county, the number of suitable spouses was so restricted that direct parental choice of a specific individual made good sense. The national marriage market of the eighteenth century greatly reduced the need to be so specific, for there were now a larger number of potential spouses who would meet the necessary financial and social qualifications. With internalized parental norms and the availability of a wide range of socially acceptable potential mates, children could safely be allowed greater freedom of access to members of the other sex, and greater freedom of choice, without threatening the long-term interests of the family in the making of a 'suitable' marriage.

Even within single families, however, individual character governed the choice of motives for marriage, so that all that can be expected is evidence for a trend, not uniformity of behaviour. Thus in 1774 Frederick Robinson, the son of Lord Grantham, wrote to his sister, asked for her help in finding him a bride, and setting out his requirements in purely economic terms. His sister was shocked, and wrote to their father, 'I should advise him not to think of so much as £60,000, and to study nothing but his happiness; he says nothing of beauty – which I don't understand.' Brother and sister within a single family were clearly poles apart in their attitudes to marriage. It was alleged that some calculating and necessitous parents deliberately exploited this ambiguity of motives in order to get a daughter off their hands at no financial cost to themselves.

How many parents are in specious circumstances, who drop artful hints of what they will do for a daughter; and when an advantageous offer appears, will encourage a young man until he has swallowed the bait, and then discountenance the connection; when, the young lady cooperating, a private match takes place, and the enraged papa or mama declares they will not give – what they never had to bestow! The poor dupe, in such case, has no remedy but to take home the wife of his bosom, and make the best he can of his bargain.[70]

Despite this evidence of a very ambiguous situation, which varied widely from family to family and generation to generation, foreign visitors in the mid and late eighteenth century were unanimous in their conviction that the English enjoyed greater freedom of choice of a marriage partner and greater companionship in marriage than was the case on the Continent. As early as 1741 Baron de Pollnitz was struck by the greater liberty English women enjoyed than those in his own country, and forty-seven years later the Duc de la Rochefoucauld had the same reactions: 'the English have much more opportunity of getting to know each other before marriage, for young folk are in society from an early age; they go with their parents everywhere. Young girls mix with the company and talk and enjoy themselves with as much freedom as if they were married.' The explanation for this practice of free and lengthy courtship he ascribed directly to the rise of the companionate marriage, which he also thought was peculiar to England, alleging that 'three marriages out of four are based on affection', and that subsequent relations remained far closer than in France. 'I am not sure whether the obligation to live constantly with one's wife does not make it necessary to marry at a later age, but I am inclined to think so. To have a wife who is not agreeable to you must, in England, make life a misery. Accordingly the Englishman makes more effort to get to know his bride before marriage; she has a similar desire, and I suppose it is on this account that marriage before the age of twenty-five or twenty-eight is rare.' [71]

There is statistical evidence to show that the median age of first marriage among the elite had risen sharply by the eighteenth century, to about twenty-four for women and twenty-eight to twenty-nine for men (Graph 4). By that age, young people know better what they are about, their identity is more firmly established, their experience of the world is larger, and their judgement more mature. Companionship *plus* economic security were the prime goals of marriage; young people of the English elite were, therefore, more likely to make satisfactory choices of mate in the late eighteenth century than they were in the seventeenth century, when the median age of marriage was only about twenty to twenty-one for women and twenty-five for men.

The other piece of statistical evidence is the prolonged fall throughout the eighteenth century from about forty per cent to about ten per cent in the proportion of all marriages of sons of peers which were made with heiresses (Graph 14). [72] If it is assumed that the principal attraction of an heiress tends to be her wealth rather than her personal qualities, this fall indicates a marked shift in marriage motives among the sons of the peerage from

PROPORTION OF SONS OF PEERS
WHO MARRIED HEIRESSES

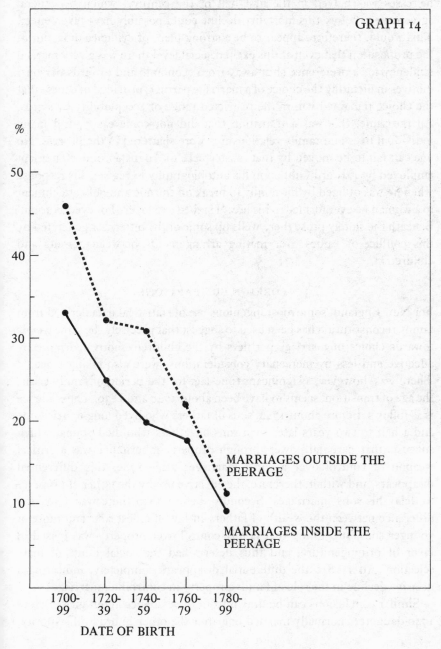

GRAPH 14

%

50

40

30

20

MARRIAGES OUTSIDE THE
PEERAGE

10

MARRIAGES INSIDE THE
PEERAGE

1700-   1720-   1740-   1760-   1780-
99   39   59   79   99

DATE OF BIRTH

interest to affection. The only other possible explanation could be a decline in the male infant and child mortality. But the proportion of marriages with heiresses was halved in the first half of the century, which by general agreement is before this mortality decline could possibly have taken effect. This would, therefore, appear to be a strong piece of evidence in favour of the proposition that even at this exalted social level there was a very marked tendency for a preference shift away from economic and towards personal motives in dictating the choice of a marriage partner, provided of course that the choice remained within the restricted range of acceptability by status. All the same, this was a transition that did not come easily, and many individual lives and family relationships were shattered in the process. No one can fail to be moved by that masterpiece of Augustan understatement employed by Edward Gibbon in his autobiography to register his response when he was obliged by his family to break off the one and only attachment to a woman he ever formed in his life: 'I sighed as a lover; I obeyed as a son.' Beneath the stately prose there wells up some of the bitterness generated by this conflict of values over mating arrangements between parents and children.

3   FOREIGN COMPARISONS

For New England, some most ingenious use of statistical data derived from family reconstitution has been used to suggest that precisely the same trends towards choice of marriage partners by the children, motivated more by affective and less by mercenary considerations, were also taking place. [73] There was, however, a significant time-lag, for the period of family crisis, the age of transition, seems to have been about 1740 and 1830. The evidence is as follows. Before about 1740, sons of fathers who lived long married one and a half to two years later than sons of fathers who died young, which suggests that parental power through property inheritance was a critical weapon of control over a son's marriage; after 1780, this differential disappears, and with it, therefore, the effective use by the father of property to delay his sons' marriages. Secondly, before 1810 there was a striking difference between the wealth of fathers-in-law of eldest sons and those of younger sons, suggesting that family control over property was biased in favor of primogeniture, and thus determined the social limits of mate selection. After 1810 the differential disappears completely, indicating a decisive decline in the role of family property in controlling marriage.

Similar conclusions can be drawn from the evidence about girls. Before 1740 daughters normally married one after the other in order of seniority, which strongly suggests parental control of decision-making in this area; after 1740, the order of marriage is more random, which indicates that many girls were making their own marital choices at times of their own choosing. Finally, before 1740, pre-marital pregnancy was very low, suggesting tight family and community control over courtship practices; after 1740, the proportion of pregnant brides shoots up to over forty per cent, which indicates a collapse of control over courtship. [74] These and other indicators all point in the same direction, towards a slow shift from parent-directed courtship and marriage to participant-directed courtship and marriage. Until the same tests have been made on an English village and town population, using family reconstitution techniques, it is impossible to tell whether or not the same pattern applies to England. But the identical startling rise in pre-nuptial pregnancies in the eighteenth century strongly suggests that the other criteria will probably also be found in England. For the moment, in the present state of knowledge, it is a reasonable hypothesis that the same change was taking place in the distribution of authority within lower middle-class and lower-class families in England in the eighteenth century as were clearly taking place in Hingham, Massachusetts, and that there was the same half-century or more time-lag behind the gentry and professional upper bourgeoisie.

In French peasant society, for example in Normandy in the eighteenth century, change took place much more slowly. Parental power remained formidable well into the nineteenth century, even if it was generally limited to a veto, while, as in England, the lower one descends in the social scale, and the less property that was at stake, the greater the freedom of choice exercised by the children. [75] In courting, initiative lay with the males, and the females could only accept or reject, while the opportunities for meeting were confined to the workplace or village festivities. The courtship process was long and tedious, and might take years to accomplish, dependent on the degree of enthusiasm exhibited by the boy. The pair began by making the short trips together to visit fairs and pilgrimage sites. Next came a purely verbal and unwitnessed offer of marriage by the boy, followed by a formal request for parental consent. If accepted, the boy began visiting the girl at home and at some point gave her a ring in the presence of witnesses. Then came the written contract, the publication of the banns, the religious ceremony and the sexual consummation. The main object of marriage for both parties was not love but co-operation and assistance in economic production and the cementing of a family alliance. The act was therefore often stimulated by the death of the boy's father and his inheritance of a piece of land. Although the initial stages of the courtship process left some initiative to the children, these marriage arrangements followed a fairly traditional pattern. In one commune in the Eure, it was not until the late nineteenth century that there is clear evidence of greater freedom of mate selection based more on affection than economic calculation and parental pressure. [76]

In the aristocracy and upper bourgeoisie, the arranged marriage lasted right through the nineteenth and even into the twentieth century, and the shift that occurred in England in the eighteenth century had little effect in France. In the sixteenth and seventeenth centuries the French state had gone much further than the English in reinforcing parental authority. Between 1566 and 1639 a series of ordinances and declarations made marriage without parental consent under the age of twenty-five for girls or thirty for men a penal offence, punishable by death and the confiscation of goods. It was treated, in fact, as the legal equivalent of rape. The only recourse against wholly unreasonable parents or guardians was an appeal to the royal courts. As a result, in the French aristocracy the most authoritarian form of arranged marriage, in which the bride and groom had not set eyes on each other before the wedding, continued to be common throughout the eighteenth century, and there is evidence that similar practices were also common among the peasantry. Unlike in England, there was no tradition built up in France of allowing the bride and groom the right of veto, much less of allowing them to choose for themselves. Writing in the 1830s about English conditions in the first decade of the eighteenth century, Lady Louisa Stuart remarked that in those far-off days 'for a young lady to interfere or to claim a right of choice was almost thought, as it is in France, a species of indelicacy.' Her conclusion about France in the early nineteenth century finds support in the novels of Balzac, where the arranged marriage figures prominently. Before marriage French girls were extremely strictly supervised, and they often married merely to escape from this constant surveillance. After marriage, however, they enjoyed a degree of sexual and intellectual freedom that far exceeded anything known in England. [77]

On the other hand, it should not be forgotten that Locke had been translated into French, and that Rousseau's works on marriage and child-rearing were widely read. Evidence of the adoption of these new attitudes towards the affective marriage by at least one member of the French bourgeoisie in the late eighteenth century as a result of reading the works of Rousseau, is provided by a letter of 1774 written to a friend from a merchant of La Rochelle, Jean Ranson, who was about to get married at the age of twenty-nine. 'I hope that it will cost me no effort to fulfil the duties . . . which I have imposed on myself. If up to the age of nearly thirty I have been able entirely to manage without a woman, although I am far from looking upon the other sex with an indifferent eye, I am fully persuaded that one will be enough for me for the rest of my life. All that friend Jean-Jacques [Rousseau] has written about the duties of married couples, of fathers and mothers, has much affected me, and I assure you that they will be the rules for my conduct.' Later on, he was delighted that his wife breast-fed their children.[78] Here is another direct illustration of nature imitating art, showing the practical effects of the written word in affecting the most intimate details of the family life of a particular individual.

There is, however, reason to doubt whether Ranson was typical of the French bourgeoisie. There is a lot of evidence to indicate that in France the older patterns of the arranged marriage and the old motives of social and economic advancement rather than companionship continued to predominate among the bourgeoisie far into the nineteenth and even into the twentieth centuries. The time-lag with England is quite astonishing. In 1806 Joseph Droz, in a popular work entitled *Essai sur l'Art d'être heureux*, which ran to seven editions by 1853, described marriage as 'in general a means of increasing one's credit and one's fortune, and of ensuring one's success in the world.' Manuals about child care in the nineteenth century continued to stress the patriarchal principles of obedience to the father as the delegate of God, the need for coldness and formality in parent–child relations, and the absolute necessity for the crushing of the will. Manuals as late as the 1880s urged that from children, as from dogs, obedience must be demanded without restriction. With regard to marriage, parental consent was legally essential according to the Code Napoléon for men up to the age of twenty-five and women up to the age of twenty-one, and up to the age of thirty and twenty-five respectively, permission had to be requested and refused three times before it could be ignored.[79] In Italy the arranged marriage, of the most authoritarian patriarchal type, continued among the nobility right through the eighteenth century, with the concomitant phenomenon of promiscuous adultery by both sexes.[80] In eastern and northern Europe, the most rigid of patriarchal attitudes continued to prevail well into the eighteenth century, if an anonymous English commentator is to be believed. According to him, in popular circles in Russia, 'the man is not permitted to see his mistress before the marriage but employs some of his relatives to view her from head to foot.

The wedding day is said to be the last pleasant day the wife has, being never allowed to stir abroad afterwards: . . . The husband exercises an absolute dominion over his wife, frequently proceeding to blows, which she is said to take very kindly from him, and will be hardly persuaded he loves her, if she does not sometimes feel the weight of his hand. The men have no other notion of adultery than the marrying of another man's wife.... The women are never suffered to advance further than the church-porch, being looked upon as too impure to enter the consecrated place.' Similarly in Sweden: 'the parents, without consulting their children, match them as they think fit, and wealth is chiefly considered in the affair: the poor girls have not so much an opportunity of being courted or admired or the lover the pleasure of communicating his flame.' In Germany, wives, 'are very obsequious to their husbands, have less command in their houses than English or French women, and are not allowed the upper end of the table.' [81]

If these reports are to be trusted, there can be little doubt that England and America were well in advance of continental Europe in the shift of power over marriage from parents to children, in the shift of motives away from economic and towards more affective considerations, and in the development of less authoritarian relations between husbands and wives in marriage. 'The dear English privilege of choosing a husband' was an established fact among the bourgeoisie, squirarchy and lesser nobility by 1770. [82]

CHAPTER 8

The Companionate Marriage

'I only know or fancy that there are qualities and compositions of qualities *(to talk in musical metaphor) which in the course of our lives appear to me in her [Mrs Boswell], that please me more than what I have perceived in any other woman, and which I cannot separate from her identity.'*
(James Boswell in *Boswell: The Ominous Years, 1774–1776*, ed. C.Ryscamp and F.A.Pottle, New York, 1963, p. 290)

I   THE RISE OF THE COMPANIONATE MARRIAGE

i. Theoretical Advice

The many legal, political and educational changes that took place in the late seventeenth and eighteenth centuries were largely consequences of changes in ideas about the nature of marital relations. The increasing stress laid by the early seventeenth-century preachers on the need for companionship in marriage in the long run tended to undercut their own arguments in favour of the maintenance of strict wifely subjection and obedience. Once it was doubted that affection could and would naturally develop after marriage, decision-making power had to be transferred to the future spouses themselves, and more and more of them in the eighteenth century began to put the prospects of emotional satisfaction before the ambition for increased income or status. This in turn also had its effect in equalizing relationships between husband and wife. Thomas Gouge, in the 1634 edition of his popular marriage manual, stated bluntly that a husband may not beat his wife, and Perkins and Baxter agreed with him. It is perhaps significant that in an episode of violent marital discord in the early seventeenth century, Viscount Fenton's wife Marjory was accused of tearing from the Bible a chapter which treated of the duties of women to their husbands.

This shift in moral theology did not affect the theoretical position in common law that a husband may administer 'moderate correction', a doctrine reasserted in court by the Solicitor-General as late as the 1730s. But in practice and by general consent this had fallen into disfavour, and it is hardly surprising that there was a great outcry in 1782, when a pedantic judge tried to revive the ancient doctrine that it was lawful for a husband to beat a wife, provided that the stick were no thicker than his thumb (plate 19).[1]

By the end of the seventeenth century, the lead in giving advice on marriage was being taken over from the clergy by the laity. In the 1690s the Presbyterian editor of the *Athenian Mercury*, John Dunton, sternly advised his readers against maltreating their wives, whatever the provocation. Asked by a reader if he could beat his nagging wife, the *Athenian Mercury* replied: 'Stripes? No sir, by no means.' Although at other times Dunton was more equivocal on the issue, he nonetheless called the legality questionable and the practice inadvisable, a safer remedy being 'the rebuke of a kiss.' The *Athenian Mercury* in general thought that there should be considerable equality in the marriage partnership, made possible by the fact that 'she has art, the man the custom.' In defiance of the law, he denied that after marriage all a wife's goods became the property of her husband, on the grounds that they jointly share the ownership. On the other hand, he admitted that a husband became responsible for his wife's obligations, so that some women 'have only married to have their husbands lie in prison for them' for their debts.[2]

Thirty years later, in 1727, another bourgeois writer, Daniel Defoe, took a similar advanced position about companionate marriage. He complained that still in his own time 'the money and the maidenhead is the subject of our meditations', the result being 'how much marriage, how little friendship.' But he believed that 'matrimony without love is the cart before the horse.' He recognized that this demand for love as the basis of marriage involved a fundamental change in power relations within the family. 'I don't take the state of matrimony to be designed ... that the wife is to be used as an upper servant in the house. ... Love knows no superior or inferior, no imperious command on the one hand, no reluctant subjection on the other.' He made the point that 'persons of a lower station are, generally speaking, much more happy in their marriages than Princes and persons of distinction. So I take much of it, if not all, to consist in the advantage they have to choose and refuse.'[3] Defoe and others saw very clearly how a shift of control of marital choice from parents to children would have significant effects upon marital relations thereafter.

It is significant of changing attitudes that one of the principal themes of George Farquhar's very successful play *The Beaux' Strategem*, first produced in 1707, is that of the miseries of an unhappy marriage, in which the husband neglects his wife and spends all his time tippling with male companions. He makes Mrs Sullen give an inimitable description of her intolerable life, buried deep in the countryside with Squire Sullen, who never even speaks to her. 'He came home this morning at his usual hour of four, wakened me out of a sweet dream of something else by tumbling over the tea table, which he broke all to pieces. After his man and he had rolled about the room, like sick passengers in a storm, he comes flounce into bed, dead as a salmon into a fishmonger's basket, his feet cold as ice, his breath hot as a furnace, and his hands and face as greasy as his flannel night cap. O matrimony!'[4] Deprived of friendship, conversation, companionship, sex and sleep by her sottish husband, her successful formal separation at the end of the play, with the enforced return by Squire Sullen of her marriage portion of £10,000, is clearly regarded as no more than moral justice.

For the English middle and upper classes in the middle of the eighteenth century, Mrs Hester Chapone summed up the prevailing opinion about the ideal relationship between husband and wife: 'I believe that a husband has a divine right to the absolute obedience of his wife in all cases where the first duties do not interfere.' On the other hand, 'I believe it ... absolutely necessary to conjugal happiness that the husband have such an opinion of his wife's understanding, principles and integrity of heart as would induce him to exalt her to the rank of his *first and dearest friend*.' In 1740 Wetenhall Wilkes published *A Letter of Genteel and Moral Advice to a Young Lady*, which ran to eight editions in the next twenty-six years. In it he further developed the view of the married state as an arena of domestic happiness. 'This state, with the affection suitable to it, is the completest image of heaven we can receive in this life; the greatest pleasures we can enjoy on earth are the freedoms of conversation with a bosom friend. ... When two have chosen each other, out of all the species, with a design to be each other's mutual comfort and entertainment, ... all the satisfactions of the one must be doubled because the other partakes in them.' Despite this high-flown and idealistic rhetoric, Wilkes took great care to spell out the limits of what was to be expected. 'The utmost happiness we can hope for in this world is contentment, and if we aim at anything higher, we shall meet with nothing but grief and disappointments.' He advised his readers to seek in a husband such qualities as 'a virtuous disposition, a good understanding, an even temper, an easy fortune, and an agreeable person.' He warned against marriage for money or title, stressed that the key quality was 'the temper', and advised that 'the conversation of a married couple cannot be agreeable for years together without an earnest endeavour to please on both sides.'[5] On the whole, the advice Wilkes offered was prudent and sensible, and except for the fact that he avoids altogether the problem of compatibility of sexual tastes and demands, his book does not differ greatly from a modern marriage manual. Its success was symbolic of the new era in family relationships. In 1762 Dr John Gregory, in an equally popular treatise, wrote that 'I have always considered your sex, not as domestic drudges, or as the slaves of our pleasures, but as our companions and equals.'[6] This was an uncompromising statement of the now conventional ideal of wifely status, the contemporary literary apotheosis of which has to be found in Oliver Goldsmith's *Vicar of Wakefield* of 1766. An early example of this new ideology among the landed elite is the monumental inscription at Yarnton, in Oxfordshire, to Catherine, wife of the Honourable George Mordaunt, who died in 1714. Her husband had inscribed on the slab a statement of his feelings recorded in marble for all time:

> With unavailing tears he mourns her end,
> Losing his double comfort, wife and friend.

By the 1770s there appeared a successful and long-lasting periodical exclusively devoted to women, *The Lady's Magazine*. Its contributors repeatedly harped on the same themes, particularly that sexual passion needed to be buttressed by sentiment to make an enduring marriage. 'If love [i.e., sex] affords some exquisite pleasures, conjugal friendship, which is shunned by so many, will furnish us with more permanent and refined ones.' Conversely, a wife was warned that 'it is not enough that a woman should be a domestic friend.' She should not neglect her appearance and become slovenly after marriage – 'the cause of much misunderstanding between married couples' – but rather should take pains to preserve her sexual attractiveness to her husband.[7]

ii   Foreign Comment

Foreign observers had no doubt that by the second half of the eighteenth century there was a clear trend to companionate marriages, particularly in the upper and the lowest levels of society. Sophie von La Roche, who visited London in 1786, regarded it as a well-known fact that 'so many love-marriages are made in England', and was not at all surprised to learn at the lunatic asylum of Bedlam that most of the young female inmates had been unhinged by thwarted love. This comment about the poor was supported by others about the rich. The Duc de La Rochefoucauld noted with surprise in 1784 that:

Husband and wife are always together and share the same society. It is the rarest thing to meet the one without the other. The very richest people do not keep more than four or six carriage-horses, since they pay all their visits together. It would be more ridiculous to do otherwise in England than it would be to go everywhere with your wife in Paris. They always give the appearance of perfect harmony, and the wife in particular has an air of contentment which always gives me pleasure.

He observed that newly married couples immediately set up house on their own, often in a different town away from their parents, and concluded that 'the Englishman would rather have the love of the woman he loves than the love of his parents.'[8] Von Archenholz, though not impressed by the legal protection afforded to women of property, nevertheless came to the conclusion that 'women rule here perhaps more than anywhere else.'

iii. Modes of Address

More concrete evidence of change is provided by the abandonment in many circles of the formal seventeenth-century modes of address between husband and wife of 'Sir' and 'Madam', and the adoption of first names and terms of endearment. When Dorothy Osborne was writing her love letters to William Temple in the middle of the seventeenth century, she began by addressing him as 'Sir', and then later got around the problem by dropping any opening at all once they were formally engaged. At no time did she address him as 'William'. In 1707, immediately after his marriage, Richard Steele addressed his wife as 'Madam', but soon slid into 'Dear creature', 'My loved creature', 'My dear'. Within a few months, however, he was writing to her as 'Dear Prue'. In 1699 the conservative John Sprint objected to the practice of women calling their husbands by their first names, 'as if they esteemed them at no higher rates than their very servants', since it signified a lack of that deference and respect he was so anxious to preserve. His female opponent defended the practice as no more than 'the effect of tenderness and freedom which will banish all the names of haughty distance and servile subjection.' It is interesting to find the same issue raised two years later by Mary Chudleigh, who makes the parson, expressing the views of the conservatives, advise a wife to

> Call him your lord, and your good breeding show
> And do not rudely too familiar grow;
> Nor like some country matrons call him names
> As John or Geoffrey, William, George or James.[9]

In around 1700 this issue of what to call a husband was clearly a widely debated issue, the conservatives realizing the egalitarian and anti-patriarchal implications of a change to the use of the first name by a wife to a husband.

During this transitional period of the early eighteenth century, the mode of address can be deceptive and may be a poor index of the true relationship between man and wife. In 1732 Catherine Banks ended her letters to her husband Joseph with 'I am, dear Mr Banks, your most affectionate C. Banks.' Two years later, however, when her husband was in Bath for his health, we find him writing to his 'dear Kitty' six days a week, and when in the same year she gave birth to a boy, he declared 'I ... hope we three shall make each others' days happier.' The pursuit of personal happiness through domestic intimacy was clearly uppermost in the mind of her husband, despite the continued use of his wife's part of the old formal mode of address. By the end of the century this formality had gone, and in 1797 Thomas Gisborne noted with satisfaction that 'the stiffness, the proud and artificial reserve, which in former ages infected even the intercourse of private life, are happily discarded.'[10] It was, however, to return later.

iv. Property Rights and Status

The hardest evidence for a decline in the near-absolute authority of the husband over the wife among the propertied classes is an admittedly limited series of changes in the power of the former to control the latter's estate and income. The seventeenth century saw a sharp rise in the size of marriage portions paid by the bride's parents to the groom's parents. This rise meant an increase in the economic stakes in marriage, and so enhanced the position of the wife. By her marriage portion she was now making a major economic contribution to her husband's finances. This was because in the eighteenth century the portion was normally invested in land to be settled on the young couple, whereas in earlier centuries it had gone straight into the pocket of the groom's father. Moreover the introduction of the practice of inserting into the marriage contract a clause about pin money now guaranteed the wife an independent fixed income at her exclusive disposal. The property of widows and heiresses was also now more carefully safeguarded against seizure and exploitation by the future husband. After 1620 the Court of Chancery intervened to enforce marriage contracts, and over the next fifty years, by judicial interpretation and practice, it virtually succeeded in creating the legal doctrine of the wife's separate estate.[11] For the commercial classes this was a welcome development, since it provided some protection against total loss from bankruptcy proceedings.

A good example of the importance of these new legal developments was the situation which arose when Mrs Alice Thornton's husband died in 1668, and appraisers came to value the furniture in the house with a view to its sale for the payment of his many debts. Although most of the furniture was not his but had been left by her mother, the appraisers pointed out to her that 'the property was in him not in the wife, being under covert bar.' They were surprised to learn, however, that her mother had anticipated this situation and had taken the precaution of conveying the personal estate not to Mrs Thornton but to feoffees for her use, in a deed so carefully drawn that it could not be overthrown. Since under this deed the property belonged to the feoffees and not to her, it could not be sold to pay her late husband's debts. All that could be taken was furniture bought by her with money which had come from her mother's estate.[12] This is a classic example of the way women were using the legal device of the conveyance of property to feoffees in trust so as to protect their property rights in marriage. It must be emphasized that these improvements in the legal position of married women only affected those restricted social groups whose marriages were accompanied by a legal settlement, and who could, if necessary, afford the cost of launching a suit in the Court of Chancery. Even so, the financial position of some of the highest women in the country was very precarious. Georgiana Duchess of Devonshire could secretly run up huge debts for which her husband would be responsible, but she owned nothing of her own. When she wrote her will in 1792 she had to ask the Duke's permission to bequeath a few trinkets to personal friends to remember her by, since 'everything I have is yours.'[13]

For the vast majority of the population, including all the poor, the limited safeguards offered to wealthy women were unknown. As Blackstone put it bluntly, 'the husband and wife are one, and the husband is that one.' As late as 1869 John Stuart Mill could accurately describe the legal position of most women in England as one of total dependence on their husbands. In terms of property, they could acquire nothing which did not automatically become their husbands'. 'The absorption of all rights, all property, as well as all freedom of action is complete. The two are called "one person in law", for the purpose of inferring that whatever is hers is his.' Similarly, by law the children belonged solely to the husband, and even after his death the widow had no rights over them, unless she was made their guardian in his will. If she should desert him, however severe the provocation, she could take nothing with her, neither her children nor her property. Her husband could, if he chose, compel her to return. Or he could at any time seize any income she might earn, or any means of support given to her by others. Only a legal separation, the cost of which put it beyond the reach of the majority, gave any protection to the deserting or deserted wife, and even then, before a change in the law in 1839, she had no claim upon her children unless her husband wanted to be rid of them.[14] Moreover, in other ways the wife remained in a legally inferior status. A man convicted of murdering his wife would be hanged, but a woman convicted of murdering her husband would by law be burned alive. This barbarous penalty was in practice disappearing in the eighteenth century, but a woman was burned alive at Tyburn for this crime as late as 1725.[15]

This is why in 1724 Defoe makes Roxana refuse a handsome offer of marriage, on the grounds that 'the very nature of the marriage contract was, in short, nothing but giving up liberty, estate, authority and everything to the man, and the woman was indeed a mere woman ever after, that is to say a slave.' Half a century later a young woman was echoing the same complaint.

The two sexes seem to be very unequally situated in the marriage state. The man only ventures the loss of a few temporary pleasures: the woman, the loss of liberty, and almost the privilege of opinion. From the moment she is married she becomes the subject of an arbitrary lord, who has her person, her friendship, her fortune, her time at his disposal. Even her children, the pledges of their mutual affection, are absolutely under his direction and authority. Severity of every kind is in his power, and the law countenances him in the use of it.[16]

These disabilities only became burdensome when the marriage was on the rocks, and their very existence gave a wife the strongest possible incentive to make her marriage a success, so that these theoretical legal handicaps would have no relevance to her life. In any case, the situation was changing, however slowly, and increasing claims were being made by married women for sharing of power. In 1709 a correspondent appealed to *The Tatler* to arbitrate a dispute between his brother and a woman being courted by him. The lady was demanding as part of the marriage contract that she be given 'an independent jurisdiction over all her female children and servants' for life, leaving her husband full authority only over all male children and servants. This was a stipulation whose novelty shocked the suitor, despite the fact that he was 'passionately in love', and they both agreed to submit the dispute to the decision of Mr Bickerstaff.[17] The mere formulation of such a demand for shared marital authority suggests that new power relationships were in process of developing between husband and wife in upper and upper-middle class circles in the early eighteenth century. Other signs of growing sexual equality are that women were regularly to be seen on the hunting field, and occasionally competed in other sports, such as cricket, rowing and running, to which they are only just being grudgingly readmitted today. There is even evidence that they could occasionally be invited to an official Oxford college Christmas feast, a thing unheard of even in the mid-twentieth century.

One important cause of the rather greater liberalism in husband-wife relations in the late seventeenth and eighteenth centuries was technological and social changes. Better transportation, in particular the spread of the sprung coach and improvements in road surfacing, now made it much easier for middle- and upper-class women to travel long distances with their husbands. Before the development of these new facilities, women who were too infirm to stand long journeys riding sidesaddle on a horse over very rough roads, and who could not afford the rare luxury of a litter, were obliged to stay at home. By the late seventeenth century, however, it was becoming increasingly common for upper-class families to retain a house in the west end of London and to spend part of the year there. By the 1820s 'the season' in London lasted from January to June, climaxing in May and June with an endless succession of routs, balls, and other entertainment for the fashionable of both sexes.[18] Now that the wife accompanied her husband to London, it was inevitable that she should play a decisive role in determining expenditure patterns and life styles.

Although statistical proof is lacking, one gets a distinct impression that wives married to impossible husbands in the upper classes were increasingly seeking formal separations, accompanied by adequate financial provisions which allowed them to continue to live active and satisfying social lives. Formal separations certainly became more common, and in January 1766 the newspaper gossip alleged – as usual with exaggeration – that seventeen couples in the world of fashion were on the point of breaking up.[19] Paradoxically enough, the rise of separations in the eighteenth century, like the rise of divorces in the twentieth, is an indication of rising emotional expectations from marriage. In periods when expectations are low, frustrations will also be low. Nor were separations always taken too seriously by high society when they did occur. In the 1760s Lady Sarah Lennox reported that 'The Duke and Duchess of Grafton are absolutely parted; he allows her £3,000 a year. She has the girl and the youngest boy with her, and they say that the reason of their parting is only that their tempers don't suit.' The extremely generous terms of the separation, with the mother keeping the girl and the youngest child and so handsome an allowance, led Lady Sarah to think 'they would soon be friends again'.[20]

v. The Honeymoon

One revealing indication of the rise of the concept of privacy and the rise of companionate and sexually bonded marriage is the new definition of the old word 'honeymoon'. Previously taken to mean no more than the month after marriage, characterized by goodwill and perhaps sexual passion, it was now re-defined as a period during which the newly married couple were expected to go away together and to be left totally alone in order to explore each other's bodies and minds without outside support or interference. In upper and middle-class society where so much stress was laid on pre-marital virginity, the bridal night in the sixteenth and seventeenth centuries had been surrounded with ritual, much of it public. The pair were brought to the bedroom in state by the relatives and friends, often accompanied with horse-play and ribald jests, and were only left alone (perhaps for the first time in their lives) once the curtains of the four-poster bed were closed and the last wedding guest and maid had withdrawn. Even then the ritual continued, for it was apparently customary on this occasion for the bride to go to bed in gloves. When in 1708 a protesting girl sent a letter to the correspondence column of *The British Apollo*, she was told that 'since it is the custom and the fashion to go into the bridal bed with gloves on, we think it not genteel to go to bed without.' One assumes that the gloves were subsequently removed, to symbolize the loss of virginity. The details of that loss was something about which the pair could often expect to be closely questioned the next morning.[21] The concept of the honeymoon as a period of holiday travel certainly existed by the end of the eighteenth century, but it is far less certain that there was general recognition of the importance of privacy and isolation, which is central to modern ideas about this experience. An early example occurred in the middle of the eighteenth century, when Mr West told Mrs Elizabeth Montagu how William Pitt and his new wife were living privately by themselves at Wickham for a few weeks for 'the free course of those pleasures which for a time at least possess the whole mind, and are most relished when most private.'[22]

In some wealthy and near-wealthy aristocratic circles, however, marriage and its aftermath in the eighteenth century were as much a public affair as they had ever been. In 1756 John Spencer, the wealthy heir to the Spencer barony, married Margaret Georgiana Poyntz, and the groom's mother insisted on the most extravagant display. After the wedding, the party set out from Althorp for London in three six-horse coaches accompanied by two hundred horsemen. So alarming was the cavalcade that villagers on the road assumed that it was a French invasion, and either turned out with pitchforks to fight the enemy, or barricaded themselves in their houses. It is significant, however, that all this publicity was 'quite disagreeable to both the young people.'[23]

When in 1770 Jacob Houblon, the heir of the Houblons of Hallingbury Place, married Susanna, heiress of the Archers of Welford, the whole affair was arranged in such a way that the newly married couple were hardly ever left alone. The two weeks of the honeymoon were spent at Welford by the assembled wedding party of parents, bridesmaids, brothers and sisters on both sides, together with some family clergymen as hangers-on, in an endless round of sightseeing trips and elaborate dinners and suppers. The trips were always in a crowd, and on the other days the groom went off with the men to shoot, to course hares or to play billiards, while the bride stayed gossiping in the drawing-room with the ladies. The pre-marital habits of single-sex bonding and association thus continued as before, and the newly married pair had apparently no privacy at all for the first two weeks of marriage except at night in their bedroom, to which they only retired very late after cards, dancing and singing until midnight or after. In the first decade of the nineteenth century, wealthy merchants were still imitating this now dying aristocratic style. Among the rich Liverpool merchants of that time, it was the custom for the newly married pair to set off on a tour of England, accompanied by two bridesmaids and two grooms. They travelled in two carriages; the married couple and one bridesmaid in one, the two grooms and one bridesmaid in the other. Every day was spent in sightseeing and every evening in large and lengthy dinner parties and supper parties. On return home, there followed the custom of the 'bride's visits' during which for three days the husband entertained the male callers in the dining-room, and the wife the female callers in the drawing-room. Only after all these formalities were completed were the thoroughly exhausted pair at last left in peace.[24]

All this was a far cry from the very private wedding of Mary Thackeray to

Mr Pryme of Cambridge in 1813, followed by a lengthy, solitary honeymoon in hotels in London, Brighton and Worthing. But even then this isolation was unusual, and a chaperone was common. When Elizabeth Robinson married Edward Montagu in 1742, they were accompanied on their honeymoon tour by her sister Sarah, and late eighteenth-century novelists confirm the persistence of this pattern in wealthy circles. In Charlotte Smith's *Celestina*, published in 1791, Mr and Mrs Molyneux make a marriage of fashion and convenience, and leave for their honeymoon accompanied by a close friend of each. They settle into a rented house, which is constantly 'filled with company', while the bride is 'fully occupied with parties all the morning and play in the evening.' After a few weeks, the whole party sets off for a tour of the western bathing places. Wherever they go the public whirl continues, with 'the constant succession of company in which Mr and Mrs Molyneux lived'. Similarly, though on a less massive scale, Jane Austen in *Mansfield Park* makes Mr and Mrs Rushworth go to Brighton for some weeks after their marriage, the latter being accompanied by her sister Julia, 'each of them exceedingly glad to be with the other at such a time.' The need for supportive female assistance in this time of psychological and physiological crisis shows how strong was the social attraction of each sex for its own company, even in those days of the companionate marriage. It was not until 1846 that an upper-class marriage manual commented, as a relative novelty, that 'the young couple take their journey, as is now the fashion, in a tête-à-tête.'[25]

The concept of the honeymoon thus passed through three stages, as the companionate marriage slowly evolved. First, it was no more than a description of the first weeks after marriage, which consisted of a non-stop, sex-segregated public party with the wedding guests, taking place in the home. Next, it became a time of travel, but in the company of others, either a group or the sister of the bride. Finally, in the late eighteenth and very early nineteenth centuries, it became a time of withdrawal and isolation away from home for private mutual exploration.

2   EARLY FEMINIST MOVEMENTS

The companionate marriage demanded a reassessment of power relations between the sexes since it depended on a greater sense of equality and sharing. Consequently, the early feminist movements have a place in this story, even if one concludes in the end that they were largely abortive and without much influence in changing public attitudes. These movements bore no relation to the traditional prominence of women in food riots, which was normal right through the Early Modern period and into the nineteenth cenury. 'All public disturbances generally commence with the clamour of women' generalized the *Leicester Journal* in 1800.[26] This was particularly because, as shoppers, women were the first to feel the effects of rising prices, and partly because their husbands encouraged them to take the lead, on the correct assumption that the forces of order would handle women more gently and cautiously than they would men. But the ideological agitation of women on a national political issue or that of sexual equality was something quite different from this recurrent phenomenon of economic protest.

i. Anne Hutchinson in Massachusetts

Both the role-model for the self-reliant woman and the religious theory to break the bonds of patriarchy were first supplied by the indomitable Anne Hutchinson in Massachusetts in 1636–37. If the individual conscience were the only test for law and obedience and if Grace were conferred equally by God on members of either sex, this idea, if carried to its logical extreme, could wreck the deferential social system of the seventeenth century, not only in Church and state, but also in the family. John Winthrop lamented that thanks to Anne Hutchinson 'All things are turned upside down among us.' As in most mystical revivalist movements since the beginning of time, the most numerous and enthusiastic supporters of Anne Hutchinson were women. They publicly complained that 'men usurp over their wives and keep them in servile subjection', while their enemies argued that by luring away women from the family church, the movement was causing 'division between husband and wife'. What particularly disturbed the lay and clerical male authorities was the overthrow of the conventional relationship between the sexes, demanding an equality between men and 'silly women laden with their lusts'. Anne was told by Hugh Peter that 'you have rather been a husband than a wife, and a preacher than a hearer, and a magistrate than a subject'. The result was that Anne was driven into exile, her followers were excommunicated and punished, and the movement collapsed. Church, state, and male domination in the family were successfully restored in Massachusetts.[27]

ii. Women in the English Civil War

A few years later, exactly the same cycle of events repeated themselves in England during the Civil War of the 1640s. Women played a very prominent role in the host of radical sects which based themselves on the extreme interpretation of the doctrine of Grace. In these independent churches, women were at last allowed to debate, to vote, to prophesy when moved by the Spirit, and even to preach. Many left the former family church without the consent of their husbands, and some even abandoned their unregenerate spouses and chose new mates who shared their new-found faith. As in New England, their opponents saw these developments as a threat to family subordination, claiming that they were demanding sexual equality of rights:

> We will not be wives
> And tie up our lives
> To villanous slavery.[28]

This was a far cry from the position of their fellow radical, John Milton. But in fact, if one looks closely, one finds that the majority of women in the sects were only asking for liberty of conscience and religion, not freedom from male control or civil authority. Just as they were willing, up to a point, to obey the 'ungodly magistrate', so they were willing, up to a point, to obey their ungodly husbands. As in New England, therefore, this outbreak of feminism encouraged by antinomian sectarianism had only a limited effect on the emancipation of women.

What is remarkable, however, is the way the breakdown of royal government in 1640, the prolonged political crisis between King and parliament of 1640–42, the Civil Wars of 1642–48, and the emergence of many extremist independent sects and of a genuinely radical political party, stimulated the women of London and elsewhere to unprecedented political activity. On 31 January and 1 and 4 February 1642, women, operating without help from fathers, husbands or other males, took independent political action on the national level as women, for the first time in English history: they petitioned the Houses of Lords and Commons for a change of public policy. They numbered some four hundred or more, and were apparently composed of working women, artisans, shop-girls and labourers, who were suffering severe financial hardship as a result of the decay of trade. When the outraged Duke of Richmond cried 'Away with these women, we were best have a Parliament of women', the petitioners attacked him physically and broke his staff of office.[29]

In August 1643 the women were back again, this time in their thousands, mobbing Parliament and demanding peace in order to stimulate the economy and give them employment. They were clearly egged on by male members of the peace party, such as the Earl of Holland, but once again they were acting alone. Since the guards were naturally reluctant to shoot women or cut them down with their swords, the latter soon realized their advantage by virtue of their sex, and held the members of the House of Commons prisoners for several hours. They massed in their thousands and became so truculent and obstreperous that in the end they had to be dispersed by a show of force by the guards and the shedding of a certain amount of female blood.[30]

The next crisis came in April and May 1649 when very severe economic hardship coincided with a political showdown between the army and Parliament and the London-based lower-middle-class radical movement of the Levellers. Once again masses of women assembled at Westminster, complaining of the economic crisis and demanding the release of the Leveller leaders who had been imprisoned. This time the House responded with disdain, telling the women that they were petitioning about matters above their heads, that Parliament had given an answer to their husbands, who legally represented them, and that they should 'go home and look after your own business and meddle with your housewifery.'[31]

By now, however, the women were not satisfied with these patronizing replies and were making statements which revealed the development of a wholly new level of feminine consciousness. 'The lusty lasses of the Levelling party' were now claiming equal participation with men in the political process, and were backing up their claims with petitions signed, so they said, by up to ten thousand women. In 1642 the petitioners had humbly emphasized that women were not 'seeking to equal ourselves with men, either in authority or wisdom', but were merely 'following the example of the men which have gone ... before us'; moreover, they frankly admitted that their intervention 'may be thought strange and unbeseeming our sex.' By 1649, however, they were rejecting the idea that they were represented by their husbands: 'we are no whit satisfied with the answer you gave unto our husbands.' They coolly faced a barrage of criticism that they were claiming to 'wear the breeches', and that 'it can never be a good world when women meddle in state's matters ... their husbands are to blame, that they have no fitter employment for them.' In reply the women quoted the example of Esther from the Bible and even rewrote history to argue that 'by the British women the land was delivered from the tyranny of the Danes ... and the overthrow of episcopal tyranny in Scotland was first begun by the women of that nation.' They claimed an equal share with men in the right ordering of the Church 'because in the free enjoying of Christ in his own laws, and a flourishing estate in the Church ... consisteth the happiness of women as well as men.' This principle they then extended to the state: 'we have an equal share and interest with men in the Commonwealth', a claim which logically led to a demand for female voting rights.[32] But 1649 was the apogee of this movement towards women's political liberation, and it is very noticeable that even the Leveller leaders always excluded women from their proposals for a greatly enlarged suffrage.

According to Lord Clarendon – not the most unprejudiced of witnesses – the result of all this egalitarian activity in the 1640s and 1650s was temporarily to overthrow the principle of subordination and deference in the family. 'All relations were confounded by the several sects in religion, which discountenanced all forms of reverence and respect, as relics and marks of superstition. Children ask not the blessing of their parents. . . . The young women conversed without circumspection or modesty. . . . Parents had no manner of authority over their children, nor children any obedience or submission to their parents.'[33] At the Restoration, the normal authority patterns were more or less restored. This feminine agitation at a time of temporary breakdown of law and order should, therefore, best be seen as a symptom rather than as a cause. The episode is significant as the first emergence on a mass level of feminist ideas among an artisan urban population, but it was a movement without a future. It certainly indicates that even at this lower social stratum, serious challenges were already developing to the traditional authority of husbands in the patriarchal family. Moreover, the sectarian demand for the separation of religion from state control accelerated the process by which the divine sanctions for the social hierarchy were undermined. Once they were gone, the way was open, first for a contract theory of the state, and then, by logical analogy, for a contract theory of the family.[34]

iii. Late Seventeenth-century Feminists

New claims concerning the status and rights of women were set in motion by the repudiation of monarchical patriarchy in the state in 1688, and were publicized by a handful of zealous feminists at the end of the seventeenth century. Most notable among them were Hannah Woolley, Aphra Behn, Mary Astell and Lady Chudleigh.

Few were as savage as the last, in her poem of 1703 addressed 'To the Ladies':

> Wife and servant are the same,
> But only differ in the name
> . . . .

When she the word 'obey' has said,
And man by law supreme has made,

. . . .

Fierce as an Eastern Prince he grows
And all his innate rigor shows.
Then but to look, to laugh, or speak
Will the nuptial contract break.
Like mutes she signs alone must make,
And never any freedom take,
But still be governed by a nod
And fear her husband as her God.

. . . .

Then shun, oh shun that wretched state
And all the fawning flatterers hate.
Value yourselves and men despise:
You must be proud if you'll be wise.[35]

In 1699 a last-ditch conservative, the Reverend John Sprint, published a wedding sermon that trotted out the most extreme of all the old dogmas about the subordination of women. He dragged in the ancient accusation that man was undone by the first woman, Eve, and went on to assert that the prime duty of a wife is to please her husband in all things and that in any case 'Subjection and obedience to their husbands is required from wives, as resolutely and pre-emptorily as unto Christ himself.' But he was quickly crushed by a woman pamphleteer, who retorted that 'he goes a little too far, when he makes it a woman's duty to lie like a spaniel at her husband's feet and suffer herself very civilly to be trampled on.' As he admitted, Sprint was not altogether in tune with the times.[36]

iv. Late Eighteenth-century Feminists

The rise of the blue-stockings a century later as leaders of salons which included the most distinguished intellects and wits of London is proof of how at any rate some women were now forcing themselves upon male society and holding their own there. Perhaps an even more striking example of the rise of female independence in the late eighteenth century was the founding in 1770 of the wholly unintellectual Female Coterie, an exclusively women's club to which men were invited only as guests. Since, so far as is known, this is the first purely female club, it was naturally subjected to ridicule, as indeed was the Blue-Stocking Club many years later in 1815.[37]

At the same time, inspired first by the American and then by the French

Revolution, there emerged a new wave of feminists far more radical in their demands, their personal behaviour and their religious attitudes than their predecessors had been a century earlier. The most prominent among them was Mary Wollstonecraft, who probably did the cause of women's rights positive harm, for her passionate claim to sexual equality, together with her sympathy for the French Revolution and her irregular personal life, merely alienated the support of all but the most tolerant of men. It was this combination of radicalism in both national and sexual politics that drove Horace Walpole to describe her as 'that hyena in petticoats'. It would be hard at any period for a man to sympathize with the ideas expressed by her fellow radical Mrs Barbauld in her doggerel poem on *The Rights of Women*, published in 1771.

> Yes, injured women, rise, assert thy right;
> Women, too long degraded, scorned, oppressed.
> . . . .
>
> Go, bid proud man his boasted rule resign
> And kiss the golden sceptre of thy reign,
> . . . .
> Make treacherous man thy subject not thy friend;
> Thou may'st command, but never can be free.

Lady Louisa Stuart was right to contrast the Christian, virtuous, loyal and essentially deferential life-style and beliefs of Mary Astell in the late seventeenth century with those of Mary Wollstonecraft, who was 'the reverse of all these things.'[38]

This latest movement was therefore soon overwhelmed in the wave of reaction to the French Revolution, and even a periodical like *The Lady's Monthly Museum*, which was dedicated to the improvement of women's rights and education, was severe in its criticism of these feminists. It denounced an anonymous *Appeal to the Men of Great Britain on Behalf of Women* of 1797 for demanding 'unqualified equality' with men. 'An opinion thus preposterous and inimical to the monarchial constitution of matrimony is one of the last qualities, almost, any man would wish to find in his wife', it pointed out in a very practical vein. It joined in a general attack on 'a Wollstonecraft, who squared her principles to her conduct' and declared that 'the champions of female equality . . . are no longer regarded as sincere and politic friends, but as base and insidious enemies.'[39] The radical feminist movement of the late eighteenth century thus died a swift and natural death, not to be revived again until the twentieth century.

It is hard to see that any of these three feminist movements of the seventeenth and late eighteenth centuries had much effect in changing attitudes towards relations between the sexes. The causes of those changes must be sought elsewhere, and the fears engendered in men by these indignant women probably inhibited change rather than speeded it up.

3. THE EDUCATION OF WOMEN

i. Educational Reform

a. Theory. In view of the greater degree of companionship in marriage that was developing in the eighteenth century, it is not surprising that considerable, and in the long run successful, efforts were made to improve the quality and quantity of female education among the upper classes.

The first fierce attack against the consciously inferior curriculum that was offered to women in the seventeenth century was published anonymously in 1640, just as the English Revolution was beginning and as ideas that were not to come to fruition for centuries were beginning to ferment. The anonymous authors rightly saw the inferiority of gentlewomen's education as a key element in their inferiority to men in terms of power and status, but the savagery of their indignation was not at all typical of the women of their age. They were largely speaking to the deaf. Their arguments, however, have an historical interest, if only because they were the first to protest so vigorously.

It hath been the policy of all parents, even from the beginning, to curb us of that benefit by striving to keep us under, and to make us men's mere vassals, even unto all posterity. How else comes it to pass that when a father hath a numerous issue of sons and daughters, the sons, forsooth, they must be first put to the Grammar School, and after perchance sent to the University, and trained up in the liberal arts and sciences, and there (if they prove not blockheads) they may in time be booklearned. . . . [But we daughters] are set only to the needle to prick our fingers; or else to the wheel to spin a fair thread for our own undoings, or perchance to some dirty and debased drudgery. If we be taught to read, they then confine us within the compass of the mother tongue, and that limit we are not suffered to pass; or if (which sometimes happeneth) we be brought up to music, to singing and to dancing, it is not for any benefit that thereby we can engross unto ourselves, but for their own particular ends, the better to please and content their licentious appetites when we come to our maturity and ripeness. . . . If we be weak by nature, they strive to make us more weak by our nurture. And if in degree of place low, they strive by their policy to keep us more under. . . .[40]

The arguments of the conservatives, who wished to keep women in a state of ignorance, were brilliantly, if satirically, summarized by Swift in the 1720s, in his essay *Of the Education of Ladies*. It is argued.

That the great end of marriage is propagation: that consequently, the principal business of a wife is to breed children, and to take care of them in their infancy, that the wife is to look on her family, watch over the servants, see that they do their work; that she be absent from her house as little as possible; that she is answerable for everything amiss in her family; that she is to obey all the lawful commands of her husband, and visit or be visited by no persons whom he disapproves; that her whole business, if well performed, will take up most hours of the day. . . .; that a humour of reading books, except those of devotion or house-wifery, is apt to turn a woman's brain; that plays, romances, novels, and love-poems, are only proper to instruct them how to carry on an intrigue; that all affection of knowledge, beyond what is merely domestic, renders them vain, conceited and pretending; that the natural levity of woman wants ballast; and when she once begins to think she knows more than others of her sex, she will begin to despise her husband, and grow fond of every coxcomb who pretends to any knowledge in books; that she will learn scholastic words, make herself ridiculous by pronouncing them wrong, and applying them absurdly in all companies; that in the meantime, her household affairs, and the care of her children, will be wholly laid aside, her toilet will be crowded with all the under-wits, where the conversation will pass in criticising the last play or poem that comes out, and she will be careful to remember all the remarks that were made, in order to retail them in the next visit, especially in company who know nothing of the matter; that she will have all the impertinence of a pedant without the knowledge, and for every new acquirement will become so much the worse.[41]

The main lines of the debate, which lasted from the late seventeenth century to the early nineteenth, were thus clearly defined on both sides at an early stage.

When serious pressure for a better education for women began in about 1675, it was led by a group of middle-class women, with a little male help from John Locke, William Law and Jonathan Swift addressing the gentry and from John Dunton and Daniel Defoe addressing the bourgeoisie. Mrs Woolley, who had herself been the mistress of a school, a governess, and the wife of a free-school usher, expressed her feelings on this subject in a bitter pamphlet in 1675: 'Vain man is apt to think we were merely intended for the world's propagation, and to keep its human inhabitants sweet and clean, but, by their leaves, had we the same literature, he would find our brains as fruitful as our bodies. . . . Most in this depraved age think a woman learned enough if she can distinguish her husband's bed from another's.' Bathsua

Makin reminded her readers that women had formerly been educated in the knowledge of the arts and tongues, and protested that now 'the barbarous custom to breed women low is grown general among us.' In 1710 Lady Mary Wortley Montagu, who had taught herself the classics in secret, protested bitterly to Bishop Burnet about the deplorably low education afforded to gentlewomen, 'whose birth and leisure only serve to render them the most useless and most worthless part of creation.'[42]

In 1706 Mary Astell put forward the argument that men were destroying the possibility of marital companionship by depriving girls of a good education. 'How can a man respect his wife when he has a contemptible opinion of her and her sex ... so that folly and a woman are equivalent terms with him?'

These women were no wild-eyed political or moral radicals, but devout Christians of impeccable virtue, and loyal subscribers to the standard doctrines about the naturally subordinate role of wives. All they wanted to see was their sex better prepared to be companions with their husbands. Mrs Makin told her female readers in no uncertain terms that their purpose in life was 'to answer the end of your creation, to be meet helps to your husbands.' Mrs Astell also emphasized, apparently in all seriousness, that 'she ... who marries ought to lay it down for an indisputable maxim that her husband must govern absolutely and entirely, and that she has nothing else to do but to please and obey.[43]

One of the few late seventeenth-century male advocates of a more academic education for women was John Locke, who geared his plan not to companionate marriage but to improving the capacity of women to educate their children for the first eight or ten years. He therefore wanted them to be able to 'read English perfectly, to understand ordinary Latin and arithmetic, with some general knowledge of chronology and history.' But in upper-class households, the education was often left to governesses and tutors, and even. Locke was forced to admit that there was 'an apprehension that should daughters be perceived to understand any learned language or be conversant in books, they might be in danger of not finding husbands, so few men, as do, relishing these accomplishments in a lady.' Locke's motive, of training the wife to be a good mother, was also that of the equally popular moral theologian William Law, writing in 1729.[44]

Naturally enough, most men who publically advocated a better education for women preferred Mrs Astell's argument that it would be to the benefit of husbands. 'I would have men take women for companions, and educate them to be fit for it', said Defoe. He foresaw a millennium of domestic bliss that would result from improved female education. 'A woman well bred and taught, furnished with the additional accomplishments of knowledge and behaviour, is a creature without comparison. . . . She is all softness and sweetness, peace, love, wit and delight. She is in every way suitable to the sublimest wish, and the man that had such a one to his portion has nothing to do but to rejoice in her and be thankful.'[45] Another male sympathizer was Swift, who in *Gulliver's Travels* and elsewhere supported more or less equal education for both sexes, while even a conventional writer like Wetenhall Wilkes urged a more scholarly curriculum for women. In his popular handbook of advice to young ladies, first published in 1740, he told them 'to cultivate and adorn your understanding with the improvements of learning (suitable to your sex).' He wanted them to read moral, religious and historical books, *The Spectator* and *The Guardian*, and to learn to speak and write fluently. He was not opposed to their learning French or Italian or even Latin (although he was not enthusiastic and his main emphasis was on English). He even included natural philosophy, such as the works of Robert Boyle, as well as 'a genteel, speculative knowledge of geography, cosmography and chronology.' On the other hand, 'novels, plays and romances must be read sparingly and with caution', to avoid contracting 'light over-gay notions' such as believing that the passion of love was an adequate basis for a marriage. All in all, this widely read work advised a more intellectual curriculum for girls than anything which had been offered since the first half of the sixteenth century. The purpose of such an education was to fit girls to make companionate wives, for as things stood Swift computed that 'half the number of well-educated nobility and gentry must either continue in a single life or be forced to couple themselves with women for whom they have no esteem.' Steele in *The Tatler* took the same position and broadened the vocational objectives, demanding an education that would 'advance the value of their innocence as virgins, improve their understanding as wives, and regulate their tenderness as parents.'[46]

b. Practice. It is very doubtful whether this barrage of propaganda had much effect on improving female education before the middle of the eighteenth century, even though it was based on the self-interest of husbands. Male education had been shifting from the intensely scholarly classical education of the late sixteenth century to the shallower and more aesthetic training in the seventeenth century of the 'virtuoso', a dabbler in many arts and sciences. Similarly, the standard female education among the aristocratic elite had also become more purely ornamental. In the 1670s

Anne Barrett-Lennard, who came from a very wealthy noble family, was regarded as very well bred. She had been taught singing by the famous Signor Morelli, and she could speak and read French and Italian. Her cousi Roger North considered her a highly educated woman, even though she apparently knew nothing of the classics, history, mathematics or the sciences. What he admired was her 'exceeding obliging temper' and 'a more than ordinary wit and fluency of discourse.'[47]

Mrs Cappe was born in 1746, the daughter of a parson from a gentry family with a private income, who had married the daughter of a younger son of an enormously wealthy family of baronets, the Winns of Nostell Priory. Her father was very opposed to female education and paid no attention to her. He spent a lot of time trying to teach her blockhead of a brother, 'but I do not recollect that he ever taught me a single lesson.' As for her mother, for all her influential family connections, she was almost illiterate, being self-taught and barely capable of reading the Bible and writing a simple letter. In 1754 the future Mrs Cappe was sent to York 'for the purpose of attending the dancing school and of learning the sort of ornamental needlework then in fashion.' Similarly in the 1730s, the second Duchess of Argyll was very ignorant, and the Duke forbade his daughters to learn French since 'one language was enough for a woman to talk in.' As a result the only education they got was in handwriting and accounts from the steward, and needlework from the governess. As for Mrs Powys, the daughter of a rich surgeon born in 1739, she was a skilled needlewoman, and she 'embroidered, worked in cloth, straw-plaited, feather-worked, made pillow-lace, paper mosaic work, etc., dried flowers and ferns, painted on paper and silk, collected shells, fossils, coins, and was a connoisseur of china, etc.' She had been taught to occupy her time in decorative but essentially frivolous ways, although she was also an excellent housekeeper and concocter of herbal remedies.[48]

Boarding-schools for girls had been fairly common in the seventeenth century, specializing in training in the social graces which it was thought would enable women both to attract husbands and to occupy their leisure hours once they were married. At a school run by a Mr Playford at Islington, 'the young gentlewomen may be instructed in all manner of curious work, as also reading, writing, music, dancing and the French language.' The 'curious work', which tended to bulk so large in the curriculum in the late seventeenth and early eighteenth centuries, consisted of embroidery and needlework, paper-cutting, wax-work, japanning, painting on glass, patchwork, shell-work, mosswork, feather-work, and similar time-consuming trivia, while the arts of housekeeping and polite conversation also figured prominently. It was a busy education, but not an intellectual one, being rather concerned with 'everything that was genteel and fashionable', and designed to provide time-consuming occupations for women of infinite leisure.[49]

Like the private schools and academies for boys, which were growing rapidly in number throughout the eighteenth century, boarding-schools for girls also increased, so much so that it was alleged that in 1759 around London '2 or 3 houses might be seen in almost every village with the inscription "Young Ladies Boarded and Educated"' written in gold letters on a blue signboard.[50] But the education these little schools provided in the early eighteenth century was no more intellectual than that of the seventeenth century. It was still primarily concerned with instruction in the social graces and such ladylike pastimes as embroidery and needlework.

Writing in the 1820s, Lady Louisa Stuart thought that in the first decades of the eighteenth century, 'the education of women had then reached its lowest ebb, and if not coquettes or gossips or diligent card-players, their best praise was to be diligent housewives.' The old school of seventeenth-century gentlewomen had been brought up to believe that they should occupy all their leisure time with needlework. The new generation of the early eighteenth century were still taught, some of these skills, but tended to abandon them once they were out of school. They were as ignorant as their grandmothers, but now devoted themselves to parties, visits, cards, and the theatre – pursuits that characterized a far more leisure-oriented and pleasure-loving society. In 1714 an angry old woman wrote bitterly about the life-style of her young nieces. 'Those hours which in this age are thrown away in dress, plays, visits and the like, were employed in my time in writing out recipes or working beds, chairs and hangings for the family. For my part I have plied my needle these fifty years, and by my good will would never have it out of my hand. It grieves my heart to see a couple of proud idle flirts sipping their tea for a whole afternoon in a room hung around with the industry of their great-grandmother.'[51] She was deploring the decline of the Puritan ethic of useful work among gentlewomen in the early eighteenth century, but had no vision of how their endless leisure hours could be put to more rewarding use.

ii. Middle-class Demand

One reason for the persistence of deportment in the boarding-school curriculum was that some of these establishments were now filling up with the daughters of the prosperous London bourgeoisie and professional men, and what these parents were seeking in return for their money was precisely training in the manners, graces and skills of a lady. By 1775 it was alleged that some of these schools now catered for the daughter of 'the blacksmith, the ale-house keeper, the shoemaker etc, who from the moment she enters these walls becomes a young lady.' Satires like D'Urfey's *Love for Money, or the Boarding School* of 1691 were quite incapable of stopping the trend, and indeed Defoe's plans in some ways tended in precisely this direction.[52]

In eighteenth-century fiction, the archetypal representative of the over-educated lower middle-class girl is Richardson's *Pamela*. Although only a poor farmer's daughter, her mother had taught her reading, writing, singing, dancing the minuet and other fashionable steps, flower arrangement, drawing, and needlework. She was thus fully equipped to be the wife of a man of quality, but hopelessly unfitted for her probable future of household drudgery among her 'milkmaid companions'. She was not trained to work. But Pamela was untypical in being both the daughter of a poor farmer and brought up at home.[53] On the other hand, there can be little doubt that the daughters of wealthy yeomen, farmers, and more especially of London tradesmen, did indeed help to fill the proliferating boarding-schools of the eighteenth century (plate 24).

As always when a class improves its position economically and socially, their wives hastened, with the encouragement of their husbands, to join the ranks of the consumers of products of a rapidly expanding leisure industry. They now occupied their time with drawing, dancing, 'fancy work', novel reading, visits to Vauxhall Gardens or the theatre, walks in the park, card parties, and excursions to some fashionable watering place.[54]

The way the rise of affluence led to the withdrawal of a middle-class wife from active engagement in the day-to-day physical and administrative tasks of the household to a life of elegant but idle gentility can be traced in minute detail in the diary of Samuel Pepys in the 1660s. When he was first married in 1655, they were very poor and could not afford a servant. His wife Elizabeth washed his clothes and did all the chores. As his wealth increased, so the domestic household grew to include a kitchenmaid, a parlourmaid and a boy, and Elizabeth, who was childless, was left with nothing to do all day. She then demanded a living-in companion of her own social class with whom she could gossip, play cards and music, sing, set hair, trim petticoats, and go visiting. But this created marital discord, first because Samuel was very unwilling to incur the expenses, and then, when he finally gave way, because Elizabeth was torn between pleasure from her companion's company and fear lest she should steal her husband's affections. She took up dancing with a dancing-master, which aroused Samuel to paroxysms of jealousy that he was being cuckolded. All in all, Elizabeth may have been happier in her earlier condition of busy housewifely poverty than in her new condition of idle genteel affluence.[55]

This transformation of the domestic life of the wife of a rising bureaucrat in the 1660s must have been a commonplace among the wealthy London tradesmen in the early eighteenth century. Mrs Pepys was exceptional in being childless, but even fertile women of the quality and the bourgeoisie now found themselves with time on their hands. The result was the creation of a whole new leisure industry. It provided employment for dancing masters, music teachers, and teachers of French; it supplied provincial towns with theatres, music-rooms, assembly-rooms, tea-rooms, and coffee-houses with the latest London newspapers. It generated the demand for the romantic novel, many of whose rapidly growing numbers were now written by women as well as for women. It created a whole new occupation for the unmarried woman as a well-bred, well-educated companion to the lady of leisure, who could share her pleasures and help her to avoid the pangs of loneliness and to while away the time while the lower servants did all the domestic work and looked after the children, and while her husband was pursuing his own business and amusements.[56] This evolution of the London middle-class wife into a status ornament waited on hand and foot by servants achieved its purpose of cutting her off completely from the class of women who had to work for their living. The gulf so deliberately created was unbridgeable. In 1864 a Victorian maid-of-all-work, Hannah, wrote a revealing comment in her journal about this cultural divide that had been so carefully built up over the previous century and a half: 'I often thought of myself and them, all they ladies sitting upstairs and talking and sewing and playing games and pleasing themselves, all so smart and delicate to what I am – though not real ladies, the missus told me – and then me by myself in that kitchen drudging all day in my dirt, and ready to do anything for them whenever they ring for me – it seems like being a different kind of creature to them, but it's always so with ladies and servants.'[57]

Criticism of the change of the bourgeois wife from a busy help-mate to an idle ornament developed both from the elite, jealous of their monopoly of cultivated leisure activities, and from the lower middle class itself. In 1724 Bernard de Mandeville staged a debate between two lower middle-class women. One argued that 'in England women are treated very respectfully as well as tenderly', while the other angrily rejected their relegation to mere functionless status objects. "Tis that respect and tenderness I hate, when it consists of only outward show. In Holland women act in their counting houses and do business, or at least are acquainted with everything their husbands do. But, says a rascal here, "No, my dear, that is too much trouble" ... with this he sends her to the playhouse.' Seventy years later, Mary Wollstonecraft was even more convinced of the evils of the downward spread of genteel education. 'In the superior ranks of life, every duty is done by the deputies. ... Women in particular all want to be ladies, which is simply to have nothing to do, but listlessly to go they scarcely care where, for they cannot tell what.'[58] In the 1770s *The Lady's Magazine* was viciously satirical about the education of grocers' wives as genteel layabouts. The next major periodical for women, *The Lady's Monthly Museum*, took exactly the same line in 1798. 'When I see a girl destined to weigh candles behind a counter or make butter in a dairy, learning to jabber a language she cannot comprehend and thrumming an instrument she has no ear to enjoy, I consider it [a] manifest infringement upon the rights of gentlemen.' Here, as well as in some bitter caricatures of the first decade of the nineteenth century, there emerges in the open naked class resentment at the invasion of genteel education by those of lower social status.[59] This created a blurring of that critical division between 'the quality' and those below them upon which eighteenth-century society laid so much stress. The former could no longer be immediately recognized by their distinctive cultural attributes, and the only benefit – if benefit it was – that the elite gained by the change was that the males could now pick up lower-class mistresses possessing some of their own social graces.

Similar criticism came from the lower middle class itself. In 1728 Defoe was lamenting the passing of the era when tradesmen's widows would carry on the shop or trade. Now, he said, they would not 'stoop to the mechanic low step of carrying on a trade.' 'The tradesman,' he explained, 'is foolishly vain of making his wife a gentlewoman, forsooth; he will ever have her sit above in the parlour, and receive visits, and drink tea, and entertain her neighbours, or take a coach and go abroad; but as to the business, she shall not stoop to touch it; he has apprentices and journeymen and there is no need of it.'[60] A century later, in 1829, that most practical of radical reformers, William Cobbett, firmly declared that 'as regards to young women, everlasting book-reading is absolutely a vice. ... They neglect all other matters. ... Attending to the affairs of the house are their proper occupations. ... To sing, to play on instruments of music, to draw, to speak French and the like are very agreeable qualifications, but ... who, then, is there left to take care of the houses of farmers and traders?...' The result is that 'the servant girls step in and supply their place.' 'I do not know ... a more unfortunate being than a girl with a mere boarding-school education and without the fortune to enable her to keep a servant when married. Of what use are her accomplishments?'[61] It seems likely that at this lower middle-class level, Cobbett was right in his strictures. What a newly educated wife gained in genteel accomplishments to catch a husband in the first place, she lost in economic functional role during marriage as mistress of the household or helper in the counting house. Complementary participation in conjugal business certainly decreased, and it is not even clear that there was a compensatory increase in joint participation in leisure activities after work. How many farmers or tradesmen really wanted their wives to sing or play music to them, or discuss the latest novel with them, in the evening after the hard day? (Plate 20.)

At the very end of the eighteenth century, feminist educational reformers like Hannah More and Maria Edgeworth also launched an attack on training in time-consuming aesthetic accomplishments.[62] The most ferocious criticism of feminine education at the end of the eighteenth century came from the pen of Mary Wollstonecraft, an educated lady whose father dissipated the family fortune and who therefore found herself and her sisters forced to eke out a living as teachers or governesses. For her, the downward spread of genteel education was nothing but a disaster. 'Strength of body and mind are sacrificed to libertine notions of beauty, to the desire of establishing themselves – the only way women can rise in the world – by marriage.' In her opinion, the real purpose of the current education of women was 'to make them alluring mistresses rather than affectionate wives and rational mothers.' She passionately objected to women being trained 'merely to gratify the appetite of man, or to be the upper servant, who provides his meals and takes care of his linen.' She classified well-educated women into two groups. The first was the 'fine ladies' who have 'been taught to look down with contempt on the vulgar employments of life', and devote themselves to a life of hedonistic social pleasure. The second was 'notable women' whose 'husbands acknowledge that they are good managers and chaste wives, but leave home to seek more agreeable ... society.' In both cases, the result was far from that ideal of companionate marriage based on rational friendship to which she aspired, and towards which she thought that female education should be redirected.[63]

Mary Wollstonecraft's criticism was, as usual, exaggerated. One clear gain in marital companionship came from the greater equality in the rural areas in reading skills between husbands and wives at the lower middle-class and respectable artisan levels. To judge from the ratio of male to female signatures (relative to marks) made by witnesses in court cases in East Anglia and London, there was an improvement from one woman to eight men in the period 1580–1640 to one woman to two or three men in the late seventeenth century. In the 1660s a sample of tax-paying householders, (which excludes the very poor), indicates that even at this level women were only about half as literate as men, to judge from the proportion who could sign their names. A century later, the proportions were a little closer; a nation-wide sample for 1754 of 274 parishes covering all social classes indicates that about sixty per cent of men could sign their names at marriage but only thirty-five per cent of women; by 1800 the gap had narrowed to sixty per cent and forty-five per cent.[64]

If the capacity to sign one's name can be taken as evidence of a capacity to read newspapers and other forms of popular literature (an assumption which seems reasonable but has yet to be proved), then the narrowing of the gap should have meant that in a rather larger number of humble families the husband and wife had more shared interests and more in common to talk about. It should have been a stimulus in these circles to a more companionate marriage pattern. The effect of the sex differential in literacy on marital relations is well brought out by Dr Johnson's recollection of his father and mother, the former being a bookseller by trade, in the first decades of the eighteenth century. He recalled that they 'had not much happiness from each other. They seldom conversed. ... Had my mother been more literate, they had been better companions.' Johnson may not have been right in his diagnosis of the basic cause of his parents' unhappy marriage, but the comment is a significant hint of a contemporary marital problem. Thomas Somerville, writing in 1813, certainly thought that 'the more liberal education given to young ladies' had resulted in 'an increase of those attractions of the fair sex which sweeten domestic and social intercourse.'[65]

iii. Changes in the Curriculum

The education that late seventeenth-century feminists like Mrs Woolley and Mrs Astell had advocated was certainly broader but shallower than the classical linguistic skills of the sixteenth-century learned lady. Mary Astell wanted women to have 'a stock of solid and useful knowledge', including religious instruction, while Defoe was even less ambitious, asking, ambiguously, that they 'should have all the advantages of learning suitable to their genius.' Mrs Hester Chapone's mid-eighteenth-century recommendations for the education of a lady included free and legible writing, common arithmetic, and some reading in geography, chronology, English history, poetry, natural and modern philosophy and novels. Optional extras were music and dancing, while the classical languages and theological controversy were strictly to be avoided.[66]

There is good reason to think that slowly over the eighteenth century their recommendations took effect, and the success of *The Tatler* and *The Spectator* in the first decade of the eighteenth century proves that there was a market, female as well as male, for semi-serious periodical literature on subjects of current interest. Indeed one female correspondent appealed to *The Spectator* for help in persuading her mother to expand her education from needlework to such things as modern English literature, French, music, dancing and mathematics. Since Colley Cibber's heroine in his play *The Refusal* 'does not read Aristotle, Plato, Plutarch or Seneca, she is neither romantic nor vain in her pedantry; and as her learning never went higher than Bickerstaff's *Tatler*, her manners are consequently natural, modest and agreeable.'[67] By the middle of the eighteenth century boarding-school girls no longer toiled over their needlework for six hours a day and no longer confined their reading to the Bible and edifying sermons. They read romances and plays and were taught the 'mode of the court and diversion of the town.'

One of the best late eighteenth-century schools for girls was that run by the Misses Lee at Bath. Sarah Butt, the daughter of a wealthy naval doctor, was sent to the school in 1798 at the age of fifteen. It was a big school with fifty-two boarders and over twenty day-girls, a permanent staff of five and other specialist teachers. The curriculum covered the traditional areas of feminine deportment, namely music, dancing, drawing and needlework. But equal stress was laid on the more academic aspects of the curriculum, which included writing and grammar, arithmetic, geography and French. So seriously was French taken that it was the only language which was allowed to be spoken during working hours. This was because 'to speak French is necessary in order to appear genteel.'[68]

In 1798 ladies were told that 'the acquisition of languages, simple mathematics, astronomy, natural and experimental philosophy, with history and criticism, may be cultivated by the sex with propriety and advantage', to say nothing of 'poetry, music, painting and statuary'. Other respectable studies included 'a knowledge of the customs and manners of different nations, geography, chemistry, electricity, botany, an investigation of the several orders of animals, gardening, turning and works of ingenuity.'[69] Practice lagged somewhat behind theory, but the product of this female educational reform was undoubtedly better adapted to the new age of leisure. She was both cause and consequence of the spread into provincial capitals of such cultural amenities as the theatre, the music room, and the bookstore.

Contemporaries were well aware that things had improved. In 1753 Lady Mary Wortley Montagu contrasted favourably the current educational advantages of her grandchildren with those available in her own day. By 1770 the feminine reading market was now so large that there appeared the first successful women's periodical, *The Ladies' Magazine, or Entertaining Companion for the Fair Sex*, while the sales and circulation of novels, written mostly for and often by women, continued to soar. 'All our ladies read now, which is a great extension,' commented Dr Johnson in 1778. As a result, he believed that 'the ladies of the present age ... were more faithful to their husbands, and more virtuous in every respect than in former times, because their understandings were better cultivated.'[70] Unlike Mary Wollstonecraft, he saw a clear correlation between improved female education in the upper and upper middle classes and the development of the companionate marriage. At the end of the eighteenth century, Thomas Gisborne praised the education then provided to women – he was presumably talking about upper-class women – compared with that which had prevailed in the late seventeenth and early eighteenth centuries. While avoiding 'the depths of erudition', female education was now providing 'a cultivated understanding, a polished taste, and a memory stored with useful and elegant information.' 'In cultivation of the female understanding, essential improvements have taken place in the present age.' Even the querulous and carping Mrs Thrale confirmed the reality of the improvement, remarking in 1778 that 'the duty of education has of late years been practised with an alacrity truly astonishing to me. Every girls' school now of decent rank has a master in pay to teach the Misses verses, criticism, geography, etc., things never dreamed of as necessary 30 or even 20 years ago.'[71] Mrs Thrale's one real objection was that the new curriculum, although now much more serious and broad-ranging, was nonetheless designed for the same old purpose – to catch a husband. She could not accept the fact that 'our great female boarding schools are so many seminaries of candidates for matrimony.'[72]

In any case, these criticisms of the purpose of late eighteenth-century female education were not altogether fair, since although husband-hunting and the making of companionate wives was a prime objective, another was radically to reshape the character and morals of the next generation through the early education of children. John Moir, for example, writing in 1798, 'Considers this as the source of whatever improvements we wish to take place in human life.... He therefore addresses himself to mothers... to teach their daughters.' Improved female education was regarded by some, from John Locke to John Moir, as the key to social progress in the future.[73]

iv. Opposition to Scholarship

Despite this clear improvement in female education, there persisted a powerful current of suspicion and dislike of the learned lady, which was widely shared by both sexes, and which had begun in the latter half of the sixteenth century. A common proverb of the seventeenth century ran 'Take heed of a young wench, a prophetess and a Latin woman.' In 1753 Mrs Carter asked: 'Since the days of Queen Elizabeth and Lady Jane Grey, whoever thought of teaching princesses Latin and Greek?' Who indeed? The deep-rooted masculine hostility to female classical learning had not been mollified by the deferential attitudes of such advocates of higher education for women in the late seventeenth century as Mrs Astell. The prejudice was probably actually reinforced by the radical claims of Catherine Macaulay and Mary Wollstonecraft in the late eighteenth century, and by the arrogant intellectual claims of the coterie of blue-stockings in their literary salons. Men felt uneasy when told that Mrs Carter, who 'talks Greek faster than any woman in England', succeeded single-handedly in tutoring her young brother Henry to gain him admittance to a Cambridge college in 1756, 'the only instance of a student at Cambridge who was indebted for his previous education to one of the other sex.' Even *The Lady's Magazine*, which was very enthusiastic about improving the quality of women's education, declared in 1773 that 'we can never wish that society should be filled with doctors in petticoats to regale us with Latin and Greek.'[74] It was far from an unreasonable position to adopt.

Men of the seventeenth and eighteenth centuries clearly felt very threatened by intellectual women and erected a whole battery of philosophical and biological arguments to protect themselves. In 1674 Malebranche had propounded the popular idea that women were intellectually inferior to men because of a basic physiological difference, the greater sensitivity of the nerve fibres in their brains. This belief in the biological inferiority of women was commonly held, and when in 1708 a reader asked *The British Apollo* whether women were as capable of learning as men, he was told that 'they are cast in too soft a mould, are made of too fine, too delicate a composure to endure the severity of study, the drudgery of contemplation, the fatigue of profound speculation.' In his widely published *Advice*, William Savile, Lord Halifax, firmly declared in 1688 that men 'had the larger share of reason bestowed upon them', and women in the eighteenth century generally accepted that they were biologically 'incapable of great attainments.' All attempts by a tiny minority of women to break through this barrier of intellectual inferiority were met with derison and mockery. Indeed from Molière's *Les Femmes Savantes* of 1672 through works of Dryden, Shadwell, Congreve, Farquhar and Gay, the next fifty years saw the regular parodying upon the English stage of the pretentiously learned lady, 'the philosophress'. Even women writers did not hesitate to make fun of them, like Mrs Centlivre's character Valeria, 'a Philosophical girl', in her play *The Basset Table* of 1705. Thomas Wright devoted a whole play to *The Female Virtuoso*, whose husband addressed her as 'my walking University, my puzzling library of flesh', and Swift admitted that 'those who are commonly called learned ladies have lost all manner of credit.'[75]

There is no doubt that there was a strongly hostile male response to any suggestion that a woman could be the intellectual equal of a man, or that she should be educated in any form of serious, especially classical, scholarship. Most ordinary women took the same view, like Mrs Cappe's aunts in the middle of the century who 'had a great horror of what they called learned ladies', and 'were continually warning me against spending my time reading.' They regarded a woman's career as leading to marriage and the home, which was factually correct, and saw no point, and indeed some positive harm, in the acquisition of useless learning, the display of which would only irritate most men. Those few women who defied the convention found it prudent to conceal their activities. Lady Mary Wortley Montagu had taught herself the classics in the early eighteenth century in the deepest secrecy. Over forty years later, in 1753, she advised her daughter to give her granddaughter a serious and scholarly education, but warned her

to conceal whatever learning she attains, with as much solicitude as she would hide crookedness or lameness; the parade of it can only serve to draw on her the envy, and consequently the most inveterate hatred, of all he and she fools, which will certainly be at least three parts in four of all her acquaintance.[76]

Dr Johnson was exceptional in claiming in 1769 that 'contrary to the common notion, a woman would not be the worse wife for being learned' –

but then he lived much with Mrs Thrale.[77]

In the late eighteenth century the radical feminist advocates were foolish enough to link educational equality with equality of power within the family – and by doing so destroyed any hope of achieving concrete change. Lady Mary Wortley Montagu was an early portent of the more strident attitude. In her earlier years she was traditionally deferential about her sex: 'We are a lower part of Creation; we owe obedience and submission to the superior sex.' In her sixties in 1753, however, she was boldly declaring that 'nature has not placed us in an inferior rank to men, no more than the females of other animals where we see no distinction of capacity.' Ten years before, Elizabeth Montagu had argued that men deliberately deprived women of education, since 'they know fools make the best slaves.'[78] It was Rousseau in *Émile* who drew most clearly the lines of battle with the women on this issue of higher education. He flatly declared that 'the woman is made specially to please the man', that she is 'always subordinate to man', and that learning in a woman is 'unpleasing and unnecessary.'[79] This was the point of view which so infuriated Mary Wollstonecraft and her fellow radicals.

v. Conclusion

By the end of the eighteenth century a consensus was emerging about the ideal education for women from the landed classes and from the higher ranks of the bourgeoisie. She was neither the frivolous, party-going, neglectful mother and possibly adulterous wife of the aristocracy, nor the middle-class intellectual blue-stocking who challenged and threatened men on their own ground of the classics. She was a well-informed and motivated woman with the educational training and the internalized desire to devote her life partly to pleasing her husband and providing him with friendship and intelligent companionship, partly to the efficient supervision of servants and domestic arrangements; and partly to educating her children in ways appropriate for their future.[80] The girls stayed under her care for a prolonged period, so that she was well placed to mould them into her own useful but subordinate sex-role; the boys stayed until the age of seven, when they passed under masculine control of tutors and schoolmasters. The education of women now covered a broad sweep of subjects, including history, geography, literature and current affairs, and some women were now boasting, with reason, of the positive superiority of their education over the narrow classical linguistic training of their brothers. In 1790 *The Ladies Monthly Magazine* claimed that 'many women have received a much better education than Shakespeare enjoyed.' 'Boys at grammar school,' remarked Mrs Eliza Fox, 'are taught Latin and Greek, despise the simpler paths of learning, and are generally ignorant of really useful matters of fact, about which a girl is much better informed.' The change in women's consciousness from a humiliating sense of their educational inferiority in 1700 to a proud claim to educational superiority in 1810 is little short of revolutionary. Men also admitted the change, and in 1791 *The Gentleman's Magazine* could observe that 'at present . . . the fair sex has asserted its rank, and challenged that natural equality of intellect which nothing but the influence of human institutions could have concealed for a moment.'[81] The standard male attitude towards woman's intellectual capacities had also been significantly modified over the previous half century.

It seems likely that this broader education of women must have played its part in leading to demands for greater freedom of choice in mate-selection and a greater share in family decision-making. It certainly resulted in a greater capacity to participate in the life and problems of the husband, and it probably also resulted in a more relaxed attitude toward sexuality within marriage, and a greater desire to restrict births. On the other hand, it presupposed a growing number of women wholly withdrawn from productive work and with a great deal of enforced leisure on their hands. There is no doubt whatever that large numbers of bourgeois and even lower-middle-class wives were now being educated like their social superiors for a life of leisure, and were being withdrawn from useful economic employment in their husbands' businesses. As Dr Gregory explained in 1762, 'the intention of your being taught needlework, knitting and such like is not on account of the intrinsic value of all you can do with your hands, which is trifling, but to enable you . . . to fill up, in a tolerably agreeable way, some of the many solitary hours you must necessarily pass at home.' Moreover, many of these now leisured and lonely wives tended to lapse into melancholia, the connection between female idleness and mental disease being commonly recognized even in the seventeenth century.[82] The critics of the lady of leisure were strongly motivated by the Puritan ethic of work, and could not imagine that a life devoted to pleasing her husband, educating her children, directing the servants, performing a variety of good works and attending parties could be fully satisfying. There is a good deal of evidence, both from correspondence and from the novels of Jane Austen, to suggest that this assumption is quite untrue.

The improved education of upper- and middle-class women during the eighteenth century transformed English culture, stimulating not only the novel, but also the provincial theatre and the circulating library. It greatly increased the companionship element in marriage, now that wives were as well read as their husbands in all fields except the classics. But it carried a cost in increased female idleness and withdrawal from the world of work. This may not have mattered too much to happily married women, but to the growing number of life-long spinsters, it was a catastrophe.

4 CASE HISTORIES

The study of intimate domestic relations involves probing into an area of the human psyche where it is extremely difficult, and sometimes impossible, to distinguish reality from image, fact from fiction. This is particularly the case when, as is usual, there has survived only a one-sided record of the relationship, sometimes written down immediately in a diary or in letters, and sometimes reconstructed later in an autobiography. Even if the facts are accurately reported, human feelings are so changeable and evanescent that interpretation of them is a most hazardous exercise.

Take, for example, the bare facts – which are all we know – of the story of the two marriages of Captain Yeo in the mid-eighteenth century. Most of the period of his first marriage was spent at sea, where he reached the rank of captain in command of a ship. In the home, on the rare occasions he was there, he was 'a bashaw, whose single nod of disapprobation struck terror into the whole family.' And yet when he heard that his wife was dangerously ill at Plymouth, he steered his ship immediately for harbour, in defiance of Admiralty orders. He arrived at Plymouth just too late, for his wife was dead and her funeral had taken place a few hours earlier. He promptly indulged in the romantic gesture of having the coffin dug up again and opened so that he could take one last look at the face of his dead wife. For the serious breach of naval discipline by directing his ship to Plymouth without permission, Captain Yeo was punished by having to wait for nine years before again being given a command at sea.

So far, the story appears to be one of remarkable marital devotion, exercised at the cost of the ruin of a professional career. A mere nine weeks later, however, he married again, with 'a giggling girl of nineteen' who bore him five more children.[83] It is an extraordinary story, and it is hard to know how to evaluate the motives of the captain and his true feelings for his first wife and the children he had by her. The difficulty is compounded by the fact that we only know the story as it is told by his daughter, who actively disliked her father.

i. The Middling Ranks

There is good reason to suppose that Oliver Goldsmith's model of the ideal companionate marriage first developed as a norm among the more pious, often nonconformist, middle-class families of the late seventeenth century. The Presbyterian Richard Baxter and his wife married one another, not with a view to worldly advancement, but for their personal qualities. When his wife died in 1681, Baxter wrote her biography, in which he departed wholly from the traditional patriarchal attitude to women of early seventeenth-century society and of most of his contemporaries. He freely admitted that in practical matters, 'her apprehension . . . was so much quicker and more discerning than mine. . . . I am not ashamed to have been much ruled by her prudent love in many things.' He even confessed that she told him – rightly – that he wrote too much, too superficially. He was also unusual in giving her free control of the disposal of her own fortune. When it was all over and she was dead, he wrote that 'these near nineteen years I know not that we ever had any breach in the point of love, or point of interest.'[84] The Baxters clearly enjoyed a most intimate spiritual, intellectual and emotional relationship.

Similar evidence is provided by another nonconformist minister of the late seventeenth century, Oliver Heywood. In 1697 he wrote, with genuine feeling: 'God has given me a pious, prudent, sweet-tempered wife, whom I love entirely, and she loves me dearly, and is exceeding tender to me, almost to excess, with whom I have lived very peaceably almost 30 years.'[85]

When the struggling Grub-street writer Richard Steele married in 1707, his affection for his new wife knew no bounds and broke through all the barriers of austere seventeenth-century convention. 'There are not words to express the tenderness I have for you,' he wrote in 1708. Two years later, 'I know no happiness in this life in any degree comparable to the pleasure I have in your person and society.' In 1716, nine years after marriage, he was still telling his wife 'I love you to distraction', including his four children in a pean of praise for the pleasures of domestic felicity. Unfortunately, however, these emotions were not fully shared by his wife, who soon became exasperated by Steele's financial irresponsibility, and the last years before her death in 1718 were full of tension caused by what Steele over-optimistically brushed aside as the 'little heats that have sometimes happened between us.'[86] For all this, however, Steele's frank and open demonstrations and assertions of love over a long period of years are clearly not hypocritical and are in striking contrast to the formal relations that were so carefully maintained in the sixteenth and early seventeenth centuries. What makes them historically important is his influence in moulding eighteenth-century squirarchy attitudes to love and marriage through the pages of *The Tatler*.

An important distinction has to be made between the life-style and familial arrangements of smallholders, shopkeepers, artisans and the labour aristocracy on the one hand, and the masses of the propertyless labouring poor on the other. The former group, anxious to preserve its precarious economic foothold one rung above the poor, were probably more concerned with capital and property accumulation as a motive for marriage than any other group in society except the highest aristocracy. Prevailing affective relations between spouses were symbolized by the customary behaviour of the nineteenth-century French peasant, who gave 'his arm to his wife the day of their marriage for the first and last time.'[87] The small shopkeepers, tradesmen and artisans in the towns were equally dependent on capital to get a start in life, and therefore equally influenced by material as much as affective considerations in marriage. Moreover, this was a social group much at the mercy of economic circumstances, which could very easily go wrong, and as a result plunge the whole family into embittered misery. Financial disaster was extremely common among them in the eighteenth century, the debtors' prison was an ever present threat, and the consequence of imprudent marriage could easily be

> a smoky house, a failing trade
> Six squalling brats and a scolding jade,

as the late eighteenth-century caricaturist James Gillray described *Les Plaisirs de Mariage*.[88]

The development of free courtship and companionate marriage at the peasant level was a direct consequence of the early economic independence of the children afforded by the rise of a cottage industry. In contrast to the rich, changing ideology played no part in this transformation of inter-personal relationships among the rural smallholders and tenant farmers. It was economic, not ideological, considerations which made possible the stratified diffusion downward of the 'erotic consciousness' first developed for other reasons among the squirarchy and the upper bourgeoisie.[89]

One small piece of evidence of this growing economic independence is the breakdown of the living-in apprenticeship system in London, which had severely restricted the matrimonial and sexual opportunities for poor apprentices. Francis Place's father, who was born in 1717, although not an apprentice but a journeyman baker, nevertheless continued to live on his master's premises even after he was married, going home to his wife only on Saturday nights. This practice, which was apparently normal among journeymen bakers in the first half of the century, certainly made the development of the companionate marriage all but impossible. As night workers, bakers were probably exceptional, but by the 1770s even the unmarried apprentices were obtaining the freedom to live in lodgings of their own choice, no longer under the watchful scrutiny of their master and mistress, who now wanted privacy in the home more than total control of the lives of their apprentices. By 1800 this practice of living in lodgings was described as 'a very common custom now'. Patriarchal control of the sexual and marital affairs of the young, urban employees was clearly breaking down, thus facilitating both extra-marital liaisons and early marriages based on affective ties.[90] Even so, many of these unions among the poor were still fairly strictly business arrangements. Place records that it was the custom among London tradesmen in the 1770s for 'almost every man who had the means to spend his evenings at some public house or tavern or other place of public amusement', thus leaving his wife and children alone to their own devices. Married couples thus still pursued sexually segregated leisure activities. In Place's childhood, collective family outings were confined to Sundays.

On the other hand, the freedom of choice in marriage made possible by easy work prospects meant that many marriages were made for affective as well as economic reasons. Place's sister married someone she despised merely in order to spite her real lover, with whom she had quarrelled. The predictable result in the latter case was acute unhappiness: 'He therefore sought consolation in drinking, and she in Methodism.' As for Place himself, in 1791 he married for love a badly educated but morally estimable girl. In 1827 when she died painfully of breast cancer, the family situation had changed from one of abject poverty to relative affluence. Place was now a well-known intellectual, a self-educated man but a close associate of Bentham and Mill; his children were all well educated, and his poor semi-literate wife was naturally torn by jealousy and resentment. Despite all this and her admittedly 'hasty temper', Place was shattered by her death and could not bring himself to attend the funeral. 'I have lost, and forever, my *friend*, my long cherished *companion* in all my various changes of life.'[91]

By the early nineteenth century the companionate marriage seems therefore to have been well established among the lower-middle classes. When in 1808 Ellen Weeton went to visit her brother, an attorney's clerk who had been married four years and produced three children, she was confronted daily with somewhat extravagant visual demonstrations of affection – perhaps laid on to impress the spinster sister with her brother's conformity with the current romantic fashion. 'Every day after dinner and supper, instead of a dessert on her table, came his wife upon his knee, and her lips to his mouth, sweeter I dare say in his opinion than the finest garden fruit, and more grateful to his heart.'[92]

To offset the over-idealized picture presented by Francis Place and Miss Weeton, the stories of Thomas Wright and Thomas Turner put matters in a more realistic perspective. A poor Methodist, Thomas Wright's first attempt at courting was when he visited a young woman 'after the family were gone to bed', while his companion wooed the maidservant. It was not a pleasurable experience and years later Wright remembered that 'I was terribly embarrassed to keep up the conversation, she not being a very talkative girl.' She was probably disappointed at Wright's lack of sexual enterprise during the long night for she later became pregnant by another suitor, followed by a forced wedding, unhappy married life, and early death: 'Farewell poor Nancy Hopkinson.' Wright's next, more serious, attempt at courting turned out no better. The girl became pregnant by an apprentice, but her parents refused to let her marry him. The child was born but fortunately died. She later married and had six children, but cuckolded her husband, who therefore left her, went off to London and bigamously married another wife, which was easy enough to do in the eighteenth century. Despite overtures from two girls and one widow, Wright finally fell in love with an eleven-year-old, Miss Birkhead. He waited several years for her to grow up, although at some point he was also courting another girl. But in 1766, when she was still only nineteen, he proposed to Miss Birkhead and was accepted. Since her parents were opposed to the marriage because of Wright's lack of financial prospects, the pair ran away to Scotland and were married in an inn by a minister for a fee of two guineas.[93]

The marriage turned out badly. His wife's parents never forgave him for the elopement, particularly since they found themselves obliged to lend him £100, interest free, to buy a lease of a small farm. But they succeeded, according to Wright, in alienating his wife's affection from him, while to add to his matrimonial troubles she took to drink, so much so that at one stage a gallon of rum a week was being consumed in the house. In 1777, eleven years after he married her, she died of galloping consumption, having given birth to seven children, three of whom died young.

After a lot of trouble with two thievish and drunken housekeepers who

cost him some £50, Wright finally realized that he had no option but to
remarry. The motives which guided his choice were illuminating.

Some people advised me to marry an old woman that would have no more children,
and talked in such a manner as if they supposed that I might accommodate my fancy
and affection to any old creature, with as much ease as I might choose a joint of meat
to get my dinner upon. These people seemed to think, that if a person has been
married once, and got some children, he must have lost all the finer feelings of the
human heart; or, at least, that he could be justified by no other motives to a future
marriage, than those mean and sordid ones, interest and convenience.... I therefore
chose to take a young woman whom I could love, and with whom I could be happy,
though attended with almost a certainty of being encumbered with more children,
rather than take an old woman, to avoid that inconvenience, whom I could not love,
and with whom I could not be happy.

So in 1781 after four years of widowhood and at the age of forty-five, he
married the fifteen-and-a-half-year-old daughter of a neighbouring farmer,
who 'had got a tolerable education, had very good hands, was very
ingenious, solid and sensible.' The growing family, and the total hostility of
the parents of his first wife, helped to drive him into deeper financial
difficulties than ever, but he claimed that he judged them worth it.[94] As
Wright tells the story, the desire for love and affection were uppermost in his
mind in both his marriages, even if the first disappointed his expectations,
and the second added to his financial troubles.

The diary of Thomas Turner, an educated and widely read shopkeeper in
the mid-eighteenth century, tends to confirm the picture drawn by Thomas
Wright. He married for love in 1751, at the age of twenty-six, with high
expectations of domestic happiness, drawn presumably from his reading of
novels. But his wife was both cross-tempered and often ill, he himself was
far from perfect, for he not infrequently came home drunk, and by the time
the diary opens three years later, he was a very disillusioned man. 'I married,
if I know my own mind, entirely to make my wife and self happy', but
domestic quarrels had grown so bitter that three years later he seriously
considered separation. He also suffered a good deal from his wife's mother,
'having a great volubility of tongue for invective, and especially if I am the
subject.' He continued to note 'nothing else but matrimonial discord and
domestic disquietude', but became increasingly solicitous of his wife as her
physical condition deteriorated. By 1761 she was 'most prodigious bad', and
finally died at the age of twenty-seven, after a long-drawn thirty-eight week
final illness, in June of that year, ten years after he had married her.[95]

Immediately, all her faults were forgotten, and all he could remember were her good points. 'In her I have lost a sincere friend, a virtuous wife, a prudent good economist in her family, and a very valuable companion.' Two years later he was still lamenting the death of 'dear Peggy', and it was not until 1765, four years after her death, that he found a suitable replacement – a girl called Molly Hicks, a farmer's daughter then in service with a neighbouring squire. Despite two nights of 'bundling' during the courtship, his diary makes it clear that this second marriage was motivated not by affection or sexual desire but rather by a combination of financial calculation and loneliness.[96]

The picture of married life among the lower middle classes as presented in these two randomly preserved records is a reasonably consistent one, in which economic calculation played an important part, but in which much weight was given to the often thwarted expectation of domestic felicity. This is a view supported by George Crabbe, the poet. He thought that although romantic love was almost unknown among the rural smallholder, companionship was common enough. He approvingly described a couple

> Blessed in each other, but to no excess,
> Health, quiet, comfort form'd their happiness.
> Love, all made up of torture and delight
> Was but mere madness in this couple's sight.

The same he thought was true of the more substantial tenant and freehold farmers.

> Our farmers too, what though they fail to prove
> In Hymen's bonds the tenderest slaves to love
> . . . .
> Yet, coarsely kind and comfortable gay.
> They heap the board and hail the happy day.[97]

The urban tradesmen and artisans and the rural smallholders of the late eighteenth century were thus probably largely unaffected by the new demands of love, generated among their betters by the romantic movement of the age, although they had recognized the need for companionship as well as for economic partnership. As Crabbe pointed out, they therefore avoided some of the inevitable disappointments that accompanied the sharp rise among the upper middle classes in expectations from the married state. In *Mansfield Park*, Jane Austen makes Mary Crawford, as the spokeswoman for worldly wisdom, declare that 'there is not one in a hundred of either sex who is not taken in when they marry. Look where I will, I see that it is so, and I feel that it *must* be so, when I consider that it is, of all transactions, the one in which people expect most from others and are least honest themselves.'[98] There was undoubtedly a good deal of truth in her diagnosis of the practical results of romantic aspirations upon marriage arrangements. There was a very marked contrast between mid-seventeenth-century patriarchy and late eighteenth-century romanticism, and the result among the upper classes was confusion and a wide diversity of ideal models of behaviour. Lower down the social scale, the contrast and the confusion were far less severe.

ii. The Squirarchy and Nobility

It is not hard to find examples of affectionate couples among the upper squirarchy and nobility at any time in history; indeed, it would be surprising if this were not the case. But a purely subjective impression – and it can be no more – is that the proportion of such couples increased in the late seventeenth and eighteenth centuries, especially in the last half of the eighteenth century. But since we are dealing with real life, most cases are full of ambivalence. For example, Elizabeth and Richard Legh of Lyme addressed each other in the fondest terms in the 1660s – 'my dearest dear', 'my dear dear', etc., – but they had no compunction whatever twenty years later in putting very great pressure on their daughters to make loveless but financially and socially advantageous marriages.[99]

A very romantic gesture towards a companionate marriage was made in his will by John Hervey, first Earl of Bristol, although it must be admitted that the gesture was posthumous and that by implication it reflected badly on the success of his second marriage. The Earl's first wife had died in 1693, and when he died in 1751, nearly sixty years later, he left instructions that he was to be buried with a packet of his first wife's letters laid beside his left cheek and a blue Turkey stone ring she had given him placed on his finger.[100]

A much more clear-cut case concerns the Duke of Newcastle and Henrietta Godolphin, whom he married in 1716. Despite the fact that this was a purely arranged marriage for money on the one side – the Duke had heavy debts to be liquidated – and for the social prestige of a dukedom on the other, the subsequent relations between the couple turned out exceptionally well, at any rate for Newcastle. The latter's political business kept him mostly in London and therefore often separated from his wife, but within two years he was writing the most affectionate letters to 'my dearest girl'. In 1759, after forty-four years of childless marriage, the now elderly pair had a serious quarrel, and the Duke wrote to 'Harriot' in near despair. 'Be the same to me you ever was. For God's sake, my dear, consider the many happy years we have by the mercy of God had together, how much our mutual happiness depends on each other. You know, you must know, how much, how sincerely, I love and esteem you. You must know that if once your affection, your dear warm heart, is altered to me, I shall never have a happy moment afterwards. All other uneasiness and affliction I can get over; from that I never can, and that is *the most solemn truth.*' This was a marriage that began as a mere mercenary arrangement, but turned out to be truly companionate, except that the pair were separated for very long periods, she in the country occupied with music and card-playing, he in London absorbed in political patronage manipulation.[101]

This was by no means the only example of a companionate marriage of the period. When the blue-stocking Elizabeth Robinson married Edward Montagu in 1742, he wrote to her as 'my dearest Angel', or 'my dearest life'. Three years later, he told her that 'the happiest days I have ever passed in my life have been with you', and on their eighth wedding anniversary, he wrote to commemorate the day 'when you made me your friend and companion.'[102]

Other marriages that began as mere business arrangements, strongly influenced by parents and motivated by matters of money and status and convenience, turned out less well. As has been seen, when Hester Lynch Salusbury married the great brewer Henry Thrale in 1762, there was no love or affection on either side. She soon brought her mother to live with her and keep her company during her husband's absences, since even household management of the staff of eighteen was out of her hands and she had nothing to do except breed and educate her regular annual babies. Later, she added Dr Johnson to the household and began to form a literary salon of her own, while her husband, a genial, tolerant and amiable man, spent his time at the brewery, at the opera and with his mistresses. It was a vicious circle, and Dr Johnson once told her bluntly that the situation was partly her own fault: 'Why should any man delight in a wife that is to him neither use nor ornament?' She neither understood his brewing business nor went out into society. 'You divide your time between your mamma and your babies, and wonder you do not by that means become agreeable to your husband.' This was a warning that for many years she either could not, or would not heed. Her children either died or grew up as cold and distant as her husband, and as a result, on her mother's death in 1773, she was so starved for affection that she felt utterly lost. Her success in saving her husband's brewing business from failure due to liquidity crises in 1772 and 1778, her active canvassing of voters to get him elected to Parliament, and her success in luring the most distinguished literary figures of London to his table increased the latter's respect for his wife's business sense and intellectual gifts. And despite his many mistresses and at least two bouts of venereal disease, he slept with her sufficiently often to keep her pregnant on the average every fourteen months. But he never showed her the slightest affection, and when she was confined to bed after a difficult childbirth, 'might visit my chamber two or three times a week in a sort of formal way', but otherwise ignored her. Towards the end of his life, he fell openly in love with one of her friends, fortunately a lady of impregnable chastity. Mrs Thrale did not care about his low-class amours, but the love of Miss Streatfeld, who was younger, more beautiful, and more learned (she knew Greek) than herself, she took very hard. She confided doubtfully to her secret diary: 'Tho' he loves Sophy Streatfeld, he has some care for *my* life, I think, *I hope so.*'

Thus Mrs Thrale never found her way to her husband's heart, nor did she feel any affection for him. The best she could say, after thirteen years of marriage, was that 'tho' little tender of her person, he is very partial to her understanding.' According to herself, however, she was the very model of wifely obedience. 'I never offer to cross my Master's fancy ... unless on some truly serious occasion where virtue, life or fortune are concerned. I have never opposed his inclination three times in the fifteen years I have been married.' This was not entirely the result of her sense of deference to patriarchal authority; it also sprang from recognition of the futility of protest. If she were to try to oppose him on small matters, 'he most undoubtedly would give me a coarse reply and an abrupt negative.' In an obviously autobiographical mood, she commented that 'the fine men of this age use their wives very ill, and then wonder at their infidelity.' Only religious faith, such as she possessed in full measure, 'will restrain a woman of a warm constitution and high health from making cuckolds of creatures who neglect their charms.'[103] But this self-pity is not altogether fair or accurate. The story is in some ways an excellent example of how almost total indifference on both sides could nevertheless be made the basis of a tolerable working partnership. Mr Thrale provided his wife with a luxurious house in which to hold a salon and to house both her mother and Dr Johnson, neither of whom were easy to live with. She saved him in financial crises, helped him in political campaigns, serviced him sexually when required, tried her best to provide him with the male heir he wanted so badly, and looked after him when he was ill. She found alternative outlets for her energies and affections in her children, her mother, her intellectual pursuits and Dr Johnson. Her marriage was by no means as unsatisfactory as she made it out to be.

When Mr Thrale finally died of repeated strokes of apoplexy in 1781, he left a healthy, wealthy widow of forty-one, frustrated of affection all her life, but burdened with responsibilities for five unmarried daughters, two of them still quite young, and with the care of the elderly Dr Johnson, now increasingly sickly and crotchety but also psychologically heavily dependent on her for support. After a year of formal mourning and a year of agony and indecision, faced with ferocious opposition from her daughters and all of her friends, including Dr Johnson, she finally decided to follow the dictates of her heart. 'I have nothing to seek but return of affection. . . . To marry for love would therefore be rational in me.' And so she married the man she loved, Gabriel Mario Piozzi, an Italian Catholic singer and composer, who had been the music teacher of her children. She abandoned her four daughters, Dr Johnson, her country, her religion and her friends, and fled with him to Italy, a gesture of high romance, selfish pursuit of her own happiness, and material imprudence, for which her children and most of her friends never forgave her.[104]

The marriage turned out reasonably well, and the Piozzis were for many years an affectionate and companionate couple. But the last decade of her life was one of increasing misery, as Mr Piozzi died slowly and agonizingly of gout, open ulcers and arthritis. In 1791, moreover, Mrs Piozzi noted in her diary of both her husbands, that if she had been together with either of them in a sinking ship, neither would have had the slightest hesitation at saving his own life without regard for her. One of the main differences between the two, she finally came to believe, was the different life styles they led. Mr Thrale was a businessman and Mr Piozzi a country gentleman, and she concluded that a companionate marriage was more likely with the latter than the former. 'The merchant's lady is never informed of her husband's circumstances any more than his whore is; she cannot be let into the mysteries of a large and complicated business', whereas the country gentleman will readily discuss with his wife the rise and fall of agricultural prices and rents. Secondly, the wife of a country gentleman 'must study to please her husband too, because she lives with him in a situation of considerable isolation.' This the merchant in London 'scarce can be said to do', since he spends his days at his business and his evenings pursuing his pleasures at the theatre, the opera and parties. This was clearly a dubious generalization from the particular of her own experience. Mrs Thrale forgot how many country gentlemen preferred the company of their dogs and horses to that of their wives, and how many slept with their serving-maids, and how many London merchants returned home every evening to the domestic hearth.[105]

Mrs Thrale/Piozzi's matrimonial ventures thus ranged over the two extreme poles of conduct, both of which were by now regarded with suspicion and moral distaste. The first marriage was an old-style one of mere convenience. Financial interests were primarily at stake, and little or no attempt was made at courtship to build up affection. The second marriage was the result of an uncontrollable passion, which she was unable to resist, despite the obvious hazards of the sacrifice of her children and the high possibilities of ultimate failure. Both her character and her marital choices were so exceptional that no generalizations can usefully be made from Mrs Thrale's story. Its value is to illustrate the wide range of options that were open in the eighteenth century.

By the late eighteenth century, the first of these matrimonial modes, arranged marriages for money, had fallen into disrepute. In 1776 Lady Sarah Lennox commented on an unhappy marriage that 'he had no more business to marry a girl he did not like than she had to accept of a man she was totally indifferent to .' This was a position to which she had arrived by bitter experience, having married at seventeen a man she could cheerfully accept and with whom she got on reasonably well. But there were no children, and her husband, though very fond of her, yet loved his racehorses more. She became dissatisfied and flirtatious, and in 1796, after six years of marriage, she eloped with a lover, only to leave him within a year to live in seclusion with her daughter by him. In 1776, the year she made the comment, she was at last divorced from her husband, and was free to remarry. On the other hand, she brought up her children by her second husband with love and discretion, and they made marriages which were based on prior attraction and developed into stable affection, all of which met with her warm approval. Even the whirlwind courtship and marriage of her son George was acceptable to her once she was satisfied that the pair were happy: 'Judge if I may not be very thankful that a sudden match of fancy should turn out so well.'[106]

A final example of the companionate marriage of the eighteenth century is that of Mary Hamilton, who was born in 1756. At the age of seventeen when she first came onto the marriage market, her guardian gave her some sound advice: not to accept the first suitor for fear of never having another and in hopes that 'love is to come afterwards', 'never to enter into engagements without the consent of her parents and friends', but also never to 'take the man her friends desire without consulting her own heart.' Hotly pursued by the Prince of Wales (later George IV), she rejected his amorous advances, but agreed to be his platonic friend and advisor. Finally, at the age of twenty-eight, she fell passionately in love with a suitably rich and virtuous young man, John Dickinson. She told him 'how much I love you', and a year later in 1785, soon after they were married, she wrote, 'I love you as much as it is possible for one human creature to love another.' When a daughter was born a year later, she lavished similar affection and attention on 'our dear girl'. It was a most happy and enduring union, and after some fifteen years of married life, in about 1800, John Dickinson wrote to her that 'I have only time to say that I love you dearly – best of women, best of wives and best of friends.'[107] Here was the epitome of the new companionate marriage among the upper classes of the late eighteenth century, exuding a warmth and an emotional commitment that is so very hard to find in the sixteenth and early seventeenth centuries, especially among men. There are fashions in love, as in everything else, and the Dickinsons were undoubtedly influenced in their use of language and in the sentiments they expressed by the rise of the sentimental and romantic novel.

By way of contrast to these enduringly successful companionate marriages, it is fitting to conclude with two which began well, but eventually turned sour. In 1761 Philip Francis, the brilliant only son of a well-connected clergyman, fell in love with Elizabeth Mackrabie, the daughter of a retired London businessman, who had by now fallen on hard times. Despite the opposition of his father, Philip married Elizabeth, and for several years they were blissfully happy. When absent, he wrote to her as 'dearest Betsy', telling her 'I promise myself the greatest pleasure of holding my dearest girl in my arms.' But his career did not develop the way it should have; he was stuck with a boring clerical job in the War Office and was short of money to live the kind of life he wished. In 1772, after eleven years of marriage, he abandoned his wife and young family and went off alone on a five-month tour of Europe. Two years later, he wangled an appointment as a Member of the Council in India, with a princely salary of £10,000 a year, and set sail for India. He left behind him a desolate wife in charge of five daughters and one son, aged between eleven and two. After he left, she wrote: 'I came home ... to my dismal house, where everything that was dear to me was fled.' During the constantly extended period of absence which began as three years and lengthened into seven, she continued to nourish her vision of marital affection. 'If it was possible, I love you more than ever', she wrote to Philip in 1777, after three years apart.

But Philip's voluntarily prolonged stay in India strongly suggests that he did not feel her absence very deeply, and no doubt he consoled himself by taking a native mistress, as was the usual custom. In 1780 Elizabeth finally faced up to reality. 'Separation, I was but too sure, for almost seven years, would make a great alteration in your affection, and indeed I am sorry to say I fear it has proved a very great one indeed.' On 30 March 1781, the seventh anniversary of his departure from England, 'I wept for four hours.' Soon afterwards Philip returned, now a rich man with an income from capital of £3,000 a year, and on the surface as affectionate as ever. But before long, he was off again on a tour of Europe, still writing to 'Dearest Betsy' and signing himself 'yours, yours, yours, yours, P.F.' By 1791, however, relations had deteriorated and he was writing to 'Dear Mrs. F', and signing off with 'And so, dear Madam, . . . I remain yours indelibly.' By 1802 things had come down to 'Dear Madam F' . . . 'Yours dutifully.' It seems that Philip found his aging and ailing wife a bore, and after his return from India in 1781, he spent relatively little time at home. Over the next twenty years, relations steadily and relentlessly cooled. Although Elizabeth stubbornly refused to recognize it, the heart had gone out of the marriage at least by 1772, at the time of Philip's first long solitary European tour.[108]

A somewhat similar story, but one in which the more affectionate of the pair was the husband, concerns Lord William Russell, younger son of the Duke of Bedford. In 1817 he made a socially suitable marriage with Miss Elizabeth Rawdon, with whom he was genuinely much in love. His father the Duke expressed his pleasure that 'you have every prospect of being happy with Miss Rawdon', and six years later, in 1823, Lord William told his wife, 'I love you more than anything in the world.' The evidence suggests that she was quite fond of him but had little respect for him, and there is little doubt that she invested all her emotional capital in her children. At the age of two in 1822, 'the child breakfasts, dines and lives with us as if he were 20 years old, to the horror and amazement of English mothers', and a year later was still sleeping in his parents' room, in his own bed, at any rate when they were travelling. As late as 1829, after twelve years of marriage, Lord William was still telling himself, perhaps to keep up his morale, that 'there is no happiness like that derived from wife and children, it makes one indifferent to all other pleasures.' It was not until 1830 that there was the first sign of marital tension, due to Elizabeth's imperious ways and her single-minded devotion to her children at the expense of her husband. It also seems that she was very anxious to limit the number of her children. At the age of two in 1822, 'the child breakfasts, dines and lives with pregnant with a third (surviving) child. Her husband's abject apology suggests that he may have forcibly raped her in his frustration, or failed to withdraw in time. 'I regret the affliction and mortification my fatal sin has brought upon you . . . I think and hope I can never again be wicked.' They did indeed have no more children.

In 1835 Elizabeth became increasingly discontented with life in England, and to please her Lord William gave up his career in the army and parliament in order to go to live abroad with her. After all this, it is hardly surprising that soon afterwards, in 1835, he fell head over heels in love with a rich German Jewess, with whom he carried on a liaison without even pretence of concealment. Thereafter the pair in practice went their separate ways, with only fleeting visits home by the father to see his children. By 1846 Lord William was dead, as dead as his marriage had been for many years.[108]

iii. The Propertyless Poor

Among the mass of the poor not yet affected by the 'respectable' morality seeping down from the bourgeoisie and lower middle class, another familial style is said by upper-class observers to have predominated. Spouses chose each other freely, without interference from parents, and pre-marital sexual relations were extremely common. Economic necessity and sexual desire on the part of the man and fear of spinsterhood on the part of the woman were perhaps the most powerful incentives for marriage. But once married, the husband was the patriarch of the household and the wife the obedient drudge, liable to abuse and even physical assault if she tried to assert herself. A girl from the labouring classes would start life in servitude to her parents in their home, would move in early adolescence to servitude for someone else in another home as living-in domestic, and would end in servitude to her husband in her own home. There was no real change in her life of drudgery for others in the tasks of domestic purification. The whitened doorstep was the only symbol of self-esteem to which she could aspire.[109] In 1869 John Stuart Mill thought that 'in the most naturally brutal and morally uneducated part of the lower classes, the legal slavery of the woman and something in the merely physical subjection to their will as an instrument, causes them to feel a sort of disrespect and contempt towards their own wife which they do not feel towards any other woman, or any other human being with whom they come in contact.'[110]

On the other hand there is some reason to think that Mill was generalizing too broadly, perhaps on the basis of the most degraded of the urban poor. One piece of evidence which tends to suggest a change in attitudes in the rural areas towards marital relations between the eighteenth and the nineteenth centuries is the shift in the type of victim of the traditional English village collective shame punishments known as 'charivaris' or 'skimmingtons'. Previously the victims had been partners in ill-assorted marriages of young and old, sexual transgressors, or women who abused and dominated their husbands. Increasingly, however, a fourth type of victim became the principal target, namely husbands who beat their wives. This change from female scolds to male wife-beaters as the subject of village disapproval indicates a major change in rural popular attitudes towards marital relations.[111] Sometimes the neighbours expressed their feelings in even more drastic fashion. In Boston in 1707 some seven or eight of both sexes lured a man out of his house 'then with the help of a negro youth, tore off his clothes and whipped him with rods to chastise him for carrying it harshly to his wife.' But at this early period this was clearly a most unusual occurrence, and the magistrate was so shocked at the idea of women whipping a man that he ordered them to be whipped in turn.[112]

5 SINGLE PERSONS

This rise of the companionate domesticated marriage was accompanied by a rise in the proportion of unmarried in the society, caused partly by the postponement of marriage to a later and later age, and partly by an increase in the proportion who never married at all.

i. Adolescents

The very late marriage age prevalent among the lower classes, rising in the eighteenth century from the mid to the late twenties for men, together with the current practice of 'fostering out', that is of sending children away from home at between ten and fourteen years of age to serve as domestic servants, agricultural servants or artisan apprentices in someone else's household, created serious problems of social control of adolescents. In Catholic countries, the animal spirits of this distinctive age-group were siphoned off into religious confraternities where they could meet and socialize with their peer-group under carefully controlled circumstances. Their exuberant surplus energies were diverted to organizing religious processions and other rituals, release of sexual tensions was achieved by the licensed outlets of May Day festivities and carnivals, patriarchal controls were strongly reinforced by state authority, and order in the towns was maintained by an organized police force. The Protestant Reformation destroyed all peer-group associations like confraternities, and suppressed such 'pagan' practices as May Day festivities and carnivals, and finally even the periodic days of social inversion, when for a brief moment the young were allowed to lord it over the old.[113] The only survivor of these customs into the eighteenth century was the *terrae filius* at the universities, who once a year, at Commencement, was allowed to insult the vice-chancellor and the faculty, but even he was soon suppressed as seditious, libellous and obscene. The only solution to the adolescent peer-group problem in post-Reformation England was therefore to make sure that all unmarried youths were living in a household under the control of an elderly married man, and that discipline in colleges was tightened, as the tutors took up the novel disciplinary function of acting *in loco parentis*, which they have only abandoned in the last few years.

A more serious problem was how to control the London apprentices, thousands of whom enrolled for seven-year terms every year. They composed by far the largest adolescent peer-group in the country and were inevitably a constant threat to social order. From the May Day Riot of 1517 through the numerous political mass street demonstrations during the mid-seventeenth-century Revolution down to the Gordon Riot of 1780, the London apprentices repeatedly disturbed the peace in the capital. The London Common Council and the various Companies did their best to control them by prohibiting their presence at dances, tennis courts, bowling alleys, cock-fights, brothels, etc., and their masters were given wide latitude to administer physical punishment. But nothing could suppress so large a number of unmarried youths clustered together, and nothing could stop the development of an adolescent sub-culture, described in 1647 as 'a kind of supernatural sympathy, a general union, which knits their hearts in a bond of fraternal affection.' They arranged informal meetings, special church services were held to cater for their needs, they organized themselves to present petitions on common grievances, and when the political storm broke in 1640, they flung themselves headlong into the fray. The special appeal of revolutionary ideology, then as now, was that it satisfied an adolescent identity crisis and gave the opportunity for the employment of bottled-up energies and frustrated longings to play a more adult role in society. But even in non-revolutionary times, the London apprentices were a well-defined group with a distinctive character. 'Belonging to a recognized economic order, possessing their own literature and their own heroes, seeking some set of ideals, sought after by reforming politicians and preachers, the apprentices developed a set of values for the sub-culture....'[114]

The problem of adolescence, and the nuisance it causes to society, were familiar enought to Europeans since the fifteenth century, especially as the time-lag between sexual maturity and marriage got longer and longer. The shepherd in Shakespeare's *A Winter's Tale* must have struck a familiar chord when he remarked, 'I would there were no age between sixteen and twenty-three, or that youth would sleep out the rest; for there is nothing in the between but getting wenches with child, wronging the ancientry, stealing, fighting.'[115] The idea that adolescence, as a distinctive age-group with its distinctive problems, was a development of the nineteenth century is entirely without historical foundation.

ii. Bachelors

During the late seventeenth and eighteenth centuries, there was a very high proportion of lifelong bachelors among younger sons of the nobility and gentry (Graph 3). Unless they were lucky enough to catch an heiress, many could not afford to get married and still maintain themselves in the life style to which they were accustomed. By this time, the property arrangements of the elite had hardened into custom: younger sons were now pushed out into the world with a small life annuity and some patronage leverage, rather than being given, usually for two lives but sometimes in perpetuity, one of the ancestral estates on which to live like country gentlemen. If they stayed in the countryside, they sometimes occupied a spare country house, but more often served in obscure caretaker jobs on the estate, not so much more rewarding or dignified than that of a bailiff except that they associated socially with the gentry. One of the recurrent characters in *The Spectator* was Will Wimble, the bachelor younger brother of a baronet: 'being bred to no business and born to no estate, he generally lives with his elder brother as superintendent of his game.' He seems to have drifted into this position for lack of talent for one of the respectable professions: 'It is not improbable that Will was formerly tried at divinity, law or physic, but finding his genius did not lie that way, his parents gave him up at length to his own inventions.'[116]

Failing this, many took to peripatetic professions such as the army, or remote and isolated ones such as service in the colonies where white women of the appropriate status were in very short supply. The result was that the proportion of sons (including some eldest sons, so that is a substantial underestimate for younger sons) who were still unmarried at fifty from the late seventeenth to the early nineteenth centuries was between one in four and one in six of the whole (Graph 3). At the same time, the median age of marriage among the children of the upper and professional classes was rising, reaching twenty-eight by 1800 (and thirty by 1870), so that even those who did eventually marry remained bachelors for some twelve or thirteen years after the time of sexual maturity (Graph 4). In 1773 *The Lady's*

Magazine complained that nowadays 'the men marry with reluctance, sometimes very late, and a great many are never married at all', the explanation offered being fear of the expense, now rendered insupportable by women's passion for caprice and extravagance. In 1799 it was alleged that

Railing at matrimony is become so fashionable a topic that one can scarcely step into a coffee-house or a tavern but one hears declamations against being clogged with a wife and a family, and a fixed resolution of living a life of liberty, gallantry, and pleasure, as it is called.[117]

This was a distortion of the harsh reality that for a younger son, early marriage was likely to increase expenses so significantly as almost to guarantee downward mobility. The exception to this rule is that marriage to an heiress or to the daughter of an influential member of his chosen profession or occupation was probably a younger son's best hope of hoisting himself back into the social and economic position in which he was born. Failing that, bachelordom was the most prudent way of life to adopt, since companionship and sexual satisfaction could be obtained far more cheaply with a lower-class mistress. Only after he had made his fortune might he try, late in life, to find a bride from the same class in which he began.

Apart from the decline in nuptiality, the first result of this economic crisis for younger sons was their invasion of the professions and their pressure on the state for a constant expansion of the higher ranges of the civil service to create jobs for them. One valuable source of employment for these younger sons was the more affluent positions in the Church. The purchase of rights of presentation to rich livings and the combining of several livings held in plurality were common devices, as a result of which there was a shrinkage of the less well paid jobs and a growing neglect of clerical services. The way these younger children were looked after in the Church is explained by Elizabeth Robinson in 1752: 'My father is going to purchase a fine living for Willy; indeed he will not enjoy it till after the death of the present incumbent, but it brings in £470 a year, a fine reversion for a younger brother, and what, joined to another moderate living, will be a comfortable subsistence.' The living in question was at Burghfield in Berkshire, the presentation to which was bought for two lives and was, therefore, occupied in due course both by William and by his son Matthew. Lord Herbert was thus not entirely joking when, on the birth of his third son in 1793, he told a friend that 'the boy is a fine, healthy, thick-headed fellow, and, in time, will make a devilish good bishop.'[118] Another alternative was as a barrister in the

Courts of Law. Total numbers were falling both at the Inns of Court and the universities, but in both places the sons of the elite were now squeezing out the sons of the poorer men.[119] More important, perhaps, were careers in the army and navy, which expanded enormously during the wars of Louis XIV, the Seven Years' War and the Revolutionary and Napoleonic Wars. These services absorbed large numbers of these upper-class younger sons, especially since offices in the army were up for sale to aspirants from the socially appropriate class. Other great sources of jobs were in the administrative services, both at home and abroad, in the ever-increasing imperial possessions and the East India Company.

It was not until the middle of the nineteenth century, by which time contraception was sharply reducing the number of elite children, that the cosy system of outdoor relief provided by the state for these social groups came under powerful attack by the advocates of meritocracy. The journalist Matthew Higgins was exaggerating, but not wildly, when in 1855 he denounced the way the 'Upper Ten Thousand' had 'hitherto monopolized every post of honour, trust and emolument under the Crown, from the highest to the lowest. They have taken what they want for themselves; they have distributed what they did not want among their relations, connections, and dependents. They have in turn paid their debts of friendship and gratitude, they have provided for their younger sons and worn-out servants with appointments in the public service.'[120] This is the language of polemics rather than of objective fact, but it is certainly true that the primogeniture system of the strict settlement among the landed classes was able to operate as smoothly as it did in part because the main victims of the system – the younger sons – could often find shelter in some area or other of government patronage, in the civil service, the army or navy, the customs service, the imperial administration, and the higher ranks of the Church and the law.

Even so, it seems clear that the supply of jobs for younger sons failed to match demand in the eighteenth and early nineteenth centuries. J.C. Hudson's *The Parents Handbook* of 1842 painted a grim picture of an excess of aspirants over places in all professional careers, and the situation was probably little different in the late eighteenth century, although the Revolutionary and Napoleonic Wars must temporarily have absorbed large numbers into the armed services.[121]

The second consequence of a system of very late marriage and a large number of permanent bachelors is more problematical. A strong case can be made that this situation leads to the development of a violence-prone society of bachelors who take out their sexual frustrations in military aggression. 'I am drunk with unsatiated love. I must rush again to war . . .', wrote William Blake, perceptively. Not only did these groups have a strong economic incentive to war and imperial conquest, but they also had a psychological incentive. Early nineteenth-century doctors were worried about the situation, and in the 1850s Dr William Acton wrote that 'I have daily cause to regret that in the present civilized age pecuniary considerations render the marriage tie so frequently beyond the reach of our patients.' All he could advise as a remedy for frustrated sexual desire was 'low diet, aperient medicine, gymnastic exercise and self-control.'[122] It is no accident that the English Public School of Thomas Arnold tried all these expedients, for Arnold was advised by Dr Acton. The results were clear enough. Wayland Young has persuasively argued that 'If every value and every force surrounding an adolescent tells him that his bodily affections must at all cost be transformed and sublimated into physical effort, intellectual prowess, competitive zeal, and manly prowess, how can he not found empires? . . . The nineteenth-century British Empire was not acquired in a fit of absence of mind, it was acquired in a fit of absence of women.'[123]

There is some reason to suppose that the rise of bachelordom was not confined to the sons of the upper classes, but also applied to the sons of small farmers, who found their opportunities similarly restricted as a result of enclosures and the consolidation of farms into larger units. In 1766 the Reverend William Cole of Bletchley in Buckinghamshire noted that in his village this process was 'making it very difficult for young people to marry, as was used; . . . . Several farmers' sons are forced to live at home with their fathers, though much wanting to marry and settle, for want of proper places to settle at.'[124]

iii. Spinsters

As a result of the shortage of suitable males, owing to the level of low nuptiality among younger sons and to the rise in the cost of marriage portions, there developed in the eighteenth century a new and troublesome social phenomenon, the spinster lady who never married, whose numbers rose from under five per cent of all upper-class girls in the sixteenth century to twenty to twenty-five per cent in the eighteenth century (Graph 3). As Moll Flanders complained, 'the market is against our sex just now.' This was especially true in the towns, and particularly London, where the sex ratio, due to the influx of young women from the countryside and perhaps the greater vulnerability of males to the plague, was thirteen women to ten men at the end of the seventeenth century. As a result, a London marriage broker of the period carried 'a catalogue of women wanting marriage, some young, some not, all tame as a city cuckold chid by his wife.' In economic theory, such an excess of supply over demand should have cheapened the price, but it did not work this way among the landed classes, where marriage portions continued to rise, causing many fathers to prefer to keep their daughters off the market altogether. A correspondent in 1710 asked *The Tatler* to draw its readers' attention to the fact that 'there are three things ... that hurt estates very much, viz. gaming, parliamentary elections and women's portions.'[125]

In the early nineteenth century, and possibly earlier, another factor which exacerbated the situation was the rising surplus of females over males in the population, caused presumably by the decline in infant and child mortality affecting the tougher females more powerfully than the more delicate males. In 1851 there was a surplus of three hundred and sixty-five thousand women over men, and from the 1800s to the 1840s the periodical literature of the day was more than usually filled with articles discussing 'what shall we do with our old maids?' One result of this situation was that in upper-class circles in the late eighteenth century, manoeuvres to marry off a daughter turned into a desperate man-hunt. A fictitious letter from a young girl to *The Lady's Monthly Museum* in 1798 gives some hint of the frantic quality of this traumatic experience:

My papa and mamma have been trying for the last three years to match me, and have for that purpose carried me from our country seat to London, from London to Brighton, from Brighton to Bath, and from Bath to Cheltenham, where I now am, backwards and forwards, till the family carriage is almost worn out, and one of the horses is become blind, and another lame, without my having more than a nibble, for I have never yet been able to hook my fish. I begin to be afraid that there is something wrong in their manner of baiting for a husband or in mine of laying in the line to catch him.[126]

The increasing number of upper-class women who were forced to remain single often found themselves in an unenviable position. Because of their high social background, they could not work and were thus deprived of any independent social and economic function. This was a fate that loomed over any girl who was too particular about whom she would accept for a husband, and the possibility therefore, severely reduced the potential use of the veto over suitors. As a spinster in Steele's *The Tender Husband* of 1705 explained: 'My dear, I was very cruel thirty years ago, and nobody asked me since. Yet,

I assure you there were [then] a great many matches proposed to me.'
Another in *The Conscious Lovers* of 1772 had been in love with 'a man who
poorly left me to marry an estate, and I am now, against my will, what they
call an old maid.'[127] Since England was a Protestant country, most English
fathers did not have the option of Florentine noblemen of the eighteenth
century, who deposited up to half their daughters in nunneries. The
paternal decision was taken when the girls were about six and the latter took
their vows of perpetual chastity as nuns at thirteen. Since this alternative –
'convenient stowage for their withered daughters', as Milton brutally
described it – was not available in England, surplus English daughters of the
upper classes had to be let loose on the society at large rather than being
safely locked up in nunneries. [128] Among the nobility and squirarchy, there
was often some household or other in which they would be welcome as part
companion, part housekeeper and part child-minder. They were certainly at
the beck and call of others and lacked financial independence, but then so
were their sisters who were wives. Some strong-minded spinsters came to
play a key role in the household, like William Blundell's sister Frances, who
lived with him at Crosby Hall, along with another sister. When she went
away for a visit in 1654, he complained to her hostess that she had 'taken
from my sister Winifred a husband, from Milly [his daughter] a tutoress, a
companion from my wife, and from myself a most excellent player of
shuttlecock.' Twenty years later Frances was still in the house, now
occupying herself with William's grandson. 'My sister Frances', he
reported, 'hath made herself his nurse, his servant, his mistress, his mother
indeed.' He paid her and her sister an annuity of £25 a year each instead of
the marriage portion assigned then by their father, and they lived in his
house until they died. These were the lucky ones, and Miss Grant recalled
that among the gentry in the early years of the nineteenth century the office
of housekeeper was 'regularly filled in every household then by such stray
maidens of the race as were in want of a home.'[129]

More unfortunate were the many who were unable to find a home where
they could be useful, and who were regarded by their relatives as unwanted
parasites. Often the victims of constant petty humiliations, these unhappy
creatures in many cases sought consolation in religious devotion and
charitable good works in the village.

Even more difficult was the fate of spinsters from the middle and lesser
country gentry, who lacked access to a range of big houses with lots of
accommodation, servants and children, but who suffered from the same
social inhibitions against work. For them, very often the only solution was a

life on a small pension in obscure and lonely lodgings in a town. In 1785 William Hayley drew a gloomy picture of a woman in this position. 'If she has received a polite education ... it is probable that after having passed the sprightly years of youth in the comfortable mansion of an opulent father, she is reduced to the shelter of some contracted lodging in a country town, attended by a single female servant, and with difficulty living on the interest of two or three thousand pounds, reluctantly and perhaps irregularly paid to her by an avaricious or extravagant brother.... Such is the condition in which the unmarried daughters of English gentlemen are too frequently found.' Mary Wollstonecraft also drew attention to these spinster ladies 'unable to work and ashamed to beg'. Usually ejected from the family home by a jealous sister-in-law soon after their brother and heir got married, they were sent 'with a small stipend and an uncultivated mind into joyless solitude.'[130] Many of these spinster ladies, who helped out in the households of their married sisters in emergencies, were naturally very willing to replace them permanently if they died, which no doubt accounts for the tremendous battle in the mid-nineteenth century over the proposal to remove the incest taboo on marriage with a deceased wife's sister.

Ellen Weeton's father, a late eighteenth-century sea captain, consequently expressed a strong desire to limit his family to sons. For 'unless a father can provide independent fortunes for his daughters, they must either be made mop-squeezers or mantua-makers, whereas sons can easily make their way in the world.' Samuel Butler reinforced the same view for a rather higher social class in the early nineteenth century in his fictional character of Christina Allaby. Aged twenty-seven and the daughter of an impoverished country clergyman, she was desperate for a husband, any husband of the right background. 'What else could she do? Run away? She dared not. Marry beneath her and be considered a disgrace to her family? She dared not. Remain at home and become an old maid and be laughed at? Not if she could help it.'[131] In the 1790s Mary Wollstonecraft and Mrs Mary Ann Radcliffe thought that it was the lack of job opportunities which drove the spinster daughters of the poor to prostitution, being faced with 'the great and shocking alternative between vice and death.'

As far back as 1739 *The Gentlemen's Magazine* proposed that at about fifteen or sixteen the daughters of the gentry should be made apprentices to 'genteel and easy trades like linen or woollen drapers, haberdashers of small wares, ... etc. Why are not these as creditable trades for the daughters of gentlemen as for their sons, and all of them more proper for women than men?'[132] But notions of gentility prevented the acceptance of this solution, and the situation deteriorated as they spread down the social scale. By the late eighteenth century among the lower middle class it was a sensible idea, but one which ran across the social prejudices of the age. It was considered respectable among the gentry to apprentice a younger son, but not a daughter, who thereby lost her gentility and with it any chance of a socially appropriate marriage.

One of the few occupations open to spinsters from lesser gentry families in the eighteenth century was that of companion to a wealthy but bored married woman. Mary Wollstonecraft, who spoke from personal experience, found the occupation an odious one, obliging the companion 'to live with strangers who are so intolerably tyrannical. . . . It is impossible to enumerate the many hours of anguish such a person must spend. She is alone, shut out from equality and confidence.' The only alternative in the eighteenth century was to serve as teacher in a girls' school, described tersely by Mary as 'only a kind of upper servant, who has more work than the menial ones.'[133]

It was not until the very end of the eighteenth century that another occupation opened up for well-educated spinsters from decent homes, when 'accomplished girls, portionless and homeless' could become governesses in wealthy households to young children under seven. That this was a fairly recent development is shown by Mrs Cappe's recollection in 1822 of the predicament of the daughter of a naval officer's wife in the middle of the previous century: 'She might have tolerably qualified for a governess in a respectable family, had this been a character at that time in request; but the fact being otherwise, no alternative remained but that of attending upon a lady.'[134] But even this new opening offered no more than a frustrating and peripatetic career with few prospects or enduring satisfactions, since the emotional bonds with the children were constantly being broken as the latter were transferred to the care of a male tutor or went off to school. Moreover, governesses suffered from both economic hardship and social stigma. They were usually very badly paid, sometimes as little as £12 to £30 a year, although those who knew French and had the right graces and connections might earn up to £100 a year 'in a family of distinction'. The work was very hard, for they were on duty seven days a week from 7 a.m. to 7 p.m. 'more a prisoner than any servant in the house'. Worst of all was that their equivocal social status deprived them of any companionship or sense of belonging. 'A governess is almost shut out of society, not choosing to associate with servants, and not being treated as an equal by the heads of the house and their visitors.' Not a relation, not a guest, not a mistress, not a servant, the

14. The formalities of court-ship, 1785.

15. Marital discord. By John Collett, 1782.

16. The middle-class companionate family, *c.* 1780.

L'APRÈS-DINÉE DES ANGLAIS

17. Sexual segregation after dinner: the men, 1814.

LES DAMES ANGLAISES APRÈS-DINÉ.

18. Sexual segregation after dinner: the women, 1814.

19. Wife-beating ('Judge Thumb').
By J. Gillray, 1782.

20. The accomplished wife and the
bored husband, 1789.

THE
CHILDRENS BIBLE:
OR, AN
History of the Holy Scriptures.

In which, the several Passages of the Old and New
Testament are laid down in a Method never before
attempted; being reduced to the tender Capacities of
the little Readers, by a lively and striking Abstract,
so as, under GOD, to make those excellent Books
take such a firm Hold of their young Minds and Memories, and leave such Impressions there, both of
Moral and Religious Virtue, as no Accidents of
their future Lives will ever be able to blot out.

To which is added,
The Principles of the Christian Religion, adapted to
the Minds of Children: With a small Manual of
Devotions fitted for their Use.
By a DIVINE of the Church of ENGLAND.
Adorned with Cuts.

LONDON: Printed, And,

DUBLIN: Re-Printed by ANN LAW, at the
REIN-DEER in MOUNTRATH-STREET.
M,DCC,LXIII.

21. Children's books for moral
improvement: *The Children's Bible*,
1763.

22. Children's books for amusement:
Will Wander's Walk, 1806.

WILL WANDER's WALK,
With both his Companions
And all of their Talk.

Says Will to his Sister
My Dog here proposes,
To take a nice Walk
And just follow our noses.

London Publish'd by J. Aldis, N.º9 Pavement, Moorfields, August 9, 1806.

23. The educated upper middle-class child: Mrs Hester Thrale and her daughter Queenie. By Sir Joshua Reynolds, 1781.

24. The educated lower middle-class child: Farmer Giles and his daughter, 1809.

25. The whipped child (the girl has thwarted her French governess by tying a papier-mâché mask of the latter's face over her buttocks), 1817.

26. The spoiled child.
By T. Rowlandson, 1808.

27. The abandoned child:
selling teeth for transplantation. By T. Rowlandson,
1787.

governess lived in a kind of status limbo. By reason of her position, she was also treated as almost sexless. Not a lower-class servant and so open to seduction, not a daughter of the house and so open to marriage offers, she was nothing. 'There are three classes of people in the world', remarked an anonymous writer in 1836, 'men, women, and governesses'.[135]

Around 1800 Mrs Catherine Mary Howard drew a vivid picture of the life of a governess: 'Cooped up in a school room in some remote part of the house, with the same books, desks, stools, back-boards, an indifferent pianoforte, a noisy canary or two, perhaps a pet cat, and a high fender which eclipses the cheerfulness of the fire. This seclusion from society tends to sour the temper and narrow the ideas, but I am happy to observe a considerable improvement in that class, who are now much more enlightened and liberal.' Mary Wollstonecraft, who had been a governess, took an even grimmer view of 'the humiliating situation'. 'Such is the blessed effect of civilization,' she concluded, 'the most respectable women are the most oppressed.' It is hardly surprising that, according to Harriet Martineau, governesses were among the largest occupational groups to be found in lunatic asylums in the early nineteenth century.[136]

At all levels of society, therefore, the spinster in 1800 was a drug on the market. Worse still, there were hints that her position was deteriorating at the end of the eighteenth century, as men invaded occupations, such as dressmaking, hitherto reserved for women.[137]

One should be careful not to exaggerate the predicament of any social group on such fragmentary evidence as is at present available. But there can be no doubt that the spinster in the early eighteenth century, when the problem first became of serious proportions, enjoyed a reputation for malice and ill-temper. 'If an old maid should bite anybody, it would certainly be as mortal as the bite of a mad dog,' remarked Defoe in 1723, and from then onward the ill-natured old maid became a permanent feature of the English novel, and a subject of hostile comment by all writers of domestic handbooks. In 1774 Dr John Gregory warned his daughters about 'the forlorn and unprotected situation of an old maid, the chagrin and peevishness which are apt to infect their tempers.' Eleven years later William Hayley declared that the worst feature of the condition was 'that coarse and contemptuous raillery with which the ancient maiden is perpetually insulted.'[138]

It was not until the very end of the century that the English upper classes began to accustom themselves to the existence of these social rejects. In 1797 Thomas Gisborne thought, perhaps a little optimistically, that 'the good sense and refinement of the present age have abated much of the contempt with which it was heretofore the practice to regard women who had attained or passed the middle period of life without having entered into the bonds of marriage.' But he was probably an optimist, for three years later the embittered Ellen Weeton, who as a spinster herself probably knew what she was talking about, was contemplating marriage merely in order to avoid 'the finger of contempt, the smile of ridicule.... An old maid is a stock for everyone to laugh at. Every article of dress, every word, every movement is satirized. Boys play tricks on them and are applauded. Girls sneer at them and are unreproved.'[139]

The three obstacles to any solution to the spinster problem were social snobbery, which made most business occupations beyond the pale for a girl of genteel upbringing; the non-vocational educational training of women; and the lack of openings in the professions, or even as clerks. In the early nineteenth century, John Stuart Mill saw the defects of female education as the root cause of the spinster problem. 'Women are so brought up, as not to be able to subsist in the mere physical sense, without a man to keep them.... They are so brought up as to have no vocation or useful office to fulfil in the world, remaining single.... A single woman, therefore, is felt both by herself and others to be a kind of excrescence on the surface of society, having no use or function or office there.'[140]

Only a few single women from really affluent families seem to have managed to carve out a satisfactory life for themselves in the late eighteenth century, filling their time with visits to friends and relatives in country houses and in lengthy correspondence with other spinster friends. Miss Elizabeth Iremonger and Miss Mary Heber were two who seem to have come to terms with life as spinsters, though both were buoyed up by very comfortable incomes and powerful connections. In 1786 Miss Iremonger admitted to her friend that marriage was best. On the other hand, she was 'clearly of the opinion that to be without a companion is far preferable to being tied to a disagreeable one.' She lived an apparently happy and interesting life by taking 'every opportunity of forming and cultivating those sort of valuable female friendships that are the best substitute for the other sort of connection.' Another such woman was Maria Louisa, eldest daughter of Lord George Lennox, who refused three attractive suitors and deliberately chose spinsterhood. 'She has seen so much unhappiness from gallantries in her own family that ... she is firmly resolved against matrimony.'[141]

6 FOREIGN COMPARISONS

Everything that is known about domestic relations in New England suggests that there the ideal of the companionate marriage spread perhaps even more widely and that the legal and practical position of wives improved at least as early as they did in England. A content analysis of five hundred and forty-six issues of the thirteen leading Colonial magazines published between 1741 and 1794 gives a good insight into the ideas and the preoccupations of their upper- and middle-class readers, who were especially drawn from New England. This is based on the not unreasonable assumption that the issues most commonly raised and the values expressed in these magazines are more or less accurate reflections of the concerns and ideas of their readers. The conclusion is that there was a very great deal of discussion of the companionate marriage, with far greater emphasis on personal happiness than on material considerations as the proper motive of choice of a spouse. Masculine superiority over women was still asserted, as it was in England, but it was recognized that women could and should exercise considerable power on the family in more subtle ways than those of direct confrontation. As in England, the double sexual standard remained as firmly rooted as ever, but there was increasing recognition of the existence of the romantic love complex. The only *caveat* about this type of evidence is that, as in England, it almost certainly exaggerates the impact of ideas about romantic love disseminated in the literature of the day. It seems likely that on both sides of the Atlantic settled affection based on a shrewd appreciation of human qualities played a larger role in courtship and marriage in real life than did the extravagant emotional posturing and stories of love at first sight which filled the romantic novels and magazines. These latter provided an unreal fantasy world, which most readers enjoyed as a form of escapism, but did not apply in practice to the management of their own affairs. Another piece of evidence is Crevecoeur's *Letters from an American Farmer* of 1782, which painted an idyllic (and no doubt idealized) version of the new family relationships, which formed the basis of the new social morality which he was preaching.[142]

In France, on the other hand, there was a time-lag of well over a century with developments in England and New England. In the nineteenth century, the wife in France suffered under extraordinary legal disabilities. She was obliged to live where her husband chose; she could not go to law without her husband's permission; under the system of community of property, her estate was merged with that of her husband and managed by him. Among the peasantry, the bourgeoisie and the aristocracy, marriages were still largely arranged by parents, and were primarily made for social and economic reasons rather than for emotional satisfaction.[143]

As a result, a companionate marriage was rare in high society. When Philip Francis was in Paris in 1783, he asked a French nobleman to take a letter to London for his wife; the jocular reply was: 'What! a letter to your wife! That is something new . . . there are no husbands like you.'[144] Under these circumstances, the double standard flourished to a degree unknown in the less patriarchal English society. In law the husband could have his wife imprisoned for adultery, while in practice, by common consent, he was free to kill her if he caught her in the act. The wife had no such freedom to punish her husband for his extra-marital activities, and he could break the law, not by the act of adultery, but only by introducing and maintaining a concubine in the home. Very many middle and upper-class girls were educated in convents where they were kept in total ignorance and fear of sex. As pious married women, they were subjected to the teachings of moral theologians urging that intercourse for mere pleasure is a sin, that 'the souce of all pain is sensualism', that 'marriage is holy and must be protected from gross sensualism' and that 'the secret of love is in the act of self-restraint'. No doubt many did not agree, but their compliance with these rules of conduct was enforced by the prurient interrogatories to which they were subjected by priests in the confession box. It is hardly surprising under such circumstances that marriages arranged for material advantage and burdened with such a load of moral guilt about the sexual act were often unable to provide either emotional or sensual satisfaction to either spouse, and that a mid-nineteenth-century popular domestic handbook by a doctor found it necessary to warn wives against 'the solitary masturbation practised by many women dissatisfied with their husbands'. For a husband, adultery was a normal recourse, either with a stable mistress, if he could afford it, or with one of the many prostitutes whose services were available. If it is possible to generalize in this obscure area, a husband in early nineteenth-century France tended to have sexual relations with his wife for the limited purpose of procreation, and with his mistress or a prostitute for pleasure. Thus the domestic life style openly practised in England almost exclusively by a handful of members of the high court aristocracy – at any rate as a normal and acknowledged ethical system – was practised in France not only by the nobility but also by very large numbers of the bourgeoisie, who each had his *petite maitresse* or call-girl, and even by the *petite bourgeoisie* who frequented the publicly regulated and inspected brothels.[145] The contrast between

English and French domestic relations in upper- and middle-class circles in the late eighteenth and early nineteenth centuries is on the surface quite striking. An English observer noted the difference in 1783, finding that English ladies were more domestic, more affectionate, and more child-oriented, while French visitors to England also agreed with this conclusion.[146]

As for the poor in France, the evidence suggests that they too only followed the English pattern with a substantial lag of a century or more. For those without property, affective and companionate marital relations did not develop before the nineteenth century, although, as in England, the absence of any economic stake allowed free mate choice considerably earlier. But as late as 1800 the peasant family was a purely economic union in which the wife was soon worn out by hard labour in the fields, ties to kin on both sides remained strong, and neighbourly interference in domestic life was close and constant. That emotional independence and isolation which is so central to the modern concept of the nuclear family had little chance to develop before the early nineteenth century.[147]

It is very interesting to see how feminist agitation during the French Revolution ran the same almost entirely abortive course, for much the same reasons, as did the similar movement in the English Revolution a hundred and fifty years earlier.[148] While the Revolution was at its height between 1789 and 1794, there was a certain amount of feminist agitation, and women were prominent participants in the great revolutionary *journées*. But the movement never took root, partly because of the sexual freedom and social pretensions of some of its main protagonists, but mainly because of the lack of appeal to the mass of ordinary women and the lack of support from male intellectual and political leaders. The feminist agitators, who were demanding better education, the franchise, and the right to political organization, were totally blocked by the male leaders of the Revolution, none of whom, with the sole exception of Condorcet, had any sympathy for these aspirations. Following Rousseau, they saw a woman's place as in the home, not as an active competitor or an equal with men in public life. As a result, the only achievements of the most radical phase of the French Revolution in advancing the cause of women lay in the granting to them of far more extensive legal rights. Women now at last obtained an equal share in inheritances, assured by law, majority status and therefore personal freedom from parental control at twenty-one, the power to contract debts and testify in civil suits, protection of their own property against interference by their husbands, equality of rights in cases of divorce, and some share in decisions affecting their children. It is clear that all that the French revolutionaries were willing and anxious to grant was greater equality of power within the home. All these newly acquired rights, however, were swept away again within ten years by the *Code Napoléon*, the only surviving element of change from the pre-revolutionary situation being the legal claim to equality in rights of inheritance. The principle and practice of patriarchy, in and out of the home, was firmly re-established in early nineteenth-century France.[149]

The dangers of relying on didactic materials as evidence of reality are well illustrated by the fact that in France in the second half of the eighteenth century there was some intensive propaganda, both in writing and in art, in favour of the affective family type, free marriage choice, marital love, sexual fulfilment within marriage – the alliance of Cupid and Hymen – and close parent-child bonding, especially maternal breast-feeding. Stemming from the ideas of Enlightenment thinkers like Rousseau and Diderot, fashionable painters like Greuze and Fragonard took up the theme in the 1760s and developed it in the portrayal of both aristocratic and peasant families.[150] Despite this, however, there is strong evidence that the practice of marriage arranged by parents for material advantages was reinforced by the legal code of both the *Ancien Régime* and Napoleon's *Code Civil*, and that all classes down to and including the urban artisans continued to send their children out to wet-nurse rather than breast-feed them themselves. In late eighteenth-century France, there appears to have been a yawning gap between theory, as registered by Enlightenment philosophers and fashionable artists, and practice, as revealed by the study of demographic statistics, family correspondence and contemporary comment.

7 CONCLUSION

i. Social Classes and Marital Types

In the eighteenth century, there developed in England several types of marriage, each most characteristic of a particular sector of society and each definable by a series of different variables. The first variable, which was discussed in the previous chapter, was inter-generational conflict about the selection of a particular spouse. This might be decided by the parents, kin and 'friends' without consulting the bride and groom. Or it might be decided by parents, kin and 'friends', but the groom, and by extension also the bride, was granted the right to reject someone whom he or she found at first sight to be physically or temperamentally wholly incompatible. Or choice was made by the spouses themselves, their parents retaining the right of veto to reject someone they regarded as unsuitable, usually on social or economic grounds. A further modification of this position was to grant to parents the right to impose a delay on a marriage which they considered unsuitable – a right conceded even by such a radical as Mary Wollstonecraft in 1792. Finally, the individual spouses might make their own choices, their parents being merely informed of what had been decided and asked for their formal blessing.

The second variable was the mixture of motives for making the selection of the particular spouse, the basic options being lineage 'interest', companionship, romantic love, sexual attraction, or need for an economic assistant.

The third variable was the distribution of authority within the family, which could range all the way from patriarchal despotism through egalitarian joint decision-making to *de facto* matriarchal dominance. This variable changed greatly over time and, like all the others, was highly class specific in its nature. The matriarchal mode, however, depended more on the relative strength of the personality of the woman than on the cultural traditions of any particular group.

The fourth variable was the character of the marital relationship. This could be stiff and formal, with little evidence of affection, and little or no privacy to permit affection to develop. Or it could be largely economic in function, a division of tasks for the management of a joint enterprise, such as a shop or a small farm at the lower level, or the administration of a household devoted to organized social entertainment at the highest. Or it could be genuinely affective, a bond of close friendship and companionship in the pains and pleasures of a shared life. Or it could be merely a habit and routine of daily existence.

The fifth variable was sexual satisfaction. The sexual drives of both man and woman might be entirely satisfied within the marriage bed. Or, especially among the high aristocracy, the husband might regard marital sex as no more than a duty for the production of legitimate children, and might direct all his libidinal energy elsewhere, on to prostitutes, serving-maids, nurses (plate 15), professional courtesans, mistresses installed in separate establishments, or the wives of his friends.

Based on these variables, it is possible to construct a set of Weberian ideal family types, each of which was predominant in a particular status or economic group at a particular period. Thus for 1800, at the end of the process that has been described in previous chapters, the most common type of marriage for the highest court aristocracy was one in which parents retained considerable influence over the choice of spouse and in which economic, social or political considerations were often still paramount. On the other hand, the sharp decline in the proportion of marriages with heiresses within this group shows that this pattern had changed very significantly. The ease and frequency of movement from place to place and the habit of correspondence preserved close contacts with relatives, so that kinship ties were closest at the top of society, where they still had political significance. The chores and responsibilities of child care were carried out by deputies, while both husband and wife were largely preoccupied with the pursuit of pleasure or politics. The marriage often had little affective, or even sexual, bonding, and both males and females indulged in widespread adultery. But the legal conditions of the marriage settlement gave the wife considerable power over her own property, as well as an independent source of income. In this class, separations were not uncommon, and they left the wife with considerable economic resources.

Among the lesser nobility, the squirarchy and gentry (end paper) and the professional and upper middle classes (plate 16), a different model predominated, the one that has been described in this and the preceding chapter. The choice of a spouse was increasingly left in the hands of the children themselves and was based mainly on temperamental compatibility with the aim of lasting companionship. The wife concerned herself with household management, entertainment and leisure activities. She also often closely supervised, in an increasingly permissive mode, the upbringing of the young children, while also maintaining contact by correspondence and visits with the closer relatives among the kin. The husband and wife were closely bonded by affective ties, and the wife was normally both faithful and obedient to her husband. The husband might well have a few extra-marital sexual adventures, but they were not allowed to break up the marriage. Many of these marriages were also accompanied by legal settlements which protected the wife's property, and decision-making power tended to be shared rather than monopolized by the husband.

Among the lower middle classes and the growing number of the 'labour aristocracy', a third model predominated. Economic considerations bulked large in motivating mate selection, since a little capital was so important in the establishment of a secure niche in this socially precarious class. Parental influence over choice varied from family to family, and it is difficult to generalize in this area. The marriage often tended to be an economic partnership for productive work, although the higher levels of the urban lower middle class were increasingly seeking to elevate their status by choosing brides educated not for work but to display all the refinements of upper-class leisure activity. Many in this class were dissenting or Methodist in religion and were very prudish in their sexual behaviour. Affective bonding was often highly developed, both between spouses and between parents and children. Relations with the latter were highly intrusive, using psychological pressures rather than physical beating, and there was no permissiveness. The husband tended to make the important decisions, and if the marriage turned sour, the lack of a legal settlement left the wife at the economic mercy of her husband.

Among the propertyless poor a fourth model predominated. Since neither had any capital to contribute to the union, parental direction was minimal, pre-nuptial sexual relations were common, and freedom of choice was the norm. The motives of choice may have been sexual or personal, but health and strength for co-operative economic support must have been critical considerations. After marriage, fairly brutal treatment of wives by husbands was normal, and the subordination of the former was almost as great as it had been centuries earlier in the higher ranks of society. Men spent much of their time in the ale-house, and drunkenness was a common recourse to induce temporary forgetfulness of the bitter realities of life. Children were often neglected, and sometimes abandoned since they could not be fed, to face almost certain death in an institution. Those who were kept and survived were liable to be roughly treated to enforce obedience to the parental will. At the earliest possible age, they were hired out to work very long hours in the most dreary and degrading of occupations, their wages going directly to their parents. This was a policy dictated by necessity, in order to keep the family income above the bare subsistence level. On the other hand, after 1780 increasing numbers of the respectable poor just above the abject poverty line were investing money in giving their children an elementary education in Sunday Schools. Francis Place was certain that his life-time had seen a marked improvement among many of the labouring classes in sobriety, cleanliness, chastity and desire for self-improvement which must have been reflected in improved domestic relations. The gap between the respectable and the non-respectable poor was therefore widening.

The difference between these co-existent models of family life in 1800, each appropriate to a different social rank and economic circumstances, were reflected in the way the response of a husband to the breakdown of the marriage and the development of positive hatred towards his wife took different overt forms in different strata of society. As *The Matrimonial Magazine* put it in 1793, 'if in low life, frequently his recourse is to the adoption of violent measures, and strives to break her bones, if not her heart; if in high life, he keeps his mistresses abroad and takes no trouble about his wife at home.' Husbands in the middle ranks, however, were barred from either solution 'on account of their fortunes or reputation', and therefore tended to resort to psychological warfare. A man would introduce 'a handsome vixen' into the house as companion for his wife (and perhaps as bed-partner for himself) and he would constantly, regardless of justice, criticize his wife's cooking, extravagant clothes, housekeeping management, etc.[151] This typology of responses to a marital crisis situation shows how behaviour depended partly on economic constraints, since only the rich could afford two establishments, and partly on the cultural norms of the status group: the rich and the poor could ignore a public scandal, but the bourgeoisie could not, while the poor tended to be more violent than the rich or the middle class.

In 1800, therefore, there were four main family types which roughly corresponded to the four major status and economic divisions of society, a situation which was reinforced by the fact that cross-class marriages were universally condemned in theory and very rare in practice. The only notable exceptions were the very infrequent occasions when a nobleman actually married his mistress, as Lord Berwick did Sophie Wilson and the Marquess of Worcester once offered to do to her sister Harriette. Dr Johnson was expressing conventional wisdom when he deplored such exogamy. His argument was the ancient one that society depends upon the principle of hierarchy and that, therefore, 'it is our duty to maintain the subordination of civilized society', and to penalize any temptation to 'that inordinate caprice which generally occasions low marriages.'[152] So far as parents were concerned, giving their children free mate-choice was predicated upon the assumption that the choice would be restricted to children of persons of the same rank and fortune.

The lead sectors of the society, where the most significant changes took place earliest and with widest impact, were the wealthy professional and landed classes. This group formed a fairly homogeneous social unit, tightly bound together for the first time by a unified culture, and by a common desire to pursue whatever was the fashionable mode. This being so, it is impossible to underestimate the importance of the writings of universally read didactic writers like Locke, Addison, Steele and others, of medical practitioners like Dr Cadogan, and of novelists like Richardson and

Mackenzie. These men created fashion, and the fashionable world followed in their wake, partly, of course, because they found the ideas congenial to their tastes, aspirations, and way of life.

ii. Positive and Negative Consequences

a. Positive. The three most significant physical symbols of these profound shifts in psychological attitudes among the elite are the ha-ha, the corridor and the dumb waiter. The ha-ha, the substitution of an invisible sunken ditch for high brick walls, marked the triumph of romanticism, for it destroyed the seventeenth-century concept of the garden as an orderly symmetrical area of enclosed space, as man-made and artificial as the house itself. In the eighteenth century, the rooms became more secluded and more private, but the external view from the windows was now thrown open to carefully contrived parkland and grazing cattle and sheep. The corridor, which was a feature of all new houses in the eighteenth century and was progressively added to older buildings, made a major contribution to the rise of physical privacy by removing the ever-present and inhibiting threat of a stranger walking through one's bedroom to reach his own room. Four walls and a door are a better protection of privacy than the curtains of a four-poster. The dumb waiter, used in the small private dining-room, made possible the intimate family meal-time conversation, not only away from the crowd of servants in the great hall, but also free of the surveillance of waiters serving at table. The desire to give the false impression of nature in the raw lapping around the portico of the Palladian villa, the desire for privacy in the bedroom, and the desire to reinforce nuclear family bonding by excluding both servants and strangers at meal-times were the factors which stimulated the invention of these three convenient devices. All three, together with the abandonment of the suite of rooms and the removal of the bedrooms upstairs, the rise of maternal breast-feeding, the use by children into adolescence and adulthood of the words 'Mamma' and 'Papa', the use of first names between husband and wife, the opposition to flogging, and some limited but significant improvements in female education, were symptoms of a whole set of new attitudes towards nature, natural instincts, privacy, the affective character of the nuclear family and the education of children. Contemporaries were well aware of this major shift in human relations. 'The behaviour of ladies in the past age was very reserved and stately. It would now be reckoned ridiculously stiff and formal.' Even public figures like admirals now boasted on their tombstones of their domestic virtues, such as 'filial reverence, conjugal attachment and parental affection.'[153]

b. Negative. Against these positive advances, there have to be set some serious negative features. In the first place, the series of developments from the sixteenth to the eighteenth centuries, including the rise of the state, the rise of Puritanism and then the rise of individualism, had the effect of stripping away from a marriage one by one many of those external economic, social and psychological supports which normally serve as powerful reinforcing agencies to hold together the nuclear family. Among the landed classes the assistance and/or interference of the kin were largely reduced, though not removed; the importance of property exchange, patrimony and dowry was undermined in all but the highest aristocracy by the quest for personal happiness. Among the middling and lower ranks, the social support of the neighbours was lessened as the intrusive and inquisitorial functions of village or parish community declined. All that was left of the old external props was the indissoluble nature of the marriage contract, and that could be evaded by concubinage by the rich or desertion and bigamy by the poor.

The nuclear family was thus left to stand far more than ever before on its own bottom, with little to hold it together but its own internal cohesion. There can be little doubt that in many cases this was not enough. Among the upper classes, the demand for romantic love and sexual fulfilment was stimulated – especially among women – by the reading of romances and love stories, which created exaggerated expectations of marital felicity which were very often frustrated. As early as 1712, long before the romantic movement got under way, *The Spectator* was complaining that the result of the 'half theatrical and half romantic' style of courting was to 'raise our imaginations to what is not to be expected in human life.' (Plate 14.) In the mid century Oliver Goldsmith was still more convinced of the damage caused by the exaggerated expectations raised by novels. 'How delusive, how destructive, are those pictures of consummate bliss. They teach the youthful mind to sigh after beauty and happiness which never existed, to despise that little good which fortune has mixed up in our cup, by expecting more than she ever. gave.' To make matters worse, the readers of novels mostly came from the middle ranks, while the subjects were usually drawn from the squirarchy or nobility.[154]

The second problem was that wives of the middle and upper ranks of society increasingly became idle drones. They turned household management over to stewards, reduced their reproductive responsibilities by contraceptive measures, and passed their time in such occupations as novel-reading, theatre-going, card-playing and formal visits. This was because they had been taught to cultivate 'that refined softness and delicate sensibility which renders its possessor incapable of performing the active duties of humanity.' The result was that the custom of turning wives into ladies 'languishing in listlessness' as ornamental status objects spread downward through the social scale. It was not long before more and more women found themselves utterly frustrated. In 1853 Marietta Grey complained in her diary that 'ladies, dismissed from the dairy, the confectionery, the store-room, the still-room, the poultry-yard, the kitchen garden and the orchard, have hardly yet found themselves a sphere equally useful and important in the pursuits of trade and art to which to apply their abundant leisure.'[155]

Thirdly, this erosion of outside supports involved a reduction of sociability, of contracts and emotional ties with persons outside the nuclear group. Friends, neighbours and relatives all receded into the background as the conjugal family turned more in upon itself. Moreover, the decline of the kin involved a serious loss of identity with the lineage, with the concept of oneself as a link between past and future generations. Fewer and fewer knew who their great-grandfathers were, and fewer and fewer cared. There was a fragmentation of the familial aspect of the Great Chain of Being, leaving the individual as an atomized unit without a past. He was no longer linked to a piece of property or to tombstones in a graveyard, or to names in a family Bible, and it is not mere modern romanticism to argue that he lost his past in the process of achieving his autonomy and self-fulfilment in the present.

Fourthly, a new tension now emerged to threaten the peace of domesticity. Many wives found themselves torn between the two sets of new affective responsibilities, towards their husbands and towards their children. This conflict appears again and again in the surviving records. Some wives, like Mrs Philip Francis and Mrs Boscawen, were left behind by their husbands, who were pursuing their professional careers at sea or abroad, and solaced their loneliness by devoting themselves obsessively to their children. Others, like Mrs Stanley, faced with a choice of living with her husband in London or with her children in the country, opted for the latter. Yet others, like Mrs Thrale and Lady William Russell, never much cared for their husbands anyway, and lavished all their attention on their children, even to the point of hardly ever leaving them to go out to dinner or the theatre for years on end. But one way or another, this conflict between duty to a husband and duty to children was a source of great domestic tension in the eighteenth century, and one which particularly affected wives.

A special manifestation of this tension must have been generated by the spread in upper- and middle-class circles of the practice of mothers breast-feeding their own children. This had always been recommended by doctors, who were equally insistent that resumption of sexual relations during lactation would spoil the milk and endanger the life of the child. The poor apparently ignored this educated opinion, although if the mother should become pregnant (as would happen to a minority), the milk would dry up altogether and the infant at the breast would die. Since breast-feeding in the seventeenth and eighteenth centuries normally lasted from twelve to eighteen months, upper-class wives were clearly faced with a difficult decision. They could hardly expect their husbands to remain chaste for this length of time, but if they gave way to their sexual demands, many presumably still believed that it might endanger the health of the child. What they did about this problem we do not know, but one solution may have been to wean the infant early, at three or four months, a compromise by which the life of the child was admittedly put at some risk, but the husband's sexual needs were satisfied after a relatively short space of time. Since sexual relations were an important component of the new companionate marriage, the dilemma of these unfortunate women torn between their husbands and their children must have been a cruel one. Nor was it one which could be resolved by contraception through *coitus interruptus*, since it was sexual excitement itself, not even leading to intercourse, which was thought to spoil the milk.[156] Perhaps the growing doubts of doctors about the truth of this medical theory helped to solve this agonizing dilemma by undercutting its alleged scientific foundations.

Another reason for the frustration of many women was that this shift of motives for marriage from the concrete ones of power, status and money to the imponderable one of affection probably worked to the benefit more of men than of women. This was because social custom dictated that the initiative in the courtship process should be with the male and not the female. The former was, therefore, free to follow his personal inclinations wherever they might lead him, but the latter was, at any rate in theory, restricted in her choice to those who made advances to her. She had great latitude to encourage or rebuff, but she could not formally initiate a courtship. Dr John Gregory pointed out this problem to his daughter in a volume published posthumously in 1762. If a man 'should become extremely attached to her, it is still extremely improbable that he should be the man in the world her heart most approved of. As, therefore, Nature has not given you that unlimited range of choice that we enjoy, she has wisely and benevolently assigned to you a greater flexibility of taste on the subject', by responding to any demonstration of interest by any man. 'If attachment was not excited in your sex in this manner, there is not one of a million of you that could ever marry with any degree of love.' Women came to the same conclusion on their own, for example a shrewd and well-educated young New England girl, Eliza Southcote, who observed in 1800: 'the female mind I believe is of a very pliable texture; if it were not we should be wretched indeed. . . . The inequality of privilege between the sexes is very sensibly felt by us females, and in no instance is it greater than in the liberty of choosing a partner in marriage; true, we have the liberty of refusing those we don't like, but not of selecting those we do.'[157] Even under the new arrangements, successful marriage thus depended on the docility and adaptability of the woman, as it had always done in the past, which is one of the reasons that some women were so vociferous in their disappointment and frustration in the eighteenth century.

A further reason for the discontent of some wives in the eighteenth century was that the rise of the concept of the affective marriage, like that of the seventeenth-century 'holy matrimony', caught the more independent-minded women in something of a double bind. This dilemma was made crystal clear by Defoe's liberated heroine Roxana, when she discussed the proposals of her Dutch suitor. He argued that where there was mutual love there could be no bondage; that there was but one interest, one aim, one design, and all conspired to make both very happy. Roxana would have none of this. 'That is the thing I complain of', she retorted, 'the pretence of affection takes from a woman everything that can be called herself: She is to have no interest, no aim, no view, but all is the interest, aim and view of the husband. She is to be the passive creature.' It was no good for the suitor to try to tell a woman like Roxana how lucky were the wives of rich men. 'The women had nothing to do but to eat the fat and drink the sweet. . . . They had indeed much the easier part . . . spending what their husbands get.' Roxana did not want to lead the life of an idle drone, and suspected that her husband's power of the purse would give him power over her will.[158]

It was almost inevitable that the trend towards greater emotional and sexual freedom for elite women in the late seventeenth century should give rise for a while to a good deal of overt misogyny, as expressed in popular male fantasies. Thus one of the most successful plays of the period was Wycherley's *The Country Wife*, whose hero, or antihero, was that insatiable adulterer, Horner. But Horner was a prisoner of sex. He derived no sensual pleasure from his conquests, only sadistic satisfaction at the seduction and then betrayal of his victims: his gratification came from their private humiliation and public ruin. That for thirty years fashionable audiences should have found this sexual cruelty so attractive to see upon the stage indicates some of the tensions and anxieties aroused by the first tentative steps towards the greater liberation of women in the late seventeenth century.[159]

Another problem that led to much marital unhappiness was caused by the education given to wealthy children. The girls were brought up permissively at home by nurses and governesses and not taught to curb their tempers or their tongues. In infancy and youth, boys were spoiled at home by doting mothers, sisters, nurses and governesses. They were then packed off to the rough-and-tumble male world of public school and college, and so deprived of experience of female company, apart from lower-class prostitutes and tavern girls. The anonymous female author of a marriage manual for the upper-middle-class young girl, published in 1846, warned her of the shock she would experience when 'her delicate and shrinking nature discovers the real and intense coarseness of the male character.' This was not a discreet allusion to the brutality of the male sexual drive, but rather to masculine selfishness, desire for autocratic domestic authority, and contempt for common little politenesses in the treatment of a wife: 'the courtesies of life soon – too soon – after marriage are changed into a careless and fluctuating attention.' A young married woman was advised to obey her husband, even if under protest, not to cry, to put on a cheerful expression and not to complain, *never* to refer to 'the rights of women', to curb her tongue and to try to avoid a quarrel, not to criticize her husband's friends or relatives, not to keep him waiting, and to be neat and elegant without being over-scrupulously fussy. It is the advice of someone with fairly low expectations of marital behaviour from a husband, and it describes a world far removed from the notions of married life supplied by the romantic novels of the time. The general conclusion is that wives make husbands unhappy through 'perverse tempers and cold hearts' and that husbands make wives unhappy through 'careless neglect', tyranny and adultery (plate 15).[160]

It is symptomatic of unresolved problems in the more companionate marriage that in the second half of the eighteenth century many of both sexes still felt more at ease in the company of their own sex, evidence of which is the persistence of the custom of the withdrawal of the women from the dining-room to the drawing-room after dinner (plate 18). In the 1720s Swift remarked that 'it has sometimes moved me with pity to see the lady of the house forced to withdraw immediately after dinner, . . . as if it were an established maxim that women are incapable of all conversation.' He attributed this social custom to the inadequacies of female education, which left them uninterested in discussing anything but clothes. Even in the second half of the eighteenth century the custom persisted, despite the improvement in female education. One possible explanation is that it was customary in England for chamber-pots to be kept in the sideboards in the dining-room and for the men to relieve themselves openly while their companions went on drinking (plate 17). Under such circumstances it was clearly desirable for the women to withdraw, to use close-stools or chamber-pots elsewhere in the house. Another possible explanation was the reluctance of well-bred women to listen to masculine postprandial bawdy conversation and to participate in their heavy drinking. Whatever the cause, the facts are clear. In 1762 it was reported that 'their drawing-rooms are deserted and after dinner and supper the gentlemen are impatient till they retire.' Another commentator remarked that 'the gloom that hangs over an English company while the ladies remain, and the reciprocal restraint that each sex seems to be upon the other, has been frequently a subject of ludicrous observation to foreigners.' In the 1770s Mrs John Parker saw relatively little of her husband while they were in London, although they were only recently married. She breakfasted upstairs in her room, he downstairs in the breakfast-room. And later, 'Mr Parker likes to play his game of whist at Boodles almost every evening, so that I have nothing else to do.' At the Duke of Devonshire's seat at Woburn Abbey in 1820, a female member of the house-party reported that 'in the evening the men play at whist or billiards, and we sit in the saloon all very well together.'[161]

In the country, the isolation of the married couple exacerbated the situation. In 1712 Lady Mary Wortley Montagu observed that 'very few people that have settled entirely in the country but have grown at length weary of one another. The lady's conversation generally falls into a thousand impertinent effects of idleness; and the gentleman falls in love with his dogs and horses and out of love with everything else.' Half a century later, Mrs Montagu confirmed these generalizations. 'Man and wife should always have something to charge with their ennui; the impertinence of society bears the blame very well; in solitude they must accuse each other of all they suffer of it.' The miseries of female isolation in the countryside was a common theme of complaint in well-to-do circles in the eighteenth century. Many husbands spent their days in outdoor sports and the hunting field, and their evenings in male company 'drinking, playing at loo or cribbage, or talking scandal, news and ribaldry. . . . A play now and then at a distant town, some modern novels from the circulating library there, was all the country afforded; and thus heavily passed the leaden hours. . . . A trip to the county races or an assembly, was all they had to live upon in the pleasurable way.'[162]

Even in London, however, things were not much better among the wealthy citizens and landowners in the mid-eighteenth century, if John Shebbeare is to be believed. 'He passes his evening in the tavern in wine and smoking tobacco, she drinks her afternoon tea in chatting with her neighbour. At night they tumble into one bed together, he drenched with wine and stinking of tobacco.'[163]

A subject which still needs much further exploration is the way in which close female bonding persisted in the eighteenth century, parallel to the familiar bonding of the men. Males of the upper classes spent much of their waking hours at their work among men, and their leisure in all-male dining clubs and stag dinner parties. Their sanctums were the billiard-room, the smoking-room and the stables, and much of their time was spent with men, horses and dogs in the hunting-field. As we have seen, even the dining-room tended to become a male preserve, at any rate as soon as the main meal was finished. Female sanctums were the drawing-room and the boudoir, where they spent much of the day in feminine company, gossiping, doing needlework, playing cards, and exchanging endless visits. Many very close female friendships developed, closer in many cases than those with husbands. On the other hand, the ubiquitous and time-consuming habit of card-playing was a bisexual leisure activity, as was attendance at assembly-rooms, balls, masquerades, visits to the theatre and the performance of amateur theatricals at home. The development after about 1780 of the intellectual salons, hosted by a number of blue-stocking ladies and attended by the cultural elite of London, was a further step towards the social integration of the sexes at this somewhat exalted level. In 1765 Almack's Club was founded, which was open to members of high society of both sexes, the men elected by the women, and vice-versa. This was apparently the first bisexual private club in London. More important were the assembly-rooms, which were springing up in the mid-century in so many provincial towns, and which provided a meeting place for both sexes which had not previously existed, thus facilitating the new mating arrangements based on prior knowledge and affection. In 1760 Lady Mary Wortley Montagu was satisfied that 'the frequency of assemblies has introduced a more enlarged way of thinking; it is a kind of public education, which I have always thought as necessary for girls as for boys.'[164] There is therefore evidence that the sexes were mingling far more freely than before within the squirarchy, although the growth of exclusively male London clubs and the habit of ejecting the women from the dining-room after dinner remained as significant exceptions to this trend.

Among the lower middle class and the respectable poor, there is a little evidence to suggest that the separation of the sexes for leisure activities was perhaps even more prevalent than among the rich. In 1793 *The Matrimonial Magazine* described the plight of two neglected and lonely wives. The first was married to the chief clerk of a banker, who was so wholly absorbed in his work that 'he dined daily at the table of his master, from whose house he seldom returned home until a late hour'; the other was married to a painter who spent much time away, staying for weeks at a time in country houses painting the portraits of the owners. His weekends he spent in drunken carousals in taverns, instead of at home. The prevalence of male drunkenness in the eighteenth century tended to divide husband and wife, since 'a coarseness of thought and language was insensibly contracted, which ... made a wider separation in domestic intercourse between the sexes.' In 1829 William Cobbett commented adversely on the habit of French husbands spending their evenings in the cafés, leaving their wives at home, and complained that 'many English husbands indulge too much in a similar habit. Drinking clubs, smoking clubs, singing clubs, clubs of odd-fellows, whist clubs, sotting clubs ... innumerable are the miseries that spring from this cause', including the expense, the damage to health, and the abandonment of wives, forcing them into societies of their own sex.[165]

Another victim of change was the aged. The decline in patriarchy involved not only a loss of authority by the old, but also a philosophical re-evaluation of the role and value of old people generally. Old age had previously been highly respected as a stage of life's progression, during which weakening physical powers were compensated for by the accumulation of wisdom and dignity; it now came to be seen as a period of decay in all faculties, as the biological organism approached death. There was a running down, not only of physical powers, but also of intellectual and moral strengths. Folly and miserliness were now regarded as predominant characteristics of the old. Decay and death were no longer at the mercy of God's will, but could be postponed by a healthy regime and by medical intervention. Thus the old did not merely lose power as the patriarchs of the lineage, they also lost respect. The rise of alms-houses and of institutionalized poor-relief to look after them, suggests that their children were increasingly shedding responsibility for their support, and transferring it to the community at large. The fate of King Lear at the hands of his daughters foreshadowed a century of change and uncertainty in family and societal attitudes towards old people.[166] Finally, the growing independence of the nuclear group tended to destroy vertical family ties. In 1828 a foreign observer noted that 'grown-up children and parents soon become almost strangers, and what we call domestic life is therefore applicable only to husband, wife and little children living in immediate dependence on their father.'[167]

There are thus many reasons to believe that the institution of marriage was undergoing very severe stresses – perhaps even a major crisis – as a result of the profound changes in domestic relationships which were taking place at this time. Affective individualism brought costs as well as benefits.

CHAPTER 9

Parent-Child Relations

'The beast and bird their common charge attend
The mothers nurse it and the sires defend.
The young dismissed, to wander earth and air,
There stops the instinct and there ends the care.
A longer care man's helpless kind demands,
That longer care contracts more lasting bonds.'
(A.Pope, *An Essay on Man*, 1733, Epistle 3, lines 26–31.)

Slowly, at a pace which varied from class to class and from individual family
to individual family within each class, there took place in England between
about 1660 and 1800 a remarkable change in accepted child-rearing theory,
in standard child-rearing practices, and in affective relations between
parents and children. As early as 1697 a French visitor could detect that a
change was taking place, and that English children were being treated in an
extraordinarily affectionate manner.[1] The new attitude was at first strictly
to the middle ranks in the society, neither so high as to be too preoccupied
with pleasure or politics to bother with children, nor so low as to be too
preoccupied with sheer survival to be able to afford the luxury of
sentimental concern for them. As will be seen, by 1800 there were six
distinct modes of child-rearing practised by different social groups. This
chapter is devoted to the emergence of the only new one among the six, the
maternal, child-oriented, affectionate and permissive mode that came to
prevail among the upper ranks of the bourgeoisie and the squirarchy.

I THE CHILD-ORIENTED, AFFECTIONATE AND PERMISSIVE MODE

i. General Indicators of Change

a. *The Nature of the New-born Child*. There are four possible views about
the nature of the new-born child, the adoption of each of which profoundly

affects the way he is treated. The first, and most common, was the traditional Christian view, strongly reinforced by Calvinist theology, that the child is born with Original Sin, and that the only hope of holding it in check is by the most ruthless repression of his will and his total subordination to his parents, schoolmasters and others in authority over him. This religious view merely reinforced the current secular position that it is the duty of inferiors, like children, to give full obedience to superiors, like parents, and that early socialization in the need for such obedience and deference is an essential preparation for life in a strictly hierarchical society.

The second view was the environmentalist one, that a child is born with a propensity towards neither good nor evil, but is a *tabula rasa*, malleable and open to being moulded by experience. As early as 1628 the Anglican John Earle observed that 'the child is . . . the best copy of Adam before he tasted of Eve or the apple. . . . His soul is yet a white paper unscribbled with the observations of the world. . . . He knows no evil.'[2]

The third view was biological, that the character and potentialities of the child are genetically determined at conception, that there is little that subsequent environmental influence and educational efforts can do except to reinforce good habits and restrain bad ones. This view was of course fundamental to astrological theory, according to which both character and fate are largely determined by the configuration of the planets at the moment of birth (or possibly conception). But in practice seventeenth century parents do not seem to have acted on this assumption, despite their faith in astrology. They continued to break the will of children in the hope of remoulding character. It was a view which only began to affect child-rearing during the eighteenth century, and in 1744 Molly Lady Hervey wrote that children 'acquire arts but not qualities; the latter whether good or bad, grow like their features; time enlarges, but does not make them.' Education, she believed, is powerless to change nature, 'yet one may certainly help it.'[3]

The fourth view was utopian, that the child is born good and is corrupted only by his experience in society. This was an idea which had been propounded by some Renaissance humanists, but it had disappeared under the onslaught of the Calvinist doctrine of Original Sin. Early evidence of its re-emergence in England appears in connection with the 'noble savage' in Mrs Aphra Behn's play *Oroonoko* in 1688: 'God makes all things good: man meddles with them and they become evil.' The suggestion was ignored, until it was put forward with far greater publicity by Rousseau in the middle of the eighteenth century. Even then, however, it seems to have had little practical influence, although *Émile* was certainly widely read in England. In eighteenth-century England the environmental theory tended to supersede the Calvinist in middle- and upper-class circles, before it was overwhelmed again in the nineteenth century.

In 1693 John Locke gave wide currency to the second – 'piece of clean paper' – point of view in his extremely popular handbook of education. His book coincided with the overthrow of Divine Right monarchy, the rejection of the doctrine of Passive Obedience, the granting of limited religious toleration and the passage of the Bill of Rights. The general relaxation of deferential and hierarchical practices in society, as reflected in these political changes, combined with Locke's *Some Thoughts upon Education* to open the way for a new era in parent-child relations, and a much more relaxed and affectionate approach to the problems of child-rearing. The book was a success because the readership was already half prepared to accept its ideas. Its time had come.

Locke warned parents against excessive permissiveness, or 'fondness' as he called it, but he argued that education had to be a stage process adapted to the growing capacities and self-development of the child. At birth the infant is merely like an animal, without ideas or morals and ready to receive any imprint, but later, as he develops both a will and a conscience, the treatment of him has to change accordingly. 'Fear and awe ought to give you the first power over their minds, and love and friendship in riper years to hold it.' The result would be that 'you shall have him your obedient subject (as is fit) whilst he is a child, and your affectionate friend when he is a man.'[4] Locke was clearly not an apostle of childish autonomy and parental permissiveness, but he differed widely from those theorists earlier in the century who advised constant distance and coldness, and the enforcement of deference and obedience by the use of force. After infancy, he advocated psychological manipulation rather than physical coercion. This is a change the significance of which should not be underestimated by those who have never been subjected to the latter, and who are obsessed with the fashionable mirage of complete childhood autonomy as an ideal goal. He also thought that parental authority ceased once the children reached the age of discretion.

The Marquess of Halifax's *Advice to a Daughter* of 1688 was on the whole a very conservative document since it was addressed to the high aristocracy, but even it made major concessions to the new trend. 'You must begin early to make them love you that they may obey you,' he advised in his cool, cynical way. On the one hand, 'You are to have as strict a guard upon yourself amongst your children as if you were among your enemies'; on the other, 'the kind and severe parts must have their several turns seasonably applied, but your indulgence is to have the broader mixture, that love, rather than fear, may be the root of their obedience.'[5]

These two cautious pieces of advice, carefully balanced between the old repressive mode and the new more permissive one, heralded a series of changes in all aspects of child-rearing among the professional and upper classes in the late seventeenth and eighteenth centuries, beginning with the treatment of the child at birth and ending with the handling of his marriage. Even in the late eighteenth century, however, attitudes towards infants wavered uncertainly between the Locke and the Rousseau positions. In the 1770s Dr Arthur Collier believed that 'one loved one's children in anticipation, one hopes they will one day become useful, estimable and amiable beings. One cannot love lumps of flesh . . . and they are nothing better during infancy.' Dr Johnson – of all unlikely people – took the Rousseauesque view, that 'one cannot help wishing whilst one fondles a baby that it would never grow up to man's estate, but always remain an innocent and amiable creature.'[6] Under the new doctrine, which was repeatedly by a conservative handbook for upper-middle-class wives and mothers as late as 1846, 'happiness is the best moral atmosphere for children.' They should never be even slapped in infancy, never left for weeks at a time in the hands of nurses or servants, punished if at all only by the mother, and not bullied into premature intellectual training, being not ready for reading or writing before the age of five or even six. The basic philosophy of the new educational methods of the professional and landed classes was utterly different from that of the seventeenth century, and from that which still prevailed among other social classes both above, among the high aristocracy, and below, among the lower middle class and the poor. It was that eighteenth-century Enlightenment ideal, the Pursuit of Happiness. 'It is . . . truly important that the period of childhood should be a happy one, that the growth of mind and body should not be impeded by the dread of punishment, the snappish, irritating word. Many a child have I seen pining under this execrable treatment.'[7] By the time these words were written, in 1846, this ideology was well past its peak of popularity, and the number of pining children was on the rise again, even in the class the anonymous author was addressing.

b. Recognition of the Child. The earliest evidence of greater attention being paid to infants and children was the tendency in England, beginning in the late sixteenth century, to record upon tombs erected decades later children who died in infancy – represented as tiny images wrapped up in swaddling clothes – or in youth – represented as children holding skulls. At Tettenhall in Staffordshire there is an Elizabethan tomb surrounded by images of no fewer than ten dead babies. At Fulham a dead wife is seated holding a dead baby, both having perished in childbirth (plate 7). It is also very revealing that the omission from genealogies of very short-lived infants among children of the aristocracy is estimated to have fallen from fifteen per cent or more in the late sixteenth century to five per cent in the mid-eighteenth century to under one per cent by the early nineteenth century.[8] This cannot be entirely due to the improvement in record-keeping which is a feature of this period in all areas; it must also reflect a greater concern to register the existence on earth, however brief, of all infants born.

There is also evidence that, for the first time, parents were beginning to recognize that each child, even if it only lived for a few hours or days, had its own unique individuality. During the middle ages and the sixteenth century, it had been common practice to give a new-born child the same first name as an elder sibling, especially if it was the traditional name for the head of the family. The habit lingered on into the first half of the eighteenth century, and Edward Gibbon records that after his birth in 1737, 'so feeble was my constitution, so precarious my life, that in the baptism of my brothers, my father's prudence successively repeated my Christian name of Edward, that, in case of the departure of the eldest son, this patronymic appellation might still be perpetuated in the family.' More frequent in the seventeenth century was the practice of substitution, of giving a new-born son the same name as one who had recently died. When Sir Christopher Wandesford's eldest son Christopher died at the age of ten, the next child to be born a few months later was also named Christopher. Similarly when John Benjamin Wesley was born in 1703, both his names were those of elder brothers, who had died in 1699 and 1700.[9] So far as I am aware, this practice died out by the late eighteenth century, indicating a recognition that names were highly personal and could not be readily transferred from child to child.

Indications of the trend towards a more child-oriented society can be found in many different areas. Special clothing, however, does not seem to have been one of them.[10] Right through the seventeenth and eighteenth centuries middle- and upper-class boys passed through a critically important *rite de passage*, when they shifted out of the long frocks of their childhood into the breeches and sword-carrying of the adult world. Among the aristocracy in the seventeenth century this took place at about six or seven, the moment when they were transferred from the care of women to the care of men. It was a great moment for a child, 'to throw off the coats and write "man"'.[11] What happened in the early eighteenth century was that the change of clothing took place at an earlier and earlier age. Boys were dressed like their fathers from the age of three or four, girls like their mothers from the age of two. Young Henry Thrale was put into breeches at two and a quarter in 1769 – an unusually early age. Conservatives complained that 'even misses at whose age their mother wore the backstring and the like, assume the dress of womanhood.' So far as girls are concerned, loose, informal clothing was developed for young children after 1760, to become the standard style of adult clothing forty years later. 'Skeleton suits' for boys also developed after 1780, and in 1782 a German noted that 'free and natural dress is worn until they are eighteen or twenty.' As for working-class boys in the late eighteenth century, Francis Place recorded that 'there was then no taste displayed in the dress of boys, no attention to their convenience in this respect, and the ugly dress of an ill-dressed man was common to them.'[12] At all times, English children have either worn special clothes, or been dressed as miniature adults. The choice seems to have depended more on whims and fashions than on deep-seated psychological shifts in the attitude towards children.

There are, however, more revealing types of evidence than clothing to prove that the eighteenth century was a turning point in the recognition of childhood as a period with its own distinctive requirements. Other than chap-books for the poor, children's literature before the mid-eighteenth century had been highly didactic and unattractive in tone. Beginning with Comenius' *Orbis Pictus* of 1650 and running through John Bunyan's *Book for Boys and Girls* of 1686 and *The Pilgrim's Progress* of 1678 and James Janeway's *A Token for Children* of 1671, they had all been filled with stories threatening divine vengeance for sin. Abraham Chear's lines of 1678:

> 'Tis pity such a pretty maid
> As I should go to Hell

aptly summarize the theme of this early children's literature.[13]

The first jolly books and rhymes especially written for the sheer entertainment of middle- and upper-class children, as opposed to their moral improvement (plate 21), were the works of a remarkable publishing entrepreneur, John Newbery, who was the first of a series of professional writers specializing in literature for children. In 1742 he published *A Little*

Pretty Pocket Book, intended for the Instruction and Amusement of little Master Tommy and pretty Miss Polly, and *Tommy Thumb's Pretty Song Book*; *Mother Goose's Melody, or Sonnets for the Cradle* followed about sixteen years later. In 1751 the enterprising Newbery actually launched what seems to have been the first, though short-lived, children's magazine in English history, *The Lilliputian Magazine*, which was intended to impart information in a manner 'more agreeable and better adapted to the tender capacities of children.' Between 1750 and 1814 some twenty professional writers of children's books produced some 2,400 different titles. Parents were now willing to spend money to buy children's books that were totally lacking in moral implications and were merely to amuse (plate 22): a wholly new demand had given rise to a new industry to supply it. By 1800 there was a very large range of children's books, costing between a penny and sixpence, and therefore accessible to the humblest artisan who wished to indulge his children. Already, however, the Evangelical Revival was spreading its influence over children's books, some of which were again becoming more uplifting and more gloomy. 'Damn them – I mean the cursed Barbauld Crew – those blights and blasts of all that is human in man and child' vainly protested Charles Lamb.[14]

Educational games that combined instruction with fun were also introduced in the mid-eighteenth century, geographical jig-saws in 1762 and a geographical or travel game played with dice in 1759. This was the time when toy-shops were springing up in provincial towns, and were doing a brisk trade selling toys that were designed merely to give pleasure to the individual child, not to gratify its parents' desire for moral or educational improvement. It was now that dolls with changeable clothing and dolls' houses were first mass produced for a commercial market (plate 15). Apart from toy soldiers and forts – a German speciality – England led the way in Europe in the manufacture of toys in the eighteenth century, and by 1780 toy-shops were everywhere.[15] The commercialization of the supply of goods specially designed for children was obviously only made possible by social and economic developments which created a large upper- and lower-middle-class market of parents with money to buy such relative luxuries in quantity for their children. As today, status competition undoubtedly also played its part in stimulating demand.[16] But what is important is that large numbers of parents were now willing to pamper their children by buying them these frivolous toys and books. England was clearly moving towards a child-oriented family type.

By the middle of the eighteenth century, there is also visual artistic evidence of a growing solidarity between parent and children, as exemplified in the growing popularity of family portrait groups, no longer stiffly and formally posed, but with the children in postures and attitudes which indicate friendly and playful association with their parents. Sir Joshua Reynolds in particular specialized in portraits of mothers with young children in their lap or playing about them. The earliest seems to have been his portrait of Jane Lady Cathcart and her one-year-old daughter, painted in 1755, but in the next thirty years Reynolds painted at least fifteen more such groups of mothers with young children ranging from one year to nine.[17] These pictures by Reynolds, and others by Zoffany, J.S.Copley and others, are a genre especially popular in England in the late eighteenth century (end paper), although its origins lay in Dutch bourgeois art of the seventeenth century. In England, as nowhere else in Europe, it was adopted and adapted by the landed classes, and additional stress was put on physical and psychological intimacy. In eighteenth-century England, this is an art form patronized not by the bourgeoisie, but by the squirarchy and nobility. It was all very well for Thackeray in 1848 to sneer at these romping family groups embalmed for posterity on the walls of country houses. 'Some few score years afterwards, when all the parties represented have grown old, what bitter satire there is in those flaunting childish family-portraits, with their farce of sentiment and smiling lies, and innocence so self-conscious and self-satisfied.'[18] Maybe so, but this is how eighteenth-century noblewomen, and even noblemen, wanted themselves to be remembered – as affectionate, even doting, mothers and fathers – and in many cases, as we shall see, the reality approximated to the ideal.

c. From Deference to Respect. Other evidence of the change in attitude, this time as it affected both young and adolescent children, is provided by the fading away of those symbolic acts of deference, the kneeling, the standing, the doffing of the hat in the parents' presence, which were so noticeable in the sixteenth and early seventeenth centuries. As early as 1663 Richard Allestree, in his widely read *Whole Duty of Man*, was condemning parents 'who think they must never appear to their children but with a face of sourness and austerity.' It is always dangerous to use the argument *in absentia* in history, since the void may be caused by chance destruction of documents or by the ignorance of the researcher, but I know of little evidence for the persistence of overt marks of deference to parents into the middle of the eighteenth century. The only known examples are recorded as exceptions to the norm. In the early 1720s the first Duke of Kingston, now a very old man, barged his way into the dressing-room of his married daughter Lady Mary Wortley Montagu. Lady Mary's little daughter, who was playing in the room at the time, recalled years later that 'to my great surprise, Lady Mary instantly starting up from the toilet table, dishevelled as she was, fell on her knees to ask his blessing. A proof that even in this great and gay world this primitive custom was still universal.' Another example, the late eighteenth-century Dean Shipley of St Asaph who 'never permitted his daughter to sit down in his presence', was now generally regarded as an anachronistic freak.[19] The first categorical statement of the new parent-child relationship came from John Locke in the late seventeenth century when he wrote: 'he that would have his son have a respect for him and his orders, must himself have a great reverence for his son.' Locke was a bachelor and a philosopher, who did not have to put his ideas to the test of practice, but this is nonetheless a very remarkable observation. It is very unlikely that such a statement could have been made at any previous period, and even now it was in advance of its time. Conservatives naturally viewed such novelties with alarm, and in 1700 one complained that 'the expressions of outward honour from children to parents by the dissoluteness of the age are almost out of fashion, viz., to bow before them and desire their blessing or prayers.' A century later, in about 1800, Mrs Catherine Mary Howard explained the change as an evitable concomitant of the greater familiarity of parents with their children. 'When children, like ours, live much with parents ... there is no longer that very great distance observed ... which engendered fear and was the bane of confidential intercourse.'[20]

Scotland was naturally well behind England in abandoning the traditional behaviour, which could therefore still be recollected in 1813 by Thomas Somerville, who was born in 1741. He remembered the time when 'austerity ... in the treatment of the young was not confined to schools but was the rule also in the family – parents keeping their children, even when grown to mature years, at a great distance and exacting from them a ceremonious attention to the forms of outward respect.' In 1797 President John Witherspoon of Princeton College, an émigré representing Scottish Enlightenment ideas in the New World, protested that 'many a free-born subject is kept a slave for the first ten years of his life....' 'Let them romp and jump about,' he urged. 'I would recommend every expression of affection and kindness to children, when it is safe, that is to say, when their behaviour is such as to deserve it.'[21]

Modes of address from children to parents also support belief in a major change in personal relationships among the squirarchy and upper bourgeoisie. As we have seen, the early seventeenth-century convention was stiff, formal and deferential, parents being addressed as 'Sir' and 'Madam'. In the 1720s, however, the young John Verney, away at school for the first time, began his letters to his father with 'Dear Pappy' or 'Dear Papa', and referred to his mother as 'dear Mamma'. Sir Richard Steele said of his five-year-old son, 'we are very intimate friends and playfellows', and told his daughters, 'my soul is wrapped up in your welfare.' By 1778, at the height of this trend to affectionate parent-child relations, the Countess of Bristol could talk ecstatically about her 'little fairies... bleating... that dear word "Mamma"'. By that time this new mode was seeping down to the upper bourgeoisie, and in 1774 *The Lady's Magazine* published a (probably fictitious) letter from a merchant's daughter complaining that her friends were shunning her because she would not stop addressing her parents as 'father' and 'mother', and start calling them by 'the pretty delicate names of papa and mama'. She expressed her mock fear that 'father' and 'mother' would soon disappear from the dictionaries as 'merely obsolete words'.[22]

Among the landed elite, the current modes of address to parents became more and more extravagantly affectionate at the height of romanticism in the early years of the nineteenth century. In 1814 Lady Caroline Capel addressed her mother, the Countess of Uxbridge, as 'Dearest, best and kindest of mothers', and signed herself 'your most devoted, affectionate, and dutiful....' Fred Douglas as a schoolboy at Westminster in 1801, and later on the Grand Tour, was clearly devoted to his mother Lady Glenbervie (who, when he was a child, had taught him his elementary maths), and the affection was warmly reciprocated. In 1780 the Earl of Pembroke, eccentric and difficult though he was, nevertheless began his letters to his eldest son with 'Dear George,' and ended them with 'ever most affectionately yours, my dearest George.' Five years earlier the Countess was beginning her letters with 'My dear George', and ending them with 'your most affectionate mother', sometimes adding a revealing little domestic touch, such as the closing remark that 'The dear little Charlotte is now waiting with impatience for my finishing my letter, to read a story to me.'[23]

On the other hand, families varied very widely in the modes of address between children and parents, and generalizations from the particular are very dangerous in this regard. In 1737 Elizabeth Robinson at the age of eighteen still addressed her parents as 'Sir' and 'Madam', and in 1747 her brother Matthew, a Cambridge undergraduate, addressed his father as 'Honoured Sir'. In 1759 Dr Johnson addressed his dying mother, to whom he was greatly attached, as 'Honoured Madam', and 'Dear Honoured

Mother'. But these seem to be exceptions to a more casually affectionate eighteenth-century norm. At the very end of the eighteenth century, however, the tide was slowly beginning to turn again, and in 1799 Richard Thackeray was addressing his parents as 'Pater' and 'Mater'.[24] These new Latin words do not preclude affection, but they certainly suggest affectation, if not renewed formality, and their popularity was to grow enormously in the course of the nineteenth century.

These changes in overt marks of deference and modes of address are symbolic of a major shift in parent-child relations. But this relaxation of manners did not necessarily imply very much weakening in belief in the obligation of children to obey their parents, except over the (admittedly crucial) issue of choice of a spouse. Defoe, who was in many ways in the vanguard of change, still harped on the need for filial piety and obedience, and he makes Robinson Crusoe admit that his original sin for which God punished him was his failure to obey parental advice.[25]

d. Growth of Contraception. Another piece of evidence of increased concern for the child as an individual is the beginning after about 1675 of contraceptive practices among the upper classes. In the sixteenth century, the upper classes had a higher rate of fertility than the lower. But between 1675 and 1775 there took place a striking decline in the fertility of the children of the nobility, just at the time when mortality was rising (Graphs 8 and 10). As a result, for a time they brought their effective generation replacement rate (the number of children reaching the age of fifteen relative to the number of adults) below the zero population growth level of 1·0. The rate fell from 1·6 in 1550–99 to 0·8 in 1700–25, rising again to 1·4 in the late eighteenth century.[26]

Causes: What induced late seventeenth-century and early eighteenth-century upper-class women and men to want to reduce the size of their families? There are four conditions to be fulfilled before contraception will be practised in a society. In the first place, it must be theologically and morally acceptable both to make planned choices rather than to trust to the will of God, and to regard sexual pleasure within marriage as a legitimate aspiration without relation to the objective of reproduction. So long as the officially accepted view remained that of Tertullian that 'to prevent a child being born is to commit homicide in advance', and so long as the story of Onan in the Book of Genesis was used as evidence of God's vengeance on those who defied this rule, there could be no prospect of any change. In any case, sixteenth- and seventeenth-century Puritans (and Anglicans) had four distinct objections to marital birth control. First, it violated God's injunction to be fruitful and multiply; second, children were a blessing of God, and fecundity was God's will; third, it would, especially if practised by Puritans, reduce the number of the Elect in the next generation; and lastly, childbirth brought honour to women and aided them to achieve salvation.[27]

The liberation of sexuality in the eighteenth century from the constraints of theology is evidence that the self and its satisfactions were now being regarded as of prime importance, even if the individual remained no more than a small cog in the huge biological machine of Nature. Few upper-class English families had reached this position before the late seventeenth century, and the attitude of helpless resignation of Mrs Alice Thornton in the 1660s was still the norm, even if her piety was of an extreme variety. After seven attempts, in 1662 she at last satisfied her husband by producing a healthy male heir, and would clearly have been more than content to have ceased childbearing then. But she endured two more painful and difficult – and futile – childbirths before her final liberation by the death of her husband. When she found she was pregnant for the ninth time at the age of forty-one in 1667, when she was in very poor health, she commented revealingly: 'if it had been good in the eyes of my God, I should much rather ... not have been in this condition. But it is not a Christian's part to choose anything of this nature, but what shall be the will of our heavenly Father, be it never so contrary to our own desires.'[28] Until conscious family planning became theologically acceptable, no progress could be made in moving to a contraceptive society. It was not until the eighteenth century that the pleasure principle began to be clearly separated from the procreative function, both in theological tracts and in the minds of husbands and wives. Well into the seventeenth century, however, the idea that sexual intercourse within marriage was only legitimate if it led to conception, modified though it was by the concession that another end was mutual comfort, was so deeply embedded in the internalized value system of most women, especially pious women, that deliberate contraceptive practices were unacceptable to them. Up to a certain point, the higher the cultural level the greater the exposure to ideas of sexual resignation. As a result of the successful christianization of the household, the sixteenth and seventeenth centuries saw the development of a lay, private, internalized morality of sexual asceticism, which spread widely in the middle and upper classes. No change was possible until this morality began to break down. The 'mutual comfort' argument might possibly lead a pious Puritan couple to continue sexual activity during pregnancy in defiance of theological advice, but it would not permit deliberate contraceptive practices like oral or manual sex or *coitus interruptus*. But by separating pleasure from procreation, however tentatively and guardedly, Protestant theology opened the way for a new, more positive attitude towards contraception as its unintended legacy to the secularized world of the eighteenth century.[29]

Secondly, husbands must begin to share in the anxieties and sufferings of their wives, subjected to the agonies and dangers of repeated pregnancies and painful childbirths, and to desire to help them. It was not enough for the wives themselves to begin to be willing to take positive steps to limit pregnancies, since what is assumed to have been the most widely practised method, *coitus interruptus*, depends on extraordinary measures of self-control on the part of the husband. By the middle of the century the ancient Biblical teaching about the sin of Oman and God's punishment of him had so far lost its strength that in Puritan Massachusetts in 1771 a young man accused in a paternity suit could openly claim in court (unsuccessfully) that he had practiced *coitus interruptus*: 'I fucked her once, but I minded my pullbacks.'[29] The companionate marriage thus helped to spread the desire for contraception from the wife to the husband.[30]

Thirdly, and equally importantly, contraception will only develop where there is a clear economic incentive to reduce births, that is where the cost of bringing up and launching a child into the world exceeds the profit to be gained from his free labour in his youth, and from his support for his parents in their old age. It is significant that the first groups in Europe to practise contraception within marriage were the aristocracy and the urban elite, who did not depend on their children for labour in the fields or shop, or for support in their old age, and who were the first to experience the rising costs of education and marriage. They were, therefore, the class with the most to gain and the least to lose by restricting births. The decline of kin responsibility for welfare threw a greater burden for the economic upkeep of children upon the father, and therefore increased his incentive to restrict numbers.

The same egocentric motives could also apply lower down the social scale, and in 1727 Defoe thought it necessary to condemn the prevalence among married women of the lower bourgeoisie without servants of 'this aversion for children, to nauseate the nursing, the watching, the squalling, the fatigue of bringing up children, which, as they call it, makes a woman a slave and a drudge all her days.' The objection to children here was apparently not only their economic cost, but also their interference with personal pleasure. This motive was felt particularly strongly by fashionable women, who resented periodic interference in their life of pleasure by the burdens and pains of pregnancy. There were always women in high society who felt like the Countess of Westmorland in 1801. 'She is again breeding, which greatly vexes her, for she hates children.' By then, however, many of her contemporaries were taking active measures to avoid this situation.

Few found it necessary to go to the lengths of the wife of the first Earl Talbot in the 1760s. After she had given birth to one child, 'declaring that she would never go through the operation a second time, she insisted upon a separation.' Lady Talbot evidently had no knowledge of or confidence in contraceptive measures – and presumably a low sex drive.[31]

The fourth factor necessary for the spread of contraception is, paradoxically enough, the development of a more child-oriented society. It is more likely to be practised if children are regarded as valuable individuals in their own right. So long as the futures of younger sons and of daughters are not a matter of primary concern to their parents, it does not matter too much how many there are. But once serious trouble has to be taken over their nurturance, maintenance, education, and launching into the world, they become competitors for a number of scarce resources, and any increase in numbers reduces the investment in quality per child. The decision to limit births is thus partly the result of a cost-benefit analysis, a trade-off between known parental resources and anticipated costs in both time spent by the mother in rearing and money spent by the father on education. It is also partly one of preference, the balance between the value placed on children as against other goods, especially that of the personal pleasures of the parents and of conspicuous consumption. Contraception is therefore only likely to happen in a child-oriented society in which bringing up the child and launching him into the world is becoming so burdensome in its demands for love, time, effort and money, that some reduction in numbers is highly desirable.[32] The issue became a live one in the late seventeenth century as the cost of girls' marriage portions rose, and came out into the open in Sedley's play *Bellamira* in 1687. Merryman promised his future wife that: 'we will have two beds, for I will not come home drunk and get girls, without I know where to get portions for them. In this age they sour and grow stale upon their parents' hands.' A character in a play of 1705 by Richard Steele complained bitterly that 'the war has fetched down the price of women; the whole nation is overrun with petticoats. Our daughters lie upon our hands. ... Girls are drugs, sir, mere drugs.'[33]

The seriousness of this problem at this particular time can be demonstrated from two examples, one from the middle class and one from the
aristocracy. The Reverend Ralph Josselin was vicar of Earl's Colne, for
some years served as schoolmaster at the local school, and was also the owner
of a significant amount of farmland; all of which brought him the modest
income of around £160 a year between 1641 and 1683. Of his total expenses
over this forty-two-year period, including the purchase of land, no less than
one-third went on the rearing, education and marriage of his ten children,
only five of whom lived to survive their parents. A third of this money was
wasted, in the sense that it was spent on children who did not live to enjoy an
adult life span.[34]

Another – admittedly extreme – example of the high cost of children in
the late seventeenth century is the arrangements made by the third Earl of
Salisbury for the provision of his ten surviving children. He died in 1683
with a gross income of £12,200 a year, out of which he set aside about half in
order to provide them all with handsome life annuities plus enormous cash
legacies. He thus effectively crippled the estate and impoverished the family
for decades to come.[35] Such affectionate generosity towards children could
only be tolerated if their numbers were limited. The other alternative,
adopted in many families, was severely to restrict expenditure on younger
sons and to leave a number of daughters unmarried, which permitted a
greater concentration of economic assets on the male heir.

It has very plausibly been argued that it was the rise in standards of
consumption for the maintenance of status, coupled with the rising costs
and duration, and the long delay in the rewards, of professional middle-class
education for boys in the middle of the nineteenth century which caused the
massive adoption of contraception by those classes at that time. These
parents could not afford to launch more than a limited number of children
into the world if they were to maintain the living standards to which they
had become accustomed. Because they were determined not to sacrifice
their children to the risks of downward social mobility, they were forced
either to beggar themselves to provide them with a lengthy and expensive
education, or else to adopt stringent contraceptive measures so as to reduce
the burden of numbers. By a fortunate coincidence, the technology of
mechnical contraception was improving at this time, information about it
was being more widely spread, and Darwinian ideas of the relation of man to
nature made its use morally acceptable.[36] Before these developments took
place towards the middle of the nineteenth century, however, there was a
severe crisis of overproduction in some middle-class families. In a semi-

fictional autobiography published in 1831, there is recorded the response of a professional parent of the late eighteenth century to an excess of children: 'Malthus had not yet enlightened the world. Every succeeding year he reluctantly registered in the family bible the birth of a living burthen. He cursed my mother's fertility.... He grew gloomy and desponding', as the economic cost of the children began to crush him.[37]

A concrete example of the enormous pressure of educational costs on an upper-middle-class parent in the early nineteenth century is provided by the case of the Reverend John Skinner of Camerton. For a period of about five years, from 1823–28, one son was passing through Winchester and Oxford, another through Winchester and Sandhurst, while the daughter was at a fashionable boarding-school for young ladies. Over this five-year period they were costing him between £400 and £500 a year, the equivalent of the total income from his church living. Worse still, it was money wasted, since one boy dropped out of Oxford and the other was more or less expelled from Sandhurst with no hope of obtaining an army commission, so that they both ended up idling away several years at home without an occupation or a future. He lamented, 'How difficult it was now for a young man to procure any situation in a respectable line of life, especially with the little interest and money I had to push him with,' and regretted the thousands of pounds he had wasted on the boys' education to no purpose.[38] But the story illustrates the connection between fewer children and better cared for, better educated, and more deeply loved children.

For a child-oriented society to develop, however, it is essential that children should be less liable to sudden and early death than they were in the early sixteenth or again in the seventeenth and early eighteenth centuries. To use the language of the economists, the value of children rises as their durability improves – although at the same time their maintenance cost also rises. There is reason to believe that the last two-thirds of the sixteenth century was a period of relatively low infant and child mortality rates, although the rates rose again sharply in the seventeenth and early eighteenth centuries.[39] One could hypothesize that the sixty years of low child mortality may have given an impetus to the growth of a new respect for, and attention to, children, which could not be arrested by a fresh relapse into the old pattern of high mortality rates in the seventeenth century. The attitude survived into the new era of sustained decline in infant and child mortality, which seems to have begun in about 1750. It was perhaps this renewed fall which provided the final stimulus for the eventual development of the permanently child-oriented, and increasingly contraceptive, family type.

Moral theology, economics, affect between spouses, and care for children were thus all involved in the growth of contraception among the elite.[40]

For those lower down the social scale, the husbandmen, artisans, small tradesmen on the one hand, and the poor cottagers and common labourers on the other, the critical variable was probably not any change in attitude towards pleasure or consumption, but a balance between two purely economic considerations. On the one hand, everyone recognized that the time would come when, if they survived, they would be unable to work at the craft or in the field, and they and their wives would need to be provided with a pension if they were not to fall into complete destitution. Given the high mortality rates of the age, five or six children would be needed to guarantee that one breadwinner would survive to look after the parents in their old age. According to this hypothesis, the supply of a cheap labour force from the children when adolescents and the expectation that they would provide a pension for the parents in their old age were the prime reasons for multiple procreation. This second incentive only works, however, for those with the foresight to look far ahead, with sufficient property, house-space and current income to be able to raise the children without economic hardship, and with the confidence of being able to place them in a situation where they will be able to afford a pension for their aged parents. In practice this means the husbandmen and small yeomen, and relatively prosperous artisans and small traders. For the propertyless, however, the cottagers and common labourers, the economic balance was different. In bad years, when the harvest failed and food prices were high, they could not afford to feed their children, while in their cramped two-room houses children were a nuisance and always underfoot. They did not cultivate land on a large enough scale to be able to put the children to useful employment, and the future job prospects were such that there was no reasonable expectation that the children would be in any position to look after their parents in their old age. Their houses would be too small to accommodate them, and their incomes too marginal and precarious to have any surplus with which to feed and clothe them. Except in clothing areas, where children from the age of four could earn their keep, the very poor had, therefore, no incentive to have many children. They procreated extensively, partly because of social tradition, and partly for lack of forethought and self-control. But semi-deliberate neglect and deliberate abandonment of infants kept the mortality rate very high, and so reduced the numbers of the survivors. All the evidence available suggests that despite their high fecundity and lack of contraception, the very poor had fewer surviving children than those who owned property. High infant mortality was caused by high marital fertility, as well as vice-versa.[41]

Methods: Just how this reduction of births was achieved is not known for certain, but since sexual abstention is unlikely, except by the very poor suffering from malnutrition and physical exhaustion, it is presumed that the principal means was *coitus interruptus*, assisted no doubt by oral, manual and anal sex. One would have supposed that these are techniques which each generation can think up for itself, without the need for transmission of information. But in eighteenth-century France, they were called *'funestes secrets,'* and in 1590 the Vicar of Weaverham in Cheshire was denounced as 'an instructor of young folks how to commit the sin of adultery or fornication and not beget or bring forth children.'[42] So *coitus interruptus* is perhaps a learned technique, transmitted by culture. In any case the practice of non-procreative sex acts and the deliberate increase of intercourse during non-procreative periods such as pregnancy, depended on the rejection of religious controls over sexuality in the eighteenth century. There are hints in Boswell's diaries that both were happening. Elizabethan cookbooks, herbals and medical treatises contain a wide variety of suggestions for limiting births. One suggested technique was to reduce sexual desire by violent vomits, purges or bloodletting until the patient felt too sick or weak for sex; another was to apply a variety of ointments to the penis to prevent an erection. Some treatises recommended vaginal douches, the effectiveness of which is unknown.[43] The exotic nature of the remedies, however, and their burial in obscure medical treatises, suggests that they had little practical utility, and were little employed.

Condoms first appeared in the late seventeenth century, but did not become common until the early eighteenth. Even then they were hard to find outside London, and were apparently reserved largely – though probably not entirely – for extra-marital affairs as protection against venereal disease. Thus a London advertiser of the sale of condoms in 1776 referred to them as 'implements of safety which secure the health of my customers', and another referred to the shop as the place where 'all gentlemen of intrigue may be supplied with those bladder policies or implements of safety, which infallibly secure the health of our customers.' It seems clear that in the eighteenth century the contraceptive function of the condom was at best secondary, and that its primary purpose was protection against venereal disease. James Boswell used them frequently, but only on one occasion for contraceptive purposes. When he was sleeping with a woman about whose health he felt reasonably secure, he preferred to promise to look after any possible child. In 1847 Mauriceau admitted that the original purpose of the condom was 'to obviate the penalty incurred by prostitution and thereby guard against the contraction of syphilis.' Although Richard Carlile claimed in 1825 that the vaginal sponge and the sheath had been used by the English aristocracy to reduce their marital fertility for at least the previous century, there is no positive evidence that these methods were indeed in common use among upper-class married couples in the eighteenth century. On the other hand, an early nineteenth-century doctor stressed that he was marketing condoms exclusively for the purpose of contraception within marriage, not to encourage extra-marital debauchery.[44]

The only other methods of restricting births were medicines offered for sale in London in the eighteenth century both for contraceptive and for abortifacient purposes. One can safely discount the efficacy of recipes for the former purpose, as advertised by an early eighteenth-century London quack: 'If the party... would not conceive, take one paper of powders in a glass of warm ale, every morning after the man has been with her, and she shall be out of danger.' More effective may perhaps have been the recipe advertised as follows: 'If she is quick with child and desires to miscarry take two papers of the powders here enclosed, night and morning... taking it twice shall bring away the conception.' The abortionist surgeon and the chemical abortionist's shop certainly existed, and were resorted to by some unmarried pregnant women. One such shop is illustrated in a contemporary engraving of 1753 where the shopkeeper is busy peddling bottles of medicine and 'Hooper's Female Pills'.[45] It seems unlikely that either these desperate chemical remedies or surgical intervention were resorted to by more than a minority, although the traditional methods of inducing abortion by hot baths, heavy purges, jumping off tables and galloping on horseback were no doubt more frequently attempted, with varying results.

Two examples of early nineteenth-century efforts at abortion will serve to illustrate the point. Mary, wife of the second Lord Alderley, had a quiverful of children who were already a severe strain on her husband's resources, when in 1847 she found herself pregnant again. She hastened to inform her husband, who was appalled. 'This your last misfortune is indeed most grievous and puts all others in the shade. What can you have been doing to account for so juvenile a proceeding: it comes very opportunely to disturb all your family arrangements. . . . I only hope it is not the beginning of another flock, for what to do with them I am sure I know not. I am afraid, however, it is too late to mend, and you must make the best of it, tho' bad is best.' But he wholly underestimated his wife's resourcefulness, for she wrote to him triumphantly the same day: 'A hot bath, a tremendous walk, and a great dose have succeeded; but it is a warning.' The next day she added reassuringly that 'I was sure you would feel the same horror I did at an increase of family, but I am reassured for the future by the efficacy of the means.' This pious Victorian lady, who devoted twenty years of her life to her children, clearly saw nothing whatever wrong in inducing an abortion. Others, however, were not so lucky, and when Mary Downall fell very ill in 1807 it was suspected that 'she took something when pregnant of her little girl, intended to fall on the child, and it has light on herself.' Abortion recipes clearly were not uncommon in the early nineteenth century, however doubtful their safety and effectiveness.[46]

ii. Changes in Child-rearing Practices

a. From Swaddling to Freedom. Sometime during the eighteenth century swaddling, like so many other traditional child-rearing practices, began to be abandoned in England. Swaddling goes back at least to Roman times, but in the late eighteenth century, both moral and medical advice in England and America was beginning to turn against it. At the end of the seventeenth century, Locke objected strongly to tight-laced stays, and had his doubts about swaddling. 'The child has hardly left the mother's womb, it has hardly begun to move and stretch its limbs when it is deprived of its freedom. It is wrapped in swaddling bands, laid down with its head fixed, its legs stretched out, and its arms by its sides, it is wound round and round with linen and bandages of all sorts, so that it cannot move.' In the 1740s Richardson's *Pamela* took Locke to be attacking swaddling directly, while strong criticisms were levelled in France by Rousseau in *Émile* and by Buffon in his *Histoire Naturelle de l'Homme*, so that complaints by intellectuals and moralists are spread over almost a hundred years.[47]

It is one thing for moralists, and even doctors, to preach, and quite another for mothers to put their advice into practice. The speed with which the new advice was followed in England is still not clear. In 1707 Mme de Maintenon expressed her approval of the English habit of removing the bands after three months, so that already England may have been in advance of the continent, at any rate in reducing the duration of the swaddling. Moreover it seems to be generally admitted that the practice was on its way out during the third quarter of the century. In 1762 Rousseau stated that in England it was already 'almost obsolete', and in 1785 *The Lady's Magazine* thought that most of its readers would not even know how it was done. The most influential books on the subject in England were the two enormously popular works on child care by Dr William Cadogan, published in 1748 (ten editions in the next twenty-five years), and Dr William Buchan, published in 1769 (twenty editions in the next fifty years). Dr Cadogan presented to the fashionable mother a horrific picture of how her infant was being handled by the wet-nurse in the village, while she enjoyed herself in town. 'At the least annoyance which arises, he is hung from a nail like a bundle of old clothes and while, without hurrying, the nurse attends to her business, the unfortunate one remains thus crucified. All who have been found in this situation had a purple face, the violently compressed chest not allowing the blood to circulate. . . . The patient was believed to be tranquil because he did not have the strength to cry out.' Twenty years later, Dr Buchan denounced in no uncertain terms the way 'the poor child, as soon as it came into the world, had as many rollers and wrappers applied to its body as if every bone had been fractured in the birth.' He admitted, however, that by now 'in several parts of Britain the practice of rolling children with so many bandages is now in some measure laid aside', an observation which was also supported by Jonas Hanway in 1762. By the end of the century the standard advice was to let infants exercise early and use their legs.[48]

In 1784 von Archenholz was surprised to find that in England 'the children are not swaddled . . . they are covered with light clothing, which leaves all their movements free', and a year later an English doctor agreed that 'the barbarous custom of swathing children like living mummies is now almost universally laid aside.' In 1821 Lady Morgan was shocked by the practice of tight swaddling used by the Italians, and noted that it had been unheard of in England for many years. The upper classes in France began to abandon the habit in the second half of the eighteenth century, but the change did not begin to affect lower-class customs before 1850. In nineteenth-century France, parents had the option of the traditional swaddling or 'the English manner.'[49] England would thus seem to have been far in advance of the rest of Europe in abandoning a practice which had been standard throughout Europe for millennia and was to persist well into the nineteenth century through most of the rest of western Europe, and into the twentieth century in Russia.

Once again, one can only speculate about the true causes of this precocious change in eighteenth-century English child-rearing practices, but it falls into line with other similar changes at the time, all tending to the liberation of the infant and the child. These changes are symptoms of a profound shift of attitudes towards family life in general, and towards children in particular. One of the most significant results of swaddling is that it prevents the mother or wet-nurse from cuddling, hugging and caressing the child. It seems clear, therefore, that the change came about for ideological rather than scientific reasons, for the benefit of the parents rather than the infants. Recent research has shown that swaddled children are indeed more tranquil, sleeping a lot, crying little, and with reduced cardiac and respiratory rates, and that there is little evidence of later physical or mental retardation due to the lack of early stimuli. Swaddling was condemned in England since it was seen as an assault on human liberty, and its early disappearance there and in America, and its survival in Russia and elsewhere into the twentieth century, must be explained on grounds of different cultures and different political, social and psychological ideals.[50] The arguments of Drs Cadogan and Buchan were not as scientifically proven as they pretended, nor those of Locke and Richardson as ethically incontrovertible as they believed.

b. From Wet-nursing to Maternal Breast-feeding. In Early Modern Europe, breast-feeding seems usually to have lasted between one year and eighteen months, and it was therefore a severe burden on a mother. The time may have shortened later, for in the middle of the eighteenth century James Nelson alleged that 'the present fashion . . . is to let children suck only three or four months', although he strongly advised six to twelve months, with nine as the ideal.[51]

Although doctors had always advised against it, it had long been the custom of upper-class mothers to put children out to paid wet-nurses.[52] There were many reasons for this practice. Many mothers were unable to produce an adequate milk supply, either because of exhaustion and sickness after childbirth or because of some congenital defect, or possibly because of psychological hostility towards the child. For others it was a painful process for the nipples, and in any case it was always a nuisance interfering with sleep, and the normal round of social engagements. As Aphra Behn pointed out in 1682 in a satirical account of marriage, handing an infant over to a wet-nurse 'means both you and your wife are freed from tossing and tumbling with it in the night', or being disturbed at teething time when it 'bawls and cries so night and day.'[53] Breast-feeding was a task entirely without social prestige, and many mothers were afraid that it would impair the shape of their 'pretty breasts, firm nipples, round and smooth', and, therefore, their sexual attractiveness. In the sixteenth century, Stephen

Guazzo complained that mothers would 'rather pervert the nature of their children' (through imbibing bad moral qualities through nurses' milk) 'than change the form of their firm, hard and round paps.'[54] The compelling reason for this practice, however, lay elsewhere. In the early seventeenth century William Gouge, and in the middle of the eighteenth James Nelson, both thought that it was the insistence of the husbands rather than the desire of the wives which was the main reason for the employment of wet-nurses: 'Many a tender mother... is prevented by the misplaced authority of a husband.'[55] This was partly so that the child at the breast would not be a competitor for his wife's attention, but mainly so that he could continue to have access to her sexual services, since according to Galen, who was followed by sixteenth and seventeenth-century doctors, husbands ought not to sleep with nursing wives since 'carnal copulation... troubleth the blood, and so by consequence the milk.' This ancient dogma was only mildly questioned by François Mauriceau, who noticed that the infants of the poor were suckled by mothers who 'lie every night with their husbands', and did not seem to be any the worse for it.[56] But the idea died hard, and there can be little doubt that wealthy fathers insisted on sending their children out to wet-nurse so that they would not be deprived of the regular sexual services of their wives for months or years on end. This was also a reason why kings and noblemen took the wet-nurse into their own house, so that sexual access to her by her husband could be effectually prevented. Henri IV of France dismissed a wet-nurse of his child merely because she was seen to be talking with her husband. In 1743, when Elizabeth Montagu dismissed the wet-nurse of her child after a year, she remarked that she 'will soon be restored to her husband.' As late as 1792, when the practice was already dying out, Mary Wollstonecraft still thought that desire for sexual relations by the fathers was the main reason for the survival of wet-nursing: 'There are many husbands so devoid of sense and parental affection that, during the first effervescence of voluptuous fondness, they refuse to let their wives suckle their children.' In 1829 William Cobbett blamed the sensuality of the mothers themselves, and their desire 'to hasten back, unbridled and undisfigured, to these enjoyments.'[57] What evidence he had for this assertion, however, is not stated.

The practice of using mercenary wet-nurses was consequently maintained by wealthy women, despite physiological difficulties and in the teeth of criticism from doctors and moralists. The principal technical problem was how to prevent the breasts from becoming painfully engorged with milk if the infant was not allowed to suck them. One early eighteenth-century solution was apparently to get an adult to suck them instead. Thus, in 1712 a Manchester wig-maker drained the breasts of his aunt, and that he did it with his mouth is proved by his comment: 'I'm dry, but will not drink till I've sucked her. I did so, then I ate breakfast well.'[58]

More formidable, but for centuries equally ineffective, was medical and moral advice. In the early seventeenth century the most popular and influential Puritan writers on household management, Perkins, Gouge, and Cleaver and Dod, strongly reinforced the traditional advice of the medical profession, and advised mothers to feed their own children. They used the functional argument that nature had provided women with breasts to supply milk, not to serve as sexually exciting erogenous zones; they used the medical argument that mother's milk was best; and they used the ancient superstitious argument that by absorbing the wet-nurses' milk, babies would also pick up their lower-class, and probably evil, character traits, whereas the mother would pass on her own good traits.[59] Even a few of the nobility began to accept these ideas in the early seventeenth century. In 1596 the ninth Earl of Northumberland declared that 'mother's teats are best answerable to the health of the child', and a generation later the Countess of Lincoln published a book which urged mothers to breast feed their children themselves.

How far this growing propaganda took effect in the seventeenth century is not entirely clear, but is significant that those mothers who fed their own children regarded it as something to boast about, as if it was an unusual occurrence. There is also some indication that it was the more puritanically inclined mothers who were the first from well-to-do families to try to nurse their own children.[60] Benjamin Brand, who died in 1636, boasted on his tombstone that his wife bore him twelve children, 'all nursed with her unborrowed milk.' In 1658 the second wife of the second Earl of Manchester had recorded on her tombstone that, of her eight children, seven 'she nursed with her own breasts. . . . Her children shall rise up and call her blessed.' In the middle of the seventeenth century, the pious, upper-gentry Mrs Alice Thornton repeatedly stressed her strong sense of obligation to try to nurse her own children, although she was often too ill after her confinements to be able to do so. Twenty-five years before, on the other hand, she and her brother had automatically been put out to a wet-nurse. It is noticeable also that in 1678 the wife of Sir John Chicheley was very unwilling to give up nursing the baby daughter, 'though I have but little milk.'[61] Even so, maternal breast-feeding continued to be a minority practice among the well-to-do. This view is supported by the comment in 1633 of the rector of a parish near London that his parish was 'filled with sucking infants' [from London], and by the statement in 1671 by the midwife Mrs Sharp that 'the usual way for rich people is to put forth their children to nurse.' [62]

In the early eighteenth century, the propaganda in favour of mothers nursing their own children was powerfully reinforced by a fierce attack in *The Spectator* on so inhuman and physically dangerous a practice as handing children over to slovenly and dirty wet-nurses, even if they did only cost between three and six shillings a week. Addison, however, admitted that 'this cruelty is supported by fashion, and nature gives place to custom', and in 1756 James Nelson in his *Essay on the Government of Children* added his voice to the chorus, but also had to confess that 'I am not insensible how little probability there is that my advice herein will be followed by persons in high life.' It seems that Nelson was right. In 1716 even so independent a woman as Lady Mary Wortley Montagu was against maternal breast-feeding: 'I grant that Nature has furnished the mother with milk to nourish her child; but I maintain at the same time that if she can find better milk elsewhere, she ought to prefer it without hesitation.' In 1748 Mrs Boscawen, who was in all respects a most devoted mother, had her child fed by a wet-nurse, apparently for the same practical reason. She also disapproved of Mrs Evelyn's plan to nurse her own baby since 'I can't think but she will make a bad nurse – at least I know I would not hire her.' Below this exalted level of the rich, however, it is probable that cost was a limiting factor, for according to Dr Cadogan a really good wet-nurse in 1748 cost £25 a year, which was a substantial sum, three times higher than Addison's estimate earlier in the century. In the 1740s Elizabeth Montagu was paying £50 a year for a very reliable wet-nurse. [63]

The conclusion seems to be, therefore, that the practice of using wet-nurses was largely confined to the wealthy classes. Although the proportion may have been declining, it seems that the majority of mothers in these classes, even devoted and child-oriented ones, were still not feeding their own children well into the middle of the eighteenth century. In 1748 Dr William Cadogan published his widely read *Essay upon Nursing and the Management of Children*. He argued that ninety per cent of children died who were reared on pap or fed by lazy wet-nurses with a poor or contaminated milk supply. He went so far as to claim that the children of the poor were healthier than those of the rich since they were breast-fed by their mothers and not kept shut up in stuffy rooms. [64]

This weight of medical opinion was supported by the memoirs of several men, who blamed their adult ill-health on the negligence of their wet-nurses. Worst of all was the experience of J.G.Stedman, who was born abroad, the son of a military officer, in 1774:

Four different wet-nurses were alternately turn'd out of doors on my account, and to the care of whom I had been entrusted, my poor mother being in too weak a condition to suckle me herself. The first of these bitches was turn'd off for having nearly suffocated me in bed; she having slept upon me till I was smothered, and with skill and difficulty restored to life. The second had let me fall from her arms on the stones till my head was almost fractured, and I lay several hours in convulsions. The third carried me under a moulder'd old brick wall, which fell in a heap of rubbish just the moment we had passed by it, while the fourth proved to be a thief, and deprived me even of my very baby clothes. Thus was poor Johnny Stedman weaned some months before the usual time.[65]

One of the few who reported favourably on the physical benefits of wet-nursing was Sir Robert Sibbald, born in 1641:

I sucked till I was two years and two months old, and could run up and down the street and speak... which long suckling proved, by a blessing of God, a means to preserve me alive. My nurse was Bessie Mason, a country woman... who had all her days a tender affection for me and both before her marriage... and after stayed most part of her life thereafter with me.[66]

In Bessie he clearly found a surrogate mother.

It was not until the second half of the eighteenth century that practice at last began to conform to propaganda, and wet-nursing quite rapidly went out of fashion. In the 1770s and 1780s one of the highest women in the country, the Duchess of Devonshire, breast-fed her eldest son for a period of nine months. In 1786 Countess Fitzwilliam was breast-feeding her infant son, and three years later the wife of Vice-Admiral F.W.Drake expressed her satisfaction that a friend was breast-feeding her child. 'I am sure it is much better for herself, as well as the child, than having a nurse, and the changing the milk is often attended with very disagreeable consequences. Indeed I ever had a great objection to a wet nurse, and had I not been able to persevere in nursing my girls, I would have brought them up by hand.' A few years later, Mrs Penyston was talking about 'my late and present avocation of nursing my last dear little babe.' That these mothers were now very numerous is confirmed by Lady Craven, who in 1789 reported that 'you will find in every station of life mothers of families who would shrink with horror at the thought of putting a child from them to nurse: a French custom with people of every degree.' 'Even women of quality nurse their children', von Archenholz remarked with surprise when he visited England in 1784, and in 1797 the popular handbook of Thomas Gisborne stated firmly that for a mother, 'the first of the parental duties ... is to be herself the nurse of her own offspring.'[67] (Plate 32.)

By 1793 it had become sufficiently standard practice for *The Matrimonial Magazine* to be able to offer its middle- and upper-class readers satirical advice, without any fear of being taken seriously: 'Should you become a mother, scorn to descend as low from the dignity of human nature as to suckle your own offspring. It would be difficult to exhibit a more vulgar mark of mere instinct and gross animal affection.' By 1846 it was taken for granted that upper-class women would breast-feed their own children, although now only for three months, unless they were physically incapable of producing an adequate supply of milk. On the other hand, it was still much resented as a tedious chore, and 'to the higher classes, and even to the luxurious among the middle classes, you might preach for hours upon the necessity of nursing at night without effecting it ... for I am sorry to say women are very selfish on this point.'[68]

As often happens, a sensible reform became a rigid social dogma, and the children of upper-class mothers who were physiologically unable to produce sufficient milk were liable to suffer from it. The novelist Maria Edgeworth, who drew her information from the 1770s and 1780s, makes Lady Delacour reminisce about how she was obliged to feed her own child.

It was the fashion in that time for fine mothers to suckle their own children; so much the worse for the poor brats. Fine nurses never made fine children. There was a prodigious point made about the matter; a vast deal of sentiment and sympathy, and compliments and enquiries. But after the novelty was over, I became heartily sick of the business; and at the end of three months my poor child was sick too – I don't much like to think of it – it died. If I had put it out to nurse I should have been thought by my friends an unnatural mother; but I should have saved its life.[69]

Despite these excesses, there can be little doubt that the growth of maternal breast-feeding as an upper-class fashion saved many infants from death at the hands of negligent wet-nurses. The other consequence, the importance of which can hardly be exaggerated was psychological. As Plutarch had pointed out in his *Moralia* centuries before, breast-feeding by the mother stimulates maternal affection. It also gives the child a greater sense of security and confidence about the world, and increases its attachment to its mother. This may well be a prime cause of that growth of affect in the eighteenth century which is central to the argument in this book. Causes of the change are obscure, but they must surely be related not only to the growing weight of medical opinion but also to the growth of more child-oriented family attitudes, and to a shift away from the patriarchal traditions of the seventeenth century expressed in many ways, from more egalitarian relations between husbands and wives to a more nurturant and loving attitude towards children. Moreover doctors were now no longer so dogmatic about the evil effects on milk of sexual activity. If wives now felt free to sleep with their husbands while nursing, which cannot be proved but seems plausible, this could have been a major cause for the rapid change.

There is reason to believe that in this shift to maternal breast-feeding, as in a number of other family matters, England was in the lead in Europe. The use of rural wet-nurses was more or less universal among all but the lowest classes in the towns and cities of eighteenth and early nineteenth-century France, causing a very high rate of infant mortality. The practice seems to have died out in France only in the late nineteenth century and in Germany only in the twentieth, to be replaced in many cases by bottle-feeding.[70]

c. Permissive Education in the Home. Children in the Home: In noble families, there was a growing practice of educating the children at home, according to the advice of Locke, who recommended a private tutor in order to avoid the crude and vulgar rough and tumble and the strong temptations to vice of a public boarding-school.[71] Home education also served to remove the noble child from social contamination by contact with those of lower social status than himself. Much more research is needed before a clear picture can be obtained of the development of this practice, but it was undoubtedly common throughout most of the eighteenth century, as the aristocracy withdrew their sons from the local grammar schools to educate them either by a private tutor in the home, or in private academies, or at one of the two most aristocratic public schools, Eton and Westminster. It was only at the very highest level of the court aristocracy that Locke's advice was ignored, and children were still largely neglected and sent early away from home.[72] Many aristocratic children still went off to boarding-school as early as the age of seven, and did not return home again for decades, spending their holidays with close relatives, uncles or grown-up brothers or sisters.

The main cause for the withdrawal of the elite from the grammar school to the home was the same one as that which caused the withdrawal from the university, namely the fear of moral contamination from other boys, especially boys of lower social status. It was widely, and rightly, feared that the eighteenth-century school and college were training-grounds of vice, which tended in the minds of many parents to outweigh the benefits of political maturity by exposure to the rough and tumble of school life. This was why Squire Allworthy had Tom Jones and Master Blifil educated at home, 'where he thought their morals would escape all that danger of being corrupted to which they would be unavoidably exposed in any public school or university.' Defoe, who was bitterly hostile to home education by a tutor, thought that the reason was mainly one of social snobbery. '"What," says the lady mother, "shall my son go to school? My son? no, indeed, he shan't go among the rabble of every trademan's boys and be bred up among mechanics." . . . And so the young gentleman has a tutor bestowed on him to teach him at home.' Later in the eighteenth century, still others believed that public schools were suitable only for the upwardly mobile, or for those already of high rank and with an assured career ahead of them. Many writers like the headmaster Vicesimus Knox and the novelist Maria Edgeworth denounced the middle-class practice of 'sending a son to school merely to form connections . . . to pay servile deference to those of his school fellows who are likely to be distinguished by rank or fortune.'[73]

Domestic Discipline: This rise of education in the home meant that teaching methods became less brutal and authoritarian. Between the remote, unfriendly attitude of early seventeenth-century upper-class parents, with their ruthless methods of crushing the will of the child, and the affectionate permissiveness of the mid and late eighteenth century, there was an intermediate stage, when the parents became affectionate towards their children, but still retained very tight control over them, now by psychological rather than physical means. It was recommended that parents now set their children an example, rather than crushing them by severe beatings.[74]

As in many other areas of domestic relations, middle-class dissenters seem to have been in advance of the rest of the society. In the late seventeenth century the Quaker William Penn advised parents to 'love them with wisdom, correct them with affection, never strike in passion, and suit the correction to their ages as well as the fault.' If children were sinful or disobedient, 'show them the folly, shame and undutifulness of their faults rather with a grieved than an angry countenance.' In 1691 John Dunton, the Presbyterian-trained editor of the *Athenian Mercury*, was advising his bourgeois readers to educate their children at home. The mother, he argued, lacks 'that magisterial sourness which sticks so close to most pedagogues, and frightens more learning out of children than ever they can whip into them.'[75]

It was not long, however, before maternal affection was spilling over into indulgence in more religiously orthodox and more wealthy families. As the trend towards home education spread, treatment of children tended to become more and more permissive. When Sarah Fielding published her novel *The Adventures of David Simple* in 1744, she thought that she was propagandizing for a new and still rare way of bringing up children. Her heroine Camilla reported that 'I spent my infancy, from the time I can remember, very different from what most children do, it being the usual method of most of the wise parents I have ever seen to use their little ones as if they were laying plots to make them take an aversion to them all of their lives afterwards.' Her father did not whip his children 'for it was not lawful to make slaves of Christians', and the standard punishment was dismissal from the parental presence. In the middle of the eighteenth century, James Nelson, in his popular handbook on the upbringing of children, advised strict moderation of chastisement in the home, although he was generally opposed to excessive permissiveness in child-rearing. His objections to brutality were both medical and social. 'Severe and frequent whipping is, I think, a very bad practice: it inflames the skin, it puts the blood in a ferment; and there is besides, meanness, a degree of ignominy attending it, which makes it very unbecoming.' Stress was laid now on the psychological carrot rather than on the physical stick. In 1798 mothers were told that 'the first object in the education of a child should be to acquire its affection, and the second to obtain its confidence.... The most likely thing to expand a youthful mind ... is praise.'[76]

This advice was certainly followed in many upper-class households in the eighteenth century. The most explicit statement of the new attitude is contained in the instructions given by Philip Francis when in 1774 he entrusted his only son to a private tutor: 'since it is my purpose to make him a gentleman, which includes the idea of a liberal character and sentiment, I cannot think it consistent with that purpose to have him brought up under the servile discipline of the rod.... I absolutely forbid the use of blows.' This was not an unusual position to adopt by then. Arthur Young, born in 1741, was only once flogged by his naturally irascible father, a well-to-do and well-connected clergyman, and then only as punishment for an act of cruelty. Mrs Eliza Fox, born in 1793, the daughter of a local barrister, 'was seldom checked or chided at home', while Mrs Boscawen's son was only whipped once in the home, when he was still a child in long coats.[77]

But there were clearly differences of opinion on this subject even among the most affectionate of parents (and indeed modern child psychologists are still far from united on the subject). The son of Robert Owen, the industrialist, who was born in 1800, recorded later that his mother, who was a Scotch Calvinist, and his father had different views on child-rearing. When as a baby he screamed for something, 'very gentle though she was, the doctrine of innate depravity, in which she had been bred, urged her to slap me into quiet.' But his father would not let her, preferring to allow the child to scream until he stopped. When he was older, his father said to him, 'I have never struck you. You must never strike anybody.' Mrs Howard of Corby Castle thought that 'the rod, if used with discretion, is of great use before they can perfectly discern right from wrong, and does much less harm to the child than a persevering cry.' The attitude to the beating of older children, however, was generally hostile. When in 1813 Ellen Weeton was employed as a governess in a wealthy industrialist's home, she struggled for some time to control 'the perverse and violent tempers of the children.' At last she 'resorted to the rod, notwithstanding it is so repugnant to the present mild system of education', and despite the 'sour looks and cool treatment' of both the parents (plate 25). In those circles, at that time, flogging in the home was clearly frowned upon.[78]

What was happening in the eighteenth century was a steady shift away from prime reliance on physical punishment in the upbringing of children to reliance on the reward of affection and the blackmail threat of its withdrawal. The root causes of the change were the rejection of the doctrine of Original Sin, and the recognition of the individuality of the child, who was no longer equated with a young animal to be broken in. The rise of individualism among the middling and upper ranks in society brought with it, as a logical corollary, the rejection of that determination to crush the child's will that had so obsessed educators and parents in the sixteenth and early seventeenth centuries. Florio's translation of Montaigne's *Essays*, published in 1603, helped to begin the slow secular shift of opinion, but because of Puritanism it was a long time before the new ideas took hold. One of the first clear repudiations of the traditional policy comes from the mid-eighteenth century, when Henry Lord Holland gave instructions for the upbringing of his son Charles James Fox: 'Let nothing be done to break his spirit. The world will do that business fast enough.' A (possibly apocryphal) story has it that when young Charles announced his intention to smash a watch, his indulgent father replied, 'Well, if you must, I suppose you must.'[79]

Evidence of Excessive Permissiveness: Some of the stories about parent-child relations in the late eighteenth century indicate a degree of indulgent permissiveness among parents and of spoilt arrogance among children which historically have no parallel except for conditions in the United States in the late twentieth century. When Mary Butt (later Mrs Sherwood) visited a doctor at Warwick in 1782, she found the son of the house lying on a carpet in front of the fire. When told by his mother to get up and greet the visitor, he replied, 'I won't', which was Mary's first introduction to this sort of licensed insubordination and bad manners. 'But I have lived to see this single specimen multiplied beyond calculation,' she added bitterly. Another woman recalled a disastrous dinner party at which 'the eldest boy was a perfect pest in the house, although only about five years old. A more uncomfortable dinner there could not be than the one we had that day, owing to the behaviour of that horrid child . . . he screaming every now and then and making such a noise. There was little conversation.' An equally disastrous dinner party was given in 1777 by Sir Joshua Reynolds for David Garrick and Mrs Thrale. Unfortunately, Mary Countess of Rothes, who was also there with her second husband, Bennet Langton, spoilt the party for Boswell by bringing along her two babies: 'they played and prattled and suffered nobody to be heard but themselves. . . . Langton and his wife with a triumphant insensibility kissed their children and listened to nothing with pleasure but what they said.' Boswell complained bitterly about the deplorable social consequences of this widespread practice.[80]

This evidence of an injudicious fondness by parents for exhibiting children in company is supported by signs that parental authority had in some cases been virtually abdicated. It was in 1762 that Henry Lord Holland wrote a letter to his son at Eton which could hardly be matched in tone of deferential supplication from father to schoolboy son at any other period in history than the late 1960s. 'I much wanted to see your hair cut to a reasonable length and gentlemanlike shortness. You and some Eton boys wear it as no other people in the world do. It is effeminate; it is ugly; and it must be inconvenient. You gave me hopes that if I desired it, you would cut it. I will, dear Ste, be much obliged if you will.' Even by the standards of the day, Lord Holland was an exceptionally permissive parent, who brought up his precocious son Charles James Fox on 'a system of the most unlimited indulgence of every passion, whim or caprice. A great dinner was given at Holland House to all the foreign ministers. The children came in at the dessert. Charles, then in petticoats, spying a large bowl of cream in the middle of the table, had a desire to get into it. Lord Holland insisted he should be gratified, and, in spite of Lady Holland's remonstrations, had it placed on the floor for the child to jump in and splash about at his pleasure.[81]

At the turn of the century, there were a few families, admittedly eccentrics, where permissiveness was carried to the ultimate extreme. In 1804 Admiral Graves and his wife at Exeter never had their children's hair cut. 'None of the children are allowed to be contradicted, and when 3 or 4 of them cry at once for the same thing and run tearing and screaming about the room together with their long tails, the effect on strangers is rather surprising.'[82] The courtesan Harriette Wilson records a visit to a married sister, who was following her own system of education of her children, which she regarded as an improvement on that of Rousseau. The children never went to school, were never left to nurses or servants, were never told about evil or deceit, and never got their way by rudeness or tears, but only by politeness and humility. Harriette saw the children romping about naked before bedtime, and noticed the two-year old girl playing with the penis of her four-and-a-half -year old brother Henry. The latter asked: '"Is Sophie to have my didoodle to keep?" "No, my love," answered mamma with calm dignity, "not to keep, only to play with."' Here was the application of the principle that 'nothing shall be called indecent which is natural, either in words or deeds', a brave attempt to return to the pristine innocence of the Garden of Eden.[83]

The conclusion one can draw from these diverse scraps of evidence is that in some high professional and landed circles in England by the late eighteenth century, there had developed an astonishingly permissive style of child-rearing. As a result, some parents were obliged humbly to cajole their adolescent children instead of ordering them about, and adult social occasions were often marred by those twin scourges of civilized conversation, the presence of undisciplined, noisy and talkative children demanding to be the centre of attention, and the habit of doting parents of 'repeating *bon mots* of babies among people of wit and understanding.'[84]

Protests against Excessive Permissiveness: The trend towards a more affectionate and permissive handling of children did not go unnoticed by contemporaries. Some welcomed the change, and in 1797 Thomas Gisborne pointed out that in the sixteenth and seventeenth centuries 'domestic manners were severe and formal. A haughty reserve was affected by the old, and an abject deference exacted from the young.' Even not so long ago, he observed, children were 'condemned to almost perpetual silence in the presence of their parents.' At the time he was writing, however, a quite different domestic atmosphere prevailed and a parent strove to 'preserve the confidence of a friend' of the children.[85]

Many others, on the other hand, were increasingly worried that affection was leading to spoiling, and permissiveness turning into licence. The first to draw attention to these potential dangers was Thomas Shadwell in 1676, although his grumbles were clearly premature. He believed that upper-class boys were becoming either domestic milk-sops or undisciplined, dissolute London rakes.[86] It was not until the 1730s, however, by which time home education was widespread, that commentators began seriously to worry that the English nobility were getting soft, being breast-fed by their mothers, pampered and spoiled in infancy, and tenderly educated at home until the early teens under the watchful eye of a loving mother. Protests against brutality, indifference and repression, especially by fathers, were now replaced by protests against excessive permissiveness, especially by mothers. By 1732 Richard Costeker was afraid that the sons of nobles were now 'degenerate into foppery and effeminacy.... Thousands are ruined by the very effect of maternal love.' Nowadays, he complained, a son was 'naturally under the conduct and tuition of his mama.' As early as 1697 a French visitor was commenting on how the English 'have an extraordinary regard ... for young children, always flattering, always caressing, always applauding what they do,' so that the native complaints do not lack corroboration.[87]

In the 1750s James Nelson, in his popular *Essay on the Government of Children*, was far more concerned about the dangers of excessive permissiveness, which he thought was current, than with the dangers of excessive strictness, which he regarded as now confined to a minority. He wasted little time in denouncing 'the cruelty of some parents who use everybody well but their own children', but devoted two hundred pages to damage done by excessive permissiveness. 'Let a child of three years old, who has been much indulged, be bid to do anything, and how ready it is to answer "I won't." And if forbid a thing, how pert to say "I will."' His advice was to enforce obedience but to follow the golden rule of moderation, and he cautioned parents 'to let their children see and feel their affection for them, and their power over them; and then regulate their actions as they find necessary.'[88]

In the early years of the nineteenth century, even the caricaturists weighed in. One drawing entitled 'The Mother's Hope', shows a small boy screaming with rage before his complaisant and helpless mother, concluding his tirade with the statement: 'I will have my own way in everything (plate

26).' Another shows two children torturing a cat and a dog, while their father remarks fondly, 'Dear little innocents, how prettily they amuse themselves.'[89]

There is an extraordinary contrast between these reiterated warnings in the eighteenth and early nineteenth centuries about excessive maternal influence and domestic affection, and the complaints in the late seventeenth century about excessive parental indifference and severity. It is a contrast that clearly had a firm basis in reality.

d. Decline of Flogging at School. Theory: One of the most impressive pieces of evidence of a kindlier attitude towards children is the late seventeenth-century revulsion in many quarters against the brutal flogging that had been standard practice earlier, especially in the public grammar schools. In terms of pedagogy and of psychology, there is an essential difference between constant flogging for academic lapses, such as stupidity, ignorance, inattention or idleness, and occasional flogging for serious moral faults, such as disobedience and lying. The prime objective of the reformers was the total elimination of the former practice, the secondary objective being to reduce the latter to the bare minimum necessary for social control and moral improvement.

The first onslaught on the extraordinary brutality of schoolmasters in the public grammar schools towards their pupils did not occur until soon after the middle of the seventeenth century. It was not only inspired by a spirit of compassion, but was also informed by a new understanding of the psychological motivation for the current practice of routinely and daily flogging boys severely for the most trivial lapses of memory or failure of understanding or performance in class. The Elizabethan poet Thomas Tusser had complained that his Eton master had once given him fifty-three stripes for 'fault but small or none at all' in learning his Latin. Critics noted that the frequency and severity of the punishment was vastly in excess of the cause, and that it took the form of beating boys with a birch on the naked buttocks while bent over and horsed on the back of another boy.[90]

Samuel Butler in *Hudibras* hinted at the explanation of this ferocity but it was left to an anonymous author to spell it out. In a pamphlet of 1669 the boys are made to point out that 'our sufferings are of that nature as makes our schools to be not merely houses of correction, but of prostitution, in this vile way of castigation in use, wherein our secret parts . . . must be the anvil exposed to the immodest and filthy blows of the smiter.' The author asked 'who can think that if the punishment were not suffered on those parts, that it were like to be so much?' Having demonstrated the homosexual sadistic motivation for the practice, he pointed out that it failed totally in its ostensible object of increasing the capacity to learn, while it was unworthy to treat a future gentleman in a manner fit only for a slave. Moreover, the terror induced could lead to stammering and other psychosomatic illnesses. He concluded, 'it is in truth a question rather worthy of the most mature deliberation whether children should ever be beaten at all about their books.' Flogging, that is, should be a rare punishment limited to moral crimes, not applied indiscriminately to minor intellectual deficiencies.[91]

At just the same time that the sadistic motivation of flogging by schoolmasters was being analysed and exposed, the psychological opposite, the stimulus to masochism in some boys, was also first brought to public attention. In his play *The Virtuoso* of 1678, Thomas Shadwell portrayed an elderly man who in a moment of sexual excitement asks his mistress: 'Where are the instruments of our pleasure?' When she produces a couple of birch rods, he explains 'I was so used to it at Westminster School I could never leave it off since. . . . Do not spare thy pains: I love castigation mightily.'[692] (Plate 34.) James Cleland included a mutual whipping episode in *Fanny Hill* in 1748, while Hogarth's print in 1732 of a whore's room in *A Harlot's Progress* showed a bundle of birch rods hanging on the wall over the bed. '*Le vice Anglais*' was well established by the eighteenth century, apparently among both sexes.[93]

The late seventeenth-century view of the sexually and educationally harmful effects of flogging to enforce education gained enormous currency by being adopted by John Locke in his best-selling treatise on education of 1693, which had gone through twenty-five editions by 1800. He approved of physical punishment, in moderation, at an early age before a child had developed powers of reasoning. After that, however, he insisted on the almost exclusive use of the psychological stimulus of competition and emulation and the psychological punishment of shame at failure. He flatly declared that flogging was wholly ineffective as a means of moral or intellectual improvement. 'The usual lazy and short way by chastisement and the rod, which is the only instrument that tutors generally know, or ever think of, is the most unfit of any to be used in education.' Under Locke's educational scheme 'there will be very seldom any need of blows.' His arguments, which closely follow those of Plutarch in his *Moralia*, were two-fold, practical and moral. The first was that it was counter-productive, because, 'this sort of correction naturally breeds an aversion to that which it is the tutors' business to create a liking to.' The second was that 'such a sort of slavish discipline makes a slavish temper', and is therefore unsuitable 'to be used in the education of those who would have wise, good and ingenuous men.'[94]

Largely as a result of Locke's powerful advocacy, these ideas slowly became the conventional wisdom of the time. In 1711 the widely read and very influential *Spectator* contributed to the chorus. Swift alleged that it had now become a popular notion 'that whipping breaks the spirits of lads well-born.' Finally in 1769 Thomas Sheridan, senior, made a lively plea, based on the new spirit of the age, for the total abolition of corporal punishment in schools for the elite. 'Away with the rod. . . . Let pleasure be their guide to allure the ingenious youth through the labyrinths of science, not pain their driver to goad them on.'[95]

These novel ideas naturally did not go without challenge from 'the party of the Thwackums'. Neither Dr Johnson nor Oliver Goldsmith was convinced by the new educational ideas, the latter concluding grimly: 'I do not object to alluring it [a child] to duty by reward, but we well know that the mind will be more strongly stimulated by pain.' On the other hand, in Smollett's *Roderick Random* of 1748, the hero led a rebellion of boys against a cruel master, on whom they turned the tables by tying him to a post and whipping him themselves – a fantasy of schoolboy revenge that must have appealed to many thousands of eighteenth-century readers.[96]

Practice : The degree to which this new approach slowly affected practice in schools is not easy to determine with precision. Flogging at the university certainly died out altogether in the 1660s – the last known case at Cambridge was in 1667.[97] It declined from a daily expectation in the classroom to a rare and solemn occasion in the fashionable public schools at some time between the post-Restoration Westminster School of Dr Busby – famous both for his pedagogic successes and for his enthusiasm for flogging – and the early nineteenth-century Rugby of *Tom Brown's Schooldays*. Neither *The Spectator* in 1711 nor Robert Campbell in 1747 thought that there had been much change, but there can be little doubt that flogging by masters was on the decline in the major elite public schools.[98] The headmaster of St Paul's School between 1748 and 1769, George Thicknesse, was famous not only for his classical scholarship but also for his kindness to his pupils, many of whom became friends for life. He took the view that 'some boys had no talent for the acquisition of dead languages, and that a master must be content with their elementary instruction, as the birch and cane would not alter nature.' Things were also changing at the other, and more socially prestigious, London public school, Westminster, as well as at Harrow.[99] As for Eton, the eighteenth-century headmaster Dr Barnard 'had a way of talking to the boys who were taking their leave of him at once so tender and so full of admonition that many of them had been known to shed tears at parting.'

One reason for the change seems to have been a change in the balance of power from the masters to the senior boys. George Hanger, who later attended Eton, observed of a sadistic master he suffered under at Reading Grammar School in the late eighteenth century, 'this brute, had he been a master of Westminster or Eton, would in less than a fortnight have been tossed in a blanket by the upper boys.'[100] But the eighteenth-century headmasters of aristocratic schools were also very different persons from the famous headmasters of the seventeenth or the nineteenth centuries, who were mostly to be remembered for the strength of their right arms. As a result, in 1747 Thomas Gray looked back on his schooldays at Eton as the best years of his life, a concept unthinkable in the seventeenth century:

> Ah, happy hills, ah, pleasing shade,
> Ah Fields beloved in vain
> Where once my careless childhood strayed,
> A stranger yet to pain.

Dr Johnson, who was on this issue extremely conservative, agreed that 'there is now less flogging in our great schools than formerly, but then less is learned there; so that what the boys get at one end they lose at the other.'

In 1803 it was said that flogging 'is obsolete in our public schools.' This was something of an exaggeration, for formal public flogging persisted at Eton as late as 1834. But it was now of a shaming rather than a brutal character, and had been 'abandoned in a great degree at other public schools.'[101] By now the worst abuses of flogging at Eton were not so much by the masters as by the senior boys, the 'fag-masters.'[102]

Academic lapses and cases of laziness were now punished at both school and university by 'impositions' – the obligation to do a piece of academic work, usually to translate lengthy passages from English into Greek or Latin, or vice-versa. As discipline tightened in the nineteenth century, the imposition became a serious burden, and in 1850 Lord Stanley complained about this development at Eton, where he had two boys. He concluded that 'it occupies their time and takes them from their usual studies. After all, the good old whipping is perhaps as good or better than anything for young boys.'[103]

All that can be said about the lesser provincial grammar schools, which were increasingly abandoned by the squirarchy to the children of the middle and lower-middle classes, is that the concept of a grammar-school master as primarily a flagellant seems to have declined. The situation clearly varied greatly from school to school, depending on the temperament and character of the master. At Bury St Edmunds Grammar School in the 1730s and 1740s, an admittedly excellent master made full use of the rod and the ferule. In the 1750s in nearby Lavenham, Arthur Young received an inferior education, but was never beaten once. At Reading Grammar School in the late eighteenth century, George Hanger was brutally beaten for academic faults: the 'tyrant did but seldom use the rod; his favourite instrument was a long rattan cane, big enough to correct a culprit in Bridewell. . . . The shrieks of the boys who were writhing beneath his blows were music to his soul. . . . I declare to God I have seen wales on the sides, ribs and arms of boys of the bigness of my finger.' At another country grammar school in the late eighteenth century, the headmaster frankly stated: 'my system is to whip, and to have done with it.' The victim thought he might have made some progress in the school 'had not the rod and cane supplied the absence of every other stimulus.'[104]

There is some reason to suppose that brutality had always been less common in the many little private schools run by clergymen as a way of augmenting their income by taking in a few upper- or middle-class boarders and teaching them the classics, as well as in the larger and more professional academies, if only because their survival depended on their popularity with their middle-class clientele. In the early eighteenth century James Frelwell, the son of a modest timber-merchant, was educated in a series of private schools and records 'I was never whipped at school by any of my masters.' It is noticeable that he records the fact as if it was an unusual occurrence, but his testimony is supported by that of others; for example, George Hanger in the late eighteenth century at the Reverend Mr Fountaine's Academy at Marylebone, where the boys were treated 'with the utmost kindness and attention, and with proper correction, but only when it appeared absolutely necessary.' By the 1780s some private academies were boasting in their advertisements in the newspapers about their reliance on 'emulation excited by proper rewards at every reasonable opportunity', rather than 'corporal punishment'.[105]

As for girls' schools, physical punishment seems also to have died out by the end of the eighteenth century in the better-run establishments for the middle and upper classes. Mrs Boscawen, who was born in 1719, 'was never whipped at school', while at the Misses Lee's school at Bath in 1797, 'no one is ever allowed to be struck.'[106]

The evidence advanced for the proposition that flogging was on the decline in eighteenth-century schools is unfortunately less clear-cut than one would wish. There were marked differences from school to school, so that one child's experience might differ widely from that of another. But what seems certain is that between the early seventeenth century and the very late eighteenth, there had been a very significant shift in the intensity and purpose of flogging as a method of academic discipline practised in most schools, and especially in the major public schools and the private schools and academies, which most of the upper classes now attended. Samuel Roberts, who was born in 1763, recollected of his childhood that 'the almost savage violence which had some years before been common in parents and masters was then greatly diminished.'[107] The method of punishment had also changed, with more beating on the hands and less on the buttocks, and a trend towards the substitution of impositions. One of the puzzles is why France, which throughout the eighteenth and nineteenth centuries was a much crueller and more authoritarian and patriarchal society than England or America, nevertheless succeeded in abolishing corporal punishment in the elite grammar schools earliest of all.[108]

e. Physical Restraints on Female Adolescents. John Locke seems to have been the first to protest vigorously against the encasing of young bodies in tight corsets reinforced with metal and whalebone. William Law, whose handbook on the upbringing of children ran to ten editions between 1729 and 1772, told the story of a mother whose daughters were laced as tightly as possible, stinted in their meals, and constantly given purges and enemas to maintain a fashionably pallid complexion. As a result not only were they all 'poor, pale, sickly, infirm creatures, vapoured through want of spirits', but the eldest daughter died at the age of twenty. At the autopsy it was found that 'her ribs had grown into her liver, and that her other entrails were much hurt by being crushed together with her stays, which her mother had ordered to be twitched so straight that it often brought tears into her eyes whilst the maid was dressing her.' Rousseau in *Émile* took a gloomy view of the biological and the aesthetic results: 'I cannot but think that this abuse, pushed in England to an inconceivable point, will cause in the end the degeneration of the race.... It is not agreeable to see a woman cut in two like a wasp.'[109]

In practice, however, this was one area in which the combined criticism of philosophers and doctors had not the slightest effect. The reason that the most cruel physical restraints continued to be employed on girls, admittedly at school rather than in the home, throughout the more permissive and affectionate period of the eighteenth century, was that they were thought absolutely essential to create the physical attributes required to catch a husband. One victim of these contrivances was Mary Butt, the daughter of a parson, who grew very rapidly up to the age of thirteen, and had a tendency to stooping. 'It was the fashion then for children to wear iron collars round the neck, with a back-board strapped over the shoulders. To one of them I was subjected from my sixth to my thirteenth year. It was put on in the morning and seldom taken off till late in the evening, and I generally did my lessons standing in stocks with this stiff collar round my neck.' A few years later Mary Somerville went through the same torture, but without any reasonable justification for it. 'Although perfectly straight and well-made, I was enclosed in stiff stays with a steel busk in front, while, above my frock, bands drew my shoulders back till the shoulder-blades met. Then a steel rod, with a semi-circle which went under the chin, was clasped to the steel busk in my stays. In this constrained state I, and most of the younger girls, had to prepare our lessons.' At about the same period Lucy Aikin underwent the same experience: 'There were back-boards, iron collars, stocks for the feet, and a frightful kind of neck-swing in which we were suspended every morning, whilst one of the teachers was lacing our stays, all which contrivances were intended and imagined to improve the figure and the air. Nothing was thought so awkward and vulgar as anything approaching to a stoop. "Hold up your head, Miss", was the constant cry. I wonder any of us kept our health.'[110] To meet the market for restraints to create this upright stance, there developed a specialized industry of stay-makers. Most of them were producing mass-consumption articles, but some were specialized experts at constructing custom-built harnesses. In late eighteenth-century London the most successful was a Mrs Lloyd Gibbon, 'famous for her stays for females who might be afflicted with curvatures of the spine etc.'[111] These experts were the affluent equivalents of the orthodontists of late twentieth-century America, who also cater for a real need as well as a desire for perfection in a certain area thought to be important for success in life.

Nor were stays and braces the only constraints imposed on fashionable girls. By the late eighteenth century, the ideal of feminine beauty and deportment was extreme slimness, a pale complexion and slow languid movements, all of which were deliberately inculcated in the most expensive boarding-schools. When Arthur Young's beloved daughter Bobbin caught tuberculosis in 1797, he blamed in part the school regime of inadequate food, no fresh air, and the forbidding of all running about or quick motions.[112]

By the late eighteenth century, the frail health induced by these constricted bodies and spare diets had become generally associated with the female sex. Women of 'the quality' were expected to be creatures whose 'whole frames [are] incessantly deranged by the most trivial shocks.' It was generally agreed that the ideal was a pale, languid and fainting belle, and that 'an air of robustness and strength is very prejudicial to beauty.' Dr Gregory advised that 'a wise woman enjoys her good health in grateful silence but never boasts of possessing it.' Not until the 1790s were there protests by some lay commentators and doctors. Gisborne and others complained about the tight lacing, the inadequate food, and the sedentary lives imposed on English girls, which led, they argued, to emaciation, listlessness and anaemia. In 1792 Mary Wollstonecraft complained that 'the sedentary life which they are condemned to live . . . weakens the muscles and relaxes the nerves. . . . I once knew . . . a weak woman of fashion . . . neglect all the duties of life, yet recline with self-complacency on a sofa, and boast of her want of appetite as a proof of delicacy that extended to, or perhaps arose from, her exquisite sensibility.' 'Sedentary employments render the majority of women sickly', she concluded, 'and false notions of female excellence make them proud of this delicacy.'[113]

By a strange twist of cultural fate, the sex which is the toughest and most resilient of the two became identified with both physical and psychological delicacy and debility – defects in fact artificially induced in the interests of conformity to the current ideal of beauty. The cultivation of feminine debility had the same symbolic significance as the crushing of the feet of upper-class Chinese women, and it survived the opposition of philosophers and doctors and was stimulated by the rise of a more child-centered society in the late eighteenth century. Loving parents now believed that their daughters' chances on the marriage market would be seriously impaired unless they had the correct, rigidly upright, posture, emaciated bodies, pallid complexion and languid airs, and were prepared to faint at the slightest provocation. The importance attached to these matters was a direct result of the decline of money and the rise of personal choice as the most important factor in the selection of a marriage partner. Girls were now competing with one another in an open market, for success in which physical and personal attributes had to a considerable degree taken over the role previously played by the size of the dowry. A straight back was now thought to be as important as a substantial cash portion in the struggle to catch the most eligible husband.

f. Control of Career Choice of Sons. It is far less certain whether the growing freedom of education and of choice of marriage partner permitted to children was also extended to freedom of choice of a career. In the landed classes the eldest son would inherit the estate, and his career was therefore not at issue. For younger sons, however, long-term planning and educational investment was necessary, especially for the Church, the law and medicine, which became increasingly respectable at this time.

In 1712 a correspondent asked Addison, in his capacity as editor of *The Spectator*, to comment on the question 'is it well for a father to become a master to his children' to the extent of forcing them into careers they disliked. The case he had in mind was of a clerical father trying to force his son to follow in his footsteps (and those of his own father) when the boy wanted to be apprenticed to a merchant. It is perhaps significant that Addison did not publish the letter, and shied away from the problem.[114] In 1758 Arthur Young's clerical father had no hesitation in apprenticing him against his will – at a cost of £400 – for a mercantile accountancy training for three years, instead of sending him to Oxford and into the Church, which he later claimed he would have preferred. There are hints, therefore that professional parents continued to exercise considerable control over the career choices of their sons right through the eighteenth century.[115]

Among the lower middle classes in London in the early eighteenth century, Robert Campbell was convinced that very little freedom of choice was allowed, and in 1747 he launched a vigorous attack on this practice. 'Pride, avarice and whim are the chief councelors of most fathers when they are deliberating the most serious concern in life, the settlement of their children in the world. . . . The genius, the natural talents nor so much as the constitution of youth are seldom or never consulted.' The result, according to Campbell, was a series of square pegs in round holes, resulting in a great deal of inefficiency and unhappiness. In particular, he was indignant that because of false snobbery, 'The lesser gentry or more substantial tradesmen think it a dishonour to put their children to any branch of business that is not termed a genteel trade.'[116] It seems, therefore, that at most levels of upper-, middle- and lower-middle-class society parents continued to determine the career choices of their children. This was the last area of parental control to go.

g. Conclusion. There can be no doubt that between 1660 and 1800 there took place major changes in child-rearing practice among the squirarchy and upper bourgeoisie. Swaddling gave way to loose clothing, mercenary wet-nursing to maternal breast-feeding, breaking the will by force to permissiveness, formal distance to empathy, as the mother became the dominant figure in the children's lives. These changes reflect a general easing of those tensions which justified the iron discipline of the post-Reformation century, and in their turn they helped to produce individuals less suspicious of the world at large, less prone to violence, and now capable of intense personal attachments to other individuals, in particular to their wives and children.

On the other hand there was a good deal of truth in the contemporary indictment of the permissive child-rearing patterns recently adopted by many middle- and upper-class parents. The critics argued that parents were failing in their prime responsibility to prepare their children to fit comfortably into the adult world that waited them, and that the result was a generation of idle rakes, mannerless boors and social misfits.[117] There was a partial breakdown of that essential process of the socialization of the child.

Particular sufferers were those boys who were suddenly wrenched out of a home environment which was almost excessively affectionate and indulgent, and thrust into one of the great public boarding-schools, where the torture of younger boys by the older ones was common. It has been suggested that this pattern of a relatively permissive domestic childhood followed by an extremely repressive experience at boarding-school may explain the frustrations and resentment which produced the revolutionary generation of the 1830s.[118] The trouble with this thesis is not only that the psychological chain of causation is obscure, but also that this sudden shift from permissiveness at home to repression at school had been a common experience of upper- and professional-class children in Europe ever since the late eighteenth century.

But what *were* the results? On the one hand, the early years at home may have provided the necessary psychological stability and self-assurance for the future, while endurance and survival of the period of repression and bullying at boarding-school may have hardened the spirit, offered an invaluable experience in dealing with others, and prepared youth for leadership in the rough and often brutal world of business, politics, the army or imperial administration. On the other hand, the experience may instead have led to a crushing of the spirit, a mindless admiration for physical strength and prowess in sports, a permanent taste for sado-masochism and/or homosexuality, and a strong sense of male bonding coupled with a resentment and suspicion of women which may have made successful marriage very difficult.

A further unfortunate consequence of the liberation of maternal love was that mothers found it almost impossible to let go of their children, especially their sons, when they reached adolescence. Childhood came to be regarded as the best years of one's life, instead of the grim purgatory it had been in the seventeenth century.

> Such, such were the joys
> When we all girls and boys
> In our youth were seen
> On the echoing green

wrote William Blake, whose attitude would have astonished John Aubrey and his contemporaries. But again and again it becomes apparent in the literature of the eighteenth century that this Golden Age of childhood under close maternal care had serious inhibiting consequences later on. As Professor Hagstrum has pointed out, 'the maternal orientation of romantic vision appears in the boyhood of the Man of Feeling', that archetypal hero of the late eighteenth century. Again and again the story is one of sexual love that goes unfulfilled, inhibited by an oedipal fixation on the mother.[119]

2 CHILD-REARING MODES AND SOCIAL CATEGORIES

It cannot be emphasized too often that the changes in child-rearing which have been described were socially highly selective in their impact, affecting primarily the professional classes and the gentry, and later the nobility. The key to the story of the evolution of child-rearing is the principle of stratified diffusion, by which new attitudes first take hold among those classes which are most literate and most open to new ideas; and which are neither so very poor that economic circumstances often compel them to neglect, exploit or abandon their children; nor so very rich that their social and political life style is too time-consuming to allow them to devote much time or trouble to child-rearing, and whose enormous economic assets encourage them to compel their children to marry persons selected for them on strictly economic or political grounds. The first to adopt the new attitudes towards children were professional people, wealthy merchants and the squirarchy, all of whom were economically entrepreneurial, often upwardly mobile, and united by a common literary culture. Parents from these classes did not personally attend to the day-to-day needs of their children, who were looked after by nurses, maids, governesses and tutors, but they did see them every day, and gave them their full attention during those periods. For many mothers, this took up a good deal of their time.

From family to family a variety of motives may have been at work to stimulate this concern for children. In some cases, easy-going affection from a happy marriage spilled over on to the children, who were lovingly cherished but encouraged to develop autonomy and responsibility at an early age. In others, bored young mothers found children from two to seven amusing pets and playthings to while away the time. In others, unhappily married mothers, or mothers whose beloved husbands were for years on end away from home on business – for example, tied to London by political responsibilities, or at sea with the navy, or in India – turned all their psychic energies upon their children as a way of escape from emotional and sexual frustration. Other women were unwilling to bear more children, and used their devotion to those they had as a shield to protect themselves from the sexual importunities of their husbands. Some fathers turned the malleability of young children to their own ends, in an attempt to get even with destiny. Some gave their daughters an intellectual education as if they were sons; others were unemployed, and filled in the time by devoting themselves to the domestic education of their children; others pressured their children into pursuing the goals they themselves were frustrated in achieving.

The first of these motivational sub-categories is the one of prime concern in this chapter, although examples of all the others are also present in abundance. To some extent they all may be found among all classes in society, but the necessity for education, leisure and a modicum of wealth means that they tended to be heavily concentrated in the upper bourgeoisie and squirarchy. Given the preponderant influence of status and income and culture, it is possible to define six ideal types of child-rearing, each of which tended to predominate in a different social category. This is a way of looking at the problem which blurs the significant differences in parental motivation, and focuses on the end-product, the pattern of child-rearing itself.

The first mode of child-rearing was confined to some elements of the higher court aristocracy. Based on an attitude of indifference, the children were more or less abandoned to the care of nurses, governesses, tutors and schoolmasters. The second mode was adopted by parents who cared, but who still believed that to spare the rod was to spoil the child, and who subscribed to the traditional faith in the early and constant use of physical punishment. The third mode, which was largely confined to the well-to-do professional and landed classes of the late eighteenth century, was now fully child-oriented, very affectionate, and, if anything, excessively permissive. In the education of daughters, this model spread far down into the upwardly aspiring lower-middle class. The fourth mode, which was primarily that of Puritan and nonconformist bourgeois and upper artisans, was one of concern and love, which rejected the use of physical punishment but substituted for it overwhelming psychological pressures of prayer, moralizing, and threats of damnation. The fifth mode, prevalent among the lower artisan class, combined traditional brutality with a care for sound education. The sixth mode, which was largely confined to the very poor, was dictated by economic circumstances. It was brutal, exploitative and indifferent, even to the extent of fairly widespread child abandonment.

i. The Aristocracy: the Negligent Mode

At the highest level of society, among the court aristocrats and among some of the wealthy squires, there were many families in the eighteenth century in which both husband and wife were too immersed in politics and the social whirl of London and the court to bother themselves with their children, who for the first six to eight years were left in the hands of wet-nurses, nurses, governesses and tutors. After that the boys were then sent off to school, the university and the Grand Tour. These were not harsh or cruel parents, merely indifferent ones who had little interest in their children and saw little of them. Between 1682 and 1698, from the age of six when he went away to school to the age of twenty-two when he was summoned back from Cambridge on the death of his elder brother, Robert Walpole had only spent a few weeks at a time, at rare intervals, at home with his parents. When Elizabeth Robinson got married in 1724, she had not seen her three younger brothers for five years, since they had been away at school and had never once returned home. When she invited them to stay with her in her new establishment, they were '*enfants trouvés* by a sister unknown to them.' Even then, they still never went home to their parents, moving on to Westminster School and then Cambridge at their parents' expense, but spending the holidays with their sister. Similarly, when John, son of the first Earl of Bute, went off to school at Eton at the age of seven, he did not return home again until he was almost a man, for he spent his holidays with his uncles, who clearly acted as surrogate parents.[120]

As these stories suggest, it was mostly sons who were early sent away from home. Of the four sons of Lord and Lady Hervey in the second quarter of the eighteenth century, the eldest went off to boarding-school at the age of six, and thence to Westminster School and Geneva, entering the army in 1739 at the age of eighteen. The second son was sent into the navy at the age of twelve, and the two youngest sons at about the same age or rather earlier were sent to live with a private tutor, and from there sent on to boarding-school at Westminster.[121]

In the late eighteenth century protests at this mode of upbringing became increasingly common. 'Nothing can justify such monstrous indifference' thundered *The Lady's Magazine* in 1774. Some aristocratic ladies joined in to reproach their friends and acquaintances. In 1789 a family friend told Georgiana, Duchess of Devonshire, 'I think it is a great disadvantage to children to have five nurses and footmen to attend them, and to see their parents but seldom, and under a sort of constraint which prevents them behaving naturally....' The most acidulous critic, as one might imagine, was that embittered ex-governess, Mary Wollstonecraft. Clearly referring to her former employer, Lady Kingsborough, she wrote scathingly that 'she who takes her dogs to bed and nurses them with a parade of sensibility when sick, will suffer her babes to grow up crooked in a nursery.' When in 1792 she wrote her violent tract *A Vindication of the Rights of Woman*, she addressed herself to 'those of the middle class, because they appear to be in the most natural state.' The rich, she declared, are full of 'false refinement, immorality and vanity.... The education of the rich tends to render them vain and helpless... they only live to amuse themselves', and neglect their maternal duties in the process. There is plenty of evidence, however, that these protests failed utterly to change the pattern of upbringing of children in these very wealthy circles, which continued unaltered at least until the Second World War.[122]

ii. The Upper Bourgeoisie and Squirarchy: the Child-oriented, Affectionate and Permissive Mode

In the course of the eighteenth century many of the professional and landed classes of England seem to have evolved a very long way towards the child-oriented society as we know it today. Not only mothers but also fathers were involved, an early example being the affection shown to his little children in the late 1680s by John, future Duke of Marlborough. 'You cannot imagine,' he wrote to his wife Sarah, 'how pleased I am with the children for, they having nobody but their maid, they are so fond of me that when I am home they will be always with me, kissing and hugging me.... Miss is pulling me by the arm that she may write to her dear Mamma, so that I will say no more, only beg that you will love me always so well as I love you, and then we cannot but be happy.' Even at this early date, the children regularly addressed their parents as Papa and Mamma. But when they grew up relations deteriorated with their imperious mother, who in the 1720s kept a book to show to her friends, entitled 'An Account of the Cruel Usage of my Children'.[123] A similar case from the third quarter of the eighteenth century is the Boswell family, where early affection also ended in hostility when the children grew up. As a professional man with little professional business to perform, James Boswell was in the exceptional position of having plenty of time at home to devote to his children. In his diary he was careful to record the lisping efforts of his young children as they learned to speak. 'Etti me see u pictur' said his little daughter Veronica. When she rubbed Boswell's sprained ankle, 'with eager affection I cried "God bless you my dearest little creature". She answered "od bless u, Papa".' The only fly in the ointment was that 'she loved her mother more than me.'[124]

He was delighted when, as he left home on a trip, the five-year-old Veronica 'cried very much and clasped her little arms around my neck, calling out "O Papa". Sandie cried too. . . .' He was equally pleased to find that on his return home 'the children were quite overjoyed to see me again. Effie and Sandie actually cried. This was very fine.' His letters to his son Sandie are both affectionate and written as one equal to another. So far as the record goes, he only beat Sandie once in his life, and this was for telling a lie. As the children increased in number and grew up, Boswell took them on special outings for their pleasure, and every Sunday he listened to them reciting psalms and the Lord's Prayer.

His favourite child was his eldest daughter Veronica, but, like most eighteenth-century parents, he could not resist frightening her with fears of death. It was not a very successful experiment. At first he only told her about Heaven, not Hell, but even so at the age of six she suddenly declared that she did not believe in God. When asked why, she explained that 'she did not like to die', and that if there was no God to accept her, then there would be no death. Boswell explained to her the fallacy of the argument, but a few weeks later told all three children about how devils would seize wicked people at their death and carry them off to the everlasting torments of Hell. The response was unfortunate: 'they were all three suddenly seized with such terror that they cried and roared out and ran to me for protection . . . and alarmed their mother.' A month later he tried again with Veronica alone. 'I was doatingly fond of her, and talked with earnest, anxious, tender apprehension of her death, how it would distress me, but that I must submit to God's will and hope to meet her in Heaven. She was quite enchanting. I prayed extempore while we knelt together.'

Two years later Boswell was more affectionate than ever, but conscious that his control over his children was weakening. He maintained his regular

Sunday practice of staying at home with his children to hear them say their hymns and prayers, and he began the habit of getting the two older girls to read him chapters from the Bible every morning. In return he read them stories from *The Arabian Nights*, played with them, and took them on outings. He found his younger son Jamie 'a delightful child', went out riding with his eldest son Sandie, and was very touched when in 1782, as he was leaving for a trip, the nine-year-old Veronica said 'Papa, write to me'. He and his wife made the Boswell home so much of a nest that the children found it difficult to leave. In 1783 the nine-year-old Phemie was sent to school in Edinburgh as a full boarder, while the ten-year-old Veronica for some reason attended only as a day boarder. But Phemie 'cried so much that after persisting for a week, we allowed her to come home every evening as well as her sister.' Three years later Boswell was busy helping Sandie with his Latin, and Veronica and Phemie with their French.[125]

By 1789 the children were growing up and going off to school, their mother had died and Boswell had moved to London where he was sinking increasingly into alcoholic and sexual dissipation, and often lay in bed half the day in a state of abject melancholia. By 1790 Sandie was off at Eton, and only the eleven-year-old Jamie remained at home. But even he was reluctant to leave his father, and 'implored to stay in my house till summer in so piteous a tone that I inwardly yielded.' When he at last went off to Westminster School 'the house seemed dull without little James.' The three elder children were now in their late teens, and were showing inevitable signs of independence, which much upset poor Boswell. Sandie was less of a problem, since he was only home during the holidays from Eton, but the two girls had left school and were now living at home. Boswell told himself 'how unhappy it is both for parents and children when there has been too much indulgence.' 'My two daughters who were with me seemed in so ill-governed a state... had so little respect for me... that I ... wished earnestly to have them stationed somewhere with propriety at a distance from me.'

All the same, it was young Jamie who picked his alcoholic father out of the gutter, and stopped him from staggering through the London streets in pursuit of cheap whores. Moreover Boswell needed his children's company to help occupy the time, for he had nothing to do, and to ward off his melancholia. Sometimes he got Janice to play draughts and talk with him all day to distract his attention from his troubles. By 1793 when the daughters were twenty-one and twenty, tension rose in the house, as they took an increasingly independent line, as their contempt grew for their drink-sodden, idle failure of a father, and as Boswell's temper deteriorated under the strain of his misfortunes. He lost his temper with them for their habit of gadding about too often and of inviting guests to the house without consulting him, but was conscious that he was himself largely to blame for his failure to exercise any consistent discipline. His old friend Temple told him frankly that 'my temper was sadly changed for the worse, especially when I was at home with my daughters, at whom I was almost perpetually fretting. He saw that they did not treat me with the respect due to a parent, but he imputed this to the unsteadiness of my behaviour, as I sometimes was too free with them, and then attempted to keep them in too much restraint.'[126] Two years later Boswell was dead.

Philip Francis was another openly affectionate and informal father. In 1774 his wife reported to him that 'the two dear children are as well as possible. Sally ate a bit of chicken with me yesterday.' A little later, when Philip was left at home, he told his wife, 'The two children and I played together this morning about half an hour on the carpet', when Sally said 'Ti-ta-to-tu' to her sister. 'The two dear childers look like little angels.' When away from home, his letters normally included some phrase like 'a thousand kisses to my sweet chickeys' or 'love to the chickens'. When he finally left for India for a prolonged stay in order to make his fortune, his wife stayed behind with the children. When he left, he instructed her to keep the children 'constantly in your company (when from school),' and she could truthfully report that she hardly ever accepted an invitation to go out since 'my girls are employment enough for me,' being now aged twelve and thirteen. The parents had pet names for all their children, and when they were grown up, their father continued to write to them in most affectionate terms. In 1801, he addressed Harriet as 'most dear Doll', and Catherine as 'most dear Babby', and 'Most dear Miss Kitty', signing himself 'your loving sire.' In 1805, however, a row broke out with his married daughter Mary, who after a disastrous visit commented, 'a most extraordinary, incomprehensible man my father is.' But at least their childhood had been enveloped in close parental affection that is without a known parallel in earlier periods.[127]

It should be emphasized that Boswell and Francis were by no means exceptional in their interest in their children, and some of the stories the former tells about others clearly prove that affectionate child-centered family attitudes had spread in the late eighteenth century even to some fathers among the highest court aristocracy. When in 1778 Boswell visited the Earl of Pembroke in his London house, there was 'coffee and tea and little Lady Charlotte climbing on her father's knee.... I was delighted with the perfection of easy fashionable behaviour.' He was equally pleased to learn that the Duke of Gloucester 'put his little daughter to bed every night... resembling myself and Veronica.' Another very affectionate and permissive father was Henry Fox, Lord Holland, who despite his heavy involvement in political affairs, found time to write anxiously about the welfare of his children and spend some time with them. When his precocious son Charles was only three, his father was already fascinated by him. 'I dined at home today *tête-à-tête* with Charles, intending to do business; but he had found me pleasanter employment. I grow immoderately fond of him.'[128] As a result, he spoilt the child, calmly ignored his temper tantrums, and refused to allow him to be disciplined. The boy grew into that charming, impetuous, wilful, brilliant, but erratic and dissipated statesman, Charles James Fox.

It is maternal rather than paternal affection which is most amply documented in the eighteenth century, and the intimate family groups of mothers and children depicted by Reynolds and Zoffany (end paper) clearly had a firm basis in reality. Many wives and mothers, when faced with the choice of personally supervising their children, or leaving them to servants, nurses and governesses and accompanying their husbands on pleasure or business, unhesitatingly chose the former, despite the recognized probability that the decision would drive the husband into the arms of a prostitute or mistress. Mrs Boswell was far from unique when in 1778 she was 'so anxious about her children that she thinks she should be unhappy if at a distance from them', and so let the highly unreliable Boswell go off to London by himself.[129]

Nothing could be more unlike the harsh and remote seventeenth-century upper-class domestic relations or the cloyingly pious and morally oppressive Victorian ones than the warmth, affection and tact which enveloped the family life of Lady Sarah Lennox, wife of the Honourable George Napier, and their children. When in her old age in about 1820, one of her daughters-in-law questioned her about her relations with her children, her reply (as reported by her interrogator) was very revealing: 'As they rose out of infancy, I left them to their father's management, and studied to become their friend, not the tutoress of my sons.... In me they trusted to find sympathy, kindness, my opinion or advice if they sought it, knowing at the same time that it was unaccompanied by the necessity of adopting it.... Then, left to decide for themselves, their actions (even if unknown to themselves) were somewhat of the hue of what they had just heard.' The reason for her influence, she thought, was that her children always recognized her as 'the object of their father's tender love and care, seeing me at the same time holding a high place in his estimation as his friend and companion.' The same warm relationships seem to have prevailed in the families of their children.[130]

An early example of the upper-class mother exclusively devoted to her children is the Honourable Mrs Edward Boscawen, the attractive and highly intelligent wife of Admiral Boscawen. One reason for her devotion to her children is clearly that they served as a surrogate for her husband, whose career in the navy, either at sea or at the Admiralty, meant that he was only rarely at home during their eighteen-year married life from 1742 to 1761. In 1747 she finished a letter to him with: 'Goodnight. The boy is a most beautiful sleeping Cupid, and the girl is pure well.' She assured him that the children 'shall be my sole care and study, and that my chief purpose and the business of my life shall be to take care of them and to procure for them a sound mind in a healthful body.' She could hardly bring herself to leave them for a single night; she carried them into Hyde Park for walks and games; and she regularly had supper with them and romped with them afterwards. When she finally went away for a week's holiday in Oxford, she left three maids with strict instructions to 'watch and attend the children night and day.' It was not until the early 1750s that she was freed from this child-centered life, the boy being sent off to Eton at the age of nine and the two girls to Mrs Bear's Polite Seminary for Young Ladies at Kensington. But for the first nine years of her marriage, she was a woman – supported, it must be admitted, by a household staff of nine servants – who in the absence of her husband found fulfilment in the upbringing of her children.[131]

Mrs Boscawen is far from being a unique example of her class and time. Despite the support of an army of nurses and governesses, these upper-class women of the late eighteenth century constantly describe themselves as unable to tear themselves away from their children lest they be neglected by the servants. In 1771 Mrs Powys wrote her husband that 'my little Tom, [aged three] at the distance he now is from me, makes me feel for him each moment, lest he should not be well as I left him.' In 1792 Lady Duncannon, in Europe for her health, constantly lamented that she was so far away from 'my dear dear children' for so long. Georgiana, Duchess of Devonshire, whose relations with her husband were far from good and who lived a giddy social life, nonetheless expressed extraordinary devotion to her children in her letters. In 1793 'I get up early to see the children sooner.' Three years later, 'I have been interrupted by the dear children saying "hear my prayers" with their dear little touching voices.' Many of these devoted mothers also kept extremely close relations with their own mothers, long after they were grown up and married. At the age of thirty-two in 1789, Georgiana wrote: 'I love you dearest M. as an adored mother, as a darling friend. . . .' 'Dear, dear, dear Mama, I cannot express all I feel about you and my dear children.'[132] Mrs Thrale was another example of a woman whose relations with her mother were much closer than those with her husband.

A good example of the new, totally child-oriented upper-class mother of the early nineteenth century is Mary Stanley, wife of Edward, future second Lord Alderley. Like Mrs Boscawen a century before her, her situation in the 1840s was a peculiar one, since her husband lived the life of a gay man-about-town and professional politician in London, while she and her growing family were left in the country seat to their own devices for most of the year. He visited them just sufficiently to procreate nine children. Mary loved her husband and longed for his presence, but was in fact totally wrapped up in the lives of her children and refused to abandon them to join her husband in London. The letters to him are filled with the maladies, misfortunes, accidents and good or bad behaviour of the children. He, on the other hand, showed relatively little interest either in her or in the children. Mary Wollstonecraft was making a shrewd point when she remarked that 'the neglected wife is, in general, the best mother', especially if the word 'best' is taken to mean a mother who pays most attention to her children, regardless of the result.[133]

iii. The Upper Bourgeoisie and the Squirarchy: The Child-oriented but Repressive Mode

Some families within this same social class followed a different mode. A remarkably well-documented example of the caring but authoritarian parent of the eighteenth century who still resorted to physical force to break the will of her children is the case of Mrs Hester Lynch Thrale (plate 23). Born in 1741 the daughter of an impoverished branch of the wealthy gentry family of the Salusburys, she was brought up as an intellectual by her father and mother, who were condemned by poverty to live very unhappily together in a remote Welsh village with nothing else to do but to educate their precocious child. 'I was their joint plaything, and although education was a word unknown as applied to females, they had taught me to read and speak and think and translate from the French till I was half a prodigy.'[134] After years in which she and her mother sponged off relatives, her fortunes changed when she was adopted by a rich, childless uncle and so became a desirable heiress. In 1763, at the age of twenty-two, the combined pressures of her mother and her uncle induced her to agree to marry a wealthy brewer, Henry Thrale, whose primary interest in her, it seems, was her £10,000 marriage portion from her uncle. In the next fourteen years, from 1764 to 1778, she had two miscarriages and produced twelve children. This was an exceptionally high fertility rate, no doubt helped by the use of wet-nurses to suckle the children, which exposed her very rapidly after birth to renewed sexual activity and liability to pregnancy. In 1779 she remarked 'five little girls and breeding again, and fool enough to be proud of it. Ah, idiot, what should I want more children for? God knows only to please my husband.'[135]

A careful record Mrs Thrale kept from 1766 to 1778 allows a unique view of one mother's relations with her children.[136] Mrs Thrale was far from being typical, but her story is firmly embedded in the culture of her time and her class. Old-fashioned views about total submission of the will by physical force – encouraged by Mrs Thrale's chief friend and advisor Dr Johnson, who spent much of his life living with the family – were coupled with a strong maternal ambition to produce a series of intellectual child prodigies. The tragedy was that her failure to breast-feed them, her harsh educational methods, and her selfish ambition to make her children exceptional in their learning and achievements alienated their affections, while her extraordinary fertility – one birth every fourteen months or so – produced a race of puny children who were constantly dying. For twelve years, however, all her energies were devoted to her children. She was lacking any emotional support from her husband, who followed his business, pursued his own gay social life and his extra-marital affairs, largely ignored his growing brood of children, and only paid sufficient attention to his wife in bed to keep her constantly pregnant in the hopes of getting a male heir to carry on his brewery. She was an energetic and dynamic woman, deprived of all emotional or functional outlets except her children, her mother, and her books. As she described it, 'We kept the finest table possible at Streatham Park, but [I] his wife was not to think of the kitchen. So I never knew what was for dinner till I saw it. . . . From a gay life my mother held me fast. Those pleasures Mr Thrale enjoyed alone. . . . Driven thus on literature as my sole resource, no wonder if I loved my books and my children.' She 'brought a baby once a year, lost some of them, and grew so anxious about the rest that I now fairly cared for nothing else but them and her' – her mother, whom she saw for several hours almost every day.[137]

When her Children's Book opens in 1766, Mrs Thrale's eldest daughter Hester, or 'Queeney', was already a child wonder. The eighteenth century was an age which encouraged child prodigies, and whose parents took pride in showing them off to visitors, and her mother treated her very much like a show animal. Queeney was indeed truly remarkable for her memory. At two and a half she could not read or write, but she already knew the compass, the solar system, the signs of the zodiac, the nations, seas and islands and European capital cities, the three Christian virtues, the first page of Lilly's *Grammar*, the names of colours, the days of the week and the months of the year, the two-times table, the Pater Noster, the Nicene Creed and the Decalogue, and could tell the stories of the Fall of Man, Perseus and Andromeda, and the Judgement of Paris. By the age of three, Queeney could repeat all the Responses, but still could not read, and was a poor speller. By four and a half she could read fairly well and knew her Latin grammar to the fifth declension.

Mrs Thrale's obsessive devotion to Queeney knew no bounds. In 1770, by which time Queeney was six, she recorded that she went to the theatre (taking Queeney with her) for the first time since the child was born. 'I have never dined out, nor ever paid a visit where I did not carry her, unless I left her in bed; for to the care of servants (except asleep) I have never yet left her an hour.' At the age of six and a quarter, in January 1771, her mother made her go through her paces before Mr Bright of Abingdon, who finally declared that if the examination had been in Latin, 'she would have qualified for a degree in the university of Oxford.' Queeney's emotional response to all this excessive maternal care and egotistical devotion – her mother was constantly showing off her child prodigy – was far from satisfactory. Her mother concluded that the girl was 'obstinate to that uncommon degree, that no punishment except severe smart can prevail upon her to beg pardon if she has offended.' 'A heart void of all affection for any person in the world, but aversion enough for many.' After ten years she noted that Queeney was 'sullen, malicious, perverse, desirous of tormenting *me*, even by hurting herself.'[138]

Among all her many children, two were her particular favourites. Lucy was 'wonderfully amiable. I am accused of a partial fondness towards her, but she is so lively one cannot resist her coaxing.' Henry 'has charity, piety, benevolence ... a desire for knowledge. ... He is so rational, so attentive, so good.' On the other hand, poor little Susanna, the premature baby, was ugly, sickly, and whining. Her mother detested the child – 'her temper is so peevish and her person so displeasing that I do not love to converse with her'

– and packed her off at the age of four to a private school in Kensington, where to her astonishment the girl immediately began to thrive. In 1775 Mrs Thrale decided to take the other girl, Sophy, back home since she was 'very amiable. I will keep her at home, Queeney and I can tutor her mighty well, and it will be an amusement.' This wholly self-centered attitude towards her children was coupled with the use of force to make herself obeyed. She beat her children with her 'Salusbury fist' to make them obey her orders at once and to learn their lessons. This aroused the disgust and hostility of their Italian teacher Baretti, who advocated an educational system based on permissiveness and love, and encouraged the children to oppose their mother. So there was constant friction in the home.[139]

It was not until 1774, after eleven years of child-rearing, that Mrs Thrale first took an extended holiday away from them. Even then, she was a prey to anxiety and wept when no letters arrived from home to tell how they were faring. What eventually soured her on her educational endeavours was partly the hostility towards her expressed especially by her prized pupil Queeney, and partly the constant attrition of the children by death. One child died within ten hours from respiratory trouble, one within two weeks of diarrhoea, one within six months of influenza; these deaths could be endured, but the beloved Lucy died at four of mastoiditis. One son, Ralph, was diagnosed as suffering from brain disease ('a thing to hide and be ashamed of whilst we live'), but fortunately died at under two; Henrietta died of measles at five; Susanna, as we have seen, was sickly and ugly, and was sent off to school at four. But their mother constantly worried about the health of the others, stayed up all night with them when they were sick, and doctored them herself to try to cure them. The greatest blow was the death in 1776, at the age of nine, of Henry, the talented, handsome and amiable only son and heir. He suddenly collapsed and died within hours of a ruptured appendix, leaving his mother 'childless with all her children – want an heir.' 'I was too proud of him,' she told herself, 'and provoked God's judgements by my folly. Let this sorrow expiate my offences, good Lord. . . . Suffer me no more to follow my offspring to the grave.' She, and even more her husband, desperately wanted a boy, if only for a simple economic reason. As her friend and advisor Dr Johnson put it, 'a son is almost necessary to the continuance of Thrale's fortune; for what can misses do with a brew-house? Lands are fitter for daughters than trades.' It was probably for this reason that she allowed herself to be constantly re-impregnated by her husband, although to no effect. 'Mrs Thrale is in hopes of a young brewer,' commented Dr Johnson when she once more became pregnant in

1777.[140]

But the events of 1776 finally broke Mrs Thrale's determination to mould the lives of her children, and to turn them all into prodigies of learning who could be put on display. Within one year she had lost three of her six children, including the only boy, and became thoroughly disillusioned. 'I have really listened to babies learning till I am half stupefied – and all my pains have answered so poorly. I have no heart to battle with Sophy. She would probably learn very well, if I had the spirit of teaching I once had. . . . I will not make her life miserable, as I suppose it will be short. . . . At present I cannot begin battling with babies – I have already spent my whole youth at it, and lost my reward at last.' Of the three surviving daughters, two were sullen and hostile to their mother.[141]

So at last, in 1776, she abandoned the struggle to subdue her children's wills and to cram book-learning down their throats, pushed the survivors off to school, and turned her energies to her literary pursuits, the cultivation of the blue-stocking coterie of London, and the creation of an intellectual salon of her own. Her children had defeated her either by dying or by ingratitude. In 1781 her husband died of apoplexy, leaving his widow with five surviving daughters (of whom one soon died). Mrs Thrale then at last faced the bitter truth: 'they are five lovely creatures to be sure, but they love not me. Is it my fault or theirs?' Two years later, she abandoned both her old friend Dr Johnson and her four surviving children for the sake of a passionate romance: she married their Italian music teacher Mr Piozzi and went off to Italy to taste, for the first time in her life, the pleasures of true married love.[142]

Even then, her efforts to mould her children to her will were not finally at an end. In 1787 she seized control of the last daughter, the nine-year old Cecilia, from Queeney, who had tried to remove her from her mother's care. At first she was overjoyed to get the girl back from school. 'I have got the child home to us. . . . I hold her to my heart all day long.' She then proceeded to drag Cecilia about the country with her and her now ailing husband, trying to teach her to be a scholar and using her as a companion to talk to. But Cecilia hated scholarship and bitterly resented the harsh pressures of her mother. She grew up a pretty, impetuous and temperamental girl, and when Mrs Piozzi refused her leave to marry when under age, she ran away to Gretna Green and married without consent (plate 4). Mrs Piozzi ended up by totally alienating the affections of her youngest surviving daughter.[143]

Even this was not the end of her efforts, for in 1798 she adopted her second husband's five-year-old nephew, John Piozzi, and brought him to England to be educated as an English gentleman. Her motives were still selfish, for she confessed: 'we will see if he will be more grateful and rational and comfortable than Miss Thrales have been to the mother they have at length driven to desperation.' At first she wanted him educated as a scholar and 'a very good one,' but later aimed merely at 'virtue, literature and manners.' Later still, when he dropped out of Christ Church, Oxford, after one year due to his hatred of book-learning, the best she could hope for was that he had acquired the values and manners – but not the literature – of an English landed gentleman. She settled her Welsh property on him so that he could live in the appropriate style, but he failed to show her affection or gratitude, and was constantly wheedling more money out of her, culminating in £6,000 given him in 1817 to buy a baronetcy, which he used for other purposes. So in the end, he too was a disappointment, like all the rest of her children.[144]

What conclusions are we to draw from this story? It concerns a woman who directed all her driving ambition on to her children, for lack of any serious support from, or interest shown in her by, her husband. Dominant, authoritarian, demanding, possessive, and wholly selfish in her pursuit of ego-gratification through her children, as a mother Mrs Thrale/Piozzi was a total failure. She had not succeeded in turning any of her children into intellectual prodigies, and she had not attracted their affection. Lucy and Henry, the two to whom she had been most attached and who seemed both most closely to match her ambitions for them and to reciprocate her love, both died young, aged four and nine respectively. The two upon whom she had lavished most attention, the eldest Queeney and the youngest Cecilia, came to resent her most and even speculated that subconsciously she actually hated them because of her hostile feelings towards their father.[145] The adopted son of her later years, John Piozzi, was too noisy and obstreperous for her to endure at home for more than short intervals, showed no inclination whatever for things intellectual, gave her little affection, and exploited her financially. The combination of the physically repressive parental mode of the seventeenth century with the child-oriented obsessions of the eighteenth, and the high intellectual ambitions of the contemporary female blue-stocking, together formed an altogether disastrous mix.

iv. The Pious Nonconformists: the Egocentric Intrusive Mode

All the evidence hitherto put forward for an increasing concern for children is strictly confined to the upper landed and high professional or bourgeois classes, and there is no evidence that this attitude penetrated much lower down the social scale. One would suppose that stern Calvinistic ideas about upbringing persisted longest among the lower-middle class, but this is largely speculation.

The most detailed example of a highly intrusive but psychologically oppressive and not at all affectionate family is provided by the diaries and writings of Cotton Mather, a middle-class, rigidly Puritan minister in Boston, who was bringing up his children between about 1690 and 1720. He was strongly opposed to physical punishment in the home, both in theory and in practice.

I wish that my children may as soon as may be, feel the principles of reason and honour working in them, and that I may carry on their education very much upon those principles. Therefore, first, I will wholly avoid that harsh, fierce, crabbed usage of the children, that would make them tremble, and abhor to come into my presence. I will so use them that they shall fear to offend me and yet mightily love to see me, and be glad of my coming home if I have been abroad at any time. I would have it looked upon as a severe and awful punishment for a crime in the family, to be forbidden for awhile to come into my presence.... I will never dispense a blow, except it be for an atrocious crime, or for a lesser fault obstinately persisted in; either for an enormity, or for an obstinacy. I would ever proportion chastisements unto miscarriages; not smite bitterly for a very small piece of childishness, and only frown a little for some real wickedness. Nor shall my chastisements ever be dispensed in a passion and a fury; but with them, I will first show them the command of God, by transgressing whereof they have displeased me. The slavish, raving, fighting way of education too commonly used, I look upon it as a considerable article in the wrath and curse of God upon a miserable world.

Instead, Mather exercised the most intense moral pressure to mould his children's wills and characters, day in and day out, year in and year out. Rarely has so much effort been put by a father into the attempt to create the perfect children. The whole effort was first directed to subordinating their wills to that of their father. The strategy he adopted was as follows: 'First I beget in them a high opinion of their father's love to them and of his being best able to judge what shall be good for them. Then I make them sensible 'tis folly for them to pretend unto any wit or will of their own; they must resign all to me, who will be sure to do what is best; my word must be their law.' The tactics were those of relentless thought control, buttressed by a fear of God's wrath and visions of eternal hell-fire for those who disobeyed. He published a book called *Ungodly Children*, which contained awful examples of sin and its consequences, a book which he thrust upon his children. He regularly called them into his study one by one, prayed with them, and examined them about their sins and their private prayers for redemption. They were instructed in the morning to consider the faults they needed to cure and to report the results of their meditations in the evening. They were also questioned each evening on what they had done during the day and were frequently told to write down the contents of their prayers for their father's inspection. Whenever they fell ill, they were reminded that the punishments of God were the wages of sin.[146]

In addition to this personal pressure, their father made it a practice of holding morning and evening family prayers, Bible readings, and psalm singings, while he used the dinner and supper times as occasions for 'instructive' conference. Whenever he met them about the house it was his practice to drop useful moral hints or tell moralizing stories – 'a continual dropping of maxims of piety', which he believed would inevitably take effect.[147]

Nor did Cotton neglect the formal, academic education of his children. He took an active part in teaching Latin and mathematics to his sons, and reading, writing, shorthand, household duties and practical skills such as medicine to his daughters. They were all constantly kept busy writing essays, making translations or taking notes in commonplace books under his direction.[148]

The results of all these efforts were not too happy. Of the fifteen born, only six survived. The eldest son, Increase, went hopelessly to the bad, and his drowning at sea was in some ways a merciful relief.[149] Moreover by the time the diary ends two of the fully-grown daughters had not yet had a conversion experience nor made their covenant with God to become full members of the church. In 1718 Cotton had some reason why 'my mind is visited with dark thoughts, lest my children should, through the just wrath of Heaven upon me, prove a miserable offspring.' Only one, the dutiful child-prodigy Samuel, turned out fully to his father's satisfaction.[150]

Whatever the practical consequences of all Cotton Mather's paternal care may have been, what is important historically is this remarkable example in about 1700 of a family in which a significant amount of the father's efforts and time were directed to the bringing up of his children within the home. Even the ne'er-do-well eldest son Increase managed to attract his father's concern to the bitter end, despite the latter's horror at the boy's behaviour and actions. This is, no doubt, an exceptional case, only possible for a father whose work was largely conducted in the home, and who had the leisure, the education and the compelling religious motivation to supervise closely the upbringing of his children. In England it could probably only be paralleled at that time in a few dissenting clerical households. On the other hand, it looks forward to the English Evangelical middle-class family of the eighteenth and early nineteenth century, for whose behaviour patterns and relationships the family of Cotton Mather provides the archetype.

It is not known how far this family type, not so much loving as intensely watchful for the sake of the parents' standing with God, and therefore highly intrusive, continued to flourish among the pious lower-middle class during the eighteenth century. The picture of his family life drawn by the son of George Crabbe, the poet, at the end of the century is far more joyous and serene than the tormented and anxious atmosphere in the household of Cotton Mather a century before.

How delightful it is to recall the innocent feelings of unbounded love, confidence and respect, associated with my earliest visions of my parents. They appeared to their children not only good, but free from any taint of the corruption common to our nature; and such was the strength of the impressions then received, that hardly could subsequent experience ever enable our judgments to modify them. Many a happy and indulged child has, no doubt, partaken in the same fond exaggeration; but ours surely had everything to excuse it. Always visibly happy in the happiness of others, especially of children, our father entered into all our pleasures, and soothed and cheered us in all our little griefs with such overflowing tenderness that it was no wonder we almost worshipped him.

Joseph Brasbridge, the silversmith, speaking of the late eighteenth century, recalled the friendly and egalitarian joshing and teasing that took place between himself and his son, using it as evidence of 'the friendly and unrestrained terms on which I lived with my family.'[151]

To what extent these are exceptional cases of upbringing among the lower-middle class of the very late eighteenth century we do not know. George Crabbe was certainly an exceptionally gentle person, but his son may not be an altogether unbiased witness, and we do not know whether Brasbridge's son would have agreed with his father's eulogy. It seems not unlikely that in many lower-middle-class homes, there was carried over from the seventeenth century the concept of the innate depravity of children and therefore the need and the incentive for an unremitting and stern effort to break the child's will and so repress his impulses to sin. There seems to have been an uninterrupted connection between the caring but authoritarian discipline of the Puritan bourgeois parent of the seventeenth century and the caring but authoritarian discipline of the Evangelical bourgeois parent of the late eighteenth and early nineteenth centuries.

The link between the two is provided by the methods of education of children adopted by John Wesley's mother Susanna at Epworth rectory in the early years of the eighteenth century and passed on by him to the Wesleyan movement. As she explained her policies in 1732, 'when turned a year old, and some before, they were taught to fear the rod and cry softly, by which means they escaped the abundance of correction they might otherwise have had, and that most odious noise of the crying of children was rarely heard in the house.' The children were drilled into strict obedience to parental instructions. 'In order to form the minds of the children, the first thing to be done is to conquer their will and bring them to an obedient temper.' 'Whenever a child is corrected, it must be conquered', for this provides 'the only strong and rational foundation of a religious education.' As a result, the children were made to eat everything that was put before them, even if it nauseated them, and were fully obedient to Susanna's wishes. She devoted her life to them, teaching them religion and the three Rs six hours a day. It was her policy to reward them for goodwill and effort, even if the results were unsuccessful, thus encouraging them to try their very best.[152] It was a discipline not too far removed from that recommended by Locke. It was strict, intrusive, but supportive, rational and predictably consistent. Where it differed from that of Locke was that the object, so far as the parents were concerned, was to please God, and to bring up the next generation to internalize the same strong sense of piety and duty. The result of this upbringing was the adult John Wesley, a compulsive perfectionist, with a persistent desire to conform to authority, but with an overwhelming sense of his own role in history as one of the chosen of God. Half a century later, in 1783, Wesley was still preaching the same doctrines in his *Sermon on the Education of Children*. Although he admitted that in his degenerate age only one parent in a hundred had the resolution to go through with it, he insisted on the need to 'break the will of your child, to bring his will into subjection to yours, that it may be afterwards subject to the will of God.'

It seems quite likely that large numbers of parents of the lower-middle classes, who had to deal with children all day and every day rather than at brief intervals of their own choosing, found that breaking the will to enforce obedience was the easiest solution. The permissive mode was a luxury reserved for those who had plenty of nurses and governesses to deal with the temper tantrums of spoilt children. This intrusive mode also had both philosophical and theological underpinnings. It was a form of child-rearing theoretically based firmly on the doctrine of Original Sin, but mitigated by care and a belief in the redeeming quality of Grace. Wesley's later Evangelical successes were with some of the most brutalized of the labouring poor, like the miners. In part this was because of his message that firm, fair, consistent, rational control of natural impulses to disorder and vice would lead to conversion and salvation. The vision of such an ordered and reasonable world, which also led to redemption, was strikingly different from his auditors' own childhood experience with unpredictable and capricious parents, sometimes terrifyingly and irrationally cruel, often aloof and indifferent, sometimes affectionate and generous. This frighteningly erratic treatment was in complete contrast with the routinized moral order offered by Wesley, which derived from his own upbringing by his mother.[153]

It is no surprise, therefore, to find a late eighteenth-century Evangelical like Hannah More, a middle-class educational reformer of the poor, echoing the ideas of Susanna Wesley, and writing in 1799 that it is a 'fundamental error to consider children as innocent beings, whose little weaknesses may perhaps want some correction, rather than as beings who bring into the world a corrupt nature and evil dispositions, which it should be the great end of education to rectify.'[154] This could be interpreted to mean that Hannah Moore thought that the 'childish innocence' theory was very common among her audience, or that she was reinforcing and repeating accepted dogma. It seems at least likely that the lower-middle classes never accepted the Lockean view of the child as a *tabula rasa* upon which society could imprint its image, much less the Rousseauesque theory that he is born naturally good. They always knew about Original Sin and acted accordingly, using a combination of physical force and moral manipulation that varied from family to family.

v. The Cottager and Artisan: the Brutal but Careful Mode

For those slightly above the line of absolute destitution, the smallholders, small tenant farmers, cottagers and artisans, children were positive economic assets, primarily for their productive labour from the age of seven until their marriage, but also as supports for the parents in old age.[155] When the factory system was introduced in the late eighteenth century, the attitude of neglect by the parents of the poor shifted to one of economic exploitation. It was not so much the capitalist employers who drove little children down mines or into factories for fourteen hours a day or more; it was the parents who eagerly pushed them into it, in part admittedly because of the fall in the price of their own labour. As Marx put it: 'Previously, the workman sold his own labour power, which he disposed of nominally as a free agent. Now he sells his wife and child. He has become a slave dealer.' In Bethnal Green in the early nineteenth century, there was a public market 'where children of both sexes from nine years of age upwards hire themselves out to the silk manufacturers', the usual terms being 15s 8d per week to the parents and 2d and tea for the child. Similarly, children were taken from the workhouse and let out at 25s 6d per week. Over two thousand children were sold by their parents for the filthy, frightening and dangerous job of chimney-sweeping. The rector of Camerton in Somerset recorded a case in 1805 of an eight-year-old boy killed in a coal-mine accident, and he blamed the covetousness of the parents and the proprietors for allowing seven-year-olds to enter into so dangerous an occupation. In 1822 he was indignant to find a widowed father in the village refusing to allow his sons to be sent away and apprenticed to a trade (the fees paid for by their grandfather), 'as they brought in fifteen shillings per week' by working down the mine.[156]

Judging from the very few working-class diaries that were written in the mid-eighteenth century, the treatment by this class of their children and their apprentices was sometimes very brutal. Thomas Holcroft was born in London, the son of a poor shoemaker-turned-peddler. He later recalled that his father 'used to beat me, pull my hair up by the roots, and drag me by my ears along the ground till they ran with blood.' But his father's moods changed fast and a little later 'he would break out into passionate exclamations of fondness.'[157]

Francis Place, who was born in 1771, recalled that his father treated his sons with calculated ferocity, although he never touched his daughters. He always carried around in his pocket a knotted rope's end; he often punched them if they got in his way in a corridor or doorway; and when really enraged, would beat them with a stick until it broke. 'Beating and that too in excess, was with him the all in all in the way of teaching.' 'In his opinion coercion was the only way to eradicate faults, and by its terror to prevent their recurrence. These were common notions, and were carried into practice not only by the heads of families and the teachers of youth generally, but by the government itself and every man in authority under it.'

But attitudes were changing, and by the time Place was writing, in the 1820s, he was convinced that an enormous change had taken place in the public and private use of physical cruelty as a means of social control. He saw very clearly the great improvements effected during his lifetime by the widespread impulse to humanitarian reform of the age, in which he himself played a prominent part. His conclusions were confirmed in 1810 by a foreign visitor, Simond, who asserted that there had taken place a vast change in the nature of human relationships, so that now 'there is no one so low as to suffer the treatment he would have born in former times ... blows and abusive epithets are known only in old novels and on the stage – the picture of obsolete manners.'[158]

vi. The Poor: The Indifferent and Exploitative Mode

Among the mass of the very poor, the available evidence suggests that the common behaviour of many parents towards their children was often indifferent, cruel, erratic and unpredictable. It is not clear whether the reason was cultural, a result of deprivation of any property stake in society and displacement far from home and kin, or whether it was economic, in the sense that more humane feelings and a greater sense of sustained concern were luxuries which they could rarely afford. The culture of poverty did not encourage foresight or providence, since the lives of those on the economic margin of existence were too much at the mercy of sheer chance – a bad harvest, unemployment or sickness – to justify rational calculation for the future. They were therefore improvident in begetting children, with no thought of how they were to be nursed and fed, and improvident and careless in disposing of them once they had arrived: easy come, easy go. They were in the habit of treating their children occasionally with rough, even extravagant affection in good times, more often with casual indifference, and not infrequently with great brutality when in drink or in bad times. If they were cruel to their children, it was because they needed to vent their frustrations on somebody, or because they failed to foresee the consequences of their actions, or because that was the way they themselves had been brought up, and they therefore regarded it as the normal and proper method of rearing children, or because they had no alternative due to economic circumstances. In a society which was generally horribly cruel to animals, children tended to be treated in a similar manner. As late as 1846, a sensible upper-class woman commented that 'anyone who has been accustomed to live in a country village must know that the children of the poor there are brought up with blows – with harsh words.' It was for this reason that she strongly advised against entrusting the power of punishment of upper-class children to a nurse or servant, since the latter would 'naturally carry the same system into execution.'[159]

The tradition of education by physical brutality was not the only cause of the treatment of their children by the poor. It is evident that many families lived so close to the absolute poverty line that they could not be expected to regard their children as much more than either impediments to the earning capacity of the wife, or hungry mouths to be got rid of as soon as possible.

> Mine greater bliss would be
> Would Heav'n take those my spouse assigns to me,

comments a poor rural labourer in George Crabbe's *Parish Register* of 1807.[160]

For those without property, security or prospects, children were often an unmitigated nuisance. There was the cost of feeding and housing them and the opportunity cost in the removal of the wife for a time from productive labour in order to breast-feed and look after the children. Even if the child could be gainfully employed after the age of seven, which was possible in many rural areas for guarding animals, collecting firewood, frightening birds, etc., and became both more common and more profitable in the early stages of the industrial revolution, there were still seven years in which it would have to be fed. If the wife produced a child every two years, the family might therefore have to support three or four unproductive mouths, which was a burden that many simply could not afford. One is torn between pity and horror at the story of the poor man near Wakefield in 1674 who 'hanged his own child to death for taking a piece of bread to eat it; another child said, "father, you'll not hang me, I took no bread."'[161]

Neglect of children was particularly prevalent in areas where female employment was high and the demand for child labour was low. The mothers went out to work every day, leaving their children at home, exposed to malnutrition and maltreatment, and often dosed with opiates to keep them quiet. In these areas, child mortality was very much higher than in others where the women stayed at home, the cause being death by negligence. Where the women stayed at home and the children survived, hunger and deprivation was their lot, and William Huntingdon, a future Methodist preacher, had bitter memories of his childhood as the son of a day-labourer earning no more than 7s to 9s a week and with eleven children to support. 'Suffering with hunger, cold and almost nakedness so embittered my life in childhood that I often wished secretly that I had been a brute, for then I could have filled my belly in the fields.'[162]

In such circumstances, infant and child mortality was extremely high. In 1687 Mrs Elizabeth Cellier lamented the vast numbers of infants who died, most of them, she thought, for lack of care, as well as 'the great number . . . which are overlaid and wilfully murdered by their wicked and cruel mothers.' In 1712 *The Spectator* was still lamenting 'what multitudes of infants have been made away with by those who brought them into the world, and afterwards were either abandoned or unable to provide for them.' Many were 'not thought of sufficient consequence to be much attended to', and therefore died almost immediately of semi-deliberate exposure or starvation. Others were killed by the alcohol or opiates given them to keep them quiet at night, either being liberally dosed with brandy, gin or rum, or else being given opium-based patent preparations such as 'Godfrey's Cordial', or 'Dalby's Carminative'.[163]

Even the industrious and sober labourer found himself in much the same plight as the feckless poor who drowned their despair in drink. Francis Place, who began his married life in the 1790s in London, living in one room in miserable poverty, repeatedly refers to the curse of many children. This was a situation which he apparently thought inevitable, for he seems to have had no knowledge whatever of contraception. He explains how desperate was the situation of the diligent labouring poor at that time, who could see no hope of improvement of their lot. 'How, as the number of their children increases, hope leaves them. How their hearts sink as toil becomes useless.' As for himself, 'I saw the certainty that I should have a large family, and that nothing but wretchedness awaited us', unless he could set himself up in business. His wife became pregnant at regular intervals, and looking after the first two children took her from productive labour as his helper. She, too, fell into despair as 'her fears of our ever doing well were increased by her again being pregnant.' Although she was up for the family dinner within three days of giving birth, the care of the children reduced her earning power, and the increase of mouths to feed dragged down the already marginal living standards of the family.[164]

Where opportunities for child labour existed, a different, but equally cruel, treatment of children prevailed. An excellent example is the rural areas of Buckinghamshire and Bedfordshire, where in the seventeenth and eighteenth centuries the pillow-lace-making and straw-plaiting trades provided gainful employment for large numbers of female children from the age of four upwards. The junior children were deposited by their parents in 'schools', where a severe disciplinarian saw to it that the children, often only five or six years old, slaved away at their allotted tasks for from four to eight hours a day. To keep them hard at work the children were obliged to keep their necks and arms bare, so that they could be 'slapped more easily'. Later the children stayed at home, working even harder – nine hours a day for eight-year-olds, ten for thirteen-year-olds, and thirteen for fourteen-year-olds were normal – under the direction of their equally severe mother. 'Some mothers are very brutish', reported a nineteenth-century Parliamentary Commission.

The effects of this employment opportunity upon the little girls were almost all harmful. It induced their parents to treat them as slave labour. It prevented them from going to school and so kept them illiterate. It undermined their health by eye-strain; painfully twisted their shoulders from hunching over the lace-pillows; and killed them early from tuberculosis due to over-crowding in small work-rooms in order to provide heat without the expense of a fire. The only benefit was that the children's wages of 1s 6d to 4s a week substantially increased the family income, although it all went to the parents to spend as they pleased. Teenage children could easily earn their own living and therefore the employment offered the bolder ones the chance of independence from this family tyranny. Many could and did leave home early. The result was not only early marriage, but also a much higher than average rate of illegitimacy, since these young girls, cast adrift from their families, were often easy prey to male sexual advances. On balance there can be little doubt that the increased affluence of labouring families in these areas was more than offset by the illiteracy, the disease, the early death, the human pain and exhaustion from overwork, and the high illegitimacy that the employment engendered. The decline of these domestic cottage industries where children were exploited ruthlessly by their parents, and its replacement by machine production in factories, was a positive contribution to family life among the poor.[165]

One consequence of the rise in the proportion of the propertyless in the society was a rise in the rates of illegitimate to legitimate births, for reasons which will be discussed later on. This rise in bastardy inevitably stimulated some deliberate infanticide and a great deal of abandonment, for the plight of an unmarried mother without means of support was enough to encourage a few desperate women to murder their newly born infants and many more to leave them in the streets either to die or to be looked after by a charitable passer-by, the parish workhouse, or a foundling hospital. There is a long history of fairly generalized infanticide in western Europe going back to antiquity, when it seems to have been extremely common. How far it remained a common deliberate policy for legitimate children in the Early Modern period is still an open question, although it is suggestive that as late as the early eighteenth century in Anjou, priests were instructed to warn their congregations in a sermon every three months of the mortal sin of killing an infant before baptism. In medieval England, infanticide was not treated as homicide and dealt with in the secular courts, but was a lesser crime left to the Church courts. These courts did not distinguish between induced abortion and infanticide, nor did they attempt to distinguish between death by neglect and death by intent – an impossible problem when many deaths occurred through suffocation by over-laying by a parent or parents in bed (and some of which were probably only the mysterious crib-deaths of today). Punishments were limited to shame – public display of guilt – and sometimes also public whipping.[166]

In the sixteenth and seventeenth centuries, as the Church strengthened its hold over the moral conduct of the population at large and enlisted the help of the state in law enforcement, infanticide became a much more serious offence. Since it deprived an infant of baptism, and so the opportunity for salvation, it now became a crime that carried with it the penalty of death. The Church in the sixteenth century was not only insisting that the sole legitimate justification for marital sex was procreation, but was also forbidding the last method of population control, namely deliberate infanticide. It therefore became a practice almost entirely confined to those most desperate of women, unmarried mothers. When the three witches in *Macbeth* were concocting their magic brew, among the many things they threw into their cauldron was a

> Finger of birth-strangled babe
> Ditch-delivered by a drab.

Finding this ingredient, which might be a little hard to come by in the twentieth century, should not have presented insuperable difficulties in Shakespearean England. The abandonment in the eighteenth century of the punishment of the mothers of illegitimate children, by making them stand publicly in church before the congregation in a white sheet, was caused, according to Colonel Hanger, by a desire, which seems to have failed, to reduce the incentive to infanticide. Bastardy was still thought shameful in the village community, and the social and economic penalties of discovery thus remained very high. As Erasmus Darwin commented in 1767, 'the cause of this most horrid crime is an excess of what is really a virtue, of sense of shame, or modesty.'[167]

Deliberate infanticide – to become 'the butcher of her own bowels' was a solution adopted by only the most desperate of pregnant mothers, and abandonment, both of illegitimate and of legitimate children, was infinitely more common. As Jonas Hanway observed in 1766, 'it is much less difficult to the human heart and the dictates of self-preservation to drop a child than to kill it.'[168]

During the eighteenth century rapidly increasing numbers of infants were simply abandoned in the streets, and left to become a charge on the parish. Most of them were sent off to the parish workhouses, which were built after 1722, where the death rate was almost as high as if they had been left in the streets. 'There is no wonder in this, when it is considered that these children were put into the hands of indigent, filthy and decrepit women, three or four to one woman, and sometimes sleeping with them. The allowance to these women being scanty, they are tempted to take the bread and milk intended for the poor infants. The child cries for food, and the nurse beats it because it cries. Thus with blows, starving and putrid air, with the addition of lice, itch, filthiness, he soon receives his quietus.' In 1757 it was alleged that 'a prodigious number of children are cruelly murdered by those infernals called nurses. These infernal monsters throw spoonfuls of gin, spirits of wine, or Hungary water down a child's throat, which instantly strangles the babe.'[169] This arrangement was often a financially profitable one for the Overseers of the Poor, who extracted a lump sum from the father, or the putative father if the infant was a bastard, and made a clear profit from the early death of the child.[170]

For the few children who lived, the prospect was a grim one. The older females were frequently handed over to 'a master who is either vicious or cruel: in the one case they fall victim to his irregular passions (plate 35); and in the other are subjected, with unreasonable severity, to tasks too hard to be performed.' These were the lucky ones, others being virtually enslaved by criminals and trained for a life of prostitution if female or of robbery and pick-pocketing if male. Some had their teeth torn out to serve as artificial teeth for the rich (plate 27); others were deliberately maimed by beggars to arouse compassion and extract alms. Even this latter crime was one upon which the law looked with a remarkably tolerant eye. In 1761 a beggar woman, convicted of deliberately 'putting out the eyes of children with whom she went about the country' in order to attract pity and alms, was sentenced to no more than two years' imprisonment. No wonder this constant flow of abandoned children was the source of the 'great numbers of nine and ten-year old harlots, and hence proceeds the constantly supplied swarm of pick-pockets, shop-lifters, thieves, and the starving crew of impudent, ignorant and insolent demanders, that infest our streets.'[171]

During the 1730s Captain Thomas Coram frequently walked from Rotherhithe through the East London slums to the City. These walks 'afforded him frequent occasions of seeing young children exposed, sometimes alive, sometimes dead, and sometimes dying, which affected him extremely.' As a result, he enlisted support from the wealthy, and in 1741 established the London Foundling Hospital, 'to prevent the frequent murders of poor miserable children at their birth, and to suppress the inhuman custom of exposing new-born infants to perils in the streets, and to take in children dropped in churchyards or in the streets, or left at night at the doors of church wardens or Overseers of the Poor.'[172] The hospital was planned to accept a limited number of children each year, but in 1756 a well-meaning Parliament threw it open to the country as a whole. The results were catastrophic. Three or four thousand infants poured in every year, being collected in baskets from all over the country by itinerant baby transporters, who dumped the contents, dead, dying or half alive, on the doorsteps of the hospital. Travelling tinkers were paid a guinea to carry a child to the hospital, while another man took four infants from Yorkshire, two in each pannier, for eight guineas the trip. Of the fifteen thousand children dumped in the hospital in the first four years, some ten thousand died. It became 'a charnel house for the dead'. The same thing happened in Dublin between 1790 and 1796, where nearly ten thousand died out of twelve thousand six hundred.[173]

Although many of this growing mass of abandoned children were illegitimate, a majority seem to have been legitimate children of couples who were financially unable to support them. Abandonment of infants was thus a product partly of rising rates of bastardy, but still more of a deepening economic crisis for the very poor. Partly also it was a population control device operating after birth for lack of knowledge of the two alternatives – abortion of the foetus while in the womb or the prevention of conception.[174] The paradox should also be noted that the practice of abandonment was partly stimulated by the setting up of charitable public institutions. It was easier for mothers to abandon their children if they knew that they would be picked up, even if the workhouses and foundling hospitals in which they were deposited in practice, and inevitably, became little more than licensed death camps.

So long as such conditions persisted, the shift in parent-child relations that occurred in the upper and middle classes was simply not conceivable. There are levels of human misery at which the intensity of the struggle to satisfy the basic need for food and shelter leaves little room for humane emotions and affective relationships. If the second basic drive, for sexual satisfaction, results in the production of greedy little competitors for an inadequate food supply, they are bound to be treated with at best neglect and at worst deliberate hostility to encourage their rapid departure from this world.

By 1820 the situation, at any rate in London, was already greatly improved. Francis Place, who was a very well-informed observer of urban poverty in the metropolis, had no doubts about the changes which had occurred in the previous fifty years. Recalling conditions he knew in the 1770s, he denounced 'the ignorance, the immorality, the grossness, the obscenity, the drunkenness, the dirtiness, and the depravity of the middling and even a large portion of the better sort of tradesmen, the artisans, and the journeymen tradesmen of London in the days of my youth.' The causes of the change he attributed to the introduction of cotton underclothing which revolutionized the problem of personal cleanliness; a higher standard of living as the benefits of the industrial revolution seeped down to the poor; a greater sense of self-respect and equality as a result of the diffusion of the ideas of Tom Paine and the French Revolution; and the moral and literary education of children provided by the Sunday Schools. The result was a general elevation of 'the manners and morals of the whole community.'[175]

So far as the treatment of children is concerned, all these factors were important in improving their lot. In 1774 Dr Lettson drew attention to medical improvements which contributed to the same effect, in particular inoculation against smallpox, better obstetric training of midwives, and improvements in 'the nurture and management of infants.' Improved marketing arrangements which made fresh cow's milk available in the cities probably also helped. By the 1820s there can be no doubt that there had been significant changes for the better. Francis Place noted in 1824 that in London 'there are no such groups of half-starved, miserable, scald-headed children with rickety limbs and bandy legs as there were in the days of my youth, neither is there anything like the same mortality amongst them.' The crude statistics of births and deaths in the London Bills of Mortality, however inadequate they may be for a variety of reasons, nevertheless point to a dramatic progressive reduction of infant mortality. The number of burials of children under two years, as a ratio of baptisms, was sixty per cent in 1730–49 and fell steadily to twenty-three per cent by 1810–29.[176] This decline is unlikely to have been due exclusively to medical improvements like smallpox inoculation, or industrial improvements like the introduction of cheap cotton goods, or nutritional improvements like the availability of cow's milk. It probably also reflects a change in attitude towards children, involving a greater concern for the preservation of infant lives. Bad as things were by the time Marx and Dickens were writing, they were very much better than they had been in the third quarter of the eighteenth century. In 1824 Francis Place had no doubt that in his lifetime, he had seen an 'increased knowledge of domestic concerns and the general maintenance of children.'[177]

vii. Foreign Comparisons

In New England a more affectionate attitude to children became common at least as early as in England, while in France it developed a good deal later. There was the same desire to subordinate and mould the child's will in New England as there was in England, but the methods used were more psychological than physical. The doctrine of the Calling, the duty to work hard at whatever vocation God has chosen for one, was quickly internalized, and made to operate as an effective control-mechanism.[178]

It would seem that first tentative and then rapid moves towards the relative liberation of the child occurred about a century earlier in England and New England than in France, at any rate in aristocratic households. The sixteenth and seventeenth centuries had seen the authority of both the state and the Counter-Reformation Church thrown in support of the most absolute claims to parental control by noblemen over the marriages of their children. Between 1639 and 1789, a noble French father had the virtually untrammelled right – which was not infrequently exercised – to order his children to be imprisoned by *lettres de cachet* of the Crown on the vaguest grounds of disobedience, dissoluteness of morals, or a menace to the honour and good name of the family. The Revolution did little to reduce this despotic power, which was reintroduced in the *Code Napoléon* for fathers of all classes over children under the age of sixteen, although the courts had the right to refuse enforcement.[179] Before the Revolution, fathers also retained wide powers to disinherit their children at will, powers which were total in the *pays de droit écrit*. Parental permission was still necessary for the marrying of women up to the age of twenty-five and of men up to the age of thirty, and parental disposal of children at will, whether in marriage or into nunneries or monasteries, appeared to be almost absolute. Even Montesquieu thought that it was 'the responsibility of parents to marry off their children.' Moreover, right up to the end of the eighteenth century the relations of parents and children remained as distant as they had ever been. The Prince de Ligne remarked in the early part of the century that 'My father did not like me; I do not know why, because we did not know each other at all.' Reminiscing about his own childhood towards the end of the century, Talleyrand declared that his parents had never set eyes on him by the time he was eight. They believed, he commented acidly, that 'too much care would have seemed pedantry; affection too openly expressed would have been regarded as quite unusual, and therefore ridiculous. Parental care had not yet come into fashion.' His sociological explanation, which was clearly correct, was that 'In the great houses, it is the family which is loved, far more than the individuals which compose it, and above all more than the young individuals who are still unknown to their parents.'[180]

If there is a clear difference of a hundred years or so in the evolution of the high aristocratic family in France and England, the evidence for a similar difference between middle-class and professional households is much less secure. But it is noticeable that books and periodicals designed to be read by children began in France in the 1780s, forty years later than in England, and that they relied heavily on English translations and plagiarisms.[181] Similarly middle-class exponents of the new child-rearing ideal in France, Diderot and Rousseau, were writing their propaganda tracts more than half a century after Locke, Dunton, Defoe, Addison and Steele had published their views in England. Moreover, it appears that Rousseau had little practical influence, although only a detailed study of French middle-class memoirs and diaries of the eighteenth and nineteenth centuries would be able to prove this point conclusively.

What is beyond doubt, however, is the enormous and indeed increasing scale of mercenary wet-nursing among the labouring and artisan classes of urban France during the eighteenth century and the first three-quarters of the nineteenth century. The result of this practice was an infant mortality rate which was as high as forty-five per cent at Rheims and sixty per cent at Lyons, which suggests a massive indifference towards children, indeed a positive desire for infanticide.[182] Rousseau's theories and French practice were thus at opposite poles of the spectrum of possible attitudes towards child-rearing, which points once again to the danger of using famous didactic works as evidence of actual behaviour. In view of the staggering mortality rate, the practice was clearly not only a product of poverty but also of a cultural pattern of indifference to children and an urgent desire to limit numbers, if necessary by this form of licensed infanticide.[183]

This growing trend by the urban middle class to infanticidal wet-nursing was coupled with a growing trend by the really poor, under the pressure of extreme economic hardship, to abandonment of their children in the streets or outside foundling hospitals. As in England, most of those picked up by these charitable institutions soon died of malnutrition and disease.[184]

On the other hand, for reasons which are very obscure, France was almost a century ahead of all other countries in Europe in the widespread adoption among the lower classes of contraceptive practices, while they were also well ahead of England in abandoning the physical punishment of school-children. The story is therefore a complicated one, and England was more advanced than France in most respects, but more backward in a few.

PART FIVE

Sex

'Knowledge gives like pleasure to the mind that Venus doth to the body.'
(Marginalia by King Charles I on a copy of F. Bacon, *Advancement of Learning* in the British Museum. I owe this reference to Dr M. Smuts.)

'I could be content that we might procreate like trees, without conjunction, or that there was any way to perpetuate the world without this trivial and vulgar way of coition; it is the foolishest act a wise man commits in all his life; nor is there anything that will more deject his cooled imagination, when he shall consider what an odd and unworthy piece of folly he has committed.'
(T. Browne, *Religio Medici*, 1642, Oxford, 1909, p. 163.)

CHAPTER 10

Upper-Class Attitudes
and Behaviour

*'The husband who, transported by immoderate love, has intercourse with his wife
so ardently in order to satisfy his passion that, even had she not been his wife he
would have wished to have commerce with her, is committing a sin.'*

(J.Benedicti, *Somme des Péchés*, 1584, quoted by J.-L.Flandrin,
'Contraception, Marriage and Sexual Relations in the Christian
West' in *Biology of Man in History*, ed. R.Forster and O.Ranum,
Baltimore, 1975, p. 35.)

*'Life can little else supply
But a few good fucks and then we die.'*

(J.Wilkes, *Essay on Woman*, 1763, ed. J.C.Hotten London
1871, p. 13.)

I INTRODUCTION: GENERAL CONSIDERATIONS

i. Biological Constants

In terms of his sexual drive, the human species lies at the extreme end of the
normal range of animal behaviour, in that the drive lasts all the year round,
and even during periods when reproduction is impossible. This is caused by
the biological fact that, at some very remote time in the past, the human
female lost the oestrus, the brief but intense period of sexual receptivity. On
the other hand, the abnormal size and development of man's cerebral cortex
means that the sexual drive is stimulated or controlled by cultural norms and
learned experience. Despite appearances, human sex takes place mostly in
the head. Thus in the history of the West, infantile sexuality has sometimes
been condoned and sometimes repressed; adolescent masturbation has
sometimes been ignored and sometimes fanatically repressed; bisexual and

homosexual instincts among men have usually been strongly condemned by the masses, but often tolerated by the elite; homosexual relations between women have usually been ignored; pre-marital sexual experiments have sometimes been tacitly tolerated and sometimes strictly forbidden; the double standard of sexual behaviour for men and women has usually, but not always, been deeply embedded in customary morality and in legal codes; incest taboos have everywhere existed, but have varied widely in scope, and in the zeal with which they have been enforced; the female sexual libido has usually been regarded as dangerously powerful, but in the Victorian middle class as virtually non-existent; women have sometimes been expected to achieve orgasmic fulfilment and sometimes to be passive and inert recipients of the semen of the male. The Freudian assumption that sex is an unchanging infrastructure, and that there has been no change in the strength of the libido over time has therefore no basis in reality, so deeply is it overlaid by cultural norms.

The sexual act has always been treated as legally essential to a valid marriage, but it has sometimes been regarded as morally legitimate solely as a means of procreation, sometimes as a means of mutual endearment and gratification in its own right, and sometimes as a supreme physical pleasure the achievement of which is the prime purpose of marriage. The male semen has usually been regarded as a vital fluid, the excessive loss of which will have serious medical consequences, and married couples have usually been advised to place limits on the frequency of marital intercourse. Limits have often also been recommended on the times in which marital intercourse should take place, on either religious or medical grounds. The many deviant manifestations of sexual gratification have usually been strongly condemned, but sometimes been regarded as morally neutral, as long as they provide pleasure to both parties. Concepts of sexual privacy and sexual shame have varied enormously over time. Because of cramped living conditions, most of the human race over most of history can never have enjoyed sexual privacy, and few seem to have felt uneasy or inhibited by the lack. On the other hand, there is widespread evidence that full nudity openly displayed in the light has very often been regarded as shameful. There has thus been an extraordinary diversity of attitudes towards sex, and extraordinary efforts have been made to channel the basic drives into many different culturally acceptable channels. Changing rules about sexual behaviour have nearly always been made by men, and have mainly defined what is acceptable behaviour by women, the variations in sexual restrictions on men being relatively small, and the penalties normally light.

ii. Disincentives

It seems very likely that the levels of marital and extra-marital sexual activity revealed in late twentieth-century surveys are far higher than those normally achieved in the Early Modern period. In the first place, the general standard of personal hygiene, even among the elite, was very low. Samuel Pepys was a successful bureaucrat and a business associate of great nobles and courtiers in London of the 1660s. Yet he regarded it as a matter of course that he should have lice in his hair, for which his maid regularly combed him, and he only expressed surprise when one day his wife found no fewer than twenty of them. He hardly ever washed his body until February 1664 when his wife suddenly went to a bathhouse, temporarily discovered the pleasures of cleanliness and refused to allow him into her bed until he too had washed. After holding out for three days, he finally gave way to her whim and bathed in hot water. As for William Byrd, sixty years later in London, he washed his feet every few weeks, but bathed only when he took a woman to a bagnio for a night of sexual enjoyment – and then not every time. As late as the 1760s Topham Beauclerk, a man of charm and wit who moved in the highest aristocratic circles, was 'remarkably filthy in his person, which generated vermin'. Despite the fact that his wife, Lady Diana, slept in a separate bed and had her sheets changed daily, he was not in the least ashamed of his condition. When at a Christmas party at Blenheim, all the ladies complained to him that he was spreading lice in their hair, he retorted casually: 'Are they so nice as that comes to? Why, I have enough to stock a parish.' One or two private bathrooms existed at the end of the seventeenth century, but only in the most up-to-date palaces of the enormously rich. For example, at Chatsworth in 1700 the Duke and Duchess of Devonshire had a sumptuous marble bathroom, with a marble bath large enough for two, fed by hot and cold water taps. The Duke and Duchess of Bedford had baths with running hot and cold water in their country seat at Woburn Abbey and their town house at Bedford House by about the middle of the century, and they installed a water-closet for themselves in 1771. But this was altogether exceptional, and most people, even in the highest social stratum, hardly ever washed anything, except their faces, necks, hands and feet.[1]

There is evidence to suggest that carelessness in personal hygiene was more common among upper-class women in England than abroad, and was something which greatly annoyed those men who took their sexual pleasures seriously. The first, and frankest, to complain was John Wilmot, Earl of Rochester, in the 1670s:

Fair nasty nymph, be clean and kind
And all my joys restore
By using paper still behind
And sponges for before.

In the early eighteenth century, Swift confirmed that English women neglected 'care in the cleanliness and sweetness of their persons', while in the middle of the century the rake John Wilkes echoed Rochester's complaint that 'the nobler parts are never in this island washed by the women; they are left to be lathered by the men.' In 1755 John Shebbeare also confirmed that among English women 'the parts concealed are more neglected than among the regions of Italy', and in 1792 Mary Wollstonecraft asserted that among English women 'that regard to cleanliness... is violated in a beastly manner.' Half a century later in 1841, Dr William Acton was still complaining that in England women 'wash every other part of the body, but, unhappily for their own comfort as well as that of their husbands, they seem averse to let clean water reach the vagina.'[2] To what extent this lack of personal cleanliness, particularly among women, acted as a disincentive to sexual play and intercourse is not an easy question to answer. It is certain that earlier societies were far less offended by smells than we are today. It is also a known fact that in the animal world female genital body odours – chemical substances called pheromones – play a critically important part in triggering male sexual responses, and that they also play some part, if only to a somewhat atrophied degree, in human sexuality. Body cleanliness is one thing, but use of the vaginal douche may well reduce rather than increase sexual desire in the male. On the other hand, contemporary complaints about the dirtiness of women, and the use of the bagnio as a place of sexual assignation, both suggest that men in the seventeenth and eighteenth centuries found cleanliness a positive asset to sexual activity. The bidet was introduced into upper-class French households in the early eighteenth century, but never spread to England. As early as 1752 it was known in England as a 'machine which the French ladies use when they perform their ablutions'; but it was not adopted. English opposition to it, which was based apparently on moral rather than hygienic objections, supports the hypothesis of an association of cleanliness with foreplay and oral sex.[3]

Another fact of Early Modern life which is easy to forget is that only a relatively small proportion of the adult population at any given time was both healthy and attractive, quite apart from the normal features of smell and dirt. Both sexes suffered long periods of crippling illness, which incapacitated them for months or years. Even when relatively well, they often suffered from disorders which made sex painful to them or unpleasant to their partners. Women suffered from a whole series of gynaecological disorders, particularly leuchorrhoea, but also vaginal ulcers, tumours, inflammations and haemorrhages which often made sexual intercourse disagreeable, painful or impossible. Both sexes must very often have had bad breath from the rotting teeth and constant stomach disorders which can be documented from many sources, while suppurating ulcers, eczema, scabs, running sores and other nauseating skin diseases were extremely common, and often lasted for years. For example, in 1635 Adam Martindale 'broke out in an ugly dry scurf, eating deep and spreading broad', and in the late eighteenth century, Samuel Bamford's 'head became entirely covered with scab', so that he had to leave school since he was too disgusting a spectacle. The doctor Richard Kay's accounts of his patients in the early eighteenth century make it clear how extremely common were various forms of open sores and other peculiarly disagreeable skin diseases. A good example of a man whose sexual drive was clearly severely reduced by constant ill health was the scientist Robert Hooke.[4]

In addition, there was the ever-present risk of venereal disease, which seems to have been spreading steadily over the centuries. As we shall see, Boswell contracted gonorrhoea at least seventeen times during his life. In 1762–63 both Charles Churchill and his mistress had it, and the former was taking the dangerous remedy of mercury treatment to cure it. In 1787 Lord Herbert got it after serving as president at a military dinner. 'Curse great English dinners and military or civil clubs', commented his father, 'all is drunkenness and pox afterwards with us.' As a result, Lord Herbert was ill for a considerable time with 'a wound in my groin which no one can persuade to heal', and which had to be cut by a surgeon five times. As we shall see, wives not infrequently found themselves sleeping with husbands suffering from venereal disease, as a result of which they developed the disease themselves. Not surprisingly, eighteenth-century newspapers were full of advertisements for such things as Dr Rock's 'Famous Anti-Venereal Grand Specific Pill.'[5]

Among the poor, all the disincentives already listed were present to an exacerbated degree. Because of the cost of soap, the lack of facilities for washing, and from traditional habit, the poor were very much dirtier than the rich. In parts of France, personal hygiene remained at medieval levels among the peasantry and even the town population as late as the end of the nineteenth century. In 1897 it was said that 'in Catholic countries hygiene of the skin is almost unknown. In France, most women die without ever once having taken a bath. It would be the same for most men, were it not for their baths during military service.' In Rennes, there was a population of seventy thousand, but only two houses with bathrooms, and only thirty public bathhouses, so that conditions were only marginally better there than in the countryside.[6]

It is possible that the English poor began to be more cleanly in their persons a century before the French, at the beginning of the nineteenth century. In the eighteenth century, however, personal hygiene was very poor. Francis Place recalled that among the lower-middle and lower classes in the late eighteenth century, bed sheets were changed three times a year at most. Women wore stays made of bone or leather, which lasted for decades and were worn day in and day out without ever being washed. They also wore quilted petticoats which were also never washed and were worn until they disintegrated. As for children, 'when I was a boy ... the children of tradesmen ... all ... had lice in their hair', which was combed once a week, while grown-ups, even in these more respectable circles, were not free from them. But in Place's opinion, the spread of cheap and easily washable cotton clothes in the early nineteenth century 'has done all but wonders in respect to the cleanliness and healthiness of women.'[7]

Because of poor diet and lack of protection from the weather, it is probable that sickness was more common among the poor than among the rich. Many of the very poor also suffered from malnutrition, especially in years of harvest deficiency, and it is known that a severely reduced level of caloric intake will somewhat reduce the sexual instinct among males, and greatly reduce it among females. Even if adequately fed, sheer physical exhaustion from labour in the fields could reduce sexual desire.[8]

At all social levels there were also psychological inhibitions as well as physical, quite apart from internalized restrictions imposed by moral theology. The poor seem in general to have been both more prudish and less imaginative about sex than the leisured classes. Reluctance to strip naked was especially prevalent among the poor. What was true of the eighteenth-century German lower-middle class was almost certainly also true of the English: 'the more exotic perversities which delighted the upper classes were doubtless unheard of and unimagined in provincial backwaters.'[9] A French doctor confirmed that foreplay was largely unknown among the peasantry. As a result, lower- and lower-middle-class sexual activity in the Early Modern period has been described as 'man on top, woman on bottom, little foreplay, rapid ejaculation, masculine unconcern for feminine orgasm.'

As such, it was a mirror of prevailing social relationships, where the patriarchal power of the husband for long remained in full force.[10]

Among all classes, the fear of unwanted pregnancy must have been a very powerful deterrent to sexual pleasure, not only for wives who found themselves repeatedly giving birth painfully and dangerously, but also for husbands who had somehow to find the money for the upkeep of the growing brood of children. The best known method of contraception, the practice of *coitus interruptus*, or withdrawal by the male before ejaculation, requires great self-control and must therefore also act as a strong inhibiting factor to the male, while possibly affording little satisfaction to the female. The latter would often have had to choose between completing the sexual act and consequently running the risk of pregnancy, or withdrawal before she reached her climax, leaving her sexually aroused but frustrated. Nineteenth-century writers went to great lengths to stress the harmful effects of this practice on women, 'whose nervous system suffers from ungratified excitement', when 'the sensibilities of the womb and the entire reproductive system are teased to no purpose.' This merely added to normal female complaints about 'the hasty ejaculation of the husband.'[11]

Furthermore it has been argued that the very late marriage pattern of north-west Europe, coupled with the low illegitimacy rate, meant that both parties at the time of marriage must have had some ten years' experience of masturbation, and that this habit was likely to inhibit satisfactory sexual relations in marriage.[12] If to this is added the fact that, before the eighteenth century, most marriages among all levels of the propertied classes were loveless contracts of convenience either arranged by parents or chosen by the spouses on economic or other prudential grounds, the chances of mutually satisfactory sexual relations must have been reduced still further. It is significant that seventeenth-century French casuists, writing instruction manuals for Catholic confessors, make two major concessions. They permit the wife to manipulate herself before intercourse, presumably to facilitate penetration; and if the husband ejaculates and withdraws before the wife has obtained satisfaction, she is permitted to masturbate to orgasm. The theory behind this tolerance was not the enhancement of the woman's pleasure, but the fulfilment of medical ideas about procreation. According to Galen, who rejected Aristotle's view of the woman as a mere receptacle for seed, the mingling of both sexual fluids may not be necessary for conception, but is desirable for the production of strong and healthy children. French medical authorities in the seventeenth century went further and argued not only that both female and male fluids were necessary for conception, but also that in any case female sexual pleasure was needed in order to open the mouth of the womb to receive the male sperm.[13]

The obstacles against the mutual achievement of full sexual satisfaction by man and wife in the Early Modern period were thus both numerous and severe, and as a result both the quantity of sexual activity and its pleasurable quality were both probably significantly lower than they are today, even among the elite. The French evidence from advice to confessors certainly suggests that the sexual act was not a means of providing mutual satisfaction, but one in which each partner operated independently, for his or her own ends. Since there are no sexual diaries written by women at this period, and since even pornographic writings purporting to represent the woman's point of view, like *Fanny Hill*, were the work of men, there are no means whatever available to the historian of testing these hypotheses. They will have to remain no more than unproven, and unprovable, speculations. On the other hand, there can be no doubt that the female orgasm was regarded as both medically desirable and morally legitimate. The idea that most women either were or were supposed to be frigid before the eighteenth century receives no support whatever from the evidence of medical literature, nor from current sayings and proverbs about the natural lustfulness of women.

iii. Peculiarities of Western Society

There were certain features of sexual behaviour which were peculiar to Western man, at any rate in the seventeenth and eighteenth centuries, and distinguished him from members of other societies. The first, and hardest to explain, was the interval of ten years or more between the age of sexual maturity and the mean age of marriage, an interval which in most other societies is relatively short. The gap was most marked among the plebs, but it was also noticeable among the elite, and it was a gap which became wider and wider throughout the seventeenth and most of the eighteenth centuries. Moreover, there was a significant proportion – about ten per cent among the plebs and rising to twenty-five per cent among the elite in the eighteenth century – who never married at all, most of the females among the latter group probably remaining virgins all their lives.

The second characteristic has been the imposition on the sexual drive of an ideological gloss known as romantic love, which, thanks to nature imitating art, at times has taken on a life of its own. Beginning as a purely extra-marital emotion in troubadour literature of the twelfth century, it was transformed by the invention of the printing press and the spread of literacy in the sixteenth and seventeenth centuries. It was a theme which dominated the poetry, theatre and romances of the late sixteenth and seventeenth centuries and found its way into real life in the mid-eighteenth century.

The third, and in some ways the most salient, characteristic has been the predominance of a religion – Christianity – which has always been more or less hostile to sex as pleasure or play, and anxious to confine its legitimacy to the functional purpose of procreation. Though mitigated somewhat by the Protestant rejection of virginity as an ideal and the substitution of holy matrimony, this suspicion nonetheless persisted as a prominent feature of moral theology throughout the sixteenth and seventeenth centuries.

2 UPPER-CLASS CULTURE IN THE SIXTEENTH AND SEVENTEENTH CENTURIES

i. Taboos

All known societies have incest taboos, and the only peculiarity about them in England was the restriction of their number at the Reformation to the Levitical degrees. On the other hand, the punishments meted out by Church courts in cases of incest in Elizabethan England were surprisingly lenient, and there is reason to think that sodomy and bestiality were more repugnant to popular standards of morality than breaking of the laws of incest, which must have been common in those overcrowded houses where the adolescent children were still at home.[14] Neither social nor ethnic exogamy was prohibited by any laws, but in practice both were strongly disapproved of. As a result, there was a high degree of social endogamy in England, and even in colonies with highly unbalanced white sex ratios, like India in the eighteenth century, it was normal to take a native mistress but unthinkable to marry her.[15] This was in marked contrast to the attitude of other European colonists in similar situations, for example the Portuguese in Brazil, the key difference being that the Portuguese were there to stay and settle, while the English were in India to make a fortune and return home.

Before the Reformation the taboo on marriage for all members of the clergy had been slowly gaining currency throughout Catholic Europe. Its symbolic purpose was to set the clergy off from lay society by this supreme act of ascetic abnegation, but the practice was less successful than the theory. Many pre-Reformation clergy settled down in comfortable concubinage with their housekeepers, while the friars in particular earned a very bad reputation as the seducers of married women. After the Reformation, all these restrictions on clerical marriage were swept away;

monasteries and nunneries were abolished; and by a peculiar quirk of historical circumstances, the taboo – now no more than a legal obligation – was maintained only for the Fellows of Oxford and Cambridge colleges. Despite efforts in the late eighteenth century to abolish it, this rule persisted down to the late nineteenth century.

A more difficult problem concerns attitudes towards homosexuality. The sixteenth century inherited from the medieval church a strong hostility to homosexuality, which over time, particularly because of the affair of the Templars and the Albigensian crusade, had become closely associated in official thinking with religious heresy. In sixteenth-century continental Europe, waves of prosecutions of homosexuals seem to be closely correlated with waves of persecutions of witches, both being regarded as dangerous deviants whose existence threatened the well-being of society. For reasons which are still obscure, however, England escaped the worst excesses of these attacks on both sodomy and witchcraft, towards which a more pragmatic attitude seems normally to have prevailed.[16]

Both in law and in public consciousness, lesbianism seems to have been ignored. As Aphra Behn put it in her poem *To the Fair Clarinda*:

> In pity to our sex sure thou wer't sent
> That we might love, and yet be innocent.
> For sure no crime with thee we can commit,
> Or if we should – thy form excuses it.

The only public notice taken of it seems to be two caricatures of 1820, showing Lady Strachan and Lady Warwick embracing, to the indignation of their husbands.[17] Officially, both Church and state in the sixteenth century regarded male homosexuality as a serious crime: an act of 1533, reissued in 1563, made buggery punishable by death, but there is no evidence of how often, if at all, it was enforced. It was generally believed to be a rare occurrence in England, but very prevalent in Italy, which was one reason why parents thought that that country should be avoided by the young traveller on the Grand Tour.

> Lust chose the torrid zone of Italy
> Where blood ferments in rapes and sodomy,

wrote Defoe in 1701, repeating two centuries of national prejudice.[18] Although homosexuality was familiar enough to the Elizabethan court, it did not become a common subject of conversation until the accession of James I. Too many of his courtiers, like the Earl of Northampton and Francis Bacon, were notorious for their proclivities; and from their public behaviour the worst was assumed – probably rightly – of the relations between the King and his favourites, like Robert Carr, Earl of Somerset, and George Villiers, Duke of Buckingham. It was one of the many factors that contributed to the undermining of confidence in divine right monarchy.[19]

On the other hand, parents, right up to the end of the seventeenth century, seem to have shown singular lack of anxiety that their sons might be subject to homosexual solicitation or attack from school-fellows or college tutors.[20]

ii. Medical Advice

Information about sexual conventions in Early Modern times, whether inside or outside the marriage bonds, is not easy to come by, since it was not a subject which contemporaries were in the habit of committing to paper. The evidence has, therefore, in the main to be derived from advice in medical treatises and didactic literature of moral theologians, or by inference from statistical data about observed behaviour. Both are risky procedures: the first since there is always a yawning gap between how people are supposed to behave and how they do in fact conduct themselves; and the second because it is highly speculative to infer motives and feelings from data about actions.

Sex manuals of the Early Modern period were few, were a compendium of received wisdom handed down from the classical authorities, and were a mixture of physiological fact and fiction. Ovid's *Art of Love* is vague and imprecise for the ignorant seeker after truth. The most popular sex manual in the West in the Early Modern period, misleadingly called *Aristotle's Masterpiece or the Secrets of Generation*, ran to edition after edition in many languages over many centuries (there were eight registered editions in eighteenth-century England alone). Unlike the Chinese manuals, neither it nor its few rivals offered any advice whatever about methods and varieties of sexual foreplay, the wide options of positions for intercourse, or ways to prolong and maximize pleasure; these matters were left in decent obscurity. Those seeking purely technical information on such subjects would have been obliged to look for it elsewhere, namely in the French, and later the English, pornographic literature, which began in the sixteenth century with Aretino and Giulio Romano's famous *Postures* and grew from a trickle to a moderate stream in the eighteenth century. As a result, the average upper-class man, much less the average woman, would have had no easy access to precise information on sexual techniques before the mid-twentieth century.

One of the very few medical treatises which dealt at all with sexual positions was that of the French Dr Venette of La Rochelle, published in 1716, and he was both vague in his descriptions, and careful not to disagree with the theologians. He therefore sided with them in disapproving of sexual positions involving standing, sitting, or lying with the woman on top. Having said all that, he concluded, somewhat paradoxically, that one can adopt any position one wishes, provided that the pleasure derived from it is not excessive, health is not endangered, and it helps rather than hinders conception. He was therefore tolerant of penetration from the rear, since although it is said to be against nature, it is customary in the animal world, it helps procreation, and it is safer during pregnancy than the standard 'missionary' position. But his book is neither very illuminating in detail, nor very positive in its attitude towards sexuality.[21]

There is nothing in Western literature to compare with the extremely elaborate, detailed and practical handbooks on sexual techniques produced by Taoist scholars in ancient China. The reason for the superiority of the Chinese texts was that sex was not frowned upon by Confucian or Taoist religion, as it was by Christianity, but was recognized as an absolute necessity for healthy existence. Since Chinese religion had no sense of guilt about sex, the handbooks were elaborately explicit about the varying postures and movements which could be adopted. Here was a wholly different civilization, with an entirely different, strongly positive, set of attitudes towards sex, but which like the West took a purely masculine point of view, and regarded the semen as a precious fluid. The Chinese example thus provides a valuable yardstick by which to measure Western attitudes.[22]

On subjects other than techniques and positions of love-making, *Aristotle's Masterpiece* was full of facts and advice – some true, some false. For women, the menarche was placed at fourteen to fifteen and the menopause at forty-four. For men, sexual activity began at sixteen to seventeen, increased in 'force and heat' to between forty-five and fifty-five, and then died away. The sexual organs of the man were described, and the clitoris was clearly identified as the 'seat of venereal pleasure' in women, without which 'the fair sex neither desire nuptial embraces nor have pleasure in them nor conceive by them.' In 1724 De Mandeville noted that 'all our late discoveries in anatomy can find no other use for the clitoris but to whet the female desire by its frequent erections.'[23] Vaginal, as distinct from clitoral, orgasm, however, was a discovery – or false hypothesis – which still lay in the future. Throughout the middle ages and the Early Modern period, woman had been regarded as the temptress, taking after her ancestress Eve, and, by her fickleness and liability to sexual arousal, as a

constant threat to the monogamous nuclear family. When in 1621 Robert
Burton asked 'of woman's unnatural, insatiable lust, what country, what
village doth not complain?' he was doing no more than repeating the
conventional wisdom of the age. Aphra Behn went so far in 1682 as to
suggest that a young wife often sexually exhausted her husband, as
evidenced by 'the paleness of his face, the lankness of his cheeks, the
thinness of his calves.' The capacity of the female for multiple orgasms far
exceeding the male ability to keep pace was a well-known fact, and provided
the physiological basis for this popular belief. 'Though they be weaker
vessels, yet they will overcome 2, 3 or 4 men in the satisfying of their carnal
appetites,' observed the misogynist Elizabethan musician Thomas
Wythorne, a proposition repeated a hundred and fifty years later by Dr
Venette.[24]

Advice about the ideal quantity of sexual activity was based on the
Aristotelian principle of moderation in all things, and on theories about the
nature of male semen, which was regarded as essential to good mental and
physical health, and therefore to be expended only in moderation. Early
marriage was therefore unwise since adolescent husbands might become 'so
enfeebled and weakened that all their vital moisture was exhausted.' Even in
adulthood, 'to eject immoderately weakens a man and wastes his spirit.' Dr
Venette declared that sexual excess shortens life, and the great Swiss mid-
eighteenth-century Dr Tissot, whose work was translated and reprinted for
a century, was only repeating an old belief, but giving it a false statistical
veneer, when he stated that the loss of one ounce of semen is the equivalent
of the loss of forty ounces of blood – apparently a new version of Avicenna's
medieval claim that one ejaculation is more debilitating than forty blood-
lettings.[25]

A second reason for moderation was the widespread and persistent
medical theory that the constitutional characteristics of the child were
determined by the physical condition of the parents at the moment of
conception. It was believed that sexually exhausted fathers and/or sexually
abused wives were likely to produce weakly children with low life
expectations. The moment of copulation should occur, therefore, when
both man and woman were in full sexual vigour, as well as being rested,
sober, and free from mental worries. Early morning was therefore a
propitious time.[26]

As a result, from the fifteenth century to the nineteenth, lay
commentators and the writers of marriage manuals unanimously
recommended very restricted sexual activity in marriage. In early fifteenth-

century Florence, Giovanni di Pagolo Morelli was advising restraint, and in early eighteenth-century France Dr Venette was doing the same. The male capacity for orgasm is physiologically limited, the latter alleged, to anything between four or five a night – a dangerous excess – and two a month, while that of a woman is almost limitless.[27] In America over a century later, in 1847, A.M.Mauriceau was advising his readers to restrict intercourse to a maximum of twice a week. The most popular French marriage manual of the mid-nineteenth century, which ran to one hundred and seventy-three editions between 1848 and 1883 and which was written by A.Debray, a retired army doctor, took much the same line. It set maximum rates of sexual intercourse based on age: less than two to four times a week in the twenties, twice a week in the thirties, once a week in the forties, once a fortnight in the fifties, and never after sixty. Much the same advice was offered at the same period in England in the very influential writings of Dr William Acton, who recommended for good health a maximum of twice a night every ten to fourteen days.[28]

In addition to this general advice about moderation, doctors advised total abstinence at the height of summer, since sex overheats the blood and 'infrigidates and dries up the body, consumes the spirits'; during menstruation, since procreation at this time was thought likely to produce diseased children (there was no knowledge of the female ovarian cycle and that conception was impossible), during the latter stages of pregnancy, since there was danger of crushing or aborting the foetus; and during the period of breast-feeding after birth, since sexual activity could spoil the mother's milk, and renewed pregnancy would cut off the milk supply altogether and so kill the infant child.[29] We do not know how seriously any of these prohibitions were taken. The last was certainly believed in by the rich, which was one reason why upper- and middle-class husbands in the sixteenth and seventeenth centuries made their wives put their children out to a wet-nurse and why they tried to prevent the husband of the wet-nurse having sexual access to her. In view of the very long period of breast-feeding – usually twelve to eighteen months – it is certain that the poor, who for lack of money to hire a nurse had to breast-feed their own children, were unable to resist the importunities of their husbands for so long. Catholic moral theologians of the sixteenth and seventeenth centuries recognized this problem and thought it better for the wife and mother to satisfy the sexual demands of their husbands, with possible danger to the health of their infants, rather than to risk driving their husbands to adultery by refusing intercourse. So much was this an issue that an advanced woman like Mme

Roland in the late eighteenth century wanted a special clause inserted in her marriage contract, which would give her the full right to breast-feed her children, and presumably, therefore, to refuse her sexual services to her husband during that period.[30]

The standard medical view of sex in the Early Modern period was based on a plumber's view of the body, the maintenance of good health being determined by a nice balance between the production and discharge of fluids in the pipes so as to maintain an equilibrium. The medical profession also had some understanding of the twentieth-century boiler-maker's view of sex, as a release-valve for the letting off of psychological steam. This meant that before the nineteenth century, when medical opinion became more radically anti-sexual, doctors were as much concerned with the dangers of abstinence as with those of excess. Galen flatly stated that 'if this natural seed be over-long kept (in some parties) it turns to poison', and led to both physical disease and melancholia (although Robert Burton thought that melancholia was also 'exasperated by venery').[31] Most doctors recognized that sexual release had important psychological as well as physical benefits and regarded it as normally necessary for mental health. As Thomas Cogan put it in 1589, 'the commodities which come by moderate evacuation thereof [semen] are great. For it procureth appetite to meat and helpeth concoction; it maketh the body more light and nimble, it openeth the pores and conduits, and purgeth phlegm; it quickeneth the mind, stirreth up the wit, reneweth the senses, driveth away sadness, madness, anger, melancholy, fury.'[32]

Just what the lay public made of all this advice from the medical profession is obscure. On the one hand, it was laity rather than doctors who took some of the most alarmist positions about the medical dangers of excess. One of the seventeenth-century lay commentators who indulged in hyperbole on medical grounds was John Evelyn, who thought that 'too much frequency of embraces dulls the sight, decays the memory, induces gout, palsies, enervates and renders effeminate the whole body, and shortens life.' This opinion was echoed in a pamphlet by Daniel Defoe, published in his crabbed old age in 1727, in which he too warned that sexual excess would lead to 'palsies and epilepsies, falling sickness, trembling of the joints, pale dejected aspects, leanness, and at least rottenness and other filthy and loathsome distempers', to say nothing of impotence in old age.[33]

On the other hand, it is very doubtful how far married couples actually practised the kind of restraint advised by *Aristotle's Masterpiece* and by Defoe in England in the early eighteenth century, or by Mauriceau in

America or Debray in France in the mid-nineteenth century. One has reason to suspect that in these matters the gap between precept and practice may have been a wide one. For example, contraception certainly grew slowly in the eighteenth century in upper- and middle-class circles, presumably primarily through *coitus interruptus*, despite the violent objections of theologians, moralists and, later, doctors. In France in the nineteenth century, it was admitted to be 'an almost universal usage' despite the enormous power over women of the Catholic Church through the confession box.[34] This example – and the two-thousand-year defiance by upper-class women of medical advice in favour of maternal breast-feeding – suggests great caution in assuming that practice follows theory in such matters.

iii. Moral Theology

The attitude of sixteenth- and seventeenth-century theologians towards sexuality was one of suspicion and hostility, only very slowly and reluctantly tempered by the rejection of the ideal of virginity at the Reformation and the substitution of 'holy matrimony'. This attitude has a long history behind it, stretching back to the early Fathers of the Church, like St Jerome, to whom all sex was unclean. Thus Anglo-Saxon Penitentials were astonishingly restrictive in their demands for marital continence: three days before communion; three days after the marriage ceremony; all church festivals (which were very numerous); Sundays and the two fast days of Wednesdays and Fridays; forty days during Lent and forty days before Christmas; and during all periods of penance, which were imposed frequently and for long periods.[35] If these regulations had been strictly and universally obeyed, it is difficult to see how the race could be propagated, but they were clearly ignored by much of the still semi-pagan population.

As a result of Church teachings in the late Anglo-Saxon period, public attitudes towards chastity also altered. To the pagans, female chastity was no more than a property value, an asset to the father before marriage and to the husband after, and violators could therefore purge themselves by the payment of damages appropriate to the status of the persons involved. By the tenth century, however, fornication and adultery had become crimes against God, and therefore offences to both Church and state: it was now souls, not property, which were at stake. By 1300, all violations of the strict rules of chastity and monogamy were in theory punishable offences, handled in courts operated not by the state but by the Church.[36]

In view of this long tradition, it is not surprising that marital sex was still regarded by early sixteenth-century theologians as a regrettable necessity, justified only if it were directed to the task of procreation. This rigid position was still firmly held by seventeenth-century Catholic theologians, for example the Jesuit Thomas Sanchez whose massive early seventeenth-century tome on marriage was an enormously influential work, since its views were disseminated in little octavo summaries for the use of priests in the confession box. Not only did he denounce all ways of preventing or diverting conception, such as masturbation or sodomy, but he even defined it as a mortal sin for a woman to stand up or urinate after intercourse in the hope of preventing conception.[37]

More remarkable still was the persistence of the view, which began with St Jerome, that any man who displayed an excess of sexual passion for his wife was no more than an adulterer. In 1584 the Franciscan theologian Benedicti repeated this position in uncompromising terms. In England, the consensus of theological opinion also stressed the prime importance of 'matrimonial chastity', as it was called, and identified breaches of it with breaches of the Seventh Commandment against adultery. This was not in conflict with the Protestant view of 'holy matrimony' as a source of mutual comfort as well as a means of satisfying lust and procreating legitimate children, although it was left to Milton to argue that 'copulation ... is an effect of conjugal love', rather than the other way around.[38]

By 'matrimonial chastity' was meant moderation of sexual passion, something which had been advocated not only by the Catholic Fathers but also by both Calvin and foreign humanists of the early sixteenth century, like Vives and Guazzo. The husband was expected to give his wife sufficient satisfaction to avoid her being obliged to seek consolation elsewhere, but not so much as to arouse her libido to the extent of encouraging her to seek extra-marital adventures.[39] Thus both Protestant and Catholic theologians condemned not only extra-marital fornication and adultery, but also the introduction of strong sexual passion into marriage itself. All passionate love-making was sinful, regardless of whether it took place inside or outside marriage. Sensuality itself, the lust of the flesh, was evil. The basic advice to a husband was that 'nothing is more impure than to love a wife like an adulterous woman.' Calvin was in agreement with the Catholics in describing 'the man who shows no modesty or comeliness in conjugal intercourse as committing adultery with his wife.'[40] As a result, there was a general theological condemnation of any excesses in quantity, or any variations in quality, of marital sexual relations.

In the first place, intercourse was forbidden during periods when there could be no conception, which at that time were believed to be limited to the nine months of pregnancy. In addition, both the forty days of Lent and Sundays were regarded as periods of ritual sexual continence for married couples. In late medieval Catholic Europe, Lent had been popularly regarded as a period of sexual abstinence, but without much official encouragement from the Church authorities. In the seventeenth century, the practice is alleged to have gradually disappeared in Catholic countries,[41] but the inhibitions continued, and were perhaps reinforced, in Protestant areas. Some seventeenth- and early eighteenth-century New England clergymen believed that a child born on a Sunday was conceived on a Sunday, and therefore refused to baptize it until the parents had publicly confessed to the sin of Sabbath-breaking. George Hanger confirmed that as late as the American Revolution, in New England 'the sinful lusts of the flesh were so abominated on that day that carnal knowledge even between husband and wife was forbidden, and no bundling whatsoever was permitted.' In England in the late eighteenth century, the period on Sunday during which respectable couples were at their devotions in church was particularly sacrosanct. A popular obscene poem of the period, about a sexually over-demanding wife who reduced her husband to a pale emaciated skeleton, ended with the lines

> And for which I am sure she'll go to Hell,
> For she makes me fuck her in church time.

For Methodists, the whole day was taboo, and there is the (perhaps apocryphal) story of a Methodist in St Martin's Lane who on Saturday nights tied together the legs of his cocks so that they could not mount his hens on Sundays. The religious prohibition on sexual activity on Sunday was also a standard part of Victorian middle-class morality, at least up to 1870. On the other hand, by 1870 some medical advisors, such as A.K.Gardner, were recommending Sunday as the ideal day of procreation on the grounds that the sense of relaxation from the weekly round of work would produce healthier children. 'Never on Sunday' therefore has a long, complicated and still somewhat obscure history, involving conflicts between moral theology, medical theory, and social convenience.[42]

Apart from restricting the times of intercourse, the theologians also interfered in the details of the sexual act. Variant sexual positions other than the standard 'missionary' position of the man on top and the woman supine underneath were rejected, since they were merely incitements to lust and designed for pleasure not procreation. Any approach from behind was condemned since it made man imitate the behaviour of animals; any position with the woman on top was condemned, partly since it inverted sex roles, making the female the dominant and active partner, and partly because it reduced the likelihood of conception, since the semen was running against gravity. For the same reasons there was total prohibition of the use of 'unnatural' orifices such as the mouth or the anus, and of contraceptive practices such as *coitus interruptus*.[43] English moral theologians seem to have avoided the more complicated question handled by Catholic casuists like Sanchez, who provided advice for priests hearing confessions on such matters as whether, acting on a sudden wave of repentance, it was right to withdraw from a whore, or whether it is legitimate to begin intercourse in the anus if it is completed in the vagina.[44]

The layman who was most puritanical and longwinded about such matters in the early eighteenth century was Daniel Defoe, addressing a bourgeois audience in 1727 on 'Conjugal Lewdness'. His book on this subject was a prolonged attack upon the theory that in the marriage bed 'nothing can be indecent, nothing improper, that there is no restraint and that no law can be broken by them.' He followed theological tradition in condemning sex during pregnancy, although he admitted that here he was going against normal practice. In his opinion, this is 'the making a necessary-house of his wife.' He prescribed one month's abstinence after birth, which he said was the normal convention. Beyond that, he urged the avoidance of 'scandalous violences on both sides', and complained that 'sodomy itself has been not only acted on but even justified in the marriage bed.' He also followed tradition in urging moderation in quantity as well as the avoidance of perversions.[45]

iv. Secular Morality: The Double Standard

Among the upper classes for most of the Early Modern period, the 'double standard' of sexual behaviour prevailed.[46] According to this convention, the husband enjoyed full monopoly rights over the sexual services of his wife, who was expected to be a virgin on her wedding night. As Fielding's Mr Modern told his wife in 1732: 'Your person is mine: I bought it lawfully in the church.' On the other hand, the man was expected to have gained some sexual experience before marriage, and any infidelities after marriage were treated as venial sins which the sensible wife was advised to overlook. Thus, both fornication and adultery were exclusively male prerogatives at this social level, despite the fact that in current physiological theory and folk tradition women were regarded as more lustful in their appetites and more fickle in their attachments than men. 'All witchcraft comes from carnal lust, which in women is insatiable', observed the authors of the *Malleus Maleficarum*, thus expressing no more than the conventional view.[47] This dichotomy between women's physiological impulses and their social obligations to pre-marital chastity and post-marital monogamy was solved by the imposition on them of the strictest standards of sexual behaviour, enforced by all the legal, moral and religious pressures of which the society was capable. The explanation of this discrepancy lies firstly in the value attached to female chastity in the marriage market of a hierarchical and propertied society, and secondly in the necessity that there should be no legal doubts about the legitimacy of the heirs to property and title. As the Marquess of Halifax explained to his daughter in 1688: 'The root and excuse of this injustice is the preservation of families from any mixture which may bring a blemish to them; and whilst the point of honour continues to be so placed, it seems unavoidable to give your sex the greater share of the penalty.' If, on the other hand, the husband is unfaithful, 'do not seem to look or hear that way ... such an indecent complaint makes a wife much more ridiculous than the injury that provoked her to it.' A century later, Dr Johnson was still saying the same thing, that upon female chastity 'all the property of the world depends' and that 'confusion of progeny constitutes the essence of the crime' of adultery. Consequently, 'wise married women don't trouble themselves about infidelity in their husbands', whereas wifely infidelity was unpardonable.[48]

The view that male fornication and adultery are venial sins to be overlooked by the wife was strengthened by the fact that before the eighteenth century most marriages among the propertied classes were arranged by the parents in the interest of family financial or political advantage. The bride and groom were not expected, and indeed were given no opportunity, to develop any prior attachment or affection. Male adultery with lower-class women and the procreation of bastards by them always tend to be regarded as moral by social groups whose marriages are arranged and not consensual. Consequently, in the sixteenth century, husbands felt free to take lower-class mistresses and to beget bastards without any sense of shame and any attempt at concealment. The children of these unions were frequently mentioned in wills and open provision was made for their upkeep and education.[49]

In the early seventeenth century, however, the public attitude towards these liaisons temporarily altered under Puritan pressure, and they became much more secretive. Bastards largely disappeared from aristocratic wills, and far greater discretion seems to have been exercised in the degree of public recognition afforded to a mistress. Even so irreligious a hedonist as Edward, Lord Herbert of Cherbury, when confessing his amours in his *Autobiography*, found it necessary to excuse them. In 1619 when he was serving as English Ambassador in Paris, he explained that his robust health 'disposed me to some follies which I afterwards repented and still do repent of. But as my wife refused to come over, and my temptations were great, I hope the faults I committed are the more pardonable. Howsoever I can truly say that ... I was never in a bawdy-house, nor used my pleasures intemperately, and much less did accompany them with that dissimulation and falsehood which is commonly found in men addicted to love women.'[50]

The second explanation of this durable phenomenon of the double standard is that women have for millennia been regarded as the sexual property of men and that the value of this property is diminished if it has been or is being used by anyone other than the legal owner. It was for these reasons that Mrs Manley's protests in the first decade of the eighteenth century that 'what is not a crime in men is scandalous and unpardonable in women' were entirely ignored. As late as 1825 Sir John Nicholls declared that 'forgiveness on the part of a wife is meritorious, while a similar forgiveness on the part of a husband would be degrading and dishonourable.' As a result the 1857 Divorce Act permitted a wife to be divorced for simple adultery, but a husband only if the act were accompanied by aggravating circumstances such as cruelty, desertion, bigamy, rape, sodomy or bestiality.[51]

A third explanation for the prevalence of the double standard lies in the stress in secular society on honour. In the sixteenth, seventeenth and eighteenth centuries, the concept of honour had a very clearly defined meaning, which was significantly different from that of today. The worst thing a man could say about another man was that he was a liar. 'Giving the lie' inevitably resulted in a challenge to a duel in genteel circles, and in a fight in peasant or artisan circles. The worst thing a woman could say about another woman was that she was unchaste, which might well result in a lawsuit for slander in an ecclesiastical court. Thus a man's honour depended on the reliability of his spoken word; a woman's honour on her reputation for chastity.[52]

But the honour of a married man was also severely damaged if he got the reputation of being a cuckold, since this was a slur on both his virility and his capacity to rule his own household. He became the joke of the village, or at a higher level of his associates, and was defamed and thought unfit for public office. The Elizabethan Thomas Wythorne remarked bitterly on the injustice of a situation in which 'a man's honesty and credit doth depend and lie in his wife's tail.'[53] In the village, the cuckolded husband and his delinquent wife were frequently victims of a 'skimmington', or public shame punishment.

This idea that female honour depended upon a reputation for pre-marital chastity and marital fidelity was one which was most effectively internalized in the middling ranks of society. Until one reaches the apex of the pyramid, the higher one goes in the society and the greater the amount of property likely to change hands with a marriage, the greater the stress on pre-marital chastity. Even in these classes, however, there were real dangers of pre-nuptial conception after the formal engagement, under the new eighteenth-century conditions of marriage for affection and greater freedom of access. In 1773 *The Lady's Magazine* found it necessary to warn its readers to be especially on their guard against seduction between the spousals and the wedding.[54] After marriage, however, and especially after the first son and heir was born, the seventeenth- and eighteenth-century aristocratic court ladies felt themselves free to take lovers if they chose, despite the problems of paternity which such behaviour could cause. This was but one aspect of the growing divorce of 'court' from 'country' in the early seventeenth century, and of the development among the members of the former of a distinct culture peculiar to an elitist minority. Although it was only under the rule of the tolerant (and homosexual) James I that the sexual morality of the court reached its nadir and became a public scandal, the situation had evidently been deteriorating in the latter years of Queen Elizabeth, despite her anxiety to prevent her entourage from enjoying those sexual pleasures which she had deliberately denied herself. As early as 1603 Lady Anne Clifford reported that 'all the ladies about the court had gotten such ill names that it was grown a scandalous place', indicating that the double standard had already collapsed in these circles. Both the royal favourites, Robert Carr, Earl of Somerset, and George Villiers, Duke of Buckingham, were notorious – and successful – pursuers of noble ladies, and Ben Jonson summed up the moral tone of the court when he remarked "'tis there civility to be a whore.'[55]

It was not until the reign of Charles I and Henrietta Maria that a serious effort was made to sublimate this sensual promiscuity in the ideal of neo-platonic courtly love, which rose above both animal lusts and the turbulent passions of love, to enter the calm arena of a spiritual union of souls. The external manifestations of this new ideal were expressed in the masques which were such a central feature of court culture of the 1630s, and which extolled the marital fidelity of the royal couple, and the sublimation of base desires. How far this intellectual movement changed actual behaviour at court rather than mere surface appearances is a matter of some doubt, and there were still those in the royal entourage who took a more earthy view. The court poet Lovelace, for example, looked back enviously at the Golden Age, when

> Lasses like autumn plums did drop
> And lads indifferently did crop
> A flower and a maidenhead.[56]

But the chaste Charles I and the flirtatious Henrietta Maria were exceptions to the rule that the double standard always applied with particular intensity to royalty, if only because marriage in these circles was so exclusively a matter of political convenience rather than personal choice. So far as is known, the English record for the production of bastards is held by Henry I, who begat at least twenty. According to William of Malmesbury, the procreations were acts of policy not pleasure, since the female children were used to obtain politically profitable marriage alliances with neighbouring princes.[57] Those of Charles II, on the other hand, who were married into the aristocracy thanks to their money, were a financial drain on the Exchequer, as well as being a moral liability to the image of kingship in more old-fashioned and puritanical circles.

Whether or not the actual practice of extra-marital relations among the landed classes temporarily declined in the early seventeenth century is of course impossible to say, but there can be little doubt that social pressure against it was building up, and Barnaby Rich was somewhat out of date when he claimed in 1622 that 'it is holden a credit to be a bastard to a great man of fame and note.'[58]

The only period in which the double standard was seriously questioned was the 1630s and 1640s. Courtiers like Sir Kenelm Digby, who led a chequered sex life, claimed that breach of chastity 'is no greater fault in them [women] than in men', while the Puritan John Milton adopted a similar position.[59] But this was a temporary phenomenon, and did not survive the Restoration and the growing respect for property. Away from the hot-house atmosphere of the court, wives of the nobility and squirarchy of the sixteenth, seventeenth and eighteenth centuries usually felt themselves obliged to follow the rules of the double standard.

Even pious and chaste upper-class women in the late eighteenth century turned a blind eye to their husband's infidelities, so long as only sexual passion and not deep emotional attachment was involved. Mrs Thrale paid no attention to her husband's many liaisons with lower-class mistresses, though she was distressed when he fell in unconsummated love with one of her friends. Years later she protested vigorously to her daughter Cecilia when reports reached her that the latter's husband was sleeping with his wife's maid. But Cecilia brushed the matter aside as something of no consequence. '"It is the way," she says, "and all who understand genteel life think lightly of such matters."'[60]

Since few men of fashion were prepared to enter into a duel to avenge their wife's honour, the only serious danger to a wealthy gentleman from an adulterous relationship with a married woman of high status in the eighteenth century was that he might be sued for damages by the aggrieved husband on an action of 'crim. con.' (criminal connection). When in the late eighteenth century Colonel Sykes had heavy damages to the husband awarded against him for his adultery with a married woman, he subsequently always referred to his ex-mistress as '*dear* Mrs Parsloe, having a right, he said, to use the word after he had paid £10,000 for her.' The standard ethics of the late eighteenth-century elite indicated that a man should be discreet in his amours, so as not publicly to humiliate his wife. As the great courtesan Harriette Wilson put it: 'a man ought to be of royal blood before he commits adultery, except in private.' On the other hand, it was alleged at the time that some aged husbands married young wives with the deliberate purpose of making money by threats of legal proceedings against the latter's lovers: 'As most of us bargain to be husbands, so some of us bargain to be cuckolds.'[61]

The prevailing attitude of women towards such matters in elite London circles in the late eighteenth century is perfectly summed up by an unknown lady who discussed the matter with Boswell one day in 1776. It shows how far the new contract theory of marriage had spread, and its consequences for the double standard. The lady

argued with me that marriage was certainly no more but a political institution, as we see it has subsisted in so many different forms in different parts of the world. 'Therefore,' said she, 'it is merely a mutual contract which if one party breaks, the other is free. Now', said she, 'my husband I know has been unfaithful to me a thousand times. I should therefore have no scruple of conscience, I do declare, to have an intrigue, and I am restrained only by my pride, because I would not do what is thought dishonourable in this century, and would not put myself in the power of a gallant.' I argued that the chastity of women was of much more consequence than that of men, as the property and rights of families depend upon it. 'Surely' said she, 'that is easily answered, for the objection is removed if a woman does not intrigue but when she is with child.' I really could not answer her. Yet I thought she was wrong, and I was uneasy....[62]

v. Attitudes to Childhood Sexuality

Since sexual matters were rarely set down in writing in the sixteenth and seventeenth centuries, our knowledge of adult attitudes towards childhood sexuality is almost entirely confined to a detailed account by Dr Jean Héroard of the upbringing of the young French dauphin, the future Louis XIII, in the first decade of the seventeenth century.[63] During his first three years, his genitals were frequently caressed and rubbed by his nurse and by visiting noblewomen.[64] At one year old, he sometimes exposed his penis, and the company would kiss it, a playful ritual which, when he was older, he occasionally initiated by himself: 'he has Monsieur de Souvré, Monsieur de Liancourt, Monsieur Zamet kiss his cock.' At the age of twenty-one months, the doctor noted Louis' habit of masturbating himself while breast-feeding, and at the age of three when he developed an erection, the child summoned his attendants to admire it: 'Zezai, my cock is like a draw-bridge; see how it goes up and down.' Between four and six Louis was taken into bed with a number of his ladies-in-waiting and nurses and was encouraged to explore their private parts, later commenting publicly on their size and degree of lubrication. He would get into bed with them while they lay with their husbands, and join in playful sexual games like whipping their buttocks. By three and a half he had evidently witnessed the sexual act, for he was climbing on a female playmate and making the external physical motions and noises of copulation with her. He was by then well aware that it was by the insertion of the penis in the vagina that children are made, although he pretended to Héroard at the age of four that he thought they were conceived through the ear-hole.

It was not until the age of six and a half that these sexual games with his female attendants ceased; Louis was put in the hands of men and was expected to begin to behave with somewhat greater propriety. The period of play was over; he was no longer a pet and plaything for the adults. He changed his clothes to those of an adult, put on a cloak and sword, and was even more severely whipped for moral lapses and disobedience. But one aspect of this adulthood was that he was urged to overcome his growing shyness and to kiss girls, and even to show his genitals to them.

It is not at all clear what one is to make of this period of sexual freedom, actively encouraged in a child aged from one to seven, and to a more limited degree thereafter. That Louis was being sexually manipulated and over-stimulated by his nurse, his governess, the ladies of his entourage, the courtiers and even his parents for their own amusement and titillation is obvious, while the objectivity of the doctor in recording these matters is not above suspicion. For example, he attributes sexual advances and actions to the boy before he could walk freely, whereas in fact he may have been manipulated with leading strings by adults, and encouraged and goaded into sexual play for the amusement of others. Moreover, the doctor's preoccupation with sexual matters seems a little peculiar in a pre-Freudian age, and some of Louis' recorded remarks, for example about the size of vaginas he had felt, sound like mere boasting to show off. But it is equally clear that many, if not all, of these events actually happened, and that the child's father Henri IV not only raised no objections to what was going on, but actively encouraged it. Indeed his father showed him the bed in which he had been conceived, and exposed himself to the child, 'stretching out his penis with his hand and saying, "behold what made you what you are."' Some of this education may have been consciously designed to follow the recommendation of the great doctor Fallopius to 'be zealous in infancy to enlarge the penis of a boy',[65] – and the penis of the dauphin was the mechanism on which the French monarchy depended for its biological survival – but the play seems to have been wholly devoid of medical or moral content. The result was that the child was familiar with the male and female sexual organs, had witnessed intercourse between adults, and had felt free to satisfy his sexual curiosity in speech or action, while still being far too young to have any understanding of the nature of erotic passion or the physiology of conception and childbirth.

Louis was also getting some confused signals from the adults, which began to make him shy and to withdraw from some of the playful sexual advances made to him by the courtiers. For example, his nurse once said to him, 'Monsieur, do not let anyone touch your nipples or your cock; they will cut them off', and for a time he took her seriously. Moreover, from the age of seven, far more modesty was expected of him and Dr Héroard now protested against his climbing into bed with married couples to engage in sexual play. At the age of fourteen, he was married and formally put to bed with the previously unseen thirteen-year-old bride his father had chosen for him, the Infanta of Spain. Although, according to his own account, he managed to penetrate her twice on that occasion – allegedly without orgasm – in later life Louis suffered long periods of impotence and was widely reputed to have homosexual tastes. It was only after twenty years of marriage that he managed to father an heir to the throne.

It certainly seems possible that his childhood of overstimulated sexual expression, followed by a period of bashfulness and guilt, and then by premature marriage to a child bride he had not even set eyes on, all contributed to his later sexual difficulties. His father, on the other hand, who sanctioned this sexual education, and therefore presumably had been brought up the same way himself in his rough rural backwater, was one of the most virile of men until his death. It is therefore inadmissible to attempt to use Freudian psychology to generalize about the later effects of this kind of education on the class as a whole, most of whom were neither dynamic men of action and promiscuous sexual athletes like Henri IV, nor obstinate, secretive, introverted stutterers and sexual cripples like his son Louis XIII.[66]

A more difficult and more important question is whether the attitudes towards infant sexuality revealed in Héroard's diary were peculiar to the court, and to the French court at that, at a particular moment in time in the first decade of the seventeenth century, or whether they represented a common European cultural pattern over the whole Early Modern period. Courts in seventeenth-century Europe had a reputation for sexual licence which was generally believed to be far in excess of that practised among the aristocracy and gentry as a whole, much less among the bourgeoisie. On the other hand, the fact that all the adults around the dauphin, both male and female, either directly encouraged or were complacently amused by his auto-erotic activity, genital exhibitionism and heterosexual inquisitiveness and play, suggests a commonly shared sense of values in which such things were neither deplored nor concealed. These nurses, governesses, doctors, aristocratic court ladies and gentlemen, and the King himself, came from different social milieux and different geographical areas. It seems hardly credible to suppose that they had shed all belief in the child-rearing practices with which they themselves had been brought up and had adopted a wholly new system of values that was exclusive to the French court. Sexual stimulation of older children was certainly practised also in England, for one day when Louis' Master of the Robe met him emerging from his bath with an erection, he proceeded to masturbate the adolescent with his hand, as 'a remedy which I have seen applied in England.'[67] It should also be remembered that Louis' attendants and courtiers were dealing with the upbringing of the future king, upon whose healthy development the stability and prosperity of the kingdom would eventually depend. It is inconceivable that they were a wholly exceptional group of sexual perverts amusing themselves by playing with a child. Their attitude towards infant and child sexuality must certainly reflect a sense of values that was not exclusively confined to French court circles. How much wider it went, we cannot say, but it must have been current in both medical and aristocratic circles of the day. Whether this also applied to gentry, bourgeois and peasant circles is, at present, very uncertain. But at least at the French court in the early seventeenth century, attitudes toward infantile and childish sexuality more closely parallel those found by Malinowski among the Trobriand Islanders than anything we are familiar with at other times and other places among the social elites of western Europe.

One of the very few pieces of direct evidence we have about the sexual behaviour of the children of the peasantry in the seventeenth century comes from the pen of a French village *curé* in 1700. He reported that it was common for boys and girls of seven to play at copulation, experiments made easy by the fact that children of both sexes were out alone in the fields for long hours tending the cattle and sheep.[68] In the early seventeenth century, another observer, J.J.Bouchard, recorded how little French children played at being adults: 'He was scarcely 8 years old when he started to clamber up on little girls.... Instead of sticking little sticks up their [rectums] as children do, pretending to give each other enemas, he lustily screwed them without knowing what he was doing.' It is obvious that this is an example of game-play in imitation of the observed behaviour of adults. Adam Martindale, a low-born English schoolmaster-minister of the same period, made his three-and-a-half-year-old daughter testify in court on a matter of life and death under cross-examination about the sexual assault by a neighbour on a six-year old girl. She must have known what it was all about, and her father was proud that she was 'so witty a girl' as to be able to testify credibly in open court in such a case.[69]

It has to be remembered that in the bottom third or so of the population, whole families were obliged to sleep in one room, which must have allowed children of this class to observe their parents in sexual intercourse, from an age when they still had no idea of its meaning. Even among those classes who lived in houses with separate bedrooms, the partitions were of thin board or lathe and plaster, through which it was often easy to see and always to hear – and vigorous coition is a noisy business. At a very early age most children must have observed their parents or others, to say nothing of animals, in sexual intercourse, and must have listened to the sexual gossip of servants and adults. The fragmentary surviving evidence, therefore, suggests that at all social levels in the seventeenth century, there was very considerable tolerance of childish sexuality, and that children were well aware of the physical facts of sexual relations between adults. The era of repression of childish curiosity and experimentation in these matters had not yet begun in the seventeenth century.

There has been much speculation on the psychological results of this early exposure to the 'Primal Scene'. One strongly supported view is that the shock of witnessing 'the beast with two backs' and the frustration imposed on the children by incest taboos leads to the development of a super-ego which is rigid, ferocious and pathogenic, thus explaining the extreme casual brutality and cruelty of the Early Modern poor in town and country. It has also been suggested that traumatic effect of the experience is greatly mitigated by a permissive attitude towards overt childish sexual activity.[70] If so, the greater privacy and perhaps greater sexual permissiveness enjoyed by children of the upper classes might help to explain their greater tolerance and less brutal behaviour in the Early Modern period than the more exposed and more repressed lower-middle and lower classes.

There are signs, however, that the seventeenth and eighteenth centuries saw a growing concern to control childish and adolescent sexuality, a concern which was a by-product of increasing care for children, and was to reach its height in the nineteenth century. One sign of this was the decline of co-education in schools, and a deliberate separation of the sexes at an early age. For example, when a school was founded at Uffington in 1637, the Founder stipulated that

Whereas it is the most common and usual course for many to send their daughters to common schools to be taught together with and amongst all sorts of youths, which course is by many conceived very uncomely and not decent, therefore the said schoolmaster may not admit any of that sex to be taught in the said school.[71]

This evident desire to break a sixteenth-century habit and to separate the sexes long before they reached puberty may perhaps be ascribed to the rising tide of Puritanism in the 1630s. But the movement continued after the decline of Puritanism in the late seventeenth and eighteenth centuries, and forms an exception to the general trend of that period towards greater permissiveness in child-rearing generally. In 1725 Isaac Watts impractically urged that children's ears be 'ever kept from all immodest stories ... wanton songs ... or amorous romances', and their eyes from 'lewd and unclean pictures.' In the mid-eighteenth century, James Nelson, in a standard work on middle- and upper-middle-class child-rearing, was calling for separation of bedrooms for boys and girls and 'an universal regard to decency both in words and actions', which 'must not be confined to the state of childhood.' This is a different cultural world from that of the court of Henry IV a century and a half earlier, a world of growing anxiety about childhood sexuality that was to grow to alarming proportions in the late nineteenth century. Indeed, by 1792 Mary Wollstonecraft was complaining that children were now too sheltered from the facts of life and asked 'why ... are they not to be told that their mothers carry and bear them,' instead of being filled up with 'ridiculous falsities' about storks?[72]

vi. Attitude to Adolescent Sexuality

With marriage delayed for ten to twelve years after puberty, and with the practice of sending children out of the home at an early age to serve as apprentices or agricultural or domestic servants, living in other people's houses, it is hardly surprising that the problems of adolescence were a common preoccupation of the Early Modern period. The idea that adolescence only became a social problem in the nineteenth century is sheer historical fantasy, and there was constant anxiety about the danger to the social and moral order of the huge numbers of unmarried apprentices in London at this period. As Thomas Wythorne put it in the late sixteenth century, 'After the age of childhood [0-15], beginneth the age named adolescency which continueth until twenty and five.... In this age Cupid and Venus were and would be very busy to trouble the quiet minds of young folk.'[73]

This being the case, official attitudes towards masturbation provide perhaps the most illuminating insight into attitudes towards adolescent sexuality in general. Although the position of moral theologians in the middle ages was that both adult and child masturbation were mortal sins, eighteenth-century Catholic confession manuals treated the latter as no more than a venial sin.[74] But the subject is not even mentioned in post-Reformation English child-rearing handbooks of the sixteenth and seventeenth centuries except in the most guarded terms. Current medical handbooks also largely ignored it, but medical theory pointed indirectly in its favour, if used in moderation. Based on the idea of balancing the humours, the standard doctrine was that for good health the human body needs occasional evacuation of superfluous fluids: blood by blood-letting; and semen by ejaculation. Both bachelors and widowers were, therefore, advised by doctors in the seventeenth century to follow a regime of moderate sexual activity. This being the case, the medical profession can hardly have disapproved of occasional pre-marital adolescent masturbation.[75]

The only direct evidence on this subject comes from obscure hints about lustful thoughts and acts by seventeenth-century youths who later underwent a conversion experience. For example, George Trosse referred to his earlier practice of 'a sin which too many young men are guilty of and look upon it as harmless, though God struck Onan dead in the place for it.' In general, however, post-conversion memoirs of the seventeenth century do not lay too much stress on adolescent masturbation, and Trosse's comment is revealing.[76] Even seventeenth-century children exposed to intense Calvinist indoctrination displayed only mild anxiety about the matter. Cotton Mather, the most fanatically pious of New England Puritan ministers of the late seventeenth century, certainly worried about the problem, but only intermittently. In 1682 at the age of twenty-one, he noted in his diary, 'Lord, I have sinned horribly, and by my early wickedness and filthiness I have provoked thee.' But the subject is not raised again in the diary until two years later when he reported that 'I found Satan buffeting me with unclean temptations.' It seems reasonable to conclude that this was not something which preyed very regularly on his mind or conscience as an unmarried young man, although in 1723 he hastened to join the rising tide of pamphleteering on the subject with a terrifying treatise against those 'who do evil with their hands.'[77]

The most detailed account comes from a lapsed Calvinist of the mid-eighteenth century. James Boswell was brought up in Scotland by a fanatically Calvinist mother, and was in his youth a most pious child, oppressed with visions of hell-fire and eternal damnation. In an autobiographical fragment written years later to show to Rousseau, he explained that he was about thirteen in 1753 when he first learned from books and from a school friend about what he called, significantly, 'the fatal practice'. He had in fact already been masturbating without knowing it by climbing trees (which is apparently a rather common cause of spontaneous ejaculation among boys). His notes on the subject read: 'In climbing trees, pleasure. Returned often, climbed, felt, allowed myself to fall from high trees in ecstasy.' He asked the gardener about it, but got no enlightenment from him. At thirteen or fourteen, 'My youthful desires became strong. I was horrified because of the fear that I would sin and be damned.' At one moment he even considered self-castration as a solution, but promptly abandoned the idea. After all, 'I thought what I was doing was a venial sin, whereas fornication was horrible.'[78]

From this very fragmentary evidence it would seem that in the seventeenth and early eighteenth centuries even the most Calvinistic of children, brought up in fear of hell-fire, nevertheless were not too deeply disturbed by the problem of handling their early sexual impulses, no more so, at any rate, than children at any period in history; and that medical theory, parental pressures and moral lectures on the subject had not yet begun to approach the intensity of the nineteenth century. In this area of sexuality, at any rate, childhood and adolescence in the Early Modern period was a time of relaxation, compared with the intensification of repression in the late eighteenth, nineteenth, and early twentieth centuries. It was a period in which, in Calvinist circles at least, the subject was not much talked about, so that a boy like Boswell could at thirteen be totally ignorant of sexual physiology. In the nineteenth century this verbal taboo seems to have collapsed, and doctors and moralists talked of little else but sex when discussing the problems of childhood and adolescence.

As the interval between puberty and marriage became longer and longer, as the age of marriage was increasingly postponed in all classes of society, the problem of masturbation inevitably loomed larger and larger. It is characteristic of the prevailing silence on the subject, and the consequent uncertainty in the public mind, that in 1704 a gentleman wrote a letter to Defoe's *Review* asking whether or not 'self-pollution' was a mortal sin. Defoe replied in the affirmative, but added prudishly that the problem 'is not more fit to be shown in public any more than to be acted in private.'[79]

The first popular pamphlet which spoke frankly about the terrible moral and physical dangers of masturbation was published in London in about 1710 by an anonymous clergyman. It was entitled *Onania or the heinous Sin of Self-pollution, and all its frightful Consequences in both Sexes considered.* Despite its vapid moralizing and implausible stories of resulting disease, the book was a great success. By 1760, thirty-eight thousand copies had been sold in nineteen English editions. It had also been translated into French and German, so that it clearly struck some hidden area of anxiety in early eighteenth-century Europe. Even Bernard de Mandeville accepted the theory and warned in 1724 that youthful masturbation, 'the first lewd trick that boys learn', could lead to impotence if practised in excess.[80] In 1764 the internationally celebrated Swiss Dr Tissot weighed in with a learned medical treatise on the subject, which gave the problem the dignity of full authoritative medical recognition. His argument was ostensibly not moral but scientific, the old theory of the dangers from excessive loss of seminal fluid, on the subject of which he assembled an impressive list of authorities from Hippocrates to Galen to Boerhaave. He cited allegedly authentic cases of masturbating youths – and maidens – falling victims to lassitude, epilepsy, convulsions, boils, disorders of the digestive, respiratory or nervous systems, and even death. All he could suggest as remedies were low diet, short sleep, vigorous exercise, and regular bowel movements, but he seems in fact to have regarded the habit as more or less incurable.[81]

This alarming statement from one of the most distinguished doctors in Europe was the start of a growing onslaught on masturbation in the late eighteenth and nineteenth centuries, which has been compared by one scholar with the witchcraft persecutions of the sixteenth century or with modern anti-semitism. So far as the English are concerned, there is no sign whatever that parents began to take drastic steps against masturbation by their adolescent children before the middle third of the nineteenth century. For what it is worth, the statistics of the number of publications on the subject of the evils of masturbation printed in France, and in the Bibliothèque Nationale in Paris, suggests a burst of anxiety in the mid-eighteenth century, followed by a lull, before the full torrent of propaganda against this menace was unleashed between about 1810 and 1850.[82] It seems likely that the English pattern ran a slightly different course, starting earlier in 1710, running at a much lower level through the eighteenth century, reaching far greater heights in the nineteenth century, and continuing high up to about 1870, whereas the French peak had begun to subside by 1840.

This rise of anxiety about adolescent masturbation in the early and mid-eighteenth century is not easy to account for, since it coincides with the period of greater general adult sexual permissiveness. The late eighteenth- and early nineteenth-century epidemic of hysteria on the subject is more easily explained, since it coincided with the rise of Evangelical doctrine and the growing sense of horror and shame about sex that was current at that time.

Some have tried to argue that there is a close causal relationship between early industrial society with its need for saving for investment and the drive against masturbation – both demanded a reduction of 'spending'. Conversely, the argument runs that the consumer society of the twentieth century must inevitably also be a sexually active 'spending' society.[83] This theory is attractive, but implausible. The drive against masturbation was led by clergymen and doctors, neither of whom can easily be identified with industrial society; the chronology is wrong since the first anti-masturbation publication was in 1710, half a century before industrialization made any impact on the scene; the propaganda was directed to the middle and upper classes, not the industrial classes; and it coincided with what was in all other respects a period of relaxation rather than a tightening of restrictions on sexual expression.

The most likely explanation of the rise of anxiety about masturbation in the early eighteenth century is that it was a by-product of the growing concern for the welfare of children and for their education to be socially and morally estimable persons. This would explain why the anxiety started first in England, which was in the vanguard in Europe in the development of the child-oriented family, and why it was repeated by Rousseau in his educational treatises. The anxiety may also have been encouraged by the rising median age of marriage, raising fears that masturbation was on the increase. More and more men were spending a longer and longer part of their sexually mature years with no other outlet for their libido but masturbation or prostitution. The rising age of marriage might help to explain the extraordinary success of Dr Tissot's learned and horrific treatise on the subject, since it was a problem of direct concern to more and more young men.

The second type of evidence about attitudes towards adolescent sexuality is provided by the degree of care taken to prevent homosexuality. In the sexually segregated academies and boarding-schools, which housed most upper- and middle-class children at that time, the children normally slept two in a bed, for reasons of economy, so that the first sexual experiments of most boys and girls may well have taken the form of mutual masturbation with a member of one's own sex, or some other form of overt homosexual activity. This is clearly what Mary Wollstonecraft was talking about when in 1792 she raised objections to sending children to boarding-schools: 'What nasty indecent tricks do they not also learn from each other, when a number of them pig together in the same bed-chamber, not to speak of the vices which render the body weak.'[84]

It is astonishing to discover how apparently indifferent seventeenth- and early eighteenth-century parents were to what today would seem to be obvious temptations for the children that were better avoided. It was not until the 1770s that parents began to worry about the problem of adolescent homosexuality, and it was noted as a special feature of an extremely expensive private school, among whose pupils were two future dukes, that all the boys slept in separate beds. One school, which charged the substantial sum of forty guineas a year in fees, found it worthwhile to advertise in 1786 that the boys would share a room, but 'each will have a bed to himself.' In more normal schools, parents who wished their boys to sleep alone had to pay extra for the privilege. One such parent was Philip Francis; when in

1774 he prepared to send his son Philip to Harrow or some other boarding-school, he wrote: 'wherever he goes I insist upon his constantly sleeping *alone* . . . for reasons that will increase with his years.' At Harrow he soon got him moved from a big house with sixty boys to the private house of the boy's tutor, where there were only six, explaining the move on the grounds that 'what I fear the most . . . is the bad examples of many bad boys.' Even in the 1770s, however, most parents were apparently perfectly content for their boys to sleep two in a bed at school, a procedure which would have been quite unthinkable seventy years later. The same was also true of girls, and in 1797 in a fashionable London boarding-school costing £80 a year, Arthur Young's daughter had to share with another girl a bed which was so narrow that they both had to sleep on the same side.[85]

Another piece of evidence of parental indifference to the dangers of adolescent homosexual contact is that in Oxford and Cambridge colleges in the sixteenth and seventeenth centuries it was normal practice for the tutor, who was usually a young bachelor in his middle twenties, to share his bedroom with several young students, aged perhaps fifteen to eighteen. One would have supposed that this was a situation which would have given great anxiety to parents, but in fact there is no evidence whatever that this is the case. In fact, parents were eager for their son to live with his tutor so that he could be more closely supervised. Only the homosexual poet John Marston seems to have drawn attention to the dangers, and he was ignored:

> Had I some snout-fair brats, they should endure
> The new found Castilian calenture
> Before some pedant tutor in his bed
> Should use my fry like Phrygian Ganymede.[86]

It is not until after 1700, by which time the drastic fall in student numbers had put an end to the need for cohabitation of tutors and students, that there is evidence of parental anxiety on this score. As early as 1666 Anthony Wood alleged that the electors to a Fellowship at All Souls had chosen a handsome young man with a view to 'kissing and slobbering' him. In 1715 Dudley Ryder reported that 'among the chief men in some of the colleges, sodomy is very usual. It is dangerous sending a young man who is beautiful to Oxford.' And in 1739 there broke out a major scandal at Wadham College in which the Warden was accused, with a wealth of supporting evidence, of attempted forcible rape of a student, with less well-documented rumours of other homosexual activity between dons and students in the College. The Warden left the country hurriedly for France, and the episode was hushed up as rapidly as possible by heads of colleges.[87] What this very fragmentary evidence suggests is that, whether or not the reality was changing, there was a growing concern among parents in the eighteenth century about the danger to their adolescent children (especially sons) of homosexual advances from fellow-students or adults.

A last test of attitudes towards adolescent sexuality is the degree to which efforts were made to keep the two sexes apart from each other. At the handful of greater English public schools in the eighteenth century, which were attended by considerable numbers of the aristocracy, it was apparently not at all difficult to indulge in heterosexual adventures. As a boy at Eton in the late eighteenth century, George Hanger 'had a most decided preference for female society, and passed as much time in the company of women as I have ever done since.' At night he used to climb out of his house to meet 'some favourite grisette of Windsor'; finally he fell in love with the daughter of a cabbage-seller, as a result of which 'Ovid's *Epistles* were totally laid aside for his *Art of Love*, in which we made considerable progress.' Nor was Hanger's experience unusual, for he noted how the senior boys made a point of going to church on Sundays at Windsor, instead of in the College chapel, in order to make assignations with their girls. It seems unlikely that Eton was unique among public schools in the ease with which the sexes could meet.

In any case, young noblemen were sent abroad on the Grand Tour at an early age, since few attended the University, and it was expected that they would return home with some sexual experience. When the seventeen-year-old Lord Herbert was touring Europe in 1776, his tutor wrote anxiously to his mother the Countess of Pembroke to urge that the proposed descent into Italy be postponed for a while. 'I would not for the world have his passions first awakened there.... In Italy they scout every idea of decency and morality, and will give him too little trouble.' Among the lower-middle classes, co-educational day schools existed in the late eighteenth century in London, which were attended by the children of respectable tradesmen. This gave Francis Place his first opportunity for sexual exploration, after the master had gone home for the day, leaving him alone with one of the girls. This was a situation which he believed could not have occurred in the stricter moral atmosphere of the 1820s.[88]

3 UPPER-CLASS BEHAVIOUR IN THE SIXTEENTH AND SEVENTEENTH CENTURIES

i. English Attitudes to Sensuality

There is some evidence to suggest that throughout the Early Modern period, English attitudes to sensuality were more free than they were in most areas of Europe. One piece of evidence of actual behaviour is the staggering number of prosecutions in Church courts for sexual offences in the Elizabethan period. No doubt many of these accusations were the result of the malice and unfounded suspicions of neighbours, but a substantial proportion must have had some basis in fact. It has been estimated that in the one county of Essex, with a population of about forty thousand adults, some fifteen thousand persons were summoned to court for sex offences over the forty-five years between 1558 and 1603.[89] This is an average of about three hundred and thirty a year, or one per cent of the sexually mature population. In an adult life span of thirty years, an Elizabethan inhabitant of Essex, therefore, had more than a one-in-four chance of being accused of fornication, adultery, buggery, incest, bestiality, or bigamy. Even if only half the charges were well founded, it still suggests a society which was both sexually very lax and also highly inquisitorial, with a great readiness to denounce one another's transgressions. That malice and back-biting were prominent characteristics of village society has already been demonstrated, and this therefore comes as no surprise. The very high level of extra-marital sex, however, is more startling. Very many cases of fornication were between maidservants and either fellow-servants in the house or their masters. This temptation was greatly aggravated by the overcrowding in bedrooms, for the maid not infrequently slept in the same room as the master and mistress of the house. Some masters were quite frank about the services they expected, like the man who offered a girl '40s. to serve him by day and 40s. to lie with him on nights.'[90]

If convicted, the Elizabethan penalties in Church courts for most sexual offences were not very severe. For fornication and adultery, they took the form of shame punishments of standing in a white sheet holding a white wand either in the town market place on market day, or in church before the full congregation. For pre-nuptial pregnancies, the penalty was open confession in church on a Sunday or at the time of marriage. As for bigamy, it was not even a civil offence at all before 1603, and many individuals ran away and married again without risk of being caught and often with a clear conscience. Thus in 1578 John Loggan formally put up the banns to marry

Mary Hewitt, arguing that his first wife Jane was 'gone from him and married to another man now dwelling in Kent, wherefore he thinketh he might marry again.' The Church court naturally thought otherwise, but there is no reason to suppose that the delinquent first wife was tracked down.[91] Apart from buggery and bestiality, which carried the death penalty, the one crime that was severely punished was not irregular sex itself, but its consequence. The production of a bastard child was likely to result in a drain on the financial resources of the parish and was, therefore, treated with exceptional severity. The father was served with a maintenance order – often very difficult to enforce – and up to about 1700 both mother and father were often stripped naked to the waist and whipped through the streets at a cart's tail. It is hardly surprising that abortion potions made from the dried tops of the savin bush, or even more drastic remedies such as physical maltreatment of the womb, or post-natal infanticide and abandonment, were sometimes resorted to by desperate mothers.[92]

Another piece of evidence of the rather casual English attitude to sensuality is the fact that even in their period of maximum authority and influence in America and England, the Puritans were either unwilling or unable to suppress the custom of bundling, the socially recognized practice of intimate pre-marital courting among the poor that was common throughout most of north-west Europe including Switzerland, parts of Germany, parts of France, all Scandinavia, Scotland, Ireland and Wales. The evidence for England is much thinner, but it exists. This indicates that Calvinist hostility to sexual play for its own sake, divorced from reproduction, failed to take deep root.

Another indication of English attitudes is that foreign visitors from the late fifteenth to the late eighteenth centuries noted with astonishment and shock the freedom with which it was the custom in England for persons of different sexes to greet each other by a kiss upon the lips. Visiting England in 1499, Erasmus found it a most attractive custom: 'wherever you come, you are received with a kiss by all; when you take your leave, you are dismissed with kisses; you return, kisses are repeated. They come to visit you, kisses again; they leave you, you kiss them all round. Should they meet you anywhere, kisses in abundance; in fine, wherever you move, there is nothing but kisses.' Over a century later, a young woman in one of Marston's plays complained that ''tis grown one of the most unsavoury ceremonies . . . any fellow . . . must salute us on the lips.' Drayton in 1613 noted that 'our kissing salutations [are] given and accepted amongst us with more freedom than in any part of the southern world.' In 1620 it was confirmed that 'for us to salute strangers with a kiss is counted but civility, but with foreign nations immodesty.'[93]

By the early eighteenth century, there were some doubts about the legitimacy of the practice, for in *The Spectator* a country gentleman, 'Rustic Sprightly', asked for 'your judgement, for or against kissing, by way of civility or salutation.' But the habit died hard and was still standard practice at the end of the eighteenth century, when a visitor observed that 'the kiss of love and the kiss of friendship are impressed alike upon the lips.' It was still 'the form of salutation peculiar to our nation.'[94]

It is also significant that in England, as elsewhere in Europe in the late sixteenth and early seventeenth centuries, it appears that many perfectly respectable women often exposed their naked breasts in public, much to the disapproval of the moral theologians. In 1616 Thomas Tuke spoke of 'the paps embossed laid forth for men's view'; in 1608 John Downham complained that 'pure virgins and chaste wives' were accustomed to 'laying out their breasts to be seen and touched'; and in 1620 an anonymous author attacked the 'bared breasts seducing'. In the 1630s some of the greatest ladies of the court, like Mary, Marchioness of Hamilton, were painted by Van Dyck in dresses which left the nipples exposed. In 1654 the habit was described as still 'too common in all places', but it seems to have died out soon after. When in the early eighteenth century Richard Steele complained about 'the naked bosoms of our British ladies', it was plunging necklines, not exposed nipples, to which he was referring. Bernard de Mandeville made the same complaint in 1724 but finally admitted that all he was talking about was 'that white vale between your breasts.' It was only in the late eighteenth century that the full topless style made a tentative and short-lived comeback (plate 32).[95] Mixed bathing still flourished in the eighteenth century, and at the baths at Bath a guidebook remarked that the crowds of half-naked bathers reminded him of the scene at the Resurrection, while another observer commented on the 'tempting amorous postures' of the bathing women. As one satirist put it:

> T'was a glorious sight to behold the fair sex
> All wading with gentlemen up to their necks.[96]

Finally there is the faint suggestion that in upper-class circles, at any rate in the late eighteenth century, the conversation was much more uninhibited than abroad. In 1784 La Rochefoucauld found after-dinner talk 'extremely free upon highly undecent subjects.... Very often I have heard things mentioned in good society which would be in the grossest taste in France.'

He was probably referring to conversation after the ladies had left the room, a practice which did not occur in France.[97]

Another piece of evidence about English attitudes towards sexuality, this time affecting all classes, is the retention in the official marriage service from the middle ages into the twentieth century of some very explicit wording which accompanies the ritual of the ring. In this ceremony, the bride and groom exchange rings, accompanied by the following words: 'With this ring I thee wed, ... and with my body I thee worship....' This was part of the marriage service in the middle ages, and was taken over by the Protestant Prayer Book in 1548. The Puritans objected to this wording in the *Admonition to Parliament* in 1572, on the not unreasonable grounds that they had not got rid of idolatry of images of the saints and the Virgin Mary in order to retain idolatry of a flesh and blood body. The issue was raised again at the Hampton Court Conference in 1603 by the Puritan bachelor John Rainolds, but he was rebuffed by King James who glossed the word 'worship' as the equivalent of 'honour', as in the phrase 'a gentleman of worship'. In 1641 a committee of the House of Lords suggested an alteration of the words to 'I give thee power over my body', and in the parliamentary *Directory* of 1644, the ceremony of the ring was omitted altogether. In the abortive Savoy Conference between Anglicans and Presbyterians in 1661, the latter asked that the ceremony be made optional, as a thing indifferent, and the Bishops conceded to alter the wording to 'with my body I thee honour.' But since the conference failed to reach agreement, the original wording was retained, and so has lasted until today.[98]

Sexual modesty was a characteristic of the lower-middle class, but it is very doubtful whether it extended to their superiors. Richardson remarked that Pamela's bashfulness showed that she was 'not of the quality', while James Cleland's Fanny Hill, a respectable country girl, was genuinely shocked to discover that some men and women took all their clothes off in daylight to make love. When seeing it practised by a Genoese, she attributed it to 'a taste, I suppose, peculiar to the heat, or perhaps the caprices of their own country.' On the other hand, it is noticeable that in Thomas Rowlandson's pornographic caricatures of the late eighteenth century, which represent the upper and middle ranks disporting themselves, the women are all more or less stripped but the men are all fully clothed, with only their breeches pulled down around their ankles to expose their genitals (plate 35). In the divorce trial of Lord Grosvenor, it emerged that he would pay substantially more to a lower-class prostitute if she was willing to strip – which some were reluctant to do – than if she merely let him penetrate her.

One who agreed to do so complained that his Lordship's breeches hurt her, which alone made him take off both them and his shoes.[99]

ii. Puritan Behaviour

A fairly sympathetic attitude towards sex in Elizabethan England is reflected in some of the characters in Shakespeare's plays, such as Juliet's nurse, the Merry Wives of Windsor, and the flirtatious couples in *As You Like It*, *The Taming of the Shrew* and *The Tempest*. Those with a more ambiguous love-hate attitude towards sex, such as Thersites in *Troilus* and Angelo in *Measure for Measure*, are not depicted as likeable or admirable persons. In the early seventeenth century, however, the attitude that sex is one of the natural pleasures of life, although like everything else bringing with it complications and side-effects, was tending to give way to the more puritanical view of sex as unfortunate evidence of the sinfulness of man. The only alternative available was the disembodied neo-platonic concepts of idealized love reflected in Ben Jonson's court masques and popular in the isolated entourage of Queen Henrietta Maria in the 1630s.[100]

The reason for the early seventeenth-century tightening of sexual attitudes must mainly be attributed to the work of Protestant, and especially Puritan, preachers. As Christianity slowly took hold, for the first time, as a result of dedicated missionary work by the newly educated clergy, the moral aspects of religion came increasingly into prominence. Protestant thought and theology laid great stress on the sanctity of marriage, which led preachers to denounce extra-marital relations and the double standard. It was part of the Puritan ethic of thrift and hard work that the pleasures of the flesh were peculiarly sinful and to be deplored. This ethic was particularly congenial to the rising urban bourgeoisie, and the success of the Puritan preachers during this period was undoubtedly helped by this social development. For a time, the nobility were under great pressure to behave like the middle classes, while both the lay Justices of the Peace and the Ecclesiastical Courts made extraordinary efforts to control and regiment the sexual behaviour of villagers and urban workers. One sign of the effects of moral Puritanism is the repeated reference by seventeenth-century autobiographers to a religious conversion as a solution to the temptations of lust in youth.[101]

Some illuminating hints about the attitude to sexuality adopted by seventeenth-century Puritans may be obtained from a close reading of the diaries of the Reverend Cotton Mather, covering the period from 1682 to 1724.[102] Mather was already something of an anachronism; a man who represented the stern Puritanism of the mid-seventeenth century, struggling vainly against the increasingly secular and materialistic society of contemporary Boston. He was also exceptional in his self-righteous religious fanaticism, but this freakishness brings out more clearly some of the inner drives of the Puritan character. Mather's diary is very discreet about sexual matters, since it was intended to be read by his children and to bring credit to him after his death, but there is enough to make possible some tentative conclusions. Cotton was a man of driving energies, one of the busiest public figures and the most active minister and preacher in New England. He was also clearly highly sexed, married three times, and father of fifteen children. As a charismatic young preacher, he found himself pursued by female parishioners, and his temptations were therefore great. In 1686, he solved his problem by marrying Abigail Philips.[103] The marriage was a success, and indeed it helped to cure his stammer that at one time threatened his career as a preacher. Between 1686 and 1701 his wife presented him with nine children, and their sex life had presumably been an active one. But in 1695 we find him reflecting on the 'manifold filthiness of my heart and life, and the horrible aggravations of that filthiness'; and when his uncle, the minister of Plymouth, was driven from the pulpit for fornication in 1697, Cotton was very much afraid that God's judgement might also light on him for his sins.[104] He had clearly been tempted to extra-marital adventures.

His wife died in December 1702, and by January 1703 he was praying that he might avoid the temptations that beset a widower – a preoccupation which worried him whenever one of his parishioners was in the same situation. In February 1703 a beautiful young girl of twenty, talented, pretty and of good and pious family, pressed herself upon him in marriage. He was much attracted, but was obliged to draw back since she had a reputation for flightiness which caused the opposition of friends, relatives and parishioners. Cotton was in deep despair, subject to 'temptations to impurities', to 'the abandonment of all religion as a mere delusion', and even to suicide. His frustrated sexual drive had clearly barely been held in check by a compliant wife and an overpowering piety. Now both were in jeopardy, as he was obliged by public opinion to refuse the girl – 'my victory over flesh and blood.'[105] But the only solution to his problem was another wife, and in June he found a discreet and respectable widow two doors down the road, with a sweet temper, only one son, and 'a very comely person.' He married her and was soon happy in 'the enjoyment of a most lovely creature.' Even so, in 1707, he found himself tempted with 'a certain impure and foolish idea' of 'incredible force', which in the end he successfully beat back by prayer. A series of children were produced from this apparently reasonably satisfactory marriage, but in 1713 'my dear, dear friend expired'.[106]

Meanwhile, Cotton was beginning to have growing doubts about the morality of the sexual act itself. In 1711 he was worried lest the virtue of his children might be corrupted by the 'inexpressible circumstances of meanness relating to their origin, their production and conception.' He prayed that 'no vileness of that nature may have any influence to render them abominable to Heaven'. After his second wife's death, by which time he was fifty-one, he decided to remain single, praying for 'purity in the widowhood'. At first he found comfort in the peace and quiet of a household without either a wife or any children under seven in it, for the first time for decades. But within two years, he was tired of his widowhood, and he married again in 1715 to a woman who had been widowed only six months before.[107] This third wife was in the end less satisfactory than the first two, for she was temperamental and volatile – perhaps a little unstable psychologically – and eventually became deeply resentful of Cotton's constant preoccupation with his political and religious activities and his prolonged withdrawals into his study to pray and write his diary.[108]

It is also possible that she suffered from Cotton's decreasing interest in sex and his increasing belief in its sinfulness; the latter no doubt a rationalization of the former, in its turn caused by increasing age. At all events in March 1718, when he was fifty-seven, he wrote in his diary (in Greek to prevent his wife from reading it) the following remarkable passage. 'The diseases of my soul are not cured until I arrive at the most unspotted chastity and purity. I do not apprehend that Heaven requires me utterly to lay aside my fondness for my lovely consort. But I must mourn most bitterly and walk humbly all my days for my former pollutions. I must abhor the least thought of regard unto any other person but this dearly beloved of my soul. I must be temperate in my conversation [meaning sexual relations] with her. And I must always propose a good and an high end in it; something that may be an expression or an evidence of my obedience to God.'[109]

If Cotton was still tempted by other women, but at the same time was enveloping his sexual relations with his wife with such an extraordinary web of religious restrictions, it is little wonder that she, who did not share her husband's fanatical piety, grew increasingly restive. Within a year, domestic quarrels became frequent, and in 1719 Cotton had to confess that his wife was a disappointment to him because of her frequent temper tantrums: 'our idols must prove our sorrows'. She was obviously jealous of his outside activities and his private life of prayer and diary-keeping in his study. She stole three years of the diary and would not let him have them back, while a further cause of friction was a godless niece she introduced into the household to keep her company, and the burden of debt of her former husband which threatened to overwhelm Cotton.[110] Moreover, the latter was becoming increasingly convinced of the sinfulness of sex. In 1724, aged sixty-one, he noted, 'Let my conversation with my consort be full of all goodness. But then, oh, let all possible purity accompany it, and let me watch against all such inordinate affection as may grieve the holy spirit of God.' In such circumstances, it is hardly surprising that late one night a few weeks later there broke out a tremendous domestic row, caused by his lack of warmth towards her. Cotton retired to pray in his study with his two children, while his wife and her niece left the house to sleep with a neighbour. Ten days later she returned home, asked for oblivion, and they prayed together, Cotton noting dispassionately that 'the tokens of the greatest enamoration on her part ensued upon it', although he discreetly omits to disclose whether he gave her any satisfaction.[111]

This evidence of Cotton Mather's attitude to sex is reinforced by his efforts to organize and sustain a 'Society for the Suppression of Disorder', whose main purpose seems to have been the shutting down of brothels in Boston;[112] by the suspension or expulsion of all members of his congregation convicted of fornication;[113] and by his constant anxiety about the temptations to which widows and widowers were exposed. To him, sex was a powerful, almost irresistible, human drive, which only the most passionate and exhaustive prayers and preaching, together with the outlet of a legal sexual partner, could possibly keep under control. 'We must kill our lusts before they kill us,' he repeatedly reminded himself. The New England marriage laws, which permitted formal divorce and remarriage of the innocent party on the grounds of adultery or prolonged desertion, also fitted into this general attitude towards sexuality.[114]

Cotton Mather was by no means the only seventeenth-century Puritan clergyman to be plagued by the problems of sex. In the middle of the century, a young Puritan minister in Yorkshire, Oliver Heywood, had a similar experience. He explained his predicament in the standard terms of Puritan theology. 'Tho' my parents were Saints, yet my birth and my nativity was in sin, and so was my conception, for they were instruments to bring me into the world not as Saints but as man and woman. . . . Therefore I am by nature . . . a limb of Satan . . . with propensity to sin.' He noted with alarm that 'from my childhood and youth my natural constitution exceedingly inclined to lust.... Temptations, backed with strong solicitations, have been so violent upon me that I look upon it as a miraculous mercy that God hath not left me to stain my profession and be a perpetual blot to myself and friends by some notorious act of prodigious uncleanness.' Driven by such hidden fires in 1655, Heywood sought the obvious remedy: 'My necessities within and without put me on seeking a suitable yoke-fellow.'[115]

There is no doubt that in the sixteenth and seventeenth centuries there were severe cultural pressures to conform to very austere patterns of sexual relations within marriage, the prime (or usually the sole) purpose of which was restricted to procreation. Sex as pleasure was something about which Puritans always felt a little guilty: it was not something to be enjoyed. On the other hand, the hostility of the Puritans to sexuality should not be exaggerated. They were realists, who accepted lust as a fact of life, unfortunately given to man by God for the purpose of perpetuating the species, and their main concern was to regulate forms of deviation which threatened the social order, like adultery or sodomy. Even so, the stress laid by the Puritans on the need for self-control and their constant harping on the moral and spiritual dangers of the lusts of the flesh makes recent attempts to present them in a more genial light less than fully persuasive.[116] In a Protestant country such as England, these pressures were confined to the advice given in handbooks by moral theologians, most of whom, but by no means all, were Puritans. In Counter-Reformation Europe, there was also the private, anonymous confession box, which was a new development and perhaps the most effective form both of safety valve for the penitent and of thought control by the clergy that has ever been devised by any society. As we have seen, the manuals prepared for confession went into far more intimate and explicit details about sexual behaviour than anything which could be or was published for the general public by Protestant moral theologians.

4 BEHAVIOUR OF 'THE QUALITY' IN THE EIGHTEENTH CENTURY

i. New Ideals

In the sixteenth and early seventeenth centuries, there had been two parallel archetypes of sexual conduct in existence: one being conjugal, primarily for the procreation of a male heir; and the other being extra-marital, exclusively for love, companionship, and sexual pleasure. What happened in the eighteenth century was that the two archetypes became increasingly fused into one in certain key social strata, as religious opposition to the second declined or was increasingly ignored, and as companionate marriages of personal choice increased. But this fusion took a very long time to spread much beyond the middling ranks and the country gentry. The second development in the eighteenth century was one of the most conspicuous results of the collapse of moral Puritanism as a dominant influence in society after 1660 and of the general secularization of society. This was a release of the libido from the age-old restraints of Christianity, which had been particularly effective in the late sixteenth and early seventeenth centuries. By the mid-eighteenth century there was emerging a new ideal, which now included sensual pleasure within its scope, if only as an unanticipated by-product of Lockean philosophy. In France some Jesuit theologians were also turning away from the doctrine of Original Sin, and urging the cultivation rather than the denial of human nature. Later some Enlightenment and post-Enlightenment thinkers, like Helvetius, Fourier and St Simon, were to make the same argument on a high philosophical plane, namely that pleasure and passion should be guides to conduct in life. It was John Wilkes, who admittedly was speaking only for a libertine minority, who put the new attitude in its grossest and crudest terms, and applied it to pure sensuality in his notorious *Essay on Woman* of 1763.[117]

A measure of the revolution in sexual attitudes that occurred in elite circles between 1660 and the early eighteenth century is to be found in Bernard de Mandeville's *Wishes to a Godson* of 1712:

> Of the handsome female fry
> May you've still variety
>
> . . . .
>
> May you never stick to one
> Or by fondness be undone;
> But have forty at a call
> And be fit to serve them all.
> May the silly creatures love ye,
> Never try to rule above ye.

Another example is Aphra Behn (taking her cue from Rochester), unblushingly referring to the vagina as:

> That fountain where delight still flows
> And gives the universal world repose.

Such frank and hedonistic eroticism was unthinkable in England before that period. Mrs Manley was only expressing current opinion when in the first decade of the eighteenth century she described sexual pleasure as 'those inestimable joys ... which ... are the greatest that human nature is capable of enjoying.' Her words were shocking to contemporaries merely because they came from the pen of a woman. The trend even affected that most prudish of classes, the *petite bourgeoisie*, and Richard Griffiths was a mid-eighteenth century lower-middle-class husband trying to have the best of both worlds when he wrote his bride a hopeful epithalamium:

> Her air coquettish but her mind a prude,
> Her body wanton but her soul not lewd.

At any rate one of the reasons for the success of the anonymous pamphlet against masturbation of 1710 was that some of its readers regarded it as titillating literature rather than an awful warning.[118]

The late eighteenth-century upper classes were deeply affected by the trend to recognize the needs of the body and even Mrs Thrale in 1790 condemned the current practice of deferred marriages on these grounds. Early marriages, she argued, 'are the best (popularly speaking) for all ranks. Why should we straggle so very far, as tis now the fashion, away from the course of nature?' Earlier, the poet William Blake had wrestled with the same problem, accepting sexuality as an essential, if subordinate, element in civilization: 'Art and Science cannot exist, except by naked beauty displayed.' It was, he felt, better to burn sexually than to suffer 'in misery supreme' the torments of ungratified desire. His final advice was 'let men do their duty, and the women will be such wonders.'[119] Freedom of sexual expression was one of the many by-products of the eighteenth-century pursuit of happiness.

It must be admitted, however, that there were some counter-currents at work in eighteenth-century culture. Daniel Defoe's *Conjugal Lewdness* of 1727 was, as has been seen, a very austere work which deliberately advised strict self-control over sensual pleasure. Wetenhall Wilkes, in *A Letter of Genteel and Moral Advice to a Young Lady*, which ran to eight editions between 1740 and 1766, told his audience that chastity – 'the great point of female honour' – includes 'a suppression of all irregular desires, voluntary pollutions, sinful concupiscence, and an immoderate use of all sensual or carnal pleasures.'

ii. New Practices: the Rise of Libertinism

a. Aristocratic Adultery. The first conspicuous results of the collapse of moral Puritanism after 1660 was not the fusion of marriage with sexual passion, but the release of the libido. A hundred years later, Sheridan commented on the extreme volatility of the English character as revealed in this sudden transformation. 'In Oliver Cromwell's time they were all precise canting creatures. And no sooner did Charles II come over than they turned gay rakes and libertines.'[120] One manifestation of the change was the dramatic upsurge of extra-marital liaisons among members of both sexes of the court aristocracy, spreading slowly down into rural elite society. Mistresses and bastards once again became a matter of common gossip and accepted normal fact of social life in these circles. The memoirs of Count Grammont are eloquent testimony to the return to patterns of extra-marital sexual licence at the court of Charles II. It was not merely that the King himself kept mistresses and spawned bastards in ostentatious profusion, to the pious horror of middle-class bureaucrats like Pepys, but that the whole court was absorbed in an endless game of sexual musical chairs. 'Lady Middleton, Lady Denham, the Queen's and the Duchess' maids of honour, and a hundred others bestow their favours to the right and to the left, and not the least notice is taken of their conduct.' Sexual promiscuity became a hallmark of fashion at court and in high political circles. Lord Keeper North was urged to keep a mistress, since otherwise he would be 'ill looked upon for want of doing so' and 'lose all his interest at court'. In 1675 it was remarked that 'adultery is common and this age gives it the soft and gentle French names of gallantry and divertisement in apology for it.' It is indeed significant of the new attitude that the crude word 'adultery' was replaced by the rather attractive euphemism 'gallantry'. A century later, when efforts at the moral reform of the upper classes were again being made, Hannah More remarked that 'the substitution of the word *gallantry* for that crime which stabs domestic happiness and conjugal virtue is one of the most dangerous of all the modern abuses of the language.'[121] At the same period, a whole new genre of adulterous court literature also sprang up, from the plays of Wycherley to the poems of Rochester.

The post-Restoration and eighteenth-century court and its aristocracy rejected the whole concept of 'matrimonial chastity' so dear to the Puritans, and regarded marriage itself as 'the clog of all pleasure, the luggage of life', as Rochester put it. In 1724 Bernard de Mandeville was still taking the same line, arguing that marriage merely 'gives a man's fancy a distaste to the particular dish, but leaves his palate as luxurious as ever.'[122] It was an artificial hot-house atmosphere, bred more of angry distaste for Puritanism than of an acceptance of man's natural instincts and a sensible recognition of the problems involved in either their total repression or their total liberation.

Throughout the eighteenth century it remained quite common in upper-class circles for men of rank, position and quality to keep a mistress or series of mistresses. Throughout the whole of the mid-eighteenth century, the monthly periodical *Town and Country Magazine* entertained its readers in each issue with an illustrated account of the irregular sex life of some man of note. These stories add up to only twelve persons a year out of a potential population of many hundred and, therefore, cannot be taken as typical of upper-class life. But what is interesting about the accounts is the uniformity of the social pattern they reveal. The girls who, in return for a fixed allowance, became the mistresses of noblemen and wealthy gentlemen were nearly all women from a well-to-do professional or merchant background whose fathers had gone bankrupt, and who found this virtually the only way of maintaining the standard of living to which they were accustomed. Between 1781 and 1784 the mistress of the Earl of Surrey was the daughter of a bankrupt attorney; of Thomas Gage the daughter of a poor parson (who had begun her career as the mistress of a naval lieutenant); of the Earl of Aldeburgh the widow of a lieutenant killed in America; of Colonel Tarleton the daughter of a bankrupt solicitor; of Sir Herbert Pakington the daughter (already pregnant by the Duke of Dorset) of an eminent brewer; of the Lord Mayor of London the widow of a bankrupt merchant; of the fifth Duke of Bedford the daughter of a bankrupt physician; of Baron Sydney, later Duke of Queensbury, the daughter of a bankrupt apothecary; of W.W.Grenville the daughter of a bankrupt musician.

The economic uncertainties of professional and mercantile life, the improvement in the education of bourgeois daughters, and the lack of alternative career opportunities for girls suddenly reduced from genteel affluence to poverty meant that there was a reasonably supply of attractive and well-bred girls to form suitable companions and mistresses for men of means. A few of these women led a distinctly chequered life. There was one, the daughter of an eminent wine-merchant who went bankrupt, who for lack of money first became the mistress of a Lord B. When his lordship married he arranged for her to marry his butler, for whom he procured a 'genteel place' in the customs service, since it clearly would not do for the girl to remain in the house. When the butler died soon afterwards, the widow became the mistress of a son of Lord North. Only a few noblemen descended lower in the social scale, taking up with the daughter of one of their tenants. The third Earl of Oxford and the third Duke of Portland were two who lived with daughters of tenants, the former remaining faithful for twenty years. A very few took on well-bred girls of dubious reputation, like G.E.Boscawen, Lord Falmouth, whose mistress had first eloped from her boarding-school with her dancing master on a false promise of marriage, and had since had a succession of lovers.[123] It is also worth noting that it was in the late eighteenth century – in 1782 to be precise – that respectable London newspapers like *The Herald* were publishing advertisements by men openly 'soliciting female friendships', a phenomenon which has only reappeared in England and America in the last few years.[124]

This free-wheeling promiscuity of the rich may have contributed to the rise of the illegitimacy rate, if a higher proportion of men from elite society were intensifying their efforts to seduce lower-class girls. A girl seduced by a man of her own class might reasonably hope that marriage might follow, but she could have no such hopes if her lover were a gentleman. When Tom Jones seduced Molly, the gamekeeper's daughter, her mother was furious with her. When Molly pointed out that her mother had given birth within a week of her own marriage, the latter became even more indignant. 'I was made an honest woman then', she replied, 'and if you was to be made an honest woman I should not be angry. But you must have to doing with a gentleman, you nasty slut: you will have a bastard, hussy, you will.' When in Aphra Behn's *Amorous Prince* the prince was asked by a courtier how he achieved his conquests, he admitted that he offered promises of marriage: 'that's your only bait. And though they cannot hope we will perform it, yet it secures their honour and my pleasure.'[125] These literary examples carry with them a strong ring of truth, which receives ample confirmation from French evidence.

The case of Mrs Pendarves shows how in the eighteenth century even an upper-class girl, if married against her will to an obviously incompatible husband, was constantly subjected to invitations to adultery by married and unmarried men of her own social status.[126] Moreover, bastards appeared once more in wills in the early eighteenth century and were tolerantly accepted into the household, at least by some wives. In his will drawn up in 1721, John, Duke of Buckingham, mentioned many bastards including a son by one mistress living abroad with a tutor in Utrecht, and two girls by another being brought up at home by his second wife with their legitimate children, and now away at boarding-school. These girls, 'to whom she has always been most generously indulgent, he left with full confidence to the care of his widow. The higher the level of society, the greater the promiscuity, and the European record for fathering illegitimate children in the eighteenth century was probably held by Augustus the Strong, Elector of Saxony and King of Poland, who had three hundred and fifty-four acknowledged bastards.[127]

This easy-going attitude to sexual promiscuity among the higher aristocracy persisted, and may even have become more common, throughout the eighteenth century. In 1724 Lady Mary Wortley Montagu alleged that not only husbands but also wives were now freely committing adultery, so that 'the appellation of rake is as genteel in a woman as a man of quality'. An anonymous author claimed in 1739 that female adultery in high circles was now 'rather esteemed a fashionable vice than a crime.' The causes of this situation he attributed to the traditional free and easy ways of the English, corruption by foreign manners, the decay of religion, permissive education with too much stress on 'ornament of the body' for girls, marriages for money or sexual passion rather than settled affection, and the infidelity of husbands. It was a plausible list, and he was undoubtedly right when he observed that 'the middling people are certainly more happy in the married state than persons of a more elevated dignity.' Forty years later, nothing had changed. In 1780 the Earl of Pembroke commented that *'nos dames, douces commes des agneaux, se laissent monter par tout le monde.'* Mrs Armstead, the mistress and later the wife of Charles James Fox, had previously been the well-established mistress successively of Lord George Cavendish, Lord Derby and Lord Cholmondeley. The children of the Countess of Oxford were known as 'the Harleian Miscellany', and in the 1790s there were brought up at Devonshire House and Chatsworth a whole collection of oddly assorted children: three were the children of the fifth Duke of Devonshire and his Duchess, Georgiana; and two were of the Duke and Lady Elizabeth Foster, the Duchess' most intimate friend and life-long companion; while one child of the Duke and Charlotte Spencer and one of the Duchess and Lord Grey were brought up elsewhere. This was a confusion of generation that left Georgiana quite unmoved. In 1784 she wrote to Lady Elizabeth Foster, 'Dear, dear Bess, you grow every day more Canis's [the Duke's] sister, and your Georgiana's friend. . . . You are Canis's child's [by Charlotte Spencer] guardian angel.'[128] A year later, 'Canis's sister' produced her own child by him.

The tenth Earl of Pembroke had children by two mistresses, and his bastard son, who had a successful naval career, was on the best of terms with the legitimate son and heir, Lord Herbert, and also with the Countess. The latter's sole request, which was respected, was that the illegitimate children should not take the family name of Herbert. She also objected when her husband hung prints of his current mistress, the actress La Bacelli, in his bedroom in Wilton House, a protest the Earl rejected, declaring that it could not be taken as an open affront 'between two people who professedly never wish to cohabit together.' In 1812 'the Duke of Manchester was repairing his fortunes abroad as governor of Jamaica; the Duchess had left home years before with one of her footmen.'[129] Both these case histories and the memoirs of famous courtesans like Harriette Wilson and Julia Johnstone provide plenty of evidence that there was a great deal of extra-marital sexual activity among many aristocratic husbands and some aristocratic wives at least as late as the first decade of the nineteenth century. Harriette Wilson, for example, was the mistress of (among others) the Dukes of Wellington, Argyll and Beaufort, the Marquesses of Worcester, Anglesey, Bath and Hertford, Lord Craven, and many more of the lesser nobility.[130] In these circles, illegitimate boys seem usually to have been well educated and to have suffered no social discrimination in terms of professional career or marriage. As Lord Mulgrave remarked in the House of Lords in 1800, 'bastardy is of little comparative consequence to the male children.' Illegitimate female children, however, 'have to struggle with every disadvantage from their rank in life', since the only career open to a woman of this class was marriage. Only a small minority were as successful as the illegitimate daughter of Sir Edward Walpole, who in 1759 married the second Lord Waldegrave, and on his death George III's brother, the Duke of Gloucester.[131]

This casual acceptance of illegitimate children in the eighteenth century spread down quite far into the professional classes. In the 1770s Erasmus Darwin, a successful and respected Cambridge doctor, fathered two illegitimate children between the death of his first wife and the marriage with his second. He brought them up openly, giving them a good education, and they remained on intimate terms with his second wife and his children by her. A century later, his grandson commented with astonishment that this irregularity in no way damaged Erasmus Darwin's professional practice as a physician. This could not have happened in the late nineteenth century, or, for the matter of that, in the early seventeenth.[132]

b. Bachelor Morality. The memoirs of Casanova and other professional libertines support the suggestion that there was a very easy-going sexual morality prevalent in the growing bachelor element among the upper classes in the eighteenth century, after the impact of seventeenth-century Puritanism had died away. There was an ethical code which was supposed to govern such lives, one which was best stated by Richardson's rakish creation, Lovelace: 'to marry off a former mistress, if possible, before I took a new one; to maintain a lady handsomely in her lying in, to provide for the little one, if he lived, according to the degree of the mother, if she died.' This was an honour code of a kind, and the memoirs of William Hickey in the late eighteenth century show it in full operation among expatriate English officials in India with regard to their native mistresses. The code implied that women of lower social class were fair game for sexual exploitation, but not ladies of one's own rank. When Major W.C. Yelverton, the son of an Irish peer, was under cross-examination in a court case in 1861 concerning his seduction of the daughter of a silk-merchant, he tried to excuse himself by reverting to eighteenth-century conventions about such matters. He argued that the degree of the moral culpability of the man depended on the social status of the woman: 'It is not laudable if the person seduced is a gentlewoman, as she has more to lose; she loses position.'[133]

c. *Libertine Excesses.* During the eighteenth century, the most striking manifestations of sexual libertinism, now heavily tinged with conscious anti-Christian ideology, occurred in France and were confined to the higher reaches of the aristocracy and some of the intellectuals. The erotic writings of Choderlos de Laclos and the Marquis de Sade are manifestations of this movement in France, while in England the Hell-Fire Club of Sir Francis Dashwood provides a notorious example of these ideas carried to extremes. Between 1779 and 1784, an ingenious quack entrepreneur, an Edinburgh medical student named James Graham, made a living from lecturing to fashionable London society on 'generation' – allegedly illustrated by a naked woman on the stage – and from renting out to the jaded rich at £50 a night his 'celestial bed'. This remarkable contrivance, first installed in a 'Temple of Health', later replaced by a 'Temple of Hymen', was marketed as a sovereign remedy for female sterility or male impotence. Harmonica, flute and organ music, 'stimulating vapours' and oriental perfumes were piped into the bedroom, where the couple was encouraged to warm up by elaborate washing, followed by singing, and drinking a patented aphrodisiac 'divine draught' costing a guinea a bottle. They were then to approach the 'electro-magnetic' bed – Graham had visited America and seen Benjamin Franklin's electrical experiments – where they were expected to perform in the light of the moon, on a mattress impregnated with the essences of Arabia, while 'magnetic fluid' wrought up their nerves and 'celestial and electric fire' was pumped into the chamber from a pressure-cylinder next door. This prototype of Masters and Johnson in the art of sex therapy ran his business with enormous success for four years before closing down in 1784.[134]

d. *Female Fashions in Clothing.* These sometimes bizarre upper-class manifestations were exaggerated reflections of more profound and widespread changes that were taking place in general attitudes and conduct. There are clear signs that during the middle years of the eighteenth century attitudes towards sex in England, especially in London, were unusually relaxed. It is an open question how far the attitude towards sexuality in a society can be judged from the amount of sexual provocation or sexual concealment in women's clothes. Assuming that there is some correlation, it is noticeable that in the mid-1780s the fashionable dress included grotesquely enlarged breasts and buttocks, the former created by wirework and the latter by cork attachments (plate 31). Elegant women resembled the callipygous statues of prehistoric art. Within a decade this fashion was replaced by the flowing see-through style in which women floated about in diaphanous veils with bosoms exposed or lightly covered, and the contours of the body fully displayed (plate 32).[135] In their very different ways, both fashions reflected an identical desire to advertise sexual attractions, the one representing unrealistic male sexual fantasies, the other exhibiting the real thing.

While perhaps equally sexually provocative, when it came to courting or dalliance the latter fashion had one obvious advantage over the former. Colonel George Hanger commented in 1801: 'I must confess, I am a great admirer of short waists and thin clothing; formerly, when the women wore strong stiff stays and cork rumps, you might as well sit with your arm round an oaken tree with the bark on, as around a lady's waist; but now, as you have seldom any more covering but your shift and gown of a cold day, your waist is extremely warm and comfortable to the feel.'[136]

e. *Sexual Aids.* The production of sexual hardware was partly the result of improved technology and greater specialization in manufacture. But their appearance is also evidence of a new demand, made possible by a new morality. It is thus no accident that it was in the 1660s that such sophisticated devices as dildoes (imported from Italy) first became available in London, along with the first condoms. The former were sold, according to Rochester, at the Sign of the Cross in St James's Street and were bought and used by aristocratic ladies of the court, although they were still unknown to the wives of the bourgeoisie further east in the city.[137] A century later they were still being imported from abroad, much to the embarrassment of the customs officials, since neither were they listed as dutiable, nor were they prohibited goods. They nonetheless ordered a consignment to be burned. They were then known as 'passo tempos for the amusement of single ladies', or by the French as '*bijoux indiscrets*', and it was argued that if they were more commonly available, fewer women would find themselves pregnant. It was also (somewhat improbably) alleged that 'scarce a lady comes from abroad without being in possession of one or two'.[138]

As for condoms, London and Paris were said to have been the only capital cities in Europe in the second half of the eighteenth century where these devices, then used primarily for prophylactic rather than contraceptive purposes, were openly manufactured, advertised, sold and used. They were clumsy affairs made of sheep gut, and were secured to the wearer at the base with a red ribbon, which was tied around the scrotum. In the 1740s they were sold by a Mrs Lewis in a shop in St Martin's Lane. Later on in the century, the monopoly passed to a Mrs Phillips, selling them in a shop first at the Green Canister in Half Moon Street, and later at 5 Orange Court, Leicester Fields. So famous was she that she figured in two caricatures of the period, one in 1773 and one in 1786, the first of which depicts a sale of all the effects of a bankrupt by auction, including 'a quantity of articles in Mrs Phillips' way, not the least the worse for wear.'[139]

f. Pornography. It is equally significant that it was only in the eighteenth century that there first developed the large-scale production of home-made English pornography, both in literature and in pictures. When in the 1660s Pepys wanted to read a pornographic book, he had to buy a French work called *L'École des Filles*, 'a lewd book, but what doth me no wrong to read for information's sake.' This was a somewhat lame excuse, for the reading gave Pepys an erection and led him to ejaculate once. He then burned the book, presumably to prevent his wife from finding it. France long continued to be a major source, and as late as 1753 there were complaints about 'that inundation of obscenity which is daily pouring in from France.'[140]

Frankly erotic English poetry certainly occurred in the early seventeenth century, such as John Donne's lyrical exploration of a woman's body: *O America! O my new found land!* Poetry only began to be more physically explicit, and even pornographic, however, with the Cavalier poets like Lovelace, as in his poem *To Amarantha*:

> Here we'll strip and cool our fire
> In cream below, in milk-baths higher.[141]

With Lovelace there surfaces a new sensibility, involving the open expression of the long-suppressed id, which paved the way for the eroticized court culture of the Restoration.

Native English pornography as a literary genre seems to have had its tentative beginnings in the scurrilous and mildly obscene poems about sexual life at the court in the 1620s, which circulated widely in manuscript. This unpublished material began again slowly after the Restoration, but became a torrent in the last years of Charles II, from 1679 to 1685. Although the authors included Lord Rochester and Sir George Etherege, the quality of the doggerel was if anything lower than before. The great difference from the output of the pre-war years, however, is in the tone, the moral sensibility displayed by the authors and the elite audience of both sexes, who avidly sought after, read and preserved this material. It was now frankly pornographic in content, both in the generalized use of four-letter words and in the explicit descriptions of different kinds of sexual activity attributed to the King and other members of the court. The two variations on normal sexual intercourse most commonly referred to were female masturbation with dildoes, and anal penetration. But it seems not unlikely that the harping on the latter may have been due partly to the poverty of imagination of the poets, and the accident that the word 'tarse' (penis) happens to rhyme with 'arse'.[142]

These manuscript poems went hand in hand with more directly political satires, and in both types the chief villain was the King, who was depicted in the former as the leader of an endless debauch. The connection between political opposition and pornographic anti-court satire was seen at the time, and a poem of 1682 makes it very clear:

> The King, Duke and State
> Are so libelled of late
> That the authors for Whigs are suspected.
> For women in scandal
> By scribblers are damned all,
> To Court and to cunt disaffected.[143]

The political significance of such material in destroying the charisma of kingship should not be underestimated. On all three occasions in Early Modern times when a King was deposed or executed – England in 1649 and 1688, France in 1793 – the event was preceded by decades of pamphlets and poems, depicting the court as a sink of financial corruption and sexual depravity, fit only to be destroyed by men of moral integrity.

In printed, as opposed to manuscript, literature, the development of native English pornography began after the Restoration with bawdy parodies of classical authors like Virgil and Lucian, followed by Edward Ward's scurrilous and obscene publications of about 1700. Output rose in the first half of the eighteenth century, and the key event was the publication in 1748 of James Cleland's *Memoirs of a Woman of Pleasure*, a lively piece of cheerful and literate hard-core pornography which was the first of its kind to be written by an Englishman, and one of the few which succeeded in being extremely graphic without the use of four-letter words. The author, printer and publisher were admittedly prosecuted, but it is noticeable that nothing serious in fact happened to them, and that the book was defended as not 'offensive to decency' by the *Monthly Review*.[144] There followed similar works, some ostensibly mere reporting, like the book about rapes and sodomies committed, 'showing all the tricks and methods used by the mollies [homosexuals]'. By 1750 the market had grown sufficiently large to justify the launching of a fortnightly pornographic magazine, but it did not last. In 1773, however, *The Covent Garden Magazine or Amorous Repository* began a more successful career. It contained sexually provocative stories, and advertisements for prostitutes and brothels, with the prices (five shillings 'for a temporary favour', and half a guinea 'for a night's lodging'). In 1795 there began publication of *The Ranger's Magazine, or the Man of Fashion's Companion*, which included, according to its own statement of contents, monthly lists of whores; annals of gallantry; the juicier parts of trials for adultery, 'crim. con.' and seduction; *doubles entendres*; choice anecdotes, warm narratives, curious fragments, animating histories of tête-à-têtes, and wanton frolics. Some years earlier, there had begun publication of *Harris' List of Covent Garden Ladies*, an annual directory of call-girls, with prices, specialities, and descriptions which combined lyrical enthusiasm with extreme anatomical precision. The issue of 1786, for example, listed a hundred and five women, the attractions of one of whom were described by an obviously well-educated hack ad-writer. Despite seven years experience in the trade, 'the coral-tipped clitoris still forms the powerful erection . . . nor has the sphincter vaginae been robbed of any of its contractive powers; the propelling labia still make the close fissure.'[145]

Another sign of the spread of the new erotic sensibility is the widespread production and distribution of pornographic prints in eighteenth-century England. An early but abortive attempt to supply the market was made by some young dons at All Souls College in 1675. They were caught in the act of using the Oxford University presses after closing hours to print off copies of Giulio Romano's engravings from Aretino's *Postures* – the most famous, indeed almost the only, illustrated how-to-do-it sex manual of the day.[146] By the early eighteenth century pornographic prints were in wide circulation and even found their way into fashionable drawing-rooms by the 1740s, if one can rely on the illustrations in Hogarth's *Marriage à la Mode* series of 1745. In the dining-room of this wealthy couple – a viscount's son and a rich merchant's daughter – there hung a pornographic illustration of some kind, discreetly covered by a curtain, while another print in the series shows the wife buying antiquities, which include some of the erotic prints of Giulio Romano. So popular was the demand that in the very late eighteenth and early nineteenth centuries – mostly in about 1812 – England's most famous caricaturist, Thomas Rowlandson, was turning out pornographic prints, some of them for special customers like the Prince Regent[147] (plate 35). Finally, we have some evidence of a phenomenon which may have been present from the days of Pompeii to the twentieth century, but which certainly varies in quantity over time and space, as travellers and elderly persons today can testify, namely the habit of scribbling obscenities in public places:

> In wicked sport they rudely scrawl
> Unseemly words on every wall,
> And underneath the well-spelt line
> The parts themselves at large design.[148]

The authors were presumably drawn from all sectors of the literate classes, including the elite.

g. *University Libertinism*. The same tolerant sexual attitudes inevitably spread to the universities. In 1698 a Visitation of Wadham College, Oxford, showed that the college had been employing a bedmaker of very ill repute. She had slept with a number of members of the college, become pregnant, and drowned herself just before delivery. At Caius, Cambridge, in 1714 the Master alleged that the Fellows 'take married persons who never were of the College, . . . and lie with them in their beds.' Thomas Hearne's *Diary* for the early eighteenth century is full of gossip about the sexual peccadilloes of the Oxford dons, such as the Warden of All Souls who, although married, 'took all opportunities of having his pleasure with whores.' He had two nieces living with him, one of whom was 'mighty desirous of men, so as to be ready to leap out at windows after them.' He also records one remarkable episode at the annual horse-race on Port Meadow in 1731 when some thirty undergraduates lay with a young woman called Cradock in the meadow 'whilst all the people in the meadow stood around to see them.'[149]

h. Homosexuality. By the eighteenth century homosexuality was apparently becoming more common, or at any rate more open, among the upper classes. It may perhaps be significant that the numbers of male heirs who inherited landed estates in three sample counties and who never married rose from about five per cent before 1650 to about fifteen per cent thereafter (Graph 2). Since the incentive of a property owner to marry, if only to produce a male heir, was very great, this may possibly indicate a rise in the number of homosexuals in this class. By the early eighteenth century, homosexual clubs existed for the upper classes in London, and throughout the century there were well-known wealthy deviants, like William Beckford, who were never brought to book. Mrs Thrale certainly believed that the practice was then becoming increasingly common in the circles in which she moved. In 1781 she described it as 'now so modish' and in 1790 remarked that 'there is a strange propensity in England for these unspeakable crimes.' The caricaturists also noticed the trend, and produced one print in 1773 entitled 'Refined Taste', showing a civilian eyeing the tight backside of a soldier, with a caption denouncing 'A crime that "spite of sense and nature reigns".' Another of 1808 showed seven owners of bawdy-houses tossing the manager of the Covent Garden Theatre in a blanket in protest against private boxes, crying 'No pretty boys. No private boxes.'[150]

Francis Place also noted the relish with which the newspapers of that period would print all 'the filthy details' brought out in the numerous trials for sodomy. But the fact that there were so many trials indicates that the forces of order still tried to punish those accused of this offence, and as late as 1772 a Captain Robert James was executed for this crime. The normal punishment for attempted sodomy was the pillory, but in more than one case this was the equivalent of the death penalty. Such was the fury of the mob, apparently mostly women, that they would sometimes pelt, stone or whip the victim to death, shouting 'cut it off', 'shave him close', 'flog him', etc. A savage print of 1763 showed the killing of a 'molly' in the pillory at Stratford in that year. The accompanying poem was addressed to:

> ye reverses of nature, each dear little creature
> Of soft and effeminate sight

and concluded grimly:

> But a race so detested, of honour divested

> The daughters of Britain invite.
> Whom they leave in the lurch, to well flog 'em with birch;
> Should they slay 'em – all in the right.[151]

It is very hard to draw any firm conclusions from this very fragmentary evidence. It certainly looks as if eighteenth-century upper-class society was becoming more tolerant of adult male homosexuality, although the violent prejudices of the poor did not alter. It also seems possible that a higher proportion of the social elite were indeed homosexuals. What is certain is that male homosexuality was practised and talked about more openly in the eighteenth century than at any previous time, except in the restricted court circles in the reign of James I. The increasing care taken by elite parents to protect their adolescent children from the homosexual advances of fellow students, college tutors or other adults also suggests a greater awareness in the society of the existence of this sexual impulse. The new precautions taken were a product of the growing concern for children, not of a growing elite hostility towards homosexuals as such, which was confined to the poor around the pillory. Taken together, this evidence points to a distinct rise in public consciousness about homosexuality. Whether or not the practice was on the increase must remain a far more open question.

i. Marital Sexuality. The second feature of eighteenth-century sexual life, the fusion of the previously separate roles of wife and mistress – the one to run the house and provide a male heir, and the other for companionship and sexual pleasure – is more difficult to document. There is evidence of an urgent female desire in the late eighteenth century to obtain full scientific knowledge of the anatomy of female sexual organs of reproduction, and public waxwork exhibitions on this subject were thronged with respectable young women (plate 36). They were representative of the modern girl,

> Who 'ere for wedlock ripe, is wild to see
> What must its joys, and what its pains must be;
> How in the womb the foetus is reclined,
> What passage thence by nature is designed.
> With every other circumstance beside
> That may inform her ere she be a bride.

She had, complained the conservatives,

> This bawdy itch of knowing secret things
> And tracing human nature to its springs.

Armed with this new knowledge, she was better equipped than any generation before her to handle the problems of marital sexuality. The quotations from correspondence provided in Chapter 9 indicate that sexual passion was an essential ingredient of many marriages among the squirarchy and professional and bourgeois classes, and it was the frequent waning of this passion which led to the rise of extra-marital liaisons during this period. Marriage was supposed to be sexually satisfying, and if it was not, husbands (and sometimes wives) sought sexual satisfaction elsewhere. It is highly significant that in *The Lady's Magazine* in the 1770s, the constant advice is, firstly that sexual attraction is ephemeral and an inadequate basis for marriage by itself, but secondly that it is an essential ingredient of marriage and something that the wife should do her utmost to keep alive. Above all, she should not, after capturing her man, allow herself to become sluttish and neglect her appearance. A letter of advice by a brother to a sister on her marriage puts it in a nutshell: 'never lose the mistress in the wife – a text of bullion sense'; the word 'mistress' being clearly defined in the context as a sexual partner, not a household manager.[152]

5   CONCLUSION

The main argument of this chapter is that the period 1660–1800 saw a remarkable release of the libido among many members of the squirarchy and aristocracy, caused primarily by the collapse of the Puritan ascetic morality which during the previous century had been both externally enforced by the authorities and also widely internalized. This change, together with concurrent changes in the way marriages were arranged, encouraged the more open admission of sexual passion into the marital relationship with a resultant reshaping of the ideal role-model of the wife to include sexual and affective functions previously performed by the mistress. It also led to the tolerated rise of extra-marital liaisons, and to the development of a wide range of sexual devices, deviations and diversions, from dildoes to homosexuality to pornography. It also inevitably led to the practice of contraception as the only way of separating sexual pleasure from the procreation of children. The trouble was that the main method employed, *coitus interruptus*, itself interfered with pleasure, while condoms seem to have been mainly reserved for extra-marital sexual activity, whether as prophylactics or as contraceptives.

On the other hand, before marriage the ideal of the double standard persisted, and continued to be translated into practice in real life. Young men of the upper classes were expected to have had some or even a good deal of pre-marital sexual experience with prostitutes, serving-maids, court-esans, or foreign married women in Europe on the Grand Tour. Young women of the same class, however, nearly all carefully preserved their virginity, since its loss seriously damaged their value on the marriage market. At the highest level of the aristocracy, marriage was still often made primarily by the parents and, in any case, was mainly with a view to the acquisition of wealth and influence; after marriage husband and wife were often too entangled in a hectic social and political whirl to have much time for each other. In these circles very many men commonly sought extra-marital sexual encounters and liaisons, and an increasing number of women, although still only a minority, followed their example. Rather lower down the social scale, among the lesser nobility and rich squirarchy, marriages were increasingly based on prior personal affection, sexual attraction or love. Of course, when that attraction eventually dried up, as it often did, many husbands sought sexual variety elsewhere, and the double standard continued to apply. Some women certainly sought sexual satisfaction in the arms of other men, but the majority of disappointed wives probably found compensatory psychic satisfaction in immersing themselves in the upbringing of their children.

The main contrast, constantly noted by contemporaries, between this situation and that abroad was with the Italian nobility, and to a lesser extent the French. There the double standard was rigidly applied before marriage; marriage itself was primarily a matter of mere business convenience, and thereafter each partner was relatively free to follow his or her own sexual inclinations. Italy was a society in which noble wives were as free to indulge in extra-marital liaisons as their husbands, and after marriage the double standard did not exist. In the 1760s Lady Morgan observed of the Italian nobility that 'the bond of marriage was one of mere accommodation. The necessity (originating in fashion) by which every man was under of neg-lecting his own wife and entering the service of his neighbour's while it undermined morality, deprived taste of its preference and passion of its excitement; and general gallantry was so blunted by authorized libertin-ism that lovers became as stupidly faithful as husbands were confessedly faithless.' It was in 1765 that James Boswell, fired up by these reports, went bounding into Italy, all eager to bag a countess. In the 1780s Mrs Thrale/ Piozzi found in Milan that 'the men of quality and *bon ton* considered me as fair game to shoot their senseless attentions at . . ., conjugal fidelity being a thing they had no conception of.' This convention of extra-marital sexual promiscuity by both husbands and wives, meaning the collapse of the post-marriage double standard, must presumably be explained by the discrepancy between the persistence of the traditional arranged marriage and the new demands of personal self-fulfilment and self-gratification by both husband and wife which spread across upper- and middle-class Europe in the eighteenth century. Mary Wollstonecraft put her finger on the key when she pointed to 'the intrigues of married women, particularly in high life, and in countries where women are suitably married according to their respective ranks, by their parents.' France she denounced as a country where 'a kind of sentimental lust has prevailed.' One result, of course, was to leave the problem of paternity very moot in the social circles where these habits were prevalent. [153]

In terms of the sexual attitudes of the upper classes, who more or less successfully imposed their values on their social inferiors, English society thus passed through several phases: a phase of moderate toleration lasting until towards the end of the sixteenth century; a phase of repression that ran from about 1570 to 1670; and a phase of permissiveness, even licence, that ran for over a century from 1670 to 1810. As will be seen, this was followed by a new wave of repression that began in 1770, was spreading fast by 1810, and reached its apogee in the mid-Victorian period. After about 1870 this wave in turn receded, to be followed by a new period of permissiveness that has perhaps reached its apogee in the 1970s. These long-term see-saw oscillations do not seem to be connected to economic or political factors, but rather to cultural – and particularly religious – changes. Both sexual repression and sexual permissiveness eventually generate extremist features, which in turn set in motion counterforces which by a process of 'social eversion' slowly turn the pendulum back in the other direction. [154] The duration of each of these swings of religio-ethical attitudes towards sexuality seems to have been about a hundred years. There is no reason to believe that there is a cyclical law in operation, for the swings can be accounted for by specific changes in religious enthusiasm, and by the time it takes for excesses to generate their own opposites.

CHAPTER 11

Gentlemanly Sexual Behaviour: Case Histories

'My wife ... said it was leaving myself embowelled to posterity.... But I think it is rather leaving myself embalmed.'

'Is it preserving evidence against oneself? Is it filling a mine which may be sprung by accident or intention?'

(James Boswell about his diary in *Boswell: the Ominous Years, 1774–1776*, ed. C.Ryscamp and F.A.Pottle, New York, 1963, pp. 174–75, and *The Private Papers of James Boswell*, ed. G.Scott and F.A.Pottle, New York, 1932–34, 13, p. 275.)

If the examination of sexual behaviour among the upper classes is to be studied in greater depth than in the previous chapter, it can only be done by taking a number of well-documented case histories and examining them in detail. This is, admittedly, a dangerous procedure for a variety of reasons. In the first place, those who kept diaries which recorded their sexual experiences and fantasies were exclusively men, and secondly, the mere fact of keeping diaries of their sex lives marks them off from their fellows. Most men at most periods do not record their sexual experiences, and the few who do are likely to be exceptional in some way or another. The mere desire to record sexual experience is usually a sign of latent anxiety, not necessarily about the writer's sexuality, but about his moral and physical performance generally.

The information provided by these diaries is therefore limited by the motivations of the authors. Byrd merely puts down a bare record of events, as coolly as he records meals and visits to friends: it is a very guarded account which discloses nothing of his emotions and no details of exactly what happened. Pepys felt guilty about his conduct, but his bubbling

interest in himself and his activities drove him to record his somewhat minor
lascivious peccadilloes, and his responses to them. But he avoids too much
detailed physical description, and rarely pauses to consider the feelings of
his sexual partners. The most revealing record of all is that of Boswell,
although he too usually steers clear of close physical description, and is so
concerned with himself that his partners only rarely come alive. The
extreme egocentricity of all the diarists blocks the reader from a full
understanding of the two-way physical and emotional relationships. On the
other hand, there is no reason to suppose that any of the diarists except
Boswell were at all exceptional in their tastes, virility or degree of
promiscuity. All, in their different ways, seem to have been fairly average
human beings, responding to a basic drive in fairly conventional ways
according to the culture of the late seventeenth and eighteenth centuries. To
this extent, they are highly revealing about the sexual conventions of their
time and class.

The number of examples from which to work for the Early Modern
period is pitifully small. Only six major sexual records kept by Englishmen
or Americans seem to have survived, all but one of them mostly confined to
activity in London. These six are, in fact, among the very first in recorded
history, so that there is nothing to compare them with for earlier periods.
Since Dr Kinsey and others have amply demonstrated the enormous variety
and range of human sexual behaviour, generalization from a handful of
individuals is obviously very hazardous. On the other hand some of them,
especially Boswell, record not only their own experiences, but also how their
male and female friends and associates reacted to their comments and
confessions about themselves. Their sense of guilt, which runs through
several of the diaries, especially those of Byrd and Boswell, is also an
illuminating indicator of current values. What interests the historian is not
what are the normal sexual responses of men and women at all times, but
what are peculiar to a given time, place and society. This chapter will
therefore narrate the sexual experiences of these six men, and will try to
distil from them such generalizations as are specific to the culture.

The first of the six diaries is that of the fashionable astrologer Simon
Forman in the 1580s and 1590s. He had two mistresses and many casual
affairs with his clients, and also for a period recorded at least the bare
statistics of his sexual relations with his wife. Next in time comes the diary of
the rising young bureaucrat Samuel Pepys in the 1660s, who was married,
but who made sexual advances of one sort or another to a wide range of
women who attracted his attention, despite continual twinges of conscience.

At almost the same time his acquaintance the scientist, technical inventor and architect, the bachelor Robert Hooke, was keeping a somewhat abbreviated record of his sexual relations with a succession of housekeepers. For the eighteenth century, there is the diary of the Virginian country gentleman William Byrd in the first half of the century, at home with his wife in his middle thirties, as a highly promiscuous widower in his forties in London after her death, and in his old age back in Virginia with an elderly second wife. There is the diary of Sylas Neville, which is barren of all sexual detail, but which illustrates the entanglements of a man too poor to marry and still maintain his status. Most revealing of all is the extraordinary diary and memoranda of James Boswell, the son of a Scottish laird, which covers all his adult life in the late eighteenth century, including his sexual adventures as a young bachelor, his relations with his wife, and his constant infidelities. He reveals everything: his failings, his lusts, his fantasies, his remorse, and his rationalizations of his conduct. He does this with a wealth of detail, absolute candour and truthfulness and an introspective insight into his own motivations which makes his record perhaps unique in the whole of human history. There has never, at any time or in any place, been anything quite like it.

I SIMON FORMAN

Simon Forman was a professional necromancer, astrologer, magician and physician, who in the 1590s built up a lucrative practice in London as a fortune-teller, serving a wide range of clients ranging from the wives of humble seamen to countesses, knights and clerical dignitaries. From his notes and diaries, a good deal can be glimpsed of his sexual activity and of those with whom he came in contact.

Born in 1552, he did not have intercourse with a woman until 1582, at the age of thirty. During the next seventeen years, before he married, however, he made up for lost time. He had two long-term mistresses, with both of whom he was more or less in love, and both of whom bore children by him. The first, Annie Young, who lived in Wiltshire, was his mistress in 1584–86, and did not finally break with him until 1595, long after her own marriage and Forman's commitment to his second mistress in London. This second mistress, with whom he took up in 1593, was the wife of a Catholic gentleman, William Allen, and their tempestuous three-year affair was carried on under her husband's nose at times when he was out of the house.[1]

Far more remarkable was the ease with which Forman managed to seduce well over a dozen of his female professional clients, who first came to him for advice about the future of a husband or lover, and ended up by sleeping with him. In social class, these women covered a very wide spectrum, from the poor to the prosperous bourgeoisie, and most of them appear to have been married. For example, there was Mrs Flower, a common seaman's wife, who consulted him about the health and prospects of her husband away on a sea voyage, and about whether she was pregnant (inevitably a very common subject of consultation). There was the frustrated Mrs Hipwell, whose husband's taste ran to sodomy. There was the wife of a schoolmaster, who allowed Forman to feel her all over and do anything but have intercourse with her in her chamber, while her husband was busy teaching downstairs. There was Mrs Condwell, wife of his friend John Condwell who had been one of the few witnesses of his wedding; there was Mrs Emilia Lanier, the ex-mistress of the Lord Chamberlain, Lord Hunsdon; there was Mrs Blague, the lascivious young wife of his friend the Dean of Rochester and mistress of Dean Wood. She and her husband were constantly consulting him about their health and the latter's prospects of clerical promotion. And there was Mrs Martha Webb, the wife of William Webb and the mother of eight or nine children, who came to ask him whether Sir Thomas Walsingham, whose mistress she was, really loved her. These were all, it seems, women who treated their marriage ties very casually.[2]

The other group who were seduced by him were his living-in servants, both one of his maids and the nurse he hired to help deal with his medical clients. The latter became pregnant and was, therefore, discharged in less than a year, while to protect himself from a possible paternity suit Forman drew up a list of the six other men he alleged she had slept with.[3]

His marriage in 1599 at the age of forty-seven to a nineteen-year-old girl of good family, who began as a servant in his household, did not put an end to his sexual interest in his clients, despite the fact that his pet name for her was 'Tronco', meaning 'body'. His sexual activity with his young wife in the spring of 1607, when he was fifty-five and she was twenty-seven, seems to have maintained a level of about two episodes a week. From time to time, however, he was spurred into extraordinary bouts of promiscuous activity. On 28 February 1596, from 3 p.m. onwards he had intercourse with – 'halek' was his mysterious word for it – three different women. On 16 January 1601, two years after his marriage, he had intercourse with his old friend and client Mrs Condwell at 9 a.m. and with his maidservant Frances Hill at midday. On 9 July 1607, he had intercourse with two different women at 8 a.m. and 3 p.m., presumably clients, and with his wife 'Tronco' at 9 p.m. It was a busy day.[4]

The striking thing about Forman's activities, and those sketches of the sex lives of others which he records, is the high level of casual fornication and adultery in these lower-middle-class, middle-class and even upper-class circles. The prospect of pregnancy seems to have been no deterrent, and despite his sexual promiscuity, Forman only got gonorrhoea once, so far as he recorded.[5] This was presumably because the disease had not yet reached the epidemic proportions of the eighteenth century, and because he never used prostitutes, always keeping to enthusiastic amateurs. Many of his clients were Roman Catholic, and he had few dealings with Puritans. But otherwise, his clients seem to have been a fair cross-section of London society of the 1590s. Since he had five clients a day for many years, the women whom he managed to seduce were only a very tiny minority of the whole. But the ease of his conquests is still surprising. One of the causes of his success was undoubtedly his personal magnetism and vitality, which comes through very clearly in his surviving papers. Another was the dominant position he deliberately cultivated over his credulous female clients from his position as the confessor of their most intimate secrets and longings, the physician for their physical complaints, and the monopolist of the secrets of the future. The few letters to him which have survived, from one aristocratic lady, begin with 'Sweet Father', and end with 'your affectionate, loving daughter'.[6] His power was that of doctor, priest and psychoanalyst rolled into one.

This power explains Forman's sexual conquests over this handful of his female clients, but his biographical sketches of the lives of other clients and acquaintances present a picture of a fairly significant number of sexually promiscuous men and women in late Elizabethan London, who were as yet untouched by the Puritan code of holy matrimony and matrimonial chastity. Many of these individuals were no more than victims of economic circumstances, and the role of poverty as a prime cause of the submission of women to sexual exploitation is very obvious – as with Defoe's Moll Flanders and Roxana over a century later. The constant seduction of the ubiquitous living-in maidservants is the most striking example of this. There was Mr Borlase's servant Joan, who 'is pregnant by her master; he hath given her some ill medicine, and gone to somebody [Forman ?] to bewitch her that she should die.' There was Clemence Scarborough, who at fifteen met a man who was wooing a widow. Having run through the widow's fortune, the man married Clemence, and then deserted her for five years. She remarried, but he unexpectedly returned, sold everything she possessed – which, as her legal husband, he had a right to do – and disappeared again, leaving her penniless with four children to support. To keep herself and her children in food, she was forced into prostitution.[7]

Other women, from a wealthier background, had more varied experiences. There was Susan Lovett of Gloucestershire, who 'had great living left her by her friends, but by marriage and adultery spoiled all. She had two or three husbands, and two or three bastards and consumed all vainly.... She was a woman thick-set, of reasonable stature, fat and very black hair; and she of a brown complexion, compacted of lechery.' Others from moderately well-to-do families had come down in the world through no fault of their own, and had to live by their sexual attractions. There was Christian, who at the age of seventeen became the kept mistress of a wealthy married knight, who gave her the generous allowance of £40 a year. Then there was Emilia Lanier, whose royal musician father died young, leaving his family impoverished. She became the kept mistress of Henry, Lord Hunsdon, the Lord Chamberlain, an elderly politician and nobleman, who gave her jewels and an allowance of £40 a year. Then 'being with child she was for colour married to a minstrel', her husband Alfonso Lanier, also a royal musician. In 1597 she consulted Forman about her husband's future, and despite his note that 'she useth sodomy', he nonetheless soon contrived to sleep with her.[8] All these women were probably the minute exception to a general rule of uneventful monogamy, but their bigamous marriages and their highly spiced and varied sexual experience are nonetheless illuminating about an aspect of Elizabethan life that is usually hidden.

This conclusion is supported by some notes made by another astrologer, Elias Ashmole, when in the early seventeenth century he was looking for a second wife. When he was wooing the young Bridget Thornborough, he dreamed that she allowed herself to lie on a bed with him and be handled sufficiently intimately for him to be satisfied that she was still a virgin. Later, Ashmole turned his attentions to a widow. Widows were perhaps a special case, being generally regarded as allowing, indeed demanding, direct physical attack, partly because they were not chaperoned, and partly because they were more likely to be suffering from sexual frustration. However this may be, in his courtship of the widow, Ashmole was freely permitted to indulge in some very close physical contacts, although falling short of full sexual intercourse.[9] One has to assume that in this period such intimacies were not normal in the wooing of young girls from respectable families, who would usually be carefully chaperoned, although, as we shall see, they were becoming standard practice among the poor.

2 SAMUEL PEPYS

i. Facts

By far the better of the two frank English sexual diaries which have been preserved from the late seventeenth century is that of Samuel Pepys (plate 28).[10] Married in 1655 at the age of twenty-three to a fifteen-year-old girl Elizabeth St Michel, his domestic life for the next fourteen years until her death was not an easy one. Samuel was a rising young official in the Navy Office, rapidly gaining money, power and reputation for himself, after an initial push from his great patron the Earl of Sandwich. Elizabeth was childless and lonely, left at home in the constantly expanding house with more and more maids to do all the work. She was frivolous, extravagant and easily aroused to anger or the sulks. One problem for her was that she loved her husband and was very jealous of other possible women in his life, with far more reason than she ever suspected.

To make matters worse, she was sexually inadequate for long periods of time. Even in his early days, before he sought other diversions, his sexual relations with his wife do not seem to have been very frequent, his only complaint occurring when once he had not slept with her for ten days or two weeks. On another occasion he slept with her before she left him for an extended stay in the country, noting that 'we have [not] lain together because of the heat of the weather a good while.'[11] The main use to which they seem to have put marital sex was to make peace after one of their not infrequent quarrels. One reason for Elizabeth's sexual inadequacy was that she was often ill. Throughout the early 1660s she suffered badly from severe menstrual cramps, which put her into bed for several days at a time every month. In 1663 she developed an abscess in the vaginal area which at times made intercourse altogether impossible and at times very painful to her.[12] Even when she was more or less cured, there were long periods when the Pepys' domestic sexual life seem to have ceased altogether while he pursued his amours elsewhere. On 12 August 1667, for example, he recorded that he had not slept with his wife for three months.

On the other hand, Elizabeth was a great beauty who was admired wherever she went and, as Pepys eventually discovered, was formally invited to a sexual liaison on at least two occasions, once by Pepys' great patron the Earl of Sandwich and once by his son Lord Hinchinbrook, both of which she virtuously refused. Pepys at times was extremely suspicious of her, especially when she was learning to dance with an attractive young dancing master. She was one of the few women of her age to wear drawers, and so jealous and irrational was her husband that he took to watching her closely as she undressed at night on days when she had been taking dancing lessons, to make sure that she was still wearing them.[13] In fact his suspicions about her were as baseless as his wife's about him were well founded.

As for Pepys himself, his sexual activity went in bursts. He rarely seems to have had intercourse more than once at a time with either his wife or any of many women. Once in 1664 he took Mrs Betty Martin twice '*sous de la chaise*' (? in the sitting position), and two years later he had intercourse with her 'forwards and backwards, which is my great pleasure.' Nine days later, he did whatever he wanted – an obscure phrase he often uses – with Mrs Martin at Westminster, and then hurried down to Deptford to sleep with his other mistress Mrs Bagwell, who was waiting for him naked in bed. After one bout with her, however, his lust was satiated, and he was overcome with shame and disgust at his behaviour.[14] He got up in the middle of the night and slunk off home.

Like most men, Pepys was an insatiable *voyeur* of pretty women. At the playhouse, he spent his time in looking at the actresses and the court ladies and royal mistresses in their boxes. Indeed, he was so taken by Charles II's beautiful mistress Lady Castlemaine that he fell in love with her, although he never even managed to speak with her. He was fascinated when he saw her underclothes hanging out to dry in the Palace garden; whenever he got a chance, he 'glutted myself with looking on her', and he bought a print of her portrait and had it mounted in his house. On one occasion he dreamed that he had her 'in my arms and was admitted to use all the dalliance that I desired with her', an episode that led him to wish that one could perhaps dream in one's grave, 'then we should not need to be so fearful of death, as we are in this plague time' of 1665. Since he had earlier been told that she 'hath all the tricks... that are practised to give pleasure' to be found in Aretino's famous illustrated sex manual, it must have been an enjoyable dream. He knew himself well and was astonished at the 'strange slavery I stand in to beauty, that I value nothing near it.' Everywhere he went, every shop he visited, every party he attended, every street he walked down, he was forever on the look-out for a pretty face. Sometimes he would follow attractive women down the street and try to take them by the hand. He did his best to strike up a close acquaintance with the pretty wives of his vintner, his bookseller, and other tradesmen.[15]

After an initial period of timidity, he grew bolder in his advances, and found to his surprise that most women were quite willing to be kissed and to allow their breasts to be seen and handled, an experience in which Pepys took enormous pleasure and over which, if he is to be believed, he could spend literally hours without proceeding to further intimacies. What he most enjoyed were prolonged tactile fondlings, leading sometimes to masturbation.

In his choice of the no fewer than fifty-odd women with whom he had some physical contact between 1660 and 1669, he was governed by four primary considerations, apart from their physical attractiveness. The first was a fear of venereal disease, which led him to avoid all relations with professional prostitutes, despite a week in which he was strongly tempted by one called Cocky of Fleet Alley. Fortunately, he had another amateur mistress available at that time. The only occasion he used a professional was some years later, when he took a slut into his coach and got her to masturbate him – a fairly safe procedure.[16]

The second consideration that guided his on the whole very prudent conduct was a fear of pregnancy. It is perfectly clear that neither he nor any of his women had any knowledge whatever of contraceptive devices, either as protection against venereal disease or as barriers to impregnation. It was for this reason that almost without exception he confined actual sexual intercourse to married women whose husbands were not too long absent, so that if pregnancy occurred he could not be held responsible. Unmarried girls, and women whose husbands were absent on board ship or on a journey, he usually would not penetrate. He contented himself with kissing, looking at, fondling, and tumbling them about, possibly to orgasm, although this is rarely clear from the diary. Thus he played to his heart's content on many occasions with his first mistress Betty Lane, the seamstress and haberdasher in a booth at Westminster Hall, but she dared not indulge in intercourse so long as she was unmarried, a resolution he praised her for. The nearest they allowed themselves to go was for Pepys to rub his penis on her breasts and belly. He therefore did his very best to get a subordinate in the Navy Office, one Mr Hawley, to marry her – 'God knows I had a roguish meaning in it' – but Hawley procrastinated, much to Pepys' irritation. The pair once succumbed to a moment of passion and had intercourse, but fortunately there was no pregnancy. It was only in 1664, after Betty had married a Mr Martin, that they were free to indulge in full sexual relations, a process that went on for years regardless of her pregnancies. On one occasion they slept together after her husband had been absent for a while, and for a week there was a panic when she thought she was pregnant and Pepys had to think wildly of some scheme to get her husband posted back home hastily from his ship, which was at sea off Scotland.[17]

The third consideration which guided Pepys, in his prudent way, was not to get so absorbed in his pursuit of sexual pleasure that he neglected his business at the office. His career was based on making a name for himself as a most capable and devoted man of business, and again and again he foreswore women, ale-houses and playhouses for a period in order to concentrate on his work. His sexual adventures were, therefore, a form of relaxation from a normal life of diligent drudgery in the Navy Office. A fourth consideration that governed him was his determination to conceal all traces of his adventures from his wife, of whose jealousy he was well aware. Although he moved in the vicinity of court circles where mistresses were openly flaunted and where wives accepted the situation and took lovers of their own, this was very far removed from the life style of the bourgeois Pepys, and he was very anxious not to have a domestic row or a separation. After several narrow escapes from detection by his wife, it was almost inevitable that sooner or later he would be found out, especially since he could not keep his hands off the chambermaids in his own house. As we shall see, in the end this was his undoing. Finally, he was constantly torn between his nagging puritanical conscience and his irrepressible sensuality and love of pleasure. Forever making good resolutions, and forever breaking them, he lacked a strong moral centre to hold him together. Meticulous to a degree in his business affairs at the Navy Office, his private life was something of a mess, possibly because he pursued women as a form of relief from the tensions in the office.

One striking aspect of Pepys' adventures is the way he used his official position to extract sexual favours, while others used their sexual favours to extract official grants from him. It is never quite clear in these exchanges who was exploiting whom. As Clerk of the Acts and Commissioner of the Navy Board, he was able to exercise patronage over a vast range of jobs, both at sea and in the dockyards, and he did not hesitate to use it for his own ends. Indeed, all the women who actually went to bed with him were in some way or another dependent on him for the professional advancement of their husbands. His first and most durable mistress, Betty Lane, married Mr Martin, for whom Pepys got an appointment as a ship's purser, despite the low opinion he had of Martin's personal capacity. Mrs Martin continued to satisfy Pepys' sexual desires whenever he was in need, and her husband continued to rise in the world. Long after the diary ceases, Martin was made consul in Algiers, where he died in 1679, after which his widow, Pepys' old love, was given a handsome government pension of £100 a year. It is hard not to believe that it was the sexual availability and attraction of his wife which formed the basis of Mr Martin's successful career. Nor is there much doubt that Martin was well aware of his wife's relationship with Pepys, and used it for his own advantage. Thus on one occasion Pepys notes 'to Mrs Martin, and did what I would with her; her husband going for some wine for us. The poor man I think would take pains if I can get him a purser's place, which I will endeavour' – and he did.

The same story at a lower social level applies to William Bagwell and his pretty young wife. Pepys first met Mrs Bagwell in 1664 when she began lobbying him in his office to obtain promotion for her husband, who was then only an ordinary carpenter, to a fifth-rate man of war, about the lowliest job a naval carpenter could have. She immediately discovered that Pepys liked kissing her, and she played her cards with calculated but measured encouragement and becoming modesty. She reproved him for his advances, but slowly gave way step by step, allowing Pepys to advance from kissing her mouth to fondling her breasts and then her vagina, at the same time continually reminding him about her husband's promotion. After some months of this sexual ballet, he got her to the stage of mutual masturbation, once in a tavern and once in her home while her husband discreetly took a walk. Finally, in February 1665, Pepys got her husband his promotion and came to the Bagwell house for his reward. There he finally got what he wanted, although Mrs Bagwell put up a token struggle in which Pepys strained his probing left forefinger. After many years of this on-and-off procedure of Mrs Bagwell's lobbying Pepys for her husband's promotion, rewarded always by semi-reluctant intercourse, Mr Bagwell ended his career as Master Carpenter of a first-rate man of war, with Pepys in 1689 still lobbying for him, now to be promoted to Assistant Shipwright. In this case, there can be no doubt that the Bagwell parents and Mr Bagwell himself were aware of what was going on, and were perfectly content to let it happen. On 1 February 1667, for example, he visited the Bagwells' house by appointment, to find Mrs Bagwell expecting him. They went upstairs and she let Pepys do whatever he wanted with her. Only later did her husband discreetly come home, took no notice of his wife and Pepys being alone together in the house, and began to talk business. As for Mrs Bagwell, she mystified Pepys, who remarked: 'strange it is to see how a woman, notwithstanding her great pretence of love to her husband and religion, may be conquered.' It does not seem to have struck him that it is very uncertain who was using whom for his or her own purposes, the only certainty being that the coin in which the bribe was made was sex. It seems likely that both parties were well satisfied with their bargains.[18]

Then there was a Mrs Burrowes, the widow of a naval lieutenant, who came to Pepys' office to get payment of a ticket (a government I.O.U. for arrears of salary) for her late husband. Pepys as usual seized the opportunity to kiss her and handle her breasts, and later saw her alone in his office and took her for rides in a coach in not unsuccessful hopes of getting his hand under her skirts.[19] There was also a Mrs Daniel, the wife of a seaman who came several times to his office to ask for promotion for her husband to a lieutenancy. Pepys was very excited by her, kissed her and played with her breasts and thrust his hand under her skirts to feel her, and once took her in a coach and got her to masturbate him, as a result of which her husband was promoted and she received eight pairs of gloves. But the market relationship was clear; for example, she once asked to borrow money from him, but he refused since he was too busy in his office to get his sexual reward that day.[20] One gets the impression that it became well known in naval circles that the best way to obtain a favour from Pepys as Commissioner of the Navy was to send a pretty wife or a daughter, who had to be prepared at the very least to be kissed and to have her breasts fondled. The young wife of the merchant Thomas Hill was kissed while lobbying for a naval cork contract for her husband. A Mrs Lowther, who was also after a favour, was similarly manhandled. Black Nan, the daughter of the paper-ruler in the office, allowed herself to be kissed as often as she appeared with paper, which no doubt helped to keep her father employed. Old Delks the waterman artfully left his daughter in Pepys' office to be felt and kissed by him, in order to get his son released from impressment into the navy.[21]

The women who fell most easy prey to his advances were tavern girls like Frances and Susan Udall of the Swan, whose mouth and breasts he would kiss until he climaxed, or Sarah and Frances Herbert, who were equally willing.[22] But there were also the wives or friends of the family or business acquaintances, like Mrs Pierce or Mrs Pennington, with whom he toyed for hours whenever he got the chance.[23] Then there were the barely nubile young daughters of respectable neighbours, like Diana Crispe, whom he once took upstairs in his empty house and played with, without meeting any serious resistance, or little Frances Tooker, whom he handled intimately several times. He then expressed surprise when his wife told him that Miss Tooker had contracted venereal disease, having been very loosely brought up by her mother, who once took a lover to bed with her while her daughter watched them.[24] He never stopped to ask himself whether in fact it had been his own explorations which had first aroused her libido and therefore contributed to her fall.

Finally, there was the succession of maids in his own house, both chambermaids and the higher-class companions to his wife. One of their duties was to comb his hair for lice and to help him dress; and on many occasions maid after maid had to put up with Pepys' hands exploring their breasts and thrusting up under their petticoats while they did their work. It should be explained that in days when women normally wore neither brassières nor underpants or drawers, these explorations met with little obstacle from clothing, so that access to bare flesh was easy. Also, a fall might have embarrassing consequences, for when one of his maids was getting into a boat, Pepys was pleased to be told by his wife that she 'did fall down and did show her arse' (plate 37).[25]

Pepys' imagination was so vivid that he could ejaculate while merely engaged in sexual fantasies. Once he did it in church on Sunday while thinking of Betty Michell, a pretty young wife with whom he fell half in love, and pursued for years without succeeding in doing more than getting the use of her hand to rub his penis now and then when sitting close together in a coach or a boat.[26] Once he even experienced orgasm while lying on his back in a boat, not using his hand but merely thinking about a woman. Much of his sexual activity was not directed to intercourse, but to dreaming about or handling women for masturbatory purposes.[27]

He only fell even superficially in love twice, and on each occasion it was because his sexual desires were thwarted. In 1664 he fell in love with Jane Walsh, the maid of his barber, who double-crossed him and failed to turn up to every assignation he made.[28] In 1668 he fell in love with his wife's young companion Deb Willett, his passion for whom at last led to the discovery by his wife of some of his doings. On 25 October, Elizabeth suddenly entered the dining-room to find Deb combing her husband's hair while one of his hands was well up under her petticoats, feeling her vagina. It was three weeks before his wife could bully Pepys into dismissing Deb from the house. The trouble was that, as he confessed to his diary, 'I love the girl'; or rather 'the truth is I have a great mind for to have the maidenhead of this girl', if only the opportunity to do so offered itself. Meanwhile, his wife Elizabeth alternately raged and stormed at him, her anger being temporarily appeased only by passionate sexual intercourse. Pepys was thoroughly bewildered by his wife's violent oscillations from fury to sexual frenzy, but noted in his usual objective manner that he had slept with her more frequently in those three weeks than in all the previous twelve months. Moreover, the quality had improved with the quantity, for his wife received this sexual activity 'with more pleasure to her than I think in all the time of our marriage before.' At last, after thirteen years of marriage, Elizabeth's discovery of just one of her husband's more minor peccadilloes had succeeded in arousing her libido.[29]

Soon after this episode, the curtain falls on Pepys' sex life since failing eyesight forced him to discontinue his diary. Two years later, his wife died of typhus, still childless and at the early age of twenty-nine. Pepys never remarried, but formed a lifelong liaison with a cultivated woman, Mary Skinner, whom he kept as his mistress for the next thirty-three years. Towards the latter end, she was openly living in his house and being treated by his friends as the social equivalent of a wife. Since Mr Bagwell and Mr Martin continued to rise in their professions, one can assume that for some years at any rate, he also maintained, if only intermittently, his sexually satisfying connections with their wives. When he died in 1703, he left Mary Skinner a handsome life annuity of £200 a year.[30]

ii. Conclusions

Pepys' diary is a unique piece of historical evidence, which could only have been kept by a very unusual man. But his activities involved large numbers of other people, and to that extent his *Diary* provides reliable and illuminating evidence about current standards of behaviour in the circles within which he moved in post-Restoration London. The first conclusion is that few women put up much resistance to his sexual advances, most of which went no further than a fondling of their erogenous zones. At first Pepys' upbringing led him to be shocked when he saw or heard about Charles II fondling his mistresses in chapel or at the theatre.[31] Later he successfully adopted the same tactics among his own circle of acquaintances. All the evidence suggests that such casual physical contacts, only rarely leading to actual intercourse, were acceptable to a wide variety of women in late seventeenth-century London, whether married or unmarried, and coming from a wide variety of social classes. Only once were his physical advances totally rebuffed, when a woman he was standing next to, listening to a sermon in St Dunstan's church, threatened to stick pins in him if he persisted in molesting her – and that may have been more a result of the unsuitability of the occasion and place than her general hostility to being touched.[32]

Secondly, there is clear evidence that Pepys did not hesitate to use his power, both as master over his servants and as Commissioner of the Navy, to obtain consent from women for his sexual advances. He saw nothing wrong in this abuse of authority, nor did they. In any case, each was using the other for his or her own purposes. Nor was he surprised or shocked when he learned that his own patron, Lord Sandwich, had tried to seduce his wife. In a world of patronage, power and deference, a woman's body was within limits at the disposal of her or her husband's superior, a fact rammed home half a century later by Defoe in his stories of Moll Flanders and Roxana. Pepys was a naturally prudent and cautious man, at the mercy of a growing sexual obsession, particularly with women's faces and breasts. It was not only his own personal charm, which was clearly considerable, but also the authority he wielded which enabled him to satisfy these longings with such a wide variety of women, from the middle, lower-middle and lower classes in post-Restoration London.

Pepys' story also points to the difficulties and inhibitions placed on extra-marital sexual life by the absence of contraceptives. The result was a great deal of very prolonged play, kissing and feeling, and in Pepys' case the careful selection only of married women with whom to have full sexual intercourse. Pepys' love of sexual play, often prolonged for hours, makes the traditional courting practice of bundling more intelligible as a way of passing the time during the long hours of darkness, while his diary makes it clear that before the introduction of the brassière and underpants in the nineteenth century, women's erogenous zones were wide open to the roving hand of any man. Women before the nineteenth century must have been accustomed to being intimately fondled as they went about their business, and being indecently exposed if they fell down (plate 37).

Pepys tried his best to be very secretive, to achieve which a good deal of his sexual activity took place in coaches, which were very secure places once the blinds were drawn, or in private rooms in ale-houses across the river in Lambeth or north in Tothill Fields where he was unlikely to meet an acquaintance.

Finally, the spread of the sexual habits of Charles II's court by rumour, observation and example downward through the social scale of London life is very clearly evidenced by Pepys' diary. He continued to express shock and disgust, but also prurient interest and envy, at the goings-on at court. And while carefully preserving his own wife from temptation from others and from knowledge of his own extra-marital activities, he slowly succumbed to the temptation to imitate – in a far more modest and guilt-ridden way – the sexual behaviour of his social superiors.

Pepys' sexual life seems not at all exceptional. He appears to have been the archetypal *homme moyen sensuel*, unusual only in the lack of satisfaction he derived from his wife and his consequent search for pleasure elsewhere. His sexual activities often went in bursts, with occasional days when he rushed frantically from one woman to another. It is not at all clear what triggered off these hectic bouts of activity, but some of them may have been caused by the build-up of tensions and conflicts at work in the Navy Office.

The diary records a ceaseless battle between the id and the superego, between Pepys' powerful appetites and his nagging, puritanical, bourgeois conscience. Unlike the court grandees with whom he associated professionally, he was unable to indulge in hedonistic adventures of sexual seduction without a twinge of guilt or remorse. He recorded what he regarded as his failings as an aid to his reformation, and at the New Year he would make futile good resolutions to be more chaste in the future. Pepys was a man at war with himself, and as such was an epitome of his time and his class. Unlike Boswell a century later, he told no-one about his exploits, neither his wife nor his most intimate male friends. This difference between Pepys and Boswell is partly one of character and class, but still more it is one of time. In the 1760s both men and women talked far more freely about sex than they did in the 1660s outside a small circle around the court.

3 ROBERT HOOKE

Pepys' story can be supported by some evidence about the sexual life of one of his contemporaries and acquaintances – the extraordinary scientific virtuoso, inventor and architect Robert Hooke, whose diary covers the years 1672 to 1680, from the ages of thirty-seven to forty-five.[33] Hooke was a pale, thin, sickly bachelor, who was constantly dosing himself with alarming quantities of vomits, purges and other dubious medical remedies. He was a man of dazzling inventiveness, scientific insight and mechanical skills, who spent an extremely busy and active life in close association with the circle of the Royal Society, for which he acted as Curator of Experiments, or director of research.

The diary consists of brief jottings, mostly about his health and his scientific activities, some of which were certainly written up later. When the diary opens in August 1672, Hooke had established what was clearly a very satisfactory arrangement with Nell, his resident maid and seamstress. She looked after him for board and lodging and a salary of £4 a year, plus extra for the sewing she did for him. She also slept with him about three times a month, for which she was not paid. Hooke was obviously much attached to her, although for variety he occasionally slept with a call-girl picked up at his favourite coffee-house, Garroway's in Change Alley, Cornhill, for which he paid five shillings. When Nell married in August 1673 and set up on her own with her husband, Hooke was very upset and could not sleep for two nights.

The marriage, and Nell's departure in September, marked the end of the phase of fairly normal sexual activity for him; he slept with her for the last time two days after her marriage, but before she and her husband set up house together.[34]

In October he hired a new maid, Doll, whom he first persuaded to sleep with him in December. She only lasted until March 1674, during which time he slept with her six times. Later, in 1679, he heard that she had had a child by her uncle. The next maid, Bette, was even less satisfactory. He first 'wrestled' with her in June, and it was not until the end of July that she capitulated. But after only two sexual episodes, she was discharged for laziness in August of that year.[35]

Instead of these unreliable girls, Hooke now decided to take in his niece Grace, the only child of his grocer brother, to act as his housekeeper-companion, while a second maid, Mary, worked under her at the usual wage of £4 a year. If the diary is complete, Hooke now passed through a two-year period of busy scientific activity but total sexual quiescence, although he was slowly becoming more and more attached to Grace. In January 1676, he had the first recorded orgasm since Bette had last slept with him in July 1674, and this appears to have been a purely solitary episode. During a sleepless night in May, he entered Grace's bedroom at 3 a.m., and in June he first slept at her side, though without orgasm. Between October 1676 and 1679 however, he intermittently allowed himself to be tempted into sleeping with Grace some fourteen times, full penetration first occurring in March 1677. But these episodes were widely scattered, and mainly concentrated in the year 1677, when there were ten. After her father's death by suicide in 1678, Hooke only slept with her twice before the diary ends in 1680. But there is evidence that he continued to be extremely jealous of any outside activities of the girl, especially of any men who showed the slightest interest in her, and he contrived to keep her cooped up at home as his housekeeper-companion until her early death in 1687. Apparently, Hooke was shattered by her death, and his hypochondria – and perhaps genuine illnesses – grew markedly worse from this time until his own death in 1703.[36]

This is a story of a brilliant scientist and active man-about-town, a man who consorted daily with the leading men of science and even with the King himself. But his body was tormented by illnesses, some probably psychosomatic and others certainly caused by the extraordinarily noxious medical remedies he was constantly taking to cure his stomach disorders, his dizziness and his headaches. He also suffered from curvature of the spine and extreme emaciation, so that he could hardly have been attractive to women. His sexual needs were small, and he seems to have expected, rightly, that they would be met by the succession of maid-housekeepers he engaged, whose relative powerlessness before their master's demands is all too clear. The only satisfactory relationship he achieved was with Nell, with whom he remained friends after her marriage. When this position was filled by his niece, however, things became more difficult. The incest taboo does not seem to have had the same strength that it possesses today, but both Hooke and his niece clearly felt guilt about their occasional physical relations, and eventually gave them up altogether. The final striking thing about Hooke's sex life, if the diary gives a complete record, is how extremely limited it was for a man in his late thirties and early forties, even if he was obsessed with his scientific research and suffering from a variety of tiresome minor ailments. Varying from zero to thirty orgasms a year, his sexual drive was far below that of the average Western man today. The central interest of his life lay not in women – not even in Nell or Grace – but in his scientific, technological and architectural pursuits. He was one of the first to describe in detail the possibilities of the microscope, and it is typical of him that one of his rare orgasms was provoked by a desire to put some of his semen under the microscope to check out Leeuwenhoek's recent discovery of the wriggling sperm, now for the first time visible in the seminal fluid. It is also typical, and a touching tribute to her loyalty to him, that Nell provided him with an aborted human foetus for dissection, presumably at his request, which she got from the poorhouse in Blackfriars.[37]

4   WILLIAM BYRD

The next diary containing sexual information is that of William Byrd, the surviving fragments of which cover the years 1709–12, 1717–21 and 1739–41. William Byrd was a Virginia gentleman with extensive English education and connections, a plentiful income of about £1,800 a year, and strong, if conventional, Anglican piety. His diary is a cold and bloodless account of the bare facts of his daily routine, the saying of his prayers morning and evening, the books he read, the food he ate, the guests he entertained, the state of his health, the movement of his bowels, and his sexual experiences. It is entirely lacking in colour, warmth, imagination, or self-revelation. It just recites the facts, apparently accurately, though often written up later, presumably from rough notes.

The first diary covers part of Byrd's life at home at Westover in Virginia with his first wife, when he was in the prime of life in his middle thirties.[38] His wife was a neurotic and difficult woman, whom Byrd seems to have treated rather as an irresponsible child, which probably did not help. Byrd's attitude to women generally was that they were intellectually and morally inferior beings, for whose weaknesses allowances had, condescendingly, to be made. The only occasions in his diary when he mentioned his wife was when they quarrelled, when she was sick, and when they had sexual relations. But their sex life over a three-year period from 1709 to 1712 was on a very modest scale indeed, amounting – if the record is complete – to no more than about twenty-five episodes a year. Byrd was not unkind to his wife, but there is no evidence that he had much affection for her, and the low level of marital intercourse perhaps supports the idea that the arranged marriage reduces sexual activity, since the husband is not physically stimulated by his wife. Intercourse mostly took place in the evening, but about a fifth in the early morning and a fifth in the afternoon (once on the trestle of the billiard table during a game). A frequent prelude was either a trip away to Williamsburg or a quarrel,[39] and an occasional one was a whipping given to one of the female domestic slaves, usually by his wife, who had clear sadistic tendencies. A frequent sequel was the reading of one of Tillotson's uplifting sermons or some Latin or Greek author. This last was a reversal of the sequence advised by Ralph Verney's Oxford tutor in 1631, when as an undergraduate he was on his honeymoon: 'Pleasures are augmented through their intermission, and the sweetness of a kiss will relish better after the cracking of a syllogism.'[40] Byrd, like Pepys, paid attention to current medical advice against sex during the heat of summer, for he only slept with his wife on two occasions in three years between 20 July and 9 September. He masturbated occasionally when away on trips to Williamsburg, apparently without any special sense of guilt and usually at a time when he had had no relations with his wife for a month or so.

The second diary covers a three-year period when Byrd was in his early forties. He was then living in London, in theory on official business for the state of Virginia, but in practice leading a life of leisure. His first wife had died of smallpox in November 1716, a year before the diary opens. By March 1717 he was deeply engaged in an effort to persuade Mary Smith, the daughter and heiress of a rich Commissioner of Excise, to marry him. But in July 1718, Mary finally married instead Sir Edward Des Bouveries, the son of an even wealthier Levant merchant, and his hopes were dashed. Up to the last minute he pursued her with love letters couched in terms of artificial and high-flown rhetoric which smack of insincerity. But he seems to have been genuinely attracted to her physically, whatever his deeper emotions may have been. In January he dreamed that Miss Smith was in bed with him and had called him dear; in March he dreamed that she kissed him a lot, and a few days later that he saw her and embraced her almost naked. Finally in August, after she was married and he had lost her, 'I dreamed I rogered my Lady Des Bouveries.'[41]

The pursuit of Miss Smith was far from being the limit of Byrd's interests at this time. He was a forty-three-year-old widower, living in London with plenty of time on his hands, and plenty of money. His wife's death and the limitless temptations of London seem to have released a quite novel flood of sexual passion. It transformed his life from one of placid, almost sexless domesticity, piety and learned scholarship in Virginia in his thirties to one devoted to an urgent, but still prudent, pursuit of lust in London in his forties. When the diary begins in December 1717 he was already suffering from a troublesome case of gonorrhoea, which kept recurring well into the summer. Both his closest friends, Mr Burton and Sir William Lawson, also had the same disease, got from a single woman.[42] His sexual activity was of three carefully specified kinds: 'playing the fool', meaning sexual play without orgasm, of which there is very little at this period; 'uncleanness' or 'pollution', meaning self-masturbation, an orgasm produced by sexual excitement at handling and kissing women, or masturbation (or perhaps fellatio) performed on him by women; and lastly, 'rogering', meaning full sexual intercourse. Because of the fear of venereal disease, the bulk of the activity took the form of 'uncleanness' with a variety of women, full sexual intercourse being mainly – but by no means entirely – restricted to a few women with whom he had a more or less regular relationship. During 1718, for example, he slept with women twenty-seven times, often performing twice a night, and sometimes three times. Some six of these women were whores whom he picked off the street and took to a tavern or the bagnio for the night, and three were mistresses on semi-permanent contract. His first mistress was a Mrs Alec, whom he paid two guineas a month to make his shirts and ruffles and to sleep with him from time to time. In June, however, he had proof of her infidelity and dismissed her.[43] Mrs Alec was soon replaced by Miss Annie Wilkinson, whom he first took to the Unicorn tavern in Longacre, 'rogered' her to his satisfaction, and then agreed to pay her £20 a year 'to take care of my linen, etc.' – the 'etc.' including sexual services, at any rate for a time. Three times in the next three weeks in July he took her to a bagnio, where they bathed, dined, and spent the night together; episodes which were repeated from time to time until August. Long after Byrd had more or less lost sexual interest in her, she continued to visit him and bring him his linen. Only very occasionally did he still use her sexually, for example, on 26 January 1719 when she brought him his linen at ten in the morning, and he seized the occasion to 'roger' her.[44]

In August 1718 he found another regular mistress, a Mrs Allen, whom he visited in her home about every two weeks. Once she was out, so he whiled away the time by getting her maid to masturbate him, and then slept with Mrs Allen when she came home. She was an expensive woman, for Byrd paid her a guinea a night. In January 1719 he found another mistress, a Mrs Betty Strand, whom he always took to a bagnio, so she may have been a married woman. The first two encounters with Mrs Strand stimulated him to his greatest feats of sexual activity, in which he performed three or four times a night, for which he gave her a guinea each time. Indeed, the next seven weeks were a period of considerable sexual excitement, in which he had twenty-five orgasms in all, with four different women. September 1719 was another period of peak activity, when he had eleven orgasms in seventeen days, also with four women, two with Mrs Smith, one with a pick-up in the street, and the last with Mrs Strand. He was not always at this peak of virility, and sometimes could not perform at all. One evening in October 1718 he picked up a woman and took her to a tavern for supper, but after the meal 'she could provoke me to do nothing because my roger would not stand up, with all she could do.'[45]

In January 1719 he finally found what he had been looking for, a discreet but expensive house of assignation in Queen Street, run by a Mrs Smith, upon whom he could rely to procure him a ready supply of wholesome girls. She was soon being referred to as 'my kind Mrs Smith', 'my friend Mrs Smith'. The first girl Mrs Smith supplied was a married woman, a Mrs Molly Courtenay, who was paid a guinea a night for her efforts, and whom on one occasion Byrd took out to the masquerade. But sometimes Byrd liked variety. On 15 February he visited Mrs Smith, but was annoyed to find 'the new girl' was absent. Mrs Courtenay was sent for but did not come, and eventually Widow Jones was sent for, who gave him what he wanted. Once in March there was a new girl at Mrs Smith's, and despite the fact that he was temporarily impotent, he gave her the large sum of three guineas. A week later the same thing happened with Molly Jones, 'to my great grief'. At other times he was triumphantly successful and could perform three times in a night. By October prices were rising at Mrs Smith's, for on the sixth he paid Molly Horton the standard two guineas, despite his inability to perform, and on another occasion soon after, when he performed twice, he paid no less than ten guineas to the girl and a guinea to Mrs Smith.[46]

All this intercourse, which Byrd coldly and drily records with hardly a sign of either pleasure or guilt, was interspersed with many episodes when he picked up a girl in the street and either got her to masturbate him in his coach or took her back to her lodgings or to a tavern for a meal, followed by the same service. With these street pick-ups, who cost only a few shillings, he was obviously extremely careful not to run the risk of disease once more. He seems to have been more or less unfamiliar with condoms as a prophylactic, only referring to them once, when he watched two friends having intercourse with a woman one after the other 'in condoms'. Whether or not he used them himself is unclear, but it seems very doubtful. The result of this cautious approach, paying either a guinea or more for a theoretically disease-free call-girl to sleep with him, or a few shillings for a street whore to masturbate him, was that he remained entirely free from infection after the first attack. It also meant, however, that before he found Mrs Smith at least half his sexual experiences were the result of masturbation rather than intercourse. Over a period of a year in 1718, he had fifty-seven orgasms; twenty-six by intercourse, twenty-seven by masturbation by a woman or as a result of kissing or petting, one by self masturbation, and three by sexual dreams. In the year 1719, on the other hand he had eighty-nine orgasms; sixty-seven by intercourse and only twenty-two by masturbation.[47] The discovery of Mrs Smith's establishment had greatly increased both the quantity and the quality of his sex life.

As 1719 drew to an end, and the time for return to Virginia approached, Byrd continued to take Mrs Strand and others to the bagnio, to sleep with a variety of women at Mrs Smith's, to pick up occasional whores in the street, and, in the very last week, to manhandle his maid and to make her feel him in return. Such was his state of sexual excitement at this period that merely kissing a pretty maid could bring on an orgasm. Back in 1718 there was a period in which he had repeatedly kissed his maid 'and my seed came from me'.

No sooner had he returned to his lonely home in Virginia in February 1720 than he laid energetic siege to his maid Annie, whom he had brought with him from England. It was a siege that was still in progress fourteen months later, when the diary ends. After some resistance, Annie was usually, but not always, willing enough to play with him to orgasm, in or out of bed, but by the time the diary ends Byrd had not yet actually had intercourse with her, despite a frequency of encounters which at times was twice a week, usually in the evening after prayers, while she was washing his feet or otherwise attending to him before retiring. It was a proceeding for which he showed some guilt, usually adding a routine 'May God forgive me' to his diary entry. Early in September 1720, he records that 'I tempted Annie to let me feel her, but she would not let me, for which she is to be commended and for which God be praised.' In December he 'resolved to forbear Annie, by God's grace', but by February 1721 his resolution had broken down again.[48]

Despite its dispassionate and frozen quality (possibly caused by its composition in shorthand), Byrd's diary reveals the irresistible tidal force of sexual passion which was driving him during these years, despite his scrupulous piety. It is clear, moreover, that a powerful secondary motive, besides middle-aged lust, was sheer loneliness. Unlike Pepys or Hooke or Boswell, he had only a moderate circle of friends and acquaintances in London, and he found time hanging heavily on his hands. Again and again he would take a girl out to a leisurely dinner followed by sex, rather than merely demand immediate satisfaction. He was prepared to pay substantial sums for women with whom he felt safe to sleep, not less than a guinea a night. Unlike James Boswell (as we shall see), he was a cautious man who looked after his health, and as a result he was obliged very often to content himself with being masturbated by these women rather than risk venereal disease by full intercourse. Despite his wealth, he was unable to find in early eighteenth-century London a regular mistress approaching his own social and intellectual level, who could provide him with both the companionship and the sexual satisfaction he so badly needed.

The third Byrd diary covers a period twenty years later, when he was in his sixties. By now, his sexual activity had virtually ceased: he had no relations of any kind with his second wife, and a diary covering two years records only one episode of masturbation, and rare occasions, about once every two months, when he 'played the fool' with his maid Sally, which clearly amounted to no more than a little superficial fondling.[49]

5 SYLAS NEVILLE

A striking example of the complicated sexual arrangements imposed by the conventions of eighteenth-century marriage and morals upon an impoverished gentleman is provided by the diary of Sylas Neville. Neville appears to have been the younger son (or possibly the illegitimate son) of Henry Neville, a wealthy Londoner. He held advanced views on religion, was a staunch Whig in politics, was intolerably priggish and a little mad. He justified his sexual behaviour on the grounds that 'a connection with women ... when indulged without invading any man's right or any woman's virtue [is] a venial offence arising from a most natural desire.' He conceded that patronizing prostitutes merely encouraged them, but characteristically comforted himself with the reflection that he had never done so without 'my earnest endeavours for their reformation.'[50]

By the time the diary opens in 1767, Neville was twenty-five years old, a silly, selfish and idle man-about-town in London, who had already dissipated most of his inheritance through gambling at the card table and on the turf. His mother was still alive in Scotland, and he was dependent on her for a remittance. Its size is unknown, although in 1771 he was hoping for a fixed annuity of £140 or £150 a year instead of these uncertain payments. Soon after the diary opens, Neville realized that he could no longer afford to live in London, and therefore decided to set up house in the country, a scheme which he supposed would be cheaper. While he was touring round England looking for a house to rent and a housekeeper to look after him, he found in Eastbourne a girl called Sarah Bradford, who was already pregnant by a passing army major. Neville noted primly in his diary, 'Some may be censorious, but my motives for this action, the taking of the girl out of her native place where her reputation is blasted, is a benevolent one.' This seems more than doubtful, for nine months later, when he had finally rented a house at Scratby in Norfolk, he awaited her arrival in London with undisguised impatience. Not that Neville had kept himself for her all these months, for he had had a warm intrigue with a married woman whose husband was in jail for debt. She had flattered him by telling him, 'you are able to seduce any woman.'[51]

Sally arrived in town on 3 June 1769, now calling herself Mrs Russell. For the next three days Neville showed her the sights of London, and on 7 June he slept with her for the first time. By the end of the month, they were settled in Scratby, along with a lavish supporting staff of other servants. But soon the trouble began, when Sally pressed Neville into allowing Poll, her little illegitimate child by her previous liaison, to join them. Neville agreed, provided that he had a free hand to punish her when he thought fit, a point Sally objected to. Neville saw himself trapped and noted, 'I wish I was rid of this connection and all its consequences.' Poll arrived and was naturally hostile to her mother's new lover. When Neville beat her 'rather more severely (I confess) than I ought to have done, her mother used me most vilely, calling me all sorts of bad names. I wish I was fairly rid of both. How miserable is the situation of a bachelor, exposed to all the bad humours of low life, deprived of those real joys which a virtuous and well-educated wife affords.' But Neville's financial situation precluded any hope of such a match.[52]

At the end of one year at Scratby, Neville discovered that he had spent four times his income, and decided, reluctantly, that he would have to work for his living and take up some profession, if he was to maintain his position and way of life as a gentleman. He therefore decided to go off to Edinburgh to take a degree in medicine, leaving Sally behind at Scratby until he could break the lease of the house. Sally was very unhappy about the separation, fearing that it meant the end of their liaison, and talked wildly of 'embezzling things on my marriage, and then of cutting her throat on that account. Lord deliver me from this connection, for it prevents my entering into every good one.' But he delayed his departure for almost a year, during which there were continual quarrels with Sally, followed by reconciliations. Neville told himself that 'the badness of my housekeeper's temper is extremely troublesome', and planned to marry a submissive wife of gentle stock, if he could find one. But in fact he was trapped, partly by his own indolence and weakness of character, partly by the responsibility he had assumed by making Sally his mistress (she pretended to her mother that she was married to Neville), partly by ties of affection and habit, partly by the impossibility of finding a suitable wife, given his financial situation.[53]

At last, in September 1771, he set off for London, preparatory to going to Edinburgh. On his return home in October, he made poor Sally swear a solemn oath, 'May God strike me blind and may my right hand rot off if I have... done anything bad by you.' A few days later, he set off for Edinburgh, leaving Sally behind in tears, while he was in his usual state of indecision: 'I feel an affection for both her and her child, notwithstanding the badness of her temper. Everything conspires to show me how dangerous it is to form any such connection. Alas, I fear I shall never know a more honourable one.' Once in Edinburgh, he was tormented by suspicions that Sally was being unfaithful to him with his manservant, while he himself occasionally frequented the whores and brothels of Edinburgh. When he returned to Scratby in the spring of 1772, he conceived the slightly bizarre scheme of slipping into the house incognito to spy on her, but had to abandon it as impractical. As he was closing down the house, he offered Sally the choice of joining him in Edinburgh or going her own way, and she chose the former. But he was still half mad with suspicion of her, and once held a pistol to her head to get her to explain a long conversation with the manservant. She told him it was only to reproach the servant for trying to go to bed with a new maid who had only been in the house a day or two. Even now, he was indecisive and toyed with the idea of marrying a virtuous innkeeper's daughter, only to reject it because of her low birth. In December

Sally at last arrived at Edinburgh, being made to swear on the gospels that she had been faithful to him. This was more than could be said for Neville, who four days later went down with gonorrhoea and had to be given a two-week treatment with mercury to cure him.[54]

A year later Neville was still living with Sally and pursuing his medical studies. Sally was now pregnant by him, a situation which did not stop him from going 'to see the harlots in an Edinburgh brothel' one evening. In February 1775 Sally, discreetly disguised as 'Mrs Turner' and in the anonymity of the city of Newcastle, gave birth to a baby girl. In July Neville again was unfaithful to her and was relieved to find that he had not picked up venereal disease again. In August 1776 the child died, while still with its wet-nurse at Newcastle, never having been seen, so far as we know, by its father.[55]

In September 1775 Neville finally obtained his medical degree and left Edinburgh, leaving behind him Sally, now pregnant by him a second time. Instead of settling down as a doctor, he for some reason went off on a three-year jaunt round Europe, during which he appears to have formed a liaison with an Italian woman. By 1780 he was back in England and engaged in a new liaison with a girl called Mary Orde, like Sally the cast-off mistress of an army officer. But he had not broken with Sally, and went to Newcastle to visit her and their daughter. For the next three years, he drifted indecisively without settling down to an occupation. He shuttled between Sally in Newcastle and later in London, Mary Orde in Norwich, and a girl called Emily in London. In the autumn of 1783, he finally decided to settle down in Norwich in order to try to establish himself in practice as a doctor, and to take Sally along with him (although on subsequent trips to London he still picked up again with Emily). Neville's hopes as a professional man lay in cultivating the patronage of the solid bourgeoisie of Norwich and the local gentry in the area. He could, therefore, afford neither to marry a lower-class girl like Sally nor to live with her openly as his mistress. Moreover, Sally was now pregnant again, a fact that would have somehow to be explained. This problem he most ingeniously solved by persuading his manservant John Read – presumably in return for a cash payment – to marry Sally, so that they could both live in his house as majo-domo and housekeeper without arousing any suspicions.[56]

The diary ceases at this point. All that is known of Neville's later life is that his attempt to set up a medical practice was a total failure and that he lived in increasing poverty on the charity of his political and noble friends, using his daughter Sarah to write pathetic begging letters for him at his dictation. Sally gave birth to two more children, but it is not known whether the father was her legal husband, the servant John Read, or her master, Neville himself. Sally certainly stayed with him until her death in 1825, while Sylas lived on to the ripe old age of ninety-nine, dying at last in 1840. In 1842 his daughter Sarah Read, now the headmistress of a girls' school, observed, 'I cannot but lament being the offspring of such a parent', one who had wasted his talents, consumed his substance, and done absolutely nothing with his life except to form this bizarre association with Sally.[57] His story, however, casts a vivid light on the difficulties of marriage for a man of gentlemanly status but little money in the eighteenth century, a situation which was a common one for younger sons. The ease with which liaisons, often long-lasting ones, could be formed with lower-class girls at this time helps to explain both the rising rate of illegitimacy in the society and the low rate of nuptiality among younger sons of the gentry.

6   JAMES BOSWELL

i. Facts

The most revealing information of all about sexual mores in the eighteenth century comes from the diaries, notes, memoranda and letters of James Boswell, which cover all his adult thirty-seven years from 1758 to his death in 1795 (plate 29).[58] Boswell, who was born in 1740, was the son and heir of an ancient and status-conscious Scottish family, and his father, the laird of Auchinleck, was a Lord of Court of Sessions and a member of the High Court of Judiciary in Scotland, one of the most respected lawyers in Edinburgh. For him, as for many young men of his time from upper bourgeois or landed backgrounds, a key figure in his early life, who decisively moulded his later character, was his mother. 'My mother was extremely pious. She inspired me with devotion. But unfortunately she taught me Calvinism. My catechism contained the doctrines of that system. The eternity of punishment was the first great idea I ever formed. How it made me shudder! . . . I thought but rarely about the bliss of heaven, because I had no idea of it.' The experience left him with a lifelong sense of guilt about the sensual pleasures he sought so avidly.

But it was his own genetic make-up which was responsible for his most pronounced characteristic – his supreme egoism, his absorbing passion in all aspects of himself, which was the cause of his compilation of so staggering a quantity of notes, memoranda and journals of such a self-revelatory and intimate a nature. 'I have a kind of strange feeling as if I wished nothing to be secret that concerns myself.'[59] He was also a manic-depressive, forever oscillating between moods of exuberant zest for life and profound melancholy. This melancholia was an inherited family trait which virtually incapacitated both his brother and an uncle. Possessing so volatile a temperament, none of his declarations of mood are to be taken too seriously, since they rarely lasted very long. But as a reporter of facts and of immediate feelings, he is beyond compare.

From the age of sixteen in 1756 to the age of twenty-nine in 1769 when he finally got married, Boswell was in the throes of a complex identity crisis, of which there were three main components. The first was the problem of religion. Brought up as a strict Calvinist, he was under great pressure from his mother to have a conversion experience. But this he could not do. He studied logic and metaphysics at the University of Edinburgh, and was temporarily converted to Methodism. He then became for a time a Pythagorean vegetarian under the influence of an old man. A little later, at the age of eighteen, he fell in love with a Catholic woman, and in 1758 suddenly fled to London and was secretly admitted by a priest into the Roman Catholic Church. This lasted only a matter of weeks before he was converted to hedonistic Deism (and the pleasures of sex) by a young Scottish friend, Lord Eglinton. Finally, five years later, on Christmas Day 1764, he was admitted to communion in the Anglican Church, although since he had had his bastard son baptized in that faith in November 1762, he had presumably more or less settled his religious problems by then. The man he admired most in the world was that bigoted Anglican Dr Johnson, but he still delighted in talking with sceptics like John Wilkes and Voltaire, while maintaining fascination for an outright atheist like David Hume and a boundless admiration for a Deist like Rousseau. His religious anxieties seem to have been mainly generated by his fear of and preoccupation with death – he rarely missed a hanging in London–and his uncertainty about an after-life.[60]

The second identity crisis concerned Boswell's career and his relations with his father. The latter was an aloof and frosty figure with whom he could never establish human contact, and who despised him for his indolence and instability of purpose. He wanted his son to stay in Edinburgh and follow the practice of Scottish law like himself, but Boswell had other plans. He loved the theatre and fine literature; he wanted to travel and to meet the intellectual world of Europe; and he wanted to become famous as a writer – just how, he did not then know. Above all, he did not want to be cooped up in the provincial town of Edinburgh under the stern and inquisitive supervision of his unsympathetic father. His first plan, therefore, was to try to get a commission in a Guards regiment, which would give him an adequate income with little to do, except an obligation to reside in London. 'I could in that way enjoy all the elegant pleasures of the gay world, and by living in the metropolis and having plenty of time, could pursue what studies and follow what whims I pleased, get a variety of acquaintances of all kinds, get a number of romantic adventures, and thus have my satisfaction of life.'[61]

The third identity crisis concerned the problem of how to deal with his sexual impulses. It was the discovery of the pleasures of the flesh which, according to his own account to Rousseau, cured him of his religious crisis by diverting his mind into other channels. His father naturally wanted him to settle down and marry a suitably rich and well-connected Scottish heiress, but this was not at all to Boswell's taste. He found himself blessed or burdened with an overwhelmingly powerful sexual drive – crude, unrefined, and urgent – and a very large member. This was a combination which regularly overcame his fear of venereal disease, his contempt for the low women he resorted to, and his recurrent moral doubts. He told himself that 'I am of a warm constitution; a complexion, as the physicians say, exceedingly amorous.' Moreover, 'I am too changeable where women are concerned. I ought to be a Turk.' As a result, he was forever plotting new sexual adventures: in 1762, 'in the midst of divine service' – in fact listening to a sermon on the topic 'Wherewith shall a young man cleanse his way' – 'I was laying plans for having women, and yet I had the most sincere feelings of religion.' When he forced himself into Rousseau's presence in 1764, the main problem he wanted to discuss was his boundless sexual fantasies. He proposed to Rousseau: 'If I am rich, I can take a number of girls. I get them with child, propagation is thus increased. I give them dowries and marry them off to good peasants who are very happy to have them. Thus they become wives at the same age as would have been the case if they had remained virgins, and I, on my side, have had the benefit of enjoying a great variety of women.... I should like to follow the example of the old Patriarchs, worthy men whose memory I hold in respect.' Rousseau would have none of these ideas, telling Boswell that fleshly pleasures were ephemeral compared with spiritual ones and that virtue has its own reward, advice which the latter followed for about a month.[62]

The trouble was that the sensual mysticism of Rousseau, the elevation of sexual passion to a kind of religious experience, was alien to Boswell's whole approach to the subject. He was driven by direct, uncomplicated physical needs, to him as simple and instinctive as urinating or excreting. He was therefore much more at home with the frank sensuality of John Wilkes, whom he met at Naples. Wilkes reassured him that sex and literary distinction went hand in hand, that dissipation and profligacy renew the mind, proof being that he had written his best pieces for *The North Briton* in bed with Betsy Green. Wilkes also told him to be grateful for his constitution. 'Thank heaven for having given me the love of women. To many she gives not the noble passion of lust.' This was the sort of thing in which Boswell fundamentally believed, although, unlike Wilkes, his Calvinist upbringing continued to worry him about the propriety and the morality of his behaviour. Once in 1764 he referred to Cupid as Satan and later told himself to 'think if God really forbids girls.' In Berlin he even tried to frighten himself by writing a discourse against fornication along the hell-fire and brimstone lines of his early education by his mother. But none of these doubts, and constant spasms of guilt and remorse, had more than temporary effects on his actual behaviour.[63]

To sum up in purely quantitative terms Boswell's sex life from the ages of twenty to twenty-nine, he laid unsuccessful siege to more than a dozen ladies of quality – Scottish, English, Dutch, German and Italian; he made three married women of quality his mistresses; he had liaisons of varying length with four actresses, and a brief but passionate affair with the lifelong mistress, friend and attendant of Rousseau; he kept at least three lower-class women as mistresses, and he produced two illegitimate children, one in 1762 and one in 1767; he made a brief but successful assault early one morning on the pregnant wife of one of the King of Prussia's guards at Potsdam; and last but by no means least, he had sexual relations with well over sixty different prostitutes in Edinburgh, London, Berlin, Dresden, Geneva, Turin, Naples, Rome, Florence, Venice, Marseilles, Paris, and Dublin. As a result, he suffered from at least ten outbreaks of gonorrhoea before his marriage, and seven after, although it is certainly possible that some of them may have been recrudescences of latent old disease rather than altogether new infections.[64]

The chronology of Boswell's sexual experiences was as follows. He lost his virginity during his first runaway visit to London to join the Roman Catholic Church at the age of twenty in March 1760. This took place in a room in the Blue Periwig in Southampton Street with a woman called Sally Forrester. This introduction into 'the melting and transporting rites of love' was an experience to which Boswell always looked back fondly,[65] and he immediately embarked, under the tutelage of his older mentors Lord Eglinton and the Duke of York, on a series of debauches which ended in his first attack of gonorrhoea, the cure for which lasted ten weeks. On his forced return to Edinburgh, he missed both the intellectual and the sensual pleasures of London. In May 1761 he consoled himself with a visit to a brothel in Edinburgh, where he promptly caught an even worse infection of gonorrhoea, which put him out of action for four months. On his recovery, he flung himself into a variety of intrigues, carrying on no fewer than four active liaisons at the same time. The first was with Mrs Jean Heron, the seventeen-year-old wife of a close friend and the daughter of one of his father's friends and his own patron, Lord Kames. She flung herself at him within a month of her marriage, and his notes contain unambiguous memoranda such as 'Tea, angel, two.' He naturally was consumed with guilt at his treachery, but Jean made a clear distinction between marriage and sexual passion, and was totally indifferent to such scruples. At the same time, he carried on active liaisons with two middle-aged actresses – one of them the wife of his second best friend – and picked up a lower-class girl as a steady mistress: one Peggy Doig, a 'curious young little pretty.' By November 1762, when he at last persuaded his father to let him go to London again to seek a commission in the Guards, Peggy was pregnant. Before he left, he made proper gentle-manly arrangements for her lying-in, the baptism of the child, and its care by a foster-mother.[66]

Boswell thus arrived in London in November, 1762, at the age of twenty-two, with a wide variety of sexual experience already behind him. He had experimented with prostitutes in two cities; he had visited a brothel; he had had two intrigues with 'that delicious subject of gallantry, an actress'; he had conquered the heart and used the body of a young married woman of his own social class; he had kept a lower-class mistress and got her with child; and he had contracted venereal disease twice. The next seven years were to be no more than variations on these established themes.

He began his visit to London full of wise resolutions: 'I determined to have nothing to do with whores, as my health was of great consequence to me.' In London he could take his pick of hired women, 'from a splendid Madam at fifty guineas a night down to the civil nymph... who tramps along the Strand and will resign her engaging person to your honour for a pint of wine and a shilling.' But he could not afford the one and planned to keep away from the other for fear of 'the loathsome distemper.' What he wanted was a renewal of what he had enjoyed in Edinburgh, 'the most delicious intrigues with women of beauty, sentiment and spirit, perfectly suited to my romantic genius.' He therefore fastened his attention upon a pretty twenty-four-year-old actress at Covent Garden Theatre, 'Louisa', or Mrs Lewis, who came from respectable parents and was separated from her

28. Samuel Pepys. By John Hayls, 1667.

29. James Boswell. By G. Willison, 1765.
30. Margaret Boswell, *c.* 1769.

In the Poke   Out the Poke

A PIG in a POKE

31. Seductive fashions: artificial breasts and buttocks, 1786.

32. Seductive fashions: the topless style and the cult of maternal breast-feeding, 1796.

33. The late eighteenth-century sexual scene: the objects for sale, besides women, include condoms, birches, pornographic books, pills and surgical instruments for VD, and aphrodisiacs. By T. Rowlandson, 1786.

34. Sexual deviations: flagellation, 1752.

35. Pornography.
By T. Rowlandson, c. 1812.

36. Sex education: exhibition of wax-work models of the reproductive system. Late eighteenth century.

37. Indecent exposure, 1800.

Pub^d July 20th 1800 by R. Ackermann N° 101 Strand

38. Lust among the poor. By T. Rowlandson, 1810.

PSALM LXXIII, V:14.

"For all the Day long have I been plagued, and chastened every Morning.

"I became also a Reproach unto them, & when they looked upon me, they shaked their heads

P: CIX . V: 25 .

Stool of Repentance

39. Venereal disease and its treatment by mercury, 1784.

40. A brothel for the upper classes. By T. Rowlandson, 1781.

41. A brothel for the lower classes, 1807.

42. Pre-nuptial pregnancy: a shot-gun wedding, 1778.

43. Pre-nuptial pregnancy: a paternity claim, 1800.

husband. On 17 December, he thought that he 'felt the fine delirium of love', and every day he pressed his suit more closely. Three days later she borrowed two guineas from him, and he offered up to ten, consoling himself with the reflection that although not cheap, 'it cost me as much to be cured of what I contracted from a whore, and that ten guineas was but a moderate expense for women during the winter.' At the end of the month, mutual attraction was clear. Mrs Lewis asked him what would happen if she became pregnant, and he promised that he would behave like a gentleman and see the child taken care of. On Sunday, 2 January 1763, while the landlady was out, she offered herself to him, but he felt impotent for a while. At last his energies revived, and he hurried her into the bedroom and 'was just making a triumphal entry when we heard her landlady coming up.' Thwarted on this occasion, Louisa promised to spend the night with him at an inn on a Saturday, since she did not have to act in the theatre on Sundays. The meeting took place on 12 January, when Boswell excelled himself. 'Five times was I fairly lost in supreme rapture', for him an unsurpassed feat of which he was extremely proud. Six days later, however, Boswell felt 'a little heat in the members of my body sacred to Cupid', and by the next day it 'too, too plain was Signor Gonorrhoea' again. When taxed with this unpleasant fact, Louisa confessed that she had been very bad three years ago, but had felt no symptoms for eighteen months, and had slept with no-one but Boswell for six. It seems more than likely that she was telling the truth and was an unsuspecting carrier, but Boswell was naturally furious and broke off all relations. 'Thus ended my intrigue with the fair Louisa . . . from which I expected at least a winter's safe copulation.'[67]

This mishap forced Boswell to retire to his room to live on bread and water and broth and to take physic for five weeks. He was visited by friends, but none of them took his predicament very seriously. The Judge Advocate of Scotland even made a pun about it, asking 'Who in the performance of a manly part would not wish to get claps?' But it spelt the end of Boswell's hopes of a liaison with an amiable and reasonably cultivated woman with whom he could both talk and make love. In March, therefore, as soon as he was cured, he visited Mrs Phillips' shop at the Green Canister in Half Moon Street and bought himself some condoms as a protection against the prostitutes he would henceforth be obliged to resort to – his 'armour', as he called them. On 25 March he went into St James's Park, picked up a whore, and 'for the first time I did engage in armour, which I found but a dull satisfaction.' Every four or five days thereafter the physical urge became irresistible again and out he would go in search of a whore and 'copulated . . . free from danger, being safely sheathed.' From time to time he made good resolutions 'against low street debauchery', but he could never put them into practice for long. Once he picked up 'a fresh agreeable young girl' and took her down a lane to 'a snug place'. 'I took out my armour, but she begged that I might not put it on, as the sport was much pleasanter without it.' Boswell was foolish enough to agree, a decision he much regretted the next day, but which fortunately brought no serious consequences. Once he found some willing amateurs, when he ran into two pretty girls 'who asked me to take them with me'. He offered them no more than his company and a glass of wine, which they accepted. He escorted them to a room in an Inn, fondled them, sang some songs, and then took them 'one after the other, according to their seniority.'[68]

Encounters of this type – one of which took place on Westminster Bridge – went on all throughout the spring and summer of 1763, despite the reproaches of his friend Temple and his own self-disgust, not at the immorality of his behaviour, but its brutishness. What he really longed for was 'a genteel girl' as a mistress, but he could not find one. It was in June that he first met and became friendly with Dr Johnson, whom he enormously admired and to whom he confided his sexual problems. Dr Johnson gave him stern moral advice, and Boswell resolutely concluded that 'Since my being honoured with the friendship of Dr Johnson . . . I have considered that promiscuous concubinage is certainly wrong.' Even this did not stop him from a few further adventures, but his moral fibre was certainly being stiffened.[69]

In August he left London on the Grand Tour of Europe, starting with Holland for the rest of 1763 and proceeding on through Germany and Switzerland in 1764 and Italy, Corsica and France in 1765–66. The moral lessons of Dr Johnson and the reproaches of his friend Temple had made a profound impression on Boswell. In Holland he was plunged into depression until on 15 October 1763 at Utrecht he drew up an 'Inviolable Plan' of moral reform and regeneration. 'For some years past, you have been idle, dissipated, absurd and unhappy,' he told himself. Henceforward, he would be industrious, purposeful, dignified, and chaste. The plan was hardly inviolable, but he certainly worked at the law at Utrecht and turned away from dabbling with whores and scheming for liaisons with ladies to a more serious study of a possible matrimonial prospect.[70] The result was that on 23 July 1764, almost a year after leaving London, he could boast to Temple that 'since I left England, I have been as chaste as an anchorite.'

By September his matrimonial schemes had collapsed and he was in

Berlin, where temptations were more plentiful. But he successfully resisted them until early one morning when a woman came to his room to sell chocolate. 'I toyed with her and found she was with child. Oho, a safe piece. Into my closet. "*Habst du ein Mann?*" "*Ja, in der Guards bei Potsdam.*" To bed directly. In a minute – over.... Bless me, have I now committed adultery?... Let it go. I'll think no more of it. Divine Being, pardon the errors of a weak mortal.'[71]

As he proceeded onward on his journey, he was torn between lust and fear of disease. 'Chase libertine fancies,' he told himself; 'Swear solemn with drawn sword not to be with women *sine* condom *nisi* Swiss lass.' In Dresden he tried to buy condoms but failed, and was, therefore, obliged to content himself with picking up girls and ejaculating between their thighs without penetration for fear of infection. His visit to Rousseau, whom he then admired as much as he did Dr Johnson, did much to fortify him with renewed good resolutions to remain chaste in his forthcoming visit to Italy and France. But, as usual, it did not last, and in December, while at Geneva preparing to cross the Alps, his concern was not with chastity but with health. He was repelled by the masturbation he had again resorted to in desperation: 'Swear with drawn sword never pleasure but with woman's aid. In Turin and Italy you will find enough. But venture not but with perfect sure people.'[72]

In Turin he attempted to gain access to two noble ladies, but he bungled both affairs and was rejected with humiliation. His approach to the Contessa di San Gillio was nothing if not direct. 'I am young, strong and vigorous. I offer my services as a duty and I think that the Comtesse de St Gilles will do very well to accept them.' She told him brutally, 'You should not attempt the profession of gallantry ... for you don't know the world.' Thus rebuffed, he consoled himself with whores, to his anxiety and disgust. From Turin he proceeded to Rome, where all scruples disappeared. 'Be Spaniard: girl every day,' he told himself – and he did. At Naples he slept with an opera singer, and others. As he confessed to Rousseau, 'I ran after girls without restraint. My blood was inflamed by the burning climate, and my passions were violent. I indulged them; my mind had almost nothing to do with it. I found some very pretty girls. I escaped all danger.'[73]

Back in Rome in time for Easter week in 1765, he was not so lucky. After a series of orgies with whores, he had to confess on 29 April, 'Alas, real disease.' The infection was mild but persistent, the beginning of a urethric condition that lasted, on and off, for the rest of his life, despite the advice of many doctors and surgeons. Undeterred by this warning symptom, he continued throughout May to make an intensive study of classical art and architecture all day and to chase girls in the evening. At Rome he became acquainted with Lord Mountstuart, the eldest son of Lord Bute, the English Prime Minister, who invited him to join his party (consisting of himself, an ex-colonel as a governor, and a crotchety Swiss historian as a tutor) on a trip to Venice. At Venice Boswell's imprudence led to serious consequences. He allowed Lord Mountstuart to accompany him 'to take a look at the girls,' as the result of which 'a pretty dancer was our common flame, and my Lord catched a tartar as well as I. A fine piece of witless behaviour.'[74]

Lord Mountstuart was soon afterwards summoned home by his father, but Boswell, defying the instructions and expectations of his father, proceeded on to Florence and then Siena in a last attempt to bag an Italian countess. He first tried Porzia Sansedoni, the wife of the Chamberlain of the Grand Duke of Tuscany, who had earlier been the mistress of his friend Mountstuart. Once again his approach was a direct one: 'I should like to be with you, late at night, and in a modest darkness, to receive a tender pledge of your favour for an eternal friend' – i.e. Mountstuart. Rebuffed in this quarter, he turned to Girolama Piccolomini, the wife of the Mayor of Siena, who promptly fell in love with him. The first encounter was not a success, according to Boswell's notes: 'Girolama. Quite agitated. Put on condom; entered. Heart beat; fell. Quite sorry, but said "A true sign of passion."'[75] Later he recovered his virility, and there followed eighteen days of passionate love-making. But, as usual, Boswell soon tired of this new love, and resolutely left Siena never to return. For Girolama, however, this was the great emotional experience of her life, and she continued to write to her unfaithful lover for at least another four years.[76]

There followed a visit to Corsica and the rebel General Paoli, his account of which was later to make Boswell famous at last. Paoli, whom he admired as much as he did Rousseau and Dr Johnson, was consulted by Boswell in his usual frank way about his sexual problems, and advised chastity and an early marriage. En route back home, Boswell stopped in December at Marseilles, where he had an introduction from a friend to a girl who had been this friend's mistress for about a year. He looked her up and, on the basis of his friendship with her ex-lover, persuaded her to spend the night with him. This episode sapped his Corsican resolve, and on his arrival in Paris he made straight for the best brothels in town, where he seems to have spent most of his time. While in Paris he met Rousseau's mistress and companion of twenty years, Thérèse Le Vasseur, who was on her way to join the philosopher in his English exile. She and Boswell therefore joined forces for the trip. Just what happened during the first eleven days of February between Paris and Dover is not known for certain since these pages of the journal have been destroyed. All that is left is Boswell's entry for 12 February, the day after their arrival at Dover: 'Yesterday morning had gone to bed very early and had done it once. Thirteen in all. Was very affectionate to her.' There seems to be no doubt that when he left Paris Boswell had no intention of seducing the lifelong companion of his hero Rousseau, but there can equally be no doubt that this is what happened. One scholar, who claimed to have read the missing pages before they were destroyed, said that the liaison began when they were forced to share a bed at an inn. After the usual period of impotence, Boswell finally succeeded. But when he boasted to her of his prowess, she told him bluntly that 'you are a hardy and vigorous lover, but you have no art' and proceeded to give him a series of lessons in the techniques of foreplay and the variations of postures. Once she rode him 'agitated, like a bad rider galloping downhill', while Boswell was vainly trying to pump her about details of her life with Rousseau.[77]

Back in London and then in Edinburgh, Boswell continued to frequent whores, all his good resolutions having disappeared. In 1766, however, he formed a serious liaison with a pretty young woman of his own class, a Mrs Dodds, whose husband had left her. This was just what Boswell wanted: 'In this manner I am safe and happy, and in no danger either of the perils of Venus or of desperate matrimony.' Moreover, 'she has the finest black hair, she is paradisial in bed.' She was his mistress for about a year, and in April 1767 she became pregnant with Boswell's second illegitimate child. Meanwhile, the latter was extremely busy both cultivating his legal practice at the Scottish Bar and at last looking for a wife in real earnest. Despite this pressure of business and despite Mrs Dodds' willingness to give him every sexual satisfaction he asked for – on one occasion dressing in black and leaving the candles lit – Boswell nevertheless from time to time indulged in the grossest and stupidest behaviour, now largely due to a new vice, a propensity to get drunk.[78]

On 8 March 1767, Boswell gave a bachelor party to pay a debt of honour to his friends with whom he had, before he left Scotland in 1762, made a bet of 'a guinea that I should not catch the venereal disorder for three years.' He got so drunk that he staggered off to a whore and spent the night with her, with the inevitable result (despite some half-hearted precautions) of a recrudescence of his gonorrhoea. Since the reaction was so fast, it seems possible that he was by now suffering from chronic gonorrhoeal infection of the prostate, which was reactivated by venereal or alcoholic excess. He still did not learn his lesson, and in June the same thing happened again. He spent the evening with his friends drinking the health of Miss Blair, his prime matrimonial choice at the time, and again got drunk and spent the night with a whore. This time the disease was really serious, and he passed it on to the now pregnant Mrs Dodds. Fortunately she recovered quickly, but it took Boswell all the summer in retreat and under a strict regime of diet and physic to clear up the infection.

In December he again slept with an Edinburgh whore, with the same result, and in January, while still infected, he was sleeping again both with whores and with Mrs Dodds. One of the whores was an illegitimate daughter of Lord Kinnaird, which gives some insight into the wide social spectrum from which the profession of prostitution was then drawn. He was no longer in love with Mrs Dodds, who in December had given birth to his daughter Sally, and was simply using her as a sexual convenience, usually after a heavy drinking party when he was inflamed with wine. On 7 February 1768 he arrived drunk at Mrs Dodds' house at 2 a.m., slept with her, and then went off to make a proposal of marriage to Miss Blair, who had the good sense to refuse him. Soon afterwards Mrs Dodds drops out of the picture, to be replaced by 'a pretty lively little girl', but one in whose constancy Boswell had no confidence. He gave her some money before he left for London, but asked two of his friends to test her by trying to seduce her, which they found only too easy. In March he was in London again, where in a manic mood he promptly 'sallied forth like a roaring lion after girls.' At first he was careful to use his 'armour', but General Clark told him that oil was a good protection, and he tried it out with a girl he had known before. He performed twice, paid her only four shillings and noted that 'I never saw a girl more expert at it', so it was a successful experiment. He had now acquired a taste for two girls at a time, and – no doubt because of his use of oil instead of condoms – he found himself re-infected for the ninth time. This time he was only cured by a retreat which lasted six weeks, and the experience inspired a vow of chastity for six months, taken in St Paul's Cathedral just before leaving for Edinburgh.[79]

By the spring of 1769 his matrimonial choice, which was still focused on an heiress with at least £10,000, had narrowed down to two; and in June he visited Dublin in pursuit of one, during which he once more had the folly to visit a brothel, with the usual result of a new gonorrhoeal infection. So severe was it this time that he had to go to London for the cure, which consisted of a camphor liniment and mercury plaster on the affected parts, a daily draught of a pint of 'Kennedy's Lisbon Diet Drink' – at half a guinea a pint – and finally some minor surgery. In October the doctors reassured him that he would recover: 'By sleeping with the same woman all would come right.' A month later, on 25 November 1769, he married his final choice, his old friend and cousin Margaret Montgomerie, to whom he had become engaged before leaving for London for medical treatment. She was an intelligent and sensible woman, two or three years older than Boswell, without fortune, but whose physical proportions well suited the latter's gross appetites: she was 'a heathen goddess painted al fresco on the ceiling of a palace at Rome.' She was also deeply devoted to him, despite his manifold defects of character which she knew only too well (plate 30).[80]

It was a marriage which permanently alienated his father, who had set his heart on some well-connected heiress who would substantially increase the family fortunes. As a cousin with a portion of a mere £1,000, Margaret brought neither wealth nor additional political connections. Boswell had married in defiance of his father's wishes, and for long-standing settled affection, not family interest. It was thus on both counts a classic example of the new marriage in the eighteenth century. If the filial challenge was common, the paternal response was unusual in its brutal psychological impact. A sixty-two-year-old widower, his father suddenly announced his intention of remarrying. Not only did he not attend Boswell's wedding, but he arranged for his own to take place on the same day. A more obvious attempt at the sexual castration of his son could hardly be imagined.

But it was not only his father who disapproved of his marriage. Even his two bachelor friends were none too enthusiastic about it at first. Temple warned him that 'you are born to a fortune not inconsiderable, of a family of some note in your country. These are circumstances you must consider.... If by marriage you do not both add considerably to your fortune and increase your influence by your wife's connections, the world will deem your generosity weakness and imprudence.' Dempster was just against marriage on principle: 'I think marriage is setting up a child-manufactory, at which one must drudge like a horse. Children are a commodity which requires great pains in the raising, and then you are miserable until you get them disposed of.'[81]

In retrospect it is clear that Boswell's marriage to Margaret Montgomerie was the most – perhaps the only – sensible thing he ever did, and for some years thereafter his life was a model of domestic virtue and happiness, monogamy, sobriety and professional diligence. She loved him deeply, understood him, and was patient with all his weaknesses and follies. In his own odd way he loved her in return, and paid her the compliment of always being frank and honest with her, confessing all – or nearly all – of his constant infidelities. He kept a notebook entitled 'Uxoriana or my Wife's excellent Sayings,' and after her death he carefully preserved her purse, a lock of her hair, her wedding-ring, and 'two stalks of lily of the valley which my dear wife had in her hand the day before she died.'[82]

She had known him and been his confidante for years, and the ties of cousinhood no doubt reinforced Boswell's narcissism. He was almost marrying himself. This is not to say that he and his wife were temperamentally identical, for they were not. She had less of a sexual drive than her husband, and lacked both his ebullience and his melancholy. She was a plain, solemn, sensible woman. Once in 1775 she complained to him that he never talked seriously to her 'but merely childish nonsense.' Boswell admitted the truth of the charge. 'The reason of it may be partly indolence, to avoid thought; partly because my wife, though she has excellent sense and a cheerful temper, has not sentiments congenial with mine. She has no superstition, no enthusiasm, no vanity; so that to be free of a disagreeable contrariety, I may be glad to keep good humour in my mind by foolish sport.'[83]

Mrs Boswell worked hard to satisfy her husband and to produce the son and heir he so badly wanted. A son was born in August 1770, but only lived two hours; a daughter Veronica arrived in March 1773; another daughter in May 1774; and at last a son Alexander in October 1775. In the next five years there followed two more sons (one of whom died almost immediately), one miscarriage and one daughter.

So happy was Boswell after his marriage that he abandoned his diary for almost three years, only taking it up again in the spring of 1772, when he left home for an extended trip to London in order to renew his association with old friends, and especially with Dr Johnson. He was reluctant 'to part with a valuable friend and constant companion,' and his wife was equally sorry to see him go. Hardly had he reached London when the old temptations presented themselves. Boswell walked up and down the Strand, looking at the whores and 'indulging speculations about... the harmlessness of temporary likings, unconnected with mental attachment.' But he controlled himself and 'resolved never again to come to London without bringing my wife along with me,' – a resolve he never kept. He was also tempted by the pretty maid at his lodging, who as she bade him goodnight would ask him, 'Do you want anything more tonight, sir?' but he kept his desires to himself. During the two months he was in London, he wrote thirty-five letters to his wife, and he only faltered once in April when for two nights he 'went with bad women a little.'[84]

On the other hand, he had a disturbing conversation with an old and intimate friend of his wife, the Honourable Mrs Stuart, wife of James Archibald Stuart, younger brother of Boswell's old travelling companion Lord Mountstuart. Somehow or other the breakfast talk got around to the subject of marital infidelity. Mrs Stuart

candidly declared that from what she had seen of life in this great town she would not be uneasy at an occasional infidelity in her husband, as she did not think it at all connected with affection. That if he kept a particular woman, it would be a sure sign that he had no affection for his wife; or if his infidelities were very frequent, it would also be a sign. But that a transient fancy for a girl, or being led by one's companions after drinking to an improper place, was not to be considered as inconsistent with true affection. I wish this doctrine may not have been only consolatory and adapted to facts. I told her I was very happy; that I had never known I was married, having taken for my wife my cousin and intimate friend and companion; so that I had nothing at all like restraint.

Despite this reassurance, Boswell was clearly thrown into some confusion by these remarks by a woman in whose judgement he had some confidence.[85]

It was not until he was back in Edinburgh in the autumn of 1772 that he committed adultery for the first time after his marriage. On this occasion, it was caused by the vice of very heavy drinking, which was growing steadily on him during these years. More and more frequently he would go off on all-night drinking bouts which would deprive him of all self-control. Because of illness after a miscarriage the previous winter, Mrs Boswell was unable to satisfy her husband's sexual needs, and in late October after a drunken evening he visited an Edinburgh prostitute. He promptly confessed his folly to his wife, who made him send for a doctor at once. 'She is my best friend and the most generous heart,' he noted, justly. In January 1773, by which time Mrs Boswell was far gone with child, he lapsed again, contracted gonorrhoea once more and had to place himself in the surgeon's hands.[86]

The birth of Veronica in March 1773 and the shame and pain of the disease seem to have made him get a grip on himself for over a year, but in the summer of 1774 alarming symptoms of loss of self-control reappeared. Six times in six weeks he went on all-night drinking orgies, returning home dead drunk to his waiting wife in the early hours of the morning. It seems likely that these drinking bouts were a substitute for sexual frustration, for he did not resume relations with his wife after the birth of the second child in May until 19 August. Boswell's sexual drive far exceeded that of his wife and she did not let him sleep with her again for another five weeks. A week before he had got dead drunk again, returned home, cursed his wife, and threw a candlestick at her with a lighted candle – an episode which filled him with contrition the next morning.[87]

She probably realized the pressures that were tormenting her husband, and in late September 1774 he persuaded her to leave the two children at home and go off with him on a brief holiday. The first night he took her three times, and once on each of the three succeeding nights. He tried, but failed through excess of alcohol, a week later, but this was the last period for a long while during which he could obtain full sexual satisfaction from his wife. If his record is complete, they slept together only four times between 23 October 1774 and 22 January 1775, although by January she was again with child. On 8 March 1775, they finally had a frank discussion about their sexual problems, the result of which was to throw poor Boswell into a flurry of indecision, with temptation battling against moral qualms, and with a host of religious and literary witness on both sides.

I was quite in love with her tonight. She was sensible, amiable, and all that I could wish, except being averse to hymeneal rites. I told her I must have a concubine. She said I might go to whom I pleased. She has often said so. I have not insisted on my conjugal privilege since this month began, and were I sure that she was in earnest to allow me to go to other women without risk either of hurting my health or diminishing my affection for her, I would go. Thus I thought; but I was not clear, for though our Saviour did not prohibit concubinage, yet the strain of the New Testament seems to be against it, and the Church has understood it so. My passion, or appetite rather, was so strong that I was inclined to a laxity of interpretation, and as the Christian religion was not express upon the subject, thought that I might be like a patriarch; or rather, I thought that I might enjoy some of my former female acquaintances in London. I was not satisfied while in this loose state of speculation. I thought this was not like Isaak Walton or Dr Donne. But then the patriarchs, and even the Old Testament men who went to *harlots*, were devout. I considered indulgence with women to be like any other indulgence of nature. I was unsettled.[88]

Ten days later, on his way to London for another extended visit, Boswell was still worrying over the morality of concubinage. He explained in a letter to his friend Temple, 'that no man was ever more attached to his wife than I was, but that I had an exuberance of amorous faculties, quite corporeal and unconnected with affection and regard, and that my wife was moderate and averse to too much dalliance. Why might I not then be patriarchal...?' As soon as he got to London, he put the problem to his friend the Honourable Mrs Stuart, who seemed to agree with him: 'the difference between men and women was that men could have connections with women without having their hearts engaged. Women could not with men.' This psychological explanation of the double standard Boswell found comforting, but not conclusive. He was as usual tempted by whores, but kept away from them. But by April his good resolutions had failed again.[89]

By May Boswell was back in Edinburgh, and in October his son Alexander was born, for whom a wet-nurse was promptly introduced into the house. In November and December he visited a woman, apparently in her room in his house, who was probably Mrs Ross, the wet-nurse to his infant son. At the same time the tensions were rising again, and he was indulging in wilder drinking bouts, after one of which he came home and smashed all the dining-room chairs, throwing them at his poor wife. Moreover a new vice of all-night gambling at cards was growing steadily upon him.[90]

Back in London on his usual spring jaunt in March 1776, he renewed relations with an old lover, probably the actress Mrs Love who had been his mistress back in 1761–62, a proceeding which he justified to himself on the grounds that 'these are Asiatic satisfactions, quite consistent with devotion and with a fervent attachment to my valuable spouse.' Not content with Mrs Love, he relapsed into casual promiscuity made easier by alcohol, picking up cheap whores in the street. The main thing he was afraid of was catching venereal disease, 'which there could be no doubt was an injury to her.' On 1 April he had another encounter with a whore and indulged in a new perversion – 'a kind of licence I never had.' By early April he had inevitably contracted gonorrhoea again and was in the hands of doctors and surgeons, who promised to cure him quickly with a new injection.[91]

Back in Edinburgh again, Boswell was acutely depressed, and plunged into an endless round of alcoholic excess, all-night card playing, and promiscuous whoring. In the eight months from August 1776 to March 1777, he was hopelessly – sometimes helplessly – drunk twenty-six times, usually followed by terrible hangovers which made him quite incapable of business. His legal career in Edinburgh was getting nowhere, and he was profoundly bored by the vulgar provinciality of his job and his existence. His wife was not well. She gave birth to a son in November 1776, who soon died; had a miscarriage the following July; and gave birth to their second son James in September 1778. In 1777 she began to spit blood, first evidence of the tuberculosis which was to kill her twelve years later. Boswell's relations with his father remained strained, and until the old man died and he came into the estate, he was condemned to drudgery at the Edinburgh Bar, a situation which merely exacerbated his inherited tendency to bouts of profound melancholia. One cause for depression was a visit he paid to the dying David Hume on 21 August 1776. He hoped to find Hume reconciled to the Christian religion, only to discover that he was stoically resigned to the prospect of everlasting annihilation. This deeply upset Boswell, who had an intense fear of death and whose hold on religion was none too secure; after the visit he 'ranged awhile in the Old Town after strumpets, but luckily met with none that took my fancy.' At other times, alcohol clouded his discrimination, and anything female would serve the purpose: on 28 August he drunkenly ranged the streets, met with 'a comely fresh-looking girl, madly ventured to lie with her on the north brae of Castle Hill. I told my dear wife immediately.' A week later he discovered that the fresh-looking girl was a common whore, which made him afraid of gonorrhoea and obliged him to stop all sexual relations with his wife for fear of passing the infection on to her in her seventh month of pregnancy. Fortunately, this was a false alarm, but meanwhile he was falling half in love with the children's nurse living in the house, his wife's penniless orphan niece Annie Cunningham. In November his child was born, but he continued to slake his appetite with casual encounters after heavy drinking bouts. Once he took 'a plump hussy who called herself Peggy Grant' in a field behind the Register Office on 'one of the coldest nights I ever remember', and on another occasion in a mason's shed in St Andrew's Square.[92]

Always confessing to his long-suffering wife, always repenting, always relapsing, Boswell dragged through a wretched year. On 8 December even his wife had had enough. She insisted on reading his journal and found not only these brutish couplings with whores, which she could forgive if not understand, but evidence of love for her niece Annie Cunningham, which she could not. She 'told me she had come to a resolution never again to consider herself as my *wife*, though for the sake of her children and mine, as a *friend* she would preserve appearances.' But a week later, as usual, she relented and forgave him. On 7 April 1777, his last day in Edinburgh before a trip to see his father, he was drunk again and met an old 'dallying companion', now pregnant, who encouraged him to penetrate her. But he contented himself with 'a lesser lascivious sport', came home to bed, stripped, 'enjoyed my dear wife excellently', and at dawn set out on his journey.[93]

In September he set out on a trip to Ashbourne in Derbyshire to meet Dr Johnson, but on the way he lost no opportunity to feel the maids in every inn. At Liverpool he toyed with the chambermaid in the evening, and the next morning while she was taking his sheets off the bed he took further liberties, but was denied full penetration. At Leek he felt both the chambermaid and the maid who brought him tea, meanwhile reflecting: 'How inconsistent... is it for me to be making a pilgrimage to meet Dr Johnson, and licentiously loving wenches by the way.' Once in the presence of the doctor, however, the latter's intellectual conversation effectively replaced 'the pleasure of enjoying women.' On October 2, he was back home and lay with his wife, but she was 'justly displeased' on reading his journal to find out about his manhandling of the maids at the inns. That winter his wife was ill again and spitting blood, but she gave him satisfaction whenever she could, on 5, 6 and 17 December. She did it again on 5 January, but this brought on an alarming fit of spitting of blood in the middle of the night. Boswell, therefore, found solace with 'a fine wench' in a room in Blackfriars Wynd, and by February 1778 he had contracted gonorrhoea again. This was the twelfth time in his life, the second since his marriage in 1769 and the first in five years. As he left for London on 12 March, he noted that when they parted 'my wife having had reason to be offended with me, we were at present in a state of coolness.'[94]

In London he renewed his acquaintance with the actress Mrs Love, his old mistress of sixteen years before, and now in her late fifties. As soon as the doctors declared him fit again, he pressed her to sleep with him, and she reluctantly agreed, saying it was 'only to oblige me or be agreeable to me or some such phrase.' As they climbed into bed, Boswell asked, 'What harm in your situation?' to which she replied, 'to be sure. Or in yours, provided it does not weaken affection at home.' Although she was clearly a very sensible and decent woman, Boswell commented unkindly to his journal, 'What a slut, to be thus merely corporeal.' But two days running Mrs Love satisfied his physical needs, and sent him on his way with the much appreciated compliment that 'I was better than formerly.' When Boswell consulted his venereal doctor Sir John Pringle before he left London, the latter got him to admit his adventure with Mrs Love. Sir John advised him to 'add one more sin and deny it to Mrs Boswell. I insisted on preserving my truth.' Boswell might have been incapable of being a faithful husband, but he still prided himself on being an honest one.[95]

Back in Edinburgh in May 1778, all was once more forgiven, as usual, and for a while Boswell lived a chaste and sober life. On 15 September, his son James was born, but only after great difficulty. Mrs Boswell had suffered so severely that she expressed a wish that 'she might have no more. I was satisfied to think that she should not.' Despite this agreement, and despite

Margaret's obviously failing health, there are no signs that Boswell took any contraceptive precautions, either by using the condoms with which he had been so familiar before his marriage or by the practice of withdrawal. Before Margaret was fit for sex again, Boswell was already sneaking off to a house in the suburb of Portsburgh, where he had found a complaisant and, he hoped, disease-free widow woman. On 11, 19, and 21 October he resumed relations with his wife. But the occasions were rare, occurring not at all in November and only twice in December and three times in January. Boswell, therefore, filled in the gaps by visits to Portsburgh, although on one occasion he had an unwelcome surprise. He had slept with his wife on 25 January 1779 and had visited Portsburgh on the 29th. But his appetite was so whetted that he was back on the doorstep at Portsburgh early the next morning between 7 and 8 a.m. Boswell's staccato notes tell the story: 'Tedious waiting for the door to open. Found man in closet. Wonderful presence of mind. Bade him to be at it. The man went off. I was going, but was allured back, and twice.'[96]

Boswell's record of the annual jaunt to London in the spring is very incomplete, but he must have been fairly chaste, for he slept with his wife the first and second day after his return home in late May. On 7 July, however, he visited a brothel called 'The Pleasance', and on the eighth came home dead drunk and was put to bed by the patient Margaret. On the ninth he was relieved to find he had not contracted disease from his visit to the brothel, but his subsequent forced abstinence from relations with his wife made her guess what had happened, and she forced him to confess. 'I was sorry for it. She was very good,' and they made it up in bed, although Margaret was angry a few days later when she found that Boswell had been cold sober when he made his unfortunate visit. He also confessed to his visits to the obliging widow at Portsburgh, but Margaret again forgave him, a forgiveness once more sealed in bed. On 15 July Boswell noted: 'I vowed fidelity. . . . It is amazing how callous one may grow as to what is wrong by the practice of it.'[97]

The autumn and winter of 1779–80 was a happy time for the Boswells. Boswell was in good health and spirits, reasonably sober, busy at his legal work, and entirely faithful, except 'only once with a coarse Dulcinea, who was perfectly safe.' By early December Margaret was pregnant again, and they slept together twenty-one times in the three months from 13 December to 14 March, despite Margaret's increasing coughing and spitting of blood. Possibly their common anxiety about the prospect of her early death may have drawn them closer; possibly the progress of the disease may have stimulated Margaret's libido; possibly the fact that she was already pregnant made her more willing to satisfy her husband's desires. In April, however, Boswell lapsed again into heavy drinking, and on the tenth he staggered through the streets of Edinburgh and 'dallied with 10 strumpets.... I told my valuable spouse when I came home. She was good humoured and gave me excellent beef-soup which lubricated me and made me feel well.' The child Elizabeth was born on 13 June 1780, and the last time Boswell slept with Margaret before the birth was 21 May. Thereafter he was on his own, and an assignation with a black prostitute a week after the birth was followed by another slight attack of venereal disease. The rest of the year was a gloomy period of melancholia, drunkenness, and whoring, which apparently ended with yet another mild dose of gonorrhoea. However on 28 December 'at night when in bed with my dear wife, I was wonderfully free from gloom, and trusting to Mr Wood's opinion that I had no infection, I prevailed upon her to allow me to enjoy her.' He then rounded out the old year triumphantly by sleeping with her on the three following nights.[98]

The spring of 1781 found Boswell back in London to renew the acquaintance of Dr Johnson, Sir Joshua Reynolds, Edmund Burke and his other literary and artistic friends. But their conversation was not enough to keep him happy, and he could not resist pursuing a variety of street girls, until once again he caught gonorrhoea. With his passion for confession, he confided his troubles to his old friend the Honourable Mrs Stuart 'and was calmly consoled.' Returned to Edinburgh, and presumably cured, he must have resumed relations with his wife, for she miscarried again in October, and was for a long time very ill as the tubercular symptoms got steadily worse. His misery, fear and sexual frustration drove Boswell back into the streets and backyards of Edinburgh, despite his own clear-headed self-appraisal: 'I am quite sensual, and that, too, not exquisitely, but rather swinishly.' On 18 February 1782 he sank to a new low of alcoholic and sexual debauchery, and he confessed on 28 February that 'I am really in a state of constant, or at least daily, excess just now. I must pull the reins. But I feel my dull insignificance in this provincial situation.' The next day his wife read the (now missing) account of the debauch on 18 February and for the second time in her life told her husband that 'all connection between her and me was now at an end, but that she would contrive to live with me only for decency's sake and for the sake of her children.' Less than a fortnight later, however, all was forgiven, and they made it up in bed.[99] Their shared fears about Margaret's health united them, and they slept together twenty-seven times between December 1781 and April 1782.

But Boswell was incorrigible, and in April slunk back to the whores, giving him symptoms which for a time made him think he had caught gonorrhoea once again. By the end of the month, he felt sufficiently reassured to sleep with Margaret again – 'Wife wonderfully good' – and in May he tried to pull himself together and keep off both the bottle and the whores. But by June he had lapsed again, largely because his wife was ill and spitting blood more than ever. In late July there was a remission in the disease, and Boswell and Margaret slept together seven times in nineteen days. 'It was a renovation of felicity', but it did not last. So they drifted through the next six months, Margaret now rallying and eagerly renewing sexual relations, and now sinking, Boswell faithful and sober for a while, and then setting out on one of his drunken sprees in pursuit of Edinburgh whores.[100]

His father's death on 30 August 1782 transformed Boswell's life, since he at last came into his substantial inheritance, and was also freed from the psychological burden of this stern, forbidding father, who regarded him as a good-for-nothing fool and wastrel. Two days later Boswell tried to sleep with Margaret, but was checked by the thought, 'What! When he who gave you being is lying a corpse?' Once the old man's body was safely underground, however, Boswell's spirits rose, and despite Margaret's constant coughing and spitting blood, he slept with her eight times between 9 September and 4 October. In February 1783, he could tell himself that he had been sober for over seven months – in fact, ever since his father died.[101] If only temporarily, a great psychological weight had been lifted off him by his father's death.

After 1783 the story now goes blank for two years until 1785, when Boswell was on another of his spring visits to London. There he struck up with a 'pleasing and honest' girl, Betsy Smith, of whom he became very fond. On one occasion they visited a friend of hers and made it a threesome: 'I insisted she should repeat the Lord's Prayer. Strange mixture. Wondrous fondness.' Two days later, 'Something not right appeared', and once again poor Boswell was in the hands of doctors, swallowing sulphurated pills and mercury pills and confined to his rooms. So concerned was he about Betsy that he paid 10s 6d to get her admitted to St Thomas's Hospital, but the girl was unhappy there, and soon went home to resume her normal career as a prostitute. 'I told her I was ashamed, but I loved her.'[102]

In the autumn and early winter of 1785, Boswell was again in London and, despite Sir Joshua Reynolds' warning, in November he became the lover of a notorious but fashionable woman, Mrs Rudd. He returned to Edinburgh on 28 December, and in the first eight days of January he slept with his wife six times. But in February he was back in London for a long stay and was a regular visitor to Mrs Rudd. During this year in London, Boswell at last tried – and failed – to establish himself at the English Bar. By July it was clear even to him that his career as a lawyer in London had no future. No one would give him a brief, and anyway he was totally ignorant of English law and made no serious effort to learn it. The next three years were ones of great misery, as Boswell busied himself mostly in London collecting materials for his *Life of Johnson*, while harassed by poverty, deeply distressed at the relentless progress of his wife's tuberculosis which was finally reaching the terminal stage, and drinking heavily. On 17 March 1788, Margaret said to him on one of his now rare visits north, 'O Mr Boswell, I fear I'm dying.' Ten months later in January 1789, she finally died alone, while Boswell was away in London in a typically foolish and hopeless effort to carve out a political career for himself by attaching himself to the entourage of the cruel and tyrannical Lord Lonsdale. Before her death he had explained his behaviour to himself: 'I sometimes upbraid myself for leaving her, but tenderness should yield to the active engagements of ambitious enterprise.'[103]

His wife's death, his failure to make a career either as a lawyer in London or as a politician, and the death of Dr Johnson all deeply depressed Boswell, and the years after 1789 are ones of increasing misery and degradation. In London in 1789, he entered into a liaison with 'C', a beautiful woman of fashion. But, as usual, when he was dealing with women of his own class, he sometimes suffered from impotence. The first encounter was a 'delicious night'. Two days later he returned home dead drunk and staggered out again into the night in pursuit of 'C', only to be fetched back home by his young son James. The next night went badly, 'with love and wine oppressed'. He was 'weakly deficient; only one; ineffectual wishes.' Although one day later the familiar indications of infection reappeared (probably the disease was now chronic, so that 'C' may not have been responsible), the liaison lasted through December. But on 21 December, Boswell dreamed of his late wife and awoke in tears: 'It seemed to me impossible that I could ever again love a woman except merely as gratifying my senses.' And yet he thought that there remained the faint chance that he might yet discover 'a sensible, good-tempered woman of fortune' to make a second wife. He consulted his old friend Temple, who in view of 'my warm propensities', thought that 'a contract with any decent woman' was 'an insurance against some very imprudent connection.'[104]

But no such paragon appeared, and Boswell became a habitual drunken lecher, a familiar figure staggering through the less reputable streets of London. Despite increasing urethric trouble, once causing total stricture necessitating surgical intervention, his sexual virility remained unimpaired – in June he visited a new girl three times in the course of a single day – but he became more and more reckless, and the attacks of gonorrhoea more frequent. To whet his now jaded palate, he once 'tried an experiment on three', although he is careful not to explain what the experiment was. Three years later, in September 1793, his friend Temple again advised him to marry, as the only way to sober him up. But he warned Boswell that any wife 'would be very unhappy with a man of such a disposition and such a life as I was.' So Boswell continued his dissolute ways, although now at rarer intervals, until the end came in May 1795, when he fell ill and died of a tumour in the bladder, probably the result of the spread of urinary tract infection. One can reasonably speculate whether the repeated ingestion of mercury pills to cure his bouts of gonorrhoea may not have contributed to his mental deterioration, while his early death was almost certainly caused ultimately by the disease.

ii. Conclusions

A man plagued by inherited manic depression, an evident failure as a husband, a father and a lawyer, driven by a lust for female flesh that he was unable to control, constantly more inebriated than was seemly, Boswell nevertheless had two extraordinary gifts. The first was for making friends, and when he died the Shakespearean editor Malone remarked, 'I ... now miss and regret his noise and his hilarity and his perpetual good humour.'[105] The second was his passionate introspective honesty, which makes his notes and diary perhaps a more revealing record of a man's life than any other of any time or any age. We now know Boswell, with all his faults, better than we know any man who has ever lived. Sometimes narcissistic, sometimes moralistic and guilt-ridden, sometimes a device to drive away his ever-threatening melancholia, the record served a variety of purposes. But above all, it carries the ring of truth, even though the final version is a polished literary product, often written up after the event from rough jottings taken down at the time. It was Boswell's greatest (and only) legacy to posterity, and he knew it. From it he quarried his published works, his account of General Paoli of Corsica, the journal of his tour of the Scottish Highlands with Dr Johnson, and his great biography of the latter. The recent discovery and publication of these records has at last brought him the fame that largely eluded him in life.

There can be little doubt that the liberation of Boswell's libido was caused by his rejection of the strict Calvinist upbringing of his youth and his rapid passage through Methodism and Catholicism into scepticism and then to a somewhat lukewarm Anglican Episcopalianism. He continued to feel guilt, embedded in him from his Calvinist past, particularly noticeable in his rejection of masturbation, which was the deepest area of conflict between Calvinism and his sexual urges during his adolescence. The result was that his attitude to his sexual behaviour oscillated wildly between those of Cotton Mather and Casanova, between lacerating self-reproach and swaggering machismo.

His main problem, with which he wrestled all his life, was his failure to link *Eros* and *Agape*: lust and love. It was a problem that did not bother him very much so long as he was a bachelor, but after his marriage in 1769 it became acute. He was deeply attached to his wife, and as late as 1776 could tell himself, 'I could not have been so happy in marriage with any other woman as with my dear wife.' She in her turn loved him, and suffered with extraordinary patience and good humour his habitual sexual infidelity, his growing alcoholism, and his growing passion for all-night gambling. On the other hand, as she frankly explained to him on 8 March 1775, she could not fully satisfy his sexual appetites, which may well have been partly a cause not only of his whoring, but also of his drowning his frustrations in alcohol and gambling. But other, perhaps more important, causes were his congenital manic-depressive melancholia, which was exacerbated by the open contempt of his father, his sense of failure as a professional man and as an author, his hatred of his job as a lawyer at the Scottish Bar and his disgust at the vulgar provincialism of Edinburgh society in comparison with the glittering intellectual circles in which he moved in London. Dr Johnson probably had Boswell in mind when he generalized that 'Melancholy and otherwise insane people are always sensual; the misery of their minds naturally enough forces them to recur for comfort to their bodies.' Boswell certainly pursued whores most avidly in his depressive troughs, and when his sense of guilt was anaesthetized by alcohol. By pursuing only the cheapest whores, with the consequent near certainty of disease, it almost looks as if he were deliberately seeking to punish himself for his sensuality.

It seems likely that what with her prolonged illness, her pregnancies, her miscarriages and her generally low libido, Margaret was for considerable periods something of a sexual disappointment to Boswell. He may have been thinking of her when he remarked in 1777, 'I have my own private notions as to modesty, of which I would only value the appearance: for unless a woman has amorous heat, she is a dull companion, and to have amorous heat in elegant perfection, the *fancy* should be warmed with lively ideas.' The only solution, and one which came easily to him, was to dissociate sexual desire and affection altogether, as two totally different human passions. He had always treated women as purely sexual objects, so this presented no problem to him. An even more extreme position on the issue was advanced on high theoretical grounds by his friend Lord Monboddo, who 'would not allow a philosopher to indulge in women as a pleasure, but only as an evacuation; for he said that a man who used their embraces as a pleasure would soon have that enjoyment as a business, than which nothing could make one more despicable.'[106] Boswell had an uneasy feeling that he might fall into that category.

What bothered Boswell most was guilt about his own infidelity to his wife, and he sought advice on the subject wherever he could find it, from his friend Temple, from the Honourable Mrs Stuart, who agreed with him, and from Dr Johnson, who took a stern moral line against adultery in any form. He tried to think through the problem rationally, but never succeeded. Once he mused: 'I thought of my valuable wife with the highest regard and warmest affection, but had a confused notion that my corporeal connection with whores did not interfere with my love for her. Yet I considered that I might injure my health, which there could be no doubt was an injury to her.'[107] This question of whether his infidelity to his wife was morally acceptable was one which always worried Boswell, and he never did resolve it to his satisfaction. On the other hand, unlike many other eighteenth-century husbands, he was scrupulous in keeping away from her when there was any fear that he might have contracted venereal disease.

The other two areas of guilt concerned the seduction of young virgins and married women. Despite his fantasy proposal to Rousseau for the use of a series of young girls of low birth, later to be married off to peasants, he was in fact unusual for his class and his time for never, so far as one can tell, attempting to seduce a virgin. In 1766 he boasted, justifiably, about 'my principle of never debauching an innocent girl.'[108]

He was always very uneasy about sexual relations with married women. Mrs Jean Heron threw herself at him, but he felt very guilty about his conduct, and followed Dr Johnson's advice to keep away from her in future. His liaison with Mrs Dodds he did not regard as adultery, since her husband had left her and was living with another woman. His sudden assault on the pregnant wife of the Potsdam guardsman seriously upset him for a while. His liaison with Girolama Piccolomini he excused on the grounds that all

Italian upper-class women were married off against their will by their parents, and it was the custom of the country for them to take lovers. Indeed, it is clear from Boswell's journals that in the high aristocratic circles of continental Europe, especially in Germany and north Italy, where the arranged marriage was still the norm, it was now as socially accepted for wives to take lovers as it was for husbands to take mistresses. The jealous monopoly of female honour, the double standard of the traditional patriarchal society, had collapsed in these circles in the mid-eighteenth century. Among the gentry of Calvinist Scotland, however, much stricter standards still prevailed.

The final area in which Boswell's sexual life was governed by a clear set of principles was concerned with the treatment of any possible illegitimate offspring. Mrs Heron assured him that she was sterile, which relieved part of his anxieties; when Peggy Doig produced a child of his, he made arrangements for the lying-in and for its maintenance with a foster-mother. When Mrs Lewis discussed the possibility with him, he reassured her that he would meet his obligations; and when Mrs Dodds gave birth to Sally, we have no reason to suppose that he did not also take responsibility for her upkeep, although she probably did not live long. With Signora Piccolomini, he was careful to use a condom. In this respect he was like most of the great aristocrats of his period, who normally took care of their illegitimate children, although there were exceptions, such as Lord Kinnaird, whose bastard daughter Boswell met in Edinburgh plying her trade as a prostitute.

On the other hand, he was very strict in refusing to treat them as social equals to legitimate children, the way his friend the tenth Lord Pembroke treated his. When Lord Chancellor Thurlow invited Boswell and his daughter to a musical soirée with his lordship's illegitimate daughter Kitty, Boswell was careful to decline to go since 'I have always disapproved of putting them on a level with those lawfully born.'[109]

There is a good deal of evidence from Boswell's diary that most women of the period accepted the double standard with resignation. Even in eighteenth-century pseudo-Calvinist Scotland these principles were more or less accepted. Boswell mused that 'an abandoned profligate may have a notion that it is not wrong to debauch my wife, but . . . if I catch him making an attempt, . . . I will kick him downstairs or break his bones.' But he regarded his own case as somehow different. Mrs Boswell knew about Boswell's affairs before she married him; she several times advised him to satisfy his sexual appetites with a concubine, and although she was often disturbed when she found out about his amours, she always forgave him.[110]

On his side, although he was constantly sexually unfaithful, he never lied to her, never infected her, and was usually prompt to tell her about his innumerable lapses. Given his nature, it was the only fidelity he could offer her, and he was remarkably scrupulous in using her as his confessor. As a result, she realized that at bottom he loved her as he loved no other woman, and she was prepared to tolerate his almost insatiable promiscuity on condition that it never spilled over into any hint of love for another woman. Right up to the end, as she was slowly being consumed by tuberculosis, she continued to provide him with what sexual pleasure she could, which sometimes fully satisfied his needs. Boswell's diary is the work of a man obsessed with himself and his feelings, who is consequently not much interested in how others felt. But despite the agonizing pregnancies, the frequent miscarriages, the slow wasting of her lungs, and the often intoxicated condition of her husband, there are indications in her husband's notes that Mrs Boswell occasionally enjoyed, as well as loyally fulfilled, her wifely duties.

What other general conclusions can be drawn from Boswell's extra-ordinary story? It is obvious that he was in very many ways, not least in his egotistical absorption in his own affairs, a most unusual man. But he moved not unsuccessfully through the noble, intellectual and professional society of western Europe, and his adventures shed a dazzling searchlight upon sexual attitudes and practices among these classes. Boswell's sexual drive was clearly very different from that of either Pepys or Byrd. Pepys was content to kiss and fondle women's lips and breasts for hours on end without orgasm. Byrd's sexual drive was relatively low, and even in the years of high sexual excitement he at all times controlled his impulses and avoided the danger of disease. Boswell's appetite was stronger and grosser. His main need was frequent and violent sexual intercourse without preliminary foreplay or even conversation. He was consequently especially attracted to the cheapest of whores, and he was liable to find himself impotent at the first sexual encounter on the rare occasions when he had to deal with women of his own social class.

Boswell was not a reticent man, and he poured out the details of his sexual life not only in his notes and journals but also in correspondence and conversation with his close friends like Temple and with the three men he most admired: Dr Johnson, Rousseau, and General Paoli. No-one seems to have been particularly shocked by his indiscretions and infidelities, or by the grossness of his appetite. Dr Johnson advised chastity; General Paoli and Temple marriage, and Rousseau a mystical view of sexual passion which would exclude his brutish couplings.

Although Boswell found it difficult to discover a regular genteel mistress in London, the level of marital infidelity among the upper classes of Europe seems to have been fairly high, as many other reminiscences confirm. Those married women who refused him were not shocked by his advances, but merely put off by his lack of tact, and a few, like Mrs Heron, Signora Piccolomini and Mrs Dodds, simply threw themselves into his arms. Some lower-class women were equally receptive, like the wife of the Potsdam guard and a woman at a Swiss inn who offered to accompany Boswell to Scotland. But pregnancy was an ever-present risk, which is why married women, and especially pregnant ones, were so much sought after, by both Pepys in the seventeenth century and Boswell in the eighteenth, although the latter always felt guilty.

The greatest risk from promiscuous sexual activity in the eighteenth century was clearly gonorrhoea, which Boswell contracted at least seventeen times, possibly more. Boswell's friends found these repeated attacks no more than a joke, although they certainly warned him to take more care. When his father complained of his son's recurrent infections to a Scottish lady, Mrs Montgomerie-Cunningham, she reassured him, 'telling him that what occasioned it was now become quite common.' Not even women took venereal disease very seriously any more, despite the fact that the medical results were quite serious. The treatment was almost as dangerous as the disease, since the most reliable cure was the ingestion of mercury, itself a dangerous poison, the other remedy being strict diet and sweating in a sweating-tub (plate 39). On the other hand, syphilis does not seem to have been a serious threat. The ubiquity of gonorrhoea and the rarity of syphilis seems to have been an established feature of England at least by the late sixteenth century.[111]

7 CONCLUSIONS

Various general conclusions about upper-class sexual behaviour and attitudes in eighteenth-century England may be drawn from these six case histories. In the first place, tolerant although at this time society was towards venereal disease, there were limits to what some wives would put up with. Mrs Boswell was far more long-suffering than other wives of their husband's venereal infections. In 1776 Mr Thrale showed his wife a greatly enlarged testicle, a condition he tried to explain away as the result of bruising when he jumped out of a carriage some months before. Mrs Thrale refused to believe this improbable story, and she immediately recalled her father's remarks when she first got engaged to Mr Thrale thirteen years back. 'If you marry that scoundrel he will catch the pox, and for his amusement set you to make his poultices,' he warned her. She told herself that 'this is now literally made out, and I am preparing poultices like he said and fomenting this elegant ailment every night and morning for an hour together on my knees.' She recalled that her husband had had a previous infection seven years before, which was cured by a surgeon for fifty guineas, and comforted herself with the thought that 'he has, I am pretty sure, not given it to me.' When the truth finally came out that the cause was indeed venereal disease and not the jump from the carriage, she commented bitterly. 'What need of so many lies about it? I am sure I care not, so he recovers to hold us all together.' But it is clear that she did care, and was deeply offended. Similarly, the famous actress Mrs Siddons took it very badly in 1792 when her husband gave her the pox. After her recovery, 'an indignant melancholy sits on her fine face, . . . ; she is all resentment.'[112]

In view of the prevalence of the disease, and the pain and mental anguish that it caused, it is hardly surprising to find that the three most common subjects in the advertisement columns of eighteenth-century periodicals were cures for venereal disease, cosmetics and books – in that order. Take, for example, two fashionable London newspapers for 1785, *The Morning Chronicle* and *The Whitehall Evening Post*. They advertised aphrodisiacs for the jaded, like 'Hunter's Restorative Balsamic Pills,' described as 'the first medicine in the world of restoring and invigorating the constitutions of persons weakened by a course of dissipated pleasures, or indeed by any other causes'; or 'The Bath Restorative', for 'those who have been almost worn out by women or wine', those who 'are not early happy in their conjugal embraces, . . . and those who have impaired their constitution by the act of self-pollution.' They also advertised the addresses of obstetricians who would take care of 'ladies whose situation requires a temporary retirement.' But mostly they advertised nostrums for venereal disease, such as 'Leake's Genuine Pills', 'The Specific', 'Lisbon Diet Drink', 'Dr Solander's Vegetable Juice' and 'Dr Keyser's Pills'.[113]

It is surprising to discover how difficult it was in the late eighteenth century, a hundred years after their introduction, to buy condoms as a prophylactic against venereal disease. Mrs Phillips' shop in London seems to have been the only place where Boswell could buy them without difficulty. He also sometimes expected his London whores to carry them, but they rarely, if ever, did.[114] In all the other capitals of Europe, he drew a blank, which was why he so constantly caught venereal disease. He did have one on him in Siena, however, which he used, interestingly enough, for contraceptive rather than prophylactic purposes during his liaison with Signora Piccolomini. By the 1760s Boswell knew all about condoms and their uses, unlike Pepys in the 1660s who was wholly ignorant of their very existence, and unlike Byrd in 1718–19 who knew about them but does not seem to have used them. On the other hand, there is no sign that Boswell used them for contraceptive purposes in relations with his own wife, despite her weakening physical condition and unwillingness to bear any more children after the first three.

Finally, the journals of Byrd and Boswell throw a flood of light on the sexual underworld of eighteenth-century London. Beginning at the top, there was always a chance of finding a respectable married woman with whom to strike up an affair, although they seem to have been in short supply. Failing that, there was the *demi-monde* of the theatre, whose actresses, then as today, seem to have led more sexually permissive lives than the rest of the population. Then there were the milliners and shirt and ruffle makers, some of whom seem to have been willing to provide occasional sexual services as well as shirts and ruffles in return for their monthly retainer. Below them there were high-class houses of assignation, like that of Mrs Smith in Queen Street, where expensive call-girls could be had. There were also both general and specialized brothels, which neither Byrd nor Boswell ever visited, like the all-black one Lord Pembroke told Boswell about in 1775 (although by then it also had some white girls) (plate 40).[115] At the bottom of the ladder of the professionals there were the common street whores, clustering along the Strand or in St James's Park, who could be picked up and taken into a coach or down a dark alley for a few minutes, or to a bagnio for a bath, dinner, and a night of pleasure. And finally, there were the poor amateurs, the ubiquitous maids, waiting on masters and guests in lodgings, in the home, in inns; young girls whose virtue was always uncertain and was constantly under attack (plate 35). These last were the most exploited, and most defenceless, of the various kinds of women whose sexual services might be obtained by a man of quality in eighteenth-century England. There were also the long-term mistresses taken on to satisfy the needs of men before marriage, like Boswell before 1769; or men financially unable to marry, like Sylas Neville; or widowers, like Pepys after 1671. Some of them were educated and respectable women, like Pepys' Mary Skinner; others were lower-class girls who had been seduced and abandoned, and were therefore more or less unmarriageable, like Neville's Sarah Bradford; others were mere sluts, like some with whom Boswell lived before his marriage. Increasingly, however, it was possible for rich men to discover for themselves well-educated and attractive women of the middling ranks, whose fathers had gone bankrupt. None of the six men in these case stories found such girls, but other evidence shows that they were not hard to find by the late eighteenth century.

Almost all aspects of the late eighteenth-century upper-class sexual scene are displayed in a caricature by Rowlandson of 1786 (plate 33). A shipload of pretty, well-dressed but impecunious girls anxious to find a rich husband or lover have just arrived on the dockside, presumably in Calcutta or Bombay, and are being inspected for purchase by wealthy nabobs and by an agent for the Governor. In the foreground are goods unloaded from the ship: one box of surgeon's instruments and seven casks of 'Leake's Pills', the best-known cure for gonorrhoea; a case of books labelled 'For the Amusement of military Gentlemen,' and containing such titles as *Fanny Hill* and *Female Flagellants*; a large bale of condoms labelled 'Mrs Phillips (the original inventor), Leicester Fields, London. For the Use of the Supreme Council'; and finally a case marked with crossed birch-rod bundles and labelled 'British Manufacture'. In the 'Warehouse for Unsaleable Goods' lie damaged barrels with broken bottles of 'Hunter's Restorative', the well-known stimulant for jaded sexual appetites. Here in one picture are young girls for sale, medicine against venereal disease, condoms, pornographic literature, aphrodisiacs, and instruments to satisfy the peculiarly English taste for sado-masochism.

CHAPTER 12

Plebeian Sexual Behaviour

When dealing with the sexual behaviour of the lower orders, the historian is forced to abandon any attempt to probe attitudes and feelings, since direct evidence does not exist. He is obliged to deduce such things from legal records, the comments of literate contemporaries, and the stark demographic facts which can be laboriously extracted from parish registers of marriages and baptisms. Since in this area practice only faintly corresponded to the ideal norms of the society, almost the only indicator available to the historian is the type and amount of extra-marital sexual activity, either before marriage or outside it altogether. Among the plebs, sex within marriage – which is where most sex inevitably took place – is a world closed to the historian. This is the reason why a chapter on plebeian sexual behaviour is almost exclusively devoted to areas which by the norms of the day were generally regarded as sinful. If it can be demonstrated that there were significant changes in the type and amount of such theoretically deviant behaviour, then it may perhaps be possible to make some deductions about changes in attitudes towards sexuality among the lower orders of society. Thus evidence can be found for a possible decline in pre-marital and extra-marital sexual activity from the sixteenth to the early seventeenth century and for a certain and a very striking increase in the late seventeenth and eighteenth centuries. Since there is no correlation with the rise and fall in the age of marriage, which one might suppose would have affected the amount of pre-marital sexual activity, the explanation of the growth first of tighter and then of very much laxer sexual behaviour must lie in changing attitudes.

As had been seen, in the middle ages, the institution of marriage was very imperfectly controlled by the Church, which meant that the lower classes were allowed a wide degree of freedom in their sexual arrangements. In the fourteenth century, betrothal followed by intercourse was recognized by the Church as a binding marriage contract; children born after betrothal but before marriage were usually recognized as legitimate; bigamy was common and almost impossible to detect, given the absence of formal marriage registers, and clandestine marriages were equally common.[1] The only comprehensive evidence for sexual behaviour in a pre-modern village comes from an area which unfortunately has certain features that may make it less than typical of the Christian West. It concerns Montaillou, a tiny village high up in the French foothills of the Pyrenees between about 1300 and 1320. Besides its isolation, the village is also atypical since it was full of Catharist heretics, who seem to have been more tolerant of sexual deviation than orthodox Catholics. Even so, it comes as a surprise to find that at least ten per cent of all couples in the village were living in unsanctified concubinage, while there was also a great deal of casual fornication by bachelors, spouses and widows. The production of an illegitimate child was no bar to the subsequent marriage of a girl. On the whole, however, the sexual monopoly rights of marriage were respected, and the amount of adultery was small, especially by wives, who were fearful of the vengeance of their husbands and their clan. Sexual propositioning, usually but not always by the male, was direct and to the point, according to the stenographic record of the peasants' confessions. As expressed in the sanitized Latin record of vernacular speech, it seems to have boiled down to a direct question and answer: 'I want to lie with you.' 'All right.' This was a world in which the sinfulness of such behaviour had not yet fully penetrated the consciousness of the peasants, partly because the village priest was himself the leading Don Juan of the neighbourhood, partly through ignorance, and partly because of heretical ideas.

In the most remote areas of the highland north extremely ancient customs may have lasted well into the sixteenth century. In the middle of the fifteenth century an Italian cleric and diplomat (later Pope Pius II), travelling from Scotland to England through Northumberland, spent the night in a village just across the Border. After dinner all the men and the children withdrew to a fortified tower, leaving the Italian and all the women to take their chance with Scottish bandits. They justified the exclusion of the women from the safety of the tower on the grounds that the worst that could happen to them was rape, which they did not count as a wrong. When the Italian retired to sleep, he was accompanied to his room (which was bare except for straw on the floor) by two young women, who proposed to sleep with him if he wished, which he found to be a customary gesture of hospitality to an honoured guest. The Italian refused the offer, for fear of having his throat cut in the night while still in a condition of mortal sin. If this account is to be believed, in Northumberland in the mid-fifteenth century men did not prize the chastity of their women, and women offered their favours freely to strangers, both attitudes which have been observed in several very primitive societies in other parts of the world.[2]

The failure of the medieval church to impose either its traditional hostility to sex except for the purpose of procreation, or its own religious ceremony as the one binding ritual to legitimate a sexual union, combined with the habitually casual ways of the population to make the medieval approach to marriage and sex very different from that of seventeenth-century England. The introduction of registers of births, marriages and deaths in 1538 was evidence of a tightening of both lay and clerical controls over the private lives of the population. The missionary activity of the Protestant Church over the following century did more than bring the institution of marriage under effective regulation by the public authorities, apparently for the first time; it also brought Puritan attitudes to sexuality to the attention of the public, and enforced them with the full sanctions of Church and state.

A final general observation that needs to be made is that for the poor sexual privacy was a luxury which they neither possessed nor could have desired. Living conditions were such that among the bulk of the population before the second half of the nineteenth century, whole families lived, worked, ate and slept in one or two rooms. In Leeds in the early nineteenth century, the typical cottage was fifteen feet square. In Nottingham, an average of five persons occupied tiny three-floor boxes, the cellar for artisan working space, the ground floor for living and eating, and the upper floor for communal sleeping.[3] Under such conditions sexual privacy for parents, or for married children living at home, was impossible, and children from an early age must have been familiar with the sight and sounds of the physical act of love. Only in summer – and then only on a dry day – was sexual privacy obtainable out of doors in the fields and woods.

i. Courting Procedures

Courting customs are obviously closely related to the amount of pre-marital sex. In many parts of north-west Europe in the seventeenth and the eighteenth centuries, there was a general practice among the labouring classes of the type of intimate courting known as 'bundling.' Bundling meant paying court to a girl, in bed, in the dark, half naked. In Wales in the eighteenth century, the man retained 'an essential part of his dress', and the women had 'her underpetticoat fastened at the bottom by a sliding knot.' In America, as an extra precaution, a wooden board was often placed in the bed to divide the pair. This practice was apparently almost universal amongst the poor on the north-western fringes of Europe, in Wales, Scotland, Holland and Scandinavia in the eighteenth and even early nineteenth centuries, as well as in Germany, Switzerland and certain limited areas of France. In 1761 John Adams was prepared to state publicly that 'I cannot wholly disapprove of bundling', and it was certainly common all over New England in the eighteenth century, and still practised in New Jersey in 1816 and on Cape Cod in 1827.[4]

The conclusion seems inescapable that 'this pleasing but dangerous habit was probably imported from abroad.' The wide prevalence of this custom in eighteenth-century New England makes it hard to believe that it was not also fairly common in England itself, although the evidence on this point is scanty. The practice of lying clothed on a bed, talking and petting, which is what bundling in its simplest form amounts to, was certainly practised in seventeenth and eighteenth-century England. It is noticeable that when Thomas Turner was courting his second wife in 1765 – a very respectable girl – he twice spent all night with her, although he was shocked at a case of pre-nuptial conception in the village. On an early visit, he sat up with her until five in the morning, and on a second visit he stayed with her again till dawn – whether seated or lying down is not stated. Turner's courting methods strongly suggest that bundling – meaning at least all-night conversations – was then a current custom in Sussex. On finding the custom in Wales in 1804, William Bingley remarked that 'within the last few years [it] was scarcely even heard of in England', which suggests that it had existed in the eighteenth century.[5]

A possible economic rationale for the practice may have been the cost of providing fuel for warmth in the long winter nights in more than one room, but it had long since hardened into a custom with its own strict code of honour.[6] In Norway, as in Wales, it was particularly practised by the young unmarried servants in their dormitories, and their masters were obliged to tolerate it, whether they approved of it or not. As in many primitive societies, it was a custom which in the seventeenth century did not lead to much pregnancy. In Wales, 'the lower orders of people do actually carry on their love affairs in bed, and . . . they are carried on honourably.' In short, in the seventeenth century it was 'a practice ancient, general and carried on without difficulty.' It also made a good deal of sense. An all-night conversation allowed both parties to explore each other's minds and temperaments in some depth, while the physical propinquity provided a socially approved means of obtaining sexual satisfaction in the decade between maturity and marriage, and of experimenting in sexual compatibility with a series of potential spouses without running the risk of pregnancy and without commitment to marriage. In late nineteenth-century France, bundling involved prolonged kissing and body contact, often including masturbation of the girl by the boy, and more rarely vice-versa. But full sexual penetration during bundling was still very rare.[7]

The origins of bundling are lost in obscurity. It is therefore uncertain whether it is a folk custom of great antiquity which survived through the period of clerical repression of the sixteenth and seventeenth centuries and was revived again in the eighteenth. If so, it presumably led to abuses in an increasing but proportionately small number of cases as the result of a decline in the old moral conventions which had prohibited full sexual intercourse. It then disappeared in England and America, but not elsewhere, at the beginning of the nineteenth century under pressure from Evangelical religious reformers. Alternatively, it was a new practice which spread rapidly in the late seventeenth and eighteenth centuries because of the greater economic independence of young people afforded by the growth of cottage industry and because of a growing demand for affection and sexual attraction as a basis for marriage. It has been argued that in Switzerland in the eighteenth century the latter is the case, and that industrialization of the countryside by the putting-out system of cloth manufacture led to a great increase both in bundling and in consequent pregnancy. A contemporary there remarked that 'bundling gets to be looked on as a right and a freedom, and to be considered nothing sinful. Marriage is always the sequel to pregnancy.' Since it was now so much easier to earn a living and get married at an early age, parental control declined, girls were less protective of their virginity, and more willing to allow pre-nuptial favours to their suitors. Under either hypothesis, it is agreed that the result was a rapid rise in population, in the amount of bundling, in pre-nuptial pregnancies, in bastards, and in the proportion of beggarly poor.[8]

ii. Pre-nuptial Pregnancy

The most reliable indicator of the level of pre-marital chastity in a society without contraceptives is the proportion of first children who are born less than eight and a half months after marriage. The index of pre-marital conceptions is as good a guide to the realities of pre-marital sexual behaviour as the historian is likely to find, particularly if the trends are sufficiently clear.[9]

But before examining the facts, it is first necessary to establish exactly what the phenomenon means. If it is to leave evidence in the historical record of parish registers, pre-marital pregnancy must involve four distinct acts. There must be conception before the wedding, and since the chances of conception from a single random act of intercourse of a healthy young couple are only between two and four per cent, this must therefore probably be the result of several weeks, and perhaps several months, of unprotected intercourse. Secondly, it involves a marriage ceremony in a church after conception, normally, but not necessarily always, with the father of the unborn child. Thirdly, the pregnancy must run its course and produce a live infant; and fourthly, that infant must be baptized, and so be recorded. It is obvious that any one of these last three steps could fail to take place. If this definition is accepted, it is evident that bastardy is merely a sub-branch of pre-nuptial conception in which intercourse before marriage took place, the child was carried to term (and was baptized), but there was no marriage.

It is possible to construct a typology of pre-nuptial pregnancies, based on the motives which might lead a couple to follow all four stages. The first type is when there was a formal betrothal in front of witnesses, followed by regular cohabitation before the church ceremony, carried on with the full knowledge and consent of parents and the community. There can be no doubt that this was a normal custom among the poor in some parts of England at this period, and probably also in New England. It probably accounts for a considerable number of those pregnancies which occurred within four months of marriage. It should be remembered that many brides who were only one or even two months pregnant may well have been unaware of their condition. In any case, these are pre-nuptial conceptions which carried with them no stigma of shame or guilt. A variant on this type could occur when the parents were obstructing the marriage. The pair could then betroth themselves in secret, begin to sleep together, and then confront their parents with the necessity for consent, since the girl was pregnant.

The second main type was the seduction of the girl by the man, with or without a secret or even public promise of marriage. The man then tried to repudiate his promise but was forced to the altar by the pressure of parents, neighbours, clergy, magistrate and the threat of legal action. This type probably includes many of the marriages of girls who were seven to nine months pregnant, and was mostly a rural phenomenon, since in the cities these pressures were more easily evaded. Another variant of this type was the result of a plot by the girl to force the man to marry her by deliberately letting herself become pregnant, relying on these community pressures to force the man into marriage later on. The third main type was when a lower-class girl, often a servant, allowed herself to become the mistress of a rich man. When she got pregnant, her master would arrange to have her married off to a poor man, perhaps his own manservant, who would be paid handsomely to take her on and to accept the child as his own. Another variant of this type, reportedly quite common in a seventeenth-century French village, was when a peasant married a girl already pregnant by another man, merely in order to lay hands on her dowry of money and sheep.[10]

It is worth noting that in France in the eighteenth century, and therefore probably also in England, the pre-nuptial conception ratio for widows was five times higher than that for first brides. It is to be presumed that the reason for this enormous discrepancy is that the libido of widows had been aroused by their first marriage, and that they were therefore more willing than young virgins to risk pre-marital sex, since they enjoyed it and missed it more.[11] There are thus many possible motives for a pre-marital pregnancy, and any explanation of change in the proportion of all births must take these various possibilities into account and weigh their significance.

It has now been established that the level of recorded pre-nuptial pregnancies in England was low in the late sixteenth century and declined lower still in the seventeenth century, certainly well below twenty per cent, while scattered evidence suggests that it was even lower, below ten per cent, in New England (Graph 15).[12] During the first half of the eighteenth century, however, a startling change took place. The rate of recorded pre-nuptial pregnancies shot up, reaching over forty per cent in the last half of the century in many places on both sides of the Atlantic. From these figures one can only conclude that among the English and American plebs in the last half of the eighteenth century, almost all brides below the social elite had experienced sexual intercourse with their future husbands before marriage. By then pregnancy was preceding – if not actually causing – marriage, not marriage pregnancy. In 1730 the minister of Brewster, Massachusetts, attributed the rise of pre-nuptial pregnancies to 'a wicked practice of young people in their courtships.' Contemporaries were thus very well aware that things had changed. The only minor corrective is that the tightening up of marriage registration in 1754 may have given an artificial boost to the

PRENUPTIAL CONCEPTION RATIO

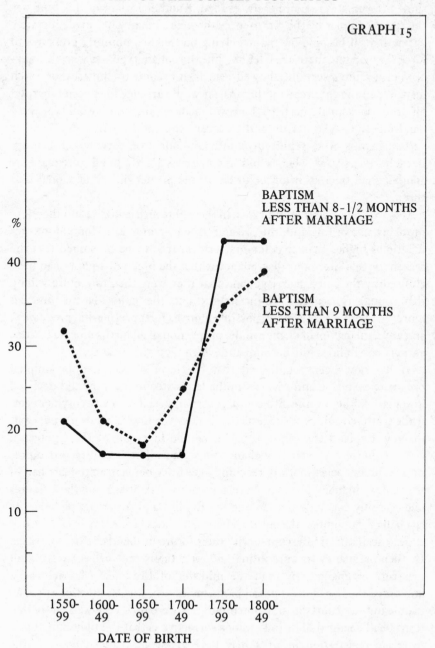

GRAPH 15

BAPTISM
LESS THAN 8-1/2 MONTHS
AFTER MARRIAGE

BAPTISM
LESS THAN 9 MONTHS
AFTER MARRIAGE

%

40

30

20

10

1550-
99

1600-
49

1650-
99

1700-
49

1750-
99

1800-
49

DATE OF BIRTH

English statistics, since previously some pregnant brides were married privately to avoid being publicly shamed.[13]

Francis Place remarked that 'want of chastity in girls was common' in late eighteenth-century London right up to the class of respectable small property owners, tradesmen and master craftsmen, and was not then regarded as a bar to marriage. By the time he was writing, however, in the 1820s, these practices were now confined to the daughters of wage-earners, journeymen and labourers, at the very bottom of the economic and social scale.[14] If Place is right, the continued rise of pre-nuptial conceptions (and illegitimacy) well into the early nineteenth century conceals a significant shrinkage of the social classes which were responsible for these statistics. More and more the respectable lower-middle class were rejecting the permissive sexual morals of the propertyless wage-earners, but the graph of pre-nuptial conceptions went on rising, owing to the great increase in the numerical size of the latter group.

The bare statistics can be fleshed out a little by the diaries of the Reverend William Cole of Bletchley, Buckinghamshire, and the Reverend John Skinner of Camerton, Somerset. In the one year 1766 the former baptized the son of the local blacksmith, whom he had married to his bride six months before; he married the pregnant maid of a local gentleman to a soldier in the Life Guards; and in a single day he married a pair, baptized their newborn baby and churched the mother, the last two rituals being carried out in the privacy of his parlour, despite the incongruity of performing a 'churching' in a private room. John Skinner, who in the early nineteenth century was rector of a large and disorderly colliery village, had to deal with a number of such situations. In the early 1800s there was an ugly scene in the church at the wedding of a girl very close to her delivery, when the groom refused to marry her unless the Overseers of the Poor gave him two guineas to do so, as a favour for getting the child off the poor rate. The blackmail was rejected and the groom was finally persuaded to go through with the ceremony. In 1823 a bride gave birth the same day as her marriage, and in 1830 Skinner married a pair of whom 'the bride was as round as a barrel', so that the christening was likely to occur during the honeymoon. On another occasion in 1831, when the bride of a miller had already given birth, the rector describes the occasion as 'after the Camerton mode'.[15] It is clear from these stories that a considerable number of these pre-nuptial pregnancies occurred long before the wedding, and therefore had nothing to do with any change of custom to cohabitation after the betrothal, but rather were caused by a breakdown of community controls on pre-marital sex.

iii. Illegitimacy

The evidence for illegitimacy is far less secure than that for pre-nuptial pregnancy since it may be affected by changes in the habits of unmarried women in practising primitive birth control, in procuring abortions, in encouraging infanticide, and in baptizing their bastards, as well as by changes in the habits of clergy both in agreeing to baptize children born out of wedlock and in recording them as illegitimate. The figures also, of course, fail to record as such the illegitimate offspring of married women. It is certain, therefore, that all the recorded levels of illegitimacy are underestimates of the reality, in some periods perhaps seriously so. In the seventeenth century, it is possible that many Puritan clergymen refused to baptize an illegitimate child, which would result in a lowering of the official figures. On the other hand, the growing indifference to organized religion among the poor in the eighteenth century and the growing indolence of the clergy make it most unlikely that there could have been any increase either in maternal desire for the baptism of their bastards or in clerical efficiency in recording them as such. If anything, one would expect the trend to be the other way, with clergymen, like the Reverend William Cole, acquiescing in a situation they deplored but could not control.[16] This suggests that the exceptionally low level of recorded bastardy in the seventeenth century may well be an underestimate, but that the striking increase in the eighteenth century probably reflects a real change, though it may well underestimate the new scale of the phenomenon.

There is only one reason why new legislation may have affected the recorded bastardy rate in the eighteenth century. A speaker in the debate in the House of Commons over the Clandestine Marriage Bill in 1753 explained how in his capacity as a country JP he was in the habit of dealing with pregnant girls brought before him by the parish officers. 'She names the father, generally some young country fellow in the neighbourhood. He is immediately sent for, and confesses his being the father. The consequence is, he must either agree to marry her or go to Bridewell. If he agrees to the first, I send them directly to church and they are presently married.' The whole matter was settled and the couple married within a matter of hours, thanks to the threat of prison under very harsh conditions, and the lack of opportunity for the man to run away. The post-1754 obligation to publish the banns for three weeks before the marriage must have made it very much easier for the father to flee the village and disappear, thus avoiding a quick shot-gun marriage and raising the rural bastardy rate. How important this new legislation was in practice in causing such a rise is at present quite impossible to evaluate.[17]

Bastardy, which is a sub-branch of pre-nuptial conceptions, also can be given a typology according to the circumstances of the conception. The first type was the result of the seduction of a girl by a fellow-servant or worker or neighbour, probably after a vague promise of marriage. When pregnancy occurred, the man repudiated the promise, if he had made one, and ran away. The second was the seduction of a girl, often a living-in maidservant, by somone of higher social status and in a position of authority over her, usually the master of the house, or one of his sons or friends. This could take place with or without a promise of marriage, the girl giving her consent for fear of losing her job. In this case, social custom made it impossible for any such promise to be honoured. If the girl became pregnant, she was either discharged or married off to another poor man who would accept her and her prospective child. The third, and rarest, type was the notoriously promiscuous girl who sooner or later became pregnant. She was liable to be repudiated and scorned by the community, and would be hard put to it to identify the father with any certainty.

It should be noted that in theory the same amount of pre-marital sexual intercourse will lead to the same aggregated amount of pre-nuptial conceptions and bastardy. Change in social conventions, moral attitudes and religious beliefs will alter the proportion, so that if bastards go up, pre-nuptial conceptions go down, and vice-versa. Thus it has been argued that in France the Counter-Reformation clergy successfully enforced marriage on pregnant couples, but were unable to stop the practice of sexual intercourse before marriage. Therefore, illegitimacy went down, and pre-nuptial conceptions went up in the seventeenth century.[18] Alternatively, there may be an increase of pre-marital sexual intercourse together with an increase in the repudiation of marriage. In this case, pre-nuptial conceptions and illegitimacy ratios will go up together, the latter being a deviant sub-category of the former, which is what happened in eighteenth-century England.

In the Elizabethan period the rural illegitimacy ratio had been running at the modest level of under four per cent. Between 1590 and 1660, however, the ratio fell steadily to the astonishingly low point of one half per cent at the height of the period of Puritan control, in the 1650s. It picked up a bit thereafter, but was still under two and a half per cent in the 1720s. It then took off, rising to four and a half per cent in the 1760s and over six per cent after 1780 (Graph 16)[19]; the explanation for the decline and the subsequent

ILLEGITIMACY RATIO

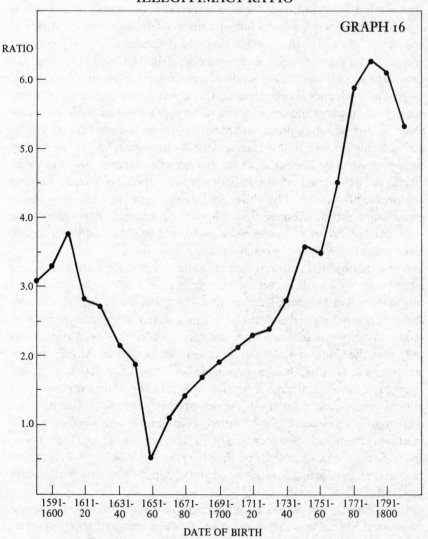

GRAPH 16

RATIO

DATE OF BIRTH

remarkable rise must be deferred until later. What should be noted, however, is that since for the majority of the population the average age of marriage was twenty-six to twenty-eight and rising, this evidence suggests that during the sixteenth, and especially the seventeenth centuries, most men must have exercised extraordinary sexual self-control during the first twelve to fourteen years of optimum male potency.

Nor is this all, for we now have reasonably good evidence to suggest that about a third of all births were not registered in baptismal registers before 1830, and that in London, whither so many unmarried mothers fled to have their babies in secrecy, non-registration in places ran as high as seventy per cent. It is not unreasonable to suppose that an abnormally high proportion of these unregistered births consisted of illegitimate children. If this is so, it means that all these figures for rural illegitimacy ratios need to be inflated significantly, although since the national average of non-registration does not seem to have altered very much over time, the correction does not alter the slope of the upward trend. It merely raises the probable illegitimacy ratio from a much higher sixteenth- and early seventeenth-century base to a much higher late eighteenth-century peak than the raw figures suggest.[20]

iv. Prostitution

Despite the rise of bundling, pre-nuptial pregnancy, and bastardy, the late and rising age of marriage meant that at all periods from the sixteenth to the eighteenth century most men of the lower classes passed twelve years or more of their most sexually virile period unmarried, and therefore in a condition of considerable sexual frustration. During the late sixteenth and early seventeenth century, internalized repression was undoubtedly aided by the moral pressures of Puritanism. This hypothesis of repression is supported by the fact that many of Napier's patients in the early seventeenth century were disturbed by accusations of sexual indiscretion, and that young women worried by pre-marital pregnancy without prospect of marriage were extremely rare. Simon Forman, the late sixteenth-century astrologer, records that he did not sleep with a woman before the age of thirty, and his case may not have been as exceptional as one might suppose.[21]

Repression was not the only solution, however, and it would be unreasonable to conclude that a low level of pre-marital conceptions necessarily meant an equally low level of all kinds of sexual activity. It has been argued that a variety of alternatives are, and probably were, available, notably lonely or mutual masturbation, oral or anal sex, homosexuality, bestiality, adultery with married women whose offspring are attributed to their husbands, and resort to prostitutes. None of these suggestions seems wholly implausible, but none but the last can be supported by more than very fragmentary and inconclusive historical evidence.[22] The 'double standard', with its toleration of male sexual experimentation and its insistence on female virginity before marriage for respectable girls, when coupled with the growth of lifelong bachelordom for younger sons of the upper classes and the general delay in marriage for young men to the age of twenty-six or more, created an acute socio-sexual problem which was partially relieved by a substantial increase of the ancient profession of prostitution.

Most of these women were concentrated in the bigger towns, which for country boys might involve a long journey and a not insignificant expense. In 1681 it was reported that Norwich swarmed with ale-houses, 'and every one of them, they tell, is also a bawdy-house.' On the other hand, Elizabethan legal records show that there was also a certain amount of casual, semi-amateur prostitution in the villages. Some poor families let out a room in their house to a whore, and the occasional married woman indulged in casual fornication in the fields for 4d a time, partly to earn money, and partly, it would seem, for mere pleasure. Sex was, therefore, rather more readily available to rural bachelor youths than one would have suspected without this evidence.[23] Prostitutes congregated in London in profusion, partly to supply the needs of the twenty to thirty thousand bachelor apprentices in the city (plate 41). The apprentices both used and abused these women, and in the seventeenth century were accustomed to work off their frustrations on Shrove Tuesday by rioting and pulling down bawdy-houses, ostensibly to remove temptation during Lent. In 1668 a panicky government reacted strongly to the rioting, which of course worsened the situation and caused two nights of serious disturbances. Charles II, himself the most practical of men, could not understand the ambivalence that underlay the apprentices' behaviour. 'Why? Why do they go to them then?' he asked, not unreasonably.[24]

The increase in the supply of prostitutes to meet the demand was generated by 'Place's Law' that 'chastity and poverty are incompatible.' Place backed up his 'law' with a number of concrete examples: of one Duke, a tailor, who was financially ruined, and therefore 'sold his niece . . . to a rich man who came from the East Indies'; of one Bury, a shopkeeper, also ruined, who sold his illegitimate daughter to a man at the age of fourteen; of one Seldon, a silk-mercer, also ruined, whose daughter ended up as a common prostitute.[25]

The ranks of the prostitutes were fed not only by poverty, but by the growing culture of sexual promiscuity in the large submerged class of the very poor. For some girls, selling their bodies was a preferable way of earning a living to working fourteen to sixteen hours a day as a seamstress or mantua-maker. Very many recruits to the profession presumably began as unwed mothers, and the rise of illegitimacy must, therefore, have increased the supply of prostitutes. Other recruits were said to be the cast-off mistresses of men of fashion, their seducers dumping them in brothels when they were tired of them. Many more, according to Defoe in 1725, were members of the huge class of young maidservants in London, who found themselves temporarily out of a job and were forced to 'prostitute their bodies or starve'. 'This is the reason why our streets are swarming with strumpets. Thus many of them rove from place to place, from bawdy-house to service, and from service to bawdy-house again ... nothing being more common than to find these creatures one week in a good family and the next in a brothel.' Defoe disapproved of this amateurish way of life, claiming that the girls 'make neither good whores nor good servants.'[26] But the harsh fact about eighteenth-century employment opportunities was that apart from slaving as a seamstress, those were the only two major occupations open to an uneducated girl from a poor family. Because of the irregularity of employment, the two often tended to get mixed up.

In 1724 Bernard de Mandeville launched a vigorous protest against the Society for the Suppression of Vice, which was then very busy trying to close down brothels and to drive prostitutes off the streets. He argued that the consequent private and unregulated prostitution was a menace to society. It led to the spread of venereal disease; it caused extravagant consumption patterns among the patrons; it tempted the girls to murder their bastard infants; and it encouraged men to tempt married women to adultery or to seduce and later abandon innocent girls, who then became common prostitutes. His solution was the establishment of publicly licensed and medically supervised brothels under state control, with different classes of girls and houses catering for different social groups, the cost varying from two shillings and sixpence to one guinea. Needless to say, his plea fell on deaf ears, and all the evils to which he drew attention became more and more common and serious as the eighteenth century progressed.[27]

In 1768 the London magistrate John Fielding turned his attention to the growing problem of these girls, whom he was convinced became whores from sheer poverty, since their bodies were all they had to sell to keep themselves alive. As proof he cited the fact that many began their careers before they were even sexually mature. He believed that in a number of cases the mothers were 'either starved by their necessities or drowned in gin' to such an extent that they 'have trepanned their own children into bawdy-houses, and shared with the bawd the gains of their own infants' prostitutions.' A survey of twenty-five girls arrested in the streets about the Strand on 1 May 1758 tended to confirm his conclusions. The age of the girls ranged from fifteen to twenty-two, with the median only eighteen. Eighteen of the twenty-five had been at the job for more than a year, although the other seven may possibly have been using prostitution as a temporary financial solution while looking for another occupation. The median age of first becoming a prostitute was sixteen and a half, while seven had begun at fourteen or less. Seventeen of the twenty-five were orphans, and another five had been deliberately abandoned by their parents and left to fend for themselves. Most of them were 'half eaten up with the foul distemper' of venereal disease. None were still active after the age of twenty-two or had been in the profession longer than six years – and most only one to three years. This shows that their careers were very short, either because they dropped out to get married, or because they rapidly became so diseased as to be unemployable, and were discharged, presumably to face an early death from venereal disease and malnutrition. In view of this evidence, Place was not exaggerating when he spoke of these women as 'common, wretched, helpless, hopeless, reckless prostitutes, the most pitiable class of persons in England, if not of Europe.'[28]

On the other hand there were clear gradations in the profession, which it is important to recognize, and which come out very clearly in the sexual diaries of men like Byrd and Boswell. The main distinctions are between the common street prostitute; the selective call-girl with her own rooms visited by gentlemanly clients; and the kept mistress set up in her own apartment, who might also make a little extra money on the side. In the 1780s Francis Place was apprenticed to a London leather-breeches-maker named Mr France, who had had three daughters by a first wife. 'His eldest daughter was and had been for several years a common prostitute. His youngest daughter, who was about seventeen years of age, had genteel lodgings where she was visited by gentlemen; and the second daughter ... was kept by a captain of an East India ship, in whose absence she used to amuse herself as such women generally do.' Mr France's three daughters thus represented all three levels of the profession.[29]

In the eighteenth century those who managed and ran this profession –

the madams of the brothels – were not regarded as respectable and respected figures in society. This disrepute was probably caused by their practice of meeting coaches from the country, luring unsuspecting and innocent village girls into their houses and then breaking them into the service of prostitution, instead of that of an ordinary domestic. In 1731 a well-known London madam, Mrs Elizabeth Needham, was put into the pillory by an energetic anti-vice magistrate, where she was so severely handled by the mob that she died of her wounds a few days later. It is not known whether the crowd which stoned her to death consisted of women, or of men anxious to transfer their guilt feelings on to her, but it was probably the latter in view of the comment of the *Grub Street Journal* that 'they acted very ungratefully, considering how much she had done to oblige them.'[30]

Despite these occasional setbacks and the earnest efforts of the various anti-vice societies at work at the end of the eighteenth and during the nineteenth centuries, the number of prostitutes continued to increase, and they were clearly serving a far wider clientele than upper-class men like Byrd and Boswell. In the late 1830s there were some seven thousand prostitutes in London, over nine hundred brothels, and eight hundred and fifty houses of ill fame, the difference between the two being that the latter provided accommodation, but without a resident staff. The problem was particularly acute in university towns, and as early as 1676 Cambridge contained no fewer than thirteen disorderly houses. Despite the vigorous efforts of the proctors, there were some forty prostitutes at work in the streets of Oxford in the course of a year in 1828.[31]

v. Conclusion

There is thus massive evidence for a large-scale trade in prostitution in the towns, running from the late seventeenth century to the mid-nineteenth century and increasing significantly in size as time went on. But these developments seem to have had little effect upon the statistically observable changes in pre-marital pregnancies. The number of prostitutes plying their trade, the number of brides led to the altar when already pregnant, and the number of bastard children born, all rose together in the eighteenth and early nineteenth centuries, and it is reasonable to assume that the three phenomena are all inter-connected. It was only in a society like Italy in which sexual promiscuity was common among married women that there was serious competition, and that prostitution was, therefore, kept at a fairly low level, since men could obtain the same satisfaction without payment.[32] The spread of prostitution as a profession in England thus helped to preserve the virginity of many respectable young girls who would otherwise have been subjected to tremendous pressures from young unmarried males. When Victorian ideas about the inhibited sexual response of women became common, resort to prostitutes may also have spared many prudish or frigid wives from submission to the grosser sexual demands of their husbands. The cost, however, was the spread of venereal disease and the creation of an under-class of an abject group of women serving a primarily middle-class market, who had little current happiness and even less rosy future prospects.[33]

vi. Annual Cycle of Sexual Activity

The only thing known about marital sexual activity among the poor is that it varied from month to month. An annual 'conception cycle', with quite strong fluctuations over the year, has been discovered in France and New England during the Early Modern period, although it has yet to be proved conclusively for England. In a society that does not use contraceptives, this cycle must reflect significant changes in the level of sexual activity among married couples. There was a fairly general trough in conceptions during March and another during August and September. The periods of peak conceptions, and therefore of peak sexual activity, were the spring and early summer, from April to July, and especially June. Only the March low can be explained by a taboo, being almost certainly the result of abstention from sexual intercourse during Lent, and to a very minor extent the absence of marriages during that period. Indications that this trough was weaker in England than in France and New England suggests that the power of the English clergy to regulate the sexual habits of their flock was weaker – which seems very plausible. The late spring and early summer peak may have been caused by the greater privacy afforded by warmer weather, but this is pure hypothesis. The low in the harvest months of the mid-summer is very puzzling: possible explanations are physical exhaustion due to very heavy labour in the fields, the separation of families for migrant labour, and malnutrition since food prices were always high before the new harvest came in. On the other hand food prices peaked as conception peaked in May and June, while the cycle applies to townspeople as well as to agricultural workers. Doctors were advising sexual abstention during the heat of summer, but it seems unlikely that this would have influenced any but the wealthy elite, who read or listened to them. Since the cycle slowly disappears with urbanization and modernization, there is no reason to suppose that the evidence supports any theory of a natural human female fertility cycle.[34] The fact is that we do not know the explanation for this curious phenomenon.

vii. Popular Libertinism

Between the late seventeenth century and the very beginning of the nineteenth, exceptional freedom was provided for the popular expression of sexuality. Compared with the Puritan period that preceded it, or the Evangelical period that followed, it was a time when the authorities made very little effort to curb displays and products that reflected the pagan admiration for virility common to all folk culture. In the late seventeenth century, the nonconformist minister Oliver Heywood was a horrified observer of what he regarded as a moral collapse in rural Yorkshire. In 1673 he noticed a large, highly obscene sign-board, erected during a 'Priapic feast' and set on posts straddling the main road from Halifax to Bradford; it depicted, it seems, a naked man and woman in, or just before, the act of copulation, and all travellers on the road were obliged to pass beneath it.[35] The huge priapic figure of the Long Man, cut into the turf on the chalk hillside at Cerne Abbas in Dorset and visible for miles around, is also thought to date from the eighteenth century.

In London this taste was catered for by the growth of a flourishing industry in popular pornography. In 1773 the energetic London magistrate Sir John Fielding protested to a grand jury about 'the exposing to sale and selling of such indecent and obscene prints and books as are sufficient to put impudence itself to the blush.' In 1756 John Shebbeare alleged that 'every print-shop has its windows stuck full with indecent prints to inflame desire through the eye, and singers in the streets charm your ears with lascivious songs to waken you to the same employment.' Francis Place confirms these reports from the point of view of the consumer. In his youth in the 1780s, respectable stationery shops sold pornography. At the one he frequented, the owner, Mrs Roach, 'used to open a portfolio to any boy or to any maidservant; ... the portfolio contained a multitude of obscene prints; ... she encouraged them to look at them. . . . This was common to other shops' (plates 34, 35, 37). Pornography, like the standard sex manual *Aristotle's Masterpiece*, was 'at that time sold openly on every stall.' Very obscene songs were commonly sung at mixed parties given by respectable tradesmen,[36] and the streets of London apparently swarmed with singers – many of them women – of 'infamous and obscene songs and ballads'. To give but one example, recalled by old men in the 1820s, there was a very popular and lengthy ballad about a hawker of sand, Sandman Joe, which was sung regularly at the Crown and Anchor Tavern in the Strand, and also out in the streets by two women. The last verses of this ballad ran:

He stared awhile, then turned his guide;
'Why blast you, Sall, I loves you!
And for to prove what I have said,
This night I'll soundly fuck you.'

'Why then,' says Sall, 'my heart's at rest,
If what you say you'll stand to.'
His brawny hands her bubbies pressed
and roaring, cried 'White sand, O.'

O, then they kissed, and then shook fist,
'My dearest Joe I know you.
As sound a dog as ever pissed,
This night, I'll doss with Joey.'

Then away they went with hearts content
To play the game you all know.
While Gallows Joe he wagged his arse
and roaring, cried 'White sand, O.'[37]

This and other ballads sung in late eighteenth-century London give some idea of the cheerfully frank flavour of the popular culture of this period of peculiar permissiveness on the part of the authorities. The two romantic heroes of the poor were the highwayman, who preyed exclusively on the rich and inevitably ended his days in the awesome ritual of the gallows; and the sexual athlete; while the greatest hero of all was the man who was both. These were antique types of hero, going back to Robin Hood and beyond, and both of them violated the moral norms of the bourgeoisie, who believed in the sanctity of property and in chastity. According to Place, these ballads were the only ones to be heard on the London streets before the moral reformers, aided by fear of the spread of French revolutionary ideas, led police and magistrates to suppress them at the end of the century. In any case by 1800 public toleration for such things was declining, as middle-class morality spread down to the respectable poor through the Sunday Schools.

2   THE CAUSES OF CHANGE

It is clear that what needs explaining is a three-stage shift in the sexual behaviour of the English poor in the seventeenth and eighteenth centuries; first to an increase of pre-marital chastity in the early seventeenth century; then in the eighteenth century to greater visual and verbal permissiveness, far more pre-nuptial intercourse (usually followed by marriage), and a more or less simultaneous increase in the proportion of couples who failed to marry after pregnancy had occurred. Later still, in the very late eighteenth and the nineteenth centuries, a new wave of sexual prudery spread downwards from the lower-middle classes to the respectable poor, leaving unaffected only the very lowest elements of the society, the *lumpen proletariat*. Throughout all these changes there was a steady rise in the number of prostitutes in the towns, though whether the rise was faster than that of the population is unknown. It certainly seems quite likely. The explanation of these changes lies in changes in two independent variables, religion and its application to ethics, and economics and its effect on the distribution of property and income. Behavioural changes are the most difficult of all to explain convincingly and treatment of so mysterious and poorly documented a subject as attitudes towards sex is fraught with danger. The economic factor alone, which will be dealt with later, provides a necessary but certainly not a sufficient explanation of these profound attitudinal shifts.

i. Culture

The shifting attitude toward sexuality in western Europe in Early Modern times can be studied at three levels, that of the official moral theologians, that of the religious radicals, and that of an increasingly secular society. It seems likely, however, that the first was of critical importance only during the early seventeenth-century Puritan drive and that thereafter it was modified to conform to attitudes among the laity, and is thus a secondary variable from 1660 until the renewed Evangelical drive after 1770. As for the second, it had little or no temporary or permanent influence whatsoever in its own time or afterwards.

a. Moral Theology before 1640. There is every reason to believe that the chief cause of the unusually high and rising standard of sexual morality in early seventeenth-century England was the external pressure of Puritan organization and Puritan preaching, which slowly affected the attitudes of nearly all the propertied classes, whether Puritan, Anglican or Arminian. It became part of the generally accepted pattern of internalized and enforced social discipline, and thus seeped downward through the social hierarchy to the plebs. To give but one example from a not especially devout Elizabethan, the gentleman musician Thomas Wythorne, he resisted the idea that he should attempt to seduce before marriage the young widow he was wooing, on the grounds that 'we should have provoked God's heavy displeasure and wrath, to have lighted upon us for our wickedness.'[38] This phrase conveys something of the sense of God's looming presence, which was so powerful a force for sexual restraint in the late sixteenth and early seventeenth centuries.

In his old age, Roger North painted an idyllic picture of the rustic simplicity and sexual innocence of life in the village of Kirtling in Cambridgeshire when he was a child in about 1665. Since it was mostly given over to dairy farming, work was not arduous. 'It was always the custom for the youth of the town, who were either men or maid servants, and children, to assemble, after horses baited, . . . on the green . . . and there all to play till milking time and supper at night. The men to football, and the maids, with whom we children commonly mixed, . . . to stool-ball, and such running games as they knew. And all this without mixing men and women . . ., no idle or lascivious frolics between them.'[39] It all sounds hardly credible, were it not supported by the extraordinarily low figures for pre-nuptial conceptions and bastardy. One hundred years of Puritan teaching, patronized by the Norths, had apparently created a model village, so far as the sexual propriety of adolescents goes.

The development by Church and state of punishments by public shame and by the infliction of humiliating physical pain is evidence of a determination to impose external constraints upon human sexuality. It reflects a hierarchy of values which placed the sins of the flesh on a level with the more socially damaging acts of economic exploitation or physical oppression. These internalized values, and the powerful system of punishments for transgression to which they gave rise, must have been the principal causes of the low level of pre-nuptial pregnancy and of illegitimacy in early seventeenth-century England.

In the late seventeenth century, however, there was both an evident decline in the enthusiasm of the upper classes to repress the sexual exuberance of the poor and a shift in attitudes of the poor themselves.

One possible explanation of this relaxation of attitudes towards sexuality is a change in moral theology, obviously mainly affecting the middle- and upper-class reading public, but also presumably penetrating down to the poor through sermons. The strict medieval Augustinian doctrine about sex was that intercourse was only lawful, even between spouses, when its purpose was procreation. Intercourse to avoid fornication was defined as a venial sin, and intercourse to satisfy lust or to enhance pleasure a mortal sin. Even before the Reformation this view had been modified by a few, not very influential, Catholic theologians, who substituted a new ideal of 'conjugal chastity' – a happy mean between nymphomania and frigidity. It was grudgingly admitted by these few progressives that 'not every copulation of spouses not performed to generate offspring is an act opposed to conjugal chastity.' But it was not until the eighteenth century that Catholic theologians finally identified the purpose of intercourse with the spiritual purpose of marriage itself as a union of two human beings for mutual comfort and support.[40]

In England, on the other hand, Protestant theologians of all persuasions had long since identified mutual comfort and endearment as two of the purposes of the sexual act within marriage. By the mid-seventeenth century, this was a common assumption of everyone from Jeremy Taylor to John Milton.[41] The explicit recognition of the legitimacy of these two objectives opened up a new stage in the evolution of official Christian attitudes to sexuality within marriage, and by extension – although not by intent – was bound eventually to have its effect on pre-marital sexuality as well. By legitimizing the sexual act within marriage for the purpose of mutual comfort and endearment, Protestant theology began the slow separation of sexual pleasure from procreation that ended in the late seventeenth-century spread of both contraception and libertinism. This was the last thing that the theologians had in mind, but it was in fact one of the legacies of the concept of holy matrimony to a more secularized world.

b. Sexual Radicalism in the 1650s. It was in the wilder fringes of sectarian extremism during the chaotic post-civil war conditions of the late 1640s and early 1650s that there emerged the first, ephemeral development of a wholly permissive attitude towards sexuality. The Seekers and Ranters believed in universal redemption, and some of them strayed easily into the heresy of antinomianism, the theory that to the pure all things are pure. In 1651 it was said that 'all the world now is in the Ranting humour', and Parliament was so concerned that it passed special legislation directed against those who believed that acts of adultery, drunkenness, swearing or theft were not intrinsically shameful, wicked and sinful. An Oxford University scholar, Abiezer Coppe, regarded property as theft, and pride, covetousness and oppression as greater crimes than adultery and uncleanness. He claimed that 'I can kiss and hug ladies and love my neighbour's wife as myself, without sin.'

Laurence Clarkson – a married man, though married by himself – carried the theory a stage further, arguing that 'what act soever is done by thee in light and love is light and lovely, though it be that act called adultery.' He proceeded to put his principle into practice, and in an extraordinary religio-sexual autobiographical essay, he recounted his triumphs.[42] He told how at Canterbury a maid 'with my doctrine was affected, and I affected to lie with her, so that night prevailed and satisfied my lust; afterwards the maid was highly in love with me.' But he avoided telling her he was already married, promised to return and marry her, and quickly moved on from place to place till at last he found in London a congenial little group which called itself 'My One Flesh'. He soon persuaded them that 'there was no sin but as man esteemed it sin', and that 'therefore till you can lie with all women as one woman, and not judge it sin, you can do nothing but sin.' Inspired by this doctrine Sarah Kullin invited him 'to make trial of what I had expressed', and with one or two other girls 'lay with me that night'. For a time he lived a strenuously happy life of charismatic preaching by day and multiple promiscuity by night, with ample 'choice of what before I had aspired after', a course of life he justified to himself by reading 'Solomon's writings ... supposing I might take the same liberty as he did.' He still supported his wife financially, but 'my body was given to other women', so much so that 'I was not able to answer all desires.'

After a time, these sexual excesses inevitably palled, and he returned for a while to his long-suffering wife in the country. But his principles remained the same, that property is the root of all evil, and that his promiscuous use of women was thus similar in inspiration to Winstanley's attempt to exploit common land on behalf of the Diggers. So he returned to London and set out again on his wanderings as a Ranter preacher, accompanied by a Mrs Star. The pair travelled as man and wife, and spent much time feasting and drinking in taverns. The well-attended meetings at which he preached were sometimes accompanied by orgiastic scenes, such as the occasion when 'Dr Paget's maid stripped herself naked and skipped among them; but being in a cook's shop, there was no hunger, so that I kept myself to Mrs Star.'

Arrested by the Privy Council in 1650, he was accused of preaching and practising free love, 'a sad principle which if not routed, all honest men will have their wives deluded.' But he was soon freed and continued his itinerant Ranting preaching, now adding astrology, healing and magic to his repertoire. Finally, however, unsuccessful efforts to raise the devil, 'so that I might see what he was', convinced him that 'there was no devil at all, nor indeed no God, but only nature. ... I really believed no Moses, Prophets, Christ, or Apostles, nor no resurrection at all.' This was the end of the religious road for Clarkson, until he met the Muggletonian John Reeve, who convinced him that Reason was damned and Faith alone remained. In 1660 he publicly renounced all his past career, declaring that 'the Ranting principle broke forth all manner of wickedness with a high hand, that did tempt such as I to break the Law as themselves.'

Another antinomian who emerged in this period of political, economic and spiritual distintegration was a Wiltshire rector, Thomas Webbe, who was accused of saying that 'it was lawful for him to lie with any woman.' Yet others, like John Pordage, believed that monogamous marriage was in itself evil. Webbe was accused of saying that 'there is no heaven but women, nor no hell save marriage', and Coppe urged his hearers to 'give over thy stinking family duties.' These men held extremely radical views, not only about the morality of sex, but also about marriage as a social institution. In addition, the chaos of the Revolution threw up a handful of open atheists, like the man who in 1653 wrote to a girl that he would rather be in bed with her than in Heaven with Jesus Christ.[43]

There can be little doubt, however, that these opinions had no effect, since they were more shocking than attractive to the great majority of their contemporaries. Admittedly, some decades later, John Dryden spoke, with clear signs of envy and a total absence of moral condemnation, about those far-off

> ... pious times e'er priest-craft did begin,
> Before polygamy was made a sin:
> When man, on many, multiply'd his kind,
> Ere one to one was, cursedly, confin'd;
> When Nature prompted, and no law deny'd
> Promiscuous use of concubine and bride.

Even if Dryden was being serious, this was no more than a tiny minority view, current only in the dissolute court circles around Charles II, and one which met with little support elsewhere. But occasional antinomian ideas continued to plague the sects, and in 1751 John Wesley had to crush a Methodist preacher who was arguing that 'a believer had a right to all women.'[44]

c. Secularization of Society after 1660. Far more important in loosening popular conventions about sexual behaviour in England was the reaction after 1660 to the Draconian imposition by military rule in the 1650s of the more austere anti-pleasure principles of the Puritans. Stage plays, horse-racing, cock-fighting, maypoles, and brothels had all been suppressed; ale-houses had been severely limited in numbers, and adultery made punishable by death. The result was exactly the opposite of what the Puritan leaders had expected. Instead of producing a regenerate nation of the godly, they created a society bitterly resentful of public interference with their normal recreations, one which regarded all enthusiasm with distaste, and which eventually came to reject the Puritan vision of man's relation to nature and God, and to deny the sinfulness of pleasure.

There are three different ways in which this cultural change may have affected the pre-marital and extra-marital sexual behaviour of the poor in the late seventeenth and eighteen centuries. The first is merely the result of the relaxation in the external controls on sexual behaviour imposed by Church and state; the second is a decline in respect by children for established moral standards of sexual behaviour expected by their parents; and the third is a change in those internalized standards themselves. According to the first, the strict code of honour which had hitherto governed the common practice of intimate courting now broke down due to a relaxation of religious and secular penalties. According to the second, there developed a severe inter-generational conflict in which children were rejecting the moral code of their parents. According to the third, there was a spread – or more likely a revival – of the recognized medieval custom by which sexual intercourse was permitted to take place immediately after the formal public betrothal, but before the wedding. Before the tightening up of religious controls over society after the Reformation and the Counter-Reformation in the mid-sixteenth century, the formal betrothal ceremony seems to have been at least as important, if not more so, than the wedding.[45] To many, the couple were from that moment 'man and wife before God', and the temptation to sexual intercourse before the marriage ceremony in the church was clearly great. The Church itself recognized this situation, and as late as 1619 in the Deanery of Doncaster a betrothal was successful as defence against an accusation in the courts of pre-nuptial fornication. Even in the 1630s this defence mitigated the penalty from public to private penance.[46]

It is at least possible that the period of religious anarchy between 1640 and 1660, and the subsequent decline of clerical enthusiasm and devotion to duty after 1660, meant that the secular ceremony of the betrothal once again became more significant to the poor than the Christian ceremony of the wedding, and that it therefore determined the moment of consummation. This was certainly the custom in parts of Leicestershire in the late sixteenth century, and may well have spread elsewhere during the late seventeenth and early eighteenth centuries.[47] But since in Leicestershire the consummation was apparently limited to a single night before the wedding, it is impossible for this particular custom to have been responsible for a pre-nuptial pregnancy rate of forty to fifty per cent since the probability of pregnancy from a single act of unprotected coitus is low.[48] Further evidence that this was not everywhere the decisive factor is that in the one eighteenth-century New England town that has been studied, between two-thirds and three-quarters of the pre-marital conceptions occurred before the filing of an intention to marry.[49]

It does appear, however, that the custom of marriage in church partly broke down after the Restoration, and when it was again universally reinforced after about 1720, and especially after the Marriage Act of 1753, it was probably no longer regarded as the decisive event in forming a union. There is one piece of evidence to suggest that clandestine marriages, contracted outside the Church altogether, were very common indeed between 1680 and 1720: in the small market town of Tetbury in Gloucestershire in the 1690s, they amounted to at least twenty per cent of the total, and possibly a good deal more.[50] There is also evidence that consensual unions were by no means unknown in mid-seventeenth-century Derbyshire, and that some of the children were duly baptized in the church as if they were legitimate. If this was the general practice, consensual unions did not add to the recorded rise of pre-nuptial pregnancy or illegitimacy, but formed a submerged part of the iceberg of legally unrecognized sexual unions and their offspring, only the tip of which is visible to the historian.

The key to the change, therefore, is a change in recognized standards of honour. The gigantic rise of pre-nuptial conceptions in the late eighteenth century was not caused by a massive violation of accepted standards of sexual behaviour, but rather by a change in those standards. Only the minor phenomenon of the rise of bastardy involved a violation of social norms. In the eighteenth century it looks as if the spousals again became the generally accepted moment at which sexual relations could begin, the marriage ceremony occurring later, often when the bride was quite far advanced in pregnancy. The man's honour was not damaged in the public conscious-ness, provided that he lived up to his promise to marry despite any possible second thoughts he might subsequently have had; and the woman's honour was not damaged in the public consciousness merely for having commenced sexual relations after the spousals but before the marriage.

If, on the other hand, the man repudiated his promise or ran away, one may legitimately assume that the honour of both was ruined in the eyes of the community: the man was then a liar, and the woman unchaste. If the woman allowed herself to be seduced without any promise, her reputation was ruined, but the man's was not. Community interest was limited to ensuring that it was the father who paid for the support of the bastard child, rather than the parish poor rate, and that the child was taught a trade by which to earn its living. The rise of pre-nuptial conceptions therefore represents primarily a shift in community standards of honour; the rise of bastardy represents social disintegration and a collapse of all standards of honour, primarily among social groups too poor to afford or comprehend such things.

The most likely explanation of the dramatic rise in pre-nuptial pregnancies is thus a change in internalized norms of honour, caused partly by the decline of Puritanism and partly by the growth of inter-generational conflict over freedom to choose a mate, caused in turn partly by the rise of individualism and a desire to put personal happiness before collective or family interests. In New England before 1670, at least half of all pre-nuptial pregnancies were detected and punished, usually by a whipping. Between 1670 and 1700, fines were increasingly substituted for whippings, while the revised statutes of Plymouth, Massachusetts, of 1671 distinguished between fornication before betrothal (fine £10) and fornication after (fine £5). After 1700 prosecutions rapidly disappear from court records, while churches abandoned the practice of confession before admission. Further efforts in New England to stem the tide of moral laxity, such as parental directions in about 1756 to confine bundling to the sofa, if anything did more harm than good, for 'the sofa in summer is more dangerous than the bed in winter.'[51]

Pre-marital pregnancy in the eighteenth century could also be used, not only by children to force the hands of their parents, but also by women to force men to marry them. Within the rural community, where traditional ideas about honour and morality persisted, there was an economic incentive for the prospective father to marry the pregnant girl since, as a commentator on Wales in 1804 remarked, 'both parties are so poor that they are necessarily constrained to render their issue legitimate, in order to secure their reputation and with it a mode of obtaining a livelihood.'[52] This economic incentive was powerfully reinforced by legislation passed in 1733. Designed to relieve the poor rate of the responsibility for maintaining bastards, it added legal to community pressures for marriage by making any man identified by the mother as the father of an illegitimate child liable to arrest to enforce payment for its upkeep. This meant that the prospective father – or alleged father – was forced to choose between marriage, imprisonment, and the payment of an allowance, which varied from one to seven shillings a week for seven years. It also meant that if he was without means, his marriage would make him eligible for a child's allowance from the poor rate in his own parish. But if it strengthened the man's incentive to marriage, the Act may also have weakened the woman's motives for pre-marital chastity. A girl now had less reason to refuse a man's sexual advances, since if she became pregnant she retained this powerful weapon to enforce marriage. As the poet Crabbe put it in 1807,

> next at our altar stood a luckless pair
> Brought by strong passions and a warrant there [plate 42].

There is even evidence of a man being brought to his wedding in handcuffs to make sure that he did not abscond before the ceremony; and James Lackington records a lucky escape from the parish constables in about 1760, after being nominated as the father by a pregnant woman. He was chased from pillar to post by the constables, but, luckily for him, the girl had a miscarriage two months later, 'so that I was never troubled for expenses.'[53]

d. Relaxation of Social Controls after 1660. The most obvious sign of this major shift of values was a progressive separation of sin from law, which resulted in a marked decline in attempts to enforce the laws concerning sexual behaviour.

Church Courts: In the half-century before the civil war, the Church courts had been more and more actively engaged in the struggle to control sexual behaviour. Cases of sexual immorality more than doubled between 1595 and 1635, and comprised anything up to half of all the business with which the courts dealt. The commonest form of penalty for fornication imposed by these courts, whether or not it led to bastardy, was shame punishment, which took the form of being forced to stand publicly, dressed in a white sheet, before the congregation on Sunday or in the market-place of the local town on market-day.[54] On the other hand, the powers of enforcement of these courts were limited. About half of all the accused preferred to live in excommunication than to obey the summons of the court, and only a small proportion of those accused of sexual deviation ever did public penance. In the face of an obstinately recalcitrant poor laity, the Church courts before the civil war were therefore of only limited effectiveness in curbing sexual immorality.[55]

In Presbyterian Scotland, however, Church control of sexual morality was a reality. An English visitor to Presbyterian Edinburgh in the middle of the century described the Church's machinery for the detection and punishment of sexual delinquents which he found there.

Those that commit fornication under colour of intended marriage, and after promise of marriage, are enjoined to sit upon the stool of repentance one day. This stool is a public and eminent seat erected towards the lower end of the church about 2 yards from the ground, either about some pillar, or in some such conspicuous place, where the whole congregation may take notice of them; this seat is capable of about 6 or 8 persons. Here this day 28 June I was at sermon in the Grey Friars, where there stood 3 women upon the stool of repentance, who are admitted to sit during the sermon.

Fornicators who did not intend to marry later were condemned to three days on the stool, and adulterers to every Sunday for a year. Since Sunday services lasted four hours in the morning and three in the afternoon, this was no light penalty.[56] Similarly in New England as late as 1713 a convicted adulteress in Boston was publicly whipped and made to stand on the gallows platform wearing the letter 'A' for 'adulteress'. It should be noted, however, that these shame punishments were not inflicted on the Governor of Massachusetts' daughter, when she too lapsed. On both sides of the Atlantic there was a due respect for authority and property in the treatment of moral transgressions.[57]

In England, the ecclesiastical courts were temporarily abolished in 1646, and the final suppression of the Court of High Commission in 1688 left the inferior courts with even less power than they had before to enforce sanctions upon sexual transgressors, although the Court of Arches remained in business until the nineteenth century. The motive behind the 1646 move was certainly not a greater toleration for the weaknesses of the flesh, but rather anti-clericalism bred of resentment of the use to which these courts had been put to persecute the godly. Indeed, the same lay Puritan leadership four years later made adultery a capital offence, although there is no evidence that the penalty was ever actually carried out. In the Middlesex Quarter Sessions between 1650 and 1660, twenty-three women and fourteen men were tried for adultery and five women and three men for fornication – the relative number of the sexes shows the persistence of the double standard. The punishments, however, are unknown, and only one pregnant woman was, in fact, found guilty of adultery. This woman, Ursula Powell, is the only known possible victim of this Draconian law, and, if she was indeed executed, the event so shocked the jurymen that at the next session all twenty-two women accused of adultery were declared not guilty. Despite Cromwell's efforts to obtain enforcement in 1655, it seems clear that the pressure of public opinion against the law was too strong for it to have had the slightest practical effect.[58]

In the late seventeenth century there took place a slow shift in attitudes, which eventually distinguished private sin from public law. This shift took place despite the continuity of values stressed by moral theologians running from Richard Baxter's *Christian Directory* of 1673 through William Law's *Serious Call to a Devout and Holy Life* of 1728 to Henry Venn's *Complete Duty of Man* of 1763. Anxious critics saw the moral dangers of an erosion of legal authority to repress sin and warned that 'if there be no power in the church sufficient to enforce a regularity of life, and the civil magistrate be remiss and negligent, great confusions and disorder will ensue in that state.' But popular though these writings were, all of them running into many editions, their readers seem to have been more the pious bourgeoisie than the landed elite who ruled the country. In the eighteenth century, the cases brought before the Church courts concerning sexual morality declined drastically as the power of the courts declined in a secularized society. In 1743 in one Yorkshire village, both parson and churchwardens were afraid to report sexual delinquents to the Archdeacon for fear of reprisals from the parishioners. Not only did the number of immorality cases drop markedly after 1660, but by 1740 shame punishments for fornication or pre-nuptial conceptions had virtually disappeared altogether. Although a thin trickle of public penances for fornication show up again after 1770, pre-nuptial conception was abolished as an offence by statute in 1787.[59]

Justices of the Peace: In England in the late sixteenth and early seventeenth centuries, the deficiencies of the Church courts were made up by the zeal of the Justices of the Peace. The problem of preventing bastardy had long attracted the attention of Parliament, where the members, most of whom were also JPs, passed Act after Act to try to deal with what they believed to be both a moral scourge and a financial burden on the community. An Act of 1576 punished both the father and the mother and ordered the father to pay maintenance, which in their capacity as JPs the gentry took to mean a weekly payment until the child reached the age of seven, and a cash sum to pay for apprenticeship to a trade. Another Act of 1609 ordered the mother to be sent to the House of Correction for a year, and a third in 1623 'to prevent the murdering of bastard children' put on the mother who concealed the death the onus of proof that the baby was born dead. In the late sixteenth and early seventeenth centuries, the justices did not hesitate to use their authority to punish mere fornication as well as bastardy. Particularly in the north of England, the woman convicted of fornication was often whipped in the nearest market town 'as a deterrent to others', while at the second offence she was often committed to the House of Correction for hard labour under the lash. Bastardy cases tended to be treated severely, although sentences varied from place to place and justice to justice. In 1601 the Lancashire Quarter Sessions condemned the father and mother of an illegitimate child to be publicly whipped and then sat in the stocks, still naked from the waist upwards, with a placard on their heads, reading 'These persons are punished for fornication.' This kind of shame punishment by public exposure in the stocks was normal practice in the north, although it was already dying out nearer London.[60]

After the Restoration in 1660, however, the gentry, in their dual capacities as JPs and MPs, were neither eager to police sexual behaviour themselves, nor willing to allow the clergy to police it for them. The private societies for the Reformation of Manners, which sprang up between 1674 and 1694 in a last-ditch effort to hold back the tide of sexual permissiveness, were only temporarily effective and died away after a few decades of activity. In any case, half their efforts were concerned with breaches of the laws enforcing Sabbatarianism.[61]

It is interesting to note that some of the clergy attributed the increase in moral laxity not only to this growing indifference of the public authorities, but also to the decline of the powers of the head of the household to exercise control over its members. In 1725 the Bishop of Coventry, disturbed by the decline of church attendance in favour of drinking, sex, cock-fighting and other secular pastimes, concluded that 'the Lord's day is now the Devil's market-day.' His explanation was that 'it went far towards keeping up the face of virtue and piety and the preventing of much wickedness, when formerly a man's house was a little oratory, when the master himself prayed with all his family and read a portion of scripture to them, when he took his children and servants to church with him on Sundays. ... It went well with this City when masters thus governed their families.'[62] Despite the idealization of a perhaps rather mythical Golden Age of household government, the Bishop's comment is a shrewd one. Moreover, the decline of religious enthusiasm in the early eighteenth century was undoubtedly accompanied by a decline in the moral control formerly exercised by heads of households over their children, apprentices and servants. It was not merely that society was more tolerant of sins of the flesh, but also that there had been a significant shift of power relationships within the household.

Purely moral repugnance at the act of fornication as such declined, and the Justices increasingly limited their concern to its practical consequences. They became exclusively preoccupied with the economic problem of transferring the maintenance costs of a bastard child from the poor rate of the parish to the father, or failing that to some other body. Shame punishments were no longer imposed; all prosecution stopped at once if the child died, and further Acts of 1662 and 1733 were exclusively concerned with the economics of child maintenance and no longer with the morality of fornication *per se*. This did not mean, however, that the situation of the unmarried mother improved. Indeed, it may have worsened, as the parish authorities tried desperately to ensure that the baby was not born within their boundaries, and thus did not become a burden on the local rates. There were frequent cases, like that recorded by Oliver Heywood in 1662, in which a pregnant mother about to deliver was hastily bundled out of town. In this case, the woman 'was delivered in the town field, in cold frost and snow; the child died, the woman is distracted.' Failing physical deportation, the parish authorities put tremendous pressure on the mother to reveal the identity of the father, who could then be required to pay for the child's maintenance. A common practice was for the midwife and some local women to cross-question the mother during labour, refusing to come to her help in her agony until she revealed the name of the father. Indeed the midwives' oath of 1726 imposed this duty upon them. The only satisfactory solution for a pregnant mother was falsely to assert that the father was some rich man, who would then be forced by the Justices to pay a generous maintenance for the upkeep of the child (plate 43).[63]

The penalties of pregnancy without marriage in the eighteenth century were thus very heavy for both mother and child. The former was likely to lose her job, might be sent to the House of Correction, and eventually be driven into prostitution. Because of the tremendous incentive to the mother to conceal the birth, the child was likely to be murdered in the first few hours, or abandoned in the street, either to die there or to be dumped in a workhouse, where the prospects of survival were not much better.

e. Foreign Comparisons. Even in the City upon the Hill in Puritan New England, the same development was at work in the late seventeenth and eighteenth centuries to undermine the strenuous efforts of the early leaders to use the law to suppress sexual misconduct. After 1670 fines were increasingly substituted for whipping as a punishment for pre-marital pregnancy, and after 1700 prosecutions for this crime rapidly disappear from court records, while the churches ceased to demand public confessions before admission. This resulted partly from disillusionment, the realization of the ineffectiveness of efforts to control and canalize the sexual drive, and partly from a growing indifference. The urgent reminders of the preachers about the divine wrath which had been visited on Sodom and Gomorrah fell on deaf ears in eighteenth-century New England.[64]

In England this secularization process was greatly accelerated, firstly by the defeat and disillusionment of the great Puritan movement after 1660, and secondly by the final establishment of the secular state in 1688. It was also aided by the rise of clerical pluralism in organization, which weakened the control of the clergy in the rural parishes by fostering absenteeism, and of a more rational theology and a decline in the emphasis on the torments of Hell in sermon literature, which weakened the impact of the threat of everlasting damnation. The best proof that this secularization of the Anglo-Saxon Protestant world was an important cause of the shift in sexual behaviour is that no such change took place in Catholic France until the very late eighteenth century. Nearly everywhere in France the rate of both pre-nuptial pregnancies and of illegitimate births remained low until the 1780s. It seems likely that tight control of popular morality through the confession box by the post-Tridentine clergy, especially the Jansenists, was the main cause of this success in bottling up sexual energy amongst the unmarried. France in the eighteenth century had Catholic – or pagan – religion and austere sexual morals.[65] In 1766 the Reverend William Cole, a country parson at Bletchley, frankly admitted that the Roman Catholic Church 'takes more care of the morals of its people, both children and grown people, than ours can pretend to'. Twenty years later Hannah More thought that little moral improvement could be hoped for as long as 'every man of the world naturally arrogates to himself the superiority of understanding over every religious man.' But already she saw signs of regeneration.[66]

ii. Economics

The second plausible explanation for the rise in the eighteenth century of pre-nuptial conceptions and illegitimate births is not cultural but economic. Anthropologists tell us that the value attached to chastity is directly related to the degree of social hierarchy and the degree of property ownership. Pre-marital chastity is a bargaining chip in the marriage game, to be set off against male property and status rights. Pre-marital female sexual repression is thus built into the social system, since male and female are bargaining on the marriage market with different goods, the one social and economic, the other sexual. The withholding of sexual favours is a woman's only source of power over men, as Aristophanes pointed out in *Lysistrata*.

The system serves the interests of both parties, since the male is guaranteed that he is purchasing new and not second-hand goods, while the female has a powerful lever to obtain marriage. This model explains the prevalence of the system of values according to which male pre-marital sexual promiscuity is not only tolerated but encouraged, while any hint of female pre-marital sexual transgression is strongly condemned. The same double standard holds true after marriage, since wifely infidelity causes uncertainty about property inheritance, while no such legal problems are caused by infidelity by the husband. 'We hang a thief for stealing sheep,' remarked Dr Johnson, 'but the unchastity of a woman transfers sheep and farm and all from the right owner.' Both the principle of pre-marital female chastity and the double standard after marriage are, therefore, functional to a society of property owners, especially small property owners.[67]

It must be stressed, however, that female 'virginity' in such a society is a relative, not an absolute, term, and the principle does not preclude various forms of sexual advertising and enticement through bundling or other traditional courting practices involving some degree of physical intimacy. The accepted, but very limited, criterion of virginity in such societies is full coitus. The woman is expected to let herself be handled sufficiently to inflame the passion of her suitor, but never in any circumstances to allow him (or anyone else) full intercourse before marriage, or at the very least before formal and morally irrevocable betrothal.

It follows that the most sexually inhibited class in the population is likely to be the lower-middle class of small property owners, among whom rigid ideas of patriarchy, extreme loyalty to the authoritarian state, and extreme sexual inhibitions tend to be the norm, among both husbands and wives.[68] The poor were under no such constraints, and the rise of a class of landless rural labourers and urban workers without either property or status meant the rise of a class to whom virginity was not important, and foresight, prudence and planning were irrelevant to their dismal economic future (plate 38). The developments of the eighteenth century, with the progress of enclosures, the amalgamation of farms, the development of cottage industries and the growth of towns, were causing a considerable increase in the size of such a class. In one rural Shropshire parish the population in 1700–05 consisted of fifty-eight per cent farmers and forty-two per cent labourers; in 1813–22 it was sixteen per cent farmers and eighty-four per cent labourers. Since the population had doubled, this means that in actual numbers the farmers had shrunk by one half, and the labourers had multiplied by four. This is an extreme case, but the trend was universal, and it alone would go far to explain the increase in pre-nuptial conceptions and bastardy; the latter rose from one to fifteen per cent in the parish in question.[69] There is here a clear connection between economic and sexual change.

Francis Place is not an entirely reliable witness, since he was writing in old age in the 1820s, as one who had pulled himself by his own efforts out of the ranks of the propertyless urban labourers. He is believable, however, when he stressed the appalling physical conditions of life of the late eighteenth-century poor, their lack of education and varieties of amusement, the economic insecurity of their lives, and the unattractive-ness of their homes, full of overworked, haggard wives and squalling children. For a member of this impoverished proletariat, Place argued, 'none but the mere animal sensations are left; to these his enjoyments are limited, and even these are frequently reduced to two – namely sexual intercourse and drinking.... Of the two ... drunkenness is by far the most desired', since it provided a longer period of escape from gloomy reflections upon present conditions, and upon future prospects of an old age spent 'in the most abject poverty and misery.'[70] Promiscuous sex was, therefore, the second best of the only two forms of recreation that allowed the poor to forget for a while the stark realities of their situation.

The second economic explanation for the dizzy rise in pre-nuptial con-ceptions lies in the spread of cottage industry, and later of factories, which enabled a young couple to earn enough to live on at an early age. They were therefore for the first time in a position to defy both their parents and community norms, and to indulge in full pre-marital sex, secure in the knowledge that if pregnancy occurred there would be no economic obstacle to an early marriage.

As has been seen, by itself this economic factor is not an adequate explanation of the enormous rise in pre-marital conceptions in the eighteenth century. Other important variables were the pre-existence of a legal system which recognized spousals as a binding contract, and of a folk custom – how widespread in England is uncertain – of bundling. Given these pre-conditions, there were needed changes in attitudes towards obedience to parents, a decline in both religious and community controls over personal morality, a relaxation of the restrictive norms governing courting procedures, and greater acceptance of sexual pleasure as something to be enjoyed without guilt. If all these things took place, the opportunity for young people of both sexes to obtain well-paid industrial work was very important both in liberating adolescents for pre-marital sexual experiment-ation and in lowering the age of marriage, as has been shown statistically for two small areas of Switzerland around Zurich and Neuchatel. 'The decay of agriculture has been followed by that of morals', lamented an observer in 1801.[71]

Economic factors thus played an important part in causing the rise of pre-nuptial conceptions. They were also influential in causing the concurrent rise of illegitimacy, although this is a subcategory with its own distinct causes. It was quite possible, for example, for one industrial village in Neuchatel to have a massive rise in pre-nuptial conceptions, while the illegitimacy ratio remained static at a mere one per cent.[72] The rise of illegitimacy was caused by fathers defying custom and evading their responsibility to marry the pregnant girls. This may be attributed in large part to the growth in number of rural landless males who were obliged by poverty to postpone marriage and so to repudiate any marriage promises they may have made. Many of this class were forced by demographic pressures to leave the village and seek casual labour in the town, while more and more young women were also forced to move further away from home to go into urban domestic service or the dressmaking trade. This drift from the countryside was accelerated by late seventeenth-century legislation which made each parish responsible for the relief of the poor who resided in or were born in their parish. This created a very strong incentive to prevent the building of houses in the parish by the poor, lest they or their children should become an economic burden. Landlords and parish officials, therefore, did their utmost to prevent the erection of new cottages. As a result, 'young men, intimidated by such cruel treatment, are unwilling to marry; and this leads them frequently to debauch young women and then leave them with child in a hopeless condition', whereupon the parish officials tried to hurry the mother out of the parish before she gave birth.[73] The legislation thus created an artificial rural housing shortage in 'closed parishes' which exacerbated the very trend the authorities were trying to curb, the rise of the indigent poor who were a charge on the parish. There is also evidence to suggest that there was a small segment of the population, at the lowest social level, which failed to conform to the prevalent norms from generation to generation: a bastardy-prone minority group. Many were drawn from the most wretched dregs of the population, those drifting homeless vagrants whose growing number had increasingly preoccupied the authorities in the late sixteenth and seventeenth centuries. Large numbers of these girls ended up on the streets of London, and the confession of one such woman, arrested and whipped for vagrancy and bastardy in Southwark in 1603, can stand for them all.

Frances Palmer, a vagrant . . ., having two children begotten and born in whoredom, says that one Thomas Wood, servant with Sir Edward Wotton, is the father of them; and the place where she was delivered was openly in the street, two or three doors off the Cross Keys; and they died and were buried in Allhallows parish in Gracechurch Street.[74]

This was the group for whom the policy of open admissions to foundling hospitals in the mid and late eighteenth century proved a godsend. If as a result of their promiscuity they became pregnant and gave birth to a child, it was morally much easier to abandon it, now that it could be disposed of (in fact mostly killed by neglect) by a charitable institution, out of sight and out of hearing. Those who argued that the system of open admissions to foundling hospitals encouraged promiscuity and illegitimacy probably had a point. Thomas Bernard commented in about 1818 that it had 'a direct and uncontrollable tendency to encourage vice and increase the mortality of our species.'[75]

An additional reason for this irresponsible behaviour may have been the great increase in the production and consumption of cheap spirits, especially gin and rum. Thomas Turner's account of village life in Sussex in the middle of the eighteenth century includes accounts of all-night drinking parties among the more respectable married couples of the village, while he himself, despite his good resolutions, from time to time got very drunk at race meetings, cricket matches and other social gatherings, some episodes lasting for several days.[76]

It is not surprising, therefore, that the traditional festivities of village life got a very bad name in this period. The May Day custom of boys and girls trooping out into the woods and commons before dawn to gather may soon came under suspicion. 'Much wickedness and debauchery are committed that night,' it was alleged in 1725. The annual wakes or week-long holidays which were – and still are – common in the north of England 'sometimes prove fatal to the morals of our swains and the innocence of our rustic maidens', it was said in 1777. The worst reputation of all, however, was held by the annual or semi-annual 'hiring fairs' where agricultural and domestic servants assembled in order to be rehired for the coming year. Such large assemblies of unmarried teenagers inevitably became riotous towards evening, and 'when bastardy cases are being adjudicated, many a poor girl declares that her ruin was affected at the last Martinmas Hirings.' Indeed, there is statistical evidence from Bromley in Kent of a significant bulge in bastardy nine months after the spring Hiring Fair.[77]

The eighteenth-century increase in the rural population thus combined with the unanticipated consequences of legislation to cause both a rise in the proportion of the propertyless in the society and a migration of more and more girls and boys to find work and housing further away from home. Here the temptation of the girls to seduction, either by masters or by fellow-workers, was great, due to psychological pressure, poverty and loneliness. At the same time, the powerful counter-pressures of family, village community and priest, which had previously forced the putative father to marry the girl, were now removed in the more rootless atmosphere of the city. Among the anonymous drifting mass of the urban proletariat of the late eighteenth century, where the only social bond seems to have been to comrades in the workshop, the men could more easily take their pleasure and run, leaving the girls to suffer the consequences. It is not surprising, therefore, that it was in the cities that the rise of illegitimacy first began.[78] One may conclude, therefore, that the principal cause of the rise of illegitimacy in England in the late eighteenth century, as in the rest of Europe, was not any change in the nature of the work young girls performed, for only a tiny minority went to work in factories, but rather to a collapse of resistance by more young women to full pre-marital intercourse due to a rise of the proportion of the propertyless with no economic stake in the value of their virginity, and a rise in the proportion of men removed from the pressures of family, community and priest which previously would have contrived to force them into marriage. There was thus a change of attitudes towards pre-marital sex on the part of some working-class women; a change of economic circumstances which left them more exposed to enticement and coercion to seduction; a change in social circumstances which deprived them of the moral stiffening provided by older relatives; and a change of economic and social circumstances which left the male seducers more free to refuse their traditional obligation to marry the girls whom they had impregnated.[79]

The story of the love life of the radical Samuel Bamford lends some support to this theory. He first fell in love with a girl called Catherine, but her mother said that 'no one should marry her daughter who could not fetch her away on his own horse', a piece of property Bamford did not possess. He then got a Yorkshire girl pregnant. It is significant of changing attitudes that the girl did not insist on marriage, and was quite content with a financial settlement for the maintenance of the child in the parish workhouse. Finally, he married another girl, but only some months after she had produced her first child by him. This was probably a not untypical story of life among the propertyless young in the late eighteenth century, involving both bastardy and pre-nuptial conception and birth.[80]

An important and tragic result of this decline of family and community protection of single girls, especially in domestic service or a small workshop, was that they were increasingly exposed to sexual exploitation. Without protection from parents, kin, neighbours, ministers or local opinion, these girls were easy victims of seduction by their masters, who then dismissed them when they became pregnant. In some French towns, there survive series of 'declarations of pregnancy' made to the authorities by unwed mothers or mothers-to-be which explain the circumstances of the impregnation. There is no reason to believe that the records for the town of Nantes, which have been analysed in detail, would not also apply to England.[81] The witnesses were mostly country girls in their early twenties from very poor homes, who had allowed themselves to be seduced, either by men of their own class, often seamen or servants, or by their masters. Half of the girls were domestic servants, half of whom had been impregnated by their masters, mostly members of the Nantes bourgeoisie. Although the claim is not necessarily to be believed, a great majority alleged that they had had a promise of marriage which was later repudiated.

There is a little English evidence to show how marital sexual difficulties between a middle-class master and mistress exposed the servants in the household to particular temptations or opportunities. In 1767 the Reverend Thomas Goodwin, parson of Loughton in Bedfordshire, was on chronically bad terms with his wife, who complained that they would lie in bed together at night for three weeks at a time, and he would never touch her. In the daytime, he was very bad-tempered to everyone, 'except to the maid, who was going away with child.' The next maid soon left, alleging that her master had offered her five guineas to sleep with him, and when she refused and gave him a black eye, he offered her ten guineas to keep her mouth shut about the episode. She also told him that his wife was sleeping with the manservant, and it was rumoured in the neighbourhood that a few years before she had offered to run away with the manservant.[82] In a household such as the Goodwins', the chastity of the servants was almost impossible to preserve. So far as the maids were concerned, bastardy was a likely result; so far as the menservants were concerned, they fathered children on their mistress who presumably passed as legitimate children of their master. In other households the close propinquity of servants of both sexes inevitably led to a good deal of pregnancy, a picture confirmed by the early nineteenth-century journals of the Reverend John Skinner. It was only in the larger houses of the Victorian period that the most elaborate architectural precautions were taken to isolate the female from the male servants.

It seems clear that the rapid rise of illegitimacy in the late eighteenth century was due to a shift in the consciousness of young unmarried women from the poorest classes. They were increasingly emancipated from both parental control and the supervision of the church, and they may even have been freeing themselves from deference to their social superiors. Illegitimate children were the product of temporary unions of a floating population of men and women, drifting about at the very bottom of the social scale, mostly but by no means entirely in the towns. What was happening was that the expansion of domestic service and migration from the countryside to the cities was shattering the traditional moral restraints of family, neighbours and church, exposing the girls to easy seduction and tempting the men to make promises of marriage which could easily be repudiated. Such was the desire to catch a husband and not to be left an old maid, that many girls were tempted to surrender their virginity as the only way they could see to secure the marital status they so much desired. Most were successful in this objective, as the statistics of bridal pregnancy show, but a growing minority failed.

iii. Biology: Increased Libidinal Drive

A third possible but unlikely cause of the growth of sexual activity in the eighteenth century is that there was an increase in the libidinal drive of the poor, due to improved nutrition and health. The age of menarche in women, their reproductive ability and lactational amenorrhoea are thought to be linked to weight relative to height, and so to calorie intake.[83] It is known that food was in short supply and dear in the sixteenth and early seventeenth centuries, and relatively cheap in the late seventeenth and the first two-thirds of the eighteenth century. We also know that by comparison with continental Europe, the English were great consumers of protein in the form of meat, both beef and mutton, the latter being a necessary by-product of an active woollen cloth industry. But there is no sign of any improvement in health – indeed, the death rate rose in the seventeenth century, so far as we can tell – and no evidence of increased calorie intake *per capita*, so that the possibility of an increase in libidinal drive after 1660 remains no more than an unproven and unprovable hypothesis.

iv. Conclusion: Sexual Change in the Eighteenth Century

a. The Stages of Change. In summarizing the stages through which sexual attitudes and behaviour passed in England between 1500 and 1800, it is necessary to distinguish between on the one hand the propertied classes, who were increasingly literate, and who were governed more by changing ideas than changing economic circumstances, and on the other the largely illiterate, propertyless poor, among whom economic and social factors predominated.

The Propertied Classes: Among moral theologians and lay writers of domestic handbooks in the Early Modern period, the three basic motives for copulation were love, lust and procreation, and it was in these terms that it was discussed. In the middle ages and the early sixteenth century, the first motive, love, was largely ignored, except as an extra-marital aristocratic artifice, and the second was regarded by the theologians as positively sinful. The exclusive legitimate purpose of the sexual act was for the procreation of children, as a result of which the stricter theologians condemned sexual activity with a pregnant woman, since it could not result in impregnation. The distinction between love and sex was not clearly defined, the latter word to describe the purely physical act not being generally employed. The phrase 'to make love' is a relic of this early linguistic ambiguity, for it covers all three purposes. In the sixteenth century, the demand by the Puritan theologians for 'holy matrimony' joined the earlier concept of extra-marital love to the marital act of procreation as the two legitimate motives for the sexual act; the third motive, the enjoyment of physical pleasure for its own sake, was still condemned. Lust was an admitted fact and marriage provided a legitimate outlet for it, but the purpose of marital sex was procreation and the expression of mutual affection, not sensual pleasure. As a result, 'matrimonial chastity', a strictly limited use of conjugal rights, in quantity and in quality and in variety, was strongly recommended. One can argue, however, that the late sixteenth and early seventeenth centuries was the only period in history when the three basic motives were more or less united in the thinking of theologians and moralists.

The next stage came with a rising dissatisfaction of women with their lot as biological reproductive machines, and their demand for freedom from the tyranny of constant childbearing. By the late seventeenth century, some social groups among the upper-middle classes of Europe, the high bourgeoisie of Geneva and the English nobility, for example, were evidently practising birth control. Even theologians admitted that poverty might be a reason for the limitation of children, and admitted the legitimacy of *coitus reservatus*, or sexual intercourse without ejaculation by the male.[84] *Coitus interruptus*, in which the male withdraws just before ejaculation, was still condemned as the sin of Onan referred to in the Book of Genesis. Not much distinction was made between it and deliberate acts to abort the foetus, or infanticide at or immediately after birth. In fact, however, all three measures were increasingly practised once men came to join with women in desiring to control the number of children, not only to ease the burden on the latter, but to enable the family to provide a better future for the children.

The eighteenth century, therefore, saw a rise in prostitution and pornography on the one hand, as well as of a more companionate, more child-oriented and more contraceptive family type on the other. There was at last a clear realization of the theoretical distinctiveness of the three components of love, lust and procreation. The new family type encouraged the identity of the first two, but increasingly separated them from the third; while the new hedonism tended to detach the second from both the others.[85] These developments were governed more by ideas than by economics, and applied almost exclusively to the middle and upper propertied classes. Thus the next wave of sexual repression, which began around 1770 and reached its full flowering in the mid-Victorian period, seems to have been motivated largely by Evangelical religion and only affected those groups who came under its influence. This included the gentry, the bourgeoisie, the lower-middle class and the respectable segment of the working class, but excluded the greater aristocracy who pursued their normal hedonistic ways, and the mass of the poor untouched by Methodism and Sunday Schools.

The Lower Classes: Among the lower classes, the evolution of sexual attitudes and behaviour between 1500 and 1800 followed a different pattern and was more strongly influenced by economic and social change. The first stage, from about 1500–1700, was characterized by a customary practice of intimate courting, but little pre-marital intercourse, and largely virgin brides. Sexuality was channelled and controlled, partly by the strong pressure of community feeling at the local level, partly by the legal pressure of Puritan magistrates and the propaganda pressure of Puritan preachers, and partly by the successful internalization of ideas about chastity and virginity. The result was a society in which a late marriage pattern co-existed with low rates of illegitimacy and of pre-marital pregnancy. It was a remarkably chaste society, the relief valve for which was intimate courting, carried out under carefully regulated conditions.

The second stage, which began in about 1700, was characterized by continued intimate courting, but a sharp rise in pre-marital intercourse, and consequently in the proportion of pregnant brides. This was caused by the collapse of the Puritan movement, the decay of institutional religion, the weakening of kin protection, the rise of a landless labourer class, which placed less value on virginity than on fertility, the rise of a rural cottage industry which made it economically easy to marry if pregnancy occurred, and perhaps a revival in the belief that the decisive ceremony was the betrothal not the wedding. Moral controls over intimate courting were greatly weakened, but local community pressure, exercised through moral suasion and legal compulsion, was still strong enough to enforce marriage on all except a handful of couples. This handful was increasing rapidly, however, and as a result the illegitimacy ratio was rising fast. This was caused by the weakening of the social controls over the seducer previously exercised by the neighbours, the parish clergy and the local community, caused in part by the isolation of migrant and propertyless young people in the big cities, and in part by the emergence of a hereditary bastardy-prone subculture among the poor.

What is unacceptable is the argument that these developments can be attributed in some way or other to capitalism. Young women had been going into domestic service or working in the textile or garment-making industries for centuries, and there was little change in this pattern before the twentieth century. In any case, the factory offered little in the way of new opportunities for their economic independence from their parents. All the latter institution did was to increase the economic profit to parents of children under ten, who could now be put to useful work, which may just possibly have made parents less anxious to abort or abandon illegitimate children. The second objection to attributing the change in sexual habits to the rise of capitalism and the spread of a market economy is that the chronology is wrong, since pre-nuptial pregnancy rates rose before industrialization. The only effect of capitalism in this respect was to increase the potentialities for the sexual abuse of young women, since early factory workers were second only to domestic servants as the mothers of illegitimate children.

Far into the nineteenth century it remained true that the largest single occupation for single women was in domestic service. This was the group most exposed to sexual abuse, and least economically capable of resistance. As William Acton remarked in 1865, 'there are few women more exposed to temptation to immorality than domestic servants, especially those serving in houses where menservants are also kept.... A woman found pregnant is usually dismissed from her employment without a reference.' 'Men who themselves employ female labour, or direct it for others, have always ample opportunity of choice, compulsion, secrecy and subsequent intimidation should exposure be probable and disagreeable. . . . They can at any moment discharge her.'[86] The rising tide of pregnant and abandoned young women, many of whom drifted into the disease-ridden and futureless profession of prostitution, were tragic victims of sexual exploitation, particularly since there is evidence of an association of pre-nuptial pregnancy not only with economic dependence and low social status but also with illiteracy. In Paris in 1836 one-third of the prostitutes were servant-girls who had been seduced by men on the promise of marriage and then abandoned.[87] These were the poorest, the most ignorant, most defenceless and most exploited of women, not the cheerful hedonistic pleasure-seekers conjured up by modern sexual romantics. The rise of pre-nuptial pregnancies and of illegitimacy among the poor have nothing to do with any new demand for 'personal freedom of action and sexuality for the sake of individual self-fulfilment.'[88] They are primarily products of increased economic deprivation and increased geographical mobility, coupled with a decline in Puritan controls over sexual behaviour.

In the very late eighteenth and early nineteenth centuries, a new factor was introduced which began to narrow the social boundaries of sexual laxity and confine it to the unregenerate, non-respectable poor. This was the secular humanitarian drive of Enlightenment thought in the late eighteenth century, one aspect of which was a detached scientific study of the causes of poverty and misery among the poor and the planning of practical measures to alleviate them. There was a new idea abroad that misery was not an inevitable consequence of God's Providence, or of original sin finding concrete expression in the alcoholism, gambling, fecklessness, filthiness and promiscuity of the poor, but was due to the operation of bad laws and a bad environment. Restraints upon the sale of alcohol and on gambling, better policing of the streets, increased prosperity, and the provision of education for the poor through Sunday Schools in the ideals of thrift, punctuality, sobriety, chastity and cleanliness would, it was hoped, transform the desperate character of working-class lives. If Francis Place is to be believed, these measures had striking effect, not least of which was the noticeable increase of chastity among the daughters of respectable tradesmen and artisans.[89] The working class was dividing between the respectable segment and the disreputable segment. The numerical, but not the proportional, size of the latter was nonetheless constantly growing, due to the enormous increase of population.

b. Conclusion. Although the details of the stage of the change, its precise manifestations and its causes vary from the propertied to the non-propertied classes, the conclusion is inescapable that in the late seventeenth and the eighteenth centuries there took place a great secular change in sexual attitudes and sexual behaviour. Sandwiched between two periods of strict moral repression, under Puritan leadership in the early seventeenth century and under Methodist and Evangelical leadership in the early nineteenth, there was rather more than a century during which both the upper and the lower classes took a remarkably relaxed and permissive attitude to sexual behaviour. It is possible, but not proven, that the lower-middle classes did not share in this cultural change, continuing to cherish Puritan and then Methodist values throughout the century without a break. It seems certain that the more pious of the Anglican upper bourgeoisie and gentry were also unaffected by the change. Some contemporaries certainly thought that this was the case, for example, a somewhat sententious correspondent in *The World* in 1753. 'There are certain vices which the vulgar call "fun", and the people of fashion "gallantry", but the middle rank, and those of the gentry who continue to go to church, still stigmatize them by the opprobrious names of fornication and adultery.'[90] For those who did not share the religious convictions of these respectable, God-fearing middle ranks, however, the eighteenth century was a period of extraordinary sexual tolerance.

Whether this in fact led to any significant increase in individual happiness, however, is quite another question. For the propertyless there was certainly a high cost to pay, as evidenced in the growing army of abandoned and murdered infants, of illegitimate children, of shot-gun marriages of pregnant brides, and of prostitutes. For the rich, the main penalty was a high rate of venereal disease, possibly leading to increased sterility, and the psychological strains imposed on marriage by extra-marital liaisons and the support of bastard children. Sexual permissiveness carried a high price-tag for both men and women in a pre-contraceptive, pre-antibiotic, pre-divorce society.

PART
SIX

Conclusion

CHAPTER 13

Facts, Interpretations, and Post-1800 Developments

'What is good for the individual can be destructive to the family; what preserves the family can be harsh on both the individual and the tribe to which the family belongs; what promotes the tribe can weaken the family and destroy the individual; and so on upward through the permutations of levels of organization.'
(E.O. Wilson, *Sociobiology: the New Synthesis*, Cambridge, Mass. 1975, p. 4).

I THE FACTS OF CHANGE, 1500–1800

i. Stable Demographic Conditions

The family as it evolved in England during the Early Modern period was always limited in its options by certain unyielding demographic facts. The first was the very high level of mortality, particularly an infant and child mortality rate of between thirty and fifty per cent, which affected all classes of society, although the poor suffered more than the rich. Until this mortality rate began to fall in the late eighteenth century, family limitation was a gamble with death, since at any moment all the children might be wiped out by an epidemic disease, leaving none to inherit the property and family name. Continued high mortality among young adults also meant that few marriages outlasted the child-rearing period. On the average, they endured for only about twenty years at most, because of the early death of husband or wife. This meant that grandparents were relatively few in number, either as a support to help in child care or as a burden in their old age. The omnipresence of death coloured affective relations at all levels of society, by reducing the amount of emotional capital available for prudent investment in any single individual, especially in such ephemeral creatures as infants. One result was the neglect of infants by their parents, which in turn reduced the latter's prospects of survival. This was a situation which encouraged the concept of the family as a group of replaceable surrogates, both spouses and more particularly children.

Secondly, this was a society with relatively low nuptiality, in which a significant and rising proportion of population, especially from the upper classes, never married at all, being forced out of the marriage market by the iron law of primogeniture and by the need to earn an arduous living in a profession if status was to be maintained. Even among the poor, some ten per cent never married, and remained bachelors or spinsters all their lives.

Thirdly, western Europe and America were unique among all known societies in the extraordinary delay in the age of marriage some ten or more years after the age of puberty, a feature of family life common to all classes, except the male heirs and the daughters of the landed nobility and gentry. Dictated by the need, itself caused by the custom of separate residence for the newly married, to inherit or accumulate some capital and furniture before marriage, this delay involved severe sexual abstinence at the period of maximum sexual drive. The sublimation of sex among young male adults may well account for the extraordinary military aggressiveness, the thrift, the passion for hard work, and the entrepreneurial and intellectual enterprise of modern Western man. The withdrawal of women from the reproductive cycle for ten of their twenty-five fertile years was a critical factor in slowing down population growth. Delayed marriage also meant that household formation from generation to generation tended to be consecutive rather than concurrent. This facilitated social and intellectual change, since the parents of those who married were often already dead, and thus no longer in a position to impose their will and their values on the new household.

ii. Changing Family Types

Changes in the family from 1500 to 1800 were limited primarily to two important status groups, the upper bourgeoisie of the towns and the squirarchy of the country. These two lead sectors in society provided a pattern which was followed, at varying intervals of time, by the propertied lower middle class and by the highest levels of the court aristocracy.

a. The Open Lineage Family 1450–1630. The late medieval and sixteenth-century family welcomed both aid and direction from the kin and the community. There was no sense of domestic privacy, and inter-personal relations within the conjugal unit, both between husbands and wives and between parents and children, were necessarily fairly remote, partly because of the ever-present probability of imminent death, partly because of cultural patterns which dictated the arranged marriage, the subordination of women, the neglect and early fostering out of children and the custom of harsh parental discipline. Child-rearing practices, especially swaddling, the lack of a single mothering figure, and the crushing of the supposedly sinful will by brute force at an early age, tended to create special psychological characteristics in adults: suspicion towards others, proneness to violence, and an incapacity to develop strong emotional ties to any one individual. The result was a family type whose characteristics of psychological distance, deference and publicity were congruent with the basic values and organization of the hierarchial, authoritarian and inquisitorially collectivist society of Early Modern England.

b. The Restricted Patriarchial Nuclear Family 1550–1700. In the late sixteenth and early seventeenth centuries, this family type was modified by the loss of a sense of trusteeship to the lineage, by the decline of kinship and clientage, and by the concurrent rise of the power of the state and the spread of Protestantism. The most important consequence was the substitution of loyalty to state or sect for loyalty to lineage or patron. This weakened the diffuse affective network of kin and neighbours which had surrounded and sustained the loosely bound family structure, and tended to isolate the nuclear core. This process exposed that core to stresses it was often not yet strong enough to sustain, despite the fact that its internal psychological cohesion was steadily improving. This cohesion was stimulated by a flood of propaganda from the pulpit and printing press, making the household responsible for, and the symbol of, the whole social system, which was thought to be based on the God-given principles of hierarchy, deference and obedience. This almost hysterical demand for order at all costs was caused by a collapse of most of the props of the medieval world picture. The unified dogma and organization of the Catholic Church found itself challenged by a number of rival creeds and institutional structures, the role of the priests as the only authorized intercessors between God and man was undermined, and the reliance upon the intellectual authority of the Ancients was threatened by the new scientific discoveries. Moreover, in England there occurred a phase of unprecedented social and geographical mobility which at the higher levels transformed the composition and size of the gentry and professional classes, and at the lower levels tore hundreds of thousands of individuals loose from their traditional kinship and neighbourhood back-grounds. Protestant preaching in the late sixteenth century caused large numbers of the English to be effectively christianized for the first time, but the concurrent high geographical mobility also left them a prey to acute insecurity and anxiety. The material world was more threatening and unpredictable than it had ever been, and the Devil and his agents were everywhere, but the ancient remedies for human ills in magic and 'wise women' were now denounced as mere satanic witchcraft.

In an atmosphere of heightened religious enthusiasm, the only hope of salvation was thought to lie in the ruthless persecution of dissidents. Traitors were hanged, drawn and quartered; religious radicals and gypsies were exterminated like vermin; witches were denounced, tortured and burned; children were beaten; wives were subjugated. Passive Obedience and the Divine Right of Kings seemed to many to be the only theories that promised hope of avoidance of political chaos. For the state, Passive Obedience to the husband and father in the home was the model for and guarantee of Passive Obedience to the king in the nation. In Protestant England there took place a partial transfer of the functions of the Church to the family, of the priest to the head of the household. The spiritual sanctity of the family was particularly stressed by the Puritans, and the gathered Churches of the sectaries finally substituted a free association of godly families for the traditional religious organization of the parish which included both saints and sinners.

Paradoxically, although the institution of marriage was becoming more sanctified in the late sixteenth century and although there was a growing stress by the moral theologians on the importance of marital and parental love, at the same time power relations within the family were being theoretically urged to become more authoritarian and patriarchal under the strong encouragement of both Church and state. The propaganda for – and the reality of – this internal authoritarianism within the family, which was so marked among the propertied classes, applied to pre-marital relations between young people, which were strictly limited and controlled by their parents, to husband-wife relations, where the principle of wifely obedience was constantly stressed, and to parent-child relations, where the breaking of the child's will was thought to be the paramount purpose of infant and child training.

In the lower-middle and the labouring classes, economic co-operation in the running of the family business dictated a certain measure of sharing of responsibility, if only for the sake of joint survival. But leisure activities were mostly conducted in sexually segregated groups and very clear status lines continued to be drawn on the basis of sex. Working wives were subjected to a crushing burden of toil, both outside the home and in household management, while still kept in a thoroughly subservient position. Engels' theory that work brought equality between the sexes, and that the subordination of wives was a product of their transformation into a kept leisured class in the home, is not supported by the historical evidence. [1] On the other hand, children in the propertyless class had greater freedom of choice in marriage. Adolescents had mostly long since left home to work as servants or apprentices in other people's homes and were, therefore, physically free to make their own mate selection, and even to indulge in some sexual experimentation during the courting process. Nor were they tied down by the burdens of property exchange and so dependent on parental consent for marriage, since neither partner had much to give.

On the other hand, since the children were also part of the family economic unit, they were probably subjected to physical and moral coercion from an early age in order to maximize their productivity before they left home. Secondly, the need to accumulate household goods and working capital to set up an independent household forced the children of the poor to postpone marriage until later and later, to some ten to sixteen years after sexual maturity. Their freedom of choice in timing and person in marriage was thus severely limited by economic considerations.

c. The Closed Domesticated Nuclear Family 1620–1800. The third stage in the evolution of the nuclear family in the middle and upper classes began in the late seventeenth century. It was characterized by a continuation of the emphasis of the boundary surrounding the nuclear unit, and a progressive decline in the influence on that unit of both the neighbourhood and the kin. This of necessity led to greater stress on internal bonding within the family both as emotional ties to outsiders diminished, and as pressures from external organized groups relaxed. On the other hand, there was a marked reversal of the previous trend towards domestic patriarchy. Neither the absolute monarch nor the patriarchal father was any longer necessary for the maintenance of the social order, as Locke deliberately pointed out in his assault on Robert Filmer's last-ditch stand in his *Patriarcha*.

By 1700 there was clearly emerging among the bourgeois and landed gentry a new family type inspired by the principle of Affective Individualism, whose particular manifestations were as follows. The strength of the kin ties had declined and those that survived were increasingly limited to close relatives. Mate selection was determined more by free choice than by parental decision and was based as much on expectations of lasting mutual affection as on calculations of an increase in money, status or power. Except in the highest aristocratic circles, the financial considerations of the dowry and the jointure became less decisive elements in marriage negotiations than the prospect of future personal happiness based on settled and well-founded affection; as a result there were fewer marriages to heiresses, fewer marriages within the ramifications of the kin, and fewer marriages of young men to significantly older women. The authority of husbands over wives and of parents over children declined as greater autonomy was granted to, or assumed by, all members of the family unit. There were the beginnings of a trend towards greater legal and educational equality between the sexes, and the claims of each child to some part of the inheritance were carefully protected, although there was no decline in the emphasis on primogeniture. Professional, upper-bourgeois and gentry families became much more child-oriented, and some adopted remarkably permissive attitudes to child-rearing. Among the upper tradesmen and shopkeepers, yeomen and tenant farmers, more and more wives were being educated in the social graces of their betters, and were withdrawing from active participation in family economic production. Instead, they were occupying themselves with the supervision of the servants, child care and a round of status enhancing leisure activites, whether time-consuming pursuits like tea parties and card playing, or good works, or visits to the local theatre and the circulating library. Although the economic dependence of these women on their husbands increased, they were granted greater status and decision-making power within the family, and they became increasingly preoccupied with the nurturing and raising of their children.

The higher social groups whose life-style these women were aping were now clearly distinguished by an elaborate set of culturally induced manners that marked them off as 'the quality'. The key was conformity to elaborate rituals of behaviour involving an increasing privatization of one's body, its fluids and its odours. The substitution of forks for fingers in eating, the supply by the host of separate plates and utensils for each course, the substitution of handkerchiefs for fingers or clothes for nose-blowing, the control of spitting, the wearing of nightclothes, the introduction of washbasins, portable bathtubs and soap, the substitution of wigs for lice-ridden natural hair, are all symptoms of the same evolution. Knowledge of the classics for men, and music, dancing and needlework for women, were additional glosses on this deeper evolution of elite manners based on the refinement and elegance of body and mind. There was now a civilization of Western manners for the elite, defined by a set of internationally recognized patterns of behaviour.

In some quarters there was a glorification of the sexual aspects of love in art, literature and life, now channelled as much inside marriage as outside it: the role-models of wife and mistress were united, and the libido was released from its long period of religious containment. Among the higher aristocracy, adultery by both sexes again became extremely common, while men of all classes made much use of the growing army of prostitutes in the cities. Among the propertyless poor, and to a lesser extent the smallholders, artisans and small tradesmen, sexual relations before marriage became normal, pre-nuptial conceptions rose as high as forty per cent and the illegitimacy ratio greatly increased from a previously very low level. The first two are evidence of a weakening of parental, clerical and community controls over old customs of pre-marital petting, and of a willingness by young girls far from home to attempt to entice men into a stable relationship by taking a promise of marriage rather than the wedding as the moment to allow full sexual relations to begin. The third is evidence that a growing minority of men were exploiting their power as masters of servants or their position as drifting and lonely fellow workers, in order to take their sexual pleasure and evade the consequences.

Among the upper bourgeoisie and squirarchy the eighteenth century thus saw the emergence of a new family type playing a new role and experiencing new internal and external relationships: a family serving rather fewer practical functions, but carrying a much greater load of emotional and sexual commitment. It was a family type which was more conjugal and less kin and community oriented; more bound by ties of affection or habit, and less responsible for the helpless, who were now looked after by public utilitarian; more internally liberal, and less patriarchal and authoritarian; less responsible for the helpless who were now looked after by public authorities, but more concerned for their well-being; more sexually liberated, preferably within marriage, and less sexually repressed; more concerned with children and their needs and less adult-oriented; more private and less public; and finally, more desirous and capable of controlling procreation, and less willing to leave such matters to the will of God.

These are, of course, trends and not absolutes, and older customs and values survived for a very long time. The degree to which, if at all, this new family type was adopted varied enormously from one class and one family to another. Most features took root first among the urban bourgeoisie, and spread a little later to the landed classes. Many never penetrated the poor at all until the nineteenth or even the early twentieth centuries. The outcome was not so much the replacement of one family type by another as the widening of the varieties. There was a growing diversity of family types, a widening pool of cultural alternatives.

Particular aspects of the new family type struck deeper and more immediate roots in some classes than in others. Thus the higher aristocracy clung longest to the arranged marriage with an eye to property, but were the first to welcome the new attitude towards sex as one of the supreme pleasures of life; the professional and bourgeois classes were probably the first to adopt the ideal of married love, but the last to build frank sexual passion into the marital relationship. The upper gentry seem to have been the pioneers in the creation of the permissive child-oriented family, and yet they continued to tolerate the brutal barbarities of English public school life. The labouring classes had long been accustomed to a family with shared economic responsibilities, but were the last to develop strong internal emotional bonds, to admit a greater sense of equality of status between husband and wife, and to invest love or money in their children.

2 INTERPRETATIONS OF THE CHANGE 1640–1800

What needs explaining is not a change of structure, or of economics, or of social organization, but of sentiment. People within the nuclear family in certain circles treated one another quite differently in 1780 from the way their great-grandparents had done in 1600, and their attitude towards outsiders, whether kin or neighbours, was also substantially different. There was a shift in a whole cultural system, defined as the growth of Affective Individualism, the symptoms and causes of which have been spelt out at length in Chapter 6.

If the facts are correct, if the change to the new family type began as early as the mid-seventeenth century, and if the lead was taken by the mercantile and professional upper bourgeoisie and by the squirarchy, then certain common explanations for the evolution of the modern family cannot be true.

a. Modernization Theory. For one thing, the early and erratic chronology and social specificity of these developments make it impossible to accept any general sociological theory of modernization as applied to the family. There are numerous definitions of modernization theory, but one of the best and most relevant, a synoptic view of a century and a half of sociological work, has been made by R. Nisbet. He has argued that there has taken place a progressive erosion of five traditional values.[2] The first of these values is the sense of community, which decays as the village neighbourhood gives way to the floating urban migrant mass. The immigrants are said to be detached physically from the ties of kin and friends and to be thus freed to evolve new values and ideologies of their own about virginity, pre-marital sex, marriage for love, individual autonomy, and so on. There seems to be a good deal of truth in this. The second value is the all-pervasive sense of authority and deference which enveloped late medieval man. This was ritualized by the repeated gesture of doffing the hat on all occasions to all superiors, and was internalized by constant indoctrination at every turn. The Great Chain of Being, the hierarchical ordering of the universe, made it natural to look on the monarch as a super-patriarch, and the father as a mini-sovereign. These values, too, were allegedly destroyed by the social, economic and political changes of the sixteenth century onwards. In fact, however, they were positively reinforced for over a century, from 1530 to 1660, as a buttress against anarchy, and they only finally gave way when the rate of change slowed down and they became superfluous to the maintenance of political stability.

Of the other traditional values, that of social stability was allegedly undermined by increased geographical, social and occupational mobility. But this is called into question when it is found that mobility among the propertied classes may have been on the decline after 1660. Increasing, not decreasing, proportions of apprentices in English towns in the late seventeenth and eighteenth centuries were admitted by virtue of their fathers' freedom of the city and membership of the guild. Urban immigration was increasingly short-range, from neighbouring areas. On the other hand more and more of the population were becoming propertyless, and as the demographic expansion of the eighteenth century picked up momentum, more and more flocked into the towns. Among these classes social disintegration certainly occurred, and to this extent the sociologists are right.

The fourth traditional value, the concept of the sacred, was certainly undermined by the secularization of society. But this is a change to be handled with extreme attention to chronology, in view of the rise of Protestant (and Catholic) religious enthusiasm between 1550 and 1650, and its revival again after 1780: secularization was squeezed in between two phases of religious zeal among all sections of the propertied classes. England in 1650 was probably less secular than it ever had been, and in 1780 it was probably more secular than it was ostensibly to be again for over a century.

The final alleged loss of traditional values, the cutting of modern man from his psychological roots, his purchase of autonomy and independence at the price of alienation and anomie, is also open to question because of faulty chronology and failure to specify the class under discussion. Familial change towards greater autonomy and equality took place among the squirarchy and upper bourgeoisie in the eighteenth century, whereas it was part of the labouring classes who were drawn into the dark satanic mills which by Marxist theory created the condition known as 'alienation.'

In view of these chronological and class discrepancies, the logic of a sociological theory based on an overarching concept of modernization marching relentlessly through the centuries appears less than convincing. It is merely one more example of the many pitfalls of any unilinear theory of history, which ignores the ups and downs of social and intellectual change, the lack of uniformity of the direction of the trends, and the failure of the various trends to synchronize in the way they ought if the paradigm is to fit. Above all, by sweeping broadly across the vast spectrum of highly distinctive national cultures, status groups and classes, these theories reduce the enormous diversity of social experience to a uniformity which has never existed in real life.

b. Gemeinschaft-Gesellschaft. Another way of looking at the evolution of the family is as a response to the slow shift in Early Modern and Modern times from the values of a small, immobile, close-knit, face-to-face, status-bound community (known to sociologists as *Gemeinschaft*) to those of a big, impersonal, bureaucratic, meritocratic, competitive, contractual individualistic society (known as *Gesellschaft*).[3] It is certainly true that the nuclear family's kin affiliations and its openness to community pressures have been undermined, that many of its economic and social functions have been taken over by larger and more impersonal institutions, such as schools and hospitals and banks, and that the trend towards atomistic individualism has increased. But everything we know about the pre-modern community, such as the village, indicates that it was riddled with competitive feuds and factions, usually organized around kinship groups. Aspects of *Gesellschaft* were thus present in the old *Gemeinschaft* world. Similarly, in the new *Gesellschaft* world of today, the nuclear family has developed and strengthened its emotional cohesion as a last *Gemeinschaft* refuge. Thus both periods have included elements of both structures and qualities, but rearranged in different ways. This evolution therefore lies less in a qualitative change, though this undoubtedly is present, than in a redistribution of the two qualities throughout the social system. Moreover, the trend was itself interrupted once, by the revival among the middle and upper classes during the Victorian period of the authoritarian patriarchal family. Even if the trend has been correctly identified, it has not been a constant linear movement.

c. Industrial Capitalism. Yet another explanation of the evolution of the new family type is that it was a product of industrial capitalism. Capitalist society, it is said, stresses achievement, uniformity, functional specificity and geographical mobility, whereas the traditional family stressed ascription, particularism, diffuseness, and geographical stability. The latter, therefore, had to be modified to fit the former. It was Engels who argued that the free-contract system of labour relations, on which industrial society in the West was based, presupposed a free-contract system of marital relations. He recognized the prior importance of Protestantism in fostering possessive individualism and personalized morality, but stressed that it was industrialization which brought the love marriage to the working classes. Under this theory he was obliged to assert that the new family type was confined to the lower classes, and, unlike all other civil rights in the society, excluded the propertied classes.[4]

There are many factual historical errors in this hypothesis, which has recently become the accepted dogma of Parsonian functionalist sociology.[5] The main objection is that the class analysis is wrong. It was among the landed, professional and upper bourgeois classes, not among the propertyless industrial poor, that an individualistic ideology first changed the character of internal and external family relationships. The second objection is that the chronology is wrong, since the <u>new family type</u> developed in New England and in England <u>well before industrialization even began</u>. Since both the social class distribution and the chronology fail to fit the model, it seems evident if there can have been no direct connection between the two developments. A third objection is that there is mounting evidence that the factory did not break up the family as an economic unit. Engels thought that 'the modern industrial family is founded on the open or concealed domestic slavery of the wife' and that the early factory caused the destruction of family life, since it drove work out of the home and separated husband, wife and children in different occupations in different locations. But it now looks as if the first phase of industrialization in the eighteenth century had little effect on the employment of married women in cottage industries in the home, and that the later stages of factory industrial-

[marginalia: But not mercantilism]

ization in the nineteenth century actually drove them back into the home.

What is certain is that the traditional female occupations of domestic service, textile manufacture and garment-making remained the three largest until the early twentieth century, while the family continued to act as a unit of production far into the nineteenth century in major areas of the economy, in domestic industry, agriculture and even in early industrial workshops. Fourthly, it is very doubtful whether the factory did much to increase the employment of married women outside the home. There are good reasons to think that in the seventeenth and early eighteenth centuries a very high proportion of married women took part in productive labour, especially in labour-intensive drudgery in agriculture, petty trading, spinning, lace-making and other cottage industries. The demand for this labour was seasonal and erratic, and the women were paid only one-half to one-third the wages of men. But the work existed, and it served to ease some of the stresses of abject family poverty. In 1690 William Petty remarked that 'all women over 7 are to labour, except among the upper tenth.' It was only in 1820, when industrialization had been under way for over forty years, that employment opportunities for women in factories increased, and then only in the cotton trade. Even so, most of these women were unmarried girls, who mostly left the factory as soon as they set up a family: only seventeen per cent were married women in 1833. The only employment for women that continued to increase through the nineteenth century was as domestic servants to the increasing number of affluent middle class, but this again was a form of employment largely confined to unmarried girls. The evidence that industrialization in the eighteenth and nineteenth centuries substantially and progressively increased the job opportunities for married women outside the home is thus on balance very dubious indeed. If this is so, the link between the new family type and industrialized society becomes extremely tenuous.[6]

It cannot be denied that for those married women who worked in factories, industrialization was highly destructive of family life. A report of 1833 noted that these girls had had little or no opportunity to learn domestic duties, and that they were forced to abandon the home for very long hours. 'Here is the young mother absent from her child about twelve hours daily. And who has the charge of the infant in her absence? Usually some little girl or aged woman, who is hired for a trifle, and whose services are equivalent to the reward.'[7] But these were a tiny minority of all married women, and a small minority even of the women who worked in factories. Although the effect of the industrial revolution on the employment opportunities of married women was not very marked, except possibly in the limited area of the cotton towns, both cottage industry and factory industry everywhere increased the earning potential of children, in the period before the introduction of child-labour laws. If children could be put to regular productive work from the age of six or seven, and if the bulk of their wages could be appropriated by their parents until their early twenties, they could be transformed from an economic burden to a major economic asset to the family: three or four children out at work could double the family income. There can be little doubt about the effects of this on raising fertility rates, increasing nutrition in the home, and generally in improving the living standards of the poor. But the improvement must have been limited to that period in the family life cycle when the children were mostly over six and under twenty-six, and to the period in time before the new laws came into force.[8]

There is no evidence as yet about the way in which this use of child-labour changed either power or affective relationships within the nuclear family or among the kindred. It should be pointed out that parental love, which was one of the central features of the new family type as it developed in the middle classes, was hardly conducive to early industrial work practices. As Marx and Engels were at pains to document, young children were exploited unmercifully in factories and mines in the early phases of industrialization. But it was their parents who consented and indeed actively encouraged this exploitation in order to obtain an early economic profit from these otherwise useless mouths that had to be fed. This is certainly true, although it is not established that the juvenile wage slaves of the factory were in fact worse off than the children employed in small family crafts carried on in the home.

The final blow to the theory that industrialization created the new family type is the recent empirical evidence which strongly indicates that the fit between the two is far less perfect than was previously supposed. Admittedly, the custom of independent residence for the nuclear family facilitates geographical mobility into new work areas and the breaking of ties with the kin. Partible inheritance facilitates the mobility of capital (although primogeniture drives younger sons out of the countryside into the city in search of work). Greater internal freedom within the nuclear family increases psychological adaptability to new situations and new work routines. But recent studies of family life among the poor during industrialization in the nineteenth century, or in the post-industrial urban world of the twentieth century, show conclusively that a variety of family types are compatible with industrialization and that kin relationships still remain very close in industrial urban societies, and indeed are positively reinforced as life-savers in times of high geographical mobility or economic hardship. A detailed case study of the relations between the family and employment in the largest textile factory in the world in Manchester, New Hampshire, in the late nineteenth and early twentieth centuries shows a very close interrelationship between the traditional family structure and modern factory needs. What emerges is the paradoxical discovery that it was the very old-fashioned family of the French Canadians, patriarchally controlled, enlarged and extended, with close kin ties and high fertility rates, which was best adapted to recruit, house and discipline a reliable labour force for this great modern industrial plant. Dependent on the changing conditions of supply and demand for labour, the modern factory managers and the traditional family patriarchs manoeuvred and bargained to control employment and recruitment to suit their own internal needs.[9] Under these hard facts, the causal model that makes industrialization the independent variable in creating the modern nuclear family collapses completely.

It does appear, however, that the new family type is first associated with the upper levels of the urban bourgeoisie and professional classes. To this extent there is certainly a connection with the spirit of capitalism, though not with industrialization. It was early commercial capitalism as it affected the wealthy patriciate, the entrepreneurs and merchants, first in Florence in the fifteenth century, then probably in Amsterdam in the early seventeenth century, then in London in the late seventeenth century, which was a necessary, although not a sufficient, cause of the emergence of the new family type.[10]

What seems to have happened in the late eighteenth and early nineteenth centuries is that the new family type already adopted by the upper-middle and landed classes now spread downward into the labouring classes. It was the Sunday Schools and other agencies which created a diligent, thrifty and sober labour force, mobile in relation to parents but centered around the family home, which was the ideal of every industrial entrepreneur. This new family type was in theory perfectly adapted to the economic changes of the period.

It is not being claimed that industrialization had no effect whatever upon family structure. As Marx demonstrated in the first volume of *Capital*, early factory industrialization was certainly destructive of cohesive family life as it then existed. Thus the modern family fitted the modern factory far better than the modern factory fitted the modern family. What is here being argued is that the relationship is not a simple one, that most of the features of the modern family appeared before industrialization and among social groups unaffected by it, and that even those exposed to it responded in different ways. Moreover meritocratic rather than patrimonial and kin-oriented systems of recruitment and promotion are not essential to the efficient working of a modern factory, as the Japanese example indicates. It is only when meritocratic values become paramount in hiring and promotion decisions that a very important aspect of traditional and early modern family structure disappears. But recent studies suggest that even in societies with rigorously impartial examination systems, there persists a strong built-in hereditary bias, which tends to preserve elite positions for children of elite families, while lower down in the class structure certain trades and occupations tend to be handed down from father to son, with the active help of modern trade unions.[11]

d. Individualism. Another explanation of the trend towards a new family type was formulated a century and a half ago by Alexis de Tocqueville, when in 1835 he surveyed the pre-industrial American scene. To him, the key to the change was what he called 'the democratic spirit', and is here called the spirit of individualism. Writing just before the Victorian revival of patriarchy, he remarked that it was now a commonplace that 'in our time the members of a family stand upon an entirely different footing towards each other: that the distance which separated a father from his sons had been lessened, and that paternal authority, if not destroyed, is at least impaired.' Here he is speaking in the same terms as Dr Johnson used about England sixty years before. He also noted the striking change in the affective character of private correspondence between family members, the change in legal obligations, and the early emancipation of young people from parental control. He flatly denied that this adolescent autonomy was achieved only as the result of a bitter oedipal struggle: it was freely conceded since it conformed to accepted social values. The causes of these changes he ascribed to the shift away from an aristocratic society in which 'the father is not only the civil head of the family but the organ of its traditions, the expounder of its customs, the arbiter of its manners. He is listened to with deference, he is addressed with respect.' Tocqueville found the change particularly noticeable in the two Anglo-Saxon societies of America and England for exactly the reasons which have here been put forward. He believed that the spirit of independence was the result of a major cultural shift, fostered by Protestantism and reinforced by the rights of self-government. 'Freedom is then infused into the domestic circle by political habits and by religious opinions.'[12] What he omitted to mention was first the enormous influence of the growth of a large, independent and self-confident middle class, equipped with a genteel education and enjoying sufficient affluence to support a life-style based on privacy and leisure; and second the cultural homogeneity of this class and the landed squirarchy since many of the former were young sons of the latter. Both are essential to explain why the lead in these vast changes in *mentalité* occurred first in England and New England.

3   POST-1800 FAMILY TYPES

i. The Nineteenth-century Reversal

Historical change is not a one-way street, and even in the West over the last five hundred years, continuous linear development has only occurred in the one field of technology. The trend towards the isolated nuclear family, greater personal autonomy, and emphasis on affective ties has not run a steady course from the sixteenth century to the twentieth. In terms of both sexual attitudes and power relationships, one can dimly begin to discern huge, mysterious, secular swings from repression to permissiveness and back again. In England an era of reinforced patriarchy and discipline lasted from about 1530 to about 1670, with the high point in the 1650s. This in turn gave way to an era of growing individualism and permissiveness which was dominant in the upper middle and upper classes from about 1670 to about 1790. The next stage in the evolution of the family was marked by a strong revival of moral reform, paternal authority and sexual repression, which was gathering strength among the middle classes from about 1770.

a. Moral Reform. The first sign of change was a drive to reform the morals first of the poor, then of the rich. This moralistic streak was visible in parliamentary legislation, in the revival of societies for the suppression of vice and in the various, perhaps more powerful, organs of social control such as family, Church, school, university and petty sessions. In 1787 George III issued a Proclamation against vice, in which he urged his subjects to join in a crusade to suppress 'excessive drinking, blasphemy, profane swearing and cursing, profanation of the Lord's day, and other dissolute, immoral or disorderly practices.' He ordered the closing of brothels and gambling houses, and the suppression of 'all loose and licentious prints, books and publications.'[13] This conformed to the growing demands, led by the Evangelicals, to suppress the deplorable folk customs of the poor, so as to make 'several million of poor labouring people sober, industrious, frugal, temperate, virtuous and happy.' The hedonistic popular culture of the rural poor in the eighteenth century was to be made to conform to urban middle-class morality. Sydney Smith was right when in 1809 he pointed out that the Society for the Suppression of Vice should more accurately 'denominate themselves a Society for suppressing the vices of persons whose income does not exceed £500 a year.'[14]

From this middle-class drive for the moral regeneration of the poor, the movement spread out to include much of the upper class and the respectable working class, perhaps reaching its peak in the middle of the nineteenth century.

*b. Paternal Authority.*The key institution upon which this new moral Puritanism was concentrated was the family. 'Home is the first and most important school of character,' remarked Samuel Smiles, a view strongly reinforced by the existence in Victoria and Albert of what Bagehot called 'a family on the throne' – the first since Charles I and Henrietta Maria, if one excludes the political alliance of William and Mary.[15] The driving force behind this movement was the spread of Evangelical piety. God was again seen as directly controlling day-to-day events within the household, in which capacity he was a severe and pitiless masculine figure. His representative on earth was the husband and father, who now acquired a new and significant title: the 'Paterfamilias', the man who by the 1840s once more led the family prayers three times a day. 'It was constantly emphasized that the will of the parent was the will of God. . . . The more religious a father was, the more likely was he to make this confusion between his own inclinations and the divine purpose.'[16]

With this reassertion of patriarchal authority in the early nineteenth century, the status of women inevitably declined, despite the hollow blast on the trumpet of female liberation issued by Mary Wollstonecraft in 1792.[17] The standard advice of the moralists was now that 'in everything that women attempt, they should show their consciousness of dependence.' The anonymous author of *The English Matron* of 1846 put the situation as follows: 'the government of a household, for the sake of all its inmates, should be a monarchy, but a limited monarchy; of all forms, a democracy is most uncomfortable in domestic life.' This was fairly moderate advice, but it was interpreted in a more authoritarian fashion. 'Rarely indeed did the wife venture upon the tiniest self-assertion, and then only with a sense of sin.'[18]

The sign of the times was the extraordinary success of Hannah More's *Coelebs in Search of a Wife* of 1809, which ran to eight editions in two months. The book celebrates the ideal woman, Lucilla Stanley, who is devoted to domestic duties, religious, modest in dress, silent unless spoken to, deferential to men, and devoted to good works. Her antithesis was Amelia Rattle, 'a mass of accomplishments without one particle of mind, one ray of common sense, or one shade of delicacy.' She threw herself into indecorous postures, exhibited a manly independence of mind and behaviour, tended to dominate the conversation, had a taste for dances, parties and the gay London life, and was also very scholarly in almost all subjects. The defenders of eighteenth-century values fought a brave but losing battle against the new trend. Sydney Smith found the moral of the book to be that 'no Christian is safe who is not dull', and Charles Lamb defiantly announced that

> If ever I marry a wife
> I'll marry a landlord's daughter
> For then I may sit at the bar
> And drink cold brandy and water.

But Sydney Smith and Charles Lamb had not the slightest effect – nor did either of them get married. The success of *Coelebs* marks the end of an era in husband-wife relations: the Amelia Rattles were out, the Lucilla Stanleys were in.[19]

The new ideal of womanhood involved total abnegation, making the wife a slave to convention, propriety, and her husband. Inevitably, this could only be achieved, if at all, at a very high psychic cost, particularly at a time when divorce was not available, and wives and husbands were living longer and longer. It has been seriously suggested that one not uncommon solution to an impossible domestic situation in early Victorian England was resort by the desperate wife or husband to the arsenic bottle in the chemist's shop.[20]

Formality was revived and by the 1830s wives were once more addressing their husbands in public, and apparently in private, as 'Mr Douglas', while in general social intercourse the use of familiar names like Dick, Tom or Jack gave way to 'Mr Darcy', 'Mr Bingley', and 'Mr Collins', as is found in the novels of Jane Austen.[21] On the other hand one important exception to the drift of patriarchy was some Parliamentary legislation, beginning with the first divorce act of 1857. The granting to deserted wives of the control of their own property in the same year, and the two Married Women's Property Acts of 1870 and 1882, at last gave wives some control over their own estates, and also legal recognition and thus the ability to sue in court.

The same patriarchal trend affected parent-child relations, while authoritarianism again became strongly marked, with a renewed stress on the pre-eminence of the father, and the subordination of the children. The family became increasingly 'a stifling fortress of emotional bonding', while relations between parents and children grew more intrusive. Supervision was more intense and oppressive since it was now motivated by an intense religious zeal. The seventeenth-century Puritan theory of the innate sinfulness of the child was revived, and Hannah More argued that it was 'a fundamental error to consider children as innocent beings whose little weaknesses may, perhaps, want some correction, rather than as beings who bring into the world a corrupt nature and evil dispositions, which it should be the great end of education to rectify.'[22] This movement began in Evangelical circles, linking up with a continuous Wesleyan tradition that in turn was rooted in late seventeenth-century Puritanism. The connection is shown by its forceful appearance as early as 1770 in a leading Evangelical publication, *The Gospel Magazine or Spiritual Library*. Its readers were told that 'in order to form the mind, the first necessary step is to conquer and effectually subdue the natural perverseness of the stubborn will.... I must insist on conquering the wills of children betimes.' The way to break their spirit was laid out in chilling detail: 'Never commend them when present. ... Let them have nothing to cry for. ... Never let them choose their victuals.... From a year old, make them do as they are commanded, if you chastise them ten times running to effect it. Let none persuade you it is cruel to do thus.... The carnal world cry loudly against this..., vainly thinking it arises from tyranny and cruelty.'[23] The similarity with the earlier advice of Susanna Wesley is very close.

These dedicated reforming Evangelists slowly but surely triumphed over the easy-going permissiveness of the eighteenth century, and as a result punishment became once again both frequent and severe. It was now less the old-fashioned flogging, except at school, but rather the newer, more devastating methods of withdrawal of affection, coupled with food and sensory deprivation. It was normal to lock a child for hours or even days in a dark room or closet on a limited diet of bread and water. Further to break the child's will, it was constantly emphasized that 'every fault of our children [is] to be felt by them as an offence against God.' 'Whatever may have been their wishes on any subject, mine have ever been paramount,' wrote a mother complacently about her daughters in a story published in 1855. John Stuart Mill lamented 'that rarity in England, a really warm-hearted mother', while the father became that remote figure known to his children as 'the governor'. Frederic Harrison recalled that in his middle-class early Victorian home, 'My father remains a blank for quite a long time.... ' He concluded that 'a boy's haziness about the personality, and of course the purport, of his male parent certainly must have been the rule rather than the exception under the Victorian usage, which so subdivided and inevitably estranged the family.'[24]

In some families, for example that of Elizabeth Grant, the daughter of a Scottish laird, lawyer and member of Parliament, these features of Victorian child-care were all visible by the first decade of the nineteenth century. They may possibly have been a seventeenth-century survival in a backward area rather than a revival, but most of the punishments were distinctively nineteenth century. The first thing in the morning, regardless of the weather, the children were plunged into a cold bath. 'A large, long tub stood in the kitchen court, the ice on the top of which had often to be broken before our horrid plunge into it.... How I screamed, begged, prayed, entreated to be saved.' There followed a breakfast of bread and milk, which had to be swallowed despite the fact that some of the children were allergic to milk, which made them feel ill all day. Indeed, the food discipline was very severe. 'The children were always forced to eat all the food on their plate, including the fat.' The stomachs which rejected milk could not easily manage fat, 'except when we were under the lash, then indeed the fat and the tears were swallowed together.' The normal punishment for obstinacy, such as refusal to eat, was to be locked in a dark closet 'where we cried for an hour or more.' Any food not eaten at one meal was produced at the next, and Elizabeth's sister Jane once went for thirty hours without food until she finally gave in and ate her spinach, which made her sick all night. When offered water gruel, Elizabeth simply could not get it down and was locked in a closet without food all day. 'Faint from hunger I lay down in the evening on the floor of the closet where I had passed the summer's day and sobbed out that I wished to die.' For other acts of disobedience or assertions of the will, the punishments were the same. The children were locked in a small room on bread and water, while for academic faults 'we were flogged too for every error, boys and girls alike', a punishment administered exclusively by the father. As for the mother, she was a remote figure, usually languishing, 'very reserved with us, not watchfully of us, nor considerate, nor consistent.' Even marriage was subject to parental control, and when Elizabeth fell in love with the son of her father's bitter enemy in 1815, the two families forced the young couple to call off the match, thus breaking Elizabeth's heart.[25] The general picture is one of a severe family discipline, flourishing in Scotland and London over thirty years before Queen Victoria came to the throne, at a time when other upper-class families were still clinging to the permissive and affectionate late eighteenth-century mode. Its basic objectives were the old seventeenth-century ones: crushing the will and assisting learning with blows. The only difference was that beating was reserved for academic lapses, and that starvation and locking in dark closets were used instead to break the will. The tide had clearly turned by 1818, with the publication of the *History of the Fairchild Family*, by Mrs Sherwood, which was an immediate and lasting best-seller as a book for children. The moral of the book is that children are by nature depraved creatures, that every slip is a grievous sin against God, and that the appropriate punishment is confinement in a dark closet. As substitutes for Cinderella, Jack the Giant Killer or Mother Goose, Mrs Sherwood's books ushered in a new era in middle- and upper-class child reading.

It has been plausibly argued that 'in the psychology of sexual repression and its ever-attendant guilt, we may ... find part of the explanation of the popularity of the myth of the innocent child and the savagery towards children in practice which seems to have existed so astonishingly – otherwise – side by side.'[26] Certainly there seems to be a link between the frantic attempts to suppress adolescent masturbation and the continued – or perhaps revived – use of whipping, even of girls, right into the 1870s and beyond, to a degree which horrified the French. Extensive correspondence in *The Englishwoman's Domestic Magazine* in 1870 proves that the whipping of girls on the bare buttocks, sometimes by men, was still a common occurrence in many schools, and that a sado-masochistic relationship not infrequently developed between the punisher and his or her victim.[27]

This subjection of children to their parents lasted well into adolescence and early manhood. At this period, middle- and upper-class sons were financially dependent on their parents well into their adult life, as the expense and duration of training for a professional career grew longer and longer. Until well into their twenties, these sons needed generous allowances from their fathers if they wished to become clergymen, doctors or lawyers in order to maintain the standards to which they were accustomed.[28]

At the same time as middle-class parents were exercising emotional pressure and economic blackmail on their children, upper- and middle-class parents were increasingly turning the whole business of socializing the child over to hired specialists operating in a physically separate part of the house, the nursery. The English nanny was as much a characteristic phenomenon of Victorian England as the railroad.[29] Several consequences resulted from this curious development. The child might find himself almost as remote from his parents as he had been in the sixteenth century, and he was very frequently subjected to the trauma of separation at an early age from the one person to whom he was closely attached, when the nanny left to take service in another household. On the other hand, the nursery and the nanny could serve as a refuge from the emotional stresses of the Victorian family, leaving the parents free, if they wished, to cultivate the intellectual life of the child. To name but two concerned nineteenth-century fathers, James Mill and Thomas Arnold, both paid a lot of personal attention to the education of their children. But such figures seem to have become increasingly rare as the century wore on.

For most boys this enclosed domestic world of the nursery was abruptly shattered at an early age by ejection from the home. Among the elite it became normal once more to dispatch boys at seven to nine years of age into the brutal experience of the boarding-school. It was admitted that the education was terrible and the discipline often atrociously cruel once more, but it was nonetheless thought to be a necessary experience for an English gentleman. As Lord William Russell put it to his brother Lord Tavistock in 1822, 'it fits a boy to be a man, to know his fellow creatures, to love them, and to be able to contend with the difficulties of life, to attach friends to him, to take part in public affairs, to get rid of his humours and caprices and to form his temper and manners, to make him loved and respected in the world – in short, it is an essential part of our constitution, and makes our patricians so superior to those of the continent.'[30] The manifest and admitted defects of the early nineteenth-century boarding-school thus became one of its merits, in that the hardships endured trained the survivors to suffer the rough and tumble of public life with controlled equanimity.

The disappearance of the open expression of emotion was the most obvious, and perhaps one of the most significant, indicators of a change in *mentalité* among the nineteenth-century English elite. As late as the Regency, it was perfectly normal for a man openly to burst into tears at some personal or public calamity, or to show signs of exuberant, and sometimes drunken, pleasure at parties and festivities, or openly to lose his temper. During the Victorian period, these expressions of violent emotion were inreasingly frowned upon and the most severe self-control upon all occasions was considered the acid test of manly behaviour. Emotionalism was a weakness left to women. This highly unnatural pattern of behaviour was carefully inculcated both in the home and in the school, and it is almost the only part of the Victorian ethic which has successfully survived into the late twentieth century. Even today, publicly to shed tears is taken as a sign of weakness and instability, and Sir Winston Churchill was the last English politician to be able to carry off such displays and not suffer for them at the polls. The conventional upper-class English ideal became, and remains, the impassive stoicism under stress of the Red Indian brave.

c. Sexual Repression. Together with these authoritarian tendencies within the family went a general hostility towards sexuality. The eighteenth-century drive for moral reform slowly evolved not only into patriarchy and sentimentality but also into paranoid prudery and sexual repression. Although it was thirty years before the tide of disapprobation began seriously to effect the actual behaviour of the elite, it was in the 1770s that counter-pressures began to develop, and a whole series of organized groups sprang up who devoted themselves to the general problem of moral reform, and the internalization of iron self-control. The obscene and atheistical aristocratic clubs like the Medmenham Monks and the Wig Club, which flourished between about 1670 and 1770, died away thereafter.[31] At Oxford and Cambridge, the students were driven back into chapel and to their books, while every effort was made to clear the streets of prostitutes.[32] In 1779 the peers in the House of Lords – of all people – actually passed a Bill introduced by a bishop to forbid the guilty party in a divorce for adultery from marrying the co-respondent in the case. Mrs Thrale thought this a feeble bill and that 'they should inflict some real punishment.' In 1809 George III at last decided that mistresses should no longer live openly in royal palaces, and ordered two of his sons, the Dukes of Kent and Clarence, to get their mistresses – who were now of twenty years' standing – out of their official residences. In the late eighteenth century, the leading squires of Cheshire had taken their pleasure in 'fox-hunting, drinking, bawling out obscene songs and whoring'; by 1827, 'they are all gone now, except one or two of the youngest.' Reserve, decorum, and dullness replaced the extrovert hedonism of the eighteenth century. As the *Edinburgh Review* remarked in 1815, 'our very advances in politeness have an undeniable tendency to repress all the extravagances of mirth or indulgence of humour, which, at an earlier period, gave a variegated and amusing aspect to society.'[33]

Even so, the open and easy ways of the eighteenth century persisted in the very highest levels of aristocratic society well into the Victorian period. A striking public display of irregular sexual relations took place in the middle of the nineteenth century when the eleventh Duke of Beaufort was deserted by his mistress. The duke openly wept and asked that the hundred-odd grooms and stableboys on his estate should attend Holy Communion with him in the local church next Sunday, as a gesture of sympathy with him in his unhappiness that 'little Nellie had left him.'[34] As a vignette of a vanishing civilization, combining obsession with horses and the chase, open sexual liaisons, the Church as an obsequious family dependency, and an atmosphere of semi-feudal deference from an army of servants, this early Victorian episode could hardly be more striking. It was already, however, hopelessly anachronistic.

Prudery reached extraordinary heights, purging English literature, the newspapers, and conversation not only of Anglo-Saxon words for sexual and excretory organs, but even of all mention of these bodily functions. James Plumtree and Thomas Bowdler went to work on the English classics to expunge any hint of sexual innuendo from Shakespeare and other great poets, playwrights and novelists of the past. They changed 'Under the greenwood tree/Who loves to lie with me', from *As You Like It*, so that it became 'Under the greenwood tree/Who loves to work with me.'

The comfortable eighteenth-century habit of both sexes bathing together (more or less fully clothed) in the King's Bath at Bath was abandoned. Such co-educational day schools as still existed in London and elsewhere for the children of respectable tradesmen were broken up into single-sex institutions.[35] By the first decade of the nineteenth century, Sabbatarianism was making the English Sunday even gloomier than it had been before, while the Society for the Suppression of Vice was actively prosecuting sexual offenders of all kinds. Pornographers were hunted down, and such was the climate of opinion that it was said that two pornographic bookstores were forced to close down for lack of customers. What was ostensibly the most sexually puritanical period in English history was well established by the first decades of the nineteenth century, its triumph being temporarily concealed by the veneer of Regency dissipation.

Hannah More tried to have it both ways, by arguing that female modesty in dress and deportment was not only right and necessary, but also 'voluptuous'. Sydney Smith retorted that if this were so, 'nudity becomes a virtue, and no decent woman, for the future, can be seen in garments.' But it was no good. Poking fun at the humourless Hannah More or the other reformers had no effect whatsoever. Thomas Gisborne warned against the sexual dangers of masquerades and dancing; Mrs Trimmer warned women to avoid 'an improper display of personal beauty or indecorous agility'; Joshua Collins advised them never to subscribe to circulating libraries since 'it is much to be questioned whether any sort of fictitious representation of life and manners should be put in the hands of youth.' By 1798 some thought that even the mid-eighteenth-century best-sellers *Clarissa Harlowe* and *Pamela* contained 'materials of such a dangerous complexion as rendered their performances totally improper for the eye of an innocent female.' The only safe activities for a girl were teaching at Sunday School, distributing Biblical tracts and visiting the poor.[36] Nakedness became as dangerous as books and in 1812 Miss Weeton thought 'it is a wrong thing in parents to inure children to be stripped entirely in the nursery while washing', even at the age of seven. In 1829 William Cobbett, who was a clear-sighted man, saw the hypocrisy of the new prudery. Both illegitimacy and prostitution were on the increase in both town and country, and yet 'farmers' wives, daughters and maids cannot now allude to, or hear named without blushing, those affairs of the homestead which they, within my memory, used to talk about as freely as of milking or of spinning.'[37]

By the early nineteenth century, nature was imitating art, with pale and fragile young ladies languidly stretched out in *chaises longues*, ready to swoon at the first suggestion of a coarse word or gesture from an impatient male. Tight corseting, inadequate diet, and a lack of fresh air and exercise were contributory factors which created real physical debility, but the root of the trouble was psychosomatic. Girls were taught by their culture to assume that they were frail and sickly, and as a result they seriously believed that they were, and in fact became so. A hard-headed female critic remarked with exasperation in 1846, 'How many suffer, or say they suffer, from debility, headaches, dyspepsia, a tendency to colds, eternal sore throats, rheumatic attacks, and the whole list of polite complaints.' She attributed this degeneration from the sturdy condition of their eighteenth-century grandmothers to the fact that imagination and sentiment were now predominant over the reasoning faculties, as a result of which 'the two prevailing diseases among females in this country [are] hypochondriasis and hysteria.'[38]

Along with the belief, derived from the fashionable cult of 'sentiment', that women were infinitely delicate creatures whose nervous systems were easily upset, went the new assumption by most of the medical profession that as a sex women were, therefore, too fragile to be susceptible to the coarse passion of lust, which was confined to men. Science thus joined hands with aesthetic and literary fashion to support the ideal of the delicate and frigid female. The two contradictory theories about women's sexual nature had found their most extreme expression in imaginative literature at just the same moment, in the 1740s. Cleland's Fanny Hill enjoyed an exuberant and inexhaustible appetite for all varieties of sexual pleasure; Richardson's Pamela fainted away at the mere hint of the most tentative of sexual advances. Fanny seemed to be winning in the eighteenth century, but thereafter, for the next hundred years or more, the future lay with Pamela and her rarefied sense of feminine 'delicacy'. In 1865 the popular medical authority Dr William Acton confidently asserted that 'the majority of women (happily for them) are not very much troubled with sexual feelings of any kind.' As a result, he regarded woman's sexual role in marriage as one of passive resignation. 'She submits to her husband, but only to please him, and but for the desire of maternity, would far rather be relieved from his attentions.' In 1869 John Stuart Mill observed that 'an oriental thinks that women are by nature particularly voluptuous.... An Englishman usually thinks that they are by nature cold.' As late as 1906 one medical view was that 'in many [women] the appetite never asserts itself.'[39]

On the other hand, some doctors were well aware that 'passion is absolutely necessary in a woman', although they tended to argue that women's pleasure is 'less acute', even if it lasts longer. A very popular American handbook by Dr George Naphey, published in 1869, denounced wives who 'plume themselves on their repugnance or their distaste for their conjugal obligations', alleged that conception was aided by simultaneous orgasms of husband and wife, and even advised the continuation of sexual relations, in moderation, during pregnancy. On both sides of the argument, much of the writing is clearly normative and moralistic rather than merely descriptive of proven biological facts.[40]

The only conclusion to be reached is that, despite internal dissension within the medical profession, for the first time in Western history there was a strong body of opinion which actually denied the existence of the sexual drive in the majority of women, and regarded the minority who experienced it to any marked degree as morally, mentally or physically diseased. A marriage manual of 1839 stated as a fact that sterility was caused by any female who displayed 'excessive ardour of desire', and advised that 'tranquility, silence and secrecy are necessary for a prolific coition.' It was very discouraging advice, almost as discouraging as that offered to married women by Mrs Ellis in 1845: 'suffer and be still.'[41] It is hardly surprising that the size of the profession of prostitution grew by leaps and bounds at

just this period, and that there developed a luxuriant and esoteric pornographic literature for distribution among a handful of wealthy men who
found these restrictions insupportable.

This increasingly suspicious attitude to sexuality also found expression in
a reinforcement of the traditional view that sexual activity was a dangerous
waste of energy for men, unless used in great moderation. In the mid
century, Dr William Acton was recommending the limit of sexual activity
within marriage as at most once every seven to ten days for the very healthy
and active, and told his readers as a physiological fact that the urge mostly
petered out at thirty-five in men and forty-five in women. Others were even
more restrictive, and advised once per lunar month.[42]

Perhaps the most bizarre manifestation of the new sexual attitude was
that the perils of masturbation developed into a major obsession not only of
moralists but also of the medical profession. As has been seen, the alarm had
been sounded in the eighteenth century, but it was only in the nineteenth
that the fear of masturbation reached paranoid proportions, and the
emphasis shifted from cure to suppression. In 1857 Dr William Acton
described in horrifying terms the fate of the youthful masturbator: 'his
health fails, he is troubled by indigestion, his intellectual powers are
dimmed, he becomes pale, emaciated, and depressed in spirits; exercise he
no longer has any taste for, and he seeks solitude.' Inspired by fears of
physical debilitation and even of insanity, some surgeons in the third
quarter of the century, especially in England and America, were performing
clitoridectomy on masturbating girls and deliberately painful circumcision
on boys, while agitated parents were attaching toothed rings to the penis and
locking adolescents into chastity belts or even in strait-jackets for the
night. So extreme were these parental reactions that it is a clear case of 'the
return of the repressed in the repressing.'[43]

d. Conclusion. The causes of this second tidal wave of moral regeneration
and repression seem to be very similar to those that caused the first between
1560 and 1660. There was a sense of social and political crisis, a fear that the
whole structure of social hierarchy and political order were in danger. In the
first period the fear had been of religious wars and peasant revolts. Now the
fear was that under the inspiration of 1789 the impoverished and alienated
masses in the industrial cities would rise up in bloody revolution. Secondly,
two rival religious factions, one established and one nonconformist, were in
competition for the allegiance of the population. In the sixteenth century, it
had been the Anglicans and the Puritans, now it was the Evangelicals and the

Methodists. In each case, both sides stressed the enforcement of patriarchy and obedience, and the crushing of the libido.

The middle classes felt strongly that the morals of the masses could only be reformed by eliminating the vices of the aristocracy, and this could only be done by reviving a zeal for the Christian religion. By 1798 'it was a wonder to the lower orders . . . to see the avenues to the churches filled with carriages', and twenty-five years later it was clear that once more 'a Christian may be a gentleman', now that 'it is not so convenient as once it was to decry seriousness as fanaticism or religious zeal as madness.' As a result, by 1827 *The Morning Chronicle* could complacently observe that 'our men of rank may occasionally *assume* a virtue which they do not have . . . but hypocrisy is, at all events, a homage offered to public opinion, and supposes the existence of a fear of the people.' As Lucy Aikin shrewdly observed, 'the precepts of Christianity have been pressed into the service of a base submission to all established power.'[44] The Christianity of the nineteenth century, like that of the sixteenth, once more exalted a stern and unforgiving masculine God whose vengeance fell inexorably on all sinners. There is a clear correlation between puritanical sexual codes and a High God of this character.

Finally the extraordinary emphasis on prudery and sexual repression both inside and outside marriage was congruent with the bourgeois values of frugality. It has been pointed out that 'spending' had both sexual and economic meanings, both pejorative. The most valued of Victorian characteristics was respectability, which took the form of moral asceticism, buttressed by Evangelical piety and reinforced by patriarchy.[45] There is reason to believe that reticence, sobriety and thrift, punctuality, self-discipline and industry, chastity, prudery and piety are qualities which had been predominant among some sections of the middling ranks uninterruptedly since the late sixteenth century. If this is so, what happened in the seventeenth century and again in the nineteenth was that these values were temporarily imposed, by a combination of repressive measures and vigorous moral and religious propaganda, upon large numbers of the upper landed elite, the lower middle class and the respectable sector of the labouring class. This would help to solve one of the main difficulties about handling ethical changes of this magnitude, which is that the beginnings of each new phase are already visible even before the existing phase reaches its apogee or signs of the preceding phase have entirely faded away. Thus, complaints about the brutal treatment of children had hardly died away by about 1720 than there appeared complaints about the excessive pampering of children by their mothers in the 1740s; similarly the collapse of the first

Society for the Reformation of Manners in 1738 was separated from the foundation of the second in 1757 by less than twenty years.[46]

There were, however, some features which were peculiar to the middle-class Victorian family. For one thing, it was the first family type in history which was both long-lasting and intimate. Child mortality had dropped markedly, and so had the mortality of young adults, so that children now survived more often, and fewer marriages were terminated prematurely by death. Moreover the practice of fostering out was now less common than it had been, except in those growing numbers who sent off their sons to public boarding-schools. Within this more durable unit, there developed a combination of repression of wives and children and an intense emotional and religious concern for their moral welfare. The subordination of women and the crushing of the sexual and autonomous drives of the children took place in a situation where the total emotional life of all members was almost entirely focused within the boundaries of the nuclear family. The psychodynamics of this family type have been well described as 'Explosive Intimacy.'[47]

There is good reason to believe that it was only those of the poor who became attracted to Methodism who got caught up in this Victorian reaction towards erotic and emotional repression and paternal authority within the home. The continued rise of illegitimacy, pre-nuptial conceptions, prostitution and consensual unions during the first two-thirds of the nineteenth century suggest that more and more of the poor were being removed from parental and communal restraints on pre-marital sexual relations by the twin actions of increasing poverty and geographical mobility. The men found it easier to seduce and run, the women were more tempted to allow sexual relations in the hope of establishing a stable family later. But by the late nineteenth century things were improving. There is evidence of a sharp decline in infant abandonment, and the decline of infant mortality perhaps indicates a rise of maternal affection, and consequent child-care. Census data show that the practice of 'fostering out' was on the decline for boys, even if their sisters were still going off in their early teens to be domestic servants or seamstresses. Illegitimacy and marital fertility were declining, more stable unions were being formed, and the treatment of working-class wives by their husbands at last became something rather better than that accorded to domestic slaves. There can be little doubt that the spread of these features of middle-class domesticity to the poor in the late nineteenth century was caused by the social and economic transformations of the age. After 1840 there is indisputable evidence of a seeping down to the proletariat of some of the economic benefits of the industrial revolution, in the form of better housing, better nutrition and more money to spend on the minor luxuries of life. The growing take-over by the state of health, welfare and education relieved the local community and the family of many of their old functions. The rapid rise of elementary education provided incentives to autonomy that had not existed among the rural illiterate. As a result, the domestic life and sexual behaviour of the poor in the late nineteenth century at last crept closer to those of the middling classes of the eighteenth. The period of growing instability, poverty and social and psychological disorientation among the poor was at last drawing to a close.[48]

ii. The Twentieth-century Reversal

After this second phase of repression, which was at its peak from about 1800 into the 1860s or later, the tide slowly turned again. Since then there has developed a second and far more intense phase of permissiveness, beginning slowly among the middle classes in the 1870s, and spreading to the social elite in the 1890s; then, in the 1920s and more dramatically in the 1960s and 1970s, spreading for the first time to all sectors of the population. The influence of the family on job placement has declined as meritocracy has increased. The influence of the parents in the determination of the marriage choices of their children has all but disappeared. Patriarchal power, of husband over wife and father over children, has been severely eroded. Love has now become the only respectable and generally admitted motive for mate selection, whatever the secret reality may be. Aspirations for sexual and emotional fulfilment through marriage have mushroomed; pre-marital sexual experimentation has become increasingly respectable, thanks partly to a dramatic improvement in contraceptive technology which has at last more or less successfully isolated sexual pleasure from procreation, and partly to a shift of attitude to one favourable first to contraception and now to abortion. The period has been characterized by rising divorce rates, moving in waves followed by periods of stability, by increasing numbers of consensual unions, by open demands for free sexual expression and unrestrained sexual fulfilment by both men and women, by growing permissiveness in child-rearing, and now by rising demands for female equality with men in all spheres of life. During this last stage the astonishing success of modern medicine in all but eliminating death among children and young adults has transformed the whole character of family life. Children no longer die, and it is worth while to lavish profound affection upon them and to invest heavily in their education, while their numbers have necessarily to be restricted by contraception. Young adults no longer die naturally, and in consequence affection is a necessary bond for persons likely to be together for a period of over fifty years, while divorce is equally necessary as a safety valve when the bond fails. Marriage is now a high-risk enterprise.

The accompanying sexual revolution has been brought about by four things. Firstly, attitudes have been transformed by popular Freudianism, which has not only enormously stimulated the trend toward sexual permissiveness in child-rearing, but has raised the level of demand for sexual fulfilment in marriage by men, and latterly also by women. The absence of sexual difficulties among the complaints of Napier's patients in the early seventeenth century, as compared with their frequency in the case-books of modern psychiatric consultants, can only be explained either by a high level of seventeenth-century prudery, or by a generally low level of sexual expectations at that time, or by exaggerated expectations today. Whatever the reasons, the contrast is a startling one. The second cause of the sexual revolution is the astonishing success of contraceptive (and abortive) technology. The third is the remarkable rise in living standards for the great majority of Western society, who can now maintain higher standards of personal health and cleanliness, and greater privacy in the bedroom, than was enjoyed even by the wealthiest of aristocrats in the past. The fourth and last factor has been the erosion of the furtiveness and shame with which for two thousand years Christian morality has surrounded the sexual drive, due mainly to the erosion of belief in Christianity itself, and to a lesser extent an adaptive evolution of first Protestant and now Catholic clergy and laity to the new cultural climate. This has been coupled with the civil libertarian drive against censorship to release a flood of literature and visual images in magazines and on film, which explicitly glorify all aspects of sexuality. Every sex handbook or marriage manual encourages polymorphous perversity. The pressure has been intensified by the development of the women's liberation movement, which has included in its platform not only a rejection of male superiority, but an imperious demand for full sexual fulfilment – a demand which has the paradoxical result of reducing many men to impotence for fear of failing to match up to their new sexual role as the virile engine which stimulates the multiple female orgasm.

4 GENERAL CONCLUSIONS: FAMILY CHANGE AND HISTORICAL DEVELOPMENT

i. Fluctuating Change, not Linear Development

The key to family change in middle- and upper-class circles is the ebb and flow of battle between competing interests and values represented by various levels of social organization, from the individual up to the nation state. The evolution of the family, from the early sixteenth and the late eighteenth century, has faithfully reflected the changing positions in the tug-of-war between these various interests and the values attached to them. At first it was recognized that the kin took priority over the state, the nuclear family and the individual: the interests of 'the house' were regarded as paramount. In the sixteenth and early seventeenth centuries, the nation state and the national Church began to assert their own claims, to undermine the authority of the kin, and to reinforce patriarchy in an increasingly nuclear family. The individual continued to be expected to subordinate his own will to the interests and desires of others, although certain ideas were already germinating in Puritan moral theology and in politico-psychological theory which were eventually to help to bring about a fairly rapid recognition of his aspirations to autonomy. At the same time, the school was taking over much of the socialization function hitherto performed by family and kin, the result being to isolate childhood and youth as a special, and increasingly prolonged, period of social moratorium, of subordination and lack of adult responsibilities. By the late eighteenth century, the happiness of the individual, his untrammelled pursuit of ego gratification, was being equated with the public good, with the good of all those older rivals for priority, the nuclear family, the patriarch, the kin, the Church and the state. This was a wholly unrealistic assumption, and in the nineteenth century the interests of the family, the patriarch, the school, the religion and the state all reasserted themselves for a while, before the final thrust of affective individualism in the twentieth century.

Because family change has depended on this eternal conflict of interests and values, with victory swaying back and forth between the various contestants for priority, it is wholly false to assume that there can have been any such thing as straightforward linear development.[49] There is no reason to assume that the end-product of affective individualism, namely the intensely self-centered, inwardly turned, emotionally bonded, sexually liberated, child-oriented family type of the third quarter of the twentieth century is any more permanent an institution than were the many family types which preceded it. This is strongly suggested by the fact that the cause of change lies in an unending dialectic of competing interests and ideas; by the historical record showing the highly erratic course of this evolution; by its very variable impact on different classes; by the strains to which it is currently being subjected; and by its very restricted geographical spread around the world. The only steady linear change over the last four hundred years seems to have been a growing concern for children, although the actual treatment has oscillated cyclically between the permissive and the repressive.

ii. Gains and Losses, not Moral Progress or Decay

There is no reason to assume that the family type which has emerged in the late twentieth century must necessarily, in all respects, be more conducive to either personal happiness or the public good than the family types which preceded it. Affective individualism is a theory which lacks any firm foundation in biological, anthropological or sociological data. As Philip Slater has pointed out, 'the notion that people begin as separate individuals, who then march out and connect themselves with others, is one of the most dazzling bits of self-mystification in the history of the species.'[50] As an ideal it has produced several unfortunate results, as well as many good ones. How else can one explain the peculiar fact that the two trends to a more individualistic family type among the middle and upper classes in the eighteenth and the twentieth centuries were both preceded and separated by two other centuries of patriarchy during the Puritan and the Victorian periods? Why is it that at least twice the lead sectors of Western society have found this family type unsuitable for their needs and incompatible with their values?

There can be no doubt that the changes themselves had serious negative as well as positive features. For one thing, power is a zero–sum game, so that increased autonomy of wives and children meant a decrease in the respect and authority previously accorded to elderly males, whose status and prospects necessarily diminished. Secondly, the decline of ties with the kin deprived the wife of much external help which had previously been available to her in the difficult tasks of adjusting to life under a husband and of child-rearing and child-care. She now lacked support in case of marital conflict, and advice in case of serious incompatibility; her life became more isolated and more tedious while the children were young for lack of relatives to share the burden of baby-sitting and education; and her existence was more empty and lacking in social or economic function when the children had left home. Thirdly, the decline in respect for lineage and ancestry, in the concept of oneself as a trustee for the handing on of blood, property and tradition, resulted in some loss of identity. Fourthly, the progressive postponement of the entry of children into the adult life of work, from seven when they started chores around the home, to fourteen when they became servants or apprentices in other households, to twenty-one when they finished their education, transformed the nature of childhood and created the problem of how to deal with large numbers of adolescent children with the drives and capacities of adults, but denied their responsibilities. Finally, the highly permissive child-rearing practised in many middle- and upper-class households in the late eighteenth century and again in the late twentieth century bred a large number of ill-disciplined and poorly socialized children who grew up to be adults with demands for instant gratification which could not be satisfied. Some wasted their lives in life-long dissipation, while others eventually found a solution in the conversion experience of Evangelical religion.

The distribution of affective ties, like that of power, is also something of a zero-sum game, although affect, unlike power, changes in quantity over time. The highly personalized, inward-looking family was achieved in part at the cost of, and perhaps in part because of, a withdrawal from the rich and integrated community life of the past, with its common rituals, festivals, fairs, feast days and traditions of charity and mutual aid. 'Privacy and community are antithetical needs and cannot simultaneously be maximized.'[51] Thus the middle and upper classes, where the affect-bonded family developed most strongly, reduced their voluntary contributions to village charity and increased their physical, social and cultural isolation from the poor. They withdrew to their own world behind their park walls or inside the grounds of their Palladian villas. By a similar psychological transference, the gentleman farmer was often kind to his family but callous to his labourers; the squire might be affectionate as a husband to his wife and as a father to his children at home, but ruthless as a JP in prosecuting poor men accused of minor robberies, and getting them sentenced to hanging or transportation. Conversely a few others, now sufficiently exceptional to excite comment, turned the other way, like the Reverend Oliver Naylor, who was described in 1767 as 'beloved of his servants, but rough and severe to his children.'[52] The poor, who in general seem to have treated their wives and families with considerable callousness, may well have preserved longest the sense of communal obligations towards neighbours. Neighbourliness often led to inquisitorial prying, backbiting and malicious gossip, but at least it involved a relationship of some sort with other people. Any solution to the problem of boundary awareness has its benefits and its drawbacks. Optimum adaptation to the outer world of kin or community is achieved only by some limitation on internal affective bonding within the nuclear family. Conversely, optional internal integration is achieved only at the cost of some mal-integration into wider social networks.[53]

Group life, as in a nuclear family, not only involves a trade-off between demands internal to the group and those external to it; it also involves a trade-off between the demands of collective affect, intimacy and intrusion within the group, and those of personal privacy and autonomy for its individual members. The triumph of affective individualism as an ideal in the eighteenth century and the twentieth century has therefore brought losses as well as gains to each member as well as to the family as a whole. It has given rise to a narcissistic obsession with personal self-fulfilment which is often inevitably self-defeating. Since the basic theme of fiction since the eighteenth century has been an unrealistic fantasy about romantic love, both husband and wife have tended to develop exaggerated expectations of sexual and emotional satisfaction from each other: disappointment is inevitable. Since self-fulfilment is the chief goal to which all else has to be sacrificed, couples with marital problems now divorce without giving much thought to the consequences on the psychological stability not only of themselves and their spouses but also of their young children. Similarly, mothers of very young children put their jobs before their duties as wives and mothers, sometimes with equally damaging consequences to their marriage and their children.

Alternatively, over-intense parent-child relationships have produced children who are obsessive over-achievers and who have experienced great difficulty in cutting the umbilical cord at the period of adolescence and emergence into the world: they have found themselves still tied to their parents by strings of love and/or hate. Despite its many virtues, the rise in the West of the individualistic, nuclear, child-oriented family which is the sole outlet of both sexual and affective bonding is thus by no means always an unmixed blessing. This intense affective and erotic bonding is no more permanent a phenomenon than were the economic ties of property and interest that united families in the past, even if this is the rough general direction in which Western society has been moving over the last three hundred years. Today parents can expect to live twenty or thirty years beyond the departure of the children from the home, the number of children is declining fast, and the number of mothers with small children who go out to work is rapidly growing. The separate economic preoccupations of each parent are beginning to detach them both from the home and from their dependence on each other. Already, moreover, the peer-group is almost as important as the family in the social life of children. It therefore seems possible that a new, more loosely structured, less emotionally and sexually cohesive, and far more temporary family type is already being added to the number of options available. The frustrated and lonely housewife, the over-possessive mother and the oedipal relationship of the son with the father may all be transient phenomena of a particular time, place and social class – to be replaced, of course, by a different set of pathological types. Furthermore, the historical record suggests that the likelihood of this period of extreme sexual permissiveness continuing for very long without generating a strong back-lash is not very great.

It is an ironic thought that just at the moment when some thinkers are heralding the advent of the perfect marriage based on full satisfaction of the sexual, emotional and creative needs of both husband and wife, the proportions of marital breakdowns, as measured by the divorce rate, is rising rapidly. Just at the moment when some thinkers are heralding the advent of the perfect parent-child relationship, based on the permissive theories of A.S. Neill, many American and English young are losing interest in children and are choosing not to have any at all. When they do have them, they are also, it seems, either turning away from treating them permissively in the home, or else dumping them in day-care centres at the earliest opportunity. The cycle of history is revolving once more.

The factors which are ripping apart husband-wife relations are firstly the isolation of the nuclear pair from external ties and friendships: the withdrawal from neighbours, friends and peer-group associates in the street, the pub, the village shop or the church, and the physical and psychological detachment from relatives, including parents. The only thing that holds the pair together is what they can get out of each other in the way of emotional and sexual satisfaction. Secondly, the pair are ceasing to bear children much earlier than ever before, and are living some twenty years longer than couples in the past. For the first time in the history of the human family, they face the prospect of some thirty years alone together after the departure from the home of the last child.

The factors that are ripping apart parent-child relations are firstly the stresses caused by the fact that sexual maturity is occurring at a younger and younger age – down by about three years over the past century – while the period of full entry into the adult world is being extended by the ever-increasing duration of specialized education. The widening gap is only partly filled by pre-marital sexual liaisons made safe by modern contraceptives. Secondly, the society is in such rapid flux that the values of each generation bear less and less relationship to one another. The result is not so much an intensification of inter-generational conflict as of an outright rejection of parental values about right and wrong.

One hundred and fifty years ago, before the transformation of the family had run the full cycle that we have now witnessed, Tocqueville was cautiously but moderately optimistic in assessing the gains and losses to mankind: 'I do not know, on the whole, whether society loses by the change, but I am inclined to believe that man individually is a gainer by it. I think that in proportion as manners and laws become more democratic, the relation of father and son becomes more intimate and more affectionate.... It would seem that the natural bond is drawn closer in proportion as the social bond is loosened.'[54] Such a cautiously favourable final judgement about the results of the rise of Affective Individualism seems best to fit the confused and conflicting evidence about the evolution of the Closed Domesticated Nuclear Family. However one assesses it in moral terms, for better or for worse, it is certainly one of the most significant transformations that has ever taken place, not only in the most intimate aspects of human life, but also in the nature of social organization. It is geographically, chronologically and socially a most restricted and unusual phenomenon, and there is as little reason to have any more confidence in its survival and spread in the future as there is for democracy itself.

Notes

ACKNOWLEDGEMENTS

1. *The Family in History*, ed. C.E.Rosenberg (Philadelphia 1975).

CHAPTER I   PROBLEMS, METHODS AND DEFINITIONS

1. S.Johnson, *The Idler* (1759), II, no. 84.
2. E.H.Carr, *What is History?* (New York 1963), p. 16.
3. P.Delany, *British Autobiography in the Seventeenth Century* (London 1969), pp. 13, 66, 110, 114, 168. See also R.Pascal, *Design and Truth in Autobiography* (London 1960); L.Trilling, *Sincerity and Authenticity* (London 1972).
4. *Autobiography of Francis Place*, ed. M.Thale (Cambridge 1972), p. 7.
5. R.Goldthwaite, *Private Wealth in Renaissance Florence* (Princeton 1968), p. 264.
6. D.Riesman, *The Lonely Crowd* (New Haven 1961), p. 38.
7. E.Erikson, *Childhood and Society* (New York 1963), ch. VII; E.Erikson, *Identity and the Life Cycle*, introduction by D.Rapoport, *Psychological Issues*, I (New York 1959); H.Hartmann, *Ego Psychology and the Problem of Adaptation* (New York 1964).
8. See A.Skolnick, 'The Family Revisited: Themes in recent Social Science Research', in *Journal of Interdisciplinary History*, V (1975).
9. *The Family in Historical Perspective*, 1970–5 (from 1976 it has become *The Journal of Family History*); *History of Childhood Quarterly* (1973–); *Annales E.C.S.* 27 (4–5) (1972), and 29 (4) (1974); *Journal of Interdisciplinary History*, II (2) (1971) and V (4) (1975). In addition, the Newberry Library in Chicago has launched a research training programme for family historians, and from 1976 to 1978 the Shelby Cullom Davis Center at Princeton will be running a research seminar on the History of the Family. P.Ariès, *Centuries of Childhood* (New York 1975); G.Snyders, *La Pédagogie en France au XVIIᵉ et XVIIIᵉ Siècles* (Paris 1965), pp. 217–342; E.Morgan, *The Puritan Family* (New York 1966); L.L.Schüking, *The Puritan Family, a Social Study from the Literary Sources*, tr. B.Battershaw (New York 1970); P. Laslett, *The World We have Lost* (London 1971); *The Family in History*, ed. T.K.Rabb and R.I.Rotberg (New York 1973); L.deMause, *History of Childhood* (New York 1974); E.Shorter, *The Making of the Modern Family* (New York 1975); *The Family in History*, ed. C.E.Rosenberg (Philadelphia 1975); J.-L.Flandrin, *Familles: Parenté, Maison, Sexualité dans l'ancienne Société* (Paris 1976).

10. C.Lévy-Strauss, *The Savage Mind* (Chicago 1968), pp. 261–2.
11. Quoted by J.L.Clifford in *Essays in Eighteenth Century Biography*, ed. P.B.Daghlian (Bloomington 1968), pp. 74–5.
12. T.Zeldin, *France 1848–1945* (Oxford 1973), p. 285.
13. P.E.Slater, *Earthwalk* (New York 1974), p. 106.
14. T.Fuller, *The Holy State and the Profane State*, ed. M.G.Walton (New York 1938), II, p. 212.
15. E.Morgan, *op. cit.*, pp. 145–6; R.H.Bremner, *Children and Youth in America* (Cambridge, Mass. 1970), I, pp. 49–50.
16. G.E.Mingay, *English Landed Society in the Eighteenth Century* (London 1963), p. 78; C.Clay, 'Marriage, Inheritance and the Rise of Large Estates in England, 1660–1815', in *Econ. Hist. Rev.*, 2nd Ser., XXI (1968), pp. 503–4.
17. P.Laslett, *Household and Family in Past Time* (Cambridge 1972), pp. 5–9, 126, table 4.12.
18. J.-L. Flandrin, *op. cit.*, p. 74; L.Berkner, 'Inheritance, Land Tenure and Family Structure in Lower Saxony at the end of the 17th Century', *Past and Present* Conference Paper (1974); Review of P.Laslett, *op. cit.* by E.Shorter in *History of Childhood Quarterly*, I (1973), pp. 344–5; A.Collomp, 'Famille nucléaire et famille élargie en Haute Provence au XVIIIᵉ siècle (1703–34),' in *Annales E.C.S.*, 27 (1972), pp. 970–1. I owe the information given about France to an unpublished article by Professor P.Goubert.
19. R.North, *Autobiography*, ed. A.Jessop (London 1887), pp. v, xiv, xv.
20. *Cavalier: Letters of William Blundell to his Friends*, ed. M.Blundell (London 1933), p. 133; J.B.Williams, *Memoirs of the Life of the Reverend Matthew Henry* (London 1865), p. 75.
21. D.V.Glass, 'London Inhabitants within the Walls 1695', in *London Record Soc.*, II (1966), p. xxxiv, note 1. See also E.A.Wrigley, *Population and History* (London 1969), pp. 132, 134.
22. R.Wheaton, 'Family and Kinship in Western Europe', in *Journal of Interdisciplinary History*, V (4) (1975), pp. 601–12; J.Goody, *The Developmental Cycle in Domestic Groups* (Cambridge 1958); O.R.Gallacher, 'Looseness and Rigidity in Family Structure', in *Social Forces*, 31 (1952), p. 333; P.C.Glick, 'The Life Cycle of the Family', in J.J.Spengler and O.D.Duncan, *Demographic Analysis* (Glencoe, Ill., 1956), p. 471; L.Berkner, 'The Stem Family and the Developmental Cycle of the Peasant Household: An Eighteenth Century Austrian Example', *American Historical Review*, LXXVII (1972), pp. 398–9, 418; P.Laslett, *Household ...*, pp. 32–4; E.Le Roy Ladurie, 'Structures familiales et coutumes d'héritage en France au XVIᵉ Siècle', in his *Le Territoire de l'Historien* (Paris 1973), p. 230; T.Harevin, 'The Family as Process: the Historical Study of the Family Cycle', in *Journal of Social History*, VII (3) (1974).
23. *Passages from the Diaries of Mrs Philip Lybbe Powys 1756–1808*, ed. E.J.Climenson (London 1899), pp. 97, 201; J.L.Clifford, *Hester Lynch Piozzi* (Oxford 1952), p. 9; R.Blunt and M.Wyndham, *Thomas Lord Lyttelton* (London 1936), p. 93.
24. I owe the information about Charles Scott to Mr Peter Clark. M.Spufford, *Contrasting Communities* (Cambridge 1974), pp. 162–4; 112–19. Exactly the same arrangements prevailed in early eighteenth-century Massachusetts (A.Keyssar, 'Widowhood in 18th Century Massachusetts: A Problem in the History of the Family', in *Perspectives in American History*, VIII [1974], pp. 104, 117).
25. J.A.Johnston, 'Probate Inventories and Wills of a Worcestershire Parish 1676–1775', in *Midlands History*, I (1971), p. 32.

26. L.Berkner, 'Rural Family Organization in Europe: A Problem in Comparative History', in *Peasant Studies Newsletter*, I (4) (1972), p. 151.

27. *Ibid.*, pp. 146–8. See also D.E.C.Eversley in *Econ. Hist. Rev.*, 2nd Ser., XX (1967), p. 170. J.Goody, 'The Evolution of the Family' in P.Laslett, *Household*, p. 119. For recent studies of this phenomenon, see: B.N.Adams, *Kinship in an Urban Setting* (Chicago 1968); M.Young and P.Willmott, *Family and Kinship in East London* (London 1957); E.Litwak, 'Geographical Mobility and Extended Family Cohesion', in *American Sociological Review*, 25 (1960); M.B.Sussman and L.Burchinal, 'Kin Family Network: Unheralded Structure in Current Conceptualizations of Family Functioning', in *Marriage and Family Living*, 24 (1962).

28. A.Macfarlane, *The Family Life of Ralph Josselin* (Cambridge 1970), p. 148.

29. R.Cleaver and J.Dod, *A Godlye Forme of Householde Government* (London 1614), no pagination; *Diary of Cotton Mather*, II, *Massachusetts Historical Collections*, 7th Ser., VIII (1912), pp. 672, 698, 702, 710, 721.

30. W.Gouge, *Of Domesticall Duties* (London 1622), p. 183; W.Perkins, 'Of Christian Oeconomie', in *Works* (London 1626), III, p. 671.

31. I owe the information about Coventry in 1623 to Mr Phythian-Adams. J.A.Williams, 'A Local Population Study at a College of Education', in *Local Population Studies*, 11 (1973), pp. 37–9.

32. P.Laslett, *Household*, p. 139, tables 4.4 and 5.1. See reviews by E.Shorter in *History of Childhood Quarterly*, I (1973), pp. 342–7 and T.Harevin in *History and Theory*, XIV (1975), pp. 242–51. It has been shown that the mean size of households in British colonies in America in the eighteenth century varied from 4·2 in the Bahamas to 43·6 in Tobago, which casts further doubt on the usefulness of this kind of calculation (R.V.Wells, 'Household Size and Composition in the British Colonies in America, 1675–1775', in *Journal of Interdisciplinary History*, IV (1974), p. 548).

33. W.H.Dunham, *Lord Hastings' Indentured Retainers* (New Haven 1955), pp. 11–14, 18–20, 41–61, 50–53; M.E.James, *A Tudor Magnate and the Tudor State: Henry 5th Earl of Northumberland*, Borthwick Papers, 30 (1966), pp. 6–9; L.Stone, *The Crisis of the Aristocracy, 1558–1641* (Oxford 1965), pp. 199–234.

34. R.H.Helmholz, *Marriage Litigation in Medieval England* (Cambridge, Mass. 1974), pp. 4–5, 25, 31–2, 166–7; J.Scammell, 'Freedom and Marriage in Medieval England', in *Econ. Hist. Rev.*, 2nd Ser., XXVII (1974), pp. 530, 532, 535; M.M.Sheehan, 'The Formation and Stability of Marriage in Fourteenth Century England: Evidence of an Ely Register', in *Medieval Studies*, 33 (1971).

35. G.E.Alleman, *Matrimonial Law and the Materials of Restoration Comedy* (Wallingford, Pa. 1942), pp. 5–13, 76; R.H.Helmholz, *op. cit.*, pp. 27–8, 34, 51; H.Swinburne, *A Treatise of Spousals or Marriage Contracts* (London 1686).

36. R.Haw, *The State of Matrimony* (London 1952), p. 33; O.D.Watkins, *Holy Matrimony* (London 1895), p. 135; M.M.Sheehan, *op. cit.*; G.Alleman, *op. cit.*, p. 8; P.Hair, *Before the Bawdy Court* (New York 1972), pp. 204, 239–42. For evidence about the late seventeenth century, see *infra*, p. 629. The most convincing evidence of the 'handfast' in the Highland zone is the high rate of civil marriages in these areas in the middle of the nineteenth century, which can only be explained as a continuation of a previous folk custom of marriage outside the church (O.Anderson, 'The Incidence of Civil Marriage in Victorian England', in *Past and Present* 66 (1975), pp. 66–7, 73.

37. It was only at the Council of Trent that the Catholic Church set itself firmly against the traditional custom of the pre-contract followed by cohabitation. It ordered 'that spouses shall not cohabit in the same house before they have received the nuptial blessing from the priest in church'. (J.Bossy, 'The Counter-Reformation and the People of Catholic Europe', *Past and Present*, 47 (1970), p. 57, note 20.)

38. W.H.Hale, *A Series of Precedents and Proceedings ... from the Act Books of Ecclesiastical Courts in the Diocese of London* (London 1847), p. 170.

39. G.E.Alleman, *op. cit.*, pp. 34, 121–2; R.H.Helmholz, *op. cit.*, pp. 59, 62, 75–9, 87.

40. G.E.Alleman, *op. cit.*, pp. 45, 48–9; M.D.George, *London Life in the Eighteenth Century* (London 1925), p. 305; J.S.Burn, *The Fleet Registers* (London 1833), pp. 1–10, 19, 25–9, 45–9, 94, 97; *Catalogue of Political and Personal Satires in the British Museum*, no. 2874.

41. *The Athenian Mercury* (London, vols. I–X, 1691–3, *passim*), *Life and Errors of John Dunton* (London 1818), pp. 189–94; J.Underhill, *The Athenian Oracle* (London 1892), pp. xxiv–xxv. Dunton admitted that 'as for the nobility and gentry, we are not much acquainted with them' (*The Athenian Mercury*, IX, 10, question 2).

42. See *infra*, ch. 12, section 1, ii.

43. *The Athenian Mercury*, V, 13, question 5; G.E.Alleman, *op. cit.*, pp. 35–8, 82.

44. *Ibid.*, p. 38.

45. J.Grego, *Rowlandson the Caricaturist* (London 1880), I, p. 171; II, pp. 190, 215; *Catalogue of Political and Personal Satires in the British Museum*, nos. 7992, 9660.

46. W.Cobbett, *Parliamentary History of England* (London 1813), XV, col. 2, note.

47. *Ibid.*, XV, cols. 6–11, 50.

48. *Ibid.*, XV, cols. 13, 15–16, 21–2, 29, 34, 40–1, 46, 60, 68, 81. See also H.Stebbing, *A Dissertation on the Power of States to deny Civil Protection to the Marriages of Minors* (London 1755); J.Sayer, *A Vindication of the Power of Society to Annul the Marriages of Minors* (London 1755).

49. Many late medieval courts had the wife inspected by other women to establish that her hymen was unbroken. A few courts also tested the husband. A group of seven women would gather round him, and try to provoke him sexually to see if he could obtain an erection (R.H.Helmholz, *op. cit.*, p. 89).

50. R.H.Helmholz, *op. cit.*, pp. 59, 62, 75, 79, 87.

51. D.Defoe, *Conjugal Lewdness or Matrimonial Whoredom* (London 1727), p. 217; *Miss Weeton's Journal of a Governess*, ed. J.J.Bagley (Newton Abbot 1969), I, p. 87.

52. J.Godolphin, *Repertorium Canonicum, or Abridgement of the Ecclesiastical Laws of this Realm* (London 1680), pp. 493–504; W.Cobbett, *Parliamentary History of England*, XXXV, col. 244; *Parliamentary Papers* (1857), Session 2, *Accounts and Papers*, vol. XLII, p. 121.

53. J.F.Pound, 'The Norwich Census of the Poor 1570', in *Norfolk Record Society*, 40 (1971), p. 95; *The Diary of Thomas Turner of East Hoathly (1754–65)* (London 1925), pp. 68–9.

54. *Autobiography of Francis Place*, pp. 134–5; *Journal of a Somerset Rector 1803–34: John Skinner*, ed. H. & P.Coombs (Bath 1971), pp. 35, 235.

55. C.Kenny, 'Wife-selling in England', *Law Quarterly Review*, 45 (1929); Anon, *The Laws Respecting Women* (London 1727), p. 55; J.von Archenholz, *A Picture of England* (London 1797), II, p. 37; *The Times* (30 March, 1796 and 18 July, 1797); see also T.Hardy, *The Mayor of Casterbridge*.

CHAPTER 2   THE DEMOGRAPHIC FACTS

1. E.Power, *Medieval English Nunneries c. 1275–1535* (Cambridge 1922), ch. 2.

2. *Memoirs of the Verney Family during the Seventeenth Century*, ed. F.P. and M.M.Verney (London, 2nd ed. abridged and corrected by M.M.Verney 1907), II, pp. 186–8.

3. D.Defoe, *Some Considerations upon Streetwalkers* (London, n.d.), pp. 6–7; T.H.Hollingsworth, 'The Demography of the British Peerage', supplement to *Population Studies*, XVIII, no. 2 (1964), table 11. Since record-keeping was improving, a more or less stable number of recorded bachelors means in practice an increase, since at earlier periods a larger number of marriages went unrecorded; L.Henry (*Anciennes Familles Genevoises* [Paris 1956], pp. 51–3) shows a sharp rise at Geneva.

4. P.Goubert, 'Legitimate Fecundity and Infant Mortality in France during the Eighteenth Century: a Comparison', in *Daedalus* (Spring 1968), p. 602; R.Deniel & L.Henry, 'La Population d'un village du Nord de la France: Sainghin-en-Melantois', in *Population*, XX (1965), p. 571; J.Houdaille, 'Un Village du Morvan: St. Agnan', *loc. cit.*, XVI (1961), p. 302; L.Henry & C.Levy, 'Quelques données sur la region autour de Paris au XVIIIᵉ siècle', *loc cit.*, XVII (1962), p. 318; P.Goubert, *Beauvais et le Beauvaisis de 1600 à 1730* (Paris 1960), pp. 42–3; P.Girard, 'Aperçus de la démographie de Sotteville-Lès-Rouen vers la fin du XVIIIᵉ siècle', in *Population*, XIV (1959), p. 489; Y.Blayo & L.Henry, 'Données Démographiques sur la Bretagne et l'Anjou de 1740 à 1829', in *Annales de Démographie Historique* (1967), p. 113; J.-M.Gouesse, 'La Formation du couple en Basse-Normandie', in *Le XVIIᵉ Siècle*, 102–3 (1974), p. 49; J.Houdaille, 'La Population de Remmesweiler en Sarre au XVIIIᵉ et XIXᵉ siècles', in *Population*, XXV (1970), p. 1186; J.Houdaille, 'La Population de Sept Villages des environs de Boulay (Moselle) au XVIIIᵉ et XIXᵉ siècles', *loc. cit.*, XXVI (1971), p. 1065; L.Roussel, 'La Nuptialité en France', *loc. cit.*, XXVI (1971), pp. 1034–5.

5. D.V.Glass and D.E.C.Eversley, *Population in History* (London 1965), p. 181.

6. For the peers, see T.H.Hollingsworth, *op. cit.*, table 17. P.Laslett, *The World We Have Lost* (London 1971), p. 86, indicates that noble bridegrooms were about five years younger than their brides in the first half of the seventeenth century. This seems hardly credible, since it runs directly contrary to evidence for squires and gentry.

7. L.Stone, *The Crisis of the Aristocracy, 1558–1641* (Oxford 1965), pp. 656–7.

8. *Ibid.*, pp. 687–702.

9. Anon, *Reflections on the Caelibacy of Fellows of Colleges* (Cambridge 1798), p. 11 (Bodleian Library, Gough Camb. 66 [11]); E.G.W.Bill, *University Reform in Nineteenth Century Oxford* (Oxford 1973), p. 166.

10. J.A.Banks, *Prosperity and Parenthood* (London 1954), p. 48; C.Ansell, *On the Rate of Mortality at the Early Periods of Life ... in the Upper and Professional Classes* (London 1874), p. 46.

11. J.Hajnal, 'European Marriage Patterns in Perspective', in D.V.Glass & D.E.C.Eversley, *op. cit.*, p. 106.

12. E.A.Wrigley, 'Family Limitation in Pre-Industrial England', in *Econ. Hist. Rev.*, 2nd Ser., XIX (1966), p. 87. (The figures for women are exceptionally high.); D.V.Glass and D.E.C.Eversley, *op. cit.*, p. 110; P.Laslett, *The World We Have Lost*, p. 86; A.D.Dyer, *The City of Worcester in the Sixteenth Century*, Leicester (1973), p. 37; R.V. Wells, 'Quaker Marriage Patterns in a Colonial Perspective', in *William and Mary Quarterly*, XXIX (1972), p. 429; J.Demos, *A Little Commonwealth* (New York 1970), p. 193;

B.Farber, *Guardians of Virtue: Salem Families in 1800* (New York 1972), pp. 38, 43. (Women seem to have married very early in Plymouth, and fairly early in Salem); For the French data see articles cited in Footnote 4: J.-L.Flandrin, 'Marriage tardif et vie sexuelle', in *Annales E.C.S.*, 27 (1972); A.Burguière, 'De Malthus à Max Weber: le mariage tardif et l'ésprit d'entreprise', *loc. cit.*, p. 1133; Tuscany in the fifteenth century was unusual in having a late marriage age for men (25), but a very early one for women (18) (C.Klapisch, 'L'Enfance en Toscane au début du XVᵉ Siècle', in *Annales de Démographie Historique* [1973], pp. 115–16).

13. R.B.Outhwaite, 'Age at marriage in England from the late seventeenth to the nineteenth century', in *Transactions of the Royal Historical Society*, 5th Ser., XXIII (1973), p. 61; P.E.Razzell, 'Population Change in Eighteenth Century England: A Reinterpretation', in *Econ. Hist. Rev.*, 2nd Ser., XVIII (1965), p. 315. These are all from marriage licences and therefore refer to classes above the labourer level. There is similar evidence for Gloucestershire:

	Males	Females
1700–3	26·4	24·2
1750–5	26·0	24·6

(Gloucester Diocesan Archives, Marriage Licences, Q 3); E.A.Wrigley's evidence for Colyton in Devonshire, *loc. cit.*, showing a higher late seventeenth-century marriage age for women than for men is so out of line from most other European data as to be very suspect. For some of the French evidence, see D.V.Glass and D.E.C.Eversley, *op. cit.*, p. 454; *Population*, XXV (1970), p. 1185; XXVI (1971), p. 1065; *Annales de Démographie Historique*, X (1968), p. 201; J.-M.Gouesse, *op. cit.*, p. 48.

14. Very little is known about the age of menarche (female sexual maturation) before the nineteenth century. In early nineteenth century Northern Europe the median age of menarche was in general remarkably late (over 17 in Norway in 1840 and varying from 18 to 20 in the 1780s in Britain. Some very poor English evidence for the same period suggests between $14\frac{1}{2}$ and $15\frac{1}{2}$ (P.Laslett, 'Age at Menarche in Europe since the Eighteenth Century', in *The Family in History*, ed. T.K.Rabb and R.I.Rotberg (New York 1973), p. 45; J.M.Tanner, *Growth at Adolescence* (Springfield, Ill. 1962), pp. 152–3. (See also E.Le Roy Ladurie, 'Famine Amenorrhoea (Seventeenth-Twentieth Centuries)', in *Biology of Man in History*, ed. R.Forster and O.Ranum (Baltimore 1975), p. 178, n. 54).

15. E.Arber, *Registers of the Stationers Company 1554–1640* (London 1875), I, pp. xli-xlii; M.G.Davies, *Enforcement of English Apprenticeship 1563–1642* (Cambridge, Mass. 1956), pp. 2–3; J.Hanway, *An Earnest Appeal for Mercy to the Children of the Poor* (London 1766), p. 107.

16. Y.Blayo and L.Henry, *op. cit.*, p. 126. Unfortunately we do not have very reliable figures for the adult mortality rates of the plebeian class. All we have at present covers a limited sample for the mid-sixteenth century when male expectation of life at 20 was 26 years for the citizens of Worcester and 34 years for the surrounding villagers (Dyer, *op. cit.*, p. 43). The expectation of life of scholars of Caius College, Cambridge, who graduated and entered the church in the early seventeenth century at about the age of 23, was on the average around 37 years. Sons of peers, who were mostly gentry, had an expectation of life at the age of 30 of about 24 years in the mid-seventeenth century, rising to 32 years a hundred years later. Since it is probable that the expectation of life of the former group

was considerably higher than that of the poor, and that of the latter group about the same, one can reasonably conclude that a poor man aged 30 could expect to live about 24 years in the mid-seventeenth century, rising to maybe 30 in the mid-eighteenth century (M.Curtis, 'Alienated Intellectuals of Early Stuart England', in *Past and Present*, 23 [1962], p. 31; T.H.Hollingsworth, *op. cit.*, p. 56).

17. G.Ohlin, 'Mortality, Marriage and Growth in Pre-Industrial Populations', in *Population Studies*, XIV (1968).

18. This was certainly common in England in the fourteenth century, but seems to have become less common later (J.A.Raftis, *Tenure and Mobility* [Toronto 1964], pp. 42–6.

19. *The Spectator* (1712), no. 324.

20. R.B.Outhwaite, *op. cit.*, pp. 61, 69–70.

21. K.H.Connell, *Irish Peasant Society* (Oxford 1968), pp. 113–18.

22. *Memoirs of the Forty-Five First Years of the Life of James Lackington* (London 1795), p. 190; J.L.Sklar, 'The Role of Marriage Behavior in the Demographic Transition: the Case of Eastern Europe around 1900', *Population Studies*, XXVIII (1974), p. 236.

23. This is argued by J.-L.Flandrin, *op. cit.*

24. A.Burguière, *op. cit.*, pp. 1134–8; J.-L.Flandrin, *op. cit.*, pp. 1351–4. On this issue I find Burguière more convincing than J.-L.Flandrin.

25. See *infra*, ch. 9.

26. J.-M.Gouesse, 'Parenté, Famille et Mariage en Normandie au XVIIᵉ et XVIIIᵉ Siècles', in *Annales E.C.S.*, 27 (1972).

27. P.H. Jacobson, *American Marriage and Divorce* (New York 1959), p. 145. The sharp rise in the divorce rate in the 1960s and 1970s may mean that American marriages today are a little more unstable than they were in Early Modern England.

28. E.A.Wrigley, *Population and History* (London 1969), fig. 1.4; C.Ansell, *op. cit.*, diagram B.

29. E.Gautier and L.Henry, *La Population de Crulai, Paroisse Normande* (Paris 1958), p. 125; G.Bouchard, *Le Village Immobile: Sennely en Sologne au XVIIIᵉ siècle* (Paris 1972), pp. 82, 121, 229–32; J.-M.Gouesse, *op. cit.*, p. 49; P.Goubert, *op. cit.*, p. 38, graph 8; Y.Castan, 'Pères et Fils en Languedoc à l'Époque Classique', in *Le XVIIᵉ Siècle*, 102–3 (1974), p. 32, n. 2; J.Fourastié, 'De La Vie Traditionelle à La Vie Tertiaire', *Population*, XIV (1958), p. 419; In France in 1900, only 54% of marriages lasted longer than 15 years, although the divorce rate was still very low indeed (T.Zeldin, *France 1848–1945* [Oxford 1973], pp. 315, 358).

Some groups in America in the Early Modern period, however, were exceptionally healthy, and so experienced very durable marriages. The median duration of Quaker marriages in the Middle Colonies in the eighteenth century rose from about 29 to about 33 years (Wells, *op. cit.*, pp. 421–2). See also Demos, *op. cit.*, p. 66, for the low adult mortality rate in America.

30. These figures were worked out for me by Professor A.Coale on the basis of the evidence on mortality and age of marriage in T.H.Hollingsworth, *op. cit.*, tables 17, 42, and 43. For some European figures of mortality, see S.Peller, 'Studies in Mortality Since the Renaissance', in *Bulletin of the History of Medicine*, XXI (1947), pp. 51–64; G.Bouchard, *op. cit.*, p. 443.

31. C.Ansell, *op. cit.*, table B (Compare the graph for 'English Life 1838–54' with that for 'Peerage Families 1800–55'). The only exception to marriages of short duration broken

by death is in New England, where ample food and much healthier living conditions created a very different situation (A.Keyssar, 'Widowhood in Eighteenth Century Massachusetts: A Problem in the History of the Family', in *Perspective in American History*, VIII (1974), p. 88).

32. R.V.Wells, 'Demographic Change and the Life Cycle of American Families', in *The Family in History*, ed. T.K.Rabb and R.I.Rotberg, p. 90.

33. T.H.Hollingsworth, *op. cit.*, table 14; P.Laslett, *op. cit.*, p. 289, n. 109. The remarriage rate among the Genevan bourgeoisie was substantially lower, but also on the decline (L.Henry, *Anciennes Familles Genevoises*, p. 57). D.V.Glass and D.E.C.Eversley, *op. cit.*, p. 181.

34. Y.Blayo and L.Henry, *op. cit.*, p. 126; G.Bouchard, *op. cit.*, pp. 83–4. As late as 1900, 45% of French children were orphaned in their teens (T.Zeldin, *op. cit.*, p. 315).

35. L.Stone, *op. cit.* (data used for Fig. 16, p. 619); P.Laslett, *op. cit.*, p. 103 (evidence for Manchester in the 1650s).

36. Figures calculated from D.Holles, *Calendar of the Bristol Apprentice Book, Part I, 1532–42. Bristol Record Society Publications*, XIV (1949); C.Blagden, 'The Stationers' Company in the Civil War Period', in *The Library*, 5th Ser., XIII (1958), p. 2, n. 1; London Guildhall Library MS 5576/1–3, 5184; P.Laslett, *op. cit.*, p. 103; J.R.Holman, 'Orphans in pre-industrial Towns: the Case of Bristol', in *Local Population Studies*, 15 (1975).

37. W.Saffady, 'The Effects of Childhood Bereavement and Parental Remarriage in Sixteenth Century England: the Case of Thomas More', in *History of Childhood Quarterly*, I (1973).

38. M.Baulant, 'La Famille en Miettes: sur un aspect de la Démographie du XVIIe siècle', in *Annales E.C.S.*, 27 (1972), pp. 967–8.

39. D.V.Glass and D.E.C.Eversley, *op. cit.*, p. 209; I owe the 1970 American figure to Susan Watkins; M.Spufford, *Contrasting Communities* (Cambridge 1974), pp. 88–90, 113–19, 162–4; A.Keyssar, 'Widowhood in 18th Century Massachusetts', in *Perspectives in American History*, VIII (1974), pp. 104, 107.

40. B.C.Blackwood, 'Marriages of Lancashire Gentry on the Eve of the Civil War', in *Genealogists' Magazine*, 16 (7) (1970), p. 322.

41. I owe this information, taken from Kent Marriage Records, to the kindness of Mrs V.B.Elliott.

42. L.Stone, *op. cit.*, pp. 623–6.

43. B.C.Blackwood, *op. cit.*, p. 322; J.P.Ferns, 'The Gentry of Dorset on the Eve of the Civil War', in *Genealogists' Magazine*, 15 (3) (1965), p. 108; J.Macky, *A Journey through England in Familiar Letters* (London 1714), p. 4.

44. From an unpublished study of the local elites in these three counties.

45. B.C.Blackwood, *loc. cit.*

46. R.Speake, 'Historical Demography of Wharton Parish before 1801', in *Lancashire and Cheshire Historical Society Transactions*, 122 (1970), pp. 50–1; B.Maltby, 'Parish Registers and the Problem of Mobility', in *Local Population Studies*, 6 (1971), pp. 41–2; B.Maltby, 'Easingwold Marriage Horizons', in *Local Population Studies*, 2 (1969), p. 37; For identical findings in Normandy, see J.-M.Gouesse, *op. cit.*, *Le XVIIe Siècle*, 102–3 (1974), p. 49; For New England, see S.N.Norton, 'Marital Migration in Essex County, Massachusetts, in the Colonial and Early Federal Periods', *Journal of Marriage and the Family*, 35 (1975).

47. H.M.Colvin, 'A Scottish Origin for English Palladianism?' in *Architectural History*, 17 (1974), p. 9.

48. P.Goubert, *op. cit.*, pp. 32–3; L.Henry, *Anciennes Familles Genevoises*, p. 88; E.Gautier and L.Henry, *op. cit.*, p. 157.

49. R.Deniel and L.Henry, *op. cit.*, *Population*, XX (1965), p. 593.

50. R.S.Schofield, 'Perinatal Mortality in Hawkshead, Lancashire, 1581–1710', in *Local Population Studies*, 4 (1970), p. 13.

51. E. and F.Van de Walle, 'Allaitement, sterilité et contraception: les opinions jusqu'au XIXᵉ siècle', in *Population*, XXVII (1972); E.A.Wrigley, *Population and History*, p. 92. For information about the effects of lactation on malnourished women, I am grateful to Professor Ansley Coale. See also *Population Growth: Anthropological Implications*, ed. B.Spooner (Cambridge, Mass. 1972), pp. 329–42.

52. The intervals doubled among completed families. J.Dupaquier, 'Sur la Population Française au XVII et XVIIIième Siècles', in *Revue Historique*, 239 (1968), p. 73; R.V.Wells, 'Quaker Marriage Patterns', p. 440, table X; P.Goubert, 'Historical Demography and the Reinterpretation of Early Modern French History', in *The Family in History*, ed. T.K.Rabb and R.I.Rotberg, p. 21.

53. E.Shorter, *The Making of the Modern Family* (New York 1975), appendix I.

54. R.E.Frisch, 'Demographic Implications of the Biological Determinants of Female Fecundity', *Harvard Center for Population Studies*, Research Paper, n. 6 (1974), p. 4; E.Le Roy Ladurie, *op. cit.*

55. C.Levy and L.Henry, 'Ducs et Pairs sous l'Ancien Régime', in *Population*, XV (1960), pp. 816–20; E.A.Wrigley, 'Family Limitation', in *Econ. Hist. Review*, 2nd Ser., XIX (1966), p. 104.

56. P.Laslett, *The World We Have Lost*, p. 97. This is a minimum figure, since there is evidence to suggest that up to one third of all births were never recorded in rural parish registers (P.E.Razzell, 'The Evaluation of Baptism as a form of birth registration', in *Population Studies*, 26 (1972), p. 131).

57. G.Vigo, 'Infant Mortality in a Pre-Industrial District', in *Journal of European Economic History*, III (1) (1974), p. 123.

58. W.H.Hale, *A Series of Precedents and Proceedings from the Act Books of Ecclesiastical Courts in the Diocese of London* (London 1847), p. 162.

59. F.West, 'Infant Mortality in the East Fen Parishes of Leake and Wrangle', *Local Population Studies*, 13 (1974), pp. 43–4; D.V.Glass and D.E.C.Eversley, *op. cit.*, p. 410; *Victoria County History, The City of York* (London 1961), p. 121; J.Hanway, *An Earnest Appeal for Mercy to the Children of the Poor*, p. 5. All the evidence from the 38 French and American family reconstitution studies has been summed up by D.S.Smith, 'A Homeostatic Demographic Regime: Patterns in Western European Family Reconstitution Studies' (unpublished paper). For the French evidence see J.-L.Flandrin, *Familles: Parenté, Maison, Sexualité dans l'ancienne Société* (Paris 1976), p. 57; P.Goubert, *Beauvais et le Beauvaisis de 1600 à 1730*, pp. 39–40; J.Dupaquier, *op.cit.*, pp. 63–4; G.Bouchard, *op. cit.*, p. 75; review of M.Bouvet and P.M.Bourdin, *A Travers la Normandie du XVIIᵉ et XVIIIᵉ siècles (Cahier des Annales de Normandie*, 6, 1968), in *Annales E.C.S.*, 27 (1974), p. 1219; review by M.Lachiver of A.Molinier, *Une Paroisse de Bas-Languedoc: Sérignan, 1650–1792*, in *Annales de Démographie Historique* (1970), p. 422; J.Houdaille, 'La Population de Sept Villages', *loc cit*, p. 1071; review by

J.Dupaquier of M.Lachiver, 'La Population de Meulan (Yvelines) du XVIIe au XIXe siècles', in *Annales de Démographie Historique* (1968), p. 205; J.Bourgeois-Pichat, 'Evolution Générale de la Population Française depuis le XVIIIe siècle', in *Population* (1951), p. 662; Y.Blayo and L.Henry, *op. cit.*, p. 135; F.Lebrun, *Les Hommes et La Mort en Anjou aux XVIIe et XVIIIe siècles* (Paris 1971), pp. 182, 187, 191; M.Térisse, 'Un Faubourg du Havre: Ingouville', in *Population*, XVI (1961), p. 292; P.Goubert, *op. cit.* in *Daedalus* (Spring 1968), p. 599; P.Goubert, *The Family in History*, p. 21.

60. See *infra*, ch. 9, section 2. vi.
61. See *infra*, ch. 9, section 1.I.B.
62. J.L.Clifford, *Hester Lynch Piozzi* (Oxford 1968), pp. 83, 94.
63. S.Goulart, *The Wise Vieillard or Old Man* (London 1621), p. 146. The figures have been adapted from those in E.Lebrun, *op. cit.*, p. 191; M.Garden, *Lyon et les Lyonnais au XVIIIe Siècle* (Paris, n.d.), graphs XVII, XVIII; E.A.Wrigley, *Population and History*, p. 9 (graph). The comparative figures for England and America were calculated for me by Mr M.A.Stolo. The figures for England 1838–54 come from C.Ansell, *On the Rate of Mortality*, diagram B.
64. *North Country Diaries*, II, Surtees Soc., CXXIV (1914), p. 52.
65. I.Cutter and H.Viets, *Short History of Midwifery* (Philadelphia 1964); K.Das, *Obstetric Forceps: Its History and Evolution* (Calcutta 1929); I owe these references, and my knowledge of the development of midwifery skills to Mr L.N.Rosenband.
66. *Private Papers of James Boswell*, ed. G.Scott and F.A.Pottle (New York 1932), 14, p. 115; T.R.Forbes, 'The Regulation of English Mid-Wives in the Eighteenth and Nineteenth Centuries', in *Medical History*, 15 (1971).
67. M.A.Beaver, 'Population, Infant Mortality and Milk', in *Population Studies*, XXVII (1973). For figures on the decline of infant mortality in London, see T.R.Edmonds, 'On the Mortality of Infants in England', in *The Lancet*, I (1835–6); E.Caulfield, *The Infant Welfare Movement in the Eighteenth Century* (New York 1931), p. 179. The percentage who died under 2 years fell from 60% in 1730–9 to 30% in 1790–1810.
68. P.E.Razzell, 'Population Change in Eighteenth Century England: A Reinterpretation', *loc. cit.*, pp. 321–31; P.E.Razzell, 'The Smallpox Controversy', in *Local Population Studies*, 12 (1974), p. 44; N.J.F.Pounds, 'John Huxham's Medical Diary', in *Local Population Studies*, 12 (1974), p. 37.
69. *Memoirs of the Verney Family during the Seventeenth Century*, *passim*.
70. *Autobiography of Mrs Alice Thornton*, Surtees Soc., LXII (1875), pedigree, p. 344.
71. *Ibid.*, pp. 49–52.
72. *North Country Diaries*, II, Surtees Soc., CXXIV (1914), p. 55.
73. J.F.D.Shrewsbury, *A History of Bubonic Plague in the British Isles* (Cambridge 1970), pp. 5, 266–70, 315–36, 372–8, 445–78, 302, 383, 417, 436, 500; For the epidemiology of plague, see J.N.Biraben and J.Le Goff, 'The Plague in the Early Middle Ages', in *Biology of Man in History*, pp. 50–5.
74. Quoted in K.V.Thomas, *Religion and the Decline of Magic* (New York 1971), p. 8.
75. See note 68.
76. *Autobiography of Mrs Alice Thornton*, pp. 6, 33, 157–9, 293
77. *Memoirs of Richard Cumberland* (London 1806), p. 67.
78. *Autobiography of Thomas Wright of Birkenshaw, 1736–1797*, ed. T.Wright (London 1864), p. 153; *Memoirs of her Life by Mrs Catherine Cappe* (London 1822), pp. 10, 392; *Poems of*

Thomas Gray, William Collins and Oliver Goldsmith, ed. R.Lonsdale (London 1969), p. 586 ('The Double Transformation').

79. *Bletchley Diary of the Rev. William Cole*, ed. F.G.Stokes (London 1931), pp. 27, 48; F.Bamford, *Dear Miss Heber* (London 1936), p. 177.

80. M. and J.Rendle-Short, *The Father of Child Care* (Bristol 1966), pp. 9, 33–4, 20, 23, 25.

81. L.Stone, *op. cit.*, p. 562.

82. *Life and Times of Anthony Wood*, ed. A.Clark, II, *Oxford Historical Soc.*, XXI (1842), p. 68; S.Pepys, *Diary*, 28 September 1665.

83. The best description of contemporary urban hygienic conditions is in F.Lebrun, *op. cit.*, pp. 263–9; M.D.George, *London Life in the Eighteenth Century* (London 1925), pp. 97, 340 n. 66, 342 n. 99, 344 n. 114, 117, 345 n. 124. The conditions in Anjou were almost certainly worse than those in England – it is significant that domestic latrines were called 'les lieux dits à l'anglaises' – which partly explains the higher death rates through epidemics in France far later than in England. But the difference in hygienic conditions should not be exaggerated, for the key difference lay rather in the greater poverty in France due to stagnant agricultural productivity, a crushing burden of taxation, and no rural poor relief except in emergencies.

84. J.Clifford, 'Some Aspects of London Life in the Mid-Eighteenth Century', in *City and Society in the Eighteenth Century*, ed. P.Fritz and D.Williams (Toronto 1973), p. 34; *Autobiography of Thomas Wright*, p. 85; *Autobiography and Selected Remains of Samuel Roberts* (London 1849), pp. 22, 24; *Autobiography of Francis Place*, p. 108; *Catalogue of Political and Personal Satires in ... the British Museum*, VI, no. 8906.

85. J.P.Peter, 'Disease and the Sick at the End of the Eighteenth Century', in *Biology of Man in History*, pp. 118–24.

86. In the early seventeenth century Napier carefully noted the effects of his purges and emetics, which frequently resulted in the ejection of worms (I owe this information to Mr Michael MacDonald). R.L.Edgeworth, *Memoirs* (London 1820), I, p. 31; *Henry, Elizabeth and George, 1734–80*, ed. Henry Lord Herbert (London 1939), p. 260; *Thraliana*, ed. K.C.Balderston (Oxford 1942), I, pp. 29–30, 117–18, 340, 504.

87. *Diaries of Oliver Heywood*, ed. J.H.Turner (Brighouse 1882), II, p. 167. The mortality rates among married couples are taken from the squirarchy and above in the three counties of Hertfordshire, Northamptonshire and Northumberland.

88. For numerous notices of accidents or deaths from falls from horses see *Yorkshire Diaries and Autobiographies in the Seventeenth and Eighteenth Centuries*, Surtees Soc., LXV (1875), *passim*; Surtees Soc., CXVIII (1910), pp. 7, 211–12, 264, 298; Surtees Soc., CXXIV (1914), p. 185; *Diary of Richard Kay 1716–51*, Chetham Soc., 3rd Ser., XVI (1968), pp. 19, 21, 23, 27, 47, 54, 113. *Diaries of Oliver Heywood*, I, *passim*.

89. *Autobiography and Correspondence of Sir Simonds D'Ewes* (London 1845), I, pp. 5, 26, 28, 30, 32, 94, 124–5, 358. For another long list of seventeenth-century childhood escapes from death, see *Diaries of Oliver Heywood*, I, pp. 203–5.

90. F.Lebrun, *op. cit.*, pp. 281–4; *Diary of Robert Hooke, 1672–1680*, ed. H.W.Robinson and W.Adams (London 1935), pp. 26, 41. Inoculation seems to have been both widespread and safe by the 1760s (*Local Population Studies*, 14 (1975), p. 58).

91. K.V.Thomas, *op. cit.*, ch. 7, 8, 10.

92. E.Shorter, *The Making of the Modern Family*, p. 175.

93. M.Baulant, 'La Famille en Miettes', in *Annales E.C.S.*, 27 (1972), pp. 959–68.

CHAPTER 3   FAMILY CHARACTERISTICS

1. *Autobiography of Mary Countess of Warwick*, ed. T.C.Croker *Percy Soc.*, XXII (1848), p. 21.

2. M.James, *Family, Lineage and Civil Society* (Oxford 1974), pp. 21–6; R.K.Marshall, *Days of Duchess Anne* (London 1973), pp. 32–3, 80–1. For an excellent example, see M.Slater, 'The Weightiest Business: Marriage in an Upper-Gentry Family in Seventeenth Century England', in *Past and Present*, 72 (1976).

3. W.S.Holdsworth, *A History of English Law* (3rd ed., London 1923), III, pp. 114–16, 172; VII, pp. 456–8.

4. *Private Papers of James Boswell*, ed. G.Scott and F.A.Pottle (New York 1932–4), 15, p. 54.

5. *Crosby Records*, ed. T.E.Gibson (London 1880), p. 67.

6. M.James, *op. cit.*, pp. 177–85.

7. M.E.James, 'Politics and the Concept of Honour in England 1485–1642', in *Past and Present*, Supplement 3 (1977).

8. M.E.James, 'The Concept of Order and the Northern Rising of 1569', in *Past and Present*, 60 (1973), pp. 54–5, 70–3.

9. H.J.Habakkuk, 'Family Structure and Economic Change in Nineteenth Century Europe', in *Journal of Economic History*, XV (1955).

10. M.Spufford, *Contrasting Communities* (Cambridge 1974), pp. 85–7, 91, 106, 137, 159.

11. This point is stressed by J.Thirsk, 'The Family', in *Past and Present*, 27 (1964), pp. 118, 122, and P.Ariès, 'Couples et Familles dans la Société d'aujourd'hui', in *Chronique Sociale de France* (Lyon 1973).

12. L.Stone, *The Crisis of the Aristocracy, 1558–1641* (Oxford 1965), pp. 223–34.

13. *Memoirs of the Verney Family during the Seventeenth Century* ed. F.P. and M.M.Verney (London 1907), II, pp. 314, 318–20, 346–64; J.Knyveton, *Diary of a Surgeon in the Year 1750–51*, ed. J.Gray (New York 1937), p. 6.

14. J.Boswell, *Life of Samuel Johnson, LLD* (Everyman ed., London 1906), I, p. 60.

15. M.D.George, *London Life in the Eighteenth Century* (London 1925), p. 24; J.M.Beattie, 'The Pattern of Crime in England 1660–1800', in *Past and Present*, 62 (1974).

16. J.Bossy, 'The Counter-Reformation and the People of Catholic Europe', in *Past and Present*, 47 (1970), pp. 55–6.

17. B.H.Westman, 'The Peasant Family and Crime in Fourteenth Century England', in *Journal of British Studies*, XIII (1974), p. 16.

18. A.L.Rowse, *Simon Forman* (London 1974), p. 14; see also the maxims of John Ferrour in A.Hassell Smith, *Country and Court* (Oxford 1974), pp. 145–6.

19. *Wentworth Papers 1597–1628*, ed. J.P.Cooper, *Camden Soc.*, 4th Ser., XII (1973), pp. 9–24.

20. I owe this suggestion to Professor Morton Smith of Columbia University.

21. *Dictionary of National Biography*, *sub* Greville, Sir Fulke; A.Macfarlane, *Family Life of Ralph Josselin* (Cambridge 1970), pp. 151, 152; *Private Papers of James Boswell*, 13, p. 234; M.Pennington, *Memoirs of the Life of Mrs Elizabeth Carter* (London 1808), I, p. 127.

22. A.Macfarlane, *op. cit.*, pp. 143, 149; M.Slater, 'The Verney Family in the Seventeenth Century' (Princeton PhD thesis 1971), pp. 57–8, 66–7; G.Holmes, *British Politics in the Age of Anne* (London 1967), p. 16.

23. *Wentworth Papers 1597–1628*, pp. 10, 23, 13, 14, 15, 19, 20, 14; Notebooks of the Rev. Richard Napier (I owe this quotation to the kindness of Mr Michael MacDonald); H.J.Perkin, 'The Social Causes of the British Industrial Revolution', in *Transactions of the Royal Historical Society*, 5th Ser., XVIII (1968), pp. 132–3; *Letters and Works of Lady Mary Wortley Montagu*, ed. Lord Wharncliffe and W.M.Thomas (London 1887), I, p. lxxxix.

24 See *infra*, ch. 4; F.G.Emmison, *Elizabethan Life: Morals and the Church Courts* (Chelmsford 1973), *passim*, especially chs 1, 2 and 9.

25. G.Bouchard, *Le Village Immobile: Sennely en Sologne au XVIIIᵉ siècle* (Paris 1972), pp. 51, 234–6, 263–4; Comment of Dr Brieude in *Histoire et Mémoires de la Société Royale de Médecine, 1782–83* (Paris 1787), p. 302, quoted by Professor Edward Shorter.

26. E.Aubry, 'Les Adieux de la Nourrice', illustrated in *Art Bulletin*, 55 (4) (1973), pl. 9 (Original in the William and Francis Clark Art Institute at Williamstown, Mass.).

27. W.Cobbett, *Advice to Young Men* (1829), ed. H.Morley (London 1887), p. 189; *Boswell: the Ominous Years, 1774–1776*, ed. C.Ryskamp and F.A.Pottle (New York 1963), pp. 164, 175, 190; I. Eibl-Eibesfeldt, *Love and Hate* (London 1971), ch. X.

28. *Memoirs of Susan Sibbald, 1783–1812*, ed. F.P.Hett (New York 1926), p. 21.

29. H.Freudenberg and A.Overby, 'Patients from an Emotionally Deprived Environment', in *Psychoanalytic Review* 56 (1969); quoted by M.H.Stone and C.J.Kestenbaum, 'Maternal Deprivation in Children of the Wealthy', in *History of Childhood Quarterly*, II (1974), p. 96; J.W.Prescott, 'Body Pleasure and the Origins of Violence', in *The Futurist*, IX (2) (1975); quoted in *History of Childhood Quarterly*, III (1975), pp. 196–7.

30. P.Laslett, 'Parental Deprivation in the Past', in *Local Population Studies*, 13 (1974), pp. 13, 16–17.

31. R.J.Lifton, 'On Death and the Continuity of Life', in *History of Childhood Quarterly*, I (1974), p. 689.

32. S.S.Tomkins, 'The Biopsychosociality of the Family', in *Aspects of the Analysis of Family Structure*, ed. M.J.Levy (Princeton 1965), pp. 219–48; G.Gorer and J.Rickman, *The People of Great Russia* (London 1949), p. 213.

33. A.Behn, *The Emperor of the Moon* (1687), Act III, Sc. ii in *Works*, ed. M.Summers (London 1915), III, p. 449.

34. J.Wells, 'Demographic Change and the Life Cycle of American Families', in *The Family in History*, ed. T.K.Rabb and R.I.Rotberg (New York 1973), pp. 90–1.

35. *Autobiography of William Stout of Lancaster, 1665–1752*, ed. J.D.Marshall (Manchester 1967), p. 128; In this bleak assessment of the normally low level of companionship in seventeenth-century arranged marriages, I find myself in some disagreement with other authorities in the field, whose data certainly indicate that some marriages were affectionate, but do not support, in my opinion, their more optimistic general conclusions. (E.Morgan, *The Puritan Family* (New York 1966), p. 60; J.Demos, *A Little Commonwealth* (New York 1970), p. 98; D.Hunt, *Parents and Children in History* (New York 1970), p. 67; A.Macfarlane, *op. cit.*, p. 106.)

36. E.Shorter, *The Making of the Modern Family*, pp. 56–61.

37. *Autobiography of Thomas Wythorne*, ed. J.Osborn (Oxford 1961), pp. 22–60, 76–105.

38. *Autobiography of Phineas Pett*, Navy Record Soc., 51, 1918, p. 9.

39. *Autobiography of Thomas Wythorne*, pp. 185–99.

40. Montaigne, quoted by P.Ariès, *Centuries of Childhood* (New York 1975), p. 39; *The*

Flemings in Oxford, I (*Oxford Historical Society*, XLIV), 1904, p. 425; Fleming also gave 3d to each of the poor who attended the funeral service, which cost him £3 6d, as well as 10s to his servants.

41. Comment by J.Walzer in *History of Childhood Quarterly*, I (1973), p. 58.
42. *Autobiography and Correspondence of Sir Simonds D'Ewes* (London 1845), II, pp. 146–7.
43. L.deMause, *History of Childhood* (New York 1974), table I, p. 36; *Montaigne's Essays*, ed. J.I.M.Stuart (London 1931), I, p. 439.
44. W.Shakespeare, *Romeo and Juliet*, Act I, Sc. iii; S.Guazzo, *The Civile Conversation*, tr. G.Pettie (London 1586), p. 143.
45. P.P.Dunn, in L.deMause, *op. cit.*, p. 398; *Journal de Jean Héroard sur l'Enfance et la Jeunesse de Louis XIII*, ed. E.Soulié and E.de Bartélemy (Paris 1868), I, p. 20.
46. A.Chamoux, 'Mise en Nourrice et Mortalité des Enfants légitimes', in *Annales de Démographie Historique* (1973), p. 421.
47. A.Macfarlane, *op. cit.*, pp. 206–10; P.Laslett, *Household and Family in Past Time* (Cambridge 1972), table 4.13; *Lay Subsidy Rolls, 1524–25*, ed. J.Cornwall, *Sussex Record Soc.*, LVI (1956), pp. 35–55; D.V.Glass, 'London Inhabitants within the Walls 1695', in *London Record Soc.*, II (1966), p. xxxv; R.S.Schofield, 'Age-specific Mobility in an Eighteenth Century Rural English Parish', in *Annales de Démographie Historique* (1970), pp. 261–2; P.Laslett, *The World We Have Lost* (London 1971), pp. 66–7; M.Anderson, *Family Structure in Nineteenth Century Lancashire* (Cambridge 1971), p. 85; For the age of apprenticeship in America (7 to 11) see B.Farber, *Guardians of Virtue: Salem Families in 1800* (New York 1972), p. 36.
48. *A Relation of the Island of England*, Camden Soc., XXXVII (1847), pp. 24–5.
49. See *infra*, ch. 6, section 3. iv.
50. *North Country Diaries*, II, Surtees Soc., CXXIV (1914), p. 52.
51. S.R.Smith, 'Religion and the Conception of Youth in Seventeenth Century England', in *History of Childhood Quarterly*, II (4) (1975); S.R.Smith, 'The London Apprentices as Seventeenth Century Adolescents', *Past and Present*, 61 (1973).
52. *Autobiography . . . of Sir Simonds D'Ewes*, I, pp. 2–111, *passim*.
53. *Cavalier: Letters of William Blundell to his Friends 1620–1698*, ed. M.Blundell (London 1933), p. 152.
54. *Autobiography of William Stout of Lancaster*, pp. 142, 178; Samuel Bamford, *Early Days* (London 1849), p. 96; G.F.Sydenham, *History of the Sydenham Family* (East Molesey 1928), pp. 529–33.
55. M.Slater, *op. cit.*, pp. 55, 64.
56. *Cavalier: Letters of William Blundell to his Friends*, ed. M.Blundell, pp. 44, 135–6, 154, 170.
57. A.Macfarlane, *op. cit.*, pp. 93, 165–7, 206–9.
58. *Life of Adam Martindale*, Chetham Soc., 1st Ser., IV (1845), pp. 212, 221.
59. G.Bouchard, *op. cit.*, pp. 75–6, 88–9; F.Lebrun, *op. cit.*, pp. 422–4.
60. *Autobiography of Mrs Alice Thornton*, Surtees Soc., LXI (1873), pp. 91–2, 94, 124, 156. It has to be remembered that this autobiography had a propaganda purpose, to prove to her posterity that the authoress was a loyal wife, a devoted mother and a pious Christian of exemplary morals. Her protestations of devotion to her husband and children have, therefore, necessarily to be taken with a grain of salt, although they do carry a strong ring of truth.

61. I owe all my information about the Rev. Richard Napier to talks with Mr Michael MacDonald, who has kindly given me permission to use his evidence.

62. *Memoirs of the Family of Guise, Camden Soc.*, 3rd Ser., XXVIII (1917), p. 114; cf. also the remarks of Charles Croke in 1667 (C.Croke, *Fortune's Uncertainty or Youth's Unconstancy* (Oxford 1959)), p. 28; Montaigne also commented that primogeniture '*détrempe merveilleusement et relâche cette soudure fraternelle*' (G.Snyders, *La Pédagogie en France au XVIIe et XVIIIe siècles* (Paris 1965), p. 251.

63. *Autobiography of Mrs Alice Thornton*, pp. 33, 66; A.Macfarlane, *op. cit.*, pp. 82, 131; *The Diaries of Sylvester Douglas (Lord Glenbervie)*, ed. F.Bickley (London 1928), II, p. 350; For another example from the seventeenth century see *Memoirs of the Verney Family during the Seventeenth Century*, II, p. 483.

64. *Letters and Works of Lady Mary Wortley Montague*, I, p. lxxxviii; E.J.Climenson, *Elizabeth Montagu, Queen of the Bluestockings* (London 1906), II, p. 88; *Retrospections of Dorothea Herbert 1790–1806* (London 1929), II, p. 392.

65. E.Le Roy Ladurie, *Montaillou: Village occitan de 1294 à 1324* (Paris 1975), ch. XI–XIII, pp. 301, 316. I draw rather different conclusions from those of Professor Le Roy Ladurie.

CHAPTER 4   THE DECLINE OF KINSHIP, CLIENTAGE AND COMMUNITY

1. *The Diary of Sir Henry Slingsby*, ed. D.Parsons (London 1836), p. 329 note.

2. *Advice to a Son*, ed. L.B.Wright (Ithaca 1962), p. 11.

3. L.Stone, *The Crisis of the Aristocracy, 1558–1641* (Oxford 1965), pp. 42–4, 187, 547, 555–7.

4. *Ibid.*, pp. 572–8.

5. *Ibid.*, pp. 228–9.

6. R.Goldthwaite, *Private Wealth in Renaissance Florence* (Princeton 1968), p. 260.

7. G.Snyders, *La Pédagogie en France au XVIIe et XVIIIe siècles* (Paris 1965), pp. 242, 305.

8. J.E.Neale, *The Elizabethan House of Commons* (London 1949).

9. Excluding the under-age, the very old and the insane, there were 119 noblemen who could have taken sides. Eighteen of these 119 split within the conjugal family, thirteen of them on father/son lines.

10. I.Carter, 'Marriage Patterns and Social Sectors in Scotland before the Eighteenth Century', *Scottish Studies*, XVII (1973), pp. 51–2.

11. G.Holmes, *British Politics in the Age of Anne* (London 1967), pp. 264, 323, 328–33, 498, n. 66.

12. *Cavalier: Letters of William Blundell to his Friends*, ed. M.Blundell, (London 1933), p. 132; H.Aveling, 'The Marriages of Catholic Recusants', in *Journal of Ecclesiastical History*, XIV (1963); B.C.Blackwood, 'Marriages of the Lancashire Gentry on the Eve of the Civil War', in *Genealogists' Magazine*, 16 (1970), pp. 326–7.

13. In Kent, where subdivisions of estate among brothers were unusually common and where mobility among the elite had been unusually low, the situation of near-universal cousinhood was arrived at as early as 1640 (A.Everitt, *The Community of Kent and the Great Rebellion, 1640–1660* (Leicester 1966), pp. 35–6); D.Brunton and D.H.Pennington, *Members of the Long Parliament* (London 1954), p. 17.

14. G.Aylmer, *The King's Servants* (London 1961), p. 82.

15. For the Treasury, see S.B.Baxter, *The Development of the Treasury, 1660–1702* (London 1957).

16. G.Aylmer, *op. cit.*, pp. 81–2.

17. A.Macfarlane, *Family Life of Ralph Josselin* (Cambridge 1970), pp. 17, 132, 137–9; 'The Diary of the Rev. John Thomlinson', in *Six North Country Diaries*, I, Surtees Soc., CXVIII (1910), pp. 67–167, *passim*.

18. J.A.Johnston, 'Probate Inventories and Wills of a Worcestershire Parish, 1676–1775', in *Midlands History*, I (1971), p. 32.

19. B.Farber, *Guardians of Virtue: Salem Families in 1800* (New York 1972), pp. 61, 178; M.Anderson, 'The Study of Family Structure' in *Nineteenth Century Society*, ed. E.A.Wrigley (Cambridge 1972); M.Anderson, *Family Structure in Nineteenth Century Lancashire* (London 1971), ch. 7, 9.

20. See *supra*, ch. 1, section 4, iii.

21. L.S.Pressnell, *Country Banking in the Industrial Revolution* (Oxford 1956), ch. X–XII.

22. F.F.Foster, 'Politics and Community in Elizabethan England', in *The Rich, the Well Born and the Powerful, Elites and Upper Classes in History*, ed. F.C.Jaher (Urbana 1973), pp. 133–7.

23. B.Winchester, *Tudor Family Portrait* (London 1955), p. 61; R.Brenner, 'The Civil War Politics of London's Merchant Community', *Past and Present*, 58 (1973), pp. 61–2, 71.

24. R.G.Wilson, *Gentlemen Merchants* (Manchester 1971), p. 184; G.Jackson, *Hull in the Eighteenth Century* (Oxford 1972), pp. 108–9, 111; in eighteenth-century Salem, Mass., kin bonding was the key to commercial associations among the merchants (B.Farber, *op. cit.*, pp. 75, 87, 195).

25. L.Stone, 'The Educational Revolution in England, 1560–1640', in *Past and Present*, 28 (1964); L.Stone, 'Literacy and Education in England, 1640–1900', in *Past and Present*, 42 (1969); M.Spufford, 'The Schooling of the Peasantry in Cambridgeshire, 1575–1700', in *Agricultural History Review* 18 (1970) (*Supplement*).

26. Quoted in P.Ariès, *Centuries of Childhood* (New York 1975), p. 355.

27. See P.Petot, 'La Famille en France sous l'Ancien Régime', in *Sociologie Comparée de la Famille Moderne* (Paris 1955).

28. L.Stone, *Crisis . . .*, pp. 267–8.

29. M.James, *Family, Lineage and Civil Society* (Oxford 1974), pp. 182–8.

30. T.More, *Utopia*, ed. E.Surtz and J.H.Hexter (New Haven 1965), pp. xli–xlv; J.T.Johnson, *A Society Ordained by God: Puritan Marriage Doctrine in the First Half of the Seventeenth Century* (Nashville 1970), pp. 67, 39, 91.

31. W. and M.Haller, 'The Puritan Art of Love', in *Huntington Library Quarterly*, V, 1941–2, pp. 235–6; L.L.Schüking, *The Puritan Family, a Social Study from the Literary Sources*, tr. B.Battershaw (New York 1966), pp. 40–50; W.Perkins, 'Of Christian Oeconomie or Household Government', in *Works* (London 1626), III, p. 689; J.Halkett, *Milton and the Idea of Matrimony* (New Haven 1970), pp. 3–30.

32. L.L.Schüking, *op. cit.*, p. 22; R.Cleaver and J.Dod, *A Godlye Forme of Householde Government* (London 1614) (no pagination); J.Milton, *The Doctrine and Discipline of Divorce*, in *Works* (New York 1931), III (2), pp. 394, 510; W.Gouge, *Of Domesticall Duties* (London 1634), Treatise 2, Sects. 8, 9.

33. N.Z.Davis, 'City Women and Religious Change in Sixteenth Century France', in *A Sampler of Women's Studies*, ed. D.G.McGuigan (Ann Arbor 1973), pp. 33–6.

34. J.T.Johnson, *op. cit.*, pp. 21–4, 151–6, 90–6; J.Halkett, *op. cit.*, pp. 10–11; R.V.Schnucker, 'Elizabethan Birth Control and Puritan Attitudes', in *Journal of*

Interdisciplinary History, V (4) (1975), p. 660; E.Morgan, *The Puritan Family* (New York 1966), p. 48, quoting from B.Wadsworth, *The Well Ordered Family* (Boston 1712), p. 36.

35. L.Stone, *op. cit.*, pp. 594-5, 599.

36. E.Morgan, *op. cit.*, pp. 42-54.

37. R.Crosse, *The Lover, or Nuptial Love* (London 1638), sec. XI, XII, XIV; Rogers and Taylor are quoted in Haller, *op. cit.*, p. 269, and in L.L.Schüking, *op. cit.*, p. 48.

38. R.Strong, *Van Dyck: Charles I on Horseback* (London 1972), p. 70.

39. J.Halkett, *op. cit.*, pp. 50-5; J.Milton, *The Doctrine and Discipline of Divorce*, in *Works*, III (2), pp. 332, 382, 388, 402, 475, 498.

40. W.J.Goode, 'The Theoretical Importance of Love', in R.L.Coser, *The Family: its Structure and Function* (New York 1964), pp. 207, 217; J.Halkett, *op. cit.*, p. 12.

41. I owe this suggestion to Professor N.Z.Davis.

42. Articles by R.Trexler, A.N.Galpern, and N.Z.Davis in *The Pursuit of Holiness in Late Medieval and Renaissance Religion*, ed. C.Trinkhaus and H.O.Oberman (Leiden 1974).

43. N.Z.Davis, 'The Reasons of Misrule: Youth Groups and Charivaris in Sixteenth Century France', in *Past and Present*, 50 (1971).

44. *Letters of Thomas Wood, Puritan, 1566-1577*, ed. P.Collinson, Special Supplement 5 to *Bulletin of the Institute for Historical Research* (1960), *passim*.

45. T.Barnes, 'County Politics and a Puritan Cause Célèbre: Somerset Churchales', in *Transactions of the Royal Historical Society*, 5th Ser., IX (1959); C.Hill, 'The Secularization of the Parish', in his *Society and Puritanism in Pre-Revolutionary England* (London 1964), ch. XII.

46. C.Hill, 'The Spiritualization of the Household', *loc. cit.*, ch. XIII; H.S.Bennett, *English Books and Readers, 1558-1603* (Cambridge 1965), pp. 147-8; *Diary of Samuel Sewall, 1674-1729*, ed. A.H.Thomas (New York 1973), I, p. 412.

47. L.L.Schüking, *op. cit.*, p. 41.

48. Quoted by C.Russell, 'Arguments for Religious Unity in England, 1530-1650', in *Journal of Ecclesiastical History*, XVIII (1967), p. 208; In Kentish towns in the early seventeenth century, four out of five males who left inventories owned a Bible, usually kept in the hall, study or parlour (I owe this information to Mr Peter Clark).

49. E.Morgan, *op. cit.*, pp. 135-9.

50. J.B.Williams, *Memoirs of the Life of Miss Sarah Savage* (London 1829), pp. 7-8; J.B.Williams, *Memoirs of the Life of the Reverend Matthew Henry* (London 1865), pp. 221-2.

51. J.Michelet, *Priests, Women and Families* (London 1845), pp. 228, 264.

52. J.Hodgson, *History of Northumberland* (Newcastle 1840), pt II, vol. iii, p. 99.

53. P.Laslett and K.Oosterveen, 'Long-term Trends in Bastardy in England', in *Population Studies*, XXVII (1973), pp. 260, 274; see also *infra*, ch. 12, section 1, iii.

54. P.Hair, *Before the Bawdy Court* (New York 1972), pp. 70, 95, 127, 143, 175, etc.; W.H.Hale, *A Series of Precedents and Proceedings from the Act Books of Ecclesiastical Courts . . .* (London 1847), pp. 179-80, 190, 199, 206, 207, 209, 212, 219, 244, 247.

55. J.Godolphin, *Repertorium Canonicum, or Abridgement of the Canon Laws of this Realm* (London 1680), p. 474; M.Dalton, *The Countrey Justice* (London 1622), cap. 124.

56. E.P.Thompson, 'Rough Music, "Le Charivari Anglais"', in *Annales E.C.S.*, 27 (1972). For eighteenth-century caricatures of skimmingtons, see *Catalogue of Political and Personal Satires in the British Museum*, nos. 441, 1703, 2149; Anon, *The Laws Respecting*

Women (London 1772), p. 22; E.Shorter, *The Making of the Modern Family* (New York 1975), pp. 188–97; 'rough music' has a history that goes back at least to the first century AD in Italy, and was still practised in the twentieth century in Oregon. See A.W.Lintott, *Violence in Republican Rome* (Oxford 1968), p. 8. I owe this reference to Dr M.H.Crawford of Christ's College, Cambridge. The reference to modern Oregon I owe to Professor W.McCaffrey of Harvard.

57. L.A.Bukatzsch, 'The Constancy of Local Populations and Migration in England before 1800', in *Population Studies*, V (1951); P.Laslett, 'Clayworth and Cogenhoe', in *Historical Essays, 1600–1750*, ed. H.E.Bell and R.L.Ollard (London 1963), p. 177; S.A.Peyton, 'Village Population in the Tudor Lay Subsidy Rolls', in *English Historical Review*, XXX (1915), p. 248; J.D.Chambers, *Vale of Trent 1670–1800, Economic History Review*, Supplement 3 (1957), p. 22; E.E.Rich, 'The Population of Elizabethan England', in *Economic History Review*, 2nd Ser., II (1949), p. 259; P.Styles, 'A Census of a Warwickshire Village in 1698', in *University of Birmingham Historical Journal*, III (1951), pp. 45–8; J.A.Johnston, *op. cit.*, *Midlands History*, I (1971), p. 29; J.Cornwall, 'Evidence of Population Mobility in the Seventeenth Century', in *Bulletin of the Institute of Historical Research*, XL (1967); P.Clark, 'The Migrant in Kentish Towns, 1580–1640', in P.Clark and P.Slack, *Crisis and Order in English Towns* (London 1972); L.Stone, 'Social Mobility in England', in *Past and Present*, 33 (1966), pp. 29–30; R.S.Schofield, 'Age-specific Mobility in an Eighteenth-Century Rural English Parish', in *Annales de Démographie Historique* (1970), pp. 261, 264; P.Spufford, 'Population Mobility in Pre-Industrial England', in *Genealogists' Magazine*, XVII (8–10) (1973–4); W.R.Prest, 'Stability and Change in Old and New England: Clayworth and Dedham', in *Journal of Interdisciplinary History*, VI (3) (1976).

58. P.Clark, *op. cit.*, p. 122; E.A.Wrigley, 'London's Importance, 1650–1750', in *Past and Present*, 37 (1967), p. 46; D.Cressy, 'Occupations, Migration and Literacy in East London, 1580–1640', in *Local Population Studies*, 5 (1970), p. 58; L.Stone, 'Social Mobility in England 1500–1700', *loc. cit.*, pp. 30–2; E.J.Bukatzsch, 'Places of Origin of a Group of Immigrants into Sheffield 1624–1799', in *Economic History Review*, 2nd Ser., II (1950).

59. W.K.Jordan, *Philanthropy in England, 1480–1660* (London 1959), pp. 18, 90, 107. Professor Jordan enormously exaggerated the significance of private charity as compared with welfare supported by public taxation: see J.Hill, 'A Study of Poverty and Poor Relief in Shropshire, 1550–1685' (MA thesis, Birmingham University 1973), pp. 89, 99–101, 116–17, 120–1, 148–51, 271–2; A.L.Beier, 'Studies in Poverty and Poor Relief in Warwickshire, 1540–1680' (PhD thesis, Princeton University 1969), p. 178.

60. For Sunday Schools see T.Laqueur, *Religion and Respectability: Sunday Schools and Working Class Culture, 1780–1850* (London 1976). The quotation (which I owe to Professor Laqueur) comes from T.Morris, *A Discourse . . . in favour of Sunday Schools* (Market Harborough 1792).

61. *Memoirs of the Verney Family during the Seventeenth Century* ed. F.P. and M.M.Verney (London 1907), II, p. 271.

CHAPTER 5   THE REINFORCEMENT OF PATRIARCHY

1. W.N.Stephens, *The Family in Cross-Cultural Perspective* (New York 1963), pp. 325–39.
2. *Political Works of King James I*, ed. C.H.McIlwain (Cambridge, Mass. 1918), p. 307;

R.Mocket, *God and the King* (London 1616), p. 3; R.Filmer, *Patriarcha*, ed. P.Laslett (Oxford 1949), p. 62.

3. R.H.Bremner, *Children and Youth in America* (Cambridge, Mass. 1970), I, p. 32.

4. G.Fagniez, *La Femme et la Société Française dans la première Moitié du XVIIe Siècle* (Paris 1929), pp. 50–66. G.Snyders, *La Pédagogie en France* . . . (Paris 1965), pp. 259–61; Montesquieu, *De L'Esprit des Lois* (Livre XVI, ch. IX) in *Oeuvres Complètes*, ed. A.Masson (Paris 1950), I, p. 357; see also P.Ariès, *Centuries of Childhood* (New York 1975), p. 351.

5. *Remarks and Collections of Thomas Hearne*, X, Oxford Historical Soc., LIX (1915), pp. 369; C.V.Wedgwood, *A Coffin for King Charles* (New York 1964), p.223.

6. G.J.Schochet, 'Patriarchalism, Politics and Mass Attitudes in Stuart England', in *Historical Journal*, XII (1969); J.G.Marston, 'Gentry Honour and Royalism in Early Stuart England', in *Journal of British Studies*, XIII (1973).

7. E.P.Thompson, 'Rough Music: Le Charivari Anglais', in *Annales E.C.S.*, 27 (1972), p. 302.

8. G.Strauss, 'Success and Failure in the German Reformation', in *Past and Present*, 67 (1975), p. 33. J.Milton, *Paradise Lost*, Bk IV, line 299. J.Bossy, *The English Catholic Community 1570–1850* (New York 1976), p. 158.

9. Quoted by A.Everitt, 'The County Community', in *The English Revolution 1600–1660*, ed. E.W.Ives (London 1968), pp. 55–6. I owe the quotation from Thomas Scott's diary to Mr Peter Clark.

10. *Autobiography of Mrs Alice Thornton*, Surtees Society LXII (1875), p. vii; C.Russell, 'Arguments for Religious Unity . . .', in *Journal of Ecclesiastical History*, XVIII (1967), pp. 205–6, quoting T.Edwards, *Gangraena* (London 1646), I, p. 156.

11. D.Defoe, *The Family Instructor* (London 1715), pp. 276, 191, 223–4.

12. L.Stone, *The Crisis of the Aristocracy* . . . (Oxford 1965), pp. 178–80.

13. A.B.Ferguson, *The Indian Summer of English Chivalry* (Durham, N.C. 1960).

14. S.Pepys, *Diary*, 5 September 1667; J.H.Wilson, *The Private Life of Mr Pepys* (New York 1959), p. 32.

15. F.Lebrun, *Les Hommes et La Mort en Anjou*, p. 263; D.Hunt, *Parents and Children in History* (New York 1970), pp. 141–4.

16. L.deMause, *History of Childhood* (New York 1974), pp. 272, 311, 319, 341, 366; E.W.Marvick, 'The Character of Louis XIII: the Role of his Physician', in *Journal of Interdisciplinary History*, IV (1974), p. 359; *Secret Diary of William Byrd, 1709–12*, ed. L.B.Wright and M.Tinling (Richmond 1941), pp. 113, 117.

17. E.W.Marvick, 'Childhood History and Decisions of State: the Case of Louis XIII', in *History of Childhood Quarterly*, 2 (1975), pp. 144–6; E.W.Marvick in L.deMause, *op. cit.*, pp. 272–3.

18. For details, see *infra*, ch. 10, section 2, v.

19. L.deMause, *op. cit.*, pp. 242, 307; D.Hunt, *op. cit.*, p. 127.

20. M.C.Rowsell, *The Life Story of Charlotte de La Trémouille, Countess of Derby* (London 1905), pp. 35–6.

21. E.L.Lipton, A.Steinschneider, J.B.Richmond, 'Swaddling, a Child Care Practice: Historical, Cultural and Experimental Observations', in *Pediatrics*, 35 (1965), pp. 521–67.

22. G.Gorer and J.Rickman, *The People of Great Russia* (London 1949), p. 98, App. I and II, pp. 197–226.

23. W.G.Hiscock, *John Evelyn and his Family Circle* (London 1955), p. 54.

24. P.Greven, *Child-Rearing Concepts, 1628–1861* (Itasca 1973), pp. 13–14.

25. H.Rashdall, *The Universities of Europe in the Middle Ages*, ed. F.M.Powicke and A.B.Emden (Oxford 1936), III, pp. 347, 358.

26. P.Ariès, *Centuries of Childhood* (New York 1975), pp. 257–8.

27. R.North, *Autobiography*, ed. A.Jessop (London 1887), p. 12.

28. J.Janeway, *A Token for Children* (London 1676), preface.

29. J.Aubrey, *Brief Lives*, ed. A.Powell (London 1949), pp. 277–82; H.Peacham, *The Compleat Gentleman* (London 1622), pp. 23, 24; C.H.Herford and P.Simpson, *Ben Jonson* (Oxford 1925), I. p. 138.

30. J.Maclean, *The Life and Times of Sir Peter Carew* (London 1857), pp. 4–5.

31. *Autobiography and Correspondence of Sir Simonds D'Ewes* (London 1845), I, pp. 63–4.

32. G.M.Edward, *Sidney Sussex College, Cambridge* (London 1899), pp. 29, 67; A.Gray, *Jesus College, Cambridge* (London 1902), p. 93; H.P.Stokes, *Corpus Christi College, Cambridge* (London 1898), pp. 95, 108; A.Clark, *Lincoln College, Oxford* (London 1898), pp. 69, 208; C.H.Cooper, *Annals of Cambridge* (Cambridge 1842–53), II, p. 277; H.L.Thompson, *Christ Church, Oxford* (London 1900), pp. 75, 133; H.W.C.Davis, *Balliol College, Oxford* (London 1899), pp. 36, 58; W.C.Costin, *St. John's College, Oxford, Oxford Historical Society*, new series, XII (1958), pp. 4, 130; C.Wordsworth, *Social Life at the English Universities in the Eighteenth Century* (Cambridge 1874), p. 441.

33. J.Aubrey, *Brief Lives*, ed. O.L.Dick (Ann Arbor 1962), pp. xxiii–iv.

34. T.Elyot, *The Book named the Governor* (1531), ed. S.E.Lehmberg (London 1962), pp. 17, 20, 23; R.Ascham, *The Scholemaster* (1570) in *Works* (London 1864), III, p. 81; R.Mulcaster, *Positions . . .* (London 1581), in *Educational Writings of Richard Mulcaster*, ed. J.Oliphant (Glasgow 1903).

35. *The Educational Writings of John Locke*, ed. J.Axtell (Cambridge 1968), p. 185.

36. S.Guazzo, *The Civile Conversation*, tr. G.Pettie (London 1586), ff. 148v, 149; *The Catechism of Thomas Becon*, ed. J.Ayre (London 1844), p. 354, quoted in I.Pinchbeck and M.Hewitt, *Children in English Society* (London 1959), I, p. 15; L.Bradner and C.A.Lynch, *The Latin Epigrams of Thomas More* (Chicago 1953), p. 231; R.Ascham, *op. cit.*

37. A.L.Rowse, *Simon Forman* (London 1974), p. 93; S.Pepys, *Diary*, 19 February 1665.

38. S.R.Smith, 'The London Apprentices as Seventeenth Century Adolescents', in *Past and Present*, 61 (1973), p. 152.

39. R.North, *Autobiography*, pp. 1, 4, 6.

40. *Gilbert Burnet's History of His Own Time: Supplement*, ed. H.C.Foxcroft (Oxford 1902), p. 454; *Journal of Richard Norwood*, ed. W.F.Craven and W.B.Hayward (New York 1945), p. 26; *Autobiography of Thomas Raymond, Camden Soc.*, 3rd Ser., XXVIII (1917), p. 19; J.Aubrey, *Brief Lives*, ed. A.Powell (London 1941), p. 11.

41. R.Burton, *Anatomy of Melancholy*, ed. H.Jackson (London 1932), I, p. 333.

42. Quoted in D.Hunt, *op. cit.*, p. 134.

43. D.Hunt, *op. cit.*, pp. 133–5, 147–9, 156, from *Journal de Jean Héroard*, ed. E.Soulié and E. de Barthélemy (Paris 1868), I, *passim*.

44. M.King-Hall, *The Story of the Nursery* (London 1958), p. 91; D.Townshend, *Life and*

Letters of Mr Endymion Porter (London 1897), p. 68.

45. B.Batty, *The Christian Man's Closet* (London 1581), p. 26, quoted by L.L.Schüking, *The Puritan Family* ... (New York 1966), p. 75.

46. J.Aubrey, *op. cit.*, ed. A.Powell, p. 11; L.Stone, *Crisis* ..., pp. 591–2; *Autobiography of Mrs Alice Thornton*, pp. vii, 64; L.L.Schüking, *op. cit.*, p. 73; I.Pinchbeck and M.Hewitt, *op. cit.*, I, pp. 18–19.

47. Letters of Thomas Legh to his father Sir Peter Legh in 1619 (Legh MSS transcripts, Brasenose College, Oxford); *Wentworth Papers, 1597–1628*, pp. 48–51, 57; *Memoirs of the Verney Family during the Seventeenth Century* ed. F.P. and M.M.Verney (London 1907), II, p. 417; see also J.B.Williams, *Memoirs of the Life of the Reverend Matthew Henry* (London 1865), pp. 28–9; *Lyme Letters, 1660–1760*, ed. E.Newton (London 1925), p. 274.

48. R.H.Bremner, *op. cit.*, I, p. 33.

49. P.Greven, *op. cit.*, p. 78.

50. G.R.M.Ward, *Oxford University Statutes* (London 1845), I, p. 155; T.G.Jackson, *Wadham College, Oxford* (Oxford 1893), p. 58.

51. J.Norris, *Spiritual Counsel: or the Father's Advice to his Children* (London 1701), p. 31.

52. *Diary of Cotton Mather*, II, *Massachusetts Historical Collections*, 7th Ser., VIII (1912), p. 25.

53. *Diary of Samuel Sewall, 1674–1729*, ed. A.H.Thomas (New York 1973), I, pp. 249, 346, 348–9, 359.

54. B.M.Berry, 'The first English Pediatricians and Tudor Attitudes towards Childhood', in *Journal of the History of Ideas*, XXXV (1974), pp. 562–6.

55. *Autobiography of Thomas Wythorne*, ed. J.Osborn (Oxford 1961), p. 10.

56. R.Cleaver and J.Dod, *A Godlye Form of Household Government* (London 1614), p. 272; R.Allestree, *The Whole Duty of Man* (London 1663), p. 296; *Diaries of Oliver Heywood*, ed. J.H.Turner (Brighouse 1882), I, p. 51.

57. L.L.Schüking, *op. cit.*, p. 73; R.M.Bremner, *op. cit.*, I, p. 37–8; A.W.Calhoun, *A Social History of the American Family from Colonial Times to the Present* (New York 1945), I, pp. 47, 120–1.

58. I owe this information to an unpublished paper by Professor J.C.Sommerville, 'The English Puritans and Children: Psychohistory or Cultural History'.

59. *Autobiography of Thomas Wythorne*, p. 9.

60. B.Batty, *op. cit.*, p. 209, quoted in L.L.Schüking, *op. cit.*, p. 75.

61. D.Hunt, *op. cit.*, pp. 153–8.

62. *Journal de Jean Héroard*, I, pp. 294, n. 2, 55; II, pp. 56, 57, 79, 111, etc.

63. D.Hunt, *op. cit.*, p. 157.

64. P.P.Dunn, in L.deMause, *op. cit.*, pp. 397–8.

65. Brasenose College, Oxford, Legh MSS transcripts; *History of Northumberland*, IV, p. 415.

66. *Memoirs of the Verney Family during the Seventeenth Century*, II, pp. 420, 422; *The British Apollo* (London 1708), no. 112.

67. R.Allestree, *op. cit.*, p. 291.

68. *Complete Poems of John Wilmot Earl of Rochester*, ed. D.M.Vieth (New Haven 1968), p. 105.

69. J.Boswell, *Life of Samuel Johnson, LLD* (Everyman ed. London 1906), I, p. 627.

70. *Memoirs of the Family of Guise, Camden Soc.*, 3rd Ser., XXVIII (1917), pp. 122–3, 127–8, 132, 134.

71. L.Stone, *op. cit.*, pp. 595–6; *North Country Wills, Surtees Soc.*, CXVI (1908), p. 246; for a late sixteenth-century restatement of absolute parental authority, see J.Stockwood, *A Bartholomew Fairing for Parentes ... shewing that Children are not to marie without the consent of their Parentes* (London 1589).

72. L.Stone, *op. cit.*, pp. 600–04.

73. P.Hair, *Before the Bawdy Court* (New York 1972), pp. 153–4; I.Pinchbeck and M.Hewitt, *op. cit.*, I, p. 16.

74. *Cavalier: Letters of William Blundell to his Friends*, ed. M.Blundell (London 1933), p. 85.

75. *Memoirs of the Verney Family during the Seventeenth Century*, II, p. 307.

76. *Proceedings of the Society of Antiquaries of Newcastle-upon-Tyne*, 3rd Ser., I (1904), pp. 149–53.

77. E.R.Wharton, *The Whartons of Wharton Hall* (Oxford 1898), p. 40.

78. *Life and Letters of Lady Sarah Lennox 1745–1826*, ed. Countess of Ilchester and Lord Stavordale (London 1902), p. 86.

79. *Letters and Journals of Lady Mary Coke*, ed. J.A.Home (Edinburgh 1889), I, pp. xix–xxi, xxxiii–xxxv, lix–lxvi, cxxiii, cxxvi.

80. *Autobiography of Mary Rich, Countess of Warwick, Percy Soc.*, XXII (1848), pp. 2, 3, 11, 13; Lismore Papers, ed. A.B.Grosart (London 1886–8), 1st Series, V, pp. 73, 101, 139, 194; 2nd Series, IV, pp. 80–1.

81. *Autobiography and Correspondence of Sir Simonds D'Ewes* (London 1845), I, pp. 308–22, 325, 352–4, 363.

82. *Lyme Letters, 1660–1760*, pp. 143, 170–4, 195–9.

83. *Wentworth Papers, 1597–1628* (ed. J.P.Cooper, *Camden Soc.*, 4th Ser., XII (1973)), p. 324.

84. *Memoirs of the Verney Family in the Seventeenth Century*, II, p.175

85. N.Luttrell, *A Brief Relation of State Affairs* (Oxford 1857), VI, p. 38.

86. J.Harrington, *The Commonwealth of Oceana*, ed. H.Morley (London 1887), p. 114; I owe this information about Napier to Mr Michael MacDonald; P.Hair, *op. cit.*, pp. 145–6; L.Stone, *op. cit.*, pp. 595–6; *Life of Adam Martindale*, Chetham Soc., 1st Ser., IV (1845), p. 16.

87. E.Shorter, *The Making of the Modern Family* (New York 1975), p. 146 and appendix III; R.Braun, 'The Impact of Cottage Industry on an Agricultural Population' in *The Rise of Capitalism*, ed. D.Landes (New York 1966), p. 55.

88. W.G.Hiscock, *op. cit.*, pp. 38–9.

89. W.Wycherley, *The Plain Dealer* (London 1677), Act V, Sc. iii; D.Defoe, *Roxana*, ed. J.Jack (Oxford 1964), p. 148.

90. C.S.Kenny, *The History of the Law of England as to the Effects of Marriage* (London 1879), pp. 60, 67, 72, 88, 52; For the arguments, see W.Gouge, *Of Domesticall Duties* (London 1634), pp. 298–306; in seventeenth-century New England, the law was significantly more liberal in this matter than it was in England. See R.B.Morris, 'Women's Rights in Early American Law', in his *Studies in the History of American Law* (New York 1930).

91. N.Z.Davis, 'City Women and Religious Change in Sixteenth Century France', in *A Sampler of Women's Studies*, ed. D.G.McGuigan (Ann Arbor 1973), p. 38; A.Clark,

Working Life of Women in the Seventeenth Century (London 1919), pp. 67-8, 95; M.Campbell, *The English Yeoman* (New Haven 1942), pp. 213, 398.

92. D.M.Stenton, *The English Woman in History* (London 1957), p. 103.

93. C.Camden, *Elizabethan Woman* (New York 1952), pp. 23-4. 'Women are made of blood, without souls', remarked a character in John Marston's *The Insatiate Countess* (1613), III, iv, and Donne found it necessary to denounce such cynics in a sermon in 1630 (*Huntington Library Quarterly*, XIV (1950-1), p. 267, n. 14).

94. L.B.Wright, *Middle Class Culture in Elizabethan England* (Chapel Hill 1935), ch. XIII; C.L.Powell, *English Domestic Relations, 1487-1653* (New York 1917), p. 161; T.Fuller, *Holy State* (London 1642), p. 9; J.Smyth, *History of the Hundred of Berkeley*, ed. J.MacLean (Gloucester 1885), p. 32; G.Wilkins, *The Miseries of Inforst Marriage* (London 1607), Act I, Sc. i; G.B.Harrison, *Advice to his son by Henry Percy, 9th Earl of Northumberland* (London 1930), p. 55.

95. J.Swetman, *The Arraignment of Lewd, Idle, Froward and Unconstant Women* (London 1616); *Esther hath hanged Haman* (London 1617); *The Wormeing of a Mad Dog* (London 1617); Rachel Speght, *A Mouzell for Melastomus* (London 1617); *Swetnam the Woman-hater arraigned by Women* (London 1620) (ed. A.B.Grosart, London 1880); J.E.Gagen, *The New Woman: her Emergence in English Drama* (New York 1954), p. 19.

96. N.Z.Davis, *op. cit.*, pp. 31, 36, 38.

97. W.Gouge, *op. cit.*, pp. 268, 273, 269, 389-92; R.Cleaver and J.Dod, *op. cit.*

98. *Certain Sermons or Homilies appointed to be read in Churches* (Oxford 1844), pp. 446-58; J.Sprint, *The Bride-Woman's Conseller* (London 1699), p. 5.

99. L.Koehler, 'The Case of the American Jezebels', *William and Mary Quarterly*, 3rd Ser., XXXI (1974), pp. 57, 58; W.Gouge, *Of Domesticall Duties* (London 1622), pp. 267-87; E.Shorter, *op. cit.*, pp. 54, 55, 59; T.Zeldin, *France, 1848-1945* (Oxford 1973), p. 21; A.Hutchinson, *Memoirs of Colonel Hutchinson* (London 1906), p. 26.

100. D.Defoe, *Roxana*, p. 132; *Great Diurnal of Nicholas Blundell*, I, Record Soc. of Lancs. and Cheshire, 110 (1968), p. 120.

101. E.Shorter, *op. cit.*, pp. 66-70.

102. For a summary statement of the role of women in lower class and lower middle-class households in pre-industrial Europe, see J.W.Scott and L.A.Tilly, 'Women's Work and the Family in Nineteenth Century Europe', in *Comparative Studies in Society and History*, 17 (1975); L.A.Tilly, J.W.Scott and M.Cohen, 'Women's Work and the European Fertility Patterns', in *Journal of Interdisciplinary History*, VI (1976); For English evidence to support this hypothesis, see M.Campbell, *op. cit.*, p. 165; W.Crump, *The Yeoman Clothier of the Seventeenth Century* (London 1932), pp. 15, 20; M.D.George, *London Life in the Eighteenth Century* (London 1925), pp. 168, 427-9 (with a list of female occupations); A.Clark, *op. cit.*, pp. 93-6, 145, 154, 164-78; F.Collier, *Family Economy of the Working Class in the Cotton Industry, 1784-1833*, Chetham Soc., 3rd Ser., XII (1965), p. 2; M.Anderson, *Family Structure in Nineteenth Century Lancashire* (Cambridge 1971), p. 96; For French evidence see O.Hufton, 'Women in Revolution 1789-96', in *Past and Present*, 53 (1971), pp. 91-3; A.Forrest, 'The Condition of the Poor in Revolutionary Bordeaux', *loc. cit.*, 59 (1973), pp. 151-2; J.-M.Gouesse, 'Parenté, famille et mariage en Normandie au XVIIᵉ et XVIIIᵉ siècles', in *Annales E.C.S.* (July-Oct. 1972), pp. 1146-7.

103. F.Engels, *The Origins of the Family, Private Property and the State* (New York 1972),

pp. 81–2.

104. E.Richards, 'Women in the British Economy since about 1700: an Interpretation', in *History*, 59 (1974), p. 341 (quoting from *Life and Letters of Hugh Miller*, ed. P.Bayne (London 1871), I, p. 115).

105. J.W.Scott and L.A.Tilly, *op. cit.*, p. 37.

106. C.S.Weiner, 'Sex Roles and Crimes in Late Elizabethan Hertfordshire', in *Journal of Social History*,, viii (1975).

107. K.Digby, *Loose Fantasies*, ed. V.Gabrielli (Rome 1968), p. 146.

108. *Vives and the Renascence Education of Women*, ed. F.Watson (London 1912), pp. 1–11; R.K.Kelso, *Doctrine for the Lady of the Renaissance* (Urbana 1956), pp. 62–77; M.Reynolds, *The Learned Lady in England, 1650–1760* (Boston 1920), p. 9.

109. D.Gardiner, *English Girlhood at School* (London 1929), pp. 173–4; *Educational Writings of Richard Mulcaster*, pp. 52, 51.

110. M.Luther, *Table Talk*, ed. W.Hazlitt (London 1857), no. 725.

111. W.Wotton, *Reflections upon Ancient and Modern Learning* (London 1694), pp. 349–50.

112. *Autobiography of Lady Anne Halkett, Camden Soc.*, 2nd Ser., XIII (1875), p. 2; *Lyme Letters, 1660–1760*, p. 13; *Lismore Papers*, ed. A.B.Grosart, 2nd Series, IV, p. 149; *Memoirs of the Verney Family during the Seventeenth Century*, I, pp. 500–1; D.Gardiner, *op. cit.*, p. 238.

113. J.Winthrop, *History of New England*, ed. J.K.Hosmer (New York 1908), II, p. 225.

114. *Autobiography of Mrs Alice Thornton*, pp. 8, 100.

115. *Life of William Cavendish, Duke of Newcastle*, ed. C.H.Firth (London, n.d.), pp. 157–8.

116. *Memoirs of the Verney Family during the Seventeenth Century*, II, pp. 312–13; *Banks Letters and Papers, 1704–1760, Lincolnshire Record Soc.*, 45 (1952), p. 27.

117. R.S.Schofield, 'Illiteracy in Pre-Industrial England', *Umea University Educational Reports*, 3 (1973), p. 17; M.Campbell, *op. cit.*, pp. 274–5.

118. B. de Mandeville, 'Letter to Mr. Angel' in his *Wishes to a Godson with other Miscellaneous Poems* (London 1712), p. 20; J.Boswell, *Life of Johnson*, II, pp. 447, 114.

119. L.Stone, *op. cit.*, pp. 572–6.

120. *Letters and Works of Lady Mary Wortley Montagu*, ed. Lord Wharncliffe and W.M.Thomas (London 1887), I, p. xcviii.

121. E.Morgan, *The Puritan Family* (New York 1966), p. 49.

122. *Life of Adam Martindale*, pp. 6, 18.

123. A.Macfarlane, *Family Life of Ralph Josselin* (Cambridge 1970), pp. 175–6.

124. *Autobiography of Mary Rich, Countess of Warwick*, ed. T.C.Croker, *Percy Soc.*, XXII (1848), pp. 17–18.

125. *Diary of Cotton Mather*, I, pp. 283, 293–4, 369; II, pp. 139, 756; C.Holliday, *Woman's Life in Colonial Boston* (Boston 1922), p. 25.

126. *Diaries of Oliver Heywood*, I, p. 41.

127. *Autobiography ... of Sir Simonds D'Ewes*, I, pp. 353–4, 362–3; II, p. 145.

128. *Autobiography of Mary Rich, Countess of Warwick*, p. 30.

129. *Diaries of Oliver Heywood*, IV, p. 169.

130. *Diary of Samuel Sewall*, I, p. 543.

131. *Diaries of Cotton Mather*, I, pp. 248, 24, 348, 366, 378, 430, 432–5, 437.

132. *Ibid.*, I, pp. 448, 451–3.

133. *Ibid.*, I, pp. 454–5; II, pp. 6–7, 187, 374.

134. *Ibid.*, II, pp. 87, 349-50, 631-9.
135. J.B.Williams, *Memoirs of the Life of the Rev. Matthew Henry.*
136. *Diary of Richard Kay, 1716-51, Chetham Soc.*, 3rd Ser., XVI (1968), pp. 9, 36, 18, 26, 57, 24, 39.
137. J.B.Williams, *op. cit.*, p. 110.
138. D.E.Stonnard, 'Death and Dying in Puritan New England', in *American Historical Review*, 78 (1973), pp. 1311-28; R.Baxter, *Practical Works*, ed. W.Orme (London 1830), XVII, p. 255. I owe this reference to Miss E.Gilliam.
139. See *infra*, ch. 6, section 3, iii.
140. B.M.Berry, *op. cit.*, pp. 562, 565, 577.

CHAPTER 6   THE GROWTH OF AFFECTIVE INDIVIDUALISM

1. For one of these wholly impersonal contracts for tombs dated 1510, and commissioned by Henry Foljambe of Chesterfield, see *Collectanea Topographica et Genealogica*, I (1834), pp. 354-5.
2. C.J.Phillips, *History of the Sackville Family* (London 1930), I, pp. 420-1.
3. For example at Castle Howard, Yorks, and West Wycombe, Bucks.
4. D.Riesman, *The Lonely Crowd* (New Haven 1961), p. 44.
5. P.Delany, *British Autobiography in the Seventeenth Century* (London 1969), pp. 12, 27, 68, 75, 108, 167-71.
6. A.Macfarlane, *Family Life of Ralph Josselin* (Cambridge 1970), ch. I: 'Diary Keeping in Seventeenth Century England'. W.Matthews, *British Autobiographies* (Berkeley 1955); W.Matthews, *British Diaries* (Berkeley 1950); W.Matthews, *Autobiography in the Seventeenth Century*, Clark Library (Los Angeles 1973), p. 3; P.Delany, *op. cit.*; M.Bottrall, *Everyman a Phoenix: Studies in Seventeenth Century Autobiography* (London 1958), pp. 18-22; *Letters of Dorothy Osborne to Sir William Temple, 1652-54*, ed. G.C.M.Smith (Oxford 1928).
7. P.Séjourné, *Aspects généraux du roman féminin en Angleterre de 1740 à 1800*, Pubs. des Annales de la Faculté de Lettres, Aix-en-Provence, n.s. 52 (1966), p. 94.
8. *The Levellers in the English Revolution*, ed. G.E.Aylmer (London 1975), pp. 68-9, 71; H.N.Brailsford, *The Levellers and the English Revolution* (London 1961), pp. 55-6; C.Hill, 'The Norman Yoke' in his *Puritanism and Revolution* (London 1958).
9. J.Milton, *Areopagitica*, in *Works* (New York 1931), IV, p. 347.
10. P.Zagorin, *The Court and the Country* (London 1969), ch. 3; J.G.A.Pococke, 'Machiavelli, Harrington and English Political Ideologies in the Eighteenth Century', in *William and Mary Quarterly*, 3rd Ser., XXII (1965), p. 565.
11. Quoted by C.Hill, 'Reason and "Reasonableness" in Seventeenth Century England', in *British Journal of Sociology*, XX (1969), p. 237.
12. *Memoirs of the Verney Family in the Seventeenth Century* ed. F.P. and M.M.Verney (London 1907), II, pp. 444-5; A.Pope, *An Essay in Man* (1733), Epistle 3, lines 305-6; R.Paulson, *Hogarth: His Life, Art and Times* (New Haven 1971), II, pl. 284.
13. S.E.Sprott, *The English Debate on Suicide from Donne to Hume* (La Salle, Ill. 1961), pp. 98, 112.
14. J.Redwood, *Reason, Ridicule and Religion: the Age of the Enlightenment in England 1660-1750* (London 1976).
15. The theory that early seventeenth-century common lawyers like Sir Edward Coke

favoured unrestricted free enterprise is no longer tenable (B.Malament, 'The "Economic Liberalism" of Sir Edward Coke', in *Yale Law Journal*, LXXVI [1967]).

16. M.Beresford, 'Habitation versus Improvement: The Debate on Enclosure by Agreement', in *Essays in the Economic and Social History of Tudor and Stuart England*, ed. F.J.Fisher (Cambridge 1961); C.Hill, 'Reason and "Reasonableness" ...', *op. cit.*, *passim*; L.Stone, 'State Control in Sixteenth Century England', in *Econ. Hist. Rev.*, XVII (1947), p. 110.

17. L.Stone, *The Crisis of the Aristocracy* (Oxford 1965), pp. 242-50; J.P.Malcolm, *Anecdotes of the manners and customs of London during the 18th century* (London 1808), p. 147. The full extent of duelling in eighteenth-century England is at present not clear. Only 36 cases were reported in the *Gentleman's Magazine* between 1731 and 1786, but this was certainly only the more notorious tip of the iceberg. It became a more dangerous pastime after about 1745, when the pistol replaced the rapier (J.D.Aylward, 'Duelling in the XVIII Century', in *Notes and Queries*, 189 (1945), pp. 32, 34).

18. C.Robbins, *The Pursuit of Happiness* (Washington, D.C. 1974) (American Enterprise Institute's Distinguished Lecture Series on the Bicentennial); S.E.Sprott, *op.cit.*, p.112.

19. G.Snyders, *La Pédagogie en France au XVIIᵉ et XVIIIᵉ Siècles* (Paris 1965), pp. 318-19; J.-M.Gouesse, 'Le Mariage en Normandie au XVIIᵉ et XVIIIᵉ Siècles', in *Annales E.C.S.*, 27 (1972), p. 1146; J.-L.Flandrin, 'Mariage tardif et vie sexuelle', in *Annales E.C.S.*, 27, p. 1390.

20. *The Lady's Magazine*, IV (1773), pp. 521, 585; J.H.Plumb, *The Commercialization of Leisure in Eighteenth Century England* (Reading 1973).

21. *Puritan Political Ideals, 1558-1794*, ed. E.S.Morgan (Indianapolis 1975), pp. 188, 194-5 (I owe this reference to Professor John Murrin); D.R.Jardine, *A Reading on the Use of Torture in the Criminal Law of England* (London 1837), p. 57.

22. J.H.Plumb, 'The New World of Children in Eighteenth Century England', in *Past and Present*, 67 (1975), pp. 82-3; R.Paulson, *op. cit.*, II, pl. 228-31c; p. 109.

23. R.S.Crane, 'Suggestions towards a Genealogy of the "Man of Feeling"', in *English Literary History*, I (1934); H.Mackenzie, *The Man of Feeling*, ed. H.Miles (London 1928), pp. 29-30.

24. G.J.Schochet, 'The Family and the Origins of the State in Locke's Political Philosophy', in *John Locke: Problems and Perspectives*, ed. J.W.Yolton (Cambridge 1969).

25. G.Miège, *The New State of England* (London 1691), part II, p. 80.

26. J.Vanbrugh, *The Provoked Wife* (London 1697), Act I, Sc. i; Lady Mary Chudleigh, *The Ladies Defence* (London 1701), p. 3; M.Astell, *Reflections on Marriage* (London, 4th ed. 1730), pp. 106-7.

27. W.Fleetwood, *Relative Duties of Parents and Children, Husbands and Wives, Masters and Servants* (London 1716), pp. 68-70, 250-1.

28. B.de Mandeville, *The Virgin Unmask'd* (London 1724), pp. 39, 179, 30.

29. J.Bunyan, *A Few Sighs from Hell*, in *Complete Works*, ed. G.Offer (Glasgow 1853), III, pp. 699-700; *Life and Errors of John Dunton* (London 1818), I, p. 310.

30. W.Cobbett, *Parliamentary History of England* (London 1813), XV, cols. 59-60, 81; *The Lady's Magazine*, IV (1773), p. 131; see *infra*, ch. 7 sect. 1, ii.

31. J.Harrington, *Oceana*, ed. H.Morley (London 1887), p. 115.

32. H.J.Habakkuk, 'Marriage Settlements in the 18th Century', in *Transactions of the Royal*

Historical Society, 4th Ser., XXXII (1950).

33. D.Defoe, *The Family Instructor* (London 1715), p. 294.

34. *Thraliana*, ed. K.C.Balderston (Oxford 1942), I, p. 318.

35. L.Stone, *Crisis* ..., p. 635; *Memoirs of the Family of Guise, Camden Soc.*, 3rd Ser., 28 (1917), pp. 152–53.

36. L.Claxton [Clarkson], *The Lost Sheep Found* (London 1660), p. 5.

37. S.Pepys, *Diary, passim*, e.g. 15 Nov. 1663; *Athenian Mercury* (London 1692), VIII, 17, questions 4, 5 and 6; Anon, *An Essay on the Happiness and Advantages of a Well-Ordered Family* (London 1794), pp. iv, 2, 13, 33, 46; D.Defoe, *The Family Instructor* (London 1715), p. 3.

38. *Private Papers of James Boswell*, ed. G.Scott and F.A.Pottle (New York 1932), 13, p. 179; see also J.Austen, *Mansfield Park*, ed. R.W.Chapman (Oxford 1933), pp. 85–7; For an American exception to the rule, see *Autobiography of Lyman Beecher*, ed. C.Beecher (New York 1864), I, p. 33.

39. M.J.Quinlan, *Victorian Prelude* (New York 1941), p. 2.

40. G.Savile, Marquess of Halifax, *The Ladys New Year's Gift or Advice to a Daughter* (1688), in H.C.Foxcroft, *Life and Letters of Sir George Savile Bart., First Marquess of Halifax* (London 1898), II, p. 393.

41. I.Pinchbeck and M.Hewitt, *Children in English Society* (London 1959), I, pp. 301–2; A.Leger, *Wesley's Last Love* (London 1910), p. 158.

42. P.Ariès, *Western Attitudes towards Death* (Baltimore 1974), ch. III.

43. *Poems of T.Gray, W.Collins and O.Goldsmith*, ed. R.Lonsdale (London 1969), pp. 103–16.

44. *Boswell in Extremes, 1776–1778*, ed. C.McC.Weis and F.A.Pottle (New York 1970), pp. 103–5.

45. *Memoirs of Richard Cumberland* (London 1806), p. 67; see also *Pembroke Papers, 1780–1794*, ed. Henry Lord Herbert (London 1950), p. 156.

46. *The Autobiography of Arthur Young*, ed. M.Betham-Edwards (London 1898), pp. 22, 277–82.

47. Earl of Bessborough, *Lady Bessborough and her Family Circle* (London 1910), p. 265; *Capel Letters, 1814–1817*, ed. Marquess of Anglesea (London 1955), p. 143.

48. *Life of Mrs Sherwood*, ed. S.Kelly (London 1854), pp. 107, 307–8; For other examples, see: *ibid.*, pp. 327–8, 349, 37; *Life of George Crabbe by his Son*, ed. E.Blunden (London 1947), p. 134; *Thraliana*, ed. K.C.Balderston, I, pp. 278–9; C.Aspinall-Oglander, *Admiral's Widow* (London 1942), p. 21.

49. *Journals and Correspondence of Thomas Sedgewick Whalley*, ed. H.Wickham (London 1863), II, pp. 58–9.

50. *Life of Thomas Holcroft*, ed. E.Colby (London 1925), I, p. 45; Earl of Bessborough, *op. cit.*, pp. 23–6; *Francis Letters*, ed. B.Francis and E.Keary (New York 1901), I, p. 196.

51. *Boswell in Extremes, 1776–1778*, p. 299; *Pembroke Papers, 1780–1794*, ed. Henry, Lord Herbert (London 1950), p. 491.

52. *Poems of George Crabbe*, ed. A.W.Ward (Cambridge 1907), I, p. 199.

53. *Letters and Works of Lady Mary Wortley Montagu*, ed. Lord Wharncliffe and W.M.Thomas (London 1887), II, p. 186.

54. P.Sangster, *Pity my Simplicity: The Evangelical Revival and the Religious Education of Children, 1738–1800* (London 1963), pp. 28, 31, 33, 34, 41, 49, 56, 132, 139.

55. Isaac Watts, *Divine Songs Attempted in Easy Language for the Use of Children*, ed. J.H.P.Pafford (London 1971), nos. X, XI, XXIII; P.Sangster, *op. cit.*, pp. 63, 67, 152–3, 137.

56. P. Ariès, *Centuries of Childhood* (New York 1957), pp. 390–3. L.Stone, *op. cit.*, pp. 212, 669.

57. P.Ariès, *op. cit.*, pp. 398–9; G.Snyders, *op. cit.*, pp. 298–300; All these developments occurred a good deal earlier in England than in France, in the first half of the seventeenth century (see M.E.James, *Family, Lineage and Civil Society* (Oxford 1974), pp. 13–15, 103, for changes in gentry houses in the North of England).

58. D.Defoe, *Everybody's Business is Nobody's Business* (London 1725), p. 14; *Boswell in Extremes, 1776–1778*, p. 266, n. 1.

59. Anon., *A New and Complete Collection of the most remarkable Trials for Adultery* (London 1780), *passim*.

60. W.G.Hoskins, 'The Rebuilding of Rural England, 1570–1640', in *Past and Present*, 4 (1953), p. 54.

61. *Life of George Crabbe by his Son*, p. 123; J.Boswell, *The Journal of a Tour to the Hebrides* (London 1785), p. 57.

62. *Autobiography of Francis Place*, ed. M.Thale (Cambridge 1972), pp. 76, 78; J.Brasbridge, *The Fruits of Experience* (London 1824), p. 26; W.Cobbett, *Parliamentary History of England*, XIV, Col. 1345; J.Obelkevich, *Religion and Rural Society: South Lindsey, 1825–1875* (Oxford 1976), p. 56.

63. E.P.Thompson, 'Patrician Society, Plebeian Culture', in *Journal of Social History*, 7 (1974), pp. 382–5, 391.

64. *Poems of George Crabbe*, I, p. 163; F.G.Emmison, *Elizabethan Life: Morals and the Church Courts* (Chelmsford 1973), p. 5; *Autobiography of Francis Place*, pp. 275, 116, 193; H.Mayhew, quoted in E.M.Sigsworth and T.J.Wyke, 'A Study of Victorian Prostitution and Venereal Disease', in M.Vicinus, *Suffer and be Still* (Bloomington 1972), p. 81; *Local Population Studies*, 7, 1971, p. 62.

65. The following paragraphs are based on Norbert Elias, *La Civilisation des Moeurs* (Paris 1973).

66. *Annual Register*, 1976, p. 206 (quoted in Séjourné, *op. cit.*, p. 33, n. 41).

67. [N.Barbon], *A Discourse of Trade* (London 1690), p. 15, quoted by J.Appleby, 'Ideology and Theory: The Tension between political and economic Liberalism in Seventeenth Century England', in *American Historical Review*, 81, 1976, p. 505.

68. *Boswell for the Defence, 1769–1774*, ed. W.K.Wimsatt and F.A.Pottle (New York 1959), p. 102.

69. P.Burke, *Venice and Amsterdam* (London 1974), pp. 30–1; I owe this point about Genoa to my colleague, Professor A.T.Grafton.

70. J.Boswell, *Life of Samuel Johnson, LLD* (Everyman ed. London 1906), II, p. 189.

71. E.P.Thompson, *op. cit.*, p. 387.

72. I owe many of the ideas in this paragraph to an unpublished paper by Professor M.L.Shanley of Vassar, 'Marriage Contract in Seventeenth Century Political Thought', 1976.

73. A.Pope, *An Essay on Man*, Epistle 3, lines 317–18; Epistle 4, lines 395–6.

74. P.Slater, *Earthwalk* (New York 1974), pp. 116–29.

CHAPTER 7   MATING ARRANGEMENTS

1. Anon., *Reflections on Marriage* (London 1703), p. 56.

2. E.Flexner, *Mary Wollstonecraft* (New York 1972), p. 76.

3. I have mislaid the reference. The phrase occurs somewhere in the voluminous papers of James Boswell.

4. F.Bacon, *Essays: Of Love* (1625); Anon., *Reflections on Marriage*, p. 19.

5. R.Blunt and M.Wyndham, *Thomas, Lord Lyttelton* (London 1936), p. 85; *The Lady's Monthly Museum*, II (1799), p. 288.

6. K.Digby, *Loose Fantasies*, ed. V.Gabrielli (Rome 1968), pp. 147, 152; *H.M.C. Buccleuch (Whitehall) MSS*, III, p. 366; Dudley Lord North, *A Forest of Varieties* (London 1645), II, p. 141; Lady Newdigate-Newdegate, *Cavalier and Puritan in the Days of the Stuarts* (London 1901), p. 348.

7. *Athenian Mercury* (1691), I, no. 13, Q. 2, 13.

8. M.Astell, *Reflections on Marriage* (London, 4th ed. 1730, New York 1970), pp. 29, 7, 30, 25.

9. D.Defoe, *Conjugal Lewdness or Matrimonial Whoredom* (London 1727), pp. 98, 99, 101, 102, 166–7, 170–1, 199. For his similar attitude in 1705, see D.Defoe, *The Little Review* (1705), pp. 46, 70; *The Review*, III (1704), Supplementary Journal no. 1, p. 9.

10. *The Spectator* (1711), nos. 261, 268, 304; *The Tatler* (1709), no. 185; R.P.Bond, *New Letters to the Tatler and Spectator* (Austin 1959), p. 189.

11. J.E.Gagen, *The New Woman: Her Emergence in English Drama* (New York 1954), pp. 123, 127; see also I.Watt, 'The New Woman: Samuel Richardson's Pamela', in his *The Rise of the Novel* (London 1957).

12. A.Behn, *The Fair Jilt* (1688) and *The Lucky Chance* (1686), Act I, sc. ii, in *Works*, ed. H.Summers (London 1915), V, p. 72, III, p. 200; D.Garrick, *Lethe* (1740) in *Dramatic Works* (London 1798), I, p. 17.

13. R.Paulson, *Hogarth: His Life, Art and Times* (New Haven 1971), I, pp. 479–89; *Catalogue of Political and Personal Satires in the British Museum*, III, i, pp. 546–83.

14. M.Astell, *A Serious Proposal to the Ladies* (1701, New York 1970), p. 35.

15. G.Savile, Marquess of Halifax, *The Lady's New Year's Gift*, in Foxcroft, *Works of Sir George Savile Bart., First Marquess of Halifax* (London 1898), II, pp. 393–401.

16. H.Fielding, *The History of Tom Jones* (Everyman ed., London 1749), I, pp. 32, 153, 246, 248, 251; II, p. 389.

17. For two excellent analyses of the meaning of this book see C.Hill, 'Clarissa Harlowe and Her Times', in his *Puritanism and Revolution* (London 1958), and I.Watt, 'Richardson as Novelist: Clarissa', in his *Rise of the Novel*.

18. Mrs Hester Chapone, *Posthumous Works* (London 1808), II, pp. 33, 45–6, 56, 59, 73, 102.

19 Defoe's *Review*, III (1704), Supplementary Journal no. 1, p. 14; *Catalogue of Political and Personal Satires in the British Museum*, VI, no. 8219.

20. Defoe's *Review*, V, *The Little Review*, pp. 10–11.

21. *Autobiography of Thomas Wythorne*, ed. J.Osborn (Oxford 1961), pp. 46, 192.

22. C.Duncan, 'Happy Mothers and Other New Ideas in French Art', in *Art Bulletin*, 55, 4 (1973), Fig. 14 and p. 579.

23. I owe this information about Napier to Mr M.MacDonald.

24. A.Macfarlane, *Family Life of Ralph Josselin* (Cambridge 1970), p. 95.

25. J.Swift, *A Letter to a Young Lady on Her Marriage* in *Works*, ed. W.Scott (Edinburgh

1814), IX, p. 421; *The Lady's Magazine*, IV (1773), p. 402; *The Lady's Monthly Museum*, II (1799), pp. 218–19; E.J.Climenson, *Elizabeth Montagu, Queen of the Bluestockings* (London 1906), II, p. 245; J.Gregory, *A Father's Legacy to his Daughters* (London 1774), p. 126.

26. P.Séjourné, *Aspects généraux du roman féminin en Angleterre de 1740 à 1800*, Annales de la Faculté de Lettres, Aix-en-Provence, n.s. 52 (1966), pp. 69–72.

27. *Bon Ton Magazine* (October 1792).

28. M.Wollstonecraft, *A Vindication of the Rights of Woman* (1792) (Everyman ed., London 1970), pp. 81, 130; *Thraliana*, ed. K.C.Balderston (Oxford 1942), I, pp. 197, 224.

29. *Memoirs of her Life by Mrs Catherine Cappe* (London 1822), pp. 65, 133.

30. *Love-Letters of Mary Hays*, ed. A.F.Wedd (London 1925), quoted in J.M.S.Tomkins, *The Polite Marriage* (Cambridge 1938), pp. 151–90 *passim*, 156.

31. *Retrospections of Dorothea Herbert, 1790–1806* (London 1929), II, pp. 335–6.

32. R.Blunt and M.Wyndham, *Thomas, Lord Lyttelton*, pp. 223–4, 227, 234, 237–8, 242–3.

33. W.Cobbett, *Advice to Young Men* (1829) ed. H.Morley (London 1887), pp. 82–8.

34. *Original and Genuine Letters to the Tatler and Spectator*, ed. C.Lillie (London 1725), p. 149.

35. M.Pennington, *Memoirs of the Life of Mrs Elizabeth Carter* (London 1808), I, pp. 28–31.

36. *Memoirs of Mrs Catherine Jemmat* (London 1771), I, pp. 47–54, 96, 101, 111, 118–20, 124–8; II, pp. 1, 9–10, 27, 33, 34, 37, 40, 43, 57–8.

37. *Memoirs of Sir Philip Francis*, ed. J.Parkes and H.Merivale (London 1867), pp. 54–8; *Francis Letters*, ed. B.Francis and E.Keary (New York 1901), I, pp. 60–4.

38. J.Brasbridge, *The Fruits of Experience* (London 1824), pp. 161–2.

39. *Memoirs of the Verney Family during the Seventeenth Century*, ed. F.P. and M.M.Verney (London 1907), II, pp. 271–3.

40. *Ibid.*, pp. 364, 371.

41. *The Life of Mrs Sherwood*, ed. S.Kelly (London 1854), pp. 3, 9–14, 62, 144, 147, 150–1; for a similar example, see *Diary of Dudley Ryder, 1715–16*, ed. W.Matthews (London 1939), pp. 327, 96, 244, 279, 310, 20.

42. R.L.Edgeworth, *Memoirs* (London 1820), I, pp. 79–85.

43. A.Macfarlane, *op. cit.*, pp. 95–7, 122–5.

44. *Life and Errors of John Dunton* (London 1818), I, pp. 47, 61, 63–5, 92–3, 298–301, 103, 73–4.

45. *Yorkshire Diaries and Autobiographies in the Seventeenth and Eighteenth Centuries*, Surtees Soc., LXV (1875), pp. 201, 212, 223.

46. *Bletchley Diary of the Rev. William Cole*, ed. F.G.Stokes (London 1931), pp. 120, 129.

47. D.Defoe, *Moll Flanders* (1721) (Everyman ed.), pp. 57–8, 52.

48. *Cumberland Letters, 1771–84*, ed. C.Black (London 1912), pp. 180, 186, 251, 221, 239.

49. A.Leger, *Wesley's Last Love* (London 1910), pp.70–8, 109, 132, 137, 140, 148.

50. *The Diary of Thomas Turner of East Hoathly (1754–65)* (London 1925), pp. 99–101. For other examples of these conflicts of motives, and their very varying consequences, see the cases of Thomas Gent and Mrs Charlotte Charke in *Life of Mr Thomas Gent* (London 1832), pp. 35, 71, 147–8, 152–3; *Narrative of the Life of Mrs Charlotte Charke* (London 1755), pp. 50–4, 76–7, 80.

51. *Life of George Crabbe by his Son*, ed. E.Blunden (London 1947), p. 36; *Poems of George Crabbe*, ed. A.W.Ward (Cambridge 1907), I, pp. 192–3.

52. J.Knyveton, *Diary of a Surgeon in the Year 1750–51*, ed. J.Gray (New York 1937), pp. 103–5.

53. *Autobiography of Francis Place*, ed. M.Thale (Cambridge 1972), pp. 99–103, 121.

54. *Diary of Samuel Pepys*, Feb. 3, Mar. 13, 24, 31, June 23–5, July 2, 5, 8, 12, 14–17, 20, 24, 31, Aug. 1, 1665; April 4, July 6, 1667.

55. *Memoirs of the Verney Family during the Seventeenth Century*, II, pp. 453–5, 234.

56. R.K.Marshall, *Days of Duchess Anne* (London 1973), pp. 147, 170.

57. R.North, *Autobiography*, ed. A.Jessop (London 1887), pp. 232–5.

58. *Great Diurnal of Nicholas Blundell*, I, *Record Society of Lancashire and Cheshire*, 110 (1968), p. 4.

59. *The Letters and Papers of the Banks Family of Revesby Abbey 1704–1760*, Lincolnshire Record Society, 45 (1952), pp. xv, 2–18.

60. R.A.Kelch, *Newcastle: a Duke without Money* (Berkeley 1974), pp. 44–7, 14–17.

61. *Henry, Elizabeth and George, 1734–80*, ed. Henry, Lord Herbert (London 1939), pp. 282, 370, 491; *Pembroke Papers, 1780–1794*, ed. Henry, Lord Herbert, London 1950), pp. 307, 316, 321, 340–4.

62. Earl of Bessborough, *Lady Bessborough and her Family Circle* (London 1940), p. 138; For other examples of very tolerant parents in the late eighteenth century, see D.M.Stuart, *Molly Lepell, Lady Hervey* (London 1936), p. 168; Earl of Bessborough, *Georgiana* (London 1955), pp. 48, 237.

63. *Autobiography of Lady Anne Halkett, Camden Soc.*, 2nd Ser. XIII (1875), pp. 2, 13, 4, 7, 8, 9, 19, 25, 32–5, 36–8, 45, 53, 65, 79, 81, 86, 89, 91, 99, 101–3.

64. *Autobiography of Mrs Alice Thornton, Surtees Soc.*, LXII (1875), pp. 61–2, 76–8, 83, 104, 146, 154–5, 214–38.

65. *Letters and Works of Lady Mary Wortley Montagu*, ed. Lord Wharncliffe and W.M.Thomas (London 1887), I, pp. xxxi–xxxiv, 56, 64–8.

66. *Autobiography and Correspondence of Mary Granville, Mrs Delany* (London 1861), I, pp. 19, 23–39, 51–5, 63, 92–4, 105–7, 240–3, 297, 333. For other examples, see *op.cit.*, pp. 155, 182 and E.J.Climenson, *Elizabeth Montagu*, I, pp. 42, 109, 110, 119.

67. Earl of Bessborough, *Lady Bessborough and her Family Circle*, pp. 31–2.

68. Mrs Thrale's Children's Book; *Thraliana*, ed. K.C.Balderston, I, pp. 55, 299–300, 303–7, 367 n. 2; II, p. 692; R.L.Clifford, *Hester Lynch Piozzi (Thrale)* (Oxford 1952), pp. 49, 97–8, 173.

69. F.Bamford, *Dear Miss Heber* (London 1936), pp. 122–3.

70. R.Fletcher, *The Parkers of Saltram, 1769–89* (London 1970), p. 14; *The Lady's Monthly Museum*, II (1799), p. 107.

71. *Lettres de Baron de Pollnitz* (London 1741), III, pp. 365–6; F.de La Rochefoucauld, *A Frenchman in England, 1784*, ed. J.Marchand (Cambridge 1933), pp. 49–50.

72. It was believed at one time that the pursuit of heiresses was intensifying; H.J.Habakkuk, 'Marriage Settlements in the Eighteenth Century', in *Transactions of the Royal Historical Society*, 4th Ser., XXXII (1950), pp. 24–5; 'English Landownership 1680–1740', in *Economic History Review*, X (1940). It is now clear, however, that it was declining rapidly throughout the eighteenth century; D.Thomas, 'Social Origins of Marriage Partners of the British Aristocracy in the 18th and 19th Centuries', in *Population Studies*, 26 (1) (1972), p. 105.

73. D.S.Smith, 'Parental Power and Marriage Patterns: an Analysis of historical Trends in

Hingham, Mass.', in *Journal of Marriage and the Family*, 35 (1973).

74. See *infra*, ch. 12, section 1, ii.

75. J.-L.Flandrin, *Les Amours Paysannes* (Paris 1975), p. 129.

76. J.-M.Gouesse, 'Le Mariage en Normandie', in *Annales E.C.S.*, 27 (1972), pp. 144–7.

77. J.-L.Flandrin, *op. cit.*, pp. 40–58; *Letters and Works of Lady Mary Wortley Montagu*, I, p. lxxxiii; P.Séjourné, *op. cit.*, p. 299, n. 57.

78. I owe this reference to Robert Darnton.

79. T.Zeldin, *France 1848–1945* (Oxford 1973), pp. 287–9, 318–21, 361.

80. *Thraliana*, II, p. 624, n. 1.

81. *A Critical Essay Concerning Marriage* by a Gentleman (London 1724) (quoted in *Local Population Studies*, 12, 1974, pp. 46–9).

82. F.Brooke, *History of Emily Montagu* (London 1874), I, p. 116 (quoted in P.Séjourné, *op. cit.*, p. 369 n. 304).

CHAPTER 8   THE COMPANIONATE MARRIAGE

1. W.Gouge, *Of Domesticall Duties* (London 1634), pp. 389–93; L.L.Schüking, *The Puritan Family* . . . (New York 1966), p. 45; P.R.O.Star Chamber 8/158/18; *Catalogue of Political and Personal Satires in the British Museum*, V, no. 6123.

2. *Athenian Mercury*, London, 1691–3, X, 25, question 2; I, 13, question 6; 1, question 6; II, 21, question 5; V, 9, question 2.

3. D.Defoe, *Complete English Tradesman* (London 1726), pp. 33, 28, 32, 26.

4. G.Farquhar, *The Beaux' Strategem* (1707), Act II, Sc. i.

5. Mrs Hester Chapone, *Posthumous Works* (London 1808), II, pp. 149, 151; W.Wilkes, *A Letter of Genteel and Moral Advice to a Young Lady* (1740) (London 1766), pp. 186, 190, 192, 197.

6. J.Gregory, *A Father's Legacy to his Daughters* (London 1774), pp. 114–16.

7. *The Lady's Magazine*, V (1774), pp. 40, 82, 83; IV (1773), pp. 183, 203–4.

8. S.von La Roche, *Sophie in London, 1786*, ed. C.Williams (London 1933), pp. 72, 170; F.de La Rochefoucauld, *A Frenchman in England, 1784*, ed. J.Marchand (Cambridge 1933), pp. 48–50. In 1741 Baron de Pollnitz, on the other hand, thought that husbands were relatively indifferent to their wives in England. Wives were unusually free, but faithful, since the English were not much given to love affairs anyway (*Lettres du Baron de Pollnitz* (London 1741), III, pp. 365–6).

9. *Letters of Dorothy Osborne to William Temple, 1652–54*, ed. G.C.M.Smith (Oxford 1928), pp. xxxvi, 72, 129, 167, 171, 202–4; *Correspondence of Richard Steele*, ed. R.Blanchard (London 1941), pp. 205, 207–9, 222; J.Sprint, *The Bride Woman's Conseller* (London 1699), p. 13; Anon., *The Female Preacher, being an answer to the late rude and scandalous wedding sermon preached by Mr John Sprint* (London 1699), p. 19; Lady Mary Chudleigh, *The Ladies Defence* (London 1701), p. 12.

10. *Banks Letters and Papers, 1704–1760*, in *Lincolnshire Record Soc.*, 45 (1952), pp. 140, 163–4; T.Gisborne, *op. cit.*, p. 277.

11. L.Stone, *The Crisis of the Aristocracy* (Oxford 1965), pp. 641, fig. 18, 634–5; H.J.Habakkuk, 'Marriage Settlements in the 18th Century', in *Transactions of the Royal Historical Society*, 4th Ser., XXXII (1950); C.S.Kenny, *The History of the Law of England as to the Effects of Marriage on Property and on the Wife's Legal Capacity* (London 1879), pp. 116, 100–3, 119.

12. *Autobiography of Mrs Alice Thornton, Surtees Soc.*, LXII (1873), pp. 246–8.

13. Earl of Bessborough, *Georgiana* (London 1955), p. 187.

14. J.S.Mill, *The Subjection of Women* (Everyman ed. London 1929), pp. 247–9; This is the situation seen from the viewpoint of the professional classes, but it does not differ in any respect from the lower-middle class assessment of William Cobbett in 1829 (*Advice to Young Men*, p. 151).

15. British Museum, Add. MSS, 27826, f. 21.

16. D.Defoe, *Roxana*, ed. J.Jack (Oxford 1964), p. 148; *The Lady's Magazine*, IV (1773), p. 23.

17. R.P.Bond, *New Letters to the Tatler and Spectator* (Austin 1959), p. 83.

18. H.L.H.von Pückler-Muskau, *Tour of England, Ireland and France 1826–29* (Philadelphia 1833), pp. 18, 53, 130, 153, 155, 229.

19. *Life and Letters of Lady Sarah Lennox, 1745–1826*, ed. Countess of Ilchester and Lord Stavordale (London 1902), p. 182.

20. *Ibid.*, pp. 151–2.

21. L.Stone, *op. cit.*, pp. 651–2; *The British Apollo* (1708), no. 80.

22. E.J.Climenson, *Elizabeth Montagu, Queen of the Bluestockings* (London 1906), II, p. 64.

23. D.M.Stuart, *Molly Lepell, Lady Hervey* (London 1936), p. 263.

24. A.Houblon, *The Houblon Family* (London 1907), II, pp. 118–50.

25. *Memorials of the Thackeray Family*, ed. J.T.Pryme and A.Bayne (London 1879), pp. 190, 204; E.J.Climenson, *op. cit.*, I, p. 117; C.Smith, *Celestina* (London 1791), I, pp. 52–61; J.Austen, *Mansfield Park*, ed. R.Chapman (Oxford 1933), pp. 203–4; Anon., *The English Matron* (London 1846), p. 15.

26. J.Stevenson, 'Food Riots in England, 1792–1818', in *Popular Protest and Public Order*, ed. R.Quinault and J.Stevenson (London 1974), p.49.

27. L.Koehler, 'The Case of the American Jezebels: Anne Hutchinson and Female Agitation during the years of the Antinomian Turmoil, 1636–40', in *William and Mary Quarterly*, 3rd Ser., XXI (1974), pp. 57–75.

28. K.V.Thomas, 'Women and the Civil War Sects', in *Past and Present*, 13 (1958), pp. 44–57.

29. P.Higgins, 'The Reactions of Women, with special reference to Women Petitioners', in *Politics, Religion and the English Civil War*, ed. B.Manning (London 1973), p. 185; B.Manning, *The English People and the English Revolution, 1640–49* (London 1976), p. 109.

30. P.Higgins, *op. cit.*, pp. 190–5.

31. *Ibid.*, p. 203.

32. *Ibid.*, pp. 200, 202, 211, 213, 215, 217.

33. E.Hyde, Earl of Clarendon, *Life* (Oxford 1857), II, p. 39–41.

34. K.V.Thomas, *op. cit.*, pp. 56–7.

35. Lady Mary Chudleigh, *Poems on Several Occasions* (London 1703), p. 40.

36. J.Sprint, *The Bride-Woman's Conseller* (London 1699), p. 13; Anon., *The Female Preacher* (London 1699), p. 17.

37. *Catalogue of Political and Personal Satires in the British Museum*, V, nos. 4847, 5065; J.Grego, *Thomas Rowlandson, Caricaturist* (London 1880), II, p. 289; *Times Literary Supplement* (11 August 1932).

38. *Horace Walpole Correspondence*, ed. W.S.Lewis (New Haven 1961), 31, p. 397; *Works of*

Anna Letitia Barbauld, ed. L.Aikin (London 1825), I, pp. 185–7; *Letters and Works of Lady Mary Wortley Montagu*, ed. Lord Wharncliffe and W.M.Thomas (London 1887), I, p. civ. For another radical feminist, see Anne Frances Randall, *A Letter to the Women of England on the Injustices of Mental Subordination* (London 1799).

39. *The Lady's Monthly Museum*, I (1798), pp. 145, 186.

40. *The Women's Sharp Revenge* (1640), pp. 37–42, quoted by M.George, 'From Goodwife to Mistress: the Transformation of the Female in Bourgeois Culture', in *Science and Society*, 37 (1973), p. 171. I do not agree with Ms George's interpretation of this document.

41. J.Swift, 'Of the Education of Ladies', in *Works*, ed. W.Scott (Edinburgh 1814), IX, pp. 476–8.

42. M.Reynolds, *The Learned Lady in England, 1650–1760* (Boston 1920), p. 281; B.Makin, *An Essay to revive the ancient Education of Gentlewomen in Religion, Manners, Arts and Tongues* (London 1673); H.Woolley, *The Gentlewoman's Companion* (London 1675), p. 1; *Letters and Works of Lady Mary Wortley Montagu*, II, p. 5; see also M.Chudleigh, *op. cit.*, pp. 15, 19; G.B.Needham, 'Mrs. Manley, an Eighteenth Century Wife of Bath', in *Huntington Library Quarterly*, XIV (1950–1), pp. 269–70.

43. M.Astell, *A Serious Proposal to the Ladies* (London 1696), pp. 17–22; and her *Reflections on Marriage* (London 4th ed. 1730, New York 1970), pp. 52, 60, 62.

44. *Educational Writings of John Locke*, ed. J.Axtell (Cambridge 1968), pp. 354–5; W.Law, *A Serious Call to a Devout and Holy Life* (London 1729), pp. 347–8.

45. D.Defoe, *Essay upon Projects* (London 1697), pp. 302–3, 294–5; For J.Dunton's reasoned defence of a learned education for women, see *Athenian Mercury* (London 1691), I, 18, question 6.

46. W.Wilkes, *op. cit.*, pp. 157, 168–72; J.Swift, *Works*, IX, p. 479; R.P.Bond, *The Tatler* (Cambridge, Mass. 1971), p. 95; see also [Sophia], *Woman not inferior to Man* (London 1739).

47. R.North, *Autobiography*, ed. A.Jessop (London 1887), pp. 28–9.

48. *Memoirs of her Life by Mrs Catherine Cappe* (London 1822), pp. 19, 55, 38, 46, 50; *Letters and Journals of Lady Mary Coke*, ed. J.A.Home (Edinburgh 1889), I, p. xxx; *Passages from the Diaries of Mrs Philip Lybbe Powys, 1756–1808*, ed. E.J.Climenson (London 1899), p. 159.

49. K.Lambley, *The Teaching and Cultivation of the French Language in England during Tudor and Stuart Times* (Manchester 1920), p. 299; D.Gardiner, *English Girlhood at School* (London 1929), p. 214; M.Reynolds, *op. cit.*, pp. 260–1; For an account of how the second Duchess of Portland occupied her time in the 1730s with these handicrafts, see E.J.Climenson, *Elizabeth Montagu*, I, p. 27.

50. R.Bayne-Powell, *The English Child in the Eighteenth Century* (New York 1939), pp. 271–81; J.P.Malcolm, *Anecdotes of the Manners and Customs of London during the Eighteenth Century* (London 1808), p. 186.

51. *Letters and Works of Lady Mary Wortley Montagu*, I, p. lxxxi; F.Bamford, *Dear Miss Heber* (London 1936), p. xxii.

52. J.H.Plumb, 'The New World of Children in the Eighteenth Century', in *Past and Present*, 67 (1975), pp. 71–6; S.von La Roche, *op. cit.*, pp. 92, 135, 247–8; *Sentimental Magazine*, I (July 1773), p. 209, quoted in M.J.Quinlan, *op. cit.*, p. 63; D.Gardiner, *op. cit.*, pp. 333–5.

53. S.Richardson, *Pamela* (1740), I, *passim*.

54. J.P.Malcolm, *op. cit.*, p. 487.

55. *Diary of Samuel Pepys*, ed. R.E.Latham and W.Matthews; J.H.Wilson, *The Private Life of Mr Pepys* (New York 1959), pp.18-19, 31-3, 48, 58-9, 49-52.

56. J.H.Plumb, *The Commercialization of Leisure in Eighteenth Century England* (Reading, 1973).

57. D.Hudson, *Munby: Man of two Worlds* (London 1972), p. 195.

58. B.de Mandeville, *The Virgin Unmask'd* (London 1724), p. 115; M.Wollstonecraft, *A Vindication of the Rights of Women* (Everyman ed., London 1970), p. 161.

59. *The Lady's Magazine*, IV (1773), p. 296; *The Lady's Monthly Museum*, I (1798), p. 138; II (1799), p. 183; *Catalogue of Political and Personal Satires in the British Museum*, nos. 9552, 10797, 11444, 11649; J.Grego, *op. cit.*, II, pp. 87, 129. For other criticism, see *Poems of George Crabbe*, ed. A.W.Ward (Cambridge 1907), I, pp. 516, 518.

60. D.Defoe, *Complete English Tradesman*, pp. 352, 355.

61. W.Cobbett, *Advice to Young Men* (1829), ed. H.Morley (London 1892), pp. 262, 264, 114.

62. M. and R.L.Edgeworth, *Practical Education* (London 1798), II, pp. 529-30; H.More, *Strictures on the Modern System of Female Education* (London 1799), I, ch. II.

63. M.Wollstonecraft, *op. cit.*, pp. 6, 3.

64. Ratios for 1580-1700 are derived from data provided in D.Cressy, 'Literacy in Pre-Industrial England', in *Societas*, IV (3) (1974), pp. 233-5; for 1754-1910, see R.Schofield, 'Illiteracy in Pre-Industrial England', in *Umea University Educational Reports*, 2 (1973), pp. 17-18; R.T.Vann, 'Literacy in Seventeenth Century England: Some Hearth Tax Evidence', in *Journal of Interdisciplinary History*, V (1974), pp. 289-90.

65. J.Boswell, *Life of Samuel Johnson LLD* (Everyman ed., London 1906), I, p. 13, n. 1; T.Somerville, *My own Life and Times 1741-1814* (Edinburgh 1861), pp. 349-50.

66. J.E.Gagen, *The New Woman: Her Emergence in English Drama* (New York 1954), pp. 42-3 and ch. VI; Mrs Hester Chapone, *Posthumous Works* (London 1808), III, pp. 155-227.

67. J.E.Gagen, *op. cit.*, p. 100; *Original and Genuine Letters to The Tatler and The Spectator* (London 1725), II, pp. 54-5.

68. *Memoirs of Susan Sibbald, 1783-1812*, ed. F.P.Hett (New York 1926), pp. 35, 44-5; *The Lady's Magazine* (1760), p. 368.

69. *The Lady's Monthly Museum*, I (1798), pp. 37-8; see also Jane Austen, *op. cit.*, pp. 18-19, 22.

70. *Letters and Works of Lady Mary Wortley Montagu*, II, pp. 237-9; B.M.Stearns, 'Early English Periodicals for Ladies', in *Publications of the Modern Language Association*, XLVIII (1933); P.Séjourné, *Aspects généraux du roman féminin en Angleterre de 1740 à 1800* (Aix-en-Provence 1966), p. 43, n. 83; J.Boswell, *Life of Johnson*, II, pp. 237, 6; D.Gardiner, *English Girlhood at School* (London 1929), p. 374.

71. T.Gisborne, *An Enquiry into the Duties of the Female Sex* (London 1797), pp. 18, 286, 62.

72. *Thraliana*, ed. K.C.Balderston (Oxford 1942), I, p. 590; E.Flexner, *Mary Wollstonecraft* (New York 1972), p. 60; *The Lady's Monthly Museum*, II (1799), p. 36. For a similar development in America, see J.S.S.Murray, 'On the Equality of the Sexes', in *Massachusetts Magazine*, II (1790) (quoted in A.S.Kraditor, *Up from the Pedestal* (Chicago 1968), p. 32); *A Girl's Life Eighty Years Ago: Letters of Eliza Southgate*

Browne, ed. C.Cook (New York 1887) (quoted in N.F.Cott, *Root of Bitterness* (New York 1972), pp. 107–9).

73. *The Lady's Monthly Museum*, I (1798), p. 68.

74. M.P.Tilley, *Dictionary of Proverbs in England in the 16th and 17th Centuries* (Ann Arbor 1950), H.375; M.Pennington, *Memoirs of the Life of Mrs Elizabeth Carter* (London 1808), I, pp. 184, 224, 157–8, 465–70; *The Lady's Magazine*, IV (1773), p. 401.

75. *The British Apollo* (London 1708), no. 71; M.Reynolds, *The Learned Lady in England 1650–1760*, pp. 373–93; *Thraliana*, I, pp. 258–9, 465; J.Swift, *Works*, IX, p. 424.

76. *Letters and Works of Lady Mary Wortley Montagu*, II, pp. 5, 236–7. In the 1770s Mary Hamilton also kept it a dark secret that she was studying Latin (E. and F.Anson, *Mary Hamilton at Court and Home* (London 1925), p. 17).

77. *Letters and Works of Lady Mary Wortley Montagu*, II, pp. 238, 252; E. and F.Anson, *op. cit.*, p. 9; M.Reynolds, *op. cit.*, p. 280; D.Gardiner, *op. cit.*, pp. 271, 273, 244, 378, 379, 381; *Memoirs of the Life of Mrs Catherine Cappe*, p. 53; E.J.Climenson, *Elizabeth Montagu*, II, pp. 60–1; I. Ehrenpreis and R.Halsband, *The Lady of Letters in the Eighteenth Century* (Los Angeles 1969), p. 35; J.Boswell, *Life of Johnson*, I, p. 359.

78. *Letters and Works of Lady Mary Wortley Montagu*, II, p. 241; E.J.Climenson, *Elizabeth Montagu*, I. p. 155.

79. J.J.Rousseau, *Émile, ou de l'Education*, ed. F. and P.Richard (Paris 1964), pp. 446, 463, 488, 518.

80. D.Gardiner, *op. cit.*, pp. 426–38; T.Gisborne, *op. cit.*, pp. 12–13.

81. *The Monthly Magazine* (1790), p. 290; *Memoirs of Mrs. Eliza Fox*, ed. F.Fox (London 1869), pp. 14, 18–19; *The Gentleman's Magazine* (March 1791), p. 255; see also M.Wollstonecraft, *op. cit.*, p. 6; *The Lady's Magazine*, IV (1773), p. 403.

82. J.Gregory, *op. cit.*, p. 51; *A Girl's Life Eighty Years Ago: Letters of Eliza Southgate Browne*, pp. 37–8 (quoted in N.F.Cott, *op. cit.*, pp. 103–4); see also S.K.Jennings, *The Married Lady's Companion or Poor Man's Friend* (New York 1808), p. 61 (quoted *op. cit.*, p. 113).

83. *Memoirs of Mrs Catherine Jemmat* (London 1771), pp. 5–11.

84. J.T.Wilkinson, *Richard Baxter and Margaret Charlton* (London 1928), pp. 126–7, 110.

85. *Diaries of Oliver Heywood*, ed. J.H.Turner (Brighouse 1882), III, pp. 270, 300; IV, p. 162.

86. *Correspondence of Richard Steele*, pp. 232, 261, 299, 315, 319, 347, 353, 369, 386.

87. T.Zeldin, *France 1848–1945* (Oxford 1973), p. 132.

88. *Catalogue of Political and Personal Satires in the British Museum*, V, no. 5938.

89. R.Braun, 'The Impact of Cottage Industry on an Agricultural Population', in *The Rise of Capitalism* (New York 1966), ed. D.Landes, pp. 56–60.

90. M.D.George, *London Life in the Eighteenth Century* (London 1925), pp. 268–9; *Autobiography of Francis Place*, ed. M.Thale (Cambridge 1972), p. 22.

91. *Ibid.*, pp. 27, 28, 92–3, 95–6, 254, 256, 262–3.

92. *Miss Weeton's Journal of a Governess*, ed. J.J.Bagley (Newton Abbot 1969), I, p. 104.

93. *Autobiography of Thomas Wright of Birkenshaw 1736–1797*, ed. T.Wright (London 1864), pp. 36, 56, 59, 69, 72–81.

94. *Ibid.*, pp. 90–1, 100–1, 129, 142–7, 151.

95. *Diary of Thomas Turner of East Hoathly 1754–65* (London 1925), pp. 6, 16–17, 20, 22, 25, 47, 48, 52, 61, 63–7.

96. *Ibid.*, pp. 66–8, 71, 74, 79, 90–1, 94, 97–102, 110–12.

97. *Poems of George Crabbe*, I, pp. 168, 191.

98. Jane Austen, *op. cit.*, p. 46.

99 *Lyme Letters, 1660–1760*, ed. E.Newton (London 1925), pp. 23, 31–2, 66; for their daughters' marriages, see *supra*, ch. 5, section 2, iv.

100. D.M.Stuart, *op. cit.*, p. 214.

101. R.A.Kelch, *Newcastle: A Duke without Money* (Berkeley 1974), pp. 13–15, 44–7.

102. E.J.Climenson, *Elizabeth Montagu*, I, pp. 127, 211, 276.

103. R.L.Clifford, *Hester Lynch Piozzi (Thrale)* (Oxford 1952), pp. 104, 98, 164, 173; *Thraliana*, I, pp. 237, 308–9, 313, 317, 356, 399, 409, 423, 432, 461, 367 n. 2, 53, 369, 373–4.

104. R.L.Clifford, *op. cit.*, pp. 176–99; *Thraliana*, I, pp. 530–1, 544–6, 549, 557–9, 564, 593–7, 611–12, 628.

105. *Thraliana*, II, pp. 808, 824–5.

106. *Life and Letters of Lady Sarah Lennox*, pp. 251, 574, 579–80, 600–2, 211–12; see *infra*, ch. 9, pp. 456–7.

107. E. and F.Anson, *op. cit.*, pp. 21, 24, 71, 258, 275, 284, 299–301, 332.

108. *Francis Letters*, ed. B.Francis and E.Keary (New York 1901), I, pp. 62, 67, 137, 145, 149, 170, 174, 299, 335, 338; II, pp. 347, 353, 402–3, 504–5; *Lord William Russell and his Wife*, ed. G.Blakiston (London 1972), pp. 1, 15, 35, 43, 52, 55–6, 66, 85, 95, 169, 200, 205, 319, 320, 341.

109. L.Davidoff, 'Mastered for Life: Servant and Wife in Victorian and Edwardian England', in *Journal of Social History*, VII (4) (1974), p. 409.

110. J.S.Mill, *op. cit.*, pp. 261–2.

111. E.P.Thompson, 'Rough Music: Le Charivari Anglais', in *Annales E.C.S.*, 27, (1972), p. 296.

112. *Diary of Samuel Sewall, 1694–1729*, ed. A.Thomas (New York 1973), I, p. 572.

113. N.Z.Davis, 'The Reasons of Misrule: Youth Groups and Charivaris in Sixteenth Century France', in *Past and Present*, 50 (1971); N.Z.Davis, 'Some Tasks and Themes in the Study of Popular Religion' in *The Pursuit of Holiness*, ed. C.Trinkhaus and H.O.Oberman (Leiden 1974), pp. 318–26.

114. S.R.Smith, 'The London Apprentices as Seventeenth Century Adolescents', in *Past and Present*, 61 (1973).

115. W.Shakespeare, *A Winter's Tale*, Act III, Sc. iii.

116. *The Spectator* (1711), no. 108.

117. C.Ansell, *On the Rates of Mortality . . .* (London 1874), p. 46; *The Lady's Magazine*, IV (1773), p. 586; *The Lady's Monthly Museum*, II (1799), p. 299.

118. *Pembroke Papers, 1780–94*, ed. Lord Herbert (London 1950), p. 486; E.J.Climenson, *Elizabeth Montagu*, II, pp. 1–2.

119. P.Lucas, 'A Collective Biography of Students and Barristers at Lincoln's Inn, 1680–1804: A study in the "Aristocratic Resurgence" of the Eighteenth Century', in *Journal of Modern History*, XLVI (1974); L.Stone, 'The Size and Composition of the Oxford Student Body', in *The University in Society: Studies in the History of Higher Education*, ed. L.Stone (Princeton 1974), table 2.

120 Quoted in W.L.Burn, *The Age of Equipoise* (New York, 1965), p. 143. For the late nineteenth-century decline in fertility, see T.Hollingsworth, 'The Demography of

the British Peerage', supp. *Population Studies*, XVIII, 2 (1964), table 19.

121. J.C.Hudson, *The Parents Handbook* (London 1842), *passim*.

122. J.H.Hagstrum, 'Babylon revisited, or the Story of Luvah and Vala', in *Blake's Sublime Allegory*, ed. S.Curran and J.A.Wittreich (Madison 1973), p. 115; W.Acton, *Functions and Disorders of the Reproductive System*, 2nd ed. (1858), pp. 18, 20.

123. W.Young, *Eros Denied* (London 1964), p. 203. For the effects of such a situation in earlier periods, see D.Herlihy, 'Some Psychological and Social Roots of Violence in the Tuscan Cities', in L.Martines, *Violence and Civil Disorder in Italian Cities, 1200–1500* (Los Angeles 1972), pp. 136–7, 141, 145–7.

124. *Bletchley Diary of the Rev. William Cole*, ed. F.G.Stokes (London 1931), p. 41.

125. D.V.Glass and D.E.C.Eversley, *Population in History* (London 1965), p. 211; C.M.Law, 'Local Censuses in the Eighteenth Century', in *Population Studies*, XXIII (1969), (1) p. 89; R.P.Bond, *New Letters to The Tatler and Spectator*, p. 115.

126. N.McKendrick, *Historical Perspectives* (London 1974), p. 156; *The Lady's Monthly Museum*, I (1798), p. 289.

127. R.Thompson, *Women in Stuart England and America* (London 1974), p. 48.

128. R.B.Litchfield, 'Demographic Characteristics of Florentine Patriciate Families', in *Journal of Economic History*, 29 (1969), pp. 197–8; L.Trexler, 'Le Célibat à la fin du Moyen-Age: Les Religieuses de Florence', in *Annales E.C.S.*, 27 (1972), pp. 1338, 1442; L.Stone, *The Crisis . . .*, p. 646; see also *The British Apollo* (London 1708), no. 51; D.Defoe, *The Little Review* (1705), p. 7.

129. *Cavalier: Letters of William Blundell to his Friends*, ed. M.Blundell (London 1933), pp. 55, 152, 154; *Memoirs of a Highland Lady, The Autobiography of Elizabeth Grant of Rothiemurchus*, ed. Lady Strachey (London 1898), p. 146.

130. [W.Hayley], *A Philosophical, Historical and Moral Essay on Old Maids* (London 1785), I, p. 7; M.Wollstonecraft, *op. cit.*, p. 72.

131. Lady Strachey, *op. cit.*, p. 146; *Miss Weeton's Journal . . .*, I, p. 6; S.Butler, *The Way of all Flesh* (New York 1959), p. 44.

132. *The Gentleman's Magazine*, IX (1739), p. 535.

133. E.Flexner, *Mary Wollstonecraft*, p. 61.

134. *Memoirs of her Life by Mrs Catherine Cappe*, p. 17.

135. M.J.Peterson, 'The Victorian Governess', in M.Vicinus, *Suffer and be Still* (Bloomington 1972), pp. 9–10; Lady Strachey, *op. cit.*, pp. 146, 202; *Miss Weeton's Journal . . .*, II, pp. 21, 67, 62.

136. [Mrs C.M.Howard], *Reminiscences for my Children* (London 1831), I, p. 38; M.Wollstonecraft, *op. cit.*, pp. 162–3; M.Peterson, *op. cit.*, p. 13.

137. *Memoirs of Mrs Mary Anne Radcliffe* (Edinburgh 1810), pp. 405, 409, 420, 428, 431, 434, 447, 457; M.Wollstonecraft, *op. cit.*, p. 162; P.Wakefield, *Reflections on the Present Condition of the Female Sex, with Suggestions for its Improvement* (London 1798); *The Gentleman's Magazine*, IX (1739), p. 535; M.A.Radcliffe, *The Female Advocate, or an Attempt to recover the Rights of Women from male Usurpation* (London 1799).

138. R.P.Utter and G.B.Needham, *Pamela's Daughters* (New York 1936), pp. 228–30; J.Gregory, *op. cit.*, p. 105; [W.Hayley], *op. cit.*, I, p. 16.

139. T.Gisborne, *op. cit.*, p. 404; *Miss Weeton's Journal . . .*, I, p. 178.

140. I.Ehrenpreis and R.Halsband, *op. cit.*, p. 6, quoting from F.A.Hayek, *J.S.Mill and Harriet Taylor* (London 1951), p. 63.

141. F.Bamford, *op. cit.*, pp. 20–2.

142. H.R.Lanz, E.C.Snyder, M.Britton, R.Schmitt, 'Pre-Industrial Patterns in the Colonial Family in America: a Content Analysis of Colonial Magazines', *American Sociological Review*, 33 (1968); R.H.Bremner, *Children and Youth in America* (Cambridge, Mass. 1970), I, p. 142; For Crevecoeur, see R.C.Darnton, 'The Gallo-American Society' (Oxford BPhil thesis 1962), ch. II.

143. G.Snyders, *La Pédagogie en France au XVIIe et XVIIIe siècles* (Paris 1965), p. 312.

144. *Francis Letters*, II, p. 354.

145. T.Zeldin, *op. cit.*, pp. 343–4, 296, 307; *Conflicts in French Society*, ed. T.Zeldin (London 1970), pp. 27–33.

146. J.Andrews, *Remarks on the French and English Ladies* (Dublin 1783), pp. 8–11.

147. E.Shorter, 'Différences de classe et de sentiment depuis 1750: l'example de France', in *Annales E.C.S.* (1974), (4).

148. See *supra*, ch. 2, section 2, ii.

149. J.Abray, 'Feminism in the French Revolution', in *American Historical Review*, 80 (1) (1975), pp. 43–62, *passim*; D.Williams, 'The Politics of Feminism in the French Enlightenment', in *The Varied Pattern: Studies in the Eighteenth Century*, ed. P.Hughes and E.Williams (Toronto 1971).

150. C.Duncan, 'Happy Mothers and Other new Ideas in French Art', in *Art Bulletin*, 55 (4) (1973).

151. *Matrimonial Magazine* (January 1793).

152. *The Game of Hearts: Harriette Wilson's Memoirs*, ed. L.Blanch (New York 1955), p. 41; J.Boswell, *Life of Johnson* (Everyman ed.), I, pp. 535–6.

153. J.Gregory, *op. cit.*, p. 40; Epitaph to Admiral Sir John Montagu (1719), at Lacock, Wilts.

154. *The Spectator* (1712), no. 479; P.Séjourné, *op. cit.*, pp. 124, n. 47; 209, n. 28.

155. *The Lady's Monthly Museum*, I (1798), pp. 55–6; J.E.Butler, *Memoir of John Grey of Dilston* (London 1869), p. 326, n. 1. For a Marxist interpretation, see M. George, 'From Goodwife to Mistress: the transformation of the Female in Bourgeois Culture', *loc. cit.*

156. J.-L.Flandrin, 'L'Attitude à l'Egard du petit Enfant et les Conduites sexuelles dans la Civilisation Occidentale', in *Annales de Démographie Historique* (1973), pp. 181–96.

157. J.Gregory, *op. cit.*, pp. 81, 83; N.F.Cott, *The Root of Bitterness*, pp. 103–4.

158. D.Defoe, *Roxana*, pp. 148–9.

159. K.M.Rogers, *The troublesome Helpmate: A History of Misogyny in Literature* (Seattle 1966), pp. 160–6.

160. Anon., *The English Matron* (London 1846), pp. 2, 16, 18, Ch. II–III, *passim*, pp. 179–82.

161. J.B.Le Blanc, *Lettres d'un Français* (The Hague 1745), I, p. 44; II, p. 104; F.de la Rochefoucauld, *op. cit.*, pp. 30–1; J.Swift, 'A Letter to a very young Lady on her Marriage' in *Works*, ed. W.Scott, IX, p. 422; J.Gregory, *op. cit.*, p. 40; J.P.Malcolm, *op. cit.*, p. 184; R.Fletcher, *The Parkers at Saltram, 1769–89* (London 1970), pp. 24, 35; *Lord William Russell and his Wife, 1815–46*, ed. G.Blakiston, p. 47. Squire Western had a maxim 'that women should come in at the first dish and go out after the first glass', and scarcely saw his wife except during meals (H.Fielding, *Tom Jones* (1749), Everyman ed., I, p. 251).

162. *Letters and Works of Lady Mary Wortley Montagu*, I, p. 72; E.J.Climenson, *Elizabeth*

Montagu, II, p. 73; *The Lady's Magazine*, IV (1773), pp. 423–4, 465.

163. J.Shebbeare, *Letters on the English Nation* (London 1755), I, p. 164.

164. *Letters and Works of Lady Mary Wortley Montagu*, III, p. 195.

165. *The Matrimonial Magazine* (June 1793), p. 9; T.Somerville, *op. cit.*, pp. 373–4; W.Cobbett, *Advice to Young Men* (1829), pp. 145–6; L.Davidoff, *op. cit.*, p. 419.

166. S.R.Smith, 'Religion and the Conception of Youth in Seventeenth-Century England', *History of Childhood Quarterly*, II (1975).

167. H.L.H.von Pückler-Muskau, *op. cit.*, p. 266.

CHAPTER 9   PARENT–CHILD RELATIONS

1. H.Misson de Valbourg, *Memoirs and Observations in his Travels over England* (London 1719), p. 33.

2. Quoted by J.E.Illick in L.deMause, *History of Childhood* (New York 1974), pp. 316–17, from R.Cleaver and J.Dod, *A Godlye Form of Household Government* (London 1621), and J.Earle, *Microcosmographie* (London 1628), pp. 1–2.

3. D.M.Stuart, *Molly Lepell, Lady Hervey* (London 1936), pp. 143–4.

4. P.Greven, *Child-rearing Concepts* (Itasca 1973), pp. 20, 26–7.

5. H.C.Foxcroft, *Life and Letters of George Savile Marquis of Halifax* (London 1898), II, pp. 404–5.

6. *Thraliana*, ed. K.C.Balderston (Oxford 1942), I, p. 12.

7. Anon., *The English Matron* (London 1846), pp. 237–8.

8. These long-dead infants are as common on late sixteenth-century English tombs as they are rare on French ones. Ariès was the first to draw attention to the psychological significance of their appearance, but he failed to observe this important national difference (P.Ariès, *Centuries of Childhood* (New York 1975), p. 40).

9. *Memoirs of the Life of Edward Gibbon, by Himself* (London 1900), p. 30; *Autobiography of Mrs Alice Thornton, Surtees Soc.*, LXII (1875), table after p. 344; J.C.Cox, *The Parish Registers of England* (London 1910), pp. 252–3; Genealogies of County Families of Hertfordshire, Northamptonshire and Northumberland. For an eighteenth-century example, see the three successive sons of Thomas Turner, all of whom were called Frederick as the previous one died (*Diary of Thomas Turner of East Hoathly (1754–65)* (London 1925), pp. 11–12).

10. This is not the view of P.Ariès, *op. cit.*, ch. III; G.Snyders, *La Pédagogie en France au XVIIᵉ et XVIIIᵉ Siècles* (Paris 1965), pp. 272–7.

11. R.North, *Autobiography*, ed. A.Jessop (London 1887), pp. 215–16.

12. P.Cunnington and A.Buck, *Children's Clothes in England* (New York 1965), pp. 108, 112, 113, 117, 119, 122, 124, 129, 134, 141, 144; C.P.Moritz, *Journeys of a German in England in 1782*, ed. R.Nettel (London 1965), p. 68; Mrs Thrale's Children's Book, 15 February 1771 (see M.Hyde, *The Thrales of Streatham Park*, Cambridge, Mass. 1977); see also *Autobiography of Francis Place*, ed. M.Thale (Cambridge 1972), p. 63; F. Bamford, *Dear Miss Heber* (London 1936), pp. 57, 146.

13. I.Watts, *Divine Songs . . .* (1715), ed. J.H.P.Pafford (London 1971), Introduction, pp. 5–13.

14. J.H.Plumb, 'The New World of Children in Eighteenth Century England', in *Past and Present*, 67 (1975), pp. 80–5; S.Roscoe, *John Newbery and His Successors 1740–1814: A Bibliography* (Wormley 1973); F.J.H.Darnton, *Children's Books in England* (Cambridge

1932); F.V.Barry, *A Century of Children's Books* (London 1922), pp. 60, 62–3; I. and P.Opie, 'Nursery Rhymes', in W.Targ, *Bibliophile in the Nursery* (New York 1957), pp. 266, 305–7; J.H.Plumb, 'The first Flourishing of Children's Books' in *Early Children's Books and their Illustration*, Pierpont Morgan Library (New York 1975), pp. xix–xxvi, xi–xii; *Lady's Monthly Museum*, I (1798), p. 66.

15. A.Fraser, *A History of Toys* (London 1972); F.G.Jacobs, *A History of Doll's Houses* (London 1954); J.H.Plumb, 'The New World of Children', *loc cit.*, pp. 87–90; J.H.Plumb, *The Commercialization of Leisure* (Reading 1973), p. 9.

16. *Ibid.*, p. 3.

17. Lady Victoria Manners and G.C.Williamson, *Zoffany* (London 1920), *passim*. E.K.Waterhouse, *Reynolds* (London 1973), plates 12, 13, 20, 21, 49, 58, 70, 119; *Reynolds* (London 1941), nos. 125, 155, 163, 187, 191, 234; see also J.H.Plumb, 'The New World of Children . . .', *loc. cit.*, p. 67.

18. R.Edwards, *Early Conversation Pictures from the Middle Ages to about 1730* (London 1954); M.Praz, *Conversation Pieces: a Survey of the Informal Group Portrait in Europe and America* (London 1971); W.M.Thackeray, *Vanity Fair* (London 1869), I, ch. XXIV, p. 254.

19. R.Allestree, *The Whole Duty of Man* (London 1663), p. 298; *Letters and Works of Lady Mary Wortley Montagu*, ed Lord Wharncliffe and W.M.Thomas (London 1887), I, p. xcviii; A.J.C.Hare, *The Years with Mother* (London 1952), p. 249.

20. *Educational Writings of John Locke*, ed. J.Axtell (Cambridge 1968), p. 171; Anon., *An Essay on the Happiness and Advantages of a Well-ordered Family* (London 1794), p. 99; [Mrs C.M.Howard], *Reminiscences for my Children* (London 1831), I, pp. 41, 47.

21. T.Somerville, *My own Life and Times 1741–1814* (Edinburgh 1861), pp. 347–8; P.Greven, *op. cit.*, pp. 84, 95.

22. *Verney Letters of the Eighteenth Century . . .*, ed. Margaret Lady Verney (London 1930), II, pp. 133–5; *Correspondence of Richard Steele*, ed. R.Blanchard (Oxford 1941), pp. 332, 401; D.M.Stuart, *Dearest Bess* (London 1955), p. 3; *The Lady's Magazine*, V (1774). p.469.

23. *Capel Letters, 1814–17*, ed. Marquess of Anglesey (London 1955), pp. 36, 46; *Diaries of Sylvester Douglas, Lord Glenbervie*, ed. F.Bickley (London 1928), I, pp. 106, 189, 214; II, p. 69; *Pembroke Papers 1780–1794*, ed. Lord Herbert (London 1950), pp. 28–9; *Henry, Elizabeth and George 1734–80*, ed. Lord Herbert, pp. 293, 485.

24. E.J.Climenson, *Elizabeth Montagu, Queen of the Bluestockings* (London 1906), I, pp. 23, 253; J.Boswell, *Life of Samuel Johnson, LLD* (Everyman ed. London 1906), I, pp. 206–8.

25. *D.Defoe*, ed. J.T.Boulton (New York 1965), pp. 196–7, quoting from *The Family Instructor* (1715).

26. T.H.Hollingsworth, 'The Demography of the British Peerage', supp. *Population Studies*, XVIII, 2 (1964), table 21. For the bourgeoisie of Geneva, see L.Henry, *Anciennes Familles Genevoises* (Paris 1956), pp. 107–10, 180; For the Venetian nobility, see R.Mols, *Introduction à la Démographie historique des Villes d'Europe du XIVe au XVIIIe Siècles* (Louvain 1954–6), II, p. 328.

27. R.V.Schnucker, 'Elizabethan Birth Control and Puritan Attitudes', in *Journal of Interdisciplinary History*, V (4) (1975), pp. 661–5; D.Defoe, *Conjugal Lewdness . . .* (London 1927), p. 155.

28. *Autobiography of Mrs Alice Thornton*, pp. 164–5.

29. A. Perrenoud, 'Malthusianisme et Protestantisme; un modèle démographique Weberien', in *Annales E.C.S.*, 29 (4) (1974), pp. 983-5; I.K. Wroth and H.B. Zebel, *The Legal Papers of John Adams* (Cambridge, Mass. 1965), I, p. 334 (I owe this reference to David H. Fischer).

30. A. Burguière, in *Annales E.C.S.*, 27 (1973), p. 1130.

31. D. Defoe, *op. cit.*, p. 133; *Wynne Diaries*, ed. A. Freemantle (Oxford 1952), p. 337; see also D.M. Stuart, *Molly Lepell, Lady Hervey*, p. 221; *Notes by Lady Louisa Stuart*, ed. W.S. Lewis (New York 1928), p. 15.

32. T.W. Schultz, 'The Value of Children: an Economic Perspective', in *Journal of Political Economy*, 81 (1973), pp. 54-8.

33. C. Sedley, *Works* (London 1722), II, p. 132 [*Bellamira*, Act III, Sc. i]; R. Steele, *The Tender Husband* (London 1705), Act I, sc. ii.

34. A. Macfarlane, *Family Life of Ralph Josselin* (Cambridge 1970), pp. 50-1, 54, 82.

35. L. Stone, *Family and Fortune* (Oxford 1973), pp. 155-6.

36. J.A. Banks, *Prosperity and Parenthood* (London 1954), *passim*.

37. Captain [E.J.] Trelawney, *Adventures of a Younger Son* (London 1831), p. 3.

38. *Journal of a Somerset Rector 1803-34: John Skinner*, ed. H. and P. Coombs (Bath 1971), pp. 234-5, 286, 293, 327, 372, 418, 421.

39. See *supra*, ch. 2, section 3. An alternative, and equally plausible, explanation is that child mortality fell because parents took more care of them (J. Dupaquier, 'Sur la Population Française ...', in *Revue Historique*, 239 (1968), p. 65).

40. This interpretation is close to, but not identical with, that of J.-F. Flandrin in his *Familles*, pp. 207-29.

41. P.A. Neher, 'Peasants, Procreation and Pensions', *American Economic Review*, 61, 1971, and the convincing criticism by G. Benecke in *Journal of European Economic History*, II (1973), pp. 417-20, using his own evidence on Germany and that of L. Berkner for Austria; The argument that ignorance, lack of foresight and adherence to convention were the key factors among the poor is developed in J.-L. Flandrin, *Familles*, ch. IV, 3.

42. E. Le Roy Ladurie, Démographie et Funestes Secrets', in his *Territoire d'Historien* (Paris 1973); E.A. Wrigley, *Population and History* (London 1969), p. 127.

43. R.V. Schnucker, *op. cit.*, pp. 656-8.

44. N.E. Himes, *Medical History of Contraception* (New York 1963), pp. 197-200; *Boswell's London Journal, 1762-63*, ed. F.A. Pottle (London 1950), pp. 227, 231, 237, 255, 262, 272 (see *supra*, pp. 576-80, 597); H. Bergues, *La Prevention de Naissance dans la Famille* (Paris 1960), pp. 320-3; G.R. Taylor, *Sex in History* (London 1953), p. 187; F. Place, *Illustrations and Proofs of the Theory of Population* (London 1822), quoted in S. Kern, *Anatomy and Destiny* (Indianapolis 1975), p. 155; J.T. Noonan, *Contraception* (Cambridge, Mass. 1966), pp. 320-40; A.M. Mauriceau, *The Married Woman's Private Medical Companion* (New York [1847], reprinted 1974), p. 144; R. Carlile, *The Republican*, X (1825), pp. 545-76, quoted by W.L. Langer, 'The Origins of the Birth Control Movement in England in the early Nineteenth Century', in *Journal of Interdisciplinary History*, V (1975), p. 671, n. 8.

45. J.-L. Flandrin, *Familles*, ch. IV, 3; J.-L. Flandrin, 'Contraception, Mariage et Relations Amoureuses dans l'Occident Chrétien', in *Annales E.C.S.*, 24 (1969), pp. 1370, 1388-90; Articles by P. Ariès and M. Riquet in *Popular Attitudes towards Birth Control in Pre-Industrial France and England*, ed. O. and P. Ranum (New York 1972); *Catalogue of*

Political and Personal Satires in the British Museum, III, pt. 2, no. 3216. For an abortionist surgeon at work, see *The Amorous Illustrations of Thomas Rowlandson*, ed. G.Schiff (New York 1969), pl. 27.

46. *The Ladies of Alderley*, ed. N.Mitford (London 1938), pp. 169–71; *Miss Weeton's Journal of a Governess*, ed. J.J.Bagley (Newton Abbot 1969), I, p. 60.

47. W.Kessen, *The Child* (New York 1965), pp. 1–2; E.Shorter, *The Making of the Modern Family* (New York 1975), pp. 196–9; D.Hunt, *Parents and Children in History* (New York 1970), p. 126; *Educational Writings of John Locke*, p. 123.

48. M.King-Hall, *The Story of the Nursery* (London 1958), p. 128; *The Lady's Magazine* 1785; W.Cadogan, *Essay upon the Nursing and the Management of Children* (London 1748), pp. 9–10; W.Buchan, *Domestic Medicine* (London 1772), p. 12; *The Lady's Monthly Museum*, I (1798), p. 50.

49. J.W.von Archenholtz, *A Picture of England* (London 1797), II, p. 158; P.Cunnington and A.Buck, *op. cit.*, pp. 103–4; M. and J.Rendle-Short, *The Father of Child Care* (Bristol 1966), pp. 17–20; L.de Mause, *op. cit.*, pp. 411–12, 387; E.Shorter, *op. cit.*, p. 197.

50. E.L.Lipton, A.Steinschneider, J.B.Richmond, 'Swaddling, a child-care practice: historical, cultural and experimental observations', in *Pediatrics*, 35 (1965), pp. 521–67.

51. D.Hunt, *op. cit.*, p. 134; L.deMause, *op. cit.*, table I, p. 36; J.Nelson, *An Essay on the Government of Children* (London 1763), p. 57; A.Macfarlane, *op. cit.*, pp. 86–7.

52. L.deMause, *op. cit.*, pp. 243, 308–9.

53. A.Behn, *The Ten Pleasures of Marriage*, ed. J.Harvey (London 1923), pp. 92, 122–4.

54. S.Guazzo, *The Civile Conversation* (London 1581), ff. 143–3v.

55. W.Gouge, *Of Domesticall Duties* (London 1622), p. 518; J.Nelson, *op. cit.*, pp. 46–7.

56. D.Hunt, *op. cit.*, pp. 107–8; L.deMause, *op. cit.*, p. 310; R.V.Schnucker, 'The English Puritans and Pregnancy, Delivery and Breast-Feeding', in *History of Childhood Quarterly*, I, (4) (1974), p. 650.

57. E.J.Climenson, *Elizabeth Montagu*, I, p. 183; D.Hunt, *op. cit.*, pp. 107–8; M.Wollstonecraft, *A Vindication of the Rights of Woman* (Everyman ed. London 1970), p. 80; W.Cobbett, *Advice to Young Men* (1829), ed. H.Morley (London 1892), p. 191.

58. H.Edmund, 'Diary of a Manchester Wig-maker', in *Chetham Soc.*, LXVIII (1866), p. 175 (I owe this reference to Professor T.Laqueur).

59. W.Perkins, 'Of Christian Oeconomie', in *Works* (London 1626), pp. 135–6; W.Gouge, *op. cit.*, pp. 513, 515; R.V.Schnucker, *op. cit.*, pp. 644–5, 649.

60. J.E.Illick in L.deMause, *op. cit.*, p. 336, n. 30.

61. L.Stone, *The Crisis of the Aristocracy* (Oxford 1965), pp. 592–3; *Autobiography of Mrs Alice Thornton*, pp. 92, 124, 144, 148, 166, 3.

62. E.Caulfield, *Infant Welfare Movement in the Eighteenth Century* (New York 1937), p. 41; Jane Sharp, *Midwives Book* (London 1671).

63. *The Spectator*, 1711, no. 246; D.Defoe, *The Compleat English Gentleman* (1729), ed. K.D.Bülbring (London 1890), pp. 71–4; J.Nelson, *op. cit.*, p. 49; *Letters and Works of Lady Mary Wortley Montagu*, II, p. 10; C.Aspinall-Oglander, *Admiral's Wife* (London 1940), pp. 75, 81, 123; M. and J.Rendle-Short, *op. cit.*, p. 25; E.J.Climenson, *Elizabeth Montagu*, I, p. 183; See also, H.Downham, *Infancy: a Poem* (London 1774).

64. W.Cadogan, *op. cit.*, pp. 7, 25.

65. *Journal of J.G.Stedman, 1744–1797, Soldier and Author*, ed. S.Thompson (London

1962), p. 5; See also *Memoirs of the Family of Guise, Camden Soc.*, 3rd Ser., XXVIII (1917), p. 112; R.L.Edgeworth, *Memoirs* (London 1820), I, pp. 21–2; *Retrospections of Dorothea Herbert* (London 1929), I, p. 13.

66. *Memoirs of Sir Robert Sibbald (1641–1722)*, ed. F.P.Hett (Oxford 1932), p. 51.

67. Earl of Bessborough, *Georgiana* (London 1955), pp. 63, 77, 175, 188; Earl of Bessborough, *Lady Bessborough and her Family Circle* (London 1940), p. 38; F.Bamford, *Dear Miss Heber*, pp. 57, 183; G.R.Taylor, *The Angel-Makers* (London 1958), pp. 288, 328; J.W.von Archenholz, *Tableau de l'Angleterre* (Gotha 1788), II, p. 156; T.Gisborne, *An Enquiry into the Duties of the Female Sex* (London 1797), p. 363.

68. *The Matrimonial Magazine* (June 1793), p. 20; Anon., *The English Matron*, pp. 231–3; The change may not have taken full root before the 1780s, for Susan Mein, who was born in 1793 as the daughter of a well-to-do naval surgeon, recalled in old age that 'in those days children were sent from home to be nursed' (*Memoirs of Susan Sibbald (1783–1812)*, ed. F.P.Hett [New York 1926], p. 21).

69. M.Edgeworth, *Belinda* (London 1833), I, p. 53; I owe this reference to Mrs C.Colvin.

70. L.Henry and C.Levy, 'Quelques Données sur la Region autour de Paris au XVIIIᵉ siècle', in *Population*, XVII (1962), p. 315; F.Lebrun, *Les Hommes et La Mort en Anjou* (Paris 1971), pp. 181, 424; J.Ganiage, 'Trois Villages d'Ile-de-France au XVIIIᵉ siècle', in *Population*, XVIII (1963), p. 130; P.Robertson, 'The Home as a Nest', in L.deMause, *op. cit.*, p. 410.

71. *Educational Writings of John Locke*, pp. 165–70.

72. See *infra* note 120.

73. H.Fielding, *The History of Tom Jones* (1749), Everyman ed., I, p. 83; D.Defoe, *op. cit.*, pp. xv–xvi; F.Musgrove, 'Middle Class Education and Employment in the Nineteenth Century', in *Economic Historical Review*, 2nd Ser., XII (1959), pp. 100–1; see also *The Lady's Monthly Museum*, I (1798), p. 53. For attitudes towards university education in the eighteenth century, see L.Stone, 'The Size and Composition of the Oxford Student Body', in *The University in Society*, ed. L.Stone (Princeton 1974), I, pp. 48–55.

74. T.Cobbet, *A Fruitful and Useful Discourse touching on the Honour due from Children to Parents and the Duty of Parents towards their Children* (London 1656), pp. 96–7, 219–20.

75. W.Penn, *Fruits of a Father's Love* (Philadelphia 1792), p. 38 (I owe this reference to Miss Susan E.Spock); *Athenian Mercury* (London 1792), V, 3, question 1.

76. S.Fielding, *The Adventures of David Simple* (London 1744), p. 253; J.Nelson, *op. cit.*, pp. 151–2; *The Lady's Monthly Museum*, I (1798), p. 54.

77. *Memoirs of Sir Philip Francis*, ed. J.Parkes and H.Merivale (London 1867), I, p. 404; *Autobiography of Arthur Young*, ed. M.Betham-Edwards (London 1898), p. 8, n. 1; *Memoir of Mrs Eliza Fox*, ed. F.Fox (London 1869), p. 6; C.Aspinall-Oglander, *op. cit.*, p. 123.

78. R.D.Owen, *Threading My Way* (London 1874), pp. 35, 42; [Mrs C.M.Howard], *Reminiscences for my Children*, p. 16; *Miss Weeton's Journal as a Governess*, II, p. 99.

79. G.O.Trevelyan, *Early History of Charles James Fox* (London 1899), p. 44.

80. *Life of Mrs Sherwood*, ed. S.Kelly (London 1854), p. 46; *Thraliana*, I, p. 108; J.Boswell, *Life of Samuel Johnson, LLD* (Everyman ed. London 1906), II, pp. 21, 95, n. 1; see also *Francis Letters*, ed. B.Francis and E.Keary (New York 1901), II, p. 537.

81. Lord Ilchester, *Henry Fox, first Lord Holland* (London 1920), II, p. 171; *Notes by Lady Louisa Stuart*, ed. W.S.Lewis, p. 31.

82. *Francis Letters*, II, pp. 590–1.

83. *The Game of Hearts: Harriette Wilson's Memoirs*, ed. L.Blanch (New York 1955), pp. 263–4.

84. *Thraliana*, I, p. 108.

85. T.Gisborne, *op. cit.*, pp. 401, 404.

86. T.Shadwell, *The Virtuoso* (1676), Act I, Sc. i, p. 2; E.Moore, *The World* (19 July 1753) (quoted L.C.Jones, *The Clubs of the Georgian Rakes* [New York 1942], p. 23).

87. R.L.Costeker, *The Fine Gentleman, or the Complete Education of a Young Nobleman* (London 1732), p. 9; H.Misson de Valbourg, *op. cit.*, p. 33; See also W.Keith, *A Collection of Papers and other Tracts* (London 1740), p. 146; J.Swift, 'An Essay on Modern Education', in *Works*, ed. W.Scott (Edinburgh 1814), IX, p. 371; Anon., *Chickens Feed Capons* (London 1731), p. 17; J.Shebbeare, *Letters on the English Nation* (London 1756), I, p. 163; D.Fordyce, *Dialogues Concerning Education* (London 1745), I, pp. 179, 198; S.Philpot, *An Essay on the Advantage of a Polite Education* (London 1747), p. 10.

88. J.Nelson, *op. cit.*, pp. 217, 18, 156, 158; see also *The Lady's Monthly Museum*, II (1799), p. 292.

89. J.Grego, *Rowlandson the Caricaturist* (London 1880), II, p. 87, 129. For similar complaints in America, see P.Greven, *op. cit.*, pp. 89, 112, 121.

90. T.Tusser, *Five Hundred Points of Good Husbandrie*, ed. W.Mavor (London 1812), p. 317

91. Anon., *The Children's Petition* (London 1669), pp. 7, 14, 17, 19, 26–8. For other contemporaries who thought the same way, see *Aubrey on Education*, ed. J.E.Stephens (London 1972), p. 32; O.Walker, *Of Education* (Oxford 1673), pp. 39–40.

92. T.Shadwell, *op. cit.*, Act III, Sc. ii, p. 46. In the nineteenth century Dr William Acton also objected to schoolmasters' whipping boys on the buttocks since it stimulated sexual excitement (W.Acton, *The Functions and Disorders of the Reproductive System* [London 1858], pp. 59–60); for a very clear and very detailed account of how the whipping of a child by women created an association in the latter's mind of whipping and sexual pleasure, see the upbringing of Louis XIII in the early seventeenth century (*Journal de Jean Héroard* [ed. 1868], I. pp. 43, 186, 294, 316, 363).

93. R.Paulson, *Hogarth: His Life, Art and Times* (New Haven, 1971), I, figs. 93, 96. There is a print of 1745, showing a strange scene of lesbian flagellation (*Catalogue of Political and Personal Satires in the British Museum*, no. 2778).

94. *Educational Writings of John Locke*, pp. 148–50, 152–3, 155, 183.

95. J.Gailhard, *The Compleat Gentleman* (London 1678), p. 15; C.Trenchfield, *op. cit.*, p. 141; R.P.Bond, *New Letters to the Tatler and Spectator*, Austin (1959), p. 148; *The Spectator* (1711), nos. 157, 168; J.Swift, 'An Essay on Modern Education', in *Works*, IX, p. 369; T.Sheridan, *A Plan of Education for the young Nobility and Gentry of Britain* (London 1769), p. 79.

96. *The Correspondence of Samuel Richardson* (London 1804), II, pp. 61–3; R.Bayne-Powell, *The English Child in the Eighteenth Century* (New York 1939), p. 50; T.Smollett, *Roderick Random* (1748) (Everyman ed.), pp. 14, 24–6.

97. L.Stone, *Crisis . . .*, p. 32; M.Pattison, *Milton* (London 1913), p. 6.

98. *The Spectator*, 1711, nos, 157, 168; R.Campbell, *The London Tradesman* (London 1747), pp. 5, 84.

99. *Memoirs of Sir Philip Francis*, I, pp. 11–12; *Boswell for the Defence, 1769–1774*, pp. 41, 111, 118; *Diaries of Sylvester Douglas ...*, I, p. 188; Earl of Bessborough, *Lady Bessborough and her Family Circle*, pp. 63, 73.

100. *Thraliana*, I, p. 59; *Gradus ad Cantabrigiam, or a Dictionary of Terms* (London 1803), p. 106; *Life, Adventures and Opinions of Colonel George Hanger* (London 1801), p. 14.

101. T.Gray, 'Ode on a distant Prospect of Eton College'; J.Boswell, *Life of Johnson*, I, pp. 415, 589; cf. also pp. 18–19, 279; Anon., *The Eton Abuses Considered* (London 1834), pp. 11–13; I. E. M., *The Confessions of an Etonian* (London 1846), pp. 18, 35, 42.

102. R.Warner, *Literary Recollections* (London 1830), pp. 137, 30; *Life and Times of Frederic Reynolds* (London 1826), pp. 61, 85; *Life of Mrs [Lucy Letitia] Cameron* (London 1862), p. 30; M.Wollstonecraft, *op. cit.*, p. 176; J.Berkenhout, *A Volume of Letters from Dr Berkenhout to his Son at the University* (Cambridge 1790), pp. 4–8.

103. G.R.Taylor, *op. cit.*, p. 188; F.W.Bamford, *Rise of the Public Schools* (London 1967), pp. 67–8; N.Mitford, *op. cit.*, p. 392.

104. *Memoirs of Richard Cumberland* (London 1806), pp. 23, 27; *Autobiography of Arthur Young*, pp. 7–8; *Life, Adventures and Opinions of Colonel George Hanger*, I, pp. 13–14; Anon., *Academic Errors, or Recollections of Youth* (London 1817), pp. 7, 32; S.Bamford, *Early Days* (London 1849), pp. 82–3.

105. *Yorkshire Diaries and Autobiographies ...*, Surtees Soc., LXV (1875), p. 185; *Life, Adventures and Opinions of Colonel George Hanger*, I, p. 17; *Morning Chronicle and Public Advertiser* (6, 7 Jan. 1786); see also *Francis Letters*, I, p. 196; *Passages from the Diaries of Mrs Philip Lybbe Powys 1756–1808*, ed E.J.Climenson (London 1899), p. 160; [H.J.C.Blake], *Reminiscences of Eton* (Chichester 1831), p. 14.

106. C.Aspinall-Oglander, *op. cit.*, p. 89; *Memoirs of Susan Sibbald*, p. 56.

107. *Autobiography and Selected Remains of Samuel Roberts*, p. 16.

108. P.Ariès, *Centuries of Childhood*, pp. 262–5.

109. *Educational Writings of John Locke*, p. 123; W.Law, *A Serious Call to a Devout and Holy Life* (London 1729), p. 354; J.-J.Rousseau, *Émile* (Paris 1964), p. 458.

110. *Life of Mrs Sherwood*, pp. 38–9; Mary Somerville, *Personal Recollections from Early Life to Old Age* (London 1873), p. 22; *Memoirs, Miscellanies and Letters of the late Lucy Aikin*, ed. P.H.Le Breton (London 1864), p. 14.

111. J.Brasbridge, *Fruits of Experience* (London 1824), p. 176; C.Aspinall-Oglander, *op. cit.*, p. 174; see also *Diary of John Baker*, ed. P.C.Yorke (London 1931), p. 136.

112. *Autobiography of Arthur Young*, pp. 263–4.

113. D.Gardiner, *English Girlhood at School* (London 1929), p. 353; W.L.Blease, *The Emancipation of English Women* (London 1913), p. 146; J.Gregory, *A Father's Legacy to his Daughters* (London 1774), p. 50; T.Gisborne, *op. cit.*, pp. 78, 90–1; M.Wollstonecraft, *op. cit.*, pp. 43, 47, 49, 84.

114. R.P.Bond, *New Letters to the Tatler and Spectator*, pp. 146–7.

115. *Autobiography of Arthur Young*, pp. 22–3.

116. R.Campbell, *op. cit.*, pp. 2–4, 12, 23.

117. M.Wollstonecraft, *op. cit.*, p. 211; R.Blunt and M.Wyndham, *Thomas, Lord Lyttelton* (London 1936), pp. 34, 206.

118. A.Esler, 'Youth in Revolt: The French Generation of 1830', in *Modern European Social History*, ed. R.Bezucha (Lexington 1972), p. 308.

119. J.H.Hagstrum, ' "Such, such were the Joys": the Boyhood of the Man of Feeling', in

Changing Taste in Eighteenth Century Art and Literature, ed. E.Miner, W.A.Clark Memorial Library (Los Angeles 1972), pp. 45-61.

120. J.H.Plumb, *Robert Walpole: the Making of a Statesman* (London 1956), pp. 87-8; E.J.Climenson, *Elizabeth Montagu*, I, pp. 121, 123; *Letters and Journals of Lady Mary Coke*, I, p. xv.

121. D.M.Stuart, *Molly Lepell, Lady Hervey*, pp. 110, 142-3.

122. *The Lady's Magazine*, V (1774), p. 147; Earl of Bessborough, *Georgiana*, p. 157; E.Flexner, *Mary Wollstonecraft* (New York 1972), p. 77; M.Wollstonecraft, *op. cit.*, p. 5. For Victorian and Edwardian examples, see A.J.C.Hare, *op. cit.*, pp. 10, 14, 2,5, K.Clark, *Another Part of the World* (New York 1974), ch. I.

123. D.Green, *Sarah Duchess of Marlborough* (London 1967), pp. 47, 89, 234-6.

124. *Boswell: The Ominous Years, 1774-1776*, ed. C.Ryscamp and F.A.Pottle (New York 1963), p. 213.

125. *Boswell in Extremes, 1776-1778*, pp. 52, 91, 114, 189, 217, 356; *Private Papers of James Boswell*, 13, pp. 158, 165, 247, 265, 281, 285, 286; 14, pp. 5-6, 14, 20, 37; 15, pp. 4, 12, 17, 23, 24, 26, 33, 38, 85, 155, 161; 16, pp. 151-2, 286-7.

126. *Ibid.*, 18, pp. 18, 43, 108, 169, 174, 178, 243, 211.

127. *Francis Letters*, I, pp. 65, 68-9, 131, 151, 163, 239; II, pp. 409, 488-95, 621, 623.

128. *Boswell in Extremes, 1776-1778*, pp. 317, 318; G.O.Trevelyan, *op. cit.*, pp. 42-4.

129. J.Boswell, *Life of Johnson*, II, p. 160.

130. *Life and Letters of Lady Sarah Lennox, 1745-1826*, ed. Countess of Ilchester and Lord Stavordale (London 1902), pp. 632-3, 599.

131. C.Aspinall-Oglander, *op. cit.*, pp. 27, 41, 54, 63, 69, 73, 76, 87, 92, 93, 98, 104, 109-10, 148, 172.

132. *Passages from the Diaries of Mrs P.L.Powys*, p. 136; Earl of Bessborough, *Lady Bessborough and her Family Circle*, pp. 75, 76, 105, 12, 61; Earl of Bessborough, *Georgiana*, pp. 202, 218, 13, 113, 145, 137.

133. *The Ladies of Alderley*, ed. N.Mitford, *passim*; M.Wollstonecraft, *op. cit.*, p. 35.

134. *Thraliana*, I, p. 281; J.L.Clifford, *Hester Lynch Piozzi* (Oxford 1968), pp. 9, 24.

135. J.L.Clifford, *op. cit.*, pp. 43-6, 49, 461; *Thraliana*, I, pp. 311, n. 4, 389.

136. Mrs Thrale's Children's Book (see M.Hyde's forthcoming publication *The Thrales of Streatham Park*); I am very grateful to Mrs Hyde for permission to see and quote from a typescript of this document.

137. *Thraliana*, I, p. 310.

138. J.L.Clifford, *op. cit.*, pp. 70-1, 79-81, 110, 133; Mrs Thrale's Children's Book, Jan. 1771.

139. J.L.Clifford, *op. cit.*, pp. 83, 113, 143, 115; *Thraliana*, I, pp. 44, 46; Mrs Thrale's Children's Book, Jan. 1775.

140. Mrs Thrale's Children's Book, July 1776; J.Boswell, *Life of Johnson*, II, pp. 68, 152; *Thraliana*, I, pp. 291, n. 2, 319.

141. J.L.Clifford, *op. cit.*, pp. 461, 82-3, 94, 110, 125-7, 136-8.

142. J.L.Clifford, *op. cit.*, pp. 145, 161-2, 216, 226; *Thraliana*, I, pp. 321, 504.

143. J.L.Clifford, *op. cit.*, pp. 304, 336, 363-4, 380-2, 387-8, 392; *Thraliana*, II, pp. 685-6, 708, 828, 887.

144. J.L.Clifford, *op. cit.*, pp. 391-2, 418, 434; *Thraliana*, II, pp. 984, 1094, n. 3.

145. J.L.Clifford, *op. cit.*, pp. 428, n. 2, 365.

146. C.Mather, *Bonifacius, an Essay upon the Good*, ed. D.Levin (Cambridge, Mass. 1966), pp. 47–8, 50; *Diaries of Cotton Mather*, Massachusetts Historical Collections, 7th Ser., VII–VIII (1912), I, pp. 239–40, 546, 595; II, pp. 25, 53, 70, 79, 81, 84, 91, 94, 207, 214, 268, 104, 124.

147. *Ibid.*, I, pp. 423, 545–6; II, pp. 16, 21, 757.

148. *Ibid.*, II, pp. 43–4, 51, 112, 149, 153, 276, 362, 379, 473, 525, 554, 652.

149. *Ibid.*, II, pp. 76, 225, 238, 451, 466, 480, 484, 528, 609, 611, 647, 664, 668, 744, 753.

150. *Ibid.*, II, pp. 275, 280, 532, 701, 770, 744, 748.

151. *Life of George Crabbe by his Son*, ed. E.Blunden (London 1947), p. 121; J.Brasbridge, *Fruits of Experience*, p. 178.

152. *Journal of the Rev. John Wesley*, ed. N.Curnock (London 1910), III, pp. 34–9.

153. R.L.Moore, 'Justification without Joy: Reflections on John Wesley's Childhood and Conversion', in *History of Childhood Quarterly*, II (1974), pp. 49–50.

154. Quoted in G.R.Taylor, *op. cit.*, p. 302.

155. R.M.Hartwell, 'Children as Slaves' in his *Industrial Revolution and Economic Growth* (London 1971); N.McKendrick, *Historical Perspectives* (London 1974), pp. 161–74.

156. K.Marx, *Capital* (New York 1906), pp. 431–40; *Journal of a Somerset Rector 1803–34: John Skinner*, pp. 25, 227.

157. *Life of Thomas Holcroft*, ed. E.Colby (London 1925), I, p. 31.

158. *Autobiography of Francis Place*, pp. 34, 59, 61–2; L.Simond, *Journal of a Tour and Residence in Great Britain 1810–11* (London 1817), II, p. 180. An identical change took place at the same time in the treatment of apprentices and domestic servants; see M.D.George, *London Life in the Eighteenth Century* (London 1925), pp. 227–33, 247; *Life of Mr Thomas Gent* (London 1832), pp. 25–6; *Autobiography and Select Remains of Samuel Roberts* (London 1849), p. 16; *Bletchley Diary of the Rev. William Cole*, ed. F.G.Stokes (London 1931), p. 253.

159. Anon., *The English Matron* (London 1846), p. 237.

160. *Poems of George Crabbe*, I, p. 171.

161. *Diaries of Oliver Heywood*, ed. J.H.Turner (Brighouse 1882), III, p. 206.

162. R.Bayne-Powell, *op. cit.*, p. 35.

163. E.Caulfield, *op. cit.*, pp. 56, 63, 29, 19, 40; *Original and Genuine Letters to the Tatler and Spectator*, ed. C.Lillie (London 1725), I, pp. 47–53. Hanway observed in 1759 that 'the custom of the common people drinking great quantities of the most inflammatory and poisonous liquor certainly created an incredible devastation among the children of the poor.' (M.D.George, *op. cit.*, p. 323, n. 47).

164. *Autobiography of Francis Place*, pp. 127, 137, 150, 158, 174, 184.

165. P.Horn, 'Child Workers in the Pillow Lace and Straw Plait Trades in Victorian Buckinghamshire and Bedfordshire', *Historical Journal*, 17 (1974).

166. W.Langer, 'Infanticide; a historical Survey', in *History of Childhood Quarterly*, I (1974); R.Trexler, 'The Foundlings of Florence', *loc. cit.*, J.Walzer, comment, *loc. cit.*, p. 58; B.Kellum, 'Infanticide in England in the Later Middle Ages', *loc. cit.*; R.H.Helmholz, 'Infanticide in the Province of Canterbury during the Fifteenth Century', *loc. cit.*, II (1975); K.Wrightson, 'Infanticide in Earlier Seventeenth Century England', in *Local Population Studies*, 15 (1975); L.deMause, *op. cit.*, pp. 25–32; F.Lebrun, *op. cit.*, p. 419; J.-L.Flandrin, 'L' Attitude a l'Égard du petit Enfant et les Conduites sexuelles dans la Civilisation Occidentale', in *Annales de Démographie*

Historique (1973).

167. J.Samaha, *Law and Order in Historical Perspective* (New York 1974), pp. 20, 21, 127; *Diaries of Oliver Heywood*, II, pp. 258, 273, 285; *Diary of Richard Kay 1716-51* Chetham Soc., 3rd Ser., XVI (1968), p. 122; *Diary of Cotton Mather*, I, p. 279; W.Shakespeare, *Macbeth*, Act IV, scene i; *Life, Adventures and Opinions of Colonel George Hanger*, p. 265; C.Darwin, *Life of Erasmus Darwin* (London 1887), p. 29.

168. *Original and genuine Letters to the Tatler and Spectator*, I, p. 54; J.Hanway, *An earnest Appeal for Mercy to the Children of the Poor* (London 1766), pp. 21-2.

169. J.Hanway, *op. cit.*, pp. 8-9, 38, 42-3; M.D.George, *op. cit.*, p. 56.

170. *Original and Genuine Letters to the Tatler and Spectator*, I, pp. 47-53; M.D.George, *op. cit.*, pp. 216-7; E.Caulfield, *op. cit.*, pp. 56, 63, 134; J.Hanway, *op. cit.*, pp. 8-9, 25, 28-9, 31-2, 42-3; *The Lady's Monthly Museum*, I (1798), p. 35.

171. *The Lady's Monthly Museum*, I (1798), p. 36; R.Bayne-Powell, *op. cit.*, pp. 143, 174; E.Caulfield, *op. cit.*, pp. 40, 137-9; J.Hanway, *op. cit.*, pp. 65-9, 138.

172. J.Brownlow, *Memoranda, or Chronicles of the Foundling Hospital* (London 1847), pp. 114-8.

173. J.Brownlow, *op. cit.*, pp. 172-5; E.Caulfield, *op. cit.*, pp. 86-7; T.Bernard, *Pleasure and Pain*, ed. J.B.Blake (London 1930), pp. 56-7. Of over 5,000 received in the infirmary, only three lived. For an account of the same development in Paris, see C.Delasselle, 'Abandon d'Enfants à Paris au XVIIIᵉ Siècle', in *Annales E.C.S.*, 30 (1975).

174. E.Caulfield, *op. cit.*, pp. 73-4, 86-8, 90; J.Hanway, *op. cit.*, p. 24.

175. *Autobiography of Francis Place*, pp. 74, 127, 137, 150, 158, 174.

176. Quoted in *ibid.*, pp. 59, 56, 406; M.A.Beaver, 'Population, Infant Mortality and Milk', in *Population Studies*, XXVII (1973); T.R.Edmonds, 'On the Mortality of Infants in England', in *The Lancet, 1835-36*, I, p. 692. The ratio of burials of children under 2 years to total baptisms are:

1730-49: 60%	1790-1809: 30%
1750-69: 50%	1810-29 : 23%
1770-89: 40%	

D.Loschky, 'Urbanization and England's Eighteenth Century Crude Birth and Death Rates', in *Journal of European Economic History*, I (1972).

177. M.D.George, *op. cit.*, p. 61.

178. J.Illick, in L.deMause, *op. cit.*, pp. 311-8, 326-31; J.F.Walzer, 'A Period of Ambivalence: Eighteenth Century American Childhood', *loc. cit.*, pp. 364-5; R.H.Bremner, *op. cit.*, I, pp. 34-5 (quoting Benjamin Wadsworth); see also the remarks by J.F.Walzer in *History of Childhood Quarterly*, I (1973), P. 59.

179. P.Ariès, *op. cit.*, pp. 270-5, 284-90; J.Gaudemet, 'Legislation Canonique et Attitudes Séculaires à l'Égard du lien matrimonial au XVIIᵉ Siècle', in *Le XVIIᵉ Siècle*, 102-3 (1974); Y.Castan, 'Pères et Fils en Languedoc à l'Epoque Classique', *loc. cit.*; J.M.Gouesse, 'La formation du Couple en Basse-Normandie', *loc. cit.*, pp. 50-8; F.Funck-Brentano, *Les Lettres de Cachet* (Paris 1926), ch. X-XII; G.Snyders, *op. cit.*, p. 255; T.Zeldin, *France 1848-1945* (Oxford 1973), p. 361.

180. G.Snyders, *op. cit.*, pp. 257, 233, 247, 242; B.W.Lorence, 'Parents and Children in Eighteenth Century Europe', in *History of Childhood Quarterly*, II (1974), pp. 1-7, 12; *History of Childhood Quarterly*, I (1974), p. 352, quoting from C.M.de Talleyrand, *Mémoires* (Paris 1895), I, pp. 5-8; see also B.de Saint Pierre, *Studies in Nature*

(Philadelphia 1808), p. 413, quoted in C.Duncan, 'Happy Mothers and other new Ideas in French Art', in *Art Bulletin*, 55 (4) (1973).

181. A.Martin, 'Notes sur *L'Ami des Enfants* de Berguin et la littérature enfantine en France aux alentours de 1780', *Le XVIIIe Siècle*, 6 (1974), pp. 299–307.

182. R.Mercier, *L'Enfant dans la Sociéte du 18e Siècle, (avant Émile)* Paris 1961); G.V.Sussman, 'The Wet-nursing Business in Nineteenth Century France', in *French Historical Studies*, IX (1975); T.Zeldin, *op. cit.*, pp. 318, 328, 295, 361; A.Chamoux, 'Town and Child in Eighteenth Century Rheims', in *Local Population Studies*, 13 (1974).

183. M.Garden, *Lyons et les Lyonnais au XVIIIe Siècle* (Paris, n.d.), p. 124.

184. C.Delasselle, *op. cit.*; A.Chamoux, 'L'Enfance abandonnée à Reims à la Fin du XVIIIe Siècle', in *Annales de Démographie Historique* (1973), p. 263; A.Armengaud, 'L'Attitude de la Société à l'Égard de l'Enfant au XIXe Siècle', in *Annales de Démographie Historique* (1973), pp. 304–11.

CHAPTER 10   UPPER-CLASS ATTITUDES AND BEHAVIOUR

1. *Diary of Samuel Pepys* 23 Jan. 1669; 21, 22, 25 Feb. 1665; *William Byrd: the London Diary, 1717–21 and Other Writings*, ed. L.B.Wright and M.Tinling (New York 1958), pp. 143, 146, 219, 221, 225; *Journeys of Celia Fiennes*, ed. C.Morris (London 1947), p. 100; *Notes by Lady Louisa Stuart*, ed. W.S.Lewis (New York 1928), p. 23; G. Scott Thomson, *The Russells in Bloomsbury 1669–1771* (London 1940), pp. 350–1. For a popular account of the bathroom, see L. Wright, *Clean and Decent* (London 1960).

2. *Complete Poems of John Wilmot Earl of Rochester*, ed. D.M.Vieth (New Haven 1968), p. 139; J.Swift, 'A letter to a very young lady on her Marriage', *Works* (Oxford 1948), IX, p. 87; J.Wilkes, *An Essay on Woman and Other Pieces* (London 1871), p. 19, note; J.Shebbeare, *Letters on the English Nation* (London 1755), I, p. 221; M.Wollstonecraft, *A Vindication of the Rights of Woman* (Everyman ed. London 1970), p. 140; W.Acton, *A Complete Practical Treatise on Venereal Disease* (London 1841), p. 29.

3. L.Wright, *op. cit.*, pp. 117–18; V.Miller, *The Man-Plant* (London 1752), p. 31.

4. *Life of Adam Martindale, Chetham Soc.*, 1st Ser., IV (1845), p. 20; Samuel Bamford, *Early Days* (London 1847), p. 79; *Diary of Richard Kay, Chetham Soc.*, 3rd Ser., XVI (1968), p. 112; *Diary of Robert Hooke 1672–80*, ed. H.W.Robinson and W.Adams (London 1935), *passim*.

5. *Correspondence of John Wilkes and Charles Churchill*, ed. E.H.Weatherby (New York 1954), pp. 39, 48, 54; *Pembroke Papers 1780–1794*, ed. Henry Lord Herbert (London 1950), pp. 323, 319; *Catalogue of Political and Personal Satires in the British Museum*, III, pt. i, p. 57.

6. G.Thuillier, 'Pour une Histoire du l'Hygiène corporelle', in *Revue d'Histoire Economique et Sociale*, XLVI (1968), p. 235, n. 20.

7. *Autobiography of Francis Place*, ed. M.Thale (Cambridge 1972), pp. 51–2, 14.

8. E.Shorter, *The Making of the Modern Family* (New York 1975), p. 76.

9. E.Shorter, 'Illegitimacy, Sexual Revolution and Social Change', in *The Family in History*, ed. T.K.Rabb and R.I.Rotberg (New York 1973), p. 51, citing H.Möller, *Die Kleinbürgerliche Familie im 18 Jahrhundert* (Berlin 1969), pp. 282–301.

10. E.Shorter, 'Capitalism, Culture and Sexuality: Some Competing Models', in *Social*

Science Quarterly, 53 (1972), p. 339. The same social difference in sexual play and inventiveness was also discovered for the twentieth century by Dr Kinsey.

11. C.N.Degler, 'What ought to be and what was: Women's Sexuality in the Nineteenth Century', in *American Historical Review*, 79 (1974), pp. 1474–5.

12. J.-L.Flandrin, 'Mariage tardif et vie sexuelle', in *Annales E.C.S.*, 27 (1972), p. 1368.

13. J.-L.Flandrin, *op. cit.*, p. 1369; D.Hunt, *Parents and Children in History* (New York 1970), pp. 80–1; The modern statistical evidence on this subject is very ambiguous. One 1907 study of women in New York State concluded that three-quarters of all those surveyed did not normally achieve orgasm (E.Shorter, *The Making of the Modern Family*, p. 253.

14. F.G.Emmison, *Elizabethan Life: Morals and the Church Courts* (Chelmsford 1973), p. 37.

15. *Memoirs of William Hickey*, ed. A.Spencer (London 1913–25), vols. III–IV (1782–1809), *passim*.

16. E.W.Monter, 'La Sodomie à l'Epoque Moderne en Suisse Romande', In *Annales*, 29 (4) (1974), pp. 1032–3.

17. A.Behn, *Works*, ed. M.Summers (London 1915), VI, p. 363; *Catalogue of Political and Personal Satires in the British Museum*, nos. 14074–5.

18. D.Defoe, ed. J.T.Boulton (New York 1965), p. 57, quoting from *The True-Born Englishman*; see also Francis Osborne, *Advice to a Son* (London 1656), p. 74.

19. L.Stone, *The Crisis of the Aristocracy* (Oxford 1965), pp. 666–7.

20. See *infra*, ch. 10, section 2, vi.

21. N.Venette, *De la Génération de l'Homme, ou Tableau de l'Amour conjugal* (Cologne 1726), pp 235–40.

22. R.van Gulik, *Sexual Life in Ancient China* (Leiden 1961), chapters I, VI.

23. B.de Mandeville, *A Modest Defence of Public Stews* (London 1724), p. 41.

24. *Autobiography of Thomas Wythorne*, ed. J.Osborn (Oxford 1961), p. 24; N.Venette, *op. cit.*, pp. 129, 165; R.Burton, *The Anatomy of Melancholy*, quoted in K.V.Thomas, *Religion and the Decline of Magic* (New York 1971), pp. 568–9; A.Behn, *The Ten Pleasures of Marriage*, ed. J.Harvey (London 1923), p. 160; see also *Diary of Dudley Ryder, 1715–16*, ed W.Matthews (London 1939), p. 85.

25. N.Venette, *op cit.*, pp. 136, 335; S.A.A.D.Tissot, *L'Onanisme: Dissertation sur les Maladies produites par la Masturbation* (Lausanne 1764), pp. 4, 68–9.

26. N.Venette, *op. cit.*, p. 178. These ideas persisted right through the nineteenth century (C.E.Rosenberg, 'The Bitter Fruit: Heredity, Disease and Social Thought in Nineteenth Century America', in *Perspectives in American History*, VIII [1974], p. 212.)

27. R.C.Trexler, 'In Search of the Father: the Experience of Abandonment in the Recollections of Giovanni di Pagolo Morelli', *History of Childhood Quarterly*, III (1975), p. 234.

28. A.M.Mauriceau, *The Married Woman's Private Medical Companion* (New York 1847), p. 153; *Conflicts in French Society* ed. T.Zeldin (London 1970), p. 45 and T.Zeldin, *France 1848–1945* (Oxford 1973), p. 296; N.Venette, *op. cit.*, pp. 191–7; W.Acton, *The Functions and Disorders of the Reproductive System*, 2nd ed. (1858), p. 23.

29. N.Venette, *op. cit.*, pp. 132–5, 170. This advice goes back to Galen (see J.Huarte Navarro, *The Examination of Men's Wits* [London 1594], p. 266). It is a curious fact that conceptions were in reality most frequent in the spring and most rare in high summer and

early fall (see *infra*, ch. 12, section 1, vi).

30. J.-L.Flandrin, 'La Cellule Familiale et l'Oeuvre de Procréation dans l'ancienne Société', in *Le XVIIe Siècle*, 102–3 (1974), pp. 12–14; *The Family in History*, ed. T.K.Rabb and R.I.Rotberg, p. 176, n. 4.

31. R.Burton, *Anatomy of Melancholy*, ed. H.Jackson (London 1932), I, pp. 234–5.

32. T.Cogan, *The Haven of Health* (London 1596), pp. 241, 252.

33. L.Stone, *op. cit.*, pp. 659–60; D.Defoe, *Conjugal Lewdness...* (London 1727), p. 91.

34. *Conflicts in French Society*, ed. T.Zeldin, p. 46.

35. In some areas of rural France in the eighteenth century it was customary for the village youth to do everything they could to prevent sexual relations on the wedding night. In other areas the sexual taboo on the first three days after marriage still existed (E.Shorter, *The Making of the Modern Family*, p. 216).

36. G.May, *Social Control of Sex Expression* (London 1930), pp. 47–8, 58, 63–4, 74–5.

37. T.Sanchez, *Compendium totius Tractatus de Sancto Matrimonii Sacramento* (Lyons 1623), pp. 478–9, 540–1, 551.

38. R.Cleaver and J.Dod, *A Godlye Form of Household Government* (London 1614), no pagination; W.Perkins, 'Of Christian Oeconomie', in *Works* (London 1631), III, p. 689; W.Gouge, *Of Domesticall Duties* (London 1622), pp. 223–6; R.Schnucker, 'La Position Puritaine à l'égard de l'adultère', in *Annales E.C.S.*, 27 (1972), pp. 1379–86; J.Milton, *Tetrachordon*, in *Works* (New York 1931) IV, p. 101.

39. A.Beiler, *L'Homme et la Femme dans la Monde Calviniste* (Geneva 1963), p. 61; G.Sinibaldi, *Rare Verities, or the Cabinet of Venus Unlocked* (London 1658) (quoted in A.Comfort, *The Anxiety-Makers* [London 1967], p. 21).

40. J.Calvin, *Institutes of the Christian Religion*, trans. H.Beveridge (Grand Rapids 1962), Bk. II, ch. viii, section 44.

41. R.Mols, *Introduction à la Démographie Historique des Villes d'Europe du XIVe au XVIIIe Siècles* (Louvain 1956), III, pp. 298–9.

42. C.F.Adams, 'Some Phases of Sexual Morality and Church Discipline in Colonial New England', in *Massachusetts Hist. Soc. Proc.*, 2nd Ser., VI (1891), p. 494; *Life, Adventures and Opinions of Colonel George Hanger* (London 1801), I, pp. 81–2; *Autobiography of Francis Place*, p. 58; *Memoirs of the Forty-Five First Years of the Life of James Lackington* (London 1795), p. 297; W.M.Dwyer, *What Everyone Knew About Sex* (Princeton 1972), p. 2.

43. J.-L.Flandrin, 'Contraception, Marriage and Sexual Relations in the Christian West', in *Biology of Man in History*, ed. R.Forster and O.Ranum (Baltimore 1975), pp. 37–8. In the early eighteenth century the French Dr Venette took almost the same attitude towards variations in sexual positions. He blamed the invention and practice of novel positions on women, whose 'passion is more violent and whose pleasure lasts longer' (N.Venette, *op. cit.*, pp. 235–7).

44. T.Sanchez, *op. cit.* (quoted in A.Comfort, *op. cit.*, p. 34).

45. D.Defoe, *Conjugal Lewdness...*, pp. 6, 62–3, 293–4, 300, 308, 319, 329, 84, 297, 91.

46. K.V.Thomas, 'The Double Standard', in *Journal of the History of Ideas*, XX (1959).

47. H.Fielding, *The Modern Husband* (1732), Act IV, scene i. J.Sprenger and H.Kramer, *Malleus Maleficarum*, trans. M.Summers (London 1928), Pt. I, Q. 6, p. 47; N.Venette, *op. cit.*, pp. 161–5.

48. K.V.Thomas, *op. cit.*, pp. 196, 209; J.Boswell, *Life of Samuel Johnson, LLD* (Everyman

ed., London 1906), II, p. 288.

49. L.Stone, *op. cit.*, pp. 662–3.

50. *Ibid.*, pp. 663–4; *Autobiography of Edward Lord Herbert of Cherbury*, ed. S.Lee (London 1907), p. 112.

51. G.B.Needham, 'Mrs Manley, an Eighteenth Century Wife of Bath', in *Huntington Library Quarterly*, XIV (1950–1), p. 272; N.McKendrick, 'Home Demand and Economic Growth; a new View of the Role of Women and Children in the Industrial Revolution', in N.McKendrick, *Historical Perspectives* (London 1974), p. 153; O.R.McGregor, *Divorce in England* (London 1957), p. 18.

52. For a detailed description of this sense of honour as it slowly eroded in a backward area of eighteenth-century France, see Y.Castan, *Honnêteté et Relations Sociales en Languedoc (1715–1780)* (Paris 1974). The evidence of the cases in the church courts of sixteenth and early seventeenth-century England suggest that English popular concepts of 'honour' were then very similar.

53. *Autobiography of Thomas Wythorne*, p. 26.

54. *The Lady's Magazine*, IV (1773), p. 176.

55. L.Stone, *op. cit.*, pp. 664–7.

56. I owe this information to Dr M.Smuts; *Poems of Richard Lovelace*, ed. C.H.Wilkinson (Oxford 1925–30), II, p. 146.

57. W.C.Hollister and T.F.Keefe, 'The Making of the Angevin Empire', in *Journal of British Studies*, XII (1973), p. 5.

58. R.V.Schnucker, 'The English Puritans and Pregnancy, Delivery and Breast-Feeding', in *History of Childhood Quarterly*, I (1974), p. 655, n. 51, quoting B.Rich, *The Irish Hubbub* (London 1622), p. 13.

59. K.Digby, *Loose Fantasies*, p. 145; J.Milton, *An Apology against a Pamphlet* (1642) in *Complete Prose Works of John Milton* (New Haven 1953), I, p. 892.

60. R.L.Clifford, *Hester Lynch Piozzi* (Oxford 1968), pp. 97–8, 173; *Thraliana*, ed. K.C.Balderston (Oxford 1942), I, pp. 356, 399, 409, 423, 373–4; II, p. 967.

61. J.Brasbridge, *Fruits of Experience* (London 1824), p. 239; *The Game of Hearts: Harriette Wilson's Memoirs*, ed. L.Blanch (New York 1955), p. 265. H.Fielding, *The Modern Husband*, Act II, scene v.

62. *Boswell: The Ominous Years, 1774–1776*, ed. C.Ryskamp and F.A.Pottle (New York 1963), p. 320.

63. *Journal de Jean Héroard*, ed. E.Soulié and E.de Bartélemy (Paris 1968), I, pp. 31, 34, 35, 38, 42–3, 45, 76, 81, 94, 100, 117, 120, 123, 147, 151–3, 186, 191, 197, 199, 250, 279, 294, 312, 315, 316, 317. These printed extracts have been used and commented on briefly by P.Ariès, *Centuries of Childhood* (New York 1975), pp. 100–2, and more extensively by D.Hunt, *op. cit.*, pp. 161–75.

64. As late as 1841 Dr William Acton was commenting, with disapproval, on 'a plan which nurses have in France of tickling the genital organs of children who are peevish' (W.Acton, *Complete Practical Treatise on Venereal Disease*, p. 27).

65. A.Comfort, *op. cit.*, p. 94.

66. For an attempt to link the influence of Louis' upbringing at the hands of Héroard to his later psychological characteristics, see E.W.Marvick, 'The Character of Louis XIII: the Role of his Physician', in *Journal of Interdisciplinary History*, IV (1974).

67. Comment by O.Ranum in *History of Childhood Quarterly*, II (1974), pp. 181, 185–6.

68. G.Bouchard, *Le Village Immobile* ... (Paris 1972), p. 325.

69. E.W.Marvick in L.de Mause, *History of Childhood* (New York 1974), p. 273; *Life of Adam Martindale*, p. 206.

70. N.Bradley, 'The Primal Scene Experience in Human Evolution ...', in *Psychoanalytic Study of Society*, IV (1967), pp. 36–40.

71. D.Gardiner, *English Girlhood at School* (London 1929), p. 200.

72. I.Watts, *Divine Songs* ... (1715), ed. J.H.P.Pafford (London 1971), p. 27; J.Nelson, *An Essay on the Government of Children* (London 1763), p. 231; M.Wollstonecraft, *A Vindication of the Rights of Woman*, p. 139.

73. *Autobiography of Thomas Wythorne*, pp. 19, 21; N.R.Hiner, 'Adolescence in Eighteenth Century America', in *History of Childhood Quarterly*, III (2) (1975), p. 259.

74. Comment by J.F.Benton in *History of Childhood Quarterly*, I (1974), p. 587; J.-L.Flandrin, *Les Amours Paysannes* (Paris 1975), p. 165.

75. J.-L.Flandrin, 'Mariage tardif et Vie sexuelle', *loc. cit*; A.Comfort, *op. cit.*, p. 70; L.Stone, *An Elizabethan: Sir Horatio Palavicino* (Oxford 1956), p. 29; L.Stone, *Family and Fortune* (Oxford 1973), p. 52.

76. S.R.Smith, 'Religion and the Conception of Youth in Seventeenth-Century England', in *History of Childhood Quarterly*, II (4) (1975), p. 508; see *infra*, ch. 13.

77. *Diary of Cotton Mather*, Massachusetts Historical Collections, 7th Ser. VII–VIII (1912), I, pp. 49, 78; N.R.Hiner, *op. cit.*, p. 261.

78. F.A.Pottle, *James Boswell: The Earlier Years, 1740–69* (London 1966), pp. 4, 30, 461; The only time he resumed masturbation was for a month eleven years later in 1764, after he had talked about his sexual problems with Rousseau and had taken a short-lived resolution to avoid debauchery with girls in the future (*ibid.*, p. 503).

79. *Defoe's Review*, V, *The Little Review*, p. 71.

80. Anon., *Onania, or the heinous Sin of Self-pollution, and all its frightful Consequences in both Sexes considered* (London c. 1710); B.de Mandeville, *op. cit.*, pp. 30–1.

81. S.A.A.D.Tissot, *op. cit.*; R.A.Spitz, 'Authority and Masturbation. Some Remarks on a Bibliographical Investigation', in *Psychoanalytical Quarterly*, XXI (1952); P.Lejeune, 'Le "dangereux supplement". Lecture d'un aveu de Rousseau', in *Annales E.C.S.*, 29 (1974); R.P.Neuman, 'Masturbation, Madness, and the Modern Concepts of Childhood and Adolescence', in *Journal of Social History*, 8 (1975), pp. 2–5.

82. *Conflicts in French Society*, ed T. Zeldin, p. 50; J.-L.Flandrin, *Les Amours Paysannes*, p. 161.

83. P.Lejeune, *op. cit.*, p. 1020.

84. M.Wollstonecraft, *A Vindication of the Rights of Woman*, p. 182.

85. J.W.von Archenholz, *A Picture of England* (London 1797), II, pp. 114–15; D.M.Stuart, *Molly Lepell, Lady Hervey* (London 1936), p. 355; *The Morning Chronicle and Public Advertiser* (14 September 1786); *Francis Letters*, ed B.Francis and E.Keary (New York 1901), I, pp. 321, 332; *Memoirs of Sir Philip Francis*, ed. J.Parkes and H.Merivale (London 1867), I, p. 406; *Autobiography of Arthur Young*, ed. M.Betham-Edwards (London 1898), pp. 263–4.

86. A.L.Rowse, *The Elizabethan Renaissance* (London 1971), p. 187.

87. A.Wood, *Life and Times*, Oxford Historical Soc., XXI (1892), II, p. 94; *Diary of Dudley Ryder, 1715–16*, p. 143; Anon., *College Wit Sharpened, or a Head of a College with a Sting in the Tail* (London 1739) (Bodl. Library, Gough Oxford 50).

88. *Life, Adventures and Opinions of Colonel George Hanger*, p. 21; *Henry, Elizabeth and George, 1734–80*, ed. Lord Herbert (London 1939), p. 71; *Autobiography of Francis Place*, p. 56.

89. F.G.Emmison, *op. cit.*, p. 1.

90. *Ibid.*, pp. 7, 13, 10–17, 28.

91. *Ibid.*, pp. 2–6, 281–3, 286–7, 168–70.

92. *Ibid.*, pp. 31, 41; For infanticide and abandonment, see *supra*, ch. 9, section 2, vi.

93. W.B.Rye, *England as Seen by Foreigners* (London 1865), pp. 90, 260–1; J.Marston, *The Dutch Courtesan* (1604), Act III, sc. i; M.Drayton, *Polyolbion* (London 1613), sig A2 v; Anon., *Hic Mulier, or the Man-Woman* (London 1620), sig B3.

94. *The Spectator*, 1711, no. 67; H.Meister, *Letters Written during a Residence in England* (London 1799), p. 288; *The Lady's Magazine*, IV (1773), p. 587; see also J.W.von Archenholtz, *op. cit.*, II, pp. 115–16.

95. C.Camden, *The Elizabethan Woman*, p. 224; Anon., *Hic Mulier, or the Man-Woman*, sig B2; R.K.Marshall, *The Days of Duchess Anne* (London 1973), plate opposite p. 33. See also the tomb effigy of Queen Anne of Denmark in Westminster Abbey, the roof paintings of Muchelney Church in Somerset, the Masque costumes at the Caroline Court, or the illustration of a middle-class dinner party in Camden (*ibid.*, p. 108); *The Guardian* (London 1713), nos. 100, 109, 119; B.de Mandeville, *The Virgin Unmask'd* (London 1724), pp. 9–11.

96. L.Wright, *op. cit.*, p. 82; J.Grego, *Rowlandson the Caricaturist* (London 1880), I, p. 341.

97. F.de la Rochefoucauld, *A Frenchman in England* (1784), ed. J.Marchand (Cambridge 1933), pp. 31–2.

98. W.Maskell, *Monumenta Ritualia Ecclesiae Anglicanae* (Oxford 1882), I, p. 58; F.Procter and W.H.Frere, *A New History of the Book of Common Prayer* (London 1902), pp. 154, 161, 185, 189, 614; W.H.Frere and C.E.Douglas, *Puritan Manifestoes* (London 1907), p. 27; E.Cardwell, *A History of Conferences ...* (Oxford 1849), pp. 200, 330, 363.

99. C.Hill, 'Clarissa Harlowe and her Times', in his *Puritanism and Revolution* (London 1958), p. 373; J.Cleland, *Memoirs of a Woman of Pleasure* (London 1749); *The Amorous Illustrations of Thomas Rowlandson*, ed. G.Schiff (New York 1969); Anon., *A New and Complete Collection of the most remarkable Trials for Adultery* (London 1780), II, pp. 121, 125, 127.

100. I owe this idea to Dr M.Smuts.

101. *Autobiography of Thomas Raymond*, Camden Soc., 3rd Ser., XXVIII (1917), p. 23; P.Delany, *British Autobiography in the Seventeenth Century*, pp. 78, 59, 71.

102. *Diary of Cotton Mather.*

103. *Ibid.*, I, pp. 49, 78, 92, 121.

104. *Ibid.*, I, pp. 184, 236.

105. *Ibid.*, I, pp. 457–8, 466–70, 474.

106. *Ibid.*, I, pp. 490, 492–3, 585; II, p. 255.

107. *Ibid.*, II, pp. 118, 269, 273, 303–4.

108. *Ibid.*, II, pp. 397, 583.

109. *Ibid.*, II, p. 523.

110. *Ibid.*, II, pp. 504, 583–5, 590, 745.

111. *Ibid.*, II, pp. 727, 749–50.

112. *Ibid.*, II, pp. 160, 229, 235, 283, 612, 767.

113. *Ibid.*, II, p. 688 n. 1; R.Middlekauf, *The Mathers: three Generations of Puritan Intellectuals, 1596–1728* (New York 1971), p. 191.

114. E.Morgan, *The Puritan Family* (New York 1966), p. 35.

115. *Diaries of Oliver Heywood*, ed. J.H.Turner (Brighouse 1883), I, pp. 153–4, 168.

116. E.S.Morgan, 'Puritans and Sex', in *New England Quarterly*, 15 (1942); C.Bingham, 'Seventeenth Century Attitudes towards deviant Sex', in *Journal of Interdisciplinary History*, I (1971).

117. J.Wilkes, *op. cit.*, p. 13; See D.Underwood, *Etherege and the Seventeenth Century Comedy of Manners* (New Haven 1957).

118. G.B.Needham, *op. cit.*, p. 273; J.M.S.Tomkins, *The Polite Marriage* (Cambridge 1938), p. 14; British Museum, Add. MSS 27825 f. 79 (advertisement for the 15th edition of *Onania* in J.Guthrie, *Account of the Behaviour ... of Malefactors* [London 1730]).

119. *Thraliana*, II, p. 761. For an extremely subtle study of Blake's attitude to sexuality, see J.H.Hagstrum, 'Babylon revisited, or the Story of Luvah and Vala', in *Blake's Sublime Allegory*, ed. S.Curran and J.A.Wittreich (Madison 1973), pp. 115–18.

120. A.I.Dasent, *Private Life of Charles II* (London 1927), p. 61.

121. R.North, *Autobiography*, ed. A.Jessop (London 1887), p. 91; 'A Letter to an M.P., 1675', in *Harleian Misc.* (London 1810), VIII, pp. 68–9; A.Hamilton, *Memoirs of Count Grammont*, ed. W.Scott (London 1905), p. 225; R.North, *Lives of the Norths* (London 1826), II, p. 164. *Boswell's London Journal, 1762–63*, ed. F.A.Pottle (London 1950), p. 103; [H.More], *Thoughts on the Importance of the Manners of the Great to General Society* (London 1788), p. 64.

122. W.Young, *Eros Denied* (London 1964), pp. 220–2; B.de Mandeville, *A Modest Defence of Public Stews*, p. ix.

123. 'History of Tête-à-Tête', in *Town and Country Magazine* (1781–4). They are listed and identified in *Catalogue of Political and Personal Satires in the British Museum*, vols. V and VI, *passim*.

124. *Diary of Sylas Neville 1767–1788*, ed. B.Cozens-Hardy (London 1950), p. 289.

125. H.Fielding, *The History of Tom Jones* (1749), I, p. 123; A.Behn, *The Amorous Prince*, Act I, sc. ii (*Works*, IV, p. 128).

126. See *supra*, ch. 7, section 2, iv b.

127. *A Character of John Sheffield, late Duke of Buckinghamshire* (London 1729), pp. 37–9; *Boswell on the Grand Tour: Germany and Switzerland 1764*, ed. F.A.Pottle (London 1953), p. 104, n. 3.

128. Philogamus, *The Present State of Matrimony or the Real Cause of Conjugal Infidelity* (London 1739), pp. 13–64; A.J.C.Hare, *The Years with Mother* (London 1952), p. 127; *Notes by Lady Louisa Stuart*, ed. W.S.Lewis, p. 44; Earl of Bessborough, *Georgiana* (London 1955), pp. 69, 2–7.

129. *Henry, Elizabeth and George, 1734–80*, ed. Lord Herbert, pp. 409, 31, 41, 394, 497–98; *Pembroke Papers (1780–94)*, pp. 14, 22, 35, 44, 50, 57, n. 1, 139, 385–6; D.M.Stuart, *Dearest Bess* (London 1955), pp. 2, 23, 42, 239; *Diaries of Sylvester Douglas, Lord Glenbervie*, ed. F.Bickley (London 1928), I, p. 3; II, pp. 15, 16, 22, 23, 39, 63, 68, 73, 81–4, 87, 104, 113–14; *Memoirs of a Highland Lady*, ed. Lady Strachey (London 1898), p. 158.

130. L.Blanch, *The Game of Hearts: Harriette Wilson's Memoirs*. In a pioneer use of the

index of a book as a weapon, Harriette described her rival Julia Johnstone as 'Julia Storer, a girl at Hampton Court, ruined on the staircase' (*ibid.*, p. 47).

131. W.Cobbett, *Parliamentary History of England* (London 1813), XXXV, col. 261; E.Climenson, *Elizabeth Montagu, Queen of the Bluestockings* (London 1906), II, p. 160.

132. C.Darwin, *Life of Erasmus Darwin* (London 1887), p. 88, note.

133. Quoted by C.Hill, *Puritanism and Revolution*, p. 376; *Memoirs of William Hickey*, vols. III–IV (1782–1809), *passim*; W.L.Burn, *Age of Equipoise* (London 1964), p. 256.

134. *Dictionary of National Biography*, sub. James Graham; J.W.von Archenholz, *op. cit.*, I, pp. 118–25; *Diary of Sylas Neville*, pp. 284, 307; *Reminiscences of H.C.W.Angelo*, ed. J.Grego (London 1904), I, pp. 97–8, 413–14; *Catalogue of Political and Personal Satires in the British Museum*, nos. 6120, 6323–5, 8247.

135. *Catalogue of Political and Personal Satires in the British Museum*, nos. 6137, 6874, 7099, 7100, 8257, 8521, 9457, 12940; D.Hill, *Mr. Gillray the Caricaturist* (London 1965), pl. 134; *Fashionable Contrasts: Caricatures by Gillray*, ed. D.Hill (London 1966), p. 83.

136. *Life, Adventures and Opinions of Colonel George Hanger*, II, p. 181.

137. B.de Mandeville, *Wishes to a Godson, with other Miscellaneous Poems* (London 1712), pp. 5–6; A.Behn, *The Disappointment*, in *Works*, VI, pp. 178–82; 'Signor Dildo' in *Collected Poems of John Wilmot Earl of Rochester*, pp. 54–9.

138. British Museum, Add. MSS 27825 ff. 117, 117v.

139. A picture of Mrs Lewis's shop appears on the frontispiece of White Kennett, *The Machine*, a pornographic poem of 1744 (I owe this information to David H.Fischer). J.W.von Archenholz, *op. cit.*, p. 230; *A Catalogue of Political and Personal Satires in the British Museum*, no. 5171 (V, p. 139); *Fashionable Contrasts: Caricatures by Gillray*, pl. 79; For handbills advertising Mrs Phillips' wares, see F.Grose, *Guide to Health, Beauty, Riches and Honour* (London 1796), pp. 10–13; von Archenholz reported in 1784 that they were only in common use in London and Paris, and only sold openly in London, at Mrs Phillips' (J.W.von Archenholz, *op. cit.*, II, p. 194).

140. S.Pepys, *Diary* (9 Feb. 1668); *The World*, 19 (10 May 1753), p. 115. *L'École des Filles* was first translated into English in 1680, for which the publisher was prosecuted for 'uttering a certain most pernicious, wicked and vicious book' (J.H.Wilson, *Court Satires of the Restoration* (Columbus, Ohio 1976), p. 67, n. 78.

141. J.Donne, *Complete Poetry and Selected Prose*, ed. J.Hayward (London 1929), pp. 96–7 (Elegy XIX); R.Lovelace, *Poems*, ed. C.H.Wilkinson, II, p. 19.

142. The pre-war poems are unpublished, but a large collection of transcripts of them was kindly placed at my disposal by my former student Mr Julian Mitchell. For a sample of the post-war satires, see J.H.Wilson, *op. cit.*

143. *Ibid.*, p. 92.

144. D.Foxon, *Libertine Literature in England, 1660–1745* (1964), pp. 52–63; *The Monthly Review* (April 1750); *Private Papers of James Boswell*, 13, p. 220.

145. This description of eighteenth-century English pornography comes from the notes on the subject written in about 1824 by Francis Place (B.M. Add. MSS. 27825, ff. 53–136 *passim*).

146. *Letters of Henry Prideaux, Camden Soc.*, 2nd Ser., XV (1875), p. 30.

147. *The Amorous Illustrations of Thomas Rowlandson*, ed. G.Schiff; I have not seen K. von Meier, *The Forbidden Erotica of Thomas Rowlandson* (Los Angeles 1970).

148. B.M., Add. MSS 27825, f. 118.

149. Lambeth Palace MS 939 ff. 3–4; J.A.Venn, *Gonville and Caius College* (Cambridge 1901), III, p. 113; T.Hearne, *Collections, Oxford Historical Soc.*, IX (1914), pp. 120–1, 181; X (1915), p. 381.

150. N.Ward, *Secret History of the London Clubs* (London 1709), pp. 28–9; M.McIntosh, 'The Homosexual Role', in *Social Problems*, 16 (1968), pp. 189–90; A.L.Rowse, *op. cit.*, pp. 180–8; *Thraliana*, I, pp. 246, 517; II, pp. 640, 740, 747, 770; *Catalogue of Political and Personal Satires in the British Museum*, nos. 5173, 11421.

151. B.M., Add. MSS 27826, ff. 22, 177; *Catalogue of Political and Personal Satires in the British Museum*, no. 3993. In 1778 Fanny Burney noted that homosexuals seemed to have infiltrated the fashionable milliners' trade in London (*Evelina*, ed. F.D.Mackinnon [Oxford 1930], p. 33).

152. *The Lady's Magazine*, IV (1773), p. 183.

153. R.Blunt and M.Wyndham, *Thomas, Lord Lyttelton* (London 1936), p. 48; F.A.Pottle, *James Boswell: The Earlier Years 1740–69* (London 1966), p. 200; M.Wollstonecraft, *op. cit.*, pp. 145, 10.

154. P.E.Slater, *Earthwalk* (New York 1974), pp. 133, 167.

CHAPTER 11   GENTLEMANLY SEXUAL BEHAVIOUR: CASE HISTORIES

1. A.L.Rowse, *Simon Forman: Sex and Society in Shakespeare's Age* (London 1974), pp. 282, 283, 34, 70, 291; 53, 58, 64–5, 290–4.

2. *Ibid.*, pp. 52, 167, 171–2, 288; 79; 78, 80, 94, 210, 297, 101–2, 118–24, 127–8, 131.

3. *Ibid.*, pp. 297, 80–1, 295.

4. *Ibid.*, pp. 92, 249, 294, 297, 250.

5. *Ibid.*, p. 285.

6. *Ibid.*, pp. 228, 258.

7. *Ibid.*, pp. 205, 214.

8. *Ibid.*, pp. 215, 99–102.

9. *Elias Ashmole*, ed. C.H.Josten (Oxford 1966), II, pp. 386, 407–12; Ashmole also had a sexual dream about the widow (p. 424).

10. *Diary of Samuel Pepys*, ed. R.B.Latham and W.Matthews (London 1970–6). This is the only unexpurgated edition. A chronological account of Pepys' love-life is to be found in J.H.Wilson, *The Private Life of Mr Pepys* (New York 1959).

11. *Diary of Samuel Pepys*, 14 April 1661; 9 July 1664.

12. *Ibid.*, 24 Oct. 1663, 22 Dec. 1661; 4, 12, 15, 16 May 1663.

13. *Ibid.*, 10 Nov. 1668.

14. *Ibid.*, 9 July 1664.

15. *Ibid.*, 14 Oct. 1660; 20 April, 23 July, 7 Sept. 1661; 21 May, 23 Aug., 20 Oct., 15 May 1663; 15 Aug. 1665; 8 May 1667; 6 Sept. 1664; 17 Feb. 1669; 13 July, 21 Aug. 1668.

16. *Ibid.*, 20–9, July 1664.

17. *Ibid.*, 18 July, 22 Dec. 1663; 3 July 1667.

18. *Ibid.*, 18 July 1663; 7 Sept., 3, 20 Oct., 15 Nov., 20 Dec. 1664; 23 Jan., 20 Feb., 15, 19 July; 8, 12, 22 Aug., 5 Oct., 8 Nov. 1665; 13 June, 12 Sept., 23 Oct., 1, 22 Nov. 1666; 1, 11 Feb., 4, 20, 31 Mar., 30 Sept., 23 Oct. 1667; 6 Jan., 16 Mar., 29 May, 2 June 1668; 29 Mar., 15 April 1669; J.H.Wilson, *op. cit.*, pp. 168–9, 228.

19. *Diary of Samuel Pepys*, 21 Dec. 1665; 15 June, 12 July, 1 Aug., 30 Nov., 3 Dec. 1666; 10 Jan., 18 Feb. 1667.

20. *Ibid.*, 20 Dec. 1665: 2 June, 11 July, 21 Dec. 1666; 23, 31 May, 22 June 1667; 25 Mar., 10 May, 22 June, 20 July, 15 Sept. 1668.

21. *Ibid.*, 23 Aug., 1665; 18 April, 2 May, 14 July 1666; 13 April 1667.

22. *Ibid.*, 2, 20 Jan., 1 June 1665; 23 Mar., 10, 12 Oct., 30 Nov., 3 Dec. 1666; 9 April, 20 May, 30 Sept. 1667.

23. *Ibid.*, 26 Nov., 4 Dec. 1665; 24 Jan. 1667.

24. *Ibid.*, 12 Aug., 2, 4, 22 Sept. 1660; 23 Nov. 1665; 5 Jan. 1666; 24 Feb., 25 Mar. 1667.

25. *Ibid.*, 4 Feb. 1664.

26. J.H.Wilson, *op. cit.*, pp. 174–5, 177; *Diary...*, 11 Nov. 1666; 16 Dec. 1665.

27. *Ibid.*, 2, 23, Dec. 1666; 6, 13, 27 Jan., 11 Feb., 20 Mar., 9 April, 17 Sept. 1667.

28. *Ibid.*, 3, 11, 12, 18 Sept. 1664; 2, 8, 20, 22 Jan. 1665.

29. *Ibid.*, 31 March, 1 April, 6, 10, 18 Aug., 13, 25–9 Oct., 1–20 Nov. 1668; I am much indebted to Dr R.B.Latham for allowing me to read proofs of the last volume of his definitive edition of the Diary before publication.

30. J.H.Wilson, *op. cit.*, pp. 229, 232–3.

31. *Diary...*, 31 Dec. 1662; 15 May, 9 Nov. 1663; 8 Feb. 1664; 16 Oct. 1665.

32. *Ibid.*, 18 Aug. 1667.

33. *Diary of Robert Hooke, 1672–1680*, ed. H.W.Robinson and W.Adams (London 1935).

34. *Ibid.*, 1–4, 8 Aug., 12, 17–19 Sept., 8, 9, 12, 17, 28, 31 Oct., 5, 28, 29 Nov., 2 Dec. 1672; 26, 30 Jan., 9 Feb., 7–9, 11 April, 1, 8, 24, 28 May, 10, 19, 29 June, 2, 5, 11, 16, 19, 29 July, 9, 13, 14, 15, 21, 30–1 Aug., 29 Sept 1673.

35. *Ibid.*, 16 Oct., 27 Dec. 1673; 7, 12, 30 Jan., 11, 26 March 1674; 12 Jan. 1679; 26 June, 25, 26 July, 15 Aug. 1674.

36. *Ibid.*, 20 Jan., 12 Feb. 1675; 18 Jan., 13 May, 14 June, 16 Oct. 1676; 15, 16, 25 Jan., 11 Feb., 3, 5, March, 17 June, 1 July, 9 Aug 1677; 27 Feb., 7 June, 26 Dec. 1678; 30 March, 19 June, 25 Oct., 2 Nov. 1679; 6 Sept. 1680; p. xxviii.

37. *Ibid.*, 21 Aug. 1678; 24 May 1674.

38. *Secret Diary of William Byrd of Westover, 1709–12*, ed. L.B.Wright and M.Tinling (Richmond 1941), *passim*. Byrd used two phrases to indicate sexual relations: 'I rogered my wife,' and 'I gave my wife a flourish.' Whether they are synonyms or whether they indicate different positions or acts is uncertain.

39. Cf. the note in the early eighteenth-century diary of John Gordon of Fechil: 'Great anger with wife – without cause – then Venus' (*Diaries of Sylvester Douglas, Lord Glenbervie*, ed. F.Bickley [London 1928], II, p. 351).

40. M.Slater, *The Verney Family in the Seventeenth Century* (unpublished Princeton PhD thesis) (1971), p. 63.

41. *William Byrd, The London Diary and Other Writings, 1717–21*, ed. L.B.Wright and M.Tinling (Richmond 1958), pp. 69, 92, 95, 160.

42. *Ibid.*, pp. 60, 138, 140, 141, 153, 155, 156, 191, 134.

43. *Ibid.*, pp. 50, 57, 60, 71, 79, 83, 117, 123, 135–6.

44. *Ibid.*, pp. 139, 142, 143, 146, 157, 161, 188–9, 210, 217, 218, 223.

45. *Ibid.*, pp. 162, 168, 181, 183, 219, 221, 225, 232, 239, 242, 248, 256, 278, 286, 315–21, 182.

46. *Ibid.*, pp. 224–5, 236, 269, 231, 243, 250, 253, 324, 327.

47. *Ibid.*, *passim*; and especially pp. 346–50, 71–2, 77, 83, 86.

48. *Ibid.*, pp. 373–4, 377, 447, 448–528 *passim*, 491, 498.

49. *Another Secret Diary of William Byrd of Westover, 1739–41*, ed. M.H.Woodfin and

M.Tinling (Richmond 1942), pp. 157, 168, 174.

50. *The Diary of Sylas Neville, 1767–1788*, ed. B.Cozens-Hardy (London 1950), p. x–xi, 144. The diary is unfortunately printed only in an expurgated version.

51. *Ibid.*, pp. 120, 44, 65–7.

52. *Ibid.*, pp. 70–2, 77–8, 81, 84–6.

53. *Ibid.*, pp. 87–9, 111, 105, 107.

54. *Ibid.*, pp. 126, 129, 142, 144, 162–3, 166, 172, 188, 193, 195.

55. *Ibid.*, pp. 206, 208, 213–14, 221–2, 246.

56. *Ibid.*, pp. 226, 260, 261, 265–7, 299, 300, 314, 320, 322, 309–11.

57. *Ibid.*, pp. 331–3.

58. This sketch of Boswell is drawn from F.A.Pottle: *James Boswell: The Earlier Years, 1740–69* (London 1966) (referred to subsequently as *BEY*); *Boswell's London Journal, 1762–1763*, ed. F.A.Pottle (London 1950) (*BLJ*); *Boswell on the Grand Tour: Germany and Switzerland, 1764*, ed. F.A.Pottle (London 1953) (*BGT I*); *Boswell on the Grand Tour: Italy, Corsica and France, 1765–6*, ed. F.Brady and F.A.Pottle (London 1955) (*BGT II*); *Boswell in Search of a Wife, 1766–9*, ed. F.Brady and F.A.Pottle (New York 1956) (*BSW*); *Boswell for the Defence, 1769–74*, ed. W.K.Wimsatt and F.A.Pottle (New York 1959) (*BFD*); *Boswell: The Ominous Years, 1774–1776*, ed. C.Ryscamp and F.A.Pottle (New York 1963) (*BOY*); *Boswell in Extremes, 1776–1778*, ed. C.McC.Weis and F.A.Pottle (New York 1970) (*BIE*); and *The Private Papers of James Boswell*, ed. G.Scott and F.A.Pottle (New York 1932–4) (*PPJB*).

59. *BOY*, p. 214.

60. *BEY*, pp. 2–30 *passim*; *BLJ*, p. 324 n. 2; *BGT I*, p. 237 n. 1.

61. *BLJ*, p. 202.

62. *BLJ*, pp. 164, 54; *BGT I*, p. 248.

63. *BGT II*, p. 59; *BEY*, p. 496.

64. The infections occurred as follows: April 1760, London (*BEY*, p. 51); May 1761, Edinburgh (*BEY*, p. 471); Jan. 1763, London (*BLJ*, p. 164); April 1765, Rome (*BGT II*, p. 75); July 1765, Venice (*ibid.*, p. 109; *BEY*, p. 232); March 1767, Edinburgh (*ibid.*, p. 319); July 1767, Edinburgh (*ibid.*, pp. 336–7, 341); December 1767, Edinburgh (*ibid.*, p. 347); April 1768, London (*ibid.*, p. 380); June 1769, Dublin (*ibid.*, p. 409); After his marriage there were at least seven further episodes: January 1773, Edinburgh (*BFD*, p. 147); February 1777, Edinburgh (*BIE*, pp. 208, 215); July 1780, Edinburgh (*PPJB*, 14, pp. 94–5, 100); December 1780, Edinburgh (*PPJB*, 14, pp. 155, 258); May 1785, London (*ibid.*, 16, pp. 89, 95, 128); November 1789, London (*ibid.*, 18, pp. 5, 10); June 1790, London (*ibid.*, 18, pp. 56, 60, 65). For a medical discussion of this problem, see W.B.Ober, 'Boswell's Clap', *Journal of the American Medical Association*, 212 (1970), pp. 92–5.

65. *BEY*, p. 47; *BLJ*, p. 215.

66. *BEY*, pp. 76, 79.

67. *BLJ*, pp. 49, 83–4, 89, 94–5, 97, 117, 139–79, 149, 155, 161.

68. *Ibid.*, pp. 198, 227, 231, 241, 262–4, 272–3, 280; *BEY*, p. 119.

69. *Ibid.*, pp. 119–20; *BLJ*, pp. 300, 304.

70. *BEY*, pp. 127–28, 135–9, 143–5.

71. *BGT I*, pp. 36, 80, 88, 92, 181.

72. *BGT II*, pp. 37 n. 3, 127 n. 1, 128 n. 3, 131–2, 146, 248–9, 262 n. 2, 278 n. 1.

73. *Ibid.*, pp. 29–38, 54, 60–1, 6.

74. *Ibid.*, pp. 69, 75, 81, 87, 109; *BEY*, pp. 218, 232, 238.

75. *BGT II*, pp. 133, 137. This effect of true love on a habitual rake had been noted by the Earl of Rochester in the late seventeenth century in his poem *The Imperfect Enjoyment*, in which he berated his drooping member:

> Didst thou e'er fail in all thy life before?
> When vice, disease and scandal lead the way
> With what officious haste dost thou obey.
> ....
> But when great Love the onset does command,
> Base recreant to thy Prince, thou dar'st not stand.

(*Complete Poems of John Wilmot Earl of Rochester*, ed D.M.Vieth (New Haven 1968), p. 39.

76. *BGT II*, pp. 142, 145, 319–33; *BEY*, pp. 239–42.

77. *BGT II*, pp. 292–94; *BEY*, pp. 277–8. Professor Pottle now suspects that Colonel Isham invented this account of the contents of the missing pages, but his argument is not entirely convincing; see D.Buchanan, *Treasurer of Auchinleck* (New York 1974), App. IV.

78. *BGT II*, pp. 298, 307; *BEY*, pp. 290–1, 318–19, 325; *BSW*, pp. 9, 24, 31, 38, 63.

79. *Ibid.*, pp. 37, 80–1, 95, 112, 117–18, 121, 123–4, 135, 140, 142–3, 158, 160, 163, 180; *BEY*, pp. 335–7, 341, 347, 349–51, 370, 376–7, 380, 385.

80. *BSW*, pp. 207, 269–70, 286–7, 294 n, 1, 317, 213; *BEY*, pp. 391, 403, 409, 414, 419, 427, 441, 563, 566.

81. *PPJB* 8, pp. 157, 169, 173, 176–7, 190, 210, 214, 222.

82. D.Buchanan, *op. cit.*, pp. 103, 317.

83. *BOY*, p. 72.

84. *BFD*, pp. 8, 29, 35, 39, 134.

85. *Ibid.*, p. 76.

86. *Ibid.*, pp. 140, 147, 224, 231.

87. *Ibid.*, pp. 269, 273, 275, 320–1, 337.

88. *BOY*, pp. 5–7, 11, 28, 35, 41, 58, 59, 74.

89. *Ibid.*, pp. 81, 82, 88, 95, 139, 146 n. 6, 147.

90. *Ibid.*, pp. 188, 191, 35, 48, 72, 165, 170, 173, 178, 190, 199, 206, 232, 238, 246.

91. *Ibid.*, pp. 263, 274, 283, 294, 304–7, 315, 326.

92. *BIE*, pp. xviii, 25, 27–9, 53, 61, 63.

93. *Ibid.*, pp. 64–5, 66, 84, 86, 107, 128–9, 132–3, 135, 140, 141.

94. *Ibid.*, pp. 146, 149, 173, 188, 189, 198, 200, 203, 206–8, 216.

95. *Ibid.*, pp. 260, 266, 308–9, 311, 317, 346–7.

96. *PPJB* 13, pp. 123, 155, 166–7, 195.

97. *Ibid.*, 13, pp. 264, 266–9.

98. *Ibid.*, 14, pp. 85, 93, 153–5.

99. *Ibid.*, 14, pp. 183, 194, 210, 211, 213, 217, 222, 226, 228, 231; 15, pp. 32, 46, 59–60, 62, 66, 69.

100. *Ibid.*, 15, pp. 71–6, 103, 111, 117–18.

101. *Ibid.*, 15, pp. 121–2, 124–5, 158.

102. *Ibid.*, 15, p. 223; 16, pp. 86, 88–9, 94–5, 97, 102, 105, 112, 128.

103. *Ibid.*, 16, pp. 122, 123, 138, 151–5, 169–79; 17, pp. i, 83, 117; M.Hyde, *The Impossible Friendship, Boswell and Mrs Thrale* (London 1973), p. 136.

104. *PPJB* 18, pp. 4, 5, 18, 36.

105. *Ibid.*, 18, pp. 48, 56, 60, 65, 181, 213, 276, 278.

106. *Thraliana*, ed. K.C.Balderston (Oxford 1942), I, p. 199; *BOY*, p. 290; *BIE*, p. 180; *PPJB* 13, p. 260.

107. *BOY*, p. 306.

108. *Ibid.*, p. 74.

109. *PPJB* 18, p. 246.

110. *BOY*, p. 278; *BSW*, p. 155–6; *PPJB* 13, pp. 267–9; 14, pp. 61, 153; 15, pp. 66, 69, 76.

111. *BLJ*, p. 49; F.G.Emmison, *Elizabethan Life: Morals and the Church Courts* (Chelmsford 1973), pp. 31–6; A.M.Waugh, 'Venereal Disease in Sixteenth Century England', in *Medical History* 17 (1973), pp. 191–8; G.Etherege, *The Comical Revenge, or Love in a Tub* (1664). This lamentable play is constructed around remedies for VD, and was very popular, being reprinted as late as 1735.

112. *BEY*, p. 542; E.Climenson, *Elizabeth Montagu, Queen of the Bluestockings* (London 1906), I, p. 134; See also *BOY*, p. 118; J.L.Clifford, *Hester Lynch Piozzi* (Oxford 1968), p. 164; Mrs Thrale's Children's Book, August 1776; W.L.Payne, *Defoe's Review* (New York 1951), p. xii.

113. W.L.Payne, *ibid.*, p. xii; *The Morning Chronicle and Public Advertiser* and *The Whitehall Evening Post* for 1785, *passim*.

114. *BLJ*, p. 49.

115. *BOY*, p. 118.

CHAPTER 12   PLEBEIAN SEXUAL BEHAVIOUR

1. M.Sheehan, 'The Formation and Stability of Marriage in the Fourteenth Century: Evidence of an Ely Register', in *Medieval Studies*, 33 (1971).

2. E.Le Roy Ladurie, *Montaillou: Village occitan de 1294 à 1324* (Paris 1975), ch. VIII–XII; *Memoirs of a Renaissance Pope: The Commentaries of Pius II*, ed. L.C.Gabel (New York 1959), p. 35.

3. S.D.Chapman, *History of Working Class Housing* (Newton Abbot 1971), pp. 21–4, 107, 136–9, 168.

4. H.R.Styles, *Bundling: its Origins, Progress and Decline in America* (Albany 1871), pp. 29, 33, 52–71, 113, 137; J.-L.Flandrin, *Les Amours Paysannes* (Paris 1975), pp. 122–4; D.H.Flaherty, *Privacy in Colonial New England* (Charlottesville 1972), pp. 78–9; *Report of the Commissioners of Inquiry into South Wales, Parliamentary Papers* (1844), *Reports from Commissioners*, vol. XVI, p. 81.

5. H.R.Styles, *op. cit.*, p. 50; P.Laslett and K.Oosterveen, 'Long Term Trends in Bastardy in England', in *Population Studies*, XXVII (1973), p. 259; *Diary of Thomas Turner of East Hoathly, 1754–65* (London 1925), pp. 97–8, 70; W.Bingley, *North Wales* (London 1804), II, p. 282.

6. An American bundling song of 1785 defended the practice on grounds of economy:

> Since in a bed a man and maid
> May bundle and be chaste,
> It does no good to burn out wood,
> It is a needless waste (Styles, *op. cit.*, p. 92.)

7. H.R.Styles, *op. cit.*, pp. 25, 28; J.-L.Flandrin, *op. cit.*, pp. 194–6. For a detailed account of the rigid conventions still surrounding the practice in mid-nineteenth century Norway, see M.Drake, *Population and Society in Norway, 1735–1865* (Cambridge 1969), pp. 141–2.

8. R.Braun, 'The Impact of Cottage Industry on an Agricultural Population', in *The Rise of Capitalism*, ed. D.Landes (New York 1966), pp. 60–1.

9. This information is derived from an examination of parish registers, by counting the months elapsed between marriage and the baptism of the first child. The cut-off point is usually taken to be $8\frac{1}{2}$ months, since the baptism was anyway a couple of weeks or more after the birth. There is no reason why this data should not be entirely reliable, although it omits those children (probably few) who never were baptized, and those marriages (which may have been more numerous before the 1753 Marriage Act) which were never publicly registered.

10. G.Bouchard, *Le Village Immobile . . .* (Paris 1972), 327.

11. L.Henry, 'Fécondité dans le Sud-est de la France', in *Annales E.C.S.*, 27 (1972), p. 999.

12. The evidence is summarized by E. Shorter in *American Historical Review*, LXXVIII (1973), pp. 636–40, and his *The Making of the Modern Family* (New York 1975), appendix II; by D.S.Smith, 'Pre-maritial Pregnancy in America, 1640–1971', in *Journal of Interdisciplinary History*, V (1975), figs 1 and 2, pp. 538 and 540; and by P.Laslett, *Family Life and Illicit Love in Earlier Generations* (forthcoming, Cambridge 1977), table 3.3.

13. E.Shorter, *op. cit.*, P.Laslett, *The World We Have Lost* (London 1971), p. 148; E.Oberholzer, *Delinquent Saints* (New York 1956), p. 141. At Groton in the 1760s, of the 200 men and women who owned the baptismal covenant, 66 confessed to having conceived children out of wedlock (H.R.Styles, *op. cit.*, p. 80); W.Cobbett, *Parliamentary History of England* (London 1813), XV, col. 18.

14. *Autobiography of Francis Place*, ed. M.Thale (Cambridge 1972), pp. 57, 73, 81, 82.

15. *Bletchley Diary of the Rev. W.Cole*, ed. F.G.Stokes (London 1931), pp. 8–9, 13, 49; *Journal of a Somerset Rector, 1803–34: John Skinner*, ed. H. and P.Coombs (Bath 1971), pp. 63–4, 256, 401, 409, 427. Skinner commented: 'this frequently happens among the lower classes of society, but I did not think those who moved a step higher adopted the fashion.'

16. *Bletchley Diary of the Rev. W.Cole*, pp. 19, 202, 204.

17. W.Cobbett, *op. cit.*, XV, col. 18.

18. J.-L.Flandrin, *op. cit.*, pp. 238–40.

19. Information kindly supplied by Mr P.Laslett; see also his *Family Life and Illicit Love in Earlier Generations*, table 3.3 for figures for 98 less well-documented parishes; for other samples, see S.Sogner, 'Aspects of the Demographic situation in 17 Parishes in Shropshire, 1711–60', in *Population Studies*, XVII (1963), p. 130; J.D.Chambers, *Vale of Trent, 1670–1800, Economic History Review Supplement* 3, p. 59; *Dymock Parish Registers, 1538–1790*, ed. I.Gray and J.E.Gethyn-Jones, *Bristol and Glos. Arch. Soc., Records Series*, IV (1960); J.C.Cox, *The Parish Registers of England* (London 1910), p. 72; C.C.Taylor, 'Population Studies in Seventeenth and Eighteenth Century Wiltshire', in *Wilts. Archaeological Magazine*, LX (1965), pp. 107–8. For similar European trends, see E.Shorter, *The Making of the Modern Family*, ch. 3; 'Illegitimacy, Sexual Revolution and Social Change', in *The Family in History*, ed. T.K.Rabb and R.I.Rotberg (New

York 1973); 'Sexual Change and Illegitimacy', in R.J.Bezucha, *Modern European Social History* (Lexington 1972); and 'Female Emancipation, Birth Control and Fertility', in *American Historical Review*, LXXVIII (1973). Although there are considerable suspicions that practices about registering bastardy may have changed, Professor Shorter's evidence seems fairly convincing; his explanations, however, are not.

20. P.E.Razzell, 'The Evaluation of Baptism as a form of Birth Registration', in *Population Studies*, 26 (1972), pp. 130–1, 145.

21. A.L.Rowse, *Simon Forman: Sex and Society in Shakespeare's Age* (London 1974), p. 34. For reasons to believe that chastity was a fact of adolescent life in the Early Modern period, see E.Shorter, *The Making of the Modern Family*, pp. 98–104.

22. J.-L.Flandrin, 'Mariage tardif et vie sexuelle', in *Annales E.C.S.*, 27 (1972), pp. 1355–8.

23. *Letters of Humphrey Prideaux, 1674–1722*, Camden Soc., 2nd Ser., XV (1875), p. 120; F.G.Emmison, *Elizabethan Life: Morals and the Church Courts* (Chelmsford 1973), pp. 20–2, 295.

24. *Pepys' Diary*, 24–5 March 1668.

25. *Autobiography of Francis Place*, pp. xxv, 87, 88.

26. *Life, Adventures and Opinions of Colonel George Hanger* (London 1801), II, pp. 250–5; D.Defoe, *Everybody's Business is Nobody's Business*, London (1725), p. 5. The same opinion was also expressed by Saunders Welch over thirty years later in his *A Proposal to render effectual a Plan to remove the Nuisance of common Prostitutes* (London 1758). This combination of poverty and amateur status continued well into the nineteenth century (J.R. and D.J.Walkowitz, 'We are not Beasts of the Field: Prostitution and the Poor in Plymouth and Southampton under the Contagious Diseases Act', *Feminist Studies* [1973], p. 83).

27. B.de Mandeville, *A Modest Defence of Public Stews* (London 1724), pp. 2–13.

28. British Museum, Add. MSS 27825, ff. 240–4: proofs of article by Place on *Drunkenness*; B.de Mandeville, *op. cit.*, p. 22. These English explanations for the supply of prostitutes are confirmed by the more scientific investigation of Parisian prostitutes in the 1830s in J.-B.Parent-Duchatelet, *De la Prostitution dans la Ville de Paris* (Paris 1836), I, pp. 9–100.

29. *Autobiography of Francis Place*, p. 71; J.Boswell, *Life of Samuel Johnson, LLD* (Everyman ed. 1906), II, p. 252; see also J.-B.Parent-Duchatelet, *op. cit.*, I, pp. 174–82.

30. R.Paulson, *Hogarth: his Life, Art and Times* (New Haven 1971), I, p. 252.

31. W.L.Burn, *Age of Equipoise* (London 1964), p. 94; G.R.Taylor, *Sex in History* (London 1953), p. 219; C.H.Cooper, *Annals of Cambridge* (Cambridge 1845), III, pp. 571–2; Bodleian Library, MS Top. Oxon. b. 163.

32. *Memoirs of Sir Philip Francis*, ed. J.Parkes and H.Merivale (London 1867), I, pp. 399, 400.

33. E.M.Sigsworth and T.J.Wyke, 'A Study of Victorian Prostitution and Venereal Disease', in M.Vicinus, *Suffer and Be Still* (Bloomington 1972), p. 87.

34. For France, see J.Dupaquier, 'Sur la Population Française ...', in *Revue Historique*, 239 (1968), p. 71; G.Bouchard, *op. cit.*, p. 67; for New England, I owe my information to an unpublished paper by Professor Kenneth Lockridge; for England, see L.Bradley, 'An Enquiry into Seasonality in Baptisms, Marriages and Burials', in *Local Population Studies*, 4, 5 (1970); M.Massey, 'Seasonality, Some Further Thoughts', in *Local Population Studies*, 8 (1972); E.Cowgill, 'Historical Study of the Season of Birth in the

City of York, England', in *Nature*, 5028 (12 March 1966). One of the problems with this data is that the evidence is taken from baptismal records, and there is reason to think that christenings in some places tended to be delayed until the warmer season for reasons of social convenience (D.R.Mills, 'The Christening custom at Milbourn, Cambs.', in *Local Population Studies*, 11 [1973]); But this would not account for the fairly similar monthly variations found in France and America and to some extent in the few parishes that have been studied in England.

35. *Diaries of Oliver Heywood*, ed. J.H.Turner (Brighouse 1883), I, pp. 359–62; see also *op. cit.*, II, pp. 284, 294.

36. J.P.Malcolm, *Anecdotes of the Manners and Customs of London in the Eighteenth Century* (London 1808), p. 119; J.Shebbeare, *Letters on the English Nation* (London 1756), I, p. 69; *Autobiography of Francis Place*, pp. 45, 51, 58; as late as 1857 there were still complaints that 'through the windows of a great number of shops, principally tobacco shops in the populous quarters, the most licentious and exciting pictures are exposed to view'. (R.Knox, *The Greatest of our Social Evils* (London 1857), p. 97, quoted in M.Vicinus, *Suffer and Be Still*, p. 84.)

37. British Museum, Add. MSS. 27825 ff. 143–54.

38. *Autobiography of Thomas Wythorne*, ed. J.Osborn (Oxford 1961), p. 192.

39. R.North, *Autobiography*, ed. A.Jessop (London 1887), p. 10.

40. J.T.Noonan, *Contraception* (Cambridge, Mass. 1966), pp. 307–8, 320–1, 328–9.

41. See *upra*, ch. 4, section 4, ii; J.Taylor, *Holy Living* in *Works*, ed. R.Heber (London 1847), III, p. 63; J.Milton, *The Doctrine and Discipline of Divorce* in *Works* (New York 1931), III, pp. 391, 394.

42. Laurence Claxton [Clarkson], *The Lost Sheep Found* (London 1660), pp. 22–35.

43. C.Hill, *The World Turned Upside Down* (London 1972), pp. 164, 167, 180, 182, 254; G.E.Aylmer, *The State's Servants* (London 1973), p. 307.

44. J.Dryden, *Absolom and Achitophel* (1681), lines 1–6; A.Leger, *Wesley's Last Love* (London 1910), p. 117.

45. See *supra*, ch. 1, section 4, iv.

46. F.G.Emmison, *op. cit.*, pp. 3, 144; R.A.Marchant, *The Church under the Law, 1560–1640* (Cambridge 1969), p. 137.

47. P.Laslett, *The World We Have Lost*, p. 150.

48. C.Tietze, 'Probability of Pregnancy resulting from a single Act of Unprotected Coitus', in *Fertility and Sterility*, 11 (1960); I owe this reference to Professor Charles Westoff.

49. D.S.Smith, 'Premarital Pregnancy in America', *loc. cit.*, p. 555.

50. E.A.Wrigley, 'Clandestine Marriage in Tetbury in the late Seventeenth Century', in *Local Population Studies*, 10 (1973), p. 15; see also *ibid.*, 11 (1973), p. 43.

51. H.R.Styles, *op. cit.*, p. 55.

52. W.Bingley, *op. cit.*, pp. 282–3; cf. A.Anderson, *Family Structure in Nineteenth Century Lancashire* (Cambridge 1971), p. 88.

53. U.R.Q.Henriques, 'Bastardy and the New Poor Law', in *Past and Present*, 37 (1967), pp. 104–6; *Poems of George Crabbe*, ed. A.W.Ward (Cambridge 1907), I, p. 184; *Report of the Commissioners of Enquiry into South Wales, Parliamentary Papers*, 1844, *Reports from Commissioners*, XVI, p. 81; *Memoirs of the Forty-Five First Years of the Life of James Lackington* (London 1795), pp. 133–4.

54. *Episcopal Visitation Book for the Archdeaconry of Buckingham, Bucks. Rec. Soc.*, VII

(1947), p. xii; I.Pinchbeck and M.Hewitt, *Children in English Society* (London 1959), I, pp. 214–15.

55. R.A.Marchant, *op. cit.*, tables 31, 32, pp. 215, 219.

56. *North Country Diaries*, II, Surtees Soc., 124 (1914), p. 33.

57. E.Morgan, *The Puritan Family* (New York 1966). p. 41; *Diary of Samuel Sewall, 1674–1729*, ed. M.H.Thomas (New York 1973), II, p. 705.

58. *Middlesex County Records*, ed. J.C.Jeaffreson (London 1888), III, pp. xvii, 252, 283–91; G.May, *Social Control of Sex Expression* (London 1930), pp. 152–5.

59. D.W.R.Bahlman, *The Moral Revolution of 1688* (New Haven 1957), p. 29; P.Hair, *Before the Bawdy Court*, pp. 25, 71, 85, 79, 180, 23; I.Pinchbeck and M.Hewitt, *op. cit.*, I, pp. 206–9.

60. P.Hair, *op. cit.*, pp. 58, 49, 63, 66, 102, 110, 158, 179; *Lancashire Quarter Sessions Records*, I, (1590–1606), Chetham Soc., LXXVII (1917), p. 74.

61. G.V.Portus, *Caritas Anglicana: An Historical Enquiry into the Religious Societies, 1678–1740* (London 1912), pp. 59, 77, 254; L.Radzinowicz, *History of English Criminal Law and its Administration* (London 1956), II, pp. 2–13, 431. J.P.Malcolm, *op. cit.*, pp. 62, 121.

62. W.B.Whitaker, *The Eighteenth Century English Sunday* (London 1940), p. 65.

63. *The Guardian* (London 1713), CV; *Diaries of Oliver Heywood*, III, p. 89; *Warwick County Records, Quarter Sessions Order Books*, ed. S.C.Ratcliffe and H.C.Johnson (Warwick 1939), IV, pp. 173, 190, 276, 293; *Catalogue of Political and Personal Satires in the British Museum*, no. 2261.

64. D.F.Flaherty, 'Law and the Enforcement of Morals in Early America', in *Perspectives in American History*, V (1971), pp. 245–53; F.Oberholzer, *op. cit.*, ch. XV.

65. The evidence for the discrepancy is to be found in E.Shorter, *op. cit.*, *American Historical Review*, LXXVIII (1973), pp. 636–40. The discrepancy is ignored by Shorter, but stressed by P.Goubert, 'Legitimate Fecundity . . .', in *Daedalus* (Spring 1968), p. 594; J.Houdaille, 'La Population de Remmesweiler en Sarre au XVIIIe et XIXe siècles', in *Population*, XXV (1970), p. 1184; J.-C.Giacchetti and M.Tyvaert, 'Argenteuil (1740–1790)', in *Annales de Démographie Historique* (1969), p. 43; A.Croix, 'La Démographie du Pays Nantais au XVIe siècle', *loc. cit.* (1967), p. 72; Y.Blayo and L.Henry, 'Données Démographiques...', *loc. cit.* 1967, p. 106; L.Henry, 'Fécondité des mariages dans le quart Sud-Ouest de la France', in *Annales E.C.S.*, 27 (1972), p. 998.

66. *Bletchley Diary of the Rev. W.Cole*, p. 23; [H.More], *Thoughts on the Importance of the Manners of the Great* (London 1788), pp. 77, 79, 112–13.

67. D.G.Berger and M.G.Wenger, 'The Ideology of Virginity', in *Journal of Marriage and the Family*, 35 (1973), pp. 667–8; J.Boswell, *Journal of a Tour of the Hebrides* (London 1785), p. 250.

68. W.Reich, *Mass Psychology of Fascism* (New York 1970), pp. 52–6, 104–6, 146, 168.

69. R.E.Jones, 'Population and Agrarian Change in an Eighteenth Century Shropshire Parish', in *Local Population Studies*, 1 (1968), pp. 10, 19.

70. B.M., Add. MSS, 27825 (proofs of essay on *Drunkenness*, pp. 1–11). For solidarity with comrades in the shop, witness the successful appeals of condemned felons to their mates to save their bodies from dissection by the surgeons after execution (P.Linebaugh, 'The Tyburn Riot against the Surgeons', in D.Hay *et al*, *Albion's Fatal Tree* (New York 1976), pp. 82–5).

71. R.Braun, 'The Impact of Cottage Industry on an Agricultural Population', in *The Rise of Capitalism*, ed. D.Landes, pp. 60–1; P.Caspard, 'Conceptions prénuptiales et Développement du Capitalisme dans la Principauté de Neuchâtel (1678–1820)', in *Annales E.C.S.*, 29 (1974); No such study has yet been carried out for England.

72. P.Caspard, *op. cit.*, p. 1001.

73. R.North, *Discourse of the Poor* (written c. 1660–88) (London 1753).

74. P.Laslett and K.Oosterveen, *op. cit.*, pp. 282–3. I owe this quotation from the Court Book of Bridewell Hospital to Dr A.L.Beier.

75. T.Bernard, *Pleasure and Pain*, ed. J.B.Blake (London 1930), p. 57. For statistics about mortality in foundling hospitals, see *supra*, ch. 9, section 2, vi.

76. *Diary of Thomas Turner*, pp. 3–4, 7, 9, 20, 28–33, 40, 42, 44, 57, 59, 65, 72, 77, 79–80, 81.

77. R.W.Malcolmson, *Popular Recreations in English Society, 1700–1850* (Cambridge 1973), pp. 77–9, 95, 97–8, 101.

78. E.Shorter, *op. cit.*, in *The Family in History*, ed. T.K.Rabb and R.I.Rotberg (compare graphs 1 and 3 with graphs 2, 4, and 5, on p. 77).

79. L.A.Tilly, J.W.Scott, and M.Cohen, 'Women's Work and European Fertility Patterns', in *Journal of Interdisciplinary History*, VI (3) (1976). My interpretation agrees with theirs in rejecting the romantic and a-historical claims of Professor Shorter that rising illegitimacy rates are an expression of the rise of economic individualism, taking the form of female sexual liberation. But it differs in attributing part of the cause to a change in attitude towards pre-marital sex as a result of the decline of Puritanism.

80. S.Bamford, *Early Days* (London 1849), pp. 207, 229, 293–4; P.Laslett and K.Oosterveen, *op. cit.*, p. 257.

81. J.Depauw, 'Amour illégitime et société à Nantes au XVIIIe siècle', in *Annales E.C.S.*, 27 (1972).

82. *Bletchley Diary of the Rev. William Cole*, pp. 9, 270–3, 279.

83. R.E.Frisch, 'Demographic Implications of the Biological Determinants of Female Fecundity', in *Harvard Center for Population Studies*, Research Paper no. 6 (1974).

84. P.Ariès, 'On the Origin of Contraception in France', in O. and P.Ranum, *Popular Attitudes towards Birth Control in Pre-Industrial France and England*, p. 19; A.Venard, 'Deux Contributions à l'Histoire des Pratiques Contraceptives', in *Population*, 4 (1954), pp. 683–98.

85. P.Ariès, 'An Interpretation to be used for a History of Mentalities', in O. and P.Ranum, *op. cit.*, pp. 116–21. My own interpretation of this development does not exactly follow that of Ariès, though it is deeply indebted to his insights.

86. W.Acton, *The Functions and Disorders of the Reproductive System* (London 1858), pp. 207, 200, 129.

87. C.G.Pearce, 'Expanding Families', in *Local Population Studies*, 10 (1973), pp. 31–2; A.Parent-Duchatelet, *op. cit.*, pp. 73–5, 93–4.

88. E.Shorter, *op. cit.*, *American Historical Review*, LXXVIII (1973). p. 616; E.Shorter, 'Illegitimacy, Sexual Revolution, and Social Change in Modern Europe', in *Journal of Interdisciplinary History*, II, pp. 245–6, 252–3.

89. *Autobiography of Francis Place*, pp. 73, 81–2.

90. *The World*, 19 (10 May 1753), p. 114.

CHAPTER 13   FACTS, INTERPRETATIONS AND POST-1800 DEVELOPMENTS

1. F.Engels, *The Origins of the Family, Private Property and the State* (New York 1979), pp. 61, 66, 81–2; The same false theory was adopted by A.Clark, *Working Life of Women in the Seventeenth Century* (London 1919), and by I.Pinchbeck, *Women Workers and the Industrial Revolution, 1750–1850* (London 1930).

2. R.Nisbet, *The Sociological Tradition* (New York 1966); see also H.-U.Wehler, *Modernizierungstheorie und Geschichte* (Göttingen 1975).

3. F.Tönnies, *Community and Society* (East Lansing 1957).

4. F.Engels, *op. cit.*

5. The main exponents of the notion that the family is a variable dependent on the occupational structure are: T.Parsons, 'Social Structure of the Family', in *The Family: its Function and its Destiny*, ed. R.N.Anshen (New York 1959), pp. 260–8; T.Parsons and R.F.Bales, *Family, Socialization and the Interaction Process* (New York 1965), ch. I; a more nuanced and sophisticated view, based on concrete evidence, is provided by N.Smelser, 'The Family and Industrialization', in *Journal of Social History*, I (1967); and *Social Change and the Industrial Revolution* (Chicago 1959), pp. 180–224.

6. F.Engels, *op. cit.*, pp. 81–2; J.W.Scott and L.A.Tilly, 'Women's Work and the Family in Nineteenth Century Europe', in *Comparative Studies in Society and History*, XVII (1975); L.A.Tilly, J.W.Scott and M.Cohen, 'Women's Work and European Fertility Patterns', in *Journal of Interdisciplinary History*, VI(3) (1976), pp. 457–63; E.Richards, 'Women in the British Economy since about 1700: an Interpretation', in *History*, 59 (1974).

7. E.Royston Pike, *Human Documents of the Industrial Revolution in Britain* (London 1966), p. 236.

8. N.McKendrick, 'Home Demand and Economic Growth: a new View of the Role of Women and Children in the Industrial Revolution', in N.McKendrick, *Historical Perspectives* (London 1974), pp. 167–71; I do not agree with Dr McKendrick's view of the productive role of married women.

9. M.Anderson, *Family Structure in Nineteenth Century Lancashire* (Cambridge 1971); M.Young and P.Willmott, *Family and Kinship in East London* (London 1957); See also M.B.Sussman, 'The isolated Nuclear Family: Fact or Fiction?', in *Social Problems*, 6 (1959); M.B.Sussman and L.Burchinal, 'Kin Family Network: unheralded Structure in current Conceptualizations of Family Functioning', in *Marriage and Family Living*, 24 (1962); E.Litwak, 'Occupational Mobility and Extended Family Cohesion', and 'Geographical Mobility and Extended Family Cohesion', in *American Sociological Review*, 25 (1960); T.Harevin, 'Family Time and Industrial Time: Family and Work in a Planned Corporation Town 1900–1924', in *Journal of Urban History*, I (1975); J.Scott and L.Tilly, *op. cit.*

10. F.Lautman, 'Différences ou Changement dans l'Organisation Familiale', in *Annales E.C.S.*, 27 (1973), p. 1191.

11. W.J.Goode, 'Industrialization and the Family', in *Industrialization and Society*, ed. B.F.Hoselitz and W.E.Moore (Paris 1963); W.J.Goode, *World Revolution and Family Patterns*, New York (1963), ch. I; S.Greenfield, 'Industrialization and the Family in Sociological Theory', in *American Journal of Sociology*, 67 (1961); F.F.Furstenberg, 'Industrialization and the American Family', in *American Sociological Review*, XXXI

(1966); H.R.Lanz *et al.*, 'Pre-industrial Patterns in the Colonial Family in America: a Content Analysis of Colonial Magazines', *loc. cit.*, XXXIII (1968); H.R.Lanz *et al.*, 'The Pre-Industrial Family in America: a further Examination of Colonial Magazines', *loc. cit.*, XXXIX (1973). I am indebted to Professor W.J.Goode for a very helpful letter on this subject.

12. A.de Tocqueville, *Democracy in America*, ed. P.Bradley (New York 1945), II, pp. 202–7.
13. L.Radzinowicz, *History of English Criminal Law and its Administration* (London 1956), III, pp. 488–506; G.V.Portus, *Caritas Anglicana* (London 1912), pp. 200–14.
14. *Edinburgh Review*, 13 (1809), p. 342.
15. W.L.Burn, *Age of Equipoise* (London 1964), pp. 246, 248.
16. E.E.Kellett, *Religion and Life in the Early Victorian Era* (London 1938), p. 69.
17. Mary Wollstonecraft, *A Vindication of the Rights of Woman* (Everyman ed. London 1970).
18. Anon., *The English Matron* (London 1846), pp. 17, 23–8; F.Sandford, *Woman in her Social and Domestic Character* (London 1831), p. 13; W.L.Burn, *op. cit.*, p. 249.
19. M.J.Quinlan, *Victorian Prelude* (New York 1941), pp. 148–53.
20. E.E.Kellett, *As I Remember* (London 1936), p. 232.
21. E.Eden, *The Semi-Attached Couple* (1860) (London 1947), p. 57. In this novel Lord Teviot calls his wife 'Helen' but she calls him 'Teviot'; M.J.Quinlan, *op. cit.*, p. 265.
22. H.More, *Strictures on the modern System of female Education*, in *Works* (New York 1835), VI, p. 36, quoted in L.deMause, *op. cit.*, p. 421). *History of Childhood* (New York 1974), p. 421.
23. *The Gospel Magazine or Spiritual Library*, V (1770), pp. 583, 586, 621, 622, 623; Professor T.Laqueur kindly drew my attention to this source.
24. P.Robertson, 'The Home as a Nest', in L.deMause, *op. cit.*, pp. 415–18, 423, 425; G.R.Taylor, *Sex in History* (London 1953), p. 311; W.L.Burn, *op. cit.*, p. 249; P.Robertson in L.deMause, *op. cit.*, pp. 423, 425; A.Harrison, *Frederic Harrison: Thoughts and Memories* (London 1926), pp. 46–9.
25. *Memoirs of a Highland Lady*, ed. Lady Strachey (London 1898), pp. 56–9, 85, 343, 292–6.
26. P.Coveny, *The Image of Childhood* (London 1967), p. 302.
27. M.S.Hartman, 'Child-abuse and Self-abuse: two Victorian Cases', in *History of Childhood Quarterly*, II (1974), pp. 240–1; see also R.D.Anderson, 'French views of the English Public Schools', in *History of Education*, II (1973), p. 166.
28. A.J.C.Hare, *The Years with Mother* (London 1952), pp. 19–20, 25–7, 31, 43–4, 61. For other descriptions of pious Victorian families at their perhaps untypical worst, see Edmund Gosse, *Father and Son* (London 1907), and Samuel Butler's fictional *The Way of All Flesh* (1903).
29. J.Gathorne-Hardy, *The Rise and Fall of the British Nanny* (London 1972).
30. *Lord William Russell and his Wife 1815–46*, ed. G.Blakiston (London 1972), pp. 75–6; F.Bamford, *Rise of the Public Schools* (London 1967), pp. 66–7.
31. L.C.Jones, *Clubs of the Georgian Rakes* (New York 1942), *passim*.
32. The best illustration of this trend in the Colleges is to be found in Trinity College, Oxford, MSS, *Liber Decani*, vol. I, and Junior Bursar's Order Book (I am grateful to Mr J.P.Cooper for drawing my attention to these documents); For the drive against prostitutes in Oxford, see Bodleian Library, MS Top. Oxon, e 242; b 163.

33. *Thraliana*, ed. K.C.Balderston (Oxford 1942), I, p. 379; M.J.Quinlan, *op. cit.*, pp. 262, 264; Earl of Bessborough, *Lady Bessborough and her Family Circle* (London 1940), p. 184.

34. K.Fitzpatrick, *Lady Henry Somerset* (London 1923), p. 96 (quoted in W.L.Burn, *op. cit.*, p. 311).

35. M.J.Quinlan, *op. cit.*, pp. 202–12, 218–21, 235; *Memorials of the Thackeray Family*, ed. J.T.Pryme and A.Bayne (London 1879), p. 181; For a Rowlandson drawing of mixed bathing at Bath in the eighteenth century, see E.J.Climenson, *Elizabeth Montagu, Queen of the Bluestockings* (London 1906), II, p. 60; *Autobiography of Francis Place*, ed. M.Thale (Cambridge 1972), p. 56.

36. M.J.Quinlan, *op. cit.*, pp. 143–5, 155, 159; *The Lady's Monthly Museum*, I (1798), p. 435.

37. *Miss Weeton's Journal of a Governess*, ed. J.J.Bagley (Newton Abbot 1969), II, p. 59; W.Cobbett, *Advice to Young Men* (1829), pp. 196–7.

38. Anon., *The English Matron*, pp. 133–5.

39. W.Acton, *Functions and Disorders of the Reproductive System*, 4th ed. (London 1865), pp. 112–13; J.S.Mill, *The Subjection of Women* (Everyman ed. 1970), p. 282; N.G.Hale, *Freud and the Americans: The Beginnings of Psychoanalysis in the United States 1876–1917* (New York 1971), pp. 39–40; A.D.Wood, ' "The Fashionable Diseases": Women's Complaints and their Treatment in Nineteenth Century America', in *Journal of Interdisciplinary History*, IV (1973); B.Barker-Benfield, 'The Spermatic Economy: a Nineteenth Century View of Sexuality', in *Feminist Studies*, I (1972); cf: P.T.Cominos, 'Innocent Femina Sensualis in Unconscious Conflict', in M.Vicinus, *Suffer and be Still* (Bloomington 1972).

40. C.N.Degler, 'What ought to be and What was: Women's Sexuality in the Nineteenth Century', in *American Historical Review* 79, (5) (1974), pp. 1469–72. Professor Degler's evidence about what American women really felt, as opposed to what they were supposed to feel, seems very ambiguous. Only a little more than half of his 45 sample women in the late nineteenth century thought that sex was a pleasure to both parties, two out of three still thought that the prime purpose of the sexual act was procreation, and only one out of three always or usually achieved orgasm (pp. 1484, 1486).

41. M.Ryan, *The Philosophy of Marriage* (London 1839) (quoted in M.M.Hunt, *The Natural History of Love* [New York 1959], p. 319); Mrs Ellis, *The Daughters of England* (London 1845), p. 73, quoted in M.Vicinus, *op. cit.*, p. x; W.Acton, *Prostitution* (London 1857), ed. P.Fryer (London 1968), pp. 33, 38; S.Marcus, *The Other Victorians* (London 1964), ch. III, IV, VII. In view of its extremely limited Victorian audience, the social significance of this pornography is being exaggerated.

42. A.Comfort, *The Anxiety-Makers* (London 1967), p. 58; W.Dwyer, *What Everyone Knew about Sex* (Princeton 1972), pp. 54–7, 86; G.R.Taylor, *op. cit.*, p. 210.

43. W.Young, *Eros Denied* (London 1964), pp. 200–1; E.H.Hare, 'Masturbatory Insanity: the History of an Idea', in *Journal of Mental Science*, CVIII (1962); R.A.Spitz, 'Authority and Masturbation. Some Remarks on a Bibliographical Investigation', in *Psychoanalytical Quarterly*, XXI (1952); R.P.Neuman, 'Masturbation, Madness and the Modern Concepts of Childhood and Adolescence', in *Journal of Social History*, 8 (1975); S.Kern, *Anatomy and Destiny* (Indianapolis 1975), pp. 101–2, 120–2; B.Barker-Benfield, *op. cit.*, pp. 48–9; R.H.Macdonald, 'The frightful Consequences of Onanism: Notes on the History of a Delusion', in *Journal of the History of Ideas*, XXVIII (1967);

C.E.Rosenberg, 'Sexuality, Class and Role in Nineteenth Century America', in *American Quarterly* (1973), pp. 134–5; A.Comfort, *op. cit.*, ch. 3; W.Acton, *The Functions and Disorders of the Reproductive System* (London, 2nd ed. 1858), p. 56.

44. M.J.Quinlan, *op. cit.*, pp. 98–100, 119; *Remarkable Passages in the Life of William Kiffin*, ed. W.Orme (London 1823), p. vi.

45. S.Marcus, *op. cit.*, pp. 23–5; P.Cominos, 'Late Victorian Sexual Respectability and the Social System', in *International Review of Social History*, VIII (1963), pp. 10–31; C.E.Rosenberg, 'Sexuality, Class and Role in Nineteenth Century America', in *American Quarterly* (1973), pp. 135–6; B.Barker-Benfield, *op. cit.*, *Feminist Studies*, I (1) (1972).

46. G.R.Taylor, *op. cit.*, p. 12.

47. S.Kern, 'Explosive Intimacy: Psychodynamics of the Victorian Family', in *History of Childhood Quarterly*, I (1974).

48. One model of the transformation of the working-class family in the nineteenth century is set out in E.Shorter, *The Making of the Modern Family* (New York 1975), ch. VII; a much more plausible model is to be found in L.A.Tilly, J.W.Scott and M.Cohen, 'Women's Work and European Fertility Patterns', in *Journal of Interdisciplinary History*, VI (3) (1976), pp. 470–6.

49. For two very simplistic linear models of the evolution of the female sex role in history, see J.Z.Giele, 'Centuries of Womanhood: an Evolutionary Perspective on the Feminine Role', in *Women's Studies*, I (1972); R.Collins, 'A Conflict Theory of Sexual Stratification', in *Social Problems*, XIX (1971). For an even more simplistic linear model of the evolution of child-rearing, see L.deMause, *op. cit.*, 'The Evolution of Childhood'.

50. P.E.Slater, *Earthwalk* (New York 1974), p. 49.

51. *Ibid.*, p. 4.

52. *Bletchley Diary of the Rev. William Cole*, ed. F.G.Stokes (London 1931), p. 300 n. 1.

53. For some theoretical analyses of this problem, see R.F.Bales, *Personality and Interpersonal Behavior* (New York 1970); P.E.Slater, *Microcosm: Structural, Psychological and Religious Evolution in Groups* (New York 1966).

54. A.de Tocqueville, *op. cit.*, II, p. 205 (Bk II, ch. 8).

Bibliography

This bibliography includes only materials relating to England, and which were found to contain useful information. A number of items span several categories, and their placement is inevitably a little arbitrary.

I. PRIMARY MATERIALS

1. Moral and Medical Tracts

Anon., *The Children's Petition, or modest Remonstrance of that intolerable Grievance our Youth lie under in the accustomed Severity of School Discipline in the Nation*, London, 1669

Anon., *The English Matron*, London, 1846

Anon., *An Essay on the Happiness and Advantages of a Well-ordered Family*, London, 1794

Anon., *Onania, or the heinous Sin of Self-pollution, and all its frightful Consequences in both Sexes considered*, London, c. 1710

Anon., *Reflections on Marriage*, London, 1703

Acton, W., *A Complete Practical Treatise on Venereal Diseases*, London, 1841

Acton, W., *The Functions and Disorders of the Reproductive System*, London, 1858, 1865

Acton, W., *Prostitution* (1857), ed. P.Fryer, London, 1968

Allestree, R., *The Whole Duty of Man*, London, 1663

Andrews, J., *Remarks on the French and English Ladies*, Dublin, 1783

Ascham, R., *The Scholemaster*, in *English Works*, ed. Wright, W.A., Cambridge, 1904

Astell, M., *Reflections on Marriage* (1706), London, 1730

Astell, M., *A Serious Proposal to the Ladies* (1694), New York, 1970

Aubrey, J., *Aubrey on Education*, ed. Stephens, J.E., London, 1972

Bacon, F., *Essays* (Of Love), 1625 (revised ed.)

Batty, B., *The Christian Man's Closet*, London, 1581

Baxter, R., *Practical Works*, ed. Orme, W., London, 1830

Behn, A., *The Ten Pleasures of Marriage*, ed. Harvey, J., London, 1923

Buchan, W., *Domestic Medicine* (1769), London, 1774

Bunyan, J., *A Few Sighs from Hell*, in *Complete Works*, ed. Offer, G., Glasgow, 1853

Cadogan, W., *Essay upon the Nursing and the Management of Children*, London, 1748

Cawdrey, R., *A Godlye Form of Household Government*, amended by Cleaver, R. and Dod, J., London, 1614

Chudleigh, M., *The Ladies Defence*, London, 1701

Cleaver, J. and Dod, R., see Cawdrey, R.

Cobbet, T., *A fruitful and useful Discourse touching on the Honour due from Children to Parents, and the Duty of Parents towards their Children*, London, 1656

Cobbett, W., *Advice to Young Men* (1829), ed. Morley, H., London, 1887

Cogan, T., *The Haven of Health*, London, 1596

Costeker, R.L., *The Fine Gentleman, or the Complete Education of a Young Noblemen*, London, 1732

Croke, C., *Fortune's Uncertainty or Youth's Unconstancy* (1667), Oxford, 1959

Crosse, R., *The Lover, or Nuptial Love*, London, 1638

Defoe, D., *Compleat English Gentleman* (1729), ed. Bülbring, K.D.,

London, 1890

Defoe, D., *Conjugal Lewdness, or Matrimonial Whoredom*, London, 1727

Defoe, D., *Essay upon Projects*, London, 1697

[Defoe, D.] *Everybody's Business is Nobody's Business*, London, 1725

Defoe, D., *The Family Instructor*, London, 1712

Defoe, D., *Some Considerations upon Streetwalkers*, London, n.d.

de Mandeville, B., *A Modest Defence of Public Stews*, London, 1724

Edgeworth, M. and R.L., *Practical Education*, London, 1798

Elyot, T., *The Book named the Governor* (1531), ed. Lehmberg, S.E., London, 1962

Elyot, T., *The Castle of Health* (1534), London, 1610

Fleetwood, W., *The Relative Duties of Parents and Children, Husbands and Wives, Masters and Servants* (1705), London, 1722

Fordyce, D., *Dialogues concerning Education*, London, 1745

Gailhard, J., *The Compleat Gentleman*, London, 1678

Gisborne, T., *An Enquiry into the Duties of the Female Sex*, London, 1797

Gouge, W., *Of Domesticall Duties*, London, 1622

Goulart, S., *The Wise Vieillard or Old Man*, London, 1621

Gregory, J., *A Father's Legacy to his Daughters* (1762), London, 1774

Grose, F., *A Guide to Health, Beauty, Riches and Honour*, London, 1796

Guazzo, S., *Civile Conversation*, trans. Pettie, G., London, 1586

Halifax, Marquess of, *The Lady's New Year's Gift, or Advice to a Daughter*, in Foxcroft, H.C., *Life and Letters of George Savile Marquis of Halifax*, London, 1898, vol. II.

Hanway, J., *An earnest Appeal for Mercy to the Children of the Poor*, London, 1766

[Hayley, W.] *A Philosophical, Historical and Moral Essay on Old Maids*, London, 1785

Hudson, J.C., *The Parent's Handbook*, London, 1842

Janeway, J., *A Token for Children*, London, 1676

Law, W., *A Serious Call to a Devout and Holy Life*, London, 1729

Locke, J., *The Educational Writings of John Locke*, ed. Axtell, J., Cambridge, 1968

Makin, B., *An Essay to revive the ancient Education of Gentlewomen in Religion, Manners, Arts and Tongues*, London, 1673

Mather, C., *Bonifacius: an Essay upon the Good*, ed. Levin, D., Cambridge, Mass., 1966

Mauriceau, A.M., *The Married Woman's Private Medical Companion*, New York, 1847

Mill, J.S., *The Subjection of Women* (Everyman ed.), London, 1929, 1970

Milton, J., *Complete Prose Works of John Milton*, New Haven, 1953

More, H., *Strictures on the Modern System of Female Education*, London, 1799

[More, H.] *Thoughts on the Importance of the Manners of the Great to general Society*, London, 1788

Mulcaster, R., *Educational Writings of Richard Mulcaster*, ed. Oliphant, J., Glasgow, 1903

Nelson, J., *An Essay on the Government of Children*, London, 1763

Norris, J., *Spiritual Counsel: or a Father's Advice to his Children*, London, 1701

North, Dudley Lord, *A Forest of Varieties*, London, 1645

Northumberland, Earl of, *Advice to his Son, by Henry Percy Earl of Northumberland*, ed. Harrison, G.B., London, 1930

Osborne, F., *Advice to a Son*, London, 1656

Peacham, H., *The Compleat Gentleman*, London, 1622

Perkins, W., *Of Christian Oeconomie or Household Government*, in *Works*, London, 1626

'Philogamus', *The present State of Matrimony, or the real Cause of Matrimonial Infidelity*, London, 1739

Philpot, S., *An Essay on the Advantages of a Polite Education*, London, 1747

Radcliffe, M.A., *The Female Advocate, or an Attempt to recover the Rights of Women from Male Usurpation*, London, 1799

Radcliffe, M.A., *A Letter to the Women of England on the Injustices of mental Subordination*, London, 1799

Sanchez, T., *Compendium totius Tractatus de Sancto Matrimonii Sacramento*, Lyons, 1623

Sharp, J., *The Midwives Book*, London, 1671

Sheridan, T., *A Plan for Education for the Young Nobility and Gentry of Britain*, London, 1769

Sprint, J., *The Bride-Woman's Conseller*, London, 1699

Stockwood, J., *A Bartholomew Fairing for Parentes ... shewing that Children are not to marie without Consent of their Parentes*, London, 1589

Swetnam, J., *The Arraignment of lewd, idle, froward and unconstant Women*, London, 1616

Swift, J., 'A Letter to a very young Lady on her Marriage', in *Works*, ed. Scott, W., Edinburgh, 1814, vol. IX.

Tissot, S.A.A.D., *L'Onanisme: Dissertation sur les Maladies produites par la Masturbation*, Lausanne, 1764

Trenchfield, C., *A Cap of grey Hairs for a green Head*, London, 1710

Venette, N., *De la Génération de l'Homme, ou Tableau de l'Amour conjugale*, Cologne, 1716

Wakefield, P., *Reflections on the present Condition of the Female Sex, with some Suggestions for its Improvement*, London, 1797

Walker, O., *Of Education*, Oxford, 1673

Whately, W., *The Bride Bush*, London, 1617

Williams, D., *Treatise on Education*, London, 1774

Wilkes, W., *A Letter of genteel and moral Advice to a young Lady* (1740), London, 1766

Wollstonecraft, M.A., *A Vindication of the Rights of Woman* (1792) (Everyman ed.), London, 1970

Woolley, H., *The Gentlewoman's Companion*, London, 1675

Wotton, W., *Reflections on Ancient and Modern Learning*, London, 1694

2. Diaries

Baker, J., *Diary of John Baker*, ed. Yorke, P.C., London, 1931

Bee, J., *Jacob Bee's Chronicle ... 1630–1711*, Surtees Society, CXXIV, 1915

Blundell, N., *Great Diurnal of Nicholas Blundell*, I, Lancashire and Cheshire Record Society, 110, 1968

Blundell, N., *Blundell's Diary*, Liverpool, 1895

Boswell, J., *Private Papers of James Boswell*, ed. Scott, G. and Pottle, F.A., New York, 1932

Boswell's London Journal 1762–63, ed. Pottle, F.A., London, 1950

Boswell on the Grand Tour: Germany and Switzerland, 1764, ed. Brady, F., and Pottle, F.A., London, 1953

Boswell on the Grand Tour: Italy, Corsica and France, 1765–1766, ed. Brady, F. and Pottle, F.A., London, 1955

Boswell in Search of a Wife 1766–9, ed. Brady, F., and Pottle, F.A., London, 1958

Boswell for the Defence 1769–1774, ed. Wimsatt, W.K. and Pottle, F.A., New York, 1959

Boswell: the Ominous Years 1774–1776, ed. Ryscamp, C. and Pottle, F.A., New York, 1963

Boswell in Extremes 1776–1778, ed. Weiss, C.McC. and Pottle, F.A., New York, 1970

Journal of a Tour of the Hebrides, London, 1785

Boyle, R., *Lismore Papers*, 1st Series, ed. Grosart, A.B., London, 1886

Byrd, W., *Secret Diary of William Byrd of Westover 1709–12*, ed. Wright,

L.B. and Tinling, M., Richmond, 1941

William Byrd: The London Diary and other Writings 1717–21, ed. Wright, L.B. and Tinling, M., Richmond, 1958

Another Secret Diary of William Byrd of Westover 1739–41, ed. Woodfin, M.H. and Tinling, M., Richmond, 1942

Cole, W., *The Bletchley Diary of the Reverend William Cole 1765–67*, ed. Stokes, F.G., London, 1931

Douglas, S., *Diaries of Sylvester Douglas, Lord Glenbervie*, ed. Bickley, F., London, 1928

Fretwell, J., *A Family History begun by James Fretwell, Surtees Society*, LXV, 1877.

Héroard, J., *Journal de Jean Héroard sur l'Enfance et la Jeunesse de Louis XIII*, ed. Soulié, E. and de Barthélemy, E., Paris, 1868

Hickey, W., *Memoirs of William Hickey*, ed. Spencer, A., London, 1913–25

Heywood, D., *Diaries of Oliver Heywood*, ed. Turner, J.H., Brighouse, 1881–3

Hooke, R., *Diary of Robert Hooke 1672–1680*, ed. Robinson, H.W., London, 1935

Kay, R., *Diary of Richard Kay, Chetham Society*, 3rd Series, XVI, 1968.

Knyveton, J., *Diary of a Surgeon in the Year 1750–51*, ed. Gray, T., New York, 1937

Mather, C., *Diary of Cotton Mather, Massachusetts Historical Collections*, 7th Series, VII–VIII, 1912

Munby, L., *Munby, Man of two Worlds*, ed. Hudson, D., London, 1972

Neville, S., *Diary of Sylas Neville 1767–1788*, ed. Cozens-Hardy, B., London, 1950

Pepys, S., *Diary of Samuel Pepys*, ed. Latham, R.B. and Matthews, W., London, 1970–6

Powys, P.L., *Passages from the Diaries of Mrs Philip Lybbe Powys 1756–1808*, ed. Climenson, E.J., London, 1899

Ryder, D., *Diary of Dudley Ryder 1715–16*, ed. Matthews, W., London, 1939

Sewall, S., *Diary of Samuel Sewall 1674–1729*, ed. Thomas, M.H., New York, 1973

Skinner, J., *Diary of a Somerset Rector 1803–34: John Skinner*, ed. Coombs, H. and P., Bath, 1971

Slingsby, H., *Diary of Sir Henry Slingsby*, ed. Parsons, D., London, 1836

Stedman, J.G., *Journal of J.G.Stedman 1744–1797*, ed. Thompson, S., London, 1962

Thrale, H.L., *Thraliana*, ed. Balderston, K.C., Oxford, 1942–51
Children's Book (MS owned by Mrs Donald Hyde)
Thomlinson, J., *Diary of the Rev. John Thomlinson, Surtees Society* CXVIII, 1910
Turner, T., *Diary of Thomas Turner of East Hoathly, 1754–65*, ed. Turner, F.M., London, 1925
Weeton, E., *Miss Weeton's Journal as a Governess*, ed. Bagley, J.J., Newton Abbot, 1969
Wesley, J., *Journal of the Rev. John Wesley*, ed. Curnock, N., London, 1909
Whalley, T.S., *Journals and Correspondence of Thomas Sedgewick Whalley*, ed. Wickham, H., London, 1863
Wood, A., *Life and Times of Anthony Wood*, II, ed. Clark, A., *Oxford Historical Society*, XXI, 1892.

3. Autobiographies

Aikin, L., *Memoirs and Letters of the late Lucy Aikin*, ed. Le Breton, P.H., London, 1864
Angelo, H.C.W., *Reminiscences of H.W.C.Angelo*, ed. Grego, J., London, 1904
Ashmole, E., *Autobiographical and Historical Notes of Elias Ashmole*, ed. Josten, C.H., Oxford, 1966, Vol. II
Bamford, S., *Early Days*, London, 1849
Baxter, R., *Reliquiae Baxterianae*, ed. Silvester, M., London, 1696
Beecher, L., *Autobiography of Lyman Beecher*, ed. Cross, B.M., Cambridge, Mass., 1961
Bernard, T., *Pleasure and Pain*, ed. Baker, J.B., London, 1930
Brasbridge, J., *The Fruits of Experience*, London, 1824
Burnet, G., *Burnet's History of his own Time: Supplement*, ed. Foxcroft, H.C., Oxford, 1902
Blundell, W., *Crosby Records, Chetham Society*, 2nd Series, XII, 1887
Cameron, L.L., *Life of Mrs [Lucy Letitia] Cameron*, London, 1862
Cappe, C., *Memoirs of her Life, by Mrs Catherine Cappe*, London, 1822
Carew, P., *Sir Peter Carew, his Life and Times*, ed. Maclean, J., London, 1857
Carter, E., *Memoirs of the Life of Mrs Elizabeth Carter*, ed. Pennington, M., London, 1808
Charke, C., *Narrative of the Life of Mrs Charlotte Charke*, London, 1755
Charlton, B., *Recollections of a Northumbrian Lady 1815–66*, ed. Charlton, L.E.O., London, 1949

Cibber, C., *An Apology for the Life of Mr Colley Cibber*, ed. Lowe, R., London, 1888

Claxton [Clarkson], R., *The lost Sheep found*, London, 1660

Cumberland, R., *Memoirs of Richard Cumberland*, London, 1806

Delany, M., *Autobiography and Correspondence of Mary Granville, Mrs Delany*, ed. Lady Llandover, London, 1861

D'Ewes, S., *Autobiography and Correspondence of Sir Simonds D'Ewes*, ed. Halliwell, J.O., London, 1845

Digby, K., *Loose Fantasies*, ed. Gabrielli, V., Rome, 1968

Dunton, J., *Life and Errors of John Dunton*, London, 1818

Edgeworth, R.L., *Memoirs of Richard Lovell Edgeworth*, London, 1820

Ellwood, T., *A History of the Life of Thomas Ellwood*, ed. C.G.Crump, London, 1900

Fox, E., *Memoirs of Mrs Eliza Fox*, ed. Fox, F., London, 1869

Gent, T., *The Life of Mr Thomas Gent*, London, 1832

Gibbon, E., *Autobiography of the Life of Edward Gibbon, by Himself*, London, 1900

Gosse, E., *Father and Son*, London, 1907

Grant, E., *Memoirs of a Highland Lady: the Autobiography of Elizabeth Grant of Rothiemurchus*, ed. Lady Strachey, London, 1898

Guise, *Memoirs of the Family of Guise, Camden Society*, 3rd Series, XXVIII, 1917

Halkett, A., *Autobiography of Lady Anne Halkett, Camden Society*, 2nd Series, XIII, 1875.

Hanger, G., *The Life, Adventures and Opinions of Colonel George Hanger*, London, 1801

Harrison, F., *Frederic Harrison: Thoughts and Memories*, ed. Harrison, A., New York, 1927

Henry, M., *Memoirs of the Life of the Rev. Matthew Henry*, ed. Williams, J.B., London, 1865

Herbert, D., *Retrospections of Dorothea Herbert 1790–1806*, London, 1929

Herbert, E., *Autobiography of Edward Lord Herbert of Cherbury*, ed. Lee, S., London, 1907

Holcroft, T., *Life of Thomas Holcroft*, ed. Colby, E., London, 1925

[Howard, C.M.], *Reminiscences for my Children*, London, 1831

Hyde, E., *The Life of Edward Earl of Clarendon*, Oxford, 1857

Jemmat, C., *Memoirs of Mrs Catherine Jemmat*, London, 1771

Kiffin, W., *Remarkable Passages in the Life of William Kiffin*, ed. Orme, W., London, 1823

Lackington, J., *Memoirs of the Forty-Five First Years of the Life of James Lackington*, London, 1795

Lilly, W., *Mr William Lilly's History of his Life and Times from the Year 1602 to 1681*, London, 1715

Lister, J., *Autobiography of Joseph Lister of Bradford in Yorkshire*, ed. Wright, T., London, 1842

Martindale, A., *Life of Adam Martindale, Chetham Society*, 1st Series, IV, 1845

North, R., *Autobiography of Roger North*, ed. Jessop, A., London, 1887

Owen, R.D., *Threading my Way*, London, 1874

Pett, P., *Autobiography of Phineas Pett, Navy Records Society*, 51, 1918

Pilkington, L., *Memoirs of Mrs Letitia Pilkington*, Dublin, 1749

Place, F., *Autobiography of Francis Place*, ed. Thale, M., Cambridge, 1972

Radcliffe, M.A., *Memoirs of Mrs Mary Ann Radcliffe*, London, 1810

Raymond, T., *Autobiography of Thomas Raymond, Camden Society*, 3rd Series, XXVIII, 1917

Reynolds, F., *The Life and Times of Frederick Reynolds written by Himself*, London, 1826

Rich, M., *Autobiography of Mary Rich Countess of Warwick, Percy Society*, XXII, 1848

Roberts, S., *Autobiography and Select Remains of Samuel Roberts*, London, 1849

Romilly, S., *Memoirs of Sir Samuel Romilly 1753–89*, London, 1840

Savage, S., *Memoirs of the Life of Mrs Sarah Savage*, ed. Williams, J.B., London, 1829

Sherwood, *Life of Mrs Sherwood*, ed. Kelly, W., London, 1854

Sibbald, R., *Memoirs of Sir Robert Sibbald (1641–1722)*, ed. Hett, F.P., New York, 1926

Somerville, M., *Personal Recollections from early Life to old Age*, London, 1873

Somerville, T., *My own Life and Times 1741–1814*, Edinburgh, 1861

Stout, W., *Autobiography of William Stout of Lancaster*, ed. Marshal, J.D., Manchester, 1967

Thackeray, *Memorials of the Thackeray Family*, ed. Pryme, J.T. and Bayne, A., London, 1879

Thornton, A., *Autobiography of Mrs Alice Thornton, Surtees Society*, LXII, 1875.

Thrale, H.L., *Autobiography, Letters and Literary Remains of Mrs Piozzi (Thrale)*, ed. Hayward, A., London, 1861

Trelawney, E.J., *Adventures of a Younger Son*, London, 1831

Warner, R., *Literary Recollections*, London, 1830

Wentworth, W., *Wentworth Papers, 1597–1628*, ed. Cooper, J.P., *Camden Society*, 4th Series, XII, 1973

Wilson, H., *The Game of Hearts: Harriette Wilson's Memoirs*, ed. Blanch, L., New York, 1955

Wright, T., *Autobiography of Thomas Wright of Birkenshaw*, ed. Wright, T., London, 1864

Wythorne, T., *Autobiography of Thomas Wythorne*, ed. Osborn, J., Oxford, 1961

Young, A., *Autobiography of Arthur Young*, ed. Betham-Edwards, M., London, 1898

4. Correspondence

Alderley, Lady M., *The Ladies of Alderley*, ed. Mitford, N., London, 1938

Blundell, W., *Cavalier: Letters of William Blundell to his Friends*, ed. Blundell, M., London, 1933

Banks, *Letters and Papers of the Banks Family of Revesby Abbey 1704–1760*, *Lincolnshire Record Society*, 45, 1952

Boyle, R., *Lismore Papers*, 2nd Series, ed. Grosart, A.B., London, 1886

Capel, *Capel Letters 1814–17*, ed. Marquess of Anglesey, London, 1955

Chapone, H., *Posthumous Works of Mrs Hester Chapone*, London, 1808

Coke, M., *Letters and Journals of Lady Mary Coke*, ed. Home, I.A., Edinburgh, 1889–96

Cumberland, G. and R., *Cumberland Letters 1771–84*, ed. Black, C., London, 1912

Fleming, *The Flemings in Oxford*, I, *Oxford Historical Society*, XLIV, 1904

Francis, P., *Francis Letters*, ed. Francis, B. and Keary, E., New York, 1901

Hamilton, M., *Mary Hamilton at Court and Home*, ed. Anson, E. and F., London, 1925

Hays, M., *The Love Letters of Mary Hays*, ed. Wedd, A.F., London, 1925

Heber, *Dear Miss Heber*, ed. Bamford, F., London, 1936

Herbert, *Henry, Elizabeth and George 1734–1780*, ed. Henry Lord Herbert, London, 1939

Herbert, *Pembroke Papers 1780–1794*, ed. Henry Lord Herbert, London, 1950

Legh, Legh Letters (MS transcripts in Brasenose College, Oxford).

Legh, *Lyme Letters 1660–1760*, ed. Newton, E., London, 1925

Lennox, S., *Life and Letters of Lady Sarah Lennox, 1745–1826*, ed. Countess of Ilchester and Lord Stavordale, London, 1902

Montagu, E., *Elizabeth Montagu, Queen of the Bluestockings*, ed. Climenson, E.J., London, 1906

Montagu, M.W., *Letters and Works of Lady Mary Wortley Montagu*, ed. Lord Wharncliffe and Thomas, W.M., London, 1887

Osborne, D., *Letters of Dorothy Osborne to Sir William Temple 1652–54*, ed. Smith, G.C.M., Oxford, 1928

Parker, J., *The Parkers at Saltram 1769–89*, by Fletcher, R., London, 1970

Prideaux, H., *Letters of Humphrey Prideaux, Camden Society*, 2nd Series, XV, 1875

Richardson, S., *Correspondence of Samuel Richardson*, London, 1804

Russell, W., *Lord William Russell and his Wife 1815–46*, ed. Blakiston, G., London, 1972

Steele, R., *Correspondence of Richard Steele*, ed. Blanchard, R., London, 1941

Tatler, The, *New Letters to the Tatler and Spectator*, ed., Bond, R.P., Austin, 1959

Tatler, The, *Original and Genuine Letters to the Tatler and Spectator*, ed. Lillie, C., London, 1725

Verney, *Memoirs of the Verney Family during the Seventeenth Century*, ed. Verney, F.P. and M.M., London, 1907

Verney, *Verney Letters of the Eighteenth Century*, ed. Verney, Lady M., London, 1930

Wilkes, J., *Correspondence of John Wilkes and Charles Churchill*, ed. Weatherby, E.H., New York, 1954

5. Biographies and Family Histories

Aspinall-Oglander, C., *Admiral's Wife* (Mrs Boscawen), London, 1940

Aspinall-Oglander, C., *Admiral's Widow* (Mrs Boscawen), London, 1942

Aubrey, J., *Brief Lives*, ed. Dick, O.L., Ann Arbor, 1962

Aubrey, J., *Brief Lives*, ed. Powell, A., London, 1949

Baxter, R., *Richard Baxter and Margaret Charlton*, ed. Wilkinson, J.T., London, 1928

Bessborough, Earl of, *Georgiana* (Duchess of Devonshire), London, 1955

Bessborough, Earl of, *Lady Bessborough and her Family Circle*, London, 1940

Blunt, R. and Wyndham, M., *Thomas Lord Lyttelton*, London, 1936

Boswell, J., *Life of Samuel Johnson LLD* (Everyman ed.), London, 1906

Butler, J.E., *Memoir of John Grey of Dilston*, London, 1869

Cavendish, M., *Life of William Cavendish Duke of Newcastle*, ed. Firth, C.H., London, n.d.

Clifford, J.L., *Hester Lynch Piozzi (Thrale)*, Oxford, 1968

Crabbe, G., *Life of George Crabbe, by his Son*, ed. Blunden, E., London, 1947

Flexner, E., *Mary Wollstonecraft*, New York, 1972

Hamilton, A., *Memoirs of Count Grammont* (1713), ed. Scott, W., London, 1905

Hiscock, W.G., *John Evelyn and his Family Circle*, London, 1955

Holles, G., *Memorials of the Holles Family 1493–1656*, Camden Society, 3rd Series, LV, 1937

Houblon, A., *The Houblon Family*, London, 1907

Hutchinson, A., *Memoirs of the Life of Colonel Hutchinson* (Everyman ed.), London, 1906

Hyde, M., *The Thrales of Streatham Park*, Cambridge, Mass., 1977

Hyde, M., *The Impossible Friendship: Boswell and Mrs Thrale*, London, 1973

Kelch, R.A., *Newcastle: a Duke without Money*, Berkeley, 1974

Leger, A., *Wesley's Last Love*, London, 1910

Macfarlane, A., *The Family of Ralph Josselin*, Cambridge, 1970

Marshall, R.K., *The Days of Duchess Anne: Life in the Household of the Duchess of Hamilton 1656–1716*, London, 1973

Neale, J.A., *The Neales of Berkeley, Yates and Corsham*, Warrington, 1907

Newdigate-Newdegate, Lady, *Cavalier and Puritan in the Days of the Stuarts*, London, 1901

North, R., *Lives of the Norths*, London, 1890

Phillips, C.J., *History of the Sackville Family*, London, 1930

Pottle, F.A., *James Boswell: the Earlier Years 1740–69*, London, 1966

Pryme, J.T. and Bayne, A., *Memorials of the Thackeray Family*, London, 1879

Rowse, A.L., *Simon Forman: Sex and Society in Shakespeare's Age*, London, 1974

Rowsell, M.C., *The Life Story of Charlotte de la Trémouille Countess of Derby*, London, 1905

Spalding, R., *The Improbable Puritan: a Life of Bulstrode Whitelocke*, London, 1975

Stuart, D.M., *Molly Lepell, Lady Hervey*, London, 1936

Stuart, D.M., *Dearest Bess*, London, 1955

Sydenham, G.F.S., *History of the Sydenham Family*, East Molesey, 1928
Townshend, D., *Life and Letters of Mr Endymion Porter*, London, 1897
Trevelyan, G.O., *Early History of Charles James Fox*, New York, 1880
Wharton, E.R., *The Whartons of Wharton Hall*, Oxford, 1898
Wilson, J.H., *The Private Life of Mr Pepys*, New York, 1959

6. Newspapers and Magazines
The Athenian Mercury, vols. 1–10, 1691–3 (ed. Dunton, J., *et al.*)
The Bon Ton Magazine, 1792
The British Apollo, 1708
The Review, 1704–13 (ed. Defoe, D.)
The Gospel Magazine or Spiritual Library, vol. V, 1770
The Gentleman's Magazine, vols. I–XXX, 1731–60
The Guardian, 1713 (ed. Steele, R., *et al.*)
The Idler, 1759 (ed. Johnson, S.)
The Lady's Magazine or entertaining Companion for the Fair Sex, vols. I–IV,
    1770–3
The Lady's Monthly Museum, vols. I–II, 1798–9
The Matrimonial Magazine, 1793
The Morning Chronicle and Public Advertiser, 1785–6
The Sentimental Magazine, 1773–7
The Spectator, 1711–12 (ed. Addison, J., *et al.*)
The Times, 1796–7
The Tatler, 1709–11 (ed. Steele, R.)
The Whitehall Evening Post, 1785–6
The World, vols. 19–20, 1753

7. Comments and Reports of Travellers and Others
Archenholz, J. von, *A Picture of England*, London, 1797
Bingley, W., *North Wales*, London, 1804
Burton, R., *Anatomy of Melancholy* (1621), ed. Jackson, H., London, 1932
Campbell, R., *The London Tradesman*, London, 1747
de la Rochefoucauld, F., *A Frenchman in England 1784*, ed. Marchand, J.,
    Cambridge, 1933
de Blanc, J.B., *Lettres d'un Français*, The Hague, 1745
Fiennes, C., *Journeys of Celia Fiennes*, ed. Morris, C., London, 1947
La Roche, S. van, *Sophie in London 1786*, ed. Williams, C., London, 1933
Macky, J., *A Journey through England in familiar Letters*, London, 1714

Meister, J.H., *Letters written during a Residence in England*, London, 1799

Miège, G., *The New State of England*, London, 1691

Misson de Valbourg, H., *Memoirs and Observations in his Travels over England* (1697), London, 1719

[Moritz, C.P.], *Journeys of a German in England in 1782*, ed. Nettel, R., London, 1965

Oglander, J., *A Royalist's Notebook: the Commonplace Book of Sir John Oglander of Nunwell 1585–1655*, ed. Bamford, F., London, 1936

Place Manuscripts (British Museum, Additional MSS 27825–26) *A Relation ... of the Island .of England ... about the year 1500*, Camden Society, XXXVII, 1847

Pollnitz, de, *Lettres du Baron de Pollnitz*, London, 1741

Pückler-Muskau, H.L.H. von, *A Tour of England, Ireland and France 1826–29*, Philadelphia, 1883

Rye, W.B., *England as seen by Foreigners*, London, 1865

Shebbeare, J., *Letters on the English Nation*, London, 1755

Simond, L., *Journal of a Tour and Residence in Great Britain 1810–11*, London, 1817

8. Novels, Plays and Poetry

Austen, J., *Mansfield Park* (1814), ed. Chapman, R.W., Oxford, 1933

Barbauld, A.L., *Works of Ann Letitia Barbauld*, ed. Aikin, L., London, 1825

Behn, A., *Works*, ed. Summers, M., New York, 1915

Burney, F., *Evelina* (1778)

Butler, S., *The Way of All Flesh* (1903)

Chudleigh, M., *Poems on Several Occasions* (1703)

Cleland, J., *Memoirs of a Woman of Pleasure* (1749)

Crabbe, G., *The Parish Register* (1807) in *Poems of George Crabbe*, ed. Ward, A.W., Cambridge, 1907

Defoe, D., *Moll Flanders* (1721)

Defoe, D., *Roxana* (1724), ed. Jack, J., Oxford, 1964

de Mandeville, B., *The Virgin Unmask'd* (1724)

de Mandeville, B., *Wishes to a Godson, and other Miscellaneous Poems* (1712)

Eden, F., *The Semi-Attached Couple* (1860)

Edgeworth, M., *Belinda* (1801)

Etherege, G., *The Comical Revenge, or Love in a Tub* (1664)

Farquhar, G., *The Beaux' Strategem* (1707)

Fielding, H., *The History of Tom Jones* (1749)

Fielding, H., *The Modern Husband* (1732)

Fielding, S., *The Adventures of David Simple* (1744)

Garrick, D., *Lethe* in his *Dramatic Works* (1798)

Gray, T., *Poems of Gray, Collins and Goldsmith*, ed. Lonsdale, R., London, 1969

Lovelace, R., *Poems of Richard Lovelace*, ed. Wilkinson, C.H., Oxford, 1925–30

Mackenzie, H., *The Man of Feeling* (1771), ed. Miles. H., London, 1928

Marston, J., *The Dutch Courtesan* (1604)

Marston, J., *The Insatiate Countess* (1613)

Pope, A., *Essay on Man* (1733–4)

Richardson, S., *Pamela* (1740)

Richardson, S., *Clarissa Harlowe* (1748)

Rochester, Earl of, *Complete Poems of John Wilmot Earl of Rochester*, ed. Vieth, D.M., New Haven, 1968

Sedley, C., *Works* (1722)

Shadwell, T., *The Virtuoso* (1676)

Shakespeare, W., *Romeo and Juliet* (1601)
A Winter's Tale (1611)

Smith, C., *Celestina* (1791)

Smollett, T., *Roderick Random* (1748)

Steele, R., *The Tender Husband* (1705)

Vanbrugh, J., *The Provoked Wife* (1697)

Watts, I., *Divine Songs attempted in easy Language for the Use of Children* (1715), ed. Pafford, J.H.P., London, 1971

Wilkins, G., *The Miseries of Inforst Marriage* (1607)

Wilkes, J., *An Essay on Woman* (1763), ed. Hotten, J.C., London, 1871

Wilson, J.H., *Court Satires of the Restoration*, Colombus, Ohio, 1976

Wycherley, W., *The Country Wife* (1672)

Wycherley, W., *The Plain Dealer* (1677)

II. SECONDARY WORKS

1. History

Anderson, M., *Family Structure in Nineteenth Century Lancashire*, Cambridge, 1971

Anderson, M., 'The Study of Family Structure', in *Nineteenth Century Society*, ed. Wrigley, E.A., Cambridge, 1972

Ariès, P., *Centuries of Childhood*, New York, 1965

Ariès, P., *Western Attitudes towards Death*, Baltimore, 1974

Bahlman, D.W.R., *The Moral Revolution of 1688*, New Haven, 1957

Banks, J.A., *Prosperity and Parenthood*, London, 1954

Barry, F.V., *A Century of Children's Books*, London, 1922

Bayne-Powell, R., *The English Child in the Eighteenth Century*, New York, 1939

Berry, B.M., 'The first English Pediatricians and Tudor Attitudes towards Childhood', *Journal of the History of Ideas*, XXXV, 1974

Blackwood, B.C., 'Marriages of Lancashire Gentry on the Eve of the Civil War', *Genealogist's Magazine*, 16, 1970

Bond, R.P., *The Tatler : the Making of a Literary Journal*, Cambridge, 1971

Bossy, J., 'The Counter-Reformation and the People of Catholic Europe', *Past and Present*, 47, 1970

Bottrall, M., *Everyman a Phoenix. Studies in Seventeenth Century Autobiography*, London, 1958

Braun, R., 'The Impact of Cottage Industry on an Agricultural Population', in *The Rise of Capitalism*, ed. Landes, D., New York, 1966

Bremner, R.H., *Children and Youth in America*, Cambridge, Mass., 1970

Brownlow, J., *Memoranda, or Chronicles of the Foundling Hospital*, London, 1847

Burn, J.S., *The Fleet Registers*, London, 1833

Burn, W.L., *The Age of Equipoise*, London, 1964

Calhoun, A.W., *A Social History of the American Family*, New York, 1945

Camden, C., *The Elizabethan Woman*, New York, 1952

Caulfield, E., *The Infant Welfare Movement in the Eighteenth Century*, New York, 1931

Clark, A., *The Working Life of Women in the Seventeenth Century*, London, 1919

Clay, C., 'Marriage, Inheritance, and the Rise of large Estates in England, 1660–1815', *Economic History Review*, 2nd Series, XXI, 1968

Collier, F., 'The Family Economy of the Working Class in the Cotton Industry 1784–1833', *Chetham Society*, 3rd Series, XII, 1965

Cominos, P., 'Late Victorian Sexual Respectability and the Social System', *International Review of Social History*, VIII, 1963

Cominos, P., 'The innocent *Femina Sensualis* in unconscious Conflict' in Vicinus, M., *Suffer and be Still*, Bloomington, 1972

Comfort, A., *The Anxiety Makers*, London, 1967

Cott, N.F., *The Root of Bitterness*, New York, 1972

Coveny, P., *The Image of Childhood*, London, 1967

Cunnington, P. and Buck, A., *Children's Costume in England*, New York,

1965

Cutter, I. and Viets, H., *A Short History of Midwifery*, Philadelphia, 1964

Daghlian, P.B., *Essays in Eighteenth Century Biography*, Bloomington, 1968

Degler, C.N., 'What ought to be and what was: Women's Sexuality in the Nineteenth Century', *American Historical Review*, 79, 1974

Delany, M., *British Autobiography in the Seventeenth Century*, London, 1969

deMause, L., *The History of Childhood*, New York, 1974

Demos, J., *A Little Commonwealth*, New York, 1970

Ehrenpreis, I. and Halsband, R., *The Lady of Letters in the Eighteenth Century*, London, 1969

Elias, N., *La Civilisation des Moeurs*, Paris, 1973

Emmison, F.G., *Elizabethan Life: Morals and the Church Courts*, Chelmsford, 1973

Ferns, J.P., 'The Gentry of Dorset on the Eve of the Civil War', *Genealogical Magazine*, 15, 1965

Flandrin, J.-L., *Les Amours Paysannes*, Paris, 1975

Flandrin, J.-L., *Familles: Parenté, Maison, Sexualité dans l'Ancienne Société*, Paris, 1976

Forster, R. and Ranum, O. (eds.), *Biology of Man in History*, Baltimore, 1975

Foxon, D., *Libertine Literature in England 1660–1745*, London, 1965

Fraser, A., *A History of Toys*, London, 1972

Gagen, J.E., *The New Woman: her Emergence in English Drama*, New York, 1954

Gardiner, D., *English Girlhood at School*, London, 1929

Gathorne-Hardy, J., *The Rise and Fall of the British Nanny*, London, 1972

George, M.D., *London Life in the Eighteenth Century*, London, 1925

Goode, W.V., 'Industrialization and the Family', in Hoselitz, B.F. and Moore, W.E., *Industrialization and Society*, Paris, 1963

Greven, P., *Child-Rearing Concepts 1628–1861*, Itasca, 1973

Habakkuk, H.J., 'Marriage Settlements in the Eighteenth Century', *Transactions of the Royal Historical Society*, 4th Series, XXXII, 1950

Hair, P., *Before the Bawdy Court*, New York, 1972

Halkett, J., *Milton and the Idea of Matrimony*, New Haven, 1970

Haller, W. and S., 'The Puritan Art of Love', *Huntington Library Quarterly*, V, 1941–2

Hill, C., 'The Spiritualization of the Household', in his *Society and Puritanism in Pre-Revolutionary England*, London, 1964

Hill, C., 'Clarissa Harlowe and her Times', in his *Puritanism and Revolution*, London, 1958

Himes, N.E., *Medical History of Contraception*, New York, 1963

Hunt, M.M., *The Natural History of Love*, New York, 1959

Hunt, D., *Parents and Children in History*, New York, 1970

Jacobs, F.G., *A History of Doll's Houses*, London, 1954

James, M.E., *Family, Lineage and Civil Society*, Oxford, 1974

Johnson, J.T., *A Society ordained by God: Puritan Marriage Doctrine in the first Half of the Seventeenth Century*, Nashville, 1970

Jones, L.C., *Clubs of the Georgian Rakes*, New York, 1942

Kelso, R.K., *Doctrine for the Lady of the Renaissance*, Urbana, 1956

King-Hall, M., *The Story of the Nursery*, London, 1958

Kraditor, A., *Up from the Pedestal*, Chicago, 1968

Lambley, K., *The Teaching and Cultivation of the French Language in England during Tudor and Stuart Times*, Manchester, 1920

McGuigan, D.G., *A Sampler of Women's Studies*, Ann Arbor, 1973

McKendrick, N., 'Home Demand and Economic Growth: a new View of the Role of Women and Children in the Industrial Revolution', in his *Historical Perspectives: Studies in English Thought and Society in Honour of J.H.Plumb*, London, 1974

Malcolm, J.P., *Anecdotes of the Manners and Customs of London during the Eighteenth Century*, London, 1808

Malcolmson, R.W., *Popular Recreations in English Society 1700–1850*, Cambridge, 1973

May, G., *Social Control of Sex Expression*, London, 1930

Morgan, E., *The Puritan Family*, New York, 1966

Noonan, J.-T., *Contraception*, Cambridge, Mass., 1966

Pinchbeck, I. and Hewitt, M., *Children in English Society*, London, 1969–73

Plumb, J.H., 'The New World of Children in the 18th Century', *Past and Present*, 67, 1975

Plumb, J.H., *The Commercialisation of Leisure*, Reading, 1973

Portus, G.V., *Caritas Anglicana*, Oxford, 1912

Powell, C.L., *English Domestic Relations 1487–1653*, New York, 1917

Quinlan, M.J., *Victorian Prelude*, London, 1940

Rabb, T.K. and Rotberg, R.I. (eds.), *The Family in History*, New York, 1973

Ranum, O. and P. (eds.), *Popular Attitudes towards Birth Control in Pre-Industrial France and England*, New York, 1972

Rendle-Short, M. and J., *The Father of Child Care*, Bristol, 1966

Reynolds, M., *The Learned Lady in England 1650–1750*, Boston, 1920

Richards, E., 'Women in the British Economy since 1700: an Interpretation', *History*, 59, 1974

Rosenberg, C. (ed.), *The Family in History*, Philadelphia, 1975

Sangster, P., *Pity my Simplicity: the Evangelical Revival and religious Education of Children*, London, 1963

Schnucker, R.V., 'The English Puritans and Pregnancy, Delivery and Breast-feeding', *History of Childhood Quarterly*, I, 1974

Schüking, L.L., *The Puritan Family*, New York, 1970

Séjourné, P., *Aspects généraux du Roman féminin en Angleterre de 1740 à 1800*, Publications des Annales de la Faculté de Lettres, Aix-en-Provence, n.s., 52, 1966

Shinagel, M., *Daniel Defoe and Middle Class Gentility*, Cambridge, Mass., 1968

Shorter, E., *The Making of the Modern Family*, New York, 1975

Slater, M., 'The weightiest Business: Marriage in an Upper-Gentry Family in Seventeenth-Century England', *Past and Present*, 72, 1976

Smelser, N., *Social Change in the Industrial Revolution*, Chicago, 1959

Smith, D.S., 'Parental Power and Marriage Patterns: an Analysis of historical Trends in Hingham, Massachusetts', *Journal of Marriage and the Family*, 35, 1973

Smith, S.R., 'Religion and the Conception of Youth in the Seventeenth Century', *History of Childhood Quarterly*, II, 1975

Smith, S.R., 'The London Apprentices as Seventeenth Century Adolescents', *Past and Present*, 61, 1973

Sprott, S.E., *The English Debate on Suicide from Donne to Hume*, La Salle, Ill., 1961

Spufford, M., *Contrasting Communities*, Cambridge, 1974

Stearns, B.M., 'Early English Periodicals for Ladies', *Publications of the Modern Language Association*, XLVIII, 1933

Stenton, D.M., *The English Woman in History*, London, 1957

Stone, L., *The Crisis of the Aristocracy 1558–1641*, Oxford, 1965

Stone, L., *Family and Fortune*, Oxford, 1973

Styles, H.R., *Bundling: its Origins, Progress and Decline in America*, Albany, 1871

Taylor, G.R., *The Angel-Makers*, London, 1958

Taylor, G.R., *Sex in History*, London, 1953

Thomas, K.V., 'Women and the Civil War Sects', *Past and Present*, 13, 1958

Thomas, K.V., 'The Double Standard', *Journal of the History of Ideas*, XX,

1959

Thomas, D., 'The Social Origins of Marriage Partners of the British Aristocracy in the Eighteenth and Nineteenth Centuries', *Population Studies*, 26, 1972

Thompson, E.P., 'Rough Music: le Charivari anglais', *Annales E.C.S.*, XXVII, 1972

Thompson, R., *Women in Stuart England and America*, London, 1974

Tilly, L.A., Scott, J.W., and Cohen, M., 'Women's Work and the European Fertility Pattern', *Journal of Interdisciplinary History*, VI, 1976

Tomkins, J.M.S., *The Polite Marriage*, Cambridge, 1938

Trinkhaus, C. and Oberman, H.O., *The Pursuit of Holiness in late Medieval and Renaissance Religion*, Leiden, 1974

Underwood, D., *Etherege and the Seventeenth Century Comedy of Manners*, New Haven, 1957

Utter, R.P. and Needham, G.B., *Pamela's Daughters*, New York, 1936

Vicinus, M., *Suffer and be Still*, Bloomington, 1972

Watt, I., *The Rise of the Novel*, London, 1957

Waugh, M.A., 'Venereal Disease in Sixteenth Century England', *Medical History*, 17, 1973

Wright, L., *Clean and Decent*, London, 1960

Wright, L.B., *Middle Class Culture in Elizabethan England*, Chapel Hill, 1935

Young, W., *Eros denied*, London, 1964

2. Demography

Ansell, C., *On the Rates of Mortality at the early Periods of Life . . . in the Upper and Professional Classes*, London, 1874

Beaver, M.A., 'Population, Infant Mortality and Milk', *Population Studies*, XXVII, 1973

Edmonds, T.R., 'On the Mortality of Infants in England', *The Lancet*, I, 1835–6

Frisch, R., *Demographic Implications of the Biological Determinants of female Fecundity*, Harvard Center for Population Studies, Research Paper 6, 1974

Glass, D. and Eversley, D.E.C., *Population in History*, London, 1965

Hollingsworth, T.H., 'The Demography of the British Peerage', Supplement to *Population Studies*, XVIII, 1964

Laslett, P., 'Clayworth and Cogenhoe', in *Historical Essays 1600–1750*, ed. Bell, H.E. and Ollard, R.L., London, 1963

Laslett, P., *Household and Family in Past Time*, Cambridge, 1972

Laslett, P., *The World we Have Lost*, London, 1971

Laslett, P., *Family Life and illicit Love in earlier Generations*, Cambridge, 1977

Outhwaite, R.B., 'Age at Marriage in England from the late Seventeenth to the Nineteenth Centuries', *Transactions of the Royal Historical Society*, 5th Series, XXIII, 1973

Razzell, P.E., 'Population Change in Eighteenth Century England: a Reinterpretation', *Economic History Review*, 2nd Series, XVIII, 1965

Smith, D.S., 'Premarital Pregnancy in America 1640–1971', *Journal of Interdisciplinary History*, V, 1975

Wrigley, E.A., *Population and History*, London, 1969

Wrigley, E.A., 'Mortality in pre-industrial England: the Example of Colyton, Devon, over three Centuries', *Daedalus*, Spring, 1968

Wrigley, E.A., 'Family Limitation in pre-industrial England', *Economic History Review*, 2nd Series, XIX, 1966

3. Law

Alleman, G.E., *Matrimonial Law and the Materials of Restoration Comedy*, Wallingford, Pa., 1942

Anon., *The Laws Respecting Women*, London, 1772

Anon., *A new and complete Collection of the most remarkable Trials for Adultery*, London, 1780

Godolphin, J., *Repertorium Canonicum, or Abridgement of the Canon Laws of this Realm*, London, 1680

Hale, W.H., *A Series of Precedents and Proceedings from the Act Books of Ecclesiastical Courts in the Diocese of London*, London, 1847

Haw, R., *The State of Matrimony*, London, 1952

Helmholz, R.H., *Marriage Litigation in Medieval England*, Cambridge, Mass., 1974

Kenny, C.S., *The History of the Law of England as to the Effect of Marriage on Property and on the Wife's Legal Capacity*, London, 1879

McGregor, D.R., *Divorce in England*, London, 1957

Maskell, W., *Monumenta Ritualia Ecclesiae Anglicanae*, Oxford, 1882

Sayer, J., *A Vindication of the Power of Society to Annul the Marriages of Minors*, London, 1755

Stebbing, J., *A Dissertation on the Power of States to deny Civil Protection to the Marriages of Minors*, London, 1755

Swinburne, H., *A Treatise of Spousals or Marriage Contracts*, London,

1686
Watkins, O.D., *Holy Matrimony*, London, 1895

4. Theory

Adams, B.N., *Kinship in an Urban Setting*, Chicago, 1968
Anshen, H.R., *The Family: its Function and Destiny*, New York, 1959
Bales, R.F., *Personality and Interpersonal Behavior*, New York, 1970
Berger, D.G. and Wenger, M.G., 'The Ideology of Virginity', *Journal of Marriage and the Family*, 35, 1973
Berkner, L., 'The Stem Family and the Developmental Cycle of the Peasant Household: an Eighteenth Century Austrian Example', *American Historical Review*, LXXVII, 1972
Coser, R. L. (ed.), *The Family: its Structure and Function*, New York, 1964
Eibesfeldt, E., *Love and Hate*, London, 1971
Engels, F., *The Origins of the Family, Private Property and the State*, New York, 1972
Erikson, E., *Childhood and Society*, New York, 1963
Erikson, E., *Identity and the Life Cycle, Psychological Issues*, I, New York, 1959
Goode, W.J., 'Industrialization and Family Changes', in Hoselitz, B.F. and Moore, W.E. (eds), *Industrialization and Society*, Paris, 1963
Goode, W.J., 'The Theoretical Importance of Love', in R.L. Coser, *op. cit.*
Goode, W.J., *World Revolution and Family Patterns*, New York, 1963
Goody, J., 'Inheritance, Property and Women: some Comparative Considerations', *Past and Present* Conference Paper, 1974
Goody, J., 'The Evolution of the Family', in *Household and Family in Past Time*, ed. Laslett, P., Cambridge, 1972
Goody, J., *The Developmental Cycle in Domestic Groups*, Cambridge, 1958
Harevin, T., 'The Family as Process: the Historical Study of the Family Cycle', *Journal of Social History*, VII, 1974
Kessen, W., *The Child*, New York, 1965
Lipton, E.L., Steinschneider, A., and Richmond, J.B., 'Swaddling, a Child Care Practice: Historical, Cultural and Experimental Observations', *Pediatrics*, 35, 1965
Levy, M. (ed.), *Aspects of the Analysis of Family Structures*, Princeton, 1965
Nisbet, R., *The Sociological Tradition*, New York, 1966
Parsons, T. and Bales, R.F., *Family, Socialization and Interaction Process*, New York, 1965
Riesman, D., *The Lonely Crowd*, New Haven, 1961

Schultz, T.W., 'The Value of Children: an Economic Perspective', *Journal of Political Economy*, 81, 1973

Shorter, E., 'Capitalism, Culture and Sexuality: some competing Models', *Social Science Quarterly*, 53, 1972

Slater, P.E., *Microcosm: Structural, psychological and religious Evolution in Groups*, New York, 1966

Slater, P.E., *Earthwalk*, New York, 1974

Smelser, N., 'The Family and Industrialization', *Journal of Social History*, I, 1967

Stephens, W., *The Family in Cross-cultural Perspective*, New York, 1963

Sussman, M.B., 'The isolated Nuclear Family: Fact or Fiction?' *Social Problems*, 6, 1959

Sussman, M.B. and Burchinal, L., 'Kin Family Network: unheralded Structure in current Conceptualization of Family Functioning', *Marriage and Family Living*, 24, 1962

Tocqueville, A.de, *Democracy in America*, New York, 1945

Tönnies, F., *Community and Society*, East Lansing, 1957

Trilling, L., *Sincerity and Authenticity*, London, 1972

Wehler, H.-U., *Modernierungstheorie und Geschichte*, Göttingen, 1975

Weinstein, M. and Platt, G., *The Wish to be free: Society, Psyche and Value Change*, Berkeley, 1969

Index